D1561362

DARI
**practical
dictionary**

DARI-ENGLISH
ENGLISH-DARI
practical
dictionary

Carleton Bulkin

Hippocrene Books
New York

**Dedicated to Carolyn Lee Walker Bulkin,
who never gave up.**

All of the author's advance proceeds from this project were donated to the International Committee of the Red Cross (ICRC) and the Turquoise Mountain Foundation toward their work in Afghanistan.

For more information on the work of the ICRC, visit www.icrc.org.

To learn more about the Turquoise Mountain Foundation, visit www.turquoisemountain.org.

Copyright © 2010 Carleton Bulkin

Dari calligraphy by Ustad Saboor Umari and illumination by Ustad Mohammad Tamim Sahebzada, courtesy of Turquoise Mountain Foundation

For information, address:
HIPPOCRENE BOOKS, INC.
171 Madison Avenue
New York, NY 10016
www.hippocrenebooks.com

Library of Congress Cataloging-in-Publication Data

Bulkin, Carleton.
  Dari practical dictionary : Dari-English/English-Dari / Carleton Bulkin.
     p. cm.
  English and Dari.
  ISBN 978-0-7818-1247-4 (alk. paper)
  1. Dari language--Dictionaries--English. 2. English
language--Dictionaries--Dari. I. Title.
  PK6876.B85 2009
  491'.56321--dc22

                                                            2009037113

Printed in the United States of America.

CONTENTS

List of Abbreviations

•	(separator bullet)
<	derived from
→, ←	(sub-entry)
=	synonymous with
&	also, and
& pers	also usable as noun referring to a person
adj	adjective
adv	adverb
Afgh	Afghan, Afghanistan
alt	alternatively
anat	anatomical
Ar	Arabic
arch	archaic
archit	architectual
astron	astronomy
aux	auxiliary
bibl	biblical
c	century
callig	calligraphy, calligraphic
cca	circa
cf	compare
coll pl	collective plural
colloq	colloquial
conj	conjunction
ctr	district center
cul	culinary
d.	died
d.o.	direct object
dim	diminutive
dist	district; distance
dual	dual plural
E	east, eastern

e.g.	for example
esp	especially
ethn	ethnic, ethnic group
excl	exclamation
f	feminine, women, woman's
fig	figurative
geog	geographical
gram	grammatical, linguistic
grp	group
hist	historical
i.e.	that is, to wit
irreg	irregular
lang	language
law	legal
lit	literary
m	masculine, men, man's
meas	measurement
med	medical
mvmt	movement
mus instr	musical instrument
neg	negative connotation
n	noun
N	north, northern
NE	northeast
NW	northwest
NWFP	NW Frontier Province (Pakistan)
o.s.	oneself
obs	obscene
P	Pashtun, Pashto
perf	perfect
pers	person
phrs	phrase
pl	plural

pol	political
pres	present
pron	pronoun
prov	proverb; province
r.	reigned
rel	religion, religious
rhet	rhetorical
S	south, southern
sb	somebody, someone
SE	southeast
seat	provincial seat or capital
sg	singular
sth	something
subj	subjunctive
sw	somewhere
SW	southwest
syn	synonym
us	usually
v	verb
vi	intransitive verb
voc	vocative
vt	transitive verb
vulg	vulgar
W	west, western
w/	with
w/o	without
Zor	Zoroastrian

Introduction

As the United States, NATO, the UN, and the European Union work with the people of Afghanistan to bring about stability and development, communication is difficult. Outsiders tend to arrive with scant knowledge of Afghanistan's rich historical, ethnic, sectarian, and linguistic mosaic; and the lack of a commercially available, birectional Dari-English dictionary using Dari script has only widened the cultural gap. This volume attempts to narrow it.

The roughly 30,000 entries and sub-entries in this volume include much basic political, economic, religious, historical, cultural, culinary, medical, and military terminology; and are drawn from published and unpublished reference sources, academic monographs, the contemporary Afghan press, official documents, the Dari blogosphere, and informal suggestions by native speakers. Ethnic and geographical terms are also highlighted. Of particular interest to aid workers will be the appendix with province and district names (the keeper of the official list of Afghan districts is the Independent Directorate for Local Governance in Kabul; local pronunciation and usage may vary).

Formatting Notes

Dari-English entries. Entries have been sorted according to the order of the Dari alphabet, which differs slightly from that of Farsi. Sub-entries are set off by an arrow (←) on separate lines.

Dari headwords that are nouns may be followed by plural suffixes and forms. The usual plural suffix or suffixes for a given noun are preceded by a hyphen and separated by diagonals and may be followed by an Arabic plural. When plural suffixes are not indicated by a noun, animate nouns may take either ان- or ها-; inanimate nouns take ها-. When a singular noun does not take

Dari plural suffixes but is pluralized by an Arabic form, that Arabic plural appears on a separate line as a sub-entry. For example:

sin *n* /ĭ´-sĭm, ĭsm; pl ā-sām/ اثم

pl ← آثام

Verb entries for non-compound verbs include the infinitive, present-tense stem (in Dari called the *first root*) and past-tense stem (called the *second root*), separated by semicolons. The first-person singular form may be represented between diagonals, *e.g.*:

مالیدن ؛ ‑مال ؛ ‑مالید‑

پالیدن ؛ ‑پال ؛ /میپالم/ ؛ ‑پالید‑

Verb government and prepositions used with other words are indicated between carets, *e.g.*:

ارتباط , ‑ات/ها/ها <به کسی/چیزی>

Phonetics. A pronunciation guide for vowels appears in the footer on each page of the Dari-English side. For consonant sounds not appearing in English or pronounced differently than in English (*gh, kh, q, r*), the learner may wish to consult a native speaker.

The phonetic transcription for a word may differ from the transliteration. The first is a guide to pronouncing the word, while the transliteration is a more practical way of representing the word in an English-language text. For example:

a-lĭf mad = alef mad
qŭr-'ān = Quran, Koran

Variant transliterations often hinge on the problem of representing Dari's short vowels, particularly /ŭ/, hence *Uruzgan, Urozgan, Oruzgan,* or *Orozgan;* or *k* versus *q*, thus either *Qur'an* or *Koran,*

Qalat or *Kalat*. Many common transliterations use double vowels for long vowels, such as *tashkeel* and *Nooha* (or, as in the French system, *Nouha*). There is no universal standard for Dari transliteration.

In the phonetic transcriptions, syllables are separated by hyphens. Word cuts are meant to ease pronunciation but not as a guide to underlying morphology. Syllables are divided within a word so that each begins with a consonant or glottal stop. No word cuts are indicated for the most frequent base verbs, such as *kardan*, *shŭdan*, *dādan*, etc., when they appear in compound-verb entries. Colloquial variant pronunciations appear in parentheses. For example:

bál-ki
way-rān (bay-rān)
id, pl. a'-yād
bā-war kardan

Stress. In Dari, stress normally falls on the last syllable of a word. Plural suffixes (-ān, -hā, -in, etc.) assume the stress from their base noun; however, the object marker (-rā) and the *ezafat* connector (-ĭ or -yĭ) do not. In phonetic transcriptions in this volume, stress is marked only when it does not fall on the final syllable of the root word – as in many adverbs (*e.g.,* al-bá-ta) and prefixed verbs (*e.g.,* bár ā-ma-dan). The *accent grave* (´) denotes secondary stress and is to be distinguished from the apostrophe ('), which denotes a glottal stop. The phonetic transcription may include related Arabic plural forms, marked by "pl"; or the first-person, present tense form of a non-compound verb when the first and second stems differ, as in *didan*.

English-Dari entries. English headwords may be followed by a clarifying note in parentheses; that note may be a synonym, a direct object, an indirect object, or an elaboration. Lastly, the

6

English part of speech is indicated. An English headword that is an adjective may be marked "(& pers)" if the Dari gloss may also be used as a noun referring to a person. For example, *feeble* may be rendered by the Dari ضعيف, which may either be *feeble* (adjective) or *a feeble person*.

For verbs, there may also be a note between carets to illustrate verb government, *e.g.,* <to sb>; that construction will also appear in the Dari between carets.

Sub-entries are set off by an arrow (→) on separate lines.

Tips to finding a word

Even among literate native speakers of Dari, multiple spellings of a given word may be common. Spoken Dari may also metathesize consonants, *e.g.,* قلف for قفل.

- /z/ may be written as ذ , ز , ض , or ظ.
- /t/ may be written as ت or ط.
- /s/ may be written as س or ص.
- /h/ may be written as ح or ه.
- /kh/ and /h/ may occur as /q/ in some words.
- A variant spelling may depend on whether a vowel is long or short, especially in the middle of a word; short vowels are usually not written in Dari.
- A spoken word beginning in /a-/ may be written as beginning with ا , ع , or آ.
- A spoken word beginning in /o-/, /u-/, or /ŭ-/ may be written as beginning with او.
- ن before ب is pronounced not as /n/ but as /m/, *e.g.,* تنبل /tam-bal/ "lazy."
- Some loan words with ژ may occur in forms that substitute ج for ژ.

7

- The glottal stop, typically represented by ع, may go unpronounced and/or unwritten.
- When looking for a word or phrase that begins with the sound /ba-/, look both under ب plus the first consonant that follows and under به (e.g., بطور and طور به).
- Other prepositions and prefixes also may or may not be followed by a space: e.g., برآمدن or بر آمدن.
- If a word ends in /-agi/, it has been spelled here as گی- rather than گی ه-, thus حملگی rather than حمله گی.
- Two *yaws* in succession may be spelled either یی or ئی , e.g., روئیدن or رویدن. Such forms as the latter are alphabetized as spelled, *i.e., hamza-yaw.*

Dari Pronunciation: Getting Started

Dari has multiple dialects, and native speakers may offer variant pronunciations of a given word in the number of syllables, in whether a vowel is long or short, or by metathesizing consonants. This dictionary attempts a broadly literary standard for Dari pronunciation, with some spoken variations indicated in parentheses. Dari consonants are much the same as in English, except for *gh, kh, q* and *r*. More challenging are the vowels. Spoken Dari has more vowels than the written language.

Dari has these vowels, plus the glides /w/ and /y/:

Written	Spoken
آ	/ā/
ا	/a/, /ā/, /ĭ/, /ŭ/
ع-ا	/ey/, /a'/
و	/o/, /u/; /w/
ی	/i/; /y/
usually not written in word-	/ĭ/, /ŭ/

8

medial position

There are seven basic vowel sounds in Dari: /a/ close to the vowel in cup,[1] /ā/ as in lost, /i/ as in feet, /ĭ/ as in bit, /o/ as in hope, /u/ as in loot, and /ŭ/ as in put. /e/ as in bet occurs almost exclusively in the diphthong *ey*; however, /ĭ/ may sound similar to /e/. The difference between /ĭ/ and /e/ never changes the meaning of a word.

There are five diphthongs: /ay/ as in pie but less flat, /ey/ as in obey, /oy/ as in toy, /uy/ as in buoy; plus /aw/ as in now but less flat. Note that /a/ always stands for the same vowel sound, whether alone or in a diphthong.

As a first principle, long vowels (/ā/, /i/, /o/, /u/) are usually written, while short vowels (/a/, /ĭ/, /ŭ/) are generally not. The letter *alef* may be pronounced variously. In written Dari, *alef mad* (آ) at the beginning of a word is pronounced /ā/. At the beginning of a word, *alef* (ا) may be pronounced as /a/ (1), /ĭ/ (2) or /ŭ/ (3). The beginner must learn the pronunciation of these words individually. In the middle or at the end of a word, ا is sounded as /ā/ (4).

Examples:

(1) جا , چای (4) ؛ امور , امید (3) ؛ انتخاب , انسان (2) ؛ اندازه , انگور

R to L: /angur, andāza, ĭnsān, ĭntĭkhāb, ŭmeyd, ŭmur, chāy, jā/

At the beginning of a word, اع- may be pronounced either as /ey/ or /a'/. (/a'/ is found mostly in Arabic plurals; in spoken Dari, initial /a'/ may sound simply as /a/. In spoken Dari, the glottal stop is more usual when aspiring to a literary standard.)

---

[1] Phonemically, this sound is equivalent to a short /a/ sound and is transliterated as such, *e.g.,* Afghanistan.

Examples: اعشاریه , اعراب , اعدام , اعلام

R to L: /eylām, eydām, a'rāb, a'shārīya/

The first sound in a word beginning with ای- is generally /i/, which is interchangeable with /ey/ (see ایستاده).

As a vowel, the letter *waw* (و) may represent /u/ (1), /o/ (2) or, less commonly, /ŭ/ (3). In some words, speakers pronounce the و variously as either /u/ or /o/ (4). When و is followed by the vowel ا, it is always /w/ (5); however, و may also sound as /w/ when followed by a consonant (6).

Examples:

بول (6) ؛ جوان (5) ؛ بوی (4) ؛ بیروبار (3) ؛ بگوتا (2) ؛ بوره (1)

R to L: /bura, bŭgotā, birŭbār, boy/buy, jawān, bawl/

The letter *yaw* (ی) is /i/ between two consonants (1) and /y/ elsewhere (2).

Examples: تقسیم , بفریح ؛ (2) پای , رادیو (1)

R to L: /taqsim, tafrih, paay, rādīyo/

The short vowel sounds /ĭ/ and /ŭ/ are normally not written, and may be found between two consonants (1), (2). However, /a/ may also occur unwritten and between two consonants (3). The *ezafat* connector sounds as /ĭ/ after a consonant and as /yĭ/ after a vowel.

Examples:

جالب (1) ؛ جانب (2) ؛ جرم , جنوب (3) ؛ جاکت , جریمه

10

R to L: /jālīb, jānīb, jūnub, jūrm, jāk̲a̲t, jarima/

Thanks and a Disclaimer

Many thanks go to Mai-Thao Nguyen for her assistance in designing, formatting, and reformatting a prototype for this dictionary. Mohamed Popal, Hafiz Latify, Hashem Hassani, Shakila Anwari, Fahima Baluch, and Amena Hamidi reviewed portions of an early version of the manuscript. The calligraphic artwork on the cover and title page is the work of Ustad Saboor Omari and was illuminated by Ustad Mohammad Tamim Sahebzada. Much gratitude goes to Subhan Fakhrizada for his careful proofreading of the final version. All errors that remain are entirely my responsibility; comments and corrections from users will be sincerely welcomed at daridictionary@yahoo.com.

Is Dari a Language or a Dialect?

"Dari is one of the official languages spoken in Afghanistan." *(Neghat, Mohammad Nasim, et al. Dari-English Dictionary. Omaha, Nebraska: University of Nebraska Press, 1993, pg. i.)*

"The two principal languages of Afghanistan are ... Persian (or Farsi) and Pashto. The 1964 Constitution names both Dari (or Afghan Farsi) and Pashto as official languages. Dari, an old term, literally means 'language of the court.' In reality, Dari (still the court language in Afghanistan as it was in Moghul India) serves as a *lingua franca*...

"Several regional Farsi dialects exist. The Hazara speak Hazaragi; the Aimaq speak Farsi with many Turkic loan words; the Tajik speak Tajiki, a Farsi dialect related to but not identical to the Tajiki spoken in the Tajikistan S.S.R. Afghans often refer to Tajiki by the name of the valley in which it is spoken; *e.g.,* Panjsheri, Andarabi.

11

Most rural Afghans still refer to the language as Farsi, not Dari. ... The Farsiwan (or Parsiwan) farmers of western Afghanistan speak Iranian Farsi, and Heratis have an urban dialect all their own. So do the Kabulis, who speak the slurred Brooklynese of Farsi dialects." *(Dupree, Louis. Afghanistan. Princeton, New Jersey: Princeton University Press, 1973, pp. 68-70.)*

"From the linguistic point of view Dari, Tadzhiki, and Farsi (Persian) are not three different languages. They are three geographical dialects of one classical language with phonological differences and differences in vocabulary, pronunciation, and intonation. They also differ in some syntactic structures, but they should not be referred to as dialects. First of all, a dialect, in its specific sense, is a form of speech different from the standard language. Secondly, each of these serve[s] as the standard and literary languages of three independent countries, while each has geographical and social dialects in its own speech community." *(Neghat, op. cit., pg. xiv.)*

The Last Word...

A shprakh iz a diyalekt mit an armey un a flot.
A language is a dialect with an army and a navy.

Yiddish linguist Max Weinreich (1893-1969), *"Der yivo un di problemen fun undzer tsayt"* (YIVO and the problems of our time), in *Yivo-bleter* 25.1, 1945, pg. 13.

Dari-English

Dari Alphabet

آ	alef mad	ص	swad
ا	alef	ض	zwad
ب	bey	ط	toy
پ	pey	ظ	zoy
ت	tey	ع	ayn
ث	sey	غ	ghayn
ج	jīm	ف	fey
ح	hey	ق	qāf
چ	chey	ک	kāf
خ	khey	گ	gāf
د	dāl	ل	lām
ذ	zāl	م	mīm
ر	rey	ن	nūn
ز	zey	و	waw
ژ	zhey	ه	hā
س	sīn	ء	hamza
ش	shīn	ی	yā

آ

آب /āb/ water n
آب کردن ← melt, cause to melt vt
آب باز , -ان/ها /āb bāz/
swimmer n
آب بازی /āb bā-zi/ swimming n
آب بازی کردن ← swim v
آب بند /āb band/
Ab Band (dist, ctr Haji Kheyl) n
آب ترازو /āb ta-rā-zo/
level (tool) n
آب چشم /āb-ĭ chá-shĭm/ tears n
آب خوردن /āb-ĭ khŭr-dan/
drinking water n
آب دهان /āb-ĭ da-hān/ saliva n
آب دهن see آب دهان /āb-ĭ da-han/
آب دیده /āb-ĭ di-da/ tears (lit) n
آب رو , -ها /āb raw/
gutter; waterway n
آب کش /āb kash/
rinsing (dishes, clothes) n
آب کش کردن ← rinse
آب کشی , -ها /āb ka-shi/
bowl for rinsing tea dishes prior to
serving n
آب کمری /āb ka-ma-ri/
Ab Kamari (dist, ctr Sang Atash) n
آب گردان /āb gar-dān/
diversion adj
بند آب گردان ← diversion dam
آب گیر , -ها /āb gir/
pool, lake; reservoir n
آب معدنی /āb-ĭ maʻ-da-ni/
mineral water n
آب میوه /āb-ĭ mey-wa/
fruit juice, juice n
آب و تاب /āb ŭ tāb/ bombast n
آب و تات داشتن ← be bombastic
آب و دانه /āb ŭ dā-na/
one's destiny n
آب و هوا /āb ŭ ha-wā/
climate, weather n
آب های بدرفت /āb-hā-yĭ bad-raft/
sewage n pl
آبا /ā-bā/ fathers [< Ar] n pl
آبا و اجداد ← ancestors

آبا و اجداد /ā-bā ŭ aj-dād/
ancestry; ancestors n
آباد /ā-bād/
abode; built-up place n; fat (colloq);
fertile, cultivated adj
آباد کردن ← build, construct
آبان /ā-bān/
Aban (month, see عقرب) n
آبد , -ات /ā-bad/
building, structure n
آبرو see آب رو n /āb-raw/, -ها
آبرو /āb-ro/ honor, respect n
آبرومند /āb-ro-mand/
honored, respected adj
آبرومندانه /āb-ro-man-dā-na/
honorably, respectably adv
آبستن /ā-bĭs-tan/
pregnant, expecting adj
آبستن شدن ← become pregnant vi
آبستن کردن <کسی را> ←
get <sb> pregnant
آبستنی /ā-bĭs-ta-ni/
pregnancy; conception n
آبشار , -ها /āb-shār/
waterfall, falls, cascade n
آبگین /āb-gin/ watery, aqueous adj
آبله /āb-la, ā-bĭ-la (aw-la)/
blister, pimple; smallpox n
آبله کوبی /āb-la ko-bi/
smallpox vaccination n
آبنا /āb-nā/ strait n
آبنوس /āb-nus/ ebony n
آبنوسی /āb-nu-si/
ebony black (color) adj
آبی /ā-bi (a-wi)/ blue (color) adj
آپرا /āp-rā/ see اوپرا n
آتش /ā-tash/ fire, conflagration n
آتش زدن ← set on fire, light a fire
آتش کردن ← ignite, fire
آتش باری /ā-tash bā-ri/
fire (artillery), volley n
آتش بس /ā-tash bas/ cease-fire n
آتش پرست , -ان/ها /ā-tash pa-rast/
Zoroastrian (pers); fire worshiper n
آتش در دادن /ā-tash dar dādan/
set on fire; light a fire v
آتش فشان /ā-tash fĭ-shān/ volcano n

آتش فشانی /ā-tash fī-shā-ni/
eruption (volcano) n

آتش كاو /ā-tash kāw/
poker (fireplace) n

آتش كده /ā-tash ka-da/
fire temple (Zor) n

آتش كو /ā-tash kaw/ n آتش كاو see

آتش گير /ā-tash gir/ fire tongs n

آتشدان /ā-tash-dān/
fireplace; brazier n

آتشك /ā-ta-shak/ syphilis n

آتشى /ā-ta-shi/
red, dark red adj; dark red pigeon;
fiery pers n

آتشين /ā-ta-shin/ fiery; ardent adj

آتن /ā-tan/ Athens n

آتى /ā-ti/ following adj; future n
اصطلاحات اتى ←
the following terms

آثار /ā-sār, sg a-sar/
n pl اثر see sg

آثام /ā-sām; sg ĭ´-sīm, ĭsm/
n pl اثم see sg

آجندا /ā-jīn-dā/ آجنده see

آجنده /ā-jīn-da/ agenda n

آچار /ā-chār/ pickle (& eggplant) n

آچار انداختن /ā-chār andākhtan/
pickle vt

آچين /ā-chin/ اچين see

آخ ! /ākh/ ouch excl

آخذه , -ها /ā-khĭ-za/
receiver (& radio) n

آخر , -ها/اوخر /ā-khĭr, pl a-wā-khĭr/
end n; final, ultimate adj

آخر /ā-khŭr/ n آخور see

آخر هفته /ā-khĭr-ĭ haf-ta/
weekend n

آخرالامر /ā-khĭ-rŭ-lá-mĭr/
finally, at last [< Ar] adv

آخرت /ā-khĭ-rat/ the hereafter n

آخر , -ها/اوخر /ā-khĭ-rin/
final, ultimate (colloq) adj

آخور /ā-khŭr (-khor)/
crib, manger n

آخند /ā-khŭnd/ n آخوند see

آخوند /ā-khund/
religious teacher n

آخوند زاده /ā-khund zā-da/
religious teacher of noble lineage n

آخیرا /ā-khí-ran, -rán/ recently adv

آداب /ā-dāb, sg a-dab/
n pl ادب see sg

آدرس /ād-ras/ address (place) n

آدم /ā-dam/
Adam (bibl); person, human being n

آدم برفی /ā-dam-ĭ bar-fi/
snowman n

آدم میخانیکی
/ā-dam-ĭ mey-khā-ni-ki/
robot n

آدم و حوا /ā-dam ŭ ha-wā/
Adam & Eve phrs

آدمیت /ā-da-mī-yat/
humanity, humaneness n

آدینه مسجد /ā-di-na mas-jĭd/
Adina Masjed see Charbolak n

آذان كردن /ā-zan kardan/
call to prayer v

آذر /ā-zar/
fire; angel of fire; see & قوس n

آذربائیجان /ā-zīr-bā-yi-jān/
Azerbaijan n

آذین /ā-zin/ decoration n

آذین بستن /ā-zin bastan/
decorate v

آر /ār/ n آهار see

آرام /ā-rām/
comfortable; quiet adj

آرام آرام /ā-rām ā-rām/
slowly; gradually adv

آرامی /ā-rā-mi/
Aramaic adj; Aramean n

آرایش /ā-rā-yĭsh/
beautification; makeup n
آرایش کردن put on makeup ←

آرایشگاه /ā-rā-yĭsh-gāh/
beauty salon, hair salon n

آرایشگر /ā-rā-yĭsh-gar/
beautician, hairstylist n

آرتست /ār-tĭst/
artist; artiste; performer n

آرتیست /ār-tist/ n آرتست see

آرد /ārd/ flour n

آردبیز /ārd-beyz/ flour sifter n

آرزو /ār-zo/ dream; hope, wish n

آرزومنّد , -ان/ها /ār-zo-mand/
hopeful; ambitious (& pers) adj, n

آرمان /ār-mān (ar-)/
desire, hope; remorse n

آرن n هارن /ā-rān/ see

آرنج /ā-rǐnj/ elbow n

آریا /ā-rī-yā/ Herat (arch) n

آریائی /ā-rī-yā-i/ Aryan adj

آریایی /ā-rī-yā-yi/ adj *see

آز /āz/ greed, avidity n

آزاد /ā-zād/ free, unfettered adj

آزادی /ā-zā-di/ freedom n

آزادی خواه /ā-zā-di khā/ liberal n

آزار دادن <کسی را> /ā-zār dādan/
annoy, pester <sb> vt

آزرده خاطر /ā-zǔr-da khā-tǐr/
خاطر آزرده adj see

آزمایش , -ها /āz-mā-yǐsh/
test, experiment n

آزمایش شده /āz-mā-yǐsh shǔ-da/
tried, tested adj

آزمایش کرده /āz-mā-yǐsh kar-da/
آزمایش شده adj see

آزمایشگاه /āz-mā-yǐsh-gāh/
laboratory, lab n

آزمایشی /āz-mā-yǐ-shi/
experimental, tentative adj

آزمند , -ان/ها /āz-mand/
greedy; avid (& pers) adj, n

آزمندانه /āz-man-dā-na/
greedily; avidly adv

آزموده /āz-mu-da/ tested, tried adj

آژانس خبری /ā-jāns kha-ba-ri/
press agency n

آسان /ā-sān/ easy adj

آسانی /ā-sā-ni/ facilitation n

آستانه /ās-tā-na/
Astana (capital); threshold n
در آستانهٔ تاریخ <—
on history's threshold

آستریا /ās-tar-yā/ Austria n

آستریایی , -ان/ها /ās-tar-yā-yi/
Austrian (& pers) adj, n

آستین /ā-stin/ sleeve (of shirt) n

آسکر n اسکار /ās-kar/ see

آسمان /ās-mān/
sky, heaven, firmament n

آسمان خراش /ās-mān kha-rāsh/
skyscraper n

آسمانسا /ās-mān-sā/
sky-high, lofty adj

آسمانگون /ās-mān-gun/
sky blue, cyan adj

آسمانی /ās-mā-ni/
celestial; holy; cyan adj
اجرام آسمانی <—
celestial bodies

آسوده خاطر /ā-su-da khā-tǐr/
خاطر آسوده adj see

آسیا /ā-sī-yā/
Asia (continent); mill n
آسیا کردن <—
mill, grind (grain)

آسیا سنگ /ā-sī-yā sang/
millstone n

آسیاب /ā-sī-yāb/ mill, water mill n
یک حجر آسیاب <— one mill

آسیابان , -ان/ها /ā-sī-yā-bān/
miller (pers) n

آسیابانی /ā-sī-yā-bā-ni/ milling n

آسیای بادی /ā-sī-yā-yī bā-di/
windmill n

آسیای جنوب شرقی
/ā-sī-yā-yī jǔ-nu-bi/
South Asia n
جنوب آسیا <—
the south of Asia

آسیای جنوب شرقی
/ā-sī-yā-yī jǔ-nub shar-qi/
Southeast Asia n

آسیای صغیر /ā-sī-yā-yī sa-ghīr/
Asia Minor n

آسیای مرکزی
/ā-sī-yā-yī mar-ka-zi/
Central Asia n

آسیای میانه /ā-sī-yā-yī mǐ-yā-na/
Central Asia n

آسیایی , -ها /ā-sī-yā-yi/
Asian (& pers) adj, n

آسیب /ā-seyb/ damage, injury n
آسیب دیدن <— sustain damage

آسیب پذیر /ā-seyb pa-zir/
vulnerable adj

آش /āsh/ pasta, noodles n

آشامنده /ā-shā-mǐn-da/ drinker n

آشامیدن ؛ -آشام- ؛ آشامید-
/ā-shā-mi-dan/
drink v

آشامندنی , -ها /ā-shā-mǐn-da-ni/
potable adj; sth to drink n

i = keep, ǐ = big, u = coop, ǔ = put, y = yet, ' = (glottal stop) 17

آشپز /āsh-paz/ n cook, chef

آشپز خانه /āsh-paz khā-na/ kitchen n

آشتی دادن /āsh-ti dādan/ reconcile, conciliate vt

آشتی کردن /āsh-ti kardan/ make peace, make up vi

آشتی ناپذیر /āsh-ti nā-pa-zir/ irreconcilable adj

آشفته خاطر /ā-shŭf-ta khā-tīr/ see خاطر آشفته adj

آشنا , -یان/ها /āsh-nā, ā-shī-nā/ acquaintance, friend n; acquainted (lit) adj

← آشنا ساختن <همرای کسی> make friends <w/sb>

← آشنا شدن <همرای کسی> become acquainted <w/sb>

آشنایی , -ها /āsh-nā-yi/ acquaintance, friendship n

← آشنایی حاصل نمودن see آشنا شدن

← آشنایی داشتن <همرای کسی> be acquainted <w/sb>

← آشنایی کردن <همرای کسی> make <sb's> acquaintance

آشک /ā-shak/ dumplings, ravioli (w/leeks & sour cream) n

آشکار /āsh-kār/ apparent, evident; obvious adj; openly adv

آشیان /ā-shī-yān/ abode (& fig); nest n

آشیانه /ā-shī-yā-na/ n see آشیان

آغا /ā-ghā/ older brother; dad n

آغا بیادر /ā-ghā byā-dar/ older brother (colloq) n

آغا لاله /ā-ghā lā-la/ brother-in-law, sister's husband n

آغا جان /ā-ghā jān/ (respectful form of address for m) n

آغا صاحب /ā-ghā sā-hīb/ (respectful form of address for m descendants of Prophet) n

آغاز شدن /ā-ghāz shŭdan/ begin, start vi

آغاز کردن /ā-ghāz kardan/ begin, start vt

آغشته به خون /ā-ghīsh-ta ba khun/ bloodsoaked adj

آغشته کردن /ā-ghīsh-ta kardan/ soak, steep vt

آغل /ā-ghīl/ n آغیل see

آغوش /ā-ghosh/ bosom; embrace, hug n

آغیل /ā-gheyl/ pen (for animals), corral n

آفاق /ā-fāq, sg ŭ-fūq/ n pl افق see sg

آفاقیت /ā-fā-qī-yat/ objectivity; objectivism n

آفتاب /āf-tāb (af-taw)/ sun n

آفتاب برآمد /āf-tāb bár ā-mad/ sunrise (colloq) n

آفتاب نشست /āf-tāb nī-shast/ sunset (colloq) n

آفتابه /āf-tā-ba (af-tā-wa)/ pitcher (w/handle, spout, us w/lid) n

آفتابی /āf-tā-bi (āf-ta-wi)/ fair, sunny (weather) adj

آفر /ā-far/ bid, offer n

← آفر کم low bid

← آفر بلند high bid

آفرین /ā-fa-rin/ acclamation, applause n; bravo excl

آفرین خواندن /ā-fa-rin khāndan/ acclaim, laud, applaud vt

آفرین گفتن /ā-fa-rin gŭftan/ acclaim, laud vt

آقا /ā-qā/ n آغا see

← خانم ها و آقایان ladies & gentlemen!

آگام /ā-gām/ n اگام see

آگاه /ā-gāh/ aware, knowledgeable adj

آگاه بودن /ā-gāh budan/ be aware (of sth) vi

آگاه شدن <از چیزی> /ā-gāh shŭdan/ become aware <of sth> vi

آگاهی حاصل کردن <از چیزی> /ā-gā-hi hā-sīl kardan/ see آگاه شدن vi

آگرا /āg-rā/
Agra (hist, Mughal capital 1526-1658) n

آگست /ā-gǐst/ August n

آلت , -ها/آلات /ā-lat, pl -lāt/
device, instrument; tool; organ, member n

آلت تناسلی /ā-lat-ǐ ta-nā-sǔ-li/
genital organ n

آلت جنسی /ā-lat-ǐ jǐn-si/
male member (anat) n

آلبالو /āl-bā-lu/ sour cherry n

آلش /ā-lǐsh/
change (of clothes) (colloq) n
← آلش شدن change clothes
← آلش کردن replace, change

آلش بدل شدن /ā-lǐsh-ǐ ba-dal shǔdan/
see v آلش شدنُ

آلمان /āl-mān/ Germany n
آلمانی /āl-mā-ni/
Germany n; German (& lang) adj, n

آلو /ā-lu/ plum n

آلو بخارا /ā-lu bǔ-khā-ra/
prune, Bokhara plum n

آلوبالو /ā-lu-bā-lu/ n see آلبالو

آلودگی /ā-lu-da-gi/
taint, contamination, soil, tarnish, n

آلودن ؛ -آلای- /ā-lu-dan/ ؛ آلود-
defile; contaminate; pollute (& environment) vt

آلوده /ā-lu-da/
defiled; polluted adj

آله , -ها/آلات /ā-la, pl -lāt/
device, instrument; tool; implement; member n

آله تانیث /ā-la-yǐ tā-nis/ pistil n
آله تذکیر /ā-la-yǐ taz-kir/ stamen n
آله مخابره /ā-la-yǐ mǔ-khā-bǐ-ra/
walkie-talkie n

آله منفجره تعبیه شده
/ā-la-yǐ mǔn-fa-jǐ-ra-yǐ tá-bǐ-ya shǔ-da/
IED, improvised explosive device n

آلهه /ā-lǐ-ha, sg ǐ-lāh/
see اله n pl sg

آلی /ā-li/ organic adj

ام /ām/ mango n

آماج /ā-māj/ target, aim, mark n

آماج گاه /ā-māj gāh/
target; target ground n

آمادگی /ā-mā-da-gi/
readiness, being equipped n
← آمادگی گرفتن
prepare, get ready v

آماده /ā-mā-da/
equipped, ready adj
← آماده ساختن equip, prepare vt
← آماده شدن get ready, prepare vi

آماده باش /ā-mā-da bāsh/
alert, call to readiness n

آمار /ā-mār/ statistics n
آماس /ā-mās/ swelling n

آماسیدگی /ā-mā-si-da-gi/ n آماس see
آماسیده /ā-mā-si-da/ swollen adj

آمال /ā-māl, sg a-mal/
see sg امل n pl

آمد آمد /ā-mad ā-mad/
beginning, start n

آمدن ؛ -آه- (-آی-) ؛ آمد-
/ā-ma-dan/
arrive, come vi

آمده /ā-ma-da/
arrived adj; event n

آمر , -ان/ها/ین /ā-mǐr/
boss, leader, department head n

آمرانه /ā-mǐ-rā-na/
bossy, imperious adj; imperiously adv

آمرزش /ā-mǔr-zǐsh/
absolution (by God) n

آمرزیدن ؛ -آمرز- ؛ آمرزید-
/ā-mǔr-zi-dan/
absolve, forgive (said only of God) vt

آمریکا /ām-ri-kā/ n امریکا see

آملت /ām-lǐt/ n املت see

آمو دریا /ā-mu dar-yā/
Amu Darya; (hist) Oxus (river) n

آموختن ؛ -آموز- ؛ آموخت-
/ā-mokh-tan (-mǔkh-)/
learn (lit) vt

آموخته /ā-mokh-ta/
used, accustomed (to) adj

آموزش /ā-mo-zǐsh/
education; learning n

آموزگار /ā-moz-gār/
teacher, instructor n

i = keep, ǐ = big, u = coop, ǔ = put, y = yet, ' = (glottal stop)　　19

amoeba n /ā-meyb/ آمیب

that adj, pron /ān/ آن

mango n /ān-bīh/ آنبه

there adv /ān-jā/ آنجا

the fact that pron /ān-chī/ ... آنچه
← نسبت به آنچه
w/respect to the fact that...

see عده n /ān-'ī-da/ انعده

/ān-hā/ آنها
they pron [& as 3rd pers sg for
dignitary, father of interlocutor];
those adj

to that degree adj /ān-ha-ma/ آنهمه

/ā-wā-ra-gi/ آوارگی
state of being displaced,
homelessness n

آواره , -گان/ها /ā-wā-ra/
displaced person, wanderer n

/ā-wā-ra sākhtan/ آواره ساختن
displace, make homeless vt

/ā-wā-ra shūdan/ آواره شدن
become displaced vi

آواز , -ها /ā-wāz/
song; sound; voice; phoneme n

/ā-wāz khān/ آواز خوان , -ان/ها
singer n

آواز خوانی /ā-wāz khā-ni/
singing n

← آواز خوانی کردن sing

/ā-wāz shī-nā-si/ آواز شناسی
phonetics (science) n

/ā-wāz-ī mar-dŭm/ آواز مردم
vox populi n

/ā-wāz na-wi-si/ آواز نویسی
transcription (phonetic) n

/ā-wā-za/ آوازه , -ها
rumor; reputation n
← آوازه کردن spread a rumor

آوردن ؛ -آور- ؛ آورد-
(آوردن ؛ -آز- ؛ آرد-)
/āwardan, -wŭr-/
bring vt

/ā-wang/ آونگ
string of vegetables (hung up) n

آویختن ؛ -آویز- ؛ آویخت-
/ā-weykh-tan/
hang, suspend; sling vt

/ā-weykh-ta/ آویخته
hanging, suspended adj

earring; pendant n /ā-wey-za/ آویزه

starch n /ā-hār (ār)/ آهار
← آهار دادن starch vt

starched adj /ā-hār dār/ آهار دار

/ā-hīs-ta-gi/ آهستگی
slowness n; slowly adv

/ā-hīs-ta (ās-tā)/ آهسته
slow, slowly adj, adv

/ās-tā bŭ-ro/ آهسته برو
Go Slowly (wedding song) n

/ā-hīs-ta raftan/ آهسته رفتن
slow down, go slow v

lime, quicklime n /ā-hak/ آهک

iron (metal) n /ā-han/ آهن

magnet n /ā-han rŭ-bā/ آهن ربا

/ā-han-ī sard koftan/ آهن سرد کوفتن
beat a dead horse, beat cold iron
(fig) v

آهنگ , -ها /ā-hang/
melody, tune; music n
← آهنگ های تصوفی Sufi melodies n pl

/ā-han-gar/ آهنگر , -ان/ها
blacksmith, smith n

/ā-ha-nin/ آهنین
iron, made of iron adj

آهو , -ان/ها /ā-hu/ deer n

/ā-hu-rā maz-dā/ آهورا مزدا
Ahura Mazda (Zor) n

/āy īs āy/ آی اس آی
ISI, Inter-Services Intelligence n

/ā´-yā/ آیا
(question marker) (lit) excl

/ā-yat/ آیت
miracle; marvel; Quranic verse n

ayatollah n /ā-ya-tŭl-lah/ آیت الله

Ireland n /āyr-land/ آیرلند

/āyr-lan-di/ آیرلندی , -ان/ها
Irish (& pers) adj, n

see آیرلند n /āyr-leynd/ آیرلیند

/āyr-leyn-di/ آیرلیندی , -ان/ها
see آیرلندی adj, n

Iceland n /āys-land/ آیس لند

/āys-lan-di/ آیس لندی , -ان/ها
Icelandic adj; Icelander (pers) n

آيس ليند /āys-leynd/ n آيس لند see
آيس ليندى , /-ان/ها /āys-leyn-di/
آيس لندى adj, n see

آيساف /āy-sāf/
ISAF, International Security
Assistance Force n

آينده , -گان/ها /ā-yïn-da/
arrival (pers); future n; next,
subsequent adj

آيودين /ā-yo-din/
iodine (element) n

آيه /ā-ya/ آيت see
religion; custom n /ā-yin/ آيين
آيين زردشتى ←
the Zoroastrian religion

آيينه mirror n /ā-yi-na (āy-na)/
آيينى metallic, shiny adj /ā-yi-ni/

ا

ابا refusal n /ī-bā/
ابا ورزيدن /ī-bā warzidan/
refuse v

ابابيل /a-bā-bil/
swallow, swift (bird) n

اباحت /ī-bā-hat/
license, freedom (when abused) n

ابتدا /ïb-tï-dā/
beginning, outset, start n

ابتدايى /ïb-tï-dā-yi/
elementary; primitive adj

ابتكار , -ات/ها /ïb-tï-kār/
initiative; innovation n
ابتكار كردن ← innovate v

ابحار /ab-hār, sg bahr/
بحر n pl see sg

ابخره /ab-khï-ra, sg bŭ-khur/
بخور n pl see sg

ابد eternity n /a-bad/
ابدال /ab-dāl, sg ba-dil/
بديل n pl see sg

ابدالى , -ان/ها /ab-dā-li/
درانى n see

ابدان /ab-dān, sg ba-dan/
بدن n pl see sg

ابر super- pref /a-bar/
ابر , -ها /á-bĭr, abr/ cloud n
ابر آلود cloudy adj /á-bĭr ā-lud/

ابر جناور /a-bar jī-nā-war/
supermonster; (fig, as invader)
Russia n

ابر قدرت /a-bar qŭd-rat/
superpower n

ابر مرد /a-bar mard/
superman; Superman n

ابرا /ïb-rā/
freeing; (law) releasing; (med)
healing n
ابرا دادن ← release; heal v

ابراز كردن /ïb-rāz kardan/
express; divulge vt

ابراهيم /ïb-rā-him/
Abraham (bibl; m name) n

ابرى cloudy adj /ab-ri/
ابريشم /ab-rey-shŭm/
silk, raw silk n

ابريشم كباب /ab-rey-shŭm ka-bāb/
silk kabob (dessert) n

ابريشمى /ab-rey-shŭ-mi/
silken, made of silk adj

ابريشمين /ab-rey-shŭ-min/
ابريشمى adj see

ابزار /ab-zār/ n افزار see
ابعاد /ab-'ād, sg bŭ'd/
بعد n pl see sg

ابليس devil, the Devil n /ïb-lis/
ابليسانه /ïb-li-sā-na/
diabolically; fiendishly adv

ابليسى /ïb-li-si/
diabolical; fiendish adj

ابن /ï´-bĭn, pl ab-nā/
son (of) [< Ar] n
ابنا ← pl

ابن السبيل /ï´-bĭn ŭs-sa-bil/
traveler [< Ar] n

ابن الوقت /ï´-bĭn ŭl-waqt/
opportunist [< Ar] adj, n

ابن سينا /ï´-bĭn-ï si-nā/
Avicenna (hist, 980-1037, Persian
med author); Canon of Medicine n

ابنا /ab-nā, sg ï´-bĭn/
ابن n pl see sg

ابناى انس و جن
/ab-nā-yĭ ïns ŭ jĭn/
sons of man & jinn n pl

i = keep, ĭ = big, u = coop, ŭ = put, y = yet, ' = (glottal stop)   21

ابنای جنس /ab-nā-yī jīns/
sons of the race n pl

ابنای زمان /ab-nā-yī za-mān/
sons of the age n pl

ابنای وطن /ab-nā-yī wa-tan/
sons of the homeland n pl

ابنیه /ab-nī-ya/ n بنا see sg
father of [< Ar] /a-bu/ ابو

ابو علی /a-bu 'a-li/
Father of Medicine (Avicenna) n

ابو البشر /a-bu-l-ba-shar/
Father of Mankind (Adam) n

ابو الفضل /abul-fá-zīl/
Abu'l Fazl (hist, 1551-1602,
Akbar's biographer) n

ابو الهول /a-bu-l-hawl/
Sphinx n

ابو بكر /a-bu bá-kīr/
Abu Bakr (hist, 573-634, first
caliph in Mecca) n

ابواب /ab-wāb, sg bāb/
n باب see sg

ابواب جمعی /ab-wāb jam-'i/
property in one's charge n

ابوین /a-ba-wayn/
parents n pl

ابهر /ab-har/
aorta n; magnificent adj

ابیض /ab-yaz/
white adj

اپارتمان /a-pārt-mān/
apartment n

اپریدی /ap-ri-di/ افریدی see

اپریل /ap-reyl/
April (month) n

ات /at (īt)/
(ending, 2nd pers sg possessive);
(ending, 2nd pers sg object)
[written ت after consonant] suff

اتاترک /a-tā-tŭrk/ Ataturk (hist) n

اتازونی /a-tā-zu-ni/
n ایالاتِ متحدهِ امریکا see

اتاق /ū-tāq/ room (in house) n

اتاق انتظار /ū-tāq-ĭ īn-tī-zār/
waiting room n

اتاق تجارت /ū-tāq-ĭ tŭ-jā-rat/
chamber of commerce n

اتاق طعام خوری
/ū-tāq-ĭ ta-'ām khŭ-ri/
n اتاق نان خوری see

اتاق خواب /ū-tāq-ĭ khāb/
bedroom n

اتاق عاجل /ū-tāq-ĭ ā-jīl/
emergency room n

اتاق نان /ū-tāq-ĭ nān/
n اتاق نان خوری see

اتاق نان خوری /ū-tāq-ĭ nān khŭ-ri/
dining room (colloq) n

اتاق نشیمن /ū-tāq-ĭ nĭ-shi-man/
living room n

اتاق دونفری /ū-tāq-ĭ yak-na-fa-ri/
double-occupancy room n

اتاق یکنفری /ū-tāq-ĭ yak-na-fa-ri/
single-occupancy room n

ایتالیا /ī-tā-lī-yā/ اتالیا see
Italian adj, n /ī-tā-li-ya-yi/ اتالیایی

اتاوا /ū-tā-wā/ Ottawa n

اتباع /at-bā/ n pl تبع , تابع see sg
following adj /ī-tī-bā/ اتباع

اتحاد /ī-tī-hād/
union, unification n
unite, unify vt اتحاد کردن →

اتحاد اروپایی /ī-tī-hād-ĭ ū-ru-pā-yi/
European Union n

اتحاد اسلامی /ī-tī-hād-ĭ īs-lā-mi/
Islamic Unity (mvmt) n

اتحاد الاسلام /ī-tī-hād-ŭl-īs-lām/
pan-Islamism (mvmt) n

اتحاد سه گانه /ī-tī-hād-ĭ sey gā-na/
Union of Three (hist, mujahedin
grp) n

اتحاد هفت گانه
/ī-tī-hād-ĭ haft gā-na/
Union of Seven (hist, mujahedin
grp) n

اتحادیه /ī-tī-hā-dĭ-ya/
union (& labor), association,
alliance n

اتحادیه اروپا
/ī-tī-hā-dĭ-ya-yī ū-ru-pā/
European Union n

اتحادیه کارگاری
/ī-tī-hā-dĭ-ya-yī kār-gā-ri/
labor union n

اتحاف /ī-tī-hāf/
giving or sending a present n

اتحاف دعا /ī-tī-hāf-ĭ dŭ-'ā/
praying for the dead n

a = cup, ā = long, aw = now, ay = sigh, e = bet, ey = obey

اتخاذ /i-tī-khāz/ *n* taking, adopting
← اتخاذ موقف taking a position
← اتخاذ تصميم adopting a resolution
← اتخاذ تدبير adopting a plan
اتخاذ سند /i-tī-khāz-ī sa-nad/
documentation (documenting) *n*
اتریش /ŭt-rish/ *n* Austria
اتفاق , -ات/ها /i-tī-fāq/
accident, event, incident; unity; agreement *n*
اتفاق , -ات/ها /i-tī-fāq/
unity; agreement; accident *n*;
← اتفاق داشتن be united
اتفاق آرا /i-tī-fāq ā-rā/ unanimity *n*
اتفاقاً /i-tī-fā´-qan, -qán/
accidentally, incidentally *adv*
اتحاد /i-tī-hād/ *n* union; unity
اتحاد شوروی /i-tī-hād-ī sho-ra-wi/
Soviet Union (hist) *n*
اتغر /at-ghar/ *n* Atghar (dist)
اتکا کردن <به کسی/ چیزی>
/i-tī-kā kardan/
depend, be contingent; rely; lean <on sb/sth>; recline, lie down *v*
اتلانتیک /at-lān-tik/ *adj* Atlantic
اتمام /it-mām/ *n* completion
اتم /a-tom/ *n* atom
اتمی /a-to-mi/ *adj* atomic, nuclear
اتن /a-tan/
atan (Afgh national dance) *n*
← اتن کردن • اتن انداختن dance the atan *v*
اتوتک /ŭ-tu-tu-tak, wŭ-/ *n* hoopoe
اتنوگرافی /ĭt-no-gī-rā-fi/
ethnography *n*
اتنولوژست , -ان/ها /ĭt-no-lo-zhĭst/
ethnologist *n*
اتنولوژی /ĭt-no-lo-zhi/ ethnology *n*
اتو /ŭ-tu/ iron, flatiron *n*
← اتو کردن iron *v*
ایتوپیا /ī-to-pī-yā/ *n* see ایتوپیه
ایتوپیه /ā-to-pī-ya/ *n* see ایتوپیا
اتوماتیک /ŭ-to-mā-tik/
automatic *adj*
← اسلحۀ اتوماتیک automatic weapons

اتهام , -ات/ها /i-tī-hām/
accusation, charge *n*
اتهام کردن <کسی را به چیزی>
/i-tī-hām kardan/
accuse <sb of sth>, charge <sb w/sth> *vt*
اثر , -ات/ها/آثار /a-sar, pl ā-sār/
effect, result, impression; mark, sign; work (of art or literature) *n*
← در اثر <چیزی> as a result <of sth>
← آثار مکتوب written works
اثم /i´-sīm, ĭsm; pl ā-sām/ *n* sin;
← آثام pl
اثمار /as-mār, sg sa-mar/ *n* see ثمر sg
اثناعشر /is-nā-'a-shar/
twelve; duodenum *n*
اثناعشری , -ان/ها /is-nā-'a-sha-ri/
Twelver, Imami Shiite believing in the twelve imams *n*
← اسماعیلی Sevener
اجاره /ī-jā-ra/
lease (farmland), charter, hire *n*
← اجاره دادن lease, hire out
← اجاره کردن lease, hire
اجاره دار , -ان/ها /ī-jā-ra dār/
leaseholder, lessee *n*
اجاره ده /ī-jā-ra dīh/ lessor *n*
اجاره دهنده /ī-jā-ra dī-hĭn-da/
n see اجاره ده
اجازت /ī-jā-zat/ *n* see اجازه
اجازه /ī-jā-za/ permission *n*
← اجازه خواستن ask permission
اجازه نامه /ī-jā-za nā-ma/
license, permit *n*
اجاغ /ŭ-jāgh/ *n* see اجاق
اجاق /ŭ-jāq/
brazier (for cooking) *n*
اجاق برقی /ŭ-jāq-ī bar-qi/
hot plate (electric) *n*
اجبار /ij-bār/
compulsion, coercion *n*
اجباراً /ij-bā-ran, -bā´-/
compulsorily, forcibly *adv*

اجبارى /ij-bā-ri/
compulsory, forced *adj*
← تعلیمات اجبارى
compulsory education
← ازدواج های اجبارى
forced marriages

اجتماع , -ات/ها /ij-tī-mā/
assembly, gathering; community, society *n*
← اجتماع کردن
assemble, gather

اجتماعى /ij-tī-mā-yi/
social; outgoing, gregarious *adj*
← خدمات اجتماعى
social services

اجتماعى اقتصادى
/ij-tī-mā-yi īq-tī-sā-di/
socio-economic *adj*

اجتناب /ij-tī-nāb/ avoidance *n*
← اجتناب کردن avoid *v*

اجتناب پذیر /ij-tī-nāb pa-zir/
avoidable *adj*

اجتناب ناپذیر /ij-tī-nāb nā-pa-zir/
unavoidable, inevitable *adj*

اجتهاد , -ات/ها /ij-tī-hād/
legal inference from Quran & hadith by mujtahed (law) *n*

اجداد /aj-dād/
ancestors, forefathers [< Ar] *n pl*

اجدادى /aj-dā-di/ ancestral *adj*

اجرا , -ات /ij-rā/
act, deed; performance, execution, fulfillment *n*
← اجرا شدن be carried out *vi*
← ثبت ازدواج ها در کابل اجرا خواهد شد
marriage registrations will be carried out in Kabul
← اجرا کردن carry out (task) *vt*

اجرت /uj-rat/
wage, wages, pay; fee (to doctor) *n*

اجرستان /aj-rīs-tān/
Ajrestan (dist; ctr Sangar) *n*

اجزا , جزء /aj-zā; sg jūz', jūzw/
ingredients; see sg جزو *n pl*

اجساد /aj-sād, sg ja-sad/
see sg جسد *n pl*

اجسام /aj-sām, sg jīsm/
see sg جسم *n pl*

اجلاس /ij-lās/
session, meeting *n*
← اجلاس کردن convene

اجلاسیه /ij-lā-sī-ya/
session, meeting *n*
← دورة اجلاسیة پارلمان
period of parliament session

اجانب /a-jā-nīb, sg aj-na-bi/
see sg اجنبى *n pl*

اجماع /ij-mā/
consensus (by Musl scholars); gathering of Islamic scholars *n*

اجمال /ij-māl/
synopsis, summary, abstract *n*

اجناس /aj-nās/
merchandise, goods, wares *n*

اجنبى , -ان/ها/اجانب
/aj-na-bi, pl a-jā-nīb/
foreigner, outsider, stranger; (law) third party; (law) non-believer *n*

اجندا see آجنده *n* /a-jīn-dā/

اجنده agenda *n* /a-jīn-da/

اجوره /ŭ-ju-ra/
wage, wages, hire, pay *n*

اجوره کار laborer *n* /ŭ-ju-ra kār/

اجیر , -ان/ها /a-jir/
mercenary (& mil), contractor, hireling *n*
← عساکر اجیر
mercenary soldiers

اچکزى /a-chak-zai/
Achakzai (P tribe) *n*

اچین /a-chin, ā-/
Achin (dist, ctr Sarqala) *n*

احادیث /a-hā-dis, sg ha-dis/
see sg حدیث *n pl*

احاطه /ī-hā-ta/
surrounded; surrounding; understanding, comprehension *adj*

احباب /ah-bāb/
see sg حبیب , حب *n pl*

احتراز /īh-tī-rāz/
avoidance; wariness *n*
← احتراز کردن be wary *vi*

احتراق , -ات/ها /īh-tī-rāq/
burning, combustion; oxidation *n*

احتراق پذیر /ĭh-tĭ-rāq pa-zir/
combustible *adj*

احتراق ناپذیر /ĭh-tĭ-rāq nā-pa-zir/
incombustible *adj*

احترام , -ات/ها /ĭh-tĭ-rām/
respect, esteem *n*

← احترام داشتن <به کسی>
respect <sb>

احترام نظامی /ĭh-tĭ-rām-ĭ nĭ-zā-mi/
salute, military honor *n*

احتراماً /ĭh-tĭ-rā´-man, -mán/
respectfully *adv*

احتفال , -ات/ها /ĭh-tĭ-fāl/
assembly, gathering *n*

احتکار /ĭh-tĭ-kār/
hoarding (esp grain) *n*

← احتکار کردن
hoard *v*

احتکاری /ĭh-tĭ-kā-ri/ hoarded *adj*

احتکاک , -ات/ها /ĭh-tĭ-kāk/
rubbing, friction *n*

← احتکاک کردن
rub (& against) *v*

احتکاکی /ĭh-tĭ-kā-ki/ frictional *adj*

احتمال , -ات/ها /ĭh-tĭ-māl/
likelihood, probability; possibility *n*

احتمال داشتن که ...
/ĭh-tĭ-māl dāshtan key/
be likely that <+ subj> *vi*

احتمالاً /ĭh-tĭ-mā´-lan, -lán/
likely, probably; possibly *adv*

احتمالی /ĭh-tĭ-mā-li/
likely, probable; possible *adj*

احتوا /ĭh-tĭ-wā/
encompassing, containment *n*

← احتوا کردن
encompass, contain

احتیاج /ĭh-tĭ-yāj/ need (urgent) *n*

← احتیاج داشتن
need (urgently) *v*

احتیاط , -ها /ĭh-tĭ-yāt/
caution, care *n*

← احتیاط کردن
be cautious/careful

احتیاط کار /ĭh-tĭ-yāt kār/
cautious, careful *adj*

احتیاطاً /ĭh-tĭ-yā´-tan, -tán/
cautiously *adv*

احتیاطی /ĭh-ti-yā-ti/
precautionary; reserve *adj*

← اقدامات احتیاطی
precautionary actions

← عسکر احتیاطی
reserve soldier

احجار /ah-jār, sg ha-jar/
see sg حجر *n pl*

احجار کریمه /ah-jār-ĭ ka-ri-ma/
gems, precious stones *n pl*

احراز /ĭh-rāz/
attaining, obtaining; retaining,
holding *n*

احزاب /ah-zāb, sg hĭzb/
see sg حزب *n pl*

احزان /ah-zān; sg hŭ´-zĭn, hŭzn/
see sg حزن *n pl*

احساس , -ات/ها /ĭh-sās/
feeling; emotion; sensation *n*

← احساس داشتن • احساس کردن
feel (emotion, sensation)

احساساتی /ĭh-sā-sā-ti/
emotional, sentimental (& pers)
adj, n

احسان , -ها /ĭh-sān/
benevolence; good deed *n*

← احسان کردن
do good *v*

احسانمند /ĭh-sān-mand/
grateful *adj*

احصائیه /ih-sā-yĭ-a/
census; statistics *n*

احصائیوی /ih-sā-yĭ-a-wi/
statistical *adj*

احصایی /ih-sā-yi/
statistical; countable *adj*

احمد /ah-mad/ Ahmad (m name) *n*

احمد آباد /ah-mad ā-bād/
Ahmadabad (dist) *n*

احمد خیل /ah-mad kheyl/
Ahmad Kheyl (dist) *n*

احمد شاه ابدالی
/ah-mad shāh-ĭ ab-dā-li/
see احمد شاه درانی *n*

احمد شاه درانی
/ah-mad shāh-ĭ dŭ-rā-ni/
Ahmad Shah Durrani (hist, Afgh
leader, 1723-1773) *n*

---

i = k<u>ee</u>p, ĭ = b<u>i</u>g, u = c<u>oo</u>p, ŭ = p<u>u</u>t, y = <u>y</u>et, ' = (glottal stop)　　25

احمق , -ان/ها /ah-maq/
fool, idiot n; stupid adj

احمقانه /ah-ma-qā-na/
foolishly, stupidly adv

احمقی /ah-ma-qi/
foolishness, stupidity n

اجنحه /aj-nī-ha, sg jī-nāh/
see sg جناح n pl

احقاق حق /ah-qāq/ n احقاق حق see
احقاق حق /ah-qāq-ī haq/
adjudication, administering justice n

احقر [< Ar] adj /ah-qar/ humbler
← احقر العباد
humbler of servants
← احقر الانام
humblest of creatures

احکام /ah-kām; sg hŭ´-kŭm, hŭkm/
see sg حکم n pl

احکام نجوم /ah-kām-ī nŭ-jum/
astrology n pl

احمال /ah-māl; sg ha-mal, há-mīl/
see sg حَمَل , حَمل n pl

احمدزی /ah-mad-zay/
Ahmadzai (P tribe) n

احوال /ah-wāl, sg hāl/
see sg حال n pl

احول /ah-wal/ cross-eyed adj

احیا /īh-yā/
restoration (& artistic); revival,
reviving n
← احیا کردن restore, revive v

احیان /ah-yān, sg hin/
see sg حین n pl

احیانًا /ah-yā´-nan, -nán/
occasionally adv

احیای مجدد /īh-yā-yĭ mŭ-ja-dad/
rehabilitation (& of pers) n

اخ ! /ŭkh/
boo (for scaring children) excl

اخبار /akh-bār, sg kha-bar/
see sg خبر n pl

اخبار , -ها /akh-bār/
newspaper n

اخبار نویس , -ان/ها
/akh-bār na-wis/
news writer, editor n

اخباری /akh-bā-ri/ journalistic adj
← سبکِ اخباری journalistic style

اختر /akh-tar/
star; planet; omen; Akhtar (m/f
name) n

اختر شب گرد /akh-tar shab gard/
moon (fig) n

اختر شمار /akh-tar shŭ-mār/
astrological adj; astrologer n

اختر شماری /akh-tar shŭ-mā-ri/
astrology n

اختر شمر /akh-tar shŭ-mar/
see اختر شمار adj, n

اختر شناس /akh-tar shĭ-nās/
see اختر شمار

اختر شناسی /akh-tar shĭ-nā-si/
see اختر شماری n

اختصار , -ات/ها /īkh-tĭ-sār/
abbreviation; contraction,
shortened form (gram);
abridgement n

اختصار کردن /īkh-tĭ-sār kardan/
abbreviate; abridge vt

اختصارًا /īkh-tĭ-sā´-ran, -rán/
briefly, in short adv

اختصاری /īkh-tĭ-sā-ri/
abbreviated; summary adj
← نام اختصاری abbreviation

اختصاص , -ات/ها /īkh-tĭ-sās/
appropriation, allotment; giving,
conferring; specialty n
← اختصاص دادن allot, set aside

اختطاف , -ات/ها /īkh-tĭ-tāf/
kidnapping, abduction n
← اختطاف کردن kidnap, abduct v

اختلاس /īkh-tĭ-lās/
embezzlement n

اختلاف , -ات/ها /īkh-tĭ-lāf/
disagreement; difference,
disparity n

اختلاف داشتن /īkh-tĭ-lāf dāshtan/
be different vi

اختلاط , -ات/ها /īkh-tĭ-lāt/
associating with; friendly
conversation n

اختلاط و امتزاج
/īkh-tĭ-lāt ŭ īm-tĭ-zāj/
admixture n

اختلاطی /ĭkh-tĭ-lā-ti/
friendly, congenial, sociable adj

اختلال , -ات/ها /ĭkh-tĭ-lāl/
disorder, disturbance; insanity n

اختلال دماغ /ĭkh-tĭ-lāl-ĭ da-māgh/
insanity, mental disorder n

اختلال کردن /ĭkh-tĭ-lāl kardan/
disturb vt

اختناق /ĭkh-tĭ-nāq/
strangulation; (loosely) violence n

اخته /akh-ta/
marinated; castrated adj

اخته کردن /akh-ta kardan/
marinate; castrate vt

اختيار , -ات /ĭkh-tĭ-yār/
authority, power; choice, option n
confer authority v اختيار دادن ←
have authority v اختيار داشتن ←
اختيار فرمودن • اختيار کردن ←
opt, choose v

اختياری /ĭkh-tĭ-yā-ri/
optional, voluntary adj

اخذ /akhz/ taking, receiving n
take, receive vt اخذ کردن ←
take a bribe رشوه اخذ کردن ←

اخراج , -ات /ĭkh-rāj/
expulsion, ouster n
اخراج شدن ←
be expelled, be ousted vi

اخراجات /ĭkh-rā-jāt/
expenses, expenditures n pl

اخطار /ĭkh-tār/
warning, notice, admonishment n
اخطار دادن ‹به کسی› ←
warn, put <sb> on notice,
admonish <sb> v

اخطاریه /ĭkh-tā-rī-ya/
warning, notice (written) n;
containing a notice or warning adj
مکتوب اخطاریه ←
a warning letter

اخلاط /akh-lāt, sg khĭlt/
see sg خلط n pl

اخلاف /akh-lāf, sg kha-laf/
see sg خلف n pl

اخلاق /akh-lāq, sg khŭlq/
see sg خلق n pl

اخلاق /akh-lāq/
morals; virtues; ethics; manners n
pl

اخلاقاً /akh-lā´-qan, -qán/
morally, virtuously adv

اخلاقی /akh-lā-qi/
moral; related to virtue; ethical adj
فسادِ اخلاقی ←
moral corruption (esp sexual vice)
ethics n pl /akh-lā-qĭ-yāt/
اخلاقيات

اخلال کردن /ĭkh-lāl kardan/
interrupt, disturb; spoil, disrupt vt

اخلال گر , -ان/ها /ĭkh-lāl gar/
spoiler, one who disturbs the
order n

اخوان /ĭkh-wān/
brothers [< Ar]; see & اخوان
المسلمين n pl

اخوان المسلمين
/ĭkh-wān´-ŭl-mŭs-lĭm-ín/
Muslim Brotherhood (mvmt) n

ادا , -ها /a-dā/
completion, fulfillment; payment;
expression, utterance; grace,
coquetry; pronunciation n
اداى نماز ←
completion of (one's) prayers
complete, fulfill ادا کردن ←
اداى کلمه شهادت ←
fulfillment of a responsibility
payment of a loan اداى قرض ←
اداى عبارت ←
expression of a phrase
اداى زن زيبا ←
grace of a beautiful woman
به تخفيفِ ادا کردن ←
soften one's pronunciation

اداره , -ها/ادارات /ĭ-dā-ra, pl -rāt/
bureau, office; administration n
administer v اداره کردن ←

اداره انکشافى بين المللى امريکا
/ĭ-dā-ra-yĭ ĭn-kĭ-shā-fi-yĭ am-ri-kā/
USAID, U.S. Agency for
International Development n
administrative adj /ĭ-dā-ri/ ادارى

i = keep, ĭ = big, u = coop, ŭ = put, y = yet, ' = (glottal stop)   27

ادامه /ī-dā-ma/
continuation, prolonging *n*
← ادامه دادن continue, prolong *v*

ادب /a-dab, pl ā-dāb/
civility, politeness, urbanity;
learning *n*
← آداب pl

ادبا /ŭ-da-bā, sg a-dib/
see sg ادیب *n pl*

ادبیات /a-da-bī-yāt/
literature, belles lettres *n*

ادبیات شناسی
/a-da-bī-yāt shī-nā-si/
literary studies *n*

ادبیات شفاهی
/a-da-bī-yāt-ī sha-fā-hi/
folklore *n*

ادخال /īd-khāl/
entering, entrance *n*

ادرار urine *n* /īd-rār/

ادراک , ـات/ها /īd-rāk/
perception *n*

ادرسکن /ad-ras-kan/
Adraskan (dist) *n*

ادعا /ī-dī-'ā/
claim, assertion; demand,
arrogation *n*
← ادعا داشتن • ادعا کردن
claim, assert; demand, arrogate *v*

ادعیا /a-dī-ya, sg dŭ-'ā/
see sg دعا *n pl*

ادغام /īd-ghām/
coalescence, insertion *n*
← ادغام کردن
coalesce, insert *v*

ادله /a-dī-la, sg da-lil/
see sg دلیل *n pl*

ادمیرال admiral *n* /ad-mi-rāl/

ادوار /ad-wār, sg dawr/
see sg دور *n pl*

ادواری /ad-wā-ri/
periodic, recurrent, coming at
intervals *adj*

ادواری /ad-wā-ri/
recurrent, periodic, coming at
intervals *adj*
← مریض ادواری
recurrent illness
← جنون ادواری
intermittent psychosis

ادویه /ad-wī-ya, sg da-wā/
see sg دوا *n pl*

ادیب , ـان/ها/ادبا
/a-dib, pl ŭ-da-bā/
author; person/man of letters,
tutor *n*; polite; smart; learned *adj*

ادیس ابابا /a-di-sa-bā-bā/
Addis Ababa *n*

اذعان کردن /ī-zān kardan/
acknowledge, admit *vt*

اذکار /az-kār; sg zī´-kīr, zīkr/
see sg ذکر *n pl*

اذن permission *n* /ī´-zīn, īzn/
اذن دادن permit *v* /ī´-zīn dādan/

اذهان /az-hān; sg zī´-hīn, zīhn/
see sg ذهن *n pl*

اذیت pestering, teasing *n* /a-zī-yat/
← اذیت رساندن
pester, tease *v*

ارابه see & عرابه *n* /a-rā-ba/

ارابه جنگی /a-rā-ba-yī jan-gi/
chariot *n*

اراده /ī-rā-da/
intention, intent; will, volition *v*
← اراده داشتن intend *v*

اراضی /a-rā-zi/
lands, territories; estates *n pl*
← اراضی تحتِ زرع
lands under cultivation

اراضی اشغالی
/a-rā-zi-yī īsh-ghā-li/
Occupied Territories (Palestinian)
n pl

ارادتاً /ī-rā-dá-tan, -tán/
intentionally, on purpose *adv*

ارائه /ī-rā-'a/
presenting, displaying; (law)
submitting to legislature or judge
for consideration *n*
← ارائه دادن • ارائه کردن
present, display *v*

ارتقایی /ĭr-tĭ-qā-yi/
rising, ascendant adj

ارث /ĭrs/ inheritance n

ارثاً /ĭr-san/ by inheritance adv

ارثی /ĭr-si/ inherited, hereditary adj

ارثیه /ĭr-sĭ-ya/
inherited adj; inheritance n

ارجاع دو جانبه /ĭr-jā-yĭ du jā-nĭ-ba/
cross-reference n

ارجاع دو طرفه /ĭr-jā-yĭ du ta-ra-fa/
see ارجاع دو جانبه n

ارجح /ar-jah/ preferable (lit) adj

ارچق /ar-chĭq/ scab (colloq) n

ارچق گرفتن → scab (colloq) v

ارچه /ar-cha/ pine (tree, wood) n

ارچی /ar-chi/ Archi (dist) n

ارحام /ar-hām, sg ra-hīm/
see sg رحم n pl

اردن /ŭr-dŭn/ Jordan n

اردو /ŭr-du/
military; Urdu (lang) n

اردوی ملی افغانستان
/ŭr-du-yĭ mĭ-li-yĭ af-ghā-nĭs-tān/
ANA, Afghan National Army n

اردوگاه /ŭr-du-gāh/
military camp n

اردی بهشت /ŭr-di bĭ-hĭsht/
see ثور n

ارز /arz/
cost, price, value n

ارزاق /ar-zāq, sg rĭzq/
see sg رزق n pl

ارزان /ar-zān/
inexpensive, cheap adj

ارزش /ar-zĭsh/
value, worth; esteem, honor;
value n

ارزش دادن → honor, esteem v

ارزن /ar-zan/ millet (grain) n

ارزیابی /arz-yā-bi/
assessment, evaluation n

ارزیابی کردن →
assess, evaluate

ارزیدن ؛ -ارز- ؛ ارزید-
/ar-zi-dan/
cost, have a cost of v

ارزیز /ar-ziz/ tin (arch) n

اربکی /ar-ba-kay/
arbakai (shura enforcers, tribal
militia) n

ارتباط , -ات/ها ‹به
کسی/چیزی›
/ĭr-tĭ-bāt/
relation <to sb/sth>; connection,
communication n

ارتباط داشتن ‹به چیزی› →
depend <on sth> vi

ارتباط جمعی /ĭr-tĭ-bāt-ĭ ja-mi/
mass communication n

ارتباط عامه /ĭr-tĭ-bāt-ĭ ā-ma/
public relations n

ارتباطی /ĭr-tĭ-bā-ti/
communications adj

ارتجاع /ĭr-tĭ-jā/
reaction, returning to an earlier
form or order n

ارتجاع کردن →
bring about reaction (pol) v

ارتجاعی , -ها/ون /ĭr-tĭ-jā-yi/
reactionary n; elastic adj

ارتحال /ĭr-tĭ-hāl/
journey, travel (lit); death, passing
away (fig, only for Prophet) n

ارتحال کردن →
journey, travel (lit); die, pass away
(fig, only for Prophet) vi

ارتداد /ĭr-tĭ-dād/ apostasy n

ارتش /ar-tīsh/ the military [< F] n

ارتشا /ĭr-tĭ-shā/
bribery; soliciting, taking or paying
a bribe n

راشی → one who bribes
مرتشی → bribe-taker

ارتعاش , -ات/ها /ĭr-tĭ-'āsh/
trembling, vibration n

ارتعاش داشتن → tremble, vibrate

ارتفاع , -ات/ها /ĭr-tĭ-fā/
altitude, elevation n

ارتقا /ĭr-tĭ-qā/
promotion; enhancement;
increase; rise, ascent n

ارتقا دادن →
promote, enhance; increase; raise
vt

---

i = keep, ĭ = big, u = coop, ŭ = put, y = yet, ' = (glottal stop)   29

ارسال /īr-sāl/
sending, remittance n

ارسطو /a-ras-tu/ Aristotle (hist) n

ارسلان /ar-sa-lān/
brave man (fig), lion n

ار سسنیک /ar-sa-nik/ arsenic n

ارشاد , -ات /īr-shād/
instruction, direction(s) n

ارشد /ar-shad/
senior; elder [< Ar] adj

مشاور ارشد ←— senior advisor

ارشدیت /ar-sha-dī-yat/
seniority; eldership n

ارشدیت داشتن v have seniority ←—

ارشمیدس /arsh-mey-dīs/
Archimedes (hist) n

ارض /arz, pl a-rā-zi/
Earth (planet), land n

اضاع /īr-zā/ wet-nursing n

ارضی /ar-zi/ territorial adj

تمامیتِ ارضی ←— territorial integrity

ارغستان /ar-ghīs-tān/
Arghestan (dist) n

ارغنج خواه /ar-ghanj-khwā/
Arghanj Khwa (dist) n

ارغند /ar-ghand/ angry, furious adj

ارغنداب /ar-ghan-dāb/
Arghandab (dist, river) n

ارغوان /ar-gha-wān/
Judas tree, redbud n

ارغوانی /ar-gha-wā-ni/
red, rosy purple adj

ارقام /ar-qām, sg ra-qam/
see sg رقم n pl

ارکان /ar-kān; sg rŭ´-kŭn, rŭkn/
staff; see & sg رکن n

ارکان حرب /ar-kān-ī harb/
general staff (mil) n

ارگ /arg/
fortress; Arg, Presidential Palace
complex (Kabul) n

ارگنج /ŭr-ganj/ Urgench (town) n

ارگو /ar-go/ Argo (dist) n

ارگون /ŭr-gun/ Urgun (dist) n

آرمان /ar-mān/ see آرمان n

ارمغان /ar-ma-ghān/
gift, souvenir n

ارمنستان /ar-mĭ-nīs-tān/ Armenia n

ارند /a-rand/ castor bean n

ارواح /ar-wāh, sg ruh/
روح sg see n pl

اروپا /ŭ-ru-pā/ Europe n

اروپایی , -ان/ها /ŭ-ru-pā-yi/
European n, adj

اوزرگان /ŭ-roz-gān/ n اورزگان see

اروس /ŭ-rus/ n روس see

اروسی /ŭ-ru-si/ adj, n روسی see

اروغ /ŭ-rugh/
belching; burping [< F] n

اروغ زدن ←— belch; burp v

اره /a-ra/ saw (tool) n

اره کردن ←— saw v

اره کش /a-ra kash/ sawyer n

اریب /ŭ-reyb/
crooked; diagonal adj

از /az/ from; to prep

از ... به این طرف
/az ... ba in ta-raf/
since (a given time) adv

از اختلاف /az īkh-tĭ-lāf/
variously adv

از آن جهت /az ān ja-hat/
therefore, hence adv

از آن سبب /az ān sa-bab/
therefore, thus conj

از این نگاه /az in nĭ-gāh/
from this view phrs

از بحث خارج /az bahs khā-rĭj/
irrelevant adj

از بهر <چیزی> /az bá-hīr(-ī)/
for; because of <sth> phrs

از بین /az bayn(-ī)/
from in between; from inside prep

از بین بردن /az bayn bŭrdan/
kill; overthrow (govt) (colloq) vt

از بین رفتن /az bayn raftan/
die, be killed v

از پای افتادن /az pāy aftādan/
fall, tire vi

از پای در آوردن
/az pāy dár āwŭrdan/
kill; defeat vt

از پهلوی /az pah-lu(-yī)/ by prep

از شمار بیرون
/az shŭ-mār bey-run/
innumerable adj

از طرف /az ta-raf(-ī)/
on behalf of prep

از طریق /az ta-riq(-ī)/
via, by way of adv

از قبیل /az qa-bil(-ī)/
such as, for example adv

از قرار ذیل /az qa-rār-ī zayl/
as follows adv

از کار افتاده /az kār af-tā-da/
out of order phrs

از مابین /az mā-bayn(-ī)/
among; between; inside, within
prep

از مسؤلیت شانه خالی کردن
/az mas-'u-lī-yat shā-na khā-li
kardan/
shirk a responsibility v

از میان /az mī-yān(ī)/
from within prep

از میان بردن /az mī-yān bŭrdan/
destroy, annihilate, exterminate vi

از میان برداشتن
/az mī-yān dāshtan/
see از میان بردن vi

از نظر افتادن /az na-zar aftādan/
see از چشم افتادن vi

ازار /ī-zār/
pajamas; izar (f garment) n

ازاربند /ī-zār-band/
pajama drawcord n

ازاله /ī-zā-la/ removal n
ازاله بکارت /ī-zā-la-yī ba-kā-rat/
defloration n

ازبک , -ان/ها /ūz-bak/
see اوزبک n

ازبکی /ūz-ba-ki/ see اوزبکی adj
ازدحام /īz-dī-hām/
crowd, mob, throng n

ازدواج , -ها /īz-dī-wāj/
marriage; wedding n
ازدواج اجباری /īz-dī-wāj-ī īj-bā-ri/
forced marriage n

ازدیاد /īz-dī-yād/
accretion, increase, increment n

از تمام جوانب
/az ta-mām-ī ja-wā-nīb/
from every side phrs

از جان گذشتگی
/az jān gŭ-zash-ta-gi/
devotion; self-sacrifice n

از جهان رفتن /az ja-hān raftan/
die, pass away vi

از جهان گذشتن
/az ja-hān gŭzashtan/
see از جهان رفتن vi

از چشم افتادن
/az chá-shīm aftādan/
fall out of favor vi

از حال رفتن /az hāl raftan/
faint, lose consciousness vi

از حصر بیرون
/az há-sīr bey-run/
see از شمار بیرون adj

از خاطریکه /az khā-tī-rī-kī, -key/
because conj

از خلال /az khī-lāl(-ī)/
across, through prep

از خود رفتن /az khŭd raftan/
become unconscious v

از خود گذری /az khŭd gŭ-za-ri/
see از جان گذشتگی n

از دست دادن /az dast dādan/
lose vt; be improbable vi

از دست رفتن /az dast raftan/
be lost vi

از راه /az rāh(-ī)/
through, by way of prep

از راه بحر /az rāh(-ī) ba-har/
by sea adv

از ره /az rah(-ī)/ see از راه prep
از ریشه کشیدن
/az ri-sha kashidan/
eradicate, get rid of vt

از سر /az sar/
again, re- (as prefix) adv

از سر آباد کردن
/az sar ā-bād kardan/
reconstruct, rebuild vt

از سوی <کسی>
/az soy(-ī), az suy(-ī)/
by, by means of prep

i = keep, ĭ = big, u = coop, ŭ = put, y = yet, ' = (glottal stop)   31

ازرق /az-raq/
blue, azure; blind *adj*; (fig) the world *n*

ازره Azra (dist) *n* /az-ra/
ازل eternity *n* /a-zal/
ازلی eternal *adj* /a-za-li/
ازواج /az-wāj/
couple (married) *n pl*

ازیموت azimuth *n* /a-zi-mut/
اژدر see اژدهار *n* /azh-dār/
اژدر dragon *n* /azh-dar/
اس basis [< Ar] *n* /ŭs/
اس اساس /ŭs-ī a-sās/
element, basic element *n*

اسارت /a-sā-rat/
captivity; captivation *n*

اساس /a-sās/
principle; foundation *n*

اساساً /a-sā´-san, -sán/
essentially, basically *adv*

اساسی /a-sā-si/
basic, fundamental *adj*

اساطیر /a-sā-tir, sg ŭs-tu-ra/
mythology; see & sg اسطوره *n pl*

اساطیری /a-sā-ti-ri/
mythological, legendary *adj*

اسالیب /a-sā-lib, sg ŭs-lub/
see sg اسلوب *n pl*

اسباب /as-bāb, sg sa-bab/
see sg سبب *n pl*

اسباق /as-bāq, sg sa-baq/
see sg سبق *n pl*

اسبق former, previous *adj* /as-baq/
اسپ horse; (chess) knight *n* /asp/
اسپانیا Spain *n* /as-pā-nī-yā, īs-/
اسپانیایی , -ان/ها /as-pā-nī-yā-yi, īs-/
Spanish (& pers) *adj, n*

اسپ دوانی /asp da-wā-ni/
horse racing *n*

اسپرغم /īs-par-gham/
n شاه اسپرغم see

اسپرم /īs-pa-ram/ *n*
see اسپرغم *n*

اسپرنگ coil, spring *n* /īs-pī-rīng/
اسپرهم /īs-par-ham/ *n* اسپرغم see
اسپغول /īs-pa-ghol/
fleawort (colloq) (plant) *n*

اسپند wild rue *n* /īs-pand/

استاد ایستاد *adj* /īs-tād/ see
استاد , -ان/ها /ŭs-tād (-tā, us-tā)/
professor *n*

استاده ایستاده *adj* /īs-tā-da/ see
استالف /īs-tā-līf/
Istalif (dist, village) *n*

استثنا , -ات/ها /īs-tīs-nā/
exception *n*

استحکام , -ات /īs-tīh-kām/
fortification; firmness *n*

استخبارات /īs-tīkh-bā-rat/
information; (mil) espionage *n*

استخدام /īs-tīkh-dām/
hiring, recruitment *n*

استخدام کردن ←
hire, recruit, employ *vt*

استخوان /ŭs-tŭ-khān (-ghān)/
bone *n*

استخوان بندی /ŭs-tŭ-khān ban-di/
skeleton *n*

استخوان شانه /ŭs-tŭ-khān-ī shā-na/
shoulder blade, scapula (anat) *n*

استخوان کتف /ŭs-tŭ-khān-ī katf/
shoulder blade, scapula (anat) *n*

استخوانی /ŭs-tŭ-khā-ni/
bony *adj*

استدلال , -ات/ها /īs-tīd-lāl/
argumentation, reasoning; deduction *n*

استراتژی strategy *n* /īs-tī-rā-tī-zhi/
استراتژیکی /īs-tī-rā-tī-zhi-ki/
strategic *adj*

استراحت relax, rest *n* /īs-tī-rā-hat/
استراحت کردن ← relax, rest *v*

استراق سمع /īs-tī-rāq-ī sam/
eavesdropping *n*

استراق سمع کردن ←
eavesdrop *v*

استرالیا Australia *n* /as-ta-rā-li-yā/
استرالیایی /as-ta-rā-li-yā-yi/
Australian (& pers) *adj, n*

استرالیه /as-ta-rā-li-ya/
see استرالیا *n*

استریا /as-tar-yā/ *n* آستریا see
استسقا /īs-tīs-qā/
dropsy; praying for rain *n*

استشاره , -ات/ها /īs-tī-shā-ra/
consultation *n*

استشاره کردن /ĭs-tĭ-shā-ra kardan/
consult v

استشهاد , -ات/ها /ĭs-tĭsh-hād/
discovery (law) n

استعاره , -ات/ها
/ĭs-tĭ-'ā-ra, pl -rāt/
allegory, metaphor (lit) n

استعجاب , -ات/ها /ĭs-tey-jāb/
admiration, amazement n

استعجابه /ĭs-tey-jā-ba/
see استعجاب n

استعداد /ĭs-tey-dād/
talent, aptitude n

استعداد داشتن be talented v

استعفا /ĭs-tey-fā/ ها-, _
resignation n

استعفا دادن resign v

استعلام , -ات/ها /ĭs-tey-lām/
enquiry, inquiry (official) n

استعلام کردن
enquire (officially) v

استعمار /ĭs-tĭ-mār/
colonialism, imperialism n

استعمار کردن colonize v

استعمار گر, -ان/ها /ĭs-tĭ-mār gar/
colonialist, imperialist n

استعماری /ĭs-tĭ-mā-ri/
imperialistic adj

استعمال /ĭs-tĭ-māl/
utilization, application n

استعمال کردن utilize, apply vt

استفاده <از چیزی> /ĭs-tĭ-fā-da/
use, exploitation <of sth>, profiting
<from sth> n

استفاده کردن <از چیزی>
use, exploit <sth> vt

استفراغ /ĭs-tĭf-rāgh/
seeking relief (lit) n

استفراغ کردن throw up, vomit v

استفراق /ĭs-tĭf-rāq/
seeking relief (colloq) n

استقبال /ĭs-tĭq-bāl/
reception (of visitor) n

استقبال کردن receive (visitor) v

استقرار /ĭs-tĭq-rār/
settling, establishing n

استقلال /ĭs-tĭq-lāl/ independence n

استقلال فکر /ĭs-tĭq-lāl-ĭ fĭ´-kĭr/
self-reliance n

استمنا /ĭs-tĭm-nā/ masturbation n
استمنا کردن masturbate

استنباط , -ات/ها /ĭs-tĭn-bāt/
inference; extraction n

استنباط کردن infer; extract

استوا /ĭs-tĭ-wā, ŭs-tŭ-/
equality; moderation n

خطِ استوا equator n

استوار /ŭs-tŭ-wār/
firm, strong, solid adj

استواری /ŭs-tŭ-wā-ri/
solidity, strength n

استیناف /ĭs-ti-nāf/
appeal (law); restarting n

استینافی /ĭs-ti-nā-fi/
appellate (court) adj

اسد /a-sad/
Asad (month); Leo; lion n
مرداد (Farsi equivalent)

اسرا /ŭ-sa-rā, sg a-sir/
see اسیر n pl sg

اسرائیل /ĭs-rā-yil/ Israel n
اسرائیلی , -ان/ها /ĭs-rā-yi-li/
Israeli (& pers) adj, n

اسرار /as-rār, sg sĭr/
see سر n pl sg

اسرافیل /ĭs-rā-fil/
seraph; seraphim n

اسراییل /ĭs-rā-yil/ Israel n
اسراییلی , -ان/ها /ĭs-rā-yi-li/
Israeli; Israelite (& pers) adj, n

اسطرلاب /ĭs-tĭr-lāb/ astrolabe n
اسطوانه /ŭs-tu-wā-na/ cylinder n
اسطوره , -ها/اساطیر
/ŭs-tu-ra, pl a-sā-tir/
legend; myth n

اسعار /as-'ār/ currency n pl
اسعار خارجی /as-'ār-ĭ khā-rĭ-ji/
foreign exchange n pl

اسعد آباد /as-'a-dā-bad/
Asadabad (seat) n

اسفار /as-fār, sg sa-far/
see سفر n pl sg

اسفالت, -/ /ĭs-fālt, as-/
asphalt, macadam n

اسفرزه /ĭs-far-za/ fleawort (plant) n
اسفناج /ĭs-fī-nāj/ spinach n
اسفنج /ĭs-fanj/ sponge n

i = keep, ĭ = big, u = coop, ŭ = put, y = yet, ' = (glottal stop)   33

اسفنجی /is-fan-ji/ spongy adj
اسفند /is-fand/ see Hut (month) n
اسقاط /is-qāt/
giving alms before burial of dead;
dropping n

اسقف /ŭs-qŭf/ bishop; diocese n
اسقف اعظم /ŭs-qŭf-ĭ a-zam/
archbishop n

اسکار /as-kār/ Oscar (award) n
اسکان /is-kān/ colony, settlement n
اسکان مجدد /is-kān-ĭ mŭ-ja-dad/
resettlement (of migrants) n

اسکلیت /is-kĭ-leyt/ skeleton n
اسکندر /is-kan-dar/
Alexander (the Great, hist); (m
name) n

اسکندری /is-kan-da-ri/
Alexandrine (hist) adj
اسکندریه /is-kan-da-rī-ya/
Alexandria n

اسکنه /is-ka-na/ chisel n
اسکورنچ /is-kŭ-rīnch/
wrench (tool) n

اسلاف /as-lāf, sg sa-laf/
see sg سلف n pl

اسلام /is-lām/
Islam; all Muslim countries;
submission to God n

اسلام آباد /is-lā-mā-bād/
Islamabad n

اسلام قلعه /is-lām qal-'a/
Islam Qala (border crossing) n

اسلحه /as-la-ha, sg sa-lāh/
see sg سلاح n pl

اسلحه /as-la-ha (was-la), sg sa-lāh/
weaponry, weapons n pl
→ سلاح sg

اسلحه خفیفه /as-la-ha-yĭ kha-fi-fa/
light weapons n pl

اسلحه ناریه /as-la-ha-yĭ nār-ya/
firearms n pl

اسلحه هسته وی
/as-la-ha-yĭ has-ta-wi/
nuclear weapons n pl

اسلوب , -ها/اسالیب
/ŭs-lub, pl a-sā-lib/
method, way n

اسم , -ها/اسما
/i'-sĭm, ĭsm; pl as-mā/
noun n

اسم جمع /i'-sĭm-ĭ jam/
collective noun n

اسم خاص /i'-sĭm-ĭ khās/
proper noun n

اسم ذات /i'-sĭm-ĭ zāt/
concrete noun n

اسم مستعار /i'-sĭm-ĭ mŭs-ta'-ār/
pen name, pseudonym n

اسم معنی /i'-sĭm-ĭ ma'-nā/
abstract noun n

اسم مفعولی /i'-sĭm-ĭ maf'u-li/
participle, verbal noun n

اسم و رسم /i'-sĭm ŭ rá-sĭm/
reputation, fame n

اسما /as-mā; sg ĭ'-sĭm, ĭsm/
see sg اسم n pl

اسماً /is'-man, -mán/
nominally adv

اسماعیل /is-mā-yil/ Ismael (bibl) n
اسماعیلی , -ان/ها /is-mā-yi-li/
Sevener n; Ismaili Shiite n, adj

اسماعیلیه /is-mā-yi-lī-ya/
Ismaili Shiites (collectively) n

اسمر /as-mar/
tawny, wheat-colored adj

اسمی /is-mi/ nominal adj
اسمیه /is-mi-ya/
noun, noun phrase n; nominal adj

اسناد /as-nād, sg sa-nad/
see sg سند n pl

اسنان /as-nān, sg sĭn/
see sg سن n pl

اسود /as-wad/ black [< Ar] adj
اسهال /is-hāl/ diarrhea n
اسهال خونی /is-hāl-ĭ khu-ni/
dysentery n

اسهالی /is-hā-li/ diarrheal adj
اسیب /a-seyb/ see أسیب n
اسیر , -ان/ها/اسرا
/a-sir, pl ŭ-sa-rā/
captive, prisoner of war n

اسیری /a-si-ri/
captivity, confinement n

a = cup, ā = long, aw = now, ay = sigh, e = bet, ey = obey

اش , ش- /ash (īsh)/
(ending, 3rd pers sg possessive);
(ending, 3rd pers sg object) [ش-
after consonant]; (ending, forms
noun from verb root) [written ش-]
suff

اشارات ترافیکی
/ī-shā-rāt-ī ta-rā-fi-ki/
traffic signal *n pl*

اشاره , ها-/اشارات
/ī-shā-ra, pl ī-shā-rāt/
pointing with hand/finger; allusion,
gesture *n*

اشاره آبرو /ī-shā-ra-yī ā-bru/
raising of eyebrows *n*

اشاره چشم /ī-shā-ra-yī chī´-shīm/
winking (meaningfully) *n*

اشتباه , ات/ها- /īsh-tī-bāh/
error, mistake *n*

اشتباه کردن /īsh-tī-bāh kardan/
make a mistake *v*

اشتباهاً /īsh-tī-bā´-han, -hán/
by mistake *adv*

اشتباهی /īsh-tī-bā-hi/
erroneous, mistaken *adj*

اشتبنی /īsh-tab-ni/
spare, substitute *adj*

اشتراک /īsh-tī-rāk/
participation; subscription *n*

اشتراک کردن <در چیزی> ←
participate <in sth>; subscribe <to
sth> *v*

اشتراک مساعی
/īsh-tī-rāk-ī ma-sā-'i/
cooperation *n*

اشتراکاً /īsh-tī-rā´-kan/
cooperatively, jointly *adv*

اشترلی /īsh-tar-lay/
Eshtarlay (dist) *n*

اشتق /ash-taq/
dried apricot; (vulg) f genitalia *n*

اشتقاق , ات/ها- /īsh-tī-qāq/
derivation (gram) *n*

اشتقاقی /īsh-tī-qā-qi/ derivative *adj*
اشتک , ها- /ūsh-tŭk/
kid, child (colloq) *n*

اشتکانه /ūsh-tŭ-kā-na/
children's; childish *adj*; childishly
adv

اشتک بازی , ها- /ūsh-tŭk bā-zi/
child's play; kid stuff; *n*

اشتکک , ها- /ūsh-tū-kak/
kid, child (colloq, dim) *n*

اشتکی /ūsh-tŭ-ki/
childhood (colloq) *n*

اشتها /īsh-tĭ-hā (īsh-tĭ-yā)/
appetite, craving *n*

اشتها آور /īsh-tĭ-hā ā-war/
appetizing *adj*

اشتهای خوب ! /īsh-tĭ-hā-yī khub/
bon appetit *excl*

اشتها تیز کردن
/īsh-tĭ-hā teyz kardan/
whet the appetite *v*

اشجار /ash-jār, sg sha-jar/
see sg شجر *n pl*

اشخاص
/ash-khās; sg shakhs, shakh-sī-
yat/
see sg شخص , شخصیت *n pl*

اشربه /ash-rī-ba/
beverages, drinks *n pl*

اشرف /ash-raf/ nobler *adj*
→ Party of the Nobility (hist)
حزبِ اشرف

اشعار /a-shār, sg shīr/
see sg شعر *n pl*

اشعری /ash-'ā-ri/
Ashari (rel, traditionalist school of
Musl theology) *n*

اشعه /ash-'a, sg shŭ-'ā/
see sg شعاع *n pl*

اشغال /īsh-ghāl/
occupation (of country) *n*

اشغالی /īsh-ghā-li/
occupied, related to occupation
(of country) *adj*

اشک /ashk/
drop; tear, teardrop *n*
اشک ریختاندن ← shed tears *v*
اشک تمساح /ashk-ī tĭm-sāh/
crocodile tear *n*

اشکاشم /īsh-kā-shĭm/
Eshkashem (dist) *n*

---

i = k<u>ee</u>p, ĭ = b<u>i</u>g, u = c<u>oo</u>p, ŭ = p<u>u</u>t, y = <u>y</u>et, ' = (glottal stop)   35

اشکاشمی , -ان/ها /ĭsh-kā-shĭ-mi/
Eshkashemi (pers, lang) *n*
اشکال /ash-kāl; sg shá-kĭl, shakl/
see sg شکل *n pl*
اشکمش /ĭsh-ka-mĭsh/
Eshkamesh (dist) *n*
اشیا /ash-yā, sg shay/
see sg شی *n pl*
اصابت /ĭ-sā-bat/
precision, hitting the mark *n*
اصالت authenticity *n* /a-sā-lat/
اصالتاً /a-sā´-la-tan/
personally, on sb's behalf *adv*
اصحاب /as-hāb/
associates, companions (of Prophet); cf. تابع *n pl*
اصحاب کهف /as-hāb-ĭ ká-hĭf/
the Seven Sleepers (lit) *n*
اصرار /ĭs-rār/
insistence, persistence *n*
← اصرار داشتن • اصرار کردن
•insist; persist *v* اصرار ورزیدن
اصطکاک , -ات/ها /ĭs-tĭ-kāk/
rubbing, friction *n*
frictional *adj* /ĭs-tĭ-kā-ki/ اصطکاکی
اصطلاح , -ات/ها /ĭs-tĭ-lāh/
idiom; term *n*
مصطلحات /ĭs-tĭ-lā-hāt/
idioms; terminology *n pl*
اصطلاحی /ĭs-tĭ-lā-hi/
colloquial; idiomatic *adj*
اصفهان /ĭs-fa-hān/
Isfahan, Esfahan (city) *n*
← اصفهان نصفِ جهان
Isfahan is half the world (saying)
اصل , -ها/اصول
/á-sĭl, asl; pl ŭ-sul/
principle; original copy *n*; noble *adj*
اصلاً /ás-lan, -lán/
in principle; at first; primarily *adv*
اصلاح , -ات /ĭs-lāh/
reform, correction *n*
اصلاح پذیر /ĭs-lāh pa-zir/
reformable *adj*
اصلاح ریش /ĭs-lāh-ĭ reysh/
beard trim *n*
haircut *n* /ĭs-lāh-ĭ sar/ اصلاح سر

اصلاح سازی رتبه
/ĭs-lāh sā-zi-yĭ rŭt-ba/
rank reform *n*
اصلاح معاشات
/ĭs-lāh-ĭ ma-'ā-shāt/
pay reform *n*
اصلاح ناپذیر /ĭs-lāh nā-pa-zir/
unreformable *adj*
اصلاح طلب , -ان/ها /ĭs-lāh-ta-lab/
reformer (pers) *n*
اصلاح طلبی /ĭs-lāh-ta-la-bi/
reformism *n*
اصلی /as-li/
common, mutual; original; key *adj*
اصم /a-sam/
deaf; (math) irrational *adj*
اصناف /as-nāf, sg sĭnf/
see sg صنف *n pl*
اصوات /as-wāt, sg sawt/
see sg صوت *n pl*
اصول /ŭ-sul; sg á-sĭl, asl/
see sg اصل *n pl*
اصولاً /ŭ-sú-lan, -lán/
in principle, by rights *adv*
اصولی , -ون/ین /ŭ-su-li/
fundamental; per rules *adj*; fundamentalist *n*
اصیل /a-sil/
authentic, genuine; of noble family/stock *adj*
اصیل زاده , -ها/گان /a-sil zā-da/
noble (& pers) *adj*, *n*
اضافه addition *n* /ĭ-zā-fa/
add, do addition *v* ← اضافه کردن
اضافه کاری /ĭ-zā-fa kā-ri/
overtime (work) *n*
← اضافه کاری کردن
work overtime *v*
اضافی additional *adj* /ĭ-zā-fi/
اضطرار /ĭz-tĭ-rār/
emergency, distress *n*
اضطراراً /ĭz-tĭ-rā´-ran, -rán/
under constraint *adv*

اضطراری /iz-ṭī-rā-ri/
related to an emergency *adj*
← دستورات لازم در مواقع اضطراری
safety instructions *n pl*

اضداد /az-dād, sg zīd/
see sg ضد *n pl*

اضلاع /az-lā; sg zŭ´-la, zŭl'/
see sg ضلع *n pl*

اضمحلال /iz-mīh-lāl/
disappearing; downfall *n*
← اضمحلال یافتن
disappear, vanish *vi*

اطاعت /ī-tā-'at/
obedience (to orders); doctrine *n*
← اطاعت کردن
obey, follow (orders)

اطاعت علو الآمر
/ī-tā'at-ī ŭ-lu al-ā´-mīr/
doctrine of obedience to pol
authority *n*

اتاق /ŭ-tāq/ *n* see اطاق

اطراف /at-rāf, sg ta-raf/
see sg طرف *n pl*

اطعمه /at-'ī-ma, sg ta-'ām/
see sg طعام *n pl*

اطفال /at-fāl; sg ṭī´-fīl, ṭīfl/
see sg طفل *n pl*

اطفال و بزرگ سالان
/at-fāl ŭ bŭ-zŭrg sā-lān/
children & adults *n*

اطفاییه /it-fā-yīa/
firefighting; fire station *n*

اطلاع , ات/ها /it-lā/
information, intelligence;
notification *n*
← اطلاع دادن
inform, notify *vt*
← اطلاع داشتن
have info, be on notice *v*
← اطلاع گرفتن
gather intelligence *v*

اطلاعیه /it-lā-yīa/
notification, notice *n*

اطلاق /it-lāq/
use, application *n*
اطلاق کردن /it-lāq kardan/
use, apply *vt*

اطلس /at-las/ *n* satin
اطلسی /at-la-si/ made of satin *adj*

اطمینان /it-mi-nān/
assurance; confidence *n*
← اطمینان دادن *v* reassure

اطناب /it-nāb/
wordiness, lengthiness *n*

اتو /ŭ-tu/ see اطو
اطوار /at-wār, sg tawr/
see sg طور *n pl*

اظهار , ات /īz-hār/ *n* statement
← اظهار داشتن • اظهار کردن
issue a statement *v*

اظهار نامه /īz-hār nā-ma/
customs declaration; tax return *n*

اعاشه /ī-'ā-sha/
provisioning; subsistence *n*

اعاشه و اباته /ī-'ā-sha wŭ ī-bā-ta/
room & board *n*

اعانت /ī-'ā-nat/ assistance, help *n*
← اعانت کردن *v* assist, help

اعانه /ī-'ā-na/
contribution, donation *n*

اعتبار , ات/ها /ey-tī-bār/
credit, credibility; trust *n*

اعتبار نامه /ey-tī-bār nā-ma/
letter of credit *n*

اعتدال /ey-tī-dāl/
moderation; equinox *n*

اعتدالی /ey-tī-dā-li/
moderate (weather) *adj*

اعتراض , ات/ها /ey-tī-rāz/
protest, objection *n*
اعتراض کردن <به ضد چیزی>
/ey-tī-rāz kardan/
protest <against sth> *vi*

اعتصاب , ات/ها /ey-tī-sāb/
strike, walkout *n*
← اعتصاب کردن
strike, go on strike (labor) *v*

اعتصاب عام /ey-tī-sāb-ī ām/
general strike *n*

اعتصابی , ون /ey-tī-sā-bi/
striker; related to labor strike *n*

اعتقاد /ey-tī-qād/
faith, belief, creed, tenet *n*

اعتلاف /ey-tī-lāf/ *n* see انتلاف

i = k<u>ee</u>p, ĭ = b<u>i</u>g, u = c<u>oo</u>p, ŭ = p<u>u</u>t, y = <u>y</u>et, ' = (glottal stop)   37

/ey-tĭ-mād/ ‏اعتماد <سر کسی>‏
trust, confidence <in sb> n
‏اعتماد داشتن ←‏
be trusted, relied upon v
‏اعتماد کردن ←‏ trust, rely on vt
‏اعتماد به نفس‏ /ey-tĭ-mād ba nafs/
self-confidence n
/ey-tĭ-mā-di/ ‏اعتمادی‏
certain, sure; confident, trusting adj
‏اعتیاد , -ات/ها‏ /ey-tĭ-yād/
addiction n
‏اعتیاد داشتن ←‏ be addicted v
‏اعدا‏ /a-dā, sg a-du/
see sg ‏عدو‏ n pl
‏اعدام , -ها‏ /ey-dām/ execution n
‏اعدام کردن ←‏
execute, put to death vt
/a'-rāb/ ‏اعراب‏ see sg ‏عرب‏ n pl
/a'-rā-bi, pl a'-rāb/ ‏اعرابی‏
Arab, Bedouin n
‏اعراب ←‏ pl
‏اعراض‏ /a'-rāz, sg a-raz/
see sg ‏عرض‏ n pl
/ey-zām/ ‏اعزام‏
deployment; dispatch n
‏اعزام کردن‏ /ey-zām kardan/
deploy; dispatch vt
‏اعشار‏ /a'-shār; sg ŭ´-shŭr, ŭshr/
see sg ‏عشر‏ n pl
‏اعشاریه‏ /a'-shā-rī-ya/
point, decimal point n
‏اعصاب‏ /a'-sāb, sg a-sab/
see sg ‏عصب‏ n pl
‏اعضا‏ /a'-zā; sg ŭ´-zwa, ŭzw/
see sg ‏عضو‏ n pl
‏اعطا کردن‏ /ey-tā kardan/
bestow, confer, give vt
see sg ‏علم‏ n pl /a'-lām/ ‏اعلام‏
‏اعلام , -ات/ها‏ /ey-lām/
declaration, proclamation n
‏اعلام کردن ←‏ declare, proclaim v
‏اعلامیه‏ see ‏اعلام‏ /ey-lā-mī-ya/
‏اعلامیه آزادی امریکا‏
/ey-lā-mī-ya-yĭ ā-zā-di-yĭ am-ri-kā/
Declaration of Independence (U.S.) n

‏اعلان , -ات/ها‏ /ey-lān/
advertisement; announcement n
‏اعلان کردن ←‏
advertise; announce v
‏اعلی‏ /a'-lā/ superior; higher adj
‏اعلی حضرت‏ /a'-lā haz-rat/
His Majesty (royal title) n
/a-'am/ ‏اعم‏
generally, in general adv; more common adj
/ey-mār/ ‏اعمار‏
building, construction n
‏اعمار کردن ←‏ build, construct vt
‏اعمال‏ /a'-māl, sg a-mal/
see sg ‏عمل‏ n pl
/ey-māl/ ‏اعمال‏
use, exercise, exertion n
‏اعمال خیر‏ /ey-māl-ī khayr/
charity, good works n
‏اعمال زور‏ /ey-māl-ī zor/
‏اعمال قوه‏ see n /ey-māl-ī qŭ-wa/
use of force n
‏اعمام‏ /a'-mām, sg am/
see sg ‏عم‏ n pl
‏اعمی‏ blind (& pers) adj, n /a'-mā/
‏اعیاد‏ /a'-yād, sg id/
see sg ‏عید‏ n pl
/a'-yā-ni/ ‏اعیانی‏
natural, having the same parents; luxurious adj
‏اغتشاش , -ات/ها‏ /īgh-tī-shāsh/
revolt, uprising n
/īgh-tī-nām/ ‏اغتنام‏
seizing; plundering n
/agh-zī-ya/ ‏اغذیه‏
foodstuffs [< Ar] n pl
‏اغر‏ mortar (stone) n /ŭ-ghŭr/
‏اغر سنگ‏ /ŭ-ghŭr sang/
pestle (stone) n
‏اغراض‏ /agh-rāz, sg gha-raz/
see sg ‏غرض‏ n pl
‏اغراق , -ها‏ /īgh-rāq/
flattery; hyperbole n
‏اغراق کردن ←‏ flatter; exaggerate v
‏اغفال کردن‏ /īgh-fāl kardan/
mislead, delude vt

اغفال کننده /īgh-fāl kŭ-nīn-da/
misleading, deluding (& pers) adj, n

افاده ها/افادات- , /ī-fā-da, pl -dāt/
expression; haughtiness n

↳ افاده کردن express, convey vt

افاضل /a-fā-zīl/ learned men n pl

افتاد /af-tād/ omen n

افتاد خانه <کسی> شدن
/af-tād-ĭ khā-na shŭdan/
drop by <sb's> house v

افتادن ؛ -افت- ؛ افتاد-
/af-tā-dan, ŭf-/
collapse; fall; lie down; (colloq) be fired vi

افتادگی /af-tā-da-gi/
humiliation; omission n

افطار /īf-tār/ iftar (festive meal) n

افتتاح /īf-tĭ-tāh/
beginning, inauguration n

افتتاحی /īf-tĭ-tā-hi/
opening, inaugural adj

↳ مراسم افتتاحی
opening ceremony n

افتتاحیه /īf-tĭ-tā-hī-ya/
see افتتاحی adj

افتخار /īf-tĭ-khār/
honor, glory; pride n

↳ افتخار داشتن be honored v

↳ افتخار کردن honor v

افتخاری /īf-tĭ-khā-ri/ honorary adj

افترا /īf-tĭ-rā/ slander; accusation n

↳ افترا کردن slander; accuse v

افتضاح ات/ها- , /īf-tĭ-zāh/
disgrace, dishonor n

افتضاح آمیز /īf-tĭ-zāh ā-meyz/
disgraceful, degrading adj

افتضاح آور /īf-tĭ-zāh ā-war/
see افتضاح آور adj

افتیدن ؛ -افت- /میافتم/ ؛ افتید-
/af-ti-dan, ŭf-; /méyŭftŭm//
fall, fall down vi

افدر /af-dar/ n see اودر

افراختن ؛ -افراز- ؛ افراخت-
/af-rākh-tan/
hoist, raise (flag) vt

افراد /af-rād, sg fard/
n pl فرد see sg

افراشتن ؛ -افراز- ؛ افراشت-
/af-rāsh-tan/
hoist, raise (flag) vt

افراط /īf-rāt/
excessive, extravagant adj

افراط کار ان/ها- , /īf-rāt kār/
extravagant person n

افراط کاری /īf-rāt kā-ri/
extravagance n

افراطی ان/ون/ها- , /īf-rā-ti/
extremist (& pers) adj, n

افراطیت /īf-rā-tĭ-yat/ extremism n

افریدی /af-ri-di/ Afridi (P tribe) n

افریقا /af-ri-qā/ Africa n

افریقای جنوبی /af-ri-qā-yĭ jŭ-nu-bi/
South Africa n

افریقایی ان/ها- , /af-ri-qā-yi/
African (& pers) adj, n

افزایش /af-zā-yĭsh/
increase; addition n

افزودن ؛ -افزای- ؛ افزود-
/af-zu-dan/
increase; add vt

افزار /af-zār (aw-)/
tool, implement n

افزون /af-zun/ many, much adj

افزون بر /af-zun bar/
besides, in addition prep

افزونی /af-zu-ni/ abundance n

افسار /af-sār (aw-sār)/
bridle, halter (of rope) n

افسار گسیخته گان/ها- ,
/af-sār gŭ-seykh-ta/
libertine, dissolute pers n

افسانه ها- , /af-sā-na (aw-)/
legend; myth; story n

افسانه یی /af-sā-na-yi/
legendary, mythical adj

افسر ان/ها- , /af-sar/
officer (army, police); crown n

افسوس /af-sos/ pity, regret; woe n

↳ افسوس <کسی> آمدن
rue, regret v

↳ افسوس است ! what a pity excl

↳ افسوس و صد افسوس !
what a great pity excl

افسون , ها- /af-sun/
deceit; magic spell; sorcery n

افسونگر , ان/ها- /af-sun-gar/
enchanting adj; magician n

افشا /if-shā/
disclosure, revelation n

افشا کردن ← disclose, reveal vt

افشاگری , ها- /af-shā-ga-ri/
disclosure, revelation n

افشار /af-shār/ Afshar (city dist) n

افشر /af-shar/ افشار see

افضل /af-zal/ more learned adj

افضلیت /af-za-lī-yat/
precedence, priority n

افعال /af-'āl, sg feyl/
فعل n pl sg see

افغان , ان/ها- /af-ghān (aw-)/
Afghan (pers) n

افغانستان /af-ghā-nīs-tān/
Afghanistan n

افغانی /af-ghā-ni (aw-)/
afghani (currency); Pashto (lang)
n; Afghan adj

افق , ها- /ŭ-fŭq, pl ā-fāq/آفاق
horizon n

افقی /ŭ-fŭ-qi/ horizontal adj

افغان ملت /af-ghān mĭ-lat/
Afghan Melat (P pol party) n

افغان ملتی , ان/ها- /af-ghān mĭ-la-ti/
adherent of Afghan Melat n

افکار /af-kār; sg fĭ́-kĭr, fĭkr/
فکر n pl sg see

افگار /af-gār (aw-)/
injured, wounded adj

افلاس /af-lās/
bankruptcy; poverty n

افلاس کردن /af-lās kardan/
go bankrupt n

افلاک /af-lāk, sg fa-lak/
فلک n pl sg see

افلاکی , ان/ها- /af-lā-ki/
planet, star; worshiper of stars &
planets; angel n

افلیج /if-lij/
paralyzed adj; paralytic n

افواه /af-wāh/ rumor, hearsay n

افواهاً /af-wā-han, -wā´-/
by rumor, by hearsay adv

افواهی /af-wā-hi/ rumored adj

افول /ŭ-ful/ setting (of stars) n

افهام /if-hām/
explain, give instruction n

افیون /af-yun/ opium n

افیونی , ان/ها- /af-yu-ni/
opium addict n

اقارب /a-qā-rĭb/ اقربا n pl see

اقامت داشتن /ī-qā-mat dāshtan/
reside, dwell, stay vi

اقامت کردن /ī-qā-mat kardan/
اقامت داشتن see vi

اقامتگاه , ها- /ī-qā-mat-gāh/
residence, dwelling n

اقای /a-qāy/
Mr. (precedes name) adj

اقتصاد /ĭq-tī-sād/
economy; frugality n

اقتصاد بازاری /ĭq-tī-sād-ī bā-zā-ri/
market economy n

اقتصاد دان /ĭq-tī-sād dān/
economist n

اقتصاد شناس /ĭq-tī-sād shī-nās/
economist n

اقتصادی /ĭq-tī-sā-di/
economic; economical adj

اقتصادیات /ĭq-tī-sād-yāt/
the economy n

اقچه /aq-cha/ Aqcha (dist) n

اقدام , ات/ها- /ĭq-dām/
action; step, measure n

اقدام کردن ← take action v

اقرار /ĭq-rār/
confession; acknowledgment n

اقرارخط /ĭq-rār-khat/
affidavit (law) n

اقراق /ĭq-rāq/ اغراق n see

اقربا /aq-ra-bā/
relatives, kinfolk n pl

اقساط /aq-sāt, sg qĭst/
قسط n pl sg see

اقسام /aq-sām; sg qĭ´-sĭm, qĭsm/
قسم n pl sg see

اقل /a-qal/ lesser adj

اقلاً /a-qa-lan/ at least (colloq) adv

اقلام /a-qa-lām, sg qa-lam/
see sg قلم n pl

اقلیت minority n /a-qa-lī-yat/

اقلیم , ـها/اقالیم climate n /īq-lim/

اقلیم شناس /īq-lim shī-nās/
meteorologist n

اقلیم شناسی /īq-lim shī-nā-si/
meteorology n

اقلیمی climactic adj /īq-li-mi/

اقوال /aq-wāl, sg qawl/
see sg قول n pl

اقوام /aq-wām, sg qawm/
relatives (esp paternal) n pl
قوم ← (sg)

اقیانوس ocean n /oq-yā-nus, ŭk-/

اقیانوس شناس , ـان/ها
/oq-yā-nus shī-nās/
oceanologist n

اقیانوس شناسی
/oq-yā-nus shī-nā-si/
oceanology n

اقیانوسی oceanic adj /oq-yā-nu-si/

اکادمی academy n /a-kā-dī-mi/

اکادمی پولیس /a-kā-dī-mi-yĭ po-lis/
police academy n

اکادمی ملی نظامی افغانستان
/a-kā-dī-mi-yĭ mĭl-li-yĭ
nĭ-zā-mi-yĭ af-ghā-nĭs-tān/
National Military Academy of
Afghanistan n

اکبر /ak-bar/
Akbar (hist, Mughal emperor
1542-1605) n

اکتاف /ak-tāf; sg kĭtf, katf/
see sg کتف n pl

اکتوبر October n /ak-to-bar, ŭk-/

اکثر most, majority n /ak-sar/

اکثر اوقات /ak-sar-ĭ aw-qāt/
mostly, often adv

اکثراً /ak-sá-ran, -rán/
see adv اکثر اوقات

اکثریت /ak-sa-rī-yat/
majority, quorum n

اکثریت مطلق
/ak-sa-rī-yat-ĭ mŭt-laq/
absolute majority n

اکسیجن oxygen n /ak-si-jĭn/

اکک magpie (bird) n /a-kak/

اکمال , ـات /ĭk-māl/
completion, perfection n

اکمالات /ĭk-mā-lāt/
supplies (mil) n pl

اکنون /ak-nun, ŭk-/
now, at present adv

اکو /ī-ko, i-/
ECO, Economic Cooperation
Organization n

اکید emphatic, strict adj /a-kid/

اکیداً /a-kí-dan, -dán/
emphatically, strictly adv

اگام Agam (ctr) n /a-gām, ā-/

اگر if <+ subj> conj /a-gar/

اگرچه /a-gár-chī/
although, even though conj

اگرنه /a-gar-na, -ney/
otherwise, if not conj

اگست August (month) n /a-gĭst/

اگه see اگر (colloq) conj /a-ga/

الا unless, except prep /ĭ´-lā(-yī)/

الا آن که /ĭ´-lā-yī ān kĭ/
unless, except that prep

الاستیک rubber band n /ĭ-lās-tik/

الاستیکی /ĭ-lās-ti-ki/
elastic, flexible adj

الاشه jaw n /a-lā-sha/

الاغ /ŭ-lāgh/
ass, donkey; ass's load n

الاق see الاغ (colloq) n /ŭ-lāq/

البته of course phrs /al-ba-ta, -bá-/

البسه /al-bĭ-sa, sg lĭ-bās/
see sg لباس n pl

التزامی /ĭl-tĭ-zā-mi/
subjunctive (gram) adj

التهاب , ـات/ها /ĭl-tĭ-hāb/
inflammation; burning n

التهاب کردن /ĭl-tĭ-hāb kardan/
be inflamed vi

التهاب لوزتین
/ĭl-tĭ-hāb-ĭ law-za-tayn/
tonsillitis n

التهابی inflamed adj /ĭl-tĭ-hā-bi/

الجزایر Algiers n /al-ja-zā-yir/

الجزیره /al-ja-zi-ra/
al-Jazeera (news agency); Algiers n

اولچک /ŭl-chak/ n الچک see
pleading, entreaty n الحاح /īl-hāh/
الحاح کردن /īl-hāh kardan/
plead, entreat v

الحاق , -ات/ها /īl-hāq/
attachment, annexation n

الحاقی /īl-hā-qi/
attached, annexed n

الحال /īl-hāl/
now, presently adv

الساى /a-la-sāy/ n اله ساى see
alef (letter) n الف /a-līf/

الف مد /a-līf mad/
alef mad (letter) n

الفبا /a-līf-bā/
alphabet; (fig) elements n

الفباى مورس /a-līf-bā-yī mors/
Morse code n

الفبایی /a-līf-bā-yi/
alphabetical adj

القاب , sg لقب /al-qāb, sg la-qab/
n pl see sg

القاح /īl-qāh/
insemination; impregnation n

القاح مصنوعى /īl-qāh-ī mas-no-'i/
artificial insemination n

القایى /īl-qā-yi/
suggestive adj

القاعده /al-qā-'ī-da/
al-Qaeda n

القدس /al-qŭds/
al-Quds (Jerusalem) n

الکترونیکس /ī-līk-tī-ro-niks/
electronics n

الکحل /al-kŭhl/ alcohol; kohl n

الکولى , -ها /al-ko-li/
alcoholic (& pers) adj, n

اللک /īl-lak/
strainer, sieve n

الله /al-lāh/ Allah, God n

المار /al-mār/ Almar (dist) n

المارى کتاب /al-mā-ri-yī kī-tāb/
bookcase n

المارى ظرف ها
/al-mā-ri-yī zarf-hā/
cupboard n

المارى , -ها /al-mā-ri/
cabinet, wardrobe n

diamond n /al-mās/ الماس

الماسک /al-mā-sak/
lightning (colloq) n

الماسى /al-mā-si/ n الماسک see

Germany n /al-mān/ المان

المانى /al-mā-ni/
Germany n; German (& lang) adj, n

fire n /a-law/ الو

hello (on phone); yes adv /a-lo/
الو

الواح , sg lawh/ الواح , sg lawh/
n pl لوحه see sg

الویت /a-la-wī-yat/ اولویت see
god, deity n /ī-lāh, pl ā-lī-ha/ اله
pl آلهه →

اله ساى /a-la-sāy/
Alasay (dist) n

divine adj /ī-lā-hi/ الهى

to; until prep /ī-lā/ الى
۴ الى ۸ دالر 4 to 8 dollars →

forever adv /ī-la-la-bad/ الى الابد

الى سکن /a-li-sa-kan/
honeysuckle (flower, colloq) n

ام /am (ŭm)/
(ending, 1st pers possessive);
(ending, 1st pers sg pres & past)
[-م after consonant] suff

ام دفعه /īm da-fa/
then, that one time adv

but, however conj /á-mā/ اما

امارات متحده
/ī-mā-rāt-ī mŭ-ta-hī-da/
United Arab Emirates n pl

امارت , -ها/امارات
/ī-mā-rat, pl ī-mā-rāt/
emirate; office of an emir n

dill porridge n /ū-māch/ اماچ

اماکن , sg مکان /a-mā-kīn, sg ma-kān/
n pl see sg

امالشرایین /ŭm-mūsh-sha-rā-yin/
aorta [< Ar] n

امام /ī-mām/
imam, rel leader, teacher; (Shia)
one of series of divinely appointed
rel examples to mankind

امام صاحب /ī-mām sā-hīb/
Imam Saheb (dist) n

امامت /ĭ-mā-mat/
imamate, rel leadership n
امامت کردن →‌ lead in prayer v
امان /a-mān/
Aman (newspaper, hist) n
امان الله /a-mā-nŭ-lā/
Amanullah (hist, Afgh king 1919-1929) n
امبولانس /am-bo-lāns/
ambulance n
امپراتور /ĭm-pa-rā-tur/ emperor n
امپراتوری /ĭm-pa-rā-tu-ri/ empire n
امپراتوری یفتلی /ĭm-pa-rā-tu-ri-yĭ yaf-ta-li/
Hephthalite Empire (hist, 460-565 AD) n
امپراطور /ĭm-pa-rā-tur/
امپراتور n see
امپراطوری /ĭm-pa-rā-tu-ri/
امپراتوری n see
امتحان , -ات/ها /ĭm-tĭ-hān/
examination, test n
امتحان داشتن →‌ have an exam v
امتزاج , -ات/ها /ĭm-tĭ-zāj/
mixture; (fig) compatibility n
امتیاز , -ات/ها /ĭm-tĭ-yāz/
privilege, distinction; job benefit n
امتیاز دادن →‌ grant a privilege v
امتیازات قومی /ĭm-tĭ-yā-zāt-ĭ qaw-mi/
tribal privileges n pl
امثال /am-sāl, sg ma-sal (-tal)/
مثل n pl see sg
امثله /am-sĭ-la, sg mĭ-sāl/
مثال n pl see sg
امداد , -ها /ĭm-dād/
aid, assistance n
امداد های اقتصادی /ĭm-dād-hā-yĭ ĭq-tĭ-sā-di/
economic aid n
امداد های تخنیکی /ĭm-dād-hā-yĭ takh-ni-ki/
technical assistance n

امر , -ها/اوامر /á-mĭr, amr; pl a-wā-mĭr/
order, command (& mil); edict (pol) n
امر دادن • امر کردن →‌ give an order v
امر رئیس جمهوری /á-mĭr-ĭ ra-'is-jam-hu-ri/
presidential decree n
امرا /ŭ-ma-rā, sg a-mir/
امیر n see sg
امراض /am-rāz, sg ma-raz/
مرض n pl see sg
امروز /ĭm-roz/ today adv
امری /am-ri/ imperative (gram) adj
امریکا /am-ri-kā/ America n
امریکای جنوبی /am-ri-kā-yĭ jŭ-nu-bi/
South America n
امریکای شمالی /am-ri-kā-yĭ sha-mā-li/
North America n
امریکای مرکزی /am-ri-kā-yĭ mar-ka-zi/
Central America n
امریکایی , -ان/ها /am-ri-kā-yi/
American (& pers) adj, n
امریه /am-rī-ya/
command, order; (f name) n
امساک /ĭm-sāk/
cheapness, stinginess n
امسال /ĭm-sāl/ this year adv
امستردام /am-star-dām/
Amsterdam n
امشب /ĭm-shab (-shaw)/
tonight adv
امضا , -ها /ĭm-zā/ signature n
امضا کردن →‌ sign vt
امکان , -ات /ĭm-kān/
opportunity; possibility n
امکان داشتن →‌ be possible v
امکانات تولید کردن /ĭm-kā-nāt taw-lid kardan/
create opportunities v
امکنه /am-kĭ-na, sg ma-kān/
مکان n pl see sg

امل /a-mal, pl ā-māl/
desire, hope, wish (lit) n
آمال pl ←
املا /īm-lā/ dictation; spelling n
املا دادن • املا گفتن ←
give dictation v
املا گرفتن ← take dictation v
املاک /am-lāk, sg mŭlk/
ملک n pl see sg
اوملیت /om-līt/ omlette; OMLT (mil) n
املت
امن /á-mĭn, amn/
safe, peaceful adj; security, peace
n
امنا /ŭ-ma-nā, sg a-min/
امین n pl see sg
امنی /am-ni/
security, related to security adj
امنیت /am-nī-yat/ security n
امنیتی /am-nī-ya-ti/
related to security adj
اموات /am-wāt, sg ma-yīt/
میت n pl see sg
امواج /am-wāj, sg mawj/
موج n pl see sg
اموال /am-wāl, sg māl/
مال n pl see sg
اموال خالصه /am-wāl-ī khā-lī-sa/
state lands n pl
اموال قاچاقی /am-wāl-ī qā-chā-qi/
contraband, smuggled goods n pl
اموال قیمتی /am-wāl-ī qi-ma-ti/
valuables n pl
امور /ŭ-mur, sg á-mĭr/
affairs n pl
امر sg ←
امور خارجه /ŭ-mur-ī khā-rī-ji/
foreign affairs n pl
امور فلکی /ŭ-mur-ī fa-la-ki/
astronomy n
امه /ŭm-ma/ Umma, all Muslims n
امیال /am-yāl, sg mayl/
میل n pl see sg
امید /ŭ-meyd/ hope, wish, desire n
امید داشتن • امید کردن ←
hope, wish, desire v

امیدوار , -ان/ها /ŭ-meyd-wār/
hopeful (& pers) adj, n
امیدوار بودن ←
be hopeful; expect a baby vi
امیدوارانه /ŭ-meyd-wā-rā-na/
hopefully, wishfully adv
امیدواری /ŭ-meyd-wā-ri/
hopefulness n
امیر , -ان/ها/امرا
/a-mir, pl ŭ-ma-rā/
emir, prince n
امیرالبحر /a-mi-rŭl-bahr/ admiral n
امیر /a-mi-rŭl-mŭ'-mī-nin/
المؤمنین
commander of the faithful (caliph)
n
امیری /a-mi-ri/
emirate; amiri (kind of apricot) n
امیل /a-meyl/ حمایل n see
trustee n /a-min, pl ŭ-ma-nā/ امین
امنا pl ←
انابت /ī-nā-bat/ repentance n
اونابه /a-nā-ba/ n see انابه
اناث /ŭ-nās/ female adj
اناجیل /a-nā-jil, sg īn-jil/
انجیل n pl see sg
انار /a-nār/ pomegranate n
انار دره /a-nār da-ra/
Anar Dara (dist) n
انبان /am-bān/
lambskin/goatskin bag n
انبر /an-bŭr/ pliers (tool) n
انبساط /īn-bī-sāt/
expanse; cheerfulness n
انبساط کردن ← expand vi
انبوه /an-boh/
thick, bushy; crowded adj;
multitude n
انبیا /an-bī-yā, sg na-bi/
نبی n pl see sg
انبیق /an-biq/ still (for distilling) n
انتحار /īn-tī-hār/ suicide n
انتخاب , -ات /īn-tī-khāb/
choice; election (esp pl) n
انتخاب کردن ←
choose, select v
انتخابات کردن ←
vote, have an election v
انتخابی /īn-tī-khā-bi/ elected adj

Internet n /ĭn-tĭr-nat, an-/ انترنت

انتشار , -ات /ĭn-tĭ-shār/
publication, issuance n

← انتشار دادن publish, issue vt

انتظار بودن /ĭn-tĭ-zār budan/
see انتظار کشیدن vi

انتظار کشیدن /ĭn-tĭ-zār kashidan/
wait vi

انتفاع , -ان/ها /ĭn-tĭ-fā/
profit n

انتفاعی /ĭn-tĭ-fā-'i/
profitable, for profit adj

انتقاد , -ات/ها /ĭn-tĭ-qād/
criticism n

← انتقاد کردن criticize vt

انتقاد سازنده /ĭn-tĭ-qād-ĭ sā-zĭn-da/
constructive criticism n

انتقادی /ĭn-tĭ-qā-di/ critical adj

انتقال , -ات/ها /ĭn-tĭ-qāl/
transfer; transportation n

← انتقال دادن transfer, direct; transport vt

انتقال خون /ĭn-tĭ-qāl-ĭ khun/
blood transfusion n

انتقالی /ĭn-tĭ-qā-li/
transitional, transitory adj

انتقام , -ات/ها /ĭn-tĭ-qām/
revenge, retaliation n

← انتقام کشیدن • انتقام گرفتن
take revenge, retaliate v

انتقام گیری /ĭn-tĭ-qām gi-ri/
vengeance, retaliation n

انتیک /an-tik/ antique n

انتیک فروش /an-tik fŭ-rosh/
antique seller n

انتیک فروشی /an-tik fŭ-ro-shi/
antique shop n

انجام /an-jām/
completion, execution n

← انجام پذیرفتن be completed vi

← انجام دادن complete, execute vt

انجامیدن ؛ -انجام- ؛ انجامید-
/an-jā-mi-dan/
complete, execute (lit) vt

انجم /an-jŭm; sg ná-jĭm, najm/
see نجم n pl sg

انجمن /an-jŭ-man/
society, group; assembly n
→ Society for the Protection of
Women's Rights (hist, 1920s)
انجمن حمایتِ نسوان

انجن /an-jĭn/ engine n

انجنیر /an-jĭn-yar/ engineer n

انجنیری /an-jĭn-ya-ri/
engineering n

انجو /ĭn-jŭ-wa/
NGO, non-governmental
organization n

انجیل, -ها/اناجیل /ĭn-jil, pl a-nā-jil/
gospel (bibl); Enjil (dist) n

انحا /an-hā, sg nahw/
see نحو sg n pl

انحراف , -ات/ها /ĭn-hĭ-rāf/
deviation, digression n

اند /and/
(ending, 3rd pers pl pres, past &
pres perf) suff

انداخت /an-dākht/
fire (from weapon) n

انداخت مستقیم
/an-dākht-ĭ mŭs-ta-qim/
direct fire n

انداختن ؛ -انداز- ؛ انداخت-
/an-dākh-tan/
throw, cast, avert vt

اندازه /an-dā-za/
extent, limit; size, measure n

اندازه گیری /an-dā-za gi-ri/
measuring n

اندام /an-dām/
figure, form; limb, member; penis
n

اندام مرده /an-dām-ĭ mŭr-da/
corpse, dead body n

اندر /an-dar/
step- (relation) adj; in, into (arch)
prep; Andar (dist, ctr Meray) n

اندراب /an-da-rāb/
Andarab (dist) n

اندرچو /an-dar-chu/
seesaw (colloq) n

اندخوی /and-khoy/
Andkhoy (dist) n

اندرز /an-darz/ advice, counsel n
← اندرز دادن advise, counsel v

اندر /an-dar/ *prep* in, into (arch)

اندرون /an-da-run/

interior; conscience, viscera; f quarters *n*

اندرونه *n* /an-da-ru-na/ see اندرون

اندری *adj* /an-da-ri/ see اندر

اندس /īn-dūs/ *n* Indus River

اندک /an-dak/ *adj* few, little, short

اندک اندک /an-dak an-dak/ little by little *adv*

اندک رنج, -ان/ها /an-dak-ranj/ touchy (& pers) *adj*, *n*

اندکس /īn-dīks/ *n* index

اندکی /an-dá-key/ a little *n*

اندلس /ŭn-dŭ-lŭs/ *n* Andalusia

اندلسی /ŭn-dŭ-lŭ-si/ Andalusian (& pers) *adj*, *n*

اندو اروپایی /īn-do-ŭ-ru-pā-yi/ *adj* see اروپایی هندی

اندو ایرانی /īn-do-i-rā-ni/ *adj* see آریانی هندی

اندوخته, -ها /an-dukh-ta/ savings, hoard *n*; saved *adj*

اندونیزیا /īn-du-ni-zī-yā/ Indonesia *n*

اندونیزیایی /īn-du-ni-zī-yā-yi/ Indonesian (& pers) *adj*, *n*

انده /an-da/ half-load, bale; (vulg) fat ass *n*

اندوه /an-doh/ grief *n*

اندوهبار /an-doh bār/ grievous, causing grief *adj*

اندوه زای /an-doh zāy/ *adj* see اندوهبار

انده /an-dŭh/ *n* اندوه see

انده /īn-da/ (ending, forms n/adj from v) *suff*

انده ماندن /an-da māndan/ reach a standstill *v*

اندیشمند, -ان/ها /an-deysh-mand/ thinker *n*; pensive *adj*

اندیشمندی /an-deysh-man-di/ contemplation *n*

اندیشناک /an-deysh-nāk/ thoughtful; worried *adj*

اندیشه /an-dey-sha/ thought, concern *n*

← اندیشه داشتن worry, be concerned *v*

← اندیشه کردن think, reflect *v*

اندیشیدن ؛ -اندیش- ؛ اندیشید- /an-dey-shi-dan/ think, reflect (formal) *v*

انزال /īn-zāl/ ejaculation *n*

← انزال شدن ejaculate *v*

انزایم /īn-zāym/ enzyme *n*

انساب /an-sāb, sg *na*-sab/ see sg نسب *n pl*

انسان, -ها /īn-sān/ human being; humanity *n*; cultured *adj*

انسان دوست, -ان/ها /īn-sān dost/ philanthropist; humanist *n*

انسان دوستانه /īn-sān dos-tā-na/ philanthropic; humanist *adj*

انسان دوستی /īn-sān dos-ti/ philanthropy; humanism *n*

انسجام /īn-sī-jām/ coordination; harmony *n*

انسداد /īn-sī-dād/ obstruction; plosive *n*

انسدادی /īn-sī-dā-di/ plosive (speech sound) *adj*

انسولین /īn-so-lin/ insulin *n*

انشاءالله /īn-shā-'al-lāh (īn-shā-la)/ God willing *phrs*

انصار /an-sār/ Companions (Prophet's) *n*

انصاری /an-sā-ri/ of the Companions *adj*

انصاف /īn-sāf/ justice, fairness *n*

← انصاف داشتن be impartial *v*

← انصاف کردن practice justice *v*

انضباط, -ات /īn-zī-bāt/ order; mil police on duty; (mil) discipline *n*

انضمام /īn-zī-mām/ addendum (to doc) *n*

انطاکیه /an-tā-kī-ya/ Antioch (hist) *n*

انعطاف /īn-'ī-tāf/ flexibility, suppleness *n*

a = c<u>u</u>p, ā = l<u>o</u>ng, aw = n<u>ow</u>, ay = s<u>igh</u>, e = b<u>e</u>t, ey = ob<u>ey</u>

انعطاف پذیر /īn-'ī-tāf pa-zir/
flexible, supple adj

انعقاد /īn-'ī-qād/
convening, holding (of meeting) n

انعکاس , -ات/ها /īn-'ī-qās/
reflection n

انعکاس صدا /īn-'ī-qās-ī sa-dā/
echo n

انعکاس صوت /īn-'ī-qās-ī sawt/
see انعکاس صدا n

انعکاس عمل /īn-'ī-qās-ī a-mal/
reaction, response n

انعکاس روحیاتی
/īn-'ī-qās-ī ru-hī-yā-ti/
reflex n

انظار /an-zār, sg na-zar/
نظر see sg n pl

انف /anf/
nose (arch) n

انفاذ /īn-fāz/
enforcement n

انفاس /an-fās, sg na-fas/
نفس see sg n pl

انفجار /īn-fī-jār/
explosion n

انفس /an-fūs, sg nafs/
نفس see sg n pl

انفصال /īn-fī-sāl/
firing, dismissal, severance n

انفکاک /īn-fī-kāk/
انفصال see n

انفلونزا /īn-flo-wīn-zā/
influenza, flu n

انفی /an-fi/
nasal adj

انقباض /īn-qī-bāz/
contraction (of muscle) n

انقباض قلب /īn-qī-bāz-ī qalb/
systole n

انقره /an-qa-ra/
Ankara n

انقلاب , -ات/ها /īn-qī-lāb/
revolution; solstice n

انقلابی , -ان/ها/ون /īn-qī-lā-bi/
revolutionary (& pers) n, adj

انقیاد /īn-qī-yād/
obedience, submission n

انکشاف /īn-kī-shāf/
development, growth n

انگریز , -ها /ang-reyz/
Englishman, -woman (colloq) n

انگشت , -ان/ها /an-gūsht/
finger; toe n

انگشت شمار /an-gūsht shŭ-mār/
small number (of sth) adj

انگشتر /an-gūsh-tar/
ring (on finger) n

انگلستان /īn-glīs-tān/
England n

انگلیس , -ها /in-glis/
Englishman, -woman n

انگلیستان /īn-glis-tān/
England n

انگلیسی /īn-gli-si/
English (lang) n; English adj

انگور /an-gur/
grape n

انگوری /an-gu-ri/
grape; made of grapes adj

انگیختن ؛ -انگیز- ؛ انگیخت-
/an-geykh-tan/
excite; provoke; stimulate vt

انگیزه , -ها /an-gey-za/
stimulus; motive, incentive n

انگیزش /an-gey-zīsh/
excitation, stimulation n

انهار /an-hār, sg nahr (nār)/
نهر see sg n pl

انهزام /īn-hī-zām/
defeat, rout (lit) n

انواع /an-wā; sg náw-'a, naw'/
نوع see sg n pl

انیس /a-nis/
Anis (newspaper; m name) n;
familiar adj

او /aw/
آب see n

او /o (u)/
he, she, it pron

اواخر /a-wā-khīr, sg ā-khīr/
آخر see sg n pl

اوامر /a-wā-mīr; sg á-mīr, amr/
امر see sg n pl

اوایل /a-wāyl/
beginning, outset, start n

اوبه /o-bal/
Oba (dist) n

اوپرا /op-rā/
opera n

اوپک /o-pīk/
OPEC (cartel) n

اوتاوا /ŭ-tā-wā/
Ottawa n

اوتوپسی /o-top-si/
autopsy n

اوج /awj/
zenith, peak n

اودر /aw-dar/
آفدر see n

اوراق /aw-rāq, sg wa-raq/
ورق see sg n pl

اورانوس /o-rā-nus/
Uranus (planet) n

اورانیوم/u-rā-nī-yum/ یورانیم see

i = keep, ĭ = big, u = coop, ŭ = put, y = yet, ' = (glottal stop)　47

bangs (f hair) n /or-bal/ اوربل

اورزگان, o- /u-rūz-gān, o-/
Uruzgan (prov) n

Jerusalem n /ur-sha-lim/ اورشليم

اورکزی /o-rak-zay/
Orakzai (P tribe) n

Urgench (town) n /or-ganj/ اورگنج

throne n /aw-rang/ اورنگ

اورنگ زیب /aw-rang zeyb/
Aurangzeb (hist, Mughal emperor
1658-1707) n

mustard (plant) n /aw-ri/ اوری

اوزبک, ان/ها- /uz-bak/
Uzbek (pers) n

/uz-ba-kīs-tān/ اوزبکستان
Uzbekistan n

Uzbek (lang) n /uz-ba-ki/ اوزبکی

اوزار n /aw-zār/ see افزار

اوس n /aws/ see بنو اوس

Avesta (Zor) n /a-wīs-tā/ اوستا

/a-wīs-tā-yi/ اوستایی
Avestan (lang, hist) n

average, median n /aw-sat/ اوسط

Oslo n /os-lo/ اوسلو

they, them (lit) pron /o-shān/ اوشان

اوصاف /aw-sāf; sg wá-sïf, wasf/
see sg وصف n pl

اوضاع /aw-zā; sg wá-za, waz/
see sg وضع n pl

اوطان /aw-tān, sg wa-tan/
see sg وطن n pl

اوعیه /aw-'ī-ya, sg wī-'ā/
blood vessels; see sg وعا n pl

اوعیه شعریه
/aw-'ī-ya-yī sha'-rī-ya/
capillaries n pl

اوقاف /aw-qāf, sg waqf/
see sg وقف n pl

oxide (chem) n /ok-sāyd/ اوکساید

اوگار adj /aw-gār/ see افگار

اوگه یی /o-ga-yi/
step- (relation) adj

اول /a-wal/
first adj; the beginning n

اولاً
/a-wa-lan, aw-wá-lan, a-wa-lā/
firstly, first of all adv

اولاد, ها- /aw-lād/
child (esp one's own) n

اولاغ n /u-lāgh/ see الاغ

اولاق (colloq) n /u-lāq/ see الاغ

اولچک /ūl-chak/
handcuffs, manacles n

اولن باتور /o-lan bā-tur/
Ulan Bator n

اولویت, ها- /aw-la-wī-yat/
precedence; priority n

اوله n /aw-la/ see آبله

اولیا /aw-lī-yā/
parents n pl

اولمپیاد /o-lam-pī-yād/
Olympiad n

اولمپیک /o-lam-pik/
olympic adj

اومنه /om-na/
Omna (dist) n

اون /un/ see آن adj, pron

اونا /u-nā/ see آنها pron

اونبه /u-na-ba/
Unaba (dist) n

اونجه /un-ja/ see آنجه adv

اونگ n /a-wang/ see هاون

اوی adj /a-wi/ see آبی

اهالی /a-hā-li; sg á-hīl, ahl/
see sg اهل n pl

اهانت /ī-hā-nat/
insult, affront, indignity n

اهانت آمیز /ī-hā-na-tā-meyz/
insulting, affronting adj

اهتمام /īh-tī-mām/
effort, diligence n

اهدا /īh-dā/
donation; presentation n

اهداف /ah-dāf, sg ha-daf/
see sg هدف n pl

اهرام /ah-rām, sg hī-ram/
see sg هرم n pl

اهرم, ها- /īh-ram/
lever n

اهریمن /ah-ri-man/
Ahriman (Zor) n

اهریمنی /ah-ri-ma-ni/
related to Ahriman adj

اهل á-hīl, ahl; pl a-hā-li/
local resident, inhabitant n
← اهالی pl

اهل حدیث /á-hīl-ī ha-dis/
Ahl-e Hadith (Salafist mvmt) n

اهل تناسخ /á-hīl-ī ta-nā-sūkh/
Holuliyya (Musl sect, hist) n

اهل سنت /á-hīl-ĭ sŭ-nat/
the Sunni community, Sunnidom n
اهل کتاب /á-hīl-ĭ kĭ-tāb/
people of the book (rel) n
اهل هنود /á-hīl-ĭ hŭ-nud/
Hinduism n
اهلی /ah-li/
tame, domesticated adj
neglect n /ĭh-māl/ اهمال
اهمیت /ah-mī-yat/
importance; status n
ائتلاف /ey-tĭ-lāf/
coalition, alliance n
ائتلاف کردن /ey-tĭ-lāf/
form a coalition n
ائتلافی /ey-tĭ-lā-fi/
coalition (govt) adj
ائتلاف شمالی /ey-tĭ-lāf-ĭ sha-mā-li/
Northern Alliance n
ای /ay/ O (w/voc) excl
ایاب /ī-yāb/ return (arch) n
ایاب و ذهاب /ī-yāb ŭ zī-hāb/
coming & going phrs
ایاغ /a-yāgh/ cup, vessel n
ایالات متحده امریکا
/a-yā-lāt-ĭ mŭ-ta-hĭ-da-yĭ am-ri-kā/
United States (of America) n
ایالت /a-yā-lat, pl a-yā-lāt/
state, territory n
← ایالات pl
ایبک /ay-bak/ Aybak (seat) n
اپریل /ay-pī-rĭl/ see اپیل
ایتالیا /i-tā-lī-yā/ Italy n
ایتالیایی , -ان/ها /i-tā-li-yā-yi/
Italian (& pers, lang) adj, n
ایتوپیا /i-to-pī-yā/ Ethiopia n
ایجاد کردن /i-jād kardan/
create; make, produce vt
ایجاز /i-jāz/
brevity, succinctness n
ایچ آی وی /eych āy wi/
HIV (virus) n
ایدز /eydz/ AIDS (disease) n
← مبتلای ایدز person w/AIDS
← مبتلا به ایدز person w/AIDS
ایدس /eyds/ n ایدز see
ایدیولوژی /i-dī-yo-lo-zhi/
ideology n

ایدیولوژیک /i-dī-yo-lo-zhik/
ideological adj
ایذا /i-zā/ harm, hurt, injury n
ایر کندشن /eyr kŭn-dī-shin/
air conditioning n
ایراد , -ات/ها /i-rād/
delivery; finding fault with n
← ایراد کردن deliver (speech) vt
ایران /i-rān/ Iran n
ایرانی , -ان/ها /i-rā-ni/
Iranian (& pers) adj, n
ایزد /ey-zīd/ God [< P] n
ایزدی /ey-zī-di/ divine [< P] adj
ایستا /eys-tā/ stationary, static adj
ایستاد /eys-tād, is- (īs-)/
standing adj; stand (position) n
← ایستاد شدن
stand up; stall, stop (of a vehicle) vi
ایستادگی /ey-stā-da-gi/
resistance, perseverance n
← ایستادگی کردن
resist, persevere vi
ایستاده /eys-tā-da, is- (īs-)/
see ایستاد n
ایستگاه /eyst-gāh, ist-/
station, stop n
ایستگاه بین المللی فضایی
/eyst-gāh-ĭ bay-nŭl-mī-la-li/
International Space Station n
ایستگاه سرویس
/eyst-gāh-ĭ sar-wis/
bus stop n
ایشان /ey-shān/
they; them (lit) pron
ایشه ! /ey-sha/
stop (said to animal) excl
ایضاح , -ات/ها /i-zāh/
explanation n
← ایضاح کردن explain v
ایضاً /áy-zan, -zán/ ibid; ditto adv
ایفا /i-fā/ doing, fulfilling n
ایفاء /i-fā/ n ایفا see
ایفای نقش /i-fā-yĭ naqsh/
performance of a role n
ایقای وظیفه /i-fā-yĭ wa-zi-fa/
doing (one's) duty n
ایطالیا /i-tā-lī-yā/ Italy n

ايطاليايى , -ان/ها /i-tā-li-yā-yi/
Italian (& pers, lang) adj, n
ايقان /i-qān/ certainty, certitude n
ايقان داشتن → be certain vi
ايكر /ey-kar/ acre n
ايكو n /i-ko/ اكو see
ايكوادور /ey-ko-wā-dor/
Ecuador n
ايكوادورى , -ان/ها
/ey-ko-wā-do-ri/
Ecuadorian (& pers) adj, n
ايلا يله adj /ey-lā/ see
ايلک /ey-lak/ sifter; sieve n
ايلک کردن → sift (flour); sieve vt
ايم /eym/
(ending, 1st pers pl possessive);
(ending, 1st pers sg or pl pres
perf) [يم- after consonant] suff
ايما /i-mā/ allusion, hint n
ايماق , -ان/ها /ay-māq/
Aimaq (ethn) n
ايمان /i-mān/
faith, belief, creed, tenet n
ايمن /ey-mīn/ safe, secure adj
ايمن ساختن /ey-mīn sākhtan/
secure, make safe vt
ايمنى /ey-mī-ni/ security, safety n
اين , -ان/ها /in/
these, this adj; this one pron
اين جا /in-jā (-ja)/
here, in this place adv
اينان /i-nān/
they (people) adj, pron
اينجانب /in-jā-nīb/
I; me (colloq) pron; this side adv
آنچنان /ín-chū-nān/
like that (colloq) adv
اينچنين /ín-chū-nin/
like this (colloq) adv
اينک /í-nak/ now adv
اينه /i-na/ here is (colloq) adv
اينها /in-hā/ these pron
اينهمه /in-ha-ma, -há-/
to this extent adv
ايوان /ay-wān/
balcony, veranda; palace n
ايور /ey-war/ husband's brother n

ايور زن /ey-war zan/
sister-in-law (husband's brother's
wife) n

ب

با /bā/ with prep
با آغوش باز /bā ā-ghosh bāz/
willingly, open-armed adv
با احترام /bā īh-tī-rām/
respectfully (& in latter) adv
با استعداد /bā īs-tey-dād/
talented adj
با امان خدا /bā a-mān-ī khŭ-dā/
goodbye excl
با تجربه , -رُ- /bā taj-rī-ba, -rū-/
experienced adj
با تدبير /bā tad-bir/
prudent; tactful adj
با تناسب(-ى) /bā ta-nā-sŭb(-ī)/
proportionate to adj
با تهديد بلند /bā tah-did-ī bī-land/
high-threat adj
با تأسف /bā ta-'a-sŭf/
unfortunately adv
با ثبات /bā sŭ-bāt/
firm, stable, steady adj
با ثمر /bā sa-mar/
fruitful; profitable adj
با جذبه /bā ja-za-ba/
spiritually influential adj
با جرئت /bā jŭ-rat, bā jŭr-'at/
brave, courageous adj
با حميت /bā ha-mī-yat/
enthusiastic; zealous adj
با حوصله /bā haw-sī-la/
patient, forbearing adj
با خدا /bā khŭ-dā/ religious adj
با رعايت(-ى) /bā rī-'ā-yat(-ī)/
in accordance with prep
با سواد /bā sa-wād/
literate, able to read adj
با شد و مد /bā shad ŭ mad/
emphatically adv
با شرف /bā sha-raf/ honorable adj
با قوت /bā qŭ-wat/
powerful, forceful adj

با مبل و فرنیچر
/bā mŭbl ŭ far-ni-char/
furnished (room) *adj*
با مزه /bā ma-za/ delicious *adj*
با معنی /bā ma'-nā/
meaningful, significant *adj*
با نام /bā nām/ called, named *adj*
با وجود(-ی)/ /bā wŭ-jud(-ī)/
despite, in spite of *prep*
با وجود آن که /bā wŭ-jud-ī key/
although, despite *conj*
با وقار /bā wĭ-qār/
dignified, respected *adj*
با هم /bā ham/ together *adv*
باب , -ها/ابواب /bāb, pl ab-wāb/
chapter (of book); door *n*
بابا /bā-bā/
father; grandfather (& fig) *n*
بابای ملت /bā-bā-yī mī-lat/
Father of the Nation (King Zaher
Shah) *n*
بابر /bā-bŭr/
Babur (hist, 1483-1530, 1st
Mughal emperor) *n*
بابل Babylon (hist) *n* /bā-bŭl/
چامومیله chamomile *n* /bā-bu-na/ بابونه
بابه کلان /bā-ba ka-lān/
grandfather *n*
باج /bāj/ tax; tribute; blackmail *n*
باج سبیل /bāj-ī sa-bil/
blackmail, extortion *n*
باج سبیل گرفتن <از کسی>
/bāj-ī sa-bil gĭrĭftan/
blackmail, extort <from sb> *v*
باجگیر , -ان/ها /bāj-gir/
blackmailer; taxman *n*
باخت /bākht/ lost *adj*
باختر /bākh-tar/
Bactria (hist, geog); Bakhtar (Afgh
news agency) *n*
باختری /bākh-ta-ri/
Bactrian (lang, hist) *n*
باختن ؛ -باز- ؛ باخت- /bākh-tan/
lose *vi*
باد be, so be it *imper v* /bād/
/bād/ باد
air; wind; pride (fig); flatulence *n*
see باد *imper v* /bā-dā/ بادا

باد بان /bād bān/ *n* see بادبان
باد پای /bād pāy/
fast, swift as wind *adj*
باد پیمانه کردن
/bād pay-mā-na kardan/
waste time *v*
/bād pay-mu-dan/ باد پیمودن
v see باد پیمانه کردن
windy *adj* /bād kheyz/ باد خیز
almond *n* /bā-dām/ بادام
بادامی /bā-dā-mi/
almond-colored *adj*
sail *n* /bād-bān/ بادبان
بادبان دار /bād-bān dār/
having sails *adj*
fan (electric) *n* /bād-pa-ka/ بادپکه
cucumber *n* /bād-rang/ بادرنگ
بادغیس /bād-ghis/
Badghis (prov) *n*
/bād-ko-ya/ بادکویه
blizzard, snowstorm *n*
/bād-gin/ بادگین
causing flatulence *adj*
بادنجان /bā-dīn-jān (bān-jān)/
eggplant *n*
بادنجان رومی /bā-dīn-jān-ī ru-mi/
tomato *n*
بادنجان سوسنی
/bā-dīn-jān-ī so-sa-ni/
n see بادنجان
بادنجانی /bā-dīn-jā-ni/
dark purple, eggplant-colored *adj*
wine (arch) *n* /bā-da/ باده
/bā-di/ بادی
air, wind *adj*; beginning *n*
/bā-di-gārd/ بادی گارد
bodyguard *n*
/bād-yān, bā-dī-yān/ بادیان
anise, aniseed *n*
/bā-dī-ya/ بادیه
desert; earthen bowl *n*
بادیه نشین , -ان/ها
/bā-dī-ya nĭ-shin/
Bedouin; nomad *n*
/bār/ بار
audience; time, repetition; bar;
load, burden *n*
grant an audience *v* ←

بازار کتاب فروشی
/bā-zār-ĭ kĭ-tāb fŭ-ro-shi/
book market n

بازار مزدوری/bā-zār-ĭ mŭz-du-ri/
labor market n

بازارک /bā-zā-rak/
Bazarak (seat, dist) n

بازتابی /bāz-tā-bi/
flashback (in film) n

بازتوانی /bāz-ta-wā-ni/
viability n

بازجویی /bāz-jo-yi/
investigation n

بازخواست /bāz-khāst (-khās)/
demand for restitution; inquiry n

بازداشت /bāz´-dāsht/
arrest; prohibition [< F] n

← بازداشت کردن
prevent, prohibit (colloq) vt

بازداشتن ؛ بازدار- ؛ بازداشت-
/bāz´-dāsh-tan/
prevent, prohibit vt

بازداشته /bāz´-dāsh-ta/
prohibited adj

بازدید نمودن <از کجا>
/bāz-did na-mu-dan/
visit <sw> (officially) v

بازرسی /bāz-ra-si/
investigation, inspection n

← بازرسی کردن
investigate, inspect v

بازرفتن ؛ باز ـر- ؛ باز رفت-
/bāz-raf-tan/
return, go back vi

بازرگانی /bā-zar-gā-ni/
trade, commerce n

بازسازی /bāz-sā-zi/
reconstruction n

← بازسازی کردن
reconstruct v

بازگشایی شدن
/bāz-gŭ-shā-yi shŭdan/
be inaugurated vi

بازگشت /bāz-gasht/
return, coming back n

بازگفتن ؛ باز ـگوی- ؛ باز گفت-
/bāz-gŭf-tan/
repeat, say again vt

بازمانده , -ها /bāz-mān-da/
remainder, rest; survivor (of deceased) n

بار اول /bār-ĭ a-wal/
for the first time adv

باران /bā-rān/ rain n

بارانداز /bā-ran-dāz/ dock, wharf n

بارانزی /bā-rān-zay/
Baranzai (P tribe) n

بارانی /bā-rā-ni/
rainy adj, raincoat n

بارجامه /bār-jā-ma/ luggage n

بارداری /bār-dā-ri/
pregnancy (colloq) n

بارش /bā-rĭsh/ rain; precipitation n

بارکش /bār-kash/
pack animal (esp horse) n

بارگاه /bār-gāh/
hall, audience hall n

بارندگی /bā-rĭn-da-gi/
rainfall, precipitation n

باروت /bā-rut/ gunpowder n

بارور /bār-war/ fruitful adj

بارومتر /bā-ro-mĭ´-tĭr/ barometer n

بارک /bā-rak/ barracks n

بارکزی /bā-rak-zay/
Barakzai (P tribe) n

← سردار
sardar (title used by Barakzai nobles) n

باریدن ؛ -بار- ؛ بارید- /bā-ri-dan/
rain vi

باریک /bā-rik/ narrow; subtle adj

باریک اندیش /bā-rik an-deysh/
perceptive, of subtle mind adj

باریکه /bā-ri-ka/ strip; stripe n

باریکه غزه /bā-ri-ka-yĭ gha-za/
Gaza Strip n

باز /bāz (wāz)/ open adj

← باز کردن open (door) vt

← باز گذاشتن leave open (door) vt

باز /bāz/ then, afterwards adv

← باز گفتن repeat, say again v

باز هم /bāz ham/ still, also adv

بازار /bā-zār/ bazaar, marketplace n

بازار آزاد /bā-zār-ĭ ā-zād/
free market n

باطنی , -ان/ها /bā-tĭ-ni/
follower of Batiniyya (rel) n
باطنیه /bā-tĭ-nĭ-ya/
Batiniyya (Shia sub-group) n
reason, cause n /bā-'ĭs/ باعث
garden n /bāgh/ باغ
باغ انگور /bāgh-ĭ an-gur/
vineyard n
باغ داری /bāgh dā-ri/
gardening; horticulture n
باغ داری کردن /bāgh dā-ri kardan/
garden, tend a garden v
باغ کاری /bāgh kā-ri/
gardening n
باغ وحش /bāgh-ĭ wahsh/
zoo n
باغبان , -ان/ها /bāgh-bān/
gardener (pers) n
باغبانی /bāgh-bā-ni/
gardening n
→ باغبانی کردن
garden v
باغران /bāgh-rān/ n بغران see
باغی /bā-ghi/
garden adj; rebel, insurgent n
بافت /bāft/
weave, texture (of carpet) n
بافتن ؛ -باف- ؛ -بافت- /bāf-tan/
weave, knit; make up v
بافندگی /bā-fin-da-gi/
weaving; knitting n
بافنده , -گان /bā-fin-da/
weaver; knitter n
باقاعده /bā-qā-'ĭ-da/
regular (gram) adj
باقی ماندن ؛ -مان- ؛ ماند- /bā-qi māndan/
remain, be left vi
باقی مانده /bā-qi mān-da/
rest n; remaining adj
Bak (dist) n /bāk/ باک
باکتریا /bāk-tĭ-rĭ-yā/ n بکتیریا see
Baku n /bā-ku/ باکو
wing n /bāl/ بال
بال دار /bāl dār/ having wings adj
بال کشیدن /bāl kashidan/
grow wings v
on, on top of prep /bā-lā(-yĭ)/ بالا(-یی)
→ بالا بردن increase vt
→ بالا رفتن increase vi
بالا بلوک /bā-lā bŭ-luk/
Bala Buluk (dist) n

بازنگر /bā-zĭn-gar/
dancer (young m) (colloq) n
بازنگری /bā-zĭn-ga-ri/
dancing (by young m) n
→ بازنگری کردن
dance (as young m) v
بازو , -ان/ها /bā-zu/
arm; armrest; (fig) help n
→ بازو دادن
help, give a hand v
بازوبند, -ها /bā-zu-band/
amulet (in armband) n
بازی /bā-zay/
Bazai (P tribe) n
بازی /bā-zi/
game, sport; deceit n
→ بازی خوردن
be deceived vi
→ بازی دادن
deceive vt
→ بازی کردن
play; dance v
بازی های اولمپیک
/bā-zi-hā-yĭ o-lam-pik/
Olympic Games n pl n
بازی گوش /bā-zi gosh/
playful, given to play adj
بازیچه /bā-zi-cha/
plaything (& pers) n
بازیگر, -ان/ها /bā-zi-gar/
performer; actor n
بازینگر see /bā-zin-gar/ n بازینگر
ancient, old adj /bās-tān/ باستان
باستان شناس /bās-tān shĭ-nās/
archaeologist n
باستان شناسی /bās-tān shĭ-nā-si/
archaeology n
باستانی /bās-tā-ni/ adj باستان see
باشنده , -گان/ها /bā-shĭn-da/
resident, inhabitant n
Basawul (ctr) n /bā-sa-wūl/ باسول
hawk (bird) n /bā-sha/ باشه
باصره /bā-sĭ-ra/
optic adj; sense of sight n
باطل کردن /bā-tĭl kardan/
throw away, discard v
باطله /bā-tĭ-la/
waste, for throwing away adj
باطله دانی /bā-tĭ-la dā-ni/
wastebasket n
mind, heart; interior n /bā-tĭn/ باطن
باطناً /bā-tĭ'-nan, -nán/
inwardly, secretly adv

بالا دست /bā-lā dīst/

senior, superior *adj* بالا زانو نشستن

/bā-lā du zā-nu nīshastan/
squat, kneel *vi*

بالا مرغاب /bā-lā mŭr-ghāb/
Bala Murghab (dist ctr) *n*

overcoat *n* /bā-lā-posh/ بالاپوش

بالاخر /bǐ'-l-ā-khīr/
finally, at last [< Ar] *adv*

/bǐ'-l-a-khas/ بالاخص
particularly, especially *adv*

/bǐ'-l-ī-rā-da/ بالاراده
voluntarily, willingly *adv*

/bǐ'-l-jŭm-la/ بالجمله
completely, wholly *adv*

/bǐ'-l-khŭ-sus/ بالخصوص
particularly, especially adv

pillow *n* /bā-līsh (-līsht)/ بالش

بالصراحه /bǐ's-sa-rā-hat/
clearly *adv*

بالضروره /bǐ'z-za-ru-ra/
necessarily *adv*

naturally *adv* /bǐ't-tab/ بالطبع

/bǐ'-l-'aks/ بالعکس
conversely, vice versa *adv*

/bǐ'-l-farz/ بالفرض
supposedly, presumably *adv*

/bǐ-l-fǐ'l, -feyl/ بالفعل
de facto *adj*; in the act *adv*

Balkans, the Balkans *n* /bāl-qān/ بالقان

/bǐ'-l-qat/ بالقطع
definitely; certainly *adv*

/bǐ'-l-qŭ-wa, -wá/ بالقوه
potential *adj*; de jure *adv*

/bǐ'-l-kŭl/ بالکل
completely, wholly *adv*

balcony *n* /bāl-kūn/ بالکن

/bǐ'-l-maq-ta/ بالمقطع
by agreement, by contract *adv*

/bǐ'-l-mŭ-wā-jī-ha/ بالمواجهه
face to face *adv*

/bǐ'-n-na-ti-ja/ بالنتيجه
consequently, therefore *adv*

/bǐ'-n-nīs-ba/ بالنسبه
relatively, comparatively *adv*

dawn, morning; roof *n* /bām/ بام

dawn, morning *n* /bām-dād/ بامداد

Bamyan (prov) *n* /bām-yān/ باميان

okra *n* /bām-ya/ باميه

/bā-neyn kī/ بانين که
let, allow (colloq) *imper*

see بادنجان *n* /bān-jān/ بانجان

bamboo *n* /bāns (bānks)/ بانس

bank (institution) *n* /bānk/ بانک
بانک انکشافی آسیا

/bānk-ī īn-kī-shā-fi-yī ā-sī-yā/
Asian Development Bank *n*

/bānk-ī ja-hā-ni/ بانک جهانی
World Bank *n*

see بانکدار *n* /bānk-dār/ بانک دار

/bānk-dār, -ān/ها/ بانکدار , -ان/ها
banker (pers) *n*

/bānk-dā-ri/ بانکداری
banking *n, adj*

see بانس *n* بانکس /bānks/

/bān-ki/ بانکی
related to banking *adj*

see بهانه *n* /bā-na/ بانه

/bā-war/ <...که / حبه کسی> باور
belief, faith, trust <in sb/that> *n*

↦ باور داشتن • باور کردن
believe

باور کننده , -گان/ها
/bā-war kŭ-nīn-da/
believer (pers) *n*

together *adv* /bā-ham/ باهم

/bā'-yad, -yád/ باید
must, ought <+ subj> *aux v*

باید داشته باشه
/bā'-yad dāsh-ta bā-sha/
should have *aux v*

/bā'-yīst, -yī'st/ بایست
must (formal) <+ subj> *aux v*

bicycle *n* /bāy-sī-kīl/ بایسکل

tiger *n* /bá-bīr, babr/ ببر

idol; beloved *n* /bŭt/ بت , -ان/ها

/bŭt pa-rast/ بت پرست
idolater *n*; idolatrous *adj*

/bŭt pa-ras-ti/ بت پرستی
idolatry, idol worship *n*

pagoda *n* /bŭt khā-na/ بت خانه

gradually *adv* /ba-tad-rij/ بتدریج

battery (for power) *n* /bīt-ri/ بتری

see بت خانه *n* /bŭt ka-da/ بتکده

بته bush, shrub *n* /bŭ-ta/

بته خار bramble *n* /bŭ-ta-yĭ khār/

بته زار thicket, copse *n* /bŭ-ta zār/

بتول /ba-tul/
virginal *adj*; virgin (only Mary & Fatima) *n*

بتی کوت /ba-ti kot/
Bati Kot (dist, ctr Nader Shah Kot) *n*

بجل بازی /bŭ-jŭl bā-zi/
gambling using astragali *n*

بجلک /bŭ-jŭ-lak/
ankle bone, astragalus *n*

بجه o'clock *adj* /ba-ja/

← یک بجه one o'clock

بچه, ها- boy; son; child *n* /ba-cha/

بچه اندر stepson *n* /ba-cha an-dar/

بچه باز child abuser, pedophile *n* /ba-cha bāz/

بچه بازی child abuse, pedophilia *n* /ba-cha bā-zi/

بچه خاله /ba-cha-yĭ khā-la/
maternal aunt's son (lit) *n*

بچه عمه /ba-cha-yĭ a-ma/
paternal aunt's son *n*

بچه ماما /ba-cha-yĭ mā-mā/
maternal uncle's son *n*

بچه کاکا /ba-cha-yĭ kā-kā/
paternal uncle's son *n*

بچه گانه /ba-cha gā-na/
boys', for boys; childish *adj*

بحث, ها-احباحث /bahs, pl ab-hās/
discussion, debate *n*

بحر, ها-ابحار /bahr, pl ab-hār/
ocean, sea *n*

بحر آرام /bahr-ĭ ā-rām/
Pacific Ocean *n*

بحر اطلس /bahr-ĭ at-las/
Atlantic Ocean *n*

بحر هند /bahr-ĭ hĭnd/
Indian Ocean *n*

بحران crisis *n* /bŭh-rān/

بحرانی critical *adj* /bŭh-rā-ni/

بحری /bah-ri/
oceanic, maritime *adj*

بحرین Bahrain *n* /bah-rayn/

بحساب رفتن /ba-hĭ-sāb raftan/
enter into consideration *v*

بحل (peyl)/ /bĭ-hĭl (peyl)/
pardon, forgiveness *n*

← بحل کردن pardon, forgive *vt*

بحمدالله /bĭ-ham-dĭl-lāh/
thank God *phrs*

بحیره sea *n* /ba-hi-ra/

بحیره احمر /ba-hi-ra-yĭ ah-mar/
Red Sea *n*

بحیره اسود/سیاه /ba-hi-ra-yĭ as-wad, sĭ-yāh/
Black Sea *n*

بحیره خزر /ba-hi-ra-yĭ kha-zar/
see بحیره کسپین *n*

بحیره رومی /ba-hi-ra-yĭ ru-mi/
Mediterranean Sea *n*

بحیره کسپین /ba-hi-ra-yĭ kas-pin/
Caspian Sea *n*

بخار steam, vapor *n* /bŭ-khār/

← بخار برآمدن erupt *vi*

← بخار کشیدن have acne *v*

بخارا /bŭ-khā-rā/
Bokhara, Bukhara (city) *n*

بخارایی, ان- /bŭ-khā-rā-yi/
Bokharan (& pers) *adj, n*

بخارست /bŭ-khā-rĭst/
Bucharest *n*

بخاری /bŭ-khā-ri/
stove (heats room) *n*; see & بخارایی *adj*

بخت /bakht/
luck, fortune, fate *n*

بخت آزمایی /bakht āz-mā-yi/
lottery *n*

بخت آور /bakht ā-war/
see بختور *adj*

بخت برگشته /bakht bar-gash-ta/
unfortunate *adj*

بختور /bakht-war/
fortunate, lucky (& pers) *adj, n*

بختی /bakh-ti/
bakhti (kind of camel) *n*

بختیار, تی-یار /bakht-yār, -tĭ-yār/
see بختور *adj, n*

بخرد, ان- /bĭkh-rad/
wise (& pers) *adj, n*

بخردی wisdom *n* /bĭkh-ra-di/

---

i = keep, ĭ = big, u = coop, ŭ = put, y = yet, ' = (glottal stop)　　55

بخش /bakhsh/
field, sector; part; fragment n
بخش کردن ← divide, distribute vt
بخشاینده /bakh-shā-yīn-da/
the Forgiver (God) n
بخشی , -ان/ها /bakh-shi/
Buddhist (pers) n
بخشیدن ؛ -بخش- ؛ بخشید- /bakh-shi-dan/
give, grant; excuse, pardon vt
بخل /bŭ´-khŭl, bŭkhl/
envy; stinginess n
بخمل /bakh-mal/ velvet (colloq) n
بخوبی /ba khu-bi/ well adv
بخور , -ات/ابخره /bŭ-khur, pl ab-khī-ra/
incense; (med) inhalation n
بخیر /ba-khayr/
OK, well, in good time adv
بخیل /ba-khil/ stingy; envious adj
بخیلانه /ba-khi-lā-na/
stingily; enviously adv
بخیلی /ba-khi-li/
stinginess; envy n
بخیلی کردن ← be stingy v
بخیه /ba-khī-ya/ suture n
بخیه زدن • بخیه کردن ← suture v
بد /bad/ bad, evil, wicked adj
بد دادن /bad dā-dan/
giving f away in marriage to compensate for a crime (Pashtunwali) n
بد شکل /bad shá-kīl/ ugly; deformed adj
بد شگون /bad shŭ-gun (-gŭm)/
inauspicious, ill-omened adj
بد قهر /bad-qahr (-qār)/
unpleasant, bad-tempered adj
بد کار /bad-kār/ sinful; adulterous adj
بد گذاره /bad gŭ-zā-ra/ see بدگذران adj
بد گذران /bad gŭ-zā-rān/
unsociable; rude, coarse adj
بد گمان /bad gŭ-mān/
doubtful, suspicious adj
بداهت /ba-dā-hat/ improvisation n

بداهتاً /ba-dā´-ha-tan, -tán/
extemporaneously adv
بدبخت /bad-bakht/
unfortunate, unlucky adj
بدبختانه /bad-bakh-tā-na/
unfortunately adv
بدبین /bad-bin/ pessimistic adj
بدتر شدن /bad-tar shŭdan/
worsen, get worse vi
بدخش /ba-dakhsh/ red garnet n
بدخشان /ba-dakh-shān/
Badakhshan (prov) n
بدر /bá-dīr, badr/ full moon n
بدررفت /ba-dar-raft/ n see بدرفت
بدرفت /bad-raft (-raf)/
drain, gutter; latrine n
بدرنگ /bad-rang/ ugly adj
بدسترس /ba-dīst-ras/
available, at hand adj
بدسترس قرار دادن
/ba-dīst-ras qa-rar dādan/
have available vt
بدعت /bad-'at/
pernicious innovation (rel) n
بدل /ba-dal/
substitute; imitation; revenge, P law of revenge n
بدل, pl ابدال /ba-dal, pl ab-dāl/ nobleman n
بدمعاش /bad-ma'-āsh (-māsh)/
hoodlum, thug n, adj
بدن, -ها/ابدان /ba-dan, pl ab-dān/
body, torso, trunk n
بدنبال /ba dŭn-bāl (dŭm-)/
following, coming after adv
بدنه /ba-da-na/ fuselage, hull n
بدو /ba-daw/
running, on the run adj
بدو /badw/ beginning, start n
بدوأ /bád-wan, -wán/
at the beginning adv
بدون /bī-dun(-ī)/ without prep
بدون استثنا /bī-dun-ī īs-tīs-nā/
without exception adv
بدون قید و شرط
/bī-dun-ī qayd ü shart/
unconditional adj

بدوى /ba-da-wi/
primitive; of the desert *adj*

بدویون /ba-da-wī-yun/
Bedouin *n pl*

بدیل /ba-dil, pl ab-dāl/
substitute (& Sufi term) *n*

ابدال ← *pl*

بدینگونه /ba-din-gu-na/
such as *adv*

بذر /bá-zīr, bazr/ seed *n*

بذر افشانى /bá-zīr af-shā-ni/
planting seeds, sowing *n*

بذرى /baz-ri/
for planting (seeds) *adj*

بر /bar/ for; on; per *prep*; high *adj*

دو بر سه ← two-thirds

بر اساس /bar a-sās(-ī)/
based on *phrs*

بر باد دادن /bar bād dādan/
inflate (balloon, tire) *vt*

بر باد کردن /bar bād kardan/
بر باد دادن see *vt*

بر پاى کردن /bar pāy kardan/
establish, set up, arrange *vt*

بر تنبه /bar tum-ba/ pushy *adj*

بر خلاف /bar khī-lāf/
on the contrary *adv*

بر خلاف <چیزى> /bar khī-lāf(-ī)/
contrary to <sth> *prep*

بر خورد , -ها <با کسى> /bar-khŭrd/
incident; treatment; encounter
<w/sb> *n*

بر خوردار /bar-khŭr-dār/
having fun; successful *adj*

بر خوردار شوید ! ← have fun!

بر خوردن ؛ برخورد- ؛ برخورد-
/bár-khŭr-dan/
encounter; offend *vi*

بر دار /bar dār/ wide, broad *adj*

بر داشتن ؛ بر -دار- ؛ بر داشت-
/bár-dāshtan/
lift, raise, pick up *vt*

بر زبان راندن
/bar za-bān rān-dan/
exclaim, utter *v*

بر سر /bar sar(-ī)/
about; over *prep*

بر سر دوراهى /bar sar-ī du-rā-hi/
at a fork in the road, undecided
adj

بر ضد /bar zĭd(-ī)/ against *prep*

برعلاوه /bar a-lā-wah(-ī)/
besides, in addition to *prep*

بر گذشتن ؛ بر -گذر- ؛ بر گذشت-
/bar gŭ-zash-tan/
return *vi*

بر مبناى /bar mab-nā(-yī)/
based on *phrs*

بر وفق <چیزى> /bar wĭfq(-ī)/
in accordance w/<sth> *prep*

برآمدن ؛ -برآى- ؛ برآمد-
/bár ā-ma-dan/
climb, ascend; come out; cope w/
vi

برآورد /bàr-ā-wŭrd/
estimate, appraisal *n*

برآورد کردن ← make an estimate

برآوردن ؛ برآور- ؛ برآورد-
/bár ā-war-dàn/
realize, carry out; pull/take out *vt*

برآورده /bar ā-war-da/
realized, come true *adj*

برآورده شدن ← come true *vi*

برآورده کردن ← carry out *vt*

برآوردى , -ان/ها /bàr ā-wŭr-di/
appraiser (pers) *n*

برابر /ba-rā-bar/
equal; times, -fold *adj*, *n*

برابر <چیزى> /ba-rā-bar(-ī)/
equal to <sth> *adj*

برابر با <چیزى> /ba-rā-bar bā/
برابر see *adj*

برابرى /ba-rā-ba-ri/
equality, equivalence *n*

برادر , -ان/ها /bĭ-rā-dar (byā-dar)/
brother *n*

برادر رضاعى /bĭ-rā-dar-ī ra-zā-'i/
foster brother *n*

برادر اندر /bĭ-rā-dar an-dar/
stepbrother, half-brother *n*

برادر خوانده /bĭ-rā-dar khān-da/
close friend (m) *n*

برادر زاده , ـگان/ها
/bĭ-rā-dar zā-da/
nephew, niece, brother's son or daughter *n*

برادر کشی /bĭ-rā-dar kŭ-shi/
fratricide *n*

برامکه
/ba-rā-ma-ka, sg bar-ma-ka/
sg of برامکه *n pl*

sharp, cutting *adj* /bŭ-rān/ بران

براوی , ـان/ها /bĭ-rā-wi/
see براهوی *n*

براهوی , ـان/ها /bĭ-rā-wi/
Brahui (ethn; & lang, pers) *n*

براهین /bŭ-rā-hin, sg bŭr-hān/
see sg برهان *n* pl

براه انداختن /ba-rāh andākhtan/
see به راه انداختن *v*

برای /ba-rāy (-ray)/
for (time period, purpose) *prep*

برای آنکه /ba-rāy-ĭ ān kĭ/
for, because *conj*

برای ابد /ba-rāy-ĭ a-bad/
forever *adv*

برای اولین بار
/ba-rāy a-wa-lin bār/
for the first time *adv*

براعظم /ba-rĭ-a'-zam/
continent, mainland *n*

برای اینکه /ba-rāy-ĭ in kĭ/
for, because *conj*

بربوط /bar-but/
barbut (mus instr) *n*

verbena (plant) *n* /bar-bi-na/ بربینه

برتانوی , ـان/ها /bar-tā-na-wi/
British (& pers) *adj*, *n*

برتانیه /bar-tā-nĭ-ya/
Britain, United Kingdom *n*

برتری /bar-ta-ri/
preference; superiority *n*

tower *n* /bŭrj/ برج

برج ایفل /bŭrj-ĭ ay-fal/
Eiffel Tower *n*

turret *n* /bŭr-jak/ برجک

برجسته /bár-jas-ta/
prominent, outstanding *adj*

برجسته کاری /bár-jas-ta kā-ri/
embossing, embossed work *n*

برجیس /bĭr-jis, bar-/
Jupiter (planet); breeches *n*

bayonet *n* /bar-cha/ برچه

برحذر /bár-ha-zar/
watchful *adj*; beware *excl*

برحسب /bar-hasb(-ĭ)/
according to *prep*

برحق /bar-haq/
true, truthful; genuine *adj*

برخاست /bár-khāst/
takeoff (of aircraft) *n*

برخاستن ؛ بر -خیز- ؛ بر خاست-
/bár khās-tan, /bár meykheyzŭm//
get up; wake up (formal) *vi*

برخوردار /bar-khŭr-dār/
successful; enjoying *adj*

برخوردار باشین !
/bar-khŭr-dār bā-sheyn/
good luck *excl*

برخورداری /bar-khŭr-dā-ri/
success; enjoyment *n*

برخی /bár-khey/
many *adj*; much time *n*

برد /bŭrd/
range, reach; victory; usage *n*

برداشت /bar-dāsht (war-)/
tolerance, patience; harvest; buying on credit; (lit) inference *n*

← برداشت داشتن • برداشت کردن
be tolerant/patient

← برداشت کردن buy on credit

برداشتن ؛ بردار- ؛ برداشت-
/bár-dāsh-tan/
lift, raise, pick up *vt*

patient *adj* /bŭr-da-bār/ بردبار

patience *n* /bŭr-da-bā-ri/ بردباری

برداری /bar-dā-ri/
lifting, raising, picking up *n*

بردگی /bar-da-gi/
slavery, serfdom; bondage *n*

بردن ؛ -بر- ؛ برد- /bŭr-dan/
carry, take; escort; win *v*

برده , ـگان/ها /bar-da/
slave, serf, bondman *n*

carried, borne *adj* /bŭr-da/ برده

بررسی /bar-ra-si/
investigation; inspect; study *n*

برگ متال /barg-ĭ ma-tāl/
Barg-e Matal (dist) n

برگ و بار /barg ŭ bār/
wealth (fig) n

برگذار شدن /bar-gŭ-zār shŭdan/
take place, happen vi

برگردان /bar-gar-dān/
translation; refrain (e.g., poem) n

برگرداندن ؛ برگردان- ؛
برگردادن-
/bár gar-dān-dan/
translate; return vt

برگرفتن ؛ بر گیر- ؛ بر گرفت-
/bár gĭ-rĭf-tan/
lift, raise; pick up vt

برگزیدن ؛ برگزین- ؛ برگزید-
/bár gŭ-zi-dan/
choose, select; prefer vt

برگزیده , -گان/ها /bar-gŭ-zi-da/
chosen; preferred (& pers) adj, n

برگشت /bar-gasht/
bad luck (colloq); return; turning n

برگشت پذیر /bar-gasht pa-zir/
revocable adj

برگشت ناپذیر/bar-gasht nā-pa-zir/
irrevocable adj

برگشتن ؛ برگرد- ؛ بر گشت-
/bár-gash-tan/
return; convert; change v

برگشته /bar-gash-ta/
bent; turned away adj

برگشته بخت /bar-gash-ta bakht/
unfortunate adj

برلین /bar-lin/ Berlin n
برما /bar-mā/ Burma, Myanmar n
برمایی , -ان/ها /bar-mā-yi/
Burmese (pers) n

برمل /bar-mal/ Barmal (dist) n
برمک/bar-mak/ Buddhist leader n
برمکی , -ان/ها/برامکه
/bar-ma-ki, pl ba-rā-ma-ka/
Barmecide (Abbasid official, hist)
n

برملا /bar-ma-lā/
public, notorious adj (& adv)

برملا شدن /bar-ma-lā shŭdan/
become public vi

بررسی کردن /bar-ra-si kardan/
investigate; inspect; study vt

برزخ /bar-zakh/
time between death & resurrection
(rel) n

برس /bors/ brush n
بررسی n /ba-ra-si/ see بررسی
برطبق(-ی)/bar-tĭbq(-ĭ)/
according to prep

برطرف /bar-ta-raf/
fired, dismissed adj

برطرف کردن → /fire, dismiss vt
برطرفی /bar-ta-ra-fi/
firing, dismissal n

برعکس /bár-aks/
opposite, contrary adv

برف /barf/ snow n
برفکوچ , -ها /barf-koch/
avalanche n

برفی /bar-fi/ snowy adj
برق /barq/ electricity; lightning n
برق دستی /barq-ĭ das-ti/
flashlight n

برقرار /bar-qa-rār/
established; functioning adj

برقع /bŭr-qa (bŭq-ra)/ veil n
برقی , -ان/ها /bar-qi/
electrician, meter-reader n

برک /bĭ-rĭk/ brake (vehicle's) n
برک زدن • برک گرفتن →
apply the brake v

برکت , -ها/برکات
/ba-ra-kat, pl -kāt/
blessing; prosperity; see & برکه n

برکنار /bar-kĭ-nār/
fired, dismissed adj

برکناری /bar-kĭ-nā-ri/
firing, dismissal n

برکه /ba-ra-ka/
blessing; (& Sufic) spiritual gifts or
power n

برکه /bar-ka/ pool, small lake n
برکه /bŭr-ka/ Burka (dist) n
برکی برک /ba-ra-ki ba-rak/
Baraki Barak (dist) n

برگ , -ها /barg/ leaf (of plant) n
برگ ریزان /barg rey-zān/
autumn, fall n

---

i = keep, ĭ = big, u = coop, ŭ = put, y = yet, ' = (glottal stop)   59

برمه /bar-ma/ n drill
↙ برمه کردن v drill
برمه کاری /bar-ma kā-ri/ n drilling
↙ برمه کاری کردن v drill
برن /barn/ n Bern
برنا، بُر/یان، -ها- /bar-nā, bŭr-/ adj, n young, youthful (& pers)
برنایی /bar-nā-yi/ n youth, youthfulness
برنامه , -ها /bar-nā-ma/ n plan
برنج /bĭ-rĭnj/ n long-grain rice
برنج لک /bĭ-rĭnj-ĭ lŭk/ n medium-grain rice
برنده , -گان/ها /ba-rĭn-da/ n winner; bearer; victorious adj
بروت /bŭ-rut/ n moustache; whiskers
برودت/ت /bŭ-ru-dat/ n cold, coldness
بروز /bŭ-ruz/ n appearance; revealing
بروسل /bŭ-ru-sĭl/ n Brussels
بروکسل /bŭ-ruk-sĭl/ n Brussels see
بروفق(-ی) /bar-wifq(-ī)/ prep according to
برونز /bŭ-ronz/ n bronze
برونزی /bŭ-ron-zi/ adj bronze
برونشیت /bron-shit/ n bronchitis
بروبی , -ان/ها /bĭ-ra-wi/ n Brahui (ethn; & lang, pers)
بره /ba-ra/ n lamb; fawn; (fig, & pers)
برهان , -ها/براهین /bŭr-hān, pl bŭ-rā-hin/ n evidence, proof; real, true
برهان قاطع /bŭr-hān-ĭ qā-tey/ Burhan-e Qatey (17th-c Dari dictionary)
برهان مسیح /bŭr-hān-ĭ ma-sih/ miracle by the Messiah
برهنه /bĭ-rah-na/ naked, nude, bare adj
↙ برهنه ساختن vt strip, denude
برهنه پای /bĭ-rah-na pāy/ barefoot adj
برهنه سر /bĭ-rah-na sar/ bareheaded adj
برای /ba-ray/ prep see بری

بری الذمه /ba-ri-yŭz-zī-ma/ acquitted (law) adj
بریان /bĭr-yān/ fried; toasted, parched adj
بریانی /bĭr-yā-ni/ biryani (kind of pilaf) n
بریتانیا /bri-tā-nī-ya/ Britain, United Kingdom n
بریج /brij/ bridge (card game) n
برید جنرال /brid jan-rāl/ brigadier general, BG n
بریدگی /brid-gay/ sergeant, SGT n
بریدمن /brid-man/ first lieutenant, 1LT n
بریدن ؛ -بر- ؛ برید-- /bŭ-ri-dan/ cut off, sever; break off vt
برین /ba-rin/ sublime, high (arch); on this adj
بز /bŭz/ goat n
بز دل /bŭz dīl/ adj see بزدل
بز کوهی /bŭz-ĭ ko-hi/ ibex, mountain goat n
بزاز /ba-zāz/ cloth dealer n
بزازی /ba-zā-zi/ dealing in cloth n
بزاق /bŭ-zāq/ saliva n
بزاقی /bŭ-zā-qi/ salivary adj
بزدل , -ان/ها /bŭz-dīl/ coward n; cowardly adj
بزرگ /bŭ-zŭrg/ big, large adj
↙ بزرگ شدن vi grow up
بزرگ داشت /bŭ-zŭrg dāsht/ commemoration n
بزغاله /bŭz-ghā-la/ kid, young goat n
بزنیس /bĭz-nis/ business n
بزودی /ba-zu-di/ soon adv
بزکشی /bŭz-ka-shi/ buzkashi (sport) n
بس /bas/ enough adj
بس /bŭs/ bus n
بست , -ها /bast/ position; cadre; arrangement n
بست /bŭst/ Bust (ancient fort) n
بستر /bĭs-tar/ bed n
بستر دریا /bĭs-tar dar-yā/ river bed n
بستر شدن /bĭs-tar shŭdan/ be hospitalized n

بستره /bĭs-ta-ra/
pallet; sleeping bag; (fig) fat ass n

بستره انداختن /bĭs-ta-ra andākhtan/
visit (sb) for a long time v

بسترى /bĭs-ta-ri/
sick, confined to bed adj

بسترى شدن /bĭs-ta-ri shŭdan/
be hospitalized (colloq) n

بستن ؛ -بند- ؛ بست- /bas-tan/
bandage; tie, fasten, close;
conclude vt

بسته /bas-ta/ closed adj; packet n
بسته شدن ← close, shut vi
بسته كردن ← tie, bind; close vt

بسكويت /bĭs-kŭ-wit/ see بسكيت
بسكيت /bĭs-keyt/ biscuit n

بسم الله كردن /bĭs-mŭl-lāh kardan/
begin, start (speaking) v

بسم الله الرحمن الرحيم
/bĭsmŭllāh-ĭ rahmān ŭl-rahim/
in the name of the Almighty &
Merciful God phrs

بسيار /bĭs-yār/
very adv; many, (too) much adj

بسيار چيزها /bĭs-yār chiz-hā(-yĭ)/
all kinds of phrs

بسيارى /bĭs-yā-rey, -ri/
many; excessive adj; much time
adv

بسيج /ba-seyj, -sij/
preparation; mobilization; Basij
(Iran) n
بسيج كردن ← prepare; mobilize v

بشدت /ba-shĭ-dat/
forcefully; intensely; harshly adv
بشدت محكوم كردن ← condemn

بشر /ba-shar/
humanity, mankind n

بشردوستانه /ba-shar dos-tā-na/
humanitarian adj

بشرشناس , -ان/ها
/ba-shar-shĭ-nās/
anthropologist n

بشرشناسى /ba-shar-shĭ-nā-si/
anthropology n

بشره /bŭsh-ra/
skin, epidermis (anat) n

بشريت /ba-sha-rī-yat/
humanity, mankind n

بشقاب /bĭsh-qāb (bŭsh-)/ plate n
بشقاب پرنده /bĭsh-qāb-ĭ pa-rĭn-da/
flying saucer n

بشمار رفتن /ba shŭ-mār raftan/
be considered v

بشكه /bĭsh-ka/
barrel (unit of measure) n

بشكك /bĭsh-kĭk/ n see بشكيك
بشكيك /bĭsh-keyk/ Bishkek n

بصارت /ba-sā-rat, bī-/
vision; insight; knowledge (arch) n

بصيرت /ba-si-rat/
vision; insight; knowledge n

بضاعت /ba-zā-'at/
wealth, capital; goods n

بضاعت مزجات
/ba-zā-'at-ĭ mŭz-jāt/
a little knowledge or wealth n

بطليموس /bat-li-mus/
Ptolemy (hist) n

بطلميوس /bat-li-mī-yus/
see بطليموس n

بطن, -ها/بطون
/bá-tĭn, batn; pl ba-tun/
interior; belly, stomach; (rel)
hidden message of the Quran n

بطور موفقانه
/ba tawr-ĭ mŭ-wa-fa-qā-na/
successfully adv

بطورى كه /ba taw-ri-kī (-key)/
as adv

بطول انجاميدن /ba tul anjāmidan/
take a long time vi

بطى /ba-ti/ sluggish, slow adj
بعد, -ها/ابعاد /bŭ'd, pl ab-'ād/
distance; dimension n

بعد /ba'd (bād, bad)/
later, then adv; subsequent adj
بعد از /ba'd az/ after adv
بعد از آن /ba'd az ān/
afterwards; consequently adv
بعد از اين /ba'd az in/
after this, hereafter adv

i = keep, ĭ = big, u = coop, ŭ = put, y = yet, ' = (glottal stop)   61

بعد از ظهر /ba'd az zŭ´-hīr/
afternoon n

بعداً /bá'-dan, -dán/
afterwards, subsequently adv

بعض /ba'z-ī/ some adj

بعض اوقات /ba'z-ī aw-qāt/
sometimes adv

بعض وخت ها /baz-ī wakht-hā/
sometimes (colloq) adv

بعضی /ba'-zey (bā-)/ some adj

بعمل آمدن /ba á-mīl āmadan/
happen, occur vi

بعنوان /ba īn-wān(-ī)/
as, in the form of; on the ground
that prep

بعینه /ba-'ay-na/
exactly; literally adv

بغ /bagh/ angel; idol; god n

بغاز /bŭ-ghāz/ strait n

بغاوت /ba-ghā-wat/
insurgency, rebellion n

بغبغه /bagh-ba-gha/ dewlap n

بغتتاً /bágh-ta-tan, -tán/
suddenly adv

بغداد /bagh-dād/ Baghdad n

بغران /bagh-rān/

بغران /ba gha-raz(-ī)/
for, in order to prep

بغل /ba-ghal/
chest, bosom; side, bank n

بغلان /bagh-lān/ Baghlan (prov) n

بغلان جدید /bagh-lān-e ja-did/
Baghlan-e Jadid (dist) n

بغند /bŭ-ghŭnd/
bump on the head; (fig) short & fat
person n

بغندی /bŭ-ghŭn-di/ n see بغند

بقالی /ba-qā-li/
grocer (pers); grocery n

بقه /ba-qa/ frog n

بقه /bŭq-qa/
bull (for breeding) n

بقیه /ba-qī-ya/ rest, remainder n

بکارت /ba-kā-rat, bī-/ virginity n

بکتیریا , -ها /bak-teyr-yā/
bacteria n

بکداشیه /bak-dā-shī-ya/
Baktashiyya, Bektashism (Sufi
order of janissaries) n

بکس جیبی /baks-ī jey-bi/
wallet, billfold n

بکس سفر /baks-ī sa-far/
suitcase n

باکو /ba-ku/ n see باکو

بکواه /bak-wā/
Bakwa (dist, ctr Sultani Bakwa) n

بگرام /bag-rām/
Bagram (dist, air base) n

بگرامی /bag-rā-mi/
Bagrami (dist) n

بگوتا /bŭ-go-tā/ Bogota n

بل /bal/ ignited, lit adj; but conj

بل /bīl/ bill n

بل کردن /bal kardan/
ignite, light v

بلا , -ها /ba-lā/
calamity; suffering; cunning pers n

بلاخره /ba-lā-khŭ-ra/
finally, in the end adv

بلادت /ba-lā-dat/
stupidity, dullness n

بلاک /bī-lāk/
bloc (pol grouping) n

بلاگک /ba-lā-gak/
devious & cunning pers n

بلاهت /ba-lā-hat/
stupidity; weak judgment n

بلبل /bŭl-bŭl/ bulbul (songbird) n

بلبلی /bŭl-bū-li/
sweetly talkative adj

بلجیم /bīl-jim/ Belgium n

بلجیمی , -ان/ها /bīl-ji-mi/
Belgian (& pers) adj, n

بلچراغ /bīl-chī-rāgh/
Belcheragh (dist) n

بلخ /balkh/ Balkh (prov) n

بلخ آب /bal-khāb/
Balkhab (dist, ctr Tarkhoj) n

بلد , -ان/بلاد <در کجا> /ba-lad/
acquainted <w/a place> adj; local
guide (pers) n

بلدرجین /bal-dar-jin/ n see بلدرچین

بلدرچین /bal-dar-chin/
quail (bird) n

بلدیه /ba-la-dī-ya/ municipality n

بلشویک /bŭl-sha-wik/ Bolshevik n

بلغارستان /bŭl-ghā-rī-stān/ n
see بلغاریا

بلغاری , -ان/ها /bŭl-ghā-ri/
Bulgarian (& pers) adj, n

بلغاریا /bŭl-ghā-rī-yā/ n Bulgaria
بلغاریه /bŭl-ghā-rī-ya/ n see بلغاریا
بلغاریایی , -ان/ها /bŭl-ghā-rī-yā-yi/
see بلغاری adj, n

بلغم /bal-gham/ n phlegm
بالکل /bǐ´-l-kŭl/ adv see بکل
بلکه /bál-kī/
but, on the contrary conj

بلگراد /bǐl-gǐ-rād/ n Belgrade
بلند /bǐī-land/
high, tall; loud adj; up adv
بلند پایه /bǐī-land pā-ya/
senior, high-ranking adj
بلند خواندن /bǐī-land khāndan/
read aloud v

بلندراژ /bǐ-lǐn-dāzh/ bunker n
بلندی /bǐ-lan-di/ altitude; height n
بلوچ /ba-luch, -loch/ n
Baluch, Baloch (ethn)
بلوچستان, -لو- /ba-lu-chǐs-tān, -lo-/
Baluchistan, Balochistan (prov) n
بلور /bǐī-lawr/
crystal; (mineral) beryl n
بلوری /bǐī-law-ri/
crystalline (lit) adj
بلورین /bǐī-law-rin/ adj see بلوری
بلوط /ba-lut/ n oak (tree)
بلوغ /bŭ-lugh/ puberty n
بلوک /bŭ-luk/
platoon; group of people n
بلی /bá-ley/
yes; hello (on phone) adv
بلیون /bǐl-yun/ billion n, adj
بم /bam/ bomb n
بم افگن , -ها /bam af-gan/
bomber n, adj
↳ طیاره بمافگن bomber plane
بم انداختن /bam andākhtan/
drop a bomb v
بم انداز, -ها /bam an-dāz/
see بمافگن n, adj
بم دستی /bam-ǐ dǐs-ti/
hand grenade n

بمانین که /bŭ-mā-neyn kī/
see بانین که imper
بمب /bamb/ n بم see
بمبارد کردن /bam-bārd kardan/ vt
see بمباردان
بمباردان /bam-bār-dān/
bombardment n
بمباردان کردن
/bam-bār-dān kardan/
bombard vt
بمباردمان
/bam-bārd-mān, bam-bār-dŭ-mān/
n بمباردان see
بمیرک /bam-bi-rak/ dragonfly n
بمبیی /bam-ba-yi/ Bombay (city) n
بمنظور(-ī) /ba man-zur(-ī)/
for, in order to prep
بن گوش /bŭn-ǐ gosh/
earlobe; area behind ear n
بنا /ba-nā/ mason, builder n
بنا , -ها/ابنیه /bǐī-nā, pl ab-nī-ya/
building n

بنا /bǐī-nā/
beginning; (gram) form n
↳ بنا کردن begin, start v
↳ بنا نهادن lay the foundation v
بنابر <چیزی> /bǐī-nā-bar(-ī)/
due to, because of <sth> prep
بنا بر آن /bǐī-nā bar ān/
therefore, for that reason adv
بنا بر این /bǐī-nā bar in/
see بنا بر آن adv
بنات /ba-nāt, sg bǐnt/
see sg بنت n pl
بنات النعش /ba-nāt-ŭn-na'sh/
Ursa Major (constellation) phrs
بناچار /ba-nā-chār/
necessarily, compulsorily adv
بنادر /ba-nā-dǐr, sg ban-dar/
see sg بندر n pl
بناگوش /bŭ-nā-gosh/
earlobe; area behind ear n
بنام /ba-nām/ called, named adj
بنایی /ba-nā-yi/
masonry; construction n
بنت /bǐnt, pl ba-nāt/
daughter (esp in documents) n
↳ pl بنات

بنت /bŭnt/ — font (printing) n

بنجارگی /ban-jā-ra-gi/ — shop; merchandise n

بنجاره /ban-jā-ra/ — retailer n

بند /band/ — dam; cord; string; joint; belt; stanza n

بند آب گردان /band-ĭ āb gar-dān/ — diversion dam n

بند امیر /band-ĭ a-mir/ — Band-e Amir (national park) n

بند انگشت /band-ĭ an-gŭsht/ — knuckle (finger or toe) n

بند باز /band bāz/ — tightrope walker n

بند برق /band-ĭ barq/ — hydroelectric dam n

بند بوت /band-ĭ but/ — shoelace n

بند پای /band-ĭ pāy/ — ankle n

بند تفنگ /band-ĭ tŭ-fang/ — sling for a rifle n

بند جراب /band-ĭ jŭ-rāb/ — garter; string of socks n

بند دست /band-ĭ dast/ — wrist n

بند سردیه /band-ĭ sar-dīh/ — Sardeh Dam (Ghazni) n

بند سلبند /band-ĭ sa-la-band/ — martingale (harness strap) n

بند بودن /band shŭdan/ — be busy vi

بند کجکی /band-ĭ ka-ja-ki/ — Kajaki Dam (Helmand) n

بند کردن /band kardan/ — attach, hang; screw (obs); fill in holes; block v

بند ناف /band-ĭ nāf/ — umbilical cord n

بند نغلو /band-ĭ nagh-lu/ — Naghlu Dam; (rhet) name of the game n

بند کجکی /band-ĭ ka-ja-ki/ — Kajaki Dam n

بنداژ /ban-dāzh/ — bandage n

بندج /ban-daj/ — see بنداژ n

بندر , ها- /ban-dar, pl ba-nā-dīr/ — port, border post n

بندر گاه /ban-dar gāh/ — harbor, port n

بندش /ban-dĭsh/ — bug, malfunction n

بندی , ان/ها- /ban-di/ — prisoner, detainee n

بندی خانه /ban-di khā-na/ — prison, penitentiary n

بندی کردن /ban-di kardan/ — arrest, take into custody vt

بنفش /bī-nafsh/ — violet (flower, color) n, adj

بنفشه /bī-naf-sha/ — violet (flower) n

بنگ /bang/ — bhang, marijuana n

بنگ دانه /bang dā-na/ — hempseed n

بنگال /bĭn-gāl/ — Bengal (geog) n

بنگال شرقی /bĭn-gāl-ĭ shar-qi/ — East Bengal (hist) n

بنگال غربی /bĭn-gāl-ĭ ghar-bi/ — West Bengal (state) n

بنگالی /bĭn-gā-li/ — Bengali adj; bangle n

بنگله دیش /bĭn-ga-la-deysh/ — Bangladesh n

بنگلی , ها- /bang-li/ — bangle n

بنگی /ban-gi/ — Bangi (dist) n

بنو /ba-nu/ — house, sons; clan, tribe [<Ar] n

بنو الخزرج ← Banu Khazraj (hist, Medinan tribe)

بنو اوس ← Banu Aws (hist, Medinan tribe)

بنو قریظه ← Banu Qurayza (hist, Medinan tribe)

بنو هاشم ← Banu Hashem (Prophet's tribe)

بنیاد /bŭn-yād/ — basis; foundation n

بنیاد بیات /bŭn-yād-ĭ ba-yāt/ — the Bayat Foundation n

بواد /bŭ-wād/ — let it be, so be it (lit) imper

بواسطه /ba-wā-sī-ta(-yī)/ — through, by way of prep

بوت /but/ — boot, shoe n

بوت ساقدار /but-ĭ sāq-dār/ — hightop boots (to calf) n

بوتل /bo-tal/ — bottle n

water bottle n /bo-tal-ĭ āb/ بوتل آب
boutique n /bo-tik/ بوتیک
با وجود conj /ba-wŭ-jud/ بوجوده
sack, gunny sack n /bu-ji/ بوجی
/bŭ-wad/ بُود
be (3rd pers sg, subj/cond form) (lit) v
existence; belongings v /bud/ بود
بود و باش کردن
/bud ŭ bāsh kardan/
live, reside, dwell v
Buddha n /bu-dā/ بودا
see بودایشت n /bu-dā-pĭst/ بودایست
Budapest n /bu-dā-pĭsht/ بودایشت
بودایی /bu-dā-yi/
Buddhism n; Buddhist n, adj
budget n /bu-dĭ-ja, bu-/ بودجه
/bu-dan/ بودن ؛ است- ؛ بود-
be vi; being n
quail (bird) n /bo-da-na/ بودنه
/bo-rān/ بوران
snowstorm, blizzard n
بورانی بادنجان
/bo-rā-ni-yĭ bā-dĭn-jān/
fried eggplant n
board (coordinative) n /bord/
بورد
بورد هماهنگی بین المللی پولیس
/bord-ĭ ha-mā-han-gi-yĭ bay-nŭl-
mĭ-la-li-yĭ po-lis/
IPCB, International Police
Coordination Board n
bourgeois adj /bor-zhŭ-wā/ بورژوا
/bor-zhŭ-wā-zi/ بورژوازی
bourgeoisie n
بورس , -ها /bors/
scholarship; bourse n
/bo-rĭk a-sid/ بورک اسید
boric acid n
borax n /bo-rĭks/ بوریکس
/bo-ra/ بوره
sugar; uncultivated soil n
sawdust n /bu-ra-yĭ a-ra/ بوره اره
/bu-ri/ بوری
burlap sack, gunny sack n
woven mat n /bu-rĭ-yā/ بوریا
/bu-rĭ-yā bāf/ بوریا باف
mat weaver n

/bu-rĭ-yā bā-fi/ بوریا بافی
mat weaving n
بوریا بافی کردن
/bu-rĭ-yā bā-fi kardan/
weave mats v
/bu-rĭ-yā ko-bi/ بوریا کوبی
housewarming party n
roan (horse) adj /boz/ بوز
/bu-zi-na/ بوزینه , -ها/گان
monkey, ape n
see بوسه n /bos/ بوس
بوسیدن ؛ -بوس- ؛ بوسید-
/bo-si-dan/
kiss vt
garden n /bos-tān/ بوستان
kiss n /bo-sa/ بوسه
/bosh/ بوش
being, existence; destiny n
/bogh band/ بوغ بند
bedding (bundled); (fig) fat pers n
/bogh-ma/ بوغمه
goiter; edema (of tree) n
/bo-qa-la-mun/ بوقلمون
chameleon (& fig); kind of silk;
turkey (bird) n
urine n /bawl/ بول
urinate vi /bawl kardan/ بول
کردن
wild leek n /bo-lān/ بولان
bolani (pastry) n /bo-lā-ni/ بولانی
bolt n /bolt/ بولت
/bum/ بوم
owl (bird); land, country; canvas n
بومی , -ان/ها /bu-mi/
native, local adj; aborigine n
بومی امریکایی
/bu-mi-yĭ am-ri-kā-yi/
Native American, Indian n
scent, smell, odor n /buy, boy/ بوی
stink vi /buy dādan/ بوی دادن
smell (sth) vt /buy kardan/ بوی کردن
/boy-na-qa-ra/ بوینه قره
Boyna Qara see Sholgara n
/ba/ به
in, at; to; in exchange for prep
quince (arch) n /bĭh/ به

به آخر /ba ā-khĭr/
finally, in the end adv
به آهستگی /ba ā-hĭs-ta-gi/
slowly adv
به اتمام رساندن
/ba ĭt-mām rasāndan/
complete v
به اتمام رسیدن /ba ĭt-mām rasidan/
be completed vi
به اجبار /ba ĭj-bār/
compulsorily, forcibly adv
به اجمال /ba ĭj-māl/
in short, in brief adv
به استثنای <چیزی>
/ba ĭs-tĭs-nā(-yĭ)/
except <for sth> prep
به اصطلاح دیگر
/ba ĭs-tĭ-lāh-ĭ di-gar/
in other words phrs
به اضافه /ba ĭ-zā-fa/
in addition phrs
به امان خدا /ba a-mān-ĭ khŭ-dā/
goodbye excl
به انضمام <چیزی>
/ba ĭn-zĭ-mām(-ĭ)/
including, along w/<sth> prep
به آن ترتیب /ba ān tar-tib/
in that way adv
به این ترتیب /ba in tar-tib/
in this way adv
به پای رفتن /ba pāy raftan/
walk, go on foot vi
bitterly adv /ba tal-khi/ به تلخی
به تمام معنی /ba ta-mām ma'-nā/
completely, in every sense adv
به تن داشتن <چیزی را>
/ba tan dāshtan/
wear <sth> (clothes) v
به تنهایی /ba tan-hā-yi/
alone, by oneself adv
به جای <چیزی> /ba jāy(-ĭ)/
instead of <sth> prep
به جای آوردن /ba jāy āwŭrdan/
obey an order; know, recognize vt
به جای کردن /ba jāy kardan/
obey an order vt
see adv به اجبار /ba já-bĭr/ به جبر

به جدیت /ba jĭ-dĭ-yat/
seriously, earnestly adv
به جهان آمدن /ba ja-hān āmadan/
be born vi
به جرئت /ba jŭ-rat, jŭr-'at/
brave, courageous adj
به چشم ! /ba chá-shĭm (chĭˇ-)/
with pleasure excl
← زنده باشین !
May you live long! (response)
به چی وسیله ؟ /ba chi wa-sĭ-la/
by what means? phrs
به حافظه سپردن
/ba hā-fĭ-za sĭpŭrdan/
memorize vt
به حیث(ی) /ba hays(-ĭ)/
with regard to; in the capacity of phrs
به خارج سفر کردن
/ba khā-rĭj sa-far kardan/
travel abroad v
به خاطریکه /ba khā-tĭ-rĭ-kĭ, -key/
because conj
به خاک سپردن <کسی را>
/ba khāk sĭ-pŭr-dan/
bury <sb> vt
به خدا /ba khŭ-dā/
by God (I swear) phrs
به خدمت شما
/ba khĭd-mat-ĭ shŭ-mā/
at your service phrs
به خطر انداختن
/ba kha-tar andākhtan/
endanger vt
conscious adj /ba khŭd/ به خود
به خود آمدن /ba khŭd āmadan/
come to, regain consciousness v
به دار آویختن <کسی را>
/ba dār āweykhtan/
hang <sb> on a gallows vt
around prep /ba dawr(-ĭ)/ به دور
به ذهن سپردن
/ba zĭ´-hĭn sĭpŭrdan/
memorize vt
fluently adv /ba rā-ha-ti/ به راحتی
به راه انداختن /ba rāh andākhtan/
begin, start <sth> vt

a = c<u>u</u>p, ā = l<u>o</u>ng, aw = n<u>ow</u>, ay = s<u>igh</u>, e = b<u>e</u>t, ey = ob<u>ey</u>

به رایگان /ba rā-ya-gān/
in vain, gratuitously adv

به رسمیت شناختن /ba ras-mī-yat shīnākhtan/
recognize (a government) vt

به رضای خدا /ba ra-zā-yī khŭ-dā/
for God's sake phrs

به رضای خدا رفتن /ba ra-zā-yī khŭ-dā raftan/
die (fig) vi

به زانو درآمدن /ba zā-nu dár āmadan/
be defeated, yield vi

به زانو درآوردن /ba zā-nu dár āwardan/
defeat vt

به زبان آوردن /ba za-bān āwardan/
mention vt

به زعم آنان /ba zam-ī ā-nān/
some people say phrs

similar to adj /ba sān(-ī)/ به سان
/ba sŭr/ به سر
in tune, in harmony adj

/ba sar bŭrdan/ به سر بردن
bear, be afflicted by (fig) v

به سر رسیدن /ba sar rasidan/
end, come to an end vi

/ba sŭr-'at/ به سرعت
fast, quickly adv

به سلامت ماندن /ba sa-lā-mat māndan/
survive (fig) vi

see بشدت adv /ba shī-dat/ به شدت
/ba shart-ī ān ki/ به شرط آن که
provided that ... phrs

/ba shŭ-mul(-ī)/ به شمول
including prep

/ba shakl(-ī)/ به شکل
in the form of prep

/ba sa-rā-hat/ به صراحت
clearly, distinctly; frankly adv

/ba sĭ-fat(-ī)/ به صفت
in the capacity of phrs

against prep /ba zĭd(-ī)/ به ضد
به عبارت دیگر /ba ĭ-bā-rat-ī di-gar/
in other words phrs

به عمل آوردن /ba á-mīl āwardan/
carry out, conduct vt

/ba ĭ-waz(-ī)/ به عوض
instead of prep

/ba gha-raz(-ī)/ به غرض
for, in order to prep

except prep /ba ghayr(-ī)/ به غیر
/ba qa-rār(-ī)/ به قرار
according to prep

به قرار گفتهٔ شما ... /ba qa-rār-ī gŭf-ta-yī shŭ-mā/
as you have said phrs

/ba qarz gĭrĭftan/ به قرض گرفتن
buy (sth) on credit vt

on purpose adv /ba qasd/ به قصد
به قوام آوردن /ba qĭ-wām āwardan/
thicken (liquid, syrup) vt

/ba qĭ-wām āmadan/ به قوام آمدن
thicken, become thicker vi

/ba qawl(-ī)/ به قول
according to; quoting (sb) prep

/ba lī-hāz-ī khŭ-dā/ ! به لحاظ خدا
for God's sake excl

/ba mĭ´-sĭl(-ī)/ به مثل
like, similar to prep

/ba mŭ-ja-rad(-ī)/ به مجرد
when, as soon as adv

به مخاطره انداختن /ba mŭ-khā-tĭ-ra andākhtan/
risk, jeopardize vt

/ba ma-rā-tĭb/ به مراتب
many times adv

/ba ma-zāh/ به مزاح
jokingly, in jest adv

به مشام رسیدن /ba ma-shām rasidan/
be perceived by smell v

به مشاهده رسیدن /ba mŭ-shā-hĭ-da rasidan/
be noticed v

/ba mī-yān āmadan/ به میان آمدن
turn up; (loosely) turn out to be vi

به میان آوردن /ba mī-yān āwardan/
create, establish; present vi

/ba nŭd-rat/ به ندرت
rarely, infrequently adv

i = keep, ĭ = big, u = coop, ŭ = put, y = yet, ' = (glottal stop)   67

/ba na-zar rasidan/ به نظر رسیدن
appear, seem, look vi

/ba na-zar-ī ká-sey rasidan/ به نظر ‹کسی› رسیدن
occur ‹to sb› vi

/ba na-zar-ī ma/ به نظر مه
in my opinion phrs

/ba naʿ-qīl(-ī)› به نقل ‹کسی›
quoting ‹sb› prep

/ba wa-si-la(-yī)/ به وسیله ‹چیزی›
by means of ‹sth› phrs

/ba waqt/ به وقت on time adv
/ba wa-qī-fa-hā/ به وقفه ها
intermittently, off & on adv

/ba wŭ-qo paywastan/ به وقوع پیوستن
happen, occur vi

/ba ha-ya-jān āmadan/ به هیجان آوردن
get excited, get agitated vi

/ba ha-ya-jān āwŭrdan/ به هیجان آوردن
excite, agitate vt

/ba yād dāshtan/ به یاد داشتن
remember, recall vt

/ba ya-qin/ به یقین
certainly, indisputably adv

/ba yakh nawīshtan ŭ dar af-tāb māndan/ به یخ نوشتن و در آفتاب ماندن
labor in vain (fig) phrs

price, cost, value n /ba-hā/ بها
/ba-hār/ بهار
spring (season); temple; bahar (flower, f name, village) n

Bihar (geog) n /bī-hār/ بهار
/ba-hār-ŭl-bar/ بهارالبر
bahar (spice) n

/ba-hā-ran/ بهاران
in the spring adv; springtime n

Baharak (dist) n /ba-hā-rak/ بهارک
/ba-hā-ri/ بهاری
spring, springtime adj

/ba-hā-na (bā-na)/ بهانه , -ها
excuse, pretext n

make an excuse v بهانه ساختن ←

/ba-hā-na joy/ بهانه جوی ,-ان/ها
one who makes excuses n

/ba-hā-na jo-yi/ بهانه جویی
making excuses n

/ba-hā-na jo-yi kardan/ بهانه جویی کردن
see بهانه ساختن v

/bīh-bud/ بهبود
well-being; improvement n

/bīh-bud yāftan/ بهبود یافتن
be in good health vi

confusion n /bŭht/ بهت
/bŭht ā-war/ بهت آور
see بهت انگیز adj

/bŭht an-geyz/ بهت انگیز
confusing adj

confused adj /bŭht za-da/ بهت زده
/bŭh-tān/ بهتان
slander, speaking ill of n

/bŭh-tān zadan/ بهتان زدن ‹کسی را›
slander, speak ill of ‹sb› vt

/bŭh-tān gŭftan/ بهتان گفتن
speak slanderously v

better, superior adj /bīh-tar/ بهتر
/bīh-tar ast/ بهتر است
had better ‹+ subj› phrs

/bīh-ta-ri/ بهتری
superiority; improvement n

best adj /bīh-ta-rin/ بهترین
/bīh-din/ بهدین
Zoroastrianism (fig, arch) n

for the sake of prep /bahr(-ī)/ بهر
/bah-rām/ بهرام
Mars (planet); Bahram (geog) n

/bah-rām-ī sha-hid/ بهرام شهید
Bahram-e Shahid (ctr Jaghatu) n

valor (arch) n /bah-rā-mi/ بهرامی
/bah-ra/ بهره
benefit; interest; share n

/bah-ra bar dā-ri/ بهره بر داری
yield (from investment) n

/bah-ra bar dā-ri kardan/ بهره بر داری کردن
exploit (mine) vt

/bah-ra-mand/ بهره مند
benefiting from adj

a = cup, ā = long, aw = now, ay = sigh, e = bet, ey = obey

بهره ور /bah-ra-war/ adj
بهره مند see

بهسود /bīh-sud/ Behsud (dist; ctr) n
بهشت , ها- /bī-hīsht/
heaven, paradise n

بهشت عدن /bĭ-hīsht-ĭ á-dĭn/
Garden of Eden n

بهشتی /bī-hīsh-ti/ heavenly adj

بهمن /bah-man/
angel for cattle (Zor); avalanche;
Bahman (m name) n

بهی /bĭ-hi/ quince n
بهی دانه /bĭ-hi dā-na/
quince seeds (med) n

بهین /bĭ-hin/ excellent; best adj
بی /bey/ without prep
بی آب شدن /bey āb shŭdan/
lose face, be disgraced vi

بی آب کردن /bey āb kardan/
cause to lose face, disgrace vt

بی اندازه /bey an-dā-za/
too, excessively adv

بی ایریا /bey ey-rī-yā/
San Francisco Bay Area n

بی بضاعت /bey ba-zā-'at/
poor, needy adj

بی بی /bi-bi/
grandmother; respected lady
(form of address for f) n

← بی بی جان dear lady
← بی بی و بیگم
admired & respected (f)

بی بی مهرو /bi-bi mah-ru/
Bibi Mahru (Kabul city district) n

بی پدر /bey pa-dar/
son of a bitch (insult); orphan n

بی پروا /bey par-wā/
indifferent, unconcerned adj

بی تجربه /bey taj-rī-ba/
inexperienced adj

بی تدبیر /bey tad-bir/
imprudent; tactless adj

بی تناسب /bey ta-nā-sŭb/
disproportionate; asymmetrical adj

بی ثبات /bey sŭ-bāt/
unstable, unsteady adj

بی حس /bey hīs/
numb; unfeeling adj

بی حمیت /bey ha-mī-yat/
unenthusiastic; lacking zeal adj

بی حوصله /bey haw-sī-la/
impatient adj

بی حیا /bey ha-yā/
shameless, not bashful adj

بی خانه /bey khā-na/ homeless adj
بی خود /bey khŭd/
unconscious adj

← بی خود شدن
lose consciousness vi

بی دین /bey din/
unbeliever, infidel n

بی روی /bey ruy/ impudent adj
بی رویی /bey ru-yi/ impudence n
بی سواد /bey sa-wād/ illiterate adj
بی سوادی /bey sa-wā-di/
illiteracy n

بی شرف /bey sha-raf/
dishonorable adj

بی شرم /bey sharm/
shameless adj

بی فایده /bey fā-yī-da/ useless adj
بی قواره /bey qa-wā-ra/
unattractive, unshapely adj

بی قیمت /bey qi-mat/
worthless, without value adj

بی گفتگو /bey gŭf-tŭ-go/
certainly, indisputably adv

بی گناه /bey gŭ-nāh/
innocent, blameless adj

بی کس و کوی /bey kas ŭ koy/
w/o friend or home adj

بی کم و زیاد /bey kam ŭ zī-yād/
exactly adv

بی نوا /bey na-wā/ poor adj
بی وقار /bey wī-qār/
undignified adj

بیابان /bī-yā-bān/
desert, wasteland n

بیابان گرد /bī-yā-bān gard/
nomad, wanderer n; nomadic adj

بیابان نشین /bī-yā-bān nī-shin/
nomad, wanderer n; nomadic adj

بیاره /bī-yā-ra/ vine n
بیان , ات/ها- /ba-yān/
statement, expression n

---

i = keep, ĭ = big, u = coop, ŭ = put, y = yet, ' = (glottal stop)   69

بیان کردن /ba-yān kardan/
make a statement *v*

بیانی /ba-yā-ni/
rhetorical, oratorical *adj*

بیانیه , ها- /ba-yā-nǐ-ya/
remarks, speech, statement *n*

بیانیه ایراد کردن
/ba-yā-nǐ-ya i-rād kardan/
deliver remarks *v*

بیانیه کردن /ba-yā-nǐ-ya kardan/
give remarks *v*

ببی *n* /bi-bi/ see ببی

بیت , ها-/ابیات /bayt, pl ab-yāt/
couplet; lyrics; house *n*

بیت الحرام /bayt-ŭl-ha-rām/
the Kaaba *n*

بیت اللحم , لام- /bayt-ŭl-lahm, -lām/
Bethlehem *n*

بیت الله /bayt-ŭl-lāh/ the Kaaba *n*

بیت المقدس /bayt-ŭl-mŭ-qa-das/
Jerusalem *n*

بیتل /bay-tal/ mare *n*

بیجاشده , گان- /bey-jā-shŭ-da/
displaced person; IDP *n*

بیجینگ /bey-jing/ Beijing *n*

بیچاره , گان/ها- /bey-chā-ra/
poor or helpless pers *n*

بیچاره گک /bey chā-ra-gak/
n بی چاره see

بیحد /bey-had/
too, excessively *adv*

بید /beyd/ willow tree *n*

بیداد /bey-dād/
injustice, oppression *n*

بیرق , ها- /bay-raq/
flag, standard, banner *n*

بیرق دار , ان/ها- /bay-raq dār/
pioneer *n*

بیرل /bey-ral/ barrel *n*

بیر /bir/ beer *n*

بیره /bi-ra/ gums *n*

بیروبار /bi-rū-bār/
busy, crowded *adj*; crowd *n*

بیروت /bey-rut/ Beirut *n*

بیرون /bi-run, bey-/
outside *adv*

بیرون کردن ←
take out, withdraw

بیز اوپراتیفی پیشراندە شدە
/beyz-ĭ o-pa-rā-ti-fi-yĭ peysh-rān-
da shŭ-da/
FOB, forward operating base (mil)
n

بیست /bist/ twenty *n, adj*

بیستم /bis-tūm/ twentieth *adj*

بیستمین /bis-tŭ-min/
twentieth (lit, oft before n) *adj*

بیست و یک /bist ŭ yak/
twenty-one *n, adj*

بیست و یکم /bist ŭ ya-kŭm/
twenty-first *adj*

بیسخن /bey-sŭ-khan/
certainly, indubitably *adv*

بیشتر <از چیزی> /beysh-tar/
more <than sth> *adj*

بیشه , ها- /bey-sha/
thicket, copse *n*

بیعت /bay-'at/ oath of allegiance *n*

بیعت کردن ← swear allegiance *v*

بیضوی /bay-za-wi/
egg-shaped, oval *adj*

بیضه , ها- /bay-za/
egg; ovum *n*

پنج بیضه تخم ← five eggs

بیضه گذاشتن • بیضه نهادن ←
lay eggs *v*

بیطار /bay-tār/ veterinarian *n*

بیطاری /bay-tā-ri/ veterinary *adj*

بیطرف /bey-ta-raf/
neutral, non-aligned *adj*

بیطرفانه /bey-ta-ra-fā-na/
neutral *adj*; neutrally *adv*

بیطرفی /bey-ta-ra-fi/
neutrality, non-alignment *n*

بیعانه /bay-'ā-na (ba-yā-na)/
down payment, earnest money *n*

بیکاری /bey-kā-ri/
unemployment *n*

بیکران /bey-kĭ-rān/
immeasurable, boundless *adj*

بیگ /beyg/
lord, prince; beg (title) *n*

بیگانگی /bey-gā-na-gi/
foreignness; alienation *n*

بیگانه , گان/ها- /bey-gā-na/
stranger; foreigner, alien *n*

بیگانه پرست /bey-gā-na pa-rast/
xenophile n; xenophilous adj

بیگفت /bey-gŭft/ disobedient adj

بیگفتی /bey-gŭf-ti/ disobedience n

بیگم /bey-gŭm/ lady (of rank) n

بیل /beyl/ shovel, spade n

بیل زدن /beyl zadan/
turn up soil w/a shovel v

بیرل /bey-lar/ n see بیلر

بیلچه /beyl-cha/ trowel, dibble n

بیلک /bey-lak/ n see بیلچه

بیلک شانه /bey-lak-ī shā-na/
shoulder blade n

بیم /bim/ fear n

بیمار , -ان/ها /bey-mār/
ill, sick adj; patient n

بیمار داری /bey-mār dā-ri/
nursing (loosely) n

بیمار غنج /bey-mār ghŭnj/
sickly, chronically sick adj

بیماری /bey-mā-ri/
sickness, illness n

بیماری مرگی /bey-mā-ri-yī mīr-gi/
epilepsy n

بیمناک /bim-nāk/
frightening, scary adj

بیمه /bi-ma/ insurance n
بیمه کردن ← insure, underwrite vt

بیمه کننده , -گان/ها /bi-ma kŭ-nīn-da/
insurer, underwriter n

بین /bayn(-ī)/ between; among adv
بین‌المللی /bayn-ŭl-mī-la-li/
international adj

بینی /bi-ni/
nose; seeing, perceiving n

بینی پوچک /bi-ni-yī po-chak/
flat-nosed adj

بینی جاری /bi-ni-yī jā-ri/
runny nose n

بیوگی /bey-wa-gi/ widowhood n

بیولوژی /bī-yo-lo-zhi/ biology n

بیوه , -ها /bey-wa/
widowed adj; widow n

بیوه زن /bey-wa zan/ widow n

پ

پا , -ها /pā (pāy)/ foot, leg n

پابوس /pā-bos/ n پای بوس see

پاپ /pāp/ pope, the Pope n

پاپی /pā-pi/ puppy n

پاچا /pā-chā/ n پاد شاه see

پاچله /pā-chap-la/ n چپلی see

پاچه /pā-cha/
foot of animal (food); trouser leg;
trouser hem n

پاختک /pākh-tak/
turtledove (bird) n

پاداش /pā-dāsh/
retaliation; reward n

پاداش دادن /pā-dāsh dādan/
give a reward n

پاداشت /pā-dāsht/ n پاداش see

پادزهر /pād-zá-hīr, -zahr/
antidote n

پادشاه /pād-shā (pā-chā)/ king n
پادشاه انقلابی ←
revolutionary monarch
(Amanullah)

پاراگراف /pā-rā-gī-rāf/
paragraph n

پارت /pārt/ Parthia (hist) n

پارتی /pār-ti/
party (pol) n; Parthian (& pers;
hist) adj, n

پارسا , -یان/ها /pār-sā/
chaste; pious (& pers) adj, n

پارسال /pār-sāl/ last year adv

پارساله /pār-sā-la/ last year's adj

پارچه /pār-cha/
brocade; piece (& mus) n

پارسل /pār-sal/ package, parcel n

پارسی /pār-si/ Persian (lang) n

پارسی باستان /pār-si bās-tān/
Old Persian (lang) n

پارسی بان , -ان/ها /pār-si bān/
Persian speaker n; Persian-
speaking adj

پارسی دری /pār-si da-ri/
Dari (lang) n

پارلمان /pār-la-mān/ parliament n

پارک /pārk/ n park (public space)
پارک کردن /pārk kardan/
park (a vehicle) vi
پارکنگ /pār-kǐng/ n parking area
پارون /pā-run/ n Parun (dist)
پاریس /pā-ris/ Paris n
پازهر, -زهر /pā-zá-hir, -zahr/ antidote n
پاس /pās/
watch, guarding; respect, consideration n
پاسبان , -ان/ها /pās-bān/
watchman, guardian n
پاسبانی /pās-bā-ni/
watching; guardianship n
پاسپورت , -ها /pās-port/
passport n
پاسپورت سیاسی /pās-port-ǐ sǐ-yā-si/
official passport n
پاستوریزه /pās-tu-rey-za/
pasteurized adj
پاسخ , -ها /pā-sǔkh/
answer, reply, response n
پاسخ خواستن /pā-sǔkh khāstan/
request a reply v
پاسخ دادن /pā-sǔkh dādan/
give an answer v
پاسخ گفتن /pā-sǔkh gǔftan/
give an oral response v
پاسدار , -ان/ها /pās-dār/
guard [< Farsi] n
پاسداران انقلاب اسلامی
/pās-dā-rān-ǐ ǐn-qǐ-lāb-ǐ ǐs-lā-mi/
Revolutionary Guards (Iran) n pl
پاسوال /pās-wāl/
major general , MG [< P] n
پاسور /pā-sur/
pasur (card game) n
پاش دادن /pāsh dādan/
scatter, sow, spray (colloq) vt
پاشا /pā-shā/
pasha (former honorific) n
پاشان /pā-shān/
scattered, sprinkled adj
پاشاندن ؛ -پاشان- ؛ پاشاند-
/pā-shān-dan/
scatter, sow, spray vt
پاشنه heel (of foot) n /pāsh-na/

پاشیدن ؛ -پاش- ؛ پاشید-
/pā-shi-dan/
scatter, sow, spray (vt, vi)
پاغنده /pā-ghǔn-da/
round object; snowflake n
پافشاری /pā-fǐ-shā-ri/
persistence n
پاک /pāk/ clean, neat adj
پاک دل /pāk dǐl/
sincere, frank (lit) adj
پاک کردن /pāk kardan/ clean vt
پاکت /pā-kat/ envelope n
پاکستان /pā-kǐs-tān/ Pakistan n
پاکستانی , -ان/ها /pā-kǐs-tā-ni/
Pakistani (& pers) adj, n
پاکی /pā-ki/
cleanness; chastity; razor blade n
پالان /pā-lān/ saddle, packsaddle n
پالایش /pā-lā-yǐsh/
filtering, straining n
پالک /pā-lak/ spinach n
پالنگ /pā-lang/
palang (decorated bed) [< P] n
پالیدن ؛ -پال- ؛ پالید- /pā-li-dan/
look for, seek vt
پامال کردن /pā-māl kardan/
پای مال کردن see vt
پامیر /pā-meyr, -mir/
Pamir (region, mtn range) n
پامیر خورد /pā-meyr-ǐ khǔrd/
Little Pamir n
پامیر کلان /pā-meyr-ǐ ka-lān/
Great Pamir n
پامیری , -ان/ها , -mi-/ /pā-mey-ri/
Pamiri (& pers, lang) adj, n
پان betel leaf n /pān/
پان اسلامیزم /pān ǐs-lā-mí-zǐm/
pan-Islamism n
پانامه /pā-nā-ma/
Panama (geog) n
پانزده /pānz-dah/ fifteen n, adj
پانزدهم /pānz-da-hǔm/
fifteenth adj
پانزدهمین /pānz-da-hǔ-min/
fifteenth (lit, used before n) adj
پانسمان /pāns-mān/
dressing (wounds) n

پایان دادن ‹به چیزی›
/pā-yān dādan/
end, finish <sth> vt
پایپ pipe n /pāyp/
پایپ‌لاین pipeline n /pāyp-lāyn/
پایتخت capital (city) n /pāy-takht/
پایدار /pāy-dār/
permanent; constant; having feet adj
پایش durability n /pā-yīsh/
پایشت /pā-yīsht/
see پایش (colloq) n
پایشی /pā-yĭ-shi/
durable, long-lasting adj
پایکی foot-operated adj /pā-ya-ki/
پایگاه /pāy-gāh/
base (mil); dignity, rank n
پایه /pā-ya/
leg (of chair); pole; pile (of money); pillar; stair n
← یک پایه تیلفون one telephone
پایی foot-operated adj /pā-yi/
پاییز autumn, fall n /pā-yeyz, -yiz/
پاییزی autumnal adj /pā-yey-zi/
پایین see پایان prep /pā-yin(-ī)/
پایینی see پایان prep /pā-yi-ni(-yī)/
پیشه automatic rifle n /pa-pa-sha/
پپوک hoopoe (bird) n /pa-puk/
پت rash (med) n /pĭt/
← پت کشیدن develop a rash v /pŭt/
covered, hidden; closed (eyes) adj
← پت کردن cover, hide; close vt
پترول /pĭt-rol/
gas, petrol; petroleum n
پتک /pa-tak/
flask, water bottle; insole n
پتک /pŭtk/
hammer, sledgehammer n
پتلون /pat-lun/
pants, trousers; pantaloon n
← پتلون پیوند کردن patch pants
پتنوس tray, tea tray n /pat-nus/
پتو /pa-tu/
blanket (coarse, woolen) n
پته /pa-ta/
rung (on ladder); step n
پتی ribbon; bandage n /pa-ti/

پانسمان کردن /pāns-mān kardan/
dress (wounds) v
پانصد n, adj /pān-sad/ see صد پنج
پانگ counterweight n /pāng/
پاو /pāw/
paw (unit of weight); quarter-hour n
پاورقی /pā-wa-ra-qi/
footnote; feuilleton n
پانین end; bottom n /pā-'in/
پانین بردن /pā-'in bŭrdan/
decrease, bring down vt
پانین رفتن /pā-'in raftan/
decrease, go down vi
پای see پا n /pāy/
پای انداز /pāy an-dāz/
runner (carpet) n
پای بازی footsie n /pāy bā-zi/
پای بازی کردن /pāy bā-zi kardan/
play footsie v
پای بست foundation n /pāy bast/
پای بند شدن /pāy band shŭdan/
become engaged vi
پای بوس foot-kissing n /pāy bos/
پای به دو گذاشتن
/pāy ba daw gŭzāshtan/
set off running v
پای پاک doormat n /pāy pāk/
پای پوش footwear n /pāy posh/
پای زیب anklet n /pāy zeyb/
پای شکسته , ـگان/ها
/pāy shĭ-kas-ta/
broken-legged; weak (& pers) adj, n
پای کوبی dance n /pāy ko-bi/
پای کوبی کردن /pāy ko-bi kardan/
dance v
پای مال کردن /pāy-māl kardan/
trample; (fig) suppress (rights) vt
پای واز /pāy-wāz/
prisoner's visitor (colloq) n
پای وازی /pāy-wā-zi/
bridal shower, engagement party by bride's family n
پایا standing; ongoing adj /pā-yā/
پایان /pā-yān/
end; bottom n; down adv
پایان below prep /pā-yān(-ī)/

پچیر و اگام /pa-chir wŭ a-gām/ Pachir wa Agam (dist) n

پخت و پز /pŭkht ŭ paz/ cooking (colloq) n

پخت و پز کردن /pŭkht ŭ paz kardan/ cook (colloq) v

پختن ؛ -پز- ؛ -پخت- /pŭkh-tan/ cook; bake v

پخته /pŭkh-ta/ cooked, baked; (in var senses) ripe adj

پخته /pakh-ta/ cotton (colloq) n

پخته کار /pakh-ta kār/ cotton grower n

پخته کردن /pŭkh-ta kardan/ cook; bake (colloq) v

پخته یی /pakh-ta-yi/ cotton-filled adj

پخچ /pakhch/ short (of stature); low adj

پخش /pakhsh/ distribution; broadcast n

← پخش کردن distribute; broadcast v

پداگوژی /pī-dā-go-zhi/ pedagogy n

پدر , -ان/ها /pa-dar, pī-/ father n

پدر خوانده /pa-dar khān-da/ father figure, mentor n

پدر کلان , -ها /pa-dar ka-lān/ grandfather n

پدران /pa-da-rān/ forefathers, ancestors (m) n pl

پدرانه /pa-dar-rā-na/ fatherly adj

پدروار /pa-dar-wār/ fatherly adj

پدری /pa-da-ri/ fatherhood n; paternal, fatherly adj

پدرود /pad-rud, pád-/ farewell; abandonment n

پدرود کردن /pad-rud kardan/ abandon vt

پدرود گفتن /pad-rud gŭftan/ bid farewell v

پدید /pa-did/ emergent; visible adj

پدید آمدن /pa-did āmadan/ emerge; become visible vi

← پدید آوردن bring into view

پدیدار شدن /pa-di-dār shŭdan/ emerge; become visible vi

← پدیدار کردن bring into view

پدیده /pa-di-da/ phenomenon n

پذیر /pa-zir/ accepting (of sth) adj

پذیرایی /pa-zi-rā-yi/ hospitality n

پذیرایی رفتن /pa-zi-rā-yi raftan/ visit, go as a guest v

پذیرایی کردن /pa-zi-rā-yi kardan/ receive guests v

پذیرش /pa-zi-rīsh/ acceptance, approval, obedience n

پذیرفتن ؛ -پذیر- ؛ پذیرفت- /pa-zi-rŭf-tan/ receive, accept, approve vt

پذیرفته بودن /pa-zi-rŭf-ta budan/ be accepted, welcomed vi

پذیرفتنی /pa-zi-rŭf-ta-ni/ acceptable adj

پر , -ها /par/ feather; playing card n

پر /pŭr/ full; loaded (gun) adj; too much adv

پرآب /pŭr āb/ juicy; tearful; full of water adj

پر افاده /pŭr ĭ-fā-da/ haughty adj

پر افگندن /par afgandan/ molt, shed feathers v

پر انداختن /par andākhtan/ see پر افگندن v

پر بار /pŭr bār/ fruitful, productive, rich adj

پر تلاطم /pŭr ta-lā-tŭm/ turbulent, tumultuous adj

پر پیچ و خم /pŭr peych ŭ kham/ curly (hair) adj

پر خمار /pŭr khŭ-mār/ languid, languorous adj

پر خوری کردن /pŭr khŭ-ri kardan/ overeat, stuff oneself vi

پر خون /pŭr khun/ bloody, bloodstained adj

پر زرق و برق /pŭr zarq ŭ barq/ gaudy, garish phrs

پر عایدات /pŭr ā-yī-dāt/ fruitful, profitable adj

پر فیض /pŭr fayz/
generous, beneficent; abundant
adj

پر کردن /pŭr kardan/ fill vt

پر ماجرا /pŭr mā-ja-rā/
adventurous adj

پر مخاطره /pŭr mŭ-khā-tĭ-ra/
high-threat adj

پر موی /pŭr muy/
hairy, hirsute (pers) adj

پرار /pī-rār/
next to last, penultimate; two (sth)
ago adj

←— پرار سال two years ago

پراشوت parachute n /pa-rā-shot/

پراشوتست /pa-rā-sho-tīst/
parachutist n

پراکرت /pa-rā-kĭ-rĭt/
Prakrit (lang) n

پراگ Prague n /prāg/

پراگندن ؛ -پراگن- ؛ پراگند-
/pa-rā-gan-dan/
scatter, disperse vt

پراگنده /pa-rā-gan-da/
scattered, dispersed adj

پراندن ؛ -پران- ؛ پراند-
/pa-rān-dan/
cause to fly; splash; blast; (colloq)
kidnap vt

پرت scratching n /part/
←— پرت کردن scratch v

پرتاب /par-tāb/
throwing, flinging; launch n

پرتاب به فضا /par-tāb ba fa-zā/
space launch n

پرتاب کردن /par-tāb kardan/
throw, fling; launch v

پرتافتن ؛ -پرت- ؛ پرتافت-
/par-tāf-tan/
throw, fling; put down vt

←— انداختن (alternative past stem)

پرتگاه pit n /part-gāh/

پرتگال Portugal n /por-ta-gāl/

پرتگالی , -ان/ها /por-ta-gā-li/
Portuguese (& lang, pers) adj, n

پرتو ray, beam; light n /par-taw/

پرچم /par-cham/
Parcham, moderate faction of
PDPA (hist); banner n

پرچم دار , -ان/ها /par-cham dār/
pioneer, standard-bearer n;
standard-bearing

پرچمن /pŭr-cha-man/
Purchaman (dist) n

پرچمی , -ان/ها /par-cha-mi/
Parcham member n; relating to
Parcham adj

پرچه piece; splinter n /par-cha/

پرچه پرچه /par-cha par-cha/
splintered; shattered adj

پرخ flurry (snow); drizzle n /pŭrkh/

پرخاش /par-khāsh/
quarreling, wrangling adj

پرخاش کردن /par-khāsh kardan/
quarrel, wrangle v

پرخچه /pa-rakh-cha/
splinter (wood) n

پرداختن ؛ -پرداز- ؛ پرداخت-
/par-dākh-tan/
pay; accomplish; wage (war) vt

پرده , -ها /par-da/
curtain; screen (& film); veil;
membrane n

پرده آهنین /par-da-yĭ ā-ha-nin/
Iron Curtain (hist) n

پرده بکارت /par-da-yĭ ba-kā-rat/
hymen (anat) n

پرده دری /par-da da-ri/
betrayal of secrets n

پرده دل /par-da-yĭ dĭl/
diaphragm (anat) n

پرده سرا /par-da sa-rā/
tent (ornate); harem n

پرده قاتکی چوبی
/par-da-yĭ qā-ta-ki-yĭ cho-bi/
folding wooden screen n

پرده گوش /par-da-yĭ gosh/
eardrum (anat) n

پرده نشین /par-da nĭ-shin/
segregated adj; veil wearer (f) n

پرده نشینی /par-da nĭ-shi-ni/
segregation of f n

پرزه , ـها /pŭr-za/
part (mechanical); note on small
paper; joke n
پرزه جات ←
(pl, colloq)
پرزه فروشی /pŭr-za fŭ-ro-shi/
auto parts shop n
پرسان /pŭr-sān/
question, inquiry n; inquisitively
adv
پرسان کردن /pŭr-sān kardan/
ask, inquire v
پرستش /pa-ras-tĭsh/
worship, veneration n
پرستش کردن /pa-ras-tĭsh kardan/
worship, venerate vt
پرستشگاه /pa-ras-tĭsh-gāh/
sanctuary, temple n
پرستنده , ـگان/ها /pa-ras-tĭn-da/
worshiper (pers) n
پرستو /pa-ras-tu/
swallow, swift (bird) n
پرسش , ـها /pŭr-sĭsh/
question; questioning n
ask, inquire v پرسش کردن ←
پرسش نامه /pŭr-sĭsh nā-ma/
questionnaire n
پرسشی /pŭr-sĭ-shi/
interrogative adj
پرسنده , ـگان/ها /pŭr-sĭn-da/
enquirer, inquirer n
پرسوناژ /par-so-nāzh/
character in a literary work n
پرسونل /par-so-nal/
personnel, manning n
پرسیدن ؛ ـپرس- ؛ پرسید-
/pŭr-si-dan/
ask, inquire v
پرکار /par-kār/
compass (for drawing) n
پرکار /pŭr-kār/
hard-working, industrious adj
پرکاری /pŭr-kā-ri/
filling (in tooth) v
fill a tooth; fill in پرکاری کردن ←
پرگنه /par-ga-na/
clan, tribe; sect; farmland tract n
پرنده , ـگان/ها /pa-rĭn-da/
bird n
پروا /par-wā/
care, concern n

پروا داشتن /par-wā dāshtan/
worry, be concerned v
پروا نداره /par-wā ná-dā-ra/
it doesn't matter; s/he doesn't
care phrs
پرواز /par-wāz/
flight (on plane) n
پروان /par-wān/
Parwan (prov) n
پروانه , ـگان/ها /par-wā-na/
moth; butterfly; propeller n
پروتستان , ـان/ها /pū-ro-tĭs-tān/
Protestant (& pers) adj, n
پروجکتر , ـها /pū-ro-jĭk-tar/
projector n
پروراندن ؛ ـپروران- ؛ پروراند-
/par-wa-rān-dan/
see پروردن vt
پروردن ؛ ـپرور- ؛ پرورد-
/par-war-dan/
nurture, cherish, foster vt
پروردگار /par-war-dĭ-gār/
Providence (God) n
پرورش /par-wa-rĭsh/
nourishment; training n
nourish, nurture پرورش دادن ←
پرورش گاه /par-wa-rĭsh gāh/
nursery n
پروریدن ؛ ـپرور- ؛ پرورید-
/par-wa-ri-dan/
nourish, nurture v
پروژکتر , ـها /pū-ro-zhĭk-tar/
see پروجکتر n
پروژه , ـها /pū-ro-zha/
project n
پروستات /pū-ros-tāt/
prostate (anat) n
پروسه , ـها /pū-ro-sa/
process n
پروگرام /pū-ro-gĭ-rām/
program n
پروگرام تحکیم صلح
/pū-ro-gĭ-rām-ĭ tah-kim-ĭ sŭlh/
Program Tahkim-e Solh, PTS n
پروین /par-win/
Pleiades (star cluster) n
پرا گراف /pa-rā-gĭ-rāf/
paragraph n
پرهیز کردن /par-hayz kardan/
abstain; diet; be chaste v
پرهیزانه /par-hay-zā-na/
diet (prescribed) n

پرهیزگار /par-hayz-gār/
abstinent; chaste (& pers) adj, n

پریان /par-yān/ Paryan (dist) n

پریدن ؛ -پر- ؛ پرید- /pa-ri-dan/
fly vi

پریروز، -ری-/ /pa-ray-roz, -ri-/
day before yesterday adv

پریشان /pī-ray-shān/
anxious; poor; disheveled adj

پریشان خاطر /pī-ray-shān khā-tīr/
adj خاطر پریشان see

پریشانی /pī-ray-shā-ni/
poverty; distress n

پریمینا /pī-ri-mey-nā/
primrose (flower) n

پزشک /pū-zīshk/
physician (arch) n

پزشکی /pū-zīsh-ki/
medicine (practice) (arch) n

پژمان /pazh-mān/ sad adj

پژمردن ؛ -پژمر- ؛ پژمرد- /pazh-mŭr-dan/
fade, wither v

پژمرده /pazh-mŭr-dan/
faded, withered adj

پژواک /pazh-wāk/
echo; Pajhwok (press agency) n

پژوهش، -ها /pa-zho-hīsh/
research n

پژوهش کردن /pa-zho-hīsh kardan/
research v

پژوهندگی /pa-zho-hīn-da-gi/
research n

پژوهنده , -گان/ها /pa-zho-hīn-da/
researcher n

پس /pas/
rear; (anat, colloq) butt n; back
adv; then, in that case conj

پس /pas(-ī)/ behind prep

پس آمدن /pas āmadan/
return (colloq) vi

پس از /pas az/ after prep

پس از آن /pas az ān/
afterwards adv

پس از آن که /pas az ān kĭ/
after (sth) conj

پس افتادن /pas aftādan/
fall behind (in task); be postponed
vi

پس انداختن ؛ پس -انداز- ؛ پس
انداخت- /pas andākhtan/
postpone; throw down/away vt

پس انداز /pa-sān-dāz/ saving(s) n

پس انداز کردن /pa-sān-dāz kardan/
save (money) v

پس پس /pŭs pŭs/ whisper n

پس پس کردن /pŭs pŭs kardan/
whisper v

پس خانه /pas khā-na/
closet (storage), back room n

پس دوزی /pas do-zi/ hemming n

پس دوزی کردن /pas do-zi kardan/
hem v

پس رفته /pas raf-ta/
shy, reticent adj

پس گردنی /pas gar-da-ni/
slap on back of neck n

پس گوش کردن /pas-ī gosh kardan/
neglect (fig); put behind ear vt

پس ماندن /pas māndan/
stay behind, stay back vi

پس مانده /pas mān-da/
underdeveloped, backward adj

پسان /pa-sān/ late, later adj, adv

پسان آمدن /pa-sān āmadan/
arrive late v

پسابند /pa-sā-band/
Pasaband (dist) n

پسانتر /pa-sān-tar/
later (colloq) adv

پساوند /pa-sā-wand/ suffix n

پست /past/
ignoble; malicious adj

پسته /pĭs-ta/ pistachio n

پستان، -ها /pĭs-tān/
breast; udder n

پستاندار , -ان/ها /pĭs-tān-dār/
mammal n

پسته یی /pĭs-ta-yi/
pistachio-colored adj

پستی /pas-ti/ malice n

پسر , -ان/ها /pĭ-sar/ son; boy n

پسر اندر /pī-sar an-dar/
stepson (lit) n

پسر خاله /pī-sar-ī khā-la/
see بچه خاله n

پسر خوانده /pī-sar khān-da/
like a son n

پسر عم /pī-sar-ī 'am/
see بچه کاکا (arch) n

پسر عمه /pī-sar-ī a-ma/
see بچه عمه n

پسر کاکا /pī-sar-ī kā-kā/
see بچه کاکا n

پسر ماما /pī-sar-ī mā-mā/
see بچه ماما n

پسرانه boys' (lit) adj /pī-sa-rā-na/
پسری filial adj /pī-sa-ri/
پسندیدن ؛ -پسند- ؛ پسندید-
/pī-san-di-dan/
choose; accept; admire vt

پسوند , -ها suffix n /pas-wand/
پسینه , -ها /pa-si-na/
postposition n

پشاور /pī-shā-wŭr (-shawr)/
Peshawar (city) n

پشت ! /pīsht/
shoo (to scare cats) excl

پشت back; reverse side n /pŭsht/
پشت(-ی) /pŭsht(-ī)/
behind, in back of prep

پشت پا زدن /pŭsht-ī pā zadan/
abandon; renounce (fig) vt

پشت پرده /pŭsht-ī par-da/
secret; veiled adj

پشت دادن /pŭsht dādan/
escape, flee; (of horse) be tame vi

پشت دق شدن /pŭsht dīq shŭdan/
miss, long for [پشت takes pers
ending for pers/object missed] v
← پشتت دق شدم I missed you

پشت رود /pŭsht rod/
Pusht Rod (dist) n

پشت سر /pŭsht-ī sar/
back of the head n

پشت سر(-ی) /pŭsht-ī sar(-ī)/
behind, in back of prep

پشت کردن /pŭsht kardan/
carry, bear v

پشت گوش انداختن
/pŭsht-ī gosh andākhtan/
see پس گوش کردن vt

پشتوانه /pŭsht-wā-na/
backup; support n

پشتو Pashto (lang) /pash-to/
پشتون , -ان/ها /pash-tun/
Pashtun (pers) n

پشتون زرغون
/pash-tun zar-ghun/
Pashtun Zarghun (dist) n

پشتون کوت /pash-tun kot/
Pashtun Kot (dist) n

پشتونستان /pash-tu-nīs-tān/
Pashtunistan n

پشتونوالی /pash-tun-wā-li/
Pashtunwali (tribal code) n

پشتی /pŭsh-ti/
cushion; support, protection; book
cover n

← پشتی کردن
support, defend, protect v

پشتیبان , -ان/ها
/pŭsh-ti-bān (-wān)/
supporter, defender (colloq) n

پشتیبانی (-وا-)/ /pŭsh-ti-bā-ni (-wā-)/
support, defense (colloq) n
← پشتیبانی کردن support vt

پشقل /pīsh-qīl/
sheep, goat, or camel dung n

پشک , -ها cat, feline n /pī-shak/
پشک /pīshk/
draft by lottery (mil); sheep, goat,
or camel dung n

پشکی draftee n /pīsh-ki/
پشم /pá-shīm, pashm/
wool; (vulg) pubic hair (esp m) n

پشم آلود /pá-shīm ā-lud/
hairy, hirsute; shaggy adj

پشمک cotton candy n /pash-mak/
پشمی /pash-mi/
woolen, made of wool adj

پشمین adj پشمی see /pash-min/
پشمینه بافی /pash-mi-na bā-fi/
wool mill n

پشمینه پوش , -ان/ها
/pash-mi-na posh/
Sufi (who wears wool) n

پشه /pa-sha/
mosquito, fly; club (cards) n

پشه بران /pa-sha bŭ-rān/
shoo-fly (yak/horse hair on stick) n

پشه خانه /pa-sha khā-na/
mosquito net; pasha khana (tree) n

پشه یی /pa-sha-yi/
Pashayi, Pashai (lang) n

یغمان /pagh-mān/
Paghman (dist) n

پف /pŭf/
boasting, bragging; puff n

پف کردن /pŭf kardan/
smoke, puff v

پفک /pŭ-fak/
blowpipe n

پکت /pakt/
treaty, pact n

پکتیا /pak-tĭ-yā/
Paktiya (prov) n

پکتیکا /pak-tĭ-kā/
Paktika (prov) n

پکنک /pĭk-nĭk/
picnic n

پکوره /pa-kaw-ra/
pakawra (dish) n

پکول /pa-kol/
cap, hat, pakol n

پکه /pa-ka/
ceiling fan, punkah n

پگاه /pa-gāh/
morning n

پگاهی /pa-gā-hi/
morning adj

پگه /pa-ga/
see پگاه n

پل /pal/
blade; razor; mark, sign n

پول /pŭl/
bridge (span) n

پل الم /pŭl-ĭ a-lam/
Pul-e Alam (seat) n

پل پای /pal-ĭ pāy/
footprint n

پل چرخی /pŭl-ĭ char-khi/
Pul-e Charkhi (prison) n

پل حصار /pŭl-e hĭ-sār/
Pul-e Hesar (dist) n

پل خمری /pŭl-ĭ khŭm-ri/
Pul-e Khumri (seat) n

پل دوستی /pŭl-ĭ dos-ti/
Friendship Bridge (to Tajikistan) n

پل سازی /pŭl sā-zi/
bridge construction n

پلاتین /pa-lā-tin/
platinum n

پلازما /pĭ-lāz-mā/
plasma n

پلاس /pa-lās/
rug without pile (colloq); pliers n

پلاستیک /pĭ-lās-tik/
plastic n

پلاستیکی /pĭ-lās-ti-ki/
plastic adj

پلان /pĭ-lān/
plan n

پلان گذاری /pī-lān gŭ-zā-ri/
planning, adopting plans n

پلپل /pĭl-pīl/
black pepper n

پلتن /pal-tan/
platoon (arch) n

پلته /pal-ta/
wick n

پلته پیش کردن /pal-ta peysh kardan/
encourage a dispute (colloq) v

پلته و چراغ گرفتن
/pal-ta w chĭ-rāgh gĭrĭftan/
find fault; pry into personal
matters (colloq) v

پلچک /pŭl-chak/
culvert n

پلخمان /pa-lakh-mān/ see فلاخن

پلستر /pa-las-tar/
plaster (material); plaster cast;
band-aid n

پلستر کاری /pa-las-tar kā-ri/
plastering n

پلک , -ها /pa-lak/
spark plug n

پلک , -ها /pĭlk/
eyelash; eyelid n

پلک زدن /pĭlk zadan/
blink v

پلک زدنی /pĭlk za-da-ni/
quickly, in the wink of an eye adv

پلک زدن /pĭl-kak zadan/
wink v

پلمه /pal-ma/
excuse, pretext; lie n

پلمه کردن /pal-ma kardan/
make an excuse v

پلنگ , -ها /pa-lang/
leopard n

پلنگ سیاه /pa-lang-ĭ si-yāh/
panther n

پلو /pa-law/
palaw, pilaf n

پلوان , -ها /pŭl-wān/
border (raised path on edge of
farm plot) n

پلوان شریک /pŭl-wān sha-rik/
farmer whose lands border
another's n

پلوتو /pŭ-lo-to/
Pluto (planet) n

پله , -ها /pa-la/
half a melon; ladder rung; step,
stair n

پله /pŭ-la/
popcorn n

پله بین /pa-la bin/
partial, biased adj

پلی /pa-li/
pod (of plant) n

پلیت /pa-leyt/
pleat; plate; epaulette n

پلیت دار /pa-leyt dār/ pleated adj

پلیت بتری /pa-leyt-ī bīt-ri/
electrode, battery plate n

پلیس /pū-lis/ n پولیس see
پناه /pa-nāh/
asylum, shelter, refuge; Panah
(ctr) n

پناه بردن /pa-nāh bŭrdan/
take refuge vi

پناه گاه , -ها /pa-nāh-gāh/
shelter, refuge n

پناه گرفتن /pa-nāh gīrĭftan/
see پناه بردن vi

پناه گزین , -ان/ها /pa-nā gŭ-zin/
see پناهنده n

پناهنده , -گان/ها /pa-nā-hīn-da/
asylum-seeker, refugee n

پنبه cotton n /pŭm-ba/
پنبه دانه cottonseed n /pŭm-ba dā-na/
پنبه خام /pŭm-ba-yī khām/
cotton wool n

پنج five n, adj /panj/
پنج ارکان /panj ar-kān/
Five Pillars of Islam n

پنج تره /panj-ta-ra/
five-cartridge gun magazine n

پنج ضلعی pentagon n /panj-zŭl-'i/
پنج یک one-fifth n /panj-yak/
پنجاب (-جاو)/pan-jāb (-jāw)/
Punjab (geog, & Bamyan dist) n

پنجال , -ها claw n /pan-jāl/
پنجاه fifty n, adj /pĭn-jā/
پنجاهم fiftieth adj /pĭn-jā-hŭm/
پنجاهمین /pĭn-jā-hŭ-min/
fiftieth (lit, often before n) adj

پنجپایک crab n /panj-pā-yak/
پنجشنبه /panj-sham-bey/
Thursday n

پنجشیر /panj-shir, -sheyr (pan-)/
Panjsheyr (prov) n

پنجگی /pan-ja-gi/
magazine (rifle); toe (shoe) n

پنجم fifth adj /pan-jŭm/
پنجمین /pan-jŭ-min/
fifth (lit, often before n) adj

پنجوایی /panj-wā-yi/
Panjwayi (dist) n

پنجه finger, toe; fork n /pan-ja/
پنجه چنار /pan-ja chī-nār/
plane tree n

پنجه خیل /pan-ja kheyl/
Panja Kheyl (ctr) n

پنجه دادن /pan-ja dādan/
confront (w/hostility) v

پنجه کش /pan-ja kash/
bread (w/hand mark) n

پنچر شدن /pan-char shŭdan/
get a flat tire v

پند advice, counsel n /pand/
پند دادن /pand dādan/
advise, counsel v

پند گرفتن /pand gīrĭftan/
take advice v

پنداشتن ؛ -پندار- ؛ پنداشت-
/pīn-dāsh-tan/
imagine, think v

پندی /pīn-di/ راولپندی see Pindi
پندیدن ؛ -پند- ؛ پندید- /pŭn-di-dan/
swell; be indignant (colloq) vi

پندیده /pŭn-di-da/
swollen, intumescent adj

پنسل pencil n /pīn-sīl/
پنسل پاک eraser n /pīn-sīl pāk/
پنهان /pīn-hān/
hidden, secret; occult adj

پنهان کردن ← hide, conceal (lit)
پنیر cheese n /pa-neyr/
پنیر مایه /pa-neyr mā-ya/
rennin, rennet n

پنیرک /pa-ney-rak/
mallow (med herb) n

پوپک /po-pak/
pompon; (arch) hoopoe n

پوپلزی /po-pal-zay/
Popalzai (Durrani P tribe) n

پوپنک mold, fungus n /po-pa-nak/
پوپنک زده بودن /po-pa-nak za-da budan/
get moldy vi

پوتاسیم potassium n /po-tā-sī-yam/
پوتاسیم پرمنگنیت
/po-tā-sī-yam par-man-ga-neyt/
potassium permanganate n

پوچ /puch/
absurd; hollow, w/o a nut *adj*

پوچ گفتن /puch gŭftan/
curse, swear; prattle *v*

پوچ مغز /puch maghz/
empty; w/o a nut; w/o character *adj*

پوچ و فحش (فاش) /puch ŭ fahsh (fāsh)/
cursing & swearing *n*

پوچاق /pu-chāq/
discarded melon rind; soap sliver *n*

پوچک /pu-chak/
empty cartridge; nut shell *n*

پود /pud/ weft, woof *n*

پودینه /pu-di-na/
wild mint, pennyroyal *n*

پودینه باغی /pu-di-na-yĭ bā-ghi/
garden pennyroyal *n*

پودینهٔ دشتی /pu-di-na-yĭ dash-ti/
wild pennyroyal *n*

پوره /pu-ra/
whole *adj*; completely, exactly *adv*

پوز /puz/
pers's nose, mouth, and jaw; (animal's) muzzle (anat) *n*

پوزبند /puz-band/
muzzle (worn) *n*

پوزخند /poz-khand/ snicker *n*
← پوزخند زدن • پوزخند کردن snicker *v*

پوزش /po-zĭsh/ apology *n*
← پوزش پذیرفتن forgive
← پوزش خواستن apologize

پوزه /po-za/ prow (ship's) *n*

پوست /post/
skin, pelt, rind, shell *n*
← پوست کردن skin, peel, shell *vt*

پوست فرهٔ قل /post-ĭ qa-ra-qŭl/
karakul sheepskin *n*

پوستر , -ها /pos-tar/ poster *n*

پوسته /pos-ta/ mail *n*

پوسته تلاشی /pos-ta-yĭ ta-lā-shi/
checkpoint *n*

پوسته سرحدی /pos-ta-yĭ sar-ha-di/
border post *n*

پوسته نظارتی /pos-ta-yĭ na-zā-ra-ti/
see پوسته تلاشی *n*

پوسته هوایی /pos-ta-yĭ ha-wā-yi/
air mail *n*

پوستین /pos-tin/
sheepskin jacket *n*

پوستین دوز , -ان/ها /pos-tin doz/
furrier (craftsman) *n*

پوستین دوزی /pos-tin do-zi/
furriery, furrier's craft *n*

پوستینچه /pos-tin-cha/
sheepskin vest *n*

پوسیده /po-si-da/
rotten (produce); decayed *adj*

پوش /posh/ cover *n*

پوش بالش /posh-ĭ bā-līsh/
pillowcase *n*

پوش کتاب /posh-ĭ kĭ-tāb/
book jacket *n*

پوشاک /po-shāk/ clothing *n*

پوشاکه /po-shā-ka/ see پوشاک

پوشال /po-shāl/ straw *n*

پوشاکه باب /po-shā-ka bāb/
see پوشاک *n*

پوشالی /po-shā-li/
straw; flimsy, fragile *adj*

پوشاندن ؛ -پوشان- ؛ پوشاند- /po-shān-dan/
dress; cover; hide *vt*

پوشش /po-shĭsh/
clothing; roofing; story (building) *n*

پوشیدن ؛ -پوش- ؛ پوشید- /po-shi-dan/
wear (clothes) *vt*

پوقانه /po-qā-na/
bubble; toy balloon *n*

پوک /pok/
hollow; bulky & light *adj*

پول /pul/
money; pul (unit of currency) *n*

پول به هوا انداختن /pul ba ha-wā andākhtan/
waste money *v*

پول پرست /pul-pa-rast/
miser *n*; miserly, stingy *adj*

پول پیشکی /pul-ĭ pey-sha-ki/
advance money *n*

پول تویانه /pul-ī to-yā-na/
brideprice n

پول خورد /pul-ī khūrd/
change (money) n

پول دوست , -ان/ها /pul dost/
miser n; stingy adj

پول دوستی /pul dos-ti/
miserliness, stinginess n

پول ساز , -ان/ها /pul-sāz/
money-maker, rich pers n

پول سازی /pul-sā-zi/
making much money n

پول سیاه /pul-ī sī-yā/
see پول خورد n

پول نقد /pul-ī naqd/
cash, ready money n

پول کاغذی /pul-ī kā-gha-zi/
banknote n

پولاد /po-lād/
steel; sword; mace, club n

پولدار /pul-dār/
rich, wealthy adj

پولی /pu-li/
monetary, pecuniary adj

پولیس /po-lis/
police, police officer n

پولیس سرحدی افغان
/po-lis-ī sar-ha-di-yī af-ghān/
Afghan Border Police, ABP n

پولیس کمکی افغان
/po-lis-ī kŭ-ma-ki-yī af-ghān/
Afghan National Auxiliary Police, ANAP (hist) n

پولیس نظم عامه ملی افغان
/po-lis-ī ná-zīm-ī ā-ma-yī mī-li-yī af-ghān/
Afghan National Civil Order Police, ANCOP n

پولیس یونفورم دار ملی افغان
/po-lis-ī yu-nī-form dār-ī mī-li-yī af-ghān/
Afghan Uniform Police, AUP n

پولیگون /po-li-gon/
polygon (math); (1978) Kabul mass gravesite n

پولند /po-land/
Poland n

پولیند /po-leynd/
see پولند n

پولندی , -ان/ها /po-lan-di/
Polish adj; Pole (pers) n

پولیندی /po-leyn-di/
see پولندی adj, n

پوهاند , -ها /po-hānd/
professor n

پوهنتون , -ها /po-han-tun/
university n

پوهنمل , -ها /po-han-mal/
assistant professor (senior to پوهنیار) n

پوهنوال , -ها /po-han-wāl/
associate professor n

پوهنیار , -ها /po-han-yār/
assistant professor (junior to پوهنمل) n

په ! /pa/ excl
wow excl

په په ! /pa pa/ excl
see په

پهره/-ه (pay-) /pah-ra/ guard, watch n
← پهره دادن • پهره داری کردن
stand guard vi
• پهره کرد

پهره دار /pah-ra dār/
guard, sentry n

پهره دار خانه /pah-ra dār khā-na/
guardhouse, guard shack n

پهلو , -ان/ها /pah-law/
Parthian, Parth (hist, empire 248 BC-224 AD); warrior, champion n

پهلو <چیزی> /pah-lu(-yī)/
next <to sth> prep

پهلو دادن /pah-lu dādan/
help, assist v

پهلو دار /pah-lu-dār/
sarcastic, snide adj

پهلو داری /pah-lu-dā-ri/
doorpost, door jamb n

پهلو زدن /pah-lu zadan/
emulate vt

پهلو گرفتن /pah-lu gīrīftan/
land, touch down v

پهلوان /pah-la-wān/
wrestler; warrior, hero n

پهلوانی /pah-la-wā-ni/
wrestling; heroism n

پهن (پام) /pahn (pām)/
wide; broad; extensive adj

پهنا /pah-nā/
width; breadth n

پهنی /pah-ni/
see پهنا n

پی /pay/
tendon, sinew; see & پای n

پی /pey(-ī)/
for; behind prep

realize v /pay burdan/ پی بردن

/pay dar pay/ پی در پی
successive adj; successively adv

/pay-ham/ پی هم adj, adv see پی در پی

/pa-yā-pay/ پیاپی see پی در پی adj, adv

پیاده , -ها /pī-yā-da/
pedestrian; pawn (chess) n; on foot adj

عسکر پیاده → infantry soldier

walk vi /pī-yā-da raftan/ پیاده رفتن

پیاده رو /pī-yā-da-raw/
sidewalk n; on foot adj

پیاده شدن /pī-yā-da shūdan/
land, touch down vi

پیاده کردن /pī-yā-da kardan/
dismount v

onion; bulb (plant) n /pī-yāz/ پیاز

پیاز نرگس /pī-yāz-ī nar-gīs/
narcissus bulb n

پیازی /pī-yā-zi/
color of layers of red onion adj

پیاله /pī-yā-la/
cup, teacup; (lit) wineglass n

یک پیاله برنج → a cup of rice

message n /pa-yām/ پیام

piano (mus instr) n /pī-yā-no/ پیانو

پیانو نواز /pī-yā-no na-wāz/
pianist n

onion soup n /pī-yā-wa/ پیاوه

pipe n /payp/ پیپ

/peych/ پیچ
screw; dysentery; wrapping n

پیچ در پیچ /peych dar peych/
complicated, intricate adj

پیچاندن ؛ -پیچان- ؛ پیچاند
/pey-chān-dan/
wrap; enfold; curl, twist vt

پیچتاب /peych-tāb/ n see پیچکش

پیچکاری /peych-kā-ri/
injection, shot; syringe n

پیچکاری کردن
/peych kā-ri kardan/
give an injection v

پیچکش /peych-kash/
screwdriver n

sidelock (f's) n پیچه /pi-cha/

پیچیدگی /pey-chi-da-gi (pi-)/
complexity, intricacy n

پیچیده /pey-chi-da (pi-)/
complicated; wrapped adj

پیخ /pikh/
bird droppings; game bird's hind toe n

پیخ زدن → deny, refuse harshly v

پیخال /pi-khā-la/
pigeon droppings, bird droppings n

evident, apparent adj /pay-dā/ پیدا

پیدا کردن → find; create; get vt

pedagogy n /pi-dā-go-zhi/
پیداگوژی

پیدایش /pay-dā-yīsh/
appearance; creation n

پیدایش زمین → creation of the world

پیدایی /pay-dā-yi/ n پیدایش see

/pir/ پیر
old (people) adj; spiritual guide, Sufi ascetic; Pir (m name) n

پیرار /pey-rār/ adj, n see پرار

پیرامن /pey-rā-mūn(-ī)/ see پیرامون prep, n

پیرامون /pey-rā-mun(-ī)/
about; around prep; environs n

پیراهن /pey-rā-han (-rān)/
shirt (m); dress (f) n

پیراهن آستین کوتاه
/pey-rā-han-ī ās-tin-ī ko-tāh/
short-sleeve shirt n

پیراهن بی آستین
/pey-rā-han bey ās-tin/
sleeveless shirt n

پیراهن خواب /pey-rā-han-ī khāb/
nightshirt n

پیراهن زنانه
/pey-rā-han-ī za-nā-na/
blouse (f) n

پیراهن مردانه
/pey-rā-han-ī mar-dā-na/
dress shirt (m) n

پیروز /pey-roz/
prosperous; triumphant adj

Peru n /pi-ro/ پیرو

i = keep, ĭ = big, u = coop, ŭ = put, y = yet, ' = (glottal stop)   83

پیرویی /pi-ro-yi/
Peruvian (& pers) adj, n

پیروزمند , -ان/ها /pey-roz-mand/
prosperous; triumphant (& pers) adj, n

پیروزه turquoise n /pey-ro-za/

پیروزه یی /pey-ro-za-yi/
turquoise-colored adj

پیروزی /pey-ro-zi/
triumph, victory n

پیروزی نصیب شدن
/pey-ro-zi na-sib shŭdan/
attain victory v

پیروی کردن /pey-ra-wi kardan/
follow, conform to vi

پیرهن (-ران) /pey-ra-han (-ran)/
shirt (m's); dress (f's) n

پیزار /pay-zār/
kind of traditional footwear n

پیزاره plinth n /pay-zā-ra/

پیزاره دیوار
/pay-zā-ra-yĭ day-wār/
socle (wall support) n

پیژنتون /pey-zhan-tun/
army personnel office n

پیژند army staff n /pey-zhand/

پیسه /pay-sa/
money; paysa (unit of currency) n

پیسه خور /pay-sa khŭr/
bribe-taker n

پیسه خوری /pay-sa khŭ-ri/
bribe-taking n

پیسی albinoism, alphosis n /pay-si/

پیش /peysh(-ĭ)/
before prep; front part n;
preceding adj

پیش آوند /peysh ā-wand/
see پیشوند n

پیش از before prep /peysh az/

پیش انداختن /peysh andākhtan/
criticize, hector; drive forward
(troops) vt

پیش برآمده /peysh ba-rā-ma-da/
protruding, sticking out adj

پیش پای بین /peysh pāy-bin/
opportunistic adj; opportunist n

پیش پای بینی /peysh pāy-bi-ni/
opportunism n

kick n /peysh pā-yi/ پیش پایی
پیش پایی زدن /peysh pā-yi zadan/
kick vt

پیش پری روز /peysh pa-ri roz/
three days ago adv

پیش پری شب /peysh pa-ri shab/
three nights ago adv

پیش خدمت , -ها /peysh khĭd-mat/
servant; waiter n

پیش خرید /peysh kha-rid/
prepayment n

پیش خود خواندن
/peysh-ĭ khŭd khāndan/
read to oneself in silence v

پیش خور /peysh khŭr/
depleted, used up (colloq) adj

پیش خور شدن ← be used up vi

پیش دستی /peysh das-ti/
anticipation; outreach n

پیش رس /peysh ras/
early; premature adj

پیش رفت /peysh-raft/
progress, advance n

پیش رفته /peysh-raf-ta/
advanced; progressive adj

پیش روی march n /peysh ra-wi/
march v پیش روی کردن ←

پیش روی /peysh-ruy(-ĭ)/
in front of, facing adj, prep

پیش شدن <به یک زن>
/peysh shŭdan/
have sex <w/f> v

پیش قبض
/peysh-qabz (-qaws,-qawz)/
dagger carried on belt (Sikh) n

پیش قدم , -ان/ها /peysh qa-dam/
forerunner, pioneer n, adj

پیش قدمی /peysh qa-da-mi/
taking the lead n

پیش قراول , -ان/ها
/peysh qa-rā-wŭl/
vanguard n

پیش کار /peysh kār/
overseer, steward; helper n

پیش کردن /peysh kardan/
close (door); serve (food); submit
(document); herd (livestock);
forward (mail) vt

پیش کش /peysh kash/
homage, gift to pers of higher rank n

پیش کش کردن /peysh kash kardan/
present, offer v

پیش گاه <کسی> /peysh gāh/
presence <of sb> n

پیش گفتار /peysh güf-tār/
foreword, preface n

پیش گویی /peysh-go-yi/
prediction, forecast n

پیش گویی کردن /peysh-go-yi kardan/
predict, foretell vt

پیش نهاد , ها- /peysh-nī-hād/
bid, offer; suggestion n

پیش نهاد دادن /peysh-nī-hād dādan/
bid, offer; suggest v

پیش نهاد کردن /peysh-nī-hād kardan/
پیش نهاد دادن see v

پیش و پس /peysh ŭ pas/
back & forth adv; ongoing adj;
front & back n

پیش و پس کردن /peysh ŭ pas kardan/
reorder, change the order vt

پیشاب /pey-shāb/
urine, (colloq) pee n

پیشاب کردن /pey-shāb kardan/
urinate, (colloq) pee v

پیشاپیش /pey-shā-peysh/
forward, in/at/to the front adv

پیشامد /pey-shā-mad/
event; treatment (of people) n

پیشانی forehead n /pey-shā-ni/

پیشانی باز /pey-shā-ni bāz/
friendly, welcoming; happy adj

پیشانی بازی /pey-shā-ni bā-zi/
friendliness n

پیشانی ترش /pey-shā-ni tŭrsh/
frowning, scowling adj

پیشانی ترشی کردن /pey-shā-ni tŭr-shi kardan/
frown, scowl v

پیشبانی /peysh-bā-ni/
support; patronage n

پیشبرد <چیزی> /peysh-bŭrd(-ī)/
contribution to the progress <of sth> n

پیشبرد /peysh-bŭrd/
improvement; fulfillment n

پیشبرده شدن /peysh-bŭr-da shŭdan/
be fulfilled, be carried out vi

پیشتر , ان- /peysh-tar/
progressive, advanced adj;
pioneer n

پیشخدمت /peysh-khĭd-mat/
waiter; attendant, servant n

پیشکی /pey-sha-ki/
advance, in advance adj, adv

پیشگیری <از بیماری> /peysh-gi-ri/
prevention <of a disease> n

پیشوا /peysh-wā/
leader (epithet for Prophet) n

پیشوند prefix n /peysh-wand/

پیشه /pey-sha/
craft, trade, profession, vocation n

پیشه ور /pey-sha-war/
artisan, craftsman, tradesman n

پیشه وری /pey-sha-wa-ri/
artisanship n

پیشینه , ها- /pey-shi-na/
preposition n; antecedent adj

پیغام message n /pay-ghām/
پیغام آوردن ← bring a message v

پیغامبر , ان/ها- /pay-ghām-bar/
messenger; prophet n

پیغله /paygh-la/
Miss (form of address) n

پیغمبر /pay-gham-bar/
پیغامبر see n

پیکار combat, battle n /pay-kār/
پیکار گاه/ها battlefield n /pay-kār gāh/

پیکان /pay-kān/
arrowhead, spearhead n

پیکپ /pay-kap/
truck, pickup truck n

پیکر تراش /pay-kar ta-rāsh/
sculptor n

پیکر تراشی /pay-kar ta-rā-shi/
sculpture (art form) *n*

پیکره /pay-ka-ra/
sculpture, statue *n*

پیگیر /pay-gir/
pursuer *n*; continuous *adj*;
continuously *adv*

پیگیرانه /pay-gi-rā-na/
continuous *adj*; continuously *adv*

پیل /peyl/ بحل see بیل
pilot, aviator *n* /pi-lot/ پیلوت
cocoon (silkworm's) *n* /pi-la/ پیله

پیما /pay-mā/
traveling; drinking *adj*

پیمان /pay-mān/
promise, vow; treaty *n*

پیمان کردن ← promise, vow *v*
پیمان شکستن ←
break a promise, renege *v*

پیمان شکن /pay-mān shĭ-kan/
promise-breaker (pers) *n*;
promise-breaking *adj*

پیمان گسل /pay-mān gŭ-sĭl/
promise-breaking *adj*

cup, bowl *n* /pay-mā-na/ پیمانه
پیمانهٔ او پر شد ←
s/he died (fig)

forehead *n* /pi-nak/ پینک
patch (shoe); callus *n* /pi-na/ پینه
پینه زدن • پینه ماندن ←
patch; repair (shoe) *v*

پینه پینه /pi-na pi-na/
having many patches *adj*

پینه دوز /pi-na doz/
cobbler, shoe repairman *n*

پینه یی /pi-na-yi/
patched (shoe, clothes) *adj*

پیوست /pay-wast/
attachment *n*; next to; adjoining
adj

پیوستن ؛ -پیوند- ؛ -پیوست-
/pay-was-tan, /méypaywandŭm//
connect, join, link *vt*, *vi*

پیوستگی /pay-was-ta-gi/
connection; continuity *n*

پیوستگی داشتن ← be connected *v*

پیوسته /pay-was-ta/
connected *adj*; continuously *adv*

پیوسته ابرو /pay-was-ta ab-ru/
monobrow, pers w/connected
eyebrows *n*

پیوند /pay-wand (pey-)/
connection, relation; patch (for
clothing); graft (botany) *n*

پیوندی /pay-wan-di/
patched; (gram) agglutinative;
grafted *adj*

fat, tallow, suet *n* /pih/ پیه

ت

تا /tā/
to; until; in order to *prep*; piece,
unit (colloq) *n*

دو تا نان ←two pieces of bread
forever *adv* /tā a-bad/ تا ابد
تا اکنون /tā ak-nun/ تا حالا see
تا حالا /tā hā´-lā/
until now, thus far *adv*

تاب /tāb (tāw, taw)/
curl; twirl, twist; shining, radiance;
warp (of wood); tolerance *n*

تاب داده /tāb dā-da/
curled, twisted *adj*

curly (hair) *adj* /tāb dār/ تاب دار
/tāb ŭ tab/ تاب و تب
pain & suffering *n*

shining *adj* /tā-bān/ تابان
تاباندن ؛ -تابان- ؛ -تاباند-
/tā-bān-dan/
illuminate *vt*

summer *n* /tā-bĭs-tān/ تابستان
summer *adj* /tā-bĭs-tā-ni/ تابستانی
radiance, shine *n* /tā-bĭsh/ تابش
تابع /tā-bey, pl at-bā/
citizen, national *n*

اتباع ←pl
تابع , -ون/ین
/tā-bey; pl tā-be-yun, -yin/
Follower (of Prophet; cf. اصحاب)
n; subordinate (& gram) *adj*

تابع ساختن • تابع کردن ←
subordinate (& gram) *vt*

تابعیت /tā-bĭ-ĭ´-yat/
citizenship, naturalization *n*

a = c<u>u</u>p, ā = l<u>o</u>ng, aw = n<u>ow</u>, ay = s<u>igh</u>, e = b<u>e</u>t, ey = ob<u>ey</u>

تابعیت <کشور> به دست آوردن /tā-bī-ĭ-yat-ĭ (kĭsh-war) ba dĭst āwardan/
naturalize, become a citizen <of a country> v

تابناک /tāb-nāk/ shining adj

تابیدن ؛ -تاب- ؛ تابیده - /tā-bi-dan/
shine, radiate vi; curl, twist; wind (thread) vt

تاتار , -ان/ها /tā-tār/
Tatar; Tartar n

تاثیر , -ات/ها /tā-sir/
effect, influence, impression n

← تاثیر بخشیدن
make an impression adj

← تاثر کردن affect, influence v

تاثیر بخش /tā-sir baksh/
impressive adj

تاج /tāj/ crown; Taj (m name) n

تاج خروس /tāj-ĭ khŭ-rus/
cockscomb (bird's flower) n

تاج دار , -ان/ها /tāj dār/
crown-bearer n; crown-bearing adj

تاجایکه /tā-jāy-kĭ, -key/
insofar as phrs

← تاجایکه می فهم
as far as I know

تاجر , -ان/ها/تجار /tā-jĭr, pl tŭ-jār (tĭ-)/
merchant, businessperson n

تاجور /tāj-war/
crown-bearing, crowned adj

تاجیک , -ان/ها /tā-jik/
Tajik (pers) n

تاجیکستان /tā-ji-kĭs-tān/
Tajikistan n

تاجیکی /tā-ji-ki/ Tajik (& lang) adj, n
تاحدی /tā-ha-di, -dey/
to a certain extent adv

ناخت و تاز /tākht ŭ tāz/ assault n

تادیه /tā-dĭ-ya, pl -yāt/ payment n
← تادیات pl
← تادیه کردن make payment v

تار /tār/ thread, string, fiber n
← تار کردن thread (a needle) vt

تار تار /tār tār/ threadbare adj
← تار تار شدن
become threadbare vi

تار داشتن have a love affair vi
تارتنک n see تار تنک /tār tŭ-nŭk/

تار دواندن /tār da-wān-dan/
extend one's circle, form contacts vi

تار گشتن /tār gashtan/
waste away, become skin & bones vi

تار و مار /tār ŭ mār/
scattered, (mil) routed adj

تار و نار /tār ŭ nār/
skinny, very thin adj

تارتنک /tār-tŭ-nŭk/ spider n

تارجلاه /tār-ĭ jo-lāh/ cobweb n

تارک الدنیا /tā-rĭk-ŭl-dŭn-yā/
see ن تارک دنیا

تارک دنیا /tā-rĭk-ĭ dŭn-yā/
hermit n

تاری /tā-ri/ stringed (mus instr) adj

تاریخ , -ها/تواریخ /tā-rikh, pl ta-wā-rikh/
history; era; day, date n

تاریخ دان , -ان/ها /tā-rikh-dān/
historian n

تاریخ دهن به دهن /tā-rikh-ĭ dān ba dān/
oral history (colloq) n

تاریخ سینه به سینه /tā-rikh-ĭ si-na ba si-na/
oral history (colloq) n

تاریخی /tā-ri-khi/
historical, historic adj

تاریخچه /tā-ri-kh-cha/
account, short history n

تاریک /tā-rik/
dark; murky; gloomy adj

تاریکی , -ها /tā-ri-ki/
darkness; gloom; (fig) ignorance n

تاز /tāz/
cicada (arch); see & ناخت و تاز n

تازه /tā-za/
fresh; refreshed; new, recent adj; newly adv

تازه به دوران رسیده /tā-za ba daw-rān ra-si-da/
parvenu, upstart n

تازه دل /tā-za dīl/
young at heart *adj*

تازه دم /tā-za dam/ *n* see تازه نفس

تازه نفس /tā-za nafs/
reinforcements (mil) *n*

تازه وارد /tā-za wā-rīd/
newcomer *n*

تازی , -ان/ها /tā-zi/
Arab (& pers) *adj*, *n*; Afghan
hound, greyhound *n*

تاس /tās/
bald *adj*; dice; sm metal bowl *n*

تاس برگ /tās barg/
petal (botanical) *n*

تاس حمام /tās-ī ha-mām/
sm metal bowl (in bathhouse) *n*

تاسف /ta-'a-sŭf/ *n* see تأسف

تاسیس , -ات /tā-sis/
establishment, foundation *n*

← تاسیس کردن
establish, found *vt*

تاسیس شده /tā-sis shŭ-da/
established, in place *adj*

تاشکند /tāsh-kĭnd/ Tashkent *n*

تاک /tāk/ grapevine *n*

تاک باغ /tāk bāgh/ *n* see تاکستان

تاکتیک /tāk-tik/ tactic; tactics *n*

تاکتیکی /tāk-ti-ki/ tactical *adj*

تاکستان /tāk-kĭs-tān/ vineyard *n*

تاکو /tā-kaw/ basement *n*

تاکوی /tā-ka-wi/ *n* see تاکو

تاکید , -ات/ها /tā-kid/
emphasis, stress *n*

تاکید کردن /tā-kid kardan/
emphasize, stress *v*

تال کار /tāl kār/ slow-working *adj*

تالاب /tā-lāb/ pool, lake *n*

تالار /tā-lār/
auditorium, hall, salon *n*

تالق داری /tā-lŭq-dā-ri/
n see تعلق داری

تالقان /tā-lŭ-qān/
Taluqan (seat, dist) *n*

تاله و برفک /tā-la wŭ bar-fak/
Tala wa Barfak (dist) *n*

تالی /tā-li/
next, following, subsequent *adj*

تالیف , -ات/ها /tā-li/
work, oeuvre (publication) *n*

تامین , -ات /tā-min/
securing; strengthening *n*

← تامین کردن
secure, strengthen *v*

تامینات /tā-mi-nāt/
collateral, escrow, guarantee,
surety *n pl*

تانسل ها /tān-sīl-hā/ tonsils *n pl*

تانک تیل /tānk-ī teyl/ gas station *n*

تاو /tāw/ *n* see تاب

تاوان /tā-wān/
damage, losses; reparations *n*

← تاوان دادن compensate *v*

← تاوان رساندن cause damages

← تاوان رسیدن • تاوان شدن
suffer losses

← تاوان کردن ask for damages

← تاوان گرفتن receive damages

تاوان جنگ /tā-wān-ī jang/
war reparations *n*

تاوانی /tā-wā-ni/ reparative *adj*

تاویذ /tā-wiz/ *n* see تعویذ

تأسف /ta-'a-sŭf/ regret *n* see

تأسف آور /ta-'a-sŭf ā-war/
regrettable *adj*

تائید /tā-yid/ *n* see تایید

تایید , -ات/ها /tā-yid/
confirmation; support *n*

تایید کردن /tā-yid kardan/
confirm, corroborate *vt*

تایید ناشده /tā-yid nā-shŭ-da/
unconfirmed *adj*

تب /tab (taw)/ fever *n*

تب بر /tab bŭr/
antipyretic, febrifuge (med) *n*

تب پر /tab pŭr/ feverish, having a high fever *adj*

تب دار /tab dār/
feverish, having a fever *adj*

تب داشتن /tab dāshtan/
have a fever *v*

تب شکن /tab-shī-kan/
antipyretic, febrifuge (med) *n*

تب کردن /tab kardan/ *v* see تب داشتن

تب لرزه /tab lar-za/ malaria *n*

تب محرقه /tab-ĭ müh-rī-qa/
typhoid fever n

تب نوبتی /tab-ĭ no-ba-ti/ malaria n

تب و تاب /tab ŭ tāb/
pain & suffering n

تبادل /ta-bā-dŭl/
exchange, interchange n

تبادل کردن /ta-bā-dŭl kardan/
exchange, interchange vt

تبادله /ta-bā-dŭ-la/
see تبادل (colloq) n

تبانی /ta-bā-ni/ collusion n

تباه کار /ta-bā kār/
spoiler, one who ruins n

تباه کاری /ta-bā kā-ri/
despoliation, ruination n

تباهی /ta-bā-hi/
destruction, damage; deterioration n

تباهی آوردن /ta-bā-hi āwardan/
bring destruction v

تباهی پذیرفتن /ta-bā-hi pazirŭftan/
be damaged v

تبت Tibet n /tĭ-bĭt, -bat/

تبتی , -ان/ها /tĭ-bĭ-ti, -ba-/
Tibetan (& pers) adj, n

تبدیل change; exchange n /tab-dil/

تبدیل در محل /tab-dil dar ma-hal/
relief in place, RIP n

تبدیل شدن /tab-dil shŭdan/
change, alter vi

تبدیل کردن /tab-dil kardan/
exchange (money) vt

تبر ax, axe n /ta-bar (-war)/

تبر دار /tab-bar-dār/
pioneer, trailblazer n

تبر زین /ta-bar-zin/
battle-ax used by dervishes n

تبرچه /ta-bar-cha/
hatchet; small ax n

تبریز Tabriz (city) n /tab-reyz/

تبریک ! /tab-rik/
congratulations excl

تبریک گفتن <به کسی>
congratulate <sb> v

تبریکی /tab-ri-ki/
congratulatory adj

smile n /ta-ba-sŭm/ تبسم , -ات/ها

smile v تبسم کردن →

تبصره , -ها /tab-sĭ-ra/
remark; commentary n

remark, comment تبصره کردن →

تبعه /tab-'a, pl at-bā/
citizen, subject, national; follower n

pl اتباع →

تبعیت /tab-'ī-yat/
following, succeeding n

تبعیت کردن /tab-'ī-yat/
follow, succeed v

exile, banishment n /tab-'id/ تبعید

تبعید گاه /tab-'id gāh/
place of exile n

تبعیدی /tab-'i-di/
related to exile adj

تبعیض , -ات/ها /tab-'īz/
discrimination n

تبعیض کردن /tab-'iz kardan/
discriminate v

تبلیغ , -ات /tab-ligh/
propaganda (esp pl); conveyance n

تبلیغات کردن /tab-li-ghāt kardan/
propagandize v

تبلیغاتی /tab-li-ghā-ti/
propagandistic adj

تبنگ /ta-bang/
tabang, grocer's tray n

تبنگ والا /ta-bang wā-lā/
tabang carrier n

heart (cards) n /ta-pān/ تپان

mound, hill n /ta-pa/ تپه

تتار , -ان/ها /ta-tār/
Tatar; Tartar n

research n /ta-ta-bo/ تتبع , -ات/ها

تتلگی /tŭt-la-gi/
stuttering, stammering n

تتله /tŭt-la/
stuttering, stammering (& pers) adj, n

supplement n /ta-tĭ-ma/ تتمه

stabilization n /tas-bit/ تثبیت

stabilize vi تثبیت شدن →

stabilize vt تثبیت کردن →

تثليث /tas-lis/
Trinity, doctrine of the Trinity (rel) n

تثنیه /tas-nī-ya/ dual (gram) adj

تجار /tū-jār (tī-), sg tā-jīr/
see تاجر sg n pl

تجارب /ta-jā-rīb; sg taj-rī-ba, -rŭ-/
see تجربه sg n pl

تجارت /tū-jā-rat/
business, trade, commerce n

تجارت خانه /tū-jā-rat khā-na/
company, firm n

تجارت کردن /tū-jā-rat kardan/
trade, do business vi

تجارتی /tū-jā-ra-ti/
commercial, mercantile adj

تجاری /tū-jā-ri/ see تجارتی

تجانس /ta-jā-nŭs/ homogeneity n
تجانس داشتن /ta-jā-nŭs dāshtan/
be homogeneous v

تجاوز , -ات/ها /ta-jā-wŭz/
aggression; transgression n

تجاوز به عصمت
/ta-jā-wŭz ba īs-mat/
rape n

تجاوز کار , -ان/ها /ta-jā-wŭz kār/
aggressor, transgressor n

تجاوز کارانه /ta-jā-wŭz kā-rā-na/
aggressively adv

تجاوز کردن /ta-jā-wŭz kardan/
offend (e.g., sb's dignity) n

تجاویز /ta-jā-wiz, sg taj-wiz/
see sg تجویز n pl

تجاهل /ta-jā-hŭl/
ignoring, disregard n

تجاهل کردن /ta-jā-hŭl kardan/
ignore, disregard v

تجدد /ta-ja-dŭd/
revival, regeneration n

تجدد پسند /ta-ja-dŭd pī-sand/
see تجدد خواه adj, n

تجدد پسندی /ta-ja-dŭd pī-san-di/
see تجدد خواهی n

تجدد خواه , -ان/ها
/ta-ja-dŭd khāh/
modernist, modern-minded adj, n

تجدد خواهی /ta-ja-dŭd khā-hi/
modernism, modern-mindedness n

تجدد طلب /ta-ja-dŭd ta-lab/
see تجدد خواه adj, n

تجدد طلبی /ta-ja-dŭd ta-la-bi/
see تجدد خواهی adj, n

تجدید /taj-did/
renewal n; renewed, refurbished adj

تجدید کردن ← renew, refurbish v

تجدید چاپ /taj-did chāp/ reprint n

تجدید روابط /taj-did-ī ra-wā-bīt/
rapprochement n

تجدید ساختمان
/taj-did-ī sākht-mān/
remodeling n

تجدید قوا /taj-did-ī qŭ-wā/
reinforcement; refreshment, revival n

تجدید نظر کردن
/taj-did-ī na-zar kardan/
revise; review vt

تجربوی /taj-rī-ba-wi/
experimental adj

تجربه , -ها/تجارب
/taj-rī-ba, -rŭ-; pl ta-jā-rīb/
experience; experiment n

تجربه دیده /taj-rī-ba di-da/
experienced (& pers) adj, n

تجربی /taj-rī-bi, taj-rŭ-bi/
experimental; experiential adj

تجزیه /taj-zī-ya/
analysis; deconstruction; disintegration; division n

تجزیه خون /taj-zī-ya-yī khun/
blood analysis n

تجزیه طلب /taj-zī-ya ta-lab/
separatist (pol) adj, n

تجزیه طلبی /taj-zī-ya ta-la-bi/
separatism (pol) n

تجزیه مملکت
/taj-zī-ya-yī mam-la-kat/
national partition n

تجزیه و تحلیل /taj-zī-ya ŭ tah-lil/
analysis n

a = cup, ā = long, aw = now, ay = sigh, e = bet, ey = obey

تجزیه و تحلیل کردن
/taj-zī-ya ŭ tah-lil kardan/
analyze v

تجلی , -ات
/ta-ja-li/
revelation; transfiguration (rel) n
← تجلی دادن • تجلی کردن
reveal; transfigure v

تجلیل /taj-lil/
celebration, honoring n

تجلیل کردن /taj-lil kardan/
celebrate (holiday) v

تجمع , -ات /ta-ja-mo/
gathering, assembly n

تجمع کردن /ta-ja-mo kardan/
gather, assemble vi

تجنب /ta-ja-nŭb/
avoidance; abstaining (from sth) n
تجنب اختیار کردن
/ta-ja-nŭb ĭkh-tĭ´-yār kardan/
avoid (sth); abstain (from sth) n

تجوید /taj-wid/
Quran reading (art) n

تجویز , -ات/ها/تجاویز
/taj-wiz, pl ta-jā-wiz/
recommendation; prescribing n

تجهیز , -ات /taj-hiz/
mobilizing; (esp pl) equipment,
gear n

تجهیزات /taj-hi-zāt/
equipment, gear; mobilizations n
pl

تحاریر , sg تحریر
/ta-hā-rir, sg tah-rir/
see sg تحریر n pl

تحایف , sg تحفه /ta-hā-yĭf, sg tŭh-fa/
see sg تحفه n pl

تحت under prep
/taht(-ĭ)/
تحت البحری /taht-ŭl-ba-hri/
submarine n

تحت السقر /taht-ŭs-sa-qar/
in hell adv

تحت صفر /taht-ĭ sĭ´-fir/
negative, minus (colloq) adj

تحت نظر <کسی>
/taht-ĭ na-zar(-ĭ)/
under <sb's> supervision adj

تحریر , -ات/ها/تحاریر
/tah-rir, pl ta-hā-rir/
editing; writing down n

تحریرات , sg tah-rir
/tah-ri-rāt, sg tah-rir/
secretariat (ministry's); writings n

تحریری /tah-ri-ri/
recorded, in writing adj

تحریم , -ات/ها <علیه یک
مملکت>
/tah-rim/
prohibition; (econ) embargo <of a
country> n

تحصیل , -ات /tah-sil/
studying (at university); gain,
acquisition n

تحصیل حاصل /tah-sil-ĭ hā-sĭl/
vain effort n

تحصیل دار /tah-sil dār/
tax collector n

تحصیل داری /tah-sil dā-ri/
tax collecting n

تحصیل کردن /tah-sil kardan/
study (at university) vi

تحصیل کرده , -گان/ها
/tah-sil kar-da/
(well-)educated (& pers) adj, n

تحصیل یافته , -گان/ها
/tah-sil yāf-ta/
see تحصیل کرده adj, n

تحصیلات عالی /tah-si-lāt-ĭ ā-li/
higher education n

تحصیلی /tah-si-li/
educational adj

تحفه , -ها/تحایف
/tŭh-fa, pl ta-hā-yĭf/
gift, present n

تحقق /ta-ha-qŭq/
realizing, coming true; certainty;
being true n

تحقیق , -ات/ها /tah-qiq/
investigation; inquest n
← تحقیق کردن
investigate; inquire into v

تحقیقات /tah-qi-qāt/
research n pl
تحقیقی /tah-qi-qi/
research-related adj

تحکیم /tah-kim/ strengthening n
← تحکیم کردن strengthen vt

تحلیل /tah-lil/ analysis n
← تحلیل کردن analyze vt

i = keep, ĭ = big, u = coop, ŭ = put, y = yet, ' = (glottal stop)   91

تحلیل گر , -ان /tah-lil gar/
analyst (pers) n
تحلیلی analytical adj /tah-li-li/
تحمل /ta-ha-mŭl/
patience; endurance n
تحمل پذیر /ta-ha-mŭl pa-zir/
tolerable adj
تحمل ناپذیر /ta-ha-mŭl nā-pa-zir/
intolerable adj
تحمیل /tah-mil/
imposition, burdening n
↵ تحمیل کردن
<چیزی را بر کسی>
impose <sth on sb> vt
تحمیلی burdensome adj /tah-mi-li/
تحول , -ات/ها /ta-ha-wŭl/
change, transformation n
تحول دادن /ta-ha-wŭl dādan/
change, transform vt
تحول کردن /ta-ha-wŭl kardan/
see تحول دادن vt
تحول یافتن /ta-ha-wŭl yāftan/
be changed vt
تحویل (تاویل) /tah-wil (tā-wil)/
delivery; deposit (money);
transition n
تحویل خانه /tah-wil khā-na/
warehouse; storage n
تحویل دار /tah-wil-dār/
warehouse custodian n
تحویل دار نقدی
/tah-wil-dār-ĭ naq-di/
cashier n
تحویل دهی /tah-wil-dĭ-hi/
delivery; handoff n
تحویل گیری /tah-wil-gi-ri/
receiving (for safekeeping) n
تخار Takhar (prov) n /ta-khār/
تخاری /ta-khā-ri/
Takhari adj; Tocharian (ancient
lang, hist) n
تخت , -ها /takht/
board; chair; throne n; flat, level
adj
تخت بام /takht bām/
upper terrace, baracoa n
تخت خواب bed n /takht-ĭ khāb/

تخت خینه /takht-ĭ khi-na/
henna tray (at wedding) n
تخت طاووس /takht-ĭ tā-wus/
Peacock Throne (hist) n
تختخک tickle n /tĭkh-tĭ-khak/
↵ تختخک دادن tickle vt
↵ تختخک خوردن be tickled vi
تختخکی ticklish adj /tĭkh-tĭ-kha-ki/
تخته /takh-ta/
board, plank; sheet (paper); unit,
piece (carpet, kilim; blanket) n
↵ تخته کردن
condense, compress; overeat v
تخته به پشت /takh-ta ba pŭsht/
on one's back adv
تخته پاک /takh-ta pāk/
eraser (felt, for blackboard) n
تخته سنگ /takh-ta-yĭ sang/
stone slab n
تخته سیاه /takh-ta-yĭ sī-yāh/
blackboard n
تخته شانه /takh-ta-yĭ shā-na/
middle of the shoulder n
تخته شطرنج /takh-ta-yĭ shat-ranj/
chessboard n
تخته شکسته بندی
/takh-ta-yĭ shĭ-kas-ta ban-di/
splint (med) n
تخته نرد /takh-ta nard/
backgammon board n
تخته یی /takh-ta-yi/
made of boards adj
تخدیر anaesthetization n /takh-dir/
تخدیر کردن /takh-dir kardan/
anaesthetize; narcotize vt
تخریب , -ات /takh-rib/
ruin; vandalism; sabotage n
تخریب کار , -ان/ها /takh-rib kār/
vandal; saboteur n
تخریب کردن /takh-rib kardan/
ruin; vandalize; sabotage vt
تخریبی /takh-ri-bi/
related to sabotage adj
تخصص /ta-kha-sŭs/
expertise, specialty n

تخصیص /takh-sis/
budget allocation n

← تخصیص دادن
allocate (in budget) vt

تخصیص یافتن vi be allocated →
تخصیصیه /takh-si-sī-ya/
see تخصیص n

تخطی , -ات/ها /ta-kha-ti/
mistake; (law) violation n

تخفیف , -ات/ها /takh-fif/
abbreviation; discount; mitigation
n

تخفیف دادن abbreviate vt →

تخفیف ادا /takh-fif-ĭ a-dā/
softening of one's pronunciation n

تخلیه کردن /takh-lī-ya kardan/
empty, vacate; unload vt

تخم /tŭ´-khŭm, tŭkhm/
egg; seed; sperm, semen n

← تخم پاشیدن • تخم دادن
sow, scatter seeds
← تخم دادن • تخم گذاشتن
lay eggs v

تخم پاشی /tŭ´-khĭm pā-shi/
planting seeds, sowing n

تخم چشم /tŭ´-khŭm-ĭ chá-shĭm/
eyeball n

تخم دان /tŭ´-khŭm dān/ ovary n
تخم گشنیز /tŭ´-khŭm-ĭ gash-niz/
coriander seeds n

تخمین , -ات/ها /takh-min/
approximation, estimation n

← تخمین زدن • تخمین کردن
approximate, estimate v

تخمیناً /takh-mi-nan, -mí-/
approximately, roughly adv

تخمینی /takh-mi-ni/
approximate, rough adj

technology n /takh-nik/ تخنیک
تخنیکر , -ها /takh-ni-kar/
technician n

تخنیکم , -ها /takh-ni-kŭm/
technical school n

تخویف , -ات/ها /takh-wif/
intimidation, bullying n

← تخویف کردن intimidate, bully
تخیل , -ات/ها /ta-kha-yŭl/
imagination; fanciful idea n

← تخیل کردن imagine v

تدابیر /ta-dā-bir, sg tad-bir/
see sg تدبیر n pl

← تدابیر گرفتن
take steps/measures v

تدارکات /ta-dā-rŭ-kāt/
supplies, provisions; preparation n
pl

تدارکاتی /ta-dār-ka-ti/
related to supplies adj

تدافع repulsion n /ta-dā-fo/
تدافعی repulsive adv /ta-dā-fŭ-'i/
تداول داشتن /ta-dā-wŭl dāshtan/
be widespread v

تداول یافتن /ta-dā-wŭl yāftan/
see تداول داشتن v

تداوی /ta-dā-wi/
therapy, treatment (med) n

تدبیر , -ات/ها/تدابیر
/tad-bir, pl ta-dā-bir/
step, measure (esp pl); planning;
tact n

تدبیر منزل /tad-bir-ĭ man-zĭl/
home economics n

تدریج /tad-rij/
gradualness, gradation n

تدریجاً /tad-rí-jan, -ján/
gradually adv

تدریجی gradual adj /tad-ri-ni/
تدریس , -ات /tad-ris/
teaching, instruction n

تدریس آموزی /tad-ris ā-mo-zi/
teaching practicum n

تدریسی instructional adj /tad-ri-si/
تدفین burial, interment n /tad-fin/
← تدفین کردن bury, inter v
تدقیق , -ات /tad-qiq/
elaboration; scrutiny n

← تدقیق کردن
elaborate; scrutinize v

تدویر /tad-wir/
taking place; recitation of Quran;
causing to function n

تذرو pheasant (bird) n /ta-zarw/
تذکار mentioning n /taz-kār/
← تذکار دادن mention v
تذکر , -ات/ها /ta-za-kŭr/
mentioning, pointing out n

← تذکر دادن mention v, point out

---

i = k<u>ee</u>p, ĭ = b<u>i</u>g, u = c<u>oo</u>p, ŭ = p<u>u</u>t, y = y<u>e</u>t, ' = (glottal stop)   93

ترانسمیتر /ta-rāns-mi-tar/
transmitter n

ترانسمیشن /ta-rāns-mey-shan/
transmission n

تراوش , -ها /ta-rā-wŭsh/
oozing n

تراوش کردن /ta-rā-wŭsh kardan/
ooze v

تراویدن ؛ -تراو ؛ تراوید- /ta-rā-wi-dan/
ooze vi

ترایی /tŭ-rā-yi/ gourd; zucchini n

تربرف /tar-barf/ wet snow n

تربند /tar-band/ compress (med) n

تربوز /tar-buz/ watermelon n

تربوزی /tar-bu-zi/
watermelon-colored, red adj

تریال /tar-pāl/ tarp n

ترت /tart/
outspoken, frank (colloq) adj

ترت گفتن /tart gŭftan/
be outspoken (colloq) v

ترتر شدن /tar-tar shŭdan/
be repeatedly ashamed v

ترتیب , -ات /tar-tib/
arranging; preparation n

← ترتیب دادن • ترتیب کردن
put in order; prepare vt

ترتیبات /tar-ti-bāt/
preparations n pl

ترجمان , -ان/ها /tar-jŭ-mān/
interpreter; translator n

ترجمانی /tar-jŭ-mā-ni/
interpretation; translation n

ترجمه , -ها/تراجم /tar-jŭ-ma, pl ta-rā-jīm/
interpretation; translation n

ترجمه کردن /tar-jŭ-ma kardan/
interpret; translate vt

ترجیح /tar-jih/
preference; superiority n

ترجیح داشتن /tar-jih dāshtan/
be superior v

ترجیح دادن <چیزی را نسبت به چیزی دیگر> /tar-jih dādan/
prefer <sth over sth else> vt

ترحیم /tar-him/
prayer for the dead n

تذکرت الشعرا /taz-kĭ-rat-ŭl-shŭ-'a-rā/
poet's biography n

تذکره , -ها/تذکرات /taz-kĭ-ra, pl -rāt/
certificate; ID card; stretcher n

تذکره ازدواج /taz-kĭ-ra-yĭ īz-dĭ-wāj/
marriage certificate n

تذکره تابعیت /taz-kĭ-ra-yĭ tā-bĭ-'ī-yat/
citizenship document n

تذکره تولد /taz-kĭ-ra-yĭ ta-wa-lŭd/
birth certificate n

تذکره وافیت /taz-kĭ-ra-yĭ wā-fī-yat/
death certificate n

تر /tar/ wet, moist, damp adj

← تر شدن get wet; be ashamed

← تر کردن moisten, dampen vt

تراب /ta-rāb/ dust, earth, soil n

ترابی /ta-rā-bi/ earth-colored adj

تراتیزک /ta-rā-tey-zak/
garden cress, pepperwort (herb) n

تراخم /ta-rā-khŭm/ trachoma n

ترازئی /tī-rā-zā-yi/ see ترازئی
/tĭ-rā-za-yi/
Terazayi (dist) n

ترازو /ta-rā-zu/
balance (device) n

ترازوی درجه دار
/ta-rā-zu-yĭ da-ra-ja-dār/
scale (for weighing) n

تراژیدی /ta-rā-zhĭ-di/ tragedy n

تراژیک /ta-rā-zhik/ tragic adj

تراس /tī-rās/ terrace (of house) n

تراشیدن ؛ -تراش- ؛ تراشید-
/ta-rā-shi-dan/
shave, scrape; erase; cut (gems);
lathe vt

تراجم /ta-rā-jīm, sg tar-jo-ma/
see sg ترجمه n pl

ترانه , -ها /ta-rā-na/
song, melody; nursery rhyme n

ترانزیستور /ta-rān-zis-tor/
transistor n

ترانسفرمر /ta-rāns-far-mar/
transformer n

تردید /tar-did/
rejection; doubt, hesitation n

← تردید داشتن doubt, hesitate v

← تردید کردن reject v

ترس fear; cowardice n /tars/

← ترس آوردن frighten v

← ترس داشتن fear, be afraid v

ترس آور /tars ā-war/
ترسناک see adj

ترسایی /tar-sā-yi/
Christianity n; Christian adj (arch)

ترسل epistolary art n /ta-ra-sŭl/

ترسناک /tars-nāk/
frightening, scary adj

ترسندوک fearful adj /tar-san-duk/

ترسو /tar-su/
coward n; cowardly adj

ترسویی /tar-su-yi/
cowardliness, timidity n

ترسیدن ؛ -ترس- ؛ ترسید- /tar-si-dan/
fear, be afraid v

ترسیم /tar-sim/
drawing; describing n

ترسیم کردن /tar-sim kardan/
draw, sketch; describe v

ترسیمی descriptve adj /tar-si-mi/

ترش /tŭrsh/
sour; morose, stern adj

ترش کردن /tŭrsh kardan/
turn sour; go bad (milk) (colloq) adj

ترشح oozing n, -ات /ta-ra-shŭh/
ترشح کردن /ta-ra-shŭh kardan/
ooze v

ترشیدن ؛ -ترش- ؛ ترشید- /tŭr-shi-dan/
ferment; turn sour vi

ترعه canal n /tŭr-'a/

ترفیع , -ات/ها /tar-fi/
promotion, advancement n

← ترفیع دادن • ترفیع کردن
promote (in job) v

ترقوه /tar-qŭ-wa/
clavicle, collarbone n

ترقی , -ات/ها /ta-ra-qi/
progress, advancement; (colloq) rise, increase n

ترقیدن ؛ -ترق- ؛ ترقید- /tar-qi-dan/
crack, split; burst, explode vi

ترک Turk (pers) n, -ان/ها /tŭrk/

ترک دادن /tark dādan/
give up, quit vt

ترک کردن /tark kardan/
leave, abandon, forsake v

ترکاری /tar-kā-ri/
vegetables (esp. salad) n

ترکمن , -ان/ها /tŭrk-man/
Turkmen (& pers) adj, n

ترکمنستان /tŭrk-ma-nīs-tān/
Turkmenistan n

ترکمنی /tŭrk-ma-ni/
Turkmen (lang) n

ترکی Turkish (lang) n /tŭr-ki/

ترکیبات /tar-ki-bāt/
ingredients; recipe n pl

ترکیه Turkey n /tŭr-kī-ya/

ترم /tŭ-rŭm/
bugle, horn, trumpet (esp mil) n

ترم جمع roll call n /tŭ-rŭm jam/

ترامیتر /tar-mā-mi-tar/
thermometer n

ترمپیت trumpet n /tŭ-rŭm-pīt/

ترمچی , -ها /tŭ-rŭm-chi/
bugle player n

ترمذ Termez (city) n /tĭr-mīz/

ترمیم , -ات/ها /tar-mim/
repair; alteration (of clothing); renovation (of building) n

ترمیم بوت /tar-mim-ī but/
shoe repair n

ترمیم شده /tar-mim shŭ-da/
repaired; renovated adj

ترمیم کردن /tar-mim kardan/
repair; alter; renovate vt

ترمیم موتر /tar-mim-ī mo-tar/
auto repair n

ترنک و جلدک /tar-nak wŭ jal-dak/
Tarnak wa Jaldak (dist, ctr Shahr-e Safa) n

ترور terror n /tĭ-ror, tŭ-/

/tí-ro-rí-zīm, tū-/ تروریزم
terrorism n

terrorist n /tī-ro-rist, tū-/ تروریست

Turwo (dist) n /tŭr-wo/ تروو

/ta-ra kheyl/ تره خیل
Tara Kheyl (ctr) n

/tar-yāq/ تریاق
treacle (antidote for poison) n

opium n /tar-yāk/ تریاک
⟵ تریاک خوردن • تریاک کشیدن
ingest opium v

/tar-yā-ki/ تریاکی
opium addict n; opium adj

Tarin (P tribe) n /ta-rin/ ترین

/ta-rin kot/ ترین کوت
Tarin Kot (seat) n

injection, shot n /taz-riq/ تزریق

/taz-riq shŭdan/ تزریق شدن
get an injection v

/taz-riq kardan/ تزریق کردن
give an injection v

code of laws n /tŭ-zŭk/ تزک
/tŭ-zŭk-ī tī-mu-ri/ تزک تیموری
Code of Tamerlane (law) n

marriage [< Ar] n /ta-za-wŭj/ تزوج
/taz-wij kardan/ تزویج کردن
marry, give in marriage v

/taz-wir/ تزویر
deceit; falsification n

/taz-wir kardan/ تزویر کردن
deceive; falsify v

increasing n /taz-yid/ تزیید
/taz-yin/ تزیین , -ات
decoration, ornamentation n

تزیین یافتن ⟨از چیزی⟩
/taz-yin yāftan/
be decorated ⟨w/sth⟩ vi

decorative adj /taz-yi-ni/ تزیینی

equality n /ta-sā-wi/ تساوی
/ta-sā-wi-yī hŭ-quq/ تساوی حقوق
equal rights n pl

/tas-bih (-bey)/ تسبیح
beads, Muslim rosary n

/ta-sa-lūt/ تسلط
rule; control; proficiency n

/ta-sa-li/ تسلی
comfort, consolation n

condolences n /tas-lī-yat/ تسلیت
⟵ تسلیت دادن • تسلیت گفتن
express condolences v

/tas-lī-yat nā-ma/ تسلیت نامه
letter of condolence n

/tas-lih kardan/ تسلیح کردن
arm, equip w/weapons vt

/tas-lim/ تسلیم , -ها
delivery, handover; surrender n
⟵ تسلیم دادن • تسلیم کردن
deliver, hand over vt
⟵ تسلیم شدن • تسلیم کردن
surrender, capitulate vi

/tas-li-mi/ تسلیمی
related to delivery adj; delivery n

/tas-ma/ تسمه
strap, belt (leather); (fig) thin &
strong pers n

/tas-mī-ya-yī taq-li-di/ تسمیه تقلیدی
onomatopoeia n

/tas-wid/ تسوید
drafting, roughing out (law) n

/tas-wid kardan/ تسوید کردن
draft, rough out (law) n

/tas-hil/ تسهیل , -ات
facilitation, easing (esp pl) n

/tash-bih (-bey)/ تشبیه , -ات/ها
comparison, simile n

/tash-bih kardan/ تشبیه کردن
compare vt

washbowl n /tasht/ تشت

/tash-ji/ تشجیع
encouragement, motivation n

/tash-khis, -ات/ها تشخیص
personification; diagnosis;
identification n

/tash-khis dādan/ تشخیص دادن
diagnose v

/tash-khi-si/ تشخیصی
diagnostic adj

/tash-khi-sī-ya/ تشخیصیه
see تشخیص n

/ta-sha-dŭd/ تشدد
hardship, difficulty n

/tash-did/ تشدید
intensification, strengthening n

/tash-rih/ تشریح , -ات/ها
description; explanation n

تشریح کردن /tash-rih kardan/
describe; explain vt

تشریف /tash-rif/
honoring; (arch) robe of honor n

تشریف آوردن /tash-rif āwŭrdan/
come (formal) vi

تشریف بردن /tash-rif bŭrdan/
go (formal) vi

تشریفات /tash-ri-fāt/
protocol; ceremonies n pl

تشریفاتی /tash-ri-fā-ti/
ceremonial, honor (guard) adj

تشعشع , ـات /ta-sha-sho/
radiation n

تشعشعات اتومی
/ta-sha-sho-'āt-ĭ a-to-mi/
see تشعشات ذروی n

تشعشعات ذروی
/ta-sha-sho-'āt-ĭ za-ra-wi/
radioactivity n

تشک /tŭ-shak/
see توشک (colloq) n

تشکان /tĭsh-kān/
Teshkan (dist) n

تشکر , ـات /ta-sha-kŭr/
gratitude n; thank you excl

تشکر کردن <از کسی>
/ta-sha-kŭr kardan/
thank <sb> vt

تشکیل , ـات /tash-kil/
establishment, formation; staffing
plan n

تشکیل دادن <چیزی را>
/tash-kil dādan/
form, comprise <sth> vt

تشکیل کردن /tash-kil kardan/
form, establish, organize vt

تشکیل مجدد /tash-kil-ĭ mŭ-ja-dad/
reconstitution n

تشناب /tash-nāb/
bathroom, toilet n

تشنگی /tŭsh-na-gi/
thirst n

تشنه , ـها/گان /tŭsh-na/
thirsty (& pers); arid (land) adj, n

تشنه بودن /tŭsh-na budan/
be thirsty vi

تشویش , ـها /tash-wish/
worry, anxiety n

تشویش داشتن /tash-wish dāshtan/
worry, be anxious vi

تشویش کردن /tash-wish kardan/
see تشویش داشتن vi

تشویق /tash-wiq/
encouragement, motivation n

تشویق کردن <کسی را به چیزی>
/tash-wiq kardan/
encourage, motivate <sb in sth>
vt

تشهیر /tash-hir/
public exposure of criminal n

ـ تشهیر کردن
public expose a criminal v

تشیع /ta-sha-yo/
Shiism; being a Shiite n

تشییع جنازه /tash-yi/
funeral procession n

تصادف , ـات/ها /ta-sā-dŭf/
chance occurrence; encounter n

تصادفاً /ta-sā-dŭ´-fan, -fán/
by chance adv

تصادفی /ta-sā-dŭ-fi/
chance adj; by chance adv

تصادم , ـات/ها /ta-sā-dŭm/
accident, collision n

تصادم سرک /ta-sā-dŭm-ĭ sa-rak/
road accident n

تصادم کردن /ta-sā-dŭm kardan/
crash; clash, conflict v

تصامیم /ta-sā-mim, sg tas-mim/
see sg تصمیم n pl

تصاویر /ta-sā-wir, sg tas-wir/
see sg تصویر n pl

تصدیق /tas-diq/
attestation; consent; belief n

تصدیق داکتر /tas-diq-ĭ dāk-tar/
doctor's note n

تصدیق نامه /tas-diq nā-ma/
certificate n

تصرف , ـات/ها /ta-sa-rŭf/
occupation (of a territory) n

تصرف قدرت /ta-sa-rŭf qŭd-rat/
occupier, occupying power n

تصریح /tas-rih/
clarification; declaring n

تصریح کردن /tas-rih kardan/
clarify; declare, state vt

تصریحاً /tas-rí-han, -hán/
clearly *adv*

تصریف , -ات/ها/ /tas-rif/
alteration; conjugation; declension
n

تصریفی /tas-ri-fi/
inflected (e.g., lang); conjugational
adj

تصفح کردن /ta-sa-fŭh kardan/
scrutinize *vt*

تصفیه /tas-fĭ-ya/
refinement; adjustment, fine-
tuning *n*

تصفیه خانه /tas-fĭ-ya khā-na/
oil refinery *n*

تصفیه نفت /tas-fĭ-ya-yĭ nĭft/
oil refining *n*

تصمیم , -ات/ها/تصامیم
/tas-mim, pl ta-sā-mim/
decision, intention *n*

← تصمیم داشتن   intend, resolve

← تصمیم گرفتن
decide, resolve (to do sth)

تصمیم انتخاب
/tas-mim-ĭ ĭn-tĭ-khāb/
decision, choice *n*

تصور , -ات/ها/ /ta-sa-wŭr/
idea; notion; imagination *n*

← تصور کردن <کسی را>
think, suppose, imagine *vt*

تصویب , -ات/ها/ /tas-wib/
approval, ratification *n*

← تصویب کردن   approve, ratify

تصویب نامه /tas-wib nā-ma/
decree (minister's) *n*

تصویر , -ها/تصاویر
/tas-wir, pl ta-sā-wir/
picture, portrait; image; effigy *n*

تضامن /ta-zā-mŭn/
joint responsibility *n*

تضامنی /ta-zā-mŭ-ni/
of joint responsibility *adj*

تضرع , -ات/ها/ /ta-za-ru/
begging, pleading *n*

← تضرع کردن   beg, plead *v*

تضعیف /taz-'if/   weakening *n*

← تضعیف کردن   weaken *vt*

تضمن /ta-za-mŭn/
inclusion, implication *n*

تضمین /taz-min/
guarantee, warranty *n*

← تضمین کردن   weaken *vt*

تضییع /taz-yi/   spoiling, wasting *n*

← تضییع کردن   spoil, go to waste

تطبیق , -ات /tat-biq/
adopting; implementation *n*

تطبیق واکسین /tat-biq-ĭ wāk-sin/
vaccination *n*

تطبیقات /tat-bi-qāt/
exercise, drill, practice *n pl*

تظاهر , -ات /ta-zā-hŭr/
demonstration, rally *n*; simulating
adj

تعابیر /ta-'ā-bir, sg ta-'bir/
see sg تعبیر *n pl*

تعادل /ta-'ā-dŭl/
balance, equilibrium *n*

تعارف /ta-'ā-rŭf/
recognition (of acquaintance) *n*

تعارف آمیز /ta-'ā-rŭf ā-meyz/
acknowledgeable; complimentary
adj

تعالی /ta-'ā-lā/
sublime, exalted (said of God) *adj*

تعالیم /ta-'ā-lim, sg ta'-lim/
see sg تعلیم *n pl*

تعامل , -ات/ها/ /ta-'ā-mŭl/
reaction (chem); precedent *n*

تعامل کیمیایی
/ta-'ā-mŭl-ĭ ki-mĭ-yā-yi/
chemical reaction *n*

تعاون /ta-'ā-wŭn/
cooperation, mutual help *n*

تعاونی /ta-'ā-wŭ-ni/
cooperative, supportive *adj*

تعبیر , -ات/ها/تعابیر
/ta-'bir, pl ta-'ā-bir/
interpretation; phrasing *n*

← تعبیر خواب
dream interpretation

تعبیر مجدد /ta-'bir-ĭ mŭ-ja-dad/
paraphrasing *n*

تعبیه /ta'-bĭ-ya/   putting, placing *n*

تعداد /tey-dād/
number (of units/people) n
← یک تعداد ‹از چیزی›
a number <of sth>

تعدد /ta-'a-dŭd/
plurality, multitude n; poly- pref

تعدد آلهه /ta-'a-dŭd-ī ā-lī-ha/
polytheism n

تعدد زوجات /ta-'a-dŭd-ī zaw-jāt/
polygamy n

تعذیب /ta'-zib/ n عذاب see
تعرض , -ات/ها /ta-'a-rŭz/
attack, assault, offensive n

تعزیر , -ات /ta-'a-zir/
discretionary punishment; rebuke;
sanction n

← تعزیراتِ اقتصادی
economic sanctions n pl

تعصب , -ات/ها /ta-'a-sŭb/
zeal, fanaticism; prejudice n

تعصب قومی /ta-'a-sŭb-ī qaw-mi/
tribalism n

تعصب نژادی
/ta-'a-sŭb-ī nī-zhā-di/
racism, racialism n

holiday, vacation n /ta'-til/ تعطیل
تعقیب , -ات /ta'-qib/
pursuit; prosecution

pursue; prosecute تعهد کردن →
تعلق , -ات/ها /ta-'a-lŭq (tā-lŭq)/
linkage, dependence n

تعلق داری /ta-'a-lŭq-dā-ri/
dependents (family) n

تعلق ‹چیزی› داشتن
/ta-'a-lŭq-ī chí-zey dāshtan/
be linked <to sth> v

تعلیق /ta'-liq/
suspension; awarding (medal);
taliq (calligraphy style) n

تعلیق کردن /ta'-liq kardan/
suspend; award (medal) vt

تعلیقات /ta'-li-qāt/
explanatory remarks; marginal
notes n pl

explanation n /ta'-lil/ تعلیل
deductive adj /ta'-li-li/ تعلیلی

تعلیم , -ات/تعالیم
/ta'-lim, pl ta-'ā-lim/
education, instruction n

تعلیم دادن → instruct, train vt
تعلیم کردن → undergo training vi

تعلیم و تربیه /ta'-lim ŭ tar-bī-ya/
education & training n

تعلیم یافته /ta'-lim yāf-ta/
educated, trained adj

تعلیمی /ta'-li-mi/
educational, instructional adj

تعمیر , -ات/ها (tā-) /ta'-mir/
building; construction n

تعمیم /ta'-mim/
generalization; popularization n

تعویذ , -ات/ها (tā-)/ /ta'-wiz/
amulet w/Quranic text n

تعویق /ta'-wiq/
postponement, delay n

تعهد , -ات/ها /ta-'a-hŭd/
promise, vow, pledge n

← تعهد دادن
promise, vow, pledge

تعهد نامه /ta-'a-hŭd nā-ma/
written promise n

تعیین , -ات /ta'-yin/
appointing, designating n

تعیین کردن → appoint, designate
تغییر /tagh-yir/
change, modification n

تغییر دادن • تغییر کردن →
change, modify vt

steam, heat n /taf (taft)/ تف
steam, heat (food) v تف دادن →
spit, saliva n /tŭf/ تف
تف انداختن ‹به کسی/چیزی› →
spit <at sb/sth> v

تفاسیر /ta-fā-sir, sg taf-sir/
see sg تفسیر n pl

تفاوت , -ها /ta-fā-wŭt/
difference, delta; disparity n

تفاوت داشتن → be different v

تفاهم /ta-fā-hŭm/
agreement, understanding n

← به تفاهم رسیدن
come to agreement v

see تف (colloq) n /taft/ تفت

---

i = keep, ĭ = big, u = coop, ŭ = put, y = yet, ' = (glottal stop)   99

تفتیش , ـها /taf-tish/
inspection, search; inspector n

← تفتیش کردن
inspect, conduct a search vt

تفرج /ta-fa-rūj/
recreation, leisure; stroll n

تفرجگاه /ta-fa-rūj-gāh/
recreation spot n

تفریح , ـات/ها /taf-rih/
recreation; rest break n

تفریحی /taf-ri-hi/ recreational adj

تفسیر , ـات/ها/تفاسیر
/taf-sir, pl ta-fā-sir/
commentary (esp on Quran);
explanation n

← تفسیر کردن comment; explain vt

تفسیری /taf-si-ri/
explanatory, expository adj

تفک /tŭ-fak/ blowpipe n

تفکر , ـات/ها /ta-fa-kŭr/
meditation, thought n

تفکیک /taf-kik/
separation; fission n

تفکیک اتوم /taf-kik-ī a-tom/
nuclear fission n

تفنگ /tŭ-fang/
gun; rifle, musket n

تفنگ بادی /tŭ-fang-ī bā-di/
air gun, BB gun n

تفنگ چره یی /tŭ-fang-ī cha-ra-yi/
shotgun, pellet gun n

تفنگ ساز /tŭ-fang-sāz/
gunsmith n

تفنگ سازی /tŭ-fang-sā-zi/
gunsmithing n

تفنگچه /tŭ-fang-cha/
gun, handgun, pistol n

تفویض /taf-wiz/
transfer, handing in n

تفهیم , ـات/ها /taf-him/
explaining; instruction n

← تفهیم کردن explain, instruct vt

تقابل /ta-qā-bŭl/
contrast, opposition n

تقاضا /ta-qā-zā/
demand; request n

← تقاضا کردن demand; request

تقاضا نامه /ta-qā-zā nā-ma/
requisition, request (form) n

تقاعد /ta-qā-'ŭd/ retirement n

تقاعدی /ta-qā-'ŭ-di/
related to retirement adj

تقبیح /taq-bih/
condemnation, denunciation n

تقبیح کردن /taq-bih kardan/
condemn, denounce n

تقدس /ta-qa-dŭs/
holiness, sanctity n

تقدم /ta-qa-dŭm/
precedence, priority n

تقدیر /taq-dir/
appreciation; destiny; (colloq)
forehead n

تقدیر نامه /taq-dir nā-ma/
letter of appreciation n

تقدیم /taq-dim/
filing, turning in, offering n

← تقدیم کردن
file, turn in, offer vt

تقرر /ta-qa-rŭr/
appointment (of officials) n

تقرر حاصل کردن
/ta-qa-rŭr hā-sĭl kardan/
gain an official appointment v

تقرر یافتن
/ta-qa-rŭr yāftan kardan/
be appointed vi

تقریباً , ـری-/ /taq-ri-ban, -rí-/
about, almost adv

تقسیم , ـات /taq-sim/
division, share, allocation n

تقسیم اوقات /taq-sim-ī aw-qāt/
schedule n

تقسیم کردن /taq-sim kardan/
divide, share, allocate; deal
(cards) v

تقصیر , ـات/ها /taq-sir/
shortcoming, fault n

تقطیر /taq-tir/ distilling n
← تقطیر کردن distill v

تقلب /ta-qa-lŭb/
deceit, fraud, trickery n

← تقلب کردن
deceive, defraud, trick v

تقلب آمیز /ta-qa-lŭb ā-meyz/
deceitful; fraudulent, tricky adj

تقلب كار /ta-qa-lūb kār/
deceiver, fraudster n

تقلبى /ta-qa-lŭ-bi/
counterfeit, fake adj

تقليد /taq-lid/
imitation; mimicry; blind obeisance (to medieval rel commentators) n

← تقليد كردن
imitate; mimic; follow blindly n

تقليدى /taq-li-di/ imitative adj

← كلمهٔ تقليدى
onomatopoeic word

تقليل /taq-lil/
reduction, diminution n

تقنين /taq-nin/
Legislative Council (within Justice Ministry) n

تقويت /taq-wĭ-yat/
strengthening, growing n

تقويم /taq-wim/
calendar, almanac n

تقويه /taq-wĭ-ya/ n see تقويت

تك كردن /tak kardan/
fire (weapon) v

تك و تك /tak ŭ tŭk/ bric-a-brac n

تكافو /ta-kā-fo/
adequacy, sufficiency n

تكامل , ات/ها- /ta-kā-mŭl/
progress, gradual perfection n

← تكامل بخشيدن • تكامل دادن
improve, perfect vt

تكان دادن /ta-kān dādan/
see تكان كردن vt

تكان كردن /ta-kān kardan/
crush, grind (in mortar); shock, shake vt

تكان برقى /ta-kān-ī bar-qi/
electroshock n

تكان دهنده /ta-kān dĭ-hīn-da/
shocking adj

تكت /tĭ-kīt (-kīs)/ ticket n

تكتانه /tĭ-kī-tā-na/
stamp tax (formalizes document) n

تكت پوستى /tĭ-kīt-ī pos-ti/
stamp, postage stamp n

تكت پولى /tĭ-kīt-ī pu-li/ dividend n

تكتيك /tak-tik/ n see تاكتيك

تكتيكى /tak-ti-ki/ adj see تاكتيكى

تكثر /ta-ka-sŭr/
growth, increase; bounty n

تكثير /tak-sir/
increase, augmentation n

تكثير كردن /tak-sir kardan/
increase, augment vt

تكذيب /tak-zib/ n denial; refutation

تكذيب كردن /tak-zib kardan/
deny; refute, disprove vt

تكر /tŭ-kŭr/
accident, stumbling (colloq); compress (med) n

← تكر خوردن stumble, trip vi

← تكر كردن apply a compress v

تكرار /tak-rār, tĭk-/
repetition, iteration n

← تكرار شدن repeat vi

← تكرار كردن repeat vt

تكراراً /tak-rā-ran, -rā´-/
repeatedly adv

تكرى /tŭk-ri/ basket (wicker) n

تكزار /tŭk-zār/ Tukzar (ctr) n

تكسى /tak-si/ taxi, cab n

تكفير /tak-fir/
excommunication, declaration of another Musl to be an apostate n

تكلم كردن /ta-ka-lŭm kardan/
speak, talk vi

تكمه , ها- /tŭk-ma/
button, switch, knob n

تكمه فشار دادن
/tŭk-ma fī-shār dādan/
press a button v

تكميل /tak-mil/
completion, perfection n

← تكميل كردن
complete, accomplish vt

تكوين /tak-win/
creation, formation n

تكه /ta-ka/
male goat that leads flock n

تكه /tĭ-ka/ cloth; piece n; torn adj

← دو تكه نان two pieces of bread

← تكه تكه
in shreds; exhausted (colloq) adj

← تكه كردن tear, rend vt

---

i = k<u>ee</u>p, ĭ = b<u>i</u>g, u = c<u>oo</u>p, ŭ = p<u>u</u>t, y = <u>y</u>et, ' = (glottal stop)

تکه و پاره /tĭ-ka ŭ pā-ra/
torn & ragged adj

تکیه /tak-ya/ n تکیه خانه see

تکیه خانه /tak-ya khā-na/
Shiite gathering place n

تگاب /ta-gāb/ n تگ آب see

تگاب Tagab (dist) n /ta-gāb, -gāw/

تگابی , -ان/ها /ta-gā-bi, -wi/
Tagabi (& pers) adj, n

تل ابیب Tel Aviv n /tĭl 'a-bib/

تلاش /ta-lāsh/
effort, serious attempt n
تلاش کردن make an effort v

تلاشی /ta-lā-shi/
search (for sth illicit) n

تلاشی منزل /ta-lā-shi-yī man-zīl/
house search n

تلاطم , -ات/ها /ta-lā-tŭm/
tumult; clash, collision n

تلافی /ta-lā-fi/
retribution; amends n

تلاوت /tĭ-lā-wat/
recitation (esp of Quran) n

تلحین /tal-hin/ modulation (mus) n

تلخ /talkh/ bitter; rancorous adj

تلخ کام /talkh-kām/
disappointed, afflicted adj

تلخ کامی /talkh-kā-mi/
disappointment, affliction n

تلخان /tal-khān/
ground dried mulberries n

تلخی /tal-khi/
bitterness; hardship n

تلخیص , -ات/ها /tal-khis/
summary n

تلف , -ات /ta-laf/
perishing; loss, waste n

تلف شدن /ta-laf shŭdan/
perish, die; be wasted vi

تلفات /ta-la-fāt/
casualties, losses n pl

تلفظ , -ات/ها /ta-la-fŭz/
pronunciation, articulation n

تلفون /tĭ-lī-fun/ telephone n

تلفون جیبی /tī-lī-fun-ī jey-bi/
cell phone, mobile phone n

تلفون چی /tī-lī-fun-chi/
long-distance operator n

تلفون کردن /tī-lī-fun kardan/
make a phone call v

تلقی , -ات/ها /ta-la-qi/
perception; contemplation n

تلقیح /tal-qih/
insemination; pollination n

تلقیح کردن /tal-qih kardan/
inseminate; pollinate v

تلقین , -ات/ها /tal-qin/
instruction, direction n

تلک /ta-lak/ trap n
تلک گردن شدن become a burden vi
تلک نشاندن lay a trap v

تلک /talk/ تلق see

تلگرام /tĭ-lī-gī-rām/
cable, telegram n

تلم /tĭ-līm/ slice (of melon) n
تلم تلم sliced; afflicted adj
تلم کردن slice, cut into slices

تلمیح /tal-mih/
allusion; insinuation n

تلمیحاً /tal-mi-han, -mí-/
indirectly, suggestively adv

تلوار /tal-wār/ sword, sabre n

تلویح /tal-wih/
allusion (& lit); insinuation n

تلویحاً /tal-wi-han, -wí-/
indirectly, implicitly adv

تلویزیون /tĭl-wiz-yun/
TV, television n
تلویزیون دیدن watch TV

تلی /tī-li/ spleen (colloq) n

تمارض /ta-mā-rūz/
feigning illness adj
تمارض کردن pretend to be sick v

تمارین /ta-mā-rin, sg tam-rin/
تمرین n pl see sg

تماثیل /ta-mā-sil, sg tam-sil/
تمثیل n pl see sg

تماس /ta-mās/
contact, touch; contiguity n
تماس داشتن be in contact, be touching vi
تماس گرفتن contact, touch vt

تماشا /ta-mā-shā/
spectacle; sightseeing n
تماشا کردن ← screen, show (film)
تماشا خانه /ta-mā-shā khā-na/
theater n
تماشابین , -ان/ها
/ta-mā-shā-bi-nān/
audience, spectators n pl
تمام /ta-mām/ all, every; entire adj
تمام شدن /ta-mām shŭdan/
turn out to be (+ adj); run out, be
depleted vi
تمام کردن /ta-mām kardan/
use up, deplete vt
تمامیت /ta-mā-mī-yat/
completeness, entirety n
تمامیت ارضی
/ta-mā-mī-yat-ī ar-zi/
territorial integrity n
تمایل , -ات/ها /ta-mā-yŭl/
inclination n
تمایل داشتن /ta-mā-yŭl dāshtan/
be inclined v
تمباکو /tam-bā-ku/ n see تنباکو
تمتراق /tŭm-tŭ-rāq/
arrogant, boastful (& pers) (colloq)
adj, n
تمثیل , -ات/ها/تماثیل
/tam-sil, pl ta-mā-sil/
acting, dramatics; depicting n
تمثیل کننده , -گان/ها
/tam-sil kŭ-nīn-da/
actor, actress n
تمثیلی /tam-si-li/
dramatic, allegorical adj
تمدد /ta-ma-dŭd/
stretching, stretch n
تمدد یافتن ← stretch vi
تمدد اعصاب /ta-ma-dŭd-ī a'-sāb/
relaxation n
تمدن /ta-ma-dŭn/
civilization; urbanity n
تمدید /tam-did/
renewal; extension n
تمدید دادن • تمدید کردن ←
renew, extend vt
تمدید شدن • تمدید یافتن ←
be renewed vi

تمرکز /ta-mar-kŭz/
focusing; centralization n
تمرکز دادن /ta-mar-kŭz dādan/
focus, concentrate vt
تمرکز یافتن /ta-mar-kŭz yāftan/
be focused vi
تمرین , -ات/ها/تمارین
/tam-rin, pl ta-mā-rin/
drill, exercise; practice n
تمساح /tĭm-sāh/
crocodile; alligator n
تمویل /tam-wil/ financing n
تمویل کردن ← finance vt
تمیز /ta-miz/
distinction, discernment n
تن /tan/ person; body, torso n
تن به تن /tan ba tan/
one-on-one (esp combat) adj
تن در دادن /tan dar dādan/
submit to v
تنازع /ta-nā-zo/
fighting; controversy n
تنازع کردن ← fight, struggle v
تناسب , -ات/ها /ta-nā-sŭb/
proportion; symmetry n
تناسخ /ta-nā-sŭkh/ reincarnation n
تناسخی , -ان/ها /ta-nā-sŭ-khi/
believer in reincarnation n
تناسل /ta-nā-sŭl/
reproduction, procreation n
تناسلی /ta-nā-sŭ-li/
reproductive, genital; venereal adj
تناظر /ta-nā-zŭr/ symmetry n
تناظر داشتن ← be symmetrical v
تنافر /ta-nā-fŭr/
mutual repulsion; dissonance n
تنافر داشتن ←
mutually repel; be dissonant v
تنافر دار /ta-nā-fŭr dār/
mutually repulsive; dissonant adj
تناقض , -ات/ها /ta-nā-qŭz/
contradiction n
تناقض داشتن ← contradict v
تناوب /ta-nā-wŭb/ alternation n
تناور /ta-nā-war/
robust, sturdy adj
تنبا /tŭm-bā/ n see تنبان
تنبان /tŭm-bān/ n pajama trousers n

تنباكو /tam-bā-ku/ n tobacco
تنبل /tam-bal/ adj lazy, sluggish
تنبور /tam-bur/ n tambur (mus instr)

تنبور نواز , -ان/ها /tam-bur na-wāz/
n tambur player

تنبورچی , -ها /tam-bur-chi/ n
tambur player

تنبه /tam-ba/
n push (colloq); door latch
← تنبه کردن
v push, shove, thrust

تنخواه /tan-khā/ n wage, salary
تنخواه خور /tan-khā-khŭr/
n wage earner (pers)
تنخواه دادن /tan-khā dādan/
v pay wages

تند /tŭnd/ adj hot, spicy (food); fast; hot-
tempered (pers)
تند خوی /tŭnd-khuy/ adj
hot-tempered (pers)
تند مزاج /tŭnd-mī-zāj/ adj
hot-tempered (pers)
تند مزه /tŭnd ma-za/ adj تند see
تند و تیز /tŭnd ŭ teyz/
phrs hot & spicy
تندرو , -ان /tŭnd-raw/ n extremist
تنزیل , -ات/ها /tan-zil/
n reduction; revelation; (fig) Quran
تنزیل رتبه /tan-zil-ī rŭt-ba/
n demotion in rank
تنزیل قیمت /tan-zil-ī qi-mat/
n devaluation
تنسته /ta-nīs-ta/ n warp; spiderweb
تنش /ta-nīsh/ n tension (& pol)
تنش زدایی /ta-nīsh zŭ-dā-yi/
n elimination of tension
تنظیف , -ات /tan-zif/ n sanitation
← مدیریتِ تنظیفات
department of sanitation
تنظیم , -ات/ها /tan-zim/
n regulation, control; organization
← تنظیم دادن vt regulate, control
← تنظیم کردن
vt arrange (meeting)

تنعم , -ات/ها /ta-na-'ŭm/
n prosperity, comfort
تنفیذ /tan-fiz/
n implementation, enforcement
← تنفیذ قانون law enforcement
← تنفیذ کردن
vt implement, carry out
← تنفیذ یافتن vi be implemented
تنقیص /tan-qis/
n decrease, reduction
← تنقیص دادن • تنقیص کردن
v decrease, reduce
تنقیط /tan-qit/ n punctuation
تنک /tŭ-nŭk/ adj sparse; thin
← تار تنک spider
← تنک کردن vt thin out
← تنک شدن vi thin out
تنک ظرف /tŭ-nŭk zarf/
n, adj blabbermouth
تنکار /ta-na-kār/
n borax (crude), tincal
تنگ /tang/ adj narrow; tight
تنگ چشم /tang chá-shīm/
adj تنگ see
تنگ گرفتن /tang gīrīftan/
vt squeeze; be tight (clothing)
تنگ نظر /tang-na-zar/
adj narrow-minded, bigoted
تنگی /tang-gi/ n gorge; narrowness
تنوع /ta-na-wo/ n variety, diversity
تنویم /tan-wim/ n lulling (to sleep)
تنویم مقناطیسی
/tan-wim-ī mīq-nā-ti-si/
n hypnotism
تنها /tan-hā/
adj only, sole; alone, lonely; adv by
oneself
تنهایی /tan-hā-yi/
n solitude; loneliness
تنی /ta-nay/ n Tanay (dist)
تنیدن ؛ -تَن- ؛ -تَنید- /ta-ni-dan/
v weave, spin
تنیس /tī-nis/ n tennis
تو /tu/ pron you (sg, informal)
تواریخ /ta-wā-rikh, sg tā-rikh/
n pl تاریخ see sg
توازن /ta-wā-zŭn/
n balance, equilibrium

توپ دافع هوا
/top-ĭ dā-fey-ĭ ha-wā/
antiaircraft artillery (mil) n

توپ دنده
/top dan-da/
top danda (game like baseball) n

توپ زدن
/top zadan/
fire a cannon or gun v

توپ کشی
/top-ka-shi/
hard work (fig) n

توپچی
/top-chi/
artillery; artilleryman adj, n

توت
/tut/
mulberry; berry n

توت بی دانه
/tut-ĭ bey dā-na/
seedless mulberry n

توت زمینی
/tut-ĭ za-mi-ni/
strawberry n

توتا
/to-tā/
parrot n

توتا چشم
/to-tā chĭ´-shĭm/
immodest (fig) (said of f) n

توته
/to-ta/
piece, morsel n

توته کردن
/to-ta kardan/
cut into pieces (food) vt

توجه , -ات/ها (-jo)/
/ta-wa-jŭh (-jo)/
attention, notice n

توجه کردن
/ta-wa-jŭh dādan/
pay attention, take notice v

توحید
/taw-hid/
unity of God (doctrine) n

توده , -ها
/to-da/
mound, pile; the masses n

توده کردن
/to-da kardan/
pile; (colloq) spill, pour (solids) vt

تودیی
/to-da-yi/
people's, of the masses adj

تور
/ta-war/
see تبر n

تورات
/taw-rāt/
Torah; Old Testament n

تورم
/ta-wa-rŭm/
swelling, intumescence n

تورم پولی
/ta-wa-rŭm-ĭ pu-li/
inflation (econ) n

تورم قیمتی
/ta-wa-rŭm-ĭ qi-ma-ti/
inflation (econ) n

تورن
/tu-ran/
captain, CPT (rank) n

تورن جنرال
/tu-ran jan-rāl/
major general, MG n

تورنتو /to-ran-to/
Toronto (city) n

توازن داشتن
/ta-wā-zŭn dāshtan/
be balanced v

تواضع
/ta-wā-zo/
humility, modesty; courtesy n

توافق , -ات
/ta-wā-fŭq/
agreement, conformity n

توافق داشتن
/ta-wā-fŭq dāshtan/
be in agreement vi

توافق نامه
/ta-wā-fŭq nā-ma/
memorandum of understanding n

توان
/ta-wān/
power, strength n

توانمندی
/ta-wān-man-di/
capability n

توانا
/ta-wā-nā/
powerful, strong adj

توانا ساختن
/ta-wā-nā sākhtan/
empower, enable vt

توانا سازی
/ta-wā-nā sā-zi/
empowering, enabling n

توانستن ؛ -توان- ؛ توانست-
/ta-wā-nĭs-tan (tā-nĭs-)/
can, be able to <+ subj> v

توبرکلوز
/to-bar-kŭ-loz/
tuberculosis n

توبره
/tob-ra/
feed bag n

توبه
/to-ba/
penitence, repentance n

توبه کردن
/to-ba kardan/
do penance, repent, be sorry v

توبه کشیدن
/to-ba kashidan/
see توبه کردن v

توبه گار
/to-ba gār/
penitent, repentant adj

توبه گفتن
/to-ba gŭftan/
apologize, express repentance v

توپ , -ها
/top/
ball; cannon, gun n

توپ بادی
/top-ĭ bā-di/
tennis ball n

توپ بازی
/top bā-zi/
top bazi (game like soccer) n

توپ دادن
/top dādan/
pitch, throw the ball v

توپ دار
/top-dār/
having artillery adj

توپ دافع تانک
/top-ĭ dā-fey-ĭ tānk/
antitank artillery (mil) n

توره بوره /to-ra bo-ra/
Tora Bora (geog) n

توزیع /taw-zi/
delivery; distribution n

توزیع کردن /taw-zi kardan/
deliver; distribute vt

توس /tus/ ace (cards) n
← توس پشه ace of clubs

توسط <چیزی/کسی>
/ta-wa-sĭt(-ī)/
through, by means of <sth/sb>
prep

توسعاً /ta-wa-sŭ-'an, -sŭ´-/
by extension, in a wider sense
adv

توسعه /taw-sĭ-'a/
expansion, broadening n

توسعه پذیر /taw-sĭ-'a pa-zir/
expandable adj

توسعه جوی , -ان/ها
/taw-sĭ-'a joy/
expansionist (& pers) adj, n

توسعه جویانه /taw-sĭ-'a jo-yā-na/
expansionist adj

توسعه جویی /taw-sĭ-'a jo-yi/
expansionism n

توسعه دادن /taw-sĭ-'a dādan/
expand, broaden vt

توسعه طلبانه
/taw-sĭ-'a ta-la-bā-na/
expansionist adj

توسعه طلبی /taw-sĭ-'a ta-la-bi/
expansionism n

توسعه یابنده /taw-sĭ-'a yā-bĭn-da/
expansionary adj

توسعه یافتن /taw-sĭ-'a yāftan/
expand, broaden vi

توسعه یافته /taw-sĭ-'a yāf-ta/
expanded adj

توسیع /taw-si/ n توسعه see

توشک /to-shak/ mattress n

توشیح /taw-shih/
approval (signed); adorning n

توشیح فرمودن
/taw-shih farmudan/
sign, approve (formal) vt

توشیح کردن /taw-shih kardan/
vt توشیح فرمودن see

توضیح , -ات/ها /taw-zih/
explanation, clarification n
← توضیح دادن • توضیح کردن
explain, clarify vt

توضیحاتی /taw-zi-hā-ti/
see توضیحی adj

توضیحی /taw-zi-hi/
explanatory adj

توطئه /taw-tĭ-'a/
conspiracy, plot, scheme n
← توطئه چیدن • توطئه کردن
conspire, plot, intrigue v

توطئه گر , -ان/ها /taw-tĭ-'a-gar/
conspirator, plotter n

توطئه جهت بدنامی <کسی>
/taw-tĭ-'a ja-hat-ī bad-nā-mi(-yī)/
smear campaign <against sb> n

توقع , -ات/ها /ta-wa-qo/
expectation; wish, hope n
← توقع داشتن
expect, anticipate

توقف , -ات/ها /ta-wa-qŭf/
stopping; pause; layover n
← توقف دادن • توقف کردن
stop; pause vt

توقیع /taw-qi/
tawqi (calligraphy style) n

توقیف , -ات/ها /taw-qif/
arrest, detention n
← توقیف کردن
arrest, detain vt

توقیف شده , -گان /taw-qif shŭ-da/
arrested adj; detainee n

توکیو /to-kī-yo/ Tokyo n

تولد /ta-wa-lŭd/ birth, childbirth n
← تولد شدن be born vi

تولدی /ta-wa-lŭ-di/
natal, related to childbirth adj

تولگ /tu-lak/ Tulak (dist) n

توله /tu-la/ flute (mus instr) n

تولی /to-lay/
company (mil); (colloq) crowd n

تولی کشف /to-lay-ā kashf/
reconnaissance unit n

تولید , -ات /taw-lid/
production; product; procreation n
← تولید کردن
produce, manufacture; procreate
vt

تولید برق /taw-lid-ī barq/
energy production *n*

تولیدی /taw-li-di/
related to production *adj*

تومور /tu-mor/ tumor (med) *n*

تون /ton/ tone (of voice) *n*

تونی /tu-ni/
permanent wave (of hair) *n*

تونی کردن /tu-ni kardan/
set hair *v*

توهین /taw-hin/
insult, affront, indignity *n*

توهین آمیز /taw-hin ā-meyz/
insulting, affronting *adj*

توهین کردن /taw-hin kardan/
insult, affront *v*

توی /toy, tuy/
wedding; wedding party *n*

تویانه /to-yā-na/ brideprice *n*

ته /ta (tā)/ bottom *n*; down *adv*

← ته رفتن go down

← ته دل bottom of the heart

ته جایی /ta-jā-yi/
ground rent for market stall *n*

ته جایی دادن /ta-jā-yi dādan/
pay rent for a market stall *v*

تهاجم , -ات/ها /ta-hā-jŭm/
attack, assault, offensive *n*

← تهاجم کردن attack, assault *v*

تهاجمی /ta-hā-jū-mi/
offensive (mil) *adj*

تهامه /tī-hā-mah/
Tihamah (geog) *n*

تهانه /ta-hā-na/
fort, outpost (border, highway) *n*

تهانه دار /ta-hā-na dār/
fort commander (border, highway) *n*

تهجی /ta-ha-ji/ spelling *n*

تهداب /tah-dāb (tā-daw)/
basis, foundation *n*

← تهداب گذاشتن
found, establish *v*

تهداب گذاری /tah-dāb gŭ-zā-ri/
founding, establishing *n*

← تهداب گذاری کردن
found, establish *v*

تهدید , -ات/ها ‹به ضد چیزی›
/tah-did/
threat, menace ‹against sth› *n*

← تهدید کردن threaten, menace

تهدید آمیز /tah-did ā-meyz/
threatening, menacing *adj*

تهدید قرار دادن /tah-did qa-rār dādan/
apply a threat *v*

تهذیب /tah-zib/
refinement; upbringing *n*

تهران /tĭ-hī-rān/ Tehran *n*

تهمت , -ها /tŭh-mat/
accusation, charge *n*

تهمت کردن /tŭh-mat kardan/
accuse, charge *v*

تهویه /tah-wĭ-ya/ ventilation *n*

تهی /tĭ-hi/ empty *adj*

تهی دست , -ان/ها /tĭ-hi dast/
empty-handed (poor) *adj*

تهی دستی /tĭ-hi das-ti/
empty-handedness (poverty) *n*

تهی مغز , -ان/ها /tĭ-hi maghz/
scatterbrained (& pers) *adj, n*

تهی کردن empty *vt* /tĭ-hi kardan/

تهی گاه /tĭ-hi gāh/ midriff (anat) *n*

تهیه /ta-hī-ya/
production, making *n*

تهیه شدن ‹طی چیزی›
/ta-hi-ya shŭdan/
consist (loosely) ‹of sth› *vi*

تهیه کردن /ta-hi-ya kardan/
produce, prepare, make *vt*

تهیه کننده , -گان/ها
/ta-hĭ-ya kŭ-nĭn-da/
producer (of film) *n*

تهییه see *n* تهیه /ta-hi-ya/

تیاتر /ta-yā-tŭr, tĭ-yā´-tĭr/ theater *n*

تیار شدن /ta-yār shŭdan/
be prepared, be ready *vi*

تیار کردن /ta-yār kardan/
prepare; fix *vt*

تیر /tayr/ tire, wheel (on vehicle) *n*

تیر /tir/
shot, bullet; arrow; beam; Tir
(month, see سرطان); (arch)
Mercury (planet) *n*

← تفنگِ شش تیره six-shooter

---

i = k<u>ee</u>p, ĭ = b<u>i</u>g, u = c<u>oo</u>p, ŭ = p<u>u</u>t, y = <u>y</u>et, ' = (glottal stop)   107

تير اشتبنى /tayr-ĭ ĭsh-tab-ni/
spare tire *n*

تير انداز , ان/ها /tir an-dāz/
sharpshooter; archer *n*

تير اندازی /tir an-dā-zi/
shooting; archery *n*

تير باران /tir bā-rān/
execution by firing squad *n*

تير پشت backbone *n* /tir-ĭ pŭsht/
شوتینگ رینج shooting range *n* /tir ras/ تير رس
تير شدن <از چیزی>
/teyr shŭdan/
pass; cross <sth>; forgive; dare;
have fun; give up *vt*

تير شده /teyr shŭ-da/
past, last, previous *adj*

تير کش /tir kash/
quiver (for arrows); embrasure *n*

تيرماه autumn, fall *n* /tir-māh/
تيره /ti-ra/
thick, viscous; dark; strained *adj*

تيره بخت , ان/ها /ti-ra bakht/
unlucky (& pers) *adj*, *n*

تيز /teyz/
quick, fast; bright, sharp *adj*, *adv*

fart (colloq) *n* /tiz/ تيز
تيز بال /teyz bāl/
sly; light-fingered (colloq) *adj*

brave *adj* /teyz chang/ تيز چنگ
تيز دو /teyz daw/
swift, fleet (running) *adj*

تيز رفتن /teyz raftan/
speed up; go fast *v*

تيز هوش /teyz hosh/
intelligent, quick-witted *adj*

تيز هوشی /teyz ho-shi/
intelligence *n*

acid *n* /tey-zāb/ تيزاب
/tey-zāb-ĭ go-gĭrd/
sulfuric acid *n*

acidic *adj* /tey-zā-bi/ تيزابی
تيزرو /teyz-raw/
swift-footed, fleet *adj*

speed, velocity *n* /tey-zi/ تيزی
/teyz-fahm/ تيزفهم
intelligent, quick to learn *adj*

thesis *n* /tey-zĭs/ تيزس
see تيزس *n* /tey-sĭs/ تيسس

تيشه adz, adze *n* /tey-sha/
تيغ sword; scimitar; razor *n* /teygh/
typhus *n* /ti-fus/ تيفوس
typhoid *n* /ti-fuyd/ تيفويد
/ti-kar/ تيکر
potsherd, broken jug *n*

تيگر /tay-gar/
tiger; large & fierce dog *n*

تيکه /tey-ka/
piecework; contract; teyka (card
game) *n*

تيکه دار /tey-ka-dār/
supplier; contractor *n*

تيکه کردن /tey-ka kardan/
work on contract *v*

fuel, gasoline *n* /teyl/ تيل
kerosene *n* /teyl-ĭ khāk/ تيل خاک
تيل دادن /teyl dādan/
fuel; lubricate, oil *vt*

تيل زغر /teyl-ĭ zĭ-ghĭr/
linseed oil *n*

تيل کشيدن /teyl kashidan/
pump oil, extract oil *v*

telephone *n* /tey-lĭ-fun/ تيلفون
تيله کردن /tey-la kardan/
push, shove, thrust *v*

تيله و تنبه کردن
/tey-la wŭ tŭm-ba kardan/
crowd, push & shove *v*

تيم باز سازی ولايتی
/tim-ĭ bāz-sā-zi-yĭ wĭ-lā-ya-ti/
PRT, Provincial Reconstruction
Team *n*

تيم رابط ناتو و مشاورين
/tim-ĭ rā-bĭt-ĭ nā-to wa mŭ-shā-wĭ-
rin/
OMLT, Operational Mentoring &
Liaison Team *n*

tending the sick *n* /ti-mār/ تيمار
تيمار خوردن /ti-mār khŭrdan/
be taken care of *v*

تيمار داری کردن
/ti-mār dā-ri kardan/
see تمار کردن *v*

تيمار داری خوردن
/ti-mār dā-ri khŭrdan/
see تمار خوردن *v*

تیمار کردن /ti-mār kardan/
take care of, nurse v

تیمم /ta-ya-mŭm/
ritual ablution using sand/earth n

تیمم زدن /ta-ya-mŭm zadan/
perform ablution with sand/earth n

تیمم کردن /ta-ya-mŭm kardan/
see تیمم زدن n

تیمن /ta-ya-mŭn/
auspiciousness, good omen n

تیمناً /ta-ya-mŭ-nán, -mŭ´-/
auspiciously adv

تیمور /ti-mur/
Tamerlane (hist, 1336-1405) n

تیموری /ti-mu-ri/
Timurid, related to Tamerlane adj

تینچر آیودین /tin-char-ĭ ā-yo-din/
tincture of iodine n

تینس /tey-nĭs/ tennis n
تینس بازی کردن
/tey-nĭs bā-zi kardan/
play tennis n

تیوره /tay-wa-ra/ Taywara (dist) n
تیوری /tĭ-yu-ri/ theory n
تیوکراسی /tĭ-yu-kĭ-rā-si/
theocracy n

ث

ثابت /sā-bĭt/ stable; constant adj
ثابت قدم /sā-bĭt qa-dam/
steadfast, resolute adj

ثابته /sā-bĭ-ta, pl sa-wā-bĭt/
fixed star n

ثوابت pl ⟶

ثاقب /sā-qĭb/ sharp, piercing adj
ثالث /sā-lĭs/ third adj
ثالث بالخیر /sā-lĭs-ĭ bĭl-khayr/
arbitrator, mediator n

ثالثاً /sā-lĭ-san, -lĭ´-/ thirdly adv
ثانوی /sā-na-wi/ secondary adj
ثانی /sā-ni/
second (ordinal) adj; equal, rival n

ثانیه , ها- /sā-nĭ-ya, pl sa-wā-ni/
second (unit of time) n

ثانیه گرد /sā-nĭ-ya gard/
second hand (clock's) n

ثبات /sŭ-bāt/
stability; endurance n

ثبات داشتن /sŭ-bāt dāshtan/
be stable, be steady vi

ثبات یافتن /sŭ-bāt yāftan/
be stable, be steady vi

ثبت /sabt/
registry, entry n; recorded adj

ثبت نام /sabt-ĭ nām/
registration, enrollment n

ثبت نام کردن ⟵ register, enroll v

ثبوت /sŭ-but/
proof, corroboration n

ثبوت کردن ⟵ prove, corroborate v

ثبوت شده /sŭ-but shŭ-da/
proven, corroborated adj

ثروت /sŭr-wat/
wealth, affluence n

ثروتمند , ان/ها- /sŭr-wat-mand/
wealthy, rich (& pers) adj, n

ثری /sa-rĭ, -rā/
earth, ground, soil n

ثریا /sŭ-ra-yā/
Suraya (f name); Pleiades
(astron) n

ثغور /sŭ-ghur/
frontiers, boundaries n pl

ثقافت /sa-qā-fat/
culture, refinement n

ثقافتی /sa-qā-fa-ti/ cultural adj
ثقافی /sa-qā-fi/ adj ثقافتی see
ثقیل /sa-qil/ heavy adj
ثلاثی /sŭ-lā-si/ tripartite adj, n
ثلث /sŭls/ suls (callig style) n
ثمر , ها-/اثمار /sa-mar, pl as-mār/
fruit; profit, benefit; result, effect,
product n

ثمر بخش /sa-mar-bakhsh/
fruit-bearing adj

ثمر دادن /sa-mar dādan/
be fruitful; be profitable v

ثمر دار /sa-mar-dār/
fruitful; profitable; effective adj

ثمر گرفتن /sa-mar gĭrĭftan/
make a profit v

i = keep, ĭ = big, u = coop, ŭ = put, y = yet, ' = (glottal stop)   109

ثمره , -ها/ثمرات
/sa-ma-ra, pl -rāt/
fruit; profit, benefit; result, effect, product; reward; offspring *n*

ثنا /sa-nā/
praise; thanks, gratitude *n*

ثناخوان /sa-nā-khān/
eulogist, panegyrist *n*

ثناخوانی /sa-nā-khā-ni/
eulogizing *n*

ثنا گفتن /sa-nā gŭftan/
praise, commend; thank *v*

ثنایا /sa-nā-yā/ *n pl*
incisors (teeth) *n*

ثواب /sa-wāb/ *n* spiritual reward *n*

ثوابت /sa-wā-bĭt, sg sā-bĭ-ta/
see sg ثابته *n pl*

ثوانی /sa-wā-ni, sg sā-nĭ-ya/
see sg ثانیه *n pl*

ثوب /sawb/
unit, piece (clothing) *n*
← یک ثوب دریشی one uniform

ثور /sawr/
bull; Taurus; Saur (month); April 1978 revolution *n*

ج

ج.ا.ا.
/jam-hu-ri-yat-ĭ ĭs-lā-lā-mi-yĭ af-ghā-nĭs-tān/
Islamic Republic of Afghanistan *n*

جا /jā (jāy)/ place *n*

جابر , -ان/ها /jā-bar/
oppressor *n*

جابرانه /jā-ba-rā-na/
oppressive *adj*; oppressively *adv*

جاپان /jā-pān/
Japan (country) *n*

جاپانی , -ان/ها /jā-pā-ni/
Japanese (& pers) *adj, n*

جاجی /jā-ji, dzā-/
Jaji (dist, ctr Ali Kheyl) *n*

جاجی میدان /jā-ji may-dān/
Jaji Maydan (dist) *n*

جادو /jā-du/ magic, sorcery *n*
← جادو کردن perform sorcery *v*

جادوگر , -ان/ها /jā-du-gar/
sorceror *n*

جادوگری /jā-du-ga-ri/
sorcery, being a sorceror *n*
← جادوگری کردن
see *v* جادو کردن

جادویی /jā-du-yi/
magical; enchanting *adj*

جاده , -ها /jā-da/
main road, avenue *n*

جاذب /jā-zĭb/
absorbent *adj*; absorber *n*

جاذبه /jā-zĭ-ba/
appeal, charm; gravity *n*

جاذبه جنسی /jā-zĭ-ba-yĭ jĭn-si/
sex appeal *n*

جاذبیت /jā-zĭ-bĭ-yat/ gravitation *n*

جارچی /jār-chi/ *n* جهرچی see

جارو /jā-ru/ broom *n*
← جارو کردن • جارو زدن
sweep *v*

جاروب /jā-rub/ *n* جارو see

جاروی برقی /jā-ru-yĭ bar-qi/
vacuum cleaner *n*

جاری /jā-ri/
current; in effect; flowing; runny (nose) *adj*

جاسوس , -ان/ها/جواسیس
/jā-sus, pl ja-wā-sis/
spy *n*

جاسوسی /jā-su-si/
spying, espionage *n*
← جاسوسی کردن spy *vi*

جاغوری /jā-ghu-ri/
Jaghuri (dist, ctr Sang-e Masha) *n*

جاکت /jā-kat/ sweater, pullover *n*

جاکت پیش باز /jā-kat-ĭ peysh bāz/
cardigan *n*

جاگارتا /jā-gār-tā/
Jakarta (capital) *n*

جلال /jā-lāl/
glory; splendor; Jalal (m name) *n*

جلال آباد /jā-lāl ā-bād/
Jalalabad (seat) *n*

جلال الدین محمد بلخی
/jā-lāl-ŭd-din mŭ-ha-mad bal-khi/
Jalaluddin Mohamad Balkhi (13th-c Dari poet) *n*

جالب /jā-lĭb/
interesting, appealing *adj*

a = cup, ā = long, aw = now, ay = sigh, e = bet, ey = obey

جالوت /jā-lut/ Goliath (bibl) *n*

جاله /jā-la/ mesh (screen, fabric) *n*

جام /jām/ bowl; goblet; flower petals *n*

جامد /jā-mĭd/ hard, solid; (gram) underived *adj*

جامدات /jā-mĭ-dāt/ solids *n pl*

جامع /jā-mey/ universal; central (mosque) *adj*

جامعه , -ها/جوامع /jā-mĭ-'a, pl ja-wā-mey/ society, community; league *n*

جامعه شناس , -ان/ها /jā-mĭ-'a shĭ-nās/ sociologist *n*

جامعه بین المللی /jā-mĭ-'a-yĭ bay-nŭl-mĭ-la-li/ the international community *n*

جامعه شناسی /jā-mĭ-'a shĭ-nā-si/ sociology *n*

جامعه ملل /jā-mĭ-'a-yĭ mĭ-lal/ League of Nations (hist) *n*

جامه عمل پوشاندن /jā-mĭ-'a-yĭ a-mal poshāndan/ put into practice *v*

جامعی /jā-mĭ-'i/ universal, comprehensive *adj*

جامعیت /jā-mĭ-'i-yat/ universality *n*

جامه دان /jā-ma dān/ box or trunk for clothes *n*

جامه بدل کردن /jā-ma ba-dal kardan/ pass away (said of rel leaders) *v*

جان /jān/ body (colloq); soul, spirit *n*

← جان باختن die, lose one's spirit

← جان دادن از گرسنگی starve to death

← جان دادن ‹برای/از چیزی› die ‹for/of sth›

← جان ‹کسی را› گرفتن kill ‹sb›

جان خراش /jān kha-rash/ distressing *adj*

جان دار /jān dār/ animate, living; loaded (gun, question) *adj*

جان فرسا /jān far-sā/ tormenting *adj*

جان کاه /jān kāh/ debilitating, exhausting *adj*

جان گداز /jān gŭ-dāz/ harrowing *adj*

جانب /jā-nĭb, pl ja-wā-nĭb/ side; party (to agreement) *n*; towards; at *prep*

← جوانب pl

جانبین /jā-nĭ-bayn, sg jā-nĭb/ see sg جانب *n dual pl*

جانب دار /jā-nĭb-dār/ partisan, supporter *n*

جانب داری /jā-nĭb-dā-ri/ partiality; partisanship *n*

جانباز /jān-bāz/ one who risks own life; gymnast *n*

جانبازی /jān-bā-zi/ risking or sacrificing one's life; athletics, gymnastics *n*

← جانبازی کردن risk or sacrifice one's life; practice athletics *v*

جاندارم /jān-dārm/ *n* see ژاندارم

جاندارمه /jān-dār-ma/ *n* see ژاندارمه

جانشین , -ان/ها /jā-nĭ-shin/ replacement; successor *n*

جانشینی /jā-nĭ-shi-ni/ replacement; succession *n*

جانور, -ان/ها /jān-war (jĭ-nā-war)/ beast; animal; monster *n*

جانی /jā-ni/ felon, criminal *n*; faithful *adj*

جانی خیل /jā-ni kheyl/ Jani Kheyl (dist) *n*

جاوا /jā-wā/ Java (island) *n*

جاودان /jā-wĭ-dān/ see جاوید

جاوید /jā-weyd/ eternal *adj*; sth eternal; Jaweyd (m name) *n*

جاویدان /jā-wey-dān/ eternal; perpetual *adj*

جاویدانگی /jā-wey-dā-na-gi/
perpetuity n

جاویدانه /jā-wey-dā-na/
eternal adj; eternally adv

جاه طلب , -ان/ها /jāh ta-lab/
ambitious (neg) (& pers) adj, n

جاه طلبانه /jāh ta-la-bā-na/
ambitious (neg; & adv) adj, adv

جاه طلبی /jāh ta-la-bi/
ambition (neg) n

جاهل , -ان/ها/جهلا
/jā-hīl, pl ja-ha-lā/
ignorant; foolish; fool n

جاهلانه /jā-hī-lā-na/
ignorant (& adv) adj, adv

جاهلی /jā-hī-li/
ignorance n; pagan, heathen (esp
pre-Musl) adj

جاهلیت /jā-hī-lī-yat, -ya/
Jahiliyyah; state of ignorance; pre-
Islamic paganism n

جا /jāy/ n see جای
جای خلوت /jā-yi khīl-wat/
hermitage n

جاي <کسی / چیزی> گرفتن
/jāy-ī <ká-sey> gīrīftan/
occupy; take the place <of sb/sth>
vt

جای مانده /jāy mān-da/
sick, confined to bed adj

جای نماز /jā-yi na-māz/
prayer rug n

جایداد /jāy-dād/
capacity; real estate n

جایداد دار /jāy-dād dár/
propertied, having property adj

جایز /jā-yīz/
allowable, permissible adj

جایزه , -ها/جوایز
/jāy-za, pl ja-wā-yīz/
prize, award n

← یک جایزه به پاس <چیزی>
an award in consideration <of
sth>

←جایزه دادن give a prize, award v
← جایزه گرفتن accept an award v

جایزه نوبل /jāy-za-yī no-bal/
Nobel Prize n

جایگاه /jāy-gāh/
dwelling; place; status n

جایگزین /jāy-gŭ-zin/
choosing an abode; placement;
superseding; replacement n

جایگه /jāy-gah/ n see جایگاه
جایی که /jā-yi kī, key/
where (introduces dependent
clause) conj

جبر /já-bīr, jabr/
force, compulsion; fatalism n

← جبر دیدن be forced v
← جبر کردن force, compel vt

جبراً /jab-ran, jáb-/
forcibly, by force adv

جبران /jīb-rān/ compensation n
← جبران کردن compensate v

جبری , -ون /jab-ri, pl –rī-yun/
fatalist, believer in predestination
n

جبریل /jīb-ra-yīl/ n see جبرییل
جبریه /jab-rī-ya/
Jabriya (fatalist school of Islamist
thought) n

جبرییل /jīb-ra-yil/ Gabriel (bibl) n
جبل /ja-bal/
mountain; crowbar n

جبل السراج /ja-bàl ŭs-sa-rāj/
Jabal us-Saraj (dist) n

جبل الطارق /ja-bàl ŭl-tā-rīq/
Gibraltar n

جبه خانه /ja-ba khā-na/
artillery depot, magazine n

جبه زار /ja-ba zār/
marsh, swamp n

جبهه , -ها/جبهات /jab-ha, pl -hāt/
forehead; (mil) front line n

جبهه متحد /jab-ha-yī mŭ-ta-hīd/
United Front (pol party) n

جبهه نجات ملی
/jab-ha-yī nī-jāt-ī mī-li/
National Liberation Front (guerrila
mvmt, hist) n

جت /jat/ jat, Asian gypsy n
جت /jīt/ jet, jet plane n
جگل داغ /jī-jīl dāgh/ cicada n
جحیم /ja-him/ hell, hellfire n

جد /jad, pl aj-dād/
grandfather; ancestor n
اجداد ← pl
جد پدری /jad-ĭ pa-da-ri/
paternal grandfather n
جد مادری /jad-ĭ mā-da-ri/
maternal grandfather n
جد /jĭd/ earnestness; attempt n
جد و جهد /jĭd ŭ jahd/
attempt & effort n phrs
جدا /jŭ-dā, jĭ-/
separate; detached adj
جدا افتادن • جدا کردن ←
separate; distinguish vt
جدا جدا /jŭ-dā jŭ-dā/
separately, one by one adv
جداگانه /jŭ-dā-gā-na/
separate adj; separately adv
جدال , -ها /jĭ-dāl/
argument; discussion; struggle n
جدران، dzad- /jad-rān, dzad-/
وزه جدران see n
جدل /ja-dal/
polemic, discussion; struggle n
جدلی /ja-da-li/
polemical adj
جوار /jad-wār/
zedoary (drug) n
جدول , -ها/جداول
/jad-wal, ja-dā-wal/
list; table; ruler n
جدول بندی /jad-wal ban-di/
tabulation n
جدول بندی کردن ←
tabulate vt
جدول تقویم /jad-wal-ĭ taq-wim/
calendar table n
جدول ضرب /jad-wal-ĭ zarb/
multiplication table n
جدول کاری /jad-wal-ĭ kā-ri/
task list n
جدول معما /jad-wal-ĭ mū-'a-mā/
جدول معمایی see n
جدول معمایی
/jad-wal-ĭ mū-'a-mā-yi/
crossword puzzle n
جده /jĭd-dah/ Jeddah (port city) n
جدی /já-di, jad-ya/
Jadi (month); Capricorn; kid (goat) n

جدی /jĭ-di/
earnest; grave adj; seriously adv
جدیت /jĭ-dī-yat/
earnestness; gravity (of situation) n
جدید /jĭ-did/ new adj
جدید الشمول /jĭ-did-ŭl-shŭ-mul/
recruit, recruited n, adj
جذاب /ja-zāb/
handsome; fascinating adj
جذام /jŭ-zām/ leprosy n
جذامی , -ان/ها /jŭ-zā-mi/
leper n; leprous adj
جذب /jazb/
attraction; captivation n
جذب کردن ←
attract; captivate
جذبه /jaz-ba/ ecstasy, rapture n
جذبه /ja-za-ba, pl -bāt/
spiritual influence n
جذبات ← pl
جذر , -ها/جذور
/já-zĭr, jazr; pl jŭ-zur/
root (math) n
جذر گرفتن ← derive a root v
جذر اصم /já-zĭr-ĭ a-sam/
irrational root, surd n
جذر تحقیقی /já-zĭr-ĭ tah-qi-qi/
rational root n
جذر مربع /já-zĭr-ĭ mŭ-ra-ba/
square root n
جذر مکعب /já-zĭr-ĭ mŭ-ka-'ab/
cube root n
جذر ناطق /já-zĭr-ĭ nā-tĭq/
جذرتحقیقی see n
جراب /jĭ-rāb, jŭ-rāb/
sock, socks (clothing) n
جراب زنانه /jĭ-rāb-ĭ za-nā-na/
pantyhose, stocking (f's) n
جراثیم /ja-rā-sim/
bacteria; germs n pl
جراح /ja-rāh/ surgeon n
جراحت , -ها/جراحات
/ja-rā-hat, pl -hāt/
cut, wound, injury n
جراحی /ja-rā-hi/
surgery n; surgical adj
راحی زیبایی /ja-rā-hi-yĭ zey-bā-yi/
cosmetic surgery n

جرايد /ja-rā-yīd, sg ja-ri-da/
see sg جريده n pl

جرايم /ja-rā-yīm, sg jūrm/
see sg جرم n pl

جرجيس /jīr-jis/
George (m name) n

جرس /ja-ras/
bell (arch, esp camel's) n

جرعه /jūr-'a/ n sip
جرعه جرعه /jūr-'a jūr-'a/
sip by sip adv

جرغات /jūr-ghāt/ yogurt n
جرقه /ja-ra-qa/ spark n
جرگه , -ها /jīr-ga/
jirga, council of elders; house of
Parliament n
جرگه کردن ←
convene a council
جرم , -ها/جرايم /jūrm, pl ja-rā-yīm/
crime, offense; Jurm (district) n
جرمنی , -ان/ها /jar-ma-ni/
German (& pers, lang); Germany
n; German adj

جرئت , جُر-'at/ /jū-rat, jūr-'at/
courage, bravery n
جرئت دادن <به کسی> ←
embolden, give courage <to sb> v
جرئت یافتن ← be courageous v
جريان , -ات/ها /jīr-yān/
flow; course, duration n
جريان داشتن ←
continue, be ongoing vi

جريب /jī-rib/
jerib (about 2000 sq m) n

جريبان /jī-ri-ban/ geranium n
جريده , -ها/جرايد
/ja-ri-da, pl ja-rā-yīd/
newspaper, gazette n

جريده نگار, -ان/ها/ها /ja-ri-da nī-gār/
journalist n
جريده نگاری /ja-ri-da nī-gā-ri/
journalism n

جريمه , -ها /ja-ri-ma/
fine, penalty, forfeiture n
جريمه نقدی /ja-ri-ma-yī naq-di/
cash fine n

جز /jūz(-ī)/ except, unless prep
جز ان که /jūz-ī ān kī/
except that conj

جزا , -ها /ja-zā/
punishment, penalty n
جزا دادن ← punish; penalize
جزای اعدام /ja-zā-yī ey-dām/
execution, death penalty n
جزای ضرب /ja-zā-yī zarb/
whipping, flogging n
جزای مرگ /ja-zā-yī marg/
see جزای اعدام n
جزای نقدی /ja-zā-yī naq-di/
fine, cash penalty n
جزايز /ja-zā-yīz, sg ja-zi-ra/
see sg جزيره n pl
جزايی /ja-zā-yi/ criminal, penal adj
جزء /jūz'/ n see جزو
جزئی /jū-zi/
minor, trivial; partial adj
جزئيات /jū-zi-yāt/
details, particulars n pl
جزئيات و کليات
/jū-zi-yāt ŭ kŭ-lī-yāt/
details & totalities n phrs
جزو /jūz', jūzw; pl aj-zā/
part; section (Quran); ingredient n
اجزا ← pl
جزو تام /jūzw-ī tām (jū-zu-)/ -ها
unit; piece; department (mil) n
جزيره , -ها/جزاير /ja-zi-ra, pl ja-zā-yīz/
island n
جزيره نشين , -ان/ها
/ja-zi-ra nī-shin/
islander (pers) n
جزيره نما /ja-zi-ra nŭ-mā/
peninsula n
جزيه /jaz-ya, jīz-/
tribute; poll tax on non-Muslims n
جست /jast/ jump, leap; zinc n
جست زدن /jast zadan/
jump, leap v
جست و جو /jūst ŭ jo/
see جستجو n
جست و خيز /jast ŭ kheyz/
capering n
جست و خيز زدن ← caper v
جستن ؛ -جو- ؛ جست- /jŭs-tan/
inquire, search v

114   a = cup, ā = long, aw = now, ay = sigh, e = bet, ey = obey

جستوجو /jŭst ŭ jo/
inquiry, search n
← جستوجو کردن
inquire, search
جسته جسته /jas-ta jas-ta/
little by little, gradually adv
جسد ها- , /ja-sad, pl aj-sād/اجساد
corpse n
جسم , ها- /jĭsm, pl aj-sām/اجسام
body (& human); solid n
جسماً /jĭs-man, jĭs´-/
physically adv
جسمانی /jĭs-mā-ni/
bodily, physical adj
جسیم /ja-sim/
bulky, huge adj
جشن /já-shĭn, jashn/
celebration, festival, feast n
← جشن کردن
celebrate, feast v
جشن عروسی /já-shĭn-ĭ a-ru-si/
wedding feast n
جشنواره /ja-shĭn-wā-ra/
جشن see n
جعبه /ja'-ba/ box; drawer n
جعد /ja'd/ forelock n
جعفری /ja-fa-ri/
marigold (flower); lambskin quilt n
جعل /ja'l/ forgery, counterfeit n
← جعل کردن
forge, counterfeit v
جغتای /ja-gha-tāy/ see n چغتای
جغتو /ja-gha-tu/
Jaghatu (dist; ctr) n
جغد /jŭghd, chŭghd/ owl (bird) n
جغرافیا /jŭgh-rā-fi-yā/
جغرافیه see n
جغرافیه /jŭgh-rā-fi-ya/
geography n
جغرافیایی /jŭgh-rā-fi-ya-yi/
geographical adj
جغل /ja-ghal/ gravel n
جغله /ja-gha-la/ see n جغل
جغه /jŭ-gha/ plume (ornamental) n
جفت /jŭft/
even number; pair; mate, spouse;
placenta n; fitting (into a space)
adj
جفت شدن /jŭft shŭdan/
mate; fit (into a space) v
جفنگ /ja-fang/ nonsense n
← جفنگ گفتن
speak nonsense v

جک /jak/
pitcher (small), jug; butter churn;
tire jack n
← جک زدن churn butter v
جک بالا کردن /jak bā-lā kardan/
jack, lift up (car) vt
جک تیر /jak-ĭ tayr/ tire jack n
جگر /jĭ-gar/
liver (anat); (fig) courage; dear
child n
جگر بند /jĭ-gar band/
pluck (of slaughtered animal) n
جگر جوشی /jĭ-gar jo-shi/
heartburn n
جگر خراش /jĭ-gar kha-rāsh/
heart-rending, harrowing adj
جگر خون /jĭ-gar khun/
grieved adj
جگر خونی /jĭ-gar khu-ni/ grief n
جگر گوشه /jĭ-gar go-sha/
lobe of liver (anat); (fig) dear child
n
جگرن /jag-ran/ [< P] n جگلن see
جگره /jag-ra/
bargaining, haggling n
← جگره کردن
bargain, haggle v
جگری /jĭ-ga-ri/ liver-colored adj
جگلن /jag-lan/ major (mil) n
جل /jal/ sunstroke; lark (bird) n
← جل زدن suffer sunstroke v
جلاب /ja-lāb/ itinerant trader n
جلاب /jŭ-lāb/
laxative; unwanted pers/task;
julep n
جلال/ل /ja-lāl/
terrible, formidable adj
جلال الدین محمد اکبر
/ja-lāl-ŭl-din mŭ-ha-mad ak-bar/
اکبر see n
جلالتماب , ان- /ja-lā-lat-māb/
Excellency (form of address) n
جلالزی /ja-lāl-zay/
Jalalzai (P tribe) n
جلالی شدن /ja-lā-li shŭdan/
get angry, become upset (colloq)
vi
جلب /jalb/
recruitment (mil); summons n

جلب نظر کردن
/jalb-ĭ na-zar kardan/
attract attention v

جلب و جذب /jalb ŭ jazb/
recruitment & absorption (mil) n
phrs

جلبی /jal-bi/ recruit; draftee n

جلترنگ /jal-ta-rang/
glass harp (mus instr) n

جلد /jŭld, jĭld/
cover (book); volume (book);
piece, unit (of hide or book); skin
n

← ۱۰۰ جلد پوست 100 hides
← ۵۰ جلد کتاب 50 copies (book)

جلد کتاب /jŭld-ĭ kĭ-tāb/
book cover n

جلدی /jŭl-di, jĭl-/
dermal, related to skin adj

جلریز /jal-reyz/ Jalreyz (dist) n
جلسه , -ها/جلسات
/jal-sa, pl ja-la-sāt/
session, meeting n

← جلسه کردن convene

جلسه وزرا /jal-sa-yĭ wŭ-za-rā/
ministerial (meeting) n

جلق /jalq/ masturbation n
← جلق زدن masturbate

جلگه /jĭl-ga/
prairie, steppe; Jelga (dist) n

جلگه نهرین /jĭl-ga nah-rin/
Jelga Nahrin see خواجه حجران n

جلوگیری /jĭ-law-gi-ri/
prevention, repression n

جلوگیری از حاملگی
/jĭ-law-gi-ri az hā-mĭ-la-gi/
birth control n

جلی /ja-li/ obvious, clear adj
← خط چلی plain handwriting

جم /jam/
many adj, n; Jam (hist/legend/Zor,
king) n

← جام جم Jam's golden bowl
← جم غفیر crowd

جماع /jĭ-mā/ sex, intercourse n
← جماع کردن have sex

جماع گسیخته/jĭ-mā-'ĭ gŭ-seykh-ta/
coitus interruptus n

جماعت , -ها/جماعات
/ja-mā-'at, pl -'āt/
group, community; congregation n

جماعت الدعوت
/ja-mā-'at ŭl-da'-wat/
see لشکر طیبه n

جمال /ja-māl/
grace, beauty; Jamal (m name) n

جمبه /jam-ba/ see جنبه n
جمپر /jam-par/ sports shirt n

جمجمه , -ها /jŭm-jŭ-ma/ skull n

جمشید /jam-sheyd/
Jamsheyd (m name; see & جم &
Jam) n

جمشیدی /jam-shey-di/
Jamsheydi (Aimaq tribe) n

جمع /jam/
group; collection; (math) addition;
(gram) plural n; compact; at ease
(mind) adj

← جمع بستن pluralize vt
← خاطر اش جمع است
his/her mind is at ease

جمع آوری /jam ā-wa-ri/
collecting, gathering together n

← جمع آوری کردن
collect, gather together v

جمع سالم /jam-'ĭ sā-lĭm/
regular plural (gram, Ar) n

جمع کل /jam-'ĭ kŭl/ grand total n
جمع مسکر /jam-'ĭ mŭ-sa-kar/
broken plural (gram, Ar) n

جمع و جوش /jam ŭ josh/
crowd (throng) n phrs

جمعاً in all adv /jam-'an, jám-/
جمعیت اسلامی
/jam-'ĭ-yat-ĭ ĭs-lā-mi/
Jamiat-e Islami (pol group) n

جملگی /jŭm-la-gi/
totality, the whole n

جمله , -ها/جملات /jŭm-la, pl -lāt/
total, whole; (gram) sentence n

← جملهٔ بسیط simple sentence
← جملهٔ بندی wording
← جملهٔ مختلف complex sentence
← جملهٔ مرکب
compound sentence

← فی الجمله in sum, in short

جمناستک /jīm-nās-tīk/
gymnastics, sport n

جمود /ja-mud/
inflexibility; stiffness n

جمود مفصل /ja-mud-ī maf-sal/
arthritis n

جمهوری /jam-hu-ri/ republican adj

جمهوریت , -ها /jam-hu-rī-yat/
republic n

جمهوریت توده یی
/jam-hu-rī-yat-ī to-da-yi/
people's republic n

جمهوریت خواه , -ان/ها
/jam-hu-rī-yat khāh/
republican; Republican n

جمهوریت خواهی
/jam-hu-rī-yat khā-hi/
republicanism n

جمیع /ja-mi/ whole, total, entirety n

جمیکا /ja-mey-kā/
Jamaica (country) n

جمیکایی , -ان/ها /ja-mey-kā-yi/
Jamaican (& pers) adj, n

جمیل /ja-mil/
handsome; pretty adj; Jamil (m name) n

جن , -ها /jīn/ jinn, genie, gin n

جناب عالی /jī-nāb-ī 'ā-li/
see جناب مبارک n

جناب مبارک /jī-nāb-ī mŭ-bā-rak/
Your Honor n

جنابت /jī-nā-bat/
unclean state after ejaculation (ablution required before prayer) n
→ غسل جنابت (the required ablution)

جناح , -ها/اجنحه
/jī-nāh, pl aj-nĭ-ha/
side, flank (mil); wing (bird's) n

جنازه , -ها /jī-nā-za/
funeral; corpse (at funeral) n

جناور , -ها /jī-nā-war/
beast; boar; monster; (fig) brutal person (colloq) n

جنایت /jī-nā-yat/ crime, felony n

جنایت کار, -ان/ها /jī-nā-yat kār/
criminal, felon n

جنایت کارانه /jī-nā-yat ka-rā-na/
criminal, felonious (& adv) adj, adv

جنایی /jī-nā-yi/
criminal, related to crime adj

جنب /jŭ-nūb (-nub)/
unclean after ejaculation adj

جنبش , -ها /jūm-bīsh/
movement (social); shaking, rocking; see & جنبش ملی n

جنبش ملی /jūm-bīsh-ī mī-li/
Junbish-e Meli (movement) n

جنبه /jam-ba/
aspect, viewpoint; (colloq) hostile group n

جنتر /jan-tar/ incantation, spell n

جنتر سرمیزی/ی /jan-tar-ī sar-mey-zi/
incantation said over table n

جنتری /jan-ta-ri/
calendar, almanac n

جنجال /jan-jāl/
bother, fuss; dispute, brawl n

جنجال‌ها-یی زندگی /jan-jāl-hā-yī zīn-da-gi/
life's inconveniences n pl

جنحه /jan-ha/ misdemeanor n

جندی /jīn-di/ demonic (colloq) adj

جنرال فرمانده
/jan-rāl-ī far-mān-da/
commanding general n

جنس , -ها/اجناس /jīns, pl aj-nās/
kind; race; breed; genus; category; gender (& gram); quality n

جنسی /jīn-si/ generic; sexual adj

جنسیت /jīn-sī-yat/
quality; sexuality n

جنگ , -ها /jang/
war, battle; fight n

جنگ آزموده , -گان/ها
/jang āz-mu-da/
battle-hardened (& pers) adj, n

جنگ آور , -ان/ها /jang ā-war/
fighter, hero, champion n

جنگ آوران آزادی
/jang ā-wa-rān-ī ā-zā-di/
freedom fighters n pl

جنگ انداختن /jang andākhtan/
incite war, foment war v

---

i = keep, ĭ = big, u = coop, ŭ = put, y = yet, ' = (glottal stop)   117

جنگ اندازی /jang an-dā-zi/
incitement to war n

جنگ تن به تن /jang-ī tan ba tan/
duel; hand-to-hand combat n

جنگ دیده , ـگان/ها /jang di-da/
battle-toughened (& pers) adj, n

جنگ زرگری /jang-ī zar-ga-ri/
scam (argument by two pers to
defraud a third) n

جنگ سالار /jang sā-lār/ warlord n

جنگ نامه /jang nā-ma/
war narrative; Jangnama (account
of First Anglo-Afghan War) n

جنگ و گریز /jang ŭ gŭ-reyz/
hit & run n

جنگ و گریز کردن
/jang ŭ gŭ-reyz kardan/
hit & run v

جنگروک /jang-rok/
quarrelsome, aggressive (child)
adj

جنگره /jan-ga-ra/
aggressive (colloq) adj

جنگل , ـها /jan-gal/
forest, jungle n; messy (colloq) adj

جنگل بان , ـان/ها /jan-gal bān/
forest ranger n

جنگل بانی /jan-gal bā-ni/
forestry n

جنگلی /jan-ga-li/
wild, uncivilized adj

جنگی /jan-gi/ martial; warlike adj
← جنگی بودن • جنگی شدن
ignore; stonewall v

جنوب /jŭ-nub/ south n

جنوب شرق /jŭ-nub sharq/
southeast n

جنوب شرقی /jŭ-nub shar-qi/
southeastern adj

جنوب غرب /jŭ-nub gharb/
southwest n

جنوب غربی /jŭ-nub ghar-bi/
southwestern adj

جنوباً , ـنۇ- /jŭ-nu-ban, -nŭ́-/
from the south adv

جنوبی /jŭ-nu-bi/ southern adj

جنوری /jan-wa-ri/
January (month) n

جنون /jŭ-nun/
insanity; rage; frenzy n

جنون آمیز /jŭ-nun ā-meyz/
foolish; maniacal adj, adv

جنی /jī-ni/ jinni, demon n

جنین , ـها- /ja-nin/
embryo, fetus n

جنینی /ja-ni-ni/ embryonic, fetal adj

جو /jaw/ barley; barleycorn n

جو به جو /jaw ba jaw/
bit by bit, gradually adv

جواب , ـات/ها /ja-wāb/
answer, reply, response n

جواب چای /ja-wāb-ī chāy/
urine (fig) n
← جواب چای رفتن
go urinate

جواب دادن /ja-wāb dādan/
answer; dismiss; fire; refuse help
v

جوابده /ja-wāb dīh/
responsible, liable adj

جوابدهی /ja-wāb dī-hi/
responsibility n

جوابی /ja-wā-bi/
retaliatory, counter; in reply adj

جوار /ja-wār/
neighborhood, proximity; corn n

جواری /ja-wā-ri/ corn, maize n

جواری پله /ja-wā-ri pŭ-la/
popcorn n

جواز /ja-wāz/ جواز نامه see

جواز تجارتی /ja-wāz-ī tŭ-jā-ra-ti/
business license n

جواز نامه /ja-wāz/
license, permit n

جواسیس , sg جاسوس /ja-wā-sis, sg jā-sus/
see sg جاسوس n pl

جوامع , sg جامعه /ja-wā-mey, sg jā-mī-'a/
see sg جامعه n pl

جوان , ـان/ها /ja-wān/
young; vigorous adj

جوان کردن /ja-wān kardan/
rejuvenate, invigorate vt

جوان مرد , ـان/ها /ja-wān mard/
brave, manly, spirited (& pers) adj,
n

جوان مرگی /ja-wān mar-gi/
untimely death n

جوانان افغان /ja-wā-nān-ĭ af-ghān/
Young Afghans (hist) n

جوانب /ja-wā-nĭb, sg jā-nĭb/
see sg جانب n pl

جوانه , ها- /ja-wā-na/
sprout; sprouts n

جوانه زدن /ja-wā-na zadan/
sprout v

جوانه گندم /ja-wā-na-yĭ gan-dŭm/
wheat sprouts n

جوانک teenager n /ja-wā-nak/
جوانی /ja-wā-ni/
youth, youthfulness; vigor n

جوانی دانه /ja-wā-ni dā-na/
acne; pimples n

جواهر , ات/ها- /ja-wā-hĭr/
jewelry; gems n

جواهر آلات /ja-wā-hĭr ā-lāt/
jewelled articles n

جواهر فروش /ja-wā-hĭr fŭ-rosh/
jeweller, gem dealer n

جواهر فروشی /ja-wā-hĭr fŭ-ro-shi/
jewelry shop, gem shop n

جواهر نشان /ja-wā-hĭr nĭ-shān/
jewelled adj

جوایز /ja-wā-yĭz, sg jāy-za/
see sg جایزه n pl

جوپه group (of people) n /jo-pa/
جوپه جوپه /jo-pa jo-pa/
in groups adv

جودر rye; grain of rye n /jaw-dar/
جور /jawr/
oppression, injustice n

← جور دادن
pester, tease, annoy v

جور fit, healthy adj /jor/
← جور آمدن
fit, be the right size v

← جور کردن
fix, repair; primp v

جور و تیار /jor ŭ ta-yār/
fit & healthy adj phrs

جوره /ju-ra/
pair; placenta n; together adv

← یک جوره بوت a pair of shoes
جوره کالا /ju-ra kā-lā/
top & bottom of clothing set n

جوری health, well-being n /jo-ri/
جوزا /jaw-zā/
Jawza (month); Gemini n

جوزجان /jawz-jān/
Jowzjan (prov) n

جوش /josh/
boiling; heat, intensity n

← جوش آمدن come to a boil vi
← جوش دادن boil vt

جوش آوردن /josh āwŭrdan/
boil; stir up, rouse, incite vt

جوش خوردن /josh khŭrdan/
heal up (bone); weld, fuse; get
along with people vi

جوشانده /jo-shān-da/
extract, decoction n

جوشیدن ؛ -جوش- ؛ جوشید-
/jo-shi-dan/
boil (formal) vi

جوقه group (of people) n /jo-qa/
جوقه جوقه /jo-qa jo-qa/
in groups adv

جوک leech n /jok/
جوک چسپاندن /jok chaspāndan/
apply leeches v

جوگی , ان/ها- /jo-gi/
yogi, supernaturalist; magician n

جولا see جولاه n /jo-lā/
جولاه /jo-lāh (-lā)/
spider; weaver n

جولاهک /jo-lā-hak (-gak)/
spider n

جولای July (month) n /jo-lāy/
جولایی see جولای n /jo-lā-yi/
جون June (month) n /jun/
جوند Jawand (dist) n /ja-wand/
جوود see یهود (colloq) n /ja-wud/
جوی /ja-wi/
atmospheric; meteorical adj

جوی irrigation ditch; brook n /joy/
جویا inquiring adj /jo-yā/
← جویا شدن inquire, ask v

جویچه /joy-cha/
ditch; brook (small) n

جویدن ؛ -جو- ؛ جوید- /ja-wi-dan/
chew v

جوین Juwayn (town) n /jŭ-wayn/
جوینده , گان/ها- /jo-yĭn-da/
seeker, inquirer n

جویه /jo-ya/
ditch for planting vines n

جهات /jī-hāt, sg ja-hat/
see sg جهت n

جهاد /jī-hād, ja-/
jihad; struggle; battle n

جهادگر , -ان/ها /jī-hād-gar/
jihadist n

جهادی /jī-hā-di/
jihad, related to jihad adj

جهاز , -ات/ها /ja-hāz, jī-/
system, apparatus n

جهاز بحری /ja-hāz-ī bah-ri/ ship n

جهاز تنفس /ja-hāz-ī ta-na-fūs/
respirator n

جهاز هاضمه /ja-hāz-ī hā-zī-ma/
digestive system n

جهاز هوایی /ja-hāz-ī ha-wā-yi/
airplane n

جهان /ja-hān/
world; universe, cosmos n

جهان آفرین /ja-hān ā-fa-rin/
the Creator n

جهان بینی /ja-hān bi-ni/
outlook; ideology n

جهان گشا /ja-hān gŭ-shā/
world-conquering adj; Jahan
Gusha (epithet) n

جهانگیر /ja-hān-gir/
Jahangir (hist, Mughal emperor) n

جهانی /ja-hā-ni/
worldly, of the world adj

جهت , -ها/جهات /ja-hat, pl jī-hāt/
direction; aspect; trend n; for the
purpose of prep

جهد /jahd/ attempt, effort n

جهر /jahr (jār)/ announcer, crier n

جهر زدن /jahr zadan/
herald, proclaim v

جهرچی /jahr-chi, jār-/
herald, messenger n

جهلا /ja-ha-lā, sg jā-hīl/
see sg جاهل n pl

جهنم /ja-ha-nŭm/ hell n

جهنمی /ja-ha-nŭ-mi/
hellish, infernal adj

جهود /ja-hud/ n see یهود

جیر /jir/ suede n

جیره /jay-ra/ porcupine n

جیره /ji-ra/ ration, small portion n

جیره بندی /ji-ra ban-di/
rationing (esp food) n

← جیره بندی کردن
ration; apportion v

جهیل /ja-hil/ lake n

جیب /jeyb/ pocket n

جیبی /jey-bi/ pocket-sized adj

جیره خور , -ان/ها /ji-ra khŭr/
rations eater; servant n

جیکر /jay-kar/
joker (card); insouciant pers n

جینوا /ji-na-wā/ Geneva (city) n

جیوه /jay-wa/
mercury, quicksilver n

چ

چابکدست (-دِست) /chā-bŭk-dast (-dīst)/
skillful adj; prestidigitator n

چاپ /chāp/ print; impression n

چاپ حروفی /chāp-ī hŭ-ru-fi/
typography n

چاپ خانه /chāp khā-na/
publishing house n

چاپ کردن /chāp kardan/ print v

چاپ سنگی /chāp-ī san-gi/
lithography n

چاپلوسی /chā-pa-lu-si/
flattery, adulation n

چاپلوسی کردن
/chā-pa-lu-si kardan/
flatter, adulate v

چاپلوس /chā-pa-lus/ flatterer n

چاپی /chā-pi/
printed adj; massage (colloq) n

چات /chāt/ perineum (colloq) n

چاتی /chā-ti/
vessel for liquids; fat person n

چادر /chā-dar/
chadar, head cover for f n

چادری /chā-da-ri/
chadari, body cover for f n

چار نعل رفتن /chār na'l raftan/
gallop vi

چاراسیاب /chā-rā-sī-yāb/
see چهار آسیاب

چاربرجک /chār-bŭr-jak/
Charburjak (dist) n

چاربولک /chār-bo-lak/
Charbolak (dist) n

چاربیتی /chār-bay-ti/
Dari poem w/two couplets n

چارپایه /chār-pā-ya/
stool, low seat n

چارتاق /chār-tāq/ Chartaq (ctr) n

چارچند /chār-chand/
quadruple, fourfold adv, n

چارچوب /chār-chob/
wooden frame; limit n

چارخانه /chār-khā-na/
checkered adj

چاردره /chār-da-ra/
Chardara (dist) n

چارراه /chār-rāh/ چارراهی n see
چارراهی /chār-rā-hi (-yi)/
crossroads, intersection n

چارزانو /chār-zā-nu/
cross-legged adj

چارسو /chār-su/
hammer (coppersmith's) n

چارسوق /chār-suq/
bazaar crossroads n

چارشانه /chār-shā-na/
broad-shouldered, tall & strong n

چارشنبه /chār-sham-bey/
چهارشنبه n see

چارسده /chār-sa-da/
Charsada (dist) n

چارق /chā-rūq/
boot used by villagers n

چارقریه /chār qar-ya/
Char Qarya (dist) n

چارک /chā-rak/
charak (unit of weight) n

چارکنت /chār-kīnt/
Charkent (dist) n

چارکنج /chār-kŭnj/
rectangular adj

چارکنجه /chār-kŭn-ja/
چارکنج adj see

چارکه /chā-ra-ka/
one-fourth; a four-pound weight n

چارمغز /chār-maghz/ walnut n

چارمغزی /chār-magh-zi/
walnut-colored adj

چارمیخ /chār-meykh/
crucifixion; tormenting n

چاره /chā-ra/
remedy; resource; helpless (pers) n

چاره پذیر /chā-ra pa-zir/
remediable adj

چاره پذیری /chā-ra pa-zi-ri/
remediability n

چاره جویی ‹برای چیزی› /chā-ra jo-yi/
seeking a remedy ‹for sth› n

چاره ساز بی چاره گان /chā-ra-sāz-ī bey-chā-ra-gān/
helper of the helpless (God) n

چاره سازی /chā-ra sā-zi/
remedying n

↵ چاره سازی کردن
remedy, cure v

چاره ناپذیر /chā-ra nā-pa-zir/
irremediable adj

چاره ناپذیری /chā-ra nā-pa-zi-ri/
irremediability n

چاریار /chār-yār/
the Prophet's four successors n

↵ یا چاریار
Geronimo (in joint attack) excl

چاریکار /chā-ri-kār/
Charikar (dist, seat) n

چاشت /chāsht/ noon n

چاشنی , -ها /chāsh-ni/
condiment; sample of food n

چاشنی گرفتن /chāsh-ni gīrīftan/
taste or sample food v

چاغ /chāgh/ چاق (colloq) adj see
چاق /chāq (chāgh)/ fat, obese adj

چاقو /chā-qu/
pocketknife, penknife n

چاقو کش /chā-qu kash/
cutthroat, thug n

چاقو کشی /chā-qu ka-shi/
thuggery n

چاقی /chā-qi/
obesity; plumpness n

چاک /chāk/ slit, opening n

چاکر /chā-kar/ servant n

چاکلیت /chāk-leyt/ chocolate n

چاکوچ /chā-kŭch/ hammer n

چال /chāl/
move (chess); pit; trick, deception;
Chal (dist) n
چال زدن ←
move (chess); trick, deceive v
چال رفتن v move (chess) ←
چالاک /chā-lāk/
tricky, deceptive adj
چالاکی دست /chā-lā-ki-yī dast/
sleight of hand n
چالش , ها- /chā-līsh/
obstacle; challenge n
چاله /chā-la/ small pit n
چانه زدن /chā-na zadan/
haggle, bargain (colloq) v
چاه /chāh/ well, deep hole n
چاه آب /chāh āb/ Chah Ab (dist) n
چاه بدرفت /chāh-ī bad-raft/
cesspool, latrine n
چاه تشناب /chāh-ī tash-nāb/
چاه بدرفت n see
چاه نفت /chāh-ī nīft/ oil well n
چای /chāy/ tea; (fig) breakfast n
چای خوردن ← eat breakfast vi
چای جوش /chāy josh/ teakettle n
چای خانه /chāy khā-na/
teahouse n
چای صاف /chāy sāf/
tea strainer n
چای صبح /chāy-ī sŭbh/
breakfast n
چایبر /chāy-bar/
teapot w/handle on top n
چاینک /chāy-nak/ teapot n
چپ /chap/ left (side) n, adj
چپ افتادن /chap aftādan/
be at sixes & sevens v
چپ باش ! /chŭp bāsh/
shut up (colloq) excl
چپ چپ دیدن /chap chap didan/
look daggers v
چپ راس /chap rās/ hinge n
چپ شدن /chap shŭdan/
be in opposition, turn away v
چپات /cha-pāt/ flat adj; slap n
چپات خوردن ← get slapped vi
چپات زدن ← slap vt

چپاتی /cha-pā-ti/
flat bread baked in a tanur n
چپاول کردن /cha-pā-wŭl kardan/
plunder, sack v
چپر /cha-par/ straw-covered hut n
چپرکت /cha-par-kat/
bedstead (metal) n
چپر هار /cha-par-hār/
Chaparhar (dist) n
چپری /cha-pa-ri/ چپر see n
چپلک /chap-lak/
sandal, slipper n
چپلی /chap-li/ men's sandal n
چپلی بوت /chap-li but/
women's sandal n
چپلی کباب /chap-li ka-bāb/
sandal kebab (cul) n
چپه شده /cha-pa shŭ-da/
upside-down; inside-out; tipped
over adj
چپه دست /cha-pa dast/
left-handed adj
چپه یخن /cha-pa ya-khan/
collar (decorative) n
چت /chat/ ceiling n
چتری /chat-ri/ umbrella n
چتل /cha-tal/ dirty, polluted adj
چتلی /cha-ta-li/ trash, garbage n
چتی /cha-ti/
ridiculous, useless adj
چخانسور /cha-khān-sur/
Chakhansur (dist) n
چخیدن ؛ خ-؛ چخید-
/cha-khi-dan/ bark v
چدن /chū-dan (cho-)/ cast iron n
چدنی /chū-da-ni (cho-)/
cast iron adj
چرا ؟ /chī-rā/ why? adv
چرا که /chī-rā kĭ (key)/
because, since conj
چراغ /chī-rāgh/ light, lamp n
چراغ برقی /chī-rāgh-ī bar-qi/
electric light n
چراغ ترافیک /chī-rāgh-ī ta-rā-fik/
traffic light n
چراغ دستی /chī-rāgh-ī dīs-ti/
flashlight n
چرب /charb/
fatty, greasy, oily adj

چرب زبان /charb za-bān/
sweet-talking; glib adj

چرب زبانی کردن /charb za-bān/
sweet-talk v

چرب کاری /charb kā-ri/
lubrication, greasing n

چرب کاری کردن
/charb kā-ri kardan/
lubricate, grease n

چربتر /charb-tar/
better (colloq); greasier adj

چربو /char-bu/
suet, tallow, animal fat n

چربی /char-bi/
fat, grease; lipid n

چربی دار /char-bi dār/
fatty, sebaceous adj

چرچرک /chĭr-chĭ-rak/
cricket (insect) n

چرخ /charkh/
wheel; pulley; circle; Charkh (dist) n

چرخ خوردن /charkh khŭrdan/
see چرخ زدن v

چرخ زدن /charkh zadan/
dance in a circle v

چرخ آب /char-khāb/
whirlpool n

چرخ باد /charkh bād/
whirlwind n

چرخ دادن /charkh dādan/
turn around, rotate, revolve v

چرخ فلک /charkh-ĭ fa-lak/
Ferris wheel; heavenly sphere n

چرخ کردن /charkh kardan/
whet knives on stone wheel v

چرخک /char-khak/
top (toy) n

چرخکی /char-kha-ki/
swivel, swivelling adj

چرخه /char-kha/
spinning wheel; reel, spool n

چرخی /char-khi/
revolving, spinning adj

چرس /chars/
hashish n

چرسی , -ها /char-si/
hashish addict (pers) n

چرک /chĭrk/
filthy, dirty adj; filth; earwax; pus n

چرک آلود /chĭrk ā-lud/
filthy, dirty adj

چرک گرفتن /chĭrk gĭrĭftan/
remove earwax n

چرک و ریم /chĭrk ŭ rim/
filth & pus n

چرکین /chĭr-kin/
filthy, dirty; squalid (lit) adj

چریک /chĭ-rik/
terrorist n

چریکی /chĭ-ri-ki/
terrorist adj

چرم /charm/
leather n

چرم باب /charm bāb/
leather goods n

چرم دوزی /charm do-zi/
leatherwork n

چره /chŭ-ra/
hernia, rupture n

چرمک /char-mak/
leather strip n

چرمگر /charm-gar/
leather worker, currier n

چرمگری /charm-ga-ri/
leather workshop n

چرمی /char-mi/
leather adj

چرمین /char-min/
see چرمی adj

چره , -ها /cha-ra/
fragment; shrapnel; pellet from gun n

چریدن ؛ -چر- ؛ چرید- /cha-ri-dan/
graze (in pasture) vi

چسان ؟ /chĭ-sān/
how? (lit) adv

چسپ /chasp/
tight, close-fitting adj

چسپاندن ؛ -چسپان- ؛ چسپاند-
/chas-pān-dan/
stick (sth onto sth) vt

چسپناک /chasp-nāk/
sticky, adhesive adj

چسپوک /chasp-pok/
see چسپناک (colloq) adj

چسپیدن ؛ -چسپ- ؛ چسپید-
/chas-pi-dan/
stick, adhere, cling vi

چشت شریف /chĭst-ĭ sha-rif/
Chesht-e Sharif (dist) n

چشتی , -ان/ها /chĭsh-ti/
member of Chishtiyya n

چشتیه /chĭsh-tī-ya/
Chishtiyya (Sufi order) n

چشک /cha-shak/
taste, small bite of food n

چشم /chá-shīm, chashm (chī´-)/
eye n

چشم انداختن ←
avert one's eyes v

چشم داشتن ← hope, desire v
چشم دوختن ← stare (fig) v
چشم شدن ←
be under the evil eye v

چشم کشیدن <سر کسی> ←
be angry <at sb> v

چشم پت /chá-shīm pŭt/
blindly, w/eyes closed adv

چشم پت شدن
/chá-shīm pŭt shŭdan/
take a little nap; (fig) die v

چشم پت کردن
/chá-shīm pŭt kardan/
close (one's) eyes v

چشم پتکان /chī´-shīm pŭ-ta-kān/
hide-and-seek (colloq) n

چشم پتکان بازی کردن
/chī´-shīm pŭ-ta-kān bā-zi kardan/
play hide & seek v

چشم تنگ /chá-shīm tang/
stingy, cheap adj

چشم تنگی /chá-shīm tan-gi/
stinginess, parsimony n

چشم چرانی /chá-shīm cha-rā-ni/
ogling n

چشم چرانی کردن ← ogle v
چشم داشت /chá-shīm dāsht/
hope, desire n

چشمک /chīsh-mak/ wink; twinkle n
چشمک زدن ← wink; twinkle v
چشمکی /chīsh-ma-ki/
eye-grille (in chadari) n

چشمه /chash-ma (chīsh-)/
origin, spring, source n

چشمه آب جوشان
/chash-ma-yĭ āb-ĭ jo-shān/
geyser n

چطو ؟ /chī-to, chŭ-/
see چطور ؟ (colloq) adv

چطور ؟ /chī-tawr (-to, chŭ-to)/
how, how about? adv

چغتی /cha-gha-tāy/
Chaghatai (13th-17th-c khanate,
hist); (& lang) n

چغچران /chagh-cha-rān/
Chaghcharan (dist, seat) n

چغر /cha-ghar/
cross-eyed (colloq) adj

چغل /chŭ-ghŭl/ gossip (pers) n
چقدر ؟ /chī-qa-dar/
how much? adv

چقدر وقت ؟ /chī-qa-dar waqt/
how long? Adv

چقر /chŭ-qŭr/ deep adj; deeply adv
چقری /chŭ-qŭ-ri/ depth; pit n
چقماق /chaq-māq/ flint & steel n
چقمق /chaq-maq/ n چقماق see

چقه ؟ /chī-qa/
how much? (colloq) adv

چک /chak/
drop (of liquid); bite of food for
dog; see & چک وردک n

چک , -ان/ها /chīk, chak/
Czech (& pers, lang) n

چک /chīk, chak/ n چخ see also
چک ! /chŭk/
chuk (sound to make camel bend
down) excl

چک انداختن /chak andākhtan/
drop; take a bite (as dog) v

چک چک /chak-chak/
applause, clapping n

چک چک کردن ← applaud vi
چک وردک /chak-ĭ war-dak/
Chak-e Wardak (dist) n

چکامه /cha-kā-ma/ ode n
چکامه سرودن ←
compose an ode

چکامه سرودن • چکامه گفتن ←
sing, recite an ode

چکر /cha-kar/ walk n
چکر زدن ← take a walk v
چکری /chŭk-ri/ rhubarb n
چکش /cha-kŭsh/ hammer n
چکش زدن ← hammer v
چکش چوبی /cha-kŭsh-ĭ cho-bi/
mallet n

چکک /cha-kak/
leaking (from roof) n

چکله /chak-la/ truck, lorry n
چکوتره /cha-ko-ta-ra/
grapefruit n

چکوسلواکیا /cha-ko-sal-wā-kĭ-yā/
Czechoslovakia (hist) n

چکوسلواکیه /cha-ko-sal-wā-kĭ-ya/
see چکوسلواکیا n

چکچ ؛ چکش see چکش n /cha-kŭsh/

چکوچ hammer n /cha-kŭch/

چکیدن ؛ چک- ؛ چکید-
crush, grind, pulp v /chŭ-ki-dan/

چگت cottonseed n /chĭ-gĭt/

چگونگی /chĭ-gu-na-gi/
detail, particular circumstance;
manner n

چگونه how? adv /chĭ-gu-na/

چل چراغ /chĭl cha-rāgh/
chandelier, candelabrum n

چلپاسه lizard (small) n /chal-pā-sa/

چلپایک centipede n /chĭl-pā-yak/

چلم /chĭ-lam, -lĭm/
water pipe, hookah n

چلم کشیدن ← smoke a water pipe
/chĭ-lam kash/

چلم کش /chĭ-lam kash/
water-pipe smoker n

چلو cooked white rice n /cha-law/

چلوصاف colander n /cha-law-sāf/

چله /chĭ-la/
wedding ring; forty-day period of
meditation; bowstring n

چلی /cha-li/
mullah's assistant (us young m) n

چلی Chile n /chĭ-li/

چلیپا /cha-li-pā/
X mark (to show sth is incorrect);
cross n

چمپانزی /cham-pān-zi/
chimp, chimpanzee n

چمتال Chemtal (dist) n /chĭm-tāl/

چمچه ladle (soup) n /cham-cha/

چمکنی /cham-ka-ni, tsam-/
Chamkani (dist) n

چمن /cha-man/
field; yard; flower garden n

چمنزار /cha-man-zār/
meadow, grassland n

چموس /cha-mus/
boot used by villagers n

چنار /chĭ-nār/
poplar, aspen (tree) n

چنار نیله /chĭ-nār-ī ni-la/
blue poplar n

چناق wishbone n /chĭ-nāq/
چناق شکستاندن ←
pull apart a wishbone v

چنان چه /chŭ-nān chĭ, chī-/
see چنان چه adv

چنان که /chŭ-nān kĭ, chī-/
as, so that adv

چنان که دیده شد
/chŭ-nān kĭ di-da shŭd/
as has been seen phrs

چنبر /cham-bar/
circle, hoop, ring n

چنبر زدن ← coil, make a circle vi

چنبری circular adj /cham-ba-ri/

چنته /chŭn-ta/
disabled (in hand) adj

چند few, not many adj /chand/

چند ؟ how many? adv /chand/

چند دفعه ؟ /chand da-fa/
how many times? Adv

چند روز پیش /chand roz peysh/
a few days ago adv

چند نشستن /chŭnd nī-shas-tan/
squat v

چنداول /chĭn-dā-wŭl (-da-)/
camp followers; rear of army;
Chendawul (city dist) n

چندم ؟ /chand-dŭm/
what number? (ordinal) adj

چندواری /chand-wā-ri/
execution by firing squad n

چندهول see چنداول /chĭn-da-wŭl/

چندی قبل /chand-ī qá-bīl/
a little while before adv

چندی pinch n /chŭn-di/

چندی کندن ← pinch v

چندی گرفتن ← take a pinch v

چندین /chan-din/
several, many adj

چندین بار /chan-din bār/
many times adv

چنگ /chang/
lyre (arch); see & چنگال n

چنگال /chan-gāl/
claw, talon; (fig) clutches n

i = keep, ĭ = big, u = coop, ŭ = put, y = yet, ' = (glottal stop)   125

چنگک /chan-gak/
hook, fishhook n

چنگک بلا شدن
/chan-gak-ĭ ba-lā shŭdan/
grappling hook n

چنگیز /chan-geyz/
Genghis Khan (1162?-1227, hist) n

چنگیزی , -ان/ها /chan-gey-zi/
related to Genghis (& pers) adj, n

چنه /cha-na/ jaw n
← چنه زدن bargain (colloq) v

چو /chaw/
yelp (as dog when beaten) excl, n
← چو زدن yelp v

چو /chu/ giddyup (to horse) excl
← چو زدن (urge a horse on) v

چوب /chob/
wood; timber, lumber n

چوب بست /chob-bast/
scaffold (wooden) n

چوب تعمیر /chob-ĭ ta'-mir/
timber, lumber (for building) n

چوب دست /chob-ĭ dast/
cane, walking stick n

چوب زدن /chob zadan/
flog, thrash (w/stick) v

چوب سوخت /chob-ĭ sokht/
firewood n

چوب صندل /chob-ĭ san-dal/
sandalwood n

چوب کاری /chob kā-ri/
wood carving n

چوبک /cho-bak/ stick (of wood) n
چوبک دندان /cho-bak-ĭ dan-dān/
toothpick n

چوپان /cho-pān/
shepherd (colloq) n

چوپانی /cho-pā-ni/ shepherding n
چوپانی کردن /cho-pā-ni kardan/
shepherd v

چوت /chot/ abacus n
چوتی /chu-ti/ braid (of hair) n
چوتی کردن /chu-ti kardan/
braid (hair) v

چوچه /chu-cha/
young, offspring (of animal) n
← چوچه دادن bear young v

چوره Chora (dist) n /cho-ra/
چوری /chaw-ri/
shoo-fly (yak/horse hair on stick) n
چوری زدن /chaw-ri zadan/
shoo flies away; flatter v

چوشیدن ؛ -چوش- ؛ چوشید-
/cho-shi-dan/
suck; suckle v

چوکات /chaw-kāt/
frame; framework; limits n

چوکات ادیب برآمدن
/chaw-kāt-ĭ a-dib bar āmadan/
the bounds of propriety n

چوکی /chaw-ki/
chair; job, position n

چوکی چرخکی
/chaw-ki-yĭ char-kha-ki/
swivel chair n

چوکیدار /chaw-ki-dār/
guard, watchman n

چوکی قاتکی /chaw-ki-yĭ qā-ta-ki/
folding chair n

چوکی وزارت
/chaw-ki-yĭ wa-zā-rat/
ministry job n

چون و چرا ها /chun ŭ chĭ-rā-hā/
whys & wherefores n phrs

چونکه /chun kĭ, key/
because, since conj

چونه lime, quicklime n /chu-na/
چه ؟ what? pron /chĭ, chi/
چه ... چه.../ /chĭ...chĭ.../
whether...or... conj

چه وقت ؟ when? adv /chi-waqt/
چهار (چار)/cha-hār (chār)/
four (see & چار) n, adj

چهار آسیاب /chār ā-sĭ-yāb/
Chahar Asyab (dist) n

چهار راه /chār rāh/
n چاراهی see

چهار زانو /chār zā-nu/
cross-legged adj, adv

چهار زانو نشستن
/chār zā-nu nĭshastan/
sit cross-legged vi

چهارده fourteen n, adj /chār-dah/
چهاردهم /chār-da-hŭm/
fourteenth adj

چهاردهمین /chār-da-hŭ-min/
fourteenth (lit, used before n) adj

چهارشنبه /chār-sham-bey/
Wednesday n

چهار ضلعی /cha-hār zŭl-'i (chār-)/
square; rectangle n; square;
rectangular adj

چهارم /cha-hā-rŭm (chā-rŭm)/
fourth adj

چهارمین /cha-hā-rŭ-min (chā-rŭ)/
fourth (lit, used before n) adj

چهره /chīh-ra/
face, appearance n

چهره خط /chīh-ra khat/
enlistment record of mil recruit n

چهره کردن /chīh-ra kardan/
enlist, take down description of
recruit v

چهل /chī-hĭl (chĭl)/
forty n, adj

چهل ستون /chĭl sŭ-tun/
Chehel Sutun (city dist) n

چهلم /chĭl-hĭ-lŭm (chĭl-lŭm)/
fortieth adj

چهلمین /chĭl-hĭ-lŭ-min (chĭl-lŭ-min)/
fortieth (lit, used before n) adj

چی؟ /chĭ, chi/
what? (colloq) pron

چی شده ؟ /chĭ shŭ-da/
what's wrong? phrs

چی ... ! /chĭ/ excl
how ... excl

← چی مقبول ! /how beautiful! !
← چشم های شما مقبول می بینه
so it is in the eye of the beholder
(response)

چیچک /chi-chak/ smallpox n

چیدن ؛ -چین- ؛ چید- /chi-dan/
pick, pluck; put in order vt

چیز , -ها /chiz/ thing; kind, sort n

چیزی /chí-zey/ something pron

چیستان /chis-tān/
riddle, conundrum n

چیغ /chigh/ shout, scream n

چیغ زدن /chigh zadan/
shout, scream (short) vi

چیغ کشیدن /chigh kashidan/
shout, scream (long) vi

چین /chin/
wrinkle, crease, fold; China n

چین خوردن /chin khŭrdan/
wrinkle vi

چین خورده /chin khŭr-da/
wrinkled; folded adj

چین دادن /chin dādan/
wrinkle; crease; fold v

چینایی , -ان/ها /chi-nā-yi/
Chinese (& pers) adj, n

چینی باب /chi-ni bāb/
china (porcelain) n

چینی بند زدن /chi-ni band zadan/
repair china v

چینی بند زن /chi-ni band zan/
china repairman n

ح

حاج , pl حجاج /hāj, pl hŭ-jāj/
hajj, Mecca pilgrimage n
← حجاج pl

حاجی , -ان/ها /hā-ji/
haji, pers who has performed the
hajj; (form of address) n

حاجی خیل /hā-ji kheyl/
Haji Kheyl (ctr) n

حادثه , -ها/حوادث /hā-dĭ-sa, pl ha-wā-dĭs/
crisis; incident; accident n

حارث /hā-rīs/
farmer; Haris (m name) n

حارمن /tsār-man/
captain, CPT (mil) n

حارنوال /tsā-ran-wāl/
public prosecutor n

حارنوالی /tsā-ran-wā-li/
public prosecutor's office n

حاسد , -ان/ها /hā-sīd/
envious (& pers) adj, n

حاسه , -ها/حواس /hā-sa, pl ha-wās/
sense (one of five) n

حاشیه , -ها/حواشی /hā-shī-ya, pl ha-wā-shi/
hem, border; footnote; margin n

حاصل , -ات /hā-sĭl/
product; result; sum n

حاصل خیز /hā-sĭl-kheyz/
fertile, rich, productive adj

حاصل خیزی /hā-sīl-khey-zi/
fertility, productivity n

حاصل کردن /hā-sīl kardan/
acquire, get, gain vt

حاضر , -ان/ها/ین/حضار /hā-zīr, pl hŭ-zār/
available, ready; willing adj;
attendant n

حاضر باش , -ها /hā-zīr bāsh/
attendant, aide (for mil officer) n

حاضر جواب /hā-zīr ja-wāb/
good at repartee, witty adj

حاضر جوابی /hā-zīr ja-wā-bi/
repartee, wit n

حاضری /hā-zī-ri/
attendance; roll, roster n

حاضری دادن ← be present v

حاضری گرفتن ← take roll v

حافظه /hā-fī-za/ memory n

حاکم , -ان/ها /hā-kĭm/
governor; ruler (hist); master n

حاکم مرزا /hā-kĭm mĭr-zā/
Hakim Mirza (Kabul ruler under
Akbar, hist) n

حاکمیت /hā-kĭ-mī-yat/
rule; sovereignty n

حاکمیت داشتن ← be sovereign vi

حاکمیت قانون /hā-kĭ-mī-yat-ī qā-nun/
rule of law n

حال /hāl, pl ah-wāl/
health; situation n

احوال ← pl

حالا /hā´-lā/ now, presently adv

حالت , -ها/حالات /hā-lat, pl -lāt/
status, condition; case (gram) n

حالت اضافی /hā-lat-ī ī-zā-fi/
genitive case (gram) n

حالت فاعلی /hā-lat-ī fā-'ĭ-li/
nominative case (gram) n

حالی /hā´-ley/ now, presently adv

حامل /hā-mĭl/ ‹چیزی›
carrying ‹st› adj; carrier ‹of st› n

حاملگی /hā-mī-la-gi/ pregnancy n

حامله /hā-mī-la/ pregnant adj

حامی , -ان /hā-mi/
supporter, patron n

حامی رعیت ← supporter of the subjects (king)

حاوی /hā-wi/
containing, comprising adj

حایض /ha-yĭz/ see حایضه adj

حایضه /ha-yĭ-za/
menstruating adj

حب /hab, pl hŭ-bub (hŭ-bu-bāt)/
grain, seed, cereal n

حبوب , حبوبات ← pl

حباب /hŭ-bāb/ bubble n

حبابی /hŭ-bā-bi/
bubble-shaped adj

حبس /habs/
confinement, imprisonment n

حبس مجرد /habs-ĭ mŭ-ja-rad/
solitary confinement n

حبشه /ha-ba-sha/
Abyssinia (hist) n

حبشی /ha-ba-shi/
Abyssinian (hist); black person
(dated term, colloq) n

حبوب /hŭ-bub, sg hab/
see sg حب n pl

حبوبات /hŭ-bu-bāt, sg hab/
see sg حب (colloq) n pl

حبیب /ha-bib, pl ah-bāb/
darling; dear friend; Habib (m
name) n

احباب ← pl

حبیب الله /ha-bi-bŭ-lā/
Habibullah (Afgh king 1901-19,
hist; m name) n

حبیبیه /ha-bi-bī-ya/
Habibia High School (founded
Kabul 1903) n

حتماً /hat-man, hát-/
definitely, must adv

حتى /hát-tā/
even if; even, also adv

حتى اگر /hát-tā a-gar/
see حتى adv

حتى الامکان /hát-tal-īm-kān/
as far as possible adv

حتى المقدور /hát-tal-maq-dur/
to the best of (one's) power adv

a = cup, ā = long, aw = now, ay = sigh, e = bet, ey = obey

حدقه , -ها/حدقات
/ha-da-qa, pl -qāt/
pupil (of eye) n

حدوث /hŭ-dus/
incidence, occurrence n
→ حدوث یافتن occur, happen vi

حدود /hŭ-dud/
approximately (lit) adv

حدیث , -ها/احادیث
/ha-dis, pl a-hā-dis/
hadith, Prophet's saying n
→ محدث student of hadiths

حدیقه , -ها/حدایق
/ha-di-qa, pl ha-dā-yĭq/
garden n

حرارت /ha-rā-rat/ temperature n

حرام /ha-rām/
prohibited (by Islam) adj

حرام خور /ha-rām khŭr/
corrupt, venal adj

حرام خوری /ha-rām khŭ-ri/
corruption, venality n

حرام مغز /ha-rām maghz/
spinal marrow n

حرام کار , -ان/ها /ha-rām-kār/
adulterer n; debauched adj

حرامی /ha-rā-mi/
illegitimate child n

حرب , -ها /harb/
battle, war, warfare n
→ حرب کردن
battle, fight, make war vi

حربی /har-bi/ military, martial adj

حرف , -ها /harf/
letter (of alphabet) n

حرفه , -ها/حرف /hĭr-fa, pl hĭ-raf/
craft, trade, vocation n

حرفه یی /hĭr-fa-yi/
vocational; professional adj

حرکات /ha-ra-kāt/
operations (mil); kinetics n pl

حرکت , -ها/حرکات
/ha-ra-kat, pl ha-ra-kāt/
movement (& social); departure n
→ حرکت دادن
move (body part) vt
→ حرکت کردن move; depart vi

حتی الوسع /hát-tal-was/
to the best of (one's) ability adv

حاج /haj/ n see حج

حجاب /hĭ-jāb/
purdah, veil; membrane; concealment n

حجاج /hŭ-jāj, sg hāj/
n pl حاج see sg

حجاز /hĭ-jāz/ Hejaz (geog) n

حجام /ha-jām/ phlebotomist n

حجامت /ha-jā-mat/ see حجامی

حجامی /ha-jā-mi/
phlebotomy, cupping n

حجت /hŭ-jat/
argument, proof; (colloq) IOU n
→ حجت آوردن
advance an argument v
→ حجت دادن pay by IOU v
→ حجت گرفتن accept an IOU v
→ حجت کردن
argue, reason; (colloq) make excuses v

حجر /ha-jar/ stone; unit ī n
→ سه حجر آسیا three watermills

حجر الاسود /ha-jar-ül-as-wad/
Black Stone (of Kaaba) n

حجره , -ها/حجرات
/hŭj-ra, pl hŭ-ja-rāt/
small room; cell (biol) n

حجروی /hŭj-ra-wi/ cellular adj

حجله /hŭj-la/ bridal chamber n

حد /had, pl hŭ-dud/
boundary, limit; (rel) punishment as prescribed by Quran n
→ حدود pl

حد اصغر /had-ĭ as-ghar/
n see حد اقل

حد اعظم /had-ĭ a'-zam/
n see حد اکثر

حد اقل /had-ĭ a-qal/ minimum n

حد اکثر /had-ĭ ak-sar/ maximum n

حد فاصل /had-ĭ fā-sīl/
boundary, demarcation n

حداد /ha-dād/ ironsmith n

حدایق /ha-dā-yĭq, sg ha-di-qa/
n pl see sg حدیقه

حدس /hads/ guess, conjecture n

حدس زدن /hads zadan/ guess v

---

i = keep, ĭ = big, u = coop, ŭ = put, y = yet, ' = (glottal stop)

حرکت اسلامی /ha-ra-kat-ī īs-lā-mi/
Harakat-e Islami (Shia mvmt) n

حرم /ha-ram/
sth prohibited; sanctuary; harem; f
area in Musl home n

حرم سرا /ha-ram sa-rā/
harem; f area in Musl home n

حرمت /hŭr-mat/
respect, esteem; holiness,
inviolability n

حرمین /ha-ra-mayn/
the two holy cities (Mecca &
Medina) n dual pl

حریت /hŭ-rī-yat/
freedom, independence n

حریر /ha-rir/
silk (lit), silk cloth/garment n

حریری /ha-ri-ri/
silk, silken; silky adj

حریص /ha-ris/ greedy; avid adj

حریصانه /ha-ri-sā-na/
greedily; avidly adv

حریف , -ان/ها /ha-rif/
opponent, rival; mate n

حریق /ha-riq/ fire, conflagration n
حریق شدن ← burn vi

حریم /ha-rim/ sanctum (sacred) n

حزب , -ها/احزاب /hĭzb, pl ah-zāb/
party (pol); group, faction n

حزب اسلامی /hĭzb-ī īs-lā-mi/
Hezb-e Islami (terrorist grp; pol
party) n

حزب جمهوری اسلامی
/hĭzb-ī jam-hu-ri-yī īs-lā-mi/
Hezb-e Jamhuri-ye Islami (hist,
Iranian pol party) n

حزب جمهوریخواهان افغانستان
/hĭzb-ī jam-hu-ri-khā-hān-ī af-ghā-
nĭs-tān/
Republican Party of Afghanistan
(pol party) n

حزب دموکراتیک خلق افغانستان
/hĭzb-ī dĭ-mo-kĭ-rā-tik-ī khalq-ī af-
ghā-nĭs-tān/
People's Democratic Party of
Afghanistan, PDPA (hist) n

حزب وحدت /hĭzb-ī wah-dat/
Hezb-e Wahdat (Shia party) n

حزبی /hĭz-bi/
party member; party-related (pol)
n, adj

حزم /há-zīm, hazm/
caution; prudence n

حزن , -ها/احزان
/hŭ´-zīn, hŭzn; pl ah-zān/
sorrow n

حزن آلود /hŭ´-zīn ā-lud/
sorrowful adj

حزن آور /hŭ´-zīn ā-war/
making sorrowful adj

حزین /ha-zin/ sorrowing adj

حس , -ها /hīs/ sense; feeling n

حس باصره /hīs-ī bā-sĭ-ra/
see حس بینایی n

حس بساوایی /hīs-ī ba-sā-wā-yi/
sense of touch n

حس بویایی /hīs-ī bu-yā-yi/
sense of smell n

حس بینایی /hīs-ī bi-nā-yi/
sense of sight n

حس چشایی /hīs-ī cha-shā-yi/
sense of taste n

حس ذایقه /hīs-ī zā-yĭ-qa/
see حس چشایی n

حس سامعه /hīs-ī sā-mĭ-'a/
see حس شنوایی n

حس شامه /hīs-ī shā-ma/
see حس بویایی n

حس شنوایی /hīs-ī shī-na-wā-yi/
sense of hearing n

حس کردن /hīs kardan/ feel v

حس لامسه /hīs-ī lā-mĭ-sa/
see حس بساوایی n

حساب , -ات/ها /hĭ-sāb/
calculation, arithmetic; account,
bank account n
حساب کردن <سر چیزی> ←
count <on sth>; calculate, count,
reckon vi

حساب پسانداز
/hĭ-sāb-ī pas an-dāz/
savings account n

حساب ده /hĭ-sāb dĭh/
accountable adj

حساب جاری /hĭ-sāb-ī jā-ri/
checking account n

حساب دهی /hĭ-sāb dĭ-hi/
accountability *n*

حسادت , ها- /ha-sā-dat/
envy, jealousy *n*

← حسادت داشتن • حسادت کردن • حسادت ورزیدن
be envious, be jealous *v*

حساس /ha-sās/
sensitive, susceptible *adj*

حساسیت , ها- /ha-sā-sī-yat/
sensitivity; allergy *n*

حسب /ha-sab/
degree, extent; value *n*

حسد /ha-sad/ envy, jealousy *n*

حسد بردن /ha-sad bŭrdan/
be envious, be jealous *v*

حسد خوردن /ha-sad khŭrdan/
be envious, be jealous (colloq) *v*

حسن /ha-san/ Hassan (m name) *n*
← حسین Husayn (dim)

حسن /hŭ´-sŭn, hŭsn/
beauty; goodness *n*

حسنه , ها- /ha-sa-na, pl -nāt/
Hasana (f name); good deed;
alms *n*; good *adj*
← حسنات pl

حسود , ان-/ها- /ha-sud/
envious, jealous (& pers) *adj, n*

حسودی /ha-su-di/ envy, jealousy *n*

حسین /hŭ-sayn/
Husayn (m name, cf. حسن) *n*

حسین خیل /hŭ-sayn kheyl/
Husayn Kheyl (ctr) *n*

حشرات /ha-sha-rāt/
vermin, pests *n pl*

حشره , ها-/حشرات /ha-sha-ra, pl -rāt/
insect, bug *n*

حشره شناس , ان-/ها- /ha-sha-ra shĭ-nās/
entomologist *n*

حشره شناسی /ha-sha-ra shĭ-nā-si/
entomology *n*

حشره کش /ha-sha-ra kŭsh/
insecticide *n, adj*

حشیش /ha-shish/ hashish *n*

حصار /hĭ-sār/
fortress, castle; enclosure *n*

حصارک /hĭ-sā-rak/
Hesarak (dist, ctr Ragha) *n*

حصبه /has-ba/ measles *n*

حصول /hŭ-sul/
achievement, attainment *n*
← حصول کردن achieve, attain *v*

حضر /há-sĭr, hasr/
counting; restriction, difficulty *n*

حصص /hĭ-sas, sg hĭ-sa/
see sg حصه *n pl*

حصه , ها-/حصص /hĭ-sa, pl hĭ-sas/
share, portion, segment *n*
← حصه ‹چیزی را› گرفتن
get a share of sth
← حصه خود را گرفتن
get one's share of sth

حصه اول بهسود
/hĭ-sa-yĭ a-wal-ĭ bĭh-sud/
Hesa-ye Awal-e Behsud (dist; ctr Zarkharid) *n*

حصه اول پنجشیر
/hĭ-sa-yĭ a-wal-ĭ panj-sheyr/
Hesa-ye Awal-e Panjsheyr (former dist) *n*

حصه اول کوهستان
/hĭ-sa-yĭ a-wal-ĭ ko-hĭs-tān/
Hesa-ye Awal-e Kohestan (dist; ctr Ezat Kheyl, alt Kohestan) *n*

حصه دوم پنجشیر
/hĭ-sa-yĭ dŭ-wŭm-ĭ panj-sheyr/
Hesa-ye Duwum-e Panjsheyr (former dist, ctr Dara-ye Hazara) *n*

حصه دوم کوهستان
/hĭ-sa-yĭ dŭ-wŭm-ĭ ko-hĭs-tān/
Hesa-ye Awal-e Kohestan (dist; ctr Ezat Kheyl, alt Keshektan) *n*

حصه گرفتن /hĭ-sa gĭrĭftan/
participate; get part (of sth) *v*

حضار کرام ! /hŭ-zār-ĭ kĭ-rām/
ladies & gentlemen *phrs*

حضرات /ha-za-rāt/
presences (title of respect for rel masters) *n pl*

حضرت عیسی /haz-rat-ĭ i-sa/
Jesus Christ (rel) *n*

حضور /hŭ-zur/
dignitary; pers of high station *n*

i = k<u>ee</u>p, ĭ = b<u>i</u>g, u = c<u>oo</u>p, ŭ = p<u>u</u>t, y = <u>y</u>et, ' = (glottal stop)

حضیض /ha-ziz/
bottom, lower extremity n

حفظ /hĭfz/
defense, protection n

حفظ الصحه /hĭfz-ŭs-sĭ-ha/
hygiene, sanitation n

حفظ قرآن /hĭfz-ĭ qŭr-'ān/
memorization of Quran n

حفظ کردن /hĭfz kardan/
memorize, learn vt

حفیظ /ha-fiz/
Hafiz (m name) n

حفیظه /ha-fi-za/
Hafiza (f name) n

حق /haq, pl hŭ-quq/
right (& pol); property n

حقوق ←
haq, pl hŭ-quq/

حق السکوت /haq-ŭs-sŭ-kut/
see حق سکوت n

حق تقدم /haq-ĭ ta-qa-dŭm/
right of way n

حق سکوت /haq-ĭ sŭ-kut/
hush money n

حقایق /ha-qā-yĭq, sg ha-qi-qat/
see sg حقیقت n pl

حقوق /hŭ-quq, sg haq/
see sg حق n pl

حقوق العبد /hŭ-quq al-'abd/
individual rights n pl

حقوق الناس /hŭ-quq al-nās/
societal rights n pl

حقوق انسان /hŭ-quq-ĭ ĭn-sān/
human rights n pl

حقوق زنان /hŭ-quq-ĭ za-nān/
women's rights n pl

حقیقت , ها- /حقایق
/ha-qi-qat, pl ha-qā-yĭq/
truth, reality; fact n

حقیقت بین /ha-qi-qat bin/
literalist adj

حقیقت بینی /ha-qi-qat bi-ni/
literalism n

حقیقت جوی /-ان/ها /ha-qi-qat joy/
truth-seeker n

حقیقتاً /ha-qí-qa-tan, -qá-, -tán/
truly, really adv

حقه /hŭ-qa/
hookah (arch) n

حقیقی /ha-qi-qi/
true, real; factual adj

حک /hak/
friction; engraving; erasing n

حک کردن ←
rub, chafe; engrave; erase v

حکاک /ha-kāk/
clever, smart (fig) (colloq);
engraver, lapidary n

حکایت , ها-/حکایات
/hĭ-kā-yat, pl pyāt/
narration, account; (lit) anecdote n

حکایت کردن ←
narrate, relate v

حکایتی /hĭ-kā-ya-ti/
narrative adj

حکم /ha-kam/
wise man; (hist) mediator n

حکم /hĭ-kam, sg hĭk-mat/
see sg حکمت n pl

حکم , ها-/احکام
/hŭ´-kŭm, hŭkm; pl ah-kām/
command, order; edict; legal
judgment n

حکم راندن ←
rule, give an order v n

حکم اعدام /hŭ´-kŭm-ĭ ey-dām/
execution order n

حکم فرما /hŭ´-kŭm far-mā/
dominant; prevalent adj

حکم فرمایی /hŭ´-kŭm far-mā-yi/
domination; prevalence n

حکم گرفتاری
/hŭ´-kŭm-ĭ gĭ-rĭf-tā-ri/
arrest order n

حکم محکمه صادر نمودن
/hŭ´-kŭm-ĭ mah-ka-ma sā-dĭr
namudan/
issue a court order v

حکمت , ها-/حکم
/hĭk-mat, pl hĭ-kam/
wisdom; science, knowledge n

حکمتیار /hĭk-mat-yār/
Gulbuddin Hekmatyar (warlord &
terrorist leader; Ghilzai P) n

حکمران , -ان/ها /hŭ-kŭm-rān/
ruler, governor n

حکمرانی کردن <در کجا>
/hŭ-kŭm-rā-ni/
rule, govern <sw> vi

حکومت , ها-/حکومات
/hŭ-ko-mat, pl -māt/
government n

حکومت کردن /hŭ-ko-mat kardan/
govern v

حل /hal/ solution (to problem) n

حل کردن /hal kardan/ solve, fix vt

حلال /ha-lāl/
permitted by Islam; legitimate;
ritually slaughtered (meat) adj

حلالی /ha-lā-li/ legitimate child n

حلزون /hal-zun/ snail, slug (lit) n

حلق /halq/ pharynx n

حلقه /hal-qa/
circle, ring; unit (for round object)
n

دو حلقه مائین ← two mines

سه حلقه فلم ← three film reels

سرکِ حلقی ← ring road

حلقه زده /hal-qa za-da/
ringed (eyes) adj

چشم های اش حلقه زده ←
she has circles under her eyes

حلقه گوش /hal-qa-yĭ gosh/
earring (hist, worn by slaves) n

حلقوم /hal-qum/ throat n

حلقی /hal-qi/ pharyngeal adj

حلوا /hal-wā/ halvah n

حلوای مغزی /hal-wā-yĭ magh-zi/
halvah w/nuts n

حلول /hŭ-lul/
approach; reincarnation n

حلول کردن /hŭ-lul kardan/
be reincarnated vi

حلول و تناسخ /hŭ-lul ŭ ta-nā-sŭkh/
reincarnation n phrs

حلولیه /hŭ-lu-lĭ-ya/
Holuliyya (Musl sect, hist) n

حلویات /hal-wĭ-yāt/
sweets; candy n

حلیم /ha-lim/
gentle, mild; patient; Halim (m
name) adj

حلیمه /ha-li-ma/
Halima (f name, Prophet's nurse)
n

حماس /ha-mās/
zeal; Hamas (terrorist group) n

حمای لکه دار /ha-mā-yĭ la-ka dār/
spotted fever (typhus) n

حماقت , -ها /ha-mā-qat/
foolishness, stupidity n

حمال /ha-māl/
porter (esp at market) n

حمام /ha-mām/
hammam, bathhouse; bath n

حمام رفتن /ha-mām raftan/
go to the hammam v

حمام کردن /ha-mām kardan/
take a bath v

حمام گرفتن /ha-mām gĭrĭftan/
see حمام کردن v

حمامی /ha-mā-mi/
bathhouse attendant n

حمایت /hĭ-mā-yat/
support; patronage n

حمایت کردن <از کسی>
support <sb> vt

حمایت گر /hĭ-mā-yat gar/
supporter, patron n

حمایل , -ها /ha-mā-yĭl (a-meyl)/
shoulder belt; sling (for arm) n

حمایوی /hĭ-mā-ya-wi/
supporting, complementary adj

حمرا /ham-rā/ the Alhambra n

حمزه /ham-za/
Hamza (m name, Prophet's uncle)
n

حمل /ha-mal, pl ah-māl/
Hamal (month); Aries; lamb n

احمال ← pl

حمل /há-mĭl, haml/
carrying; transport n

حمل کردن /há-mĭl kardan/
carry; transport vt

حمل و نقل
/há-mĭl ŭ ná-qĭl, haml ŭ naql/
transportation (of goods) phrs

حمله , -ها/حملات
/ham-la, pl ha-ma-lāt/
attack, assault, offensive n

حمله آوردن /ham-la āwŭrdan/
attack, assault v

حمله قلبی /ham-la-yĭ qal-bi/
heart attack n

حمله کردن /ham-la kardan/
attack, assault v

حمله کننده /ham-la kŭ-nīn-da/
see حمله ور n, adj

حمله ور /ham-la war/
attacker n; offensive (mil) adj

حمله ور شدن /ham-la war shŭdan/
go on the offensive v

حمیت /ha-mī-yat/
zeal; enthusiasm; passion n

حمیت مند /ha-mī-yat mand/
zealous; enthusiastic adj

حمید /ha-mid/ Hamid (m name) n

حمیده /ha-mi-da/
Hamida (f name, Akbar's mother,
hist) n

حمیرا /hŭ-may-rā/
Humayra (f name) n

حنا /hī-nā (khi-na)/ henna n

حنا بستن /hī-nā bastan/
dye w/henna v

حنابله /ha-nā-bī-la, sg ham-ba-li/
see sg حنبلی n pl

حنبل /ham-bal/
short, fat m n

حنابله/ها/ان- , حنبلی
/ham-ba-li, pl ha-nā-bī-la/
Hanbalitic (rel) adj; Hanbalite n

حنجره /han-ja-ra/
larynx; (fig) voice n

حنظل /han-zal/
colocynth, bitter apple n

حنظله /han-za-la/
Hanzala (8th-c Dari poet) n

حنفا /hŭ-na-fā, sg ha-nif/
see sg حنیف n pl

حنفی , ها/ان- /ha-na-fi/
Hanfitic adj; Hanafite n

حنفیه /ha-na-fī-ya/
the Hanafites coll pl n

حنیف ,-ان/حنفا/ /ha-nif, pl hŭ-na-fā/
Hanif (pre-Musl Arab monotheist)
n

حوا /ha-wā/ Eve (bibl) n

حوادث /ha-wā-dīs, sg hā-dī-sa/
see sg حادثه n pl

حواری , -ون/ین- /ha-wā-ri/
disciple; apostle; follower n

حواس /ha-wās, sg hā-sa/
see sg حاسه n pl

حواس پنجگانه
/ha-wās-ī panj-gā-na/
the five senses n phrs

حواشی /ha-wā-shi, sg hā-shī-ya/
see sg حاشیه n pl

حواله /ha-wā-la/
money transfer; hawala (banking
system); entrusting n

حوت /hut/
Hut (month); Pisces; fish; whale n

حور , -ان/ها /hur/ see حوری n

حوری , -ان /hu-ri/
houri; (fig) voluptuous, beautiful f
n

حوزه /haw-za/
basin; area, region n

حوصله /haw-sī-la/
patience; fortitude n

حوصله دار /haw-sī-la-dār/
patient, forbearing adj

حوصله داشتن /haw-sī-la dāshtan/
be patient vi

حوض /hawz/
pool, reservoir n

حوض آبازی /hawz-ī āb-bā-zi/
swimming pool n

حوضچه /hawz-cha/
small pool n

حوضک /haw-zak/ see حوضچه n

حومه /haw-ma/
environs, outskirts n

حویلی /ha-wey-li (aw-li)/
yard; courtyard n

حی /hay/
alive, living (& attribute of God)
adj; (arch) tribe n

حیا /ha-yā/ bashfulness n

حیات /ha-yāt/ life n

حیدر /hay-dar/
Haydar (m name); lion n

حیران /hay-rān/
amazed; perplexed adj

حیران شدن /hay-rān shŭdan/
be amazed n

حیرانی /hay-rā-ni/
amazement; perplexity n

حیرت /hay-rat/ see حیرانی n

حیز /hayz/
aspect, view; extent, scope n

حيثيت /hay-sī-yat/
prestige, standing n

حيض /hayz/
menstruation, period n
↳ حيض داشتن menstruate v

حيف /hayf/
damage, harm; injustice n
حيف است ! /hayf ast/
it is a pity excl

حيف و ميل /hayf ŭ mayl/
embezzlement n
↳ حيف و ميل كردن embezzle v

حيله /hi-la, hey-/
trick, stratagem, wile n

حيله باز , -ان/ها /hi-la bāz/
trickster, deceitful person n

حيله ساختن /hi-la sākhtan/
play a trick v

حيله كردن /hi-la kardan/
v حيله ساختن see

حين /hin/ when conj
حينى كه /hi-ney ki/ during adv

حيوان , -ات /hay-wān/ animal n
حيوان اهلى /hay-wān-ĭ ah-li/
domesticated animal n
حيوان درنده /hay-wān-ĭ da-rĭn-da/
predatory animal n
حيوان شناسى /hay-wān shī-nā-si/
zoology n
حيوان ناعمه /hay-wān-ĭ nā-'ĭ-ma/
mollusc n
حيوان وحشى /hay-wān-ĭ wah-shi/
wild animal, beast n

خ

خاتم سازى /khā-tīm sā-zi/
n خاتم كارى see
خاتم كارى /khā-tīm kā-ri/
seal, signet ring; inlaid work n
↳ خاتم كارى كردن do inlaid work
خاتمه , -ها /khā-tĭ-ma/
end; epilogue (book's) n
↳ خاتمه دادن <به چيزى>
end, conclude <sth> vt
↳ خاتمه يافتن end, conclude vi
خاتمه يافته /khā-tĭ-ma yāf-ta/
over, ended, finished adj

خاتون , -ان/ها/خواتين
/khā-tun, pl kha-wā-tin/
wife (Hazara); (arch, & title) lady n
خاد /khād/
KhAD (secret police, hist) n
خادم , -ان/ها/ين/خدام
/khā-dĭm, pl khŭ-dām/
servant; mosque attendant n
↳ خادم ملت servant of the nation
خار /khār/ thorn, prickle n
خارا /khā-rā/ granite n
خارپشت /khār-pŭsht/
hedgehog n
خارپشتك /khār-pŭsh-tak/
hedgehog (dim) n
خارج /khā-rīj/
outside; overseas n; foreign;
irrelevant adj
↳ خارج شدن
be ousted; be fired v
↳ خارج كردن
oust, fire; remove v
خارج شدن اضطرارى
/khā-rīj shŭdan-ĭ ĭz-tĭ-rā-ri/
evacuation n
خارج قسمت /khā-rīj-ĭ qĭs-mat/
quotient (math) n
خارجى , -ان/ها /khā-rĭ-ji/
dissenter, rebel; foreigner n;
external; foreign adj
خاردار /khār-dār/
thorny, prickly; barbed adj
↳ سيم خاردار barbed wire
خارش /khā-rīsh/
itch, itching, itchiness n
خارش /khā-rīsh/
↳ خارش داشتن have an itch v
خارق العاده /khā-rīq-ŭl-'ā-da/
adj خارق عادت see
خارق عادت /khā-rīq-ĭ ā-dat/
extraordinary; not customary adj
خارنوال /tsā-ran-wāl/
see حارنوال
خاريدن ؛ -خار- ؛ خاريد-
scratch vt /khā-ri-dan/
خاستن ؛ -خيز- ؛ خاست-
/khās-tan (kheys-); méykheyzŭm/
get up, rise, arise vi

i = keep, ĭ = big, u = coop, ŭ = put, y = yet, ' = (glottal stop)   135

خاسع /khā-sey/
humble, submissive *adj*

خاش /khāsh/
mother-in-law; quarrelsome pers;
Khash (geog, & dist) *n*

خاش خاش /khāsh khāsh/
خشخاش see *n*

خاش رود /khāsh rod/
Khash Rod (dist, ctr Lokhi) *n*

خاشنه /khāsh-na (khī-yāsh-)/
sister-in-law, wife's sister *n*

خاشه /khā-sha/
small amount of sth *n*

خاص /khās/
personal; particular; unique *adj*

خاص اورزگان /khās u-rūz-gān/
Khas Uruzgan (dist) *n*

خاص و عام /khās ŭ 'ām/
everyone, the high & the low *phrs*

خاصاً /khā´-san, -sán/
privately *adv*

خاصتاً /khā-sá-tan, -tán/
particularly, especially *adv*

خاصره /khā-sī-ra/
hip *n*

خاصه , -ها/خواص
/khā-sa, pl kha-wās/
characteristic; essence; high-
profile pers *n*; see & خاص *adj*

خاصیت , -ها /khā-sī-yat/
characteristic; virtue *n*

خاضع /khā-zey/
humble, submissive *adj*

خاطر , -ها/خواطر
/khā-tĭr, pl kha-wā-tĭr/
mind, heart; memory; sake *n*

خاطر آزرده /khā-tĭr ā-zŭr-da/
melancholy (& pers) *adj, n*

خاطر آسوده /khā-tĭr ā-su-da/
at ease (& pers) *adj, n*

خاطر آشفته /khā-tĭr ā-shŭf-ta/
perturbed *adj, n*

خاطر پریشان /khā-tĭr pĭ-ray-shān/
deranged; afflicted (& pers) *adj, n*

خاطر پسند /khā-tĭr pĭ-sand/
affable, likeable (& pers) *adj*

خاطر جمع /khā-tĭr jam/
assured, composed *adj*

خاطر جمعی دادن
/khā-tĭr ja-mi dādan/
assure, comfort *vt*

خاطر <کسی را> خواستن
/khā-tĭr-ī <ká-sey-ra> khāstan/
care about sb *v*

خاطر خواه /khā-tĭr khāh/
caring; accommodating (& pers)
adj, n

خاطر گرفته /khā-tĭr gĭ-rĭf-ta/
displeased (& pers) *adj, n*

خاطر نشان ساختن
/khā-tĭr nī-shān sākhtan/
خاطر نشان کردن see *vt*

خاطر نشان کردن
/khā-tĭr nī-shān kardan/
remark; remind; notify *vt*

خاطرات /khā-tī-rāt/
diary; reminiscences *n, n pl*

خاطره , -ها/خاطرات /khā-tī-ra/
memory, reminiscence *n*

خاقانی /khā-qā-ni/
Khaqani (Dari poet, 1120-1190) *n*

خاک /khāk/
dirt, soil, dust; (fig) grave *n*

خاک آلود /khāk ā-lud/
dirty, soiled; dusty *adj*

خاک انداز /khāk an-dāz/
dustpan; trash heap; outhouse *n*

خاک باد /khāk bād/
sandstorm *n*

خاک بخارا /khāk-ī bŭ-khā-rā/
Earth of Bokhara (mounds) *n*

خاک پر /khāk pŭr/
dirty, soiled; dusty (colloq) *adj*

خاک توده /khāk to-da/
dirt mound *n*

خاک جبار /khāk-ī ja-bār/
Khak-e Jabar (dist) *n*

خاک سفید /khāk-ī sa-feyd/
Khak-e Safeyd (dist) *n*

خاک و دود کردن
/khāk ŭ dud kardan/
waste (fig) *vt*

خاکروبه /khāk-ro-ba/
trash *n*

خاکریز /khāk-reyz/
Khakreyz (dist) *n*

خاکسار /khāk-sār/
humble pers *n*; dirty *adj*

خاکساری /khāk-sā-ri/
humility, meekness n

خاکستر /khā-kĭs-tar/ ash n

خاکستر دانی /khā-kĭs-tar dā-ni/
ashtray n

خاکستری /khā-kĭs-ta-ri/
ash-colored adj

خاکنا /khāk-nā/ isthmus n

خاکه /khā-ka/
dust; soil; sketch, outline n

خاکی /khā-ki/
khaki, earth-colored adj

خاگینه /khā-gi-na/
scrambled eggs n

خال /khāl/
beauty mark; mole; uncle,
mother's brother n

خال بینی /khāl-ĭ bi-ni/ nose stud n

خال خال /khāl khāl/
once in a while adv

خال خالی /khāl khā-li/
speckled, spotted adj

خال زدن /khāl zadan/
vaccinate against smallpox;
tattoo; a beauty mark vt

خال کردن /khāl kardan/
see خال زدن vt

خال کوبی /khāl ko-bi/
see آبله کوبی n

خالد /khā-lĭd/ Khaled (m name) n

خالص /khā-lĭs/
pure; net (weight) adj

خالصاً /khā-lĭ´-san, -sán/
purely; only, merely adv

خالصانه /khā-lĭ-sā-na/
pure; sincere (& adv) adj, adv

خالصه /khā-lĭ-sa/
f form of خالص adj

← اموال خالصه
state lands

خاله , ها- /khā-la/
aunt, mother's sister; (form of
address to older f) n

خاله خشو /khā-la khŭ-shu/
mother-in-law's sister n

خاله زاده , گان/ها /khā-la zā-da/
cousin, child of mother's sister n

خالی /khā-li/
empty; blank, mere adj

خالی کردن /khā-li kardan/
empty; evacuate; unload vt

خالی گاه پر کردن
/khā-li gāh pŭr kardan/
fill in a blank v

خام /khām/
raw; unripe; (fig) immature adj

خام خواب /khām khāb/
not having enough sleep adj

خام کار /khām kār/
inexperienced, unskillful n

خام کوک /khām kok/
stitch, basting n

خام کوک کردن /khām kok kardan/
stitch, baste v

خامه /khā-ma/
unpaved (road) adj

خاموش , ان-/ها /khā-mosh/
quiet; silent; reticent; (fig) dead
adj

خاموشی /khā-mo-shi/
quiet, silence n

خاموش ساختن <کسی را>
/khā-mosh sākhtan/
quiet <sb> (down); turn off (radio)
vt

خامک دوزی /khā-mak do-zi/
Afgh embroidery w/geometric
shapes n

خان , ان-/ها/خوانین
/khān, pl kha-wā-nin/
khan; feudal landlord; (honorific) n

خان آباد /khān ā-bād/
Khanabad (dist) n

خان چارباغ /khān-ĭ chār-bāgh/
Khan-e Charbagh (dist) n

خان سالار /khān sā-lār/
kitchen master in Mughal imperial
household (hist) n

خان علوم /khān-ĭ ŭ-lum/
supervisor of rel instruction; chief
justice n

خان ملا خان /khān mŭ-lā khān/
head mullah in royal household n

خان نشین /khān nĭ-shin/
Khan Neshin (dist) n

---

i = keep, ĭ = big, u = coop, ŭ = put, y = yet, ' = (glottal stop)   137

خبر , ـها/خبار/اخبار
/kha-bar, pl -bār, akh-bār/
news, information *n*
← خبر دادن ‹از چیزی›
announce ‹sth›, inform ‹of sth›
←خبر کردن ‹کسی را به چیزی›
let ‹sb› know ‹about sth›
خبر چینی /kha-bar chi-ni/
gossiping *n*
خبر کشی /kha-bar ka-shi/
gossiping *n*
خبرنگار , ـان/ها /kha-bar-nī-gār/
journalist, reporter *n*
خت muddy *adj*; mud *n* /khīt/
ختا /khī-tā/ *n* خطا see
Cathay (hist) *n* /khī-tāy/
ختک Khatak (P tribe) *n* /kha-tak/
ختم /khá-tīm, khatm/
end; termination *n*
ختنه circumcision *n* /khat-na/
← ختنه کردن circumcize *n*
ختنه سوری /khat-na su-ri/
circumcision ceremony *n*
ختنه شده /khat-na shŭ-da/
circumcized *adj*
خجالت /khī-jā-lat/
bashfulness; shame *n*
خجالت آور /khī-jā-lat ā-war/
embarrassing, shameful *adj*
خجالت دادن ‹به کسی›
/khī-jā-lat dā-dan/
embarrass, shame ‹sb› *v*
خجالت کش /khī-jā-lat kash/
bashful *adj*
خجالت کشیدن /khī-jā-lat kashidan/
be embarrassed *v*
خجالتی bashful *adj* /khī-jā-la-ti/
خجلت /khī-jā-lat/ *n* خجالت see
خجند Khujand (city) *n* /khŭ-jand/
خجول bashful *adj* /kha-jul/
خدا God *n* /khŭ-dā/
← خدا بزنت ! may God strike you!
← خدا بشر ماندت! God damn you!
← خدا رحمت کنه God bless !
← خدا حافظ ! goodbye, farewell !
← خدا کنه که ... I hope ‹+ subj›
خدا پرست /khŭ-dā pa-rast/
devout, pious (& pers) *adj, n*

خان خانان /khān khā-nān/
imperial army chief under
Mughals (hist) *n*
خاندود /khān-dud/
Khandud (ctr) *n*
خانقا /khā-na-qā/ خانقاه see
خانقاه /khā-na-qāh, -nī-/
Sufi headquarters; Khanaqa (dist)
n
خانم /khā-nŭm/
Mrs. (before name); wife; lady *n*
← خانم ها و آقایان
ladies & gentlemen!
خانه /khā-na/
home, house; nest, lair *n*
خانه به دوش /khā-na ba dosh/
vagabond; homeless pers *n*
خانه به دوشی /khā-na ba do-shi/
vagabondage *n*
خانه تکانی /khā-na ta-kā-ni/
housecleaning *n*
خانه جنگی /khā-na jan-gi/
civil war *n*
خانه خدا /khā-na-yī khŭ-dā/
Kaaba; mosque *n*
خانه خلوت /khā-na-yī khīl-wat/
خلوت خانه see
خانه دار /khā-na dār/
married; settled *adj*
خانه شطرنج /khā-na-yī shat-ranj/
square on a chessboard *n*
خانه گلی /khā-na-yī gī-li/
mud house *n*
خانوادگی /khā-na-wā-da-gi/
domestic life *n*
خانواده /khā-na-wā-da/
family; household; dynasty (takes
pl v) *n pl*
خاو /khāw/ *n* خواب see
east *adj*; Orient *n* /khā-war/
خاور میانه /khā-war-ī mī-yā-na/
Middle East *n*
caviar; roe *n* /khā-wī-yār/
← ماهی خاویار sturgeon
خاین , ـان/ها/ین /khā-yīn/
treacherous *adj*; traitor *n*
baker *n* /kha-bāz/ خباز , ـان/ها
bakery *n* /kha-bā-zi/ خبازی

138   a = c<u>u</u>p, ā = l<u>o</u>ng, aw = n<u>ow</u>, ay = s<u>igh</u>, e = b<u>e</u>t, ey = ob<u>ey</u>

خدا ترس /khŭ-dā tars/
God-fearing adj

خدا داده /khŭ-dā dā-da/
wealthy (& pers) adj, n; godsend n

خدازده /khŭ-dā za-da/
damned; disgraced adj

خدا شرمانده /khŭ-dā shar-mān-da/
see خدازده adj

خدا شناس /ا-ان/ها, /khŭ-dā shī-nās/
God-knowing adj; theist n

خدا شناسی /khŭ-dā shī-nā-si/
knowing God; theism n

خدا ناترس /khŭ-dā nā-tars/
brutal, cruel adj; atheist n

خدا ناشناس /khŭ-dā nā-shī-nās/
see خدا ناترس adj, n

خداوند /khŭ-dā-wand/
God, Allah n

خداوندگار /khŭ-dā-wand-gār/
see خداوند n

خداوندگار بلخ /khŭ-dā-wand-gār-ĭ balkh/
Khodawandgar-e Balkh (13th-c. Dari poet) n

خداوندی /khŭ-dā-wan-di/
divinity, godhood n; divine adj

خدشه /khad-sha/
anxiety; doubt (lit) n

خدمت , ها-/خدمات /khĭd-mat, pl -māt/
service, assistance n

← خدمت کردن
serve, assist v

خدمتگار , ان/ها- /khĭd-mat-gār/
servant n

خدمه /kha-da-ma, sg khā-dĭm/
crew coll n

← خادم sg

خدنگ /kha-dang/
poplar (white); (lit) arrow n

خدیجه /kha-di-ja/
Khadija (f name; Prophet's first wife) n

خدیر /kha-dir/ Khadir (dist) n

خدیو /khĭ-dayw, kha-/
khedive (hist, Egyptian viceroy) n

خر /khar/
ass, donkey; (fig) stupid pers n

خراب /kha-rāb/
damaged; wrecked; destroyed; out of order; worthless adj

← خراب شدن
break down; be ruined; be upset; get drunk vi

← خراب کردن
damage, destroy, ruin vt

خراب کار , ان/ها- /kha-rāb kār/
vandal; saboteur n

خراب کاری /kha-rāb kā-ri/
vandalism, sabotage n

خرابات /kha-rā-bāt/
Kharabat, performers' home in old Kabul n

← خرابات کردن
spend prodigally (colloq) n

خرابی /kha-rā-bi/
ruin, destruction; breakdown n

خراد /kha-rād/ see خراط n

خراسان /khŭ-rā-sān/
Khorasan (Afghanistan, hist) n

خراط /kha-rāt/ lathe worker n

خراطی /kha-rā-ti/
working a lathe n

← خراطی کردن work a lathe v

خرافه , ها-/خرافات /kha-rā-fa, pl -fāt/
superstition n

خرافی /kha-rā-fi/ superstitious adj

خرام /khĭ-rām/
sauntering, graceful walk n

خرامیدن ؛ خرام- ؛ خرامید-
/khĭ-rā-mi-dan/
saunter, walk gracefully vi

خربوزه /khar-bu-za/ melon n

خرج /kharj (kharch)/
expenditure, outlay n

← خرج کردن spend (money) v

خرج خانه /kharj-ĭ khā-na/
household expense n

خرج سفر /kharj-ĭ sa-far/
per diem n

خرچ /kharch/ see خرج (colloq) n

خرچنگ /khar-chang/ crab n

خرچنگ دراز /khar-chang-ĭ da-rāz/
lobster n

---

i = keep, ĭ = big, u = coop, ŭ = put, y = yet, ' = (glottal stop)   139

خرد /khĭ-rad/
mind; wisdom; reason n

خرداد /khŭr-dād/
see جوزا (month) n

خردل /khar-dal/ mustard n

خردمند /khĭ-rad-mand/
wise; judicious (& pers) adj, n

خردمندانه /khĭ-rad-man-dā-na/
wisely, intelligently adv

خردمندی /khĭ-rad-man-di/
wisdom, intelligence n

خرطوم /khar-tum/
Khartoum; elephant's trunk n

خرفه /khŭr-fa (khŭf-)/
purslane (edible weed) n

خرفهم /khar-fahm/
thick, slow to understand adj

خرفهم کردن /khar-fahm/
explain for a dummy phrs

خرق عادت /kharq-ĭ ā-dat/
extraordinary; supernatural adj

خرقه /khĭr-qa/
Khirqa (shrine); dervish's garb n

خرقه پوش , -ان/ها /khĭr-qa posh/
dervish n, adj

خرک /kha-rak/
small donkey; trestle; bridge
(music) n

خرکار , -ان/ها /khar-kār/
donkey driver; farm worker n

خرگاه /khĭr-gāh/
tent; halo (moon); yurt n

خرگاه زدن pitch tent v

خرگری /khar-ga-ri/
stupidity, foolishness (colloq) n

خرگوش /khar-gosh/ hare n

خرگوش اهلی /khar-gosh-ĭ a-ha-li/
see خرگوش خانه گی n

خرگوش خانگی
/khar-gosh-ĭ khā-na-gi/
rabbit n

خرم /khŭ-ram/
Khuram (m name) n

خرم و سرباغ
/khŭ-ram wŭ sar-bāgh/
Khuram wa Sarbagh (dist) n

خرما /khŭr-mā/ date (edible) n

خرمایی /khŭr-mā-yi/
date-colored adj

خرمست /khar-mast/
very drunk (& pers) adj, n

خرمستی /khar-mas-ti/
drunkenness; (colloq) horseplay n

خرمن /khĭr-man/ harvest n

خروار /khar-wār/
kharwar (unit of weight; dist) n

خروتی /kha-ro-ti/
Kharoti (P tribe) n

خروج /khŭ-ruj/
exit; transitioning n

خروجی /khŭ-ru-ji/
exit, related to exiting adj

خروس /khŭ-rus (-rās, -rāz)/
cock, rooster n

خروس جنگی /khŭ-rus jan-gi/
cockfighting n

خرید /kha-rid/ shopping n

خرید کردن /kha-rid kardan/
buy, purchase, shop v

خریدار , -ان/ها /kha-ri-dār/
buyer; customer n

خریداری /kha-ri-dā-ri/
buying, purchase n

خریداری شدن →
be bought vi

خریدن ؛ -خر- ؛ خرید-
/kha-ri-dan/
buy, purchase, shop v

خریطه /kha-ri-ta (khal-ta)/
bag, sack n

خریطه ریگ /kha-ri-ta-yĭ reyg/
sandbag n

خز /khaz/
marten (animal); creeper n

خزان /kha-zān/ autumn, fall n

خزر , -ان/ها /kha-zar/
Khazar (& pers, hist) adj, n

خزرج بنو الخزرج /khaz-raj/ see

خزیدن ؛ -خز- ؛ خزید-
creep, sneak vi /kha-zi-dan/

خسارات جانی /khĭ-sā-rāt-ĭ jā-ni/
casualties n pl

خساره , -ها/خسارات
/khĭ-sā-ra, pl -rāt/
damage, loss n

خسته /khas-ta/
weary, tired; boring adj
خسته باب /khas-ta-bāb/
nuts (edible) n
خسته کن /khas-ta kŭn/
wearisome, tiresome adj
خسر father-in-law n /khŭ-sŭr/
خسرو /khĭs-raw, khŭs-/
Khusraw (m name) n
خسک /kha-sak/
low-quality adj; bedbug n
خسوف lunar eclipse n /khŭ-suf/
خشت /khĭsht/
brick; diamond (cards) n
خشخاش /khash-khāsh/
poppy seed (& food) n
خشم /khá-shĭm, khashm/
anger, rage; indignation n
خشم آگین /khá-shĭm ā-gin/
see خشم آلود adj
خشم آلود /khá-shĭm ā-lud/
angry, full of anger adj
خشمناک /khà-shĭm-nā´k/
angry, enraged adj
خشو mother-in-law n /khŭ-shu/
خشونت , -ها /khŭ-shu-nat/
violence; harshness; rudeness n
خشونت کردن be rude v
خشونت های خانوادگی
domestic violence
خشونت آمیز /khŭ-shu-nat ā-meyz/
rude, harsh adj
خشک dry; dried; arid adj /khŭshk/
خشک سالی /khŭshk sā-li/
drought, dry year n
خشک و تر /khŭshk ŭ tar/
dry & wet; good & the bad n
خشکه land n /khŭsh-ka/
خشکه شوی /khŭsh-ka shuy/
dry cleaning n
خصم , -ها /khá-sĭm, khasm/
enemy, adversary n
خصمانه /khas-mā-na/
hostile adj; hostilely adv
خصوص /khŭ-sus/
specificity, specific n
خصوصاً /khŭ-sú-san, -sán/
especially, particularly adv

خصوصی /khŭ-su-si/
special; private, personal adj
خصوصیت , -ها/خصوصیات
/khŭ-su-sī-yat, pl -yāt/
specialty; particular n
خصی /kha-si/
gelded; castrated adj
خصی کردن geld; castrate v
خط , -ها /khat/
calligraphy; drawn line; letter
(mail); beard n
خط برآوردن • خط آوردن
sprout a new beard
خط کشیدن draw a line v
خط , -ها/خطوط /khat, pl khŭ-tut/
line; route; track n
خط آهن /khat-ĭ ā-han/
see ریل n
خط دیورند /khat-ĭ dī-yu-rand/
Durand Line (geog) n
خط ریل /khat-ĭ reyl/
railroad line, railroad track n
خط مشی /khat-ĭ mash/
guideline; policy; procedure n
خط هوایی /khat-ĭ ha-wā-yi/
air route n
خطا , -ها ‹چیزی از چیزی›
/kha-tā/
mistake ‹sth for sth› n
خطا کردن make an error v
دست از پای خود را خطا کردن
(fig) be confused v
خطا see ختایا n /khĭ-tā/
خطاب /khĭ-tāb/
speech, address n
خطاب کردن make a speech v
خطابه /khĭ-tā-ba/
lecture; oratory; preaching n
خطاط , -ان/ها /kha-tāt/
calligrapher n
خطاطی /kha-tā-ti/
calligraphy, penmanship n
خطاکار , -ان/ها /kha-tā-kār/
sinful; guilty adj; sinner; guilty pers
n
خطاکاری /kha-tā-kā-ri/
sinfulness; guilt n
خطای see ختایا n /khĭ-tāy/

خطبا /khŭ-ta-bā, sg kha-tib/
see sg خطیب n pl

خطبه , -ها /khŭt-ba/
sermon (esp on Friday) n

خطر , -ها /kha-tar/
danger, hazard, risk n

خطرناک /kha-tar-nāk/
dangerous, risky n, adj

خطمی /khat-mi/ marshmallow n

خطوط , sg خط /khŭ-tut, sg khat/
see sg خط n pl

خطوط مواصلاتی
/khŭ-tut-ĭ mŭ-wā-sĭ-lā-ti/
network (transport, supply) n pl

خطی /kha-ti/ handwritten adj

خطیب , -ان/ها/خطبا
/kha-tib, pl khŭ-ta-bā/
preacher, orator n

خفک /kha-fak/
choking, suffocating adj

خفک کردن /kha-fak kardan/
choke, suffocate vt

خفیف /kha-fif/
light; slight; weak; mild adj

خلا , -ها /kha-lā/
deficiency; gap, vacuum n

خلا داشتن /kha-lā dāshtan/
be deficient v

خلاص شدن /kha-lās shŭdan/
end, finish; run out vi

خلاصه /khŭ-lā-sa/ summary n

خلاصه این که /khŭ-lā-sa in kĭ/
in summary, briefly adv

خلاصه کلام آن که
/khŭ-lā-sa-yĭ ka-lām ān kĭ/
see خلاصه این که adv

خلاء /kha-lā/ see خلا n

خلافت , -ها /khĭ-lā-fat/
caliphate, succession; Khilafat
(Sufi order) n

خلال /khĭ-lāl/
shredded carrot or orange peel;
toothpick; interstice n

خلال کردن /khĭ-lāl kardan/
shred carrot or orange peel v

خلط /khalt/
mixing, blending; confusing n

خلط شدن با مردم
/khalt shŭdan bā mar-dŭm/
mingle with people v

خلط /khĭlt, pl akh-lāt/ phlegm n
← اخلاط humors n pl

خلطه /khal-ta/ see خریطه n

خلع /khál-'a, khal'/
deposition, dethronement n

خلع سلاح /khál-'a-yĭ sa-lāh/
disarmament n

خلعت /khĭl-'at/
robe of honor (Mughal emperor's
gift, hist) n

خلف /kha-laf, pl akh-lāf/
descendant; successor n; worthy
of father's name adj
← اخلاف pl

خلفا /khŭ-la-fā, sg kha-li-fa/
see sg خلیفه n pl

خلق /khalq/
Khalq (hardline PDPA faction,
hist); people, masses n

خلقت /khĭl-qat/
Creation, the universe n

خلقی , -ان/ها /khal-qi/
Khalq adherent (pers) n; of the
masses adj

خلل , -ها /kha-lal/
disturbance, upset n

خلل پذیر /kha-lal pa-zir/
unstable adj

خلل ناپذیر /kha-lal nā-pa-zir/
solid, firm, steady adj

خلل دماغ /kha-lal-ĭ da-māgh/
insanity, derangement n

خلم /khĭlm/ mucus, snot n

خلم /khŭlm/ Khulm (dist) n

خلمی /khĭl-mi/ snotty adj

خلمی /khŭl-mi/ Khulmi see خلم n

خلوت /khĭl-wat/
empty, deserted adj; privacy;
seclusion n

خلوت خانه /khĭl-wat khā-na/
secluded house or room n

خلوت گاه /khĭl-wat gāh/
hermitage n

خلوت نشین /khĭl-wat nĭ-shin/
hermit, recluse n; secluded adj

bay, gulf n /kha-lij/ خليج , ها-
Persian Gulf خليج فارس ←
/kha-li-fa, pl khŭ-la-fā/ خليفه
caliph; successor n
pl خلفا ←
/kha-li-fa-jān/ خليفه جان
(form of address for driver or
workman) n
/kha-liq/ خليق
polite, well-mannered adj
/kha-lil/ خليل
friend; Khalil (m name, P tribe) n
/kham/ خم
bend, curve, crook; curl n
/kham dādan/ خم دادن
bend, curve vt
/khŭm/ خم
large earthen vessel for liquids n
/kha-mār/ خمار
wine seller (arch) n
/khŭ-mār/ خمار
hangover; tipsiness; languor n
/khŭ-mār ā-lud/ خمار آلود
tipsy; languid adj
/khŭ-mā-ri/ خمارى
charming; tipsy adj; Khumari (f
name) n
/khŭm-bŭk/ خمبک
small earthen vessel; (fig) fat
person n
twig, wicker n /khĭm-cha/ خمچه
/khá-mĭr, khamr/ خمر
wine (arch) n
/khŭm-ra/ خمره
small earthen vessel for milk or
yogurt n
/kham-rī-ya/ خمريه
bacchanalian verse n
fifth, one fifth n /khŭms/ خمس
/kha-mul/ خمول
anonymity, obscurity n
/kha-mī-yāb/ خميياب
Khamyab (dist) n
/kha-mir/ خمير
dough; (fig) nature, character n
/kha-mir tŭrsh/ خمير ترش
starter (for bread) n

/kha-mir ra-si-da/ خمير رسيده
leavened dough n
/kha-mir mā-ya/ خمير مايه
leavening, yeast n
/kha-mir kardan/ خمير كردن
make/knead dough v
/kha-nā-zir, sg khĭn-zir/ خنازير
scrofula n; see sg خنزير n pl
diphtheria n /khŭ-nāq/ خناق
/khŭn-sā/ خنثى
neutral; androgynous adj
/khŭn-sā sākhtan/ خنثى ساختن
deactivate, neutralize (& n) vt, n
← خنثى ساختن مين ها demining
/khĭnj/ خنج
Khenj (dist, ctr Char Qarya) n
Khenjan (dist) n /khĭn-jāni/ خنجان
dagger (curved) n /khan-jar/ خنجر
/khan-dā-war/ خنداور
funny, humorous adj
خنده <كسى> آمدن
/khan-da-yĭ <ká-sey> āmadan/
laugh vi
خنده اش آمد →
s/he laughed vi
/khan-da ā-war/ خنده آور
see خنداور adj
/khan-da kardan/ خنده كردن
laugh vi
خنديدن ؛ -خند- ؛ خنديد-
laugh (formal) vi /khan-di-dan/
خنزير , ها-/khánzir/
/khĭn-zir, pl kha-nā-zir/
pig, swine, boar, hog n
pinky (anat) n /khĭn-sar/ خنصر
cold, coldness n /khŭ-nŭk/ خنک
feel cold vi خنک خوردن →
catch a cold vi خنک زدن →
cold, coldness n /khŭ-nŭ-ki/ خنكى
/khĭng/ خنگ
horse; white horse; (colloq)
shame n; chalk-white adj
/khĭng bŭt/ خنگ بت
Blue Idol (Bamyan Buddha) n
see خواب n خواب /khaw/ خو
OK, okay (colloq) excl /kho/ خو

خواب /khāb (khaw, khāw)/
sleep; dream n
خواب بودن ←
be asleep
خواب گزاردن ←
interpret dreams
خواب آلود /khā-bā-lud/
sleepy, drowsy adj
خواب بردن /khāb bŭrdan/
sleep, fall asleep; get pins &
needles v
خوابش برد ← s/he fell asleep
خواب برده /khāb bŭr-da/
heedless, thoughtless adj
خواب خرگوش /khāb-ĭ khar-gosh/
negligence, inadvertence n
خواب گاه /khāb gāh/
bedroom; bullet holder n
خواب گزاری /khāb gŭ-zā-ri/
dream interpretation n
خواب مقناطیسی
/khāb-ĭ mĭq-nā-ti-si/
hypnotism n
خواب نامه /khāb nā-ma/
book of dreams n
خوابیدن ؛ ـخواب ؛ ـخوابند۔
/khā-bi-dan/
sleep (formal) vi
خواتم /kha-wā-tīm, sg khā-tīm/
see sg خاتم n pl
خواتین /kha-wā-tin, sg khā-tun/
see sg خاتون n pl
خواجه /khā-ja (kho-)/
lord, master; Khaja (m name);
(form of address for descendants
of Abu Bakr); eunuch (hist) n
خواجه بهاءالدین
/khā-ja ba-hā-wŭ-din/
Khaja Bahawuddin (dist) n
خواجه دو کوه /khā-ja du ko/
Khaja Du Koh (dist) n
خواجه سبز پوش
/khā-ja sabz posh/
Khaja Sabz Posh (dist) n
خواجه سرا /khā-ja sa-rā/
eunuch, harem attendant (hist) n
خواجه عمری /khā-ja ŭ-ma-ri/
Khaja Umari (dist) n

خواجه غار /khā-ja ghār/
Khaja Ghar (dist) n
خواجه هجران /khā-ja hĭj-rān/
Khaja Hejran (dist) n
خواهر n /khwār/ see خوار
خوارج /khwā-rĭj, sg khā-rĭ-ji/
see sg خارجی n pl
خوارزم /khā-rá-zīm/
Chorasmia (empire 11th c-1220
AD, hist) n
خوارزمی , -ان/ها /khā-raz-mi/
Chorasmian (& pers, lang) adj, n
خوازه /kha-wā-za/ scaffold n
خواست خدا /khāst-ĭ khŭ-dā/
God willing phrs
خواستار /khās-tār/
applicant n; requesting; awaiting
adj
خواستگار , -ان/ها
/khāst-gār, khās-tī-/
suitor n
خواستگاری /khāst-gā-ri/
marriage proposal n
خواستگاری کردن ←
propose marriage v
خواستن ؛ ـخواه ؛ ـخواست۔
/khās-tan/
want, wish, request <+ subj>;
summon v
خواسته , -ها /khās-ta/
wish, demand, desire n
خواص /kha-wās, sg khā-sa/
see sg خاصه n pl
خواطر /kha-wā-tīr, sg khā-tīr/
see sg خاطر n pl
خوان /khān/ reading; singing n
خوانا /khā-nā/
legible, readable adj
خوانچه /khān-cha (khŭn-)/
small tray n
خواندن ؛ ـخوان۔ ؛ ـخواند۔
/khān-dan/ read, recite; sing v
خوانندگی /khā-nīn-da-gi/
literacy n
خواننده , ـگان/ها /khā-nīn-da/
reader; singer n; literate adj

خواننده و نویسنده /khā-nīn-da wŭ na-wi-sīn-da/
literate *phrs*

خوانین , sg خان /kha-wā-nin, sg khān/
see sg خان *n pl*

... خواه ... خواه /khā ... khā .../
either ... or ... (conj)

خواه مخواه /khāh ma-khāh/
willy-nilly *adv*

خواهان <چیزی/کسی> /khā-hān/
fond, desirous <of sth/sb> *adj*;
Khwahan (dist) *n*

خواهر (خوار) /khā-har (khwār)/
sister; (form of address for f) *n*

خواهر اندر /khā-har an-dar/
half-sister; stepsister *n*

خواهر زاده , -گان/ها /khā-har zā-da/
nephew, niece (sister's child) *n*

خواهرخانه /khā-har-khān-da/
girlfriend (not romantic), best
friend (f) *n*

خواهش , -ها /khā-hīsh/
request; wish, desire *n*

خواهش کردن <چیزی را از کسی> /khā-hīsh kardan/
request, ask <sth from sb> *vt*

خواهشمند , -ان /khā-hīsh-mand/
desirous; wishful (& pers) *adj, n*

خوب /khub/
good; suitable; pleasant; attractive
adj; properly *adv*

خوب کردن ←
do well; cure, heal *v*

خوب شدن ← get well *vi*

خوب و بد /khub ŭ bad/
the good & the wicked *n*

خوب و خراب /khub ŭ kha-rāb/
the good & the bad *n*

خوبتر /khub-tar/ better *adj*

خوبترین /khub-ta-rin/ best *adj*

خوبی کردن /khu-bi kardan/
do good, render a service *v*

خود /khŭd/
oneself, self (takes pers endings)
pron

خود آگاه /khŭd ā-gāh/
self-conscious *adj*

خود به خود /khŭd ba khŭd/
automatic, spontaneous (& adv)
adj, adv

خود بین /khŭd-bin/
selfish; conceited (& pers) *adj, n*

خود پرست /khŭd pa-rast/
conceited, self-worshipping *adj*

خود خواه /khŭd-khāh/
self-centered *adj*

خود داری /khŭd dā-ri/
composure, poise; distancing self
n

خود داری ورزیدن /khŭd dā-ri warzidan/
be self-composed *v*

خود رای /khŭd-rāy/
obstinate, opinionated *adj*

خود ساخت /khŭd-sākht/
handmade *adj*

خود ساز /khŭd-sāz/
pretentious (colloq) *adj*

خود ستا /khŭd-sī-tā/
boastful *adj*; braggart *n*

خود ستایی , -ان /khod sī-tā-yi/
self-aggrandizer *n*

خود سر /khŭd sar/
headstrong, stubborn *adj*

خود غرض /khŭd gha-raz/
self-interested *adj*

خود غرضی /khŭd gha-ra-zi/
self-interest *n*

خود فروش /khŭd fŭ-rosh/
prostitute *n*

خود فروشی /khŭd fŭ-ro-shi/
prostitution *n*

خود کار /khŭd kār/
automatic *adj*; ballpoint pen *n*

خود کشی /khŭd kŭ-shi/ suicide *n*

خود نمایی کردن /khŭd nŭ-mā-yi kardan/
show off *v*

خودسوزی /khŭd-so-zi/
self-immolation *n*

خودش /khŭ-dīsh/
himself, herself *pron*

خودم /khŭ-dŭm/ myself *pron*

خودی /khŭ-di/ ego; egotism n

خور خوری , -ان/ها /khor khŭ-ri/ snoring adj; snorer n

خور زدن /khor zadan/ snore vi

خوراندن ؛ -خوران- ؛ خوراند- /kho-rān-dan/ feed (sb); force to eat vt

خوراک , -ها /kho-rāk/ food; meal, portion n

خوراکه /kho-rā-ka/ edible n, adj

خوراکه باب /kho-rā-ka bāb/ foodstuffs n pl

خورد /khŭrd (khord)/ small adj

خورد ضابط /khŭrd zā-bĭt/ NCO; sergeant n

خورد ضابط قطعه /khŭrd zā-bĭt-ĭ qĭt-ta/ conscript NCO n

خورد ضابط مکتبی /khŭrd zā-bĭt-ĭ mak-ta-bi/ career NCO n

خوردن ؛ -خور- ؛ خورد- /khŭr-dan/ eat; drink; erode; hit; touch; take; experience v

خورشید /khŭr-sheyd/ sun; Khursheyd (m/f name) n

خورشیدی /khŭr-shey-di/ solar (year) adj

خوست /khost/ Khost (prov, seat) n

خوست میله /khost mey-la/ Khost Meyla (ctr) n

خوست و فرنگ /khost wŭ fĭ-rĭng/ Khost wa Fereng (dist) n

خوش <به چیزی> /khŭsh/ happy <at sth>; enjoyable adj

خوش آمد گوی /khŭsh ā-mād goy/ flatterer n

خوش <چیزی / کسی> آمدن /khŭsh āmadan/ like <sth/sb> vt

← این خوش ام نمیآید I don't like this one

← خوش آمدید ! welcome!

خوش باور /khŭsh bā-war/ gullible, credulous adj

خوش بخت /khŭsh bakht/ lucky, fortunate adj

خوش تیپ /khŭsh tip/ handsome (colloq) adj

خوش داشتن <چیزی را> /khŭsh dāshtan/ like <sth> vt

← مه این را خوش ندارم I don't like this one

خوش قواره /khŭsh-qa-wā-ra/ shapely ,attractive adj

خوش مزه /khŭsh-ma-za/ delicious, tasty adj

خوش نما /khŭsh-nŭ-mā/ attractive, nice-looking adj

خوش نویس , -ان/ها /khŭsh na-wis/ calligrapher n

خوش نویسی /khŭsh na-wi-si/ calligraphy n

خوشا به حال تان ! /khŭ´-shā ba hāl-ĭ tān/ bless you excl

خوشبختانه /khŭsh-bakh-tā-na/ fortunately adv

خوشبین /khŭsh-bin/ optimistic, positive adj

خوشحال <به چیزی> /khŭsh-hāl/ happy <at sth> adj

خوشحال خان /khŭsh-hāl khān/ Khushhal Khan (P leader, d. 1689, hist; city dist) n

خوشحال خان ختک /khŭsh-hāl khān kha-tak/ see خوشحال خان n

خوشنود /khŭsh-nud/ happy, content; satisfied adj

خوشنود ساختن /khŭsh-nud sākhtan/ please, satisfy vt

خوشنودی /khŭsh-nu-di/ happiness, satisfaction n

خوشی /khŭ-shi/ Khushi (dist) n

خوشی بخش /khŭ-shi bakhsh/ delightful adj

خوف /khawf/ fear n

خوف داشتن /khawf dāshtan/ be afraid v

خوف کردن /khawf kardan/
frighten v

خوفناک /khawf-nāk/
frightening adj

خوک , ها- /khuk/
pig, swine, boar, hog n

خوک وحشی /khuk-ī wah-shi/
wild boar, warthog n

خوگیانی /khu-gī-yā-ni, kho-/
Khugeyani (dist) n

خون , ها- /khun/
blood; killing n

خون آشام /khun ā-shām/
bloodthirsty, murderous adj

خون آلود /khu-nā-lud/
bloody, bloodstained adj

خون به جوش آمدن
/khun ba josh āmadan/
become enraged, infuriated vi

خون به جوش آوردن
/khun ba josh āwŭrdan/
enrage, infuriate vt

خون بها /khun ba-hā/
blood money n

خون پر /khun pŭr/
bloody, bloodstained adj

خون جگر /khun-ī jī-gar/
grieved adj

خون جگری /khun-ī jī-ga-ri/
grief n

خون جگر خوردن
/khun-ī jī-gar khŭrdan/
grieve vi

خون خوار /khun khār/
bloodthirsty adj

خون خواهی /khun khā-hi/
vengeance n

خون خوردن /khun khŭrdan/
grieve vi

خون دل خوردن
/khun-ī dīl khŭrdan/
grieve; try hard v

خون ریختن /khun reykhtan/
murder; shed blood; hemorrhage
v

خون ریز /khun reyz/
murderous; ferocious adj

خون ریزی /khun-rey-zi/
bloodshed; hemorrhage n

خون شریکی /khun sha-ri-ki/
blood relationship n

خون کردن /khun kardan/ kill v

خونین /khu-nin/
bloody, bloodstained; sorrowful
adj

خوی , ها- /khuy, khoy/
habit; good character;
temperament n

خویش , ان/ها- /kheysh/
relative, kin n; self pron

خویشآوند /khey-shā-wand/
relative by marriage n

خویشتن /kheysh-tan/
self, the self n; self pron

خویشتندار /kheysh-tan-dār/
self-possessed adj

خویشی /khey-shi/
relationship, kinship n

← خویشی داشتن be related v
← خویشی کردن
ally with sb by marriage v

خی /khey/ so (before clause) excl

خیاشنه /khī-yāsh-na/
sister-in-law, wife's sister n

خیاط /kha-yāt/ tailor n

خیاط زنانه /kha-yāt-ī za-nā-na/
dressmaker n

خیاطی کردن /kha-yā-ti kardan/
work as a tailor, sew v

خیال , ات/ها- /khī-yāl/
imagination; thought; vision;
Kheyal (m name) n

← به خیالم ... I imagine that...

خیال باف , ان/ها- /khī-yāl bāf/
dreamer, daydreamer n

خیال بافی /khī-yāl bā-fi/
daydream, reverie n

خیال پرست /khī-yāl pa-rast/
fantasist n

خیال داشتن /khī-yāl dāshtan/
intend v

خیال کردن /khī-yāl kardan/
muse; suppose, guess v

خیالات خام پختن
/khĭ-yā-lāt-ĭ khām pŭkhtan/
build castles in the air (fig) v

خیالی
/khĭ-yā-li/
imaginary; conceptual adj

خیام /kha-yām/
Omar Khayyam (12th-c Dari poet) n

خیام /khĭ-yām, sg khay-ma/
see sg خیمه n pl

خیانت , -ها /khĭ-yā-nat/
betrayal, treachery; fraud n

خیانت به وطن
/khĭ-yā-nat ba wa-tan/
treason n

خیانت پیشه
/khĭ-yā-nat pey-sha/
see خیانت کار n

خیانت کار , -ان/ها
/khĭ-yā-nat kār/
disloyal, treacherous adj; traitor n

خیبر /khay-bar/
Khyber (geog) n

خیر , -ات /khayr/
alms (esp pl); blessing; benefit n;
good; OK adj

خیر /khir/
disrespectful, impudent; hostile
adj

خیر اندیش , -ان/ها
/khayr an-deysh/
benevolent (& pers) adj, n

خیر اندیشانه
/khayr an-dey-shā-na/
benevolently adv

خیر چشم /khir chá-shĭm/
stubborn, obstinate adj

خیر خور /khayr khŭr/
charity-taker (insult) adj, n

خیر مقدم /khayr-ĭ mŭ-qa-dam/
welcoming address n phrs

خیر و شر /khayr ŭ shar/
good & evil phrs

خیرات /khay-rāt/
alms, charity; blessing n pl

خیرات خور نیستم ←
I don't take charity

خیرخانه /khayr-khā-na/
Khayr Khana (1-3, city dists) n

خیرخواه /khayr-khāh/ ها/ان-
benevolent (& pers) adj, n

خیرو /khay-ru/ see خیری n

خیره /khi-ra/
faint, not bright; astonished adj

خیره چشم /khi-ra chá-shĭm/
stubborn, obstinate adj

خیره خیره /khi-ra khi-ra/
gloweringly, glaringly adv

خیری /khay-ri/ marshmallow n

خیریت /khay-rī-yat/
well-being; safety, security n

خیز /kheyz/
jump, leap n

خیز با نیزه /kheyz bā nay-za/
pole vault n

خیز زدن /kheyz zadan/
jump, leap (once) vi

خیز کردن /kheyz kardan/
jump, leap (& repeatedly) vi

خیز و جست /kheyz ŭ jast/
capering n

خیز و جست کردن
/kheyz ŭ jast zadan/
caper, jump around v

خیزاندن ؛ -خیزان- ؛ -خیزاند
/khey-zān-dan/
rouse, cause to stir vt

خیستن ؛ -خیز- ؛ -خیست
/kheys-tan/
see خاستن vi

خیشاوه /khey-shā-wa/
weeding n

خیشاوه کردن
/khey-shā-wa kardan/
weed, remove weeds v

خیل /kheyl/
group, bunch; swarm; flock (of
birds); khel (tribal subdivision);
clan n

خیل کبوتران • خیل کبوتر ←
یک خیل کبوتر •
a flock of pigeons

عروس خیل ←
bride's entourage

داماد خیل ←
groom's entourage

خیل خیل /kheyl kheyl/
in groups adv

خیلگی /khey-la-gi/ silliness n

خیله /khey-la/ silly, stupid adj

خیلی <از چیزی> /khéy-ley/
very *adv*; group, bunch <of sth> *n*

خیلی از سواران
/khéy-ley az sa-wā-rān/
posse, group of horsemen *n*

خیمه , -ها/خیام
/khay-ma, pl khī-yām/
tent *n*

→ خیمه زدن pitch a tent *v*

خیوا /khey-wā/ Khiva (city) *n*

خیوه /khey-wa/ *n* خیوا see

د

داخل /dā-khīl(-ī)/ inside *prep*

داخل شدن /dā-khīl shŭdan/ enter *v*

داخلی /dā-khī-li/
civil; native; interior *adj*; inside *n*

داخلی , -ها /dā-khī-li/
native (pers) *n*

داد /dād/ justice *n*

داد گاه عالی /dād-gāh-ĭ ā-li/
Supreme Court [< F] *n*

دادستان /dā-dīs-tān/
Attorney General [< F] *n*

دادن ؛ -ده- (-ت-) ؛ داد- /dā-dan/
give *vt*

دادو /dā-do/ Dado (ctr) *n*

دادول /dād-wal/ Dadwal (ctr) *n*

دار /dār/ gallows, gibbet *n*

دارا /dā-rā/ having; wealthy *adj*

→ دارا و نادار
the rich & the poor

دار الامان /dār-ŭl-a-mān/
Darulaman (city dist) *n*

دار الانشا /dār-ŭl-īn-shā/
secretariat *n*

دار الایتام /dār-ŭl-ay-tām/
orphanage *n*

دار البقا /dār-ŭl-ba-qā/ Paradise *n*

دار البیضا /dār-ŭl-bay-zā/
Casablanca (city) *n*

دار التادیب /dār-ŭt-tā-dib/
juvenile prison *n*

دار الترجمه /dār-ŭt-tar-jŭ-ma/
translation office *n*

دار الحکومه /dār-ŭl-hŭ-ko-ma/
provincial seat (arch) *n*

دار الخلافه /dār-ŭl-khī-lā-fa/
caliph's seat (arch) *n*

دار السلطنه /dār-ŭs-sal-ta-na/
royal residence *n*

دار السلام /dār-ŭs-sa-lām/
Dar es Salaam (city) *n*

دار العلوم /dār-ŭl-ū-lum/
Dar ul-Ulum (rel/Arabic institute) *n*

دار الفنا /dār-ŭl-fa-nā/
the perishable world *n*

دار الکتاب /dār-ŭl-kī-tāb/
library (arch) *n*

دار المجانین /dār-ŭl-ma-jā-nin/
insane asylum (arch) *n*

دار المساکین /dār-ŭl-ma-sā-kin/
poor house (arch) *n*

دار المعلمین /dār-ŭl-mŭ-'a-lī-min/
teacher training college *n*

دار الملک /dār-ŭl-ma-līk/
capital city (arch) *n*

دار الوکاله /dār-ŭl-wī-kā-la/
law office *n*

دار المکافات /dār-ŭl-mŭ-kā-fāt/
the perishable world *n*

دارایی /dā-rā-yi/ possessions *n*

دارباز /dār-bāz/ acrobat *n*

داربازی /dār-bā-zi/ acrobatics *n*

دارچینی /dār-chi-ni/ cinnamon *n*

دارکوب /dār kob/ woodpecker *n*

دارو , -ها /dā-ru/
medicine cure, remedy; (colloq)
gunpowder *n*

داروغه /dā-ru-gha/
sheriff [< F]; see & *n* داروغه عدالت

داروغه عدالت /dā-ru-gha-yĭ a-dā-lat/
prosecutor of justice *n*

داره /dā-ra/ band, horde *n*

داریم /dā-ra-yīm/ Darayem (dist) *n*

داس /dās/ sickle *n*

داس دسته دراز /dās-ĭ dĭs-ta-yĭ da-rāz/
scythe *n*

داستان , -ها /dās-tān/
story; legend; novel; tall tale *n*

داستان پرداختن
/dās-tān par-dākh-tan/
brag, boast; tell a tall tale *vi*

داستان پرداز , -ان/ها
/dās-tān par-dāz/
braggart; storyteller n

داستان پردازی /dās-tān par-dā-zi/
wordiness; braggadocio n

داستان زندگی /dās-tān-ĭ zĭn-da-gi/
biography n

داستان نویس , -ان/ها
/dās-tān na-wis/
storyteller n

داستان نویسی /dās-tān na-wi-si/
storytelling n

داستان کوتاه /dās-tān-ĭ ko-tāh/
short story n

داستان کوچک /dās-tān-ĭ ko-chak/
novella n

داستانی /dās-tā-ni/
legendary; fictional adj

داش , -ها /dāsh/ stove, oven n

داش خلالی /dāsh-ĭ khĭ-lā-li/
pottery kiln n

داش نان پزی /dāsh-ĭ nān pa-zi/
bread oven n

داشتن /dāshtan/
have vt ؛ -دار- ؛ داشت-

داشته باشه ←
(irreg subj)

داشی /dā-shi/ oven-baked adj

داعی /dā-'ĭ, pl dŭ-'āt/
one who prays for another n

دعات ← pl

داعیه /dā-'ĭ-ya/
motive; desire n

داغ /dāgh/
hot adj; brand; mark; scar n

داغ جگر /dāgh-ĭ jĭ-gar/
see داغ دل

داغ دل /dāgh-ĭ dĭl/
grief, sorrow n

داغ زدن /dāgh zadan/
mark, stain, blot v

داغ کردن /dāgh kardan/
brand, burn in a mark v

داغی /dā-ghi/
stained; disgraced; damaged adj

دافع /dā-fey/
sth that deters or repels n

دافع تانک ← antitank gun
دافع هوا ← antiaircraft artillery

دافعه /dā-fī-'a/
deterrent, repelling adj

قوۀ دافع ← deterrent force

داکتر /dāk-tar/ , -ان/ها doctor n

داکتر اعصاب /dāk-tar-ĭ a'-sāb/
neurologist n

داکتر چشم /dāk-tar-ĭ chĭ´-shĭm/
ophthalmologist n

داکتر دندان /dāk-tar-ĭ dan-dān/
dentist n

داکتر عمومی /dāk-tar-ĭ ŭ-mu-mi/
general practitioner, GP n

داکتر نسایی /dāk-tar-ĭ nĭ-sā-yi/
gynecologist n

داکتر ولادی /dāk-tar-ĭ wĭ-lā-di/
obstetrician n

داکتر ولادی ونسایی
/dāk-tar-ĭ wĭ-lā-di ŭ nĭ-sā-yi/
OB-GYN doctor n

داکتری /dāk-ta-ri/
doctorate, Ph.D. n

دیپلوم داکتری ← doctoral degree

دال /dāl/ dal (side dish); lentils n

دالر /dā-lar/ dollar n

دام , -ها /dām/ trap, snare n

دام نشاندن /dām nīshāndan/
lay a trap v

دام نهاندن /dām nīhāndan/
see دام نشاندن v

داماد /dā-mād/
groom, bridegroom n

دامان /dā-mān/ n دامن see

دامن /dā-man/
skirt; margin, outer edge; Daman
(dist) n

دامنه /dā-ma-na/
slope; scope, range n

دامنه دار /dā-ma-na dār/
broad, extensive adj

دامنه کوه /dā-ma-na-yĭ koh/
foothill, mountain slope n

دان /dān/ n دهان see
دانستن /dā-nĭs-tan/
know; know as vt ؛ -دان- ؛ دانست-

دانش /dā-nĭsh/ knowledge n

دانشمند /dā-nĭsh-mand/ , -ان/ها
expert, specialist n

دانشمند امور فلکی
/dā-nīsh-mand-ĭ ŭ-mur-ĭ fa-la-ki/
astronomist n

دانه /dā-na/ unit, piece n
چند دانه ؟ ↩ how many?

دانه شطرنج /dā-na-yĭ shat-ranj/
chess piece n

دانه نشان /dā-na nĭ-shān/
jewelled (colloq) adj

داو /dāw, daw/
bid; bet, stakes; swear word n

داو بالا کردن /dāw bā-lā kardan/
raise one's bid/stakes v

داو زدن /dāw zadan/
bet, stake; curse, swear v

داود n /dā-wud/ see داوود

داوطلب , -ان/ها /dāw-ta-lab/
bidder; bettor; contestant;
candidate; volunteer n

داوطلبانه /dāw-ta-la-bā-na/
voluntary adj; voluntarily adv

داوود /dā-wud/
Mohamad Daoud (hist, Afgh pres
1973-78); David (bibl, m name) n

داؤد /dā-wud/ n داوود see

داهیه , -ها /dā-hĭ-ya/
disaster, calamity n

دایچوپان /dāy-cho-pān/
ده چوپان n see

دایر شدن /dā-yĭr shŭdan/
work, function; happen vi

دایرة المعارف
/dā-yĭ-rat-ŭl-ma-'ā-rĭf/
encyclopaedia n

دایرکت کردن /dāy-rĭkt kardan/
direct (film) v

دایرکتر /dāy-rĭk-tar/
director (film) n

دایره , -ها/دوایر
/dā-yĭ-ra, pl da-wā-yĭr/
circle; tambourine; office n

دایره زدن /dā-yĭ-ra zadan/
play the tambourine v

دایره کشیدن /dā-yĭ-ra kashidan/
draw a circle v

دایروی /dā-yĭ-ra-wi/
circular, annular adj

دایکندی /dāy-kūn-di/
Daykundi (prov, dist) n

دایم /dā-yīm/
constant; lasting adj; always
(colloq) adv

دایماً /dā-yĭ-man, -yĭ´-/
always, constantly adv

دایمالخمر /dā-yĭm-ŭl-khá-mĭr/
habitually drunk adj

دایمی /dā-yĭ-mi/ دایم see adj
generator n /dāy-na-mo/ داینمو

دایه , -گان/ها /dā-ya/
wet nurse, midwife n

دایمیرداد /dāy-mir-dād/
Daymirdad (dist, ctr Miran) n

دایی /dā-yi/ دایه n see

دبلین /dab-lin/ Dublin (capital) n

دبر /dŭ-būr/ buttocks, backside n

دبی /dŭ-bay/ Dubai (city) n

دبنگ /da-bang/
funny-looking (pers); stupid adj

دبیر /da-bir/
clerk, secretary; teacher (arch) n

دبیر انجم /da-bir-ĭ an-jŭm/
Mercury (arch) n

دیپلوم , -ها /dĭp-lom/
degree, diploma n

دیپلوم داکتری /dĭp-lom-ĭ dāk-ta-ri/
Ph.D. n

دیپلوم لیسانسه /dĭp-lom-ĭ lāy-sān-sa/
B.A.; B.S. n

دیپلوم ماستری /dĭp-lom-ĭ mās-ta-ri/
M.A. n

دیپلومات , -ان/ها /dĭp-lo-māt/
diplomat n

دیپلوماسی /dĭp-lo-mā-si/
diplomatic adj

دیپوزت deposit n /dĭ-po-zĭt/

دجال /da-jāl/
Antichrist, Imposter n

دجله /daj-la/ Tigris (river) n

دچار /dŭ-chār/ دو چار see

دخالت /da-khā-lat/
intervention; interference n

دخالت داشتن <در چیزی>
/da-khā-lat dāshtan/
be involved <in sth> v

دخانیات /dŭ-khā-nĭ-yāt/
tobacco products n pl

i = keep, ĭ = big, u = coop, ŭ = put, y = yet, ' = (glottal stop)   151

دختر , -ان/ها /dŭkh-tar/
daughter; girl n

دختر خاله /dŭkh-tar-ĭ khā-la/
cousin, mother's sister's daughter
n

دختر خوانده /dŭkh-tar khān-da/
foster daughter n

دختر عم /dŭkh-tar-ĭ am/
cousin, father's brother's daughter
n

دختر عمه /dŭkh-tar-ĭ a-ma/
cousin, father's sister's daughter n

دختر کاکا /dŭkh-tar-ĭ kā-kā/
see دختر عم n

دختر ماما /dŭkh-tar-ĭ mā-mā/
cousin, mother's brother's
daughter n

دختری /dŭkh-ta-ri/
virginity (f); maidenhood n

دخل /dá-khĭl, dakhl/
cash drawer (in shop) (colloq) n

دخول /dŭ-khul/
entry; admission; consumption n

دخیل /da-khil/
involved; loaned, borrowed adj

در /dar (da)/ in, at prep

در , -ها /dŭr/ pearl n

در آن صورت /dar ān sŭ-rat/
in that case phrs

در اثر /dar a-sar(-ĭ)/
as a result of phrs

در آغوش کشیدن
/dar ā-ghosh kashidan/
embrace, hug vt

در آغوش گرفتن
/dar ā-ghosh gĭrĭftan/
see در آغوش کشیدن vt

در اسرع وقت /dar a-sar-ĭ waqt/
fast, quickly; ASAP adv

در اطراف /dar at-rāf(-ĭ)/
around prep

در اول /dar a-wal/
initially, at first adv

در این حالت /dar in hā-lat/
meanwhile, meantime adv

در این ضمن /dar in zĭmn/
see در این حالت adv

در باب /dar bāb(-ĭ)/
about, concerning prep

در باره /dar bār(-ĭ)/
about, concerning prep

در بالای /dar bā-lā(-yĭ)/
over, on top of prep

در بدل /dar ba-dal(-ĭ)/
instead of prep

در بر داشتن /dar bar dāshtan/
contain vt

در برابر /dar ba-rā-bar(-ĭ)/
in front of prep

در به در /dar ba dar/
vagrant, homeless adj

در به دری /dar ba da-ri/
vagrancy n

در به دیوار /dar ba dey-wār/
next-door adj

در بین /dar bayn(-ĭ)/ inside prep

در پرده /dar par-da/
screen, partition n

در پشت /dar pŭsht(-ĭ)/
behind prep

در پیرامون /dar pey-rā-mun(-ĭ)/
concerning; around prep

در پیشروی /dar peysh-ĭ-ruy(-ĭ)/
in front of prep

در حال /dar hāl/
now, right now adv

در حالی که /dar hā´-ley kĭ/
while, at the same time adv

در خلوت /dar khĭl-wat/
privately, in private adv

در حقیقت /dar ha-qi-qat/
in fact, as a matter of fact phrs

در خاتمه /dar khā-tĭ-ma/
finally, in conclusion adv

در خلال /dar khĭ-lāl(-ĭ)/
during prep

در دادن /dar dādan/
fire up, make a fire v

در ذیل ‹چیزی› /dar zayl(-ĭ)/
under; at the end of prep

در راس ‹چیزی› /dar rās(-ĭ)/
at the head of <sth> phrs

---

a = cup, ā = long, aw = now, ay = sigh, e = bet, ey = obey

در رکاب <کسی> رفتن
/dar rĭ-kāb-ĭ ká-sey raftan/
accompany <sb> as servant (fig)
v

در زنبور خانه دست زدن
/dar zan-bur khā-na dast zadan/
stir up trouble, endanger o.s. (fig)
v

در زیر /dar zeyr(-ī)/
below, under prep

در سر /dar sar(-ī)/
about; over prep

در سعی و تلاش به سر بردن
/dar sa'y ŭ ta-lāsh ba sar bŭrdan/
try, strive v

در صدد <چیزی> بودن
/dar sa-dad-ĭ chí-zey budan/
intend to do <sth> v

در صورت لزوم
/dar su-rat-ī lŭ-zum/
in case, if required phrs

در عرض /dar arz(-ī)/
along, in the course of prep

در عین حال /dar ayn hāl/
while; meanwhile adv

در فوق /dar fawq/
abovementioned (colloq) adj

در قبال /dar qĭ-bāl(-ī)/
alongside prep

در قبال داشتن /dar qĭ-bāl dāshtan/
accompany v

در کنار next to prep /dar kĭ-nār(-ī)/
در کنار این که /dar kĭ-nār-ī in key/
given that, while on the one hand
conj

در کنج و کنار /dar kŭnj ŭ kĭ-nār/
everywhere (fig) adv

در گذشت death n /dar-gŭ-zāsht/
در گرفتن /dár-gĭrĭftan/
ignite, catch fire (& fig); burn vi

درگیران /dar-gi-rān (-gī-)/
kindling n

در مابین /dar mā-bayn(-ī)/
among; between; inside, within
prep

در مجموع /dar maj-mu/
altogether, in sum adv

در مدت /dar ma-dat(-ī)/
for (length of time) prep

در مورد /dar maw-rĭd(-ī)/
about, concerning (lit) prep

در نتیجه /dar na-ti-j(-ī)/
as a result of phrs

در نخست /dar nŭ-khŭst/
at first (colloq) adv

در نظر داشتن /dar na-zar dāshtan/
consider; have in mind vt

در واقع /dar wā-qey/
actually, really, in fact adv

در وقت /dar waqt(-ī)/
during, in the time of adv

در هر حال /dar har hāl/
در هر صورت see phrs

در هر صورت /dar har su-rat/
in any case phrs

دراز long, lengthy adj /da-rāz/
دراز کشیدن ← lie down, rest vi
/da-rāz mŭ-dat/ دراز مدت
long-term adj

دراز نویسی /da-rāz na-wi-si/
verbosity n

درازی length n /da-rā-zi/
درازی عمر /da-rā-zi-yĭ ŭ´-mŭr/
longevity n

درآمد /dar ā-mad/
income; earnings n

درآمدن /dar ā-ma-dan/
start to; turn into; convert; enter vi

درام see درامه n /dĭ-rām/
درامه drama n /dĭ-rā-ma/
درامه نویس , -ان/ها
dramatist n /dĭ-rā-ma na-wis/

درانی , -ان/ها /dŭ-rā-ni/
Durrani (P tribal confederacy) n

درآوردن /dar ā-wŭr-dan/
bring in; convert vt

دراین اواخر /dar in a-wā-khĭr/
lately; recently adv

دربابا /dŭr-bā-bā/
Dur Baba (dist) n

دربست /dar-bast/
whole adj; as a charter adv

درج /darj/
recording, writing down n

درج کردن /darj kardan/
record, write down v

درجه /dar-ja/
degree (unit of heat) n

درجه بندی /da-ra-ja ban-di/
categorization n

درجه بندی کردن
/da-ra-ja ban-di kardan/
categorize, classify vt

درخت , -ها /da-rakht/ n tree
درخت پیوند کردن
/da-rakht pay-wand kardan/
graft (a branch) onto a tree v

درخشان /dŭ-rŭkh-shān/
shining, glowing; glittering adj

درخشان داشتن
/dŭ-rŭkh-shān dāshtan/
shine, glow, glitter v

درخواست /dár-khāst/
application, request n

درد /dard/ hurt, pain, ache n
درد آلود /dard ā-lud/
painful; distressing adj

درد داشتن /dard dāshtan/
hurt, ache, be painful vi

درد کردن /dard kardan/
vi درد داشتن see

دردناک /dard-nāk/
painful; distressing adj

درزاب /dar-zāb/ n (dist) Darzab
درس /dars/ lesson n
درس خواندن /dars khāndan/
study v

درس دادن /dars dādan/ teach v
درست /dŭ-rŭst/
correct; true; honest; proper adj

درست کار , -ان/ها /dŭ-rŭst-kār/
honest (& pers) adj, n

درست کاری /dŭ-rŭst-kā-ri/
honesty n

درشت /dŭ-rŭsht/
coarse, rough; rude adj

درشتی /dŭ-rŭsh-ti/
coarseness; rudeness n

درفش , -ها /da-rafsh (-rawsh)/
shoemaker's awl n

درقد /dar-qad/ n (dist) Darqad

درک /da-rak/
bottom; trace; viewpoint n

درک /dark/
understanding, perception n

درک کردن/dark kardan/ v realize
درگاه /dar-gāh/
threshold; palace entryway n

درگذشت /dár-gŭ-zasht/
death (formal) n

درگذشتن ؛ درگذر ـ ؛ درگذشت ـ
/dár-gŭ-zash-tan/
cross, pass; relinquish; forgive;
die vt

درگیر , -ها /dar-gir/
involved, embroiled adj; flare-up n

درمان /dar-mān/ cure, remedy n
درمان کردن /dar-mān kardan/
cure, remedy v

درمان ناپذیر /dar-mān nā-pa-zir/
incurable adj

درمانده , -گان/ها /dár-mān-dà/
helpless, distressed (& pers) adj, n

درماندگی /dar-mān-da-gi/
helplessness n

درنده , -گان/ها /da-rīn-da/
predatory adj; predator n

درنگ /da-rang/ delay n
← درنگ کردن delay v

درو /da-raw/ reaping n
← درو کردن reap v

درواز /dar-wāz/ n (dist) Darwaz
دروازه /dar-wā-za/ door, gate n
دروازه بان (-وان)/dar-wā-za-bān (-wān)/
doorkeeper, gatekeeper n

دروغ /dŭ-rogh/
lie n; false, untrue adj

← دروغ بافتن make up lies v
← دروغ برآمدن
prove to be false v

← دروغ پرداختن
tell lies, weave stories v

← دروغ گفتن lie, tell a lie v
دروغ باف , -ان/ها /dŭ-rogh bāf/
liar n

دروغ پرداز , -ان/ها
liar n /dŭ-rogh par-dāz/

دروغ گو /dŭ-rogh go/
liar (colloq) n

دروغی/dŭ-ro-ghi/ false, untrue adj
درون (-ī)/da-run/ inside prep
← درون آمدن come in (room/house) v
← درون کردن penetrate, enter into v
درون گرا /da-run gī-rā/ introverted adj
درونی /da-ru-ni/ inner, interior adj
درویزه /dar-wey-za/ begging, beggary n
درویش , -ان/ها /dar-weysh , -ān/hā/ dervish; poor person n
درویش صفت /dar-weysh sī-fat/ humble, undemanding; like a dervish adj
درویش نهاد /dar-weysh nī-hād/ see درویش صفت adj
درویشانه /dar-wey-shā-na/ see درویش صفت adj
دره /da-ra/ valley; canyon; Dara (dist) n
← درۀ پیچ Dara-ye Peych (ctr)
← درۀ صوف Dara-ye Suf (ctr)
← درۀ صوف بالا Dara-ye Suf-e Bala (dist)
← درۀ صوف پایین Dara-ye Suf-e Payin (dist)
← درۀ نور Dara-ye Nur (dist, ctr Panja Kheyl)
← درۀ هزاره Dara-ye Hazara (ctr)
درهم /dar-ham/ dirham (currency) n; confused adj
درهم و برهم /dar-ham ŭ bar-ham/ complicated, all mixed up adj
دری /da-ri/ Dari (lang) n
دریا /dar-yā/ river n
دریاچه /dar-yā-cha/ lake n
دریا دل , -ان/ها /dar-yā dĭl/ generous (& pers) adj, n
دریای پنج /dar-yā-yī panj/ Five Rivers (middle & upper Amu Darya) n
دریافت /dar-yāft/ receiving; perception n
دریافت داشتن /dar-yāft dāshtan/ get, obtain; receive v

دریافت کردن /dar-yāft kardan/ see دریافت داشتن v
دریافتن ؛ -دریاب- ؛ دریافت- /dar-yāf-tan/ perceive; (arch) help v
دریافتی /dar-yāf-ti/ received adj
دریایی /dar-yā-yi/ of/from a river adj
دریچه /da-ri-cha/ small door/window; hatch n
دریش ! /dī-reysh/ stop excl
دریشی /dī-rey-shi/ uniform; suit (& m dress suit) n
دریشی خواب /dī-rey-shi-yī khāb/ pajamas n
دریغ /dī-reygh/ denial; remorse; distress n
دریغ داشتن <چیزی را از کسی> /dī-reygh dāshtan/ deny, refuse <sth to sb> v
دریم بریدمن /dray-yŭm brid-man/ third lieutenant n
دریم خارن /dray-yŭm tsā-ran/ see دریم سارن n
دریم سارن /dray-yŭm sā-ran/ third lieutenant n
دریور , -ان/ها /dī-ray-war/ chauffeur, driver n
ریوری کردن /dī-ray-wa-ri kardan/ drive (vehicle) (lit) vi
دزد , -ان/ها /dŭzd (dŭz)/ thief, robber, burglar n
دزدی /dŭz-di/ theft, stealing n
دزدیدن ؛ -دزد- ؛ دزدید- /dŭz-di-dan/ steal v
دزی /dŭ-zi/ theft, stealing (colloq) n
دسایس /da-sā-yīs, sg da-si-sa/ see sg دسیسه n pl
دست /dast (dīst)/ hand n
← دست زدن touch v
← دست خوردن be touched v
دست آورد , -ها /dast ā-ward/ achievement n
دست افزار /dast af-zār/ tool, implement n
دست انداز /dast an-dāz/ tyrant, oppressor n

دست انداز‌ی /dast an-dā-zi/
tyranny, oppression n

دست اندر کار , -ان/ها
/dast an-dar kār/
worker, employee n

دست بافت /dast-bāft/
handwoven, hand-knitted adj

دست برد /dast-bŭrd/
embezzlement; robbery; (mil) raid n

دست برد زدن /dast-bŭrd zadan/
carry out a raid v

دست بند /dast-band/
bracelet; difficul handiwork n

دست پاک /dast-pāk/
small hand towel n

دست پناه /dast pa-nāh (dīs-pa-nā)/
trowel (for masonry) n

دست خالی /dast-ĭ khā-li/
empty-handed adj

دست خوش ‹چیزی›
/dast khŭsh(-ĭ)/
susceptible, prey ‹to sth› adj

دست خوش ‹چیزی› شدن
/dast khŭsh(-ĭ) ‹chí-zey› shŭdan/
fall prey ‹to sth› adj

دست دادن /dast dādan/
shake hands v; handshake n

دست درازی /dast da-rā-zi/
see دست اندازی n

دست داشتن ‹با چیزی›
/dīst dāshtan/
be involved ‹with sth› v

دست کم /dīst kam/
at least (colloq) adv

دست مزد /dast-mŭzd (dīs-mŭz)/
wage n

دست نشانده /dast nĭ-shān-da/
henchman, puppet n

دست نویس /dast na-wis/
handwritten adj; manuscript n

دست نویسی /dast na-wi-si/
handwriting n

دست و پای بودن
/dast ŭ pāy budan/
be exhausted; become disabled v

دست و پای خود را گم کردن
/dast ŭ pāy-ĭ khŭd-rā gŭm kardan/
panic v

دست و پای شکسته
/dast ŭ pāy shĭ-kas-ta/
decrepit, broken-down adj

دست و پایی /dast ŭ pā-yi/
bold, aggressive, enterprising adj

دست و دهان
/dast ŭ da-hān (dīst ŭ dān)/
hand-to-mouth adv

دست و دهان بودن
/dast ŭ da-hān budan/
live hand-to-mouth v

دستار /dīs-tār/ turban n

دستار بندی /dīs-tār ban-di/
coronation ceremony n

دستخط , -ها /dast-khat/
signature (colloq) n

دسترخوان /dīs-tar-khān/
tablecloth (& on ground); (fig) table n

دسترسی داشتن ‹به چیزی›
/dīst-ra-si dāshtan/
have available, have access ‹to sth› v

دستاز /dīs-tāz/
see دستاس (colloq) n

دستاس /dīs-tās/ hand mill n

دستکش /dast-kash (dīs-)/ glove n

دستکول /dast-kawl (dīst-)/
purse, handbag n

دستکی /dīs-ta-ki/
handmade; hand-operated adj

دستگاه /dast-gāh/
apparatus, plant; strength; wealth n

دستگاه برقی /dast-gāh-ĭ bar-qi/
power plant n

دستگاه تهویه /dast-gāh-ĭ tah-wĭ-ya/
ventilator n

دستگاه فرستنده
/dast-gāh-ĭ fĭ-rĭs-tĭn-da/
transmitter n

دستگاه مرسله
/dast-gāh-ĭ mŭr-sĭ-la/
see دستگاه فرستنده n

دستگیر /dast-gir/
captured (criminal) adj; helper;
handle n

دستگیر کردن capture vt
/dast-gir dar-wā-za/
door handle n

دستمال , ـها /dast-māl (dĭs-)/
handkerchief, kerchief n

دستمال بینی /dast-māl-ĭ bi-ni/
blindfold n

دستمال سر /dast-māl-ĭ sar/
scarf (on f head) n

دستمال کاغذی
/dast-māl-ĭ kā-gha-zi/
napkin (paper) n

دستمال گردن
/dast-māl-ĭ gar-dan/
scarf (around m neck) n

دسته /das-ta (dĭs-)/
group; category; handle n

دسته موسیقی /das-ta-yĭ mu-si-qi/
band; orchestra (mus) n

دسته هاون /das-ta-yĭ hā-wan/
pestle n

دسته دسته /das-ta das-ta/
in bunches, in groups adv

دسته گل /das-ta-yĭ gŭl/
bouquet of flowers n

دستور , ـات/ها /das-tur/
order; regulation; statute;
grammar n

دستور دادن <به کسی>
give an order <to sb> v

دستور نویس , ـان/ها
/das-tur na-wis/
grammarian n

دستوری /das-tu-ri/
prescribed; grammatical adj

دستی /dĭs-ti/
handmade; hand-operated adj

دستیاب کردن /dast-yāb kardan/
find; get, receive vt

دستیابی /dast-yā-bi/
finding; getting, receiving n

دسمبر December n /dĭ-sīm-bar/

دسیسه , ـها/دسایس
/da-si-sa, pl da-sā-yĭs/
conspiracy, plot n

دسیسه ساختن conspire, plot v

دسیسه باز , ـان/ها /da-si-sa-bāz/
conspirator, plotter n

دشت desert; wilderness n /dasht/

دشت برچی /dasht-ĭ bar-chi/
Dasht-e Barchi (city dist) n

دشت قلعه /dasht-ĭ qal-'a/
Dasht-e Qala (dist) n

دشمن , ـان/ها /dŭsh-man/
enemy, foe, adversary n

دشمن درجه اول
/dŭsh-man-ĭ da-ra-ja-yĭ a-wal/
archenemy n

دشمن وطن /dŭsh-man-ĭ wa-tan/
traitor (to country) n

دشمنانه
/dŭsh-ma-nā-na/
hostile (& adv) adj, adv

دشمنی /dŭsh-ma-ni/
enmity, hostility n

دشمنی وطن
treason n /dŭsh-ma-ni-yĭ wa-tan/

دشنام دادن /dash-nām dādan/
curse, swear (colloq) vi

دشنه dagger n /dash-na/

دشوار /dŭsh-wār/
hard, difficult, arduous adj

دعا , ـها/ادعیا /dŭ-'ā, pl a-dĭ-ya/
prayer; benediction n

دعا کردن pray vi

دعات /dŭ-'āt, sg dā-'i/
see sg داعی n pl

دعاگوی , ـان/ها /dŭ-'ā-goy/
intercessor through prayer n

دفعتاً /dá-fa-tan, -tán/
suddenly, abruptly adv

دعوا , ـها /da'-wā (dā-wā)/
lawsuit; claim; entreaty n

دعوا داشتن <به چیزی>
have a claim <to sth> v

دعوا کردن <به ضدِ کسی>
bring suit <against sb> v

دعوت /da'-wat/
invitation; summons; gathering n

دعوت کردن invite vt

دعوت سلفی /da'-wat-ī sa-la-fi/
Salafism (mvmt) n

دعوت نامه /da'-wat nā-ma/
invitation letter n

دغا /da-ghā/
deceit, deception, trickery n

دغا باز , -ان/ها /da-ghā bāz/
deceitful (& pers) adj, n

دغا بازی /da-ghā bā-zi/
deceipt, deception n

دغدغه anxiety n /dagh-da-gha/

دغل /da-ghal/
deceit, dishonesty; corruption n

دغل بازی /da-ghal bā-zi/
deceit, dishonesty n

دغل بازی کردن
/da-ghal bā-zi kardan/
deceive, be dishonest v

دغلی see دغل n /da-gha-li/

دغلی کردن /da-gha-li kardan/
deceive, be dishonest n

دف , -ها /daf/
tambourine n

دف زدن /daf zadan/
play the tambourine v

دفاتر /da-fā-tīr, sg daf-tar/
see sg دفتر n pl

دفاع defense; vindication n /dī-fā/

دفاع از جان /dī-fā az jān/
self-defense n

دفاع کردن defend v /dī-fā kardan/

دفاعی /dī-fā-'i/
related to defense adj

دفاین /da-fā-yīn, sg da-fi-na/
see sg دفینه n pl

دفتانگ diphthong n /dīf-tāng/

دفتر, -ها/دفاتر /daf-tar, pl da-fā-tīr/
office (place); account book n

دفتر مسافرتی/ـی /daf-tar-ī mŭ-sāf-rī-ti/
travel office n

دفتری diphtheria n /dīf-tī-ri/

دفع /daf/
deterring, repelling n

→ دفع کردن
deter, repel, put off v

دفع الوقت /daf-'ŭl-waqt/
procrastination n

دفع الوقت کردن
/daf-'ŭl-waqt kardan/
procrastinate, buy time n

دفعه , -ها/دفعات /da-fa, pl da-fāt/
time, instance, repetition n

دفن /dá-fīn, dafn/
burial, interment n

→ دفن کردن bury, inter vt

دفینه , -ها/دفاین
/da-fi-na, pl da-fā-yīn/
trove, buried treasure n

دق /dīq/
bored; sad; snubbed adj

→ دق آوردن be bored v

→ دق آوردم I was bored

دق الباب n see دق تق /daq-ŭl-bāb/

دق الباب کردن/daq-ŭl-bāb kardan/
see v دق تق کردن

دق تق /daq taq/
knocking (at door) n

→ دق تق کردن knock (at door) v

دقایق /da-qā-yīq, sg da-qi-qa/
see sg دقیقه n pl

دقت ! /da-qat/
attention (mil order) excl

دقیق /da-qiq/
precise, accurate; careful adj

دقیقاً /da-qí-qan, -qán/
precisely, accurately adv

دقیقه , -ها/دقایق
/da-qi-qa (da-qa), pl da-qā-yīq/
minute (time); subtlety n

دکان , -ها/دکاکین /dŭ-kān (do-)/
shop, store n

دکان دار , -ان/ها /dŭ-kān dār/
shopkeeper n

دکتاتور dictator n /dīk-tā-tor/

دکتاتوری /dīk-tā-to-ri/
dictatorship n; dictatorial adj

دکشنری dictionary n /dīk-shī-na-ri/

دکمه n تکمه see /dŭk-ma/

دگر see & دیگر adj /dī-gar/

دگرجنرال /da-gar-jan-rāl/
lieutenant general, LTG n

دگرمن /da-gar-man/
lieutenant colonel, LTC n

دگروال /da-gar-wāl/
colonel, COL n

دل آرام reassuring adj /dīl ā-rām/

دل آزرده /dīl ā-zŭr-da/
offended adj

دل <کسی را> خوش کردن
/dīl-ĭ ká-sey-rā khŭsh kardan/
please <sb> v

دل دادن /dīl dādan/ fall in love v

دل درد /dīl dard/
having a stomach ache adj

دل دل زار /dīl dal zār/
marsh n; marshy adj

دل زدن /dīl zadan/ hesitate vi

دل <کسی را> سرد کردن
/dīl-ĭ ká-sey-rā sard kardan/
discourage <sb> vt

دل <کسی> سرد شدن
/dīl-ĭ ká-sey sard shŭdan/
become discouraged vi

دل <کسی را> شکستن
/dīl-ĭ ká-sey-rā shīkastan/
disappoint <sb> v

دل شکسته /dīl shī-kas-ta/
heartbroken adj

دل فریب /dīl fĭ-reyb/
fascinating, charming adj

دل کردن /dīl kardan/ dare vi

دل کش /dīl kash/ attractive adj

دل کشا /dīl kŭ-shā/
Delkusha (Palace building) n

دل گیر /dīl gir/
depressing, gloomy adj

دل ناخواه /dīl nā-khāh/
unwilling (& adv) adj, adv

دل <کسی> یخ کردن
/dīl-ĭ <ká-sey> yakh kardan/
get one's revenge v

← دلم یخ کرد I got my revenge

دلاک /da-lāk/ barber n

دلاکی /da-lā-ki/
barbering n; barber's adj

دلال /da-lāl/
broker; procurer; (lit) ogling n

دلال زن /da-lāl zan/ n دلاله see

دلاله /da-lā-la/
procuress, madam n

دلالی /da-lā-li/
brokerage; broker's fee n

دلاور /dī-lā-war/
brave, courageous adj

دلاورانه /dī-lā-wa-rā-na/
brave adj; bravely adv

دل آسا کردن /dīl ā-sā kardan/
reassure, calm (sb) down vt

دل از دست دادن /dīl az dīst dādan/
fall in love v

دل انداختن /dīl andākhtan/
become discouraged v

دل انگیز /dīl an-geyz/ exciting adj

دل انگیزی /dīl an-gey-zi/
excitement n

دل باختن /dīl bākhtan/ fall in love v

دل باخته , ـگان/ها /dīl bākh-ta/
lover, pers in love n

دل بد /dīl bad/ nauseous adj

دل بد شدن /dīl bad shŭdan/
throw up, vomit vi

← دلم بد شد I threw up

دل بر , ـان /dīl bar/ sweetheart n

دل بند /dīl band/
dear, beloved (esp child) adj

دل به دست آوردن
/dīl ba dĭst āwŭrdan/
gratify, humor vt

دل پاک /dīl pāk/
sincere, candid (colloq) adj

دل پذیر /dīl pa-zir/
pleasant, agreeable adj

دل پسند /dīl pī-sand/
likeable, affable adj

دل تنگ /dīl tang/
depressed, sad adj

دل خراش /dīl kha-rāsh/
heart-rending, harrowing adj

دل چسپ /dīl chasp/ adj دلچسپ see

دل خواه /dīl khāh/ adj دلخواه see

دل خواستن /dīl khāstan/
feel like (doing sth) <+ subj> vi

← دلم می خوایه که برم I feel like going

دل خود را خالی کردن
/dīl-ĭ khŭd-rā khā-li kardan/
get one's revenge v

دل خود را یخ کردن
/dīl-ĭ khŭd-rā yakh kardan/
avenge v

دل خوش /dīl khŭsh/
happy, merry adj

دلایل /da-lā-yīl, sg da-lil/
pl دلیل see sg

دلچسپ /dīl-chasp/ interesting adj
دلخواه /dīl-khāh/
favorite, beloved adj,
دلستان /dīl-sī-tān/ sweetheart n
دلسوزی داشتن /dīl-so-zi dāshtan/
be sympathetic n

دلک پای /dī-lak-ī pāy/ calf n
دلک گوش /dī-lak-ī gosh/ earlobe n
دلگی /dīl-gay/ squad (mil) n
دلگی مشر /dīl-gay mī´-shīr/
corporal n

دلو /dalw/
Dalw (month); Aquarius; leather bucket n

دله /da-la/
cuckold; homosexual's father n

دله خفک /da-la kha-fak/
marten (animal) n

دلیر /dī-leyr/
brave, courageous adj
دلیرانه /dī-ley-rā-na/
brave adj; bravely adv
دلیری /dī-ley-ri/ دلیری bravery, courage n
دلیل , -ها/ادله/دلایل
/da-lil; pl a-dī-la, da-lā-yīl/
reason, cause n

دلیه /dīl-ya/ dahlia (flower) n
دم /dam/
breath; pause; instant; bellows; edge n

دم /dŭm/ tail n
دم به دم /dam ba dam/
incessantly adv

دم پخت /dam pŭkht/
steamed (cul) adj
دم دم /dam dam/ n دم see
دم دمی /dam-da-mi/ fickle adj
دم زدن /dam za-dan/
breathe; speak v
دم ساز /dam sāz/
intimate, very close adj
دم و دستگاه /dam ŭ dast-gāh/
wealth; power; authority n
دم و دعا /dam ŭ dŭ-'ā/
incantation (rel) n
incessantly adv دمادم/da-mā-dam/

دماغ /da-māgh (-māq)/
arrogance; brain; nose n
دماغ اصغر /da-māgh-ī as-ghar/
cerebellum n
دماغ اکبر /da-māgh-ī ak-bar/
cerebrum n
دماغ <کسی> خراب شدن
/da-māgh-ī <ká-sey> kha-rāb shŭdan/
become mentally ill vi
دماغ داشتن /da-māgh dāshtan/
be arrogant v
دماغ سوختن /da-māgh sokhtan/
get upset v
دماغه /da-mā-gha/
cape, promontory n
دماغی /da-mā-ghi/
arrogant; cerebral adj
دماق /da-māq/ n دماغ see
دمبال /dŭm-bāl/ n دنبال see
دمبوره /dam-bu-ra/
dambura (mus instr) n
دمشق /da-mīshq/
Damascus (capital) n
دمن /da-man/ n دامن see
دموکراسی /dī-mo-kī-rā-si/
democracy n
دن /dan/ n دهان see
دنبال /dŭm-bāl/
rear, hind part; tail n
دنبال کردن /dŭm-bāl kardan/
continue; follow vt
دنباله /dŭm-bā-la/
continuation; tail, trail n
دنبوره /dam-bu-ra/ n دمبوره see
دنبه /dŭm-ba/ n دنبه گوسفند see
دنبه دار /dŭm-ba dār/
ass, buttocks (colloq) n
دنبه داشتن /dŭm-ba dāshtan/
be fat v
دنبه کردن /dŭm-ba kardan/
get fat v
دنبه گوسفند /dŭm-ba-yī gos-fand/
sheep's tail n
دند /dand/ pool, pond; puddle n
دند و پتان /dand wŭ pa-tān/
Dand wa Patan (dist, ctr Ghunday) n

دندان , -ها tooth n /dan-dān/

دندان آلاشگی
/dan-dān-ĭ a-lā-sha-gi/
molar (tooth) n

دندان بر جگر گذاشتن
/dan-dān bar jĭ-gar gŭ-zāsh-tan/
grin & bear sth v

دندان تیز کردن
/dan-dān teyz kardan/
covet, hanker after sth n

دنده stick, bat, club n /dan-da/

دنمارک
Denmark (country) n /dan-mārk/

دنمارکی , -ان/ها /dan-mār-ki/
Danish adj; Dane (pers) n

دنی low, base; inferior adj /da-ni/

دنیا /dŭn-yā/
world, Earth; this world n

/dŭn-yā-yi/
worldly, of the world adj

دو two n, adj /du, dŭ/

دو آب Du Ab (dist) n /du āb/

دو آبی Du Abi (ctr) n /du ā-bi/

دو باره /du bā-ra/
twice, two times; again adv

/du ba-rā-bar/
double adj, adv

دو به دو /du ba du/
in private, one on one adv

دو بیتی , -ها /du bay-ti/
Dari poem with two couplets n

/du pĭ-yā-za/
dupeyaza (cul) n

/du pay-kar/
Gemini; (arch) twin n

دو تار /du tār/ dutar (mus instr) n

دو چار /du chār/
encounter, meeting n

double adj, adv /du chand/

/du chand kardan/
double (sth) vt

دو دفعه
twice, two times adv

دو دل /du dĭl/
uncertain, undecided adj

دو دلی /du dĭ-li/
uncertainty, indecision n

دو زدن v /daw zadan/ see داو زدن

دو گانگی /du gā-na-gi/
twin; disunity, dissension n

دو گانه /du gā-na/
binary; with two genuflections
(prayer) adj

دو لینه /du lay-na/
Du Layna (dist) n

دو منزله /du man-zĭ-la/
two-story (house) adj

دو نقطه /du nŭq-ta/
colon (punctuation) n

bisyllabic adj /du hĭ-jā-yi/ دو هجایی

دوا , -ها/ادویه /da-wā, pl ad-wĭ-ya/
medicine n

← دوا خوردن • دوا گرفتن
take medicine v

← دوا دادن give medicine v

دوای مسکن /da-wā-yĭ mŭ-sa-kĭn/
analgesic; sedative, tranquilizer n

دوازده /dŭ-wāz-dah (dwāz-da)/
twelve n, adj

دوازدهم /dŭ-wāz-da-hŭm/
twelfth adj

دوازدهمین /dŭ-wāz-da-hŭ-min/
twelfth (lit, oft before n) adj

دواساز , -ان/ها /da-wā-sāz/
pharmacist n

دوافروشی /da-wā fŭ-ro-shi/
pharmacy n

دوام /da-wām/
continuation; durability n

دوام دار /da-wām-dār/
continuous; durable, lasting adj

دوان /da-wān/ running adv

دوان آمدن /da-wān āmadan/
come running (lit) v

دواير /da-wā-yĭr, sg dā-yĭ-ra/
see sg دایره n pl

دوباره /du bā-ra/ adv دو باره see

دوبی /du-bay/ n دبی see

دوختن ؛ -دوز- ؛ دوخت-
sew, do needlework v /dokh-tan/

دوختن ؛ -دوش- ؛ دوخت-
milk (an animal) v /dokh-tan/

دود /dud/ smoke n

دود دادن <به چیزی> /dud dādan/
smoke <sth> v

i = keep, ĭ = big, u = coop, ŭ = put, y = yet, ' = (glottal stop)   161

دود شدن /dud shŭdan/
go up in smoke, vanish v

دود کش /dud kash/
chimney; smokestack n

دور adv far /dur/

دور /dawr, pl ad-wār/
period, era, time n

← ادوار pl

دور /dawr(-ĭ)/ around prep

دور ‹چیزی/کسی را› گرفتن
/dawr-ĭ ‹chí-zey-rā› gĭrĭftan/
surround ‹sth/sb› vt

دور خوردن /dawr khŭrdan/
turn; rotate v

دور کردن /dawr kardan/ recur vi

دوران /daw-rān/ circulation n

دوران سر /daw-rān-ĭ sar/
dizziness, vertigo n

دوراندیش , -ان/ها /dur an-deysh/
farsighted, prudent (& pers) adj, n

دوراندیشی /dur an-dey-shi/
prudence n

دوراهی /du-rā-hi/
fork in the road n

دوردست , -ها /dur-dast/
remote adj; remote area n

دوررس /dur-ras/
long-range; far-reaching adj

دورگ /du-rag/ mongrel adj

دورگه /du-ra-ga/ see دورگ adj

دورمنزل /dur-man-zĭl/
see دوررس adj

دورنگ /dŭ-rang/
insincere; hypocritical adj

دورنگی /dŭ-ran-gi/
insincerity, hypocrisy n

دورنما /dur-nŭ-mā/
outlook, prospects; vista n

دورنمای /dur-nŭ-māy/
see دورنما n

دوروی /dŭ-ruy/
insincere; hypocritical adj

دورویی /dŭ-ru-yi/
insincerity; hypocrisy n

دوره /daw-ra/
period, age, time; reign n

← دورۀ سنگ • دورۀ حجر
Stone Age

← دورۀ مکلفیت
conscript's term

دوزخ /do-zakh/ hell; inferno n

دوزخی , -ان/ها /do-za-khi/
infernal; fiendish adj; fiend n

دوزی /do-zi/ sewing n

دوست , -ان/ها /dost/ friend n

دوست داشتن /dost dāshtan/
love vt

دوست محمد /dost mŭ-ha-mad/
Dost Muhamed (19th-c Kabul emir,
hist) n

دوستانه /dos-tā-na/ friendly adj

دوستی /dos-ti/
friendship; affection n

دوسیه /du-sĭ-ya/
file, folder, dossier n

دوش /dosh/ shoulder (lit) n

دوشاخه /du-shā-kha/
pitchfork (tool) n

دوشنبه /du-sham-bey/
Monday; Dushanbe (capital) n

دوشک /do-shak/ see توشک n

دوشی /do-shi/ Doshi (dist) n

دوشیدن ؛ -دوش- ؛ دوشید-
/do-shi-dan/ v
milk (an animal) v

دوطرفه /du-ta-ra-fa/
mutual; bilateral; round-trip adj

دوغ /dogh/ buttermilk n

دول /dol/ bucket; drum n

دولت /daw-lat/
state, country; government n

دولت آباد /daw-la-tā-bād/
Dawlatabad (dist) n

دولت پوشالی /daw-lat-ĭ po-shā-li/
puppet state n

دولت دار , -ان/ها /daw-lat-dār/
rich; lucky (& pers) adj, n

دولت شاه /daw-lat shāh/
Dawlat Shah (dist) n

دولت یار /daw-lat-yār/
Dawlatyar (dist) n

دولتزی /daw-lat-zay/
Dawlatzai (P tribe) n

دولتمند , ‑ان/ها /daw-lat-mand/
rich; lucky (& pers) adj, n
دولتی /daw-la-ti/ governmental adj
دولمه /dol-ma/ dolma (cul) n
دوله /do-la/ bucket n
دوم /dŭ-wŭm (-yŭm)/ second (ordinal) adj; secondly adv
دوهم بریدمن /dwa-hŭm brid-man/
2LT n see دوهم خارن
دوهم خارن /dwa-hŭm tsā-ran/
second lieutenant, 2LT n
دوهم سارن /dwa-hŭm sā-ran/
see دوهم خارن n
دویدن ؛ ‑دو‑ ؛ دوید‑ /da-wi-dan/
run vi
ده /dah/
ten n, adj; in, at (colloq) prep
ده , ‑ات/ها /dĭh/ village n
← ده بالا
Deh Bala (dist, ctr Kotwal)
ده بوری /dĭh bu-ri/
Deh Buri (city dist) n
ده راود /dĭh rā-wod/
Deh Rawod (dist) n
ده سبز /dĭh sabz/
Deh Sabz (dist) n
ده ساله /dĭh sā-la/ Deh Sala (dist) n
ده چوپان /dĭh cho-pān/
Deh Chopan (dist) n
ده یک /dah yak/ tenth, one-tenth n
ده یک /dĭh yak/
Deh Yak (dist, ctr Ramak) n
دهاقین /dĭ-hā-qin, sg dĭh-qān/
see sg دهقان n pl
دهان /da-hān (dān)/
mouth; aperture, opening n
دهدادی /dĭh-dā-di/
Dehdadi (dist) n
دهری /dah-ri/
atheist, freethinker; dahri (rel) n
دهشت /dah-shat/ terror, horror n
دهشت افگن , ‑ان/ها
/dah-shat af-gan/
terrorist n; terrifying adj
دهشت افگنی /dah-shat af-ga-ni/
terrorism n
دهشت آور /dah-shat ā-war/
terrifying, horrific adj

دهشت زده , ‑گان/ها
/dah-shat za-da/
terrified (& pers) adj, n
دهشتناک /dah-shat-nāk/
terrible, dreadful adj
دهقان , ‑ان/ها/ها
/dĭh-qān, pl dĭ-hā-qin/
farmer, peasant n
دهکی , ‑ها /dĭ-ha-ki/ villager n
دهگان , ‑ان/ها /dĭh-gān (-gān)/
Tajik (local usage) n
دهگانی /dĭh-gā-ni (-gā-ni)/
Dehgani, Deygani (Dari dialect) n
دهل , ‑ها /dŭ-hŭl (dol)/
drum (mus instr) n
← دهل زدن beat a drum
دهل زن /dŭ-hŭl zan/ drummer (lit) n
دهل نواختن /dŭ-hŭl nawākhtan/
play the drum v
دهل نواز /dŭ-hŭl na-wāz/
drummer n
دهلچی /dŭ-hŭl-chi (dol-chi)/
drummer (colloq) n
دهلی جدید /dĭh-li-yĭ jĭ-did/
New Delhi n
دهلی نو /dĭh-li-yĭ naw/
see دهلی جدید n
دهلیز , ‑ها /dĭh-leyz/
hallway, corridor n
دهم /da-hŭm/ tenth adj
دهمین /da-hŭ-min/
tenth (lit, oft before n) adj
دهن /dan/ n دهان see
دهنه غوری /da-ha-na-ye gho-ri/
Dahana-ye Ghori (dist) n
دهه /da-ha/ decade; ten days n
دی /day/ n جدی see
دی کندی /day-kŭn-di/
see دای کندی n
دی وی دی /di wi di/
DVD n
دیابت /dĭ-yā-bĭt/ diabetes n
دیاپزن /dĭ-yā-pa-zan/ tuning fork n
دیافرام /dĭ-yā-fĭ-rām/ diaphragm n
دیالوگ /dĭ-yā-log/ dialogue n
دیباچه /day-bā-cha/ preface n
دیپلومات/دپلومات /dip-lo-māt/ n see

i = keep, ĭ = big, u = coop, ŭ = put, y = yet, ' = (glottal stop)   163

دیپلوماسی /dip-lo-mā-si/
see دیپلوماسی adj

دپوزت n /di-po-zit/ see دیپوزیت

دیدار /di-dār/ visit n

دیدگاه /did-gāh/
viewpoint; scheme, vision n

دیدن ؛ -بین- ؛ دید-
see; visit vt /di-dan, méybinŭm//

دیدن کردن /di-dan kardan/ visit v

دیر /dayr/ monastery, convent n

دیر /deyr/ late (not on time) adv

دیر آشنا /dey-rāsh-nā/
shy, slow to befriend adj

دیر باور /deyr-bā-war/
skeptical (& pers) adj, n

دیر دیر /deyr deyr/
rarely, infrequently adv

دیر مانده /deyr mān-da/ stale adj

دیرپای /deyr-pāy/
lasting, enduring adj

دیررس /deyr-ras/
far-reaching, long-term adj

دیرک /di-rak/ pole; mast (ship's) n

دیروز /di-roz/ yesterday adv

دیروزه /di-ro-za/ adj see دیروزی

دیروزی /di-ro-zi/ yesterday's adj

دیزانتری /di-zāyn-tĭ-ri/
dysentery n

دیزاین /di-zāyn/ design n

دیزل /di-zal/ diesel n

دیشب /di-shab (-shaw)/
last night adv

دیشبه /di-sha-ba/ last night's adj

دیشو /di-sho/ Disho (dist) n

دیفتری /dif-tĭ-ri/ diphtheria n

دیگ /deyg/ pot (for cooking) n

دیگ بخار /deyg-ĭ bŭ-khār/
pressure cooker; pimple n

دیگ پایه /deyg pā-ya/
trivet for cooking pot n

دیگ پختن /deyg pŭkh-tan/
cook, do the cooking vi

دیگر , -ان/ها /di-gar (dĭ-ga)/
other, another (& pers); else;
other; next adj, n

دیگر سبا /di-gar sa-bā/
day after tomorrow adv

دیله /di-la/ Dila (dist) n

دین , -ان/ها /din/
religion, faith, creed n

دین الهی /din-ĭ ā-lā-hi/
Din-e Ilahi (mvmt, hist) n

دین به /din-ĭ bĭh/ n see بهدین

دین نسطوری /din-ĭ nas-tu-ri/
Nestorianism (hist) n

دیندار , ان/ها /din-dār/
religious (& pers) adj, n

داینومو /day-na-mo/ n see دینمو

دینیات /di-nĭ-yāt/
theology, religion (school subject)
n

دیو , -ان/ها /deyw/
evil spirit, demon; (fig) strong m n

دیوار /di-wār/ (colloq) n see دیوال

دیوال /di-wāl (-wār)/ wall n

دیوال موج شکن
/di-wāl-ĭ mawj-ĭ shĭ-kan/
breakwater n

دیوان /dey-wān, di-/
office; room, hall; revenue
collector (hist); divan n

دیوان عالی /dey-wān-ĭ 'ā-li/
high court [< F] n

دیوان عام /dey-wān-ĭ 'ām/
hall of public audiences n

دیوان خاص /dey-wān-ĭ khās/
hall of private audiences n

دیوانگی /dey-wā-na-gi/
craziness; fury; foolishness n

دیوانه , -گان/ها /dey-wā-na/
crazy; furious; foolish adj, n

دیوانه عشق /dey-wā-na-yĭ ĭshq/
madly in love adj

دیوانه وار /dey-wā-na-wār/
frenzied adj; frantically adj

دیوانی /dey-wā-ni/
administrative adj; Deywani (callig
style) n

دیوبندی /dey-ban-di/
Deobandi (mvmt) n

دیوزده /deyw-za-da/
possessed by evil spirit; lazy (&
pers) adj, n

دیوسرشت /deyw-sĭ-rĭsht/
adj see دیوصفت

ديوصفت /deyw-sĭ-fat/
cruel, wicked; fiendish adj

ديويزيون /di-wiz-yun/
division (mil) [< Eng] n

ذ

ذات البينى /zāt-ŭl-bay-ni/
interpersonal adj

ذات الريه /zāt-ŭr-rī-ya/
pneumonia n

ذايقه /zā-yĭ-qa/
sense of taste; flavor n

ذخاير /za-khā-yir, sg za-khi-ra/
see sg ذخيره n pl

ذخيره/ها , ذخاير /za-khi-ra, pl za-khā-yir/
reserve; repository n
← ذخيرة پولى reserve fund
← ذخيره كردن
stockpile, accumulate n

ذروى /za-ra-wi/
nuclear, atomic adj

ذره بين /za-ra-bin/
magnifying glass; microscope n

ذره ذره /za-ra za-ra/
bit by bit; in detail adv

ذريعه /za-ri-'a/
means n
← به ذريعه <چيزى> by means of

ذريه /zŭr-ya/
offspring, progeny n

ذغال /zŭ-ghāl/ n زغال see

ذقن/ها , /za-qan/
chin (lit) n

ذكا /za-kā/ n ذكاوت see

ذكاوت /za-kā-wat/
intelligence, acumen n
← ذكاوت داشتن be intelligent v

ذكر/ها , /zĭ´-kĭr, zĭkr/
mention, naming; reputation; dhikr n
← ذكر شدن • ذكر رفتن
be mentioned vi
← ذكر كردن mention vt

ذكر /za-kar/ penis (obs) n

ذكور /zŭ-kur/ male adj

ذكور و اناث /zŭ-kur ŭ a-nās/
male & female adj phrs

ذكى /za-ki/
intelligent, clever, bright adj

ذمه /zĭ-ma/ responsibility n

ذمه وار دار /zĭ-ma-wār dār/
ذمه دار see (colloq) adj

ذمه دار /zĭ-ma dār/
responsible (for sth) adj

ذمى /zĭm-mi/
dhimmi (Jews, Christians; people of the book) n

ذوالفقار /zŭl-fĭ-qār/
Zulfiqar (Ali's sword) n

ذوالقرنين /zŭl-qar-nayn/
two-horned (epithet of Alexander the Great) n

ذواللسانين /zŭl-lĭ-sā-nayn/
bilingual adj

ذوب /zawb/ melting n
ذوب شدن /zawb shŭdan/ melt vi
ذوب كردن /zawb kardan/ melt vt

ذوجنسين /zu-jĭn-sayn/
hermaphrodite n

ذوحياتين /zu-ha-yā-tayn/
amphibian n

ذوزنقه /zu-zan-qa/ trapezoid n

ذوق/ها , /zawq/
taste, preference; sophistication n

ذوقمند/ان , /zawq-mand/
interested (in sth) (& pers) adj, n

ذوى الارحام /za-wi-ŭl-ar-hām/
maternal relatives n pl

ذوى العقول /za-wi-ŭl-'ŭ-qul/
endowed with intellect, human adj

ذهاب /zĭ-hāb/ n ایاب و ذهاب see

ذهن/ها , اذهان /zĭ´-hin, zĭhn; pl az-hān/
mind, intellect n

ذهنى /zĭh-ni/
mental, intellectual; subjective adj

ذهنيت/ها , ذهنيات /zĭh-nĭ-yat, pl -yāt/
mentality n

ذى حق /zi haq/ rightful adj

ذى حيات /zi ha-yāt/
living, animate adj

ذى روح /zi ruh/ adj ذيروح see

ذيربط /zeyr-bat/ relevant adj

/zi-ruh/ ذیروح
living, having a soul adj

/zayl/ ذیل
following; below adj; end (of
page); appendix (of book) n

as follows adv /zay-lan, záy-/ ذیلاً

ر

/rā-bīṭ/ رابط
liaison, intermediary adj

رابطه , -ها/روابط
/rā-bī-ta, pl ra-wā-bīṭ/
relation; tie, link n

Rabeya (f name) n /rā-bī-ya/ رابعه
report n /rā-por/ راپور , -ها
/rā-jey ba/ راجع به
about, concerning prep

/rā-hat/ راحت
comfort, rest n; comfortable adj
/rā-hat ta-lab/ راحت طلب , -ها/ان
couch potato, sybarite n

radio n /rā-dī-yo/ رادیو
/rā-dī-yo-ak-tif/ رادیواکتیف
radioactive adj

/rā-dī-yo-lo-zhi/ رادیولوژی
radiology n

radium n /rā-dī-yom/ رادیوم
/rā-dī-yo-yi/ رادیویی
related to radio adj

secret, mystery n /rāz/ راز , -ها
keep a secret v ← راز پوشیدن
/rāz nī-gāh kardan/ راز نگاه کردن
keep a secret v

/rāz-dār/ راز دار , -ان/ها
confidant n; able to keep secrets
adj

/rāz-dā-ri/ راز داری
secrecy, confidence n

/rā-zīq/ رازق
Provider (God); Raziq (m name) n
/rāz ŭ nī-yāz/ راز و نیاز
prayerful supplication; billing &
cooing n

← راز و نیاز کردن
supplicate prayerfully; bill & coo v

/rā-zī-yā-na/ رازیانه
anise, aniseed (arch) n

/rās/ راس
head (of delegation); of animal) n
5 head of sheep گوسفند← ۵ راس
/rā-san, rā´-/ راساً
directly, straightaway adv
raspberry n /rās-ba-ri/ راسبری
/rāst/ راست
right (not left); true; direct adj
be right (colloq) vi راست گفتن ←
right side n راست طرفِ ←
/rāst-kār/ راست کار , -ان/ها
righteous, honest, just (& pers)
adj, n
/rāst-kā-ri/ راست کاری
righteousness, honesty n
/rāst-kar-dār/ راست کردار
adj راست کار see
field (of work) n /rās-tā/ راستا
by the way adv /rās-ti/ راستی
really? excl /rās-ti/ راستی ؟
bribe-giver n /rā-shi/ راشی
/rā-zi/ راضی
satisfied, content; willing, ready
adj
/rā-zi kardan/ راضی کردن
satisfy; persuade, convince vt
Ragha (ctr) n /rā-gha/ راغه
/rā-kīb/ راکب , -ین
passenger (esp pl) n
/rā-kīṭ/ راکت , -ها
rocket, missile (larger than مزایل)
n
← راکتِ آر پی جی
rocket-propelled grenade
rocket launcher راکتِ انداز ←
ballistic missile راکتِ بالستیکی ←
← راکتِ رهبری شده
guided missile
missile launcher راکتِ لنچر ←
Ramak (ctr) n /rā-mak/ رامک
/rān/ ران
thigh, calf (of leg) (anat) n
/rān-dan/ راندن ؛ -ران- ؛ راند-
push, drive, urge vt
/rā-nīn-da/ راننده , -گان/ها
driver (of vehicle) n

راولپندی /rā-wal-pīn-di/
Rawalpindi (city, Pakistani mil headquarters) n

راه /rāh/ road, way, path n
راه بند /rāh-ī band/ roadblock n
راه حل /rāh-ī hal/ solution (to problem) n
راه خامه /rāh-ī khā-ma/ dirt road, unpaved road n
راه رفتن /rāh raftan/ walk, go vi
راه گیر /rāh-gir/ bandit, highwayman n
راه میان /rāh-ī mī-yān/ shortcut n

راهب , - ان/ها/ين/رهبان /rā-hīb, pl rŭh-bān/
monk (Christian) n

راهبه , -ها/راهبات /rā-hī-ba, pl rā-hī-bāt/
nun (Christian) n

راهرو , -ها /rāh-raw/
hallway; walkway; traveler of the path (Sufi) n

راهنما , -ها/يان /rāh-nŭ-mā/
guide; guidebook n

راهنمایی /rāh-nŭ-mā-yi/
guidance, act of guiding n

رهنمای معاملات /rāh-nŭ-mā-yī mŭ-'ā-mī-lāt/
realty, real estate n

راهی /rā-hi(-yī)/
en route to, on the way to adv
← راهی شدن
embark on a journey v
← راهی کردن send vt

رای , -ها /rāy/
vote; opinion; (Musl law) subjective opinion n
← رای دادن vote v

رای اعتماد /rāy-ī ey-tī-mād/
confidence vote n

رای غیر اعتماد /rāy-ī ghayr-ī ey-tī-mād/
no-confidence vote n

رای دهنده , -گان/ها /rāy dī-hīn-da/
voter n; voting adj

رایت , -ها/رایات /rā-yīt, pl rā-yāt/
flag, banner (lit) n

رایحه , -ها/روایح /rā-yī-ha, pl ra-wā-yīh/
scent, fragrance n

رایگان /rā-ya-gān/
free, gratis adj

رب /rŭb/
sauce, paste (& < fruit) n

ربا /rī-bā/
usury, excessive interest n

ربا /rŭ-bā/ abductor, snatcher n

رباب /rŭ-bāb/ rubab (mus instr) n

رباب نواز /rŭ-bāb na-wāz/
rubab player n

ربابی /rŭ-bā-bi/ رباب نواز see

ربایندگی /ra-bā-yīn-da-gi/
kidnapping n

رباینده , -گان /ra-bā-yīn-da/
kidnapper n

رباعی , -ات/ها /rŭ-bā-'i/
quadrilateral; quatrain n

ربانی , -ون/ین /ra-bā-ni/
divine; pious adj; divinity scholar (Musl); Rabani (m name) n

ربایش /ra-bā-yīsh/ kidnapping n
رباینده /ra-bā-yīn-da/ kidnapper n
ربح /rībh/ interest (on money) n

ربودن ؛ -ربای- ؛ ربود-
/ra-bu-dan/, /méyrŭbāyŭm//
abduct, kidnap; attract vt

رتب /rŭ-tab, sg rŭt-ba/
رتبه n pl see sg

رتبه , -ها/رتب /rŭt-ba, pl rŭ-tab/
rank; standing n

رجحان /rŭj-hān/
preference; superiority n
← رجحان دادن prefer v
← رجحان داشتن be superior v

رجعت /rŭj-'at/
return; relapse; (Musl law) revoke n
← رجعت دادن • رجعت کردن
return; relapse; (law) revoke v

رجعی /rŭj-'i/
retroactive; (law) revocable adj

رجم /rá-jīm, rajm/ stoning n
← رجم کردن stone v

i = keep, ĭ = big, u = coop, ŭ = put, y = yet, ' = (glottal stop)   167

رجوع /rŭ-jo/
looking up (in book); turning to (for help) n
رجوع دادن →/ look up (in book) v
رجوع کردن →/
look up (in book); turn to (for help) v

رحلت /rīh-lat/
passing away (fig; only for Prophet); (lit) journey n
رحلت کردن →/
pass away (fig; only for Prophet); (fig) travel vi

رحم , -ها/ارحام
/ra-hĭm, pl ar-hām/
uterus, womb; kinship ties n

رحمان /rah-mān/
merciful adj; the Merciful (God) n

رحمت /rah-mat/
mercy, compassion n

رحیم /ra-him/ Rahim (m name) n
رحیمه /ra-hi-ma/
Rahima (f name) n

رخ /rŭkh/
rook (chess); cheek; side n

رخ دادن /rŭkh dādan/
happen, take place (lit) vi

رخت /rakht/
clothes, clothing; cloth n

رخت خواب /rakht-ĭ khāb/
bedding, bedsheets n

رخت شوی /rakht-shoy/
launderer, launderess n

رخسار /rŭkh-sār/ face (lit) n
رخساره /rŭkh-sā-ra/ cheek (lit) n

رخشانه /rakh-shā-na/
Roxanne (Alexander's wife, hist) n

رخصتی /rŭkh-sa-ti/
holiday, vacation n

رخنه /rakh-na/
penetration; gap, breach n

رخه /rŭ-kha/ Rukha (dist) n

رد /rad/ rejection, denial n
رد کردن →/
reject, repudiate, deny vt

رده /ra-da/ line, row; trace n

رذالت /ra-zā-lat/ depravity n

رذایل /ra-zā-yīl, sg ra-zi-lat/
see sg رذیلت n pl

رذیلت , -ها/رذایل
/ra-zi-lat, pl ra-zā-yīl/
depravity, vice n

رزاق /ra-zāq/
Provider (God); Razaq (m name) n

رزق , -ها/ارزاق /rĭzq, pl ar-zāq/
subsistence, sustenance, daily needs n

رزگی , -ها /rĭz-gi/
crumb; chip, bit (colloq) n

رزم /rá-zĭm, razm/
fight, battle, combat n

رزمگاه /razm-gāh/ battlefield n
رزمگه /razm-gah/ see رزمگاه

رزمنده , -گان/ها /raz-mĭn-da/
figher, combatant n; combat adj

رزمی /raz-mi/
epic; related to battle adj

رزمیدن ؛ -رزم- ؛ رزمید-
/raz-mi-dan/
fight, do battle v

رژیسور /rī-zhi-sor/
director (film/theater) n

رژیم /rī-jĭm/
regime, government; diet n

رسام , -ان/ها /ra-sām/
draftsman n

رسامی کردن /ra-sā-mi kardan/
draft (draw) v

رسانه های خبری
/ra-sā-na-hā-yĭ kha-ba-ri/
the media n pl

رستاق /rŭs-tāq/ Rustaq (dist) n
رستگاری /ras-ta-ga-ri/
salvation, redemption n

رستم /rŭs-tam/
Rustam (m name) n

رستوران /ras-tu-rān/ restaurant n

رسل /rŭ-sŭl, sg ra-sul/
see sg رسول n pl

رسم /rasm, pl rŭ-sum/
custom, rule; drawing n
رسوم pl →
رسم کردن • رسم کشیدن →
draw, sketch v

رسم و رواج /rasm ŭ ra-wāj/
traditions, customs n

رسماً /ras-man, rás-/
officially, formally adv

رسمی /ras-mi/
official; formal, ceremonial adj

رسمیاً /ras-mī-yan, rás-/
see رسماً adv

رسن , -ها /ra-san/ rope n

رسوا /rŭs-wā/
dishonored, disgraced adj

رسوا کردن ←
dishonor, disgrace v

رسوایی /rŭs-wā-yi/
scandal, dishonor, disgrace n

رسوایی آور /rŭs-wā-yi ā-war/
see رسوایی آمیز adj

رسوایی آمیز /rŭs-wā-yi ā-meyz/
scandalous, disgraceful adj

رسوب , -ات/ها /rŭ-sub/
sediment, deposit n

رسوبی /rŭ-su-bi/
sedimentary; alluvial adj

رسول , -ان/ها/رسل
/ra-sul, pl rŭ-sŭl/
messenger; Rasul (m name) n

رسوم /rŭ-sum, sg rasm/
see sg رسم n pl

رسید /ra-sid/ receipt (bill) n

رسید کردن ←
enter receipts on books v

رسیدن ؛ -رس- ؛ رسید/
/ra-si-dan/-rasid-/
arrive, come; reach vi

رسیدگی /ra-si-da-gi/
ripeness; mental development;
audit; investigation n

رسیده /ra-si-da/
ripe; mentally developed;
unshaven adj

رشاد /ra-shād/
integrity; maturity; (m name) n

رشادت /ra-shā-dat/
valor, bravery n

رشته , -ها /rīsh-ta/
string; bond; relation; field of study
n

رشته تسبیح /rīsh-ta-yĭ tas-bih/
Muslim rosary n

رشته شاقول
/rīsh-ta-yĭ shā-qol, -qul (-wul)/
plumb line n

رشته های خویشاوندی
/rīsh-ta-hā-yĭ khey-sha-wan-di/
kinship ties n pl

رشته های صوتی
/rīsh-ta-hā-yĭ saw-ti/
vocal cords n pl

رشد /rŭshd/ growth; maturity n

رشوه /rīsh-wa/ see رشوت n

رشوت /rīsh-wat/ bribe n

رشوت خواستن ←
solicit a bribe

رشوت خوردن • رشوت گرفتن ←
take a bribe

رشید , -ان/ون /ra-shid/
rightly-guided (rel) adj, n; Rashid
(m name) n

رشیدان /ra-shi-dān/
Rashidan (dist) n

رشیده /ra-shi-da/
Rashida (f name) n

رعایت /rī-'ā-yat/
compliance with; regard n

رعایه /rī-'ā-ya/ n see رعایت

رعب /ra'b/ fright, fear, alarm n

رعد /ra'd/ thunder; thunderstorm n

رعد آسا /ra'd ā-sā/
thunderous adj

رضا /ra-zā/ satisfaction; assent n

رضا دادن ←
satisfy; gratify v

رضا نامه /ra-zā nā-ma/
testimonial (letter) n

رضا کار , -ان/ها /ra-zā-kār/
volunteer n

رضاعی /ra-zā-'i/
having a foster relationship adj

رضایت /ra-zā-yat/
satisfaction; assent n

رضایت بخش /ra-zā-yat bakhsh/
satisfactory adj

رطوبت /rŭ-tu-bat/
humidity; moisture n

رعایا , sg رعیت /rī-'ā-yā, sg ra-'ī-yat/
see sg رعیت n pl

رعیت /ra-'ī-yat, pl rī-'ā-yā/
subject (of monarchy); subjects (coll pl) n
رعایا ← pl
رف /raf/ ledge, mantle n
رفاه /rī-fāh/
prosperity; well-being n
رفتار /raf-tār/ see رفتاری
رفتاری /raf-tā-ri/
behavior; act; pace (of sb/sth) n
رفتن ؛ -ر- ؛ رفت- /raftan/
go; leave; die; keep doing (sth) vi
رفته , گان/ها /raf-ta/
gone; deceased (& pers) adj, n
رفته رفته /raf-ta raf-ta/
gradually adv
رفری /rĭf-ri/ referee n
رفع /raf', ráf-'a/
elimination, removal n
رفع شدن ← disappear, go away vi
رفع کردن ← eliminate, get rid of vt
رفقا /rŭ-fa-qā, sg ra-fiq/ n pl رفیق see sg
رفورم /rī-form/ n see ریفورم
رفیق /ra-fiq, pl rŭ-fa-qā/
friend; (pol) comrade n
رفقا ← pl
رفیقه /ra-fi-qa/
friend (m); girlfriend n
رقاب /rī-qāb, sg ra-qa-ba/ n pl رقبه see sg
رقابت /rī-qā-bat/
competition; jealousy n
رقابت داشتن ← be jealous vi
رقاص /ra-qās/
dancer (m); pendulum n
رقاصه /ra-qā-sa/ dancer (f) n
رقاع /rī-qā/ riqa (callig style) n
رقبا /rŭ-qa-bā, sg ra-qib/ n pl رقیب see sg
رقبه /ra-qa-ba, pl rī-qāb/
cervix; neck; region n
رقاب ← pl
رقت /rī-qat/
pity, sympathy; dilution n
رقت آور /rī-qat ā-war/ pitiful adj

رقت بار /rī-qat bār/
رقت آور adj see
رقص /raqs (rakhs)/
dance, dancing n
رقص کردن ← dance (colloq)
رقصیدن ؛ -رقص- ؛ رقصید- /raq-si-dan/
dance vi
رقم , -ها/ارقام /ra-qam, pl ar-qām/
figure, number; writing; kind, type n
رقیب , -ان/ها/رقبا /ra-qib, pl rŭ-qa-bā/
competitor, rival n
رقیه /rūq-ya/
charm, spell, incantation n
رکاب /rī-kāb/
stirrup; pedal, treadle n
رکن , -ها/ارکان /rŭ´-kŭn, rŭkn; pl ar-kān/
pillar; basic element n
رگ , -ها /rag/
vein (& bot, geol, anat) n
رگ زن /rag zan/ phlebotomist n
رگ زنی /rag za-ni/
phlebotomy, cupping n
رگ سرخ /rag sŭrkh/ artery n
رل /rŭl/ n see رول
رمال /ra-māl/ geomancer n
رمالی /ra-mā-li/ geomancy n
رمالی کردن • رمل انداختن ← practice geomancy v
رمبا /rŭm-bā/ rumba (dance) n
رمز , -ها/رموز /ramz; pl rŭ-muz (ra-)/
allegory; hint; symbol n
رمضان /ra-ma-zān/ Ramadan (month) n
رمضانی /ra-ma-zā-ni/ song of Ramadan n
رمل /rá-mīl, raml/ n see رمالی
رمل انداز /rá-mīl an-dāz/ n see رمال
رمه /ra-ma/ flock (sheep/goats) n
رموز /rŭ-muz (ra-), sg ramz/ n pl رمز see sg
رنج /ranj/ suffering; toil n

رنج بر , -ان/ها /ranj-bar/
proletarian; laborer n

رنج بران /ranj-bar-ān/
proletariat n pl

رنج بردن /ranj bŭrdan/ suffer vi

رنجش /ran-jīsh/
offense, indignation n

رنچ /rĭnch/ wrench (tool) n

رند /rĭnd/ cunning, sly adj; Sufi n

رندانه /rĭn-dā-na/ see رند adj

رنده /ran-da/
grater; plane (tool) n

رنده شده → grated

رنده کردن → grate; scrape

رندی /rĭn-di/ cunning n

رنگ /rang/ color; paint; dye; ink n

رنگ شده → colored; painted

رنگ کردن → color; paint

رنگین /ran-gin/ colorful adj

رنگین کمان /ran-gin ka-mān/
rainbow n

رو /raw/ going; pedestrian n

رو /ru, ro/ see روی n

رو آوردن <به طرف کسی>
/ru āwardan/
head for (sw); turn to <sb> v

رو برقی /raw-ĭ bar-qi/
electrical current n

رو به راه /ru-ba-rāh/
ready to go adj

رو به رو کردن <کسی>
/ru-ba-ru kardan/
cross-examine, confront <sb> vt

رو به روی <چیزی>
/ru-ba-ru(-yī)/
facing <sth> adj; straight ahead adv

رو به <چیزی> گذاشتن
/raw ba <chí-zey> gŭzāshtan/
tend towards <sth> v

رو گرم /raw-ĭ garm/ gulf stream n

روابط , sg رابطه /ra-wā-bĭt, sg rā-bĭ-ta/
see sg رابطه n pl

رواش /ra-wāsh/ rhubarb n

رواق , -ها /ra-wāq/
porch, balcony, veranda n

روان /ra-wān/
going, running; current; fluent (adj, & adv); soul, spirit n

روان شناس , -ان/ها /ra-wān shĭ-nās/
psychologist n

روان شناسی /ra-wān shĭ-nā-si/
psychology n

روان کردن /ra-wān kardan/
send (colloq) vt

روانی /ra-wā-ni/
good style, fluency n; psychological adj

روایات ضعیفه /ra-wā-yāt-ĭ za-'i-fa/
obscure rules n pl

روایت , -ها/روایات /rĭ-wā-yat, pl -yāt/
narrative n

روباه /ro-bāh/
fox; (fig) clever person n

روباه خانه /ro-bāh khā-na/
ventilation system n

روباه صفت /ro-bāh sĭ-fat/
cunning, clever adj

روبل, ru- /ro-bŭl, ru-/
ruble (currency) n

روپیه /ro-pī-ya/
rupee; (colloq) afghani n

روت /rot/ rot (kind of bread) n

روجایی /ru-jā-yi/ bedsheet n

روح , -ها/ارواح /ruh, pl ar-wāh/
soul, spirit; core, essence; (sg) breath of God, Universal Spirit n

روح الامین /ruh-ŭl-a-min/
faithful spirit (archangel Gabriel) n

روح القدس /ruh-ŭl-qŭds, -qŭ-dŭs/
Holy Spirit n

روح الله /ruh-ŭl-lāh/
spirit of God (Jesus) n

روح اللهی /ruh-ŭl-lā-hi/
having to do w/Jesus adj

روحانی , -ان/ون /ru-hā-ni/
rel leader n; sacred adj

روحانیت /ru-hā-nī-yat/
spirituality, sanctity n

روحیلا /ro-hi-lā/ see روهیلا n

روحیه /ru-hī-ya, pl -yāt/ attitude, mindset; morale n
→ روحیات pl
روحیه جهادی /ru-hī-ya-yĭ jī-hā-di/ jihad mentality n
روحیه هماهنگی /ru-hī-ya-yĭ ha-mā-han-gi/ esprit de corps n
رود /rod/ river; (mus instr) rod n
رودات /ro-dāt/ Rodat (dist, ctr Shahi Kot) n
روده /ro-da/ intestine, gut n
روده خورد /ro-da-yĭ khŭrd/ small intestine n
روده کلان /ro-da-yĭ ka-lān/ large intestine n
روز , -ها /roz/ day n; during the day adv
روز تولد /roz-ī ta-wa-lŭd/ birthdate n
روز بازپرس /roz-ī bāz-pŭrs/ see روز باز خواست n
روز بازخواست /roz-ī bāz-khāst/ Judgment Day n
روزانه /ro-zā-na/ see روزمره adj, adv
روزگار /roz-gār/ times; era adv
روزمره /roz-ma-ra/ daily, everyday adj; every day adv
روزنامه /roz-nā-ma/ newspaper; journal n
روزنامه نگار /roz-nā-ma nĭ-gār/ newspaper journalist n
روزنامه نویس /roz-nā-ma na-wis/ newspaper editor n
روزه /ro-za/ fasting, fast n
→ روزه باز کردن
• روزه خوردن
break a fast v
→ روزه داشتن be fasting v
→ روزه گرفتن fast v
روزی /ro-zi/ daily bread; Rozi (m name) n
روس , -ها /rus (ū-rus)/ Russian (pers) n
روسپی /ros-pi/ harlot, whore (arch) n
روستا , -ها /ros-tā/ village n

روستا زاده , ـگان /ros-tā-zā-da/ villager n; rural adj
روستایی , -ان/ها /ros-tā-yi/ villager n; rural adj
روسی , -ها (ū-)/ /ru-si/ Russian (& pers, lang) adj, n
روسیه /ru-sī-ya/ Russia (country) n
روش , -ها /ra-wĭsh/ way, manner; approach, method n
روش تدریس /ra-wĭsh-ī tad-ris/ instructional method n
روشن /ro-shan/ clear, obvious; bright adj
روشن دل , -ان/ها /ro-shan dĭl/ see روشن دل adj, n
روشن فکر , -ان/ها /ro-shan fĭ-kĭr/ open-minded (& pers) adj, n
روشن کردن /ro-shan kardan/ light; switch on (light) vt
روشنی /rosh-ni/ light; brightness n
روغن /ro-ghan/ oil (for cooking) n
روغن جواری /ro-ghan-ī ja-wā-ri/ corn oil n
روغن خوک /ro-ghan-ī khuk/ lard n
روغن داغ /ro-ghan dāgh/ pan, saucepan n
روغن زرد /ro-ghan-ī zard/ ghee, clarified butter n
روغن زیتون /ro-ghan-ī zay-tun/ olive oil n
روک /ra-wak/ drawer (in table) n
رول /rol/ role, part; steamroller n
رول بازی کردن /rol bā-zi kardan/ play a role v
رولت /ro-lĭt/ roller skates n
روم /rum/ Roman Empire (hist) n
روم شرقی /rum-ī shar-qi/ Byzantine Empire (hist) n
روما /ro-mā/ Rome (capital) n
روماتزم /ro-mā-tey-zŭm/ rheumatism n
رومان /ro-mān/ novel n
رومانیا /ro-mā-nĭ-yā/ Romania (country) n

رومانیایی , -ان/ها /ro-mā-nī-yā-yi/
Romanian (& pers) adj, n

رومانیه n /ro-mā-nī-ya/ see رومانیا

رومی /ru-mi/
Rumi (13th-c poet) n; Roman,
Mediterranean adj

بحیرۀ رومی ←
Mediterranean Sea

روند /ra-wand/
course; progression n

رونق /raw-naq/
flourish; liveliness n

رونق دادن /raw-naq dādan/
flourish, grow well or abundantly v

روهینا rohina (steel) n /ro-hi-nā/

روئیدن ؛ -روی- ؛ -روید
/ro-yi-dan/
grow (e.g., plant, crop) vi

روهیلا /ro-hi-lā/
Rohilla (P group, hist) n

روی zinc (arch) n /roy/

روی /ruy, roy/
reason; surface; face n

روی آوردن <به چیزی>
/ruy āwŭrdan/
convert to (rel); take (sth) up v

روی پاک hand towel n /ruy-pāk/

روی پت /ruy-pŭt/
face covered (m) adj

روی جایی bedsheet n /ruy-jā-yi/

روی داد n /ruy dād/ see رویداد

روی دادن /ruy dādan/
happen; (colloq) support vi

روی دار /ruy dār/
respected, in good standing adj

روی کش /ruy kash/
bedspread; cover; plating n

روی گرداندن <از چیزی>
/ruy gardāndan/
shun, evade <sth> v

روی لچ /ruy lŭch/
face uncovered (f) adj

روی هم رفته /ruy-ī ham raf-ta/
altogether adv

رویه n /ra-wī-ya/ see روش

رویا , -ها /ro-yā/
dream; Roya (f name) n

رویاندن ؛ -رویان- ؛ -رویاند-
/ro-yān-dan/
grow, make (sth) grow vt

رویداد , -ها /ruy-dād/
event (& current) n

رویبدن vi /ro-yi-dan/ see روئیدن

رها کردن /rĭ-hā kardan (ey-lā)/
release; divorce (lit) vt

رهایی /rĭ-hā-yi/
relief; deliverance n

هایی بخشیدن /rĭ-hā-yi bakhshidan/
relieve, give relief to vt

رهبان /rŭh-bān, sg rā-hĭb/
see sg راهب (& used as sg) n pl

رهبانیت /rŭh-bā-nī-yat/
monasticism; monks' order n

رهبر , -ها/ان /rah-bar/
leader (& pol); guide n

رهبری /rah-ba-ri/
leadership (& pol) n

رهسپار /rah-sĭ-pār/
proceeding; start of journey adj

رهنمای /rah-nŭ-mā-yĭ/
guidance; guide n

رهنمای تلفون
/rah-nŭ-mā-yĭ tĭ-lĭ-fun/
phone book n

رهنمایی کردن
/rah-nŭ-mā-yi kardan/
guide vt

رهی adj /ra-hi/ see راهی

رؤسا /rŭ-'a-sā, sg ra-'is (re-yis)/
see sg رئیس n pl

رئیس , -ان/ها/رؤسا
/ra-'is (re-yis), pl rŭ-'a-sā/
chief; president; manager n

رئیس بلدیه /ra-'is-ī ba-la-dī-ya/
mayor n

رئیس پارلمان /ra-'is-ī pār-la-mān/
Speaker of Parliament n

رئیس پولیس /ra-'is-ī po-lis/
police chief n

رئیس جمهور /ra-'is jam-hur/
president (of republic) n

رئیس جمهوری /ra-'is jam-hu-ri/
presidential adj

رئیس فابریکه /ra-'is-ī fāb-ri-ka/
general manager (factory) n

رئیس قبیله /ra-'is-ĭ qa-bi-la/
tribal chieftain n

رئیس مجلس /ra-'is-ĭ maj-lĭs/
رئیس پارلمان see n

رئیس هیئت /ra-'is-ĭ hay-'at/
chief of staff n

ریا /rĭ-yā/ hypocrisy, insincerity n

ریاست , -ها /rĭ-yā-sat/
office, department; leadership n

ریاست ضبط احوالات
/rĭ-yā-sat-ĭ zabt-ĭ ah-wā-lāt/
Intelligence Department (hist) n

ریاست مستقل ارگان های محلی
/rĭ-yā-sat-ĭ mŭs-ta-qĭl-ĭ ar-gān-hā-yĭ ma-ha-li/
Independent Directorate of Local
Goverance, IDLG n

ریاست استخبارات
/rĭ-yā-sat-ĭ ĭs-tĭkh-bār-āt/
intelligence department (mil,
espionage) n

ریاست جمهوری
/rĭ-yā-sat-ĭ jam-hu-ri/
office of the presidency n

ریاست مصونیت ملی
/rĭ-yā-sat-ĭ ma-su-nĭ-yat-ĭ mĭ-li/
National Directorate of Security,
NDS n

ریاض /rĭ-yāz/ Riyadh (capital) n

ریاضی /ri-yā-zi/
math, mathematics; mathematical
n, adj

ریاضی دان , -ان/ها /ri-yā-zi dān/
mathematician n

ریاضیات /ri-yā-zĭ-yāt/
ریاضی see n

ریاکار /rĭ-yā-kār/
insincere; hypocritical adj

ریال /rĭ-yāl/ riyal (currency) n

ریحان /rey-hān/
sweet basil; reyhan (callig style) n

ریختاندن ؛ -ریزان- ؛ ریختاند-
/reykh-tān-dan/
pour; spill; shed (blood) vt

ریختن ؛ -ریز- ؛ ریخت-
/reykh-tan/
pour; shed; spill; secrete vi

ریخته گری /reykh-ta ga-ri/
foundry n

ریزرف /ri-zarf/ reservation n
← ریزرف کردن
make a reservation

ریزش /rey-zĭsh/
pouring; cold, catarrh n

ریزش <کسی را> گرفتن
/rey-zĭsh gĭrĭftan/
catch <sb's> cold v

ریزه /rey-za/
small piece, bit n; small adj
← ریزه کردن chop, dice vt

ریسمان /reys-mān/ rope n

ریسمان غرغره
/reys-mān-ĭ ghar-gha-ra/
noose n

ریش , -ها /rish/ beard n
← ریش کشیدن grow a beard v

ریش /reysh/
wound n; wounded adj

ریش سفید , -ان/ها /rish-ĭ sa-feyd/
elder n; gray-bearded adj

ریشخند /reysh-khŭnd/
ridicule, mockery n; ridiculed adj
← ریشخند زدن • ریشخند کردن
• ریشخندی کردن
ridicule, mock v

ریشخندی /reysh-khŭn-di/
ریش خند see n

ریشه , -ها /ri-sha/ root, stem n

ریشه دواندن /ri-sha dawāndan/
take root vi

ریشه شماره دو
/ri-sha-ĭ shŭ-ma-ra-yĭ du/
past tense stem n

ریشه شماره یک
/ri-sha-ĭ shŭ-ma-ra-yĭ yak/
present tense stem n

ریشه شناس, -ان/ها/ri-sha shĭ-nās/
etymologist n

ریشه شناسی /ri-sha shĭ-nā-si/
etymology n

ریشه کردن /ri-sha kardan/
take root vi

ریفورم /ri-form/ reform n

ریگ /reyg/
sand; Reyg (dist, see & خان نشین)
n

ریگستان /rey-gīs-tān/
Reygestan (dist); see ریگ n

ریگویدا /rig-wi-dā/
Rigveda (Hindu text) n

ریگی /rey-gi/
sandy; made of sand adj

ریل /reyl/ railway; railroad train n

ریم /rim/ pus n

ریه , -ها /rī-ya/ lung n

ریوی /rī-ya-wi/ pulmonary adj

ز

زابل /zā-būl/ Zabul (prov) n

زادگاه /zād-gāh/
birthplace, homeland n

زار /zār/
vile; weak; bitter adj; czar n

زارع , -ان/ین /zā-rey/
farmer, peasant n

زاری /zā-ri/
lamentation, mourning;
supplication; Zari (dist) n

زاری کردن /zā-ri kardan/
lament, mourn; supplicate v

زاج /zāj-ĭ sabz/
vitriol, sulfate n
زاج سبز ferrous sulfate ←
زاج سفید zinc sulfate ←
زاج کبود copper sulfate ←

زاغ , -ان/ها /zāgh/
crow, raven (bird) n; black &
shiny; cunning adj

زاغ آبی /zā-ghā-bi (-wi)/
cormorant (bird) n

زاغچه /zāgh-cha/
jackdaw (bird) n

زاغنول /zāgh-nol/
pick; pliers (tool) n

زانو /zā-nu/ knee n
زانو خم /zā-nu kham/
joint (pipe) n
زانو زدن /zā-nu zadan/ kneel vi

زاویه , -ها/زوایا
/zā-wī-ya, pl -wā-yā/
angle; corner, nook, alcove n
زاویه حاده acute angle ←
زاویه قایمه right angle ←
زاویه منفرجه obtuse angle ←

زاهد , -ان/ها /zā-hĭd/
hermit, ascetic n; austere adj

زاهد فریب /zā-hĭd fī-reyb/
very beautiful (lit) adj

زاهدانه /zā-hī-dā-na/
austere, hermit-like (& adv) adj,
adv

زاهدی /zā-hī-di/
austerity, hermit's life n

زایاندن ؛ زایاند- ؛ -زایان-
/zā-yān-dan/
assist in childbirth vt

زاید <از چیزی> /zā-yĭd/
surplus <to sth> adj

زایده , -ها /zā-yī-da/ appendage n

زایر , -ان/ین/زوار /zā-yĭr, pl za-wār/
visitor, pilgrim n

زایشگاه /zā-yīsh-gāh/
maternity ward/hospital n

زایمان /zāy-mān/ childbirth n

زاییدن ؛ زایید- ؛ -زای-
/zā-yi-dan/
give birth to (d.o. does not take
را- marker); bear young; bring
forth vt

زبان , -ها /za-bān (zŭ-, -wān)/
tongue; language n
زبان اصطلاحی colloq lang ←
زبان علامه یی sign lang ←
زبان مادری native lang ←

زبان آور /za-bān ā-war/
eloquent adj

زبان بریده /za-bān bŭ-ri-da/
mute, silent (& defiantly) adj

زبان بسته /za-bān bas-ta/
silenced (forcibly) adj

زبان دادن /za-bān dādan/
promise (fig) v

زبان دار /za-bān dār/ eloquent adj

زبان دراز /za-bān da-rāz/
indiscreet; insolent adj

زبان شناس , -ان/ها
/za-bān shī-nās/
linguist n

زبان شناسی /za-bān shī-nā-si/
linguistics n

زبان کردن /za-bān kardan/
revile, speak ill of vt

زبان گرفتگی /za-bān gǐ-rǐf-ta-gi/
stuttering, stammering n

زبان محاوره
/za-bān-ǐ mū-hā-wǐ-ra/
see زبان اصطلاحی n

زبانی /za-bā-ni/
oral, verbal; insincere; linguistic
adj

زبده /zǔb-da/
choice, best adj; (vulg) gist n

زبرجد /za-bar-jad/
chrysolite, olivine n

زبرجد هندی /za-bar-jad-ǐ hǐn-di/
yellow topaz n

زبردست , -ان/ها /za-bar-dast/
superior; strong; oppressive (&
pers) adj, n

زبردستی /za-bar-das-ti/
superiority n

زبور Psalms (bibl) n /za-bur/
زبیده /zǔ-bay-da/
Zubayda (f name; kind of
calendula) n

زپ zipper n /zǐp/
زجاجیه crystal lens n /zǔ-jā-jǐ-ya/
زچه /za-cha/
post-partum (& pers) adj, n

زحل Saturn (planet) n /zǔ-hal/
زحمت , -ها/زحمات
/zah-mat, pl za-ha-māt/
trouble, bother n

زحمت کش -,ان/ها /zah-mat kash/
laborer n; hard-working adj

زحمت کشیدن /zah-mat kashidan/
bother, take the trouble to v

زخ knot (on tree); wart n /zakh/
زخ بلوط /zakh-ǐ ba-lut/
knot on oak tree; (fig) ugly &
coarse pers n

زخم /zá-khǐm, zakhm/
injury, wound n

زخمه plectrum (arch) n /zakh-ma/
زخمی , -ها /zakh-mi/
injured, wounded (& pers) adj, n

زد و خورد /zad ǔ khǔrd/
fighting (fig) n

زد و خورد کردن →
fight (fig) v

زدگی /za-da-gi/
bruise (on fruit); hole (in clothing)
n

زدن ؛ -زن- ؛ -زد-
/zadan; /méyzanǔm//
hit, beat, strike vt

زر gold; (fig) riches n /zar/
زراعت /zǐ-rā-'at/
agriculture, farming n

زراعت علمی /zǐ-rā-'at-ǐ ǐl-mi/
agronomy n

زراعت کار farmer n /zǐ-rā-'at kār/
زراعت کردن /zǐ-rā-'at kardan/
farm vi

زراعتی /zǐ-rā-'a-ti/
agricultural; arable adj

زرتشت see زردشت n /zar-tǔsht/
زرتشتی see زردشتی /zar-tǔsh-ti/
زرخرید /zar-kha-rid/
Zarkharid (ctr) n

زرخیز /zar-kheyz/
fertile, productive adj

زرد yellow adj /zard/
زردآلو apricot n /zar-dā-lu/
زردچوبه /zard-cho-ba/
turmeric (spice) n

زردشت /zar-dǔsht, -dasht/
Zoroaster, Zarathustra n

زردشتی , -ان/ها
/zar-dǔsh-ti, -dash-/
Zoroastrian (& pers) adj, n

زردک carrot n /zar-dak/
زردی jaundice, icterus n /zar-di/
زرشک barberry n /zǐ-rǐshk/
زرشویی /zar-sho-yi/
gold panning n

زرشویی کردن →
pan for gold v

زرع /zá-ra, zar/
sowing, cultivation n

زرع کردن →
sow, cultivate vt

زرغول see زرشک n /zar-ghol/

زرغون /zar-ghun/
tonic (med); Zarghun (m name) *n*

زرغون شهر /zar-ghun shār/
Zarghun Shahr (dist) *n*

زرغونه /zar-ghu-na/
Zarghuna (f name; Kabul f high school) *n*

زرغونی /zar-ghu-ni/
tonic (med) *n*

زرق /zarq/ injection; hypocrisy *n*
← زرق کردن inject *v*

زرق و برق /zarq ŭ barq/
gaudiness, garishness *phrs*
← زرق و برق داشتن
be gaudy, be garish *v*

زرق و برق دار /zarq ŭ barq dār/
gaudy, garish *phrs*

زرکول /zar-kol/ Zarkol (lake) *n*

زرگر /zar-gar/
goldsmith, silversmith *n*

زرگری /zar-ga-ri/
goldsmithing; goldsmith's shop *n*

زرمت /zŭr-mat, -mal/
Zurmal (dist) *n*

زرمل /zŭr-mal/ see زرمت

زرنج /za-ranj/ Zaranj (seat) *n*

زرنگ /za-rang/
clever, smart; cunning *adj*

زرنگی /za-ran-gi/
cleverness; cunning *n*

زرورق /zar-wa-raq/
gold leaf, gold foil *n*

زره /zĭ-rĭh/ armor; chain mail *n*

زره پوش /zĭ-rĭh-posh/
armored, ironclad *adj*

زره دار /zĭ-rĭh-dār/
armored, armor-plated *adj*

زرین /za-rin/ golden *adj*

زشت /zĭsht/
crude, rough; ugly *adj*

زشت گوی /zĭsht-goy/
crude, vulgar *adj*

زشت گویی کردن /zĭsht-go-yi kardan/
be crude, be vulgar *adj*

زعامت /za-'ā-mat/
leadership (esp pol) *n*

زعفران /za'-fa-rān/
saffron (herb) *n*

زعفرانی /za'-fa-rā-ni/
saffron-colored; pale *adj*

زعم /zam/ claim, allegation *n*

زعما /zŭ-'a-mā, sg za-yim/
see sg زعیم *n pl*

زعیم , -ها/زعما /za-yim, pl zŭ-'a-mā/
leader, prominent pers (pol) *n*

زغاره /za-ghā-ra (zŭ-ghā-la)/
dough for one loaf *n*

زغال /zŭ-ghāl/ charcoal *n*

زغال چوب /zŭ-ghāl-ĭ chob/
wood charcoal *n*

زغال سنگ /zŭ-ghāl-ĭ sang/
coal *n*

زغاله /zŭ-ghā-la/ see زغاره

زغر /zĭ-ghĭr/ flax (plant) *n*

زغن /za-ghan/ kite (bird) *n*

زفاف /zŭ-fāf/ wedding *n*

زفیر /za-fir/ exhalation *n*

زقوم /zŭ-qum (-qŭm)/
cactus; zuqum (tree) *n*

زکات /za-kāt/
zakat, alms tax *n*

زکات دادن /za-kāt dādan/
donate, give zakat *v*

زکریا /zĭk-rĭ-yā/
Zechariah (bibl; m name) *n*

زلانیه /zŭ-lā-nĭ-ya/
aqueous humor *n*

زلزله /zĭl-zĭ-la/ earthquake *n*

زلزله سنج /zĭl-zĭ-la sanj/
seismograph *n*

زلزله شناسی /zĭl-zĭ-la shĭ-nā-si/
seismology *n*

زلف, -ان/ها /zŭlf/ lock (of hair) *n*

زلیخا, -زی /zŭ-lay-khā, zĭ-/
Zuleyka (f name, Potiphar's wife) *n*

زمام /zĭ-mām/
reins; (fig) control *n*

زمام دار, -ان/ها /zĭ-mām-dār/
statesman; pers in charge *n*

زمام داری /zĭ-mām dā-ri/
statesmanship; being in charge *n*

زمان /za-mān/
time; age; (gram) tense *n*
→ زمان آینده • زمان مستقبل
future tense
→ زمان حال present tense
زمان ساز /za-mān sāz/
turncoat, opportunist *n*
زمانی /za-mā-ni/
chronological *adj*
زمبار /zam-bār/ Zambar (ctr) *n*
زمرد /za-ma-rūd/ emerald *n*
زمردین /za-ma-rū-din/
emerald-colored *adj*
زمره /zūm-ra/ group (of people) *n*
زمستان /zī-mīs-tān, za-/ winter *n*
زمستانی /zī-mīs-tā-ni/ winter *adj*
زمین /za-min/
land; the Earth; floor; territory *n*
زمین جنب /za-min-jūmb/
earthquake *n*
زمین دار , -ان/ها /za-min dār/
landowner; farmer *n*
زمین داری /za-min dā-ri/
landowning; farming *n*
زمین لرزه /za-min lar-za/
earthquake *n*
زمینه , -ها /za-mi-na/
basis, base, ground *n*
زمینه آماده ساختن
/za-mi-na ā-mad sākhtan/
prepare the ground for *v*
زمینه برابر کردن
/za-mi-na ba-rā-bar kardan/
see زمینه آماده ساختن *v*
زن , -ان/ها /zan/
woman; wife *n*
زن ایور /zan ey-war/
sister-in-law (husband's brother's wife) *n*
زن گرفتن /zan gīrīftan/
marry, take as a wife *vt*
زن و شوی /zan ŭ shuy/
husband & wife *n*
زنا کردن /zī-nā kardan/
fornicate, commit adultery *vi*
زنادقه /za-nā-dī-qa, sg zan-diq/
see sg زندیق *n pl*
زنادیق /za-nā-diq/ *n pl* see زنادقه

زناکار , -ان/ها /zī-nā-kār/
adulterer *n*; debauched *adj*
زنبق /zam-baq/ iris (flower) *n*
زنبور , -ان/ها /zam-bur/ wasp *n*
زنبور خانه /zam-bur khā-na/
wasp's nest *n*
زنبور عسل /zam-bur-ī a-sal/
bee *n*
زنبور گاو /zam-bur gāw/ hornet *n*
زنجبیل /zan-ja-bil (-fil)/ ginger *n*
زنجیر , -ها /zan-jir/ chain, fetters *n*
زنجیر و زولانه
/zan-jir ŭ zaw-lā-na/
chains & shackles *n*
زنچه /zīn-cha/ effeminate *adj*
زنخ /za-nakh (-naq)/ chin *n*
زنخدان /za-nakh-dān/ see زنخ *n*
زند /zand/ forearm bone, ulna *n*
زندار /zan-dār/ married (of m) *adj*
زندان /zīn-dān/ prison, jail *n*
زندانی , -ان/ها /zīn-dā-ni/
prisoner *n*; captive *adj*
زندانی جنگ /zīn-dā-ni-yī jang/
prisoner of war *n*
زندقه /zan-da-qa/ atheism (lit) *n*
زندگی /zīn-da-gi/ life *n*
زندگی داشتن /zīn-da-gi dāshtan/
see زنده بودن *v*
زندگی کردن /zīn-da-gi kardan/
see زنده بودن *v*
زنده , -گان/ها /zīn-da/
alive *adj*; living being *n*
زنده بودن /zīn-da budan/
live, be alive *vi*
زنده جان , -ها /zīn-da-jān/
living creature; Zenda Jan (dist) *n*
زندیق
/zan-diq; pl za-nā-dī-qa, za-nā-diq/
atheist (lit) *n*
→ زنادقه • زنادیق pl
زنق /za-naq/ *n* see زنخ
زنگ /zang/
bell; gong; ringing; rust *n*
زنگ خطر /zang-ī kha-tar/
alarm (sound) *n*
زنگ دار /zang-dār/
having an alarm *adj*

زنگ دروازه /zang-ĭ dar-wā-za/
doorbell n

زنگ زدن /zang zadan/
rust, corrode v

زنگ زده /zang za-da/
rusted, rusty adj

زنگار /zan-gār/
verdigris (color) (lit) adj

زنگوله /zan-go-la/
bell (small); icicle n

زنگیر /zang-gir/
head (of camel) n

زنه خان /za-na khān/
Zana Khan (dist) n

زنی /za-ni/ womanhood n

زنیه /zĭn-ya/ zinnia (flower) n

زوار /za-wār/ pl زایر n sg see

زوایا /za-wā-yā, sg zā-wī-/
زاویه n pl sg see

زوج /zawj, pl az-wāj/
husband; couple; even (number) n
ازواج ←
pl

زوجه, -ها/زوجات /zaw-ja, pl -jāt/
wife n

زود /zud/
soon, early; quickly adv

زود آشنا /zu-dāsh-nā/
friendly, sociable adj

زود باور /zud-bā-war/
gullible, credulous adj

زود رنج /zud-ranj/
touchy, oversensitive adj

زود گذر /zud-gŭ-zar/
fleeting, ephemeral adj

زودتر رفتن /zud-tar raftan/
hurry up v

زودتر شدن /zud-tar shŭdan/
see زودتر رفتن v

زور /zor/ strength, power, force n

زور آور /zor ā-war/
strongman, oppressor n

زورق /zaw-raq/ rowboat, skiff n

زوف /zuf/
plantain (& seed, med) n

زولانه /zaw-lā-na/
shackle, manacle, fetter n

زولوجی /zu-lo-ji/ zoology n

زون /zon/ zone, region, area n

زه /zĭh/ string, catgut string n

زهار /zĭ-hār/ pubis, pubes n

زهدان /zĭh-dān/
womb, uterus (anat) n

زهر /zá-hĭr, zahr/
poison; venom n

← زهر خوردن be poisoned v

← زهر دادن poison vt

← زهر داشتن be poisonous v

زهر آلود /zá-hĭr ā-lud/
poisoned, poisonous adj

زهر آگین /zá-hĭr ā-gin/
see زهر آلود adj

زهر چشم /zá-hĭr chĭ´-shĭm/
venomous looks n

زهروی /zŭh-ra-wi/ venereal adj

زهره /zŭh-ra/
Zuhra (f name); Venus (planet) n

زهریت /zah-rī-yat/ toxicity n

زیاد /zĭ-yād (zyāt)/
much, many adj; too much adv

زیاد و کم /zĭ-yād ŭ kam/
more or less phrs

زیادت /zĭ-yā-dat/
increase, growth, excess n

زیادتاً /zĭ-yā-da-tan, -dá-/
in addition adv

زیادتر <از چیزی> /zĭ-yād-tar/
more <than sth> adj

زیادتی /zĭ-yā-da-ti/
surplus, excess adj

زیاده /zĭ-yā-da/
more; excessive adj

زیاده از حد /zĭ-yā-da az had/
excessively, too much adv

زیاده بر <چیزی> /zĭ-yā-da bar/
adv زیاده از حد see

زیارت , -ها/زیارات
/zĭ-yā-rat, pl -rāt/
shrine; pilgrimage; formal visit n

زیارت کردن /zĭ-yā-rat kardan/
make a pilgrimage v

زیارت گاه /zĭ-yā-rat gāh/ shrine n

زیان /zĭ-yān/ harm, detriment n

زیان آور /zĭ-yān ā-war/
harmful, detrimental adj

زیبا /zey-bā/
beautiful; graceful adj

زیباک /zey-bāk/ Zeybak (dist) n

زیباکی , -ان/ها /zey-bā-ki/
Zeybaki (pers, lang) *n*

زیبایی /zey-bā-yi/
beauty *n*; cosmetic *adj*

زیبایی شناس ، -ان/ها /zey-bā-yi shī-nās/
aesthete, aesthetician *n*

زیبایی شناسی /zey-bā-yi shī-nā-si/
aesthetics *n*

زیتون /zay-tun/ olive *n*

زیر /zeyr(-ī)/
under *prep*; below, down *adv*

زیر /zir/ high-pitched *adj*

زیر بغل /zeyr-ī ba-ghal/
underarm, armpit *n*

زیر بنا /zeyr bī-nā/ infrastructure *n*

زیر بنایی /zeyr bī-nā-yi/
infrastructural *adj*

زیر خانه /zeyr khā-na/
basement, cellar *n*

زیر دست , -ان/ها /zeyr dast/
inferior, subordinate (& pers) *adj*, *n*

زیر گوش /zeyr gosh/ earring *n*

زیر نگین آوردن /zeyr-ī nǐ-gin āwūrdan/
subjugate, bring under control *vt*

زیرا /zi-rā/ because *conj*

زیرا که /zi-rā kī, key/
see زیرا *conj*

زیرپوش /zeyr-posh/ underwear *n*

زیرپیراهنی /zeyr-pay-rā-ha-ni/
undershirt *n*

زیرجامه /zeyr-jā-ma/
underclothes *n*

زیروک /zi-ruk/ Ziruk (dist) *n*

زیره /zi-ra/ cumin (spice) *n*

زیره یی /zi-ra-yi/
cumin-colored *adj*

زین /zin/ saddle; seat *n*

زینه /zi-na/ ladder; stairs, steps *n*

زینه دورانی /zi-na-yǐ daw-rā-ni/
escalator *n*

زیور , -ها /zey-war/
jewelry; ornament; Zeywar (m name) *n*

ژ

ژاد /zhād/ *n* [< F] jade

ژاری /zhā-rii/ *n* see ژری

ژاژ خایی /zhāzh khā-yi/
babbling, prattling *n*

ژاژ خایی کردن ←
babble, prattle

ژاله /zhā-la/
hail; starch (for cooking); ice floes *n*

ژاندارم /zhān-dārm/ gendarme *n*

ژاندارمه /zhān-dār-ma/
gendarmerie *n*

ژرف /zharf/ deep *adj*

ژرف نگر /zharf nǐ-gar/
see ژرفبین *adj*

ژرفا /zhar-fā/ depth *n*

ژرفبین /zharf-bin/
wise, insightful *adj*

ژری /zhī-ri/ Zheri (dist) *n*

ژنده /zhan-da/
worn-out (clothes) *adj*

ژنده پوش /zhan-da posh/
dervish *n*; clothed in rags *adj*

ژنیو /zhū-nayw/ Geneva (city) *n*

ژوبین /zho-bin/ javelin (arch) *n*

ژورنال /zhor-nāl/ journal *n*

ژورنالیست /zhor-nā-list/
journalist, reporter *n*

ژورنالیستی /zhor-nā-lis-ti/
journalistic *adj*

ژوند /zha-wand/ *n* see جوند

ژیان /zhī-yān/ angry, fierce *adj*

ژیری /zhi-ri/ *n* see ژری

ژیکلور /zhik-lor/
spray nozzle, spritzer *n*

ژیگولو /zhi-go-lo/
gigolo, fop, dandy *n*

ژیولوژست /zhī-yo-lo-zhīst/
see جیالوجست

ژیولوژی /zhī-yo-lo-zhi/
see جیالوجی *n*

س

سابق /sā-bīq/ former, previous *adj*

سابقاً /sā-bǐ´-qan/
formerly, previously *adv*

سابقه دار /sā-bǐ-qa dār/
experienced, longtime *adj*

سابقه دارتر , -ان/ها <از کسی>
/sā-bǐ-qa-dār-tar/
senior <to sb> *adj*

سابقه داری /sā-bǐ-qa-dā-ri/
experience, seniority *n*

← سابقه داری داشتن
be experienced, be senior *v*

سات /sāt/ ساعت see *n*

ساتنمن /sā-tan-man/
sergeant, NCO (police) *n*

ساتونکی /sā-tun-kay/
patrolman (police) *n*

ساحر , -ان/ها /sā-hǐr/
sorcerer *n*; enchanting *adj*

ساحرانه /sā-hǐ-rā-na/
enchanting *adj*; magically *adv*

ساحره , -ات/ها /sā-hǐ-ra, pl -rāt/
sorceress, witch *n*

ساحوی /sā-ha-wi/
regional *adj*

ساحه , -ها/ساحات
/sā-ha, pl -hāt/
region, area *n*

ساختار , -ها /sākh-tār/
sector; structure *n*

ساختگی /sākh-ta-gi/
artificial; false *adj*

ساختمان /sākht-mān, sākh-tǔ-/
construction; structure *n*

ساختن ؛ -ساز- ؛ ساخت-
/sākhtan/
make; build; suit, agree with;
counterfeit *vt*

ساخته کاری /sākh-ta kā-ri/
forgery *n*

← ساخته کاری کردن
forge, counterfeit *v*

سادات , sg sa-yǐd /sā-dāt/
see sg سید *n pl*

سادو /sā-du/
flatterer; rel storyteller *n*

ساده /sā-da/
foolish; simple; plain *adj*

ساده دل , -ان/ها /sā-da dǐl/
sincere, open (& pers) *adj, n*

سارا /sā-rā/ Sara (f name) *n*

ساربان , -ان/ها /sār-bān (-wān)/
camel driver *n*

سارق , -ین /sā-rǐq/ burglar *n*

سارمن /sār-man/ captain, CPT *n*

سارنگ /sā-rang/
sarang (mus instr) *n*

سارنگی /sā-ran-gi/
sarang player *n*

سارنمن /sā-ran-man/
commissioned police officer *n*

ساری /sā-ri/
infectious *adj*; sari *n*

ساز , -ها /sāz/
music; musical instrument *n*

← ساز کردن make music *v*

ساز تاری /sāz-ǐ tā-ri/
string instrument *n*

ساز دمی /sāz-ǐ da-mi/
wind instrument *n*

ساز ضربی /sāz-ǐ zar-bi/
percussive instrument *n*

ساز و آواز /sāz ǔ ā-wāz/
music & singing *n phrs*

ساز و برگ /sāz ǔ barg/
equipment; tools *n*

ساز و سامان /sāz ǔ sā-mān/
see ساز و برگ *n*

سازش /sā-zǐsh/
compromise; agreement *n*

← سازش کردن
compromise; agree *v*

سازمان , -ها /sāz-mān/
organization *n*

سازمان بیرون حکومت
/sāz-mān-ǐ bey-run-ǐ hǔ-ko-mat/
non-governmental organization *n*

سازمان پیمان اتلانتیک شمالی
/sāz-mān-ǐ pay-mān-ǐ at-lān-tik-ǐ
sha-mā-li/
NATO, North Atlantic Treaty
Organization *n*

سازمان صحی جهان
/sāz-mān-ǐ sǐ-hi-yǐ ja-hān/
WHO, World Health Organization *n*

سازمان غیر انتفاعی
/sāz-mān-ǐ ghayr-ǐ ǐn-tǐ-fā-'i/
non-profit organization *n*

سازمان غیر دولت /sāz-mān-ī ghayr-ī daw-lat/
n سازمان بیرون حکومت see

سازماندهی /sāz-mān-da-hi/
planning n

← سازماندهی کردن
make plans v

سازمانی /sāz-mā-ni/
organizational adj

سازنده , ـگان /sā-zīn-da/
musician; manufacturer n

ساسانی , ـان/ها /sā-sā-ni/
Sassanid n; Sassanian adj (hist)

ساعت , ـها/ساعات /sā-'at (sāt), pl -'āt/
clock, watch; time n

ساعت تیری , ـها /sā-'at-ī tey-ri/
festivity, fun; pastime n

ساعت درسی /sā-'at-ī dar-si/
classroom hour, lesson n

ساعت ریگی /sā-'at-ī rey-gi/
hourglass n

ساغر /sā-ghar/
Saghar (dist); wine bowl (lit) n

ساغری /sāgh-ri/
rump, croup n

ساق /sāq/
calf (of leg); shank n

سال , ـها/سالیان /sāl, pl sā-lī-yān/
year; age n

سال خورده /sāl khūr-da/
long-lived adj

سالار , ـان/ها /sā-lār/
leader; commander n

سالار جنگ /sā-lār-ī jang/
warlord n

سالانه /sā-lā-na/
annual, yearly adj; annually adv
← بودجۀ سالانه
annual budget

سالروز /sāl-roz/ n مدت see

سالک , ـان /sā-līk/
follower (Sufi); wayfarer n

سالگرد /sāl-gard/ n سالگره see

سالگره /sāl-gī-ra/
anniversary n

سالگره تولد /sāl-gī-ra-yī ta-wa-lūd/
birthday n

سالنگ /sā-lang/ Salang (dist) n

سالون /sā-lun/ living room n

ساله /sā-la/
of (a given) age adj
← طفل دو ساله
two-year-old child

سالیان /sā-lī-yān, sg sāl/
n سال sg pl see

سامان /sā-mān/
furnishings; utensils; order n

← سامان دادن
arrange, put in order v

سامانه /sā-mā-na/
ostentation, pomp n

← سامانه کردن
preen, engage in pomp

سامانی , ـان/ها /sā-mā-ni/
Samanid n; Samanian adj (hist)

سامعه /sā-mǐ-'a/ n hearing (sense)

سامی , ـان/ها /sā-mi/
Semite (pers) n

سامی /sā-mi/
Semitic adj

سان /sān/ calico; type, sort n

سانتی گراد /sān-ti-gī-rād/
Celsius, centigrade adj

سانتی گرید /sān-ti-gī-reyd/
adj سانتی گراد see

ساواک /sā-wāk/
SAVAK (Iranian Shah's intelligence service) n

سایر , ـین /sā-yīr/ rest, remaining n

سایقه , ـها/سایقات /sā-yī-qa, pl -qāt/
incentive, motive; stimulus n

سایه /sā-ya/
shadow; ghost; gloom n

سایه بان /sā-ya-bān/
awning, canopy n

سایه روشن /sā-ya ro-shan/
contrast; light & shadow n

سبب , ـها/اسباب /sa-bab, pl as-bāb/
cause, reason; means n

سبد /sa-bad (-bat)/
basket (esp wicker) n

سبت /sa-bat/ n سبد see

سبز /sabz (sawz)/ green adj, n

سبز پوش /sabz posh/
n خواجه سبز پوش see

سبزه /sab-za/
grass n; dark-skinned adj

182   a = cup, ā = long, aw = now, ay = sigh, e = bet, ey = obey

سبزه زار /sab-za zār/
meadow, grassland n

سبزی , -ها/جات /sab-zi/
herb; vegetable; spinach n

سبزی پالک /sab-zi-yī pā-lak/
spinach n

سبق , -ها/اسباق /sa-baq, pl as-bāq/
lesson; taking lead in race n

← سبق خوردن
learn one's lesson (& fig)

← سبق دادن
teach a lesson (& fig)

سبک style n /sabk/

سبک /sŭ-bŭk/
light, not heavy; frivolous adj

سبک دوش /sŭ-bŭk dosh/
laid off; lightly laden adj

← سبک دوش کردن
lay off; fire vt

سبک دوشی /sŭ-bŭk do-shi/
unemployment n

سبک رفتار /sŭ-bŭk-raf-tār/
swift, light-footed adj

سبک سر /sŭ-bŭk-sar/
silly, frivolous adj

سبک سری /sŭ-bŭk-sa-ri/
silliness, frivolity n

سبک سیر /sŭ-bŭk sayr/
سبک رفتار see adj

سبک مغز /sŭ-bŭk-maghz/
foolish, crackbrained adj

سبوس bran n /sa-bos/

سبوس دار /sa-bos dār/
whole-wheat adj

سبوسک dandruff n /sa-bo-sak/

سپاس /sĭ-pās/
gratitude, thanks; praise n

سپاس گزار /sĭ-pās gŭ-zār/
grateful, thankful adj

سپاس گزاری /sĭ-pās gŭ-zā-ri/
gratitude n

سپاه army, host n /sĭ-pāh/

سپاهی (-یی) /sĭ-pā-hi (-yi)/
sepoy; soldier n

سپاهی گم نام /sĭ-pā-hi-yī gŭm nām/
Unknown Soldier n

سپتمبر September n /sĭp-tĭm-bar/

سپر shield n /sĭ-par/

سپر انداختن /sĭ-par andākhtan/
escape, run; surrender v

سپردن ؛ -سپار- ؛ سپرد-
/sĭ-pŭr-dan/
entrust, give vt

سپرز spleen (colloq) n /sĭ-pŭrz/

سپیره n /spī-ra/ see

سپری کردن /sĭ-pa-ri kardan/
pass through; spend (time) v

سپس afterwards (lit) adv /sĭ'-pas/

سپنج temporary adj /sĭ-panj/

سپند n /sĭ-pand/ اسپند see

سپورت sports n /sĭ-port/

سپورت مین , -ها /sĭ-port-mayn/
sportsman n

سپورت مینی /sĭ-port-may-ni/
sportsmanship n

سپورتی sports adj /sĭ-por-ti/

سپاه see n /sĭ-pah/ سپه

سپه سالار /sĭ-pah sā-lār/
commander in chief (arch) n

سپهر firmament, sky n /sĭ-pĭ'-hīr/

سفید adj /sa-peyd/ سپید see

سپیده /sa-pey-da/
brightness (esp dawn) n

سپیده داغ /sa-pey-da dāgh/
سپیده دم see n

سپیده دم dawn n /sa-pey-da dam/

سپیره Spira (dist) n /spi-ra/

سپین بولدک /spin bol-dak/
Spin Boldak (dist) n

ستار sitar (mus instr) n /sĭ-tār/

ستاره /sĭ-tā-ra/
star; horoscope; f movie star;
asterisk; starfish n

ستاره شمار /sĭ-tā-ra shŭ-mār/
ستاره شناس see adj, n

ستاره شمر /sĭ-tā-ra shŭ-mar/
ستاره شمار see adj, n

ستاره دنباله دار
/sĭ-tā-ra-yī dŭm-bā-la dār/
comet n

ستاره شناس /sĭ-tā-ra shī-nās/
astrological adj; astrologer n

ستاره شناسی /sĭ-tā-ra shī-nā-si/
astrology n

ستایش /sĭ-tā-yĭsh/
praise, commendation n

ستایش آمیز /sī-tā-yīsh-ā-meyz/
laudatory adj
← ستایش کردن praise, commend
ستایشگر /sī-tā-yīsh-gar/
eulogist, panegyrist n
ستر /sá-tīr, satr/
covering; concealing n
← ستر عورت seclusion of women
استراتژی /ĭs-tĭ-rā-tĭ-zhi/ strategy n
استراتژی انکشاف ملی افغان
/ĭs-tĭ-rā-tĭ-zhi-yĭ ĭn-kĭ-shāf-ĭ mĭ-li-yĭ
af-ghān/
Afghan National Development
Strategy, ANDS n
استراتژیک /ĭs-tĭ-rā-tĭ-zhik/
strategic adj
استر درستیز /ĭs-tar di-rīs-tiz/
general staff n
استره محکمه /ĭs-ta-ra mah-ka-ma/
Supreme Court n
استر واخفا /sat-rŭ-wĭkh-fā/
camouflage n
ستم /sĭ-tam/
oppression, injustice n
ستم آمیز /sĭ-tam ā-meyz/
oppressive adj
ستم اندیش , -ان/ها
/sĭ-tam an-deysh/
see ستمگر adj, n
ستم دیدن /sĭ-tam didan/
be oppressed vi
ستم دیده , -گان/ها /sĭ-tam di-da/
oppressed (& pers) adj, n
ستم کار , -ان/ها /sĭ-tam kār/
see ستمگر adj, n
ستم گار , -ان/ها /sĭ-tam gār/
see ستم گر adj, n
ستم گر , -ان/ها /sĭ-tam gar/
oppressive (& pers) adj, n
ستم ملی /sĭ-tam-ĭ mĭ-li/
Setam-e Meli (pol party) n
ستمی , -ان/ها /sĭ-ta-mi/
Setam-e Meli member n
ستون /sŭ-tun/ pillar, column n
ستون فقرات /sŭ-tun-ĭ fŭ-qa-rāt/
spinal column n
ستوه /sŭ-toh/
harassment n; harassed adj

ستیز /sī-teyz/
struggle, strife; quarrel n
ستیزه /sī-tey-za/
anger; strife; quarrel n
← ستیزه کردن struggle, strive
ستیزه جو(ی) , -ان /sī-tey-za jo(y)/
obstinate; contentious (& pers) adj,
n
سجاده prayer rug n /sa-jā-da/
سجده /saj-da/
touching forehead to ground in
Musl prayer n
سجره /sa-ja-ra/ n شجره see
سجود /sŭ-jud/ n سجده see
سحاب, -ها /sa-hāb/ cloud n
سحار /sa-hār/ alluring, enticing adj
سحر /sa-har/ dawn; morning n
سحر /sĭ´-hīr, sĭhr/
magic, sorcery; enchantment n
سحر آمیز /sĭ´-hīr ā-meyz/
magical; enchanting adj
سحرگاه /sa-har gāh/
just before dawn (lit) n
سحرگه /sa-har gah/ n سحرگاه see
سخت /sakht/
hard, not soft; difficult adj
سخت جان /sakht-jān/
tough, hardy adj
سختگیر /sakht-gir/ strict, stern adj
سختگیری کردن /sakht-gi-ri kardan/
be strict, be stern vi
سخن /sŭ-khan/
speech, public address n
سخن ران /sŭ-khan rān/
n سخن گوی see
سخن گوی /sŭ-khan goy/
speaker; spokesperson n
سخن راندن /sŭ-khan rāndan/
speak, give a speech v
سخن رانی /sŭ-khan-rā-ni/
see سخن n
← سخن رانی کردن • سخن گفتن
سخن راندن see
سخی /sa-khi/
generous (& pers); Sakhi (m name)
adj, n
سده /sa-da/ century n

سر /sar/
head (& fig); chief; beginning; top;
id n

سر /sar(-ĭ)/ on; at; over prep

سر , ها-/اسرار /sĭr, pl as-rār/
secret, mystery n

سُر /sŭr/ key, mode; note (music) n

سر آسیمه /sar ā-si-ma/
confused, jumbled adj

سر از /sar az/ starting from prep

سر <کسی> از گردن بریدن
/sar-ĭ ká-sey az gar-dan bŭ-ri-dan/
behead <sb> vt

سر باختن /sar bākhtan/
lose, risk (one's head) v

سر باز زدن /sar bāz zadan/
refuse (to do sth) v

سر بالا /sar bā-lā/
uphill, upward adj, adv

سر پای (خود) /sar pā-yĭ (khŭd)/
independent (takes pers endings)
adj

سر پایی /sar pā-yi/
shoes (esp sandals) n

سرپستان /sar-ĭ pĭs-tān/
pregnant (cow) adj; nipple n

سر <چیزی> دادن
/sar-ĭ <chí-zey> dādan/
compare vt

سر پل /sar-ĭ pŭl/ Sar-e Pul (prov) n

سر پناه /sar-pa-nāh/
shelter, dwelling, abode n

سر تکان دادن /sar ta-kān dādan/
nod v

سر تکانی کردن
/sar ta-kā-ni kardan/
make excuses v

سر تیار /sar ta-yār/ haircut n

سر تیار کردن cut (m's) hair

سر چرخ /sar charkh/
lightheaded, dizzy adj

سر چشمه /sar chash-ma/
origin, source; reference book n

سر چشمه گرفتن
originate, stem from vi

سر حوضه /sar haw-za (-raw-za)/
Sar Hawza (dist) n

سر دادن /sar dādan/
divorce; withhold discipline v

سر درد /sar-dard/
having a headache adj

سر درد بودن have a headache

سر رفتن /sar raftan/
get angry; boil over vi

سر زدن /sar zadan/
behead vt; sprout; rise (sun) vi

سرزنش /sar za-nĭsh/
rebuke, reproach n

سرزنش کردن rebuke, reproach

سرزمین /sar za-min/
homeland, country; land n

سرزور /sar zor/
pushy, headstrong adj

سر سبزی /sar sab-zi/
foliage, verdure n

سرسپردگی /sar sĭ-pŭr-da-gi/
devotion n

سرسپرده , گان-/ها /sar sĭ-pŭr-da/
devoted adj; devotee n

سر ستون /sar sŭ-tun/
capital (on column) n

سر ستونی /sar sŭ-tu-ni/
see سر ستون n

سر سخت /sar sakht/
persistent; powerful adj

سرسری /sar sa-ri/
cursory, perfunctory adj

سر شار /sar shār/
very full; carefree; drunk adj

سر شماری /sar shŭ-mā-ri/
census n

سر شناس /sar shĭ-nās/
famous, well-known adj

سر کار /sar-ĭ kār/ at work phrs

سر کار رفتن go to work

سر مامور /sar mā-mur/
police chief, commissioner n

سر مقاله , ها-/سر مقالات
/sar mŭ-qa-la, pl -lāt/
editorial, lead article n

سر معلم /sar mŭ-'a-lĭm/
principal (in elementary school) n

سر منشی /sar mün-shi/
secretary general n

سر وظیفه /sar-ī wa-zī-fa/ on duty phrs

سراب /sa-rāb/ mirage n

سراج /sa-rāj/ saddler n

سراچه /sa-rā-cha/ outbuilding, small house n

سرازیر /sa-rā-zeyr/ descending, sloping adj

سراسر /sa-rā-sar/ entire, whole adj

سرافراز /sa-rāf-rāz/ honored adj

← سرافراز کردن honor v

سرامیک /sī-rā-mik/ ceramic adj

سرانجام /sa-rān-jām/ end n; after all adv

سرانگشت , -ان/ها /sa-ran-gūsht/ fingertip n

سرای /sa-rāy/ caravanserai, market; inn; warehouse; poet n

سرای دار /sa-rāy dār/ see سرایبان n

سرایبان (-وان)/ /sa-rāy-bān (-wān)/ innkeeper; manager of سرای n

سرایت کردن /sa-rā-yat kardan/ infect; spread vi

سرب /sūrb/ lead (metal) n

سرباز /sar-bāz/ soldier n

سربازی /sar-bā-zi/ soldiering; courage n

سربی /sūr-bi/ leaden, made of lead adj

سرپایان /sar-pā-yān/ downhill, sloping adj

سرپایانی /sar-pā-yā-ni/ slope, grade n

سرپرست /sar-pa-rast/ caretaker; guardian (of minor); acting (pol) n

سرپوش /sar-posh/ cover, lid; top n

سرپوشیده /sar-po-shi-da/ covered adj

سرتاپا /sar-tā-pā/ top to bottom, head to toe adv

سرتاسر /sar-tā-sar/ whole n; wholly adv

سرتنبه /sar-tam-ba/ pushy; stubborn adj

سرج /sarj/ cheviot (fabric) n

سرجایی /sar-jā-yi/ bedspread; counterpane n

سرحد , -ها /sar-had/ border n; bordering adj

سرخ /sūrkh/ red; very hot adj

سرخ باد /sūrkh-bād/ erysipelas (disease) n

سرخ پارسا /sūrkh-ī pār-sā/ Surkh-e Parsa (dist) n

سرخ رود /sūrkh rod/ Surkh Rod (dist, ctr Sultanpur) n

سرخ شدن /sūrkh shūdan/ blush; be upset; turn red vi

سرخ شده /sūrkh shū-da/ fried; upset, agitated adj

سرخ کردن /sūrkh kardan/ fry (food); upset; redden (sb) vt

سرخ رگ , -ها /sūrkh rag/ artery n

سرخکان /sūr-kha-kān/ measles n

سرد /sard/ cold; (fig) indifferent adj

← سرد کردن <دل کسی را> discourage <sb> vt

سردار /sar-dār/ commander (title used & by Barakzai nobles) n

سردخانه /sard-khā-na/ cold storage, large refrigerator n

سردرختی /sar-da-rakh-ti/ fruit n

سردردی /sar-dar-di/ headache n

سردرگم /sar-dar-gūm/ confused; indistinct adj

سرده /sar-dīh/ see بند سرده n

سردی /sar-di/ cold; (fig) indifference n

سرسارمن /sar-sār-man/ senior captain n

سرسبز /sar-sabz/ lush, verdant adj

سرش /sī-rīsh (shī-)/ glue, paste n

سرشیر /sar-ī shir/ cream (from milk) n

سرطان /sa-ra-tān/ Saratan (month); cancer (med, zodiac) n

سرطان سینه /sa-ra-tān-ī si-na/ breast cancer n

سرعت /sūr-'at/ speed, velocity n

cough n /sŭr-fa (sŭl-)/ سرفه
cough vi سرفه کردن ←
سرقت , ـها /sĭr-qat/
burglary; theft; robbery n
سرقت شده • به سرقت رفته ←
stolen adj
به سرقت بردن • سرقت کردن ←
steal vt
سرقت ادبی /sĭr-qat-ī a-da-bi/
plagiarism n
plagiarize v سرقت ادبی کردن ←
سرقفلی /sar-qŭf-li/
key money (for shop) n
Sarqala (ctr) n /sar-qa-la/ سرقلعه
street, road n سرک , ـها /sa-rak/
سرک حلقی /sa-rak-ī hal-qi/
Ring Road n
سرک دایروی /sa-rak-ī dā-yī-ra-wi/
see سرک حلقی n
head clerk n سرکاتب /sar kā-tīb/
سرکار /sar-kār/
ruler, master, sovereign n
سرکاری /sar-kā-ri/
governmental adj
سرکانی /sĭr-kā-nay/
Serkanay (dist) n
سرکردگی /sar-kar-da-gi/
leadership n
سرکرده /sar-kar-da/
chief, commander n
سرکسازی /sa-rak-sā-zi/
road construction n
سرکش /sar-kash/
disobedient, rebellious (& pers) adj,
n
سرکشی /sar-ka-shi/
disobedience, rebelliousness n
سرکشی کردن • سرکشیدن ←
disobey, rebel v
سرکشاده /sar-kŭ-shā-da/
unsealed (letter) adj
vinegar n سرکه /sĭr-ka/
سرگردان /sar-gar-dān/
confused, errant adj
سرگردانی /sar-gar-dā-ni/
confusion n
سرگرم /sar-garm/
busy; intent; slightly drunk adj

سرگرمی /sar-gar-mi/
concentration; pastime n
confused adj /sar-gash-ta/ سرگشته
سرگین /sar-gin/
cow dung (& for fuel) n
سرما خوردن /sar-mā khŭrdan/
catch a cold vi
سرمایه /sar-mā-ya/
wealth, fund, capital n
سرمایه دار /sar-mā-ya-dār/
capitalist, rich pers n
سرمایه گذاری , ـان/ـها /sar-mā-ya gŭ-zā-ri/
investor (pers); investment n
invest vi سرمایه گذاری کردن ←
سرمد /sar-mad/
eternity n; eternal adj
سرمدی /sar-ma-di/
eternal, everlasting adj
سرمنزل /sar-man-zīl/
destination, goal n
kohl (cosmetic) n /sŭr-ma/ سرمه
سرمه از چشم دزدیدن
/sŭr-ma az chá-shĭm dŭz-di-dan/
steal skillfully (fig) v
سرمه یی /sŭr-ma-yi/
dark blue, navy blue adj
tablecloth n /sar-mey-zi/ سرمیزی
سرندیپ /sa-ran-deyp/
Ceylon (now Sri Lanka) n
سرنگون /sar-nī-gun/
upside down; capsized; overthrown
(govt) adj
overturn; capsize سرنگون شدن ←
overturn; overthrow (govt) سرنگون کردن ←
سرنوشت /sar-na-wĭsht/
fate, destiny n
surna (mus instr) n /sŭr-nā/ سرنا
see سرنا n /sŭr-nāy (-nay)/ سرنای
سرنایچی /sŭr-nāy-chi/
surna player n
سرنگ /sŭ-rŭng, -rang/
blast (from explosives) n
سرنگ پراندن / sŭ-rŭng parāndan/
blast (with explosives) v
سرنگ پرانی / sŭ-rŭng pa-rā-ni/
blasting (with explosives) n

i = keep, ĭ = big, u = coop, ŭ = put, y = yet, ' = (glottal stop)   187

سرنا /sŭr-nay/ see سرنی
سرنایچی /sŭr-nay-chi/
see n سرنایچی
سرو /sarw/ n cypress (tree)
سروبی /sŭ-ro-bi, sa-, -bay/
Surobi, Sarobi (dist) n
سرود /sŭ-rud/ n anthem, hymn
سرودن ؛ -سرای- ؛ سرود-
/sa-ru-dan/
sing; compose (ode) v
سرور /sar-war/
leader, chief, head n
سرور /sŭ-rur/
joy, happiness, delight n
سروری /sar-wa-ri/ n leadership
سروی /sar-wey/
survey, questionnaire n
سروی کردن ←
canvass v
سرویس /sar-weys, -wis/
bus; hospital department; service n
سرویس کردن ←
serve (food); (sports) serve v
سره رود see n سرخ رود /sĭ-ra rod/
سره میاشت /sa-ra-mĭ-yāsht/
Red Crescent
سری لانکا /sĭ-ri lān-kā/
Sri Lanka (country) n
سریانی /sŭr-yā-ni/
Syriac (lang, hist) n
سریاور /sar-yā-war/
aide de camp n
سریر /sa-rir/ n throne
سریع /sa-ri/ fast, quick adj, adv
سریع الاثر /sa-ri-'ŭ-la-sar/
effective, efficacious adj
سریع الانتقال /sa-ri-'ŭ-lĭn-tĭ-qāl/
quick of study adj
سریع التأثر /sa-ri-'ŭt-ta'-sŭr/
impressionable adj
سرین /sŭ-rin/
buttocks; rump, croup n
سرینا /sa-ri-nā/
Serena (Kabul hotel) n
سرینگر /sĭ-ri-nĭ-gar/
Srinagar (city) n
سزا /sa-zā/
worthy, deserving; appropriate adj;
punishment n

سزاوار /sa-zā-wār/
worthy, deserving; appropriate adj
سزاوار ستایش
/sa-zā-wār sĭ-tā-yĭsh/
praiseworthy, laudable adj
سزیدن ؛ -سز- ؛ سزید- /sa-zi-dan/
be deserving; be appropriate vi
سست /sŭst/
soft; weak; loose; slow adj; slowly
adv
سطح , -ها/سطوح
/sát-ha, sath; pl sŭ-tuh/
surface; plane; level n
سطح بحر /sát-ha-yĭ ba-har/
sea level n
سطح زندگی /sát-ha-yĭ zĭn-da-gi/
standard of living n
سطح مرتفع /sát-ha-yĭ mŭr-ta-fey/
plateau n
سطحی /sat-hi/
trivial; unsubstantiated adj
سطوح /sŭ-tuh; sg sát-ha, sath/
see sg سطح n pl
سعدی /sa-'a-di/
Sadi (Persian poet, 1184-1293?) n
سعی /sa'y/ n effort, attempt
سفارت /sa-fā-rat, sĭ-/
embassy; mediation n
سفارت خانه /sa-fā-rat khā-na/
embassy n
سفاین /sa-fā-yĭn, sg sa-fi-na/
see sg سفینه n pl
سفر , -ها/اسفار /sa-far, pl as-fār/
journey, travel, trip n
سفر کردن ←
travel v
سفر بخیر ! /sa-far-ĭ ba-khayr/
bon voyage excl
سفر خرج /sa-far kharj/ n per diem
سفرا /sŭ-fa-rā, sg sa-fir/
see sg سفیر n pl
سفربری /sa-far-ba-ri/ mobilization n
سفر بری کردن ← mobilize (mil) v
سفره , -ها /sŭf-ra/
tablecloth (& on ground) n
سفلیس /sĭ-fĭ-lis/ n syphilis
سفید /sa-feyd/ white adj

سكندیناوی , -ان/ها
/sī-kan-di-nā-wi/
Scandinavian (& pers) adj, n
سكندیناویا /sī-kan-di-nā-wī-yā/
Scandinavia (region) n
سكنى /sak-nā/ dwelling n
سكوپیه /īs-ko-pī-ya/
Skopje (capital) n
سكوت /sū-kut/
quiet; silence; reticence n
سكونت dwelling n /sū-ku-nat/
سكه /sa-ka/
having a blood relationship adj
سكه , -ها /sī-ka/ coin n
↳ سكه زدن mint, coin v
سكه شناس , -ان/ها /sī-ka shī-nās/
numismatist n
سكه شناسى /sī-ka shī-nā-si/
numismatics n
سكى /sī-ki/ ski n
سكى بازى skiing n /sī-ki bā-zi/
سكى خوردن ski v /sī-ki khūrdan/
سكى زدن /sī-ki zadan/
see سكى زدن v
سگ , -ان/ها /sag/
dog; (& insult) wretch n
سگ تیگر /sag-ī tay-gar/
large & fierce dog n
سگ لاوو beaver n /sag-lā-wu/
سگ ماهى /sag-mā-hi/
sturgeon; sheatfish n
سگ و سگر /sag ŭ sū-gŭr/
wretch (insult) n phrs
سگر /sū-gŭr/ porcupine n
سگرت /sīg-rīt/ cigarette n
سگرت كشیدن /sīg-rīt kashidan/
smoke (cigarettes) v
سگك /sa-gak/
buckle; small dog n
سگور /sū-gur/ porcupine n
سل /sīl/ tuberculosis n
سلاته /sa-lā-ta/ salad n
سلاح , -ها/اسلحه
/sa-lāh, pl as-la-ha/
weapon n
سلاح دار armed adj /sa-lāh-dār/
سلاست /sa-lā-sat/
stylistic fluency n

سفید پوست , -ان/ها /sa-feyd post/
white pers, Caucasian n, adj
سفید چشم /sa-feyd chá-shīm/
impudent (fig) adj
سفید شدن /sa-feyd shŭdan/
turn white; turn gray (hair) v
سفیدار /sa-fey-dār/
poplar, aspen (tree) n
سفیده face powder n /sa-fey-da/
↳ سفیده كردن powder one's face v
سفیر , -ان/ها/سفرا
/sa-fir, pl sŭ-fa-rā/
ambassador; mediator n
سفینه , -ها/سفاین
/sa-fi-na, pl sa-fā-yīn/
boat, ship n
سفینه فضایی /sa-fi-na-yī fa-zā-yi/
spaceship; space shuttle n
سقر hell n /sa-qar/
سقف , -ها ceiling n /saqf/
سقط شدن /sa-qat shŭdan/
drop dead, founder (horse) vi
سقط جنین /sīqt-ī ja-nin/
miscarriage n
سقوط fall, downfall n /sŭ-qut/
سقوط طیاره /sŭ-qut-ī ta-yā-ra/
plane crash n
سك , -ان/ها /sīk/
Sikh (& pers) adj, n
سكاتلند n /sī-kāt-land/ see سكات لند
Scotland n /sī-kāt-leynd/
سكاتلیندى , -ان/ها /sī-kāt-leyn-di/
Scot, Scotsman n; Scottish adj
سكا , -یان/ها /sa-kā/
Scythian (pers, hist) n
سكایى /sa-kā-yi/
Scythian (hist) adj
سكتور sector n /sak-tor/
سكر intoxication n /sŭ´-kŭr, sŭkr/
سكرآور /sŭk-rā-war/
intoxicating adj
سكرتر /sī-kar-tar/
secretary; clerk n
سكستن n /sŭ-kŭs-tan/ see گسیختن
سكسفون /sak-sa-fon/
saxophone (mus instr) n

سلاسل /sī-lā-sīl, sg sīl-sī-la/
see sg سلسله n pl

سلامت /sa-lā-mat/
healthy adj; intactness n

سلجوقی , -ان/ها/سلاجقه
/sal-ju-qi, pl sa-lā-jī-qa/
Seljuk (pers, hist) n

سلجوقیان /sal-ju-qī-yān/
Seljuk Dynasty (hist) n

سلدراج /sīl-dī-rāj (-tī-)/
underwear (m's) n

سلسله , -ها/سلاسل
/sīl-sī-la, pl sī-lā-sīl/
line, ancestry; series; range
(mountains) n

سلسله مراتب /sīl-sī-la-yĭ ma-rā-tĭb/
chain of command; procedure n

سلسله نسب /sīl-sī-la-yĭ na-sab/
pedigree; family tree n

سلف /sa-laf, pl as-lāf/
ancestor, predecessor n

اسلاف ← pl

سلفر /sal-far/
sulfur (element) n

سلفیزم /sa-la-fí-zīm/
Salafism (mvmt) n

سلفی , -ان/ها /sa-la-fi/
Salafist n

سلفیه /sa-la-fíy-ya/ سلفیزم n see

سلطان , -ان/ها /sŭl-tān, sal-/
sultan, king n

سلطان بکواه /sŭl-tān-ĭ bak-wā/
Sultan-e Bakwa (ctr) n

سلطانپور /sal-tān-pur/
Sultanpur (ctr) n

سلطانه , -ها /sŭl-tā-na/
sultana, queen; Sultana (f name) n

سلطانی /sŭl-tā-ni/
monarchic adj

سلطنت /sal-ta-nat/
sultanate, kingdom n

سلطنت طلب , -ان/ها
/sal-ta-nat ta-lab/
monarchist adj

سلطنی /sal-ta-ni/
monarchic adj

سلم /sa-lam/
deposit, advance money n

سلمانی /sal-mā-ni/
barber n

سلوک /sŭ-luk/
behavior; (rel) following the path n

سلوک کردن ← behave

سلول /sŭ-lol/
cell (var senses) n

سلولاید /sŭ-lo-lāyd/
celluloid n

سلولوز /sŭ-lo-loz/
cellulose n

سلی /sī-li/
slap n

سلی خوردن ← be slapped vi

سلی زدن ← slap v

سلیطه /sa-li-ta (sha-)/
nagging, abusive adj

سلیقه /sa-li-qa/
talent, instinct; preference n

سلیکا /sī-li-kā/
silica n

سلیکات /sī-li-kāt/
silicate n

سلیکان /sī-li-kān/
silicon (element) n

سلیمان /sŭ-lay-mān/
Solomon (bibl, m name) n

سلیمان خیل /sŭ-lay-mān kheyl/
Suleiman Khel (tribe) n

سلیمانی /sŭ-lay-mā-ni/
Solomonic adj

سم , -ها/سموم /sam, pl sŭ-mum/
poison; venom n

سم /sŭm/
hoof n

سم زدن ← dance, hoof it (colloq) v

سما /sa-mā/
sky, firmament n

سماروق /sa-mā-rŭq/
mushroom n

سماع کردن /sa-mā/
sing & dance to ecstasy (as dervish) v

سماعت /sa-mā-'at/
hearing (law) n

سماعی /sa-mā-'i/
irregular (gram) adj

سماوی /sa-mā-wi/
celestial adj

سمبول /sīm-bol/
symbol n

سمپاشی /sam-pā-shi/
aerial spraying n

سمت /samt/
side, direction; region; azimuth
(astron) n

سمت شمالی /samt-ĭ sha-mā-li/
Northern Province (Afgh, hist) n

سمت مشرقی /samt-ĭ mash-rī-qi/
Eastern Province (Afgh, hist) n

سمتی /sam-ti/
regional, provincial adj

سمستر /sī-mīs-tar/
semester n

سمرقند /sa-mar-qand/
Samarkand (city) n

سمنبر /sa-man-bar/
jasmine-white *adj*

سمنبوی /sa-man-buy/
jasmine-scented *adj*

سمنت /sī-mīnt/ cement *n*

سمنگان /sa-man-gān/
Samangan (prov) *n*

سمور /sa-mur/ sable *n*

سموم /sū-mum, sg sam/
see sg سم *n pl*

سمونمل /sa-mun-mal/
lieutenant colonel, LTC *n*

سمونوال /sa-mun-wāl/
colonel, COL *n*

سمونیار /sa-mun-yār/ major, MAJ *n*

سمی /sa-mi/ poisonous, toxic *adj*

سمی کلن /sī-mi ko-lan/
semi-colon *n*

سمیت /sa-mĭ-yat/ toxicity *n*

سن /sīn/ age; stage (of sth) *n*

سن پیری /sīn-ĭ pi-ri/ old age *n*

سن جوانی /sīn-ĭ ja-wā-ni/
youth (time of life) *n*

سنا /sa-nā/
senna plant (med); senate;
brilliance *n*

سناتور , -ان/ها /sa-nā-tor/
senator *n*

سناچ /sa-nāch/
lamb/goatskin bag; (insult for m) *n*

سناریست /sī-nā-rist/
scriptwriter, scenarist *n*

سناریو /sī-nā-rī-yo/
screenplay, script *n*

سناریو نویس /sī-nā-rī-yo na-wis/
see سناریست *n*

سنان , -ها /sī-nān/ spearhead *n*

سنایی غزنوی /sa-nā-yi ghaz-na-wi/
Sanayi Ghaznawi (11th-12th-c Sufi
poet, hist) *n*

سنبل /sŭm-bŭl/ hyacinth (flower) *n*

سنبله /sŭm-bŭ-la/
Sunbula (month); Virgo; ear of grain
n

سنبیدن ؛ -سنب- ؛ سنبید-
/sŭm-bi-dan/
pierce, drill through *vt*

سنت /sŭ-nat/
circumcision; (colloq) beard
trimming *n*

سنتی /sŭ-na-ti/
circumcision (act) *n*; traditional *adj*

سنت پتربربرگ /sant-pĭ-tīr-bŭrg/
St. Petersburg (city) *n*

سنبره /san-ta-ra/ tangelo (fruit) *n*

سنتکس /sīn-tīks/ syntax *n*

سنتور /san-tur/ santur (mus instr) *n*

سنج /sanj/ sanj (mus instr) *n*

سنجاب /sīn-jāb/
grey squirrel (& pelt) *n*

سنجاق /sīn-jāq/ pin *n*

سنجاق سینه /sīn-jāq-ĭ si-na/
brooch *n*

سنجد /sīn-jīd (-jīt)/ oleaster (olive) *n*

سنجدک /sīn-jī-dak (-tak)/
small oleaster; (vulg) clitoris *n*

سنجش /san-jīsh/
weighing, measurement *n*

← سنجش کردن weigh, measure *v*

سند , -ها/اسناد /sa-nad, pl as-nād/
deed, document; bond; (esp pl)
authenticating link in hadith
transmission *n*

← سند فراغت diploma *n*

← سند مالکیت title, deed *n*

ش /sīnd/
Indus River; Sind (prov) *n*

سند /sŭnd/ rayon *n*

سندان /san-dān/ anvil *n*

سنگ /sang/ rock, stone *n*

سنگ آبی /sang-ā-bi/ turtle *n*

سنگ آتش /sang ā-tash/
fire stone; Sang Atash (ctr) *n*

سنگ آهک /sang-ĭ ā-hak/
limestone *n*

سنگ آهن /sang-ĭ ā-han/ iron ore *n*

سنگ باران /sang bā-rān/
throwing stones *n*

← سنگ باران کردن
stone, throw stones *v*

سنگ بقه /sang ba-qa/
see شنگ پشت (colloq) *n*

سنگ پشت /sang pŭsht/ tortoise *n*

سنگ تخت /sang-ĭ takht/
Sang-e Takht (dist) *n*

---

i = k<u>ee</u>p, ĭ = b<u>i</u>g, u = c<u>oo</u>p, ŭ = p<u>u</u>t, y = <u>y</u>et, ' = (glottal stop)

سنه /sŭn-na/
Sunna (way/manners of Prophet) *n*

سنه /sŭ-nŭh (-no)/
daughter-in-law *n*

سنی , -ان/ها /sŭ-ni/
Sunni (& pers) *adj, n*

سواد /sa-wād/ literacy *n*

سوار /sa-wār/
horseman, rider *n*; mounted *adj*

← سوار شدن mount; board; get on

سوار کار , -ان/ها /sa-wār kār/
horseman; jockey *n*

سوال , -ات/ها /sa-wāl/
question *n*

← سوال کردن ask, inquire *v*

سوال و جواب /sa-wāl ŭ ja-wāb/
conversation (fig) *n phrs*

سوالیه /sa-wā-lī-ya/
question mark *n*; interrogative *adj*

سوانح /sa-wā-nīh (-ney)/
biography (brief) *n*

سوت /sut/ sut (1/8 inch) *n*

سوته /so-ta/ cudgel *n*

سوچ /sī-wĭch/ switch *n*

← سوچ زدن switch off, turn off *vt*

← سوچ کردن switch on, turn on *vt*

سوختاندن ؛ -سوزان- ؛ سوختان- /sokh-tān-dan/
burn *vt*

سوختن ؛ -سوز- ؛ سوخت- /sokh-tan/
burn *vi*

سوخته /sokh-ta/ burnt *adj*

سوختگی /sokh-ta-gi/
burn (injury); fire, conflagration *n*

سود (سوت) /sud (sut)/
interest, usury; ill gain *n*

← سود گرفتن • سود خوردن
charge interest *v*

سودا /saw-dā/
merchandise; groceries; bargain, deal *n*

سودا واتر /so-dā wā-tar/
soda water *n*

سوداگر , -ان/ها /saw-dā-gar/
merchant, trader *n*

سوداگری /saw-dā-ga-ri/
trade, business *n*

سودان /su-dān/ Sudan (country) *n*

سنگ تراش /sang ta-rāsh/
stonecutter (pers) *n*

سنگ چارک /sang-chā-rak/
Sangcharak (dist, ctr Tukzar) *n*

سنگ چل /sang chĭl/
pebble, small stone *n*

سنگ دان /sang dān/ gizzard *n*

سنگ دل , -ان/ها /sang dĭl/
stubborn, hardhearted (& pers) *adj, n*

سنگ ریزه /sang rey-za/ gravel *n*

سنگ سرمه /sang-ĭ sŭr-ma/
antimony (cosmetic) *n*

سنگ فرش /sang farsh/
pavement (stone) *n*

سنگ قبر /sang-ĭ qá-bĭr/
gravestone, tombstone *n*

سنگ محک /sang-ĭ ma-hak/
touchstone *n*

سنگ نوشته /sang-ĭ na-wĭsh-ta/
inscription in stone *n*

سنگ کاری /sang-kā-ri/
stonework, masonry *n*

سنگ لاخ /sang lākh/
stony *adj*; stony place *n*

سنگ ماشه /sang-ĭ mā-sha/
Sang-e Masha (ctr) *n*

سنگر /san-gar/
trench, parapet; Sangar (ctr) *n*

سنگر بندی /san-gar ban-di/
entrenchment *n*

سنگر سرای /san-gar sa-rāy/
Sangar Saray (ctr) *n*

سنگسار /sang-sār/
stoning (to death) *n*

← سنگسار کردن stone (to death)

سنگناک /sang-nāk/
see سنگ لاخ *adj*

سنگی /san-gi/
stone, made of stone *adj*

سنگین /san-gin/
heavy; oppressive; serious *adj*;
Sangin (dist) *n*

سنو /sŭ-no/
see سنه (daughter-in-law) *n*

سنوی /sa-na-wi/ annual, yearly *adj*

سنه /sa-na/ year *n*

← سنۀ هجری year of the Hegira

سودانی , ان/ها /su-dā-ni/
Sudanese (& pers) adj, n

سودجو /sud-jo/
profiteer n; profiteering adj

سودجوی /sud-joy/
see سودجو n, adj

سودجویی /sud-jo-yi/
profiteering n

سودخوار /sud-khār/
see سودخور n, adj

سودخواری /sud-khā-ri/
n see سودخوری

سودخور , ان/ها /sud-khŭr/
usurer n; usurious adj

سودخوری /sud-khŭ-ri/
usury n

سودمند /sud-mand/
profitable; favorable adj

سوده /su-da/
powdered adj

سودیم /so-dī-yam/
sodium (element) n

سودیم کاربونیت →
sodium carbonate

سوراخ /su-rākh/
hole, cavity n

سوراخ بینی /su-rākh-ĭ bi-ni/
nostril n

سوراخ سوراخ /su-rākh su-rākh/
see سوراخی adj

سوراخ سوزن /su-rākh-ĭ so-zan/
eye of a needle n

سوراخ گوش /su-rākh-ĭ gosh/
ear canal n

سوراخی /su-rā-khi/
full of holes adj

سورت /sort/
sort, kind n

← سورت کردن
sort by type vt

سورت بندی /sort ban-di/
sorting n

سورت کاری /sort kā-ri/
n see سورت بندی

سورریالیزم /su-rī-yā-li´-zīm/
surrealism n

سوره /su-ra/
sura, chapter of Quran n

سوری /su-ri/
Suri (12th-c Ghor ruler, hist); red rose n

سوریایی /su-rī-yā-yi/
Syrian adj

سوریا /su-rī-yā/
Syria (country) n

سوریایی /su-rī-yā-yi/
Syrian adj

سوریه /su-rī-ya/
n see سوریا

سوز /sawz/
see سبز adj

گونوریا /so-zāk/
gonorrhea n

سوزان /so-zān/
hot, burning adj

سوزش /so-zīsh/
inflammation, irritation n

← سوزش کردن
be inflamed vi

سوزمه قلعه /soz-ma qal-'a/
Sozma Qala (dist) n

سوزن /so-zan/
needle; syringe n

سوزن خیاطی /so-zan-ĭ khī-yā-ti/
sewing needle n

سوزن دوزی /so-zan do-zi/
needlework n

سوزن زدن /so-zan zadan/
inject, give an injection v

سوژه /so-zha/
subject, theme n

سوسمار /sus-mār/
lizard n

سوسمار آبی /sus-mār-ĭ ā-bi/
crocodile n

سوسن /so-san/
purple lily n

سوسن آزاد /so-san-ĭ ā-zād/
white lily n

سوسن سفید /so-san-ĭ sa-feyd/
dark purple, lily-colored adj

سوسنی /so-sa-ni/
n see سوسن آزاد

سوسیالست /so-sī-yā-līst/
socialist n

سوسیالستی /so-sī-yā-līs-ti/
socialist adj

سوغات /saw-ghāt/
souvenir, traveler's present n

سوغات فروشی /saw-ghāt fŭ-ro-shi/
souvenir shop n

سوف /suf/
hole; tunnel n

← سوف زدن
dig a hole v

سوفسطایی , ان/ها /su-fīs-tā-yi/
sophist (pers) n

سوق الجیشی /sawq-ŭl-jay-shi/
strategy n

سوق دادن «به نیرو ها» /sawq dādan/
mobilize <troops>; compel vt

سوق گردیدن /sawq gardidan/
be mobilized vi

سوق و اداره /sawq ŭ ī-dā-ra/
command & control n phrs

سوق یافتن /sawq yāftan/
vi see سوق گردیدن

i = keep, ĭ = big, u = coop, ŭ = put, y = yet, ' = (glottal stop)   193

سوگ /sog/
grief, sorrow; mourning n
← سوگ داشتن grieve, mourn v
سوگند /saw-gand/ oath n
← سوگند خوردن take an oath v
← سوگند دادن administer an oath v
سوگند دروغ /saw-gand-ī dŭ-rogh/
perjury n
سوگوار /sog-wār, su-gŭ-/
mourning adj; mourner n
سوال , -ها /sa-wāl/
question, inquiry n
← سوال کردن ask, inquire v
سوم /sum/ sum (currency) n
سوم /sĭ-wŭm, sŭwwm (say-yŭm)/
third (ordinal) adj; thirdly adv
سومال /so-māl/ Somalia n
سومالی /so-mā-li/ Somali adj
سومر /so-mar/
Sumer (empire, hist) n
سومری , -ان/ها /so-ma-ri/
Sumerian (& pers) adj, n
سومی /sĭ-wŭ-mi/
third adj; the third one n
سومین /sĭ-wŭ-min/
third (oft used before n) adj
سوء استفاده
/su-'ī ĭs-tĭ-fā-da (sa-wĭ-)/
misuse, improper use n
سوء استعمال
/su-'ī ĭs-tey-māl (sa-wĭ-)/
misuse, misapplication n
سوء تفاهم /su-'ī-ta-fā-hŭm (sa-wĭ-)/
mutual misunderstanding n
سوء ظن /su-'ī-zan (sa-wĭ-)/
suspicion; low opinion n
← سوء ظن داشتن
suspect (sth neg to be true) v
سوی /soy(-ī), suy(-ī)/
toward prep; side; direction n
سویدن /sŭ-wi-dan/ Sweden n
سویدنی , -ان/ها /sŭ-wi-da-ni/
Swedish adj; Swede n
سویز /sŭ-weyz/ Suez (geog) n
سویس /sĭ-wis/ Switzerland n
سویسی , -ان/ها /sĭ-wi-si/
Swiss (& pers) adj, n
سویه /sa-wĭ-ya/ level, standard n

سویه زندگی /sa-wĭ-ya-yĭ zīn-da-gi/
standard of living n
سه پارچه /sey pār-cha/
school transfer document n; in
triplicate adj
سه شنبه /sey-sham-bey/ Tuesday n
سه ضلعی /sey zŭl-'i/
triangle n; triangular adj
سه کوه /seyk-wa/ Seykwa (ctr) n
سه ماهه /sey mā-ha/
quarterly, trimonthly adj
سهل /sahl/ easy, not difficult adj
سهل انگار /sah-lan-gār/
careless, nonchalant adj
سهم , -ها /sahm (sām)/
participation; share (stock) n
← سهم داشتن • سهم گرفتن
participate (in sth) vi
سهم دار /sahm dār/
participating adj; shareholder n
سهواً /sáh-wan, -wán/
inadvertently adv
سهولت , -ها /sŭ-hu-lat/
facilitation, easing n
سهیم بودن /sa-him budan/
be involved in vi
سی /si/ thirty n, adj
سی اس تی سی الف /si ĭs ti si a-līf/
CSTC-A, Combined Security
Transition Command-Afghanistan n
سی دی , -ها /si di/
CD, compact disc; DVD n
سیاح , -ان/ها /sa-yāh/
traveler, tourist n
سیاحت /sa-yā-hat/ travel, tourism n
سیاحتی /sa-yā-ha-ti/
related to tourism adj
سیاره , -گان/ها/سیارات
/sa-yā-ra, pl -rāt/
planet n
سیاست /sĭ-yā-sat/
policy; politics; administration n
سیاست خارجی /sĭ-yā-sat-ī khā-rĭ-ji/
foreign policy n
سیاست مدار , -ان/ها
/sĭ-yā-sat-ma-dār/
politician, statesman n

سیاسی /sī-yā-si/
political; diplomatic adj
سیاق context n /sī-yāq/
سیاه /sī-yāh/
black; dark, wicked; dire adj
سیاه بخت /sī-yāh bakht/
bad luck n phrs
سیاه بخش , -ان/ها /sī-yāh bakhsh/
unfortunate (& pers) adj, n
سیاه پوش , -ان/ها /sī-yāh posh/
bereaved (& pers) adj, n
سیاه چال n /sī-yāh chāl/ سیاه چاه see
سیاه چاه /sī-yāh chāh/
pit, dungeon n
سیاه دانه /sī-yāh dā-na/
wild fennel seeds n
سیاه دل , -ان/ها /sī-yāh dīl/
wicked (& pers) adj, n
سیاه رگ /sī-yāh rag/
vein n
سیاه رنگ /sī-yāh rang/
black (in color) adj
سیاه زخم /sī-yāh zá-khīm/
anthrax n
سیاه فام /sī-yāh fām/
سیاه رنگ see adj
lynx n /sī-yāh gosh/ سیاه گوش
سیاهی /sī-yā-hi/
nightmare (colloq); blackness n
apple n /seyb/ سیب
سیب زمینی /seyb-ĭ za-mi-ni/
potato [< F] n
set; seat, couch n /sit/ سیت , -ها
seech (vegetable) n /sich/ سیچ
skewer, spit n /sikh/ سیخ
← سیخ زدن
be on pins & needles
ramrod n /sikh-ĭ tŭ-fang/ سیخ تفنگ
سیخ تنور /sikh-ĭ ta-nur/
poker (for starting fire) n
bobby pin n /si-khak/ سیخک
on a skewer adj /si-khi/ سیخی
سید , -ها/سادات
/sa-yĭd (sayd, sa-yid), pl sā-dāt/
sayed (title for descendants of
Prophet, before name) n
سید آباد /sa-yĭd ā-bād/
Sayedabad (dist) n
سید خیل /sa-yĭd kheyl/
Sayed Kheyl (dist) n

سید کرم /sa-yĭd ka-ram/
Sayed Karam (dist) n
سیر /sayr (sayl)/
movement; sightseeing n; following
a spiritual path adj
← سیر کردن
sightsee; look around, window-
shop; watch TV
سیر /seyr/
full, not hungry adj; seyr (16 lbs) n
garlic n /sir/ سیر
سیر دریا /sir dar-yā/
Syr Darya; (hist) Jaxartes (river) n
fill up vi /sir shŭdan/ سیر شدن
serum n /si-rŭm/ سیرم
thirteen n, adj /seyz-dah/ سیزده
سیزدهم /seyz-da-hŭm/
thirteenth adj
سیزدهمین /seyz-da-hŭ-min/
thirteenth (oft before n) adj
system n /sis-tūm/ سیستم
Sayghan (dist) n /say-ghān/ سیغان
سیغه n صیغه see /si-gha/
sword, sabre, rapier n /sayf/ سیف
سیکوه n سه کوه /seyk-wa/ see
cigar n /si-gār/ سیگار
سیل (colloq) n /sayl/ سیر see
سیل , -ها flood, inundation n /seyl/
سیلاب /sey-lāb/
flood water; syllable n
سیلابی /sey-lā-bi/
related to floods; syllabic adj
سیلی n سلی /si-li/ see
سیم /sim/
string (on mus instr); wire, line n
سیم خاردار /sim-ĭ khār-dār/
barbed wire n
سیم کارت /sim kārt/
SIM card (cell phone) n
سیماب /si-māb/
mercury, quicksilver n
Sinai (peninsula) n /si-nā/ سینا
سینما /si-na-mā/
movie theater, cinema n
chest; breast; bosom n /si-na/ سینه
سینه بند /si-na band/
brassiere; saddle strap n

سینه کشتی /si-na-yĭ kĭsh-ti/
bow, prow (of ship) n
سینه کوه /si-na-yĭ koh/
mountainside n
سینه و بغل /si-naw-ba-ghal/
pneumonia (colloq) n
سینه و بغل شدن ←
get pneumonia
سینی /si-ni/ round copper tray n
سیه /sī-yah/ adj سیاه see
سییم /si-yŭm/ adj thirtieth
سییمین /si-yŭ-min/
thirtieth (oft before n) adj

ش

شاخ /shākh/
branch (tree); horn (animal) n
شاخ دار /shākh-dār/
having horns; bald (lie) adj
شاخچه /shākh-cha/ شاخه see
شاخه /shā-kha/ twig n
شاخی /shā-khi/
pitchfork n; horned adj
شادی /shā-di/ monkey, ape n
شارتی برق /shār-ti-yĭ barq/
short circuit n
شارح , -ان/ین /shā-rīh/
interpreter (expounder) n
شارحه /shā-rī-ha/
شارح f of; colon (punctuation) n
شارژدافیر /shārzh-dā-feyr/
chargé d'affaires n
شاروال , -ها /shār-wāl/ mayor n
شاروالی /shār-wā-li/
mayoralty; municipality n
شاش /shāsh/ piss (vulg) n
شاش کردن ← piss, take a piss v
شاشه /shā-sha/ شاش see
شاعر , -ان/ها/شعرا
/shā-'ĭr, pl shŭ-'a-rā/
poet n
شاغلی /shāʹ-gha-ley/
Mr., mister; sir (before name) adj
شافعی , -ان/ها /shā-fĭ-'i/
Shafiitic (Sunni school of thought)
adj; Shafiite (pers) n
شافعیه Shafiites coll n /shā-fĭ-'ī-ya/

شاقول , -qul (-wul)/ شاقول /shā-qol
رشته شاقول see n
شاکی /shā-ki/ complainer n
شاگرد , -ان/ها/ /shā-gĭrd/
student, pupil; disciple n
شاگرد گریز پای
/shā-gĭrd-ī gŭ-reyz pāy/
truant student n
شال /shāl/ shawl n
شام /shām/
Syria; Damascus; the north;
evening n; in the evening adv
شامپو /shām-po/ shampoo n
شامل /shā-mĭl(-ī)/
including prep, adj; participant n
شامه /shā-ma/ sense of smell n
شانداری /shān-dā-ri/
splendid, magnificent adj
شاندن ؛ -شان- ؛ شاند- /shān-dan/
plant vt
شانزده /shānz-dah/ sixteen n, adj
شانزدهم /shānz-da-hŭm/
sixteenth adj
شانزدهمین /shānz-da-hŭ-min/
sixteenth (used before n) adj
شانه /shā-na/
shoulder; comb; weaver's card n
شانه دادن ← help, assist v
شانه بالا انداختن
/shā-na bā-lā andākhtan/
shrug v
شانه خالی کردن
/shā-na khā-li kardan/
shirk, avoid work n
شاور /shā-war/ shower n
شاور گرفتن ← take a shower vi
شاه , -ان /shāh/
king (& chess, cards), shah n
شاه اسپرغم /shāh īs-par-gham/
sweet basil (arch) n
شاه پسند /shāh pī-sand/
verbena (plant) n
شاه پور /shāh pur/ prince n
شاه تره /shāh ta-ra/
fumitory (med herb) n
شاه توت /shāh tut/ boysenberry n

شاه جهان /shāh ja-hān/
Shah Jahan (Mughal emperor, hist) n

شاه دانه /shāh dā-na/ hempseed n
شاه دخت /shāh dŭkht/ princess n
شاه دختر /shāh dŭkh-tar/
see شاه دخت

شاه رگ /shāh rag/ jugular vein n
شاه گرد /shāh-gĭrd/
Shahgerd (ctr) n

شاه مات /shāh māt/
checkmate (chess) n

شاه نامه /shāh nā-ma/
Shahnama (10th-c epic poem) n

شاه ولی کوت /shāh wa-li kot, wa-/
Shah Wali Kot (dist) n

شاهجوی /shāh-joy/ Shahjoy (dist) n
شاهد , -ان/ها/شهود
/shā-hĭd (shā-yĭd), pl shŭ-hud/
witness n

شاهد حساس /shā-hĭd-ĭ ha-sās/
Shahed-e Hasas (dist) n

شاهد عینی /shā-hĭd-ĭ ay-ni/
eyewitness n

شاهراه /shāh rāh/ highway n
شاهنشاه /shā-hĭn-shāh/ emperor n
شاهنشاهی /shā-hĭn-shā-hi/
empire n; imperial adj

شاهی /shā-hi/
kingdom, monarchy n; royal adj

شاهی کوت /shā-hi kot/
Shahi Kot (ctr) n

شاید /shā´-yad, -yád/
may, might <+ subj> v

شایسته سالاری /shā-yĭs-ta sā-lā-ri/
experience; qualifications n

شایعه , -ها/شایعات
/shā-yĭ-'a, pl -'āt/
rumor, hearsay (lit) n

شب , -ان/ها /shab (shaw)/
night, evening n; at night adv

شب پره /shab-pa-ra (shaw-pa-rak)/
bat (mammal) n

شب حنا /shab-ĭ hĭ-nā/
wedding night n

شب گردی /shab-gi-ri/ curfew n
شب کور /shab-kor/
night-blind (& pers) adj, n

شب کوری /shab-ko-ri/
night blindness n
شب کوری داشتن ←
be night-blind

شبان /shŭ-bān/ shepherd n
شبانی /shŭ-bā-ni/ shepherding n
شبرغان /shĭ-bĭr-ghān, sha-bar-/
Sheberghan (seat) n

شبکه /sha-ba-ka/
network, system n

شبکیه /sha-ba-kĭ-ya/ retina n
شبنم /shab-nam/ dew n
شبه جزیره /shĭbh-ī ja-zi-ra/
peninsula n

شبیه /sha-bih/ alike, similar adj
شپ /shŭp/ sip n
شپ کردن ← sip, take a sip v
شپیدن ؛ شپل- ؛ شپلید-
/shĭp-li-dan/
squeeze (colloq) vt

شپو /sha-po/ hat, chapeau n
شتا /shī-tā/ winter n
شتایی /shī-tā-yi/ winter adj
شتر /shŭ-tŭr/ camel n
۲ زنگیر شتر ← 2 head of camel
شتر جنگی /shŭ-tŭr jan-gi/
camel fighting n

شتر مرغ /shŭ-tŭr mŭrgh/ ostrich n
شتر کینه /shŭ-tŭr ki-na/
vindictive, spiteful adj

شتل /shŭ-tŭl/ Shutul (dist) n
شجاعت /shŭ-jā-'at/
bravery, courage n

شجر /sha-jar, pl ash-jār/ tree n
اشجار ← pl

شجره /sha-ja-ra (sa-)/
family tree n

شحم /shá-hĭm, shahm/
fat, grease; lipid n

شحمی /shah-mi/
fatty, sebaceous adj

شخص , -ها/اشخاص
/shakhs, pl ash-khās/
person (VIP, gram) n

شخص رئیس جمهور ←
the President himself
شخص اول 1st person (gram)
شخص دوم 2nd person (gram)

شخص انتحار کننده
/shakhs-ĭ ĭn-tĭ-hār kŭ-nĭn-da/
suicide bomber (colloq); (mil)
PBIED, Personnel-Borne
Improvised Explosive Device n

شخص حقیقی /shakhs-ī ha-qi-qii/
legal person (law) n

شخص حکمی /shakhs-ī hŭ-kŭ-mi/
corporation (law) n

شخص سیاسی /shakhs-ī sī-yā-si/
politician, statesman n

شخصاً /shákh-san, -sán/
personally adv

شخصی /shakh-si/
personal, private adj

شخصیت , -ها/اشخاص
/shakh-sĭ-yat, pl ash-khās/
personality; VIP; fictional character
n

شخصیت حقیقی
/shakh-sĭ-yat-ī ha-qi-qi/
legal personality (& sb/sth) n

شد و مد /shad ŭ mad/
correct pronunciation; emphasis n

شدت /shĭ-dat/
forcefulness, intensity, harshness n

شدگار /shŭd-gār/ n شیار see

شدن ؛ -شو- (-ش-) ؛ شد-
/shŭdan, /méyshawŭm (méyshŭm)//
become vi

شدنی /shŭ-da-ni/
possible, practicable adj

شدیار /shŭd-yār/ n شیار see

شدید /sha-did/
intense, severe; violent adj

شدیداً /sha-dí-dan/
intensely; violently adv

شر /shar/
evil, wickedness; damage n

شراب /sha-rāb/
wine; liquor n

شراب ارغوانی
/sha-rāb-ī ar-gha-wā-ni/
red wine n

شراب انگوری /sha-rāb-ī an-gu-ri/
grape wine n

شرار /sha-rār/ sparks; flame n

شرارت /sha-rā-rat/ doing evil n

شرارت آمیز /sha-rā-rat ā-meyz/
evil (deed) adj

شرارت پیشه /sha-rā-rat pey-sha/
wicked, evil (pers) adj

شراره /shŭ-rā-ra/
spark; (colloq) flame n

← شراره کردن
flame, flare; get angry v

شراع /shĭ-rā/ sail (lit) n

شراعی /shĭ-rā-'i/ for sailing (lit) adj

شرافت /sha-rā-fat/
honor, moral distinction n

شرافتمند /sha-rā-fat-mand/
honorable (pers) adj

شرافتمندانه /sha-rā-fat-man-dā-na/
honorable (deed) adj; honorably
adv

شراکت /sha-rā-kat/ partnership n

شرایط /sha-rā-yĭt, sg shart/
conditions; stipulations; wager; see
شرط n pl & sg

شرایین /sha-rā-yin, sg shĭr-yān/
شریان n pl see sg

شربت /shar-bat/ juice; fruit syrup n

شربت سرفه /shar-bat-ī sŭr-fa/
cough syrup n

شرح , -ها/شروح
/shár-ha, sarh; pl shŭ-ruh/
description, explanation n

← شرح دادن • شرح کردن
describe, explain vt

شرحه /shár-ha/ n شرح see

شرر /sha-rar/ n شرار see

شرشر /shar-shar/ murmur; rustle n

شرشم /shar-sham (shal-)/
mustard n

شرط , -ها/شرایط
/shart, pl sha-rā-yĭt/
condition, proviso; wager n

← شرط کردن
stipulate; make a bet v

شرط نامه /shart nā-ma/
contractual terms n

شرطی /shar-ti/ conditional adj

شرع /shár-'a, shar/
Sharia, Islamic law n

شرعاً /shár-'an/
lawfully (under Islam) adv

شرعی /shar-'i/
lawful (under Islam) n

شرق /sharq/ east adj; the East n

شرق میانه /sharq-ī mī-yā-na/
Middle East n

شرقاً /shár-qan, -qán/
from the east adv

شرک /shĭrk/
apostasy; polytheism n

شرکا /shŭ-ra-kā, sg sha-rik/
see sg شریک n pl

شرکت /shĭr-kat/
company, firm; venture n

شرکت مختلط
/shĭr-kat-ī mŭkh-ta-lat/
joint venture n

شرافت /sha-raf/ n شرف see

شرفا /shŭ-ra-fā, sg sha-rif/
see sg شریف n pl

شلشم /shal-sham/ n شرشم see

شرک /sha-rak/ n شهرک see

شرک /shĭrk/
polytheism; apostasy (obscuring
God's oneness); shirk n

شرم /sharm/ modesty; shame n

← شرم آمدن be ashamed v

← شرم است ! that's too bad excl

شرم اندام /sharm an-dām/
pudendum, f genitals n

شرمگاه /sharm-gāh/
genitals, privates n

شرمگاه مرد /sharm-gāh-ī mard/
penis (fig) n

شرمناک /sharm-nāk/
disgraceful adj

شرن /sha-ran/ Sharan (seat) n

شرنگ /sha-rang/
colocynth; clang, jangling n

شرنه /sha-ra-na/ n شرن see

شروح /shŭ-ruh; sg shár-ha, sharh/
see sg شرح n pl

شروع /shŭ-ro/
start, beginning, outset n

← شروع شدن start, begin vi

← شروع کردن start, begin vt

شریان , -ها/شرایین
/shĭr-yān, pl sha-rā-yin/
artery n

شریانی /shĭr-yā-ni/ arterial adj

شریعت /sha-ri-'at/
Sharia (Islamic law) n

شریف /sha-rif, pl shŭ-ra-fā/
aristocrat; Sharif (m name) n;
exalted adj

← شرفا pl

شریک , -ان/ها/شرکا
/sha-rik, pl shŭ-ra-kā/
partner; (law) accomplice n

← شریک کردن share vt

شریکی /sha-ri-ki/
jointly (colloq) adv; joint adj

شصت n, adj /shast/ see

شست و شو /shŭst ŭ sho/
washing n

← شست و شو دادن / کردن
wash (thoroughly) v

شست و شوی /shŭst ŭ shoy/
n شست و شو see

شستن ؛ -شوی- /-shŭ-wayem/ ؛ شست-
/shos-tan; méyshŭyŭm//
wash, clean vt

شش six n, adj /shash/

شش lung n /shŭsh/

شش ضلعی /shash zŭl-'i/
hexagon n; hexagonal (& verse) adj

شش کباب /shĭsh-ka-bāb/
kabob (on skewer) n

ششته /shŭsh-ta/ washed away adj

ششم /sha-shŭm/ sixth adj

ششمی /sha-shŭ-mi/
sixth adj; the sixth one n

ششمین /sha-shŭ-min/
sixth (used before n) adj

شصت sixty n, adj /shast/

شصتم /shas-tŭm/ sixtieth adj

شصتمین /shas-tŭ-min/
sixtieth (used before n) adj

شطرنج /shat-ranj/
chess; shatranj n

شطرنجی /shat-ran-ji/
related to chess adj

شعار /shŭ-'ār/
slogan, motto; distinguishing mark n

← شعار دادن sloganeer v

شعاع , -ها /shŭ-'ā/ radius n

شعاع , ‌ها-/اشعه /shŭ-'ā, pl ash-'a/
ray, beam n

شعبه , ‌ها-/شعبات
/sho-ba, pl sho-bāt/
office; department (university) n

شعبه سیاسی /sho-ba-yĭ sĭ-yā-si/
political section (embassy) n

شعبه وثایق /sho-ba-yĭ wa-sā-yĭq/
documents office (court) n

شعر , ‌ها-/اشعار /shĭr, pl a-shār/
poem, poetry; verse n

شعله /shŭ-'la (sho-)/
flame, flare, blaze n

→ شعله زدن
blaze, flame, flare v

شعله جاوید /shŭ'-la jā-weyd/
Shola Jaweyd (Afgh Maoist party) n

شعله جاویدی /shŭ'-la jā-wey-di/
شعله یی see

شعله ور /shŭ'-la-war/
blazing; (of pers) determined adj

شعله یی , ‌ها/ان- /shŭ'-la-yi/
member of Shola Jaweyd (pers) n

شعور /shŭ-'ur/
Jethro (pers, bibl) n

شغال /sha-ghāl/ jackal n

شغر /sha-gŭr/ porcupine n

شغل /shŭ'-ghŭl, shŭghl/
profession; job n

شغنی , ‌ها/ان- /shĭgh-ni, shŭgh-/
pers from Shighnan; Shigni (Pamir
lang) n

شفا /sha-fā/ cure, recovery n
→ شفا دادن cure, treat
→ شفا یافتن recover (from illness)

شفاخانه /sha-fā khā-na/ hospital n

شفاخانه عقلی و عصبی
/sha-fā khā-na-yĭ ŭ-qa-li ŭ as-bi/
hospital for the mentally ill n

شفاف /sha-fāf/
clear, transparent adj

شفافیت /sha-fā-fĭ-yat/
clarity; transparency adj

شفاهی /sha-fā-hi/ oral, verbal adj

شفق /sha-faq/ twilight n

شفیق /sha-fiq/
kind, compassionate adj

شق , ‌ها- /shaq/ split n
→ شق شدن split vi
→ شق کردن split vt

شق , ‌ها-/شقوق /shaq, pl shŭ-quq/
branch; subdivision; field of study n

شقاق /shĭ-qāq/ discord, disunity n

شقوق /shŭ-quq, sg shaq/
شق see sg n pl

شقه /sha-qa/
part; split, tear, rip n
→ شقه کردن split, tear, rip v

شقه /shŭ-qa/ piece (paper) n

شقیقه /sha-qi-qa/
temple (anat); sideburns n

شک /shak/
doubt, uncertainty n
→ شک داشتن doubt, have doubts

شک آور /shak ā-war/
controversial, dubitable adj

شکار /shĭ-kār/
hunting; game, prey n
→ شکار کردن hunt v

شکار افگن /shĭ-kār af-gan/
شکاری see n

شکاری /shĭ-kā-ri/ hunter n

شکایت /shĭ-kā-yat/
complaint, grievance n
→ شکایت کردن complain v

شکایت آمیز /shĭ-kā-yat ā-meyz/
complaining, plaintive adj

شکر /sha-kar/ sugar n

شکر /shŭ-kŭr/
praise; thanks, gratitude n
→ شکر خدا ! thank God!
→ شکر کردن thank (sb) vt

شکر پاره /sha-kar pā-ra/
shakar para (kind of dried apricot) n

شکردره /sha-kar-da-ra/
Shakardara (dist) n

شکر گزار /shŭ-kŭr gŭ-zār/
grateful, thankful adj

شکرک /sha-ka-rak/
honeydew (on leaves) n

شکری /sha-ka-ri/
sugar-brown n

شکست /shĭ-kast/ defeat, rout n
→ شکست خوردن be defeated vi
→ شکست دادن defeat v

شکستاندن ؛ شکنان- ؛ شکستاند-
/shĭ-kas-tān-dan,
/méyshĭkanānŭm//
break, crack; smash vt

شکستن ؛ ـشکن ؛ ـشکست ـ
/shĭ-kas-tan, /méyshĭkanŭm//
break, crack; be smashed vi

شکسته /shĭ-kas-ta/
broken adj

شکسته دل /shĭ-kas-ta dĭl/
heartbroken adj

شکل , ـها/اشکال
/sha´-kĭl, shakl; pl ash-kāl/
form; way; picture; appearance n

← شکل دادن <به چیزی>
form, give form <to sth> v

← شکل گرفتن
form, take form v

شکلی /shak-li/
formal, procedural adj

شکل مصدری /sha´-kĭl-ĭ mas-da-ri/
infinitive (gram) n

شکلیات /shak-lĭ-yāt/
formalities n pl

شکم /shĭ-kam (ĭsh-kam)/
belly; (colloq) womb n

← شکم کردن
get pregnant (colloq)

شکم دار /shĭ-kam dār/
pregnant (colloq) adj

شکم درد /shĭ-kam dard/
having a stomach ache adj

شکم رو /shĭ-kam-raw/
having diarrhea adj

شکنجه /shĭ-kan-ja/
torture, torment; clamp n

← شکنجه دادن • شکنجه کردن
torture (sb) vt

شکنندگی /shĭ-ka-nĭn-da-gi/
fragility, frailty n

شکننده /shĭ-ka-nĭn-da/
fragile, frail adj

شکوفه /shŭ-ku-fa/ blossom n
← شکوفه کردن
blossom; (colloq) vomit vi

شکوه /shĭk-wa/ complaint n
← شکوه کردن
complain v

شکی /shĭ-ki/ Sheki (dist) n
شکیب /shĭ-keyb/
patience; forbearance; Shikeyb (m
name) n

شکیبا /shĭ-key-bā/
patient adj

شکیبایی /shĭ-key-bā-yi/
patience n

شکیل /sha-kil/
handsome adj; Shakil (m name) n

شکیلا /sha-ki-lā/
Shakila (f name) n; handsome adj

شگال /sha-gāl/ jackal n

شگفتا ! /shĭ-gĭf-tā/
wow! (for sth surprising or strange)
excl

شگوفه n شکوفه see /shŭ-gu-fa/

شگون /shŭ-gun (-gum, -gŭm)/
bad omen n

شلاق /sha-lāq/
whip, lash (for flogging) n

شلاق قرار دادن
/sha-lāq qa-rār dādan/
whip, lash v

شلشم n شرشم see /shal-sham/

شلغم /shal-gham/ turnip n

شلک /shŭ-lŭk/ leech n

شلند /shĭ-lĭnd/ lizard (small) n

شلوک n شلک see /shŭ-luk/

شله /shŭ-la (sho-)/
shola (Afgh dish) n

شلیطه /sha-li-ta/
nagging, shrewish (colloq) adj

شلیک /sha-lik/
gunshot, salvo, volley n

شلیک پی در پی
/shĭ-lik-ĭ páy dar páy/
fusillade n

شلیل /sha-lil/
nectarine; (N Afgh) reconstituted
dried apricots n

شما /shŭ-mā/
you (sg formal, pl) pron

شماره /shŭ-mā-ra/
number, numeral; digit n

شمال /sha-māl/
north; wind n

شمال شرق /sha-māl sharq/
northeast n

شمال شرقی /sha-māl shar-qi/
northeastern adj

شمال غرب /sha-māl gharb/
northwest n

شمال غربی /sha-māl ghar-bi/
northwestern adj

شمالاً /sha-mā-lan, -mā´-/
from the north adv

شمس /shams/
sun; Shams (m name) n

شمسی /sham-si/ solar (year) adj

شمشیر /sham-sheyr/ sword, sabre, rapier n
← شمشیر زدن wield a sword v
← شمشیر کردن show courage (colloq) v

شمشیر باز /sham-sheyr bāz/ fencer n

شمشیر بازی /sham-sheyr bā-zi/ fencing n

شمشیر زن /sham-sheyr zan/ swordsman; combatant n

شمع /sham/ wax; candle; support n
شمعدان /sham-dān/ candlestick n
شمعدانی n /sham-dā-ni/ شمعدان see
شمعریز /sham-reyz/ candle maker n
شمعه /sham-'a/ watt n

شمل /sha-mal/ Shamal (dist) n
شمولزی /sha-mol-zay/ Shamolzai (dist) n
شمن /sha-man/ shaman n
شمول /shŭ-mul/ inclusion; participation; enrollment n

شنا کردن /shī-nā kardan/ swim vi

شناخت /shī-nākht/ knowledge, acquaintance n
← شناخت داشتن <همرای کسی> be acquainted <w/sb> v

شناختاندن ؛ -شناختان- ؛ -شناختاند- /shī-nākh-tān-dan/ introduce (sb to sb else) vt

شناختن ؛ -شناس- ؛ -شناخت- /shī-nākh-tan/ know, recognize; identify vt

شناسایی /shī-nā-sā-yi/ acquaintance n

شناور , -ان/ها /shī-nā-war/ swimmer n

شنایی n /shī-nā-yi/ شناخت see
شنبه /sham-bey/ Saturday n
شنگرف /shan-garf/ vermilion, cinnabar adj

شنوا /shī-na-wā/ able to hear adj
شنوایی /shī-na-wā-yi/ hearing (sense) n

شنونده , -گان/ها /shī-na-wīn-da/ listener, hearer n

شنونده گان /shī-na-wīn-da-gān/ audience n pl

شنیدن ؛ -شنو- ؛ شنید- , شنفت- /shŭ-ni-dan/ /méyshĭnawŭm// listen, hear, pay attention to v

شنیدنی /shŭ-ni-da-ni/ interesting, worth hearing adj

شو n شب /shaw/ see
شواک /sha-wāk/ Shawak (dist) n
شوال /shaw-wāl/ Shawal (month) n
شوخ /shokh/ naughty; playful; impudent adj

شور /shor/ salty adj; zeal; commotion n
← شور بودن be very salty vi
← شور خوردن complain v
move; make a commotion v
← شور کردن salt, add salt to v
← شور نخو ! don't move!

شورا /sho-rā/ shura, assembly n
← شورای دولت State Council

شورابک /sho-rā-bak/ Shorabak (dist) n

شورای امنیت /sho-rā-yĭ am-nī-yat/ Security Council (UN) n

شورای متحد ملی /sho-rā-yĭ mŭ-ta-hĭd-ĭ mĭ-li/ Council for National Unity (NGO) n

شورای مشرقی /sho-rā-yĭ mash-rĭ-qi/ Eastern Shura (hist, ca. 1997) n

شورای ملی /sho-rā-yĭ mĭ-li/ National Assembly, Parliament n

شورای نظار /sho-rā-yĭ na-zar/ Supervisory Council (hist, 1990s) n

شورای ولایتی /sho-rā-yĭ wĭ-lā-ya-ti/ provincial council n

شوربا /shor-bā (shŭr-wā)/ soup n
شورتیپه /shor-tey-pa/ Shorteypa (dist) n

شورش /sho-rĭsh/ insurgency; rebellion, riot n

شورشی , -ان /shor-shi/ insurgent, rebel n

شوره /sho-ra/ niter, saltpeter n

شوروی , -ان/ها /sho-ra-wi/ USSR (hist, colloq) n; Soviet (& pers) n, adj

شوره زار /sho-ra-zār/
salt marsh *n*

شوری /sho-ri/
saltiness, savoriness *n*

شوریک /shur-yak/
Shuryak (valley) *n*

شوکران /shok-rān/ hemlock *n*

شولگره /shol-ga-ra/
Sholgara (dist) *n*

شوله /sho-la/ pest, nag *n*

شوم /shum/
ill-omened; nefarious *adj*

شوهر /shaw-har (sha-war, shuy)/
husband *n*

شوهر دار /shaw-har-dār/
married (f) *adj*

شوی /shoy/ washing *n*
→ شوی کردن wash, clean *vt*

شوی /shuy/ *n* شوهر see

شهادت /sha-hā-dat/
testimony; attestation (of faith); martyrdom *n*
→ شهادت دادن
testify; attest (& to faith) *v*
→ شهادت یافتن be martyred *vi*

شهدا /shŭ-ha-dā, sg sha-hid/
see sg شهید ; Shuhada (rel) *n pl*

شهدا /shŭ-ha-dā/ *n pl* شهید see sg

شهر /shahr (shār)/ city, town *n*

شهر صفا /shahr-ī sa-fā/
Shahr-e Safa (ctr) *n*

شهر کهنه /shahr-ī kŭh-na/
Shahr-e Kuhna (city dist) *n*

شهر نو /shahr-ī naw/
Shahr-e Naw (city dist) *n*

شهرت /shŭh-rat/
fame, reputation; identity *n*
→ شهرت داشتن be famous *v*

شهرزاد /shá-hīr-zād/
Scheherazade (1001 Ar Nights, cf شیرزاد)

شهرستان /shah-rīs-tān/
Shahrestan (dist) *n*

شهرک /shah-rak/ Shahrak (dist) *n*

شهرک حیرتان /shah-rak hay-ra-tān/
Shahrak Hayratan (dist) *n*

شهروند /shahr-wand/
citizen, national *n*

شهریور /shah-ray-war/
Shahraywar (month, see سنبله) *n*

شهلا /shah-lā/
Shahla (f name) *n*; bluish-black *adj*

شهوت /shah-wat/ lust, lechery *n*

شهوت انگیز /shah-wat an-geyz/
provocative, lascivious; aphrodisiac *adj*

شهوت ران /shah-wat rān/
lecherous *adj*

شهوت رانی /shah-wat rā-ni/
lecherousness *n*

شهوتی /shah-wa-ti/
lecherous, lewd (colloq) *adj*

شهود /shŭ-hud, sg shā-hīd/
see sg شاهد *n pl*

شهید , -ان/ه/شهدا /sha-hid, pl shŭ-ha-dā/
martyr *n*
→ شهید شدن be martyred *vi*

شهید در عملیات /sha-hid dar a-ma-lī-yāt/
n see شهید در محاربه

شهید در محاربه /sha-hid dar mŭ-hā-rī-ba/
KIA, killed in action *n*

شهید عشق /sha-hid-ī īshq/
martyr of love *n*

شهیر /sha-hir/
famous, renowned *adj*

شهیق /sha-hiq/ inhalation *n*

شئون /shŭ-'un/ matters, affairs *n pl*

شی /shay, pl ash-yā/
object, thing; pl goods *n*
→ اشیا pl

شیاد /sha-yād/ impostor *n*

شیار /shī-yār/ furrow, wrinkle *n*

شیاف /shī-yāf (shāf)/ suppository *n*

شیاطین /sha-yā-tin, sg shay-tān/
see sg شیطان *n pl*

شیب کوه /shib koh/
Shib Koh (dist) *n*

شیبر /shi-bar/ Shibar (dist) *n*

شیخ , ها/شیوخ
/sheykh, pl shŭ-yukh/
sheik, sheykh; old man; head of Sufi order n

شیخ علی /sheykh a-li/
Sheykh Ali (dist) n

lion; (zodiac) Leo n /sheyr/ شیر

شیر شاه سوری /sheyr shāh su-ri/
Sher Shah Suri (P leader, hist) n

milk n /shir/ شیر

شیر برنج /shir bĭ-rĭnj/
rice pudding n

شیر چای /shir-chāy/
milk tea (drink) n

شیر چوشک /shir-cho-shak/
baby bottle n

شیر خشت /shir-khĭsht/
laxative manna n

شیر خشک /shir-ĭ khŭshk/
powdered milk n

شیر خط /shayr khat/
see شیر یا خط n

شیر خوار (-خور) /shir-khār (-khor)/
infant, nursling adj

lukewarm adj /shir garm/ شیر گرم

milkfish n /shir-mā-hi/ شیر ماهی

شیر و خط انداختن
/shayr ŭ khat andākhtan/
flip a coin v

شیر یا خط /shayr yā khat/
heads or tails n

شیردهن (شیردان)
/shir-da-han (shir-dān)/
tap, faucet n

شیرزاد /sheyr-zād/
Sheyrzad (dist, ctr Mama Kheyl) n

lukewarm adj /shir-garm/ شیرگرم

ice cream n /shir-yakh/ شیریخ

شیرین /shi-rin/
sweet; pleasant (& adv) adj, adv

licorice n /shi-rin bu-ya/ شیرین بویه

شیرین تگاب /shi-rin ta-gāb/
Shirin Tagab (dist) n

شیرینی /shi-ri-ni (shīr-ni)/
candy, sweets; sweetness n

شیرینی خوری /shi-ri-ni khŭ-ri/
engagement party (for f) n

schist (rock) n /shist/ شیست

شیشتن ؛ -شیشت- ؛ شین- /shish-tan/
sit (colloq) vi

sissoo (tree) n /shi-sham/ شیشم

شیشه /shi-sha/
glass (material); bottle n

شیشه بر /shi-sha bŭr/
glass cutter; glass cutting n

شیشه دل /shi-sha dĭl/
coward n; timid adj

شیشه یی /shi-sha-yi/
glass, made of glass adj

شیطان , -ها/شیاطین /shay-tān, pl sha-yā-tin/
devil; (fig) bad pers n; naughty adj

شیطانت /shay-tā-nat/
treachery; devilry n

شیطانت آمیز /shay-tā-nat ā-meyz/
treacherous; devilish adj

شیطانت بار /shay-tā-nat bār/
see شیطانت آمیز adj

شیطانی /shay-tā-ni/
diabolical; fiendish; naughty adj; mischief n

شیعه , -ها /shi-'a (shĭ-ya, shu-ya)/
Shiite; disciples (rel) n

شیعی , -ان /shi-'i/
Shiite (& pers) adj, n

شیگل و شلتن /shay-gal wŭ shĭl-tan/
Shaygal wa Sheltan (dist) n

hollow n /shi-la/ شیله

شیمه /shi-ma/
power, strength (colloq) n

شینکی /shin-kay/
Shinkay (dist) n

شینوار /shin-wār/
Shinwar (dist, ctr Ghani Kheyl) n

شینواری /shin-wā-ri/
Shinwari (dist) n

شیندند /shin-dand/
Shindand (dist) n

شیوخ /shŭ-yukh, sg sheykh/
see sg شیخ n pl

شیون /shey-wan/
wail, lament n

← شیون کردن
wail, lament v
/shey-wa/ شیوه

downhill adv; slope; manner; custom; Sheywa (ctr) n

شیوه دار /shey-wa dār/
polite, urbane adj
شیهه /shi-ha/ neigh n
← شیهه کشیدن neigh v

ص

صابون /sā-bun/ soap n
صاحب /sā-hĭb (-yĭb)/
sir, mister (form of address, follows name); master adj, n
صاحب خانه /sā-hĭb khā-na/
master of the house n
صاحب منصب , -ان/ها
/sā-hĭb man-sab/
military officer n
صادر , -ات /sā-dĭr/
export; issuance n
← صادر کردن export; issue v
صادر کننده , -گان/ها
/sā-dĭr kŭ-nĭn-da/
exporter n
صادراتی /sā-dĭ-rā-ti/
exportable, for export adj
صادق /sā-dĭq/
loyal; honest (& pers); Sadeq (m name) adj, n
صادقانه /sā-dĭ-qā-na/
loyally; honestly adv; unfeigned adj
صاف /sāf/
pure, clear; sincere adj; strainer n
صافی /sā-fi/
purity; Safi (P tribe) n
صالح /sā-lĭh/
proper; virtuous; Saleh (m name) n
صالحه /sā-lĭ-ha/ Saleha (f name) n
صامت , -ها /sā-mĭt/ consonant n
صایت , -ها /sā-yĭt/ vowel n
صبا /sa-bā/
east wind, pleasant wind n
صباح /sa-bāh/
tomorrow adv; morning n
صباحی /sa-bā-hi (-yi)/
morning adj; in the morning adv
صباوت /sa-bā-wat/ childhood n
صبح /sŭbh (sob)/
morning adj; in the morning adv
صبح دم /sŭbh-dam/
dawn, daybreak n

صبحانه /sŭb-hā-na/
in the morning adv
صبحکی /sŭb-ha-ki/
in the morning (colloq) adv
صبحگاه /sŭbh-gāh/ daybreak (lit) n
صبحگاهی /sŭbh-gā-hi/
morning adj
صبر /sá-bĭr, sabr/
patience, forbearance n
← صبر کردن
wait; be patient, endure v
صبری /sa-ba-ri/
Sabari (dist, ctr Zambar) n
صبیه /sa-bī-ya/ daughter (lit) n
صحابه /sa-hā-ba/
the Companions (Prophet's) n pl
صحاری /sa-hā-ri/
see sg صحرا n pl
صحاف /sa-hāf/ bookbinder n
صحافت /sa-hā-fat/ bookbinding n
صحبت /sŭh-bat (sŭw-)/
conversation; companionship n
← صحبت کردن talk, converse vi
صحت /sĭ-hat/ health n
صحتمند /sĭ-hat-mand/ healthy adj
صحرا , -ها/صحاری
/sah-rā, pl sa-hā-ri/
desert n
صحرا نشین /sah-rā nĭ-shin/
nomad n; nomadic adj
صحرا نورد /sah-rā na-ward/
desert traveler n
صحرایی /sah-rā-yi/
of the desert; uncivilized adj
صحنه /sah-na/
arena (& fig); spectacle n
صحنه تمثیل /sah-na-yĭ tam-sil/
stage (theater) n
صحنه جنگ /sah-na-yĭ jang/
staging ground (war) n
صحوه /sah-wa/
Sahwa, Muslim revival since Six-Day War n
صحه گذاشتن /sĭ-ha gŭzāshtan/
approve, sign, ratify vt
صحی /sĭ-hi/
health; hygienic; medical adj
← صحیه f form

صحيح /sa-hih/ true, correct *adj*
← صحيحه f form
صخره /sakh-ra/
boulder, large rock *n*
صد /sad/ hundred *n, adj*
صدا /sa-dā/ noise, sound; voice *n*
صدای امریکا /sa-dā-yĭ am-rī-kā/
Voice of America *n*
صدارت /sa-dā-rat/
prime ministership *n*
صدای <کسی> گرفته بودن
/sa-dā-yĭ ká-sey gĭ-rĭf-ta bu-dan/
have laryngitis *v*
صدد /sa-dad/
aim, purpose, intention *n*
صدر /sá-dĭr, sadr/
chest; beginning; top man *n*
صدر اعظم /sadr-ĭ a'-zam/
prime minister, premier *n*
صدر شهر /sadr-ĭ shahr/
senior cleric overseeing waqfs & rel
law *n*
صدف /sa-daf/
oyster; mother-of-pearl; shell *n*
صدفی /sa-daf/ made of shell *adj*
صدقه , -ها /sa-da-qa/
charity; alms tax (Musl law) *n*
← صدقه خواستن beg for alms *v*
← صدقه دادن give alms *v*
صدم /sa-dŭm/ hundredth *adj*
صدمه , -ها/صدمات
/sa-da-ma, pl -māt/
damage, harm; injury *n*
← صدمه زدن
damage; injure, harm *v*
صدمه دیده /sa-da-ma di-da/
damaged *adj*
صدمین /sa-dŭ-min/
hundredth (used before n) *adj*
صدور /sŭ-dur/ export; issuance *n*
صراحت /sa-rā-hat/
clarity; frankness *n*
صراحتاً /sa-rā-há-tan, -tán/
clearly; frankly *adv*
صراط /sĭ-rāt/
way, path, road (esp fig) *n*
صراف /sa-rāf/
cashier; money changer *n*

صرافی کردن /sa-rā-fi kardan/
change money *v*
صرب , -ها /sŭrb, sarb/
Serb, Serbian (pers) *n*
صربستان , -sar /sŭr-bĭs-tān/
Serbia (country) *n*
صربی , -sar /sŭr-bi/
Serbian *adj*; Serb, Serbian (pers,
lang) *n*
صرع /sar'/ seizure; epilepsy *n*
صرف /sĭrf/ mere, only *adj*
صرف /sarf/
turning away, averting *n*
صرف اسم /sarf-ĭ ĭ'-sĭm/
noun declension *n*
صرف فعل /sarf-ĭ feyl/
verb conjugation *n*
صرف نظر کردن <از چیزی>
/sarf-ĭ na-zar kardan/
ignore <sth>; change one's mind *vt*
صرف و نحو /sarf ŭ nahw/
morphology & syntax, grammar *n*
صرفاً /sĭ'r-fan, -fán/
merely, only *adv*
صغیر /sa-ghir/
small; juvenile *adj*; child *n*
صغیره /sa-ghi-ra/
small; juvenile (f form) *adj*; minor
transgression *n*
← نکاح صغیره child marriage *n*
صف , -ها/صفوف /saf, pl sŭ-fuf/
line, row; rank, array *n*
صف شکستاندن /saf shĭkastāndan/
break ranks *v*
صفاری /sa-fā-ri/
Saffarid (hist) *adj, n*
صفاریان /sa-fā-rī-yān/
Saffarid dynasty (hist) *n pl*
صفت , -ها/صفات /sĭ-fat, pl -fāt/
adjective *n*
صفت اشاره /sĭ-fat-ĭ ĭ-shā-ra/
demonstrative adjective *n*
صفت تفضلی /sĭ-fat-ĭ taf-zī-li/
comparative adjective *n*
صفت عالی /sĭ-fat-ĭ 'ā-li/
superlative adjective *n*
صفت مفعولی /sĭ-fat-ĭ maf-'u-li/
participle, verbal adjective *n*

صفتى /sĭ-fa-ti/ adjectival adj

صفحه , -ها/صفحات /saf-ha, pl -hāt/ page n

صفر /sĭ´-fĭr, sĭfr/ zero; cipher; nonentity
↪ صفر بودن be of no importance

صفرا /saf-rā/ rage, anger; bile, gall n

صفرا بر /saf-rā bŭr/ adj صفرا شكن see

صفرا شكن /saf-rā shĭ-kan/ ambitious adj

صفراوى /saf-rā-wi/ choleric; bilious adj

صفرايى /saf-rā-yi/ adj صفراوى see

صفورا /sa-fu-rā/ Zipporah (f name, & bibl) n

صفوف /sŭ-fuf, sg saf/ صف n pl see sg

صفوى /sa-fa-wi/ Safavid (hist; & Sufi sect) n

صفويان /sa-fa-wi-yān/ Safavid dynasty (hist) n pl

صلات /sa-lāt, pl -la-wāt/ prayer (Musl, five times daily) n
↪ صلوات pl

صلاح دادن /sa-lāh dādan/ advise; recommend, suggest v

صلاحيت /sa-lā-hǐ-yat/ responsibility; authority, competency n

صلاحيت دار /sa-lā-hǐ-yat dār/ responsible adj

صلبيه /sŭl-bī-ya/ sclera (anat) n

صلح /sŭlh (sŭl)/ peace; reconciliation n
↪ صلح كردن reconcile, make peace v

صلح كل /sŭlh-ĭ kŭl/ peace with all (Akbar's ideal) (hist) n

صلوات /sa-la-wāt, sg sa-lāt/ صلات n pl see sg

صليب /sa-lib/ cross; the Cross n

صليب احمر /sa-lib-ĭ ah-mar/ صليب سرخ n see

صليب سرخ /sa-lib-ĭ sŭrkh/ Red Cross n

صليبى /sa-li-bi/ of the cross adj
↪ جنگ های صليبى the Crusades (hist)

صمد /sa-mad/ Samad (m name) n; eternal (God) adj

صميم /sa-mim/ core, interior; bottom n

صميمانه /sa-mi-mā-na/ friendly, cordial (& adv) adj, adv

صميمى /sa-mi-mi/ friendly, cordial adj

صميميت /sa-mi-mǐ-yat/ friendliness, cordiality n

صناعت , -ها/صنايع /sa-nā-'at, pl -yey/ industry; skill; vocation n

صنايع /sa-nā-yey; sg sŭn-'at, sa-nā-'at/ صنعت n pl see sg

صندل /san-dal/ sandalwood n

صندوق /san-duq (-dŭq)/ chest, box, case, crate n

صندوق پس انداز /san-duq-ĭ pas an-dāz/ cashbox n

صندوق پوستى /san-duq-ĭ pos-ti/ mailbox n

صندوق وجهى بين المللى /san-duq-ĭ waj-hi-yĭ bay-nŭl-mĭ-la-li/ International Monetary Fund, IMF n

صنعا /san-'ā/ Sanaa (capital) n

صنعت /sŭn-'at, pl sa-nā-yey/ workmanship; see & صناعت n
↪ صنايع pl

صنعت دست /sŭn-'at-ĭ dast/ handiwork n

صنعتكار /sŭn-'at-kār/ صنعتگر n see

صنعتگر /sŭn-'at-gar/ artisan, craftsman n

صنعتى /sŭn-'a-ti/ industrial adj

صنف , -ها/اصناف /sǐnf, pl as-nāf/ trade, guild n

صنف , -ها/صنوف
/sĭnf, pl sŭ-nuf/
class, grade; classroom n

صنوبر /sa-naw-bar/
pine (tree); Sanawbar (f name) n

صنوف /sŭ-nuf, sg sĭnf/
see sg صنف n pl

صوبه /so-ba/
province n

صوت , -ها/اصوات
/sawt, pl as-wāt/
sound; phone (speech sound) n

صوتی /saw-ti/
phonetic adj

صور /sur/
sur (mus instr) n

صور /sŭ-war, sg su-rat/
see sg صورت n pl

صورت , -ها/صور
/su-rat, pl sŭ-war/
shape; face, appearance n

← صورت پذیرفتن / گرفتن
/su-rat pa-zir/
happen, take place vi

صورت پذیر /su-rat pa-zir/
possible, feasible adj

صورت حساب /su-rat-ĭ hĭ-sāb/
account statement, invoice n

صورت و معنی /su-rat ŭ ma'-nā/
form & meaning n phrs

صوفی , -ان/ها /su-fi/
Sufi, Musl mystic; (title of respect) n

صوفیانه /su-fĭ-yā-na/
Sufic, Sufist, mystical adj; as a Sufi
adv

صوفیه /su-fĭ-ya/
Sufism; the Sufis; Sofia (capital) n

صومعه /so-mĭ-'a/
monastery, cloister n

صومعه نشین /so-mĭ-'a nĭ-shin/
monk, hermit n

صهیون /sah-yun/
Zion; Israel n

صیاد /sa-yād/
Sayad (dist) n

صیام /sĭ-yām/
fasting, fast n

صیغه /si-gha/
form (& gram); temporary marriage
n

ض

ضابط , -ان/ها /zā-bĭt/
lieutenant n

ضابط اول /zā-bĭt-ĭ a-wal/
first lieutenant, 1LT n

ضابط اعاشه /zā-bĭt-ĭ ĭ-'ā-sha/
commissary, officer in charge of
foods n

ضابط امر /zā-bĭt-ĭ á-mĭr/
aide-de-camp n

ضایع /zā-yey/
wasted, lost; futile adj

← ضایع کردن
waste, lose (time)

ضایعه , -ها/ضایعات
/zā-yey-yī-'a, pl -'āt (zā-ya, pl -yāt)/
waste, loss n

ضبط /zabt/
confiscation; writing down n

← ضبط کردن
confiscate, seize; record v

ضبطی /zab-ti/
confiscated, seized; recorded adj

ضد , pl az-dād /zĭd/
opponent; contrast n; opposite adj

← اضداد pl

ضد شورش /zĭd sho-rĭsh/
counterinsurgency n

ضد عفونی /zĭd-ĭ a-fu-ni/
disinfection n

← ضد عفونی کردن disinfect vt

ضد و نقیض /zĭd ŭ na-qiz/
contradictory adj

ضدیت /zĭ-dī-yat/
opposition; contrariness n

ضراب خانه /za-rāb khā-na/
see صرب خانه n

ضرب /zarb/
hitting; shooting; multiplication n

← ضرب کردن
multiply, do multiplication v

ضرب المثل , -ها /zarb-ŭl-ma-sal/
proverb, adage n

ضرب خانه /zarb khā-na/
mint (produces money) n

ضربت /zar-bat/ see ضربه

ضربه /zar-ba/
blow, strike; (mil) thrust n

← ضربه زدن hit, strike v

ضربه فنی /zar-ba-yĭ fī-ni/
knockout blow n

ضربى /zar-bi/
percussive (mus instr) adj

ضرر /za-rar/ damage, harm n
ضررناك /za-rar-nāk/
damaging, harmful adj

ضرور /za-rur/
necessary; urgent adj

ضرورت /za-ru-rat/
need, urgency n

← ضرورت داشتن ‹به چيزى›
need, require ‹sth› vt

ضرورتاً /za-ru-rá-tan, -tán/
necessarily adv

ضرورى /za-ru-ri/
necessary, required adj

ضروريات /za-ru-rī-yāt/
requirements n pl

ضعفا /zŭ-'a-fā, sg za'-if/
see sg ضعيف n pl

ضعيف , -ان/ها/ضعفا
/za-'if, pl zŭ-'a-fā/
weak, feeble; senile adj

← ضعيف ساختن / كردن
weaken, enfeeble vt

ضلع /zŭ-la, zŭl'/
district (Pakistan); (math) side n

ضمانت /za-mā-nat/
surety, collateral, bail n

ضماير /za-mā-yīr, sg -mir/
see sg ضمير n pl

ضمن /zīmn/ interior n

ضمناً /zĭ'm-nān, -nā'n/
inherently; tacitly adv

ضمنى /zĭm-ni/
inherent; tacit; included adj

ضمير , -ها/ضماير
/za-mir, pl -mā-yīr/
conscience; (gram) pronoun n

ضمير اشاره /za-mir-ī ĭ-shā-ra/
demonstrative pronoun n

ضيافت /zī-yā-fat/
banquet, party; invitation n

ط

طابع /tā-bey/ printer n
طاس /tās/ see تاس
طاعون /tā-'un/ plague; calamity n

طاغى /tā-ghi/ rebel; despot n
طاق /tāq/ odd (math) adj; arch n
طاق ظفر يغمان
/tāq-ī za-far-ī pagh-mān/
Victory Arch of Paghman n

طاقت /tā-qat/
patience; endurance n

طاقت فرسا /tā-qat far-sā/
unbearable adj

طالب , -ان/ /tā-lĭb/
Talib (member of Taliban) n

طالب , -ها/طلاب/طلبه
/tā-lĭb; pl tŭ-lāb, ta-la-ba/
student (esp of Islam); seeker n

طالب , -ين /tā-lĭb/ claimant n
طالب العلم /tā-lĭ-bŭl-'ĭ'-lĭm/
Islamic scholar n

طالبان /tā-lĭ-bān/
Taliban (extremist mvmt) n pl

طالع /tā-ley/
fortune, fate; horoscope n

طالعمند /tā-ley-mand/
fortunate (& pers) adj, n

طاووس /tā-wus/
peacock; Tawus (m name) n

طالب , -ان/ها /tā-lĭb/ seeker n
طاليب /tā-lĭb/ n see طالب
طاليبان /tā-lĭ-bān/ n pl see طالبان
طايفه , -ها/طوايف
/tā-yī-fa, pl ta-wā-yīf/
sect; clan; group n

طب /tĭb/
medicine, medical science n

طب وقايه وى /tĭb-ī wĭ-qā-ya-wi/
preventive medicine n

طبابت /ta-bā-bat/
practice of medicine n

← طبابت كردن treat (med) v
طباخ /ta-bākh/ cook, chef n
طباخى /ta-bā-khi/ cooking adj
طباعت /ta-bā-'at/
printing, art of printing n

طباعتى /ta-bā-'a-ti/
related to printing adj

طبايع /ta-bā-yey, sg -bi-'at/
see sg طبيعت n pl

طبخ /tabkh/ cooking, cookery n
← طبخ كردن cook v

i = keep, ĭ = big, u = coop, ŭ = put, y = yet, ' = (glottal stop)   209

طبع /táb-'a, tab'/
nature; printing, press n
→ طبع کردن print v
طبع حروفی /táb'-ī hŭ-ru-fi/
typography n
طبع دوم /táb-'a dŭ-wŭm/
reprint; reprinting n
→ طبع دوم کردن reprint v
طبع سنگی /táb'-ī san-gi/
lithography n
طبعاً /táb-'an, -'án/
naturally; of course adv
طبق /tĭbq(-ī) according to prep
طبق /ta-baq/ see تبنگ n
طبقات الارضی /ta-ba-qāt-ŭl-ar-zi/
geological adj
طبقاتی /ta-ba-qā-ti/
class (& social) adj
طبقه , -ها/طبقات /ta-ba-qa, pl -qāt/
class (social); floor, story; layer n
طبقات الارض /ta-ba-qāt-ŭl-arz/
geological strata n pl
طبقه بالا /ta-ba-qa-yĭ bā-lā/
upstairs n
طبقه پایین /ta-ba-qa-yĭ pā-yin/
downstairs n
طبقه رنج بران
/ta-ba-qa-yĭ ranj-bar-ān/
proletariat n
طبلیسی /tĭ-bī-li-si/
Tbilisi, Tiflis (capital) n
doctor, physician n طبیب /ta-bib/
طبیبی /ta-bi-bi/
medical treatment n
طبیعت /ta-bi-'at, pl -bā-yey/
nature (var senses); disposition n
→ طبایع pl
طبیعتاً /ta-bí-'a-tan/
by nature, naturally adv
طبیعی /ta-bi-'i/
natural; intrinsic; ordinary adj
طبیله /ta-bey-la/ see طویله n
طحال /ta-hāl/
spleen (esp animal's) n
طراح , -ان/ها /ta-rāh/
planner; designer n
طراحی کردن /ta-rā-hi kardan/
plan; design v

freshness n /ta-rā-wat/ طراوت
→ طراوت داشتن be fresh vi
طرح /tár-ha, tarh/
plan; design; draft; subtraction;
foundation n
→ طرح ریختن • طرح افگندن
lay a foundation v
→ طرح کردن
plan; subtract v
طرح ریزی /tár-ha rey-zi/
planning; foundation laying n
طرد /tard/
firing, dismissal (& for cause) n
→ طرد شدن <از وظیفه>
be fired <from a job> vi
manner, way; style n /tarz/ طرز
طرز استعمال /tarz-ī ĭs-tey-mal/
directions for use n
طرز العمل /tarz-ŭl-'a-mal/
policy, course of action n
طرز تفکر /tarz-ī ta-fa-kŭr/
mindset, way of thinking n
طرز زندگی /tarz-ī zĭn-da-gi/
lifestyle n
طرزی /tar-zi/
Tarzi (19th -c Dari poet) n
طرف
/ta-raf, pl at-rāf, dual pl ta-ra-fayn/
side; party; direction; (in pl)
suburbs; provinces
→ اطراف pl
→ طرفین dual pl
طرف /ta-raf(-ī)/
in the direction of prep
طرف دعوا /ta-rafī da'-wā/
party (to a lawsuit) n
طرفدار , -ان/ها /ta-raf-dār/
supporter, partisan n
novel, very new adj طرفه /tŭr-fa/
طرق /tŭ-rŭq, sg ta-riq/
see sg طریق n pl
طره /tŭ-ra/ forelock n
طریق , -ها/طرق /ta-riq, pl tŭ-rŭq/
path, way; method n
طریقت , -ها /ta-ri-qat/
Sufi order (general term) n
→ شیخ (طریقت) sheykh (head of

طریقه , -ها/طریقات
/ta-ri-qa, pl -qāt/
see طریق n

طعام , -ها/اطعمه
/ta-'ām, pl at-'ī-ma/
food, meal n

طعام بخش /ta-'ām bakhsh/
serving spoon, spatula n

طعام چاشت /ta-'ām-ī chāsht/
lunch n

طعام خانه /ta-'ām khā-na/
mess hall n

طعام شب /ta-'ām-ī shab/
dinner, supper n

طعمه /tŭ-'ma/
bait; (fig) bribe n
← طعمه دادن
bait, bribe v

طعن /ta'n/ see طعنه n
طعنه /ta'-na/
sarcasm; fault-finding n
← طعنه کردن • طعنه زدن
find fault with v

طغیان /tŭgh-yān/
riot, mutiny; rising river n

طفل , -ها/اطفال /tĭ´-fīl, tĭfl; pl at-fāl/
child; baby; fetus n

طفل پیش رس /tĭ´-fīl-ī peysh ras/
premature baby n

طفلانه /tĭf-lā-na/
children's; childish adj; childishly
adv

طفلک /tĭf-lak/
kid, child (colloq, dim) n

طفلی /tĭf-li/ childhood; infancy n
طفولیت /tŭ-fu-lī-yat/
childhood; infancy n

طلا /tĭ-lā/ gold n
طلای سفید /tĭ-lā-yī sa-feyd/
platinum n

طلا کاری /tĭ-lā-kā-ri/ gold plating n
← طلا کاری شده gold-plated adj
← طلا کاری کردن gold-plate v

طلاب /tŭ-lāb, sg tā-lĭb/
see sg طالب n pl

طلاق /ta-lāq/ divorce n
← طلاق دادن • طلاق کردن
divorce (by m) v
← طلاق گرفتن divorce (by f) v

طلاق خط /ta-lāq khat/
divorce decree n

طلاق رجعی /ta-lāq-ī rŭj-'i/
revocable divorce (Musl law) n

طلاق نامه /ta-lāq nā-ma/
divorce decree n

طلاقی /ta-lā-qi/ divorced (f) adj
طلبگار , -ان/ها /ta-lab-gār/
suitor n

طلبگاری /ta-lab-gā-ri/
marriage proposal n

طلبه /ta-la-ba, sg tā-lĭb/
see sg طالب n pl

طلق /talq/ talcum powder n
طلوع /tŭ-lo/ rising n
← طلوع کردن rise (esp sun) v
طلوع آفتاب /tŭ-lo-yī āf-tāb/
sunrise n

طلوع بامداد /tŭ-lo-yī bām-dād/
see طلوع صبح n

طلوع صبح /tŭ-lo-yī sŭbh/
daybreak n

طماع /ta-mā/
greedy; avid adj

طمانینت /ta-mā-ni-nat/
calmness, composure n

طمانیت /ta-mā-nī-yat/
see طمانینت (colloq) n

طمث /tams/
monthly period (f's) n

طمطراق /tŭm-tŭ-rāq/
pomp; grandiloquence n

طمع /ta-ma/ greed; strong desire n
← طمع داشتن covet, be greedy v
طمع کار /ta-ma kār/
greedy person n

طناب /ta-nāb/ rope (small), cord n
طنز /tanz/ derision; satire n
طنز آمیز /tanz ā-meyz/
derisive; satirical adj

طنز نویس , -ان/ها /tanz na-wis/
satirist n

طنین دار /ta-nin dār/
voiced (gram) adj

طواف /ta-wāf/
fruit seller; walking around (sth) n

طوایف /ta-wā-yĭf, sg tā-yĭ-fa/
see sg طایفه n pl

طور /tawr, pl at-wār/
way, manner n

اطوار pl →
طوريکه /taw-ri-key/
thus, in this way adv

طوطا see توتا /to-tā/ n طوطا
طوعاً و کرهاً /taw-'an ŭ kar-han/
willy-nilly adv

طوفان /tu-fān/ storm, tempest n
طوفان انقلابی /tu-fān-ī īn-qī-lā-bi/
uproar; uprising n

طوفان بحری /tu-fān-ī bah-ri/
hurricane; typhoon n

طوفان ریگ /tu-fān-ī reyg/
sandstorm n

طوفان نوح /tu-fān-ī nuh/
the Flood (bibl) n

طوق /tawq/ necklace; ruffle n
طول /tul/ length n
طولانی /tu-lā-ni/
lengthy, long adj

طومار /to-mār/
scroll; (colloq) amulet w/Quranic
text n

طوی /toy, tuy/
wedding; wedding party (colloq) n

طویل /ta-wil/ adj طولانی see
طویل العمر /ta-wil-ŭl-ū´-mīr/
long-lived, longevous adj

طویل المدت /ta-wil-ŭl-mū-dat/
long-term adj

طویله /ta-wey-la (-bey)-/ stable n
طهارت /ta-hā-rat/
ritual ablutions; cleanliness n

طهماسپ /tah-māsp/
Tahmasp I (hist) n

طی /tay/
through prep; going through n

طی مراحل /tay-ī ma-rā-hīl/
screening, vetting n

طیاره , -ها/طیارات
/ta-yā-ra, pl -rāt/
airplane, aircraft, plane n

طیاره جنگی /ta-yā-ra-yī jan-gi/
fighter plane n

طیاره دوباله /ta-yā-ra-yī du bā-la/
biplane n

طیاره شکاری /ta-yā-ra-yī shī-kā-ri/
طیاره جنگی see n

ظ

ظالم , -ان/ها /zā-līm/
despot, tyrant n; cruel; unjust adj

ظالمانه /zā-lī-mā-na/
despotic, cruel adj; cruelly adv

ظلمانی /zŭl-mā-ni/
dark; gloomy; murky adj

ظاهر /zā-hīr/
apparent, obvious adj; outside n

ظاهر داری /zā-hīr dā-ri/
ceremoniousness n

ظاهر سازی /zā-hīr sā-zi/
sham, pretense n

ظاهر شاه /zā-hīr shāh/
Zahir Shah (Afgh king 1933-1973,
hist) n

ظاهراً /zā-hī´-ran, -rán/
apparently; theoretically adv

ظاهربین /zā-hīr-bin/
shallow, superficial (& pers) adj, n

ظرف(-ی) /zarf(-ī)/
during, within (formal) prep

ظرف , -ها/ظروف /zarf, pl zū-ruf/
vessel, receptacle n

ظرف شوی /zarf-shoy/
kitchen sink; dishwasher n

ظرف ها /zarf-hā/ dishes n pl
ظرفیت /zar-fī-yat/ capacity n
ظرفیت تولید /zar-fī-yat-ī taw-lid/
production capacity n

ظروف /zŭ-ruf, sg zarf/
see sg ظرف n pl

ظریف /za-rif/
fine; elegant, graceful adj

ظفر /za-far/ triumph, victory n
ظفر یافتن → triumph, be victorious
ظفر مند /za-far-mand/
triumphant, victorious adj

ظل /zīl/
shade, shadow; protection, support
n

ظلم , -ها /zŭ´-llm, zŭlm/
tyranny, injustice, cruelty n

ظلم آمیز /zŭ´-llm ā-meyz/
oppressive adj

ظلمانی /zŭ-lĭ-mā-ni/
dark, murky *adj*
ظلمت , -ها /zŭ-lĭ-mat/
darkness, murkiness; ignorance *n*
ظهر /zŭ´-hŭr, zŭhr/
noon, midday *n*
ظهر نویسی /zŭ´-hŭr na-wi-si/
endorsement (of check) *n*
ظهور /zŭ-hur/
appearance, advent; (med) outbreak *n*
ظهیر /za-hir/
supporter; Zahir (12th-c Dari poet) *n*

ع

عابد , -ین/عباد /ā-bĭd, pl ĭ-bād/
worshiper; hermit, recluse *n*
عابد فریب /ā-bĭd fĭ-reyb/
very beautiful (lit) *adj*
عاج /āj/ ivory *n*
عاجز , -ان/ها /ā-jĭz/
humble; weak; incapable (& pers) *adj, n*
عاجل /ā-jĭl/ immediate, urgent *adj*
عادت , -ها/عادات /ā-dat, pl ā-dāt/
custom, habit *n*
← عادت داشتن have a habit *v*
← عادت کردن
get used to; be addicted to *vi*
← عادت گرفتن take up a habit *v*
عادت شراب خوری
/ā-dat-ĭ sha-rāb khŭ-ri/
alcoholism *n*
عادتاً /ā-dá-tan, -tán/
customarily, habitually *adv*
عادل /ā-dĭl/
fair, just, righteous (& pers) *adj, n*
عادلانه /ā-dĭ-lā-na/
fair; legitimate; righteous (& adv) *adj, adv*
عادی /ā-di/ common, ordinary *adj*
عار /ār/
shame, disgrace, dishonor *n*
عارض , -ان/ها/ین /ā-rĭz/
cheek (anat); petitioner *n*
← عارض شدن • عارض کردن
charge, bring a complaint *n*

عارضه , -ها/عوارض
/ā-rĭ-za, pl a-wā-rĭz/
incident; illness; mechanical defect *n*
← عارضه داشتن
be mechanically defective *v*
عارضی /ā-rĭ-zi/
incidental, occasional *adj*
عارضین /ā-rĭ-zayn/ cheeks *dual pl*
عارف , -ان/ها/ین/عرفا
/ā-rĭf, pl ŭ-ra-fā/
mystic; gnostic; Sufi *n*
عارفانه /ā-rĭ-fā-na/
mystical; Sufic *adj*; mystically *adv*
عاری <از چیزی> /ā-ri/
devoid, free <of sth> *adj*
عاری از حقیقت /ā-ri az ha-qi-qat/
baseless, unsubstantiated *adj*
عاری از کوکنار /ā-ri az kok-nār/
poppy-free *adj*
عاریت /ā-rĭ-yat/ loan *n*
← عاریت خواستن borrow *vt*
← عاریت دادن loan, lend *vt*
← عاریت گرفتن borrow *vt*
عاریتاً /ā-rĭ-yá-tan, -tán/
on loan *adv*
عاریتی /ā-rĭ-ya-ti/
loaned; borrowed *adj*
عازم /ā-zĭm/
bound for, headed for *adj*
عاشق , -ان/ین/عشاق
/ā-shĭq, pl ŭ-shāq/
lover; Asheq (m name) *n*
عاشق <کسی> /ā-shĭq(-ĭ)/
in love with <sb> *adj*
عاشور /ā-shur/
Muharram; Ashur (m/f name) *n*
عاشورا /ā-shu-rā/
Ashura (day of Husayn's martyrdom, 10th of Muharram) *n*
عافیت /ā-fĭ-yat/
good health, well-being *n*
عاقبت /ā-qĭ-bat, pl a-wā-qĭb/
end; result *n*
← عواقب pl
عاقبت <چیزی> /ā-qĭ-bat(-ĭ)/
at the end <of sth> *prep*

عاقبت انديش /ā-qī-bat an-deysh/
nearsighted adj

عاقل , -ان/ها/عقلا /ā-qil, pl ŭ-qa-lā/
intelligent, wise (& pers) adj, n
← عاقلانه intelligently, wisely adv
عالم /ā-lam/ world n
عالم , -ان/ها/علما /ā-lim, pl ŭ-la-mā/
scholar, scientist n; learned, erudite adj

عالم اقتصاد /ā-līm-ĭ ĭq-tĭ-sād/
economist n

عالم سياست /ā-līm-ĭ sĭ-yā-sat/
political scientist n

عالی /ā-li/
high; exalted, sublime adj

عالی رتبه /ā-li rŭt-ba/
high-ranking adj

عام , pl a-wām/ /ām
common, general, public adj;
commoner n
← عوام pl

عامل /ā-mīl/
executive, executing adj

عامل , -ين/عمال /ā-mīl, pl ŭ-māl/
factor, agent; perpetrator (of crime) n

عامه /ā-ma, pl a-wām/
the public, the masses n
← عوام pl

عايدات /ā-yī-dāt/
income, revenue, returns n

عايشه /ā-yī-sha/
Ayesha (f name; hist, Prophet's wife) n

عايق /ā-yīq/ obstacle, hindrance n
عايق دار /ā-yīq dār/ insulated adj
عايق كاری /ā-yīq kā-ri/ insulation n
عايله /ā-yī-la/ family, household n
عبا /a-bā/ aba (cloth) n
عباد /ī-bād, sg ā-bīd/
عابد n pl see sg

عبادت , -ها/عبادات
/ī-bā-dat, pl -dāt/
worship, veneration; rel service n
← عبادت كردن
worship; conduct a service v

عبادت خانه /ī-bā-dat khā-na/
temple; Ibadat Khana (Akbar's
house of rel debate, hist) n

عبادتگاه /ī-bā-dat-gāh/
temple, sanctuary n

عبارت , -ها/عبارات /ī-bā-rat, pl -rāt/
expression, phrase n

عبارت اسمی /ī-bā-rat-ĭ ĭs-mi/
noun phrase n

عبارت بودن <از چيزی>
/ī-bā-rat-ĭ budan/
consist <of sth> vi

عبارت پردازی /ī-bā-rat par-dā-zi/
wordiness n
← عبارت پردازی كردن
blather v

عبارت ساختن /ī-bā-rat sākhtan/
phrase, word v

عبارت سازی /ī-bā-rat sā-zi/
phrasing, wording n

عباسی , -ان /a-bā-si/
Abbasid (hist, & pers) adj, n

عباسيان /a-bā-sī-yān, sg a-bā-si/
Abbasid dynasty (hist) n pl

عبدال رحمان خان
/ab-dur rah-mān khān/
Abdur Rahman Khan (Afgh emir,
hist) n

عبداله /ab-dā-la/ عبدالله n see
عبدالله /ab-dŭ-la/
Abdullah (m name) n

عبرانی , -ها/ان /īb-rā-ni/
Hebrew (& pers, lang) adj, n

عبری /īb-ri/ عرانی adj, n see
عبور و مرور /ŭ-bur ŭ mŭ-rur/
traffic, coming & going n
← عبور و مرور كردن
pass through vi

عبور و مرور منع
/ŭ-bur ŭ mŭ-rur-ĭ man'/
roadblock; curfew n

عبوری /ŭ-bu-ri/ interim (govt) adj
عبهر /ab-har/
narcissus (flower) (lit) n

عتيقه /a-ti-qa/ antique, relic n, adj
عثمان /ŭs-mān/
Osman, Usman (caliph, hist) n

عثمانی /ŭs-mā-ni/
Ottoman (hist) adj

عجالتا /í-jā´-la-tan, -tán/
now, at present adv

عجله /a-ja-la/ haste, hurry n

← عجله کردن hurry v

عجیب و غریب /a-jib ŭ gha-rib/
funny, strange, weird adj

عدالت /a-dā-lat/ justice, fairness n

← عدالت کردن administer justice

عدت /í-dat/
waiting period for widow to remarry
(Musl law) n

عدد , -ها/اعداد /a-dad, pl a'-dād/
number; figure; digit n

عدد اصلی /a-dad-ĭ as-li/
cardinal number n

عدد ترتیبی /a-dad-ĭ tar-ti-bi/
ordinal number n

عدد رومی /a-dad-ĭ ru-mi/
Roman numeral n

عدد کسری /a-dad-ĭ kas-ri/
fraction n

عدد صحیح /a-dad-ĭ sa-hih/
integer, whole number n

عدس /a-das/ lentil n

عدسیه /a-da-sĭ-ya/ lens n

عدل /á-dīl/
justice; fairness; half-load n;
(colloq) properly adv

عدلی /ad-li/ judicial, juridical adj

عدلیه /ad-lĭ-ya/
administration of justice n

عدم /a-dam/ lack, absence n

عدم اجرا /a-dam-ĭ ĭj-rā/
non-performance n

عدم توافق /a-dam-ĭ ta-wā-fŭq/
disagreement n

عدن /a-dan/ Aden (former capital) n

عدن /á-dīn, adn/ Eden, Paradise n

عدو /a-du, pl a'-dā/
enemy, foe, adversary n

← اعدا pl

عده /í-da/ number, quantity n

عذاب /a-zāb/
torture, suffering; pain n

← عذاب دادن ‹کسی را›
torture ‹sb› vt

← عذاب کردن
annoy, pester; torture vt

عذاب روحی /a-zāb-ĭ ru-hi/
mental anguish n

عذر /ŭ´-zŭr, ŭzr/
forgiveness, pardon; apology,
excuse n

← عذر خواستن • عذر کردن
apologize

← عذر قبول کردن
forgive, pardon

عذرا /ŭz-rā/ virgin n, adj

عرابه /a-rā-ba/
wheel (vehicle's); oxcart n

عراده /a-rā-da/
vehicle unit; gun carriage (lit) n

← سه عراده موتر three vehicles

عراق /í-rāq/ Iraq (country) n

عراقی , -ان /í-rā-qi/ Iraqi n, adj

عرایض , sg -ریزه /a-rā-yĭz, sg -ri-za/
see sg عریضه n pl

عرب , -ها/اعراب /a-rab, pl a'-rāb/
Arab (pers) n

عرب شناس /a-rab shĭ-nās/
Arabist (scholar) n

عربستان سعودی
/a-ra-bĭs-tān-ĭ sa-'u-di/
Saudi Arabia (country) n

عربی /a-ra-bi/ Arabic (lang) n

عرشه /ar-sha/ deck (ship's) n

عرصه , -ها /ar-sa/
field, area; arena (& fig) n

عرض , -ها/اعراض /a-raz, pl a'-rāz/
symptom n

عرض /arz/
width, breadth; petition n

عرض /írz/
honor, dignity; reputation n

عرض البلد /arz-ŭl-ba-lad/
latitude n

عرضه /ar-za/
delivery; offer, supply n

← عرضه کردن
deliver; offer, supply vt

i = keep, ĭ = big, u = coop, ŭ = put, y = yet, ' = (glottal stop)   215

عرضه و تقاضا /ar-za ŭ ta-qā-zā/
supply & demand *n*

عرف /ŭrf/
customary law (versus Musl law) *n*

عرفا /ŭ-ra-fā, sg ā-rĭf/
see sg عارف *n pl*

عرفان /ĭr-fān/
cognition, knowledge; (esp Sufi, Shia) mysticism; Sufism; gnosis *n*

عرفانی /ĭr-fā-ni/
cognitive; mystical; Sufic; gnostic *adj*

عرفی /ŭr-fi/
admitted by customary law; Urfi (16th-c Dari poet) *adj*

عرق /a-raq/ sweat, perspiration *n*
← عرق ریختن sweat, perspire *v*
عرق /īrq/ root *n*; race *n*
عرق /īrq, pl ŭ-ruq/ blood vessel *n*
← عروق *pl*
عرق گیر /a-raq gir/
undershirt; handkerchief (sweat) *n*
عرقناک /a-raq-nāk/ sweaty *adj*
عروس /a-rus/ bride *n*
عروسی /a-ru-si/
marriage; wedding *n*
← عروسی کردن get married *v*
عروق /ŭ-ruq/ blood vessels *n pl*
عروق شعریه /ŭ-ruq-ĭ sha'-rī-ya/
capillaries *n pl*

عریان /ŭr-yān/
bare, naked, nude *adj*
عریض /a-riz/ wide, broad *adj*
عریضه , -ها/عرایض /a-ri-za, pl a-rā-yīz/
petition, application; memorandum *n*

عزا /a-zā/ mourning *n*
← عزا گرفتن mourn *v*
عزا دار /a-zā dār/ in mourning *adj*
عزت خیل /ĭ-zat kheyl/
Ezat Kheyl (ctr) *n*

عزل /á-zĭl, azl/
removal (from office) *n*
← عزل کردن depose *vt*
عزیز /a-ziz/
dear, beloved (& pers) *adj, n*
عسل /a-sal/ honey *n*

عسکر , -ها/عساکر
/as-kar, pl a-sā-kar/
soldier; army *n*

عسکر پیاده /as-kar-ĭ pī-yā-da/
infantry, foot soldier *n*

عسکر قوای بحری /as-kar-ĭ qŭ-wā-yĭ bah-ri/
sailor (mil), seaman *n*

عسکر قوای هوایی /as-kar-ĭ qŭ-wā-yĭ ha-wā-yi/
airman (mil) *n*

عسکری /as-ka-ri/ military *adj*

عشاق /ŭ-shāq, sg ā-shĭq/
see sg عاشق *n pl*

عشایر /a-shā-yĭr, sg a-shi-ra/
see sg عشیره *n pl*

عشر , -ها/اعشار /ŭ´-shŭr, ŭshr; pl a'-shār/
tenth; Musl tithe *n*

عشق /ĭshq/ love, passion *n*
عشق بازی /ĭshq bā-zi/ love affair *n*
عشق ورزی /ĭshq war-zi/
lovemaking *n*

عشوه /ĭsh-wa/ flirtation *n*
عشوه ساز /ĭsh-wa-sāz/
flirtatious *adj*
عشوه سازی /ĭsh-wa-sā-zi/
flirtatiousness *n*
عشوه گر /ĭsh-wa-gar/ flirtatious *adj*
عشوه گری /ĭsh-wa-ga-ri/
flirtatious *adj*

عشیره , -ها/عشایر
/a-shi-ra, pl a-shā-yīr/
clan; tribe *n*

عصا /a-sā/ cane, walking stick *n*
عصای پیری /a-sā-yĭ pi-ri/
mainstay of one's old age (fig) *n*
عصای موسی /a-sā-yĭ mu-sā/
rod of Moses (bibl) *n*

عصاره /ŭ-sā-ra/ extract; juice *n*
عصب , -ها/اعصاب /a-sab, pl a'-sāb/
nerve (anat) *n*
عصب باصره /a-sab-ĭ bā-sĭ-ra/
optic nerve *n*
عصبی /a-sa-bi/ nervous *adj*

عصر , -ها/اعصار
/á-sǐr, asr; pl a'-sār/
time; era; reign; late afternoon n

عصری /a-sǐ-ri/
modern; high-tech adj

عصمت /ǐs-mat/ purity, chastity n

عضلاتی /a-za-lā-ti/ muscular adj

عضله , -ها/عضلات
/a-za-la, pl -lāt/
muscle n

عضو , -ها/اعضا
/úz´-wa, ŭzw; pl a'-zā/
member; limb; organ n

عضوی /úz-wi/ organic adj

عضویت /úz-wǐ-yat/
membership; organism n

عضویت حاصل کردن
/úz-wǐ-yat hā-sǐl kardan/
join, become a member v

عطار /a-tār/
perfume/spice merchant; Atar (10th-
11th-c Sufi poet) n

عطارد /a-tā-rŭd/
Mercury (planet) n

عطر /á-tǐr, atr/
perfume, scent, attar n

عطر پاش /á-tǐr pāsh/
atomizer (for perfume) n

عطسه /at-sa/ sneeze n

← عطسه زدن sneeze v

عفو /áf-wa, afw/
forgiveness, pardon; (Musl law)
waiver of punishment n

عفو عمومی /áf-wa-yǐ ŭ-mu-mi/
amnesty n

عفونی /a-fu-ni/ infectious adj

عقاید /a-qā-yǐd, sg a-qi-da/
see sg عقیده n pl

عقب /a-qab/ rear, back part n

عقب افتادن /a-qab aftādan/
lag behind, straggle v

عقب افتاده /a-qab af-tā-da/
backward, underdeveloped adj

عقب انداختن /a-qab andākhtan/
postpone, defer vt

عقب نشستن /a-qab nǐshastan/
see عقب نشینی کردن v

عقب نشینی /a-qab nǐ-shi-ni/
retreat, withdrawal (mil) n

← عقب نشینی کردن
retreat, withdraw (mil) v

عقبی /a-qa-bi/ back, rear adj

عقبی /ŭq-bā/ the hereafter n

عقد /aqd/
conclusion (contract); bond
(marriage), knot n

← عقد بستن form a bond v

← عقد کردن conclude a contract v

عقد , -ها/عقود /ǐqd, pl ŭ-qud/
necklace n

عقده /ŭq-da/ problem, difficulty n

عقده حقارت /ŭq-da-yǐ ha-qā-rat/
inferiority complex n

عقده دل /ŭq-da-yǐ dǐl/
depression, the blues n

عقده دل گشودن
/ŭq-da-yǐ dǐl gŭshudan/
get sth off one's chest v

عقده کهتری /ŭq-da-yǐ kǐh-ta-ri/
see عقده حقارت n

عقرب /aq-rab/
Aqrab (month); Scorpio; scorpion n

عقل , -ها/عقول /á-qǐl, aql; pl ŭ-qul/
wisdom; intellect, intelligence n

عقلا /ŭ-qa-lā, sg ā-qǐl/
see sg عاقل n pl

عقلی /ŭ-qa-li/
mental; intellectual, rational adj

عقود /ŭ-qud, sg ǐqd/
see sg عقد n pl

عقول /ŭ-qul; sg á-qǐl, aql/
see sg عقل n pl

عقیده , -ها/عقاید
/a-qi-da, pl a-qā-yǐd/
belief, opinion; creed, faith n

عقیق /a-qiq/ agate; carnelian n

عقیم /a-qim/
barren, sterile, infertile adj

عکاس /a-kās/ photographer n

عکاس خانه /a-kās khā-na/
photography studio n

عکاسی /a-kā-si/ photography n

عکس /aks/ photograph, picture n

← عکس کردن • عکس گرفتن
photograph v

عکک /a-kak/ see اکک n

---

i = keep, ǐ = big, u = coop, ŭ = put, y = yet, ' = (glottal stop)   217

عکه n /a-ka/ اکک see

علاقه /a-lā-qa, pl a-lā-yīq/
interest, concern; fond regard;
relation, affiliation n

← pl علایق

← علاقه داشتن ‹به چیزی›
be interested ‹in sth› v

علاقه مند , -ان /a-lā-qa-mand/
interested, concerned; affectionate
(& pers) adj, n

علاقه دار , -ان/ها /a-lā-qa dār/
sub-district governor, pers in
charge (official) n

علاقه داری /a-lā-qa dā-ri/
district, subdistrict n

علامت , -ها/علامات/علایم
/a-lā-mat, pl a-lā-yīm/
mark, sign, symbol; symptom,
indication; signal n

علامت ترافیکی
/a-lā-mat-ī ta-rā-fi-ki/
traffic signal n

علامت سوال /a-lā-mat-ī sa-wāl/
question mark n

علامت ندا /a-lā-mat-ī nī-dā/
exclamation point n

علامه /a-lā-ma/
most learned (title); see & علامت n
علامه مشخص

علامه یی مشخص /a-lā-ma-yĭ mŭ-sha-khas/
diacritical mark n

علاهده different adj /a-lā-hĭ-da/

علاوتاً /a-lā´-wa-tan, -tán/
furthermore, besides, in addition
adv

علاوه addition, increase n /a-lā-wa/

← علاوه کردن add (in speaking) vt

علاوه بر /a-lā-wa bar/
besides, in addition prep

علایق /a-lā-yīq, sg a-lā-qa/
see sg علاقه n pl

علایم /a-lā-yĭm, sg -mat/
see sg علامت n pl

علت , -ها/علل /ī-lat, pl ī-lal/
cause, reason; defect; (colloq) pus
n

علف fodder; grass n /a-laf/

علف چر pasture land /a-laf char/

علف خوار /a-laf khār/
herbivorous (lit) adj

علف هرزه weed n /a-laf-ī har-za/

علفزار /a-laf-zār/
pasturage, grassland n

علل see sg علت n pl /ī-lal, pl ī-lat/

علم , -ها /a-lam/
flag; Alam (m name) n

علم /a-lam, pl a'-lām/
noun; distinguished pers n

← pl اعلام

علم , -ها/علوم /ī´-līm, īlm; pl ŭ-lum/
knowledge, science n

علم آوری کردن /ī´-līm ā-wa-ri kardan/
make sure, make certain v

علم اخلاق /ī´-līm-ī akh-lāq/
ethics (field) n

علم اشتقاق /ī´-līm-ī īsh-tī-qāq/
etymology n

علم اقتصاد /ī´-līm-ī īq-tī-sād/
economics n

علم الاصوات /ī´-līm-ūl-as-wā´t/
phonetics n

علم الامراض /ī´-līm-ŭl-am-rā´z/
pathology n

علم الجمال /ī´-līm-ŭl-ja-māl/
aesthetics n

علم الحشرات /ī´-līm-ŭl-ha-sha-rāt/
entomology n

علم الحیات /ī-līm-ŭl-ha-yāt/
biology n

علم الکلام /ī-līm-ŭl-ka-lām/
see علم کلام n

علم الهی /ī´-līm-ī ī-lā-hi/
theology (field) n

علم بلاغت /ī´-līm-ī ba-lā-ghat/
rhetoric n

علم تربیه /ī´-līm-ī tar-bī-ya/
pedagogy n

علم ثروت /ī´-līm-ī sŭr-wat/
economics n

علم حشرات /ī´-līm-ī ha-sha-rāt/
see علم الحشرات n

علم حیوانات /ī´-līm-ī hay-wā-nāt/
zoology n

علم سیاست /ī´-līm-ī sī-yā-sat/
political science n

علم طبقات الارض
/ĭ´-lĭm-ĭ ta-ba-qā-tŭ-larz/
geology n

علم كلام /ĭ-lĭm-ĭ ka-lām/
Musl scholastic theology n

علم نباتات /ĭ´-lĭm-ĭ na-bā-tāt/
botany n

علم نجوم /ĭ´-lĭm-ĭ nŭ-jum/
astronomy n

علم وظایف الاعضا
/ĭ´-lĭm-ĭ wa-zā-yĭf-ŭl-a´-zā/
physiology n

علم هیئت /ĭ´-lĭm-ĭ hay-'at/
astronomy n

علما /ŭ-la-mā, sg ā-lĭm/
see sg عالم n pl

علماً /ĭ´l-man, -mán/
scientifically adv

علو /ŭ-lu/ highness, exaltedness n
علو الآمر /ŭ-lu al-á-mĭr/
the rightful ruler n

علوم /ŭ-lum; sg ĭ´-lĭm, ĭlm/
see sg علم n pl

علوم و فنون ← arts & sciences
علی /a-li, 'a-/
Ali (m name; hist, 4th caliph) n;
exalted, sublime adj

علی آباد /a-li ā-bād/
Ali Abad (dist) n

علی خیل /a-li kheyl/
Ali Kheyl (ctr) n

علیا حضرت /ŭl-yā haz-rat/
Her Majesty (for queen) n

علیت /ĭ-lĭ-yat/
causality, causation n

علیرغم <چیزی> /a-lir-gham(-ĭ)/
in spite of <sth> prep

علیشنگ /a-li-shĭng, -shang/
Alisheng (dist) n

علینگار /a-lin-gār/
Alingar (dist, river) n

علیه against prep /a-leyh(-ĭ)/
علیه /a-lĭ-ya/
exalted, sublime (f form) adj

عم /am, pl a'-mām/
uncle (paternal) (lit) n

اعمام ← pl

عماد /ĭ-mād/
pillar; support; (part of name) n

عمارت , -ها/عمارات
/ĭ-mā-rat, pl -rāt/
building, edifice n

عماری howdah n /ĭ-mā-ri/

عمال /ŭ-māl, sg ā-mĭl/
see sg عامل n pl

عمان Amman (capital) n /am-man/

عمداً /ám-dan, -dán/
deliberately, on purpose adv

عمده main, principal adj /ŭm-da/
عمده فروش /ŭm-da fŭ-rosh/
wholesaler n

عمر /ŭ´-mŭr, ŭmr/
age (of pers); life, lifetime n

او چند سال عمر داره ؟ ←
how old is s/he?

او چند سال عمر کرد ؟ ←
how old was s/he? (of deceased)

عمر /ŭ-mar/
Omar (m name; hist, 2nd caliph) n

عمر به سر رسیدن
/ŭ´-mŭr ba sar rasidan/
die (fig) vi

عمر خیام /ŭ-mar kha-yām/
Omar Khayyam (12th-c Dari poet) n

عمرزی /ŭ-mar-zay/
Omarzai, Umarzai (small P grp) n

عمران /ĭm-rān/
building, construction; Amraan
(bibl) n; related to building adj

عمری /ŭ-ma-ri/ n خواجه عمری see

عمل /a-mal, pl a'-māl/
act, deed, course of action n

اعمال ← pl
عمل کردن ←
act, take action; operate, perform
surgery v

عمل کرد /a-mal-kard/
profit, return; product, yield n

عملاً /a-ma-lan, -má-/
in practice; pragmatically adv

عملی /a-ma-li/
applied; practical, pragmatic adj

---

i = keep, ĭ = big, u = coop, ŭ = put, y = yet, ' = (glottal stop)   219

عملیات /a-ma-lī-yāt/
operations (& mil, used as if sg);
surgery, operation (med) n pl
↳ عملیات • عملیاتِ جراحی
operation (med) n

عملیاتی /a-ma-lī-yā-ti/
operational (& mil) adj

عمليه , -ها /a-ma-lī-ya/
process; (math) operation n

عمو /a-mu/ uncle (paternal) n
عمو زاده , -گان/ها /a-mu zā-da/
cousin (by paternal uncle) n

عمود /a-mud/
perpendicular line/plane n

عمودی /a-mu-di/ vertical adj
عموماً /ŭ-mú-man, -mán/
in general adv

عمومیت /ŭ-mu-mī-yat/
generality; generalization n

عمه /a-ma/ aunt (paternal) n
عمه خشو , -ها /a-ma khŭ-shu/
father-in-law's sister n

عميق /a-miq/ deep; profound adj
عميقا /a-mí-qan, -qán/
deeply; profoundly adv

عنان /ī-nān/
reins, bridle; (fig) control n
عنان اختيار /ī-nān-ĭ ĭkh-tī-yār/
self-control (fig) n
عنان گسسته /ī-nān gŭ-sīs-ta, -sas-/
see عنان گسیخته adj
عنان گسیخته /ī-nān gŭ-seykh-ta/
out of control (fig) adj
عناوین /a-nā-win, sg ĭn-wān/
see sg عنوان n pl
عنبر /am-bar/ ambergris n
عنبر آگین /an-bar ā-gin/
fragrant with ambergris adj
عندالضرورت /ĭnd-az-za-ru-rat/
as necessary adv
عندالضروره /ĭnd-az-za-ru-ra/
see عندالضرورت adv
عندالطلب /ĭnd-at-ta-lab/
on demand adv
عندالطلبه /ĭnd-at-ta-la-ba/
see عندالطلب adv
عندالللزوم /ĭnd-al-lŭ-zum/
see عندالضرورت adv

عندالله /ĭnd-al-lāh/
honestly; before God adv
عندليب , -ان/ها /an-da-lib/
nightingale (bird) n
عندالموقع /ĭnd-ŭl-maw-qey/
simultaneously adv
عنصر , -ها/عناصر
/an-sŭr, pl a-nā-sĭr/
element (& chem); component n
عنصری /an-sŭ-ri/
Ansuri (11th-c Dari poet) n
↳ خنگ بت و سرخ بت
The Blue Idol & the Red Idol
(poem)
عنعنه , -ها /a-na-na/ tradition n
عنعنوی /a-na-na-wi/ traditional adj
عنف /anf/ force, violence n
عنقريب /an-qa-rib/
almost, nearly (lit) adv
عنکبوت /an-ka-but/ spider n
عنوان , -ها/عناوين
/ĭn-wān, pl a-nā-win/
heading, title; basis n
عوارض /a-wā-rīz, sg ā-rī-za/
see sg عارضه n
عواقب /a-wā-qīb, sg ā-qī-bat/
see sg عاقبت n pl
عوام /a-wām; sg ām, ā-ma/
see sg عامه n pl
عوام پسند /a-wām pī-sand/
popular adj
عوام فريب /a-wām fī-reyb/
demagogue n; demagogic adj
عوام فريبانه /a-wām fī-rey-bā-na/
demagogically adv
عوام فريبی /a-wām fī-rey-bi/
demagoguery n
عود /awd (awt)/
recurrence (& med) n
عود /ud/
aloeswood (tree); ud (mus instr) n
عودت /aw-dat/ return n
↳ عودت کردن return v
عورت /aw-rat/
genitals (f); woman n
↳ ستر عورت seclusion of women
عوض /ī-waz/
replacement, substitution n

عهد /ahd (ād), pl ŭ-hud/ عهود/ها -ه-,
promise, vow; agreement; treaty *n*

عیار /a-yār/
carat; standard (for gold & coins)
(lit) *n*

عیب /ayb, pl ŭ-yub/ عیوب/ها -,
flaw, fault; disgrace; weakness of
character *n*

عیب جو(ی) /ayb-jo(y)/ ان-,
faultfinder (pers) *n*

← عیب جو(ی) کردن find fault *v*

عیبناک /ayb-nāk/ disgraceful *adj*

عید /id, pl a-'yād/ اعیاد/ها -,
Eid (Musl feast) *n*

← عید شما مبارک ! Happy Eid!

← عید کردن celebrate Eid

عید اضحی /id-ī ŭz-hā/
Feast of Immolation (marking
Abraham's sacrifice) *n*

عید الفطر /id al-fĭ'-tĭr/
Festival of Breaking the Fast (rel) *n*

عید قربان /id-ī qŭr-bān/
see عید اضحی *n*

عیدی /i-di/
Eid gift/money/greetings *n*

عیسوی /i-sa-wi/
Christian (& pers) *adj, n*;
Christianity *n*

عیسی /i-sā/ Jesus; Joshua (bibl) *n*

عین /ayn/ same *adj*; eye *n*

عین /ayn, pl ŭ-yun/
spring, source *n*
← عیون *pl*

عیناً /áy-nan, -nán/
exactly; literally *adv*

عینک /ay-nak/
eyeglasses, glasses *n*

← ٤ قاب عینک 4 pairs of glasses

← عینک گذاشتن • عینک ماندن
put glasses on *v*

عینک آفتابی /ay-nak-ī āf-tā-bi/
sunglasses *n*

عینک زانو /ay-nak-ī zā-nu/
kneecap, patella (anat) *n*

عینک ساز /ay-nak sāz/ optician *n*

عینکی /ay-na-ki/
wearing glasses *adj*

عینی /ay-ni/
ocular; objective; having the same
parents *adj*

عینیت /ay-nĭ-yat/
objectivity; objectivism *n*

عیوب /ŭ-yub, sg ayb/
see sg عیب *n pl*

عیون /ŭ-yun, sg ayn/
see sg عین *n pl*

غ

غار /ghār/ hole, cavity; cave *n*

غار غار /ghār ghār/
holey, full of holes *adj*

غار نشین /ghār nĭ-shin/
cave dweller *n*

غارت کردن /ghā-rat kardan/
loot, plunder, pillage *v*

غارتگر /ghā-rat-gar/ ان/ها-,
looter, pillager *n*

غاز /ghāz/ ات/ها-,
gas (not solid/liquid) *n*

غازی /ghā-zi/
vanquisher of infidels; (form of
address); rouge *n*

غاصب /ghā-sĭb/ ان/ین-,
usurper *n*; usurping *adj*

غافل /ghā-fĭl/ ان/ها-,
unaware, negligent (& pers) *adj, n*

غافل گیر شدن /ghā-fĭl gir shŭdan/
be surprised *vi*

غافل گیر کردن /ghā-fĭl gir kardan/
surprise *vt*

غالب /ghā-lĭb/
predominant; usual *adj*

غالباً /ghā-lĭ'-ban, -bán/
often; usually *adv*

غالبیت /ghā-lĭ-bĭ-yat/
predominance *n*

غالمغال /ghāl-ma-ghāl/
noise, ruckus *n*

غامض /ghā-mĭz, pl gha-wā-mĭz/
complication *n*; complicated *adj*

← غوامض *pl*

غامضه /ghā-mĭ-za/ see غامض *n*

غايب , -ان/ين /ghā-yīb/
absent (& pers); hidden; 3rd pers (gram) n

غايت /ghā-yat/ end, tip n

غايط /ghā-yīt/ stool, feces n

غايطه /ghā-yī-ta/ fecal adj

→ مواد غايطه fecal matter

غايه /ghā-ya/ goal, objective n

غايى /ghā-yi/ final adj

غبار /ghŭ-bār/ dust cloud; fog, mist n

غبار آلود /ghŭ-bār ā-lud/ foggy, misty adj

غبار خاطر /ghŭ-bār-ī khā-tīr/ depression; sorrow n

غبار دل /ghŭ-bār-ī dīl/ see غبار خاطر n

غباوت /gha-bā-wat/ ignorance; stupidity n

غبغب /ghab-ghab/ double chin n

غبطه /ghīb-ta/ envy n

→ غبطه خوردن envy v

غبى /gha-bi/ ignorant; stupid adj

غچى /ghŭ-chi/ swallow, swift (bird) n

غدد /ghŭ-dad, sg -da/ see sg غده n pl

غدوات /ghŭ-da-wāt/ colloq see sg غده n pl

غدود /ghŭ-dud, gha-/ tumor; (colloq) gland; a little bit n

غده , -ها/-ها /ghŭ-da (-dud, gha-), pl -dad/ gland n

غده پروستات /ghŭ-da-yĭ pŭ-ros-tāt/ prostate gland n

غدير /gha-dir/ pool, lake n

غذا , -ها/اغذیه /ghĭ-zā, pl agh-zĭ-ya/ food n

→ غذا خوردن eat v

→ غذا دادن feed v

غذایی /ghĭ-zā-yi/ nutritious adj

غرایز /gha-rā-yīz, sg gha-ri-za/ see sg غریزه n pl

غرب /gharb/ west; Occident n

غرباً /ghár-ban, -bán/ from the west adv

غربت /ghŭr-bat/ exile; poverty n

غرس /ghars/ planting saplings n

غرش /ghŭ-rīsh/ roar; thunder, boom n

→ غرش کردن thunder v

غرامت , -ها/غرامات /gha-rā-mat, pl -mat/ compensation for losses n

→ غرامت دادن compensate v

غرامت جنگ /gha-rā-mat-ī jang/ reparations (mil) n

غرایب /gha-rā-yīb/ peculiarities n pl

غربال /ghīr-bāl/ sifter (for grains) n

غربی , -ان/ها /ghar-bi/ Westerner; European n

غرجستان /ghar-jīs-tān/ Gharjistan (prov, hist) n

غرچستان /ghar-chīs-tān/ see غرجستان n

غرض /gha-raz, pl agh-rāz/ interest, self-interest; purpose n

→ اغراض pl

غرغره /ghar-gha-ra/ hanging (from gallows); gargling n

→ غرغره کردن hang, gargle vt

غرق /gharq/ drowning, drowned; sinking, sunk (ship) (& fig) adj

→ غرق شدن drown (pers); sink (ship) vi

غرقاب /ghar-qāb/ deep water n

غرقه /ghar-qa/ drowning, drowned adj; foundation stone n

غروب آفتاب /ghŭ-rub-ī āf-tāb/ sunset n

→ غروب کردن set, go down (esp sun) vi

غرور /ghŭ-rur/ conceit, vanity; pride n

غرور جوانی /ghŭ-rur-ī ja-wā-ni/ prime of youth n

غریب /gha-rib/ poor adj

غریبی /gha-ri-bi/ poverty; being in exile n

غریدن ؛ -غر- ؛ -غرید- /ghŭ-ri-dan/ roar (& animal) vi

غریزه , -ها/غرایز
/gha-ri-za, pl gha-rā-yīz/
instinct n

غریزی /gha-ri-zi/
innate, inborn; instinctive adj

غریق /gha-riq/
drowning, drowned (& pers/fig) adj

غزا /gha-zā/ war against infidels n
← غزا کردن
wage war against infidels v

غزال , -ان/ها /ghĭ-zāl/ gazelle n

غزل , -ها /gha-zal/
love poem, lyric poem n
← غزل خواندن
recite/sing a lyric poem v

غزلی /gha-za-li/ lyric adj

غزنوی , -ان /ghaz-na-wi/
Ghaznavid (& pers, hist) adj, n

غزنویان /ghaz-na-wī-yān/
Ghaznavid Dynasty (hist) n pl

غزنه /ghaz-na/ n see غزنی
غزنی /ghaz-ni/
Ghazni (prov; seat) n
غره /gha-za/ n see باریکه غره

غژدی /ghĭzh-di/
nomadic Pashtun black tent n
← غژدی زدن
pitch a black tent v

غژگاو /ghazh-gāw/ yak n

غسل /ghŭ´-sŭl, ghŭsl/
ablution (Musl); washing of body n
← غسل کردن • غسل دادن
perform ablutions, wash body v

غسل تعمید /ghŭ´-sŭl-ĭ ta'-mid/
baptism n
← غسل تعمید دادن baptize vt

غشا /ghĭ-shā/ membrane n
غشای مخاطی
/ghĭ-shā-yĭ mŭ-khā-ti/
mucous membrane n

غضب /gha-zab/
anger, rage; indignation n

غضب آلود /gha-zab ā-lud/
angry, enraged; indignant adj

غضبناک /gha-zab-nāk/
adj see غضب آلود

غضروف /ghaz-ruf/
cartilage; gristle n

غضروفی /ghaz-ru-fi/
cartilaginous; gristly adj

غضنفر /gha-zan-far/
Ghazanfar (m name); lion n

غفور /gha-fur/
oft-forgiving (God); Ghafur (m name) adj

غلام /ghŭ-lām/
slave; servant; (cards) jack n

غلت خوردن /ghalt khŭrdan/
roll, be rolled vi

غلت زدن /ghalt zadan/
roll, make (sth) roll vt

غلتاندن ؛ -غلتان- ؛ غلتاند-
/ghal-tān-dan/
demolish, level, raze vt

غلتیدن ؛ -غلت- ؛ غلتید-
/ghal-ti-dan/
collapse; fall vi

غلزایی /ghĭl-zā-yi/
Ghilzai, Ghiljai adj

غلزی /ghĭl-zay/
Ghilzai, Ghiljai (P tribal confederacy) n

غلجایی /ghĭl-jā-yi/ n see غلزایی
غلجی /ghĭl-jay/ n see غلزی
غلچه /ghal-cha/
Ghalcha (Tajik highlanders in Badakhshan) n

غلط /gha-lat/
false, mistaken (statement) adj

غلط فهمی /gha-lat-ĭ fah-mi/
misunderstanding n

غلطی , -ها/اغلاط
/gha-la-ti, pl agh-lāt/
mistake; (colloq) dishonesty n

غلطی چاپی /gha-lat-ĭ chā-pi/
typographical error n

غله , -ها/غلات/(غلجات)
/gha-la, pl -lāt (-la-jāt)/
cereal, grain n

غلیان /ghŭ-lĭ-yān/ boiling (& fig) n
غلیظ /gha-liz/ thick, viscous adj
غم , -ها /gham/ sorrow, grief n
غم شریک /gham sha-rik/
compassionate, sympathetic adj

غم شریکی /gham sha-ri-ki/
compassion, sympathy n

غوریان /gho-rī-yān/
Ghorid dynasty (hist) n pl; Ghoriyan (district) n

غوزه /gho-za/
cocoon; cotton pod n

غوغا /ghaw-ghā/
clamor, tumult, noise n

← غوغا کردن • غوغا بریا کردن
clamor, make noise v

غوغا گر /ghaw-ghā gar/
noisy (& pers) adj, n

غوغایی /ghaw-ghā-yi/
see غوغا گر adj, n

غول /ghul/
ghoul; giant n; stupid, ignorant adj

غول بی شاخ و دم
/ghul bey shākh ŭ dam/
giant w/o horns or tail n

غولک /gho-lak/
slingshot n /gho-lak/

غیب /ghayb/
the invisible, the supernatural n

← غیب شدن
disappear, vanish vi

غیبت /ghay-bat/
absence; gossiping, backbiting n

غیبی /ghay-bi/
invisible; mysterious adj

غیر /ghayr, pl agh-yār/
stranger; foreigner n

← اغیار pl

غیر /ghayr(-ĭ)/
except prep

غیر اقصادی /ghayr-ĭ ĭq-tĭ-sā-di/
uneconomical adj

غیر ذیروح /ghayr-ĭ zi-ruh/
inanimate, not living adj

غیر سیاسی /ghayr-ĭ sĭ-yā-si/
non-political adj

← غیر سیاسی ساختن
depoliticize
غیر سیاسی سازی
/ghayr-ĭ sĭ-yā-si sā-zi/
depoliticization n

غیر صحی /ghayr-ĭ sĭ-hi/
unhealthy adj

غیر عضوی /ghayr-ĭ ŭz-wi/
inorganic adj

غیر قابل برگشت
/ghayr-ĭ qā-bĭl-ĭ bar-gasht/
irrevocable adj

غم گزار , -ان/ها /gham gŭ-zār/
friend; sweetheart (fig) n

غمخور /gham-khŭr/
sympathetic adj

غمگین /gham-gin/
sad, sorrowful, grieved adj

غنا /ghĭ-nā/
riches, wealth n

← غنا ساختن
enrich vt

غنا سازی /ghĭ-nā sā-zi/
enrichment, getting rich n

غنایم /gha-nā-yĭm, sg -ni-mat/
see sg غنیمت n pl

غنایی /ghĭ-nā-yi/
lyric (poem) adj

غنج /ghŭnj/
flirtation, coquetry n

غنج و دلال /ghŭnj ŭ da-lāl/
flirtation & ogling n phrs

غند /ghŭnd, ghĭnd/
regiment (army); wing (air force) n

غند مشر /ghŭnd mĭ´shĭr/
lieutenant colonel, LTC n

غندی /ghŭn-day/
Ghunday (ctr) n

غنه /ghŭ-na/
twang (nasal) n

غنی /gha-ni/
rich adj; Ghani (m name) n

غنی خیل /gha-ni kheyl/
Ghani Kheyl (ctr) n

غنیمت /gha-ni-mat, pl gha-nā-yĭm/
spoils; windfall, godsend n

← غنایم pl
← غنیمت بودن
be profitable
← غنیمت گرفتن
appropriate, take

غواص , -ان/ها /gha-wās/
diver n

غواص مروارید
/gha-wās-ĭ mŭr-wā-rid/
pearl diver n

غواصی /gha-wā-si/
diving n

غوامض /gha-wā-mĭz/
unsolved problems n pl

غور /ghor/
Ghor (prov) n

غوربند /ghor-band/
Ghorband (dist, ctr Shahgerd) n

غورک /gho-rak/
Ghorak (dist) n

غورماچ /ghor-māch/
Ghormach (dist) n

غوری , -ها /gho-ri/
platter (for serving) n; Ghorid adj

فاتح /fā-tīh/
victorious, triumphant *adj*;
conqueror *n*
↳ فاتح شدن triumph *vi*
فاتحانه /fā-tī-hā-na/
victorious, triumphant (& adv) *adj*,
adv
فاتحه /fā-tī-ha/
beginning; exordium; funeral prayer
for the dead *n*
فاجعه /fā-jī-'a/
disaster, catastrophe *n*
فاجه /fā-ja/ yawn (colloq) *n*
فاتحه /fā-tī-ha (-yā)/ funeral *n*
فاحش /fā-hīsh/ gross, flagrant *adj*
فاحشگی /fā-hī-sha-gi/ prostitution *n*
فاحشه , -ها/فواحش
/fā-hī-sha, pl fa-wā-hīsh/
prostitute *n*
فاخته /fākh-ta/ turtledove (bird) *n*
فارسی /fār-si/
Farsi (lang); Persian (pers) *n*
فارغ , -ان /fā-rīgh/
graduate (pers) *n*; carefree *adj*
فارقه /fā-rī-qa/
distinguishing; distinctive *adj*
فارنهایت /fā-rīn-hāyt/
Fahrenheit *adj*
فاریاب /fār-yāb/ Faryab (prov) *n*
فاژه /fā-zha (-ja)/ yawn *n*
↳ فاژه کشیدن yawn *v*
فاسد /fā-sīd/ rotten; corrupt *adj*
فاسفور /fās-for/ phosphorus *n*
فاسولیه /fā-su-lī-ya/ *n* see فاصولیه
فاش /fāsh/ (colloq) *adj* see فحش
فاصل /fā-sīl/
demarcating, separating *adj*
فاصله , -ها/فواصل
/fā-sĭ-la, pl fa-wā-sīl/
distance; blank space (printing);
interval (time) *n*
↳ فاصله دادن insert a blank space
فاصولیه /fā-su-lī-ya/
green bean, string bean *n*
فاضل /fā-zīl/
surplus; excess *n*; learned (& pers)
adj, *n*

غیر قابل اجتناب
/ghayr-ĭ qā-bĭl-ĭ ĭj-tĭ-nāb/
inevitable *adj*
غیر قابل احتراق
/ghayr-ĭ qā-bĭl-ĭ ĭh-tĭ-rāq/
incombustible *adj*
غیر قابل تحمل
/ghayr-ĭ qā-bĭl-ĭ ta-ha-mŭl/
intolerable *adj*
غیر قابل تردید
/ghayr-ĭ qā-bĭl-ĭ tar-did/
non-rejectable *adj*
غیر قابل قبول
/ghayr-ĭ qā-bĭl-ĭ qa-bul/
unacceptable *adj*
غیر قانونی /ghayr-ĭ qā-nu-ni/
illegal *adj*
غیر قیاسی /ghayr-ĭ qĭ-yā-si/
irregular (gram) *adj*
غیر محرم /ghayr-ĭ mah-ram/
unclassified (document) *adj*
غیر مترقب /ghayr-ĭ mŭ-ta-ra-qĭb/
unexpected *adj*
غیر متعدی /ghayr-ĭ mŭ-ta-'a-di/
intransitive (verb) *adj*
غیر مجاز /ghayr-ĭ mŭ-jāz/
prohibited, impermissible *adj*
غیر مقدره /ghayr-ĭ mŭ-qa-da-ra/
out of bounds *adj*; punishment not
prescribed by Quran (law) *n*
غیر ممکن /ghayr-ĭ mŭm-kĭn/
impossible *adj*
غیر موجه /ghayr-ĭ mŭ-wa-jah/
unacceptable, unreasonable *adj*
غیره و غیره /ghay-ra wa ghay-ra/
et cetera *phrs*
غیظ /ghayz/
anger, fury, wrath; indignation *n*
غین /ghayn/ ghayn (letter) *n*
غین /ghin/ dick (vulg), penis *n*

ف

فابریکه /fāb-ri-ka/ factory *n*
فابریکه برق /fāb-ri-ka-yĭ barq/
power station (electric) *n*

فاطمه /fā-tǐ-ma/
Fatima (f name; Prophet's daugher) n

فاعل /fā-'īl/
perpetrator; (gram) subject n

فاعلى /fā-'ī-li/
nominative (gram) adj

فاقد <چیزی> /fā-qǐd(-ī)/
devoid of <sth> adj

فاقد تهذیب /fā-qǐd-ī tah-zib/
rude; uncouth adj

فاقد سلاح ذر وی
/fā-qǐd-ī sa-lāh-ī za-ra-wi/
nuclear-free adj

فاقد شرایط /fā-qǐd-ī sha-rā-yǐt/
unconditional adj

فاکولته faculty, college n /fā-kol-ta/
فال omen, auspice n /fāl/
فال بین fortuneteller n /fāl bin/
فال دیدن fortunetelling n /fāl didan/
فالتو spare, extra adj /fāl-tu/
فالنامه Book of Omens /fāl-nā-ma/
فالوده faluda (pudding) n /fā-lu-da/
فامیل family n /fā-mil/
فامیلی familial adj /fā-mi-li/
فایده , ها-/فواید
/fā-yǐ-da, pl fa-wā-yǐd/
benefit; profit; interest, return n

فبروری February n /fǐb-ru-wa-ri/
فت foot (unit of length) n /fūt/
فتاوا /fa-tā-wā, sg fat-wā/
see sg فتوا n pl
فتح Fatah (pol party) n /fa-tah/
فتح , ها-/فتوحات/فتوح
/fá-tǐh, fath; pl fū-tu-hāt, fa-tuh/
conquest; Fateh (m name) n
← فتح کردن conquer, win v
فتنه /fǐt-na/
schism, discord; fitna (Musl civil war) n

فتوا /fat-wā, pl fa-tā-wā/
fatwa (us not recognized by P) n
فتاوا pl
فتوحات /fū-tu-hāt, sg fath/
see sg فتح n
فتور languor, listlessness n /fū-tur/
فتور رخ دادن /fū-tur rūkh dādan/
flag, become listless vi

فتور واقع شدن
/fū-tur wā-qey shūdan/
see فتور رخ دادن vi
فتیله wick n /fa-ti-la/
فجایع /fa-jā-yey/
disasters; atrocities n pl
فجی /fa-ji/
disastrous, calamitous adj
فحاش foul-mouthed adj /fa-hāsh/
فحاشا debauchery n /fū-hā-shā/
فحش /fahsh (fāsh)/
obscene language n
← فحش گفتن curse, swear v
فحشا /fah-shā/
prostitution, harlotry n
فدا sacrifice, giving up for n /fǐ-dā/
فدایت شوم /fǐ-dā-yat sha-wūm/
I'd sacrifice my life for you phrs
فدراسیون /fǐd-rā-sī-yun/
federation, league n
فدرال /fǐd-rāl/ فدراسیون see
فدرالی /fǐd-rā-li/
federal, federative adj
فرا گرفتن acquire vt /fa-rā gǐrǐftan/
فرات Euphrates (river) n /fǐ-rāt/
فراخ /fa-rākh/
wide, broad; spacious adj
فراخ بنیاد /fa-rākh būn-yād/
broad-based adj
فرار escape, flight; exile n /fa-rār/
← فرار کردن flee, escape vi
فراری , ان/ها- /fa-rā-ri/
escapee n; related to flight or exile adj
فراشتروک /fa-rāsh-ta-ruk/
swallow, swift (bird) n
فراشغان /fa-rāsh-ghān/
فرشغان see
فراعنه /fǐ-rā-'a-na, sg fǐr-'awn/
see sg فرعون n pl
فراغت /fa-rā-ghat/
graduation (school); leisure n
فراموش کردن /fa-rā-mosh kardan/
forget vt
فرامین /fa-rā-min, sg far-mān/
see sg فرمان n pl
فرانسه /fa-rān-sa/
France (country) n

فرانسوی , -ان/ها /fa-rān-sa-wi/
French (pers, lang)

فراه /fa-rāh/ Farah (prov, seat) n

فراهم کردن /fa-rā-ham kardan/
collect, gather; provide vt

فرایض /fa-rā-yīz, sg fa-ri-za/
see sg فریضه n pl

فربه /far-bīh (-bey)/ fat, obese adj

فربهی /far-bī-hi/ obesity n

فرج , -ها/فروج /farj, pl fū-ruj/
vulva (anat) n

فرجام /far-jām/ end, conclusion n

فرخار /far-khār/ Farkhar (dist) n

فرد /fard, pl af-rād/
person, individual; (mil) private,
soldier (mil); officer (police) n

افراد ← pl /af-rād/

فردا /far-dā/ tomorrow adv, n

فرزند , -ان/ها /far-zand/
child (m, f) n

فرزندی گرفتن /far-zan-di gīrīftan/
adopt a child v; adoption n

فرزه /far-za/ Farza (dist) n

فرستادن ؛ -فرست- ؛ فرستاد-
/fī-rīs-tā-dan/
send; transmit (lit) vt

فرسنگ /far-sang/
farsang (unit of distance) n

فرسوده /far-su-da/ worn-out adj

فرش /farsh/ floor covering n

فرشغان /fa-rash-ghān, -rāsh/
Farashghan (mountains) n

فرشی /far-shi/ portulaca (flower) n

فرشته /fī-rīsh-ta/ angel n

فرصت /fīr-sat/
opportunity, chance; spare time n

فرض /farz/
assumption, supposition; duty
(rel/moral) n

فرضاً /fár-zan, -zán/
supposedly, presumably adv

فرضی /far-zi/ hypothetical adj

فرضیه /far-zī-ya/
hypothesis, theory n

فرع /fá-ra, far'/
secondary part of sth n

فرعی /far-'i/ secondary adj

فرعون /fīr-'awn, pl fī-rā-'a-na/
pharaoh n

فراعنه ← pl

فرعون , -ان/ها /fīr-'awn/ tyrant n

فرعونی /fīr-'aw-ni/ tyranny n

فرق /fī-raq, sg fīr-qa/
see sg فرقه n pl

فرق داشتن ←
matter, make a difference vi

فرقوی /fīr-qa-wi/ sectarian adj

فرقه , -ها/فرق /fīr-qa, pl fī-raq/
sect (rel); (mil) division n

فرمان , -ها/فرامین /far-mān, pl fa-rā-min/
command (& mil), order (in
restaurant); edict (ruler's) n

فرمان بردن v ← obey, comply w/

فرمان دادن v ← order; decree

فرمان بردار /far-mān bŭr-dār/
obedient, compliant adj

فرمان روا /far-mān ra-wā/
ruler, sovereign n

فرمانده , -ان /far-mān-dīh/
commander n

فرمایش دادن /far-mā-yīsh dādan/
order (in restaurant) v

فرمودن ؛ -فرمای- ؛ فرمود-
/far-mu-dan/
do (lit); order; say v

فرنگ /fa-rang/
abroad (esp Europe) n

فرنگی /fa-ran-gi/
foreigner; non-Muslim n

فرنی /fīr-ni/ firni (pudding) n

فرنیچر far-ni-char/ furniture n

فرهنگ /far-hang/
culture, civilization n

فرهنگی /far-han-gi/
cultural, educational adj

فرو /fū-ro, fī-/ downward v prefix

فرو گذاشت /fū-ro gŭzāsht/
negligence n

فرو گذاشت کردن v ← neglect

فروتن /fŭ-ro-tan/
humble, submissive (& pers) adj, n

فروج /fū-ruj, sg farj/
see sg فرج n pl

فروختن ؛ -فروش- ؛ فروخت-
/fū-rokh-tan/
sell (lit) vt

فروردین /far-war-dīn/
see Hamal (month) n

فروش /fū-rosh/
selling; (in combinations) seller n
→ فروش کردن sell v
→ کتاب فروش bookseller n

فروشگاه /fū-rosh-gāh/ store, shop n
فروشنده /fū-ro-shǐn-da/
seller, vendor n

فروماندگی /fū-ro-mān-da-gi/
poverty, helplessness n

فرومانده /fū-ro-mān-da/
needy, helpless adj

فروند /far-wand/
unit (ship, airplane) n
→ ۱۰ فروند کشتی 10 ships

فرهاد Farhad (m name) n /far-hād/
فریاد /far-yād/
shout, call; cry for help n
→ فریاد بر آوردن cry for help vi
→ فریاد زدن shout, cry, call out vi
فریاد رس far-yād ras/
protector, savior n

فریب deceit; seduction n /fī-reyb/
فریب داده /fī-reyb dā-da/
deceived; seduced adj

فریب کار , -ان/ها /fī-reyb kār/
deceitful (& pers) adj, n
فریب کارانه /fī-reyb kā-rā-na/
deceitful (& adv) adj, adv

فریبندگی /fī-rey-bǐn-da-gi/
lure, charm n

فریبنده /fī-rey-bǐn-da/
alluring, enticing adj

فرید /fa-rid/
Farid (m name) n; unrivaled adj
فریده Farida (f name) n /fa-ri-da/
فریضه , -ها/فرایض
/fa-ri-za, pl fa-rā-yíz/
religious duty n

فریفتن ؛ -فریب- ؛ فریفت-
/fī-reyf-tan/
deceive; seduce v

فریضه see فرض n /fa-ri-za/
فزیک physics n /fī-zik/

فریمانت
Fremont (city) n /fri-mānt/
فزیولوژی /fī-zī-yo-lo-zhi/
physiology n

فساد /fa-sād (fī-sāt)/
corruption, depravity; disturbance n
فساد اخلاقی /fa-sād-ī akh-lā-qi/
vice (esp sexual) n

فسخ /faskh/
cancellation, abrogation n

فش فشی , -ان/ها /fīsh fī-shi/
breathy, wheezy (& pers) adj, n
فشار , -ها /fī-shār/
pressure, stress; accent n
فشار سنج /fī-shār sanj/
manometer n

فشردن ؛ -فشر- , فشار- ؛ فشرد-
/fī-shǔr-dan/
press, squeeze vt

فشرده /fī-shǔr-da/
summarized; condensed adj

فصاحت /fa-sā-hat/
fluency, stylistic purity n

فصحا /fū-sa-hā, sg fa-sih/
see sg فصیح n pl

فصل , -ها/فصول
/fá-sǐl, fasl; pl fa-sul/
season (annual); chapter; pause n
فصلی seasonal adj /fas-li/
فصول /fa-sul; sg fá-sǐl, fasl/
see sg فصل n pl

فصیح , -ان/فصحا
/fa-sih, pl fū-sa-hā/
fluent, stylistically adept (& pers)
adj, n

فصیح /fa-sih/
literary, standard (usage); pure,
clear (style) adj

فضا /fa-zā/
atmosphere, climate (fig); space,
universe; sky n

فضا پیما fa-zā pay-mā/
spacecraft n

فضا نورد /fa-zā na-ward/
astronaut n

فضای روز /fa-zā-yī roz/
atmospherics n

فضایی /fa-zā-yi/
space, cosmic; air adj

فضل /fá-zīl, fazl/
culture, refinement; Fazil (m name)
n

فضل فروش /fá-zīl fū-rosh/
pretentious *adj*

فضل فروشی /fá-zīl fū-ro-shi/
pretensions *n*

فضله , -ها/فضلات /fúz-la, pl -lāt/
trash; excrement *n*

فضولی کردن /fū-zu-li kardan/
meddle *v*

فضیحت *n* /fa-zi-hat/ see افتضاح

فطر /fí-tǐr, fītr/ breaking of fast *n*

فطیر /fa-tir/ unleavened *adj*

فعال /fa-'āl/
active *adj*; actor, agent *n*

→ فعال شدن • فعال گردیدن
activate, become active *vi*

فعالیت , -ها /fa-'ā-lī-yat/
activity; effect *n*

→ فعالیت داشتن • فعالیت کردن
function, be in effect *v*

فعل , -ها/افعال /feyl, pl af-'āl/
act, deed; verb *n*

فعل معاونت /feyl-ĭ mŭ-'ā-wĭn-at/
auxiliary verb *n*

فعلا /féy-lan, -lán/
now, presently (lit) *adv*

فعلی /fey-li/ current, present *adj*

فغفور چین /fagh-fur-ĭ chin/
fine rider in a procession (lit., King
of China) *n*

فقاریه /fa-qā-rī-ya/ vertebrate *adj*

فقدان /fīq-dān/
lack, shortage; loss *n*

فقر /fá-qīr, faqr/ poverty *n*

فقرا /fū-qa-rā/
n pl see sg فقیر

فقرات /fū-qa-rāt/ spinal column *n*

فقرالدم /faq-rŭd-dam/ anemia *n*

فقره /fa-qa-ra/ clause (gram) *n*

فقط /fa-qat/
only, merely, solely *adv*

→ نه فقط ... بلکه ... هم
not only...but also...

فقه /fíqh/ Muslim jurisprudence *n*

فقها /fū-qa-hā, sg fa-qih/
n pl see sg فقیه

فقیه , -ان/فقها /fa-qih, pl fū-qa-hā/
faqih (expert in Musl law) *n*

فقیر , -ان/فقرا /fa-qir, pl fū-qa-rā/
poor (& pers, esp dervish or Sufi)
adj, n

فکاهی , -ات/ها /fa-kā-hi/
humor, joke *n*; funny, witty *adj*

فکاهی نویس /fa-kā-hi na-wis/
humorist *n*

فکتور /fak-tor/
factor (math, biol); gene *n*

فکر , -ها/افکار /fí´-kīr, fīkr; pl af-kār/
thought, idea, concept; opinion;
(Sufism) mystical contemplation *n*

→ فکر کردن
think, believe; consider *v*

فکرا /fí´k-ran, -rán/ mentally *adv*

فلاخن /fa-lā-khŭn/ sling, slingshot *n*

فلاکت /fa-lā-kat/
misfortune, misery *n*

فلان /fī-lān/
a certain, some *adj*; so-and-so;
genitals *n*

فلانی /fī-lā-ney/ see فلان *adj, n*

فلج /falj/ paralysis *n*; paralyzed *adj*

→ فلج بودن be paralyzed *vi*

→ فلج شدن become paralyzed *vi*

فلز , -ات/ها /fī-lĭz/ metal *n*

فلز کار /fī-lĭz kār/ metalworker *n*

فلز کاری /fī-lĭz kā-ri/ metalwork *n*

فلزی /fī-lī-zi/ metal, metallic *adj*

فلسطین /fa-las-tin/
Palestine (territories) *n*

فلسطینی , -ان/ها /fa-las-ti-ni/
Palestinian (& pers) *adj, n*

فلفل /fīl-fīl/ pepper, black pepper *n*

فلک , -ها/افلاک /fa-lak, pl af-lāk/
planet, star, heavenly sphere *n*

فلک زده , -گان/ها /fa-lak za-da/
star-crossed (& pers) *adj, n*

فلکی /fa-la-ki/
astronomical; celestial *adj*

فلم /fí´-līm, film/
film (& material); movie *n*

فلم بردار /fĭ´-līm bar dār/
cameraman; filmmaker n
← فلم برداری کردن shoot a film v
← فلم برداری ویدیویی کردن
videotape v

فلم برداری ویدیویی
/fĭ´-līm bar dā-ri-yĭ wi-dī-yu-yi/
video recording n

فلم گیری /fĭ´-līm gi-ri/
see فلم برداری v

فلم مستند /fĭ´-līm-ĭ mŭs-ta-nad/
documentary (film) n

فلمساز , -ان/ها /fĭ´-līm sāz/
filmmaker n

فلوت flute (mus instr) n /fū-lut/
← فلوت نواختن play the flute v

فلیپین /fĭ-li-pin/
Philippines (country) n

فلیپینی , -ان/ها /fĭ-li-pi-ni/
Filipino, Filipina (pers); (lang)
Tagalog n; Philippine adj

فن , -ها/فنون /fan, pl fū-nun/
craft, art; skill; trade; technique
(artistic); device (literary); trick,
artifice n
← علوم و فنون arts & sciences

فنا /fa-nā/
passing away; (Sufism) fanaa, loss
of self through gnosis n
← فنا شدن pass away; lose self vi

فنا پذیر /fa-nā pa-zir/
mortal, perishable adj

فنا ناپذیر /fa-nā nā-pa-zir/
immortal, imperishable adj

فنا ناپذیری /fa-nā nā´-pa-zi-ri/
immortality, imperishability n

فنر spring (coil) n /fa-nar/
فنلند /fĭn-land/ n فنلیند see
فنلندی /fĭn-lan-di/ n فنلیندی see
Finland (country) n /fĭn-leynd/ فنلیند
فنلیندی /fĭn-leyn-di/
Finnish adj; Finn (pers) n
فنون /fū-nun, sg fan/ فن n pl see sg
فنون ظریفه /fū-nun-ĭ za-ri-fa/
fine arts n pl

فنیقی , -ان/ها /fĭ-ni-qi/
Phoenician (& pers, hist) adj, n
Phoenicia (hist) n /fĭ-ni-qĭ-ya/ فنیقیه

فواحش /fa-wā-hĭsh, sg fā-hĭ-sha/
see sg فاحشه n pl

فواره /fa-wā-ra/
fountain; gush, spurt n
← فواره زدن • فواره کردن
gush, spurt v

فواصل /fa-wā-sĭl, sg fā-sĭ-la/
see sg فاصله n pl

فواید /fa-wā-yĭd, sg fā-yĭ-da/
see sg فایده n pl

فوت death n /fawt/
← فوت کردن die (naturally) v

فوتوکاپی photocopy n /fo-to-kā-pi/
فوراً /fáw-ran, -rán/
immediately; suddenly adv

فوراً ظاهر شدن
/fáw-ran zā-hĭr shŭdan/
emerge, become known vi

فوری /faw-ri/
immediate, urgent adj

فوسیل fossil n /fo-sil/
فوسیل شناس /fo-sil shĭ-nās/
paleontologist n

فوسیل شناسی /fo-sil shĭ-nā-si/
paleontology n

فوق above adj; top n /fawq/
فوق الذکر /fawq ŭl-zĭ´-kĭr/
abovementioned adj

فوق الطبیعی /fawq ŭl-ta-bi-´i/
supernatural adj

فوق العاده /fawq ŭl-´ā-da/
extraordinary adj

فوقانی upper adj /faw-qā-ni/
فولاد steel n /fo-lād/
فولادی /fo-lā-di/
steel; gray adj

فونتکس phonetics n /fo-nĭ-tiks/
فونولوجی phonology n /fo-no-lo-ji/
فونیم phoneme n /fo-nim/
فونیم شناسی /fo-nim shĭ-nā-si/
phonemics n

فهارس /fa-hā-rĭs, sg fĭh-rĭst/
see sg فهرست n pl

فهرست , -ها/فهارس
/fĭh-rĭst, pl fa-hā-rĭs/
list, catalogue, index, table n

فهرست اعلام /fĭh-rĭst-ĭ a´-lām/
index, table (esp in book) n

فهرست مندرجات
/fīh-rīst-ī mün-dar-jāt/
table of contents n

فهرست موضوعات
/fīh-rīst-ī maw-zo-'āt/
see فهرست مندرجات n

فهم /fahm/
understanding, comprehension,
knowledge n

فهمیدن ؛ -فهم- ؛ فهمید-
/fah-mi-dan/
understand, know vt

فهیم intelligent, "gets it" adj /fa-him/

فهیمه Fahima (f name) n /fa-hi-ma/

فی per, for each, for every n /fi/

فی الجمله /fí-l-jüm-la/
in general; in short adv

فی المثل /fí-l-ma-sal/
for example adv

فی الواقع /fí-l-wā-qey/
really, actually adv

فی صد percent adv /fi-sad/

فیته ribbon; tape n /fi-ta/

فیثاغور /fi-sā-ghor/ see فیثاغورس n

فیثاغورس /fi-sā-ghors/
Pythagoras (hist) n

فیر /fayr/
fire, discharge (from weapon) n

فیر کردن ‹بالای کسی›
fire, open fire ‹on sb›, shoot,
discharge (weapon) v

فیروز see پیروز adj /fey-roz, fi-/

فیروزکوه /fi-roz-koh/
Firozkoh (mountain range; Ghorid
capital, hist) n

فیروزکوهی /fi-roz-ko-hi/
Firozkohi (Aimaq tribe) n

فیروزنخچیر /fi-roz nakh-chir/
Firoz Nakhchir (dist) n

فیروزه see پیروزه n /fey-ro-za/

فیصد percent adv /fi-sad/

فیصدی percentage, rate n /fi-sa-di/

فیصله /fay-sa-la/
decision, resolution n

فیصله شدن ←‏ be decided vi

فیصله نامه /fay-sa-la nā-ma/
resolution (by assembly) n

←‏ فیصله نامه شورای امنیت ملل متحد
UN Security Council Resolution n

فیض /fayz/
generosity, beneficence;
abundance n

فیض آباد /fay-zā-bad/
Fayzabad (seat) n

فیل elephant; (chess) bishop n /fil/

فیل پایه /fil pā-ya/
pedestal (base of column) n

فیلد مارشال /fild mār-shāl/
field marshal n

فیل مرغ turkey n /fil-mürgh/

فیلسوف , -ان/ها/ /fey-la-suf/
philosopher n

فیوز fuse (electrical) n /fī-yuz/

ق

قاب /qāb/
case; frame; plate; dish; unit n

←‏ ۳ قاب ساعت 3 watches

←‏ ۲ قاب عینک 2 pairs of glasses

قابل(-ی) worthy of ‹sth› adj /qā-bīl(-ī)/

قابل qualified, talented adj /qā-bīl/

قابل اجتناب /qā-bīl-ī īj-tī-nāb/
avoidable adj

قابلیت احتراق /qā-bīl-ī īh-tī-rāq/
combustible, flammable adj

قابل استعمال /qā-bīl-ī īs-tey-māl/
fit, usable adj

قابل استفاده /qā-bīl-ī īs-tī-fā-da/
see قابل استعمال adj

قابل اعتماد /qā-bīl-ī ey-tī-mād/
trustworthy adj

قابل انعطاف /qā-bīl-ī īn-'ī-tāf/
flexible, supple adj

قابل انعکاس /qā-bīl-ī īn-'ī-kās/
reflective, reflecting adj

قابل برگشت /qā-bīl-ī bar-gasht/
revocable adj

قابل تحمل /qā-bīl-ī ta-ha-mül/
tolerable adj

قابل تردید /qā-bīl-ī tar-did/
rejectable adj

قابل تشکر نیست !
/qā-bĭl-ĭ ta-sha-kŭr neyst/
you're welcome excl

قابل توجه /qā-bĭl-ĭ ta-wa-jŭh/
noteworthy adj

قابل توسعه /qā-bĭl-ĭ taw-sĭ-'a/
expandable adj

قابل تیر شدن /qā-bĭl-ĭ teyr shŭdan/
passable (road) adj

قابل ستایش /qā-bĭl-ĭ sĭ-tā-yĭsh/
praiseworthy, laudable adj

قابل سماعت /qā-bĭl-ĭ sa-mā-'at/
cognizable (law) adj

قابل قبول /qā-bĭl-ĭ qa-bul/
acceptable adj

قابل مقایسه /qā-bĭl-ĭ mŭ-qā-yĭ-sa/
comparable adj

قابل ملاحظه /qā-bĭl-ĭ mŭlā-hĭ-za/
considerable, remarkable adj

قابل نشر <به کسی>
/qā-bĭl-ĭ ná-shĭr/
releaseable (document) <to sb> adj

قابلی /qā-bĭ-li/ qabeli (rice dish) n

قابلیت /qā-bĭ-lĭ-yat/
ability, capability; qualification n

قابیل /qā-bil/ Cain (bibl) n

قابیل و هابیل /qā-bil ŭ hā-bil/
Cain & Abel phrs

قات /qāt/ fold, layer n

قات کردن ←
fold; close, shut (book); bend
(knee) vt

قاتکی /qā-ta-ki/ folding adj

قاطر /qā-tĭr/ mule n

قاتل , -ان/ها/ین /qā-tĭl/
murderer, assassin n; deadly, fatal
adj

قاجار /qā-jār/
Qajar (hist, Iran 1794-1925) n

→ سلسله قاجار Qajar dynasty n

قاچاق /qā-chāq/ smuggling n

→ قاچاق کردن smuggle v

قاچاقبر , -ان/ها /qā-chāq-bar/
smuggler n

قاچاقچی , -ان/ها /qā-chāq-chi/
n قاچاقبر see

قاچاقی /qā-chā-qi/
smuggled, hot adj

قادری , -ان/ها /qā-dĭ-ri/
member of Qadiriyya n

قادریه /qā-dĭ-rĭ-ya/
Qadiriyya (Sufi order) n

قادس /qā-dĭs/ Qades (dist) n

قادیان /qā-dĭ-yān/
Qadeyan (Pakistani town; hist,
sectarian leader) n

قادیانی /qā-dĭ-yā-ni/
Qadeyani (sect) n

قار /qār/ قهر n see

قاره /qā-ra/ continent n

قاری /qā-ri/ reciter of Quran n

قاری /qā-ri/
Qari, Abdullah (20th-c Dari poet) n
(alt name) عبدالله ملک الشعرا ←

قاسم /qā-sĭm/ Qasem (m name) n

قاش /qāsh/ slice (melon) n

قاش کردن ←
slice, cut into slices v

قاش ابرو /qāsh-ĭ ab-ru/ eyebrow n

قاش زین /qāsh-ĭ zin/ saddlebow n

قاشق /qā-shŭq/ spoon n

قاصد /qā-sĭd/ messenger; herald n

قاصر /qā-sĭr/
incapable, unable; limited adj

قاضی , -ان/ها/قضات
/qā-zi, pl qŭ-zāt/
judge, magistrate n

قاط /qāt/ قحط n see

قاطع /qā-tey/
decisive; intersecting; (math)
secant n

قاغ /qāgh/ قاق (colloq) adj see

قافله , -ها/قوافل
/qā-fĭ-la, pl qa-wā-fĭl/
caravan, convoy n

قاق /qāq (qāgh)/
dried (fruit); dry (firewood); stale adj

قالمقال /qāl-ma-qāl (ghāl-ma-ghāl)/
dispute, controversy; uproar n

قالین /qā-lin/ carpet (w/pile) n

قالین بافی /qā-lin bā-fi/
carpetmaking n

قالین تکانی /qā-lin ta-kā-ni/
carpet cleaning n

قالینچه /qā-lin-cha/
carpet, rug (small) n

قاموس /qā-mus/
dictionary, lexicon n

قانع /qā-ney/ satisfied, content adj
← قانع ساختن <کسی را>
satisfy <sb> vt

قانون , -ها/قوانین /qā-nun, pl qā-wā-nin/
law, statute; rule; qanun n

قانون اساسی /qā-nun-ī a-sā-si/
constitution, basic law n

قانون جرایم /qā-nun-ī ja-rā-yīm/
criminal law/code n

قانون حاکم /qā-nun-ī hā-kīm/
law of the land (ruler's) n

قانون گذار , -ان/ها /qā-nun gŭ-zār/
legislator n; legislative adj

قانون گذاری /qā-nun gŭ-zā-ri/
legislating, lawmaking n
← قانونی گذاری کردن legislate v

قانونی /qā-nu-ni/ legal, statutory adj
← قانونی ساختن legalize vt

قانونیت /qā-nu-nī-yat/ legality n

قاهره /qā-hī-ra/ Cairo (capital) n

قاید /qā-yīd/ leader n

قایق /qā-yīq/
kayak, skiff, small boat n

قایم /qā-yīm/
vertical; perpendicular; steadfast adj

قباحت /qa-bā-hat/
petty misdemeanor; indecency n

قبال /qī-bāl/ prep در قبال see

قباله /qa-bā-la/ deed (document) n

قبایل , sg قبیله /qa-bā-yīl, sg qa-bi-la/
see sg n pl

قبر /qá-bīr/ grave, tomb n

قبرستان /qab-rīs-tān/
graveyard, cemetery n

قبرغه /qa-bŭr-gha/ rib n

قبرس /qīb-rīs/ Cyprus (country) n

قبرسی /qīb-rī-si/ Cypriot adj

قبضه /qab-za (qaw-)/
hilt; unit (sword); taking possession;
bunch (vegetables) n
← دو قبضۀ شمشیر two swords

قبط /qībt/ Copt (hist) n

قبطی /qīb-ti/ Coptic adj

قبل از <چیزی> /qá-bĭl az/
before <sth> prep

قبل از آن که /qá-bĭl az ān kī/
before <+ subj> adv

قبل از ظهر /qá-bĭl az zŭ´-hŭr/
a.m. adv; morning n

قبل التاریخ /qà-bĭl-ŭt-tā-ríkh/
prehistoric adj

قبل المیلاد /qà-bĭl-ŭl-mi-lā´d/
B.C., B.C.E. adv; pre-Christian adj

قبل الولاده /qà-bĭl-ŭl-wī-lā-dá/
prenatal adj

قبل بر /qá-bĭl bar/ prep see قبل از

قبلاً /qáb-lan, -lán/
before, formerly adv

قبله /qĭb-la/
kiblah, direction of Mecca n

قبله نما /qĭb-la nŭ-mā/
kiblah indicator, compass n

قبلی /qab-li/ former, previous adj

قبول کردن /qa-bul kardan/
accept; approve, consent (to);
convert (to rel) vt

قبولی /qa-bu-li/ acceptance n

قبیل /qa-bil/ type, kind, sort n

قبیله , -ها/قبایل /qa-bi-la, pl qa-bā-yīl/
tribe n

قبیله یی /qa-bi-la-yi/ tribal adj

قیقان /qap-qān/ trap n

قتل /qá-tĭl, qatl/
murder, homicide, assassination
(lit) n

قتل عام /qá-tĭl-ī 'ām/ massacre n

قتل عمد /qá-tĭl-ī 'amd/
homicide (deliberate) n

قتیل /qa-til/ killed, slain adj

قچ /qŭch/ ram (m sheep) n

قچ جنگی /qŭch jan-gi/
ram fighting n

قحط /qaht (qāt)/
drought; famine; shortage n

قحطی و قیمتی /qah-ti wa qi-ma-ti/
feast & famine (lit) phrs

قد /qad/
height; length (jacket, pants) n
← قد کشیدن grow tall quickly v

قد علم کردن /qad a-lam kardan/
stand one's ground *v*

قدامت /qī-dā-mat/
antiquity, being ancient *n*

قدامت دار /qī-dā-mat-dār/
ancient, very old *adj*

قدر /qá-dīr, qadr/
in combinations /qa-dar/
amount, quantity *n*
→ چقدر ? how many?
→ آن قدر , این قدر that/this many
→ چقدر وقت ? how long (time)?

قدرت /qŭd-rat/
power (& pol), strength *n*

قدرتمند /qŭd-rat-mand/
powerful (& pol), strong *adj*

قدردان /qa-dīr-dān/
grateful, appreciative *adj*

قدردانی /qa-dīr-dā-ni/
gratitude, appreciation *n*

قدر دانی ابراز کردن
/qa-dīr-dā-ni īb-rāz kardan/
express gratitude *v*

قدر شناس /qá-dīr shi-nās/
see قدر دان *adj*

قدس /qŭds/ *n* القدس see

قدغن /qad-ghan/
ban, prohibition *n*
→ قدغن کردن ban, prohibit *v*

قدم /qa-dam/
pace; step; (fig) short distance *n*
→ قدم زدن stroll (for pleasure) *v*
قدم رو /qa-dam raw/ march *n*
→ قدم رو کردن march *v*

قدما /qŭ-da-mā, sg qa-dim/
the ancients *n pl*

قدمت /qī-da-mat/ *n* قدامت see

قدیس , -ین /qī-dis/
saint (Christian) *n*

قدیسه , -ها/قدیسات
/qī-di-sa, pl -sāt/
saint (Christian, f) *n*

قدیفه /qa-di-fa/ *n* قطیفه see

قدیم /qa-dim/
ancient, old; the Eternal (attribute of God) *adj*

قدیمی /qa-di-mi/
ancient, aged; old-fashioned *adj*

قرا /qŭ-rā, sg qar-ya/
see sg قریه *n pl*

قرا باش ! /qa-rā bāsh/
shut up! (colloq) *excl*

قرار /qa-rār/
order, arrangement; rest, tranquility *n*
→ قرار دادن apply, put, set *vt*
→ قرار داشتن be located (sw) *v*
→ قرار گرفتن be decided; be put/applied *v*
قرار /qa-rār(-ī)/ according to *prep*

قرار داد /qa-rār dād/
contract, agreement *n*

قرار دادی /qa-rār dā-di/
contractor *n*

قرار ملاقات /qa-rār-ī mŭ-lā-qāt/
appointment (time) *n*
→ قرار ملاقات گذاشتن
make an appointment *v*

قرارگاه headquarters *n* /qa-rār-gāh/

قرائت /qī-rā-'at/
recitation (esp of Quran); reader (textbook) *n*

قرآن Quran *n* /qŭ-rān, qŭr-'ān/
قرآنی Quranic *adj* /qŭr-'ā-ni/

قرب /qŭrb/
closeness, proximity, vicinity; confidence *n*
→ قرب <کسی> داشتن
have <sb's> confidence *v*

قرباغ /qa-ra-bāgh/ *n* قره باغ see

قربان /qŭr-bān/
sacrifice, immolation *n*

قربانی /qŭr-bā-ni/
victim *n*; for sacrifice or immolation *adj*
→ قربانی دادن • قربانی کردن
sacrifice; victimize *vt*

قرت /qŭrt/ sip *n*
→ قرت کردن swallow *v*

قرح /qarh/ *n* قرحه see
قرحه ulcer *n* /qar-ha/

قرخت /qa-rakht/ *adj* کرخت see

قرص /qŭrs/
disk; flat, round loaf of bread *n*

قره /qa-ra/
black adj; spade (cards) n

قره باغ /qa-ra-bāgh/
Qarabagh (dist) n

قره قش /qa-ra qŭsh/
black starling (bird) n

قره قل /qa-ra-qŭl/
karakul sheepskin n

قريب /qa-rib/
close, near (& adv) adj, adv

قريب الوقوع /qa-rib-ŭl-wŭ-qo/
imminent adj

قريش /qŭ-raysh/
Quraysh (hist, Arabian/Prophet's
tribe; f name, rare) n

قريشه /qŭ-ray-sha/
Quraysha (f name, rare) n

قريشى , -ان/ها /qŭ-ray-shi/
Qurayshi (member of Quraysh) n

قريظه بنو قريظه n /qŭ-ray-za/ see

قريه , -ها/قرا /qar-ya, pl qŭ-rā/
village n

قريه دار , -ان/ها /qar-ya dār/
village chief/elder n

قريه دارى /qar-ya dā-ri/
system of tax collection by village
elder n

قز /qaz/ silk (arch) n

قزاقستان /qa-zā-qis-tān/
Kazakhstan n

قزل /qĭ-zĭl/ bay (horse) n

قزلباش /qĭ-zĭl-bāsh/ Qizilbash n

قساوت /qa-sā-wat/
cruelty, mercilessness n

قسط , -ها/اقساط /qĭst, pl aq-sāt/
installment; paying in installments n

قسم /qa-sam/ oath n

قسم /qĭ´-sĭm, qĭsm; pl aq-sām/
kind, sort, variety n

اقسام pl ←

قسم كه /qĭsm-ĭ key/
as adv

قسماً /qĭs´-man, -mán/
partially, partly adv

قسمت /qĭs-mat/
kismet, destiny, fate; portion, part;
piece, section n

قوش تيپه /qush tey-pa/
Qush Teypa (dist) n

قرض , -ها/قروض /qarz, pl qŭ-ruz/
debt; loan n

قرض دادن ←
loan, make a loan v
قرض كردن • قرض گرفتن ←
borrow (money), take out a loan v

قرض دار , -ان/ها /qarz-dār/
debtor n; indebted adj

قرض دار /qarz-dār/
indebted adj; debtor n adj, n

قرض دارى /qarz-dā-ri/
indebtedness n

قرضه /qar-za/ government loan n

قرضه بلا عوض
/qar-za ba-lā ĭ-wāz/
grant n

قرطاسيه /qĭr-tā-sĭ-ya/
stationery; office supplies n

قرطاسيه فروشى
/qĭr-tā-sĭ-ya fŭ-ro-shi/
stationery store n

قرعه /qŭr-'a/ lots n
قرعه انداختن ← cast lots v
قرعه كشى كردن
/qŭr-'a ka-shi kardan/
draw lots v

قرعه كشى /qŭr-'a ka-shi/
drawing (lottery) n

قرغان /qŭr-ghān/ Qurghan (dist) n

قرغز /qĭr-ghĭz/
Kyrgyz, (arch) Kirghiz n

قرغزستان /qĭr-ghĭ-zĭs-tān/
Kyrgyzstan n

قرغزى , -ان/ها /qĭr-ghĭ-zi/
Kyrgyz (& pers, lang) adj, n

قرغه يى /qar-gha-yi/
Qarghayi (dist) n

قرقين /qar-qin/ Qarqin (dist) n

قرمقول /qa-ram-qol/
Qaramqol (dist) n

قرن , -ها/قرون /qarn, pl qŭ-run/
century n

قرنفل /qa-ran-fŭl/ clove (spice) n

قرنيه /qar-nĭ-ya/ cornea n

قروت /qŭ-rut/ dried yogurt ball n

قروض /qŭ-ruz, sg qarz/
قرض n pl see sg

قرون /qŭ-run, sg qarn/
قرن n pl see sg

---

village n /qīsh-lāq/ قشلاق , ها-

villager n /qīsh-lā-qi/ قشلاقی

قشله /qīsh-la/

base (mil); barracks n

قشله عسکری /qīsh-la-yī as-ka-ri/
military base; barracks n

قشنگ /qa-shang/

beautiful, pretty; elegant, fine adj

قشون /qŭ-shun/

army, armed forces n

قصاب /qa-sāb/ , ان/ها-
butcher n

قصابی /qa-sā-bi/
butcher shop; butchering n

قصاص /qī-sās/

reprisal, retaliation (for murder) n

قصبت الریه /qa-sa-ba-t ŭr-rī-ya/
trachea, windpipe n

قصبه /qa-sa-ba, pl -bāt/ , ها-/قصبات
small town, large village n

قصد /qasd/
intention, purpose n

→ قصد داشتن intend v

قصداً /qás-dan, -dán/
on purpose adv

قصر /qá-sĭr, qasr; pl qŭ-sur/ , ها-
mansion, palace n

قصر ریاست جمهوری
/qasr-ĭ rĭ-yā-sat-ĭ jam-hu-ri/
Presidential Palace n

قصر سفید /qá-sĭr-ĭ sa-feyd/
White House n

قصور /qŭ-sur, sg qá-sĭr, qasr/
see sg قصر n pl

قصه /qī-sa, pl qī-sas/ , ها-/قصص
tale, story; account n

قصه جن و پری
/qī-sa-yī jĭn ŭ pa-ri/
fairy tale n

قضات /qŭ-zāt, sg qā-zi/
see sg قاضی n pl

قضاوت /qa-zā-wat/
verdict, opinion, judgment n

→ قضاوت کردن render a verdict v

قضایا /qa-zā-yā, sg qaz-ya/
see sg قضیه n pl

قضایی /qa-zā-yi/
judicial, judiciary; (rel) making up
missed prayer adj

قضیب /qa-zib/ penis n

قضیه /qaz-ya, pl qa-zā-yā/ , ها-
affair; issue, problem (& math),
case, lawsuit n

قطار /qa-tār/ line, row n

قطار پیش /qa-tār-ĭ peysh/ frontline n

قطب /qŭ'-tūb, qŭtb/
pole; one of two antithetical ideas;
axis of Sufism n

قطب جنوب /qŭ'-tūb-ĭ jŭ-nub/
South Pole n

قطب شمال /qŭ'-tūb-ĭ sha-māl/
North Pole n

قطب نما /qŭ'-tūb-ĭ nŭ-mā/
compass, pole indicator n

قطبی /qŭt-bi/ polar n

قطره /qat-ra/ drop (liquid) n

قطره چکان /qat-ra-yī cha-kān/
dropper, pipette n

قطع /qá-ta, qaťˈ/
cutting; discontinuation n

→ قطع کردن
cut; break off, discontinue vt

قطع نواری /qat-ˈī na-wā-ri/
ribbon cutting n

قطع عضو /qá-ta-yī ŭzw/
amputation n

قطع نامه /qá-ta nā-ma/
resolution (document) n

قطعاً /qat-ˈan, qáṭ-/
absolutely, certainly adv

قطعه /qī-ta/ , ها-/قطعات
unit (& mil); fragment, piece;
playing card n

قطعی /qat-ˈi/ decisive, definite adj

قطعیت /qat-ˈi/ definiteness n

قطغن /qa-ta-ghan/
Qataghan (hist, prov) n

قطی /qa-ti/
box (small); can, tin can n

قطیفه /qa-ti-fa/ towel, bath towel n

قفاق /qa-fāq/ slap n

→ قفاق زدن slap vt

قفس /qa-fas/ cage n

قفقاز /qaf-qāz/
Caucasus (region) n

قفقازی /qaf-qā-zi/
Caucasian; Caucasoid (& pers) adj, n

قفل /qŭ´-fŭl, qŭfl (qŭlf)/
lock, padlock n

← قفل شدن be locked vi

← قفل کردن lock, padlock vt

قلاب /qŭ-lāb/ hook, fishhook n

قلات /qa-lāt, ka-/
Qalat (seat, dist) n

قلابی /qŭ-lā-bi/ see تقلبی adj

قلاچ /qŭ-lāch/
arm's length (unit of measurement) n

قلب ، ها- , pl قلوب /qŭ-lŭb/
/qalb, pl qŭ-lŭb/
heart; middle; (Sufism) soul;
metathesis n; dishonest adj

قلع و قمع کردن
/qal' ŭ qam' kardan/
eradicate; exterminate vt

قلعه (قلا) /qal-'a (qa-lā)/
fort, fortress; castle; Qala (ctr) n

قلعه بست /qal-'a-yĭ bŭst/
Bust (ancient fort) n

قلعه ذال /qal-'a-yĭ zāl/
Qala-ye Zal (dist) n

قلعه کاه /qal-'a-yĭ kāh/
Qala-ye Kah (dist) n

قلعه نعیم /qal-'a-yĭ na-'im/
Qala-ye Na im (ctr) n

قلعه نو /qal-'a-yĭ naw/
Qala-ye Naw (dist, seat) n

قلعه وزیر /qal-'a-yĭ wa-zir/
Qala-ye Wazir (city dist) n

قلف /qŭlf/ see قفل n

قلم /qa-lam, pl a-qa-lām/
entry, item n

← اقلام pl

قلم ، ها- /qa-lam/
pen; style n

قلم <کسی> /qa-lam(-ĭ)/
written by <sb> adj

قلم ابرو /qa-lam-ĭ ab-ru/
eyebrow pencil n

قلم خودرنگ /qa-lam-ĭ khŭd-rang/
fountain pen n

قلم خودکار /qa-lam-ĭ khŭd-kār/
ballpoint pen n

قلم رو /qa-lam-raw/
territory, dominion n

قلندر /qa-lan-dar/
Qalandar (dist, ctr Khost Meyla) n

قلوب /qŭ-lub, sg qalb/
see sg قلب n pl

قم /qŭm/ Qom, Qum (city, river) n

قمار /qĭ-mār/
risk; gamble, bet n

← قمار زدن risk, gamble, bet v

قمار باز /qĭ-mār bāz/
gambler n

قمار بازی /qĭ-mār bā-zi/
gambling n

← قمار بازی کردن gamble v

قمری /qa-ma-ri/
lunar (year) adj

قناعت /qĭ-nā-'at/
satisfaction, contentment n

← قناعت دادن <به کسی>
satisfy; convince, persuade <sb> vt

← قناعت داشتن • قانع بودن
be satisfied v

قناعت بخش /qĭ-nā-'at bakhsh/
satisfying adj

قنات ، ها- /qa-nāt, pl qa-na-wāt/
canal (underground) n

قنوات /qa-na-wāt, sg qa-nāt/
see sg قنات n pl

قند /qand/ lump sugar n

قند خشتی /qand-ĭ khĭsh-ti/
cube sugar n

قند مخروطی /qand-ĭ makh-ru-ti/
cone sugar n

قندز /qŭn-dŭz (-duz)/ see کندز n

قندهار /qan-da-hār (-dār)/
Kandahar (prov, seat) n

قنسل /qŭn-sŭl/
consul; attache n

قندیل /qan-dil/
candelabrum, chandelier n

قنسلگری /qŭn-sŭl-ga-ri/
consulate n

قنسول /qŭn-sul/ see قنسل n

قو ، ها- /qu/ swan n

قوا /qŭ-wā, sg -wa/ see sg قوه n pl

قواره /qa-wā-ra/
shape; figure (body) n

قوافل /qa-wā-fil, sg qā-fī-la/
see sg قافله n pl

قوام /qĭ-wām/
consistency, thickness (liquid), firmness n

قوانین /qa-wā-nin, sg qā-nun/
قانون n pl see sg

قوای امنیتی مساعدت بین المللی
/qŭ-wā-yĭ am-nĭ-ya-ti-yĭ mŭ-sā-‘ĭ-dat-ĭ bayn-ŭl-mĭ-la-li/
ISAF, International Security Assistance Force n

قوای بحری /qŭ-wā-yĭ bah-ri/
navy, naval forces n pl

قوای زمینی /qŭ-wā-yĭ za-mi-ni/
army, ground forces n pl

قوای واکنش سریع
/qŭ-wā-yĭ wā-kŭ-nĭsh-ĭ sa-ri/
QRF, Quick Reaction Force n

قوای هوایی /qŭ-wā-yĭ ha-wā-yi/
air force n pl

قوت /qut/ daily meal n

قوت لایموت /qut-ĭ lā-ya-mut/
ration, scanty meal n

قوت /qŭ-wat/
force, strength, power n

قوت های امنیتی ملی افغان
/qŭ-wat-ha-yĭ am-nĭ-ya-ti-yĭ mĭ-li-yĭ af-ghān/
ANDF, Afghan National Security Forces n

قوت های مشترک وظیفوی
/qŭ-wat-ha-yĭ mŭsh-ta-rak-ĭ wa-zi-fa-wi-yĭ/
CJTF, Combined Joint Task Force n

قوتمند /qŭ-wat-mand/
strong, powerful adj

قوچ /qoch/ چ n see

قورباغه /qor-bā-gha/ frog n

قورمه /qor-ma/ korma, stew n

قوس /qaws, dual pl qaw-sayn/
parenthesis; arc n

← قوسین dual pl

قوس /qaws/
Qaus (month); Sagittarius n

← آذر (Farsi equivalent)

قوس خورد /qaws-ĭ khŭrd/
quotation mark n

← قوسین خورد dual pl

قوس قزح /qaws-ĭ qa-zah/
rainbow n

قوس کوچک /qaws-ĭ ko-chak/
قوس خورد n see

قوسین /qaw-sayn, sg qaws/
قوس n pl see sg

قوضه /qaw-za/ n قبضه see

قوطی /qu-ti/ can, container n

قول , اقوال/ها- /qawl, pl aq-wāl/
promise, word; speech n

← قول دادن promise v

← قول گرفتن accept a promise v

قول شرف /qawl-ĭ sha-raf/
word of honor n

قول و عمل /qawl ŭ a-mal/
word & deed phrs

قول /qol/ arm (upper) n

قول اردو /qol-ĭ ŭr-du/
headquarters; corps n

قوم , اقوام/ها- /qawm, pl aq-wām/
tribe, clan; ethnicity; race; fellow tribesman; paternal relatives n

قوماندان /qŭ-mān-dān/
commanding officer n

قوماندان امنیه
/qŭ-mān-dān-ĭ am-nĭ-ya/
chief of police n

قوماندان عمومی
/qŭ-mān-dān-ĭ ŭ-mu-mi/
commanding general, CG n

قوماندانی /qŭ-mān-dā-ni/
command headquarters n

قوماندانی مشترک امنیتی انتقالی افغانستان
/qŭ-mān-dā-ni-yĭ mŭsh-ta-rak-ĭ am-nĭ-ya-ti-yĭ ĭn-tĭ-qā-li-yĭ af-ghā-nĭs-tān/
CSTC-A, Combined Security Transition Command-Afghanistan n

قومانده /qŭ-mān-da/
command, order (mil) n

← قومانده دادن give an order v

قومی /qaw-mi/
tribal; ethnic, racial adj

قومیت /qaw-mĭ-yat/
tribal affiliation n

قونسل /qon-sŭl/ n قنسل see

قونسول /qon-sul/ n قنسل see

قوه , ‫ها‬- /qŭ-wa, pl qŭ-wāl/ قوا
power; energy; troop, soldier, (mil)
unit *n*

قوه باه /qŭ-wa-yī bāh/
generative power *n*

قوه خرید /qŭ-wa-yī kha-rid/
purchasing power *n*

قوه افاده /qŭ-wa-yī ī-fā-da/
speaking ability *n*

قوی /qŭ-wi/ forceful, powerful *adj*

قویته /qŭ-wey-ta, kŭ-/
Quetta (city) *n*

قهار /qa-hār/ vanquishing (God) *adj*

قهر /qahr (qār)/
anger, fury, wrath; indignation *n*;
angry, furious *adj n, adj*

‫قهر بودن ‹با کسی›‬ —
be angry; be at odds <with sb> *vi*

قهراً /qáh-ran, -rán/
forcibly, by force *adv*

قهرمان , ‫ان/ها‬- /qah-ra-mān/
hero (novel/drama); champion;
warrior *n*

قهرمانی /qah-ra-mā-ni/
championship *n*

قهقهه /qah-qa-ha/
laughter (loud), guffaw *n*

قهوه /qah-wa/ coffee *n*

قهوه یی /qah-wa-yi/
brown, coffee-colored *adj*

قی /qay/ vomit *n*

‫قی کردن‬ — vomit, throw up *v*

قی آور /qay ā-war/
emetic, vomitive (med) *adj*

قیاس /qī-yās/
comparison; deduction; reasoning
by analogy; measurement *n*

‫قیاس کردن‬ — compare; deduce *v*

قیاسی /qī-yā-si/ regular (gram) *adj*

قیام /qī-yām/
revolt; protest; standing *n*

‫قیام کردن‬ — revolt, protest *vi*

قیام گرسنگی /qī-yām-ĭ gĭ-rīs-na-gi/
hunger strike *n*

قیامت /qī-yā-mat/
marvel, wonder; the Resurrection;
tumult *n*

‫قیامت شدن‬ — be resurrected *vi*

قیچی /qay-chi/ scissors *n*

‫قیچی کردن‬ — cut with scissors *v*

قید , ‫ها‬- /qayd, pl qŭ-yud/
bond, tie; imprisonment; custody;
adverb; written record, entry; safety
position (on gun) *n*

قیر /qir/ asphalt *n*; paved *adj*

قیراط /qi-rāt/ carat, karat *n*

قیسی /qay-si/
qaysi (sweet apricot) *n*

قیصار /qay-sār/
Qaysar (dist); see & قیصر *n*

قیصاریه /qay-sā-rī-ya/
Caesarea (hist, city) *n*

قیصر /qay-sar/
Caesar, emperor *n*

قیف /qif/ funnel *n*

قیل و قال /qil ŭ qāl/
cry, shout; uproar *n*

قیم /qa-yĭm/ custodian, caretaker *n*

قیم /qī-yam, sg qi-mat/
see sg قیمت *n pl*

قیماق /qay-māq (-māgh)/
cream (from milk) *n*

قیمت , ‫ها‬- /qi-mat, pl qĭ-yam/قیم
cost, price, value *n*; expensive *adj*

قیمت بها /qi-mat ba-hā/
expensive *adj*

قیمت عوضی /qi-mat-ĭ ī-wa-zi/
exemption fee *n*

قیمتی /qi-ma-ti/
cost of living *n*; expensive *adj*

قیود , /qŭ-yud, sg qayd/
see sg قید *n pl*

ک

کابل /kā-bŭl/
Kabul (capital, prov, seat) *n*

کابلی , ‫ان/ها‬- /kā-bŭ-li/
Kabuli *adj*; Kabul resident *n*

کابین /kā-bin/ brideprice (arch) *n*

کابینه /kā-bi-na/
cabinet, council of ministers *n*

کاپیتالزم /kā-pi-tā-lĭ´-zĭm/
capitalism *n*

کاپیتالست , ‫ان/ها‬- /kā-pi-tā-lĭst/
capitalist *n*

---

i = k<u>ee</u>p, ĭ = b<u>i</u>g, u = c<u>oo</u>p, ŭ = p<u>u</u>t, y = <u>y</u>et, ' = (glottal stop)   239

کاپیتالستی /kā-pi-tā-līs-ti/
capitalist, capitalistic *adj*

کاپیسا Kapisa (prov) *n* /kā-pi-sā/

کاتب /kā-tīb/
clerk; secretary (& at embassy) *n*

کاتولیک , -ان/ها /kā-to-lik/
Catholic (& pers) *adj, n*

کاج pine (tree); buttonhole *n* /kāj/

کاخ mansion, palace *n* /kākh/

کاخ سفید /kākh-ī sa-feyd/
White House *n*

کار work, employment *n* /kār/
← کار دادن hire, employ *vt*
← کار داشتن
need; own, possess (colloq) *v*
← کار کردن work, labor *v*
← کار گرفتن <از چیزی>
make use of, exploit <sth> *vt*

کار خانگی /kār khā-na-gi/
homework *n*

کار خانه /kār khā-na/
kitchen (colloq) *n*

کار خیر /kār-ī khayr/
charity, good works *n*

کار دستی /kār-ī dīs-ti/
handicraft *n*

کار نامه , -ها /kār-nā-ma/
epic, great deed *n*

کار آمد /kār ā-mad/
useful, needed *adj*

کاراکم /kā-rā-kŭm/
Karakum (desert) *n*

کاربن carbon *n* /kār-bŭn, -bon/

کارت , -ها /kārt/
card (business, greeting) *n*

کارت سوار شدن به طیاره /kārt-ī sa-wār shŭ-dan ba ta-yā-ra/
boarding pass (for plane) *n*

کارتل , -ها cartel *n* /kār-tal/

کارتوس , -ها cartridge *n* /kār-tus/

کارتون , -ها cartoon *n* /kār-tun/

کارته , -ها /kār-ta/
district, quarter (city) *n*

کارته پروان /kār-ta-yī par-wān/
Karta-ye Parwan (city dist) *n*

کارته چهار /kār-ta-yī chār/
Karta-ye Chahar (city dist) *n*

کارته سخی /kār-ta-yī sa-khi/
Karta-ye Sakhi (city dist) *n*

کارته سه /kār-ta-yī sey/
Karta-ye Sey (city dist) *n*

کارته نو /kār-ta-yī naw/
Karta-ye Naw (city dist) *n*

کارخانه , -ها/جات /kār-khā-na/
workshop, factory; (colloq) kitchen *n*

کارد , -ها knife *n* /kārd/

کاردان /kār-dān/
skilled, expert, savvy in business *adj*

کارروا /kār-ra-wā/
useful, suitable to the task *adj*

کارزار /kār-zār/
battlefield; battle, combat *n*

کارشکنی /kār-shī-ka-ni/
hindrance; obstructionism *n*

کارفرما , -ان/ها /kār-far-mā/
employer; proprietor *n*

کارک , -ها cork *n* /kārk/

کارکن /kār-kŭn/
hard-working, assiduous *adj*

کارکنان /kār-kŭ-nān/
employees, personnel *n pl*

کارگر , -ان/ها /kār-gar/
laborer, worker *n*

کارگردان /kār-gar-dān/
director; producer (film) *n*

کارگزار اصلی /kār-gŭ-zār-ī as-li/
mastermind *n*

کارمند , -ان/ها /kār-mand/
employee *n*

کاروان /kār-wān/
caravan; convoy *n*

کاروان سرای /kār-wān-sa-rāy/
caravanserai *n*

کاریز , -ها /kā-reyz/
canal (underground) *n*

کاژه Kazha (ctr) *n* /kā-zha/

کاسب , -ان/ها/کسبه /kā-sīb, pl kas-ba/
artisan, craftsman *n*

کاسد sluggish, dull *adj* /kā-sīd/

کاسنی /kās-ni/
chicory (med herb) *n*

کاسه , -ها /kā-sa/
bowl (us metal) *n*

كاسه ليس , -ان/ها /kā-sa leys/
parasite; sycophant (fig) n

كاش /kāsh/
if only, would that <+ past subj> adv

كاش كه see كاش adv /kāsh kĭ, key/

كاشتن ؛ -كار- ؛ كاشت- /kāsh-tan/
plant, sow v

كاشغر /kāsh-ghar/
Kashgar (geog; oasis) n

كاشف , -ان/ها /kā-shĭf/
explorer, discoverer n

كاشكى see كاش adv /kāsh key/

كاشى /kā-shi/
tile (& glazed) n

كاشى كارى /kā-shi-kā-ri/
tiled surface; tiling work n

كاغذ /kā-ghaz/
paper (material) n

كاغذ باطله /kā-ghaz-ĭ bā-tĭ-la/
wastepaper n

كاغذ پران /kā-ghaz pa-rān/
kite n

كافر , -ان/ها/كفار /kā-fĭr, kā-far; pl kŭ-fār/
infidel, unbeliever, non-Muslim n

كافى /kā-fi/
coffee; café n; enough adj

كافيتريا /kā-fi-tĭr-yā/
cafeteria n

كافيين /kā-fĭ-yin/
caffeine n

كاكا /kā-kā/
uncle (father's brother) n

كاكاو /kā-kāw/
cocoa, cacao n

كاكر /kā-kar/
Kakar (P tribe, dist) n

كاكل see كاكر /kā-kal/

كالا /kā-lā/
clothes, clothing n

كامديش /kām-deysh/
Kamdeysh (seat, dist) n

كامره /kā-ma-ra/
camera n

كامل /kā-mĭl/
entire, complete; thorough adj

كاملا /kā-mĭ'-lan, -lán/
entirely, utterly adv

كامه , -ها /kā-ma/
Kama (dist, ctr Sangar Saray);
comma n

كامياب /kām-yāb/
successful adj

كامياب شدن /kām-yāb shŭdan/
succeed vi

كان /kān/
mine (deposit); rich source n

كان عزت /kān-ĭ ĭ-zat/
Kan-e Ezat (ctr) n

كانادا /kā-nā-dā/
Canada n

كانادايى , -ان/ها /kā-nā-dā-yi/
Canadian (& pers) adj, n

كانال /kā-nāl/
canal; (anat) duct, tube n

كاناليزاسيون /kā-nā-li-zā-sī-yun/
sewer system n

كانتين /kān-tin/
canteen, snack bar n

كانج /kānj/
cross-eyed, strabismic n

كانديد /kān-did/
candidate; nominee n

كانديدا see كانديد n /kān-di-dā/

كانسرت /kān-sart/
concert n

كانسرت دادن ←
give a concert v

كانكريت /kān-kreyt/
concrete n

كانكريتى /kān-krey-ti/
concrete adj

كانكور /kān-kor/
competition n

كانكورس /kān-grĭs/
congress n

كانگورو /kān-gŭ-ru/
kangaroo n

كانونشن /kān-wĭn-shan/
convention n

كاواك /kā-wāk/
hollow adj

كاوش /kā-wĭsh/
excavation; research n

كاوش كردن ←
excavate, dig; research n

كاه /kāh/
hay, straw n

كاهدان /kāh-dān/
hay barn n

كاهش /kā-hĭsh/
decrease, diminution n

كاهش دادن ←
decrease vt

كاهش يافتن ←
decrease vi

كاهش يافته /kā-hĭsh yāf-ta/
diminished adj

كاهل /kā-hĭl/
lazy, sluggish; pacific adj

كاهن , -ان/كهنه /kā-hĭn; pl ka-hĭ-na, -ha-/
soothsayer (pre-Musl) n

كاهو /kā-hu/
lettuce n

كباب /ka-bāb/
kabob n

كباب كردن ←
barbeque; broil, grill v

كباب خويش را پختن
/ka-bāb-ĭ kheysh-rā pŭkhtan/
pursue one's own interests v

كبد /ka-bad/
liver n

كبرا /kŭb-rā/
cobra n

كبوتر , -ان/ها /ka-bu-tar/
pigeon, dove n

كبود /ka-bud (-but)/ blue, azure adj

كپچه مار /kap-cha mār/ see كفته مار n

كپرى /ka-pa-ray/ Kaparay (ctr) n

كپيتاليزم /ka-pi-tā-lí´-zīm/ capitalism n

كپيتالست , -ان/ها /ka-pi-tā-līst/ capitalist n

كپيتاليستى /ka-pi-tā-līs-ti/ capitalist, capitalistic adj

كتاب , -ها /kĭ-tāb/ book n

كتاب أشپزى /kĭ-tāb-ĭ āsh-pa-zi/ cookbook n

كتاب خانه /kĭ-tāb khā-na/ see كتابخانه n

كتاب درسى /kĭ-tāb-ĭ dar-si/ textbook n

كتاب طباخى /kĭ-tāb-ĭ ta-bā-khi/ see كتاب آشپزى n

كتاب فروش , -ان/ها /kĭ-tāb fŭ-rosh/ bookseller n

كتاب فروشى /kĭ-tāb fŭ-ro-shi/ bookstore n

كتاب مقدس /kĭ-tāb-ĭ mŭ-qa-das/ the Bible n

كتابچه /kĭ-tāb-cha/ notebook, pamphlet n

كتابچه چك /kĭ-tāb-cha chak/ checkbook n

كتابخانه /kĭ-tāb-khā-na/ library n

كتاره /ka-tā-ra/ rail fence; handrail, railing n

كتان /ka-tān/ cotton; linen, flax cloth n

كتانى /ka-tā-ni/ cotton; linen adj

كتبى /kat-bi/ written, recorded adj

كتره /kat-ra/ innuendo, snide remark n

كتره و كنايه /kat-ra wa wŭ kĭ-nā-ya/ implication & innuendo phrs

كتف , -ها/اكتاف /kĭtf, katf; pl ak-tāf/ shoulder (lit) n

كتل /kŭ-tal, ko-/ pass, defile n

كتل خيبر /kŭ-tal-ĭ khay-bar/ Khyber Pass n

كتمندو /kat-man-du/ Kathmandu (capital) n

كتى /ká-ti/ with (colloq) conj

كتيره /ka-ti-ra/ tragacanth gum n

كثافت /ka-sā-fat/ dirtiness; density n

كثيف /ka-sif/ dirty, polluted adj

كج /kaj/ tilted, crooked, slanted adj

كجا ؟ /kŭ-jā (-ja)/ where? pron

كجاوه /ka-jā-wa/ large wicker basket; howdah n

كجايى ؟ /kŭ-jā-yi/ what nationality? adv

كجران /kaj-rān/ Kajran (dist) n

كجكى /ka-ja-ki/ Kajaki (dam, dist) n
← بند كجكى Kajaki Dam

كجه ؟ /kŭ-ja/ where? (colloq) pron

كچالو /ka-chā-lu/ potato, spud n

كچك /kŭ-chŭk/ puppy n

كچكك /kŭ-chŭ-kak/ uvula n

كحل /kŭhl/ kohl (& cosmetic) n

كد /kad/ house n

كد بانو /kad bā-nu/ lady of the house n

كد خدا /kad khŭ-dā/ master of the house n

كدال /kŭ-dāl/ pickaxe, pick n

كدام /kŭ-dām/ no, not any (w/neg v) adj

كدام ؟ /kŭ-dām/ which? adj

كر , -ان/ها /kar/ deaf (& pers); heedless adj, n
← كر شدن go deaf vi

كرا /kĭ-rā/ rent (money) n
← كرا دادن <چيزى را به كسى>
rent (out) <sth to sb> v
← كرا گرفتن <چيزى از به كسى>
rent <sth from sb> v

كرا نشين /kĭ-rā nĭ-shin/ renter, tenant n

كراچى /ka-rā-chi/ cart, handcart; Karachi (city) n

كرام /kĭ-rām/ honorable, respectable adj

كرامت /kĭ-rā-mat/ dignity, honor n

كرامت , -ها/كرامات
/kĭ-rā-mat, pl ka-rā-māt/
miracle (by Musl saint) n
— كرامت كردن • كرامت دادن
work a miracle v
كران /kĭ-rān/
end, limit, margin, boundary n
كران و منجان /kĭ-rān wŭ mŭn-jān/
Keran wa Munjan (dist) n
كرانه n كران see /kĭ-rā-na/
كرايه rent (money) n /kĭ-rā-ya/
كرايى rented; for rent adj /kĭ-rā-yi/
كرتى /kŭr-ti/
waist-length coat; tunic n
كرج Karaj (city) n /ka-raj/
كرخ Karukh (dist) n /ka-rŭkh/
كرخت /ka-rakht (qa-)/
numb, unfeeling adj
— كرخت شدن go numb vi
كرد , -ان/ها Kurd (pers) n /kŭrd/
كرد , -ها /kard/
plot (of cultivated land) n
كرد گل flower bed n /kard-ĭ gŭl/
كردستان /kŭr-dĭs-tān/
Kurdistan n
كردن (كدن) ؛ -كن- ؛ كرد- (كد-)
/kar-dan (ka-)/
make, do v
— بكن- (كن-) (imper/subj)
كردى Kurdish (lang) n /kŭr-di/
كرك quail (bird) n /ka-rak/
كرك dislike n /kĭrk/
— كركِ ‹كسى› آمدن
dislike <sb> vt
كرك goat fluff (& fabric) n /kŭrk/
كرگدن rhinocerous n /kar-ga-dan/
كرگس vulture n /kar-gas/
كرنگ /kŭ-rang/
reddish-brown horse n
كرسى /kŭr-si/
stool; pedestal; university chair n
كرفس celery n /ka-rafs/
كرم /ka-ram/
cabbage; generosity, friendliness n
كرم worm n /kĭ´-rĭm, kĭrm/
/kĭ´-rĭm-ĭ ab-rey-shŭm/
silkworm n
كرم پيله silkworm n /kĭ´-rĭm-ĭ pi-la/

كرم قز silkworm n /kĭ´-rĭm-ĭ qaz/
كرنگل /kŭ-rĭn-gal, ko-/
Kurengal (valley) n
كرور ten million n, adj /kŭ-ror/
كروكى rough draft n /kŭ-ro-ki/
كروه /kŭ-roh/
kuroh (unit of distance) n
كروى /kŭ-ra-wi/
spherical adj; corpuscle n
كرويات corpuscles n /kŭ-ra-wĭ-yāt/
كرويت sphericity n /kŭ-ra-wĭ-yat/
كره , -ها wide bracelet n /ka-ra/
كره , -ها/كرات /kŭ-ra, pl -rāt/
sphere n
كره , -ها colt, foal n /kŭ-ra/
كره ارض globe n /kŭ-ra-yĭ arz/
كره زمين /kŭ-ra-yĭ za-min/
n كره ارض see
كرى heel n /kŭ-ri/
كريت /kŭ-rit, -reyt/
Crete (geog) n
كريدت credit n /kĭ-ray-dĭt/
— كريدت كارت credit card n
كريم /ka-rim/
Karim (m name) n; generous adj
كريم cream (from milk) n /kĭ-rim/
كريمه Karima (f name) n /ka-ri-ma/
كريمى /kĭ-ri-mi/
cream-colored, off-white adj
كژدم n گژدم see /kazh-dŭm/
كژه n كاژه see /ka-zha/
كس , -ان/ها /kas/
person, individual n
— بى كس w/o relatives adj
— نا كس plebeian adj
كس cunt (obs); vulva n /kŭs/
— كس دادن put out (obs) v
— كس كردن fuck (w/f) (obs) v
كس و كوى /kas ŭ koy/
milieu, kith & kin n
كساد /ka-sād/
depression (econ); slow market n
كسادى n كساد see /ka-sā-di/
كسالت slight illness n /ka-sā-lat/
— كسالت داشتن
be under the weather v
كسالت آور /ka-sā-lat ā-war/
tedious adj

i = k<u>ee</u>p, ĭ = b<u>i</u>g, u = c<u>oo</u>p, ŭ = p<u>u</u>t, y = <u>y</u>et, ' = (glottal stop)   243

کسانی که /ka-sā-nī key/
someone, anyone *pron*

کسب /kĭsb (kĭsp)/
craft, trade (colloq); acquisition *n*

کسبه /kas-ba, sg kā-sĭb/
n pl کاسب see sg

کسبی /kĭs-bi (-pi)/
artisan, craftsman, tradesman (colloq) *n*

کسپ /kĭsp/ *n* کسب see

کسپی /kĭs-pi/ *n* کسبی see

کسپین /kas-pin/ *adj* Caspian

کست , -ها /ka-sĭt/
cassette tape *n*

کسر , -ها/کسور
/ká-sĭr, kasr; pl kŭ-sur/
break, fracture; (math) fraction; deficit *n*

← کسر کردن
break, fracture *vt*

کسر بودجه /ká-sĭr-ĭ bo-dĭ-ja/
deficit, budget deficit *n*

کسور /kŭ-sur; sg ka-sĭr, kasr/
n pl کسر see sg

کسی /ká-sey, kĭ´-sey/
somebody, someone *pron*

کسیل کردن /ka-sil kardan/
send, dispatch *vt*

کش کردن /kash kardan/
tow (car) *v*

کش و گیر /kash ŭ gir/
fight, scuffle *n*

← کش و گیر کردن
fight, scuffle *v*

کشاف , -ان/ها /ka-shāf/
scout (mil) *n*

کشاندن ؛ -کشان- ؛ کشاند-
/ka-shān-dan/
drag, pull along *vt*

کشت /kĭsht/
planting, sowing; check (chess) *n*

← کشت شدن
grow (crop) *vi*

← کشت کردن
farm *vi*

کشت للمی /kĭsht-ĭ lal-mi/
dry farming *n*

کشت و مات /kĭsht ŭ māt/
checkmate (chess) *n*

کشتار /kŭsh-tār/
carnage, massacre; slaughter (livestock) *n*

کشتزار /kĭsht-zār/
farm; field *n*

کشتزار مین /kĭsht-zār-ĭ mayn/
minefield *n*

کشتن ؛ -کش- ؛ کشت-
/kŭsh-tan/
kill *vt*

کشته /kŭsh-ta/
killed, slain *adj*

← کشته شدن
be killed *vi*

کشته طلا /kŭsh-ta-yĭ tĭ-lā/
kushta-ye tela (aphrodisiac) *n*

کشتی , -ها /kĭsh-ti/
boat, ship *n*

کشتی جنگی /kĭsh-ti-yĭ jan-gi/
battleship, gunship *n*

کشتی طیاره بردار
/kĭsh-ti-yĭ ta-yā-ra bar-dār/
aircraft carrier *n*

کشتی طیاره دار
/kĭsh-ti-yĭ ta-yā-ra dār/
کشتی طیاره بردار see *n*

کشتی ماهیگیری
/kĭsh-ti-yĭ mā-hi-gi-ri/
fishing boat *n*

کشتی نوح /kĭsh-ti-yĭ nuh/
Noah's Ark *n*

کشف /kashf/
reconnaissance (mil); discovery, detection *n*

← کشف کردن /kashf kardan/
discover, detect, find; reconnoiter *vt*

کشک /kŭshk/ Kushk (dist) *n*

کشک کهنه /kŭshk-ĭ kŭh-na/
Kushk-e Kuhna (dist) *n*

کشکتان /kĭ-shĭk-tān/
Keshektan (ctr) *n*

کشم /kĭ-shĭm/ Keshem (dist) *n*

کشمش /kĭsh-mĭsh/
raisin; currant *n*

کشمکش /kash-ma-kash/
skirmish, scuffle *n*

کشمیر /kash-mir/ Kashmir (prov) *n*

کشمیری /kash-mi-ri/
cashmere; Kashmiri (& lang, pers) *adj, n*

کشنده /kĭ-shĭn-dĭh/
Keshendeh (dist) *n*

کشور , -ها /kĭsh-war/ country *n*

کشور های مشترک المنافع
/kĭsh-war-hā-yĭ mŭsh-ta-rak-ŭl-ma-nā-fey/
commonwealth (pol) *n*

كعبره radius (anat) n /ka-ba-ra/
كعبه the Kaaba (rel) n /ka-ba/
كف /kaf (qaf)/
cuff (sleeve); palm (hand); sole (foot, shoe); lather n
← كف کردن
soap up; make a lather v
كفار /kŭ-fār; sg kā-fīr, kā-far/
see sg كافر n pl
كفتار hyena n /kaf-tār/
كفتر /kaf-tar/ see كبوتر
كفچه /kaf-cha/
rice server (utensil) n
كفچه مار (kap-)/ /kaf-cha mār
cobra n
كفر /kŭ-fŭr/
blasphemy, profanity; infidelity, unbelief n
كفران ingratitude n /kŭf-rān/
كفش slippers n /kafsh/
كفش کن /kafsh kan/
entrance hall, foyer n
كفل croup, rump (lit) n /kĭ´-fīl, kĭfl/
كفن /ka-fan/
shroud, winding sheet n
← كفن کردن enshroud v
كفو peer, equal (pers) n /kŭfw/
كفيدن ؛ -كف- ؛ كفيد- /ka-fi-dan/
explode, burst vi
كفيل acting executive n /ka-fil/
كفيل وزير /ka-fil wa-zir/
acting minister n
كل bald adj; bald person n /kal/
← كل شدن go bald vi
← كل کردن shave (face) (colloq) v
كل all n /kŭl(-ī)/
كلات see قلات /ka-lāt, qa-/
كلاغ crow, raven (bird) n /ka-lāgh/
كلال potter n /kŭ-lāl/
/kŭ-lā-li/
pottery; potter's shop n
كلام /ka-lām/
speech, spoken language; clause; sentence n
كلام الله /ka-lām-ŭl-lāh/
Word of God (Quran) n

كلان /ka-lān/
big, large; great adj; adult, elder (pers) n
← كلان شدن grow up vi
← كلان کردن rear (a child) vt
كلان سال , -ان/ها /ka-lān sāl/
elder n; old, aged adj
كلان کار /ka-lān kār/
conceited, vain adj
كلان کارى /ka-lān kā-ri/
conceit, vanity n
كلانتر /ka-lān-tar/
elder, chief (district) n
كلاوه , -ها /ka-lā-wa/
skein, coil (yarn, thread) n
كلاه , -ها cap, hat n /kŭ-lāh/
كلبه , -ها hut, shack n /kŭl-ba/
كلپ , -ها paper clip, clip n /kĭ-lĭp/
كلتور culture, refinement n /kŭl-tur/
كلچه , -ها /kŭl-cha/
cookie, biscuit n
كلچه پز , -ان/ها /kŭl-cha paz/
pastry chef, baker n
كلچه فروش , -ان/ها
/kŭl-cha fŭ-rosh/
pastry seller n
كلچه فروشى , -ها
/kŭl-cha fŭ-ro-shi/
pastry shop, bakery n
كلدار /kal-dār/
rupee, kaldar (currency); Kaldar (dist) n
كلدانى , -ان/ها /kal-dā-ni/
Chaldean (& pers) adj, n
كلده Chaldea (geog) n /kal-da/
كلسيم /kal-sī-yam/
calcium (element) n
كلفگان Kalafgan (dist) n /ka-laf-gān/
كلک finger (esp pinky) n /kĭlk/
كلكان Kalakan (dist) n /ka-la-kān/
كلكسيون /kŭ-lĭk-sī-yun/
collection (art) n
كلمه , -ها/كلمات /ka-lĭ-ma, pl -māt/
credo, creed (esp Musl); word n
← اداى كلمه شهادت
recitation of the Musl creed
كلمه به كلمه /ka-lĭ-ma ba ka-lĭ-ma/
word for word phrs

i = keep, ĭ = big, u = coop, ŭ = put, y = yet, ' = (glottal stop)   245

کلمه دخیل /ka-lĭ-ma-yĭ da-khil/
loan word n

کلمه ربط /ka-lĭ-ma-yĭ rabt/
conjunction (gram) n

کلمه متضاد /ka-lĭ-ma-yĭ mŭ-ta-zād/
antonym n

pickaxe n /ka-land, kŭ-/ کلند, -کلنگ

کلنگ /ka-lang/
crane (bird); pickaxe; firing hammer
(musket's) n

club, nightspot n /kĭ-lub/ کلوب, -ها
window n /kĭl-kin/ کلکین, -ها
ball-shaped adj /kŭ-lol/ کلول

کلوله /kŭ-lo-la/
ball n; ball-shaped adj

کلوله پشته /kŭ-lo-la pŭsh-ta/
Kulola Pushta (city dist) n

head (animal's) n /ka-la/ کله, -ها
cap, hat n /kŭ-la/ کله, -ها
کلید, -ها /kĭ-lid (-lĭ)/
key (& to door) n

key, critical adj /kĭ-li-di/ کلیدی

church n /ka-li-sā/ کلیسا, -ها

کلیفورنیا /ka-li-for-nĭ-yā/
California (geog) n

clinic n /kli-nĭk/ کلینک, -ها

کلینک صحی
/kli-nĭk-ĭ sĭ-hi, kĭ-li-nĭk-ĭ sĭ-hi/
health clinic n

کلینیک n /kli-nik/ see کلینک

renal, nephritic adj /kĭl-ya-wi/ کلیوی
kidney n /kĭl-ya/ کلیه
کلیه, -ها /kŭ-lĭ-ya/
principle, axiom, rule n

کم /kam/
a little n; to (time expressions) adv

کم از کم /kam az kam/
anyway; at least; as usual adv

narrow adj /kam bar/ کم بر
کم بین, -ان/ها /kam-bin/
low-vision, partially-sighted (& pers)
adj, n

narrow adj /kam arz/ کم عرض
shallow adj /kam ŭmq/ کم عمق
a little n /kam kam/ کم کم
کم و بیش /kam ŭ beysh/
more or less phrs

blanket n /kam-pal/ کمپل

pharmacist n /kam-po-dar/ کمپودر
as usual adv /ka-mā-kān/ کماکان
کمال /ka-māl/
craft, skill, art; perfection; maturity;
Kamal (m name) n

کمان /ka-mān/
arch, vault (bridge); bow (weapon)
n; curved adj

کمانچه, -ها /ka-mān-cha/
bow (violin) n

کماندو, -ها/یان /kŭ-mān-do/
commando n

کمان رستم /ka-mān-ĭ rŭs-tam/
rainbow (fig, colloq) n

کمایی /ka-mā-yi/
gain, profit, earnings n

کمایی کردن →
gain, profit v

کمبود /kam-bud/
insufficient adj; shortage n

camp; bivouac n /kamp/ کمپ, -ها
کمپنی, -ها /kam-pa-ni/
company, firm n

کمپیوتر, -ها /kam-pĭ-yu-tar, kom-/
computer n

کمتر <از چیزی> /kam-tar/
less <than sth> adj

anemic adj /kam-khun/ کمخون
anemia n /kam-khu-ni/ کمخونی
کمر, -ها /ka-mar/
belt; waist; loins n

belt, fasten a belt v کمر بستن →
کمربند, -ها /ka-mar-band/
belt, cummerbund; seatbelt n

کمرنگ /kam-rang/
light, weak (in color) adj

کمره, -ها /kam-ra, ka-ma-ra/
camera n

کمره ویدیویی
/kam-ra-yĭ wi-dĭ-yu-yi/
video camera n

کمسیون /kŭ-mĭs-yun/
see کمیسیون n

کمشنری /kŭ-mĭsh-na-ri/
commissioner n

کمشنری عالی سازمان ملل متحد در
امور پناهنده گان
/kŭmĭshnari-yĭ āli-yĭ sāzmān-ĭ mĭlal-
ĭ mŭtahĭd dar ŭmur-ĭ panāhĭnda-
gān/
UNHCR, United Nations High
Commissioner for Refugees n

کمک help, assistance n /kŭ-mak/
← کمک کردن ‹به کسی›
help, assist ‹sb› vt

کمک بلا عوض
/kŭ-mak bĭ-lā ĭ-waz/
grant n

کمک عاجل /kŭ-mak-ĭ ā-jĭl/
first aid n

کمک کننده , ـگان/ها
/kŭ-mak kŭ-nĭn-da/
assistant, aide; helper n

کمونزم /ka-mo-nĭ´-zĭm/
communism n

کمونست , ـان/ها /ka-mo-nĭst/
communist n

کمونستی /ka-mo-nĭs-ti/
communist adj

کمونیزم /ka-mo-ni´-zĭm/
see کمونزم n

کمونیست , ـان/ها /ka-mo-nĭst/
see کمونست n

کمونیستی /ka-mo-nĭs-ti/
see کمونستی adj

کمی /ka-mi/
shortage, lack; decrease n

کمیت quantity n /ka-mĭ-yat/

کمیته , ـ‌ها /kŭ-mi-ta/
committee n

کمیته انکشاف و ولایتی
/kŭ-mi-ta-yĭ ĭn-kĭ-shāf-ĭ wĭ-lā-ya-ti/
Provincial Development Committee,
PDC n

کمیسیون /kŭ-mis-yun/
commission n

کمیسیون اروپا
/kŭ-mĭs-yun-ĭ ŭ-ru-pā/
European Commission n

کمیک /kŭ-mik/ see کومیک adj

کمین , ـ‌ها /ka-min/
ambush, lying in wait n
← کمین کردن ambush vt

کنار /kĭ-nār/
bank, shore; embrace n

کنار دریا /kĭ-nār-ĭ dar-yā/
riverbank n

کنایه /kĭ-nā-ya/
implication; metonymy n

کنایه آمیز /kĭ-nā-ya ā-meyz/
insinuating adj

کنایه یی /kĭ-nā-ya-yi/
metonymic adj

کنب /ka-nab/
cannabis, marijuana, pot n

کنبره /kam-bĭ-ra/
Canberra (capital) n

کنترول check, control n /kŭn-trol/
← کنترول کردن check, control vt

کنترولر , ـان/ها /kŭn-tro-lar/
comptroller, auditor n

کنج , ـ‌ها corner, nook n /kŭnj/

کنج کاو /kŭnj kāw/
curious; nosy, snoopy adj

کنجد sesame n /kŭn-jĭd/

کندز /kŭn-dŭz, qŭn- (qŭn-duz)/
Kunduz (seat, prov) n

کندک , ـ‌ها battalion n /kan-dak/

کندک استحکام
/kan-dak-ĭ ĭs-tĭh-kām/
sapper battalion n

کندک مشر /kan-dak mĭ´-shĭr/
major (mil) n

کندن ؛ ـکن- ؛ کند-
/kan-dan/
dig; pluck, pick; extract v

کندن کاری روی چوب
/kan-dan kā-ri-yĭ ruy-ĭ chob/
woodcarving n

کندو /kan-du/
hive; vessel (flour, grain) n

کندوی زنبور عسل
/kan-du-yĭ zam-bur-ĭ a-sal/
beehive n

کنر Kunar (prov) n /kŭ-nar/

کنسرت /kan-sart/ see کانسرت n

کنسل /kŭn-sŭl/ see قنسل see

کنسلگری /kŭn-sŭl-ga-ri/
see قنسلگری n

کنش /kŭ-nĭsh/
action, deed; custom n

---

i = keep, ĭ = big, u = coop, ŭ = put, y = yet, ' = (glottal stop)   247

كنشت /kŭ-nīsht/
custom; temple; synagogue *n*

كنفدراسيون /kŭn-fīd-rā-sī-yun/
confederation *n*

كنفرانس /kan-fa-rāns, kŭn-fī-rīns/
conference *n*
← كنفرانس دادن
hold a conference

كنگ Kang (dist) *n* /kang/
كنگوره /kan-gu-ra (-go-ra)/
battlement *n*

كنگهم /kan-gī-hīm/
Kangihim (hist, Chinese philologist)
n

كنوانسيون /kan-wān-sī-yun/
convention *n*

كنون now, presently *adv* /kŭ-nun/
كنونى /kŭ-nu-ni/
present, current *adj*

كنه /kŭnh/
core, essence, substance *n*

كنه tick (parasite) *n* /ka-na/
كنياك cognac *n* /kŭn-yāk/
كنيز , -ان/ها /ka-niz/
servant, slave (girl) *n*

كنين quinine *n* /kŭ-nayn/
كوارتز quartz *n* /kŭ-wārtz/
كواسه /ka-wā-sa/
great-grandchild *n*

كواكب /ka-wā-kīb, sg kaw-kab/
كوكب see sg *n pl*

كوالا لمپور /kŭ-wā-lā lam-pur/
Kuala Lumpur (capital) *n*

كوبالت cobalt (element) *n* /ko-bālt/
كوپنهگن /ko-pīn-ha-gīn/
Copenhagen (capital) *n*

كوت Kot (dist) *n* /kot/
كوتاه short (in length) *adj* /ko-tāh/
كوتاه مدت /ko-tāh mŭ-dat/
short-term *adj*

كوتل /ko-tal, kŭ-/
mountain pass, defile *n*

كوتوال /kot-wāl/
security officer; Kotwal (ctr) *n*

كوته /ko-ta/
room (inn, fort, prison); highway
outpost *n*

كوته قلفى /ko-ta-yī qŭl-fi/
prison cell *n*

كوچ couch, sofa *n* /kawch/
كوچ /koch/
move (change of residence);
(colloq) wife *n*
← كوچ كردن
move (change residence) *vi*
كوچ كشى كردن
/koch ka-shi kardan/
كوچ كردن see *vi*

كوچگى , -ان/ها /ko-cha-gi/
neighbor on same street *n*
كوچه lane, alley *n* /ko-cha/
كوچه گرد /ko-cha gard/
wanderer *n*; wanton *adj*
كوچه گردى /ko-cha gar-di/
wandering; wantonness *n*
كوچه گشت /ko-cha gasht/
كوچه گرد see *n*
كوچه گشتى /ko-cha gash-ti/
كوچه گردى see *n*
كوچه مرغها /ko-cha-yī mŭrgh-hā/
Chicken Street (Kabul) *n*
كوچك small, little *adj* /ko-chak/
كوچكى smallness *n* /ko-cha-ki/
كوچى , -ان/ها /ku-chi/
Kuchi (social group) *n*

كود dung, manure; code *n* /kod/
كود كيمياوى /kod-ī kim-yā-wi/
chemical fertilizer *n*

كودك , -ان/ها /ko-dak/
child; baby, infant *n*
كودكانه /ko-da-kā-na/
childlike, immature (& adv) *adj, adv*
كودكستان /ko-da-kīs-tān/
kindergarten *n*
كودكى /ko-da-ki/
childhood; infancy *n*

كودن /kaw-dan/
stupid, silly, slow-witted *adj*
كودنى /kaw-da-ni/
stupidity, silliness *n*
كودى cowrie shell *n* /kaw-di/
كور , -ان/ها /kor/
blind (& pers); corps *adj, n*
كور ديپلوماتيك /kor dīp-lo-mā-tik/
diplomatic corps *n*
كور كورانه /kor ko-rā-na/
blind (& adv) *adj, adv*

choir, chorus n /ko-ras/ کورس
/kors, kurs/ کورس
course (of study) n
forge; reactor n /ko-ra/ کوره
Korea (country) n /ko-rī-yā/ کوریا
/ko-rī-yā-yi/ , -ان/ها کوریایی
Korean (& pers, lang) adj, n
/kuz kŭ-nar/ کوز کنر
Kuz Kunar (dist, ctr Sheywa) n
pot; jug n /ko-za/ کوزه
large drum (arch) n /kus/ کوس
/ko-shā-ni/ , -ان/ها کوشانی
Kushan (& pers, hist) adj, n
attempt, effort n /ko-shīsh/ کوشش
try <+ subj> v کوشش کردن ←
/ko-shak/ کوشک
mansion, palace n
کوشیدن ؛ -کوش- ؛ کوشید-
/ko-shi-dan/
endeavor, try (lit) vi
کوفتن ؛ -کوب- ؛ کوفت-
/kof-tan/
hit; pound; hammer; crush vt
کوفته /kof-ta/
ground meat, meatball n
foster brother n /ko-kā/ کوکا
/kaw-kab, pl kaw-ā-kīb/ کوکب , -ها/کواکب
star; planet; Kawkab (f name) n
trachoma n /kok-ra/ کوکره
/kok-nār/ کوکنار
poppy (head, pod); opium n
foster sister n /ko-ki/ کوکی
cholera n /ko-la-ra/ کولرا
/ko-lam-bo/ کولمبو
Colombo (capital) n
/ko-lam-bī-yā/ کولمبیا
Colombia (country) n
/ko-lam-bī-yā-yi/ کولمبیایی
Colombian adj
colon (punctuation) n /ko-lan/ کولن
/kom-pī-yu-tar/ کومپیوتر
see کمپیوتر n
/ko-mak/ کومک see کمک n
cheek (colloq); jowl n /ko-ma/ کومه
comedy n /kŭ-mey-di/ کومیدی
/kŭ-mey-dī-yan/ , -ان/ها کومیدین
comedian n

/ko-mik/ کومیک
comical, comic adj
کون /kawn/
existence (philosophical) n
کون /kun/
butt; ass (obs); bottom (of sth) n
bottom (obs) v کون دادن ←
/kŭn-sŭl-ga-ri/ کونسلگری
consulate n
homosexual (obs) n /ku-ni/ کونی
mountain n /koh/ کوه
foothill n /koh pā-ya/ کوه پایه
/koh pay-mā-yi/ کوه پیمایی
see کوه گردی n
/koh-ī sā-fi/ کوه صافی
Koh-e Safi (dist, ctr Mullah
Mohamed Kheyl)
hiking n /koh gar-di/ کوه گردی
hike, go hiking v کوه گردی کردن
/koh nī-shin/ , -ان/ها کوه نشین
mountaineer; highlander n
/koh na-ward/ , -ان/ها کوه نورد
mountain climber n
/ko-hīs-tān/ کوهستان
Kohestan (dist; & w/ctr Qala) n
/ko-hīs-tā-nāt/ کوهستانات
Kohestanat (dist) n
/ko-hīs-tā-ni/ کوهستانی
mountainous adj
Kuwait (country) n /kŭ-weyt/ کویت
/kŭ-wey-ti/ , -ان/ها کویتی
Kuwaiti (& pers) adj, n
/kŭ-wey-ta/ n کویته see
coil (electrical) n /kŭ-wayl/ کویل
moth, clothes moth n /ku-ya/ کویه
hay, straw n /kah/ که
/kī/ (key) که
that; when; because, since; in order
to conj
/kŭh/ کوه n see که
/kīh-ta-ri/ کهتری
minority, being under legal age;
inferiority n
Kuhsan (dist) n /kŭh-sān/ کهسان
Kahmard (dist) n /kah-mard/ کهمرد
/ka-hī-na, -ha-; sg kā-hīn/ کهنه
see sg کاهن n pl

i = keep, ĭ = big, u = coop, ŭ = put, y = yet, ' = (glottal stop)   249

کهنه /kŭh-na/
old, made long ago; used, worn-out (thing) adj

کهنه خیال /kŭh-na khĭ-yāl/
conservative, old-fashioned adj

کی ؟ when, at what time? adv /key/
کی ؟ who? pron /ki/

کیبل cable, cable TV n /key-bal/
کیتی Kiti (dist) n /ki-ti/
کیسه pocket; pouch n /ki-sa/
کیسه بر pickpocket n /ki-sa bŭr/
کیسه صفرا /ki-sa-yĭ saf-rā/
gall bladder n

کیش belief, faith, religion n /keysh/
کیف /kayf/
pleasure, delight; intoxication n

کیف داشتن be high; be drunk v →
کیف کردن get high; get drunk v →

کیفر /kay-far/
punishment, retribution n

کیفی qualitative adj /kay-fi/
کیفیت /kay-fĭ-yat/
state, condition; quality n

کیک flea n /kayk/
کیک cake n /keyk/
کیلو see کیلوگرام n /ki-lo/
کیلوگرام kilogram n /ki-lo-gĭ-rām/
کیله banana n /key-la/
کیمیا chemistry n /ki-mĭ-yā/
کیمیا دان chemist n /ki-mĭ-yā-dān/
کیمیاوی see کیمیایی adj /kim-yā-wi/
کیمیایی chemical adj /ki-mĭ-ya-yi/
کینه spite; rancor, grudge n /ki-na/
کینو /ki-no/
tangerine; mandarin orange n

کیوان Saturn (planet) n /key-wān/
کیهان /key-hān/
universe, cosmos; world n

گ

گاراج garage n /ga-rāj/
گارد guard /gārd/
گارد تشریفاتی /gārd-ī tash-rĭ-fā-ti/
honor guard n

گاز gas (& natural); gauze n /gāz/
گاز اشک آور /gāz-ī ashk ā-war/
tear gas n

گال millet (grain) n /gāl/
گام , -ها step, stride, pace n /gām/
گام سپردن step, stride, pace v →
گاو cow, ox, bull n /gāw/
گاو کراچی oxcart n /gāw ka-rā-chi/
گاو میش /gāw meysh/
buffalo (Asia, Africa) n

گاوک snail, slug n /gā-wak/
گاه place; time n /gāh (gah)/
گاه گاه /gāh gāh/
from time to time adv

گاهی /gāh-ī (gā-yī)/
ever, at any time <+ pres perf > adv
بولانی را گاهی خوردی ؟ →
have you ever eaten bolani?

گای fuck; fucker (pers, obs) n /gāy/
گایی see گاهی adv /gā-yī/
گاییدن ؛ -گای- ؛ گایید- /gā-yi-dan/
fuck (obs) v

گپ talk, conversation n /gap/
گپ زدن talk, speak, converse →
گپ ساختن defame, vilify →
گپ ساز , -ان/ها /gap sāz/
defamer, vilifier n

گپ شنو /gap shĭ-naw/
obedient, dutiful adj

گپ گوی /gap goy/
backbiting (& pers) adj, n

گپ ناشنو /gap nā-shĭ-naw/
disobedient adj

گچ gypsum plaster n /gach/
گد mixing; shuffling n /gad (gat)/
گد کردن mix; shuffle (cards) v →
گدا beggar, mendicant n /ga-dā/
گداختن ؛ -گداز- ؛ گداخت- /gŭ-dākh-tan/
melt vt, vi

گدازش /gŭ-dā-zĭsh (-yĭsh)/
morning sickness n

گدام /gŭ-dām/
warehouse (& for grain) n

گدایش /gŭ-dā-yĭsh/ n گدازش see
گدایی /ga-dā-yi/
گدایی کردن beg (colloq) vi →
گدایگر /ga-dāy-gar/ n گدا see
گداییگری /ga-dāy-ga-ri/
n گدا یی see

a = cup, ā = long, aw = now, ay = sigh, e = bet, ey = obey

گدود /gad-wad/
messy, cluttered (colloq) adj

گدی /gŭ-di/ doll; kite n
گدی پران /gŭ-di pa-rān/
kite (colloq) n

گذارش , -ها /gŭ-zā-rĭsh/
report, statement n

گذاشتن ؛ -گذار- ؛ گذاشت-
/gŭ-zāsh-tan/
lay, place, put; leave; abandon vt

گذرگاه /gŭ-zar gāh/
pass; crossing, ford n

گذشتن ؛ -گذر- ؛ گذشت-
<از چیزی> /gŭ-zash-tan/
cross, pass <sth> vt

گذشته /gŭ-zash-ta/
last, previous adj

گر /gar/ see اگر conj
گر /gŭr/ brown sugar n
گراج /ga-rāj/ garage n
گراف قلب /gĭ-rāf-ĭ qalb/
electrocardiogram, EKG n

گران /gĭ-rān/
expensive, valuable; heavy adj

گران بها /gĭ-rān ba-hā/
expensive adj

گربز /gŭr-bŭz/ Gurbuz (dist) n
گربه /gŭr-ba/ feline, cat (lit) n
گربه مسکین /gŭr-ba-yĭ mĭs-kin/
humble pers (compliment) n

گرج /gŭrj/ Georgian (pers) n
گرجستان /gŭr-jĭs-tān/
Georgia (country) n

گرجی , -ان/ها /gŭr-ji/
Georgian (& pers, lang) adj, n

گرچه /gár-chĭ/
although, even if conj

گرد /gard/ dust, powder n
گرد /gĭrd/
round, circular; spherical adj

گرد آب /gard āb/ whirlpool n
گرد آلود /gard ā-lud/
dusty (neg) adj

گرد باد /gard bād/
sandstorm; whirlwind n

گردان /gar-dān/
conjugation (gram); revolving,
rotating n

گرداندن ؛ -گردان- ؛ گرداند-
/gar-dān-dan/
turn (& page); revolve, rotate; bring
(sb) back vt

گرد باد , -ها /gĭrd-bād/
whirlwind; dust storm n

گردش , -ها /gar-dĭsh/
movement, change; rotation;
circulation n

← گردش کردن
stroll (for pleasure) vt

گردن , -ها /gar-dan/ neck n
گردن بند , -ها /gar-dan band/
necklace n

گردن کش /gar-dan kash/
intractable adj

گردیدن ؛ -گرد- ؛ گردید-
/gar-di-dan/
become; turn; revolve; stroll vi

گردیز /gar-deyz/ Gardeyz (seat) n
گرده /gar-da/
dust; pollen; powder n

گرده /gŭr-da/ kidney n
گرده دار /gŭr-da-dār/
gutsy, has guts adj

گردهمایی , گردیه- /gar-dah-mā-yi, gĭr-dĭh-/
assembly, gathering n

گرزوان /gŭr-zī-wān/
Gurzewan (dist) n

گرسنگی /gŭ-rĭs-na-gi/
hunger, starvation n

گرسنه /gŭ-rĭs-na (gŭsh)-/
greedy, avid; hungry adj

گرسنه چشم /gŭ-rĭs-na chá-shĭm/
insatiable (colloq) adj

گرشک /gĭ-rĭshk/ Gereshk (dist) n
گرفتار /gĭ-rĭf-tār/
captured; enraptured; infected
(med) adj; capture; captive n

← گرفتار شدن
be captured vi

گرفتار و بازداشت
/gĭ-rĭf-tār ŭ bāz-dāsht/
capture & detention phrs

گرفتاری /gĭ-rĭf-tā-ri/ captivity n
گرفتگی /gĭ-rĭf-ta-gi/
dejection; eclipse n

گرفتن ؛ -گر- ؛ گرفت- /gĭ-rĭf-tan/
take, catch, get, consume vt

گرفته خاطر /gī-rīf-ta khā-tīr/
see گرفته خاطر adj, n

گرگ scabies, mange n /garg/

گرگ wolf n /gŭrg/

گرگ آتشی /gŭrg-ī ā-ta-shi/
hypocrite (fig) n

گرگانج /gŭr-gā-nīj/
Urgench (town) n

گرگنج see گرگنج n /gŭr-ganj/

گرگی scabrous, mangy adj /gar-gi/

گرگین see گرگی adj /gar-gin/

گرم warm adj /garm/

گرمابه bathhouse; bath n /gar-mā-ba/

گرمابه بان /gar-mā-ba bān/
bathhouse attendant n

گرمسیر /garm-seyr (-seyl)/
Garmseyr (dist) n

گرمی temperature n /gar-mi/

گرنگ see گران adj /gī-rang/

گرو /gī-raw/
collateral, surety (trad, credit) n

گروپ /gŭ-rup/
group (& mil); light bulb n

گروگان hostage n /gī-raw-gān/

← گروگان گرفتن take hostage vt

گروه group n /gŭ-roh/

گرویده , ـگان /gī-ra-wi-da/
believer (rel); pers in love n;
enamored adj

گره knot n /gī-rīh (gī-ri)/

گریبان /gī-rey-bān/
neckline (of garment) n

گریپ flu, grippe n /gī-rip/

گریختن ؛ ـگریز ؛ ـگریخت-
/gŭ-reykh-tan/
flee, escape vi

گریز پای fugitive adj /gŭ-reyz pāy/

گریزی smuggled adj /gŭ-rey-zi/

گریال gong n /ga-rī-yāl/

گریلا guerrilla (mil) n /ga-rī-lā/

گریلایی guerrilla adj /ga-rī-lā-yi/

گریه /gīr-ya/
tears, crying, weeping n

گزاب see گزاب n /gī-zāb/

گزارش , ـها /gŭ-zā-rīsh/
news; report; explanation;
interpretation; translation n

← گزارش کردن • گزارش دادن
make a report <to sb>; translate v

گزارش نامه /gŭ-zā-rīsh nā-ma/
platform (pol) n

گزاره /gŭ-zā-ra/
predicate (gram); see & گزره n

گزرگاه نور /gŭ-zar-gāh-e nur/
Guzargah-e Nur (dist) n

گزره Guzara (dist) n /gŭ-za-ra/

گزمه /gaz-ma/
patrol; patrolling n

← گزمه گشتن patrol v

گزمه سوار /gaz-ma-yī sa-wār/
mounted patrol n

گزند injury, harm n /ga-zand/

← گزند رساندن injure, harm v

← گزند یافتن sustain injury v

گزیر cure, remedy n /gŭ-zir/

گزیدن ؛ ـگز - ؛ گزید- /ga-zi-dan/
bite; sting vt

گزیده /ga-zi-da/
bitten, stung adj

گزیدن ؛ ـگزین- ؛ گزید- /gŭ-zi-dan/
pick, choose; prefer vt

گژدم scorpion n /gazh-dŭm/

گستاخ /gŭs-tākh/
insolent, impudent adj

گستاخانه /gŭs-tā-khā-na/
impudent, insolent (& adv) adj, adv

گستاخی /gŭs-tā-khi/
impudence, insolence n

← گستاخی کردن
insult, be impudent v

گستردن ؛ ـگستر - ؛ ـگسترد-
/gŭs-tar-dan/
spread, stretch, expand vt

گستراندن ؛ ـگستران- ؛ گستراند-
/gŭs-ta-rān-dan/
spread, stretch, expand vt

گسترش /gŭs-ta-rīsh/
spread, deepening; popularization n

← گسترش دادن popularize vt

گسستن /gŭ-sīs-tan, -sas- (sŭ-kŭs-)/
see گسیختن vi, vt

گسیختن ؛ -گسل- ؛ گسیخت
/gŭ-seykh-tan (sŭ-kŭs-),
/méygŭsĭlŭm//
separate *vi, vt*; tear *vt*

گشا /gŭ-shā/
conqueror *n*

گشاد /gŭ-shād/
wide; loose (clothes) *adj*

گشادن ؛ -گشای- ؛ گشاد-
/gŭ-shā-dan/
see گشودن *v*

گشاده ابرو /gŭ-shā-da ab-ru/
unconnected eyebrows *n*

گشاده دست /gŭ-shā-da dast/
openhanded, generous *adj*

گشاده دستی /gŭ-shā-da das-ti/
generosity *n*

گشاده دل /gŭ-shā-da dĭl/
openhearted; cheerful *adj*

گشاده دلی /gŭ-shā-da dĭ-li/
see گشاده دستی *n*

گشاده روی /gŭ-shā-da ruy/
open-faced, cheerful *adj*

گشاده رویی /gŭ-shā-da ru-yi/
see گشاده دستی *n*

گشاده زبان /gŭ-shā-da za-bān/
eloquent *adj*

گشاده زبانی /gŭ-shā-da za-bā-ni/
eloquence *n*

گشایش /gŭ-shā-yĭsh/
opening; inauguration *n*
← گشایش دادن open, inaugurate *vt*
← گشایش یافتن start *vi*

گشتاندن ؛ -گشتان- ؛ گشتاند-
/gash-tān-dan/
see گدراندن *vt*

گشتن ؛ -گرد- ؛ گشت- /gash-tan/
see گردیدن *vi*

گشنه /gŭsh-na/ hungry (colloq) *adj*
گشنیچ /gash-nich/ see گشنیز *n*
گشنیز /gash-niz (-nich)/
fresh coriander, cilantro *n*

گشودن ؛ -گشای- ؛ گشود-
/gŭ-shu-dan/
start; unwrap, unfold; open; reveal;
release *vt*

گفت و گو /gŭft ŭ go/
saying & stating *phrs*

گفتار /gŭf-tār/ talk, conversation *n*

گفتاری /gŭf-tā-ri/
spoken, conversational *adj*

گفتگو see گفت و گو *phrs* /gŭft ŭ go/

گفتن ؛ -گ- ؛ گفت- /gŭf-tan/
say; tell; call, name; declare, state
vt

گفته ها و ناگفته ها
/gŭf-ta-hā wŭ na-gŭf-ta-hā/
spoken & unspoken *phrs*

گل /gĭl/ mud, clay *n*

گل /gŭl/
flower; leukoma *n*; switched off *adj*
← گل افتادن get leukoma *v*
← گل داشتن have leukoma *v*
← گل شدن be switched off *vi*
← گل کردن
bloom; emerge, come forth;
extinguish; switch off; erase *v*

گل آلود /gĭl ā-lud/ muddy (neg) *adj*

گل چین /gŭl chin/
gardener *n*; chosen w/care *adj*

گل خانه /gŭl khā-na/ *n* see گلخانه

گل فروش /gŭl fŭ-rosh/
florist, flower seller *n*

گل فروشی /gŭl fŭ-ro-shi/
flower shop *n*

گل کار , -ان/ها /gĭl kār/hā/
mason, builder *n*

گل کاری /gĭl kā-ri/ masonry *n*

گل کرم /gŭl-ĭ ka-ram/ cauliflower *n*

گل نافرمان /gŭl-ĭ nā-far-mān/
sage, salvia; snapdragon *n*

گلاب /gŭ-lāb/
rosewater; native pink rose; Gulab
(m name) *n*

گلاباتون /gŭ-lā-bā-tun/
thread (gold or silver) *n*

گلابی /gŭ-lā-bi/ pink *adj*

گللی /gŭ-lā-ley/ Gulaley (f name) *n*

گلان /gĭ-lān/ see گیلان (dist) *n*

گلبدن /gŭl-ba-dan/
Gulbadan (hist, Babur's dtr) *n*

گلپاشی /gŭl-pā-shi/
silver, long-necked bottle for
rosewater *n*

گلپی /gŭl-pi/ cauliflower *n*

i = k<u>ee</u>p, ĭ = b<u>i</u>g, u = c<u>oo</u>p, ŭ = p<u>u</u>t, y = <u>y</u>et, ' = (glottal stop)   253

گلخانه /gŭl-khā-na/
greenhouse; House of Flowers (at Palace) n

گلدره /gŭl-da-ra/ Guldara (dist) n
گلران /gŭl-rān/ Gulran (dist) n
گلستان /gŭ-līs-tān/ Gulestan (dist) n
گلگون /gŭl-gun/
rosy, pink; like a rose adj

گلم /gī-lam/
kilim, rug without pile; blanket n
گلو /gŭ-lu (-lun)/ throat n
گلوبند /gŭ-lu-band/
necklace; neckerchief n
گلودرد /gŭ-lu-dard/ sore throat n
گلوله /gŭ-lo-la (go-la)/
bullet; cannonball n
گلون n گلو see /gŭl-lun/
گله /ga-la/
cattle, livestock; herd (horses) n
گله مند n گله see /gī-la/
→ گله کردن v گله مند بودن see
گله آمیز /gī-la ā-meyz/
mildly plaintive adj
گله بان , -ان/ها /ga-la bān/
horse herder n
گله داری /ga-la dā-ri/
horse breeding n
گله گزاری /gī-la gŭ-zā-ri/
گله مند n see
گله مند /gī-la mand/
mild complaint n
→ گله مند بودن v complain mildly
گلی /gī-li/ mud, earthen, clay adj
گلیم n گلم see /gī-lim/
گم /gŭm/ lost, misplaced adj
→ گم شدن get lost vi
→ گم کردن lose vt
گماشتن ؛ -گمار- ؛ گماشت-
/gŭ-māsh-tan/
hire; authorize, appoint vt
گماشته , -گان/ها /gŭ-māsh-ta/
representative, authorized agent n
→ گماشته شدن
be hired, be authorized vi
گمان /gŭ-mān/
assumption, opinion n
گمان بد /gŭ-mān-ĭ bad/
suspicion, mistrust n

گمراه , -ان/ها /gŭm-rāh/
heretic, one who strays n
گمراهی /gŭm-rā-hi/
heresy, going astray n
گمرک /gŭm-rŭk/
customs; customshouse n
گمشده , -گان/ها /gŭm-shŭ-da/
lost, disappeared (& pers) adj, n
گمگشته /gŭm-shŭ-da/
گمشده see adj, n
گمنام /gŭm-nām/
anonymous, obscure (pers) adj
گمنامی /gŭm-nā-mi/
anonymity, obscurity n
گناه /gŭ-nāh/ fault; crime; sin n
گناه کار /gŭ-nāh kār/
at fault; guilty; sinful adj
گناهگار , -ان/ها /gŭ-nāh-gār/
sinner n; sinful adj
گنبد /gŭm-bad (-baz)/
dome, vault, cupola; firmament;
(obs) ass, butt n
گنبدی /gŭn-ba-di/
domed, vaulted adj
گنج /ganj/ treasure (& hidden) n
گنجایش /gŭn-jā-yĭsh/ capacity n
گنجشک , -ها /gŭn-jĭshk/
sparrow (bird) n
گنجفه /gan-jĭ-fa/
ganjifa (card game); playing card
(hist) n
گنجیدن ؛ -گنج- ؛ گنج- <در کجا>
/gŭn-jĭ-dan/
fit <sw>; be appropriate n
گندم /gan-dŭm/ wheat n
گندمی /gan-dŭ-mi/
wheat-colored adj; (colloq) black
pers n
گنداب /gan-dāb/ sewage n
گندنه /gan-da-na/ leek n
گنده /gan-da/
rotten, stinking; (fig) low, base, dirty
adj
گنده بغل /gan-da ba-ghal/
stinky armpit n
گندهارا /gand-hā-ra/
Gandhara (hist) n

گوشت ران خوک /gosht-ĭ rān-ĭ khuk/ ham *n*

گوشت گو /gosht-ĭ gaw/ beef *n*

گوشت گوساله /gosht-ĭ go-sā-la/ veal *n*

گوشت گوسفند /gosht-ĭ gos-fand/ lamb; mutton (meat) *n*

گوشت مرغ /gosht-ĭ mŭrgh/ chicken (meat) *n*

گوشته /gosh-ta/ Goshta (dist) *n*

گوشوار /gosh-wār/ earring *n*

گوشواره /gosh-wā-ra/ fuschia (plant); earring *n*

گوشه /go-sha/ corner; area; secluded spot *n*

گوگرد /go-gĭrd/ sulfur; matches *n*

گول /gol/ round; curved *adj*; goal *n*
← گول زدن • گول کردن score a goal *v*

گولایی /go-lā-yi/ curve, bend (road) *n*

گوله /go-la/ *n* گلوله see

گولی /go-li/ pill, pellet *n*

گوم /go-wam/ reindeer *n*

گومل /go-mal/ Gomal (dist) *n*

گونه /gu-na/ cheek; manner, way *n*

گویایی /go-yā-yi/ faculty of speech *n*

گویش /go-yĭsh/ dialect *n*

گوینده , -ها/گان /go-yĭn-da/ narrator; spokesperson *n*

گوهر /gaw-har/ jewel, gem, precious stone *n*

گوهری /gaw-ha-ri/ jeweler *n*

گه /gah/ *n* گاه see

گه /gŭh (go)/ shit, excrement, dung (& fig) *n*

گهواره /gah-wā-ra/ cradle *n*

گهواره جنبان /gah-wā-ra jŭm-bān/ praying mantis *n*

گهواره جنبانی کردن /gah-wā-ra jŭm-bā-ni kardan/ rock a cradle *v*

گیان /ga-yān/ Gayan (dist) *n*

گیاه , -ها /gĭ-yāh/ plant; herb *n*

گیاه شناس , -ان/ها /gĭ-yāh shĭ-nās/ botanist *n*

گندهاری /gand-hā-ri/ Gandharan *adj*

گنگس /gangs/ dizzy, giddy (colloq) *adj*
← گنگس شدن get dizzy *vi*

گنه /gŭ-nah/ *n* گناه see

گه /go/ *n* گه see

گوار /gŭ-wār/ *adj* گوارا see

گوارا /gŭ-wā-rā/ agreeable, pleasant *adj*

گوارش /gŭ-wā-rĭsh/ alimentation, digestion (arch) *n*

گواه , -ان/ها /gŭ-wāh/ witness *n*

گواهی /gŭ-wā-hi/ testimony; proof, evidence *n*

گوت /got/ spool (for thread) *n*

گوتک /go-tak/ spool (w/o thread) *n*

گور /gor/ grave, tomb *n*
← گور کردن plant, cover w/earth; bury, inter *vt*

گوراسپ /go-rasp/ zebra *n*

گوریلا /go-ri-lā/ gorilla; guerrilla *n*

گوز /goz/ fart (vulg) *n*
← گوز زدن fart, break wind *vi*

گوزن /ga-wá-zĭn/ reindeer *n*

گوزوک /go-zuk/ flatulent pers *n*

گوساله /go-sā-la/ calf; (fig) dolt, dullard *n*

گوسپند /gos-pand/ *n* گوسفند see

گوسفند /gos-fand/ sheep *n*
← ۵ راس گوسفند 5 head of sheep

گوسفند نر /gos-fand-ĭ nar/ ram *n*

گوسفندی /gos-fan-di/ sheep's; (fig) sheepish, submissive *adj*; Gosfandi (dist) *n*

گوش /gosh/ ear *n*

گوش خراش /gosh kha-rāsh/ heart-rending (sound) *adj*
← گوش گرفتن • گوش کردن listen *v*

گوش خزک , -ها /gosh kha-zak/ centipede *n*

گوشت /gosht/ meat *n*

گوشت خوار /gosht khār/ predatory, carnivorous *adj*

گوشت خوک /gosht-ĭ khuk/ pork *n*

گیاه شناسى /gī-yāh shī-nā-si/
botany n

گیاهى /gī-yā-hi/
botanical; herbal adj

گیج /gij (gich)/ dizzy, giddy adj

گیچ /gich/ (colloq) see گیج adj

گیت /geyt/ bolt (rifle) n

گیتار /gi-tār/ guitar n

گیتى /gi-ti, gay-/ world n

گیرا , ها- /gi-rā/
attractive; fascinating; clamp, grip;
hair clip n

گیرنده /gi-rĭn-da/
receiving; attractive; fascinating adj;
recipient n

گیرو /gi-ro/ Giro (dist, ctr Panah) n

گیروان /gir-wān/ Girwan (ctr) n

گیزاب /gi-zāb/ Gizab (dist) n

گیسو , ان/ها- /gi-su, gey-so/
braid; f's long hair n

گیلاس , ها- /gey-lās/
drinking glass; cherry n

گیلان /gi-lān/ Gilan (dist) n

گیلن /gey-lan/ gallon n

گیلنه /gey-la-na/
gas can (gallon-sized) n

گیهان /gey-hān/ world n

ل

لاابالى /lā-ŭ-bā-li/
negligent, careless adj

لابد /lā´-bŭd/
necessarily, certainly adv

لابراتوار /lāb-rāt-wār/
laboratory, lab n

لابراتوارى /lāb-rāt-wā-ri/
laboratory adj

لابه /lā-ba/ pleading, entreaty n
← لابه کردن plead, entreat v

لایتر /lāy-tar/ lighter n

لاتین /lā-tin/ Latin (lang) n

لاتینى /lā-ti-ni/ Latin adj

لثه /lī-sa/ see بیره

لاجواب /lā-ja-wāb/
speechless, unable to answer adj
← لاجواب ماندن leave speechless

لاجورد /lāj-ward/ lapis lazuli n

لاجوردى /lāj-wār-di/
lapis-colored; azure; inlaid with
lapis adj

لاچی /lā-chi/ cardamom n

لاحق کردن /lā-hĭq kardan/
follow, come next vi

لاحقه , ها- /lā-hĭ-qa/
suffix; appendage n

لاحول کردن /lā-hawl kardan/
drive away (devil) vt

لاخ /lākh/
nipple; teat; (suffix) abundance of n

لارى /lā-ri/ truck, lorry n

لازم /lā-zīm/
necessary, vital; (gram) intransitive
adj

لازم و ملزوم /lā-zīm ŭ mal-zum/
vital & inseparable phrs

لازمه /la-zī-ma, pl la-wā-zīm/
necessity n
← لوازم pl

لازمى /lā-zī-mi/ see لازم adj

لاش /lāsh/
precipice; steep slope; corpse n

لاش و جوین /lāsh wŭ jŭ-wayn/
Lash wa Juwayn (dist) n

لاطایل , ات- /lā-tā-yīl/
futile (& st) adj, n

لاغر /lā-ghar/ thin, skinny adj

لاغراندام /lā-gha-ran-dām/
slim, slender adj

لاغرى /lā-gha-ri/
thinness, slimness n

لاف زدن /lāf zadan/
brag, boast (colloq) vi

لافوک /lā-fok/ braggart n

لافیدن ؛ لاف- ؛ لافید- /lā-fi-dan/
boast, brag (formal) vi

لاکن /lā´-kīn/
however, but conj

لال /lāl/
heart (cards); lal (grape) n; mute
adj
← ده لال ten of hearts

لال خان آباد /lāl khā-nā-bād/
see خان آباد n

لال و سرجنگل /lāl wŭ sar-jan-gal/
Lal wa Sarjangal (dist) n

لالا /lā-lā/
brilliant adj; (form of address to
older m) n

لالتین /lāl-tayn/ lantern w/candle n

لاله /lā-la/ tulip, corn poppy n

لالى /lā-lay/
see لالا (dim of form of address, esp in Logar) n

لاما /lā-mā/ lama (rel); llama n

لامح /lā-mīh/ shining, gleaming (lit) adj

لامسه /lā-mī-sa/ touch, sense of touch n

لامع /lā-mey/ adj see لامح

لاهه /lā-ha/ The Hague (capital) n

لاوس /lā-wŭs/ Laos (country) n

لایتر /lāy-tar/ lighter n

لایحه /lā-yī-ha, pl la-wā-yīh/ standard, norm; bylaw n
← لوایح pl

لایق /lā-yīq/ suitable; worthy; able, talented adj

لب , ها/ان- /lab/ lip n /lab/, -ān/hā

لب بحر /lab-ĭ ba-har/ beach, seashore n

لب خند /lab-khand/ smile n

← لب خند زدن smile vi

لب دریا /lab-ĭ dar-yā/ river bank n

لب سرک /lab- ĭ sa-rak/ road shoulder n

لب سرین /lab-sĭ-rin/ lipstick n

← لب سرین زدن apply lipstick v

لباس , ها- /lĭ-bās, pl al-bĭ-sa/ clothes, apparel, attire n

لبلبو /lab-la-bu/ beet n

لبنان /lĭb-nān/ Lebanon (country) n

لبنانى /lĭb-nā-ni/ Lebanese adj

لبنیات /la-ba-nĭ-yāt/ dairy/milk products n

لت زدن /lat zadan/ stir, whip, mix vt

لت خوردن /lat khŭrdan/ get beat up vi

لت و کوب /lat ŭ kob/ battery, beating n

← لت و کوب کردن • لت کردن beat (sb) up v

لتوگرافى /lĭ-to-gĭ-rā-fi/ lithography n

لجام /lŭ-jām/ reins; bridle n

لجوج /la-juj/ stubborn, obstinate adj

لچ /lŭch/ naked, nude, bare adj

← لچ شدن undress vi

لچک /lŭ-chak/ punk, runt (insult) n

لحاف /lĭ-hāf (-yāf)/ quilt (blanket) n

لحاظ /lĭ-hāz (-yāz)/ regard, respect n

لحد /la-had/ grave, tomb n

لحظه , ها- /lĭ-hza, pl la-ha-zāt/ moment, instant n

لحیم /la-heym (leym)/ solder n

← لحیم کردن solder v

لحیم کارى /la-heym kā-ri/ soldering n

لخ /lŭkh/ bulrush, cattail n

لخته /lakh-ta/ colt n

لخشیدن /lakh-shi-dan/ see لغزیدن

لذا /lĭ´-zā/ hence, therefore adv

لذت , ها-/لذات /lĭ-zat, pl -zāt/ pleasure, delight n

← لذت داشتن be delicious v

لذیذ /la-ziz/ delicious, succulent adj

لرزان /lar-zān/ shaking, quivering adj

لرزاندن ؛ لرزان- ؛ لرزاند- /lar-zān-dan/ shake, cause to shake vt

لرزانک /lar-zā-nak/ shaky, unsteady; vibrating adj

لرزش /lar-zīsh/ shakiness; vibration n

لرزه /lar-za/ shiver, shudder n

لرزیدن ؛ لرز- ؛ لرزید- /lar-zi-dan/ shake, shudder vi

لرزیده /lar-zi-da/ adj see لرزان

لزوم /lŭ-zum/ necessity, exigency n

لزوماً /lŭ-zú-man, -mán/ necessarily adv

لژه احمد خیل /la-zha ah-mad kheyl/ n see احمد خیل

لسان , ها- /lĭ-sān, pl al-sĭ-na/ language n

لسانى /lĭ-sā-ni/ linguistic adj

لست , ها- /lĭst/ list n

لست أموال /lĭst-ĭ am-wāl/ bill of lading n

لست غذا /lĭst-ĭ ghĭ-zā/ menu n

لشکر /lash-kar/ army (levied); (colloq) crowd n

لشکر طیبه /lash-kar-ĭ tay-ba/ Lashkar-e Tayyeba (Islamist militant org) n

لشکر کشی /lash-kar ka-shi/
deployment; expedition (mil) n
← لشکر کشی کردن deploy (mil) v
لشکر گاه /lash-kar-gāh/
Lashkar Gah (seat) n
لشکری , -ان soldier n /lash-ka-ri/
لشم /lá-shīm, lashm/
slippery, smooth (& fig); double-
dealing adj
لطف /lŭtf/
favor, courtesy, kindness n
← لطف کردن do a favor v
لطف آمیز /lŭtf ā-meyz/
pleasant, courteous adj
لطفاً /lŭt´-fan, -fán/
please (w/requests) adv
لطیف /la-tif/
graceful, fair; delicate, fine; friendly,
agreeable adj
لطیفه , -ها/لطایف
/la-ti-fa, pl la-tā-yīf/
pun, quip, subtlety n
لعاب /lŭ-'āb/
glaze, enamel; cooking juices;
mucus n
← لعاب دادن glaze, apply glaze v
لعاب دهن /lŭ-'āb-ī da-han/ saliva n
لعابی /lŭ-'ā-bi/
glazed, enameled adj
لعبت /lŭ-'bat/ doll; (fig) beloved n
لعل /la'l (lāl)/
spinel; garnet n; red (lit) adj
لعل پور /lāl pur/ Lal Pur (dist) n
لعل پیازی /la'l-ī pī-yā-zi/ amethyst n
لغت see لگت n /la-ghat/
لغت , -ها/لغات /lŭ-ghat, pl -ghāt/
word n
لغت شناس , -ان/ها
/lŭ-ghat shī-nās/
lexicographer n
لغت نامه /lŭ-ghat nā-ma/
lexicon, dictionary n
لغز enigma (lit) n /lŭghz, lŭ-ghaz/
لغزش /lagh-zīsh/
stumble, fall, mistake n
لغزیدن ؛ ـلغز ـ ؛ لغزید-
/lagh-zi-dan/
stumble, fall vi

لغمان Laghman (prov) n /lagh-mān/
لفاظ verbose; pedantic adj /la-fāz/
لفاظی /la-fā-zi/
verbosity; pedantry n
لفافه /lī-fā-fa/
wrapping; envelope, letter; perianth
(plant) n
لفظ , -ها/الفاظ /lafz, pl al-fāz/
word; betrothal n
لفظ به لفظ /lafz ba lafz/
word for word phrs
لفظاً literally adv /láf-zan, -zán/
لق /laq/
shaky (colloq); loose (tooth) adj
← لق شدن loosen, become loose v
لقک see لق adj /la-qak/
لق لق /laq laq/
lapping up, drinking (as dog) n
لقب /la-qab, pl al-qāb/
title, honorific; nickname n
← القاب pl
لقمه /lŭq-ma (lŭgh-)/
mouthful, morsel n
← لقمه زدن take large bites v
لک one hundred thousand n /lak/
لکات loquat (fruit, tree) n /lŭ-kāt/
لکلک stork (bird) n /lak-lak/
لکن /lá-kīn/
however, but (colloq) conj
لکنت stutter n /lak-nat/
← لکنت داشتن stutter v
لکه /la-ka/
spot, blot, stain; stigma n
← لکه کردن mark, stain, blot v
لگام bridle; reins n /lŭ-gām/
لگد /la-gad (-ghat)/
kick; recoil (gun) n
← لگد انداختن • لگد پراندن
• لگد زدن kick vt
← لگد خوردن
take a hit, suffer a loss; stagger,
stumble vi
← لگد کردن step on vt
لگد خور /la-gad khŭr/
downtrodden adj
لگلگ see لکلک n /lag-lag/
لگن washbasin n /la-gan/

258   a = cup, ā = long, aw = now, ay = sigh, e = bet, ey = obey

لگن خاصره /la-gan-ĭ khā-sī-ra/
pelvis (anat) n

للمه /lal-ma/ dry farming n

للمی /lal-mi/ non-irrigated adj

للو /la-lo/ lullaby n

لمبر /lam-bar/ number n

لمبه /lam-ba/ flame n

لمف , -ها /lĭmf/
lymph, lymph node n

لمری بریدمن /lŭm-ray brid-man/
first lieutenant, 1LT n

لندن London (capital) n /lan-dan/

لنگ lame adj /lang/

لنگ leg (colloq) (anat) n /lĭng/

لنگ loincloth n /lŭng/

لنگان lamely adv /lan-gān/

لنگر /lan-gar/
anchor; poor house (esp Sufi) n

لنگر انداختن /lan-gar andākhtan/
cast anchor v

لنگر گاه /lan-gar gāh/
place of anchorage n

لنگوته turban n /lan-go-ta/

لنگی lameness n /lan-gi/

لنگی turban (colloq) n /lŭn-gi/

لنگیدن ؛ لنگ- ؛ لنگید- /lan-gi-dan/
limp, hobble vi

لوا brigade n /lī-wā/

لواطت /lī-wā-tat/
sodomy, homosexuality n

لوا مشر /lī-wā mĭ′shĭr/
brigadier general, BG n

لوازم /la-wā-zīm, sg la-zī-ma/
pl of لازمه n pl

لوایح /la-wā-yīh, sg lā-yī-ha/
pl of لایحه n pl

لوبیا red kidney beans n /lu-bĭ-yā/

لوتفا /lot-fā/
LOTFA, Law & Order Trust Fund for Afghanistan n

لوث /laws/ see آلودگی n

لوح , -ها/الواح /lawh, pl al-wāh/
board, tablet n

لوح قبر /lawh-ĭ qá-bĭr/
gravestone, tombstone n

لوحه , -ها/الواح /law-ha, pl al-wāh/
board, tablet (small); sign; page of calligraphy n

لوخی Lokhi (ctr) n /lo-khi/

لوده /law-da/
blockhead, dolt (insult) n

لودهی /lod-hi/
Lodhi, Lodi (P tribe) n

لوزتین tonsils dual pl /law-za-tayn/

لوزه tonsil n /law-za/

لوژستیک logistics n /lo-zhĭs-tik/

لوژستیکی /lo-zhĭs-ti-ki/
logistical adj

لوش sludge n /lush/

لوط Lot (bibl) n /lut/

لوطی /lu-ti/
sodomite, homosexual n

لوک Luke (bibl) n /luk/

لوکوموتیف /lo-ko-mo-tif/
locomotive, train n

لوگر Logar (prov) n /lo-gar/

لولو , -ها /lo-lo/
pearl (rare) n

لولی , -ان/ها /lu-li/
Asian gypsy; courtesan; shrew n

لومری څاران /lo-ma-ri tsā-ran/
first lieutenant, 1LT n

لوی /loy/ high, great [< P] adj

لوی پاسوال /loy pās-wāl/
lieutenant general, LTG n

لوی څارنوال /loy tsā-ran-wāl/
Attorney General n

لوی درستیز /loy dī-rīs-tiz/
Chairman of the Joint Chiefs of
Staff [< P] n

لویه جرگه /lo-ya jĭr-ga/
loya jirga, Great Council n

لهجه , -ها/لهجات /lah-ja, pl –jāt/
dialect; tone of voice n

لهذا /lī-hā′-zā/
hence, therefore adv

لهیب /la-hib/
flame, flare, blaze n

لیاظ /lī-yāz/ (colloq) n see لحاظ

لیاقت /lī-yā-qat/
suitability; merit; ability, talent n

لیاقت داشتن ← be suitable v

لیتر /ley-tar/
liter (unit of measure) n

لیتوانیا /leyt-wā-nĭ-yā/
Lithuania (country) n

لیتوانیایی , -ان/ها /leyt-wā-nĭ-yā-yi/
Lithuanian (& lang, pers) adj, n

ليسانس /ley-sāns/
Bachelor of Arts; Bachelor of
Sciences n

لست /list/ n see ليست
snail, slug (colloq) n /ley-sak/ ليسک
ليسه /ley-sa/
high school; plane (tool) n
ليسيدن ؛ -ليس- ؛ ليسيد- /ley-si-dan/ -
lick vt

however, but conj /lāy-kīn/ ليکن
night n /layl/ ليل
ليل و نهار /layl ū na-hār/
night & day; the world's vicissitudes
n

auction, public sale n /li-lām/ ليلام
ليلام کننده /li-lām kŭ-nīn-da/
auctioneer n

Layla (f name) n /lay-lā (-li)/ ليلى
ليليه /lay-lī-ya/
dorm; boarding school n

lemon; lime n /li-mu/ ليمو
lemonade n /li-mu-nād/ ليموناد
lemon yellow adj /li-mu-ni/ ليمونى
line, row; cable, wire n /layn/ لين
power cable n /layn-ī barq/ لين برق

م

we pron /mā/ ما
following, next adj /mā-ba'd/ مابعد
/mā-ba'd-ŭt-ta-bi-'a/ مابعد الطبيعه
supernatural n
/mā-ba'd-ŭt-ta-bi-'i/ مابعد الطبيعى
supernatural adj

/mā-bayn/ مابين
center, middle, inside n
/mā-bayn(-ī)/ مابين
among; between; within prep
/mā-bay-ni/ مابينى
middle, intermediate adj

/māt/ مات
surprised, amazed adj; (chess)
mate n
← مات بودن be surprised vi
/mā-taht/ ماتحت
base, bottom; butt (arch) n
/mā-taht(-ī)/ ماتحت
below, under prep

/mā-ta-qa-dam/ ماتقدم
previous, former adj
queen (cards) n /māt-ka/ ماتكه
← ماتكة قره queen of spades
/mā-tam/ ماتم
mourning (for Shiites, esp
martyrdom of Husayn) n
← ماتم داشتن • ماتم کردن
mourn, be in mourning v
bereaved adj /mā-tam dār/ ماتم دار
/mā-tam di-da/ ماتم ديده
adj ماتم دار see
/mā-tam za-da/ ماتم زده
adj ماتم دار see
/mā-tam sa-rā/ ماتم سرا
house of mourning n
adventure; event n /mā-ja-rā/ ماجرا
/mā-ja-rā joy/ ماجرا جوى
adventurous adj; adventurer n
/mā-ja-rā jo-yi/ ماجرا جويى
adventurousness n

Magog (bibl) n /mā-juj/ ماجوج
kiss (colloq) n /māch/ ماچ
← ماچ دادن • ماچ کردن
kiss (colloq) v

/mā-cha khar/ ماچه خر
donkey (f); (fig, insult for f) n
/mā-cha sag/ ماچه سگ
bitch, dog (f); (fig, insult for f) n

/mā-ha-sal/ ماحصل
result, outcome, upshot n
/mā-hawl/ ماحول
environment, surroundings n

ماخذ , -ها/مآخذ
/mā-khaz, ma'-; pl ma-'ā-khīz/
source, reference n
/mā-khuz, ma'-/ ماخوذ
loaned, borrowed (& gram) adj

/mād/ ماد
female (colloq); Mede (hist) n
cow n /mād gāw/ ماد گاو
/mā-dām/ مادام
madam (form of address) n
mother n /mā-dar/ مادر , -ان/ها
/mā-dar an-dar/ مادر اندر
stepmother n
/mā-dar ka-lān/ مادر كلان
grandmother n

ماشین کالا شوی /mā-shin-ī kā-lā shuy/
washing machine n

ماشین مولد برق /mā-shin-ī mū-wa-līd-ī barq/
generator n

ماصل n محصل n /mā-síl/ see محصل

ماضی past, bygone adj /mā-zi/

ماطل adj /mā-tīl/ see معطل

مافوق /mā-fawq/
senior, superior adj

مافوق beyond prep /mā-fawq(-ī)/

مافوق سرعت /mā-fawq-ī sŭr-'at/
supersonic adj

ماقبل تاریخ /mā-qá-bīl-ī tā-rīkh/
prehistory n

مال , -ها/اموال /māl, pl am-wāl/
goods, merchandise; property n

مآل اندیش /māl an-deysh/
nearsighted adj

مال دار cattle owner n /māl-dār/

مال داری /māl-dā-ri/
breeding & raising (cattle) n

مالامال /māl-lā-māl/
full to the top adj

← مالامال کردن fill to the top v

مالته orange n /māl-ta/

مالچه /māl-cha/
pasture; pasturage n

مالستان /mā-līs-tān/
Malestan (dist) n

مالک , -ان/ین /mā-līk/
owner, proprietor n

مالک خانه /mā-līk-ī khā-na/
master of the house n

مالکی , -ان/ها /mā-lī-ki/
Malikite (rel; & pers) adj, n

مالکیت ownership n /mā-lī-kī-yat/

مالی financial; fiscal adj /mā-li/

مالیات taxes n pl /mā-lī-yāt/

مالیات بر عایدات /mā-lī-yāt bar ā-yī-dāt/
income taxes n pl

مالیدن ؛ -مال- ؛ مالید- /mā-li-dan/
rub; massage; chafe vt

مالیزیا /mā-ley-zī-yā/
Malaysia (country) n

مادگی /mā-da-gi/
buttonhole, groove, slot n

مادون /mā-dun/
inferior, subordinate adj

ماده , -ها/مواد /mā-da, pl ma-wād/
article (& law); entry (dictionary);
stuff, substance n; female adj

مادی , -ون /mā-di/
material, substantial adj; materialist
n

مادیان mare n /mād-yān/

مار snake, serpent n /mār/

مار کفچه cobra n /mār kaf-cha/

مارچ March (month) n /mārch/

مارچوبه asparagus n /mār-cho-ba/

مارخور /mār-khūr/
markhor (wild goat) n

مارشال marshal n /mār-shāl/

مارکسزم Marxism n /mārk-sī´-zīm/

مارکسست Marxist n /mārk-síst/

مارکسستی Marxist adj /mārk-sīs-ti/

مارکیت market n /mār-keyt/

مارگیر /mār-gir/
snake charmer; (fig) swindler n

مارماهی eel n /mār-mā-hi/

مارمول Marmul (dist) n /mār-mul/

ماروف n معروف n /mā-ruf/ see معروف

مازاد surplus n /mā-zād/

ماس see ماست (colloq) n /mās/

ماست yogurt n /māst (mās)/

ماستری Master of Arts n /mās-ta-ri/

ماسکو Moscow n /mās-kaw/

ماسوره /mā-su-ra (mŭsh-la)/
spool, bobbin n

ماش mung beans, vetch n /māsh/

ماشاءالله ! /mā-shā-'al-lāh (-shāl-la)/
God's will be done excl

ماشوره n ماسوره /mā-shu-ra/ see ماسوره

ماشه trigger n /mā-sha/

ماشین engine n /mā-shin/

ماشین حساب /mā-shin-ī hī-sāb/
calculator, adding machine n

ماشین خیاطی /mā-shin-ī kha-yā-ti/
sewing machine n

ماشین دار /mā-shin dār/
machine gun n

ماه عسل /māh-ī a-sal/
honeymoon n
ماهانه monthly adj /mā-hā-na/
ماهتاب moon n /māh-tāb (-taw)/
ماهر /mā-hīr/
talented, skillful; adroit adj
ماهوار monthly adj /māh-wār/
ماهی , -ان/ها fish n /mā-hi/
ماهی بحری /mā-hi-yī bah-ri/
saltwater fish n
ماهی خال دار /mā-hi-yī khāl-dār/
trout n
ماهی خاو یار /mā-hi-yī khā-wī-yār/
sturgeon n
ماهی وال whale n /mā-hi-yī wāl/
ماهی گیر , -ان/ها /mā-hi-gir/
fisherman n
ماهی گیری /mā-hi-gi-ri/
fishing; fishery n
ماهیت essence n /mā-hī-yat/
ماهیچه /mā-hi-cha/
muscle (calf, arm) n
مایع , -ات /mā-ya/
liquid, fluid n; liquefied adj
ماین mine (explosive) n /māyn/
مایندر stepmother n /māyn-dar/
مایو swimsuit n /mā-yo/
مایوس disappointed adj /mā-yus/
مایوس کننده /mā-yus kŭ-nīn-da/
disappointing adj
مایوس see مایوس adj /mā-yus/
مایوسی /mā-yu-si/
disappointment n
مایه origin, root, source n /mā-ya/
مایه خمیر /mā-ya-yī kha-mir/
yeast, leavening, ferment n
مبادا /má-bā-dā (ná-)/
may it not be (& w/subj) adv
مبارز /mŭ-bā-rīz/
fighter, champion n; fighting, militant adj
مبارزه , -ها/مبارزات
/mŭ-bā-rī-za, pl -zāt/
fight, struggle; campaign n
مبارزه برای سواد
/mū-bā-rī-za bā-rāy sa-wād/
literacy campaign n

مالیزیایی , -ان/ها /mā-ley-zī-yā-yi/
Malaysian (& pers) adj, n
مالیه tax n /mā-lī-ya, pl -yāt/
→ pl مالیات
→ tax, collect taxes v مالیه گرفتن
مالیکول molecule n /mā-li-kul/
ماما /mā-mā/
uncle, mother's brother; (form of address, & fig) n
ماما خیل /mā-mā kheyl/
Mama Kheyl (ctr) n
مامور , -ین /mā-mur/
bureaucrat; official n
ماموریت /mā-mu-rī-yat/
assignment, mission, office n
مانا /mā-nā/ معنی n see
ماندن /mān-dan/ ؛ -مان- ؛ ماند-
place, put vt; stay, remain vi
ماندول /mān-dol/ n مندول see
مانده نباشین ! /mān-da ná-bā-sheyn/
welcome excl
مانع /mā-ney, pl ma-wā-ney/
barrier; obstacle; prevention n; preventing adj
→ pl موانع
مانند /mā-nīnd(-ī)/ like, similar to adj
مانوی , -ان/ون/ها/ین /mā-na-wi/
Manichaean (& pers) adj, n
مانویت /mā-na-wī-yat/
Manichaeanism (hist) n
مانی /mā-ni/ Manes (hist) n
مانیلا /mā-ni-lā/ Manila (capital) n
ماوراء الطبیعه
/mā-wa-rā'-ūt-ta-bi-'a/
the supernatural; metaphysics n
ماوراء النهر /mā-wa-rā'-ŭn-ná-hīr/
Transoxiana n
ماورای ابحار /mā-wa-rā-yī ab-hār/
overseas adv
ماورای بنفش
/mā-wa-rā-yī bī-nafsh/
ultraviolet, UV adj
ماورای حمره /mā-wa-rā-yī hŭm-ra/
infrared adj
ماورای سرخ /mā-wa-rā-yī sŭrkh/
see ماورای حمره adj
ماه /māh/ moon; month n

مبارزه طبقاتی
/mŭ-bā-rĭ-za-yĭ ta-ba-qā-ti/
class struggle n

مبارزه علیه تروریزم
/mŭ-bā-rĭ-za a-layh-ĭ tĭ-ru-rí-zĭm/
War on Terror n

مبارک /mŭ-bā-rak/
blessed, auspicious adj

مبارک باشه ! /mŭ-bā-rak bā-sha/
congratulations excl

مبالغ /ma-bā-lĭgh, sg mab-lagh/
pl of مبلغ n pl

مبالغه/ها , -غات /mŭ-bā-lĭ-gha, pl -ghāt/
exaggeration, hyperbole n

← مبالغه کردن
exaggerate, overdo v

مبالغه آمیز /mŭ-bā-lĭ-gha ā-meyz/
exaggerated, hyperbolic adj

مبانی /ma-bā-ni, sg mab-nā/
pl of مبنا n pl

مبتلا , -یان <به چیزی>
/mŭb-ta-lā, pl -yān/
afflicted <by sth>, suffering <from
sth> adj

مبتلا به ایدز /mŭb-ta-lā ba eydz/
PWA, person with AIDS n

مبتلای ایدز /mŭb-ta-lā-yĭ eydz/
see n مبتلا به ایدز

مبرهن /mŭb-ra-han/
obvious, evident, proved,
demonstrated adj

مبسوط /mab-sut/
elaborate, detailed adj

مبصر , -ان/ین /mŭ-ba-sĭr/
commentator, pundit n

مبل و فرنیچر /mŭbl ŭ far-ni-char/
furniture n

مبلغ /mab-lagh, pl ma-bā-lĭgh/
amount, sum (money) n

← مبالغ pl

مبلغ , -ان/ها /mŭ-ba-lĭgh/
missionary; propagandist n

مبلغ مذهبی /mŭ-ba-lĭgh-ĭ maz-ha-bi/
missionary n

مبنا /mab-nā, pl ma-bā-ni/
basis, principle n

← مبانی pl

مبنی <بر چیزی> /mab-ni/
based <on sth> adj

مبهم /mŭb-ham/
broad; ambiguous, obscure; (gram)
indefinite adj

متا /ma-tā/ n متی see

متا خان /ma-tā khān, ma-ta/
Mata Khan (dist) n

متابولزم /ma-tā-bo-lĭ´-zĭm/
metabolism n

متاهل , -ان/ین /mŭ-tā-hĭl/
married (man; & pers) adj, n

متارکه /mŭ-tā-rĭ-ka/
truce, armistice n

← متارکه کردن declare a truce v

متاع /ma-tā/ , -ها/امتعه
merchandise n

متاثر /mŭ-ta-'a-sĭr/ adj متأثر see

متاخیر /mŭ-tā-khĭr/
late, recently deceased adj

متاخیر /mŭ-ta-'a-khĭr/ adj متأخر see

متافیزیک /ma-tā-fĭ-zik/
metaphysics n

متان /ma-tān/
methane, marsh gas n

متبحر /mŭ-ta-ba-hĭr/
learned, erudite adj

متبدل /mŭ-ta-ba-dĭl/ changeable adj

متبرک /mŭ-ta-ba-rĭk/
sacred, holy adj

متبسم /mŭ-ta-ba-sĭm/
smiling, smiley adj

← متبسم شدن smile vi

متبلور /mŭ-ta-bal-wĭr/
crystallized adj

← متبلور شدن crystallize vi

متجاوز , -ان/ها/ین /mŭ-ta-jā-wĭz/
aggressive adj; trespasser n

متجاوز به عصمت
/mŭ-ta-jā-wĭz ba ĭs-mat/
rapist n

متحد , -ین /mŭ-ta-hĭd/
ally n; united, allied adj

متحد الشکل /mŭ-ta-hĭ-dŭsh-shá-kĭl/
identical; alike adj

متحد المرکز /mŭ-ta-hĭd-ŭl-mar-kaz/
concentric adj

متحدین /mŭ-ta-hī-din/
alliance n; allies n pl

متحول /mŭ-ta-ha-wĭl/
changing, evolving adj

متحیر /mŭ-ta-ha-yĭr/
amazed; perplexed adj

متخاصم /mŭ-ta-khā-sĭm/
conflicting; hostile adj

متخصص , -ان/ها/ین
/mŭ-ta-kha-sĭs/
expert, specialist n

متخصص زراعت
/mŭ-ta-kha-sĭs-ĭ zĭ-rā-'at/
agronomist n

gradual adj /mŭ-ta-da-rĭj/ متدرج
/mŭ-ta-da-rĭ´-jan, -ján/ متدرجاً
gradually adj

متدین /mŭ-ta-da-yin/
pious, devout, religious adj

متذکر شدن /mŭ-ta-za-kĭr shŭdan/
remind, point out v

متذکره /mŭ-ta-za-kĭ-ra/
abovementioned adj

متر /mĭ´-tĭr/
meter (unit of length); meter stick n
← متر کردن
measure w/meter stick vt

متر green peas n /ma-tar/
مترادف , -ات/ها /mŭ-ta-rā-dĭf/
synonym n; synonymous adj

مترجم , -ان/ین /mŭ-tar-jĭm/
translator n

مترسل , -ان/ها /mŭ-ta-ra-sĭl/
epistolarian (lit) n

مترصد , -ان/ین /mŭ-ta-ra-sĭd/
lookout (mil) n; watchful adj

مترقی /mŭ-ta-ra-qi/
progressive, advancing adj

مترولوژی /mĭt-ro-lo-zhi/
meteorology n

متزلزل /mŭ-ta-zal-zĭl/
unstable, shaky adj

متساوی /mŭ-ta-sā-wi/
see مساوی adj

متساوی الاضلاع
/mŭ-ta-sā-wi-ŭl-az-lā/
equilateral adj

متساوی الساقین
/mŭ-ta-sā-wi-ŭs-sā-qayn/
isosceles adj

متشابه /mŭ-ta-shā-bĭh/
similar; ambiguous; analogous adj;
homonym n

متشبث /mŭ-ta-sha-bĭs/
enterprising; tenacious adj

متشرع /mŭ-ta-sha-rey/
versed in Sharia law adj

متشنج /mŭ-ta-sha-nĭj/
tense; suspenseful; convulsive,
spastic adj

متصل <(به) چیزی> /mŭ-ta-sĭl/
bordering; connected, linked <to
sth> adj

متصل <(به) چیزی> /mŭ-ta-sĭl(-ī)/
connected, next <to sth> prep

متصوف , -ان/ین /mŭ-ta-sa-wĭf/
mystic (generally) adj; Sufi n

متصوفه /mŭ-ta-sa-wĭ-fa/
the Sufis (collectively) n

متعاقب /mŭ-ta'-ā-qĭb(-ī)/
after, subsequent to prep

متعاقباً /mŭ-ta'-ā-qĭ´-ban, -bán/
afterwards, subsequently adv

numerous adj /mŭ-ta-'a-dĭd/ متعدد
متعدی /mŭ-ta-'a-di/
transitive (gram) adj

متعرض /mŭ-ta-'a-rĭz/
aggressive, offensive adj

متعصب , -ها/ین /mŭ-ta-'a-sĭb/
fanatic, bigoted; obstinate, stubborn
(& pers) adj, n

متضاد /mŭ-ta-zād/
opposite, contrary adj; antonym n
متضاعف doubled adj /mŭ-ta-zā-'ĭf/
متضمن /mŭ-ta-za-mĭn/
including; implying adj

متعادل /mŭ-ta-'ā-dĭl/
balanced; in harmony adj

متعال /mŭ-ta-'āl/
exalted, supreme (God) adj

devout, pious adj /mŭ-ta'-bĭd/ متعبد
متعلق <(به) چیزی/کسی>
/mŭ-ta-'a-lĭq(-ī)/
related; referring <to sth>;
dependent <of sb> n

متعلقات /mŭ-ta-'a-lī-qāt/
attachments, appurtenances n pl
متعلقین /mŭ-ta-'a-līq-in/
relatives, dependents n pl
متعلم , -ان/ها/ین /mŭ-ta-līm/
pupil, student n
متعلمه /mŭ-ta-lī-ma/ n f form of متعلم
متفاوت /mŭ-ta-fā-wĭt/
different, dissimilar, disparate adj
↳ متفاوت بودن be dissimilar vi
متفکر , -ان/ین /mŭ-ta-fa-kĭr/
thinker n; thoughtful, meditative adj
متفکرانه /mŭ-ta-fa-kĭ-rā-na/
thoughtfully, meditatively adv
متقلب , -ان/ین /mŭ-ta-qa-lĭb/
deceiver, fraudster n
متقی /mŭ-ta-qi/ God-fearing adj
متکلف /mŭ-ta-ka-lĭf/
difficult, artificial (esp style) adj
مثل /ma-tal/ n see مثل
متلاشی /mŭ-ta-lā-shi/
disintegrated, destroyed adj
↳ متلاشی کردن disintegrate vt
متمادی /mŭ-ta-mā-di/
prolonged, protracted adj
متمایل <به چیزی> /mŭ-ta-mā-yĭl/
disposed, inclined <toward sth> adj
متمول , -ان/ین /mŭ-ta-ma-wĭl/
wealthy, rich (& pers) adj, n
متن , -ها/متون /má-tĭn, matn; pl mŭ-tun/
text (document); wording n
متنازع /mŭ-ta-nā-zey/
clashing, conflicting adj
متنازع فیه /mŭ-ta-nā-zey-fí-hī, -fih, -fi-hey/
disputed, controversial, under litigation adj
متناسب /mŭ-ta-nā-sĭb/
proportional; symmetrical adj
متناقض /mŭ-ta-nā-qĭz/
contradictory, incompatible adj
متناقض گویی /mŭ-ta-nā-qĭz go-yi/
self-contradiction n
متناوب /mŭ-ta-nā-wĭb/
alternate; intermittent adj
متوازی /mŭ-ta-wā-zi/
parallel adj; parallel bars n

متوازی الاضلاع /mŭ-ta-wā-zi-yŭl-az-lā/
parallelogram n
متوازی الاسطوح /mŭ-ta-wā-zi-yŭl-sŭ-tuh/
parallelopiped n
متوالی /mŭ-ta-wā-li/
consecutive, in a row adj; shrine custodian n
متوجه /mŭ-ta-wa-jīh/
aware, observant (of sth) adj
↳ متوجه شدن find out (about sth), become aware (of sth) vi
↳ متوجه کردن pay attention, observe v
متوجه <کسی> /mŭ-ta-wa-jīh(-ī)/
directed; addressed (to) adj
↳ سخنم متوجهِ شما است my speech is addressed to you
متود /mī-tod/ method, approach n
متودولوژی /mī-to-do-lo-zhi/ methodology n
متودیک /mī-to-dik/ methodical, systematic adj
متورم /mŭ-ta-wa-rĭm/ swollen, intumescent adj
متوسط /mŭ-ta-wa-sĭt/ middle, intermediate adj
متوسل <به چیزی> /mŭ-ta-wa-sĭl/ turning <to sth> (for recourse) n
↳ متوسل <به چیزی> شدن turn <to sth> v
متوقف /mŭ-ta-wa-qĭf/ stopping, ending n
↳ متوقف شدن stop, end vi
↳ متوقف کردن stop, end vt
متولد /mŭ-ta-wa-lĭd/ born, begotten adj
متولوژی /mī-to-lo-zhi/ mythology n
متون /mŭ-tun; sg má-tĭn, matn/ pl of متن (rare); see & خوست n pl
متأهل /mŭ-ta'-hīl/ see متاهل adj, n

مجار , -ان/ها /ma-jār/
Hungarian (& pers) adj, n; Hungary (country) n

مجاری /ma-jā-ri, sg maj-rā/
pl of مجرا n pl

مجاز /ma-jāz/
illusion, unreality; figurative expression n

مجاز see مزاج n /mĭ-jāz/

مجاز /mŭ-jāz/
permitted, allowed adj

مجازاً /ma-jā´-zan, -zán/
figuratively adv

مجازات punishment n /mŭ-jā-zāt/

مجازی /ma-jā-zi/
figurative; unreal, illusory adj

مجال /ma-jāl/
opportnity, possibility n

مجالس /ma-jā-līs, sg maj-līs/
pl of مجلس n pl

مجامع /ma-jā-mey, sg maj-ma/
pl of مجمع n pl

مجامعت /mŭ-jā-mī-'at/
intercourse, sex, coitus n

مجانبت /mŭ-jā-nī-bat/
avoidance; being at sb's side n

مجانست similarity n /mŭ-jā-nī-sat/
→ مجانست داشتن resemble v

مجانی free, gratis adj /mŭ-jā-ni/

مجانین pl of مجنون n pl /ma-jā-nin/

مجاهد , -ان/ین /mŭ-jā-hīd/
mujahed, holy warrior, fighter n

مجاهدت , -ها/مجاهدات
/mŭ-jā-hī-dat, pl -dāt/
effort, struggle n

مجبریه /mŭ-jab-rī-ya/
Mujabriya (fatalist school of Islamist thought) n

مجبور /maj-bur/
compelled, forced; obliged, made (to do sth) adj

→ مجبور بودن
must, have/ought to <+ subj> vi

→ مجبور ساختن
make, oblige; force, compel (sb do sth) vt

مجتهد , -ات/ین /mŭj-ta-hīd/
eminent Musl jurist (issues اجتهاد) n

متهم , -ین /mŭ-ta-ham/
accused, suspected adj; the accused; suspect n

→ متهم کردن <کسی را به چیزی>
blame <sb for sth>; accuse <sb of sth>, charge <sb with sth> vt

متأثر /mŭ-ta-'a-sír/
sad, depressed; affected <by sth> adj

متأسف /mŭ-ta-'a-sĭf/
sorry, regretful adj

متأسفانه /mŭ-ta-'a-sĭ-fā-na/
unfortunately adv

متی Matthew (bibl) n /ma-tā/

متیقین /mŭ-ta-ya-qĭn/
certain, sure, positive adj

مثال , -ها/امثله /mĭ-sāl, pl am-sĭ-la/
example, model n

مثانه /ma-sā-na/
bladder, vesica (anat) n

مثبت /mŭs-bat/
positive, plus, affirmative adj

مثقال /mĭs-qāl/
misqal (unit of weight, = 4.6 g) n

مثل , -ها/امثال /ma-sal (-tal), pl am-sāl/
proverb, adage n

مثل /mĭ´-sīl(-ī), mĭsl(-ī)/
like, similar to prep; equivalent n

مثل از see مثل prep /mĭ´-sīl az/

مثلاً /ma-sa-lan, má-/
for example adv

مثلث /mŭ-sa-las/
triangle n; triangular adj

مثلثات /mŭ-sa-la-sāt/
trigonometry n

مثمر /mŭs-mīr/
profitable; fruitful adj

مثمن /mŭ-sa-man/
octagon n; octagonal adj

مثنوی , -ات/ها /mas-na-wi/
couplet; Masnawi (13th-c Dari poem) n

مجادله , -ها/مجادلات
/mŭ-jā-dī-la, pl -lāt/
fight, argument n

→ مجادله کردن <همرای کسی>
fight, argue; struggle <w/sb> v

مجدد /mŭ-ja-dad/
renewed, renovated, restored *adj*

مجدداً /mŭ-ja-da-dan, -já-/
afresh, anew, again *adv*

مجذور /maj-zur/
squared (math) *adj*

مجرا , -ها/مجاری
/maj-rā, pl ma-jā-ri/
channel, duct, passage *n*

مجرا /mŭj-rā/
carried out, enforced *adj*

← مجرا کردن carry out, enforce *vt*

مجرب /mŭ-ja-rab/
skillful; experienced; tried & true *adj*

مجرد , -ات /mŭ-ja-rad/
abstraction, sth abstract *n*

مجرد , -ان/ها /mŭ-ja-rad/
single, unmarried; abstract *adj*

مجرم , -ان/ها/ين /mŭj-rĭm/
criminal *n*; guilty (of crime) *adj*

مجرمی /mŭj-rĭ-mi/ *n* مجرميت see

مجرميت /mŭj-rĭ-mĭ-yat/
guilt (of crime) *n*

مجروح , -ان/ين /maj-ruh/
injured, wounded (& pers) *adj, n*

مجسمه /mŭ-ja-sa-ma/
statue, sculpture *n*

← مجسمه ساختن sculpt *v*

مجسمه ساز , -ان/ها
/mŭ-ja-sa-ma sāz/
sculptor *n*

مجلس , -ها/مجالس
/maj-lĭs, pl ma-jā-lĭs/
meeting, session; house (of parliament) *n*

مجلس ترحيم /maj-lĭs-ĭ tar-hĭm/
wake (service) *n*

مجلس سنا /maj-lĭs-ĭ sa-nā/
Senate *n*

مجلسين /maj-lĭ-sayn/
houses (of parliament) *dual pl*

مجلل /mŭj-la-lal/
splendid, magnificent *adj*

مجله , -ها/مجلات /mŭ-ja-la, pl -lāt/
magazine, journal *n*

مجمع /maj-ma, pl ma-jā-mey/
assembly, meeting *n*

← مجامع pl

مجمع الجزاير /maj-ma ŭl-ja-zā-yir/
archipelago *n*

مجمع الكواكب /maj-ma ŭl-ka-wā-kĭb/
constellation *n*

مجمعه /maj-ma-'a (-ma)/
round copper tray *n*

مجمو /maj-mu/
total, sum, whole *n*

مجموعاً /maj-mú-'an, -'án/
altogether, in sum *adv*

مجموعه /maj-mu-'a/
collection; assembly, gathering *n*

مجموعی /maj-mu-'i/
collective; total *adj*

مجنون , -ين /maj-nun, pl ma-jā-nin/
madman, lunatic *n*

مجهز /mŭ-ja-haz/
complete, entire, whole; completed *adj*

مجهول /maj-hul/
anonymous; (gram) passive *adj*

مجيد /ma-jid/
splendid, great *adj*; Majid (m name) *n*

مچ /mŭch/ sprain (colloq) *n*

← مچ خوردن get a sprain *v*

← پايش مچ خورد she sprained her foot

محاذ , -ات/ها /ma-hāz/
battlefront, front *n*

محاربوی /mŭ-hā-rĭ-ba-wi/
combat, related to combat *adj*

محاربه , -ها/محاربات /mŭ-hā-rĭ-ba, pl -bāt/
combat, warfare; battle, fight *n*

محاسب /mŭ-hā-sĭb/
accountant, bookkeeper *n*

محاسبه /mŭ-hā-sĭ-ba/
accounting; calculation *n*

← محاسبه كردن calculate; keep books *v*

محاصره /mŭ-hā-sĭ-ra/
seige, blockade *n*

← محاصره كردن beseige, blockade; sequester; seal off *vt*

محاط /mū-hāt/
surrounded, encircled adj

محاط به خشکه /mū-hāt ba khŭsh-ka/
landlocked adj

محافظ , -ان/ها/ين /mū-hā-fīz/
guard, watchman n

محافظت guarding n /mū-hā-fī-zat/

محافظه کار , -ان/ها /mū-hā-fī-za kār/
conservative (& pers) adj, n

محافظه کاری /mū-hā-fī-za kā-ri/
conservatism n

محافل /ma-hā-fīl, sg mah-fīl/
pl of محفل n pl

محافل حاکمه /ma-hā-fīl-ī hā-kĭ-ma/
ruling circles n pl

محاکم /ma-hā-kĭm, sg mah-ka-ma/
pl of محکمه n pl

محاکمه , -ها/محاکمات /mū-hā-kĭ-ma, pl -māt/
hearing, trial n

put <sb> on trial v محاکمه کردن →

محال /ma-hāl, sg ma-hal/
pl of محل (rare) n pl

محال , -ات /mū-hāl/
impossible adj; impossibility n

محاوره /mū-hā-wĭ-ra/
talk, conversation n

محاوره یی /mū-hā-wĭ-ra-yi/
conversational adj

محبت /mū-ha-bat/
affection; intimate attraction n

be affectionate v محبت داشتن →

محبت آمیز /mū-ha-bat ā-meyz/
affectionate adj

محبس , -ها/محابس /mah-bas, pl ma-hā-bīs/
penitentiary, prison n

محبوب /mah-bub/
popular; beloved adj; sweetheart n

محبوبیت /mah-bu-bī-yat/
popularity n

محبوس , -ان/ها/ين /mah-bus/
prisoner, captive n

محتاج <کسی/چیزی(-ی)> /mŭh-tāj(-ī)/
dependent <on sb/sth>; poor, needy adj

محتاط /mŭh-tāt/
careful, cautious; prudent adj

محتاطانه /mŭh-tā-tā-na/
cautiously adv

محتال /mŭh-tāl/
trickster, deceitful person (arch) n

محترم /mŭh-ta-ram/
honorable, esteemed adj

محترمانه /mŭh-ta-ra-mā-na/
respectfully (& in letter) adv

محتسب /mŭh-ta-sīb/
supervisor of public morals (arch) n

محتمل /mŭh-ta-mīl/ adj see احتمالی

محتملاً /mŭh-ta-mī´-lan, -lán/
see احتمالاً adv

محتویات /mŭh-ta-wĭ-yāt/
contents, content n pl

محدث , -ان/ين /mū-ha-dīs/
student of hadiths n

محدود /mah-dud/
limited, bounded adj

limit, bound vt محدود کردن →

محدودیت /mah-du-dī-yat/
limitation, restriction n

محدودیت تجارتی /mah-du-dī-yat-ī tŭ-jā-ra-ti/
trade sanction(s) n

محذوف /mah-zuf/
deleted, omitted adj

محرقه typhoid n /mŭh-rī-qa/

محرک , -ات /mū-ha-rīk/
instigator; seditionist; catalyst, dynamic n; incentive adj

محرم /mah-ram, pl ma-hā-rīm/
unmarriageable relative (Musl law); servant w/access to harem n

pl محارم →

محرم /mū-ha-ram/
Muharram (month) n

محرم اسرار /mah-ram-ī as-rār/
confidant (of secrets) n

محرم راز /mah-ram-ī rāz/
see محرم اسرار n

محرمانه /ma-ha-ra-mā-na/
confidential adj

محروقات /mah-ru-qāt/
heating fuel n pl

268   a = cup, ā = long, aw = now, ay = sigh, e = bet, ey = obey

محرومی ‹از چیزی› /mah-ru-mi/
be enjoined ‹from sth› (due to cost, rel scruples); deprivation n

محرومیت ‹از چیزی› /mah-ru-mī-yat/
see محرومیت n

محسوب کردن /mah-sub kardan/
take into account vt

محسود /mah-sud/
Mahsud (P tribe) n

محسوس /mah-sus/
perceptible; tangible adj

محصل , -ان/ها/ین /mŭ-ha-sĭl (mā-sĭl)/
university student n

محصول , -ات/ /mah-sul (mā-)/
duty, custom; production, output; result n

↪ محصول دادن produce v
↪ محصول گرفتن collect duties v

محصولات /mah-su-lāt/
harvest n pl

محصولات ضمنی /mah-su-lāt-ĭ zĭm-ni/
byproducts n pl

محضر /mah-zar/
presence; attestation (statement) n

↪ در محضر عام
before the people, in public adv

محفظه /mah-fa-za/
case, container, chest, trunk n

محفل , -ها/محافل /mah-fĭl, pl ma-hā-fĭl/
group, circle; gathering, party n

↪ محفل میزان و تحقیقات
High Religious Council

محفوظ /mah-fuz/ safe, secured adj

محفوظات /mah-fu-zāt/
memorized material n pl

محقق /mŭ-ha-qaq/
muhaqaq (callig style) n

محقق , -ان/ین /mŭ-ha-qĭq/
researcher, scholar n

محققانه /mŭ-ha-qĭ-qā-na/
scholarly adj

محک /ma-hak/
touchstone; standard, criterion n

محکم /mah-kam/
firm, sturdy; steadfast adj

↪ محکم کردن ‹چیزی را کجا›
maintain, keep ‹sth sw› vt

↪ محکم گرفتن ‹چیزی را›
grasp ‹sth› firmly, take hold of ‹sth› vt

↪ محکم گرفتن ‹خود را در کجا›
stay put ‹sw› vt

محکمه , -ها/محاکم /mah-ka-ma, pl ma-hā-kĭm/
court, tribunal n

محکمه عالی /mah-ka-ma-yĭ 'ā-li/
Supreme Court n

محکمه تمیز /mah-ka-ma-yĭ ta-miz/
see محکمۀ عالی n

محکمه مرافعه /mah-ka-ma-yĭ mŭ-rā-fĭ-'a/
appellate court n

محکمه نظامی /mah-ka-ma-yĭ nĭ-zā-mi/
military court n

محکوم /mah-kum/
convicted, sentenced; condemned (& pers) adj, n

↪ محکوم کردن
condemn; convict, sentence vt

محکومیت /mah-ku-mī-yat/
conviction, sentencing; submission n

محل , -ها/محال /ma-hal, pl -hāl/
place; locale, locality n

محل تولد /ma-hal-ĭ ta-wa-lŭd/
birthplace n

محل پذیرایی مقام /ma-hal-ĭ pa-zi-rā-yi-yĭ ma-qām/
chancery (embassy) n

محل کار /ma-hal-ĭ kār/ workplace n

محلول , -ات/ها /mah-lul/
mixture, solution n; dissolved adj

↪ محلول شدن dissolve vi

محلی /ma-ha-li/
indigenous, native (& pers) adj, n

محمد /mŭ-ha-mad/
Mohamed (m name) n

محمد آغا /mŭ-ha-mad ā-ghā, -gha/
Mohamed Agha (dist) n

محمد شهيد /mŭ-ha-mad sha-hid/
Mohamed Shahid (geog, Ghazni) n

محمدزی /mŭ-ha-mad-zay/
Mohamedzai (P tribe) n

محمل /mah-mĭl/ howdah n

محمود راقی /mah-mud-ĭ rā-qi/
Mahmud-e Raqi (seat) n

محمول , ـات /mah-mul/
cargo, load; (logic) predicate n

محموله /mah-mu-la/ cargo n

محن /mĭ´-hĭn, sg mĭh-nat/
pl of محنت n pl

محنت , ـها/محن
/mĭh-nat, pl mĭ´-hĭn/
suffering n

← محنت دیدن • محنت کشیدن
suffer v

محنت بار /mĭh-nat bār/
difficult, full of suffering adj

محو /mahw/
abolishment; eradication, erasure;
fascination n

محور /mĭh-war/ pivot; axis; axle n

محوطه /mah-wa-ta/
enclosure, yard; building compound
n

محیط /mŭ-hit/
perimeter, circumference; (fig)
environment n

محیط زیست /mŭ-hit-ĭ zist/
living environment n

محیطی /mŭ-hi-ti/ environmental adj

مخابره , ـها/مخابرات
/mŭ-khā-bĭ-ra, pl -rāt/
transmission, communication n

مخاصم , ـان/ین /mŭ-khā-sĭm/
adversary, enemy, foe n

مخاطب /mŭ-khā-tab/
2nd pers (gram); addressee n

مخاطره , ـها/مخاطرات
/mŭ-khā-tĭ-ra, pl -rāt/
hazard; risk; threat n

مخاطی /mŭ-khā-ti/ see غشا adj

مخالف /mŭ-khā-lĭf(-ī)/
against, contrary to prep

مخالف , ـان/ین /mŭ-khā-lĭf/
adversary, opponent n; opposed;
resistant adj

مخالفت /mŭ-khā-lĭ-fat/
opposition, resistance; enmity n

مخبر , ـان/ها/ین /mŭkh-bĭr/
agent, spy; informer n

مخبری /mŭkh-bĭ-ri/
espionage, spying n

← مخبری کردن
spy v

مختلط /mŭkh-ta-lat/
joint (venture); complex (sentence)
n

مختلف /mŭkh-ta-lĭf/
different; various, diverse adj

مختلف الاضلاع
/mŭkh-ta-lĭf-ŭl-az-lā/
scalene (math) adj

مختلف المرکز
/mŭkh-ta-lĭf-ŭl-mar-kaz/
eccentric (math) adj

مختنق /mŭkh-ta-nĭq/
suppressed; strangled adj

مخدرات /mŭ-kha-dĭ-rāt/
narcotics n pl

مخرب /mŭ-kha-rĭb/
destructive; subversive adj

مخرج , ـها /makh-raj/
denominator (math); point of
articulation (gram) n

مخروط /makh-rut/ cone (shape) n

مخروطی /makh-ru-ti/ conical adj

مخصوص /makh-sus/
special, particular adj

مخصوصاً /makh-sú-san, -sán/
especially, particularly adv

مخطوط /makh-tut/ handwritten adj

مخفی /makh-fi/
secret, concealed, clandestine adj

← مخفی کردن /makh-fi-gāh/
hide, conceal vt

مخفیگاه
cache; hiding place n

مخلوط /makh-lut/
blend, mixture n; blended, mixed
adj

← مخلوط کردن
blend, mix vt

مخمل /makh-mal (bakh-)/ velvet n

مخمور /makh-mur/
drunk; tipsy; hung over; languid adj

مد /mad/ tide; (diacritic) mad n

flatterer; panegyist n /ma-dāh/ مداح
flatter vt → مداح کردن
مداحی /ma-dā-hi/
flattery (of powerful) n
مداخله , -ها/مداخلات /mŭ-dā-khĭ-la, pl -lāt/
interference; intervention n
مداخله کردن <به چیزی> →
interfere; intervene <in sth> vi
مدار /ma-dār/
center, core; orbit (in space); pivot n
مدار گرد /ma-dār gard/
satellite (in space) n
مدارا /mŭ-dā-rā/
leniency, gentleness n
مدارا کردن → be lenient v
مدارج /ma-dā-rĭj/
stages, steps (esp pl); paths, ways n pl
pl of مدرسه n pl /ma-dā-rīs/ مدارس
defense n /mŭ-dā-fĭ-'a/ مدافعه
medal, order n /mĭ-dāl/ مدال
مدام /mŭ-dām/
always, continually adv
مدت , -ها /mŭ-dat/
period of time, interval n
مدت /mŭ-dat(-ī)/
for, for the duration of prep
help; relief, aid n /ma-dad/ مدد
help; relieve, aid v → مدد کردن
diuretic adj /mŭ-dĭr/ مدر
مدرس , -ان/ین /mŭ-da-rīs/
teacher, tutor (rel school) n
→ مدرس باشی
rel school headmaster
مدرسه , -ها/مدارس /mad-ra-sa, pl ma-dā-rīs/
madrasa n
مدرک /mad-rak, pl ma-dā-rīk/
document (as evidence); income source n
→ مدارک pl
perceptible adj /mŭd-rak/ مدرک
/mŭd-rĭ-ka/ مدرکه
perceptive, of perception adj

مدعی , -ان/ها /mŭ-da-'i/
claimant; plaintiff; (colloq) adversary, enemy n
مدعی العموم /mŭ-da-'i-ŭl-ŭ-mum/
public prosecutor n
مدعی علیه /mŭ-da-'i a lay-hey/
defendant n
مدلل /mŭ-da-lal/
substantiated, supported by evidence adj
مدنیت /ma-da-nĭ-yat/
civilization, urbanity n
مدوامت /mŭ-da-wā-mat/
continuation; durability n
مدور /mŭ-da-war/
round, circular; spherical adj
compiled adj /mŭ-da-wan/ مدون
compiler n /mŭ-da-wĭn/ مدون
horrifying adj /mŭd-hīsh/ مدهش
horrified adj /mŭd-hosh/ مدهوش
panegyric (ode) n /ma-di-ha/ مدیحه
مدیر , -ان/ها /mŭ-dir/
director, manager n
مدیر روزنامه /mŭ-dir-ĭ roz-nā-ma/
editor-in-chief n
مدیر مکتب /mŭ-dir-ĭ mak-tab/
principal, school director n
مدیره /mŭ-di-ra/
managerial; editorial adj
board of directors n هیئت مدیره →
مدیریت , -ها /mŭ-di-rī-yat/
directorate, department, office; directorship n
مدیریت امنیتی ملی
/mŭ-di-rī-yat-ī am-nī-yat-ī mī-li/
National Directorate of Security n
مدیریت مکلفیت
/mŭ-di-rī-yat-ī mŭ-ka-la-fī-yat/
enrollment directorate (mil) n
Medina (city) n /ma-di-na/ مدینه
/ma-zāq/ مذاق
preference, pers taste n
مذاکرات /mŭ-zā-kĭ-rāt/
negotiations, talks n pl
→ مذاکرات کردن
negotiate, hold talks v

مذاکره , ـها/مذاکرات
/mŭ-zā-kĭ-ra, pl -rāt/
negotiation n

مذاهب /ma-zā-hĭb, sg maz-hab/
pl of مذهب n pl

مذکر /mŭ-za-kar/
masculine (gram) adj

مذکور /maz-kur/
abovementioned adj

مذهب , ـها/مذاهب
/maz-hab, pl ma-zā-hĭb/
sect, denomination; confession;
religion n

مذهبی /maz-ha-bi/
sectarian, religious adj

مرا /má-rā (-ra)/
me, to me (1st pers sg pron + object
marker) n

مرآت /mĭr-'āt/ mirror n
مراتب /ma-rā-tĭb/ pl of مرتبه n pl
مراتع /ma-rā-tey/ pastures n pl
مراجع /ma-rā-jey, sg mar-ja/
pl of مرجع n pl

مراجعه کردن <به کسی/چیزی>
/mŭ-rā-jĭ-'a kardan/
consult; refer <to sb/sth> vt

مراحل /ma-rā-hĭl, sg mar-ha-la/
pl of مرحله n pl

مرادف /ma-rā-dĭf/
analogous; synonymous adj

مراسم /ma-rā-sĭm/
ceremony; etiquette n

مراعات /mŭ-rā-'āt/
consideration, regard; compliance
with (regs, duties) n pl

← مراعات کردن
consider, regard; comply with (regs,
duties) n pl

مرافعه /mŭ-rā-fĭ-'a/ appeal (legal) n
مراقب /mŭ-rā-qĭb/
observation, close watch adj

مراقب حقوق بشر
/mŭ-rā-qĭb-ĭ hŭ-quq-ĭ ba-shar/
Human Rights Watch (NGO) n

مراقبت /mŭ-rā-qĭ-bat/
oversight; maintenance, sustaining
n

مراکز /ma-rā-kīz, sg mar-kaz/
pl of مرکز n pl

مراکش /ma-rā-kĭsh/
Morocco (country) n

مرام /mŭ-rām, ma-/
goal, object, purpose n

مرام نامه /mŭ-rām nā-ma/
platform, program (pol) n

مربا /mŭ-ra-bā/
jam, fruit preserves n

مربع /mŭ-ra-ba/
square n; squared adj

← دو مربع two squared

مربوط <به کسی/چیزی> /mar-but/
belonging <to sb>; dependent <on
sth> adj

مربوطات /mar-bu-tāt/ suburbs n pl
مربوطین /mar-bu-tin/
associates; dependents n pl

مرتاض /mŭr-tāz/ n جوگی see
مرتبه , ـها/مراتب
/mar-ta-ba, pl ma-rā-tĭb/
rank, grade, degree n

مرتجع , ـین /mŭr-ta-jey/
reactionary n

مرتشی /mŭr-ta-shi/ bribe-taker n
مرتفع /mŭr-ta-fey/
high, tall, elevated (mountain) n

مرتکب , ـین /mŭr-ta-kĭb/
perpetrator n

مرتکب جرم شدن
/mŭr-ta-kĭb-ĭ jŭrm shŭdan/
commit a crime v

مرجان /mar-jān/ coral n
مرجع /mar-ja, pl ma-rā-jey/
agency, authority; reference book n

← مراجع pl

مرجع پرداخت /mar-ja-yĭ par-dākht/
payer, paying authority n

مرجع تنظیم فعالیت
/mar-ja-yĭ tan-zim-ĭ fa-'ā-lĭ-yat/
regulating authority n

مرجع حقوقی /mar-ja hŭ-qu-qi/
legal center n

مرچ /mŭrch/
pepper, chili (veg, spice); Murch
(ctr) n

مرچ دولمیی /mürch-ĭ dol-ma-yi/
bell pepper n

مرحله , -ها/مراحل
/mar-ha-la, pl ma-rā-hīl/
step; stage, phase n

مرحله اول step one ⮜
مرحوم /mar-hum/
the late adj; deceased n

مرحومه
f form of مرحوم adj, n

مرد , -ان/ها /mard/
man; (colloq) husband; brave pers n

مردار /mür-dār/
dirty, unclean, filthy adj

مردار دانه /mür-dār-dā-na/
herpes n

مرداری /mür-dā-ri/
dirt, filth; fecal matter n

مردانه /mar-dā-na/
men's, relating to men; manly adj

مردانه وار /mar-dā-na-wār/
brave, manly adj; bravely, in a manly way adv

مردم , -ان/ها /mar-dŭm/
people; nation n

مردم داری /mar-dŭm-dā-ri/
tact, diplomacy n

مردم شناس /mar-dŭm shĭ-nās/
ethnographer n

مردم شناسی /mar-dŭm shĭ-nā-si/
ethnography n

مردم فریب /mar-dŭm-fĭ-reyb/
demagogue n

مردم فریبی /mar-dŭm-fĭ-rey-bi/
demagoguery n

مردمک /mar-dŭ-mak/
pupil (anat) n

مردن ؛ -مر- , -میر- ؛ مرد-
/mür-dan/, /méymürüm, -mir-//
die, expire vi

مردنی /mür-da-ni/
goner n; done for adj

مرده , -گان/ها /mür-da (mor-)/
dead, expired (& pers); extinguished adj, n

مرده دار /mür-da-dār/
bereaved, having dead pers in home adj

مرده داری کردن
/mür-da-dā-ri kardan/
make funeral arrangements v

مردیان /mar-dĭ-yān/
Mardyan (dist) n

مرز /marz/
border, frontier; land, country n

مرزا /mĭr-zā/
prince (Timurids, hist); nobleman n

مرزا غلام احمد
/mĭr-zā ghŭ-lām ah-mad/
Mirza Ghulam Ahmad (hist, leader of Qadiyani sect) n

مرزا سلیمان /mĭr-zā sŭ-lay-mān/
Mirza Suleyman (hist, Babur's cousin) n

مرزبان /marz-bān/
satrap, provincial governor, vice-regent (arch) n

مرزنگوش /mar-zan-gosh/
marjoram (arch) n

مرستون /ma-ras-tun/ poor house n
مرسل /mür-sal/
mursal (rose variety) n

مرض , pl am-rāz /ma-raz/
disease n

امراض pl ⮜
مرض شکر /ma-raz-ĭ sha-kar/
diabetes n

مرضی /ma-ra-zi/
morbid, pathological; (colloq) sickly adj

مرطوب /mar-tub/
damp, moist; humid adj

مرغ , -ها /mürgh/
bird (lit); chicken; poultry n

مرغ بریان /mürgh-ĭ bĭr-yān/
fried chicken n

مرغ پگاهی /mürgh pa-gā-hi/
nightingale n

مرغ جنگی /mürgh jan-gi/
chicken fighting n

مرغ داری /mürgh dā-ri/
poultry farming n

---

i = keep, ĭ = big, u = coop, ŭ = put, y = yet, ' = (glottal stop)   273

مرغ دشتی /mŭrgh-ĭ dash-ti/
pheasant n

مرغ دل , -ان/ها /mŭrgh dĭl/
coward n; cowardly adj

مرغ سحری /mŭrgh sa-ha-ri/
nighingale; rooster n

مرغ سلیمان /mŭrgh sŭ-lay-mān/
hoopoe, Solomon bird n

مرغ نوروزی /mŭrgh-ĭ naw-ro-zi/
seagull n

مرغاب /mŭr-ghāb/
Murghab (dist, river); see & بالا
مرغاب

مرغابی /mŭr-ghā-bi/
duck n

مرغانچه /mŭr-ghān-cha/
chicken coop n

مرغزار /margh-zār/
grassland, meadow n

مرفه /mŭ-ra-fa/
comfortable, prosperous adj

مرقس /mar-qŭs/
Mark (bibl) n

مرکب , -ان/ها /mar-kab/
donkey n

مرکز , -ها/مراکز
/mar-kaz, pl ma-rā-kĭz/
center; capital (city), seat (of prov)
n

مرکز بهسود /mar-kaz-ĭ bĭh-sud/
Markaz-e Behsud (dist, ctr Behsud)
n

مرکز تعلیمی ساحوی
/mar-kaz-ĭ ta'-li-mi-yĭ sā-ha-wi/
RTC, Regional Training Center n

مرکز سوق و اداره پولیس ملی
/mar-kaz-ĭ sawq ŭ ĭ-dā-ra-yĭ po-lis-ĭ
mĭ-li/
NPCC, National Police Command
Center n

مرکز گرمی /mar-kaz-gar-mi/
central heating n

مرکز هماهنگی مشترک ساحوی
/mar-kaz-ĭ ha-mā-han-gi-yĭ mŭsh-
ta-rak-ĭ sā-ha-wi/
JRCC, Joint Regional Coordination
Center n

مرکز هماهنگی پولیس ملی
/mar-kaz-ĭ ha-mā-han-gi-yĭ po-lis-ĭ
mĭ-li/
n مرکز سوق و اداره پولیس ملی see

مرکز هماهنگی مشترک ولایتی
/mar-kaz-ĭ ha-mā-han-gi-yĭ mŭsh-
ta-rak-ĭ wĭ-lā-ya-ti/
JPCC, Joint Provincial Coordination
Center n

مرکز هماهنگی نظامی ملی
/mar-kaz-ĭ ha-mā-han-gi-yĭ nĭ-zā-
mi-yĭ mĭ-li/
NMCC, National Military Command
Center n

مرکزی /mar-ka-zi/ central adj
مرگ /marg/ death n
مرگ <به کسی> ! /marg/
death <to sb> excl

مرگی /mĭr-gi/ seizure n
مرمر /mar-mar/ marble (material) n
مرمر سبز /mar-mar-ĭ sabz/
malachite; ophite n

مرمر سبز /mar-mar-ĭ sabz/
ophite; malachite n

مرمر سیاه /mar-mar-ĭ si-yāh/
basalt, black marble n

مرمر فولادی /mar-mar-ĭ fo-lā-di/
diabase, grey marble n

مرمی , -ها /mar-mi/
bullet, projectile, shell n

مرو /marw/ Merv (city) n
مرواری /mŭr-wā-ri/ pearl (colloq) n
مروارید /mŭr-wā-rid (-ri)/ pearl n
مروت /mar-wat/ Marwat (P tribe) n
مرور /mŭ-rur/
traffic; passage (time); overview,
review n

← مرور کردن
review; scan (read) v

مروره /ma-ra-wa-ra/
Marawara (dist) n

مروزی /mar-wa-zi/
مروی adj, n see

مروی /mar-wi/
Mervian adj; pers from Merv n

مرهم /mar-ham (ma-lam)/
balm; ointment, salve n

مرئی /mar-'i/
visible, perceptible adj

مری /mĭ-ray/ Meray (ctr) n
مری /mĭ-ri/ esophagus, gullet n
مریخ /mĭ-rikh/ Mars (planet) n

مرید, -ان/ها /mŭ-rid/
disciple, student, Sufi novice or follower n

مریدی /mŭ-ri-di/
discipleship, Sufi novitiate n

مریض, -ان/ها /ma-riz/
sick, ill (& pers) adj, n

مریضی /ma-ri-zi/
illness, sickness n

مریضی پرواز /ma-ri-zi-yĭ par-wāz/
airsickness n

مریم /mar-yam/
Maryam (f name); Mary (bibl) n

مزاج /mĭ-zāj/
nature, temperament n

مزاح /ma-zāh (-zāq)/
joke, jest, pun n

← مزاح کردن
joke, jest, banter, kid vi

مزاحم, -ها/ین /mŭ-zā-hĭm/
rude, bothersome (& pers) adj, n; interrupter n

مزاحمت ایجاد کردن
/mŭ-zā-hĭ-mat i-jād kardan/
see v مزاحمت کردن

مزاحمت کردن
/mŭ-zā-hĭ-mat kardan/
bother; interrupt v

مزاحی /ma-zā-hi (-qi)/
joker, jokester n

مزار, -ات/ها /ma-zār/
shrine; (colloq) Mazar-e Sharif n

مزار شریف /ma-zār-ĭ sha-rif/
Mazar-e Sharif (seat) n

مزارع /ma-zā-rey, sg maz-ra-'a/
pl of مزرعه n pl

مزارعه /mŭ-zā-rī-'a/
temporary sharecropping contract n

مزاق /ma-zāq/ n مزاح see

مزاقی /ma-zā-qi/ n مزاحی see

مزامیر داوود /ma-zā-mir-ĭ dā-wud/
Psalms (bibl) n

مزایده /mŭ-zā-yĭ-da/
auction, public sale n

مزایده کننده, -گان
/mŭ-zā-yĭ-da kŭ-nĭn-da/
auctioneer; highest bidder at auction n

مزایل /mĭ-zā-yĭl/
missile, rocket n

مزایل زمین به هوا
/mĭ-zā-yĭl-ĭ za-min ba ha-wā/
surface-to-air missile n

مزایل ضد هوا
/mĭ-zā-yĭl-ĭ zĭd-ĭ ha-wā/
anti-aircraft missile n

مزبور /maz-bur/
abovementioned adj

مزد /mŭzd/
wage, remuneration n

مزدا /maz-dā/
Supreme Being (Zor) n

مزدایی /maz-dā-yi/
Mazdean, Zoroastrian adj

مزدحم /mŭz-da-ham/
crowded, thronged adj

مزدور, مزـ /mŭz-dur, maz-/
see مزدور کار n

مزدور کار /mŭz-dur kār/
laborer, worker; domestic servant n

مزرعه, -ها/مزارع
/maz-ra-'a, pl ma-zā-rey/
farm; country estate n

مزمن /mŭz-mĭn/
chronic (disease) adj

مزه دار /ma-za-dār/
delicious, tasty adj

مزید /ma-zid/
additional, further; supplementary adj

مزیداً /ma-zí-dan, -dán/
additionally adv

مزیدن؛ -مزـ؛ مزید
/ma-zi-dan، -مزید -/
taste (arch) vt

مژده /mŭzh-da/
good news; (colloq) reward for good news n

مژه, -ها /mŭ-zha, mĭ-zha (mĭ-ja)/
eyelash n

مژه بر هم زدن
/mŭ-zha bar ham zadan/
blink vi

مس /mĭs/ copper n

مسابقه /mŭ-sā-bī-qa, pl -qāt/
contest, race n

← مسابقات pl

مساجد /ma-sā-jīd, sg mas-jīd/
pl of مسجد n pl

i = keep, ĭ = big, u = coop, ŭ = put, y = yet, ' = (glottal stop)   275

مساح /ma-sāh/ land surveyor n
مساحت /ma-sā-hat/
area; acreage; floor space n
مساحتى /ma-sā-ha-ti/
land surveying n
مساعد /mŭ-sā-'id/
suitable, proper; favorable adj
مساعدت /mŭ-sā-'ī-dat/
aid, assistance, help n
← مساعدت کردن aid, assist v
مساعدت بلا عوض
/mŭ-sā-'ī-dat ba-lā ī-waz/
grant, aid n
مساعى /ma-sā-'i/ efforts n pl
مسافر , -ان/ها/ین /mŭ-sā-fir/
passenger, traveler; (colloq)
itinerant beggar n
مسافرى /mŭ-sā-fi-ri/
for passengers adj
مسافه , -ها/مسافات
/ma-sā-fa, pl -fāt/
distance, interval n
مساکین /ma-sā-kīn, sg mas-kan/
pl of مسکن n pl
مساکین /ma-sā-kin, sg mīs-kin/
pl of مسکین n pl
مساله /ma-sā-la, pl -bāb (-jāt)/
seasoning, spice n
← مساله باب • مساله جات pl
مساله دیگ /ma-sā-la deyg/
see مساله n
مسالک /ma-sā-līk, sg mas-lak/
pl of مسلک n pl
مسامات /ma-sā-māt/
pores (skin) n pl
مساوات /mŭ-sā-wāt/
equality, parity n
مساوى equal adj /mŭ-sā-wi (ma-)/
مسایل /ma-sā-yīl, sg mas-'a-la/
pl of مسئله n pl
مست , -ان/ها /mast/
drunk; sexually aroused (& pers)
adj
← مست شدن become aroused vi
مستانه /mas-tā-na/
drunk; amorous (& adv) adj, adv
مستبد , -ان/ها/ین /mŭs-ta-bīd/
tyrant, despot n

مستتر /mŭs-ta-tar/
hidden, concealed adj
مستثنا /mŭs-tas-nā/ see مستثنى adj
مستثنى /mŭs-tas-nā/
excluded, excepted adj
مستحق , -ان/ها/ین /mŭs-ta-haq/
needy; deserving (& pers) adj, n
مستحکم /mŭs-tah-kam/
solid, strong adj
مسترى /mīs-ta-ri/ auto mechanic n
مستعار /mŭs-ta'-ār/
borrowed; imaginary adj
مستعفى /mŭs-ta-'fi/
pers who resigns from position n
مستفاد /mŭs-ta-fād/
understood, clear adj
مستفید <از چیزی> /mŭs-ta-fid/
using, enjoying, benefiting from
<sth> adj
← مستفید شدن <از چیزی>
use, enjoy, benefit from <sth> vi
مستقبل /mŭs-taq-bal/
future (& gram) adj
مستقر /mŭs-ta-qar/
based; settled, established adj
← مستقر شدن get settled vi
مستقل /mŭs-ta-qīl/
independent; self-reliant;
autonomous adj
مستقلا /mŭs-ta-qī-lan, -qī´-/
independently adv
مستقیم /mŭ-sta-qim/
straight, direct adj; straight ahead
adv
مستمع , -ان/ین /mŭs-ta-mey/
listener, hearer n
مستوره /mas-tu-ra, pl -rāt/
chaste adj; (arch) veiled f n
← مکتب مستورات girls school
مستوفى /mŭs-taw-fi/
provincial taxman; (hist) imperial
comptroller n
مستوفیت /mŭs-taw-fī-yat/
provincial tax office n
مستوى /mŭs-ta-wi/
flat, even, smooth adj
مستى intoxication n /mas-ti/

مستی آور /mas-ti ā-war/
intoxicating *adj*

مسجد , -ها/مساجد
/mas-jĭd, pl ma-sā-jĭd/
mosque *n*

مسجد پل خشتی
/mas-jĭd-ĭ pŭl-ĭ khĭsh-ti/
Brick Bridge Mosque (Kabul) *n*

مسخ /más-kha, maskh (mŭskh)/
metamorphosis; plagiarism *n*

مسخره /mas-kha-ra (-qa-)/
clown, buffoon; masquerade *n*;
ridiculous *adj*

مسخره باز /mas-kha-ra bāz/
see مسخره *n*

مسخره بازی /mas-kha-ra bā-zi/
clowning around, buffoonery *n*

مسدس /mŭ-sa-das/
hexagon *n*; hexagonal (& verse) *adj*

مسدود /mas-dud/
blocked; closed, shut *adj*

← مسدود شدن
be blocked; close, shut *vi*

← مسدود کردن
block; close, shut *vt*

مسرت /mŭ-sĭ-rat/
joy, happiness, delight *n*

مسرور /mas-rur/ happy, glad *adj*

مسروری /mas-ru-ri/ happiness *n*

مسری /mas-ri/ see ساری *adj*

مسطحه /mŭ-sa-tah/
plane, planar *adj*

← هندسۀ مسطحه
plane geometry

مسعود /ma-sud/
happy, lucky; Massoud (P tribe) *adj,*
n

مسقره /mas-qa-ra/ *n* مسخره see
Muscat (capital) *n* /mas-qat/ مسقط

مسقط الرأس /mas-qat-ŭr-rās/
homeland, birthplace *n*

مسکر /mŭs-kĭr/
liquor, alcoholic drink *n*

مسکن /mas-kan, pl ma-sā-kĭn/
residence, abode *n*

مسکن اختیار کردن
/mas-kan ĭkh-tĭ-yār kardan/
settle (sw) *v*

مسکن گردیدن /mas-kan gardidan/
v مسکن اختیار کردن see

مسکن , -ها /mŭ-sa-kĭn/
analgesic; sedative, tranquilizer *n*;
calming *adj*

مسکن گزین /mas-kan gŭ-zin/
settling down *n*

مسکنت /mas-ka-nat/ poverty *n*

مسکو /mas-kaw/ *n* ماسکو see

مسکوت /mas-kut/
hushed, left unsaid *adj*

مسکه /mas-ka/ butter *n*

مسکین , -ان/ها/مساکین
/mĭs-kin, pl ma-sā-kin/
beggar *n*; poor *adj*

مسکینت /mas-ki-nat/ poverty *n*

مسگر /mĭs-gar/ coppersmith *n*

مسلح /mŭ-sa-lah/ armed (mil) *adj*

مسلح ساختن /mŭ-sa-lah sākhtan/
arm (mil) *vt*

مسلک , -ها/مسالک
/mas-lak, pl ma-sā-lĭk/
profession, occupation *n*

مسلکی /mas-la-ki/ professional *adj*

مسلم , -ین /mŭs-lĭm/
Muslim (pers) *n*

مسلمان , -ان/ها /mŭ-sŭl-mān/
n مسلم see

← مسلمان ساختن • مسلمان کردن
Islamize; convert (sb) to Islam *vt*

← مسلمان شدن convert to Islam *n*

مسلمانی /mŭ-sŭl-mā-ni/
being a Muslim; Islamism *n*

مسما کردن /mŭ-sa-mā kardan/
vt مسمی see

مسموم /mas-mum/ poisoned *adj*

← مسموم ساختن • مسموم کردن
poison *vt*

مسمومیت غذایی
/mas-mu-mī-yat-ĭ ghĭ-zā-yi/
food poisoning *n*

مسمی کردن <کسی/چیزی را>
/mŭ-sa-mā kardan/
nominate, name <sb, sth> *vt*

مسند /mas-nad/
seat (for monarch, judge) *n*

مسند /mŭs-nad/ predicate (gram) *n*

مسند اليه /mŭs-nad-ĭ layh/
subject (gram) n

مسند نشين /mas-nad nĭ-shin/
dignitary n

مسوده /mŭ-sa-wĭ-da/
draft, rough copy n

مسووليت /mas-'u-lĭ-yat/
مسئوليت see مسئوليت n

مسهل , -ات /mŭs-hĭl/
laxative, purgative, cathartic n

مسئله /mas-'a-la, pl ma-sā-yĭl/
problem (& math); issue n

← pl مسایل

مسئول , -ان/ین /mas-'ul/
accountable, in charge (& pers) adj,
n

مسئول مطبوعات
/mas-'ul-ĭ mat-bo-'āt/
information officer n

مسئوليت /mas-'u-lĭ-yat/
accountabilty, responsibility n

← مسئوليت داشتن be responsible v

مسی /mĭ-si/ copper adj

مسیح /ma-sih/
Messiah, Christ n

مسیحا /ma-si-hā/ مسیح see n

مسیحی , -ان/ها /ma-si-hi/
Christian n, adj

مسیحیت /ma-si-hĭ-yat/
Christianity; Christendom n

مسیر /ma-sir/
course, route, direction; itinerary n

مشابه /mŭ-shā-bĭh/ alike, similar adj

مشاجره , -ها/مشاجرات
/mŭ-shā-jĭ-ra, pl -rāt/
difference of opinion n

← مشاجره کردن
differ, dispute mildly v

مشاور , -ان/ها/ین /mŭ-shā-wĭr/
advisor, counselor n

مشاور اقتصادی
/mŭ-shā-wĭr-ĭ ĭq-tĭ-sā-di/
economic counselor n

مشاور سیاسی
/mŭ-shā-wĭr-ĭ sĭ-yā-si/
political counselor n

مشاوره /mŭ-shā-wĭ-ra/
consultation, deliberation n

← مشاوره دادن advise, counsel v

← مشاوره کردن
consult, deliberate v

مشاهد /ma-shā-hĭd, sg mash-had/
pl of مشهد (rare) n pl

مشاهده /mŭ-shā-hĭ-da, pl -dāt/
contemplation; viewing; observation
v

← مشاهدات pl

مشایخ /ma-shā-yĭkh, sg sheykh/
pl of شیخ n pl

مشت /mŭsht/
blow, punch; fist; handful n

← مشت زدن punch, strike vt

← مشت کردن knead (dough) vt

مشت و مال /mŭsht ŭ māl/
massage n

مشتبه /mŭsh-ta-bĭh/
doubtful, suspicious adj

← مشتبه بودن doubt, suspect vi

مشترک /mŭsh-ta-rak/
shared, common, joint adj

مشترک , -ان/ین /mŭsh-ta-rĭk/
participant; subscriber n

مشترک المنافع
/mŭsh-ta-ràk-ŭl-ma-nā-fey/
sharing interests adj

مشترکاً /mŭsh-ta-rá-kan, -kán/
together, jointly adv

مشتری , -ان/ها /mŭsh-ta-ri/
buyer; customer; Jupiter (planet) n

مشتق , -ات /mŭsh-taq/
derivative (gram) n

مشتمل بودن <بر چیزی>
/mŭsh-ta-mĭl budan/
consist <of sth> vi

مشتهی /mŭsh-ta-hi/ appetizing adj

مشخص /mŭ-sha-khas/
specific, distinctive adj

← مشخص کردن
determine, distinguish vt

مشخصه , -ها/مشخصات
/mŭ-sha-kha-sa, pl -sāt/
characteristic n

مشرانو جرگه /mĭsh-rā-no jĭr-ga/
Meshrano Jirga (pol) n

detailed adj /mŭ-sha-rah/ مشرح

مشرف /mŭ-sha-raf/
honorable, honored adj

مشرف /mŭsh-rĭf/
overlooking, rising over adj

مشرق /mash-rĭq/
east, place of sunrise n

مشرق زمین /mash-rĭq za-min/
Orient, eastern regions n

eastern n /mash-rĭ-qi/ مشرقی

مشرک , -ان/ها /mŭsh-rĭk/
polytheist n

مشروب , -ات /mŭsh-rub/
drink, alcoholic beverage n

مشروب /mŭsh-rub/
potable; irrigated adj

conditional adj /mash-rut/ مشروط
مشروط بر آن که
/mash-rut bar ān kĭ/
provided that ... phrs

مشروطه /mash-ru-ta/
constitutional (monarchy) adj

مشروطه خواهان
/mash-ru-ta khā-hān/
Constitutionalists (pol movement,
hist) n

مشروطیت /mash-ru-tĭ-yat/
conditionality n

مشروع /mash-ro/
lawful under Sharia, legitimate adj

مشروعیت /mash-ro-'ĭ-yat/
compliance w/Sharia, legitimacy n
مشروعیت داشتن
be legitimate under Sharia v

مشغول /mash-ghul/
busy; employed adj

مشغولیت /mash-ghu-lĭ-yat/
occupation, profession n

مشفق /mŭsh-fĭq/
kind, compassionate adj

مشق /mashq/
practice, exercise; drill (mil); callig
model n

مشقت , -ها/مشقات
/mŭ-sha-qat, ma-/
difficulty, trouble n

مشقت دیده /mŭ-sha-qat di-da/
suffering, afflicted adj

مشک /mashk/
wineskin; inflatable skin n

musk n /mŭshk/ مشک

مشک بید /mŭshk beyd/
Egyptian willow n

مشکل /mŭsh-kĭl/
difficult adj; problem n

مشکل پسند /mŭsh-kĭl-pĭ-sand/
choosy, picky adj

مشکلات /mŭsh-kĭ-lāt/
difficulties, problems n pl

مشکوک /mash-kuk/
suspicious, distrusted; doubtful adj

مشکوله /mash-ko-la/
hot-water bottle n

black (horse) adj /mŭsh-ki/ مشکی

مشکین /mŭsh-kin/
musky (scent); musk-colored
(black) adj

field pea n /mŭ-shŭng/ مشنگ

مشورت /mash-wa-rat/
advice; consultation; deliberation n
↳ مشورت دادن • مشورت کردن
‹سر چیزی›
advise, counsel <on sth> v

مشورتی /mash-wa-ra-ti/
advisory adj

مشوره n /mash-wa-ra/ see مشورت
مشوره دهی /mash-wa-ra dĭ-hi/
mentoring n

مشوق /mŭ-sha-wĭq/
incentive (for reward); pers who
encourages n

مشهد /mash-had, pl ma-shā-hĭd/
place of martyrdom n
↳ مشاهد pl

مشهد /mash-had/
Mashad, Mashhad (city) n

مشهور ‹به چیزی› /mash-hur/
famous, celebrated; notorious <for
sth> adj

مشیمه /ma-shi-ma/
placenta, afterbirth n

interview n /mŭ-sā-hĭ-ba/ مصاحبه
↳ مصاحبه کردن interview vt

مصادر /ma-sā-dĭr, sg mas-dar/
pl of مصدر n pl

مصطلحات /mŭs-tĭ-lā-hāt/
terminology, terms n pl

مصغر /ma-sa-ghar/
diminutive (of noun) n

مصلا /mŭ-sa-lā/ prayer rug n

مصلح , -ان/ين /mŭs-līh/
reformer; peacemaker n

مصنوع /mas-no/
manufacured; artificial (style) adj

مصنوعات /mas-no-'āt/
products, goods n pl

مصنوعی /mas-no-'i/
imitation; manmade adj

مصوت /mŭ-sa-wĭt/ vowel n

مصول /ma-sul/ n محصول see

مصون /ma-sun/
safe; inviolable; immune adj

مصونيت /ma-su-nī-yat/
safety; inviolability; immunity n

→ مصونيت بر آوردن
waive immunity v

مصونيت دپلوماتيک
/ma-su-nī-yat-ī dī-plo-mā-tik/
diplomatic immunity n

مصونيت قانون گذارى
/ma-su-nī-yat-ī qā-nun gŭ-zā-ri/
parliamentary immunity n

مصئون /mas-'un/ adj مصون see

مصيبت /mŭ-si-bat/
disaster, misery n

مصيبت بار /mŭ-si-bat bār/
disastrous, calamitous adj

مصيبت زاى /mŭ-si-bat zāy/
adj مصيبت بار see

مضار /mŭ-zār, sg mŭ-zī-rat/
pl of مضرت n pl

مضاربت /mŭ-zā-rī-bat/
silent/limited partnership n

مضارع /mŭ-zā-rey/
in present/future tense adj

مضارعه /mŭ-zā-rī-'a/
partnership btwn landowner & workers n

مضاف /mŭ-zāf/
head word in possessive construction (gram) n

مصادره , -ها/مصادرات
/mŭ-sā-dĭ-ra, pl -rāt/
confiscation; ban n

→ مصادره كردن
confiscate; ban v

مصادف <با چيزى> /mŭ-sā-dĭf/
coinciding <with sth> adj; chance meeting n

مصارف /ma-sā-rĭf, sg mas-raf/
pl of مصرف n pl

مصافحه /mŭ-sā-fĭ-ha/
handshake (rare) n

→ مصافحه كردن
shake hands (rare) v

مصالح تعميراتى
/ma-sā-līh-ī ta'-mi-rā-ti/
building materials n

مصالحه /mŭ-sā-lī-ha/
reconciliation, peace n

مصحب , -ان/ين /mŭ-sa-hĭb/
proofreader n

مصدر , -ها/مصادر
/mas-dar, pl ma-sā-dīr/
infinitive (verb); origin, source n

مصدرى /mas-da-ri/
infinitive, infinitival adj

مصر /mĭ´-sīr, mĭsr/ Egypt n

مصر القاهره /mĭ´-sīr ŭl-qā-hī-ra/
Cairo (capital) n

مصرف /mas-raf, pl ma-sā-rĭf/
expenditure; consumption n

→ مصارف pl
→ مصرف كردن
• به مصرف رساندن
spend, consume vt

مصرفى /mas-ra-fi/
expendable; consumable n

مصروف /mas-ruf/
busy, occupied adj

→ مصروف بودن be busy v

مصروفيت /mas-ru-fī-yat/
occupation, profession; being busy n

→ مصروفيت داشتن
be busy; have an occupation v

مصرى , -ان/ها /mĭs-ri/
Egyptian (& pers) adj, n

مصطلح /mŭs-ta-lah/
idiomatic; colloquial adj

مضاف اليه /mŭ-zāf-ĭ layh/
dependent in possessive
construction (gram) n

مضامين /ma-zā-min, sg maz-mun/
pl of مضمون n pl

مضبوط /maz-but/
precise; sturdy, firm adj

مضر /mŭ-zīr/
harmful, detrimental adj

مضراب plectrum n /mīz-rāb/

مضرت /mŭ-zī-rat; pl -rāt, mŭ-zār/
harm, detriment n

↳ مضرات/مضار pl

مضمون , -ها/مضامين
/maz-mun, pl ma-zā-min/
text, article; document (& on
computer); meaning n

مصيبت /mŭ-si-bat/
disaster, misfortune n

مصيبت بار /mŭ-si-bat bār/
disastrous adj

مصيبت زده /mŭ-si-bat za-da/
disaster-stricken adj

مطابع /ma-tā-bey, sg mat-ba-'a/
pl of مطبعه n pl

مطابق accordance n /mŭ-tā-bīq/
مطابق(ی) /mŭ-tā-bīq(-ī)/
in accordance with prep

↳ مطابق بودن
conform w/, be consistent w/ v

مطابق خواهش شما
/mŭ-tā-bīq-ĭ kha-hĭsh-ĭ shŭ-mā/
as you wish phrs

مطابقت /mŭ-tā-bī-qat/
agreement (gram) n

↳ مطابقت داشتن
agree (gram) v
↳ مطابقت کردن <به چیزی>
correspond <to sth> vi

مطالب /ma-tā-līb, sg mat-lab/
pl of مطلب n pl

مطالبه , -ها/مطالبات
/mŭ-tā-lĭ-ba, pl -bāt/
claim, demand n

مطالعه /mŭ-tā-lĭ-'a/ study; perusal n
مطایبه , -ها/مطایبات
/mŭ-tā-yĭ-ba, pl -bāt/
teasing remark, banter n

مطبعه , -ها/مطابع
/mat-ba-'a (-ba), pl ma-tā-bey/
printing press n

مطبوع printed adj /mat-bo/
مطبوعات /mat-bo-'āt/
the press n pl

مطبوعاتی /mat-bo-'ā-ti/
related to the press adj

مطبه /mat-ba/ n مطبعه see

مطرب , -ان/ها /mŭt-rĭb/
minstrel (lit) n

مطربی /mŭt-rĭ-bi/ minstrelsy (lit) n

مطرح کردن /mat-rah kardan/
propound, set forth vt

مطلا gilded, gilt adj /mŭ-ta-lā/
مطلایی blonde adj /mŭ-ta-lā-yi/
مطلب /mat-lab, pl ma-tā-līb/
aim, goal, intention n

↳ مطالب pl
مطلب آشنا /mat-lab āsh-na/
insincere; self-interested adj

مطلع place of sunrise n /mat-la/
مطلع /mŭ-ta-ley/
aware, well-informed,
knowledgeable adj

↳ مطلع نمودن
inform, make aware vt

مطلق /mŭt-laq/
absolute, unlimited; absolutist adj
مطلقاً /mŭt-lá-qan, -qán/
absolutely adv

مطلقه /mŭ-ta-la-qa/ adj طلاقی see
مطمح goal, aim n /mat-mah/
مطمح نظر /mat-mah-ĭ na-zar/
n مطمح see

مظاهره /mŭ-zā-hĭ-ra/
demonstration (pol) n
↳ مظاهره کردن demonstrate v
مظاهره کننده , -گان/ها
/mŭ-zā-hĭ-ra kŭ-nĭn-da/
demonstrator (pol) n

مظفر triumphant adj /ma-za-far/
مظنون /maz-nun/
suspicious; dubious adj; suspect n

مع هذا /ma-'á hā-zā/
nonetheless, however (lit) adv

معابر /ma'-ā-bĭr, sg ma'-bar/
pl of معبر n pl

i = keep, ĭ = big, u = coop, ŭ = put, y = yet, ' = (glottal stop)   281

معادل /mŭ-'ā-dĭl/
equivalent, equal *adj*

معادله /mŭ-'ā-dĭ-la/
balance; (math) equation *n*

معادن /ma-'ā-dĭn, sg ma-'dan/
pl of معدن *n pl*

معارک /ma-'ā-rĭk, sg ma'-rĭ-ka/
pl of معرکه (rare) *n pl*

معاش /ma-'āsh/, ـات
wage, salary; living *n*

معاش تقاعدی /ma-'āsh-ĭ ta-qā-'ŭ-di/
retirement pension *n*

معاصر /mŭ-'ā-sĭr/
modern, current *adj*

معاصی /ma-'ā-si, sg ma'-sī-yat/
pl of معصيت *n pl*

معافی /mŭ-'ā-fi/
pardon (by president) *n*

معافيت ‹از یک مرض›
/mŭ-'ā-fī-yat/
exemption, excuse; immunity (med)
n

→ معافيت داشتن ‹از یک مرض›
be immune ‹to disease› *vi*

معالج /mŭ-'ā-lĭj/
attending, treating (doctor) *adj*

معالجوی /mŭ-'ā-lĭ-ja-wi/
therapeutic, curative *adj*

معالجه /mŭ-'ā-lī-ja/
treatment, therapy (med) *n*

→ معالجه کردن treat (a patient) *v*

معامله , ـها/معاملات
/mŭ-'ā-mĭ-la, pl -lāt/
transaction; (pl) dealings *n*

معامله گر /mŭ-'ā-mĭ-la-ga-gar/
wheeler-dealer (& pers) *adj, n*

معانی /ma-'ā-ni, sg ma'-nā (mā-nā)/
pl of معنی *n pl*

معاودت return *n* /mŭ-'ā-wĭ-dat/

معاون /mŭ-'ā-wĭn/
assistant, aide; deputy *n*; tributary;
auxiliary *adj*

معاونت /mŭ-'ā-wĭ-nat/
aid, assistance, help *n*

→ معاونت کردن aid, help *vt*

معاهده , ـها/معاهدات
/mŭ-'ā-hĭ-da, pl -dāt/
treaty, pact *n*

معاينه /mŭ-'ā-yĭ-nat, pl -nāt/
examination, inspection, (med)
check-up *n*

↪ معاينات pl
↪ معاينه کردن
examine, inspect, (med) perform a
check-up *n*

معاينه خانه /mŭ-'ā-yĭ-na khā-na/
doctor's office (checkups) *n*

معایير /ma-'ā-yir, sg mī'-yār/
pl of معیار *n pl*

معبر , ـها/معابر
/ma'-bar, pl ma'-ā-bīr/
pass; crossing, ford *n*

معبود /ma'-bud/
diety, god; idol *n*; adored,
worshiped *adj*

معبود بر حق /ma'-bud-ĭ bar haq/
the true God *n*

معتاد , ـان/ها/اين /mo-tād/
addict *n*; addicted *adj*

معتبر , ـان/ها/اين /mo-ta-bar/
authority, authoritative pers *n*;
credible, reliable *adj*

معتدل /mo-ta-dĭl/
moderate, temperate *adj*

معتزله /mŭ'-ta-zĭ-la/
Mutazila (hist, rationalist Sunni
school of theology) *n*

معتزلی , ـان/ها /mŭ'-ta-zĭ-li/
Mutazilite (hist, follower of
mu'tazila) *n*

معتمد /mo-ta-mad/
reliable, trustworthy *adj*; trusted
agent *n*

معجزه , ـها/معجزات /mo-jī-za/
miracle (prophet's) *n*

معدن , ـها/معادن
/ma'-dan, pl ma-'ā-dĭn/
mine, deposit (geol) *n*

معده stomach *n* /mī'-da/

معذرت /ma-'zī-rat/
forgiveness, pardon *n*

↪ معذرت خواستن apologize *v*

معرض /ma'-raz/
place where sth is displayed or
exposed *n*

معرف /mŭ-'a-rĭf/
presenter, introducer n

معرفت , -ها /ma'-rĭ-fat/
acquaintance, familiarity (w/pers); knowledge n

معرفت داشتن ←
be acquainted (w/sb); be conversant (on sth) v

معرفه /ma'-rĭ-fa/ definite (gram) n
معرفی /ma'-rĭ-fi/
acquainted, introduced adj

معرفی کردن <کسی را به کسی> ←
introduce <sb to sb> vt

معروف /ma'-ruf/
famous, renowned adj

معروفیت /ma'-ru-fĭ-yat/
fame, renown n

معرکه , -ها/معارک
/ma'-rĭ-ka, pl ma-'ā-rīk/
battlefield n

معروف /ma'-ruf/ Maruf (dist) n
معزول /ma'-zul/
deposed adj

معصوم /ma'-sum/
innocent, sinless adj

معصومانه /ma'-su-mā-na/
innocent (& adv) adj, adv

معصومیت /ma'-su-mĭ-yat/
innocence n

معصیت , -ها/معاصی
/ma'-sĭ-yat, pl ma-'ā-si/
sinfulness, sin n

معضله , -ها/معضلات
/mŭ'-zĭ-la, pl -lāt/
problem, difficulty n

معطل /mŭ-'a-tal (mā-tĭl)/
delayed, postponed adj

معطل <کسی> /mŭ-'a-tal(-ĭ)/
kept waiting <for sb> adj

معطل بودن ←
be kept waiting v

معطل شدن ←
be delayed v

معطل کردن • منتظر ماندن ←
delay <sb>, keep <sb> waiting vi

معطلی /mŭ-'a-ta-li (mā-tĭ-li)/
delay, postponement n

معقول /ma'-qul/
reasonable; intelligible adj

معکوس /ma'-kus/
inverted, upside-down adj

معکوس کردن • معکوس ساختن ←
invert, turn upside-down vt

معکوساً /ma'-kú-san, -sán/
inversely adv

معلق /mŭ-'a-laq/
hanging, suspended adj; somersault n

معلق زدن ←
turn a somersault v

معلم , -ان/ها/ین /mŭ-'a-līm/
teacher, instructor, tutor n

معلمه , -ها /mŭ-'a-lī-ma/
f form of معلم n

معلوم /ma'-lum/
certain, known; (gram) active adj

معلوم دار /ma'-lum dār/
of course, naturally adv

معلوم شدن ←
seem, appear; seem likely; be visible vi

معلوم شوان /ma'-lum sha-wan/
outward appearance n

معلومات /ma'-lu-māt/
information, data; knowledge n pl

معلومات دادن ←
inform v

معما , -ها /mŭ-'a-mā/
puzzle, riddle, conundrum n

معمار /mĭ'-mār/
architect, builder; mason n

معماری /mĭ'-mā-ri/
architecture; masonry n

معمر /mŭ-'a-mar/
long-lived, old adj

معمور , -ین /ma'-mur/
civil servant n

معمول /ma'-mul/
usual, ordinary adj /ma'-mul/

معمولاً /ma'-mu-lan, -mú-/
usually, ordinarily adv

معنایی /ma'-nā-yi/
semantic adj

معنی , -ها/معانی
/ma'-nā (mā-), pl ma-'ā-ni/
meaning, sense n

معنی دار /ma'-nā-dār/
meaningful, significant adj

معیار , -ها/معاییر
/mĭ'-yār, pl ma-'ā-yir/
standard, criterion; norm n

معیت /ma-'ī-yat/ escort, company n

deputy, assistant n /mū-'in/ معين

معيوب , -ان/ها/ين /ma'-yub/
disabled, handicapped (& pers); defective adj, n

/ma'-yu-bī-yat/ معيوبيت
disability, handicap n

/mūgh/ مغ
Zoroastrian priest, Mede; (arch) tavernkeeper n

مغاره , -ها /ma-ghā-ra/
cave, cavern, grotto n

مغازله /ma-ghā-zī-la/
flirting, amorous play (lit) n

supermarket n /ma-ghā-za/ مغازه

/mū-ghā-yīr/ مغاير
contrary, completely different adj

see مقبول adj /magh-bul/

Maghreb; west n /magh-rīb/ مغرب

مغروق , -ان/ين /magh-ruq/
drowning, drowned; sunken adj

core, kernel; brain n /maghz/ مغز

/maghz-ī ŭs-tŭ-khān/ مغز استخوان
bone marrow n

/magh-zi/ مغزى
brain; having kernels adj

nuts (edible) n /magh-zī-yat/ مغزيت

/mū-ghŭl/ مغل , -ان/ها
Mongolian; Mongol, Mughal n, adj

see مقلد n /mū-gha-lat/ مغلت

/mū-ghŭ-līs-tān/ مغلستان
Mongolia (country) n

complicated adj /mūgh-laq/ مغلق

/magh-lub/ مغلوب
defeated, vanquished adj

be defeated vi مغلوب شدن ←

defeat vt مغلوب کردن ←

/magh-lu-bī-yat/ مغلوبيت
defeat, state of defeat n

/magh-mun/ مغموم
sad, unhappy, sorrowful, grieved adj

/ma-fād/ مفاد
advantage, profit; loan interest; meaning n

/mū-fā-jā/ مفاجا
surprise, sudden event n

مفاجات see مفاجا /mū-fā-jāt/

/ma-fā-sīd/ مفاسد
corruption, heinous acts n pl

pl of مفصل n pl /ma-fā-sīl/ مفاصل

/ma-fā-him, sg maf-hum/ مفاهيم
pl of مفهوم n pl

free; dirt cheap adj /mūft/ مفت

/mūft khor/ مفت خور
parasite, sponger n

proud adj /mūf-ta-khīr/ مفتخر

mufti n /mūf-ti/ مفتى

singular (gram) adj /mūf-rad/ مفرد

/mūf-ra-dāt/ مفردات
details, elements n pl

bronze n /maf-ragh, mīf-/ مفرغ

مفصل , -ها/مفاصل
/maf-sal, pl ma-fā-sīl/
joint, articulation (anat) n

detailed adj /mūf-fa-sal/ مفصل

/maf-sá-lan, -lán/ مفصلاً
in detail adv

object (gram) n /maf-'ul/ مفعول

مفعول غير مستقيم
/maf-'ul-ī ghayr-ī mŭs-ta-qīm/
indirect object (gram) n

مفعول مستقيم /maf-'ul-ī mŭs-ta-qīm/
direct object (gram) n

/maf-'u-li/ مفعولى
objective (gram) adj

lost, missing adj /maf-qud/ مفقود

thinker n /mū-fa-kīr/ مفکر , -ان/ين

/mū-fa-kī-ra/ مفکره
capacity for thought n

/maf-ku-ra/ مفکره , -ها
thought, idea; opinon n

/maf-ku-ra-yī ām/ مفکره عام
public opinion n

مفلس , -ان/ها/ين /mūf-līs/
poor, indigent (& pers) adj, n

مفلس و خوشحال
/mūf-līs ŭ khŭsh-hāl/
poor & content phrs

مفهوم , -ها/مفاهيم
/maf-hum, pl ma-fā-him/
concept, idea; meaning n

/mū-fid/ مفيد
advantageous, beneficial, useful adj

مقابل /mŭ-qā-bīl(-ī)/
facing, opposite adj, prep; in exchange for prep

مقابله /mŭ-qā-bī-la/
conflict, confrontation; encounter n

مقاتله /mŭ-qā-tī-la/
carnage (in battle) n

مقادیر /ma-qā-dir, sg mīq-dār/
pl of مقدار n pl

مقاربت /mŭ-qā-rī-bat/
sex, intercourse n

مقاربتی /mŭ-qā-rī-ba-ti/
venereal adj

مقاصد /ma-qā-sīd, sg maq-sad/
pl of مقصد n pl

مقاله , -ها/مقالات /mŭ-qā-la, pl -lāt/
article, essay n

مقاله نویس /mŭ-qā-la na-wis/
essayist n

مقام , -ات/ها /ma-qām/
position, job; place n

مقام , -ها /mŭ-qām/
residence; stay, sojourn; musical tone/mode n

مقامات /ma-qā-māt/
senior govt officials n

مقاوم /mŭ-qā-wīm/
resistant, withstanding; durable adj

مقاومت /mŭ-qā-wī-mat/
resistance; durability n
→ مقاومت withstand; endure v
مقاومت منفی
/mŭ-qā-wī-mat-ī man-fi/
passive resistance (pol) n

مقایسه /mŭ-qā-yī-sa/ comparison n
→ مقایسه کردن compare v

مقبره /maq-ba-ra, pl ma-qā-bīr/
tomb, mausoleum (formal) n
→ مقابر pl

مقبل /mŭq-bīl/
fortunate, prosperous (& pers) adj, n

مقبول /maq-bul (magh-)/
attractive; pretty adj

مقتدا /mŭq-ta-dā/ head, leader n
مقتدا به /mŭq-ta-dā bīh/
example to be followed (esp rel) n

مقتضا , -یات /mŭq-ta-zā/
necessity; requirement n

مقتول , -ان/ین /maq-tul/
murder victim n

مغتوله /maq-tu-la/ f form of مقتول

مقدار , -ها/مقادیر
/mīq-dār, pl ma-qā-dir/
amount, quantity n

مقدس , -ات /mŭ-qa-das/
holy, sacred; venerable (& pers);
Muqadas (m name) adj, n
→ کتاب مقدس the Bible

مقدسه /mŭ-qa-da-sa, pl -sāt/
sth sacred n
→ مقدسات pl

مقدم /mŭ-qa-dam/
prior adj; antecedent n

مقدمات /mŭ-qa-da-māt/
preliminaries, preparatory measures n pl

مقدماتی /mŭ-qa-da-mā-ti/
preliminary, preparatory adj

مقدمتاً /mŭ-qa-da-ma-tan/
first of all, by way of introduction adv

مقدمه /mŭ-qa-da-ma/
prologue, introduction n

مقدونی , -ان/ها /maq-du-ni/
Macedonian (& pers) adj, n

مقدونیه /maq-du-nī-ya/
Macedonia (country); Macedon (hist) n

مقر /ma-qar/
seat, center; headquarters n

مقر /mŭ-qĭr/ avowing, confessing n
مقر /mŭ-qŭr/ see مقهور n
مقر فرمان دهی
/ma-qar-ī far-mān dī-hi/
command headquarters n

مقراض /mīq-rāz/ scissors (lit) n

مقرب , -ان/ین /mŭ-qa-rab/
confidant (dignitary's) n

مقرر /mŭ-qa-rar/
appointment, assignment n
→ مقرر کردن appoint; hire vt

مقرره /mŭ-qa-ra-ra, pl -rāt/
rule, regulation, stipulation n
→ مقررات pl

i = keep, ĭ = big, u = coop, ŭ = put, y = yet, ' = (glottal stop)

مكاشفه /mŭ-kā-shĭ-fa/
apocalypse, revelation, disclosure
(mystical) n

مكالمه , -ها/مكالمات
/mŭ-kā-lĭ-ma, pl -māt/
conversation, dialogue n
← مكالمه كردن converse v

مكان , -ها/اماكن/امكنه
/ma-kān; pl a-mā-kĭn, am-kĭ-na/
place, site; (colloq) privy, latrine n

مكانزم /mĭ-kā-nĭ´-zĭm/
mechanism n

مكانزه شده
/mĭ-kā-nĭ-za shŭ-da/
mechanized adj

مكتب , -ها/مكاتب
/mak-tab, pl ma-kā-tĭb/
school n
← مكتب خواندن go to school v

مكتب ابتدايى /mak-tab-ĭ ĭb-tĭ-dā-yi/
elementary school n

مكتب السنه /mak-tab-ĭ al-sĭ-na/
see مكتب زبان n

مكتب زبان /mak-tab-ĭ zĭ-bān/
language school n

مكتب حكام /mak-tab-ĭ hŭ-kām/
civil servants' training academy n

مكتب عالى /mak-tab-ĭ ā-li/
high school n

مكتب قضات /mak-tab-ĭ qŭ-zāt/
judges' training academy n

مكتب گريز /mak-tab gŭ-reyz/
truant student n

مكتب گريزى /mak-tab gŭ-rey-zi/
truancy n

مكتب متوسط
/mak-tab-ĭ mŭ-ta-wa-sĭt/
junior high school, middle school n

مكتب مستورات
/mak-tab-ĭ mas-tu-rāt/
girls' school n

مكتشف n /mŭk-ta-shĭf/ كاشف see

مكتوب , -ات/ها/مكاتيب
/mak-tub, pl ma-kā-tĭb/
letter, epistle n; written, recorded
adj

مكث /maks/
pause (esp in speech) n
← مكث نمودن pause v

مقصد /maq-sad, pl ma-qā-sĭd/
goal, purpose; intention n
مقاصد pl ←

مقصر , -ان/ين ‹از يك جرم›
/mŭ-qa-sĭr/
guilty (& pers) adj, n; fault n

مقصود /maq-sud/
see مقصد &; Maqsud (m name) n

مقطع /maq-ta/ cross section n
مقطع /mŭ-qa-ta/
interrupted; segmental adj

مقعد /maq-'ad/
ass, buttocks; anus (lit) n

مقعر /mŭq'-ar/ concave adj
مقفل /mŭ-qa-fal/
closed; locked (lit) adj

مقلد , -ان/ين
/mŭ-qa-lĭd (mŭ-gha-lat)/
imitator, mimic n

مقناطيس /mĭq-nā-tis/ magnet n
مقناطيس برقى /mĭq-nā-tis-ĭ bar-qi/
electromagnet n

مقناطيسى /mĭq-nā-ti-si/
magnetic adj

مقناطيسيت برقى
/mĭq-nā-ti-sĭ-yat-ĭ bar-qi/
electromagnetism n

مقوا /mŭ-qa-wā/ cardboard n
مقوايى /mŭ-qa-wā-yi/ cardboard adj
مقوله , -ها/مقولات
/ma-qu-la, pl -lāt/
saying; category (philos) n

مقهور /maq-hur (mŭ-qŭr)/
Maqhur (lake, dist) n

مقيد /mŭ-qa-yad/
restricted; bound adj
← مقيد ساختن restrict; bind v

مكاتب /ma-kā-tĭb, sg mak-tab/
pl of مكتب n pl

مكاتيب /ma-kā-tib, sg mak-tub/
pl of مكتوب n pl

مكار /ma-kār/ cunning, shrewd adj
مكارم /ma-kā-rĭm, sg mak-ra-mat/
pl of مكرمت n

مكاره /ma-kā-ra/ f form of مكار adj
مكارى /ma-kā-ri/
cunning, shrewdness n

a = cup, ā = long, aw = now, ay = sigh, e = bet, ey = obey

guile, cunning n /má-kĭr, makr/ مکر

microphone n /mĭk-rā-fun/ مکرافون

repeated adj /mŭ-ka-rar/ مکرر

/mŭ-ka-rá-ran, -rán/ مکرراً
repeatedly adv

/mŭ-ka-ram/ مکرم
venerable (Mecca) adj

مکرمت , -ها/مکارم
/mak-ra-mat, pl ma-kā-rīm/
noble deed n

/mŭ-ka-ra-ma/ مکرمه
f form of مکرم adj

microbe n /mĭk-rob/ مکروب

/mĭk-rob-shĭ-nās/ مکروب شناس
microbiologist n

/mĭk-rob-shĭ-nā-si/ مکروب شناسی
microbiology n

/mĭk-ro-skop/ مکروسکوپ
microscope n

/mĭk-ro-sko-pi/ مکروسکوپی
microscopic adj

/mĭk-ro-fun/ مکروفون
microphone n

مکروه , -ات /mak-roh/
disgusting, distasteful (food, thing) adj, n

/mak-si-ko/ مکسیکو
Mexico (country) n

مکسیکویی , -ان/ها /mak-si-ko-yi/
Mexican (& pers) adj, n

/mŭ-ka-'ab/ مکعب
cube (shape, math) n; cubed adj

دو مکعب ← two to the third power

obliged adj /mŭ-ka-laf/ مکلف

/mŭ-ka-la-fī-yat/ مکلفیت, -ها
obligation n

مکلفیت داشتن ← be obliged v

/mŭ-ka-mal/ مکمل
complete; concluded adj

Mecca (city) n /ma-ka/ مکه

مکیدن ; -مک- ; مکید-
/ma-ki-dan/
suck; suckle v

but; except conj /má-gar/ مگر

exception (colloq) n /ma-gar/ مگر

/ma-gas (man-)/ مگس
fly, housefly n

/ma-gas bŭ-rān/ مگس بران
shoo-fly (yak/horse hair on stick) n

/ma-gas kŭsh/ مگس کش
flyswatter n

/ma-go/ مگو
unspeakable, unutterable adj

/má-go (na-)/ مگو !
do not say (neg imper) v

/mal pās-wāl/ مل پاسوال
brigadier general, BG n

crowd (arch) n /ma-lā/ ملا

ملا , -ها/یان /mŭ-lā/
mullah, rel teacher n

/mŭ-lā bā-shi/ ملا باشی
head mullah in royal household n

ملا محمد خیل
/mŭ-lā mŭ-ha-mad kheyl/
Mullah Mohamed Kheyl (ctr) n

ملاح , -ان/ها/ین /ma-lāh/
sailor (arch) n

appeal, savor n /ma-lā-hat/ ملاحت

/ma-lā-hĭ-da, sg mŭl-hīd/ ملاحده
pl of ملحد n pl

/mŭ-lā-hĭ-za, pl -zāt/ ملاحظه
consideration; observation; remark n

ملاحظات pl ←
/mŭ-lā-hĭ-za kār/ ملاحظه کار
circumspect, prudent adj

/mŭ-lā-hĭ-za kā-ri/ ملاحظه کاری
circumspection, prudence n

malaria n /ma-lā-rī-yā/ ملاریا

/mŭ-lā-zay/ ملازی
Mullazai, Malazai (P tribe) n

uvula n /ma-lā-za/ ملازه

/ma-lāq/ ملاق
loop (aviation); somersault n

ملاق خوردن • ملاق زدن ←
loop; somersault v

/mŭ-lā-qāt/ ملاقات
meeting, encounter n

ملاقات کردن ←
meet, have a meeting v

ladle n /ma-lā-qa/ ملاقه

ملاک , -ها /ma-lāk/
criterion, standard n

ملاک , -ان/ها/ین /ma-lāk/
landowner n

ملال /ma-lāl/
annoyance; boredom; sadness *n*

ملال انگیز /ma-lāl an-geyz/
annoying; boring *n*

ملالت /ma-lā-lat/ *n* see ملال

ملامت /ma-lā-mat/
blame, censure *n*
← ملامت کردن • ملامتی کشیدن
blame, censure *vt*
← مه را ملامت نکو !
don't blame me!

ملامتی /ma-lā-ma-ti/
blameworthy, guilty (& pers) *adj, n*; (hist) member of Malamat Sufi order *n*
← ملامتی کشیدن blame, censure *v*

ملایا Malay peninsula *n* /ma-lā-yā/

ملایک /ma-lā-yīk, sg ma-lak/ pl of ملک *n pl*

ملبس /mū-la-bas/
dressed, clothed *adj*
← ملبس شدن dress, get dressed *vi*

ملبوس خاص /mal-bus-ī khās/
robe of honor given by Mughal emperor (hist) *n*

ملبوسات /mal-bu-sāt/
clothes, clothing *n pl*

ملت , -ها/ملل /mī-lat, pl mī-lal/
nation, people *n*

ملحد -ان/ها/ین/ملاحده
/mūl-hīd, pl ma-lā-hī-da/
apostate, infidel *n*

ملحق /mūl-hīq/
added, attached, joined *adj*

ملحقات /mūl-hī-qāt/
additions, supplements, appendices *n pl*

ملخ locust, grasshopper *n* /ma-lakh/

ملخک small locust *n* /ma-la-khak/

ملزوم inseparable *adj* /mal-zum/

ملزم convicted *adj* /mūl-zam/

ملعبه toy, plaything *n* /mal-'a-ba/

ملک angel *n*, pl ma-lā-yīk /ma-lak/
← ملایک pl

ملک , -ان/ها /ma-līk/
chieftain; elder (village, khel, tribe); prince, ruler *n*

ملک , -ها /mūlk/
nation, country, state; estate *n*

ملک الحارس /ma-lak-ūl-hā-rīs/
guardian angel *n*

ملک الشعرا /ma-līk-ūsh-sh-'ū-rā/
poet laureate *n*

ملک الموت /ma-lak-ūl-mawt/
angel of death *n*

ملکوت /ma-la-kut/
realm, empire (esp of heavens) *n*

ملکوتی /ma-la-ku-ti/
divine, heavenly *adj*

ملکه /ma-lī-ka/
queen; widow of king *n*

ملکه زیبایی /ma-lī-ka-yī zey-bā-yi/
beauty queen *n*

ملکی civilian *adj* /mūl-ki/

ملل pl of ملت /mī-lal, sg mī-lat/

ملل متحد /mī-lal-ī mū-ta-hīd/
UN, United Nations *n*

ملم (colloq) *n* /ma-lam/ see مرهم

ململ /mal-mal/
malmal (muslin for chadar) *n*

ملنگ /ma-lang/
malang (kind of dervish) *n*

ملوک /mū-luk, sg ma-līk/ pl of ملک *n pl*

ملوک الطوایف /mū-lu-kūt-ta-wā-yīf/
petty kings & princes *n pl*

ملی national; nationalistic *adj* /mī-li/

ملی /mū-li/
daikon, Japanese horseradish *n*

ملی جرگه /mī-li jīr-ga/
National Council *n*

ملی سرخک /mū-li sūr-khak/
radish *n*

ملیارد billion *n, adj* /mīl-yārd/

ملیاردر billionaire *n* /mīl-yār-dar/

ملیت /mī-lī-yat/
nationality; people, nation *n*

ملیون million *n* /mīl-yun/

ملیونر millionaire *n* /mīl-yu-nar/

ممات death *n* /ma-māt/

مماثل similar *adj* /mū-mā-sīl/

مماثلت similarity *adj* /mū-mā-sī-lat/
← مماثلت داشتن be similar *v*

ممالک /ma-mā-līk, sg mam-la-kat/
pl of مملکت *n pl*

مماليک /ma-mā-lik, sg mam-luk/
Mamluks (hist) n pl

ممانعت /mŭ-mā-nĭ-'at/
prohibition, ban, injunction n

ممتحن , -ان/ها/ين /mŭm-ta-hīn/
examiner, tester n

ممسک /mŭm-sīk/
cheap, stingy (& pers) adj, n

ممسکی /mŭm-sĭ-ki/
cheapness, stinginess n

ممکن /mŭm-kĭn/
possible adj; maybe, perhaps adv

مملکت , -ها/ممالک
/mam-la-kat, pl ma-mā-līk/
country, state n

مملو /mam-lu/ full adj

مملوک /mam-luk/ n ممالیک see

ممنوع /mam-nu/
prohibited, forbidden adj

من /man (ma)/ I pron

من بعد /mĭn-ba-'ad (mĭm-bād)/
henceforth adv

منابر
/ma-nā-bīr, sg mĭn-bar (mŭm-)/
pl of منبر n pl

منابع /ma-nā-bey, sg man-ba/
pl of منبع n pl

منار /ma-nār/ monument n

منازل /ma-nā-zīl, sg man-zīl/
pl of منزل n pl

منازعه /mŭ-nā-zĭ-'a/
struggle; litigation, legal dispute n

مناسب /mŭ-nā-sĭb/
appropriate, suitable; reasonable;
fair adj

مناسبت , -ها/مناسبات
/mŭ-nā-sĭ-bat, pl -bāt/
relationship, relation; occasion,
opportunity n

مناصب /ma-nā-sīb, sg man-sab/
pl of منصب n pl

مناطق /ma-nā-tīq, sg man-ta-qa/
pl of منطقه n pl

منافذ /ma-nā-fīz, sg man-faz/
pl of منفذ n pl

مناقشه , -ها/مناقشات
/mŭ-nā-qī-sha, pl -shāt/
dispute, arguing; discussion n

مناقشه آميز /mŭ-nā-qī-sha ā-meyz/
controversial adj

مناقصه /mŭ-nā-qĭ-sa/
tender; notice of tender n

منامه /ma-nā-ma/
Manama (capital) n

منبر , -ها/منابر
/mĭn-bar (mŭm-), pl ma-nā-bīr/
pulpit in a mosque n

منبع , -ها/منابع
/man-ba, pl ma-nā-bey/
source, spring n

منبعد /mĭn-ba-'ad (mĭm-bād)/
من بعد see adv

منبه , -ات /mŭ-na-bīh/
stimulus, stimulant n

منبهه /mŭ-na-bī-ha/ n منبه f form of
منتخب /mŭn-ta-khab/
elected, chosen adj

منتخبات /mŭn-ta-kha-bāt/
selected works (author's) n pl

منتشر /mŭn-ta-shīr/
published, issued adj

← منتشر شدن be published vi
← منتشر کردن publish, issue vt

منتظر , -ان/ين /mŭn-ta-zīr/
waiting, expecting (& pers) adj, n
← منتظر <کسی> بودن
wait, expect <sb> vi
← منتظر ماندن <کسی را>
keep <sb> waiting vt

منتظريت /mŭn-ta-zī-rī-yat/
waiting, waiting around n

منتقل /mŭn-ta-qĭl/
transferred (detainee) adj
← منتقل کردن transfer v

منتقم , -ان/ين /mŭn-ta-qĭm/
avenger n

منتو /man-tu/ mantu (cul) n

منج /mŭnj/
Munj (village, people); munj grass n

منجانی /mŭn-jā-ni/ n, adj منجی see

منجم , -ان/ها/ين /mŭ-na-jīm/
astrologer n

منجنيق /man-ja-niq/ capapult n

منجی , -ان/ها /mŭn-ji/
Munji (pers, lang) n; made from
munj grass adj

i = keep, ĭ = big, u = coop, ŭ = put, y = yet, ' = (glottal stop)   289

منحنی curved adj /mŭn-ha-ni/
/mŭn-hays(-ī)/ منحيث
as, in the capacity of prep
مندرج /mŭn-da-rīj/
included, inserted, contained adj
مندرجه /mŭn-da-rī-ja/
f form of مندرج adj
مندرجات /mŭn-dar-jāt/
contents (book) n pl
مندرس worn-out adj /mŭn-da-rīs/
مندمج see مندرج adj /mŭn-da-mīj/
مندو زائی /man-do zā-yi/
Mando Zayi (dist, ctr Dadwal)
مندول Mandol (dist) n /man-dol/
مندوی /man-da-wi/
wholesale market (for type of
goods) n

منزل , -ها/منازل
/man-zīl, pl ma-nā-zīl/
house, residence; floor, story; goal
n
منزل /mŭn-zal/
heavenly (revelation) adj
منزل بالا /man-zīl-ī bā-lā/
upstairs n
منزل پايين /man-zīl-ī pā-yin/
downstairs n
منسجم /mŭn-sa-jam/
organized; harmonious adj
منسوبين /man-su-bin/
members; relatives n pl
منشويک /man-sha-wik/
Menshevik (hist) n
منشی secretary n /mŭn-shi/
منشی عمومی /mŭn-shi-yī ŭ-mu-mi/
Secretary General (UN) n
منصب , -ها/مناصب
/man-sab, pl ma-nā-sīb/
office, commision; rank n
منصب دار , -ان/ها /man-sab-dār/
commissioned military officer; (hist)
high-ranking official n
منضرف شدن /mŭn-sa-rīf shŭdan/
change one's mind v
منصه /man-sa/
place of appearance n

منطقه , -ها/مناطق
/man-ta-qa, pl ma-nā-tīq/
area, region, belt, zone n
منطقوی /man-ta-qa-wi/
regional, local, zonal adj
منطقی /man-tī-qi/
reasonable, logical adj
منظره /man-za-ra/
view, vista, landscape n
منظم /mŭ-na-zam/
organized, methodical, systematic
adj
منظور /man-zur/
aim, intention, design n; authorized
adj
منظور کردن authorize vt
/man-zu-ri/ منظوری
authorization, approval n
منظومه /man-zu-ma/
system; story in verse n
منظومه شمسی
/man-zu-ma-yī sham-si/
solar system n
منع /man'/
prohibition, ban, injunction n
منع کردن prohibit, ban v
منع توقف /man' ta-wa-qŭf/
no parking (sign) phrs
منعم , -ان/ين /mŭn-'īm/
wealthy pers; benefactor n
منفجره explosive adj /mŭn-fa-jī-ra/
منفذ , -ها/منافذ
/man-faz, pl ma-nā-fīz/
aperture, orifice; pore n
منفرجه /mŭn-fa-rī-ja/
obtuse (angle) adj
منفعت , -ها/منافع
/man-fī-'at, pl ma-nā-fey/
interest (esp pl); advantage, profit n
منفی negative, minus adj /man-fi/
منفی کردن subtract v
منفی باف /man-fi bāf/
naysayer, nitpicker n, adj
منقار /mīn-qār/
beak, bill (bird's) (lit) n
منکر و نکير /mŭn-kar ŭ na-kir/
angel-examiners of the dead in
their graves n

a = cup, ā = long, aw = now, ay = sigh, e = bet, ey = obey

منگجک /mĭn-ga-jĭk/
Mengajek (dist) n

منگس n مگس see /man-gas/

منگنيز /man-ga-nĭz/
manganese (element) n

منور /mŭ-na-war/
enlightened; illuminated; Munawar
(m name) n

← علمای منور
the progressive mullahs

منوط بر <چيزی> /ma-nut bar/
dependent on, conditioned on
<sth> adj

منهدم /mŭn-ha-dĭm/
demolished, destroyed adj

منيلا /ma-ni-lā/ Manila (capital) n

مواد /ma-wād, sg mā-da/
pl of ماده n pl

مواد چرب کاری
/ma-wād-ĭ charb kā-ri/
lubricant; lubricants n pl

مواد خوراکه /ma-wād-ĭ kho-rā-ka/
foodstuffs n pl

مواد سوخت /ma-wād-ĭ sokht/
fuel (heating, cooking) n

مواد مخدر /ma-wād-ĭ mŭ-kha-dĭr/
narcotics n pl

مواد منفجر /ma-wād-ĭ mŭn-fa-jĭr/
explosive materials n

مواد منفجرناشده
/ma-wād-ĭ mŭn-fa-jĭr nā-shŭ-da/
UXO, unexploded ordnance n

مواد منفجره جابجا شده با در شخص
انتحار کننده
/ma-wād-ĭ mŭn-fa-jĭ-ra jā-ba-jā shŭ-
da bā shakhs-ĭ ĭn-tĭ-hār kŭ-nĭn-da/
PBIED, Personnel-Borne
Improvised Explosive Device (mil);
(colloq) suicide bomber n

موارد /ma-wā-rĭd, sg maw-rĭd/
pl of مورد n pl

موازنه /mŭ-wā-zĭ-na/
balance, equilibrium n

موازنه تجاری
/mŭ-wā-zĭ-na-yĭ tŭ-jā-ri/
scale (merchant's) n

موازی /mŭ-wā-zi/ parallel adj

موازين /ma-wā-zin/
standards, criteria n pl

مواصلات /mŭ-wā-sĭ-lāt/
communications n pl

← مواصلت کردن arrive together v

مواصلاتی /mŭ-wā-sĭ-lā-ti/
related to communications adj

مواضع /ma-wā-zey, sg maw-zey/
pl of موضع n pl

مواطن /mŭ-wā-tĭn, sg maw-tĭn/
pl of موطن n pl

مواعد /ma-wā-'ĭd, sg maw-'ĭd/
pl of موعد n pl

مواعيد /ma-wā-'ĭd, sg mi-'ād/
pl of ميعاد n pl

موافق /mŭ-wā-fĭq/
agreeing, concordant adj

← موافق بودن <با کسی>
agree <w/sb> vi

موافقت /mŭ-wā-fĭ-qat/
agreement; consent n

← موافقت کردن
agree, reach agreement v

موافقه n موافقت see /mŭ-wā-fĭ-qa/

مواقف /ma-wā-qĭf, sg maw-qĭf/
pl of موقف n pl

موالد /ma-wā-lĭd, sg maw-lĭd/
pl of مولد n pl

مواليد /ma-wā-lid, sg maw-lud/
pl of مولود n pl

موانع /ma-wā-ney, sg mā-ney/
pl of مانع n pl

موتر /mo-tar/ motor; automobile n

موتر تيز رفتار
/mo-tar-ĭ teyz raf-tār/
automobile n

موتر کرايی /mo-tar-ĭ kĭ-rā-yi/
rental car n

موتر کش کننده
/mo-tar-ĭ kash kŭ-nĭn-da/
tow truck n

موترران , -ها /mo-tar-rān (-wān)/
driver, chauffeur n

موترسيکل /mo-tar-sĭ-kĭl/
motorcycle n

موترسيکل /mo-tar-si-kĭl/
see مترسکل n

موتروان /mo-tar-wān/
n موترران see

موتروانی کردن
/mo-tar-wā-ni kardan/
drive (vehicle) vi

موتور /mo-tor/ engine, motor n

موثر /mŭ-wa-sīr/
effective; impressive adj

موثق /mŭ-wa-saq/
reliable, trustworthy adj

موثوق /mŭ-wa-suq/ adj موثق see

موج , -ها/امواج /mawj, pl am-wāj/ n
wave, surge (& fig) n

موج دار /mawj-dār/
wavy; watered (fabric) adj

موج دراز /mawj-ī da-rāz/
long-wave (radio) adj

موج شکن /mawj-ī shī-kan/
breakwater adj, n

موج کوتاه /mawj-ī ko-tāh/
shortwave (radio) adj

موج متوسط /mawj-ī mŭ-ta-wa-sīt/
medium-wave (radio) adj

موجه /maw-ja/ n موج see

موجب , -ات /mo-jīb, maw-jīb/
reason, cause, motive n

موحد , -ان/ها/ین /mŭ-wa-hīd/
monotheist n

موجز /mo-jaz/
concise, succinct, terse adj

موجود /maw-jud/
available, at hand adj; living being n
موجود بودن ←
be present; be available vi

موجودی /maw-ju-di/ inventory n

موجودیت /maw-ju-dī-yat/
availability, existence n

موجه /mŭ-wa-jah/
reasonable, acceptable, well-
founded adj

موخرمایی /mo-khŭr-mā-yi/
brunet(te), brown-haired adj

موخره /mŭ-wa-kha-ra/ rear guard n

موچی /mu-chi/
shoe repairman, cobbler n

مود /mod/ fashion, mode, vogue n

مودب /mŭ-wa-dab/
polite, civil, courteous adj

مودبانه /mŭ-wa-da-bā-na/
politely, courteously adv

مودت /mŭ-wa-dat/ friendship n

مودت آمیز /mŭ-wa-dat ā-meyz/
friendly adj

موذین /mŭ-wa-zin/ muezzin n

مور /mur/ caterpillar n

مورچل /mor-chal/
trench, parapet n

مورچه , -ها/گان /mŭr-cha/ ant n

مورچه خانه /mŭr-cha khā-na/
anthill n

مورخ , -ان/ها/ین /mu-rīkh/
scribe; historian n

مورخ /mŭ-wa-rakh/
dated, produced on a given date
adj

مورخه /mŭ-wa-ra-kha/
f form of مورخ

مورد , pl موارد /maw-rīd, pl ma-wā-rīd/
case, instance, occasion n
موارد ←
pl

مورد نظر /maw-rīd na-zar/
goal, aim n

مورفین /mor-fin, mo-rŭ-fin/
morphine (drug) n

مورم /mo-rŭm/ myrtle (shrub) n

موروث /maw-rus/
inherited, hereditary adj

موروثی /maw-ru-si/ adj موروث see

موریانه /mu-rī-yā-na/
termite; rust n

موزاییک /mo-zā-yik/ mosaic n

موزه /mo-za/
knee-length boots; museum n

موزیک /mu-zik/ n موسیقی see

موزیم /mo-zī-yam/ museum n

موزیک /mo-zik/ music n

موزیکال /mo-zi-kāl/
musical (production) n

موسس , -ان/ین /mŭ-wa-sīs/
founder, establisher n

موسسه , -ها/موسسات
/mŭ-wa-sī-sa, pl -sāt/
organization; institution; company,
firm n

موسسه خدمات خارجه
/mŭ-wa-sī-sa-yī khīd-māt-ī
khā-rī-ja/
Foreign Service Institute, FSI n

موسسه امنیتی خصوصی
/mŭ-wa-sĭ-sa-yĭ am-nĭ-ya-tĭ-yĭ khŭ-su-sĭ/
private security company n

موسوی , -ان/ها
/mu-sa-wĭ/
Jewish pers, Jew n; Mosaic adj

موسهی , -sā-, -hĭ/
/mu-sa-yĭ
Musayi (dist) n

موسی /mu-sā/
Moses (bibl, & m name) n

موسی خیل /mu-sā kheyl/
Musa Kheyl (dist) n

موسی قلعه /mu-sā qal-'a/
Musa Qala (dist) n

موسیقی /mu-si-qĭ/ n music
موسیقی دان , -ان/ها /mu-si-qĭ dān/
musicologist n

موسیقی نواز /mu-si-qĭ na-wāz/
musician, instrumentalist n

موسینی n /mu-sā-yĭ/ موسهی see
موش /mush/ n mouse
موش پران /mush-ĭ pa-rān/
flying squirrel, gray squirrel n

موش خرما /mush-ĭ khŭr-mā/
weasel; brown squirrel n

موش خور /mush khŭr/
mice-eater (insult) n

مشوش /mŭ-sha-wāsh/
anxious; unkempt adj

موصوف /maw-suf/
abovementioned n; characterized adj

موضع , -ها/مواضع
/maw-zey, pl ma-wā-zey/
place; situation; (mil) position n

موضوع , -ات/ها /maw-zo/
subject, topic, theme; subject matter n

موطن /maw-tĭn, pl mŭ-wā-tĭn/
hometown n

مواطن pl
موظف , -ین /mŭ-wa-zaf/
officer, official n; assigned; on duty adj

موعد /maw-'ĭd, pl ma-wā-'ĭd/
deadline, appointed time n

مواعد ← pl

موفق /mŭ-wa-faq/ successful adj
موفق بودن • موفق شدن ←
succeed vi

موفقانه /mŭ-wa-fa-qā-na/
successfully adv

موفقیت /mŭ-wa-fa-qĭ-yat/ success n
موقت /mŭ-wa-qat/
temporary, provisional, interim adj

موقتاً /mŭ-wa-qá-tan, -tán/
temporarily, provisonally adv

موقعیت /maw-qĭ-'ĭ-yat (-qĭ-yat)/
location, situation; status (social) n

موقعیت داشتن ‹در کجا›
/maw-qĭ-'ĭ-yat dāshtan/
be located ‹sw› v

موقف , -ها/مواقف
/maw-qĭf, pl ma-wā-qĭf/
situation; status n

موقوف /maw-quf/
suspended, fired, removed from office adj

موقوف کردن ←
suspend, fire, remove from office vi

موقوفی /maw-qu-fĭ/
suspension, firing, removal from office n

موکول /maw-kul/
postponed; pending adj
موکول کردن /maw-kul kardan/
postpone, put off vt

مولا master, lord; God n /maw-lā/
مولانا /maw-lā-na/
maulana, maulvi n

مولد /maw-lĭd, pl ma-wā-lĭd/
birthplace, homeland n

موالد ← pl
مولف , -ان/ها/ین /mŭ-wa-lĭf/
author, writer n

مولود /maw-lud, pl ma-wā-lid/
birth; birthday; creature n

موالید ← pl
مولود شریف /maw-lud-ĭ sha-rĭf/
the Prophet's Birthday n

مولوی /maw-la-wĭ/
maulvi, maulana n

موم wax, beeswax n /mum/
موم جامه /mum jā-ma/
oilcloth; wax paper n

مومند دره /mu-mand da-ra, mo-/
Mumand Dara (dist, ctr Basawul) n

مومی /mu-mi/ wax, waxen adj

مومیا /mu-mĭ-yā/ mummy n

مومیایی /mu-mĭ-yā-yi/
bitumen n; mummified adj

→ مومیایی کردن mummify vt

مونث /mū-wa-nas/
feminine (& gram) adj

مونولوگ /mo-no-log/
monologue, dramatic soliloquy n

مؤثر adj /mū-'a-sīr/ see مؤثر

موظف adj /mū-wa-zaf/ see موظف

موی , موی /muy, moy/
hair (esp f's); bristle n

موی بر /muy-bar, moy-/
depilatory agent n

موی تیار کردن /muy ta-yār kardan/
hair styling (for f) vt

موی چینک /muy chi-nak/
tweezers n

موی ساختگی /muy-ĭ sākh-ta-gi/
see موی عاریتی n

موی عاریتی /muy-ĭ ā-rĭ-ya-ti/
wig n

مه /ma/ (colloq) pron I

مهابل /ma-hā-bīl, sg mah-bal/
pl of مهبل (rare) n pl

مهاجر , -ان/ها/ین /mū-hā-jīr/
emigrant; immigrant n; emigrating adj

مهاجرت /mū-hā-jĭ-rat/
emigration; immigration; migration n

→ مهاجرت کردن
emigrate; immigrate; migrate v

مهاجم , -ان/ها/ین /mū-hā-jīm/
assailant, attacker n; attacking adj

مهار /ma-hār/
halter (camel's); (fig) control n

→ مهار کردن
bring under control (fig) v

مهاراجه /ma-hā-rā-ja/ maharaja n

مهارت /ma-hā-rat/
skill; proficiency n

→ مهارت داشتن
have a skill; be proficient v

مهبل , -ها/مهابل /mah-bal, pl ma-hā-bīl/
vagina n

مهبلی /mah-ba-li/ vaginal adj

مهتر , -ان /mīh-tar/
chief, leader; groom, stableman n

مهتر لام /mīh-tar lām/
Mehtarlam (seat) n

مهدی /mīh-di, mah-/
Mahdi (for Shias, a messiah) n

مهدویه /mah-da-wĭ-ya/
Mahdawiyya (hist, ascetic Musl sect) n

مهذب /mū-ha-zab/
cultured, polite adj

مهر /ma´-hīr, mahr/
divorce settlement as agreed prenuptially n

مهر /mī´-hīr, mīhr/ see میزان n

مهر /mū´-hīr, mūhr/
seal, stamp; signet ring; muhr (hist, gold coin) n

→ مهر کردن seal, stamp vt

مهربان /mīh-ra-bān/
kind; compassionate, merciful adj

مهربانی /mīh-ra-bā-ni/
kindness; compassion, mercy n

مهره /mūh-ra/
bead; vertebra; chess piece n

مهره دوزی /mūh-ra do-zi/
beading, beaded embroidery n

مهریه /mah-rī-ya/ seal, stamp n

مهم /mū-hīm/
important adj; (esp pl) important matter n

مهمات /mū-hĭ-māt/
ammunition; equipment; important matters n pl

مهمات ثقیله /mū-hĭ-māt-ĭ sa-qi-la/
heavy equipment n pl

مهماتِ جنگی /mū-hĭ-māt-ĭ jan-gi/
materiel (mil) n pl

مهمان , -ان/ها /mīh-mān/
visitor, guest n; visiting adj

→ مهمان کردن invite for a meal vt

مهمان خانه /mīh-mān khā-na/
guesthouse; guest room n

مهمان دار /mīh-mān dār/
hospitable adj; steward(ess) n

مهمان نواز /mīh-mān na-wāz/
hospitable, welcoming adj

مهمان نوازی /mīh-mān na-wā-zi/
hospitality n

مهمانی /mīh-mā-ni/
banquet, party; invitation n

مهمیز /mah-meyz/ spur (& bot) n

مهمیز دار /mah-meyz dār/
spurred, having spurs (& bot) adj

مهندس , -ان/ها/ین
/mŭ-han-dīs (man-dīs)/
architect n

مهندسی /mŭ-han-dī-si/
architecture n

مهناز /mah-nāz/ Mahnaz (f name) n

مئین /ma-yin/ n مین see

می /may/ wine (arch) n

می /mey, may/ May (month) n

میادین /ma-yā-din, sg may-dān/
pl of میدان n pl

میان /mī-yān/
interior; center, middle n

میان /mī-yān(-ī)/
between; among; within prep

میان اداری /mī-yān ĭ-dā-ri/
interagency adj

میان بر /mī-yān-bŭr/ shortcut n

← میان بر کردن take a short cut v

میان تهی /mī-yān-tī-hi/
hollow; w/o validity adj

میان جگری /mī-yān-jī-ga-ri/
mediation, arbitration;
intermediation n

← میان جگری کردن mediate v

میان خالی /mī-yān-khā-li/
میان تهی see adj

میان نشین /mī-yān nĭ-shin/
Meyan Neshin (dist) n

میان وند /mī-yān-wand/
infix (gram) n

میانجی /mī-yān-ji/
mediator, arbiter; intermediary n

میانگی /mī-yān-gi/ n میانجی see

← میانگی کردن mediate v

میانه /mī-yā-na/
average, mean, medium; central,
middle adj

میانه رو /mī-yā-na raw/
moderate (& pol) adj

میانه روی /mī-yā-na ra-wi/
moderation n

میانه سال /mī-yā-na sāl/
middle-aged adj

میت /ma-yĭt, pl am-wāt/
corpse, cadaver n

اموات pl ←

میثاق /mi-sāq/ treaty, pact n

میخ /meykh/
nail; peg, picket, stake n

میخانیک /mey-khā-nik/ mechanic n

میخانیکی /mey-khā-ni-ki/
mechanical adj

میخچه /meykh-cha/ callous, corn n

میخوش /may-khŭsh/
winey, w/complex flavors adj

میخک /mey-khak/ clove (spice) n

میدان , -ها/میادین
/may-dān, pl ma-yā-din/
field; public square n

میدان تعلیم /may-dān-ĭ ta'-lim/
training grounds/field n

میدان تینس /may-dān-ĭ tey-nīs/
tennis court n

میدان جنگ /may-dān-ĭ jang/
battlefield, field of war n

میدان شهر /may-dān shahr (shār)/
Maydan Shahr (seat) n

میدان قریه /may-dān-ĭ qar-ya/
village square n

میدان وردک /may-dān war-dak/
Maydan Wardak (prov) n

میدان هوایی /may-dān-ĭ ha-wā-yi/
airport, airfield n

میده کردن /may-da kardan/
pulverize vt

میر /mir/
mir (title for Prophet's
descendants); death n

میر بچه کوت /mir ba-cha kot/
Mir Bacha Kot (dist) n

میر واعظ /mir wā-'ĭz/
head preacher in capital n

میراث , -ها /mi-rās/
legacy, inheritance, patrimony;
heritage n

میراثی /mi-rā-si/
inherited, hereditary adj

میل بحری /mayl-ĭ bah-ri/
nautical mile n

میران Miran (ctr) n /mi-rān/
میرزا see /mir-zā/ n
میرمن /mir-mŭn/
Mrs., Madame (form of address) n
/mi-ra-mor/
Miramor (dist) n
میز table; desk n /meyz/
میزبان host n /meyz-bān/
میزبانی /meyz-bā-ni/
hosting, being a host n
میز تحریر /meyz-ĭ tah-rir/
desk, writing desk n
میز کار /meyz-ĭ kār/
desk, work table n
میزان /mi-zān/
Mizan (month, dist); Libra; balance;
measure n
← مهر (Farsi equivalent)
میزان الحراره /mi-zān-ŭl-ha-rā-ra/
thermometer n
میزان الهوا /mi-zā-nŭl-ha-wā/
barometer n
میزان مرگ و میر
/mi-zān-ĭ marg ŭ mir/
mortality rate n
میش ewe, f sheep n /meysh/
میعاد /mi-'ād, pl ma-wā-'id/
due date, cutoff; rendezvous n
← مواعید pl
میکانزم /mey-kā-nĭ´-zĭm/
مکانزم see n
میکانزه شده /mey-kā-nī-za shŭ-da/
مکانزه شده see adj
میکاییل Michael (bibl) n /mey-kā-yil/
میکرو /mi-kro/ مکرو pref & see
میکرو رایون /mik-ro-rā-yon/
میگذره Mikrorayon (1-4, city dists) n
/méy-gŭ-za-ra (mĭg´-za-ra)/
not bad, so-so phrs
میگون /may-gun/
wine-colored (lit) adj
میل , ـها/امیال /mayl, pl am-yāl/
desire, wish; inclination, tendency n
میل mile n /mayl, mil/
میل /mil/
bar, rod, shaft; unit, piece (artillery)
n

میل تفنگ /mil-ĭ tŭ-fang/
gun barrel; unit (gun) n
← ۵ میل تفنگ 5 rifles
← ۳۰ میل اسلحه مختلف انواع
30 various weapons
میل هوایی /mayl-ĭ ha-wā-yi/
air mile n
میل یونیورسل /mil-ĭ yu-ni-war-sal/
drive shaft n
میلاد /mi-lād/
birth; time of birth; birthday
(Prophet & Jesus only) n
میلادی /mi-lā-di/
A.D. (Anno Domini), C.E. adj
← سال ۱۹۸۱ میلادی (سال ۱۳۶۰
خورشیدی)
1981 A.D. (solar year 1360)
میلان /may-lān/
incline, slope; trend n
میله /mey-la/ picnic; fair, festival n
← میله کردن • میله رفتن
picnic, have a picnic v
میمنه /may-ma-na/
Maymana (seat) n
میمون /may-mun/ monkey, ape n
مین /mayn/ mine (explosive) n
مین بی جا کردن /mayn bey jā kardan/
mine clearance n; clear mines v
مین پاکی /mayn pā-ki/
mine clearance n
مین دار /mayn dār/ minefield n
مین گذاری /mayn gŭ-zā-ri/
laying mines n
مینو /mi-nu/ menu n
مینی ژوپ /mi-ni-zhop/ miniskirt n
میوزیک /mī-yu-zik/ موسیقی see
میوه , ـباب/جات /mey-wa, pl -bāb/jāt/
fruit (& coll) n
میوه دار /mey-wa-dār/
fruit-bearing adj
میوه دانی /mey-wa dā-ni/
fruit bowl n
میوه فروش /mey-wa fŭ-rosh/
fruit seller n

میه نشین /mī-ya nī-shin/
n میان نشین see

میهن /may-han/
homeland, fatherland n

ن

نا گفته نمانه /nā gŭf-ta na-mā-na/
by the way, incidentally phrs

نا ممکن /nā-mŭm-kĭn/
impossible adj

ناآرامی , -ها /nā-ā-rā-mi/
problem, difficulty; discomfort n

نامید /nā-ŭ-meyd/
discouraged, w/o hope adj

نامید شوی ! /nā-ŭ-meyd sha-wi/
may you become hopeless! (insult
used by f) phrs

نامید کننده /nā-ŭ-meyd kŭ-nĭn-da/
discouraging, disappointing n

نامیدی /nā-ŭ-mey-di/
hopelessness, disappointment n

نابرید /nā-bŭ-rid/
uncircumcised (& pers; & insult) adj,
n

نابود /nā-bud/
destroyed, annihilated adj

نابود کردن ←/ destroy, annihilate vt
نابودی /nā-bu-di/
destruction, annihilation; non-
existence n

نابغه , -ها/نوابغ
/nā-bĭ-gha, pl na-wā-bĭgh/
genius n

ناتو /nā-to/ NATO (mil) n
ناتوان /nā-ta-wān/
weak, powerless adj

ناجنس /nā-jĭns/
mongrel, not pedigreed; of poor
quality adj

ناجو /nā-ju/ pine (tree) n
ناجور /nā-jor/ sick, ill, unhealthy adj
ناچار /nā-chār/
compelled, forced adj; compulsorily;
necessarily; inevitably adv

ناچیز /nā-chiz/
insignificant; worthless adj

ناحق /nā-haq (nāq)/ unjust adj

ناحیه , -ها/نواحی
/nā-hĭ-ya (nā-ya), pl na-wā-hi/
area, region; city district n

ناخدا /nā-khŭ-dā/
ship captain (arch) n; w/o fear of
God adj

ناخاسته /nā-khās-ta/ unwilling adj
ناخن /nā-khŭn/
fingernails, toenails n

ناخن گرفتن ← trim/clip nails v
ناخنک /nā-khŭ-nak/
plectrum (worn on index finger) n

ناخنگیر /nā-khŭn-gir/ nail clipper n
ناخوان /nā-khān/ illiterate adj
ناخوانده /nā-khān-da/
uninvited; unread adj

ناخودگاه /nā-khŭ-dā-gāh/
subconscious adj

ناخوش /nā-khŭsh/
sick, ill; unhappy; unpleasant adj

ناد علی /nād a-li/ Nad Ali (dist) n
نادار /nā-dār/ poor, indigent adj
نادان /nā-dān/
ignorant, unwise; foolish adj

نادانسته /nā-dā-nīs-ta/
accidentally, inadvertently adv

نادانی /nā-dā-ni/
ignorance, foolishness n

نادر /nā-dīr/
rare, uncommon; Nader (m name)
adj, n

نادر شاه /nā-dīr shāh/
Nader Shah (hist, 20th-c Afgh king;
18th-c Persian king) n

نادر شاه کوت /nā-dīr shāh kot/
Nader Shah Kot (dist, ctr Kaparay)
n

نادره /nā-dī-ra; pl -rāt, na-wā-dīr/
rarity; extraordinary pers; Nadira (f
name) n

نادرات • نوادر ← pl forms
نادیدگی /nā-di-da-gi/
parvenu, upstart, nouveau riche n

نادیده /nā-di-da/ adj نودولت see
ناراض /nā-rāz/
angry; annoyed; dissatisfied adj

ناراض کردن ← anger; annoy vt

i = keep, ĭ = big, u = coop, ŭ = put, y = yet, ' = (glottal stop)   297

ناسیسم /nā-sí-sīm/ see نازیزم

ناسیونالست /nās-yu-nā-līst/
nationalist (pers) n

ناسیونالستی /nās-yu-nā-līs-ti/
nationalistic adj

ناشر , -ان/ها/ين /nā-shĭr/
publisher n

ناشر کتاب /nā-shĭr kĭ-tāb/
book publisher n

ناشتا /nāsh-tā/ breakfast n

ناشتایی /nāsh-tā-yi/
newlyweds' feast (sent by bride's parents) n

ناشی /nā-shi/ resulting, arising adj

ناصر /nā-sĭr/ Nasir (P tribe) n

ناصره /nā-sĭ-ra/ Nazareth (city) n

ناصری /nā-sĭ-ri/ Nasiri (P tribe) n

ناطقه /nā-tĭ-qa/ faculty of speech n

ناظر , -ان/ين /nā-zĭr/
observer; overseer n

ناظر سیاسی /nā-zĭr-ĭ sī-yā-si/
pundit n

ناعلاج /nā-'ĭ-lāj/
compelled, forced adj

ناعلاج ساختن ← compel, force vt

ناعلاجی /nā-'ĭ-lā-ji/ compulsion n

ناعم /nā-'ĭm/ soft adj

ناعمه /nā-'ĭ-ma/ f form of ناعم adj

ناف /nāf/
center, middle (fig); navel; umbilical cord n

نافذ /nā-fíz/
in force, in effect (laws); penetrating adj

نافذه /nā-fī-za/ f form of نافذ adj

نافرجام /nā-far-jām/
useless; inconclusive adj

نافرمان /nā-far-mān/
disobedient adj; snapdragon n

نافرمانی /nā-far-mā-ni/
disobedience n

نافرمانی کردن ← disobey v

نافع /nā-fey/
profitable; favorable adj

نافه /nā-fa/
musk; deer's musk gland; stamen n

ناقص /nā-qīs/
incomplete, imperfect; defective adj

نارس /nā-ras/
raw; unripe; immature adj

نارسیده /nā-ra-si-da/ see نارس adj

نارضایت /nā-ra-zā-yat/
annoyance, dissatisfaction n

نارنج /nā-rīnj/ sour orange n

نارنجی /nā-rīn-ji/
orange-colored adj

ناروی /nār-wey/
Norway (country) n

نارویژی , -ان/ها /nār-wey-zhi/
Norwegian (& pers, lang) adj, n

ناری /nā-ray/ Naray (dist) n

ناری /nā-ri/ fiery, related to fire adj

ناریال /nār-yāl/ coconut n

ناریه /nā-rī-ya/ f form of ناری adj

ناز /nāz/ conceit; flirtation n

ناز دادن ← pamper, coddle v

ناز دانه ← spoiled, pampered adj

نازا /nā-zā/ see نازای adj

نازای /nā-zāy/
barren, sterile, infertile adj

نازبو /nāz-bo/ basil, sweet basil n

نازبوی /nāz-boy/ see نازبو n

نازل /nā-zīl/
low (price); base, mean adj

نازک /nā-zŭk/
delicate, fine; tender adj

نازک اندام /nā-zŭk an-dām/
frail, of delicate constitution adj

نازک خیال /nā-zŭk khī-yāl/
perceptive, of subtle mind adj

نازک دل /nā-zŭk dīl/
sensitive, tender-hearted adj

نازی /nā-zi/
Nazi (f name); Nazi (hist, pol) n

نازیان /nā-zī-yān/ Nazeyan (dist) n

نازیزم /nā-zí-zīm/ Nazism n

ناس /nās/
nation, society (lit); (colloq) snuff n

ناسا /nā-sā/ NASA n

ناسپاس /nā-sĭ-pās/ ungrateful adj

ناسپاسی /nā-sĭ-pā-si/ ingratitude n

ناسکه /nā-sa-ka/
step- (relationship) adj

ناسوت /nā-sut/
humanity, human nature; material world n

ناقص اندام /nā-qĭs an-dām/
malformed adj

ناقص خرد /nā-qĭs khĭ-rad/
imbecile n

ناقل , -ان/ین /nā-qĭl/
carrier, vector (med); conductor n

ناقوس /nā-qus/ n (church) bell
pear n /nāk/ ناک

ناکاره /nā-kā-ra/
useless, good for nothing adj

ناکام /nā-kām/
unsuccessful, failed adj

← ناکام شدن fail vi

ناکامی , -ان/ها /nā-kā-mi/
failure (& pers) n

ناگاه /nā-gāh/ adj see ناگهان

ناگاهان /nā-gā-hān/ adj see ناگهان

ناگزیر /nā-gŭ-zir/
necessarily, certainly adv

ناگهان /nā-ga-hān/
sudden, abrupt adj

ناگهانی /nā-ga-hā-ni/ adj see ناگهان

ناگوارا /nā-gŭ-wā-rā/
disagreeable, unpleasant adj

نال /nāl/ n (pen, stylus) reed

نالان /nā-lān/
plaintive, moaning (& adv) adj, adv

نالش /nā-lĭsh/ n whining; moaning
← نالش کردن whine; moan v

نالیدن ؛ -نال- ؛ -نالید- /nā-li-dan-/
complain; moan; lament v

نام /nām/ name; reputation n
← نام گذاشتن name vt

نام آور , -ان /nām ā-war/
renowned, famous (& pers) adj, n

نام آوری /nā-mā-wa-ri/
renown, fame n

نام اختصاری /nām-ĭ ĭkh-tĭ-sā-ri/
abbreviation, short form n

نام بد /nām bad/
infamous, notorious adj

نام بدی /nām ba-di/
infamy, notoriety n

نام مستعار /nām-ĭ mŭs-ta-'ār/
pen name, pseudonym n

نام نویسی /nām na-wi-si/
enrollment, registration n
← نام نویسی کردن enroll, register

نام نهاد /nām nĭ-hād/ so-called adj
نام نهادن /nām nĭhādan/
نامبرده /nām-bŭr-da/ adj see نام گذاشتن
abovementioned (pers) adj

نامرد , -ان/ها /nā-mard/
coward, cad n; cowardly adj

نامزاد /nām-zād/ n see نامزد
نامزد /nām-zad (-zād, -zāt)/
fiancé(e); candidate n
← نامزد کردن nominate vt

نامزدی /nām-za-di/ n engagement

نامگذاری /nām-gŭ-zā-ri/
renaming (when converting to Islam) n

نامور /nā-war/ adj نام آور see

ناموس /nā-mus/
dignity, pride; honor, chastity (f's) n

ناموس /nā-mus, pl na-wā-mis/
law, principle; f family member n
← نوامیس pl

نامه /nā-ma/
document; letter; (in combined forms) official paper; publication n

نامه نگار /nā-ma nĭ-gār/
reporter, correspondent; letter writer n

نامی /nā-mi/
famous, renowned; infamous adj

نان , -ها /nān/
food; meal; (fig) a living n

نانا /nā-nā/ n see نعنا
نانبای /nān-bāy/ n see نانوا
نانبایی /nān-bā-yi/ n see نانوایی
نان بحری /nān-ĭ bah-ri/ seafood n
نان چاشت /nān-ĭ chāsht/
lunch, noon meal n

نان خشک /nān-ĭ khŭshk/ bread n
نان شب /nān-ĭ shab/
dinner, supper n

نان شب مانده /nān-ĭ shab mān-da/
leftovers (food) n

نانوا , -ها/یان /nān-wā/ baker n
نانوای /nān-wāy/ n see نانوا
نانوایی /nān-wā-yi/ bakery n
ناور /nā-wūr/
Nawur (dist, ctr Du Abi) n

i = keep, ĭ = big, u = coop, ŭ = put, y = yet, ' = (glottal stop)   299

نپتون /nīp-tun/
Neptune (planet, f name) n

نت /nat/ nut (mechanical) n

نت و بولت /nat ŭ bolt/
nut & bolt phrs

نتایج /na-tā-yīj, sg na-ti-ja/
pl of نتیجه n pl

نتیجه , ها- /na-ti-ja, pl na-tā-yīj/
result, consequence, outcome n

نتیجه بخش /na-ti-ja baksh/
useful, efficacious adj

نتیجه گیری کردن /na-ti-ja gi-ri kardan/
conclude, infer, deduce v

نثر /ná-sīr, nasr/ prose n

نثری /nas-ri/ prosaic adj

نجات <از چیزی> /nī-jāt/
escape; rescuing; liberation <from sth> n

← نجات دادن <کسی/چیزی را>
rescue, save <sb/sth> vt

نجار /na-jār/ carpenter; joiner n

نجارک /na-jā-rak/
woodpecker; unskilled carpenter n

نجاری /na-jā-ri/ carpentry n

نجبا /nŭ-ja-bā/
nobility, aristocracy n pl

نجد /najd/ plateau; Najd (region) n

نجراب /nīj-rāb/ Nejrab (dist) n

نجم
/ná-jīm, najm; pl an-jūm, nŭ-jum/
star; planet n

← انجم • نجوم pl

نجوم /nŭ-jum; sg ná-jīm, najm/
pl of نجم n pl

نجومی , ان/ها- /nŭ-ju-mi/
astrologer n; astrological adj

نجیب /na-jib/
exalted, noble adj; Najib (m name);
Najibullah (hist) n

نجیب الدوله /na-jib-ŭd-daw-la/
Najib ud-Dawla (hist, Rohilla
Pashtun leader) n

نجیبه /na-ji-ba/
Najiba (f name) n; noble, corrosion-
resistant (metal) adj

نحل /ná-hīl, nahl/ bee (lit) n

ناوقت (-وخت) /nā-waqt (-wakht)/
late, tardy (& adv) adj, adv

ناول /nā-wŭl/ novel n

ناوه /nā-wa/ Nawa (dist) n

ناوه بارکزی /nā-wa-yī bā-rak-zay/
Nawa-ye Barakzai (dist) n

ناهمخوانی , ها- /nā-ham-khā-ni/
discrepancy, difference n

ناهمگون /nā-ham-gun/
dissimilar, different adj

ناهید /nā-hid/
Nahid (f name); Venus (planet) n

نایاب /nā-yāb/ unobtainable adj

نایب الحکومه
/nā-yī-bŭl-hŭ-ko-ma/
see والی n

نایتروجن /nāy-tro-jan/
nitrogen n

نایجیر /nāy-jeyr/ Niger (country) n

نایجیری , ان/ها- /nāy-jey-ri/
Nigerois, Nigerien adj, n

نایجیریا /nāy-jey-rī-yā/
Nigeria (country) n

نایجیریایی , ان/ها-
/nāy-jey-rī-yā-yi/
Nigerian (& pers) adj, n

نایره /nā-yī-ra/ flame (& fig) n

نایل شدن <به چیزی>
/nā-yīl shŭdan/
attain <sth>; succeed <at sth> v

نبات , ات- /na-bāt/
plant; herb; hard candy n

نبات شناس /na-bāt shī-nās/
botanist n

نبات شناسی /na-bāt shī-nā-si/
botany n

نباتات /na-bā-tāt/
vegetation, plant life n pl

نبادا /ná-bā-dā/ see مبادا adv

نبرد /na-bard/
battle, combat, fight, war (lit) n

نبرد آزموده /na-bard āz-mu-da/
battle-hardened adj

نبض /nabz/ pulse; (fig) inclination n

← نبض دیدن take a pulse v

نبی /na-bi, pl an-bī-yā/
prophet; Prophet (Mohamed) n

← انبیا pl

نبیره /na-bi-ra/ (great-)grandchild n

---

a = cup, ā = long, aw = now, ay = sigh, e = bet, ey = obey

نحو , ها-/انحا /nahw, pl an-hā/
way; method; (gram) syntax n

نحیف /na-hif/ weak adj

نخ /nŭkh/ thread, string n

← نخ تابیدن • نخ رسیدن
wind thread v

نخاس /na-khās/
cattle market; (formerly) slave market n

نخاع /nŭ-khā/ spinal marrow n

نخاع شوکی /nŭ-khā'-ī shaw-ki/
spinal cord n

نخاعی /nŭ-khā-'i/
spinal, vertebral adj

نخت /nakht/ نقد n see

نخچ /nakhch/ نقش n see

نخچه /nakh-cha/
strange, odd, funny adj

نخچیر /nakh-chir/
hunt (arch); game, prey; nakhchir (deer) n

← نخچیر افگندن • نخچیر کردن
hunt (arch) v

← فیروز نخچیر
Firoz Nakhchir (dist) n

نخست /nŭ-khŭst/ first; foremost adj

نخش /nakhsh/ نقش n see

نخص /nŭkhs/ نقص n see

نخل /ná-khīl, nakhl/
palm tree, date palm n

نخلستان /nakh-lĭs-tān/ palm grove n

نخود /na-khod/
chickpea, garbanzo bean n

نخودی /na-kho-di/
chickpea-colored adj

نخی /na-khi/
cotton, made of cotton adj

نخیر /na-khayr/ no adv

نخیل /na-khil/ نخل n see

ندا /nĭ-dā/
exclamation, interjection n

ندانسته /na-dā-nĭs-ta/
accidentally, inadvertently adv

ندایه /nĭ-dā-yīa/
exclamation point n

ندبه /nad-ba/
mourning, lamentation; weeping n

← ندبه کردن
mourn; weep n

نذر /ná-zĭr, nazr/
votive offering; cash gift to ruler or noble n

نر /nar/ male; manly, virile adj

نراد /na-rād/
cunning, sly adj; backgammon player n

نرخ /nĭrkh/
rate; cost per unit; tariff; Nerkh (dist, ctr Kan-e Ezat) n

نرخ بازار /nĭrkh-ī bā-zār/
market rate n

نرخ تبادل /nĭrkh-ī ta-bā-dĭl/
exchange rate n

نرخ نامه /nĭrkh-nā-ma/
price list; rate schedule n

نرد /nard/ backgammon n

نردبان /nard-bān/ ladder n

نرس , ها-/ان /nars/ nurse n

نرگس /nar-gĭs/
narcissus (flower); Nargis (f name) n

نرم /narm/ soft adj

نرمتن , ان- /narm-tan/ mollusc n

نرمش /nar-mĭsh/
flexibility; gentleness n

نرمش پذیر /nar-mĭsh pa-zir/
flexible, adaptable adj

نرمش پذیری /nar-mĭsh pa-zi-ri/
flexibility, adaptability n

نرمه گوش /nar-ma-yī gosh/
earlobe n

نرمی گوش /nar-mi-yī gosh/
نرمه گوش see n

نرنگ /nar-rang/ Narang (dist) n

نره /na-ra/
male (animal) adj; penis (of slaughtered animal); stalk, stem (plant) n

نزار /nĭ-zār/ skinny; weak adj

نزاع /nĭ-zā/ struggle, fighting n

← نزاع کردن struggle, fight v

نزد /nazd(-ī)/
next to; for, with, in the opinion of prep

نزده /nŭz-dah/ nineteen n, adj

نزدهم /nŭz-da-hŭm/ nineteenth adj

نزدهمین /nŭz-da-hŭ-min/
nineteenth (lit, oft before n) adj

نزدیک /naz-dik(-ī) (nīz-)/
close to, near (to) prep

نزدیکان /naz-di-kān (nīz-)/
kinfolk, relatives n pl

نزول /nŭ-zul/
decline, slump (prices); revelation (of Quranic verse) n

نزولی /nŭ-zu-li/ declining adj

نژاد /nī-zhād/
race; lineage; subspecies; breed, strain n

نژاد شناس /nī-zhād shī-nās/
ethnologist n

نژاد شناسی /nī-zhād shī-nā-si/
ethnology n

نساجی /na-sā-ji/ textile, weaving adj

نسب /na-sab, pl an-sāb/
lineage, stock n

← انساب pl

← نسب داشتن <به کسی>
be related <to sb> v

نسب نامه /na-sab nā-ma/
family tree; pedigree n

نسبت <چیزی> /nīs-bat(-ī)/
due <to sth> prep

نسبت به /nīs-bat ba/
compared to, relative to, than prep

نسبتاً /nīs-ba-tan/
comparatively, relatively adv

نسبی /nīs-bi/ relative adj

نسبیت /nīs-bī-yat/ relativity n

نسترن /nas-ta-ran/
eglantine, sweetbriar (white; flower) n

نستعلیق /nas-ta'-liq/
nastaliq (callig style) n

نسخ /naskh/
copying, transcription; naskh (callig style) n

نسخه ، -ها /nŭs-kha/
copy, duplicate; prescription; recipe n

← نسخه را نوشتن
prescribe, write a prescription v

نسخه خطی /nŭs-kha-yī kha-ti/
manuscript (handwritten) n

نسخه عکس /nŭs-kha-yī aks/
print (photo) n

نسر طایر /ná-sīr-ī tā-yīr/
Altair (double star) n

نسرین /nas-rin/
jonquil, yellow narcissus; Nasrin (f name) n

نسطور /nas-tur/ Nestor (hist) n

نسطور ، -ان/ها /nas-tu-ri/
Nestorian (hist) n

نسک /nask/
lentil; chapter of Avesta n

نسل /ná-sīl, nasl/
breed, stock; offspring; generation n

نسل گیری /ná-sīl gi-ri/
animal husbandry, breeding n

نسلی /nas-li/ purebred adj

نسوار /nas-wār/ snuff n

نسوار دهن /nas-wār-ī dān/
snuff for oral intake n

نسواری /nas-wā-ri/
brown, snuff-colored adj; snuff addict n

نسوان /nīs-wān/ women [< Ar] n pl

نسی /nŭ-say/ Nusay (ctr) n

نسیم /na-sim/
breeze; pleasant scent; Nasim (m name) n

نسیمه /na-si-ma/ Nasima (f name) n

نشان /nī-shān/ mark; target n

← نشان دادن <چیزی را به کسی>
show; indicate <sth to sb> vt

← نشان زدن
practice target shooting v

← نشان گرفتن aim, take aim v

نشان انگشت کردن <به کسی>
/nī-shān-ī an-gŭsht kardan/
make an impression <on sth> v

نشان دهنده /nī-shān dī-hīn-da/
indicator, indication, sign n

نشان زن /nī-shān zan/
sharpshooter n

نشان زنی /nī-shān za-ni/
marksmanship n

نشان گیری /nī-shān gī-ri/
aiming, taking aim n

نشان نگاه /nĭ-shān nĭ-gāh/
target, bullseye; sight (on gun) n
نشانچی /nĭ-shān-chi/
sharpshooter n
نشاندن ؛ -نشان- ؛ نشاند-
/nĭ-shān-dan/
seat, set; plant, transplant; mount;
set, lay (trap) vt
نشانه /nĭ-shā-na/
sign, mark; target; sight (on gun);
index; (gram) marker; symptom n
نشانه اضافت /nĭ-shā-na-yĭ ĭ-zā-fat/
adjective marker n
نشانی /nĭ-shā-ni/ نشانه n see
starch n /nĭ-shā-yĭs-ta/ نشایسته
نشایسته یی /nĭ-shā-yĭs-ta-yi/
starchy adj
نشر , -ات /ná-shĭr, nashr/
spread, dissemination; broadcast;
publication n

نشر اسلحه هسته وی
/ná-shĭr-ĭ as-la-ha-yĭ has-ta-wi/
nuclear proliferation n

نشریه , -ها/نشریات
/nash-ri-ya, pl -yāt/
publication; flier, handbill n
نشست /nĭ-shast/
session, meeting; landing (of
aircraft) n

نشست و برخاست
/nĭ-shast ŭ bar-khāst/
takeoff & landing phrs
نشستن ؛ -نشین- ؛ نشست-
/nĭ-shas-tan/
sit; perch; occupy a dwelling; laze vi
growth; development n /nashw/ نشو
نشه /nĭ-sha/
drunk, inebriated adj; drunkenness
n

نشیده /na-shi-da/
verse, poem; song n
نشیمن /nĭ-shi-man/
dwelling, abode; sitting n
نشیمن گاه /nĭ-shi-man gāh/
n نشیمن see
نشیمن گه /nĭ-shi-man gah/
n نشیمن see

نصارا /na-sā-rā, sg nas-rā-ni/
pl of نصرانی n pl
نصایح /na-sā-yĭh, sg na-si-hat/
pl of نصیحت n pl
installation, setup n /nasb/ نصب
install vt نصب کردن ←
/nasb ŭ mŭn-tāzh/ نصب و منتاژ
installation & setup phrs
نصپ n /nĭsp/ نصف see
نصرانی , -ان/ها/نصارا
/nas-rā-ni, pl na-sā-rā/
Nazarene, Christian n; related to
Nazareth adj
نصرانیت /nas-rā-nĭ-yat/
Christianity, Christendom n
middle; half n /nĭsf (nĭsp)/ نصف
midnight n /nĭsf-ĭ shab/ نصف شب
نصواری /nas-wā-ri/ نسواری adj see
/na-sib/ نصیب
part, portion, share; fate, fortune n
نصیحت , -ها/نصایح
/na-si-hat (-yāt), pl na-sā-yĭh/
advice, admonition n
advise v نصیحت کردن ←
نصیحت آمیز /na-si-hat ā-meyz/
advisory, admonitory adj
نصیحت پذیر /na-si-hat pa-zir/
receptive to admonition adj
نصیحت شنو /na-si-hat shĭ-naw/
adj نصیحت پذیر see
Nasir (m name) n /na-sir/ نصیر
see همایون n نصیر الدین همایون ←
نطاق , -ان/ها /na-tāq/
orator; newscaster; spokesperson n
/nŭt-fa/ نطفه
offspring; embryo; sperm n
speech, oration n /nŭtq/ نطق
speak, orate v نطق کردن ←
/nŭtq i-rād kardan/ نطق ایراد کردن
v نطق کردن see
نظار /na-zār/
oversight, supervision n
supervisory council هیئتِ نظار ←

نظارت /na-zā-rat/
oversight, supervision; scrutiny, surveillance *n*

← نظارت کردن
oversee, supervise; scrutinize, surveil *v*

نظارت خانه /na-zā-rat khā-na/
detention center (pre-trial) *n*

نظافت cleanliness *n* /nī-zā-fat/

نظام /nī-zām/
system, structure, order; regime *n*

نظام نامه /nī-zām nā-ma/
legal code (arch) *n*

نظامی , -ان/ها /nī-zā-mi/
military, martial *adj*; member of military *n*

نظایر /na-zā-yīr/
examples; the like *n pl*

← و نظایر آن
and the like

نظر /na-zar/
vision, eyesight; look, glance; opinion *n*

نظر باز ogler (pers) *n* /na-zar bāz/
نظر بازی ogling *n* /na-zar bā-zi/
← نظر بازی کردن ogle *v*
نظر به <چیزی> /na-zar ba/
depending on <sth> *prep*

← نظر داشتن have an opinion *v*
← نظر دوختن stare *v*
← نظر شدن
be/come under the evil eye *vi*

نظری /na-za-ri/
theoretical; speculative *adj*

نظریات /na-za-rī-yāt, sg -ya/
pl of نظریه *n pl*

نظریه , -ها /na-za-rī-ya, pl -yāt/
opinion, comment; theory; theorem; speculation, abstract reasoning *n*

نظم /ná-zīm, nazm/
arrangement, order; discipline *n*

← نظم دادن
arrange, order; discipline *v*

نظیر alike, similar *adj* /na-zir/
نعره shout, call *n* /na'-ra (nā-)/
← نعره زدن shout (once) *v*
← نعره کشیدن cry out (at length) *v*
← نعره کردن call out (to sb) *v*

نعش corpse *n* /na'sh/
نعناع spearmint, mint *n* /na'-nā/
نعیم /na-'im/
comfort; amenity; Naim (m name) *n*

نغز /naghz/
nice, good; marvelous; nimble *n*

نغزک /nagh-zak/
marvel (dim); mango *n*

نغمه , -ها/نغمات
/nagh-ma, pl na-gha-māt/
tune, melody *n*

نغمه خوان /nagh-ma khān/
see نغمه سرا *n, adj*

نغمه زن singer (f) *n* /nagh-ma zan/
نغمه سرا /nagh-ma sa-rā/
singer; songwriter *n*; singing *adj*

نفاذ implementation *n* /nī-fāz/
نفت oil, petroleum *n* /nīft/
نفت و گاز oil & gas *phrs* /nīft ŭ gāz/
/nafkh/
bloat, bloating; blowing (on mus instr) *n*

← نفخ کردن bloat (stomach) *vi*
نفر , -ها /na-far/
person, individual; (mil) soldier, private *n*

نفر پذیرش /na-far-ī pa-zi-rīsh/
receptionist *n*

نفرت hatred, antipathy *n* /naf-rat/
← نفرت داشتن • نفرت کردن <به کسی/چیزی>
hate <sb/sth> *v*

نفرت آمیز /naf-rat ā-meyz/
hateful, showing hatred *adj*

نفرین /naf-rin/
curse; damnation, doom *n*

← نفرین شدن
be cursed; be doomed *vi*

← نفرین کردن
curse; damn, doom *vt*

نفرین شده /naf-rin shŭ-da/
cursed; doomed *adj*

نفس , -ها/انفاس /na-fas, pl an-fās/
breath; pause, moment *n*

← نفس کشیدن breathe *vi*

نفس , ـها/نفوس/انفس
/nafs; pl nŭ-fus, an-fŭs/
nature, essence; soul, spirit,
(Sufism) self, ego; psyche; mind;
breath n

نفس الامر /na-fàs-ŭl-á-mĭr/
essence of the matter n

نفس تنگی asthma n /na-fas tan-gi/

نفس کوتاهی /na-fas ko-tā-hi/
see نفس تنگی n

نفسانی /naf-sā-ni/
mental, psychological adj

نفع /naf-'a, naf'/
advantage, benefit; gain, profit;
interest n

نفقه /na-fa-qa, pl -qāt/
support (material; & of one's
household) n

← نفقات pl
← نفقه دادن • نفقه کردن
support (materially) vt

نفوذ /na-fuz/
influence, prestige; infiltration,
penetration n

← نفوذ داشتن ‹سر کسی/چیزی›
have influence ‹on sb/sth› vi

نفوذ پذیر /na-fuz pa-zir/
malleable, open to argument adj

نفوذ ناپذیر /na-fuz nā-pa-zir/
impervious to argument adj

نفوس /nŭ-fus, sg nafs/
pl of نفس n pl

نفوس /nŭ-fus/
population; inhabitants n

نفوس شماری /nŭ-fus shŭ-mā-ri/
census n

نفیر cry for help (arch) n /na-fir/
← نفیر کشیدن cry for help v

نفیس /na-fis/
delicate, fine; exquisite; precious,
costly adj

نق whining, nagging n /nĭq/
← نق زدن whine, nag v

نقاب /nĭ-qāb/
mask, veil; helmet visor n

← نقاب پوشیدن wear a mask/veil v

نقاش , ـان/ها /na-qāsh/
artist, painter, portraitist n

نقاشی painting adj /na-qā-shi/

نقاط /nŭ-qāt, sg nŭq-ta/
pl of نقطه n pl

نقاط نظامی /nŭ-qāt-ĭ nĭ-zā-mi/
military objectives, strategic
locations n pl

نقال cheater (on exam) n /na-qāl/

نقب /ná-qĭb, naqb (ná-qĭm)/
tunnel, mine, sap (mil) n

← نقب زدن • نقب کندن
dig a tunnel (mil) v

نقد /naqd (nakht), pl nŭ-qud/
cash; criticism n; on hand (money)
adj; in cash adv

← نقود pl
نقداً in cash adv /náq-dan, -dán/

نقرس gout (med) n /nĭq-rīs/

نقره silver n /nŭq-ra/

نقره کار , ـان/ها /nŭq-ra kār/
silver-plated adj; silversmith n

نقره گون /nŭq-ra gun/
silver-colored, silvery adj

نقره یی /nŭq-ra-yi/
silver, made of silver; silver-colored
adj

نقسیه /na-qŭ-sĭ-ya/
Nicosia (capital) n

نقش /naqsh (nakhch, nakhsh)/
drawing, painting; pattern; role n

نقش کردن draw/paint a picture
نقش بازی کردن
/naqsh bā-zi kardan/
play a role v

نقش بندی , ـان/ها /naqsh ban-di/
Naqshbandiyya member n

نقش بندیه /naqsh ban-dī-ya/
Naqshbandiyya (Sufi order) n

← حضرت hazrat
(title for Naqshbandiyya leaders)

نقشه /naq-sha/
layout, scheme; blueprint; map n

نقشه کش /naq-sha kash/
cartographer n

نقشه کشی /naq-sha ka-shi/
cartography; designing, planning n

i = keep, ĭ = big, u = coop, ŭ = put, y = yet, ' = (glottal stop)   305

نقص /nŭqs (nŭkhs)/
defect, flaw; shortcoming; harm, damage; business loss *n*
← نقص داشتن be defective *vi*
← نقص کردن take a loss *vi*
نقصان /nŭq-sān (nŭkh-)/
miscarriage (fetus) *n*
← نقصان کردن miscarry (fetus) *v*
نقض /naqz/
violation, breach (law, principle) *n*
نقطه , -ها/نقاط /nŭq-ta, pl nŭ-qāt/
point, decimal point; period; dot; place *n*
نقطه گذاری /nŭq-ta-yĭ gŭ-zā-ri/
punctuation *n*
نقطه گذاشتری
نقطه گذاری see /nŭq-ta-yĭ gŭ-zāsh-ta-ri/ *n*
نقل /ná-qĭl, naql/
copy; quote; cheating (on exam); transportation; change of residence *n*
نقل almond candy *n* /nŭ´-qŭl, nŭql/
نقم see نقب /ná-qĭm, naqm/
نقیض /na-qiz/
contradictory, incompatible *adj*
نکاح /nĭ-kāh/
wedding (ceremony); marriage contract *n*
← نکاح صغیره child marriage *n*
نکاح خط /nĭ-kāh khat/
marriage certificate *n*
نکره indefinite (gram) *adj* /na-kĭ-ra/
نکتایی tie, necktie *n* /nĭk-tā-yĭ/
نکل /nĭ´-kĭl, nĭkl/
nickel (metal, U.S. coin) *n*
نکلی nickel *adj* /nĭk-li/
نکوتین nicotine *n* /nĭ-ko-tin/
نکوهش /nĭ-ko-hĭsh/
reproach, rebuke *n*
نکوهیده /nĭ-ko-hi-da/
contemptible *adj*
نگار painting, drawing *n* /nĭ-gār/
نگارش , -ها writing *n* /nĭ-gā-rĭsh/
← اصول نگارش principles of writing
← نگارش تفسیری expository writings

نگارگر painter, artist *n* /nĭ-gār-gar/
نگاه , -ها /nĭ-gāh/
guarding, watching; look; keeping, holding *n*
← نگاه داشتن preserve; keep *v*
← نگاه دوختن stare (fig) *v*
← نگاه کردن watch, guard; hold, keep; store, save; preserve; raise (animals) *vt*
نگاه دار /nĭ-gāh dār/
conservator; protector *n*
نگاه داری /nĭ-gāh dā-ri/
conservation; preservation, maintenance; protecting *n*
نگاه داشت
نگاه داری see
نگاه هوس آلود
/nĭ-gāh-ĭ ha-was ā-lud/
leer, lustful gaze *n*
نگاهبان /nĭ-gāh-bān/
guard, watchman; guardian, protector *n*
نگاهبانی کردن
/nĭ-gāh-bā-ni kardan/
keep guard, stand watch; work as a guard *vi*
نگران /nĭ-ga-rān/
anxious, uneasy *adj*; observer, watchman; bus conductor *n*
نگرانی /nĭ-ga-rā-ni/
anxiety, nervousness; observation, supervision *n*
← نگرانی داشتن
‹راجع به چیزی›
worry; be concerned ‹about sth› *vi*
نگو ! /ná-go/
do not say (neg imper, colloq) *v*
نگون /nĭ-gun/
upside-down, inverted (arch) *adj*
نگون بخت /nĭ-gun bakht/
unfortunate, unlucky *adj*
نگه see نگاه *n* /nĭ-gah/
نگهت fragrance (lit) *n* /nĭg-hat/
نگین /nĭ-gin/
ring set with jewels; main gem in a ring *n*
نل pipe, tube *n* /nal/
نل دوان plumber *n* /nal da-wān/

306   a = c<u>u</u>p, ā = l<u>o</u>ng, aw = n<u>ow</u>, ay = s<u>igh</u>, e = b<u>e</u>t, ey = ob<u>ey</u>

نل دوانی /nal da-wā-ni/
plumbing, plumber's work n

نل های بدرفت /nal-hā-yī bad-raft/
sewer pipes/system n pl

نم /nam/
dampness, moisture (surface);
tears n

نما /nŭ-mā/
look, appearance; facade n

نماز /na-māz/ prayer (Musl) n
← نماز خواندن /na-māz/ v
pray (Musl)

نماز جمعه /na-māz-ī jŭm-'a/
Friday prayers n

نمایان /nŭ-mā-yān/
apparent; obvious adj

نمایاندن ؛ -نمایان- ؛ نمایاند-
/nŭ-mā-yān-dan/
indicate, show; depict, portray vt

نمایانگر /nŭ-mā-yān-gar/
guide; indicator n

نمایش , -ها /nŭ-mā-yīsh/
display, screening (film), exhibition,
play (theater) n

نمایشگاه /nŭ-mā-yīsh-gāh/
exhibition, fair n

نماینده , -گان/ها /nŭ-mā-yīn-da/
representative, agent, proxy;
exhibitor n

نمبر /nam-bar/ number n

نمبر پلیت /nam-bar pĭ-leyt/
license plate (vehicle) n

نمدار /nam-dār/ moist, damp adj

نمره , -ها/نمرات /nŭm-ra, pl -rāt/
number; score, grade n

نمره اول /nŭm-ra a-wāl/
first-rate, excellent n

نمک /na-mak/
salt; (fig) flavor, savor n
← نمک انداختن • نمک پاشیدن
salt vt

نمک آب /na-ma-kāb/
brine; Namak Ab (dist) n

نمک حرام /na-mak ha-rām/
disloyal, unfaithful adj

نمک حلال /na-mak ha-lāl/
loyal, faithful adj

نمکدان /na-mak-dān/
salt container, salt shaker n

نمکدانی /na-mak-dā-ni/
see نمکدان n

نمکی /na-ma-ki/
salty; (colloq) attractive adj

نمودن ؛ -نمای- ؛ نمود-
/na-mu-dan/, /méynŭmāyŭm//
do, make (lit); exhibit, show; seem,
appear v

نمونه /na-mu-na/
example, model; sample; prototype
n

ننگ /nang/
honor (Pashtunwali); shame,
disgrace, dishonor n

ننگرهار /nan-gar-hār/
Nangarhar (prov) n

ننگی /nan-gi/
disgraceful, shameful adj

ننگین /nan-gin/ see ننگی adj
mom, mother (colloq) n /na-na/ ننه

ننو /na-nu/
sister-in-law, husband's sister n

نو /naw/
new, recent; modern (& adv) adj,
adv

نو /no/ نه see

نو به دولت رسیده
/naw ba daw-lat ra-si-da/
نودولت see adj

نو بهار /naw ba-hār/
Naw Bahar (dist) n

نو عروس /naw 'a-rus/
newlywed f; (fig) blossom, flower n

نو محافظه کار , -ان/ها
/naw-mŭ-hā-fī-za-kār/
neoconservative n

نو محافظه کاری
/naw-mŭ-hā-fī-za-kā-ri/
neoconservatism n

نو وارد /naw wā-rīd/
newly-arrived (& pers) adj, n

نوا /na-wā/
melody; sound; prosperity n

نوابغ /na-wā-bīgh, sg nā-bi-gha/
نابغه pl of n pl

نواحی /na-wā-hi, sg nā-hī-ya/
ناحیه pl of n pl

i = keep, ī = big, u = coop, ŭ = put, y = yet, ' = (glottal stop)   307

نواختن ؛ -نواز- ؛ نواختـ
/na-wākh-tan/
cherish; play, perform (mus instr) vt

نوادر /na-wā-dīr, sg nā-dī-ra/
pl of نادره n pl

نواده , -گان/ها /na-wā-da/
grandchild (lit) n

نوار /na-wār/ ribbon n

نوازندگی /na-wā-zīn-da-gi/
performance (mus) n

نوازنده , -گان/ها /na-wā-zīn-da/
performer (mus) n

نواسه /na-wā-sa/ grandchild n

نوامبر /na-wām-bar/ n see نومبر

نوامیس /na-wā-mis, sg nā-mus/
n pl of ناموس

نوامیس طبیعت
/na-wā-mis-ī ta-bi-'at/
laws/principles of nature n pl

نوبت /no-bat/
turn (in a game); instance, time n

نوبتی /no-ba-ti/
intermittent (fever) adj

نوح /nuh/ Noah (bibl) n

نوخاسته /naw-khās-ta/
adolescent, teenage (& pers) adj, n

نوخان /naw-khān/ adj, n see نوخاسته

نود /na-wad/ ninety n, adj

نودم /na-wa-dūm/ ninetieth

نودمین /na-wa-dŭ-min/
ninetieth (lit, oft before n) adj

نودولت /naw-daw-lat/
nouveau riche adj

نوده /naw-da/ sprout, shoot n

نور /nawr/ decoy n

نور /nur/
light; brightness; (fig) awareness n

نور چشم /nur-ī chá-shīm/
eyesight; beloved child n

نورزی /nur-zay/
Nurzai, Noorzai (P tribe) n

نورستان /nu-rīs-tān/
Nurestan (prov) n

نورسیده /naw-ra-si-da/
adj, n see نوخاسته

نورستانی /nu-rīs-tā-ni/
Nurestani (lang) n

نورسته /naw-rŭs-ta/
newly-sprouted adj

نورسیده /naw-ra-si-da/ newborn adj

نورگل /nur-gal/ Nurgal (dist) n

نورگرم /nur-ga-ram, -rām/
Nurgaram (dist) n

نورمال /nor-māl/ normal adj

نوروز /naw-roz/ New Year's Day n

نوروزی /naw-ro-zi/
New Year's adj; New Year's present n

نورولوژست /no-ro-lo-zhīst/
neurologist n

نورولوژی /no-ro-lo-zhi/
neurology n

نوزاد /naw-zād/
newborn, newborn baby; larva, grub; Nawzad (dist) n

نوسان , -ات/ها /naw-sān/
wavering, vacillation; oscillation n

نوش پیاز /nosh-pyāz/
green onions n

نوش جان کنین !
/nosh-ī jān kŭ-neyn/
bon appetit excl

نوشادر /naw-shā-dīr/
ammonia, ammonium chloride n

نوشتن ؛ -نویس- ؛ /مینویسم/ ؛ نوشتـ
/na-wīsh-tan; méynawisŭm//
write (formal) v

نوشته /na-wīsh-ta/
written; formal (lang) adj
← نوشته کردن write (colloq) v

نوشیدن ؛ -نوش- ؛ نوشید-
/no-shi-dan/
drink, imbibe vt

نوشیدنی , -ها /no-shi-da-ni/
drink, beverage n

نوع , -ها/انواع
/náw-'a, naw'; pl an-wā/
kind, sort, type n

نوع بشر /náw-'a-yī ba-shar/
humanity, mankind n

نوع حیوان /náw-'a-yī hay-wān/
species n

نوعیت /naw-'ī-yat/
specification, detailing n

نوقت /na-waqt (-wakht)/
see ناوقت adv

نوکر /no-kar/
servant, domestic; low-ranking
government employee n

نوکری /no-ka-ri/
service, servant's duties n

نوکیسه /naw-ki-sa/ adj see نودولت

نول /nol/
beak, bill (bird's) n

نول زدن ← peck; work briefly v

نومبر /na-wam-bar, -wĭm-/
November (month) n

نویس /na-wis/
writer n; written adj

نویسنده , گان/ها- /na-wi-sīn-da/
writer, author n

نه /nah (no)/
nine n, adj; no, not adv

نه ... بلکی ... /na ... bál-ki .../
not ... but ... phrs

نه ... مگر ... /na ... má-gar .../
see ... بلکی ... نه phrs

نه ... نه ... /na ... na .../
neither ... nor ... phrs

نهاد /nĭ-hād/
foundation, fund; nature,
disposition; inside; (gram) subject n

نهار /na-hār/ day n

نهاری /na-hā-ri/ daytime adj

نهال , ها- /nĭ-hāl (nyāl)/ sapling n

نهال شانی /nĭ-hāl shā-ni/
planting saplings (colloq) n

نهال نشانی /nĭ-hāl nĭ-shā-ni/
see نهال شانی n

نهالی /nĭ-hā-li/ seedling n

نهایت , pl یات- /nĭ-hā-yat, pl -yāt/
end, extremity n; extremely adv

نهایات ← pl

نهر , ها-/انهار /nahr (nār), pl an-hār/
irrigation canal n

نهر سراج /ná-hĭr-ĭ shā-hi/
Nahr-e Saraj (dist) n

نهر شاهی /ná-hĭr-ĭ shā-hi/
Nahr-e Shahi (dist) n

نهرین /nah-rin/ Nahrin (dist) n

نهفت /nĭ-hŭft/
secret, covert (& adv) adj, adv

نهفتگی /nĭ-hŭf-ta-gi/ concealment n

نهفته /nĭ-hŭf-ta/
secret, covert; concealed, hidden
adj

نهم /nŭ-hŭm (no-wŭm)/ ninth adj

نهمین /nŭ-hŭ-min/
ninth (lit, oft before n) adj

نهنگ /nĭ-hang/
alligator; crocodile n

نهی /náh-ya, nahy/
ban, prohibition; (gram) negative
imperative n

نی /nay/
pipe, tube; reed (& mus instr) n

نی /ney (na)/ no adv

نیا , کان- /nī-yā/
ancestor, forefather; grandfather n

نیاز /nī-yāz/
need; desire, wish n

نیاز داشتن <به چیزی> ←
need, require <sth> vt

نیاز مند , ان- /nī-yāz-mand/
needy (pers) n

نیاز مندی , ها- /nī-yāz-man-di/
requirement n

نیازی /nī-yā-zi/ Neyazi (P tribe) n

نیال /nyāl/ see نهال n

نیایش /nī-yā-yīsh/
worship, veneration; praise n

نیایش کردن ←
worship, venerate; praise v

نیپیدو /nay-pyi-daw/
Naypyidaw (capital) n

نیپال /ni-pāl/ Nepal (country) n

نیرو , ها- /ni-ro, nay-/
force (troop) n

نیرو های ملی امینتی افغان
/ni-ro-hā-yĭ mĭ-li-yĭ am-nī-ya-ti-yĭ af-
ghān/
Afghan National Security Forces,
ANSF n

نیز /nĭz/ also, too adv

نیزه /nay-za/
spear; lance; javelin; nayza (unit of
meas) n

نیست /neyst/ is not v

نیستی /neys-ti/
absence, non-existence n

نیش /neysh/
sting (insect); fang (snake); point (needle) n

نیش زدن ←
sting, prick; deride; sprout vt

نیش خند /neysh khand/
angry smile n

نیش دار /neysh dār/
derisive, jeering adj

نیشاپور /ni-shā-pur/
Nishapur (city in NE Iran) n

نیشکر /nay-sha-kar/ sugar cane n

نیفه /ni-fa/
drawcord slot at pajama waist n

نیک , -ان /neyk/
good, w/positive qualities (& pers) adj, n

نیک انجام /neyk an-jām/
auspicious adj

نیک اندیش /neyk an-deysh/
see نیکو کار adj, n

نیک نام /neyk nām/ reputable adj

نیک و بد /neyk ŭ bad/ phrs
good & bad

نیکر /nay-kar/ shorts (sports) n

نیکو , -ان/یان /ney-ko/
good; beautiful, pretty (f) (& pers) adj, n; well, nicely adv

نیکو کار , -ان/ها /ney-ko kār/
benevolent (& pers) adj, n

نیکه /ney-ka/ grandfather (colloq) n
نیکه /ni-ka, nay-/ Nika (dist) n
نیکه و نبیره /ney-ka wŭ na-bi-ra/
grandfather & grandchild phrs

نیکی /ney-ki/
benevolence, goodness n

نیل /nil/
indigo plant/dye; Nile River n

نیلاب /ni-lāb/ indigo solution n
نیلگون /nil-gun/ indigo (color) adj
نیلوفر /ni-lo-far/
lotus, nenuphar (plant) n

نیلوفر آبی /ni-lo-far-ī ā-bi/
water lily n

نیلوفر هندی /ni-lo-far-ī hĭn-di/
nelumbo, Indian lotus n

نیلوفری /ni-lo-fa-ri/
lotus-colored, blue adj

نیله چنار /ni-la chĭ-nār/
blue poplar n

نیلی /ni-li/
indigo (color) adj; Nili (dist, seat) n

نیم /nim/ half; middle n
نیم باز /nim bāz/
ajar, half-open adj

نیم پخته /nim pŭkh-ta/
half-cooked adj

نیم جوش /nim josh/
poached adj

نیم خواب /nim khāb/
half-asleep adj

نیم دایره /nim dā-yĭ-ra/ semicircle n

نیم رخ /nim rŭkh/ profile n

نیمروز /nim-roz/ Nimroz (prov) n

نیم رویه /nim ru-ya/
in profile; sunny side up (eggs) adj

نیم سری /nim sa-ri/
migraine (colloq) n

نیم سوخته /nim sokh-ta/
charred, half-burnt adj

نیم کاره /nim kā-ra/ unfinished adj

نیم کره /nim kŭ-ra/
hemisphere (& geog) n

نیم گرم /nim garm/ lukewarm adj

نیمه افراشته /ni-ma af-rāsh-ta/
at half-mast adj

نیم کش /nim kash/ see نیم باز adj

نینوا /nay-na-wā/ Nineveh (hist) n

نینواز /nay-na-wāz/ piper n

نیوترون /nī-yo-tron/ neutron n

نیورسل /ni-war-sal/
universal joint (colloq) n

نیو یارک /nī-yu yārk/
New York (city, state) n

نیی /na-yi/
wicker, made of reeds adj

نیین /na-yin/ see نیی adj

و

و /wa, ŭ, wŭ/ and conj

و اما /wa a-mā/ but, & yet conj

و غیره /wa ghay-ra/
et cetera, & so forth phrs

و قسم على هذا /wa qīs a-lā há-zā/
& so on, & so forth phrs

و یا /wa yā/ and/or, or conj

وابستگان /wā-bas-ta-gān/
relatives; dependents n pl

وابستگی , ها- /wā-bas-ta-gi/
relation; connection n
واپسی /wā-pa-si/ backwardness n
واپسین /wā-pa-sin/
final, last (lit) (comes before n) adj
واتر پمپ /wā-tar pamp/
water pump n

واثق /wā-sīq/
certain, sure; confident, trusting adj
واجب /wā-jīb/ necessary adj
واجبات /wā-jīb-āt/
duties, obligations; requirements n pl

واجب القتل /wā-jīb-ŭl-qá-tīl/
deserving of death adj
واجد <چیزی> /wā-jīd/
possessing <sth> adj, n
واحد sole adj; unit n /wā-hīd/
واحد صوت /wā-hīd-ī sawt/
phoneme n
واحد صوتی /wā-hīd-ī saw-ti/
phonemic adj
واحد قیاسی /wā-hīd-ī qī-yā-si/
unit of measurement n
واحد مسکونی /wā-hīd-ī mas-ku-ni/
residential unit, habitat n
واخ ! ouch excl /wākh/
واخان Wakhan (geog) n /wā-khān/
واخن see واخان /wā-khan/
واخی , ان/ها- /wā-khi/
Wakhi, Pamiri, Mountain Tajik (&
pers, lang, ethn grp) adj, n
وادی valley n /wā-di/
وادی خاموشان
/wā-di-yī khā-mo-shān/
cemetery (fig) n
وارد /wā-rīd/
arrived, entering, incoming;
knowing, informed adj
وارد آمدن ← happen, take place vi
وارد ساختن ← train, teach vt
وارد شدن ← arrive, come, enter vi
وارد کردن ← import v
واردات imports n pl /wā-rī-dāt/
وارداتی imported adj /wā-rī-dā-ti/
وارس Waras (dist) n /wa-ras/
وارسا Warsaw (capital) n /wār-sā/

وارستگی /wā-ras-ta-gi/
deliverance, salvation n
وارسته /wā-ras-ta/
delivered, saved adj, n
واز open (colloq) adj /wāz/
واز کردن ← open (door) vt
وازه خوا /wā-za khā/
Waza Khwa (dist) n
واژگون /wāzh-gun/
upside-down, inverted adj
واژون see واژگون adj /wā-zhun/
واژگونه /wāzh-gu-na/
f form of واژگون adj
واژه word n /wā-zha/
واسطه /wā-sī-ta/
mediation, patronage, recourse n
واسطه داشتن ← have patronage v
واسع /wā-sey/
far-reaching (God); heir to the
Prophet (hist) adj, n
واسکت vest, waistcoat n /wās-kat/
واسکت جان /wās-kat-ī jān/
lifejacket n
واشل /wā-shal/
washer (small disk) n
واشیر Washir (dist) n /wā-shir/
واشنگتن /wā-shīn-tan/
see واشینگتن n
واشینگتن /wā-shin-tan/
Washington, DC (capital) n
واصل /wā-sīl/
received (letter, file) adj
واصله f form of واصل adj /wā-sī-la/
واضح /wā-zīh/
clear, distinct; evident, plain,
obvious adj
واضحات /wā-zī-hāt/
obvious matters n pl
واضع , ان/ین- /wā-zey/
enactor (law) n
واعظ , ان/ین- preacher n /wā-'īz/
میر واعظ ← head preacher in capital n
واعظ شهید /wā-'īz sha-hid/
see جغتو n
واغز see واغظ n /wā-ghaz/
واغظ Waghaz (dist) n /wā-ghaz/

واقع /wā-qey/
located; happening; real, actual, true *adj*

واقع بودن ← /be located (sw) vi

واقع شدن ← /happen, take place vi

واقع بین , -ان/ها /wā-qey bin/
realist, rational thinker (& adj) *n, adj*

واقع بینی /wā-qey bi-ni/
realism, objectivity *n*

واقعاً /wā-qĭ´-'an, -'án/
actually, really *adv*

واقعه , -ها/واقعات /wā-qĭ-'a, pl -āt/
accident; event; battle *n*

واقعی /wā-qĭ-'i/
actual, factual, real, true *adj*

واقعیت , -ها/واقعیات /wā-qĭ-'ī-yat, pl -yāt/
actuality, reality *n*

واقعیت گرای , -ان /wā-qĭ-'ī-yat gĭ-rāy/
realist (art) (& adj) *n, adj*

واقعیت گرایی /wā-qĭ-'ī-yat gĭ-rā-yi/
realism (art) *n*

واکسین /wāk-sin/ vaccine *n*

واکسینیشن /wāk-si-ney-shan/
vaccination *n*

واکنش /wā-kŭ-nīsh/ reaction *n*

واگذار کردن /wā-gŭ-zār kardan/
leave, give over *vt*

واگذاشتن ؛ واگذار ـ ؛ واگذاشت ـ /wā´-gŭ-zāsh-tan/
see

واگذار کردن

وال /wāl/ valve; whale *n*

والا /wā-lā/
high, exalted; possessing *adj*

والا حضرت /wā-lā haz-rat/
His Highness (royal) *adj*

والد /wā-lĭd/ father (lit) *n*

والده /wā-lĭ-da/ mother (lit) *n*

والدین /wā-lĭ-dayn/ parents *n pl*

والی , -ان/ها /wā-li/
provincial governor *n*

واما /wā-mā/ Wama (dist) *n*

وانمود کردن /wā-na-mud kardan/
pretend, make out to be *v*

وانیلا /wā-ni-lā/ vanilla *n*

واول /wā-wŭl/ vowel *n*

واولی /wā-wŭ-li/ vocalic *adj*

واه واه ! /wāh wāh/
wow (admiring; & ironic) *excl*

وای ! /wāy/
woe, alas *excl*

وایگل /wāy-gal/ Waygal (dist) *n*

وبا /wŭ-bā/
epidemic disease; cholera *n*

وته پور /wa-ta-pur/ see

وتپور *n*

وتر /wá-tīr, watr/
string (mus instr); chord; (math) hypotenuse *n*

وتوتک /wŭ-tu-tak/ hoopoe *n*

وته پور /wa-ta-pur/
Watapur (dist) *n*

وثایق /wa-sā-yīq, sg wa-si-qa/
pl of وثیقه *n pl*

وثوق /wŭ-suq/
trust, confidence *n*

وثیقه , -ها/وثایق /wa-si-qa, pl wa-sā-yīq/
legal document *n*

وثیقه شرعی /wa-si-qa-yī shar-'i/
Musl legal document *n*

وجاهت /wa-jā-hat/ beauty *n*

وجایب /wa-jā-yīb/ see واجبات *n pl*

وجب /wa-jab/ span *n*

وجب کردن ← span *v*

وجد /wajd/
delight, joy; Sufic ecstasy *n*

وجدان /wĭj-dān/ conscience *n*

وجداناً /wĭj-dā-nan, -dā´-/
in all conscience *adv*

وجدانی /wĭj-dā-ni/
mental, psychic *adj*

وجنات /wa-ja-nāt/ cheeks *n pl*

وجود /wŭ-jud/
existence, being; presence; body, organism *n*

وجود داشتن ←
exist; be present; be available; take place *vi*

وجوه /wŭ-juh, sg wajh/
pl of وجه *n pl*

وجه /wajh, pl wŭ-juh/
way, manner; reason; (gram) mood *n*

وجوه ←
pl

وجه اخباری /wajh-ī īkh-bā-ri/
indicative mood (verb) *n*

وجه التزامی /wajh-ĭ ĭl-tĭ-zā-mi/
subjunctive mood (verb) n

وجه امری /wajh-ĭ am-ri/
imperative mood (verb) n

وجه شرطی /wajh-ĭ shar-ti/
conditional mood (verb) n

وجه مصدری /wajh-ĭ mas-da-ri/
infinitive mood (verb) n

وجه وصفی /wajh-ĭ was-fi/
adjectival mood (verb) n

وجهی /waj-hi/ monetary adj

وحدت /wah-dat/ accord; unity n

وحدت فکر /wah-dat-ĭ fí´-kĭr/
likemindedness n

وحشت /wah-shat/
brutality, savagery, barbarity n

وحشتناک /wah-shat-nāk/
brutal, savage adj

وحشیانه /wah-shĭ-yā-na/
brutal, savage (& adv) adj, adv

وحشیگری /wah-shi-ga-ri/
brutality, savagery n

وحی /wahy/ revelation (rel) n

وحید /wa-hid/ Wahid (m name) n

وحیده /wa-hi-da/ Wahida (f name) n

وخ ! /wakh/ ouch excl

وخت /wakht/ وقت see

وخم /wá-khĭm, wakhm/ وقف see n
وخم شاندن ←
plant fruit trees for Musl endowment
(colloq) v

وخمی /wakh-mi/ وفقی adj see

وداع ! /wĭ-dā/ farewell (lit) excl
وداع کردن • وداع گفتن ←
say farewell v

وراثت /wa-rā-sat/
inheritance; heredity n

ور ممی /wŭr ma-may, -māy/
Wur Mamay (dist) n

ورد /ward/ rose (lit) n

ورداشت /war-dāsht/ برداشت see
ورداشتن ؛ وردار- ؛ ورداشت- ←
/wár-dāsh-tan/
lift, raise, pick up (& fig) vt

وردک /war-dak/
Wardak (prov, P tribe) n

وردوج /war-duj/ Warduj (dist) n

ورزش /war-zĭsh/
athletics, sport; gymnastics n

ورزش کار , -ان/ها /war-zĭsh kār/
athlete; gymnast n

ورزیده /war-zi-da/
skillful, experienced adj

ورس /wa-ras/ n واراس see

ورسج /war-saj/ Warsaj (dist) n

ورشکست /war-shĭ-kast/
bankrupt, insolvent adj
ورشکست شدن ←
go bankrupt vi

ورشکستگی /war-shĭ-kas-ta-gi/
bankruptcy, insolvency n

ورشکسته /war-shĭ-kas-ta/
ورشکست adj see

ورق , -ها/اوراق /wa-raq, pl aw-rāq/
leaf, sheet (paper) n

ورقه /wa-ra-qa/
document (official), paper n

ورقه هویت /wa-ra-qa-yĭ hŭ-wĭ-yat/
ID card, papers n

ورکشاپ /wark-shāp/
workshop; repair shop, garage n

ورم /wa-ram/ swelling n
ورم کردن ←
swell vi

ورم کرده /wa-ram kar-da/
swollen adj

ورود /wŭ-rud/ arrival; entrance n

ورودی /wŭ-ru-di/ for entry adj
دروازه ورودی ←
entry door n

ورید /wa-rid/ vein n

وزارت /wa-zā-rat/ ministry n

وزارت خانه /wa-zā-rat khā-na/
وزارت see n

وزرا /wŭ-za-rā, sg wa-zir/
وزیر of pl n pl

وزن , -ها/اوزان
/wá-zĭn, wazn; pl aw-zān/
weight, heaviness; weighing n
وزن باختن ← lose weight v
وزن کردن ← weigh vt
وزن گرفتن ← gain weight v
بم به وزن ۲۰۰۰ پوند ←
• بم ۲۰۰۰ پونده
a 2000-lb bomb n

وزن بردارى /wá-zīn bar-dā-ri/
weightlifting; dumbbell n
وزن بردارى کردن ←
lift weights v
وزن خالص /wá-zīn-ī khā-līs/
net weight n
وزه جدران /wū-za ja-drān/
Wuza Jadran (dist) n
وزیر /wa-zir, pl wū-za-rā/
minister; (chess) queen; Wazir (P tribe) n
وزرا ← pl
وزیر مشاور /wa-zir-ī mū-shā-wīr/
minister w/o portfolio n
وساطت /wa-sā-tat/
mediation, arbitration n
وسایط /wa-sā-yīt/
equipment; means; vehicle n pl
۳ عرادۀ وسایط ←
3 transport vehicles
وسایل /wa-sā-yīl, sg wa-si-la/
see sg وسیله n pl
وسط /wa-sat/ center, middle n
وسطی /wa-sa-ti/ central, middle adj
وسع /wá-sa, was/ ability n
وسعت /was-'at/
width, expanse; widening n
وسعت دادن /was-'at dādan/
expand, widen; develop v
وسله /was-la/ weapons (colloq) n
وسمه /was-ma/ woad (plant, dye) n
وسیع /wa-si/ wide, broad adj
وسیله, -ها/وسایل /wa-si-la, pl wa-sā-yīl/
means; mediation; support n
وسیم /wa-sim/
handsome adj; Wasim (m name) n
وصایا /wa-sā-yā, sg wa-sī-yat/
pl of وصیت n pl
وصایای ده گانه /wa-sā-yā-yī dah gā-na/
the Ten Commandments (bibl) n pl
وصفی /was-fi/ adjectival (gram) adj
وصل /wa-sīl, wasl/
connection, linkage n
وصل کردن ← connect, link n

وصلت /was-lat/
matrimony, union n
وصلت کردن ←
marry, unite in matrimony v
وصول /wū-sul/
achievement; arrival n
وصی /wa-si/
legal guardian; executor (will) n
وصیت نامه /wa-sī-yat nā-ma/
will (document) n
وضع /wá-za, waz; pl aw-zā/
situation, condition; mores; establishment (rule, law) n
اوضاع ← pl
وضع کردن ←
establish, introduce (rule, law); subtract vt
وضع حمل /wáz-'ī há-mīl/
childbirth, delivery n
وضعی /waz-'i/
rotational, rotating adj
وضعیت /waz-'ī-yat/
situation, condition, status; manners n
وضو /wū-zu/
ablutions before prayer n
وضو کردن perform ablutions v
وطن, -ها/اوطان /wa-tan, pl aw-tān/
homeland, fatherland; hometown n
وطن دار /wa-tan dār/
compatriot; fellow townsman n
وطن خواه /wa-tan khāh/
see وطن دوست n
وطن دوست /wa-tan dost/ patriot n
وطن دوستی /wa-tan dos-ti/
patriotism n
وطن دشمن /wa-tan dūsh-man/
traitor (to country) n
وطن دشمنی /wa-tan dūsh-ma-ni/
treason n
وطن فروش /wa-tan fū-rosh/
traitor (to country) n
وطن فروشی /wa-tan fū-ro-shi/
treason n
وطنی /wa-ta-ni/
native; domestically-produced adj

وظايف /wa-zā-yĭf, sg wa-zi-fa/
pl of وظيفه n pl

وظيفه, ها-/وظايف
/wa-zi-fa, pl wa-zā-yĭf/
duty, task, obligation (moral, rel,
mil); position, job n

وظيفه جلالى /wa-zi-fa-yĭ ja-lā-li/
divine obligation (period of severe
fasting, solitude & prayer) n

وظيفه جمالى /wa-zi-fa-yĭ ja-mā-li/
divine obligation (period of fasting,
solitude & prayer) n

وعا /wĭ-'ā, pl aw-'ī-ya/
blood vessel n

اوعيه ←← pl

وعده /wa'-da (wā-)/
promise, vow; (colloq) deadline n

وعده دادن • وعده کردن ←←
<چيزى را به کسى>
promise <sth to sb> vt

وعده شکستن ←←
renege, break a promise v

وعده خلاف /wa'-da khĭ-lāf/
characterized by breach of promise
adj

وعده خلافى /wa'-da khĭ-lā-fi/
breach of promise n

وعده دار /wa'-da dār/
pers making promise; pers
receiving promise n

وعده شکنى /wa'-da shĭ-ka-ni/
see وعده خلافى n

وعده گاه /wa'-da gāh/
an agreed meeting place n

وعده ملاقات /wa'-da-yĭ mŭ-lā-qāt/
appointment (meeting) n

وعده و وعيد /wa'-da wŭ wa-'id/
promise & threat (by God) phrs

وعظ /wa'z (wāz)/
preaching, sermon n

وعظ کردن ←←
preach, give a sermon v

وعظ و تبليغ /wa'z ŭ tab-ligh/
preaching & propagandizing phrs

وعيد /wa-'id/ threat n

و غيره /wa-ghay-ra/ phrs see و غيره

وفا /wa-fā/
loyalty, fidelity; fulfillment (of
promise) n

وفا دار /wa-fā dār/ loyal, faithful adj

وفا دارى /wa-fā dā-ri/
loyalty, faithfulness n

وفات /wa-fāt, pl wa-fī-yāt/ death n

وفات کردن ←← die v

وفيات ←← pl

وفد /wafd/ delegation n

وفق /wĭfq/
accordance, agreement n

وقار /wĭ-qār/ dignity, gravity n

وقار داشتن ←←
be dignified, be respected v

وقايوى /wĭ-qā-ya-wi/
preventive adj

وقايه /wĭ-qā-ya/
prevention, protection; dust jacket
(book) n

وقت /waqt (wakht)/
time n; early adv, adj; already adv

وقت دادن ←←
make an appointment v

وقتاً فوقتاً /wáq-tan fá-waq-tan/
occasionally adv

وقتر /waq-tar/ already, earlier adv

وقتى که /waq-tey-kĭ/
when, while, at the time that conj

وقع /wá-qa/
consideration, regard n

وقع گذاشتن <به چيزى> ←←
take into consideration <in sth> vt

به سخان او وقعى نگذاشت ←←
he did not take her words into
consideration

وقف /waqf (wá-khĭm); pl aw-qāf/
waqf, charitable foundation;
dedication, commitment n

اوقاف ←← pl

وقف نشاندن ←←
plant fruit trees for waqf v

وقف نامه /waqf nā-ma/
deed to waqf's endowment n

وقفه , -ها /wa-qī-fa/
pause, break, stop, interval;
intermission n

← وقفه اقتصادی
recession; depression (econ) n

وقفی /waq-fi (wakh-mi)/
of the waqf adj

وقوع /wŭ-qo/
happening, occurrence n

← وقوع یافتن • به وقوع پیوستن
happen, occur v

وقیح /wa-qih/ shameless adj

وکالت خط /wī-kā-lat khat/
power of attorney n

وکیل /wa-kil/
attorney, lawyer; representative;
(hist) imperial household chief of
staff n

وکیل دعوا /wa-kil-ī da'-wā/
see وکیل n

وکیل مدافع /wa-kil-ī mŭ-dā-fey/
see وکیل n

ولا /wī-lā/
region, territory n

ولادت /wī-lā-dat/ birth, childbirth n

← ولادن دادن <زن را>
deliver <f> of a child vt

← ولادت کردن
give birth, deliver v

ولادی /wī-lā-di/ obstetric adj

ولایت /wī-lā-yat/
province, vilayet n

← ولایت الفقیح
wilayat al-faqih (Iran pol system) n

ولایتی /wī-lā-ya-ti/ provincial adj

ولتاژ /wŭl-tāzh/ ولتیج see

ولتیج /wŭl-teyj/ voltage n

ولچک /wal-chak/
handcuffs, manacles n

ولسوال , -ها /wŭ-lŭs-wāl/
district governor n

ولسوالی , -ها /wŭ-lŭs-wā-li/
district n

ولسی جرگه /wŭ-lī-si jīr-ga/
Wolesi Jirga n

ولی /wá-ley/ but, however conj

ولی /wa-li/ Wali (m name) n

ولیک /wa-leyk/ ولی conj see

وهاب /wa-hāb/
giving, endowing (God) adj

وهابی , -ان/ها /wa-hā-bi/
Wahhabi, Wahhabist adj, n

وهابیت /wa-hā-bī-yat/
Wahhabism (Sunni sect) n

ویانا /wī-yā-nā/ Vienna (capital) n

ویتنام /weyt-nām/ Vietnam n

ویتنامی , -ان/ها /weyt-nā-mi/
Vietnamese (& pers) adj, n

ویدا /wi-dā/
Veda, sacred knowledge n

ویدایی /wi-dā-yi/ Vedic adj

ویران /way-rān (bey-)/
destroyed, demolished adj

← ویران شدن be destroyed vi

ویران کار /way-rān kār (bey-)/
junkman, scrapmonger n

ویرانگر /way-rān-gar/
destructive, ruinous adj

ویرگول /wir-gul/ comma n

ویروس /wi-rus/ virus n

ویزه /wi-za/ visa n

ویزه بیماری /wi-za-yī bey-mā-ri/
"medical visa" (does not exist) n

ویزه تحصیلی /wi-za-yī tah-si-li/
student visa n

ویزه نامزدی /wi-za-yī nām-za-di/
fiancé(e) visa n

وینتیان /win-tī-yān/
Vientiane (capital) n

ه

هابیل /hā-bil/ Abel (bibl) n

هارپ /hārp/ harp (mus instr) n

هارپ نواز /hārp na-wāz/
harpist, harp player n

هارن /hā-ran (ā-ran)/ horn (car) n

← هارن کردن honk the horn v

هارون /hā-run/ Aaron (bibl) n

هاشم /hā-shīm/
Hashem (m name; see & بنو هاشم) n

هاشمی , -ان /hā-shī-mi/
Hashemite n

هاضمه /hā-zī-ma/
digestive adj; ability to digest n

هاکی /hā-ki/ hockey n

هاگ /hāg/ The Hague (capital) n

هالند /hā-land/
the Netherlands, Holland n

هالندی , -ان/ها /hā-lan-di/
Dutch (& lang, pers) adj, n

هالیند /hā-leynd/ n see هالند

هالیندی /hā-leyn-di/
see هالندی adj, n

هان /hān (ān, ā), hayn/
behold, beware excl

هاندوراس /hān-du-rās/
Honduras (country) n

هاندوراسی , -ان/ها /hān-du-rā-si/
Honduran (& pers) adj, n

هانگ کانگ /hāng kāng/
Hong Kong (territory) n

هاوان /hā-wān/ mortar (& mil) n

هاوانا /hā-wā-nā/ Havana n

هاون /hā-wan (a-wang)/
mortar (vessel) n

هایدروجن /hāyd-ro-jan/ hydrogen n

هایدروجنی /hāyd-ro-ja-ni/
hydrogen, hydrogenous adj

هجا /hī-jā/
syllable; satiric poem; derision, scoffing n

هجایی /hī-jā-yi/ syllabic; satiric adj

هجرت /hīj-rat/
exodus, emigration; move; Hegira n

← هجرت کردن emigrate; move vi

هجری /hīj-ri/
related to the Hegira adj

هجو /háj-wa, hajw/
satire, defamation; mocking, scoffing n

← هجو گفتن mock, deride, scoff v

هجوم /hŭ-jum/
attack, offensive, assault n

← هجوم آوردن attack, assault vt

← هجوم بردن come under attack v

هجومی /hŭ-ju-mi/
offensive (mil) adj

هجونامه /hajw-nā-ma/
satiric poem; defamatory poem n

هجوی /haj-wi/
satiric; defamatory adj

هخامنشی , -ان /ha-khā-ma-nĭ-shi/
Achaemenid (& pers; hist) adj, n

هخامنشیان /ha-khā-ma-nĭ-shī-yān/
Achaemenid dynasty (hist) n pl

هدایا /hī-dā-yā, sg. had-ya/ pl of هدیه n pl

هدایت , -ها/هدایات /hī-dā-yat, pl -yāt/
instruction; directive, order n

← هدایت کردن instruct; direct, order v

← هدایت گرفتن <از کسی>
take <sb's> direction v

هدایت نامه /hī-dā-yat nā-ma/
instruction, directive (document) n

هدف , -ها/اهداف /ha-daf, pl ah-dāf/
aim, goal, objective n

هدهد /hŭd-hŭd/ hoopoe (bird) n

هدیه , -ها/هدایا /had-ya, pl hī-dā-yā/
gift, present; price of copy of Quran n

هذا /hā´-zā/ this adj

هذیان , -ات/ها /haz-yān/
drivel; delirium n

← هذیان گفتن blather v

هر /har/ each, every adj

هر جایی /har-jā-yi/
promiscuous adj

هر چند /hár-chand/
although, despite the fact that; even if, though conj

هر چه /hár-chĭ, har-chi/
anything, whatever pron

هر دو /har-du, har-dŭ/
both adj, pron

← هر دو یک چیز اس
both are the same phrs

هر روز /har roz/ every day adv

هر کس /hár-kas/
everybody, everyone pron

هر که /hár-kĭ, har-ki/
see هر کس pron

هر گز /har-gĭz/
never, not at all, in no way adv

هرات /hī-rāt/
Herat (prov in W Afgh; & city) n

← آریا (ancient name) n

هراتی , -ان/ها /hĭ-rā-ti/
Herati (& pers, dialect) adj, n

هراس /ha-rās/ fear, fright n

← هراس داشتن v fear, be afraid

هراس آور /ha-rās ā-war/
frightening, scary adj

هراسان /ha-rā-sān/
afraid, scared adj

هراسناک /ha-rās-nāk/
هراس آور see adj

هراسیدن ؛ -هراس- ؛ هراسید-
/ha-rā-si-dan/
fear, be afraid v

هرج و مرج /harj ŭ marj/
tumult, turmoil phrs

هرقدر /hár-qa-dar/ as much as adv

هرگاه /hár-gāh/ whenever adv

هرگه /hár-gah/ هرگاه see adv

هرم , -ها/أهرام /hĭ-ram, pl ah-rām/
pyramid n

هرودوت /hĭ-ro-dot/
Herodotus (hist) n

هرکدامشه /hár-kŭ-dām-sha/
every way, any way (colloq) adv

هزار /ha-zār/ thousand n, adj

هزار سموچ /ha-zār sŭ-much/
Hazar Sumuch (dist) n

هزارم /ha-zā-rŭm/ thousandth adj

هزارمین /ha-zā-rŭ-min/
thousandth (lit, oft before n) adj

هزارگی /ha-zā-ra-gi/ Hazara adj

هزاره /ha-zā-ra/
Hazara (pers); millenium n

هزاره جات /ha-zā-ra-jāt/
Hazarajat (geog) n

هزل /há-zīl, hazl/ joke, jest (lit) n

← هزل گفتن make a jest (lit) n

هزل آمیز /há-zīl ā-meyz/
jocular, facetious (lit) adj

هزلی /haz-li/ humoristic (lit) adj

هزیمت /ha-zi-mat/ defeat (lit) n

← هزیمت دادن vanquish (lit) vt

هزیمتی , -ان /ha-zi-ma-ti/
defeated (& pers; mil) adj, n

هزینه /ha-zi-na/ budget n

هژده /haj-dah/ eighteen n, adj

هژدهم /haj-da-hŭm/ eighteenth adj

هژدهمین /haj-da-hū-min/
eighteenth (lit, oft before n) adj

هسپانوی , -ان/ها /has-pā-na-wi/
Spanish (lang, pers) n

هسپانیه /has-pā-nī-ya/ Spain n

هستوی /has-ta-wi/ هسته یی see adj

هست /hast/ is see v

هستن /has-tan/ are see v بودن

هسته یی (-wi)/ /has-ta-yi
nuclear, atomic adj

هشت /hasht/ eight n, adj

هشت ضلعی /hasht zŭl-'i/
octagon n; octagonal adj

هشت نفری /hasht na-fa-ri/
mil recruitment (1 out of 8, hist) n

هشتاد /hash-tād/ eighty n, adj

هشتادم /hash-tā-dŭm/ eightieth adj

هشتادمین /hash-tā-dŭ-min/
eightieth (lit, oft before n) adj

هشتم /hash-tŭm/ eighth adj

هشتمین /hash-tŭ-min/
eighth (lit, oft before n) adj

هشدار /hŭsh-dār/ warning n

← هشدار دادن warn vt

هضم /há-zĭm, hazm/
alimentation; assimilation,
understanding n

هضمی /haz-mi/
alimentary, digestive adj

هفت /haft/ seven n, adj

هفت سیاره /haft sa-yā-ra/
the 7 celestial bodies (Mercury,
Venus, Moon, Sun, Mars, Jupiter,
Saturn) n

هفت قلم /haft qa-lam/
7 types of calligraphy; 7 types of
makeup n

هفتاد /haf-tād/ seventy n, adj

هفتادم /haf-tā-dŭm/ seventieth adj

هفتادمین /haf-tā-dŭ-min/
seventieth (lit, oft before n) adj

هفتالی , -ان/ها /haf-tā-li/
Hephthalite, Ephthalite, White Hun
(hist) n

هفتلی , -ان/ها /haf-ta-li/ هفتالی see

هفتم /haf-tŭm/ seventh adj

هفتمین /haf-tŭ-min/
seventh (lit, oft before n) adj

هفتگی weekly adj /haf-ta-gi/
هفته week n /haf-ta/
هفته نامه /haf-ta nā-ma/
weekly magazine n
هفته وار adj /haf-ta wār/ هفتگی see
هفده /haf-dah (ab-da)/
seventeen n, adj
هفدهم /haf-da-hŭm/
seventeenth adj
هفدهمین /haf-da-hŭ-min/
seventeenth (lit, oft before n) adj
هکتار hectare n /hĭk-tār/
هکک hiccup, hiccough n /hĭ-kak/
← هکک زدن hiccup, hiccough vi
هلاک dead; exhausted adj /ha-lāk/
← هلاک شدن be killed vi
هلسنگی /hal-san-gi/
Helsinki (capital) n
هلمند /hĭl-mand/
Helmand (prov, river) n
هلند n هالند see /hŭ-land/
هله ! hurry, get going excl /há-la/
هلی کوپتر /ha-li kop-tar, hĭ-/
helicopter n
هلیله /ha-ley-la/
myrobalan, Indian almond n
هلیله کابلی /ha-ley-la-yĭ kā-bu-li/
هلیله n see
هلیم halim (rice dish) n /ha-lim/
هلینستی /hĭ-ley-nĭs-ti/
Hellenistic (hist) adj
هلینیزم /hĭ-ley-ní-zĭm/
Hellenism (hist) n
هلینی Hellenic (hist) adj /hĭ-ley-ni/
هلیکوپتر /ha-li-kop-tar, hĭ-/
helicopter n
هم also, too adv /ham/
هم ... هم ... /ham ... ham .../
both ... and ... adv
هم آواز unanimous adj /ham ā-wāz/
هم آوازی /ham ā-wā-zi/
unanimity n
هم اتاق /ha-mŭ-tāq, hŭ-/
roommate n
هم این حالا /ham in hā-ley/
recently (colloq) adv
هم پیاله /ham-pĭ-yā-la/
drinking buddy n

هم جنس باز , -ان/ها /ham jĭns-bāz/
homosexual n, adj
هم جنس بازی /ham jĭns-bā-zi/
homosexuality n
هم چند /ham chand/
equivalent, equal adj
هم دوره /ham daw-ra/
schoolmate; contemporary (of sb else) n
هم دین /ham din/
coreligionist n; being of the same religion adj
هم کار /ham kār/
colleague, coworker, associate n
هم کاری /ham kā-ri/
cooperation, collaboration n
هم کیش /ham keysh/
هم دین see n, adj
هم گون similar adj /ham gun/
هم مانند similar adj /ham mā-nĭnd/
هم مذهب /ham maz-hab/
هم دین see n, adj
هم مرکز /ham mar-kaz/
concentric adj
هم مسلک /ham mas-lak/
colleague, associate (from same profession) n
هم مکتب /ham mak-tab/
schoolmate, fellow alumnus n
هم معنی /ham ma'-nā/
synonymous adj
هم میهن /ham may-han/
compatriot n
هم مسلک /ham mas-lak/
colleague (professional) n
هم نام /ham nām/
having the same name (another pers) adj
هم نشین /ham nĭ-shin/
companion, associate n
هما /hŭ-mā/
huma (legendary bird); Huma (f name) n
همان /ha-mān (-mu)/
the very same, that very adj
← همان روز the very same day

i = keep, ĭ = big, u = coop, ŭ = put, y = yet, ' = (glottal stop)   319

هماهنگ /ha-mā-hang/
coordinated, harmonious *adj*
← هماهنگ دادن • هماهنگ ساختن
coordinate, harmonize *v*

هماهنگی /ha-mā-han-gi/
coordination, agreement; (mus)
harmony *n*

← همآهنگی داشتن
be coordinated *vi*

همایون /hŭ-mā-yun/
Humayun (Mughal emperor, hist; m
name) *n*

همبازی /ham-bā-zi/ playmate *n*

همبستر /ham-bĭs-tar/
bedmate, lover *n*

همبستگی /ham-bas-ta-gi/
correlation; solidarity; connectivity *n*

همبسته /ham-bas-ta/ correlated *adj*

همپایه /ham-pā-ya/
peer, equal, person of equal dignity
& rank *n*

همتا /ham-tā/
counterpart, equal, peer *n*

همچنان /hám-chŭ-nān/
so, this way; as usual *adv*

همچنان /ham-chŭ-nān/
also, too *adv*

همچنین /hám-chŭ-nìn/
so, in that way; as usual *adv*

همخانه /ham-khā-na/
housemate, cohabitant *n*; living
together *adj*

همخوابه /ham-khā-ba/
wife, bedfellow; unmarried
cohabitant *n*

همدست /ham-dast/
partner; collaborator, accomplice *n*

همدستی /ham-das-ti/
partnership; collaboration;
complicity *n*

همراه /ham-rāh (-rāy)/ with *prep*
همراهی کردن <کسی را>
/ham-rā-hi/
accompany <sb> (travel, mus) *vt*

همرای /ham-rāy/
see همراه (colloq) *prep*

همرزم /ham-rá-zĭm/
brother in arms, fellow soldier *n*

همرنگ /ham-rang/
of the same type *adj*

همرنگ جماعت شدن
/ham-rang-ĭ ja-mā-'at shŭdan/
go with the flow *v*

همزمان /ham-za-mān/
simultaneous (& adv) *adj, adv*

همزمانی /ham-za-mā-ni/
simultaneity *n*

همسایه , ‫ گان/ها /ham-sā-ya/
neighbor *n*; neighboring *adj*

همسر /ham-sar/
spouse; subsidiary (corporation) *n*

همسنگر /ham-san-gar/
brother in arms, trenchmate *n*

همشان /ham-shān/ *n* see همپایه

همشهری , -ان/ها /ham-shah-ri/
fellow citizen *n*

همشیره /ham-shi-ra/ sister *n*

همصحبت /ham-sŭh-bat/
interlocutor; frequent conversation
partner *n*

همصنف , -ان/ها /ham-sĭnf (-sĭn-fi)/
classmate *n*

همصنفی /ham-sĭn-fi/ see همصنف

همطراز /ham-tĭ-rāz/ *n* see همپایه

همکار /ham-kār/
colleague, coworker *n*

همکاری /ham-kā-ri/
collaboration, cooperation *n*

← همکاری کردن
collaborate, cooperate *vi*

همنبرد /ham-na-bard/ *n* see همرزم

همنوا /ham-na-wā/ unanimous *adj*

همنوایی /ham-na-wā-yi/ unanimity *n*

همو /ha-mu/
that very, selfsame, the very same
(colloq) *adj*

هموار /ham-wār/
flat, level, smooth; widespread *adj*;
laying out (carpet) *n*

← هموار کردن
lay out, spread out *vt*

همواره /ham-wā-ra/
always, continuously; every time
adv

هموطن /ham-wa-tan/ compatriot *n*

همه /há-ma/
every, each *adj*; entirety *n*
همهٔ ما ←— every one of us
همه حقوق محفوظ است ←—
all rights reserved
همه مردم /há-ma mar-dúm/
everyone *pron*
همهٔ مردم /há-ma-yĭ mar-dúm/
all the people *phrs*
همی /ha-mí/
this very, the very same (colloq) *adj*
همیشه /ha-mey-sha/
always, continually *adv*
همین (-می)/ /ha-mín (-mi)/
this very, the very same *adj*
همین که /ha-mín-kĭ/
as soon as *conj*
هند /hĭnd/ India *n*
هندسه /han-da-sa/ geometry *n*
هندسهٔ تحلیلی ←—
analytical geometry *n*
هندسهٔ ترسیمی ←—
descriptive geometry *n*
هندسهٔ مسطحه ←—
plane geometry *n*
هندسی /han-da-si/ geometric *adj*
هندو , -ان/ها/هنود
/hĭn-du, pl hŭ-nud/
Hindu (pers) *n*
هندوچین /hĭn-du-chin/
Indochina (geog) *n*
هندوچینی /hĭn-du-chi-ni/
Indochinese (& pers) *adj, n*
هندوستان /hĭn-dus-tān/ India *n*
هندویزم /hĭn-du-yĭ´-zĭm/
Hinduism *n*
هندی , -ان/ها /hĭn-di/
Indian, Hindi; Hindi (lang) *n*
هندی آرامی /hĭn-di ā-rā-mi/
Indo-Aramean *adj*
هندی آریانی /hĭn-di ā-rī-yā-ni/
Indo-Aryan, Indo-Iranian *adj*
هندی اروپایی /hĭn-di ŭ-ru-pā-yi/
Indo-European *adj*
هنر /hŭ-nar/
art; artwork; art form; guile *n*
هنر باز /hŭ-nar bāz/ cunning *adj*

هنرپرور /hŭ-nar-par-war/
art patron *n*
هنرپروری /hŭ-nar-par-wa-ri/
art patronage *n*
هنرپیشگی /hŭ-nar-pey-sha-gi/
acting (craft) *n*
هنرپیشه , -گان/ها /hŭ-nar-pey-sha/
actor, actress; thespian *n*
هنرمند , -ان/ها /hŭ-nar-mand/
artist; artiste; performer *n*
هنرمندانه /hŭ-nar-man-dā-na/
artistic; skillful (& adv) *adj, adv*
هنرمندی /hŭ-nar-man-di/ artistry *n*
هنرنمایی /hŭ-nar-nŭ-mā-yi/
artistic performance, entertainment
n
هنرهای زیبا /hŭ-nar-hā-ī zey-bā/
fine arts *n pl*
هنری /hŭ-na-ri/
artistic, related to art *adj*
هنگام /han-gām(-ī)/
when, at the time of <sth> *prep*
هنگامه /han-gā-ma/
noise, uproar, tumult *n*
هنگامی که /han-gā-mey kĭ/
when (lit) *conj*
هنود /hŭ-nud, sg. hĭn-du/
pl of هندو *n pl*
هنوز /ha-noz/
still; (w/neg of pres perf) yet *adv*
هنی سکل /ha-ni-sa-kal/
honeysuckle (flower) *n*
هوا /ha-wā/
air; weather; desire, longing *n*
هوا پیما , -ها /ha-wā pay-mā/
airplane, aircraft *n*
هوا خوری /ha-wā khŭ-ri/
taking a walk; excursion, outing *n*
هوا خوری کردن ←— take a walk
هوا خوری رفتن ←— take a trip
هوا سنج /ha-wā sanj/ barometer *n*
هوا شناسی /ha-wā-shī-nā-si/
meteorology *n*
هوا کش /ha-wā kash/ vent *n*
هوا و هوس /ha-wā wŭ ha-was/
desire & longing *phrs*
هواخواه /ha-wā-khāh/
supporter, partisan (pers) *n*

هوادار /ha-wā-dār/ n هواخواه see

هواسنج /ha-wā-sanj/ n barometer

هوانورد /ha-wā-na-ward/
aviator, pilot n

هوانوردی /ha-wā-na-war-di/
aviation n

هوایی /ha-wā-yi/ air, aerial adj

هوتک /ho-tak/ n Hotak (P tribe)

هوتکی , -ان/ها /ho-ta-ki/
Hotaki (& pers) adj, n

هوتل /ho-tal/ n hotel

هودج /haw-daj/ n هوده see

هوده /haw-dah/ n howdah

هورمون /hor-mon/ n hormone

هوزیله /ho-zi-la, -si-/
Hozila (hist; region) n

هوس /ha-was/
desire, craving; lust, passion n

هوس آلود /ha-was ā-lud/ lustful adj

هوس انگیز /ha-was an-geyz/
provocative, lust-provoking adj

هوس بار /ha-was bār/ adj هوس آلود see

هوسناک /ha-was-nāk/
passionate; flighty; lusty adj

هوسیله /ho-si-la/ n هوزیله see

هوش /hush/
intellect; consciousness n

هوشدار /hush-dār/ see هشدار

هوشمند /hush-mand/ adj, n هوشیار see

هوشیار /hu-shī-yār/
intelligent; prudent; sober (& pers)
adj, n

هوشیاری /hu-shī-yā-ri/
intelligence; prudence; sobriety n

هون , -ان/ها /hun/ n Hun (hist)

هویت /hū-wī-yat/
identity, identification n

هیاهو /ha-yā-hu/ noise, hue & cry n

هیجان , -ات/ها /ha-ya-jān/
excitement n

هیجان آمیز /ha-ya-jān ā-meyz/
exciting adj

هیچ /heych/
no, not any, not one adj
nowhere adv /heych-jā/ هیچ جا

هیچ جای /heych-jāy/
see هیچ جا adv

هیچ چیز /heych chiz/ nothing pron

هیچ وقت /heych waqt/ never adv

هیچ کار /heych kār/
impractical, inefficient adj

هیچ کدام /heych kŭ-dām/

هیچ کس /heych kas/ pron هیچ کس see

nobody, no one pron

هیچ گاه /heych gāh/
never, not at all, in no way;
nowhere adv

هیچ گه /heych gah/ adv هیچ گاه see

هیچ یک /heych yak/
see هیچ کس pron

هیروئین /hey-ro-yin/ n heroin

هیزم /hey-zŭm (-ey)/
firewood, brushwood n

هیزم کش /hey-zŭm kash/
firewood seller n

هیزم کش دوزخ
/hey-zŭm kash-ī do-zakh/
gossiper (fig) n

هیکل /hay-kal/ figure, body n

هیکل تراش /hay-kal ta-rāsh/
sculptor n

هیکل تراشی /hay-kal ta-rā-shi/
sculpture n

هیل /heyl (eyl)/ cardamom n

هین ! /hayn/ behold, beware excl

هیولا /ha-yu-lā/
monster; primordial matter n

هیأت /hay-'at/
board; commission; delegation n

هینت /hay-'at/
board (editors); staff; body, corps n

هینت تحریر /hay-'at-ī tah-rir/
editorial board n

هینت تمیز /hay-'at-ī ta-miz/
Religious Council n

هینت طبی /hay-'at-ī tī-bi/
medical corps n

هینت مدیره /hay-'at-ī mŭ-di-ra/
board of directors n

هینت وزرا /hay-'at-ī wŭ-za-rā/
cabinet (pol) n

هیهات ! /haĭ´-hāt/ alas excl

ی

یا /yā/ or *conj*; O (voc) *excl*
یابنده, گان/ها- /yā-bīn-da/
procurer; finder *n*

یابو /yā-bu/
draft horse, pack horse *n*

یاجوج /yā-juj/ Gog (bibl) *n*
→ یاجوج و ماجوج
Gog & Magog (bibl) *phrs*

یاد /yād/ memory *n*
→ یاد <کسی> آمدن
remember *v*
→ یاد ام آمد که...
I remembered that...
→ یاد دادن <به کسی>
teach <sb> *v*

→ یاد داشتن
know how to, be able to *vt*
→ یاد <کسی> رفتن
forget *v*
→ یاد ام رفت که...
I forgot that... ...
→ یاد کردن
note, mention, recall *v*
→ یاد گرفتن learn, study *vt*
یاد آور شدن /yād ā-war shŭdan/
note, mention *v*
یاد آوری /yād ā-wa-ri/
reminder; reminding *n*
→ یاد آوری کردن remind *v*
یاد داشت, ها- /yād dāsht/
note; memorandum *n*

یاد گار /yād gār/
memory, reminiscence; monument;
memorial *n*
→ به یاد گار
in memory of (sb/st)
یادداشت /yā-dāsht/ *n* note see یاد داشت
یادگار monument *n* /yād-gār/
یازده /yāz-dah/ eleven *n, adj*
یازدهم /yāz-da-hŭm/ eleventh *adj*
یازدهمین /yāz-da-hŭ-min/
eleventh (lit, oft before n) *adj*
یازنه /yāz-na/
brother-in-law, sister's husband *n*
یاس /yās/
hopelessness, despair;
disappointment; lilac *n*
یاسمن /yā-sa-man/
jasmine (flower) *n*

یاسمن انگریزی
/yā-sa-man-ĭ ang-rey-zi/
lilac (flower) *n*
یاسمین /yā-sa-min/ *n* see یاسمن
یاسین /yā-sin/ Yasin (sura) *n*
یاغی /yā-ghi/
rebel, insurgent *n*; uncontrollable
adj
یاغیگری /yā-ghi-ga-ri/
rebelliousness; insurgency *n*
یافا /yā-fā/ Jaffa (city) *n*
یافتن ؛ یاب- . (یافت-) ؛ یافت-
/yāftan /méyyābŭm, méyyāfŭm//
find, come upon *vt*
یافث /yā-fīs/ Japheth (bibl) *n*
یاقوت /yā-qut, -gut/ ruby *n*
یاقوت آتشی /yā-qut-ĭ ā-ta-shi/
n see یاقوت سرخ
یاقوت احمر /yā-qut-ĭ ah-mar/
n see یاقوت سرخ
یاقوت ازرق /yā-qut-ĭ az-raq/
n see یاقوت کبود
یاقوت سرخ /yā-qut-ĭ sŭrkh/
ruby (red) *n*
یاقوت زرد /yā-qut-ĭ zard/
topaz (yellow); yellow sapphire *n*
یاقوت کبود /yā-qut-ĭ ka-bud/
sapphire *n*
یاقوتی /yā-qu-ti, -gu-/
ruby red *adj*
یال /yāl/ mane *n*
بالان /yā-lān/ cape (f's) *n*
یائسگی /yā-'ĭ-sa-gi/ menopause *n*
یائسه /yā-'ĭ-sa/ menopausal *adj*
→ یائسه شدن become menopausal
یتیم, ها-/ایتام /ya-tim, pl ay-tām/
orphan (w/o father) *n*
یتیم خانه /ya-tim-khā-na/
orphanage *n*
یثرب /yas-rĭb/ Mecca (orig name) *n*
یحیی /yah-yā/
John the Baptist (bibl); Yahya (m
name) *n*
یحیی خیل /yah-yā kheyl/
Yahya Kheyl (dist) *n*
یخ /yakh/ ice; cold (temperature) *n*
→ یخ زدن freeze *vt*
→ یخ کردن
cool, get cold (food, limb) *vi*

frostbite n /yakh za-da-gi/ یخ زدگی

/yakh mā-lak/ یخ مالک

ice skating n

ice skate v یخ مالک زدن ←

/yakh-chāl/ یخچال

refrigerator, ice chest n

lapel; neckline n /ya-khan/ یخن

/yī-rāq/ یراق

jewelry; tack (horse's gear) n

jaundice, icterus n /yar-qān/ یرقان

God [< P] n /yaz-dān/ یزدان

divine [< P] n /yaz-dā-ni/ یزدانی

Jesus n /ya-su/ یسوع

Jesuit n /ya-su-'i/ یسوعی , ان/ها-

/yá-shīm, yashm/ یشم

jasper, green chalcedony n

jasper green adj /yash-mi/ یشمی

/ya'-ney/ یعنی

see یعنی که pron, adv

/ya'-ney kĭ/ یعنی که

that, which; i.e., that is pron, adv

/yaf-tal/ یفتل

Yaftal (geog; cf. هفتالی) n

/yaf-ta-li/ یفتلی

Yaftali; (hist) Hephthalite adj

certainty, certitude n /ya-qin/ یقین

be certain vi یقین داشتن ←

/ya-qi-nan, ya-qí-nan/ یقیناً

certainly, indisputably adv

/ya-qi-ni/ یقینی

certain, indisputable adj

one (number) n, adj /yak/ یک

/yak bār/ یک بار

once, one time adv

/yak bār-ĭ di-gar/ یک بار دیگر

again, once again; (prefix) re- adv

/yak ba-gha-la/ یک بغله

crooked, lopsided, leaning over adj

/yak pah-lu/ یک پهلو

adamant, inflexible adj; on one side
adv

یک تعداد زیاد

/yak tey-dād-ĭ zyād(-ĭ)/

many, a large number adj

یک تعداد زیاد شان ←

many of them

/yak jā-nī-ba/ یک جانبه

unilateral adj; unilaterally adv

/yak da-fa/ یک دفعه

once, one time adv

soulmate adj /yak díl/ یک دل

/yak di-gar/ یک دیگر

each other, one another pron

/yak za-bān/ یک زبان

unanimous adj

/yak rang/ یک رنگ

frank, honest, straighforward;
monochromatic adj

/yak sān/ یک سان

uniform, identical adj

uniformity n /yak sā-ni/ یک سانی

/yak ta-ra-fa/ یک طرفه

one-way adj, adv

/yak ká-mey/ یک کمی

slightly adv; a little adv, n

/yak man-zī-la/ یک منزله

single-story (house) adj

/yak na-wākht/ یک نواخت

monotonous adj

/yak na-wākh-ti/ یک نواختی

monotony n

/yak hĭ-jā-yi/ یک هجایی

monosyllabic adj

/yak yak/ یک یک

one by one, one each adv

با یک یک قبضهٔ سلاح ←

with one weapon each

/ya-kāw-lang/ یکاولنگ

Yakawlang (dist) n

/yak-tā pa-rast/ یکتا پرست

monotheist n

/yak-tā pa-ras-ti/ یکتا پرستی

monotheism n

/yak-tā-yi/ یکتایی

oneness (& of God) n

یکجا see adv /yak-jā, yák-/ یکجای

/yak-jāy, yák-/ یکجای

together; simultaneously adv

Sunday n /yak-sham-bey/ یکشنبه

first (ordinal) adj /ya-kŭm/ یکم

alone, single, solo adj /ya-ka/ یکه

/ya-ka wŭ tan-hā/ یکه و تنها

all by oneself phrs

/ya-ka ya-ka/ یکه یکه

see یک یک adv

one (of sth) n, adj /ya-ki/ یکی

یکی یکی /ya-ki ya-ki/
see یک adv یک

یگانگی /ya-gā-na-gi/
oneness, cohesiveness (& God's) n

یگانه /ya-gā-na/
sole, only; unrivaled; unique adj

یگانه پرستی /ya-gā-na pa-ras-ti/
see یکتا پرستی n

یلدا /yal-dā/
winter solstice; Christmas n

یله /ya-la (ey-lā)/
divorced; freed; abandoned adj

← یله کردن
divorce; release, set free vt

یمگان /yam-gān/ Yamgan (dist) n
یمن /ya-man/ Yemen (country) n
ینگه /yan-ga/
sister-in-law, brother's wife n

ینگی قلعه /yan-gi/
Yangi Qala (dist) n

ینیچری , -ان /ya-ni-cha-ri/
janissary (hist, Ottoman slave
soldier) n

یوحنا /yu-hī-nā, -ha-/ John (bibl) n
یورانیم /yu-rā-nī-yam/
uranium n

یورانیوم /yu-rā-nī-yum/ یورانیم see
یورت /yort/ yurt (n)
یورو /yu-ro/ euro (currency) n
یوروپا /yŭ-ru-pā/ Europe n
یوروپایی , -ان/ها /yŭ-ru-pā-yi/
European (& pers) adj, n

یورولوژی /yo-ro-lo-zhi/ urology n
یوزپلنگ /yuz-pa-lang/ cheetah n
یوسف /yo-sŭf/
Yosuf, Yusuf (m name) n

یوسف خیل /yo-sŭf kheyl/
Yusuf Kheyl (dist) n

یوسفزی /yo-sŭf-zay/
Yusufzai (P tribe) n

یوغ /yogh/ yoke n
یوگوسلاویا /yu-go-slā-wī-yā/
Yugoslavia (hist) n

← یوگوسلاویای سابق
the former Yugoslavia n

یوناما /yu-nā-mā/
UNAMA, United Nations Assistance
Mission-Afghanistan n

یونان /yu-nān/ Greece n
یونانی , -ان/ها /yu-nā-ni/
Greek adj; Greek (pers, lang) n

یونانی باختری /yu-nā-ni bākh-ta-ri/
Greco-Bactrian (hist) adj

یونانی بودایی /yu-nā-ni bu-dā-yi/
Greco-Buddhist (hist) adj

یونسکو /yu-nīs-ko/
UNESCO, United Nations
Educational, Scientific & Cultural
Organization n

یونئه چی /yŭ-'ī-chi/
Yuezhi, Yüeh-Chih (hist) n

یونیسف /yu-ni-sīf/
UNICEF, United Nations
International Children's Emergency
Fund n

یونیفارم /yu-ni-fārm/ یونیفورم n see
یونیفورم /yu-ni-form/ uniform (mil) n
← مه یوینفورم پوشیدیم
I wear a uniform

یونیورسل
/yu-ni-war-sal (ni-war-sal)/
universal joint n

یهود /ya-hud/ Jewish pers n
یهودی , -ان/ها /ya-hu-di/
Jewish pers n; Jewish, Judaic adj

یهودیت /ya-hu-dī-yat/
Judaism; Jewishness n

English-Dari

A

A.D. (Anno Domini) adj • میلادی • مسیحی

A.H. (Hegira year) adj سنه هجری

a.m. adv قبل از ظهر

Aaron (bibl) n هارون

Ab Band (dist) n آب بند

Ab Kamari (dist) n آب کمری

aba (cloth) n عبا

abacus n چوت

Aban (month, see Aqrab) n آبان

abandon vt گذاشتن • پدرود کردن •
→ (fig) پشت پا زدن

abandonment n پدرود

Abbasids, the (hist) n آل • عباسیان •
عباس

abbreviate vt اختصار کردن

abbreviated adj اختصاری

abbreviation n نام اختصاری •
اختصار • تخفیف

abduct vt اختطاف کردن • ربودن

abduction n اختطاف • ربایش •
ربایندگی

abductor n رباینده • ربا

Abdullah (m name) n عبدالا •
عبدالله

Abdur Rahman Khan (hist, king r.
1880-1901) n عبدالرحمان خان

Abel (bibl) n هابیل

abide vi اقامت کردن • اقامت داشتن

ability n وسع • قابلیت • لیاقت
→ to the best of (one's) ability
حتی الوسع • حتی المقدور
→ be able to (can) <+ subj>
توانستن
→ be able to (know how) یاد
داشتن

ablution (Musl ritual) n غسل
→ perform ablutions وضو کردن
→ ritual ablution using sand/earth
if no water is available تیمم
→ ritual ablutions before prayer
وضو • طهارت
→ ritual ablutions طهارت • پاکی

abode n مسکن • اقامتگاه • نشیمن •
نشیمن گاه • نشیمن گه • آشیان •
آشیانه • آباد

abolishment n محو

aborigine n بومی

abort (fetus) v سقط جنین کردن

abortion n سقط جنین

abortive (futile) adj ضایع

about (almost) adv تقریباً • به
صورت تقریبی • به طور تقریبی •
تخمیناً • از روی تخمین
→ (lit) حدود

about (concerning) prep راجع به •
درباب • درباره • در پیرامون •
پیرامون • پیرامن • بر سر • به سر
• در سر • سر
→ (lit) در مورد

above & below phrs تحت و فوق

above adj فوق

abovementioned adj • فوق الذکر
متذکره • مذکور • مزبور
→ (colloq) در فوق
→ (about pers) موصوف • نامبرده

ABP see Afghan Border Police

Abraham (bibl; m name) n ابراهیم

abridge vt اختصار کردن

abridgement n اختصار

abroad adv در خارج

abroad n خارج

abroad (esp Europe) n فرنگ

abrupt adj
ناگهان • ناگهانی • ناگاه • ناگاهان

abruptly adv
دفعتاً • فوراً • بطور • ناگاه • ناگهان

absence (lack) n غیبت • عدم

absence (non-existence) n نیستی

absent (& pers) adj, n غایب

absolute (unlimited) adj مطلق

absolutely (certainly) adv • قطعاً
مطلقاً

absolutist adj مطلق

absolve (only God may) vt
آمرزیدن

absorbent adj جاذب

absorber n جاذب

abstain v پرهیز کردن

abstain (from sth) v تجنب اختیار
کردن

abstinence (from sth) n تجنب

abstinent (& pers) adj, n پرهیز گار

abstract adj مجرد

abstract (synopsis) n • اجمال
خلاصه

abstract noun (gram) n اسم معنی

abstraction (sth abstract) n مجرد

abstruse *adj* • پیچیده مغلق

absurd *adj* • پوچ • چتی

Abu Bakr (hist, caliph 573-634) *n* • ابو بکر

→ (form of address for Abu Bakr's descendants) خواجه

Abu'l Fazl (hist, chronicler 1551-1602) *n* ابو الفضل

abundance *n* • افزونی • برکت • فیض

abundant *adj* بسیاری • برخی • پر • فیض

abusive (colloq) *adj* شلیطه • سلیطه • لولی

Abyssinia (hist) *n* حبشه

acacia (tree, flower) *n* اکاسی

academy *n* اکادمی

accent (stress) *n* فشار

accept *vt* قبول کردن • پذیرفتن

→ be accepted پذیرفته بودن

acceptable *adj* قابل قبول • پذیرفتنی • موجه

acceptance *n* قبولی • پذیرش

accepting (of sth) *adj* پذیر

accessory (law) *n* شریک جرم

accident *n* • تصادم • اتفاق • واقعه • حادثه • تکر

accidental *adj* تصادفی

accidentally *adv* تصادفاً • تصادفی • اتفاقاً • نادانسته • ندانسته

acclaim *vt* آفرین خواندن • آفرین گفتن

accommodate (have room for) گنجیدن <در کجا> *v* <sw>

accommodating (& pers) *adj, n* خاطر خواه

accompany <sb> *v* در قبال داشتن • در رکاب <کسی> بودن • در رکاب <کسی> رفتن • همراهی کردن <کسی را>

accomplice (law) *n* شریک جرم

accomplice (partner) *n* • شریک • همدست

accomplish *vt* مجرا کردن • تکمیل کردن • دست آوردن • پرداختن

accomplishment *n* تکمیل • انجام • اکمال • دست آورد

accord *n* • هماهنگی • موافقت • موافقه • وحدت

accordance (compliance) *n* وفق • رعایت • رعایه • مراعات • مطابق

→ in accordance <w/sth> بر وفق • به موجب • مطابق <چیزی>

according to *prep* مطابق • برحسب • برطبق • بروفق • قرار • به قرار • به گفته • طبق • بر طبق • به قول • به نقل <کسی>

account (fund) *n* حساب

→ take into account محسوب کردن • محسوب نمودن

account (story) *n* قصه • حکایت

account book *n* دفتر

accountability *n* • حساب دهی • مسئولیت

accountable (& pers) *adj, n* حساب ده • مسئول

accountant *n* محاسب

accounting *n* محاسبه

accretion *n* ازدیاد • افزایش

accurate *adj* دقیق • مضبوط

accurately *adv* دقیقاً

accursed *adj* خدا شرمانده • خدازده • نفرین شده

accusation *n* تهمت • اتهام

accuse *vt see* blame

accused (& pers) *adj, n* متهم

accustomed (to) *adj* آموخته

→ be accustomed to عادت کردن

ace (cards) *n* توس

Achaemenid (& pers) *adj, n* هخامنشی

Achaemenids, the (hist, dynasty 559-300 B.C.) *n pl* هخامنشیان

Achakzai (P tribe) *n* اچکزی

achieve *v* حصول کردن • وصول کردن

achievement *n* • دست آورد • حصول • وصول

Achin (dist) *n* اچین

acid *n* تیزاب

acidic *adj* تیزابی

acknowledge *vt* اذعان کردن

acne *n* جوانی دانه

→ have acne بخار کشیدن

acquaintance (w/sb) *n* • شناسایی • شناخت • آشنایی • معرفت • آشنا

acquainted <w/sw (region, road)> (& pers) *adj, n* بلد <در کجا>

330

acquainted *adj* معرفی
→ be acquainted <w/sb> شناخت • داشتن • شناسایی داشتن • شناختن <همرای کسی>
→ get acquainted <w/sb> آشنا شدن • آشنایی حاصل نمودن <همرای کسی>
acquiesce *v* تن دادن
acquiescent *adj* فرمان بردار • فرمان دار • مطیع • تن ده
acquire *vt* حاصل کردن • حاصل نمودن • فرا گرفتن
acquitted (law) *adj* بری الذمه
acre *n* ایکر
acrobat *n* دارباز
acrobatics *n* داربازی
across *prep* از خلال
act (deed) *n* عمل • فعل • اجرا
act (legislation) see & law, decree
act (stage, film) *v* تمثیل کردن
act (take action) *v* عمل کردن
acting (minister) *adj, n* کفیل • سرپرست
acting (stage, film) *n* هنرپیشگی • تمثیل
action (deed) *n* اقدام • کنش
→ take action عمل کردن • اقدام کردن
activate (go into effect) *vi* فعال شدن • فعال گردیدن
active (gram) *adj* معلوم
active (in effect) *adj* فعال
activity (effect) *n* فعالیت
actor (agent) *n* فعال
actor *n* تمثیل کننده • هنرپیشه • بازیگر
actress see actor
actual (real) *adj* واقعی • حقیقی
actuality (reality) *n* واقعیت • حقیقت
actually (really) *adv* در فی الواقع • در واقع • واقعاً
adage (proverb) *n* ضرب المثل • مثل
Adam (bibl) *n* آدم • ابو البشر
→ Adam & Eve آدم و حوا
adamant *adj* یک پهلو
adaptability *n* نرمش پذیری
adaptable *adj* نرمش پذیر
add *vt* افزودن • علاوه کردن

added (attached) *adj* ملحق
addenda *n pl* ملحقات
addendum *n* انضمام
addict *n* معتاد
addicted *adj* معتاد
→ be addicted to عادت کردن
addiction *n* اعتیاد
Addis Ababa *n* ادیس ابابا
addition (increase) *n* علاوه • زیادت
addition *n* اضافه
→ in addition علاوتاً • به علاوه به • اضافی •
additional *adj* مزید
additionally *adv* مزیداً • زیادتاً
address (place) *n* آدرس
address (speech) *n* نطق • سخن • سخن رانی
addressee *n* مخاطب
Aden (former capital) *n* عدن
adept *adj* ماهر • تادست • لایق
adequacy *n* تکافو • کفایت
adhere (sth to sth) *vt* چسپاندن
adhere *vi* چسپیدن
adhesive *adj* چسپناک • چسپوک
Adina Masjed see Charbolak
adjectival *adj* صفتی
adjectival mood (verb) *n* وجه وصفی
adjective marker *n* نشانه اضافت
adjective *n* صفت
→ comparative adj صفت تفضلی
→ demonstrative adj صفت اشاره
→ superlative adj صفت عالی
adjoining *adj* پیوست
adjudication *n* احقاق • احقاق حق
adjustment *n* تصفیه
administer *v* اداره کردن
administering *n* سیاست
administration (office) *n* اداره • دفتر
administrative *adj* اداری • دیوانی
admiral *n* ادمیرال • امیرالبحر
admiration *n* استعجاب • تعجب • استعجابه
admission (entry) *n* دخول • در آمد • ورود
admit *vt* اذعان کردن

331

admittance (confession) *n* • اقرار • مقر

admixture *n* • اختلاط و امتزاج

admonish *v* • نصیحت کردن • اخطار دادن ‹به کسی›

admonition *n* • اخطار • نصیحت • اندرز • پند

admonitory *adj* • نصیحت آمیز

adolescent (& pers) *adj, n* • نوخاسته • نوخان • نورسیده • جوانک

adopt (child) *v* • فرزندی گرفتن

adopt (creed) *v* • روی آوردن ‹به چیزی›

adopt (practice) *vt* • ورداشتن • برداشتن

adoption (child) *n* • فرزندی گرفتن

adoption (policy) *n* • تطبیق

adore (& rel) *v* • عبادت کردن

Adraskan (dist) *n* • ادرسکن

adroit *adj* • ماهر • تادست • لایق

adulation *n* • چاپلوسی

adult *n* • کلان • بزرگ

adulterer *n* • حرام کار • زنا کار

adulterous *adj* • بد کار

→ commit adultery • زنا کردن

advance (progress) *n* • پیش رفت • پیشرفت • ترقی

advance (promote) *vt* • ارتقا دادن

advance *adj* • پیشکی

→ in advance • پیشکی

advanced (& pers) *adj, n* • پیشتر • پیش رفته • مترقی

advancement *n* • ارتقا • ارتقاء

advantage *n* • مفاد • نفع • منفعت

advantageous *adj* • سودمند • مفید • نافع

adventure *n* • ماجرا

adventurer *n* • ماجرا جوی • پر ماجرا • ماجرا جویانه

adventurous *adj* • ماجرا جوی • پر ماجرا • ماجرا جویانه

adventurousness *n* • ماجرا جویی

adverb *n* • قید

adversary (law) *n* • مدعی

adversary *n* • دشمن • خصم • مخاصم • عدو • ضد

advertise *v* • اعلان کردن

advertisement *n* • اعلان

advice *n* • پند • اندرز • نصیحت • مشورت • مشوره • مشاوره

advise *v* • نصیحت • مشوره دادن • صلاح دادن • کردن

advisor *n* • مشاور

advisory *adj* • مشورتی • نصیحت آمیز

adz *n* • تیشه

aerial *adj* • هوایی

→ aerial photograph • تصویر هوایی

→ aerial spraying • سمپاشی از طریق هوایی • سمپاشی

aesthetics *n* • زیبایی شناسی • زیبا شناسی • علم الجمال

affable (& pers) *adj, n* • خاطر پسند • دل خاطر • دل پسند

affair (matter) *n* • قضیه

→ love affair • عشق بازی

affairs (matters) *n pl* • امور • شئون

affected ‹by sth› *adj* • متأثر ‹از خاطر چیزی›

affection (fond regard) *n* • علاقه • تعلق • محبت • دوستی • مهر

affectionate *adj* • شفیق • مشفق • مهربان • شفیق • محبت آمیز • علاقه مند • علاقمند

affidavit *n* • اقرارخط

affiliation *n* • علاقه • علاقه یی • دل چسپی

affirmative (positive) *adj* • مثبت

afflicted ‹by sth› (& pers) *adj, n* • مبتلا ‹به چیزی› • مشقت دیده

affront *n* • اهانت • توهین

Afghan (pers) *n* • افغان

Afghan Border Police *n* • پولیس سرحدی افغان

Afghan hound *n* • تازی

Afghan Melat (pol party) *n* • افغان ملت

Afghan National Army *n* • اردوی ملی افغانستان

Afghan National Auxiliary Police (hist) *n* • پولیس کمکی افغان

Afghan National Civil Order Police *n* • پولیس نظم عامه ملی افغان

Afghan National Development Strategy *n* • ستراتژی انکشافی ملی افغان

Afghan National Security Forces n
قوت های امنیتی ملی افغان • نیرو
های ملی امینتی افغان
Afghan Uniform Police n پولیس
یونفورم دار ملی افغان
afghani (currency) n روپیه • افغانی
Afghanistan n افغانستان
aforementioned adj • مذکور
متذکره • مزبور • در فوق
afraid adj هراسان
→ be afraid ترس داشتن • ترسیدن
afresh adv مجدداً
Africa n افریقا
→ South Africa افریقای جنوبی
African (& pers) adj, n افریقایی
Afridi (P tribe) n اپریدی • افریدی
Afshar (Kabul city dist) n • افشار
افشر
after <sth> conj بعد از آن که • پس
از آن که
after <sth> prep بعد از •
متعاقب <چیزی>
→ after all سرانجام
after prep پس از
afterbirth n مشیمه • جفت • جوره
afterlife, the n عقبی • آخرت
afternoon n بعد از ظهر
→ late afternoon عصر • دیگر
afterwards adv بعد • بعد از آن بعداً
• پس از آن • از آن پس • باز •
سپس • پس از آن • متعاقباً
again adv یک بار دیگر • یک بار
دگر • از سر • دوباره • مجدداً
against prep بر ضد • به ضد •
مقابل
against prep به ضد • بر ضد • علیه
• مخالف • مقابل
Agam see Pachir wa Agam
agate n عقیق
age (of pers) n عمر
→ of (a given) age ساله
age (time period) n • دوره • عصر
سال
agency (authority) n مرجع
agenda n آجنده • آجندا
agent (authorized representative) n
گماشته • نماینده • وکیل
agent (factor) n عامل
agent (spy) n جاسوس • مخبر

agglutinative (gram) adj • پیوندی
التصاقی
aggression n تجاوز
aggressive adj متعرض • متجاوز
• جنگره • جنگروک • دست و پایی
aggressively n تجاوز کارانه
aggressor n تجاوز کار
agitate (excite) vt به هیجان آوردن
agitated (upset) adj سرخ شده
agitating (exciting) adj هیجان آمیز
agitation n هیجان
Agra (hist, Mughal capital) n آگرا
agree (compromise) v سازش
کردن • موافقت کردن • موافقه
کردن
agree (concur) <w/sb> vi موافق
بودن <با کسی>
agree (gram) v مطابقت داشتن
agreeable (friendly) adj گوار
گوار • لطیف • لطف آمیز • دل پذیر
agreeing (concordant) adj موافق
agreement (conformity) n • توافق
موافقت • موافقه
agreement (consent) n • موافقت
موافقه
agreement (contract) n قرار داد
agreement (gram) n مطابقت
agreement (likemindedness) n
وحدت فکر
agreement (understanding) n تفاهم
agreement n عهد • تعهد • پیمان •
میثاق • عقد
→ by agreement بالمقطع
agricultural adj زراعتی
agriculture n زراعت
agronomist n متخصص زراعت
agronomy n زراعت علمی
Ahl-e Hadith (hist, mvmt) n اهل
حدیث
Ahli Shirzi (16th-c Persian poet) n
اهلی
Ahmad (m name) n احمد
Ahmad Abad (dist) n احمد آباد
Ahmad Kheyl (dist, alt Lazha
Ahmad Kheyl) احمد خیل
Ahmad Shah Abdali see Ahmad
Shah Durrani

Ahmad Shah Durrani (hist, king 1723-1773) *n* احمد شاه درانی • احمد شاه ابدالی

Ahmad Shah Massoud (hist, fighter 1953-2001) *n* احمد شاه مسعود • احمد شاه مسعود

Ahmadiyya (sect) *n* احمدیه

Ahmadzai (P tribe) *n* احمدزی

Ahriman (rel) *n* اهریمن

Ahura Mazda (rel) *n* آهورا مزدا • اهورا مزدا

Aibak (seat) *n* ایبک

aid *n* مساعدت • امداد • مدد • معاونت • کمک

aid *v* مساعدت کردن • معاونت کردن • مدد کردن

aide (assistant) *n* کمک کننده

→ aide-de-camp • ضابط امر سریاور • حاضر باش

AIDS *n* ایدز • مرض ایدز • ایدس

ailing (sick) (& pers) *adj, n* مریض • بیمار

ailment *see* illness

aim (goal) *n* هدف • مطلب • مطمح • منظور • صدد • نظر • مورد نظر

aim (take aim) *v* نشان گرفتن • نشانه گرفتن • هدف گرفتن

aim (target) *n* آماج • آماج گاه • هدف • هدف گاه • نشان • نشان گاه • نشانه

Aimaq (ethn grp) *n* ایماق

air (space) *adj* فضایی

air (wind) *adj* بادی

air *adj see* & aerial

air conditioning *n* ایر کندیشن • ایر کندیشن

air force *n pl* قوای هوایی

air mail *n* پوسته هوایی

air mile *n* میل هوایی

air *n* هوا • باد

air route *n* خط هوایی

aircraft carrier *n* کشتی طیاره بردار • کشتی طیاره دار

airfield *n* میدان هوای

airman *n* عسکر قوای هوایی

airplane *n* طیاره • هوا پیما • جهاز هوایی

→ fighter plane • طیاره جنگی • طیاره شکاری

334

airport *n* میدان هوایی

airsickness *n* مریضی پرواز

ajar *adj* نیم باز • نیم واز • نیم کش

Ajrestan (dist) *n* اجرستان

Akbar (hist, Mughal emperor 1542-1605) *n* اکبر • جلال الدین محمد اکبر

Akbarnama (hist, narrative of 1st Anglo-Afgh war) *n* اکبر نامه

Akhtar (m/f name) *n* اختر

akhund (rel teacher) *n* آخند • آخوند

akhundzada (akhund born of family of akhunds) *n* آخوند زاده

alarm (fright) *n* رعب • بیم • ترس • خوف

alarm (sound) *n* زنگ خطر

→ alarm clock • ساعتِ زنگ دار

alas *excl* وای • هیهات • افسوس

Alasay (dist) *n* اله سای • السای

albinoism *n* پیسی

alcohol *n* شراب • الکول • باده • می

alcoholic (& pers) *adj, n* الکولی

alcoholic beverage *n* مشروب • مسکر

alcoholism *n* عادت شراب خوری

alef (letter) *n* الف

alef mad (letter) *n* الف مد

alert *n* آماده باش • گوش به آواز

→ on the alert

Alexander (m name, hist) *n* اسکندر

→ Alexander the Great (epithet) اسکندر ذوالقرنین

Alexandria (hist) *n* اسکندریه

Alexandrine (hist) *adj* اسکندری

Algeria *n* الجزایر

Algiers *n* الجزایر • الجزیره

Alhambra, the *n* حمرا

Ali (m name) *n* علی

Ali Abad (dist) *n* علی آباد

Ali Kheyl (ctr) *n* علی خیل

alien (foreign) *adj* بیگانه

alienation (foreignness) *n* بیگانگی • بیگانگی

alike *adj* مانند • متشابه • نظیر • شبیه • مشابه • متحد • الشکل

alimentary *adj* هضمی

alimentation *n* هضم • گوارش

Alingar (dist, river) *n* علینگار

Alisheng (dist) n علیشنگ

alive adj زنده • ذی حیات • حی
→ (having a soul) ذی روح •
ذیروح

al-Jazeera n الجزیره

all by oneself phrs یکه و تنها

all kinds of phrs بسیار چیزها

all n کل • تمام • همه
→ all of the people همهٔ مردم
→ all of us همهٔ ما
→ all rights reserved همه حقوق
محفوظ است
→ by all means به تمام معنی

all right adj خیر • به خیر

Allah n الله • خدا • خداوند •
خداوندگار • ایزد • یزدان

allegation n دعوا • زعم

allegiance (oath) n بیعت
→ show allegiance بیعت کردن

allegorical (dramatic) adj تمثیلی

allegory n رمز

allergy n حساسیت

alleviation n تخفیف

alley (lane) n کوچه • سرک • جاده

alliance n متحدین • اتحادیه
→ (coalition) ائتلاف

allied (united) adj متحد

alligator n تمساح • نهنگ •
سوسمار آبی

allocate (funds) vt تخصیص دادن

allocation (apportioning) n تقسیم

allocation (funds) n تخصیص

allot v اختصاص دادن

allotment n حصه

allow v بان که • بانین که

allowable adj جایز

allowed adj مجاز

alluring adj فریبنده • سحار

allusion (hint) n ایما

allusion (indication) n اشاره

alluvial adj رسوبی

alluvium (geol) n رسوب

ally n متحد

almanac n تقویم • جنتری • سال
نامه

Almar (dist) n المار

almond n بادام
→ Indian almond هلیله

almond-colored adj بادامی

almond candy n نقل

almost adv تقریباً •
به صورت تقریبی • بطور تقریبی •
به طور تقریبی • حدود • عنقریب

alms n pl خیرات

almsgiving n صدقه
→ almsgiving to poor before burial
of dead اسقاط

aloeswood (tree) n عود

alone adv تنها • به تنهایی • یکه

along prep در عرض

alongside prep در قبال

alphabet n الفبا

alphabetical adj الفبایی

alphosis n پیسی

alpinist n کوه نورد

al-Qaeda n القاعده

already adv وقت • وقتر • پیشتر

also (still) adv باز هم

also (too) adv نیز • هم • همچنان

Altair (double star) n نسر طایر

alter (mend) vt ترمیم کردن

alteration n ترمیم • تصریف •
صرف • گردان • تبدیل

alternate adj متناوب

alternately adv به تناوب • بالتناوب

alternating adj متناوب

although (sth) conj هر چند •
اگرچه • گرچه • با وجودیکه • با'یه
وجودی که • با وجود آن که

altimeter n ارتفاع سنج • آله ارتفاع
سنج

altitude n ارتفاع • بلندی

altogether adv مجموعاً • در
مجموع • روی هم رفته

always adv همیشه • مدام • همواره
• دایماً • دایم

Aman (hist, newspaper) n امان

Amanullah (m name, hist, king
1919-1929) n امان الله

amass vt توده کردن

amazed adj حیران • متحیر • مات

amazement n استعجاب • تعجب •
استعجابه

ambassador n سفیر

ambergris n عنبر
→ fragrant w/ambergris عنبر آگین

ambiguous adj متشابه • مبهم

ambition (neg) n جاه طلبی

335

ambition (pos) *n* آرزو

ambitious (neg) (& adv) *adj, adv* جاه طلبانه

ambitious (neg) (& pers) *adj, n* جاه طلب

ambitious (pos) (& pers) *adj, n* آرزومند • امیدوار

ambitious *adj* صفرا بر • صفرا شکن

ambulance *n* امبولانس

ambush *n* کمین

ambush *vt* کمین کردن

amends *n* تلافی • جبران

amenity (comfort) *n* نعیم

America *n* امریکا • آمریکا • ایالات متحده امریکا

American (& pers) *adj, n* امریکایی • آمریکایی

amethyst *n* لعل پیازی

Amman *n* عمان

ammonia *n* نوشادر

ammonium chloride *see* ammonia

ammunition *n pl* مهمات

amnesty *n* عفو عمومی

amoeba *n* آمیب

among *prep* بین • میان • مابین • از مابین • در مابین

amorous (drunk) (& adv) *adj, adv* مستانه

amount (quantity) *n* قدر • مبلغ • مقدار

amount (sum of money) *n* مبلغ • مقدار

amphibian *n* ذوحیاتین

amputation *n* قطع عضو

Amraan (bibl) *n* عمران

Amsterdam *n* امستردام

Amu Darya (river) *n* آمو دریا • دریای آمو • دریای پنج • جیحون

amulet (armband) *n* بازوبند

amulet (charm, us w/Quranic text) *n* تعویذ • طومار

ANA *see* & Afghan National Army

Anaba (dist, alt Unaba) *n* انابه

anaesthetization *n* تخدیر

anaesthetize *vt* تخدیر کردن

analgesic *adj, n* مسکن • دوای مسکن

analogous *adj* متشابه • مرادف

336

analogy *n* قیاس

analysis *n* تجزیه • تحلیل • تجزیه و تحلیل

→ blood analysis تجزیه خون

analytical *adj* تحلیلی

analytical geometry *n* هندسه تحلیلی

analyze *v* تجزیه کردن • تجزیه و تحلیل کردن

ANAP (hist) *see* Afghan National Auxiliary Police

Anar Dara (dist) *n* انار دره

ancestor *n* نیا • سلف • جد

ancestors (m) *n pl* پدران • اجداد • آبا و اجداد

ancestry (lineage) *n* سلسله

anchor *n* لنگر

ancient (from antiquity) *adj* قدیمی

→ the ancients قدما • مردم قدیم

ancient (old) *adj* باستان • باستانی • قدیم • قدامت دار

ANCOP *see* Afghan National Civil Order Police

and *conj* و

and/or *conj* و یا

Andar (dist) *n* اندر

Andarab (dist) *n* اندراب

Andijan (Uzbek city) *n* اندیجان

→ Andijan Timurids (see & Chaghatai) اندیجان تیموریان

Andkhoy (dist) *n* اندخوی

androgynous *adj* خنثی

ANDS *see* Afghan National Development Strategy

anecdote (lit) *n* حکایت

anecdote *see* & joke

anemia *n* کمخونی • فقرالدم

anemic *adj* کمخون

anew *adv* مجدداً

angel *n* ملک • فرشته • افلاکی • بغ

→ angel of cattle (Zor) بهمن

→ angel of fire (Zor) آذر

→ two angels who try faith of dead in their graves منکر و نکیر

anger (annoy) *vt* ناراض کردن

anger *n* خشم • قهر • غضب • غیظ • صفرا • ستیزه

angle *n* زاویه

angry (annoyed) *adj* ناراض

angry (furious) *adj* • خشمناک • غضبناک • خشم آگین • خشم آلود • غضب آلود • ارغند • ژیان

angry (quarrelsome) (& pers) *adj, n* • ستیزه جو(ی) • ستیزه خوی(ی) • ستیزه کار • ستیزه گر

→ get angry سر رفتن • دماغ سوختن • جلالی شدن • چشم کشیدن <سر کسی>

animal (beast) *n* جانور • حیوان

animal husbandry *n* نسل گیری

animal *n* حیوان

→ animals transformed from human state مسخ

→ domesticated animal حیوان اهلی

→ animal cub چوچه

→ wild animal حیوان وحشی • وحش

animate (living) *adj* جان دار

animate (w/soul) *adj* ذیروح

animosity *n* دشمنی • خصومت • عداوت

Anis (newspaper,m name) *n* انیس

anise *n* بادیان • رازونیاز

Ankara *n* انقره

ankle bone *n* بجلک

ankle *n* بند پای

anklet *n* پای زیب

annexation *n* الحاق

annexed *adj* الحاقی

annihilate *vi* از بین بردن • از میان بردن • نابود کردن

annihilated *adj* از بین برده • از میان برده • نابود

annihilation *n* نابودی • محو

anniversary (& birthday) *n* سالگره • سالگرد

announce <sth> *vt* خبر دادن <از چیزی>

announcement *n* اعلام • اعلامیه

announcer *n* گوینده • سخن گوی • سخن ران • نطاق

announcing *n* جهر • جار

annoy (sb) *vt* آزار دادن • اذیت رساندن • عذاب کردن • ناراض کردن

annoyance (dissatisfaction) *n* ملال • ملالت • نارضایت

annoyance (pestering) *n* آزار • عذاب • اذیت

annoyed *adj* ناراض

annoying *adj* ملال انگیز • ملالت انگیز

annual (& adv) *adj, adv* سالانه • سنوی

anonymity *n* خمول • گمنامی

anonymous (pers) *adj* گمنام

anonymous *adj* مجهول

another (& pers) *adj, n* دیگر • دگر

ANSF *see* Afghan National Security Forces

Ansuri (hist, 11th-c Dari poet) *n* عنصری

answer *n* جواب • پاسخ

→ unable to answer لاجواب

answer *v* جواب دادن

ant *n* مورچه

antagonism *n* دشمنی • خصومت • عداوت

antecedent *adj* پیشینه

antecedent *n* مقدم

anthem *n* سرود

anthill *n* مورچه خانه

anthrax *n* سیاه زخم

anthropologist *n* بشرشناس

anti-aircraft missile *n* مزایل ضد هوا

Antichrist (Imposter) *n* دجال

anticipation *n* پیش دستی

antidote *n* پادزهر • پازهر • تریاق

antidote *see* & treacle

antimony (eye liner) *n* سنگ سرمه

Antioch (hist, city) *n* انطاکیه

antipathy *n* نفرت

antipyretic (med) *n* تب بر

antique *adj, n* انتیک • عتیقه

antique seller *n* انتیک فروش

antique shop *n* انتیک فروشی

antiquity (being ancient) *n* قدامت • قدمت

antonym *n* کلمه متضاد • متضاد

anus *see* buttocks

anvil *n* سندان

337

نگرانی • تشویش • anxiety *n*
دغدغه
خدشه (lit) →
مشوش anxious *adj*
نگران • پریشان • anxious *adj*
مشوش
کسانی که anyone *pron*
هر چه anything *pron*
کم از کم anyway (at least) *adv*
ابهر • امالشرایین aorta *n*
اپارتمان apartment *n*
خون سرد apathetic *adj*
شادی • بوزینه • میمون ape *n*
دهان • دهن • منفذ aperture *n*
شهوت انگیز aphrodisiac *adj*
دوای شهوت انگیز aphrodisiac *n*
an aphrodisiac made w/gold →
dust کشته طلا
مکاشفه apocalypse (revelation) *n*
apologize (ask pardon) *vi* عذر
خواستن • معذرت خواستن • توبه
گفتن • پوزش خواستن
apologize (refuse politely) *v* عذر
خواستن • عذر کردن
عذر • معذرت • پوزش apology *n*
ارتداد apostasy *n*
شرک apostasy (polytheism) *n*
ملحد apostate (infidel) *n*
declaration of another (us fellow →
Musl) to be an apostate تکفیر
حواری apostle *n*
دستگاه • جهاز apparatus *n*
لباس • کالا • رخت apparel *n*
آشکار • نمایان • apparent *adj*
ظاهر
ظاهراً apparently *adv*
مرافعه • استیناف appeal (law) *n*
به میان آمدن • به appear (arise) *vi*
منصه ظهور رسیدن • فوراً ظاهر
شدن • طلوع کردن
به نظر رسیدن • appear (seem) *vi*
معلوم شدن • نمودن
ظهور • appearance (advent) *n*
بروز
place of appearance منصه →
شکل • appearance (form, look) *n*
صورت • نما • قیامه
استینافی appellate (law) *adj*
محکمه مرافعه appellate court *n*
338

لاحقه • پس وند appendage *n*
ملحقات appendices *n pl*
ذیل appendix (supplement) *n*
اشتها appetite *n*
اشتها آور • مشتهی appetizing *adj*
applaud *vt* آفرین خواندن • آفرین
گفتن
چک چک applause (clapping) *n*
آفرین applause *n*
سیب apple *n*
حنظل • bitter apple (colocynth) →
ترب وز ابو جهل • شرنگ
خواستار applicant *n*
درخواست • application (request) *n*
عریضه
اطلاق • application (use) *n*
استعمال
عملی applied (practical) *adj*
قرار دادن apply (put, set) *vt*
apply (use) <sth> *vt* کردن استعمال
<چیزی را>
مقرر کردن • گماشتن appoint *vt*
مقرر appointment (assignment) *n*
• تعیین
قرار appointment (for meeting) *n*
ملاقات • وعده ملاقات
make an appointment وقت →
دادن
برآورد appraisal (estimate) *n*
برآوردی appraiser *n*
قدردانی appreciation (gratitude) *n*
• تقدیر
قدردان • قدر appreciative *adj*
شناس
شاگرد apprentice *n*
apprentice's master ماستر →
حلول approach (coming) *n*
روش approach (method) *n*
لایق • ماهر appropriate *adj*
چابکدست • مناسب • مساعد
غنیمت گرفتن appropriate (take) *vt*
appropriation (allotment) *n*
اختصاص
قبولی • approval (acceptance) *n*
پذیرش
منظوری approval (authorization) *n*
تصویب approval (ratification) *n*
توشیح • approval (signature) *n*
امضا

approve (accept) vt • قبول کردن • پذیرفتن

approve (authorize) vt منظور کردن

approve (ratify, sign) vt تصویب کردن • به تصویب رساندن • توشیح کردن • به توشیح رساندن • صحه گذاشتن •

approved (authorized) adj منظور

approving n تجویز • تصویب

approximate adj تخمینی

approximate v تخمین زدن • تخمین کردن

approximately adv تقریباً • به صورت تقریبی • بطور تقریبی • به طور تقریبی • تخمیناً • از روی تخمین

→ (lit) حدود

approximation n تخمین

apricot n زردآلو

→ a kind of dried apricot شکر پاره

→ qaysi (sweet apricot) قیسی

→ dried apricot w/o stone اشتق

→ large, reddish-yellow apricot امیری

→ reconstituted dried apricots شلیل

April n اپریل

aptitude n استعداد

Aqcha (dist) n اقچه

Aqrab (month) n عقرب

Aquarius (zodiac) n دلو

aqueous adj آبگین

Arab (& pers) adj, n عرب • تازی

→ desert Arab (Bedouin) اعرابی

Arab (pers) n see & Arabian

Arabia n عربستان

→ Arabian peninsula جزیرت العرب • جزیرة العرب

→ Saudi Arabia عربستان سعودی

Arabian (& pers) adj, n عربی • تازی

Arabic adj see Arabian

Arabic (lang) n عربی

Arabist (scholar) n عرب شناس

arable adj زراعتی • قابل زرع • مزروعی

Aramaic adj آرامی

Aramean n آرامی

arbakai (shura enforcers) n اربکی

arbiter see mediator

arbitrate see mediate

arbitration see mediation

arbitrator see mediator

arch (archit) n طاق • کمان

archaeologist n باستان شناس • آرکیالوجیست

archbishop n اسقف اعظم

archenemy n دشمن درجه اول

archer n تیر انداز

archery n تیر اندازی

Archi (dist) n ارچی

Archimedes (hist) n ارشمیدس

archipelago n مجمع الجزایر

architect n مهندس • معمار • بنا • گل کار

architecture n مهندسی • معماری • بنایی • گل کاری

ardent adj آتشین

area (acreage) n مساحت

area (field) (& fig) n عرصه

area (neck of the woods) n گوشه

area (region) n منطقه • ساحه • زون • حوزه

→ area of a city ناحیه

→ jerib (unit of area) جریب

→ hectare (unit of area) هکتار

arena (field) n صحنه

arena (fig) n عرصه

Arghandab (dist) n ارغنداب

Arghanj Khwa (dist) n ارغنج خواه

Arghestan (dist) n ارغستان

Argo (dist) n ارگو

argue (mildly) v مشاجره کردن

argue (quarrel) <w/sb> v مجادله کردن <همرای کسی>

argue (reason) v حجت کردن

argument n جدال

argument (mild) n مشاجره

argument (quarrel) n مجادله

argument (reason) n حجت

argumentation n استدلال

Aries (zodiac) n حمل

arise (appear) vi به میان آمدن • طلوع کردن

arise (get up) vi خاستن • خیستن • برخاستن

aristocracy n pl نجبا

339

aristocrat *n* شریف
aristocratic *adj* شریف
Aristotle (hist) *n* ارسطو
arithmetic *n* حساب
ark *n* کشتی
→ Noah's Ark کشتی نوح
arm *n* بازو
arm (forearm & hand) *n* دست
arm (upper) *n* قول
arm (w/weapons) *vt* تسلیح کردن •
مسلح ساختن
arm's length (unit of meas) *n* قلاچ
armament *n* تسلیح
armband (esp w/amulet) *n* بازوبند
armed *adj* سلاح دار • مسلح
Armenia *n* ارمنستان
arming (w/weapons) *n* تسلیح
armistice *n* متارکه
→ declare armistice متارکه کردن
armor *n* زره
armor-clad *adj* زره پوش
armor-plated *adj* زره دار
armpit *n* زیر بغل
→ stinky armpit گنده بغل
armrest *n* بازو
army *n* اردو • عسکر • سپاه •
سپاهی • لشکری • قشون • قوای
زمینی
→ Afghan National Army اردوی
ملی افغانستان
→ army personnel office پیژنتون
→ army staff پیژند
→ levied army لشکر
around (near) <sth> *prep* پیرامون •
در پیرامون ‹چیزی›
around *prep* دور • به دور • در
اطراف
aroused (& pers) *adj, n* مست
arrange (order) *v* سامان دادن •
ترتیب دادن • نظم دادن
arrange (set up) *v* بر پای کردن •
تنظیم • ترتیب •
قرار • نظم
arrest *n* بازداشت • توقیف
arrest *vt* بندی کردن
arrival (coming) *n* ورود • وصول •
حصول
arrival (pers) *n* آینده

arrive (come) *vi* آمدن • رسیدن •
مواصلت کردن
arrive (document) *vi* واصل شدن
arrive (enter) *vi* وارد شدن • آمدن
arrived (come) *adj* آمده
arrived (document) *adj* واصل •
واصله
arrived (entering) *adj* وارد
arriviste *n* تازه به دوران رسیده •
نو به دولت رسیده • نو کیسه •
arrogance *n* نادیدگی • نادیدگی • آدم نادیده
arrogant (& pers) *adj, n* دماغ •
دماغی • طمطراق
arrow *n* تمتراق •
تیر
→ (lit) خدنگ
arrowhead *n* پیکان
arsenic *n* ار سنیک
art (craft) *n* کمال • فن • صناعت •
صنعت • هنر
art (var senses) *n* هنر
→ art patron هنرپرور
→ patronage of the arts
هنرپروری
arterial *adj* شریانی
arteriosclerosis *n* تصلب شرایین
artery *n* سرخرگ • رگ سرخ •
شریان
article (essay) *n* مقاله
article (law) *n* ماده
articulation (anat) *n* مفصل
articulation *n* تلفظ
→ point of articulation مخرج
artifice (trick) *n* حیله
artificial (false) *adj* ساختگی
artificial (manmade) *adj* مصنوعی
→ artificial insemination القاح
مصنوعی
artificial (style) *adj* مصنوع •
متکلف
artillery *adj* توپچی
artillery *n* توپ دافع
→ antiaircraft artillery توپ دافع
هوا
→ antitank artillery توپ دافع تانک
→ artillery depot جبه خانه
→ having artillery توپ دار
artilleryman *n* توپچی

كاسب • پیشه ور • artisan *n*
صنعتگر • صنعتکار
کسبی (colloq) ←
هنرمند • artist (performer) *n*
هنرور • آرتست • آرتیست
نقاش • نگارگر artist (pictorial) *n*
آرتست • آرتیست artiste *n*
هنری artistic (related to art) *adj*
artistic (skillful) (& adv) *adj, adv*
هنرمندانه
هنرمندی artistry *n*
علوم و فنون arts & sciences *phrs*
آریانی • آریایی Aryan *adj*
قسم که as (in same way) *adv*
as (in such a way) *adv* بطوری که
• به طوری که • چنان چه • چنانچه
• چنان که
منحیث • به as (in capacity of) *prep*
حیث
بعنوان • به as (in form of) *prep*
عنوان
تاجایکه as far as *phrs*
ذیلاً • از قرار ذیل as follows *phrs*
چنان که as has been seen *phrs*
دیده شد
به زعم آنان as they claim *phrs*
به زعم آنان as they say *phrs*
اسد Asad (month) *n*
اسعد آباد Asadabad (seat, dist) *n*
در اسرع وقت ASAP *phrs*
برآمدن ascend *vi*
ارتقایی ascendant *adj*
ارتقاء • ارتقا ascent *n*
مشخص کردن ascertain *vt*
زاهد ascetic (& pers) *adj, n*
خاکستر ash *n*
خجالت زده • ashamed *adj*
سرافگنده
شرم آمدن • تر be ashamed ←
شدن • سرافگنده بودن
ترتر be repeatedly ashamed ←
شدن
Ashari (rel, traditionalist school of
Musl theology) *n* اشعاری
عاشق Asheq (m name) *n*
اشرف Ashraf (m name) *n*
خاکستر دانی ashtray *n*
عاشور Ashur (m/f name) *n*

Ashura (day of Huseyn's
martyrdom) *n* عاشورا
آسیا Asia *n*
آسیای صغیر Asia Minor ←
آسیای جنوب Southeast Asia ←
شرقی
آسیایی Asian *adj*
بانک Asian Development Bank ←
انکشافی آسیا
پرسان کردن • ask (inquire) *v*
پرسیدن • سوال کردن
ask (request) <sth from sb> *vt*
خواهش کردن • خواستن <چیزی را
از کسی>
اجازه خواستن ask permission ←
خواب asleep *adj*
اسمار Asmar (ctr) *n*
مارچوبه asparagus *n*
جهت aspect (direction) *n*
جنبه • حیث aspect (view) *n*
چنار aspen (tree) *n*
سفیدار • چنار aspen (tree) *n*
اسفالت • قیر asphalt *n*
آرزو aspiration (dream) *n*
ass (backside) *n see* buttocks
خر • مرکب • الاغ ass (donkey) *n*
• اولاغ • اولاق
خر (& fig, pers) ←
حمله کننده • مهاجم assailant *n*
قاتل assassin *n*
به قتل رساندن assassinate *vt*
تهاجم • هجوم • حمله • assault *n*
تعرض • تاخت و تاز
تهاجم کردن • هجوم • assault *v*
آوردن • حمله کردن • حمله آوردن
• تاخت و تاز کردن
اجتماع • assembly (group) *n*
احتفال • گردهمایی • انجمن •
مجموعه
جرگه assembly (jirga) *n*
مجمع assembly (meeting) *n*
شورا assembly (shura) *n*
ادعا کردن • ادعا داشتن assert *v*
ارزیابی کردن assess *vt*
ارزیابی assessment *n*
کار کن • پرکار assiduous *adj*
مقرر کردن assign (task) *vt*
assigned (detailed) (& pers) *adj, n*
موظف • وظیفه دار

assignment (position) n ماموریت
assignment n مقرر
assimilation n هضم
assist <sb> v <به> کمک کردن
<کسی> • مساعدت کردن • مدد
کردن • معاونت کردن • اعانت
کردن • شانه دادن
assistance n کمک • کومک •
امداد • مدد • مساعدت • اعانت •
معاونت • خدمت • نوکری
assistant n کمک کننده • معاون •
معین
associate (companion) n هم نشین
• هم صحبت
→ associates (pl only) اصحاب
associate (coworker) n هم کار •
همکار
associate (member) n مربوط
associate (same profession) n هم
مسلک
association n اختلاط • امتزاج •
اتحادیه
assumption n فرض • فریضه •
گمان
assurance (certainty) n اطمینان
assure (comfort) vt خاطر جمعی
دادن
assured (comforted) adj خاطر
جمع
Astana n آستانه
asterisk n ستاره
asthma n نفس تنگی • نفس کوتاهی
• ضیق النفس
astonished adj خیره • حیران •
متحیر
astonishment n استعجاب • تعجب
• استعجابه
astrolabe n اسطرلاب
astrologer n منجم • اختر شناس •
اختر شمار • اختر شمر • ستاره
شمار • ستاره شناس • نجومی
astrological adj نجومی • اختر
شمار • اختر شمر • ستاره شمار
astrology n احکام نجوم • نجوم •
اختر شماری • ستاره شناسی
astronaut n فضا نورد
astronomical (celestial) adj فلکی
astronomist n دانشمند امور فلکی

astronomy n امور فلکی • علم نجوم
• نجوم
asylum n پناه
asylum-seeker n پناه گزین •
پناهنده
asymmetrical adj بی تناسب
at prep در • سر
→ (colloq) ده
at ease adj جمع
→ his/her mind is at ease خاطر
اش جمع است
atan (Afgh national dance) n اتن
Atar (hist, Sufi poet, 1161-1239
A.D.) n عطار
Ataturk (hist) n اتاترک
Atghar (dist) n اتغر
atheism n زندقه
Athens n آتن
athlete n ورزش کار
athletics n ورزش • جمناستک •
سپورت
Atlantic adj اتلانتیک
→ Atlantic Ocean بحر اطلس
atmosphere (climate) n فضا
atmosphere (environment) n محیط
atmospheric adj جوی
atmospherics (fig) n فضای روز
atom n اتوم
atomic adj اتومی • ذروی • هسته
یی • هسته وی
atomizer (perfume) n عطر پاش
atrocities (used in pl) n pl فجایع
attach v بند کردن
attache (official) n قنسل • قونسول •
قونسل • قونسول • کنسل
attached n ملحق • الحاقی • الحاق
attachment (annexation) n الحاق
attachment (document) n انضمام
attachment (linkage) n تعلق •
علاقه • سروکار • پیوست
attachments (accessories) n pl
متعلقات
attack n تهاجم • تعرض • هجوم •
حمله
attack vt هجوم آوردن • تهاجم
کردن • حمله کردن • حمله آوردن
attacker n حمله ور • حمله کننده •
مهاجم

342

attain <sth> v ‹به چیزی› نایل شدن

attain n حصول کردن • وصول کردن

attaining n احراز

attainment n حصول • وصول

attempt n کوشش • جهد • اهتمام • سعی

→ attempt & effort phrs جد و جهد

attempt vi کوشیدن • کوشش کردن

attend (be present) v حاضری دادن

attend (listen) v شنیدن

attendance n حاضری

attendance see & participation

attendant (at mosque) n خادم

attendant (to mil officer) n حاضر باش

attending (physician) adj معالج

attention (care, caution) n احتیاط

attention (heed, notice) n توجه • نظر

→ attention (mil order) دقت

→ attract attention جلب نظر کردن

→ fail to pay attention صرف نظر کردن

→ pay attention شنیدن • احتیاط کردن • متوجه کردن • توجه کردن

→ pay serious attention (to a problem) توجهِ جدی کردن

→ w/due attention <to sth> با توجه ‹به چیزی›

→ worthy of attention قابل توجه

attest v شهادت دادن

attestation n تصدیق

attitude n روحیه • روش

Attorney General n • څارنوال • څارنوال • لوی څارنوال • دادستان کل

→ Office of the Attorney General څارنوالی • څارنوالی

attorney n وکیل • وکیل مدافع • وکیل دعوا

attract v جذب کردن

→ attract notice جلب نظر کردن

attraction n جذب

attractive adj جذاب • مقبول • خوش قواره • خوش نما • خوب • گیرنده • گیرا • دل کش

→ نمکی (colloq)

attractiveness n جاذبه

aubergine n بادنجان • بادنجان سوسنی

auction n لیلام • مزایده

auctioneer n لیلام کننده • مزایده کننده

audience n pl شنونده گان • تماشابینان • تماشاچیان • تماشاگران

→ grant an audience بار دادن

audit n رسیدگی

auditor n کنترولر

auditorium n تالار

augmentation n تکثیر

August n آگست • اگست

aunt (father's sister) n عمه

aunt (mother's sister) n خاله

aunt (mother-in-law's sister) n خاله خشو

AUP see Afghan Uniform Police

Aurangzeb (hist, Mughal emperor 1658-1707) n اورنگ زیب

auspice (omen) n فال

auspiciously adv تیمناً

→ be auspicious قدم داشتن

auspiciousness n تیمن

austere (& adv) adj, adv زاهدانه

austere adj زاهد

austerity n تشدد

Australia n استرالیه • استرالیا

Australian (& pers) adj, n استرالیایی

Austria n آستریا • استریا • اتریش

authentic adj اصیل

authenticity n اصالت

author n نویسنده • ادیب • مولف

authoritative adj با نفوذ

authority (agency, source) n مرجع

authority (competency) n صلاحیت

authority (influence) n نفوذ

authority (pers) n معتبر

authority (power) n اختیار

→ authorities (govt) مقامات • بالا جای

authorization (approval) n منظوری

343

authorizaton (license) n • جواز • جواز نامه

authorize (approve) vt منظور کردن

authorize (empower) vt گماشتن

authorized (approved) adj منظور

auto parts shop n پرزه فروشی

automatic adj اتوماتیک • خود کار

automatically adv خود به خود • به خودی خود

automobile n موتر • موتر تیز رفتار

autonomous adj مستقل

autonomously adv مستقلاً

autopsy n اوتوپسی

autumn n خزان • تیرماه • پاییز • برگ ریزان

autumnal adj خزانی • پاییزی

→ autumnal equinox اعتدال خزانی

auxiliary adj معاون

availability n موجودیت

available adj موجود • بدسترس • به دست رس • حاضر

→ be available (exist) وجود داشتن • موجود بودن

→ have available دسترسی داشتن <به چیزی>

avalanche (snow) n برفکوچ

avalanche n بهمن

avenge v دل خود را یخ کردن

avenger n منتقم

avenue (road) n جاده

average (mean) adj میانه

average n اوسط

avert vt گرداندن • انداختن

averting n صرف • گردان

Avesta (Zor) n اوستا

→ chapter of Avesta نسک

Avestan (hist, lang) n اوستایی

aviation n هوانوردی • هوا نوردی

aviator n هوانورد • هوا نورد • پیلوت

Avicenna (hist, med author 980-1037 A.D.) n ابن سینا • ابو علی

avid (& pers) adj, n آزمند • حریص • گرسنه • گشنه • طماع

avidity n آز • حرص • طمع

avidly adv آزمندانه • حریصانه

avoid (sth) v احتراز کردن • تجنب اختیار کردن

avoid v اجتناب کردن

avoidable adj قابل اجتناب • اجتناب پذیر

avoidance (of sth) n • احتراز • تجنب

avoidance n اجتناب • تجنب • مجانبت • احتراز

award n جایزه

→ accept an award جایزه گرفتن

→ an award in consideration of <sth> یک جایزه به پاس <چیزی>

→ awarding a medal تعلیق مدال

→ give an award جایزه دادن

aware adj آگاه • با خبر • مطلع • واقف

awareness (spiritual) n نور • روشنی

awareness n آگاهی • اطلاع • با خبری • وقوف

awkward (artificial) (style) adj مصنوع • متکلف

awl (shoemaker's) n درفش

awning n سایه بان

Aws (hist, Arabian tribe) n اوس

axe n تبر

axiom n کلیه

axis n محور

axle n محور • اکسل

ayatollah (rel) n آیت الله

Aybak (dist) n ایبک

Ayesha (f name) n عایشه

Azerbaijan n آذربایجان

azimuth n ازیموت

azimuth (astron) n سمت

Azra (dist) n ازره

azure adj لاجوردی • ازرق

B

B.A. see Bachelor of Arts

B.C. (before Christ) adj قبل المیلاد

B.S. see Bachelor of Sciences

babble v ژاژ خاییدن کردن

babbling n ژاژ خایی

Babur (hist, Mughal emperor 1483-1530) n بابر • بابر شاه

Baburnama (hist, autobiography) *n* بابرنامه

baby *n* طفل • کودک

baby bottle *n* شیر چوشک

Babylon (hist) *n* بابل

Bachelor of Arts *n* لیسانس • دپلوم لیسانس

Bachelor of Sciences *see* Bachelor of Arts

back (rear) *adj* عقبی

back *adv* پس

back (& anat) *n* پشت
→ on one's back تخته به پشت

back (rear) *n* عقب

back & forth *adv* پیش و پس

backbiter (pers) *n* گپ گوی

backbiting *adj* گپ گوی

backbiting *n* غیبت

backbone *n* تیر پشت

backgammon *n* نرد
→ backgammon board تخته نرد
→ backgammon player نراد

backup *n* پشتوانه

backward *adj* عقب افتاده

backwardness *n* واپسی

bacteria *n* بکتیریا • جراثیم

Bactrian (hist, & lang) *n* باختری

bad (wicked) *adj* بد
→ that's too bad شرم است

Badakhshan (province) *n* بدخشان

Badghis (province) *n* بادغیس

bag *n* خریطه • خلطه
→ whole lamb- or goatskin bag سناچ • انبان

Baghdad *n* بغداد

Baghlan (province) *n* بغلان

Baghlan-e Jadid (dist) *n* بغلان جدید

Baghran (dist) *n* بغران • باغران

Bagram (dist, air base) *n* بگرام

Bagrami (dist) *n* بگرامی

bahar (flower) *n* بهار

bahar (spice) *n* بهارالبر

Bahar (f name, village) *n* بهار

Baharak (dist) *n* بهارک

Bahman (m name) *n* بهمن

Bahrain *n* بحرین

Bahram-e Shahid (dist) *n* بهرام شهید

bail *n* ضمانت

bait *n* طعمه

bait *v* طعمه دادن

Bak (dist) *n* باک

bake *v* پختن • پخته کردن

baker (pastry chef) *n* کلچه پز

baker *n* نانوا • نانوای • خباز
→ (colloq) نانبای

bakery (pastry shop) *n* کلچه فروشی

bakery *n* نانوایی • خبازی
→ (colloq) نانبایی

Bakhtar (Afgh news agency) *n* باختر

bakhti (kind of camel) *n* بختی

Baktashiyya (hist, Sufi order of janissaries) *n* بکداشیه • البکداشیه

Baku *n* بکو • باکو

Bakwa (dist) *n* بکواه

Bala Buluk (dist) *n* بالا بلوک

Bala Murghab (ctr) *n* بالا مرغاب

balance *n* موازنه • توازن • معادله • تعادل

balanced *adj* متعادل

balcony *n* بالکن • رواق • ایوان

bald (& pers) *adj, n* کل • تاس
→ go bald کل شدن

Balkans, the (geog) *n* بالقان

Balkh (province) *n* بلخ

Balkhab (dist) *n* بلخ آب

ball *n* توپ

ballistic *adj* بالستیکی
→ ballistic missile راکت بالستیکی

balloon (toy) *n* پوقانه • بالون

ballpoint pen *n* قلم خودکار • خود کار

balm *n* مرهم

Baloch *see* Baluch

Balochistan *see* Baluchistan

Baluch (ethn grp) *n* بلوچ

Baluchistan (geog) *n* بلوچستان

bamboo *n* بانس

Bamyan (province) *n* بامیان

ban *n* منع • ممانعت • نهی • قدغن • مصادره

ban *v* منع کردن • مصادره کردن • دست دادن

banana *n* کیله

band (gang) *n* دسته

band-aid *n* پلستر

Band-e Amir (park) *n* بند امیر

bandage پتی • بنداژ

bandage *vt* بستن •
→ (colloq) بسته کردن

bandit *n* راگیر

Bangi (dist) *n* بنگی

Bangladesh *n* بنگله دیش

bangle *n* بنگلی • چوری

bangs (f hair) *n* اوربل

banishment *n* تبعید • فرار

bank (institution) *n* بانک

bank (shore) *n* کنار • کران • لب
دریا

bank draft *n* حواله بانکی

banker (pers) *n* بانک دار • بانکدار

banking *n* بانک داری • بانکداری
→ related to banking بانکی

banknote *n* پول کاغذی

bankrupt ورشکست •
ورشکسته
→ go bankrupt ورشکست شدن •
ورشکسته شدن

bankruptcy *n* ورشکستگی • افلاس

banned *adj* ممنوع

banner *n* بیرق • پرچم • علم •
درفش
→ (lit) رایت

banquet *n* ضیافت • دعوت •
مهمانی

banter (joke) *vi* مزاح کردن

banter (teasing remark) *n* مطایبه

baptism *n* غسل تعمید

baptize *vt* غسل تعمید دادن

bar (for serving drinks) *n* بار

bar (rod) *n* میل

Bar Kunar (dist) *n* بر کنر

Baraki Barak (dist) *n* برکی برک

Barakzai (P tribe) *n* بارکزی

Baranzai (P tribe) *n* بارانزی

barbarian (non-Arab) *n* عجم

barbaric (& adv) *adj, adv* وحشیانه •
وحشتناک

barbaric (non-Arab) *adj* عجمی

barbarity *n* وحشت • وحشیگری

barbed *adj* خاردار
→ barbed wire سیم خاردار

barbeque *v* کباب کردن

barber *n* سلمانی • دلاک

346

barbering *n* دلاکی
→ related to barbering دلاکی

barbut (mus instr) *n* بربوط

bare *adj* برهنه • لچ • عریان

barefoot *adj* برهنه پای

bareheaded *adj* برهنه سر

Barg-e Matal (dist) *n* برگ متال

bargain *n* سودا

bargain (colloq) *v* چانه زدن • چنه
زدن • جگره کردن

bark *v* چخیدن

barley (barleycorn) *n* جو

Barmal (dist) *n* برمل

Barmecide (hist) *n* برمکه

barn (for hay) *n* کاهدان

barometer *n* هوا سنج • بارومتر •
میزان الهوا

barracks *n* قشله • قشله عسکری •
بارک

barrel (unit of meas) *n* بشکه

barrel *n* بیرل • بیلر

barren *adj* عقیم • نازای • خاره

barrier *n* مانع

basalt *n* مرمر سیاه

Basawul (ctr) *n* باسول

base (bottom) ماتحت

base (ignoble) *adj* پست • دنی •
نازل • گنده

base (mil) *n* پایگاه • قشله • قشله
عسکری

base, low *adj* دنی

baseball (Afgh version) *n* توپ دنده
• توپ بازی

based (sw) *adj* مستقر

based <on sth> *adj* بر اساس • بر
مبنای • مبنی بر <چیزی>

baseless *adj* عاری از حقیقت

basement *n* تاکو • تاکوی

basement *n* زیر خانه

bashful *adj* خجالت کش • خجالتی •
خجول • دیر آشنا
→ (colloq) شرمندوک

bashfulness *n* خجالت • خجلت

basic (fundamental) *adj* اساسی

Basij (Iran) *adj* بسیج

basil (sweet) *n* نازبو • نازبوی •
ریحان • شاه اسپرغم • شاه اسپرم •
شاه سپرم • شاه سپرهم

basin (pool) *n* حوزه

basis n اساس • زمینه • مبنا • بنیاد
• تهداب • اصل • عنوان • رکن

basket (wicker) n سبد • تکری
→ large wicker basket کجاوه

bat (club) n دنده

bat (mammal) n شب پره

bath n حمام • گرمابه
→ take a bath حمام گرفتن • حمام
کردن

bathhouse n حمام • گرمابه
→ bathhouse attendant حمامی •
گرمابه بان

bathroom n تشناب

Bati Kot (dist) n بتی کوت

Batiniyya (Shia sub-grp) n • باطنیه
اسماعلیه

battalion n کندک

battery (beating) n لت و کوب

battery (for power) n بتری

battle n جنگ • رزم • پیکار •
حرب • نبرد • محاربه • واقعه
→ related to battle رزمی

battle vi حرب کردن

battlefield n میدان جنگ • رزمگاه
• رزمگه • کارزار • معرکه • پیکار
گاه • آورد گاه

battlefront n جبهه • محاذ

battle-hardened (& pers) adj, n
جنگ آزموده • جنگ دیده • نبرد
آزموده

battlement n کنگره

battleship n کشتی جنگی

bay (geog) n خلیج
→ San Francisco Bay Area بی
ایریا

bay (horse) n قزل

bayonet n برچه

bazaar n بازار

Bazai (P tribe) n بازی

Bazarak (seat, dist) n بازارک

be vi بودن
→ (3rd pers sg, subj/cond form) (lit)
بود
→ be located <sw> قرار داشتن •
واقع شدن <در کجا>
→ so be it بادا • بادا
→ so be it (lit) بواد

beach n لب بحر

bead n مهره
→ Musl rosary beads تسبیح

beak (bird's) n نول • منقار

beam (ray) n شعاع • پرتو

beam (wooden) n تیر

bean (red kidney) n لوبیا

beard n ریش
→ newly-grown black beard خط

beard trimming n • اصلاح ریش
سنت

bearing (carrying) n حمل

beast n جانور • حیوان
→ wild beast جناور • جانور

beat (mix) v لت کردن

beat (sb) up v لت و کوب کردن •
لت کردن

beat (strike) vt زدن • کوفتن
→ beat a dead horse (fig) آهن
سرد کوفتن

beat (w/stick) vt see & flog, thrash

beating n لت و کوب • ضرب •
چوب کاری
→ (w/stick)

beautician n آرایشگر

beautiful adj زیبا • مقبول • نیکو •
عابد فریب • زاهد فریب • قشنگ

beauty mark (esp tattooed) n خال

beauty n زیبایی • جمال • حسن •
وجاهت

beauty queen n ملکه زیبایی

beauty salon n آرایشگاه

beaver n سگ لاوو

because <of sth> prep نسبت • بنابر
< از بهر <چیزی>

because conj از خاطریکه • به
خاطریکه • چرا که • زیرا • زیرا
که • چونکه • چون که • چون •
برای آنکه • برای اینکه

become vi شدن • گردیدن

bed n تخت خواب • بستر
→ travel bed بستره

bedbug n خسک

bedding n رخت خواب

bedding when bundled up n بوغ
بند

bedfellow n همخوابه • همبستر •
هم بستر

Bedouin n بادیه نشین • عرب بایده
نشین
→ Bedouin (pl) بدویون

347

bedroom *n* اتاق خواب • خواب گاه

bedsheet *n* روی جایی • روجایی

bedspread *n* روی کش • سرجایی

bee *n* زنبور عسل
→ (lit) نحل

beef *n* گوشت گو

beehive *n* کندوی زنبور عسل

beeswax *n* شمع

beet *n* لبلبو

before (previously) *adv* پیش • قبلاً • چندی قبل

before (prior to) <+ subj> *adv* قبل از آن که • قبل بر آن که • پیش از آن که

beg (for alms) *v* گداییگری کردن

beg (plead) *v* تضرع • لابه کردن • الحاح کردن • زاری کردن

beg (title) *n* بیگ

beget *vt* تولید کردن

beggar *n* گدا • گداییگر • مسکین
→ beg for alms صدقه خواستن
→ itinerant beggar مسافر

begging (beggary) *n* گداییگری • درویزه

begging (pleading) *n* لابه • تضرع • الحاح • زاری

begin *vi* شروع شدن • آغاز کردن • به راه انداختن • گشودن • بنا کردن
→ begin speaking بسم الله کردن

beginning *n* شروع • آغاز • ابتدا • اوایل • اول • افتتاح • گشایش • فاتحه • آمد آمد • بدو • سر • بادی • بنا
→ (fig) طلوع

begotten *adj* متولد

behalf of <sb> *prep* از طرف • از جانب <کسی>

behavior *n* رفتار • رفتاری • رویه • سلوک

behead <sb> *vt* سر <کسی> گردن بریدن • سر زدن

behind *prep* پس

behind *prep* پشت • در پشت • از پشت • پشت سر • در پشت سر • پی

behold (lit) *excl* هان • هین

Behsud (dist, ctr) *n* بهسود

beige *adj* کریمی

Beijing *n* بیجینگ • پیکنگ

being (existence) *n* بودن • بوش

348

being (living) *n* موجود

Beirut *n* بیروت

belch (> F) *v* اروغ زدن • بشدت بیرون انداختن

Belcheragh (dist) *n* بلچراغ

Belgian (& pers) *adj, n* بلجیمی

Belgium *n* بلجیم

Belgrade *n* بلگراد

belief (creed, opinion) *n* کیش • آیین • عقیده • عقیدت • نظریه • اعتقاد • ایمان

belief (trust) <in sb/sth/that...> *n* باور <به کسی / چیزی / که...>

believe (think) *v* فکر کردن

believe (trust) *v* باور کردن

believer (rel) *n* گرویده

bell (church) *n* ناقوس

bell (small) *n* زنگوله

bell *n* زنگ • جرس • ناقوس

bell pepper *n* مرج دولمه یی
→ stuffed bell pepper دولمه

belles lettres *n* ادبیات

bellows *n* دم

belly *n* شکم • معده
→ (& fig) بطن

belonging <to sb/sth> *adj* مربوط <به کسی/چیزی> • متعلق <(به) چیزی / کسی>

beloved (fig) *n* عزیز • محبوب • لعبت • گدی

below *prep* زیر • در زیر • تحت • پایان • ماتحت • پائین • پایین • پایینی (colloq)

belt (leather) *n* تسمه

belt *n* کمر • بند • کمربند
→ shoulder belt حمایل
→ shoulder belt (colloq) حمایل

belt *v* کمر بستن

bend (curve) *n* خم

bend (in road) *n* گولایی

bend *vt* قات کردن

beneath *prep* زیر • در زیر • تحت • پایان • ماتحت

benefactor *n* منعم • کمک کننده

beneficence *n* فیض

beneficent *adj* پر فیض

beneficial *adj* مفید

benefit (employment) *n* امتیاز

benefit from (use) <sth> vi مستفید شدن ‹از چیزی›

benefit n بهره • فایده • ثمره • خوبی • نفع • منفعت

benefiting from adj بهره مند • بهره ور • مستفید

benevolent (& pers) adj, n خیر اندیش • نیک اندیش • نیکو کار

benevolently adv خیر اندیشانه

Bengal (geog) n بنگال
→ East Bengal (hist) بنگال شرقی
→ West Bengal بنگال غربی

Bengali adj بنگالی

bent adj دوقات • کمان • برگشته

bequeath vt میراث ماندن

bereaved adj مرده دار • سیاه پوش • ماتم دار • ماتم دیده • ماتم زده • سوکوار • عزادار

Berlin n برلین

Bern n برن

berry n توت

beryl n بلور

besides <sth> prep علاوه بر • بر علاوه • افزون بر ‹چیزی›

besides adv علاوتاً • به علاوه

bespectacled adj عینکی

best (choice) (vulg) adj زبده

best adj بهین

best adj خوبترین • بهترین

bestow vt بخشیدن • اعطا کردن

bet n قمار • داو • شرط • شرایط

bet v قمار زدن • قمار بازی کردن • داو زدن • شرط کردن

betel leaf n پان

Bethlehem n بیت اللحم

betrayal n خیانت
→ betrayal of secrets (fig) پرده دری

betrothal (fig) n لفظ

better adj بهتر • اعلی
→ (colloq) چربتر

betting n قمار بازی

bettor n قمار باز • آدم قمار باز

between prep بین • میان • مابین • از مابین • در مابین

beverage n نوشیدنی

beverages n pl اشربه

beware excl برحذر • برحذر باش • هان • هین

bewildered adj سرگشته • سرگردان • حیران • متحیر • بهت زده

bewildering adj بهت آور • بهت انگیز

bewilderment n بهت

beyond prep مافوق

bhang n بنگ • کنب

bias n طرف داری • جانب داری

biased adj طرف دار • جانب دار • پله بین

Bibi Mahru (Kabul city dist) n بی بی مهرو

Bible, the n کتاب مقدس

bicycle n بایسکل

bid (auction) n داو
→ make a higher bid داو بالا کردن

bid (tender) n آفر • پیش نهاد • پیشنهاد

bid farewell v بدرود گفتن • وداع کردن • وداع گفتن

bidder n داوطلب • داو طلب
→ highest bidder at auction مزایده کننده

big adj کلان • بزرگ

bigoted adj تنگ نظر • متعصب

Bihar (geog) n بهار

bilateral adj دوطرفه

bile n صفرا • زرد آب

bilingual adj ذواللسانین

bilious adj صفراوی • صفرایی

bilking (customers) n بازار تیزی

bill (bird's) n نول • منقار

bill (invoice) n بل

bill & coo v رازونیاز کردن

bill of lading n لست اموال

billfold n بکس جیبی

billion adj, n بلیون • ملیارد

billionaire n ملیاردر

billow n موج • موجه

binary adj دو گانه

bind vt بستن • مقید ساختن
→ (colloq) بسته کردن

binoculars n دوربین

biography n داستان زندگی
→ bio (brief) سوانح
→ biography of poet تذکره • تذکرت الشعرا • تذکره شاعران

biology n بیولوژی • علم الحیات

349

biplane *n* طیاره دوباله	Black Sea *n* بحیره اسود • بحیره سیاه

biplane *n* طیاره دوباله
bird *n* پرنده • طایر • طیر
→ (lit) مرغ
→ hind toe of game bird پیخ
bird call *n* نغمه سرایی
bird droppings *n* پیخ • پیخال
birth certificate *n* تذکره تولد
birth *n* تولد • مولود
→ childbirth ولادت
→ give birth to (d.o. does not take marker) زائیدن را-
→ related to childbirth ولادتی
→ time of birth میلاد
birthday *n* سالگره تولد • روز تولد • مولود
→ Prophet's/Jesus' birthday میلاد
birthplace *n* محل تولد • مولد • مسقط الراس • زادگاه
biscuit *n* بسکیت • بسکویت • بشکک
Bishkek *n* بشکک
bishop (chess) *n* فیل
bishop *n* اسقف
bisyllabic *adj* دو هجایی
bit by bit *phrs* ذره ذره
bit, chip; crumb (colloq) *n* رزگی
bitch (f dog; & fig, insult) *n* ماچه • سگ
bite (as dogs do) *v* چک انداختن
bite (morsel) *n* لقمه
bite (sting) *vt* گزیدن
bite *v* چک زدن
bitten (stung) *adj* گزیده
bitter (& fig) *adj* تلخ • زار
→ sth bitter; tree w/bitter fruit زقوم
bitterly *adv* به تلخی
bitterness *n* تلخی
bitumen *n* مومیایی
bivouac *n* کمپ
blabbermouth *n* تنک ظرف
black & shiny *adj* زاغ
black (& fig) *adj* سیاه • سیه
black (color) *adj* سیاه • سیاه رنگ • سیاه فام • قره • اسود
→ black (horse) مشکی
→ ebony black آبنوسی
→ musk-colored (black) مشکین
black pers (colloq) *n* گندمی • حبشی

Black Sea *n* بحیره اسود • بحیره سیاه
Black Stone (of Kaaba) *n* حجر الاسود
blackboard *n* تخت • تخته سیاه
blackmail *n* باجسبیل
blackmailer *n* باجگیر
blackness *n* سیاهی
blacksmith *n* آهنگر
bladder (anat) *n* مثانه
blade *n* تیغ • پل • پاکی
→ well-tempered (blade) جوهردار
blame (censure) *n* ملامت
blame (censure) *vt* ملامت کردن
→ be blamed *vi* ملامت شدن
blame <sb for sth> *vt* متهم کردن <کسی را از چیزی>
blameless *adj* معصوم • معصومانه • بیگناه
blameworthy *adj* ملامتی • ملامتی
blank *adj* خالی
blanket (kilim) *n* گلم • گلیم
blanket (quilt) *n* لحاف
blanket (woolen) *n* پتو • کمپل
blasphemy *n* کفر
→ speak blasphemies کفر گفتن
blast (from explosives) *n* سرنگ
blast *v* سرنگ پراندن • سرنگ پرانی کردن
blasting *n* سرنگ پرانی
blather *v* عبارت پردازی کردن • هذیان گفتن
blaze *n* شعله • لهیب
blaze *v* شعله زدن
blazing (& fig) *adj* شعله ور
bleeding *n* خون ریزی
blend *n* مخلوط
blend *vt* مخلوط کردن
blended *adj* مخلوط
blessing *n* خیر • برکت
blessing (from God) (rel) *n* برکه
blind (& pers) *adj, n* کور • اعمی • ازرق
blindfold *n* دستمال بینی
blink *v* پلک زدن • مژه بر هم زدن
blister *n* آبله
blithe *adj* سهل انگار

blizzard n بوران
→ (colloq) بادکویه • باد کویه
bloat n see bloating
bloat vi نفخ کردن
bloating n نفخ
bloc (pol grouping) n بلاک
block (obstruct) v مسدود کردن • بسته کردن • بند کردن
blockade n محاصره
blockade vt محاصره کردن
blocked adj مسدود • بسته
→ be blocked مسدود شدن • بسته شدن
blockhead (insult) n گوساله • لوده
blonde adj مطلایی
blood money n خون بها
blood n خون
blood relationship n خون شریکی
→ having a blood relationship سکه
blood vessel n وعا • رگ • عرق
bloodshed n خون ریزی
bloodsoaked adj آغشته به خون
bloodstained adj خون آلود
bloodthirsty (& pers) adj, n خون آشام • خون خوار • خون ریز
bloody adj خونین • پر خون • خون پر
bloom v گل کردن • شکوفه کردن
blossom n شکوفه • شگوفه
→ (fig, f) نو عروس
blossom v گل کردن • شکوفه کردن
blot (& fig) n لکه
blow (hit) n ضربه • مشت
blow up (explode) vt پراندن
blowing on (mus instr) n نفخ
blowpipe n پفک • تفک
blue (color) adj آبی
→ azure کبود • ارزق • لاجوردی
→ bluish-black (eye color) شهلا
→ cyan (sky blue) آسمانگون • آسمانی
→ indigo blue نیلگون • نیلی
→ lotus-blue نیلوفری
→ navy blue سرمه یی
blueprint n نقشه • خریطه
blues, the n عقده دل
blush vi سرخ شدن

boar n خوک • خنزیر • جناور • جناور بد
→ wild boar خوک وحشی
board (commission) n هیئت • هیأت • بورد
→ board of directors هیئت مدیره
board (& wood plank) n تخته
→ made of wood boards تخته یی
board (tablet) n لوح • لوحه
board (embark) vi سوار شدن
boarding school n لیلیه
boarding pass (airplane) n کارت سوار شدن به طیاره
boast (lit) vi لافیدن
→ (colloq) لاف زدن
boastful adj خود ستا • تمتراق • طمطراق
boasting n پف
boat n کشتی • سفینه
bobbin n ماسوره • ماشوره
bobby pin n سیخک
bodily adj جسمانی
bodkin for drawing pajama drawcord through waist n بند کش
body (& human) n جسم
→ (colloq) جان
body (chassis) adj بادی
body (figure) n اندام • بدن • تن • هیکل
body (organism) n وجود
bodyguard n بادی گارد
bog n باتلاق • مرداب
Bogota n بگوتا
boil (boiling) n جوش
→ (& fig) غلیان
boil vi جوشیدن
→ boil over (& fig) سر رفتن
→ come to a boil جوش آمدن
boil vt جوش دادن
→ bring to a boil جوش آوردن
Bokhara (city) n بخارا
Bokharan adj بخارایی
bolan (wild leek) (cul) n بولان
bolani (pastry) n بولانی
bold adj دست و پایی • مردانه وار • مردانه • دلاور • دلیر • به جرئت • با جرئت • تیز چنگ • تیز چنگال
Bolshevik (hist) n بلشویک
bolt (rifle) n گیت

351

bolt (screw) n پیچ
→ nut & bolt خشت و پیچ
bolt n بولت
bomb n بم
bombard v بمبارد کردن • بمباران کردن
bombardment n بمباردان • بمباردمان
bombast n آب و تاب
Bombay (city) n بمبیی
bomber (plane) adj, n بم افگن • طیاره بم افگن • بم انداز
bon appetit excl نوش جان کنین
bon voyage excl سفر بخیر
bond (document) n سند
bond (tie) n عقد • رشته
bone n استخوان
bony adj استخوانی
boo (to scare children) excl اخ
boo-boo (slight error) n تخطی
book cover n پشتی
book jacket n پوش کتاب • وقایه
book market n بازار کتاب فروشی
book n کتاب
→ notebook کتابچه
→ people of the book اهالی کتاب
Book of Omens n فالنامه
book publisher n ناشر کتاب
bookbinder n صحاف
bookbinding n صحافت
bookcase n الماری کتاب
bookkeeping n محاسبه
booklet n کتابچه
bookseller n کتاب فروش
bookstore n کتاب فروشی
boot (shoe) n بوت
→ boot from ankle to knee ساق
→ boot polish رنگ
→ homemade boot used by villagers چارق • چموس
→ knee-length boots موزه
booty n غنیمت
borax (crude, native) n تنکار
borax n بورکس
border n سرحد • مرز
border police n پولیس سرحدی افغان
border post (land) n پوسته سرحدی
border post (port) n بندر

bordering <sth> adj سرحد • متصل <به چیزی> • متصل <چیزی>
bored adj دق
boredom n ملال • ملالت
boric acid n بورک اسید
boring n خسته • ملال انگیز • ملالت انگیز
born (begotten) adj متولد
→ be born تولد شدن • به جهان آمدن • به جهان چشم باز کردن
borne (carried) adj برده
borrow (money) vt قرض کردن • قرض گرفتن
borrow vt عاریت خواستن • عاریت گرفتن
borrowed adj عاریتی • ماخوذ • دخیل • مستعار
bosom n آغوش • بغل • سینه
boss n آمر
bossy adj سرتنبه • امرانه
botanical adj گیاهی
botanist n گیاه شناس • نبات شناس
botany n گیاه شناسی • علم نباتات • نبات شناسی
both adj, pron هر دو
both ... and ... adv هم ... هم ...
bother (go to trouble) v زحمت کشیدن
→ don't bother زحمت نکشین
bother (harass) v به ستوه آوردن
bother (interrupt) v مزاحمت کردن • مزاحمت ایجاد کردن
bother n زحمت • رنج • مشقت • جنجال
bother v see & annoy
bothered adj خاطر آشفته • آشفته خاطر
bothersome (& pers) adj, n مزاحم
bottle n بوتل • شیشه
→ baby bottle شیر چوشک
→ long-necked silver bottle for rosewater گلابپاشی
bottom n زیر • پایان • حضیض • درک • صمیم
bottom (sexually, obs) v کون دادن
boulder n صخره
boulevard n جاده
bound (tied) adj مقید
bound for adj عازم

boundary n • کران • حد فاصل • کرانه

→ boundaries (frontiers) ثغور

boundless adj بیکران • بی کران

bouquet n دسته گل

bourgeois adj بورژوا

bourgeoisie n بورژوازی

bourse n بورس

boutique n بوتیک • دکان

bow (for violin) n کمانچه

bow (prow) n سینه کشتی

bow (weapon) n کمان

bowl (for drinking) n ایاغ

bowl (sm, metal) n تاس

bowl (us metal) n کاسه

→ bowl (goblet) جام

→ bowl for drinking wine (lit) ساغر

→ bowl for rinsing tea dishes آب کشی

→ earthen bowl بادیه

bowstring (arch) n چله

box n صندوق • قطی • جعبه

boy n بچه • پسر

→ boys', for boys بچه گانه

Boyna Qara see Sholgara

boys' (lit) adj پسرانه

boysenberry n شاه توت

bra n سینه بند

bracelet n دست بند

→ glass bracelet بنگلی • چوری

→ wide bracelet (& jeweled) کره

brag (lit) vi لافیدن

→ (colloq) لاف زدن

→ brag (tell tall tales) داستان پرداختن

braggart n لافوک • خود ستا • داستان پرداز

bragging (fig) n پف

Brahui (ethn grp, lang, pers) n براوی • بروبی

braid (hair) n چوتی • گیسو

braid v بافتن

braid (hair) v چوتی کردن

brain n مغز • دماغ

→ endowed w/brains ذوی العقول

→ related to the brain مغزی

brake (of vehicle) n برک

bramble n بته خار

bran n سبوس

branch (subdivision) n شق

branch (tree) n شاخ

brassiere n سینه بند

brave adj مردانه وار • مردانه • دلاور • دلیر • به جرئت • با جرئت • تیز چنگ • تیز چنگال

→ brave man (lionheart) ارسلان

bravery n جرئت • شجاعت • رشادت

→ show bravery in battle (fig) شمشیر زدن

bravo excl آفرین

brazier (cul) n اجاق • اجاغ • آتشدان

breach n نقض

→ breach of promise وعده خلافی • وعده شکنی

breach see & gap

bread n نان خشک

→ daily bread (fig) قوت

→ flat, round loaf of bread قرص

→ long, flat bread with hand mark پنجه کش • دستکی

→ round, flat, thick, sweet bread روت

→ thin, large, round bread baked in a tanur چپاتی

breadth n عرض • پهنا • پهناوری • پهنی • بر

break (fracture) n کسر

break (pause) n تقریح • وقفه

break vi شکستن

→ break (fracture) کسر کردن

→ break down خراب شدن

break vt شکستاندن

→ break off قطع کردن • بریدن

→ break ranks صف شکستاندن

breakable adj شکننده

breakfast n چای صبح • چای • ناشتا

→ eat breakfast چای خوردن

breakwater adj, n موج شکن • دیوار موج شکن

breast n سینه • پستان

→ breast cancer سرطان سینه

breastwork n مورچل • سنگر

breath n دم • نفس

353

breathe *vi* • دم زدن • نفس کشیدن
→ breathing in بخور
→ breathing out زفیر
breathy (& pers) *adj, n* فش فشی
breeches (mil) *n* برجیس
breed *n* جنس • نژاد • نسل • عرق
breeding (animal husbandry) *n*
نسل گیری
→ horse breeding گله داری
breeze *n* نسیم
bribe (proposal) *v* طعمه دادن
bribe *n* رشوت • رشوه • طعمه
bribe-giver *n* راشی
bribery *n* ارتشا
bribe-taker *n* مرتشی
bric-a-brac *n* تک و تک • تک و پک
brick *n* خشت
→ Brick Bridge Mosque (Kabul)
مسجد پل خشتی
bridal chamber *n* حجله
bridal shower *n* پای وازی
bride *n* عروس
bridegroom *n* داماد
brideprice *n* تویانه • پول تویانه • کابین
bridge (card game) *n* بریج
bridge (music) *n* خرک
bridge (span) *n* پل
→ bridge construction پل سازی
bridle (of rope, for donkey) *n* افسار
bridle *n* عنان • زمام • لجام • لگام
briefly *adv* اختصاراً • با الختصار • مختصراً
brigade *n* لوا
brigadier general *n* مل پاسوال • برید جنرال • لوا مشر
bright *adj* روشن • تیز • ذکاوت داشتن
→ be bright روشنی
brightness *n* نور
brilliant *adj* ابهر • لالا
brine *n* نمک آب
bring *vt* آوردن
bring in *vt* درآوردن • در آوردن
bringing *n* جلب
brisket *n* سینه
briskness *n* رونق
bristle *n* موی
Britain *n* برتانیه • بریتانیا

British (& pers) *adj, n* برتانوی
broad (extensive) *adj* • دامنه دار پهن • مپهن
broad (wide) *adj* • عریض • وسیع پهن • پهناور • دریای پهناوری • مپهن • فراخ • بر دار
broad-based *adj* فراخ بنیاد
broadcast *n* نشر • پخش
broadcast *vt* پخش کردن • منتشر کردن
broaden *vi* توسعه یافتن
broaden *vt* توسعه دادن
→ (colloq) بزرگ ساختن
broadening *n* توسعه • توسیع
broad-minded (& pers) *adj, n* روشن فکر • روشن دل
brocade *n* پارچه
broil (cul) *v* کباب کردن
broken *adj* شکسته • خراب • دست و پای شکسته
broker *n* دلال
bronchitis *n* برونشیت
bronze *n* برونز • مفرغ
brooch *n* سنجاق سینه
brook *n* جویچه • جوی • نهر
broom *n* جارو • جاروب
brother *n* برادر
→ (colloq) بیادر
→ foster brother کوکا
→ killing one's brother برادر کشی
→ older brother آغا • آقا
brother in arms *n* همرزم • همنبرد • همسنگر
brother-in-law (husband's brother) *n* ایور
brother-in-law (sister's husband) *n* یازنه • آغا لاله
brother-in-law (wife's brother) *n* خسر بره
brown (snuff-colored) *adj* نسواری
→ (colloq) نصواری
→ almond brown بادامی
→ coffee brown قهوه یی
→ cumin brown زیره یی
→ sugar-brown شکری
→ walnut brown چارمغزی
→ wheat-brown اسمر
brown sugar *n* گر
brown-haired *adj* موخرمایی

354

bruise (on fruit) n زدگی

brunet(te) adj موخرمایی

brush n برس

Brussels n بروسل • بروکسل

brutal adj وحشیانه • وحشتناک • خدا ناشناس • خدا ناترس

brutality n وحشت • وحشیگری

bubble n پوقانه • حباب

→ bubble-shaped حبابی

Bucharest n بخارست

bucket n دول • دوله

→ leather bucket دلو

buckle n سگک

Budapest n بوداپشت • بوداپست

Buddha n بودا

Buddhism (rel) n بودایی • آیین

بودایی • کیش بودایی • دین بودایی

Buddhist adj بودایی

Buddhist (pers) n بودایی • بخشی

buddy n رفیق • دوست

budget n بودجه • هزینه

→ budget allocation تخصیص

buffalo n گاو میش

buffoon n مسخره • مسخره باز

buffoonery n مسخره بازی

bug (insect) n حشره

bug (pester) <sb> vt آزار دادن

<کسی را> • عذاب کردن

bug see malfunction

bugle (esp mil) n ترم

build vt ساختن • آباد کردن

→ build castles in the air خیالات

خام پختن

builder n معمار • بنا • گل کار

building (construction) n اعمار

building (structure) n تعمیر •

عمارت • عمران • آباد

→ small building ساختمان

→ outbuilding سراچه

building adj تعمیراتی

→ building materials مصالح

تعمیراتی

Bukhara see Bokhara

Bukharan see Bokharan

bulb (plant) n پیاز

→ light bulb گروپ

bulbul (songbird) n بلبل • عندلیب

Bulgaria n بلغاریا • بلغاریه •

بلغارستان

Bulgarian (& lang, pers) adj, n

بلغاریایی • بلغاری

bulky & lightweight adj پوک

bull n گاو • ثور

→ breeding bull بقه

bullet n گلوله • مرمی • تیر

bullseye n نشان نگاه

bully v تخویف کردن

bullying n تخویف • ارعاب

bulrush n لخ

bump on the head n بغند • بغندی

bunch n دسته

→ bunch (of vegetables) قبضه

→ in bunches دسته دسته

bunker n بلنداژ

burden n بار

→ become a burden (to sb) تلک

گردن شدن

burdening n تحمیل

burdensome adj تحمیلی • سنگین

bureau n ریاست • اداره • دیوان •

→ (colloq) دفتر

bureaucrat n مامور

burglar n دزد • سارق

burglary n دزدی • سرقت

Burhan-e Qatey (17th-c Dari dictionary) n برهان قاطع

burial (interment) n دفن • تدفین

→ burial ground وادی خاموشان

Burka (dist) n برکه

Burma n برما

Burmese (& pers) adj, n برمایی

burn (injury) n سوختگی • حریق

burn vi سوختن • حریق شدن •

حریق گردیدن

burn vt سوختاندن • در گرفتن

burning n احتراق

burning (inflammation) n التهاب

burning hot adj سوزان • داغ

burnt adj سوخته

burp (< F) v اروغ زدن • بشدت

بیرون انداختن

burqa n برقع • چادری

burst vi ترقیدن • کفیدن

bury <sb> vt دفن کردن • گور

کردن • به خاک سپردن <کسی را>

bury <sth> vt گور کردن <چیزی

را>

bus conductor n نگران

355

bus n • بس • سرویس
bus stop n ایستگاه سرویس
bush n بته
bushy adj انبوه
business n • بزنیس • تجارت • بازارگانی • سوداگری
→ savvy in business کاردان
business license n • جواز تجارتی • جواز نامه تجارتی
businessperson n تاجر
→ (colloq) تجار
Bust (hist, city) n بست • قلعه بست
busy (crowded) adj • بیروبار • ازدحام
busy (intent) adj سرگرم
busy (occupied) adj • مصروف • مشغول
→ be busy (be tied up) بند بودن
→ state of being busy • مصروفیت • مشغولیت
but conj اما • مگر • لاکن • لیکن • لکن • ولی • و اما • بلکه
butcher n قصاب
butcher shop n قصابی
butchering n قصابی
butchering see & massacre
butt (anat, colloq) n پس
butt see & buttocks
butter n مسکه
butter churn n جک
butterfly n پروانه
buttermilk n دوغ
buttocks n • دبر • گنبد • سرین
→ (arch) ماتحت
→ (colloq) دنبه دار
→ (lit) مقعد
→ (obs) کون
button (knob) n • تکمه • دکمه
buttonhole n • مادگی • کاج
buy v خریدن
→ (colloq) خرید کردن
→ buy on credit به قرض گرفتن
→ برداشت کردن
→ buy time دفع الوقت کردن
→ buying & selling خرید و فروش • بیع و شرا
buyer n • خریدار • مشتری
buying time n دفع الوقت
buzkashi (sport) n بزکشی

by prep • توسط • به توسط • به وسیله • از سوی • از پهلوی
by the way adv • راستی • نا گفته • نمانه
by way of prep بواسطه
bygone adj ماضی
bylaw n لایحه
byproduct n محصول فرعی
byproducts n pl محصولاتِ ضمنی
Byzantine Empire (hist) n روم شرقی

C

C.E. (Common Era) adj • میلادی • مسیحی
cab n تکسی
cabbage n کرم
cabinet (armoire) n الماری
cabinet (government) n • کابینه • هیئت وزرا
cable (telegram) n تلگرام
cable (wire) n لین
cable TV n کیبل
cacao n کاکاو
cache n • مخفیگاه • مخفی گاه
cactus n زقوم
cad n نامرد
cadaver see corpse
Cadiz (city) n قادس
cadre n بست
Caesar (& hist) n قیصر
Caesarea (city, & hist) n قیصاریه
café n کافی
cafeteria n • کافیتریا • کانتین
caffeinated adj با کافیین
caffeine n کافیین
cage n قفس
Cain (bibl) n قابیل
→ Cain & Abel قابیل و هابیل
Cairo n • قاهره • مصر القاهره
cake n کیک
calamitous adj • مصیبت بار • مصیبت زای
calamity see disaster
calcium (element) n کلسیم
→ calcium oxide آهک

calculate vi محاسبه کردن • محاسبه کردن

calculation n محاسبه • حساب

calculator n ماشین حساب

calendar n سال نامه • جنتری • تقویم • جدول تقویم

calendula (zubayda) n زبیده

calf (anat) n ساق
→ (colloq) دلک پای

calf (animal) n گوساله

California (state) n کلیفرنیا

caliph n خلیفه
→ caliph's seat (hist) دارالخلافه
→ commander of the faithful (caliph) امیر المؤمنین

caliphate n خلافت

call (summons) n دعوت • دعوت نامه • نعره
→ assembly call (bugle) ترم جمع
→ call to prayer v آذان کردن

call (name) vt گفتن

called (named) adj بنام • با نام

calligrapher n خوش نویس • خطاط • مشاق

calligraphy n خوش نویسی • خطاطی • خط
→ the seven styles of calligraphy هفت قلم

calling (vocation) n مسلک

callus (corn) n میخچه • پینه

calm adj خون سرد

calm (sb) down vt دل آسا کردن

calming adj, n مسکن

calmness n طمانینت
→ (colloq) طمانیت

calumniate see & slander

calumniate v افترا کردن

calumny n افترا

calumny see & slander

camel n شتر
→ (sound to make camel bend down) چک
→ bakhti (kind of camel) بختی
→ seat on camel's back عماری • کجاوی • محمل

camel driver n ساربان

camel fighting n شتر جنگی

camera n کمره • کامره

cameraman n فلم بر دار

camouflage n ستر واخفا

camp (bivouac) n کمپ
→ camp followers چنداول

campaign (struggle) n مبارزه

can (container) n قوطی
→ tin can قطی

can <+ subj> v توانستن

Canada n کانادا

Canadian (& pers) adj, n کانادایی

canal (& anat) n کانال • ترعه
→ irrigation canal (manmade) نهر

Canberra n کنبره

cancellation n فسخ

cancer (med, zodiac) n سرطان

candelabrum n چل چراغ • قندیل

candid adj دل پاک • پاک دل

candidate n داوطلب • داو طلب • نامزد • کاندید
→ (nominee) کاندیدا

candle n شمع

candle maker n شمعریز

candlestick n شمعدان • شمعدانی

candy n شیرینی
→ almond candy نقل
→ candy (esp halvah) حلویات
→ rock candy نبات • گیاه

cane (support) n چوب دست • عصا

cannabis n کنب • بنگ

cannon n توپ

cannonball n گلوله • مرمی

canopy n سایه بان

canteen (snack bar) n کانتین

canvas (for painting) n بوم

canvass v سروی کردن

canyon n دره

cap (hat) n کلاه • کله
→ pakol cap پکول

capability n توانمندی • قابلیت

capacity n ظرفیت • جای داد • گنجایش
→ in the capacity of منحیث • به صفت • به حیث

cape (f clothing) n یالان

cape (geog) n دماغه

capillaries n pl عروق شعریه • اوعیه شعریه

capital (archit) n سرستون • سر ستونی

357

capital (city) *n* • مرکز • پایتخت
→ (arch) دارالخلافه
capital (wealth) *n* • سرمایه • بضاعت
capitalism *n* کاپیتالزم • کپیتالزم
capitalist *adj* کاپیتالستی • کپیتالستی
capitalist *n* • کاپیتالست • کپیتالست • سرمایه دار
Capricorn (zodiac) *n* جدی • سرنگون شدن
capsize *vi* سرنگون شدن
captain (mil) *n* تورن • څارمن • سارمن
→ senior captain • سرڅارمن • سرسارمن
captain (ship's; arch) *n* ناخدا
captivation *n* اسارت • محو
captive (& pers) *adj, n* • دستگیر • گرفتار • بندی • زندانی • اسیر • محبوس
captivity *n* اسارت • گرفتاری • قید
capture *vt* گرفتن
capture & detention *phrs* گرفتار و بازداشت
car *n* موتر • موتر تیز رفتار
→ sports car موتر سپورتی
carat *n* قیراط • عیار
caravan *n* کاروان • قافله
caravanserai *n* • کاروان سرای • سرای
carbon *n* کاربن
carbonate (chem) *n* کاربونیت
card (business, greeting) *n* کارت
→ credit card کریدت کارت
→ ID card • تذکره • تذکره نفوس • ورقه هویت
→ SIM card سیم کارت
card (playing card) *n* • پر • قطعه
→ bridge (card game) بریج
→ ganjifa (hist, card game) گنجفه
→ pasur (card game) پاسور
→ shuffle cards گد کردن
→ teyka (card game) تیکه
card (weaver's) *n* • شانه • دوش • کتف
cardamom *n* • هیل • هیل کلان
→ common cardamom لاچی
cardboard *adj* مقوایی
cardboard *n* مقوا
carder (of cotton) *n* نداف
358

cardigan *n* جاکت پیش باز
cardinal number *n* عدد اصلی
carding (of cotton) *n* ندافی
→ carding machine ماشین ندافی
care (concern) *n* پروا
care (for sb medically) *v* • تیمار داری کردن • تیمار کردن
care (not be indifferent) *v* پروا داشتن • بی پروا نبودن
care <about sb> (emotionally) *v* خاطر <کسی را> خواستن
carefree (& pers) *adj, n* • سر شار • فارغ • فارغ التحصیل
careful (cautious) *adj* • احتیاط کار • محتاط
careful (precise) *adj* دقیق
carefulness (caution) *n* احتیاط
careless (blithe) *adj* سهل انگار
careless (negligent) *adj* • لاابالی • بی پروا
caretaker *n* قیم
→ caretaker of garden باغبان
→ temporary caretaker (& pol) سرپرست
caretaker *see* & custodian
cargo *n* • محموله • محمولات
caring (& pers) *adj, n* خاطر خواه
carnage *n* • مقاتله • کشتار
carnelian (stone) *n* عقیق
carnivorous *adj* گوشت خوار
carpenter *n* نجار
carpentry *n* نجاری
carpet (w/pile) *n* قالین
→ flat-weave carpet • گلم • گلیم
→ runner پای انداز
→ small carpet قالینچه
→ two carpets دو تخته قالین
carpet cleaning *n* قالین تکانی
carrier (med) *n* ناقل
carrier <of sth> *n* حامل <چیزی>
carrot *n* زردک
→ shredded carrot خلال
→ stick & carrot (fig) وعده و وعید
carry *v* بردن
carry out (accomplish) *vt* • انجام دادن • انجامیدن • برآوردن • بر آورده کردن
carry out (enforce) *vt* • تنفیذ کردن • مجرا کردن

carrying (bearing sth) adj حامل

carrying (bearing sth) n حمل

carrying out (enforcing) n • تنفیذ نفاذ

cart (ox-drawn) n گاو کراچی • عرابه

cart (pushcart) n کراچی
→ oxcart گاو کراچی

cartel n کارتل

cartilage n غضروف

cartilaginous غضروفی

cartographer n نقشه کش

cartography نقشه کشی

cartoon n کارتون

cartridge n خواب گاه • کارتوس
→ empty cartridge پوچک

Casablanca (city) n دارالبیضا

cascade n آبشار

case (gram) n حالت

case (instance) n صورت • مورد
→ in any case در هر حال • در هر صورت
→ in case (of sth happening) در صورتی که

case (large container) n صندوق • محفظه

case (protective) n قاب

cash n نقد • پول نقد
→ cash gift (votive offering) نذر

cash drawer (colloq) n دخل

cashbox n صندوق پس انداز

cashier (bank, market) n صراف

cashier (government) n تحویل دار • تحویل نقدی

cashmere adj کشمیری

Caspian Sea n بحیره خزر • بحیره کسپین

cassette tape n کست

cast (plaster) n پلستر

cast (throw) vt انداختن
→ cast anchor لنگر انداختن
→ cast lots قرعه انداختن • قرعه کشی کردن

castle • قلعه • حصار

castrate v اخته کردن

castrated adj اخته • خصی

casualties n pl تلفات

cat n پشک
→ (lit) گربه

catalogue n فهرست

catapult n منجنیق

catarrh n ریزش

catastrophe n فاجعه

catch vt گرفتن
→ catch <sb's> cold ریزش <کسی را> گرفتن

categorization n درجه بندی

categorize vt درجه بندی کردن

category (philos) مقوله

category n دسته

caterpillar n مور • مورچه

cathartic adj, n مسهل • جلاب

Cathay (hist) ختای

Catholic (& pers) adj, n کاتولیک

cattail n لخ

cattle n گله
→ cattle market نخاس
→ cattle owner مال دار

Caucasian adj, n قفقازی • سفید پوست

Caucasus (region, range) n قفقاز

cauliflower n گلپی • گل کرم

causality n علیت

cause (reason) n دلیل • باعث • موجب • علت • روی

caution n احتیاط • حزم

cautious adj احتیاط کار • محتاط

cautiously adv احتیاطاً • محتاطانه

cave dweller n غار نشین

cave n مغاره • غار

caviar n خاویار

cavity n سوراخ • غار

CD n سی دی

cease vi متوقف شدن

cease vt متوقف کردن

cease-fire n آتش بس

ceiling n چت • سقف

celebrate (feast) vi جشن کردن

celebrated (renowned) adj معروف • سرشناس • شهیر • مشهور • نام دار • نامور

celebration n جشن • تجلیل

celebrity (distinguished pers) n خاصه

celery n کرفس

celestial (astronomical) adj فلکی

celestial (divine) adj آسمانی • سماوی

cell (biol, prison) *n* حجره • سلول
→ locked cell کوته قلفی
cell phone *n* تیلفون جیبی •
تلفون جیبی
cellar *n* زیر خانه
cellular *adj* حجروی
celluloid *n* سلولاید
cellulose *n* سلولوز
Celsius *adj* سانتی گراد • سانتی
گرید
cement *n* سمنت
cemetery *n* قبرستان
→ (fig) وادی خاموشان
censure *n* ملامت
censure *vt* ملامت کردن • ملامتی
کشیدن
census *n* نفوس شماری • سر
شماری • احصاییه
center *n* مرکز • میان • مابین •
مدار • وسط
→ (fig) ناف
centigrade *adj* سانتی گراد • سانتی
گرید
centipede *n* چلپایک • گوش خزک
central *adj* مرکزی • میانه • وسطی
→ Central America امریکای
مرکزی
→ Central Asia • آسیای مرکزی
آسیای میانه
centralization *n* تمرکز
centralize *vt* تمرکز دادن
century *n* قرن • سده
ceramic *adj* سرامیک
cereal (grain) *n* حب • دانه • غله
cereals *n pl* حبوب
→ (colloq) حبوبات
cerebellum *n* دماغ اصغر
cerebral *adj* دماغی
cerebrum *n* دماغ اکبر
ceremonial *adj* رسمی
→ ceremonial formalities تشریفات
ceremoniousness *n* ظاهر داری
ceremony *n* مراسم
certain (known) *adj* معلوم • یقینی
certain (particular) *adj* فلان • فلانی
• بعض
→ to a certain extent تاحدی

certain (sure) *adj* • اعتمادی • واثق
متیقین
→ be certain یقین داشتن
→ make certain علم آوری کردن
certainly *adv* حقیقتاً • بیسخن • بی
گفت وگو • قطعاً • یقیناً • به یقین •
لابد • ناچار • ناگزیر • بالقطع
certainty *n* یقین • ایقان • اطمینان
certificate *n* تصدیق نامه
cervix (anat) *n* رقبه
cesspool *n* چاه بدرفت • چاه تشناب
Ceylon *see* Sri Lanka
chadar (f head cover) *n* چادر
chafe *vt* مالیدن • حک کردن
Chaghatai (hist; pers, khanate,
lang, people) *n* جغتای • چغتی
→ Andijan Timurids • اندیجان
تیموریان
Chaghcharan (seat) *n* چغچران
Chah Ab (dist) چاه آب
Chahar Asyab (dist) *n* چهار آسیاب
Chahar Dara *see* Chardara
Chaharikar (seat, dist) *n* چاریکار
chain (series, mtn range) *n* سلسله
→ chain of command سلسله
مراتب
chain *n* زنجیر
→ chains & shackles زنجیر و
زولانه
→ chain (sb) up به زنجیر کشیدن
chair *n* چوکی
→ (pers) رئیس
→ (stool; & at university) کرسی
→ (throne, seat) تخت
Chairman of the Joint Chiefs of
Staff (mil) *n* لوی درستیز
chairperson *n* رئیس
Chak-e Wardak (dist) *n* چک
وردک • چک
Chakhansur (dist) *n* چخانسور
Chal (dist) *n* چال
chalcedony (green) *n* یشم
→ (agate) عقیق
Chaldea (hist, region) *n* کلده
Chaldean (& pers) *adj, n* کلدانی
challenge (obstacle) (fig) *n* چالش
chamber (& parliament) *n* مجلس
→ chamber of commerce اتاق
تجارت

chameleon (& fig) n بوقلمون

Chamkani (dist) n چمکنی

chamois *see* suede

chamomile n بابونه

champion n • قهرمان • مبارز •
جنگ آور • جنگ آزما • جنگ جو
• رزم آزما • رزم آور • رزم جو •
پیکار گر

championship n قهرمانی

chance (opportunity) n فرصت

chancery (building) n محل پذیرایی •
مقام
→ (hist) دیوان

chandelier n چل چراغ • قندیل

change (alteration) n تبدیل • تغییر
• تغئیر • صرف • تصریف •
گردش • گردان

change (belief, opinion) v برگشتن
→ change one's mind صرف نظر
کردن • منضرف شدن

change (exchange) n تبدیل • آلش •
تحول
→ change of clothes آلش بدل
→ change of residence نقل

change (exchange) v آلش کردن

change (money) n • پول خورد •
پول سیاه
→ work as money changer
صرافی کردن

change (transform) vi • درآمدن • در
آمدن

change (transform) vt • تحول دادن •
تحول کردن

change (transformation) n تحول

changeable adj متبدل

changing (evolving) adj متحول

channel n • انتقال • تفویض
→ (duct) مجرا
→ (gutter) آبرو • آب رو

Chapa Dara (dist) n چپه دره

Chaparhar (dist) n چپرهار

chapter n فصل • باب

Char (in place names, alt Chahar)
n چار

Char Qarya (ctr) n چار قریه

character (in book) n • شخصیت •
پرسوناژ

character (nature) n • شخصیت •
خوی
→ (fig) خمیر

characteristic n • مشخصه • خاصه •
خاصیت

characterized adj موصوف

Charbolak (dist) n چاربولک

Charburjak (dist) n چاربرجک

charcoal n • زغال • انگشت
→ (colloq) ذغال

Chardara (dist) n چاردره

charge (accusation) n • اتهام • تهمت
→ bring a charge • عارض شدن •
عارض کردن
→ in charge (& pers) مسئول

charge <sb with sth> vt متهم کردن
<کسی را از چیزی>

chargé d'affaires n شارژدافیر

chariot n ارابه جنگی

charity (alms) n • خیر • خیرات
→ charity-taker (insult) خیر خور
→ charity tax (Musl law) صدقه

charity (good works) n • کار خیر •
اعمال خیر

charity (Musl endowment) n وقف

Charkent (dist) n چارکنت

Charkh (dist) n چرخ

charm (attractiveness) n جاذبه

charm (lure) n فریبندگی

charm (spell) n رقیه

charm (talisman) n تعویذ
→ (colloq) طومار

charming (& adv) adj, adv ساحرانه

charming adj • ساحر • افسونگر •
جادوگر • دل فریب • خماری

charmingly adv افسونگرانه

charred adj نیم سوخته

Charsada (dist) n چارسده

Chartaq (ctr) n چارتاق

chassis (car, truck) n بادی

chaste (& f) adj, n • پرهیز گار •
پارسا • بتول
→ be chaste پرهیز کردن

chastity n • ناموس • عصمت • پاکی
• پل • تیغ

chauffeur n • دریور • راننده •
موتران
→ (colloq) موتروان

Chawkay (dist) n چوکی

361

cheap (inexpensive) adj ارزان
→ dirt cheap مفت
cheap (stingy) adj بخیل • تنگ چشم • ممسک
cheapness (stinginess) n بخیلی • بخل • امساک • ممسکی • چشم تنگی
cheater (on exam) n نقال
cheating (on exam) n نقل
check (control) vt کنترول کردن
check (in chess) n کشت
checkbook n کتابچه چک
checkered adj چارخانه
checking account n حساب جاری
checkmate (chess) n شاه مات • شه مات • شهمات • کشت و مات
checkpoint n پوسته تلاشی • پوسته نظارتی
check-up (med) n معاینه • معاینات
cheek (anat) n عارض • گونه
→ (colloq) کومه
→ (lit) رخساره
cheeks (anat) n pl عارضین • وجنات
cheerful adj گشاده دل • گشاده دست • گشاده روی
cheerfulness adj گشاده دلی • گشاده رویی
cheese n پنیر
cheetah n یوزپلنگ
chef n آشپز • طباخ
Chehel Sutun (Kabul city dist) n چهل ستون
chemical adj کیمیایی • کیمیاوی
chemist n کیمیا دان
chemistry n کیمیا
Chemtal (dist) n چمتال
cherish vt پروردن • پروراندن • نواختن
cherry n گیلاس
→ sour cherry آلبالو
→ sour cherry (colloq) آلوبالو
Chesht-e Sharif (dist) n چشت شریف
chess n شطرنج
→ chess move چال
→ chess piece • دانه شطرنج مهره
→ chess playing شطرنج باز
362

chessboard n تخته شطرنج
→ chessboard square خانه شطرنج
chest (anat) n آغوش • بغل • سینه • صدر
chest (box) n صندوق • محفظه
cheviot n سرج
chew v جویدن
chicken (bird) n مرغ
→ chicken coop مرغانچه
→ chicken fighting مرغ جنگی
chicken (meat) n گوشت مرغ
→ fried chicken مرغ بریان
Chicken Street (Kabul) n کوچه مرغها
chickpea n نخود
chickpea-colored adj نخودی
chicory (med herb) n کاسنی
chief n سر • سالار • سردار • کله • مهتر • سرور • رئیس
→ Arab chieftain شیخ
→ dist chief کلانتر
→ police chief قوماندان امنیه • رئیس پولیس
→ tribal chieftain رئیس قبیله
→ village chief قریه دار
→ village/khel/tribal chief ملک
chief n سرکرده
chief of staff n رئیس هیئت
→ (hist, in Mughal imperial household) وکیل
child abuser n بچه باز
child n بچه • کودک • فرزند • اولاد
→ (colloq) اشتک
→ (fig) نور چشم
→ child (baby) طفل
→ illegitimate child حرامی
→ legitimate child حلالی
→ small child اشتکک • طفلک
child's play n اشتک بازی
childbirth n ولادت • تولد • زایمان • وضع حمل
childhood n طفلی • طفولیت • کودکی • صباوت
→ (colloq) اشتکی
childish (& adv) adj, adv کودکانه • طفلانه • بچه گانه

children & adults *phrs* اطفال و بزرگ سالان

children's *adj* کودکانه • طفلانه • بچه گانه

children's home (orphanage) *n* یتیم خانه

Chile *n* چلی

chili (pepper) *n* مرچ

chimney *n* دود کش

chimpanzee *n* چمپانزی

chin *n* زنخ • زنخدان • ذقن
→ (colloq) زنق
→ double chin غبغب

china (porcelain) *n* چینی باب
→ china manufacture چینی سازی
→ china repairman چینی بند زن
→ repair china چینی بند زدن

China *n* چین • ختای • ختا • خطای • خطا

Chinese (& pers) *adj, n* چینایی • چینی

chip, bit; crumb (colloq) *n* رزگی

chisel *n* اسکنه

Chishtiyya (Sufi order) *n* چشتیه

chlorate (chem) *n* کلوریت

chloride (chem) *n* کلوراید

chocolate *n* چاکلیت

choice (best) *adj* زبده

choice (decision) *n* تصمیم انتخاب

choice (option) *n* اختیار

choir *n* کورس

choking *adj* خفک

cholera *n* کولرا • وبا

choleric *adj* صفراوی • صفرایی

choose (select) *v* اختیار کردن • اختیار فرمودن • پسندیدن • برگزیدن • گزیدن

choosy *adj* مشکل پسند

chop (chop up) *vt* ریزه کردن

Chora (dist) *n* چوره

Chorasmia *see* Khwarazm

chord (math) *n* وتر • تار

chosen (elected) *adj* منتخب • انتخابی

chosen (selected) (& pers) *adj, n* برگزیده
→ chosen with care گل چین

Christ (Jesus) *n* حضرت عیسی

Christendom *n* عیسویت • مسیحیت • نصرانیت

Christian (& pers) *adj, n* عیسوی • مسیحی • نصرانی
→ (arch) ترسا • ترسایی

Christianity *n* عیسویت • مسیحیت • نصرانیت
→ (arch) ترسایی • دین ترسایی

Christmas (1st of Jadi) *n* یلدا

chronic (med) *adj* مزمن

chronicle *n* تاریخ

chronological *adj* زماین

chrysolite *n* زبر جد

church (building) *n* کلیسا

churn (for butter) *n* جک

cicada *n* جغل داغ • تاز

cigar *n* سیگار

cigarette *n* سگرت

cilantro *n* گشنیز

cinchonine *see* quinine

cinema *n* سینما

cinnabar (color) *adj* شنگرف

cinnamon *n* دارچینی

cipher *n* صفر

circle *n* دایره • حلقه

circular *adj* دایروی • دایره وی • مدور • کروی • گرد • چنبری

circulation *n* دوران • گردش
→ (of publication) تیراژ

circumambulation *n* طواف

circumcision (act) *n* سنتی • ختنه
→ (colloq) سنت

circumcize *n* ختنه کردن

circumcized *adj* ختنه شده

circumference *n* محیط

circumspect *adj* احتیاط کار • محتاط • ملاحظه کار

circumspection *n* احتیاط کاری • ملاحظه کاری

circumstance (detail) *n* چگونگی • چگونگی

circumstance (situation, health) *n* حال

circumstances (conditions) *n pl* شرایط

citizen *n* شهروند • تابع • تبعه • اتباع
→ fellow citizen همشهری

citizenship n تابعیت
→ citizenship certificate تذکره • تابعیت
city n شهر • شاروالی
civil (native) adj داخلی
civil (polite) adj مودب
civil servant n معمور
→ civil servants training academy مکتب حکام (hist)
civilian adj ملکی
civility n ادب
civilization n فرهنگ
→ (urbanity) ثقافت • مدنیت • تمدن • کلتور
civilized (urbane) adj انسان
CJTF-101 n قوت های مشترک وظیفوی ۱۰۱
claim (demand) n زعم • ادعا • مطالبه • طلب
claim v ادعا کردن • ادعا داشتن
claimant n مدعی
clamor v غوغا کردن
clamp n گیرا
clan n عشیره • طایفه • پرگنه
→ (khel) خیل • خل
→ (tribe) قوم
clan (sons; clan) n بنو
clandestine adj مخفی • پنهان
clang n شرنگ
clapping (applause) n چک چک
clarification n تصریح • تشریح • توضیح
clarify (elucidate) vt تصریح کردن
clarify (explain) vt توضیح کردن • توضیح دادن
clarity n شفافیت • صراحت • صافی
clash n تصادم • تلاطم
clashing adj متنازع
class (category) n دسته
class (room, grade) n صنف
→ class hour ساعت درسی
class (social) n طبقه
→ class struggle مبارزه طبقاتی
→ related to social classes طبقاتی
classification n درجه بندی
classify (categorize) vt درجه بندی کردن

classmate n همصنف
→ (colloq) همصنفی
clause (gram) n فقره • کلام
clavicle n ترقوه
claw n چنگال • چنگ
clay adj گلی
clay n گل
clean adj پاک
clean vt شوی کردن • پاک کردن • شستن
cleanliness n نظافت • پاکی • طهارت
cleansing (ritual ablution) n طهارت
clear (evident) adj روشن • واضح
clear (pure) adj صاف
clear (transparent) adj شفاف
clear (understood) adj مستفاد
clearly adv تصریحاً • بالصراحه • به صراحت • صراحتاً • صریحاً
clerk n کاتب • سکرتر
→ (arch) دبیر
→ head clerk سرکاتب
clever adj ذکی • حکاک • زرنگ • نراد
→ (fig) روباه صفت • آتش پاره • آتش پرچه
→ be clever ذکاوت داشتن
→ clever pers (fig) روباه
cleverness n زرنگی
climate n آب هوا • آب و هوا • هوا • اقلیم
→ (fig) فضا
climb vi برآمدن
cling vi چسپیدن
clinic n کلینک • کلنیک
→ health clinic کلینک صحی • کلنیک صحی
clip (paper clip) n کلپ
→ hair clip گیرا
clip nails v ناخن گرفتن
clitoris (vulg) n سنجدک
clock n ساعت
→ o'-clock بجه
close (intimate) adj دم ساز
close (near) adj, adv نزدیک • قریب
close prep نزدیک • در نزدیک • نزدیک به • قریب

364

close *vt* بسته کردن • بستن • پیش کردن • مسدود کردن • پت کردن • قات کردن

closed *adj* بسته • مسدود • مقفل

closeness *n* قرب

closet (storage) *n* پس خانه

cloth *n* تکه • قماش • پارچه

clothed *adj* ملبس

clothes *n* کالا • لباس • رخت • پوشاک • پوشاکه • پوشش • پوشاک • پوشاک • پوشاکه باب • ملبوسات

clothing see clothes
→ suitable for clothing (fabric) پوشاکی

cloud *n* ابر • سحاب

cloudy *adj* ابری
→ (neg) ابر آلود

clove (spice) *n* میخک • قرنفل

clown *n* مسخره • مسخره باز
→ clowning around مسخره بازی

clownish *adj* مسخره • مسخره باز

club (cards) *n* پشه

club (nightspot) *n* کلوب

club (stick) *n* دنده

clutches (fig) *n* چنگال • چنگ

cluttered (colloq) *adj* گدود

coal *n* زغال سنگ
→ (colloq) ذغال سنگ

coalesce *v* ادغام کردن

coalescence *n* ادغام

coalition *n* ائتلاف
→ form a coalition ائتلاف کردن

coat (waist-length) *n* کرتی

cobalt *n* کوبالت

cobbler *n* موچی • پینه دوز

cobra *n* کفچه مار • مار کفچه • کبرا

cobweb *n* تارجلاه

cock (rooster) *n* خروس • مرغ سحری

cock a gun <at sb> *v* سر <کسی را> ماشه کردن

cockfighting *n* خروس جنگی

cockscomb (flower) *n* تاج خروس

cocoa *n* کاکاو

coconut *n* ناریال

cocoon *n* پیله • غوزه

coddle *v* ناز دادن

coddled *adj* ناز دانه

code *n* کود
→ code of laws تزک

code (legal, arch) *n* نظام نامه
→ Women's Code (hist, 1920s) نظام نامه نسوان

coercion *n* اجبار • جبر

coffee *n* قهوه • کافی

cognac *n* کنیاک

cognition *n* عرفان

cognitive *adj* عرفانی

cognizable (law) *adj* قابل سماعت

cognizant *adj* آگاه • با خبر • مطلع • واقف

cohabitant (& pers) *adj, n* همخانه

cohesiveness (& of God) *n* یگانگی • یگانگی • یکتایی

coil (electrical) *n* کویل

coil (spring) *n* اسپرنگ

coin (money) *v* سکه زدن

coin *n* سکه

coinciding <with sth> *adj* مصادف <با چیزی>

coitus *n* جماع • مجامعت
→ coitus interruptus جماع گسیخته

colander *n* چلوصاف

cold (& fig) *n* سردی • برودت • خنکی • یخی

cold (catarrh) *n* ریزش
→ catch cold خنک زدن • سرما خوردن

cold (temp) *adj* سرد • خنک • یخ
→ cold storage سردخانه
→ feel cold خنک خوردن

cold-blooded *adj* خون سرد

collaborate *vi* همکاری کردن

collaboration *n* همکاری • همدستی • تعاون

collaborator (partner) *n* همدست

collapse *vi* افتادن • غلتیدن

collar (decorative) *n* چپه یخن

collarbone *n* ترقوه

collateral *n* ضمانت • تضمین • تمینات • گرو
→ put <sth> up for collateral ضمانت دادن • ضمانت گذاشتن • تضمین کردن

colleague *n* همکار
→ (in same field) هم مسلک

365

collect *vt* • جمع آوری کردن • فراهم کردن

collection *n* مجموعه • کلکسیون

collective *adj* مجموعی
→ collective noun (gram) اسم جمع

collectively *adv* به صورت مجموعی

college *n* فاکولته

collision *n* تصادم

colloquial *adj* اصطلاحی • مصطلح
→ colloquial language زبان محاوره • زبان اصطلاحی

collude *v* سازش کردن

collusion *n* سازش

colocynth *n* حنظل • تربوز ابو جهل • شرنگ

Colombia *n* کولمبیا

Colombo *n* کولمبو

colon (punctuation) *n* کولن • دو نقطه • علامه شرحه

colonel (COL) *n* دگروال
→ (colloq) کرنیل
→ lieutenant colonel دگرمن • غند مشر

colonialism *n* استعمار

colonizer *n* استعمار گر

colony *n* اسکان

color *n* رنگ

colorful *adj* رنگین

colt *n* لخته • کره

column (archit) *n* ستون
→ (support) رکن • عماد
→ column base (pedestal) فیل پایه
→ capital (column top) • سرستون • سر ستونی
→ frontier column پایه

column (feuilleton) *n* پاورقی

column (in table) *n* جدول

comb (bird's) *n* تاج خروس

comb *n* شانه

combat *adj* محاربوی • رزمنده

combat *n* محاربه • جنگ • پیکار • حرب • رزم • نبرد • کارزار • واقعه

combatant *n* رزمنده • شمشیر زن

Combined Joint Task Force 101 see CJTF-101

Combined Security Transition Command-Afghanistan see CSTC-A

combustible *adj* قابل • احتراق پذیر احتراق

combustion *n* احتراق

come (arrive) *vi* آمدن • وارد شدن • رسیدن • تشریف آوردن
→ come back بازگشتن
→ come out برآمدن
→ come true برآورده شدن

come to, regain consciousness *v* به خود آمدن

comedian *n* کومیدین

comedy *n* کومیدی

comet *n* ستاره دنباله دار

comfort (amenity) *n* نعیم

comfort (consolation) *n* تسلی

comfort (ease) *n* راحت • رفاه

comfort *vt* خاطر جمعی دادن

comfortable *adj* آرام • مرفه
→ comfortable life تنعم

comforted *adj* خاطر جمع

comical *adj* کومیک • کمیک

coming & going *phrs* آمد و رفت

coming (approach) *n* آمد • ورود • حلول

coming back *n* بازگشت • عودت • مراجعت

comma *n* کامه • ویرگول

command (order) (mil) *n* فرمان • قومانده • حکم • امریه
→ command & control سوق و اداره
→ command headquarters قوماندانی

command *v* فرمودن
→ (colloq) فرمایش دادن

commander *n* قوماندان • سردار • سر دار • سر کرده • سالار • فرمانده
→ commander in chief (arch) سپه سالار
→ fort commander تهانه دار

commanding general (CG) *n* قوماندان عمومی • جنرال فرمانده

commandment (bibl) *n* وصیت
→ the Ten Commandments وصایای ده گانه

commando n کماندو
commence vt به راه انداختن
commend vt ستایش کردن • ثنا
گفتن
commendable adj قابل ستایش •
سزاوار ستایش
commendation n ستایش
commendatory adj ستایش آمیز
comment n نظریه • تبصره •
ملاحظه • یاد داشت
comment (esp on Quran) v تفسیر
کردن
comment (remark) v نظر دادن
commentary (esp on Quran) n
تفسیر
commentator n مبصر
commerce n تجارت • بازارگانی •
سوداگری
commerce see & buying & selling
commercial adj تجارتی • تجاری
commissary (pers, mil) n ضابط •
اعاشه
commission (board) n هیأت •
هئیت • کمیسیون
commission (rank, office) n منصب
commissioner n کمشنری
→ see & UNHCR
→ police commissioner سرمامور
commit a crime v مرتکب جرم
شدن
commitment n تعهد • عهد • پیمان
committee n کمیته • مجلس
→ advisory committee مجلس
مشوره
common (general) adj عام
common (ordinary) adj عادی
common (shared) adj مشترک •
شریکی • اصلی
commoner (pers) n عام
commonwealth n کشور های
مشترک المنافع
commotion n شور
communication n ارتباط • مخابره
→ lines of communication خطوط
مواصلاتی
communications adj ارتباطی •
مواصلاتی

communications n pl مواصلات
→ mass communications ارتباط
جمعی
communism n کمونزم • کمونیزم
communist adj کمونستی •
کمونیستی
→ communist organization memb
(hist) سازمانی
→ Khalq communist faction خلق
→ Parcham communist faction
پرچم
→ Shola Jaweyd communist
faction شعله جاوید
communist n کمونست • کمونیست
→ Khalq communist خلقی
→ Parcham communist پرچمی
→ Shola Jaweyd communist شعله
یی
community n اجتماع • جامعه •
جماعت
commute vi سر کار رفتن
compact adj جمع
compact n see pact, treaty
companion n هم نشین • هم صحبت
• رفیق • دوست
→ companions (pl only) اصحاب
Companions, the (Prophet's) n pl
انصار • صحابه
company (firm) n تجارت خانه •
کمپنی • شرکت • موسسه
company (mil) n تولی
company (other people) n معیت
comparable adj قابل مقایسه
comparative adj تفضلی
→ comparative adj صفت تفضلی
comparatively adv نسبتأ
compare v مقایسه کردن • قیاس
کردن • سر <چیزی> دادن
comparison n مقایسه • قیاس
→ in comparison to • نسبت به
نظربه
compass (for drawing) n پرکار
compass (shows kiblah) n قبله نما
compass (to north) n قطب نما
compassion (mercy) n رحمت •
مهربانی
compassion (sympathy) n غم
شریکی

367

compassionate (merciful) adj
مهربان

compassionate (sympathetic) adj
غم شریک • مشفق • شفیق
→ be compassionate دلسوزی
داشتن

compatibility (fig) n امتزاج

compatriot n هموطن • وطن دار •
هم میهن

compel vt مجبور ساختن • ناعلاج
ساختن • سوق دادن

compelled adj مجبور • ناچار •
ناعلاج

compensate (for losses) v غرامت
دادن • تاوان دادن • جبران کردن

compensation (for losses) n
غرامت • تاوان

competency (authority) n صلاحیت

competition (& econ) n رقابت

competition (contest) n مسابقه •
کانکور

competitor n رقیب

compiled adj مدون

compiler n مدون

complain (lament) v نالیدن

complain (lightly) v گله کردن

complain (to official) n عارض شدن
• عارض کردن

complain v شکوه کردن • شکایت
کردن

complainer n شاکی

complaining (lament) n نالش

complaining (light) n گله • گله
گزاری

complaining (lightly) adj گله مند

complaining adj شکایت آمیز

complaint n شکایت • شکوه

complementary adj تعارف آمیز

complete adj کامل • مجهز • مکمل
• پوره

complete v تکمیل کردن • به اتمام
رساندن

completely (in every sense) adv به
تمام معنی

completely adv کاملا • به کلی •
کلا • بالکل • بالجمله • جملتاً

completion n تکمیل • انجام • اکمال
• اتمام • ادا

complex (sentence) adj مختلط

368

complex adj پیچیده • مغلق

complexity n پیچیدگی

compliance with (regulations) n
رعایت • رعاعه • مراعات
→ non-compliance خود داری

compliant adj فرمان بردار • فرمان
دار • مطیع

complicated (mixed up) adj در هم و
بر هم

complicated adj مغلق • پیچیده •
پیچ در پیچ

complication n غامض

complicity n همدستی

comply (w/sth) v مراعات کردن •
فرمان بردن

component (mechanical) n پرزه

component n عنصر

compose (poem) v سرودن
→ compose an ode چکامه سرودن

composition (mus) n پارچه

composure n خود داری
→ having composure خویش تن
دار

compound (building) n محوطه

comprehension n فهم • احاطه

comprehensive adj جامعی

comprehensiveness n جامعیت

compress (med) n تربند • تکر
→ apply a compress تکر کردن

compress (condense) v تخته کردن

comprise <sth> v تشکیل دادن
<چیزی را>

compromise (agree) v سازش
کردن

compromise (agreement) n سازش

comptroller n کنترولر
→ chief imperial comptroller (hist)
مستوفی

compulsion n جبر • اجبار •
ناعلاجی

compulsorily adv اجبارا • به اجبار
• جبراً • به جبر

compulsory adj اجباری • ناچار

computer n کمپیوتر

comrade (pol) n رفیق

concave adj مقعر

conceal (colloq) vt پت کردن
مخفی کردن • پنهان کردن (lit) →
پوشاندن

concealed *adj* • پنهان • مخفی • مستتر • پوشیده • پوشانده • نهفته • نهفت

concealment *n* • برقع • حجاب • پرده • روی بند • نقاب • نهفتگی • ستر

conceit *n* ناز • غرور • → (colloq) کلان کاری

conceited (& pers) *adj, n* خود بین • خود پرست • خود خواه • کلان کار

concentrate *vt* تمرکز دادن

concentration *n* تمرکز

concentration (mental) *n* سرگرمی

concentric *adj* متحد المرکز • هم مرکز

concept *n* مفهوم • اندیشه • تصور • تخیل • مفکوره • فکرت • فکر

conception (med) *n* آبستنی

conceptual *adj* خیالی

concern *n* علاقه • دل چسپی • پروا

concerned (& pers) *adj, n* علاقه مند

→ be concerned نگرانی داشتن <راجع به چیزی>

→ be seriously concerned توجه جدی دادن

concerning (about) *prep* راجع به • درباب • درباره • به لحاظ • دایر بر <چیزی>

→ (lit) در مورد

concert *n* کانسرت • کنسرت

concise *adj* اختصاری • هموجز

conciseness *n* ایجاز

conclude (agreement) *n* • بستن • عقد کردن

→ (colloq) بسته کردن

conclude (deduce) *v* نتیجه گیری کردن

conclude (end) <sth> *vt* خاتمه دادن <به چیزی>

conclude (end) *vi* • پایان دادن • خلاص شدن • خاتمه یافتن

conclusion (agreement) *n* عقد

conclusion (end) *n* • خاتمه • ختم • فرجام

concrete *adj* کانکریتی

concrete *n* کانکریت

concrete noun (gram) *n* اسم ذات

concurrence *n* همزمانی

concurrent (& adv) *adj, adv* همزمان

condemn (convict) *vt* محکوم کردن

condemn (denounce) *v* تقبیح کردن

condemnation *n* تقبیح

condense (compress) *v* فشردن • تخته کردن

condensed *adj* فشرده • تخته کرده

condiment *n* چاشنی

condition (proviso) *n* شرط

condition (quality) *n* کیفیت

condition (state) *n* • حالت • وضع • وضعیت

conditional *adj* مشروط • شرطی

→ conditional mood (of verb) وجه شرطی

conditionality *n* مشروطیت

conditioned on *adj* منوط بر <چیزی>

condolences *n* تسلیت

conduct *n* رفتار • رفتاری • سلوک

conductor (orchestra) *n* رهبر • پیشوا • قاید

conductor (phys) *n* ناقل

cone (shape) *n* مخروط

confederation *n* کنفراسیون

conference *n* جلسه • مجلس • نشست • کنفرانس

conferring (giving) *n* اختصاص

confession (avowal) *n* اقرار

confession (rel) *n* مذهب

confidant *n* محرم اسرار • محرم راز • راز دار • محرم

→ (of dignitary) مقرب

confidence (certainty) *n* اطمینان

confidence (trust) *n* وثوق • اعتماد <سر کسی>

→ self-confidence اعتماد به نفس

confident *adj* واثق • اعتمادی

confidential *adj* محرمانه

confinement (custody) *n* حبس

confirm *vt* تایید کردن

confirmation *n* تایید • تائید

confiscate *vt* ضبط کردن

confiscated *adj* ضبطی

confiscation *n* ضبط • مصادره

conflagration *n* آتش • آذر • حریق • سوختگی

conflict *n* تصادم • مقابله

conflicting *adj* متخاصم • متنازع

369

conform (w/sth) v مطابق بودن

confront < sb> vt رو به رو کردن
<کسی>
→ (in hostile manner) پنجه دادن

confused adj سرگشته • سرگردان
• سردرگم • حیران • متحیر • سر
آسیمه • بهت زده • درهم
→ (fig) be confused v دست از پای
خود را خطا کردن

confusing adj بهت آور • بهت
انگیز

confusion n بهت • سرگردانی

congratulations excl تبریک •
مبارک باشه

congregation n جماعت

congress n کانگرس

Congress Party (India) n کانگرس

conical adj مخروطی

conjecture n حدس

conjecture v حدس کردن

conjugation (gram) n تصریف •
صرف • گردان

conjugational adj تصریفی

conjunction (gram) n کلمه ربط

connect v وصل کردن • پیوستن

connected <to sth> adj متصل •
پیوسته • مربوط • متعلق <به
چیزی>

connection n وصل • پیوند •
پیوستگی • وابستگی

connectivity (Internet) n همبستگی

conquer v فتح کردن

conquering adj فاتح
→ (epithet of God) قهار

conqueror n فاتح • گشا

conquest n فتح

conscience n وجدان • ضمیر
→ freedom of conscience (belief)
آزادی عقیده
→ in all conscience وجداناً

conscious adj به خود

consciousness n هوش

consecutive adj متوالی

consensus (by Musl scholars) n
اجماع

consent n موافقت • موافقه •
تصدیق • رضایت • رضا • تن دهی

consent v تن دادن

consenting adj تن ده

consequence n نتیجه • عاقبت

consequently adv بعد از آن • پس
از آن • سپس • بالنتیجه • در نتیجه •
نتیجتاً

conservation n نگاه داری •
نگاهداری • نگه داری • نگاه داشت
• نگه داشت

conservatism n محافظه کاری

conservative (& pers) adj, n
محافظه کار • کهنه خیال

conservator n نگاه دار • نگاهدار •
نگه دار • نگهدار

conserve v نگاه داشتن

consider v مراعات کردن • در
نظر داشتن • سنجیدن • فکر کردن
→ be considered بشمار رفتن •
بحساب رفتن

considerable adj قابل ملاحظه

consideration n ملاحظه • پاس •
مراعات • رعایت • تفکر
→ an award in consideration of
یک جایزه به پاس <چیزی> <sth>
→ be taken into consideration <in
sth> در وقع گذاشتن <به چیزی>

consist <of sth> vi مشتمل بر
<چیزی> بودن • عبارت بودن <از
چیزی> • تهیه شدن

consistency n قوام

consolation n تسلی

consonance n هماهنگی

consonant (sound) n صامت •
کانسوننت

conspiracy n دسیسه • توطئه

conspirator n دسیسه باز • دسیسه
کار • توطئه گر

constant adj دایم • دایمی

constellation n مجمع الکواکب

constitution (law) n قانون اساسی
→ constitutional & parliamentary
مشروطه

Constitutionalists (hist, pol mvmt) n
مشروطه خواهان

constraint n اضطرار
→ under constraint اضطراراً

construct vt آباد کردن • ساختن

construction adj عمرانی

construction n تعمیر • بنایی •
اعمار • عمرانی
→ road construction سرکسازی

consul *n* • قنسل • قونسل • قونسول • کنسل

consulate *n* قنسلگری • قنسولگری • کنسلگری • کونسلگری

consult <sb/sth> *vt* مراجعه کردن <به کسی / چیزی>

consult *vi* مشاوره کردن • استشاره کردن

consultation *n* مشوره • مشورت • استشاره

consultative *adj* مشورتی

consumable *adj* مصرفی

consume *vt* مصرف کردن • به مصرف رساندن • گرفتن

consummation (Musl law) *n* دخول • در آمد • ورود

consumption *n* مصرف • خرج

contact (have contact) <w/sb> *vi* بر خوردن <با کسی>

contact *n* تماس
→ form contacts (fig) تار دواندن

contagious *adj* ساری
→ (colloq) مسری

contain *vt* در بر داشتن

contained *adj* مندرج • مندمج

container (can) *n* قوطی

container (chest) *n* محفظه

containing *adj* شامل • حاوی • متضمن

containment *n* احتوا

contaminate *vt* آلودن

contamination *n* آلودگی • لوث

contemplation *n* مشاهده

contemplation (Sufism) *n* فکر

contemporaneity *n* همزمانی

contemporaneous (& adv) *adj, adv* همزمان

contemporary (pers) *n* هم دوره

contemptible *adj* نکوهیده

contend (struggle) *v* ستیزه کردن

content *adj* خوشنود • راضی • قانع

contentious (& pers) *adj, n* ستیزه جو • ستیزه جوی • ستیزه خو • ستیزه خوی • ستیزه کار • ستیزه گر • جنگی

contentment *n* رضایت • رضا • قناعت

contents (of sth) *n pl* محتویات • مندرجات

contest *n* مسابقه

contestant *n* داوطلب • داو طلب

context *n* سیاق

continent *n* براعظم • قاره

continually *adv* مدام • همیشه • دایماً
→ (colloq) دایم

continuation *n* ادامه • دوام • مدوامت • دنباله

continue *v* ادامه دادن • دنبال کردن • تعقیب کردن

continuity *n* پیوستگی

continuous (& adv) *adj, adv* پیگیرانه • پیوسته

continuous *adj* دوام دار

continuously *adv* همواره • همیشه • پیگیرانه • پیوسته

contorted *adj* پیچ خورده

contortion *n* پیچ خوردگی

contraband *n pl* اموال قاچاقی

contract *n* قرار داد
→ by contract بالمقطع
→ contractual terms شرط نامه • تیکه

contract (shrink) *vi* جمع شدن

contraction *n* اختصار • انقباض

contractor *n* قرار دادی • تیکه دار • اجیر

contradict *v* تناقض داشتن • تضاد داشتن

contradiction *n* تناقض • تضاد
→ self-contradiction متناقض گویی

contradictory *adj* متناقض • نقیض • ضد و نقیض

contrary *adj* مخالف • متضاد • بر عکس • مغایر • ضد
→ on the contrary *adv* بر خلاف • بالعکس • به عکس • بر عکس • بلکه

contrary to (sth) *prep* مخالف

contrast (& fig) *n* تقابل • ضد
→ (light & shadow) سایه روشن

contribution *n* اعانه
→ (zakat) زکات
→ contribution to (sth's) progress پیشبرد

371

control (regulate) *vt* کنترول کردن
→ bring under control (fig) مهار کردن • عنان • مهار آوردن
control (regulation) *n* تنظیم
→ (fig) زمام • عنان • مهار
→ out of control (fig) عنان گسیخته • عنان گسسته

controversial (provocative) *adj* مناقشه آمیز
→ (disputed) متنازع فیه
→ (dubious) شک آور • حساس

controversy (strife) *n* تنازع • نزاع • منازعه • قالمقال • قیل و قال
→ (colloq) غالمغال

conundrum *n* چیستان • معما

convene *v* جلسه کردن • اجلاس کردن

convening *n* انعقاد • اجلاس

convent (rel) *n* دیر • صومعه

convention *n* کانونشن • کنوانسیون

conversant *adj* معرفت دار

conversation *n* مکالمه • صحبت • محاوره • گفتار • گپ
→ (fig) سوال و جواب

conversational *adj* محاوره یی • گفتاری

converse *v* مکالمه کردن • گپ زدن

conversely *adv* بالعکس • به عکس • بر عکس

conversive *adj* معرفت دار

convert (to a religion) *v* روی آوردن ‹به چیزی› • قبول کردن
→ convert to Islam *vi* مسلمان شدن • به دین اسلام روی آورد
→ convert (sb) to Islam *vt* مسلمان ساختن

convert *vi* درآمدن • در آمدن

convert *vt* درآوردن • در آوردن

convey (express) *vt* افاده کردن

conveyance *n* افاده • تبلیغ • پروپاگند

convict (law) *vt* محکوم کردن

convicted *adj* محکوم • ملزم

conviction *n* محکومیت

convince *vt* قناعت دادن • رضایت دادن ‹به کسی› • راضی کردن

convoy *n* قافله • کاروان

convulsive *adj* متشنج

cook (pers) *n* آشپز • طباخ

cook *v* پختن • دیگ پختن • طبخ کردن
→ (colloq) پخته کردن

cookbook *n* کتاب طباخی • کتاب آشپزی

cooked *adj* پخته
→ badly cooked (half-cooked) نیم پخته

cookie *n* کلچه

cooking *adj* طباخی • آشپزی

cooking *n* طبخ • پخت و پز
→ (colloq) پخت و پز

cool (cool off) *vi* یخ کردن

cooperate *vi* همکاری کردن

cooperation *n* همکاری • هماهنگی • تعاون • اشتراک مساعی
→ (collusion) تبانی

coordinate *v* هماهنگ ساختن • هماهنگ دادن

coordinated *adj* هماهنگ

coordination *n* هماهنگی • انسجام

cope *vi* برآمدن

Copenhagen *n* کوپنهگن

copper *adj* مسی

copper *n* مس
→ copper sulfate زاج کبود

coppersmith *n* مسگر

copse *n* بیشه • بته زار

Copt (hist) *n* قبط

Coptic (hist) *adj* قبطی

copy *n* نسخه • نقل
→ photocopy فوتوکاپی

copying *n* نسخ

copyright (all rights reserved) *phrs* همه حقوق محفوظ است

coquetry *n* غنج • عشوه • ناز

coral *n* مرجان

cord *n* طناب • بند

cordial (& adv) *adj, adv* صمیمانه

cordial *adj* صمیمی

cordiality *n* صمیمیت

core *n* روح • جان • مغز • صمیم • کنه • مدار

coreligionist *n* هم کیش • هم دین • هم مذهب

coriander (fresh) *n* گشنیز
→ coriander seeds تخم گشنیز

cork *n* کارک

372

cormorant (bird) *n* زاغ آبی
corn (callus) *n* میخچه
corn (maize) *n* جواری • جوار
corn oil *n* روغن جواری
corn poppy *n* لاله
cornea (anat) *n* قرنیه
corner *n* کنج • گوشه • زاویه
coronation *n* دستار بندی
corporal (mil) *n* دلگی مشر
corporation (law) *n* شخص حکمی
corps *n* هیئت
→ corps (mil) قول اردو
corpse *n* مرده • اندام مرده • متن • جسد • نعش
→ (& slaughtered animal's) لاش
→ (at funeral) جنازه
corpuscle *n* کروی
→ corpuscles کرویات
corral *n* آغیل • آغل
correct *adj* درست • صحیح
correct *v* اصلاح کردن
→ erasing & correcting حک و اصلاح
correction *n* اصلاح
correlated *adj* همبسته • هم بسته
correlation *n* همبستگی
correspond <to sth> *vi* مطابقت کردن <به چیزی>
correspondent *n* نامه نگار
corridor *n* دهلیز
corroborate *vt* تایید کردن
corroboration *n* تایید • تأیید
→ (proof) ثبوت
corrode *v* زنگ زدن
corrosion *n* زنگ
→ corrosion-resistant نجیبه
corrupt *adj* فاسد • حرام خور • دغل • دغل باز
corruption *n* فساد • مفاسد • حرام خوری • دغل • دغل بازی • دغلی
cosmetic *adj* زیبایی • جمال • حسن
→ cosmetic surgery جراحی زیبایی
cosmetics *n* آرایش
→ apply cosmetics آرایش کردن
cosmic *adj* فضایی
cosmonaut *n* فضا نورد
cosmos *n* کیهان • فضا • جهان • عالم

cost (have a cost of) *v* ارزیدن
قیمت • ارزش • بها cost *n*
→ cost of living قیمتی
→ unit cost نرخ
costly *adj* قیمت
cotton *adj* نخی
→ (linen) کتانی
→ gleaned (cotton) محلوج
→ cotton-filled پخته یی
cotton *n* پنبه
→ (colloq) پخته
→ (linen) کتان
→ cotton candy پشمک
→ cotton farmer پخته کار
→ cotton ginner حلاج
→ cotton pod غوزه
→ cotton wool پنبه خام
→ one who cards cotton نداف
cottonseed *n* پنبه • چگت
couch *n* کوچ • سیت
couch potato *n* راحت طلب
cough *n* سرفه
cough *vi* سرفه کردن
cough syrup *n* شربت سرفه
council *n* شورا
→ Council for National Unity (NGO) شورای متحد ملی
→ council of elders جرگه
→ Great Council لویه جرگه • انجمن بزرگ
→ High Religious Council محفل میزان و تحقیقات
→ National Council ملی جرگه
→ Religious Council هیئتِ تمیز
→ State Council شورای دولت
counsel (advice) *n* مشورت • مشوره • مشاورت • مشاوره • اندرز • پند • نصیحت
counsel <on sth> *v* مشورت دادن • مشاوره دادن • صلاح دادن <سر چیزی>
counselor *n* مشاور
→ economic counselor مشاور اقتصادی
→ political counselor مشاور سیاسی

373

count <on sth> v حساب کردن <سر چیزی>
→ be counted • بحساب رفتن • به حساب رفتن
countenance n قواره
counter (retaliatory) adj جوابی
counterfeit adj تقلبی • قلابی
counterfeit n جعل
counterfeit v جعل کردن • جعل کاری کردن • ساخته کاری کردن • ساختن
counterinsurgency n ضد شورش
counterpart n کفو • همتا
counting n حضر
country n کشور • مملکت • دولت • ملک
→ country of origin وطن • موطن • سر زمین • میهن
countryman n هموطن
couple (mate) v جفت شدن
couple n زوج • جوره • جفت
→ married couple ازواج
couplet n بیت • مثنوی
courage n جرئت • شجاعت • سربازی
courageous adj دلیر • دلاور • به جرئت • با جرئت
→ courageous man مرد
course (process) n روند
course (route) n مسیر
→ course of study کورس
→ of course البته
court (royal) n دیوان عالی
court (tribunal) n محکمه • داد گاه
→ appellate court محکمه مرافعه
courteous adj لطف آمیز • مودب
courteously adv مودبانه
courtesan n لولی
courtesy n لطف • تواضع
courtyard n حویلی

cousin n
→ father's brother's daughter دختر عم • دخترکاکا
→ father's brother's son بچه کاکا • پسر کاکا
→ father's brother's son/daughter عمو زاده
→ father's sister's daughter دخترعمه
→ father's sister's son بچه عمه • پسر عمه
→ mother's brother's daughter دختر ماما
→ mother's brother's son بچه ماما • پسر ماما
→ mother's sister's daughter دختر خاله • خاله زاده
→ mother's sister's son بچه خاله • پسر خاله
→ mother's sister's son/daughter خاله زاده
cousin, paternal uncle's son (arch) n پسر عم
cover n پوش • پشتی
→ (lid) سرپوش
→ bed cover روی کش • سر جایی
→ book cover جلد • پشتی
cover vt پت کردن • مخفی کردن • پنهان کردن • پوشاندن
→ cover w/a shroud کفن کردن
covered adj سرپوشیده
→ (wearing chadari) روی پت
covering (concealing) n ستر
covert (& adv) adj, adv نهفت
covert adj نهفته • پنهان • پوشیده • مخفی
covet v دندان تیز کردن
→ (be greedy) طمع داشتن
covetous (& pers) adj, n آزمند • حریص • طماع
covetously adv آزمندانه • حریصانه
cow n گاو • ماد گاو
→ cow dung (for fuel) سرگین
cowardice n ترس • ترسویی • خوف • سهم
cowardly (& adv) adj, adv نامردانه وار

cowardly (& pers) adj, n • ترسو •
بزدل • مرغ دل • شیشه دل
coworker n همکار
cowrie (shell) n کودی
crab n پنج پا یک • خرچنگ
crack vi شکستن • ترقیدن
crack vt شکستاندن
cradle n گهواره
craft n فن • کسب • کسب و کار •
کمال • حرفه • پیشه • صنعت •
صناعت
craftsman n کاسب • صنعتگر •
صنعتکار
→ (colloq) کسبی
crafty adj مکار
crane (bird) n کلنگ
cranium (anat) n جمجمه
crate n صندوق
craving n میل • میلان • اشتها
craziness n دیوانگی • جنون
crazy adj, n دیوانه • مجنون
crazy pers n مجنون • دیوانه
cream (dairy) n کریم • قیماق •
سرشیر
crease n چین
creased adj چین خورده
create vi ایجاد کردن • پیدا کردن •
ساختن • به میان آوردن
creation n تکوین • پیدایش
→ (God's) خلقت
Creator, the (rel) n جهان آفرین
credible (& pers) adj, n معتبر
credit (banking, etc.) n کریدت
→ credit card n کردیت کارت
credit (trust) n اعتبار
credo (Musl) n کلمه
credulous adj زود باور • خوش
باور
creed n عقیده • نظریه • اعتقاد •
ایمان
→ (rel) دین
creep vi خزیدن
Crete (geog) n کریتُ
crew n خدمه
crib (manger) n آخور • آخر
cricket (insect) n چرچرک
crime n جرم • جنایت • گناه
→ commit a crime مرتکب جرم
شدن

criminal adj • جزایی • جنایی •
جنایت کارانه
→ criminal code/law قانون جرایم
criminal n مجرم • مرتکب • عامل
• جانی • جنایت کار
criminally adv جنایت کارانه
crimson (color) adj قرمزی
crisis n حادثه • بحران
criteria n pl موازین • معاییر
criterion n معیار • نورم • ستندرد •
ملاک • محک
critical (key) adj کلیدی • بسیار مهم
criticism n انتقاد • نقد
criticize vt انتقاد کردن
→ (nitpick) پلته و چراغ گرفتن
→ (severely) پیش انداختن
crocodile n تمساح • نهنگ •
سوسمار آبی
crooked adj کج • اریب • وریب •
یک بغله
cross (& rel) n صلیب
→ Red Cross صلیب احمر •
صلیب سرخ
cross (X mark) n چلیپا
cross <sth> vt تیر شدن • گذشتن
<از چیزی>
crossbeam (of gallows) n چوبه
cross-examine < sb> vt رو به رو
کردن <کسی>
cross-eyed n کانج • احول
→ (colloq) چغر
crossing n گذر • گذر گاه • معبر
cross-legged adj, adv چهار زانو •
چار زانو
cross-reference n ارجاع دو جانبه
• ارجاع دو طرفه
cross-reference v ارجاع دو جانبه
کردن • ارجاع دو طرفه کردن
cross-referencing see cross-
reference n
crossroads n چارراهی • چارراه •
چهار راهی
cross section n مقطع
crossword puzzle n • جدول معما •
جدول معمایی
croup n ساغری • سرین
→ (lit) کفل
crow n زاغ • کلاغ
crowbar n جبل

375

crowd *n* جم • بيروبار • ازدحام
جمعيت • غفير
→ (arch) ملا
→ (colloq) بيروبار • لشكر •
عسكر • جمع و جوش
crowd *v* تيله و تنبه كردن
crowded *adj* بيروبار • مزدحم
crown *n* افسر • تاج
crowned *adj* تاجور
crucifixion *n* چارميخ
crucify *v* چارميخ كردن
crude (rude) *adj* بد • بد گذاران •
گذاره • زشت • زشت گوی
cruel *adj* ستمگر • بيداد گر • ظالم •
خدا • ديوسيرت • ديوسرشت
ناشناس • خدا ناترس
cruelty *n* جور • بيداد • ظلم •
قساوت • ستم
crumb (colloq) *n* رزگی
Crusades, the (hist) *n pl* جنگ های
صليبی
crush *n* چك • تكان
crush *vt* چكيدن • كوفتن
cry (shout) *n* قالمقال • قيل و قال •
نعره
→ (colloq) غالمغال
→ loud cry for help نفير • فرياد
cry (weep) *v* ندبه كردن • گريه كردن
كردن
cry for help *vi* فرياد بر آوردن
crying *n* ندبه • گريه
crystal *n* بلور
crystalize *vi* متبلور شدن
crystalized *adj* متبلور
crystalline *adj* بلوری • بلورين
CSTC-A *n* الفا سی اس تی سی
سی اس تی سی الف • قوماندانی
مشترک امنیتی انتقالی افغانستان
cube (shape, math) *n* مكعب
cube root *n* جذر مكعب
cube sugar *n* قند خشتی
cubed (volume) *n* مكعب
cuckold *n* دله
cucumber *n* بادرنگ
cudgel *n* سوته
cuff (of sleeve) *n* كف
culpable (& pers) *adj, n* مقصر
cultivate (land) *vt* زرع كردن
cultivation *n* زرع
376

cultural *adj* فرهنگی
culture (civilization) *n* فرهنگ
culture (refinement) *n* ثقافت •
تهذيب • فضل • كلتور
cultured (polite) *adj* مهذب
cultured (urbane) *adj* شيوه دار
culvert *n* پلچک
cumin (spice) *n* زيره
cummerbund *n* كمربند
cunning *adj* روباه صفت • مكار •
هنر باز • رند • رندانه • نراد • زاغ
cunning (guile) *n* مكر • مكاری •
زرنگی
cunning pers *n* بلا • بلاگک
cunt see vagina
cup (as phlebotomist) *v* خون
گرفتن
cup *n* پيمانه • پياله • اياغ
cupboard *n* الماری ظرف • الماری
ها
cupful (unit of meas) *n* پياله
cupola *n* گنبد
cupping (med) *n* حجامت • حجامی
• رگ زنی
cure (recovery) *n* شفا
cure (remedy) *n* گزير • دارو •
چاره
cure *v* خوب كردن • شفا دادن
curfew *n* عبور و • شب گردی •
مرور منع
curious (nosy) *adj* كنج كاو
curl *n* حلقۀ زلف • تاب • خم
curl *vt* پيچاندن
curly (hair) *adj* خم و پيچ پر
currant *n* كشمش
currency *n* اسعار
current *adj* معاصر • روان • جاری •
كنونی • فعلی
current *n* رو
currier see leather worker
curse (damn) *vt* نفرين كردن
curse (damnation) *n* نفرين
curse (swear word) *n* داو
curse (swear) *vi* فحش • داو زدن •
گفتن • پوچ گفتن
→ (colloq) دو زدن • دشنام دادن
cursed *adj* نفرين شده
cursing *n* فحش • پوچ
→ cursing & swearing فحش و پوچ

cursory (& adv) adj, adv سرسری
curtain n پرده
curve n خم
→ (in road) گولایی
curved adj منحنی • گول • کمان
→ curved upwards برگشته
custodian n تحویل دار • قیم
→ shrine custodian متولی
custody n توقیف • بندی
→ take into custody بندی کردن
custom (excise) n محصول
custom (habit) n عادت • شیوه • خوی • کنش • کشت
custom (tradition) n رسم • آیین • دین • مذهب (rel) →
customarily adv عادتاً
customary adj معمول
→ customary law عرف
customer n خریدار • مشتری
customs (customshouse) n گمرک
→ customs form اظهار نامه
cut (injury) n جراحت • زخم • ریش
cut vt قطع کردن • بریدن
→ (gems) تراشیدن
→ (into pieces) توته کردن
→ (with scissors) قیچی کردن
cutthroat n چاقو کش
cutting n قطع
cyan adj آسمانگون • آسمانی
cyanide (chem) n سیاناید
cylinder n اسطوانه
cypress (tree) n سرو
Cypriot (& pers) adj, n قبرسی
Cyprus n قبرس
czar n زار • تزار
Czech (& pers, lang) adj, n چک
→ Czech Republic جمهوریتِ چک
Czechoslovakia (hist, country) n چکوسلواکیا • چکوسلواکیه

D

dad n بابه • بابه گک • آغا • آقا
Dado (ctr) n دادو
Dadwal (ctr) n دادول

dagger n دشنه
→ (curved) خنجر
→ Sikh dagger (on belt) پیش قبض
Dahana-ye Ghori (dist) n دهنه غوری
dahlia (flower) n دلیه
dahri (doctrine) n دهری
daikon n ملی
Daikondi (province, seat) n دایکندی
daily adj, adv روزمره • روزانه
dairy products n لبنیات
Dalw (month) n دلو
dam (for power) n بند برق • بند • سد
damage (harm) n زیان • ضرر • مضرت • صدمه • حیف • افسوس • دریغ • آسیب • خساره • نقص (colloq) →
damage (loss) n تاوان • خساره
→ ask compensation for damages تاوان کردن
→ compensate for damages تاوان دادن
→ suffer damages تاوان رسیدن • تاوان شدن
damage vt خراب کردن • صدمه زدن
damaged adj خراب • صدمه دیده
damaging adj زیان آور • ضرر ناک • مضر
Daman (dist) n دامان • دامن • دمن
Damascus n دمشق • شام
dambura (mus instr) n دمبوره
damn vt نفرین کردن
damnation n نفرین
damned adj نفرین شده
→ (by God) خدا شرمانده • خدازده
damp adj تر • مرطوب • نمدار
dampen vt تر کردن
dampness n نم
dance n پای کوبی
dance vi رقصیدن
→ (colloq) رقص کردن • بازی کردن • دانس کردن
→ circular dance چرخ
→ dance (hoof it) سم زدن
→ dance the atan اتن انداختن • اتن کردن

377

dancer (m) *n* رقاص
→ (young m) بازنگر • بازینگر
dancing *n* رقص
Dand wa Patan (dist) *n* دند و پتان
dandruff *n* سبوسک
Dane (pers) *n* دنمارکی
Dangam (dist) *n* دانگام
danger *excl* برحذر باش
danger *n* خطر
dangerous *adj* خطرناک
→ put o.s. in a dangerous situation
در زنبور خانه دست زدن
Danish *adj* دنمارکی
Daoud (hist, Afgh president 1973-
78) *n* داوود • محمد داوود
Dar es-Salaam (city) *n* دارالسلام
Dar ul-Ulum (institute for advanced
Arabic & rel studies) *n* دارالعلوم
Dara (dist) *n* دره
Dara-ye Hazara (ctr) *n* دره هزاره
Dara-ye Nur (dist) *n* دره نور
Dara-ye Peych (dist) *n* دره پیچ
Dara-ye Suf (ctr) *n* دره صوف
Dara-ye Suf-e Bala (dist) *n* دره
صوف بالا
Dara-ye Suf-e Payin (dist) *n* دره
صوف پایین
Darayem (dist) *n* داریم
dare *vi* دل کردن
dare *vt* تیر شدن
Dari (lang) *n* دری • پارسی دری
dark *adj* تاریک • ظلمانی • سیاه • تیره
→ dark-complected سبزه • علف
darkness (& fig) *n* تاریکی • ظلمت
darling *n* حبیب
Darqad (dist) *n* درقد
Darulaman (dist, Kabul city dist) *n*
دارالامان
Darwaz (dist) *n* درواز
Darwaz-e Bala (dist) *n* درواز بالا
Darzab (dist) *n* درزاب
dash (punctuation) *n* خط فاصله
dash *v see* run, hurry
Dasht-e Barchi (Kabul city dist) *n*
دشت برچی
Dasht-e Qala (dist) *n* دشت قلعه
data *n pl* معلومات
date (day) *n* تاریخ
378

date (edible) *n* خرما
→ date palm نخل • نخیل • درخت
خرما
dated (having a calendar date) *adj*
مورخ • مورخه
datura (med herb) *n* داتوره
daughter *n* دختر
→ (in official documents) بنت
→ (lit) صبیه
→ like one's daughter دختر خوانده
daughter-in-law *n* سنه • سنو •
عروس
David (bibl) *n* داوود
→ David & Goliath داوود و جالوت
Dawlat Shah (dist) *n* دولت شاه
Dawlat Yar (dist) *n* دولت یار
Dawlatabad (dist) *n* دولت آباد
Dawlatzai (P tribe) *n* دولتزی
dawn *n* صباح • صبح • صبح دم •
بام • بامداد • سحر • سپیده دم •
سپیده داغ • سفیده داغ
→ just before dawn سحرگاه •
سحرگه • سپیده گم • صبحگاه
day *n* روز • نهار • بود
→ ten days دهه
daybreak *n* طاوع بامداد • طلوع •
صبح • صبحگاه
Daychopan (dist, alt Deh Chopan)
n دایچوپان
daydream *n* خیال بافی
daydream *v* خیال کردن
Daykundi (province) *n* دایکندی •
دی کندی
Daymirdad (dist, alt Jelga) *n*
دایمیرداد
dazzled *adj* خیره
de facto *adj, adv* بالفعل
de jure *adj, adv* بالقوه
deactivate *vt* خنثی ساختن
deactivation *n* خنثی ساختن
dead (& pers) *adj, n* مرده
→ (fig) رفته
→ almost dead مردنی
→ dead tired هلاک
deadline *n* وعده • موعد
deadly (& fig) *adj* قاتل • کشنده •
مهلک
deaf (& pers) *adj, n* کر • اصم

deal (trade) n سودا
→ dealings معاملات
→ double-dealing لشم
→ wheeler-dealer معامله گر
deal (distribute) v تقسیم کردن
dear (beloved) (& pers) adj, n
عزیز • دل بند
→ dear child (fig) جگر • جگر
گوشه
→ Dear Sir (salutation in letter) با
عرض سلام و ادب
death (formal) n درگذشت
death n فوت • مرگ • ممات •
موت • وفات • میر
→ (fig) در گذاشت
→ (fig, only for Prophet) ارتحال •
رحلت
→ angel of death ملک الموت
→ at the hour of death
اجل رسیده
→ death & mortality مرگ و میر
→ death <to sb>! مرگ <به> !>
کسی>
→ death certificate تذکره وافیت
→ deserving of death واجب القتل
→ hour of death اجل
→ time between death &
resurrection (rel) برزخ
→ untimely death جوان مرگی
debate n بحث • مناقشه • جدال •
جدل
→ house of rel debate under
Akbar (hist) عبادت خانه
debauched adj حرام کار • زنا کار
debauchery (esp f promiscuity) n
فحشا
debilitating adj جان کاه
debt n قرض
debtor n قرض دار
decade n دهه
decay n فساد
decay vi خراب شدن
deceased adj خاموش
→ the deceased مرحوم
deceit n دغا • دغل بازی • دغلی •
فریب • تزویر • تقلب • بازی •
افسون
deceitful adj دغل • دغل باز • تقلب
آمیز • افسون گر

deceitful (& adv) adj, adv فریب
کارانه
deceive v دغلی کردن • دغل بازی
کردن • بازی دادن
→ be deceived بازی خوردن
→ (seduce) فریفتن
deceived (seduced) adj فریب داده
deceiver (pers) n دغا • آدم دغا •
باز • حیله باز • حیله ساز • حیله گر
• متقلب • محتال • محیل • فریب
کار
December n دسمبر
decide (resolve to do sth) v فیصله
کردن • تصمیم گرفتن
→ be decided فیصله شدن • قرار
گرفتن
decimal point n اعشاریه • نقطه
decision (resolution) n فیصله •
تصمیم
decisive adj قطعی • قاطع
deck (ship's) n عرشه
declaration n اعلام • اعلامیه •
تصریح • تشریح • توضیح
declare vt اظهار کردن • اظهار
داشتن • تصریح کردن
declension (gram) n تصریف •
صرف • گردان
decline (in prices) n نزول
declining adj نزولی
decoction n جوشانده
decorate vt آذین بستن
decoration n آذین • تزیین
decorative adj تزیینی • تزییناتی
decoy n نور
decrease n کاهش • تقلیل • تنقیص
• کمی
decrease vi کاهش یافتن • پائین
رفتن • پایان رفتن • پائین بردن •
پایان بردن
decrease vt کاهش دادن • پائین
دادن • تنقیص دادن • تنقیص کردن
decree (official) n تصویب نامه
decree v فرمان دادن
decrepit adj دست و پای شکسته
deduce v قیاس کردن • نتیجگیری
کردن
deduction n قیاس • استدلال
deductive adj تعلیلی

379

deed (act) n • عمل • فعل • کنش • اجرا

→ story of martyr's great deeds کار نامه

deed (to property) n • سند • قباله مالکیت

deep (& adv) adj, adv • عمیق • چقر • ژرف

→ deep water غرقاب

deeply adv عمیقاً

deer n آهو

→ nakhchir (kind of deer) نخچیر

defamatory adj • هجایی • هجوی

→ defamatory poem هجونامه

defame (colloq) vt گپ ساختن

defamer n گپ ساز

defeat n شکست

→ (lit) • هزیمت • انهزام

→ state of defeat مغلوبیت

defeat vt مغلوب کردن

→ (fig) • به زانو درآوردن • از پای در آوردن

→ (lit) هزیمت دادن

→ be defeated مغلوب شدن

→ be defeated (fig) • به زانو درآمدن

→ defeat & follow پیش انداختن

defeated adj مغلوب

→ (lit) هزیمتی

defect n • عیب • علت • نقص • ضرر • زیان

defective adj • عیبناک • ناقص • شرمناک

defend v • دفاع کردن • پشتی کردن • پشتیبانی کردن

defendant (law) n مدعی علیه

defender (patron) n • حمایت گر • پشتیبان • حامی

→ (colloq) پشتیوان

defender (savior) n فریاد رس

defense n • دفاع • حفظ • محافظت • حفاظت • پشتیبانی

→ (colloq) پشتیوانی

defense n مدافعه

defensive (mil) adj دفاعی

defer vt عقب انداختن

deficit (in budget) n کسر بودجه

defile (contaminate) vt آلودن

defile (pass) n • گذر گاه • معبر

380

defilement n • آلودگی • لوث

definite adj قطعی

→ (gram) معرفه

definitely adv • حتماً • بالقطع • قطعاً

definiteness n قطعیت

defloration n ازاله بکارت

deformed adj بد شکل

defraud v • تقلب کردن • حقه بازی کردن

degree (diploma) n • دیپلوم • سند فراغت

degree (extent) n حسب

degree (rank) n مرتبه

degree (unit of heat) n درجه

Deh Bala (dist) n ده بالا

Deh Buri (Kabul city dist) n ده بوری

Deh Chopan (dist) n ده چوپان

Deh Rawod (dist) n ده راود

Deh Sabz (dist) n ده سبز

Deh Salah (dist) n ده ساله

Deh Yak (dist) n ده یک

Dehdadi (dist) n دهدادی

Dehgani (Dari dialect) n دهگانی

deity n • اله • معبود

dejection n گرفتگی

delay n • معطلی • تعویق • درنگ

→ w/o delay • بی درنگ • در اسرع وقت

delay v • معطل کردن • منتظر ماندن • درنگ کردن

delayed adj • معطل • درنگ کرده

delegation n • هیأت • هئیت • وفد

deleted adj محذوف

deliberate v مشاوره کردن

deliberately adv • عمداً • قصداً

deliberation n • مشاوره • مشوره • مشورت

delicate (fine) adj • لطیف • نازک • نفیس • ظریف

delicious adj • خوش مزه • مزه دار • با مزه لذیذ

deliciousness n • لذت • تمتع • حظ

delight n • لذت • تمتع • حظ • سرور • مسرت • خوشی • شادمانی

→ Sufic delight وجد

delightful adj خوشی بخش

delirium n هذیان

deliver (give birth) v ولادت کردن

deliver (hand over) vt تسلیم دادن • تسلیم کردن

deliver (speech) vt ایراد کردن

deliver (supply) vt عرضه کردن

deliver <f> of a child vt ولادت دادن <زن را>

deliverance (salvation) n وارستگی • رستگاری

delivered (saved) (& pers) adj, n وارسته • رستگار

delivery (handover) n تحویل • تحویل دهی • تسلیم • تسلیمی • ایراد • توزیع

delivery (of child) n وضع حمل

delivery (supply) n عرضه

delivery adj تسلیمی

Delkusha (building) n دل کشا

delphinium (flower) n دلفون

delta (mil) n تفاوت • اختلاف • فرق

delude vt اغفال کردن

Deluge, the (bibl) n طوفان نوح

demagogic adj عوام فریب

demagogically adv عوام فریبانه

demagogue n مردم فریب • عوام فریب

demagoguery n مردم فریبی • عوام فریبی

demand (claim) n مطالبه • طلب

demand (request) n خواسته • تقاضا
→ demand for restitution بازخواست

demand (request) vt تقاضا کردن
→ on demand عندالطلب • عندالمطالبه

demand v ادعا کردن • ادعا داشتن

democracy n دموکراسی

demolish vt غلتاندن

demolished adj منهدم

demon (evil spirit) n دیو

demon (jinni) n جنی

demonic (fiendish) adj دیوسرشت • دیوسرست • جنی
→ (colloq) جندی

demonstrate (rally) v مظاهره کردن

demonstrate <sth to sb> vt نشان دادن <چیزی را به کسی>

demonstration (rally) n مظاهره • تظاهر

demonstrative adj اشاره
→ demonstrative adj صفت اشاره
→ demonstrative pron ضمیر اشاره

demonstrator (at rally) n مظاهره کننده

demotion n تنزیل رتبه

denial (refusal) n رد • دریغ
→ be in denial دریغ داشتن

denial (refutation) n تکذیب

Denmark n دنمارک

denomination n مذهب

denominator (math) n مخرج

denounce n تقبیح کردن

density n کثافت

dentist n داکتر دندان

denude vt برهنه ساختن

denunciation n تقبیح

deny (refuse) v پیخ زدن

deny (reject) vt رد کردن

deny <sth to sb> v دریغ کردن <کسی را از چیزی>

Deobandi (mvmt) n دیوبندی

depart vi حرکت کردن • رفتن

department n ریاست
→ (mil) جزوتام • قطعه
→ (university department) شعبه

departure n حرکت

depend (rely) <on sb/sth/God> v اتکا کردن <به کسی / چیزی / خدا>

depend <on sth> vi ارتباط داشتن <به چیزی>

dependence (linkage) n تعلق • علاقه • سروکار

dependent (& gram) adj تابع

dependent (poor) adj محتاج

dependent <of sb> n متعلق <(به)> کسی>
→ (relatives) وابسته گان • متعلقین • متعلقان
→ (spouse & children) تعلق داری

dependent <on sth> adj منوط بر <چیزی> • متعلق <(به) چیزی>
→ dependent word in poss construction (gram) مضاف الیه

depending <on sth> phrs نظر <به چیزی>

381

depict vt نمایاندن

depilatory agent n موی بر

deplete vt تمام کردن

depleted (colloq) adj پیش خور

deploy vt اعزام کردن • اعزام نمودن

→ deploy troops • لشکر کشیدن • لشکر کشی کردن

deployment n اعزام

→ troop deployment لشکر کشی

depoliticization n غیر سیاسی سازی

depoliticize vt غیر سیاسی ساختن

depose vt عزل کردن

deposed adj معزول

deposit (advance money) n سلم • دپزت • دیپوزیت

deposit (alluvium) n رسوب

deposit (for safekeeping) n تحویل

deposit (ore) n کان • معدن

deposit (remittance) n تحویل

depraved (& pers) adj, n حرام کار • زنا کار

depraved (& pers) n رذیل

depravity see & debauchery

depravity (vice) n رذیلت

depressed adj خاطر آزرده • آزرده خاطر • دل تنگ

→ become depressed دل انداختن

depressing adj سرد • خنک • یخ • دل گیر

depression (econ) n وقفه اقتصادی • کساد • کسادی

depression (sorrow) n غبار خاطر • غبار دل • گرفتگی

deprivation <from sth> n محرومی • محرومیت <از چیزی>

depth n عمق • ژرفا • ژرفی • چقری

deputy n معین • معاون

deranged (& pers) adj, n خاطر پریشان • پریشان خاطر

derangement n خلل دماغ • اختلال

deride vt نیش زدن • هجو گفتن

derided adj ریش خند

derision n ریش خند • طنز • هجو • هجا

derisive adj طنز آمیز • نیش دار

derivation n اشتقاق

derivative adj اشتقاقی

derivative (gram) n مشتق

dermal adj جلدی

dervish n درویش • خرقه پوش • ژنده پوش

→ characteristic of a dervish درویش صفت • درویش نهاد

→ dervish dance سماع

→ dervish garb خرقه

→ dervish's battle-axe تبر زین • تبرزین

→ like a dervish درویشانه

→ malang (kind of dervish) ملنگ

→ mendicant dervish فقیر

→ Rumi (dervish poet) رومی

descendant n خلف

descending adj سرازیر

describe (explain) vt تشریح کردن • تشریح دادن • شرح دادن

describe (portray) v ترسیم کردن

description (drawing) n ترسیم

description (explanation) n تشریح • شرح

descriptve adj ترسیمی

→ descriptive geometry هندسه ترسیمی

desert n بادیه • صحرا • بیابان

→ desert traveler • صحرا نورد • بیابان نورد

→ desert wilderness دشت

→ of/from the desert بدوی

deserted adj خلوت

deserve v سزیدن

deserving (& meritorious) adj سزا

deserving (needy) (& pers) adj, n مستحق

deserving (of sth) adj قابل • لایق • ماهر • چابکدست

→ deserving of death واجب القتل

design (intent) n منظور

design (plan) n طرح • دیزاین

design (plan) v طراحی کردن

designed to adj بمنظور <چیزی> ایجاد

designer n طراح

designing (planning) n نقشه کشی

desire (avidity) n طمع • حرص • آز

382

desire (hope) *n* • آرزو • امید
آرمان
← امل (lit)
desire (hope) *v* • امید کردن • امید
داشتن
desire (passion) *n* • هوس • هوا
← desire & longing • هوس و هوا
desire (wish) *n* • نیاز • خواسته
میل • میلان
desirous <of sth/sb> *adj* • خواهان
<چیزی/کسی>
← vainly desirous • خام طمع
desk (worktable) *n* • میز • میز کار
desk (writing table) *n* • میز تحریر
desolation (wilderness) *n* • دشت
خلوت
despair *n* • یاس
despite <sth> *prep* • با • بوجود
وجود • علیرغم <چیزی>
despite the fact that *conj* • با
وجودیکه • به وجودی که • با وجود
آن که • هر چند که
despot *n* • طاغی • مستبد • ظالم
despotic (& adv) *adj, adv* • ظالمانه
despotic *adj* • ظالم
destination *n* • منزل • سر منزل
destiny *n* • تقدیر • قسمت • سرنوشت
• بوش
← one's destiny (fig) • آب و دانه
destroy *vt* • از بین بردن • از میان بردن
بردن • خراب کردن • نابود کردن
destroyed *adj* • نابود • ویران
خراب • متلاشی
← (colloq) • بیران
destruction *n* • نابودی • تخریب
خرابی • تباهی
destructive *adj* • ویرانگر • مخرب
detached *adj* • جدا
detail *n* • چگونگی
← details • مفردات • جزئیات
← in detail • ذره ذره • مفصلاً
detailed *adj* • مشرح • مفصل
مبسوط
detain *vt* • بندی کردن • توقیف کردن
detainee *n* • اسیر • بندی • زندانی
محبوس • توقیف شده
detect *vt* • کشف کردن

detention (arrest) *n* • بازداشت
توقیف
← pre-trial detention center
نظارت خانه
determination (resolution) *n* • تصمیم
determine (distinguish) *vt* • مشخص
کردن
determined (pugnacious) *adj* • شعله
ور
← be determined (resolute)
تصمیم داشتن
deterrence (defense) *n* • دفع
detriment *n* • ضرر • زیان
مضرت
detrimental *adj* • مضر • زیان آور
ضررناک
devaluation *n* • تنزیل قیمت
develop *v* • وسعت دادن
developed *adj* • پیشرفته • پیش رفته
• مترقی
development *n* • نشو • انکشاف
رشد
deviation (digression) *n* • انحراف
device *n* • ابزار • آلت • آله
← (colloq) • اوزار
devil (& the Devil) *n* • ابلیس • شیطان
← Ahriman (Zor) • اهریمن
← drive away the devil • شیطان را
لاحول کردن
devilish *adj* • شیطان • شیطانی
• اهریمنی • ابلیسی
devilishly *adv* • ابلیسانه
devilry *n* • شیطانی
devious *see* cunning
devoid <of sth> *adj* • <از عاری
چیزی>
devoted *adj* • جانی
devoted (& pers) *adj, n* • سرسپرده
devotion *n* • از جان • سرسپردگی
گذشتگی • از خود گذری
devout (& pers) *adj, n* • خدا پرست
پارسا
devout *adj* • دین • بادیانت • متدین
دار • متعبد
dew *n* • شب نم • شبنم
dewlap *n* • غبغب • بغبغه
Deygani *see* Dehgani
deywani (callig style) *n* • دیوانی •
خط دیوانی

383

dhikr (remembrance of God; Sufi prayer ritual) *n* ذکر

dhimmi (Jews, Christians; people of the book) *n* اهل الذمی • ذمی

diabase *n* مرمر فولادی

diabetes *n* مرض قند • مرض شکر • دیابت

diacritical mark *n* علامه مشخص

diagnosis *n* تشخیصیه • تشخیص

diagnostic *adj* تشخیصی

diagonal *adj* وریب • اریب

dialect *n* گویش • لهجه

dialogue *n* مکالمه • دیالوگ

diamond *n* الماس
→ (cards) خشت

diaphragm (anat) *n* پرده دل • حجاب حاجز • دیافرام

diarrhea *n* پیچش • اسهال
→ having diarrhea شکم رو

diarrheal *adj* اسهالی

diary *n* خاطرات

dice (chop) *vt* ریزه کردن

dice (for gaming) *n* تاس

dick (vulg) *n* ذکر • غین

dictation (of text) *n* املا

dictator *n* دکتاتور

dictatorial *adj* دکتاتوری

dictatorship *n* دکتاتوری

dictionary *n* قاموس • دکشنری • فرهنگ • لغت نامه
→ (17ᵗʰ-c Dari dictionary published in India) برهان قاطع

die (fig) *vi* پیمانه ‹کسی› پر شدن

die (naturally) *vi* مردن
→ (be killed) کشته شدن • هلاک شدن • از بین رفتن
→ (colloq) فوت کردن
→ (fig) رفتن • از جهان رفتن • از جهان گذشتن • چشم پت شدن • به رضای خدا رفتن • عمر به سر رسیدن • جان باختن
→ (only for Prophet) ارتحال کردن • رحلت کردن
→ (said of rel leaders) جامه بدل کردن
→ ‹for sth› جان دادن ‹برای چیزی›
→ ‹of sth› جان دادن ‹از چیزی›
→ drop dead سقط شدن

384

diesel *n* دیزل

diet (food) *n* پرهیز • پرهیزانه

diet *v* پرهیز کردن

differ (in opinion) *v* مشاجره کردن

differ (not same) *vi* متفاوت بودن

difference (discrepancy) *n* ناهمخوانی

difference (of opinion) *n* مشاجره • اختلاف • عدم توافق

difference *n* اختلاف • فرق • تفاوت
→ make a difference فرق داشتن

different *adj* مختلف • ناهمگون • متفاوت • علاهده

difficult *adj* مشکل • سخت • دشوار • محنت بار • متکلف

difficulty (problem) *n* مشکل • مشقت • ناآرامی • معضله
→ difficulties مشکلات

dig *v* کندن • کاوش کردن
→ dig a tunnel (mil) نقب زدن

digestion *n* هضم • گوارش
→ (arch) هاضمه

digestive *adj* هاضمه • هضمی
→ digestive ability هاضمه
→ digestive system جهاز هاضمه

digit *n* رقم • عدد • شماره

dignified (respected) *adj* با وقار

dignitary *n* مسند نشین • حضور

dignity (prestige) *n* وقار • کرامت • حیثیت • پرستیژ

dignity (pride) *n* ناموس

dignity (rank) *n* پایگاه

digression *n* انحراف

Dila (dist) *n* دیله

dill porridge *n* اماج

dilution *n* رقت

dimension *n* بعد

diminish *vi* کاهش یافتن • پائین رفتن

diminish *vt* کاهش دادن • پائین دادن

diminution *n* کاهش • تقلیل

diminutive (gram) *adj* مصغر

Din-e Ilahi (hist, rel mvmt founded by Akbar) *n* دین الهی

dining room *n* اتاق نان • اتاق نان خوری • اتاق طعام خوری

dinner *n* نان شب • طعام شب

diocese *n* اسقف

diphtheria n خناق • دفتری

diphthong n دفتانگ

diploma n سند فراغت • دیپلوم • دیپلوم

diplomacy n دیپلوماسی • مردم داری

diplomat n دیپلومات • دیپلومات

diplomatic (political) adj سیاسی

diplomatic adj دیپلوماسی

→ diplomatic corps کور دیپلوماتیک

→ diplomatic immunity مصونیت دیپلوماتیک

direct adj مستقیم

→ direct object مفعول مستقیم

direct (film) v دایرکت کردن

direct (order) v هدایت کردن

directed <toward sb> adj متوجه <کسی>

direction (instruction) n ارشاد

→ directions for use طرز استعمال

direction (side) n طرف • جهت • سمت • مسیر

→ in the direction of به • طرف • جانب • به جانب

directive (order) n هدایت

→ (document) هدایت نامه

directly adv مستقیم • راساً

director (film/stage) n رژیسور • دایرکتر • کارگردان • کار گردان

director (manager) n مدیر

directorate (office) n مدیریت

dirham (currency) n درهم

dirigible n سفینه فضایی • کشتی فضایی

dirt (filth) n مرداری

dirt (soil) n خاک

→ dirt road راه خامه • سرک خامه

dirty (base) (fig) adj گنده

dirty (filthy) adj چرک • چرک آلود • چرک آلوده

→ (lit) چرکین

dirty (soiled) adj خاکسار • مردار • چتل • کثیف

disability n معیوبیت

disabled (& pers) adj, n معیوب

→ become disabled بی دست و پای بودن • از دست و پای ماندن

disabled (in hand) adj چنته

disagreeable adj ناگوارا

disagreement n مشاجره • اختلاف • عدم توافق

disappear vi غیب شدن • رفع شدن

disappearance n اضمحلال • نابودی

disappeared (& pers) adj, n گمشده • گمگشته

disappoint <sb> v دل <کسی را> شکستن

disappointed adj مایوس • ناامید • تلخ کام

disappointing adj مایوس کننده • ناامید کننده

disappointment n مایوسی • یاس • ناامیدی

disarmament n خلع سلاح

disaster n مصیبت • فاجعه • بلا • طاعون • داهیه

→ disasters فجایع

disaster-stricken adj مصیبت زده

disastrous adj مصیبت بار • مصیبت زا • مصیبت زای • فجی • سیاه • سیه

disc n قرص

→ compact disc سی دی

discard v باطل کردن

disciple (follower) n شاگرد • متعلم • تلمیذ • حواری

→ disciple of Sufi order مرید

→ Prophet's four disciples چاریار

discipleship (Sufi) n مریدی

discipline (order) n نظم • انضباط

→ (mil)

discipline (order) v نظم دادن

disclose vt افشا کردن

disclosure n افشاگری • افشا

discomfort n ناآرامی

discontinue vt قطع کردن

discord n شقاق

discord (schism) n فتنه

discount n تخفیف

discourage <sb> vt دل <کسی را> سرد کردن

→ get discouraged دل انداختن • دل <کسی> سرد شدن

discouraged adj مایوس • ناامید

discouraging adj ناامید کننده • مایوس کننده • یاس آور

385

discover (find) vt کشف کردن
discoverer n کاشف • مکتشف
discovery n کشف
→ (law) استشهاد
discrepancy n ناهمخوانی
discrimination n تبعیض
discussion (debate) n بحث • مناقشه • جدال
disease n مرض
→ epidemic disease وبا
disgrace n افتضاح • فضیحت • رسوایی • عار • عیب
→ (in Pashtunwali) ننگ
disgrace vt رسوا کردن
→ (fig) بی آب کردن
disgraced adj رسوا
→ (before God) خدا شرمانده • خدازده
→ be disgraced بی آب شدن
disgraceful adj شرمناک • افتضاح آمیز • افتضاح آمیز • فتضح آمیز • فتضح آور • رسوایی آمیز • رسوایی آور • عیبناک
→ (in Pashtunwali) ننگین • ننگی
disgusting (food) adj, n مکروه
dish (plate) n قاب • بشقاب
→ dishes ظرف ها
disheveled (hair) adj پریشان
disheveled see & unkempt
Disho (dist) n دیشو
dishonest adj قلب
dishonesty (colloq) n غلطی
dishonorable adj بی شرف
dishonored adj رسوا
dishwasher n ظرف شوی • ماشین ظرف شویی
disinfect vt ضد عفونی کردن
disk n قرص
dislike n کرک
dislike v کرک <کسی> آمدن
→ I dislike this از این چیز کرکم می آید
disloyal (& pers) adj, n خیانت کار • خاین • خیانت پیشه • نمک حرام
disloyalty n خیانت
dismiss (fire) v جواب دادن

dismissal (firing) n برطرفی • برکناری • انفصال • انفکاک
→ dismissal for cause طرد
→ dismissal from service طرد • ملازمت
dismissed (fired) adj برطرف • برکنار
dismount v پیاده کردن
disobedience n نافرمانی • بیگفتی • سرکشی
disobedient (& pers) adj, n نافرمان • سرکش • بیگفت • گپ ناشنو • گردن کش • عاصی • یاغی
disobey v نافرمانی کردن • سرکشی کردن • سرکشیدن
disorder (disturbance) n اختلال
dispassionate adj بی حمیت
dispatch n ارسال
dispatch vt کسیل کردن • روان کردن
→ (deploy) اعزام کردن • اعزام نمودن
disperse vt پراگندن
dispersed adj پراگنده
displaced pers n بیجاشده • بی جا شده • آواره • آواره گرد
→ state of being displaced آوارگی • آواره گردی • بیجاشدگی
display <sth to sb> v نشان دادن <چیزی را به کسی> • ارائه دادن • ارائه کردن
display n نمایش • ارائه
displeased (& pers) adj, n خاطر گرفته • گرفته خاطر
disposed (inclined) adj متمایل
disposition (nature) n طبیعت • نهاد • مزاج • مجاز
disproportionate adj بی تناسب
dispute (mildly) v مشاجره کردن
dispute n مشاجره • مناقشه • قالمقال • قیل و قال • جنجال
→ (colloq) غالمغال
→ reignite a dispute that has ended پلته پیش کردن
disputed adj متنازع فیه
disregard n تجاهل
disregard v see ignore
disrespect vt پای مال کردن • پامال کردن

386

disrespectful *adj* • بی احترامانه • خیر

dissatisfaction *n* نارضایت

dissatisfied *adj* ناراض

dissenter *n* خارجی

dissenting *adj* خارجی

dissimilar *adj* ناهمگون • نا هم گون • مختلف

dissolve *vi* محلول شدن

dissolved (chem) *adj* محلول

dissonance *n* تنافر

dissonant *adj* تنافر دار

→ be dissonant تنافر داشتن

distance *n* فاصله • مسافه • بعد

distant (& place) *adj, adv* دوردست

distill *v* تقطیر کردن

distillation *n* تقطیر

distinct (separate) *adj* جدا

distinctive *adj* مشخص

distinguish *vt* مشخص کردن

distinguished *adj* معزز • عزیز

distinguished pers *n* علم

distinguishing *adj* فارقه

distress *n* • اضطرار • پریشانی • تشویش

distressed (& pers) *adj, n* درمانده • پریشان • مشوش

distressing *adj* دردناک • دردآلود
→ (fig) جان خراش

distribute (spread) *vt* پخش کردن

distribution (delivery) *n* توزیع

distribution (spread) *n* پخش

district (in city) *n* ناحیه • کارته

district (provincial) *n* • ولسوالی • ضلع
→ dist governor ولسوال
→ subdistrict علاقه داری

disturb *vt* اخلال کردن • اخلال نمودن • خراب کردن

disturbance *n* خلل

ditch (irrigation) *n* • جوی • جویچه • نهر
→ (for planting vines) جویه

ditto *adv* ایضاً

diuretic *adj* مدر

divan *n* دیوان

diver *n* غواص

diverse *adj* مختلف • متفاوت • ناهم گون

diversion (of water) *adj* آب گردان
→ diversion dam بند آب گردان

diversity *n* تنوع

divert (water) *vt* گرداندن

divide (distribute) *vt* بخش کردن
→ do division (math) تقسیم کردن

divine *adj* • خداوندی • آسمانی • سماوی • الهی
→ divine obligation (time of fasting & prayer) وظیفه جمالی
→ divine obligation (more severe than وظیفه جمالی) وظیفه جلالی

divine *n* ایزدی • یزدانی

divinity *n* خداوندی
→ scholar of divinity ربانی

division (mil) *n* فرقه • دیویزیون

division (share, math) *n* تقسیم

divorce (from f) *v* • طلاق دادن • طلاق کردن

divorce (from m) *v* طلاق گرفتن

divorce (spouse) *v* رها کردن • سر دادن
→ (colloq) یله کردن

divorce *n* طلاق
→ divorce decree • طلاق خط • طلاق نامه
→ divorce settlement مهر • مهریه • کابین
→ revocable divorce (Musl law) طلاق رجعی

divorced (said of f) *adj* • طلاقی • مطلقه

divorced *adj* رها
→ (colloq) یله

divulge *vt* افشا کردن

dizziness *n* دوران سر

dizzy *adj* گیج • سر چرخ
→ (colloq) گنگس
→ be dizzy سر ‹کسی› دور خوردن

do *v* کردن • نمودن • فرمودن (lit)
→ carry out اجرا دادن • انجام دادن • به عمل آوردن • انجامیدن

dock *n* بارانداز

doctor *n* داکتر • دکتور • طبیب
→ (arch) پزشک
→ general practitioner داکتر عمومی

doctor's office *n* معاینه خانه

doctoral degree (Ph.D.) *n* • داکتری
دپلوم داکتری • دیپلوم داکتری

doctrine *n* اطاعت
→ doctrine of obedience to pol
authority اطاعتِ علو الآمر

document (computer) *n* مضمون

document (official) *n* • ورقه • نامه •
مکتوب
→ legal document وثیقه
→ (written instrument) سند

document (proof, evidence) *n*
مدرک
→ documents office (law) شعبه
وثایق

documentary (film) *n* فلم مستند

documentation (recording) *n* اتخاذ
سند

dog *n* سگ
→ female dog ماچه سگ
→ large & fierce dog (fig) • تیگر •
سگ تیگر

doll *n* گدی • لعبت

dollar *n* دالر

dolma *n* دولمه

dolt (insult) *n* لوده • گوساله

dome *n* گنبد

domed *adj* گنبدی

domestic (servant) *n* • نوکر •
خدمتگار • چاکر

domestic *adj* داخلی
→ domestic violence خشونت های
خانوادگی
→ domestically-produced وطنی

domesticated (animal) *adj* • اهلی •
خانگی

dominant *adj* • حکم فرما • متسلط •
مسلط
→ be dominant • تسلط داشتن •
تسلط یافتن

domination *n* • حاکمیت • حکم
فرمایی • تسلط

dominion *n* • حاکمیت • تسلط
→ (territory) قلمرو

donate (give zakat) *v* زکات دادن

donation *n* • اعانه • اهدا

done *adj* مجرا

done for (& pers) *adj, n* مردنی

donkey driver *n* خرکار

388

donkey *n* • مرکب • خر • الاغ •
اولاغ • اولاق
→ female donkey ماچه خر
→ load carried by donkey الاغ
→ small donkey خرک

doomed *adj* نفرین شده

door *n* • دروازه • باب
→ door jamb پهلو دری
→ door latch/bar تنبه
→ small door دریچه

doorbell *n* زنگ دروازه

doorkeeper *n* دروازه بان
→ (colloq) دروازه وان

doormat *n* پای پاک

doorpost *n* پهلو دری

dormitory *n* لیلیه

Doshi (dist) *n* دوشی

dossier *n* دوسیه

Dost Muhamed (hist, 19th-c Kabul
emir) *n* دوست محمد

dot *n* نقطه

double *adj, adv* دو برابر • دو چند
→ double-dealing لشم

doubled *adj* متضاعف

doubling *n* تضاعف • تضاعف مقاد

doubt (anxiety) (lit) *n* خدشه

doubt (have doubts) *v* شک داشتن

doubt (hesitate) *v* تردید داشتن

doubt (hesitation) *n* تردید

doubt (suspect) *vi* مشتبه بودن

doubt *n* شک

doubtful (suspicious) *adj* • مظنون •
مشتبه • بد گمان • مشتبه

doubtful (uncertain) *adj* مشکوک

doubtful (skeptical) (& pers) *adj, n*
دیر باور

dough (& fig) *n* خمیر
→ loaf-sized lump of dough زغاره
→ starter dough • خمیر ترش •
خمیر مایه

douse *see* extinguish, soak

dove *n* کبوتر

down *adv* • زیر • پایان
→ (colloq) • پائین • پایین
→ coming down *adj* سرازیر

down <w/sb> *excl* مرگ <به
کسی>

down payment *n* بیعانه

downfall *n* سقوط • اضمحلال

downhill *adj* • سرپایان • سراشیب •
سرنشیب

downhill *adv* شیوه

downpour *n* ریزش

downstairs *n* منزل پایین • طبقه
پایین

downtrodden *adj* لگد خور

downward (v prefix) فرو

draft (mil) *n* پشک

draft (outline) *n* مسوده • طرح •
کروکی • سکیچ • خاکه

draft (rough out) *v* تسوید کردن

draft horse *n* یابو

draftee *n* جلبی • پشکی

drafting (roughing out) *n* تسوید

drag *vt* کشاندن

dragoman *see* interpreter

dragon *n* اژدر

dragonfly *n* بمبیرک

drain *n* بدررفت

→ drain under a road پلچک

drama *n* درامه • درام

dramatic *adj* تمثیلی

draw (breath) *vi* نفس کشیدن

draw (lots) *v* قرعه کشی کردن

draw (picture) *v* رسم کشیدن • رسم
کردن • ترسیم کردن • نقش کردن

drawcord (pajamas) *n* ازاربند

drawer (in table) *n* جعبه • روک

→ cash drawer دخل

drawing (art) *n* رسم • ترسیم • نقش

drawing (lottery) *n* قرعه کشی

dream *n* رویا • خواب

→ (hope) آرزو

→ book of dreams خواب نامه

→ interpret a dream خواب
گزاردن

dreamer *n* خیال باف • خیال پرست

dregs *n* رسوب

dress (fs) *n* پیراهن • پیرهن

→ (colloq) پیران • پیرن

dress (wounds) *v* پانسمان کردن

dress *vi* ملبس شدن

dress *vt* پوشاندن

dressed *adj* ملبس

dressmaker *n* خیاط زنانه

dried *adj* قاق • خشک

drill (esp mil) *n* مشق • تمرین •
تطبیقات • جمع نظام

drill (through) *vt* سنبیدن

drill *n* برمه

drill *v* برمه کردن

drilling *n* برمه کاری

drink (alcoholic) *n* مشروب

drink (beverage) *n* نوشیدنی

→ drinks اشربه

drink *v* نوشیدن • خوردن •
درکشیدن • آشامیدن

drink water *vt* آب خوردن

drinkable *adj* مشروب • آشامیدنی

drinking (as a dog) *n* لق لق

drinking companion *n* همپیاله • هم
پیاله

drinking water *n* آب خوردن

drive (urge on) *vt* راندن

→ drive away the devil شیطان را
لاحول کردن

drive (vehicle) *vi* موتروانی کردن

→ (lit) دریوری کردن

drive shaft *n* میل یونیورسل

drivel *n* هذیان

driver (of vehicle) *n* موترران •
راننده

→ (colloq) موتروان

→ (lit) دریور

drizzle (water) *n* پرخ

drop (fall) *vi* افتیدن • غلتیدن

drop (of liquid) *n* چک • اشک • آب •
چشم • آب دیده • سرشک • قطره

drop by (sb's house) *v* افتاد خانه
<کسی> شدن

droplet (dew, water) *n* پرخ

dropper (pipette) *n* قطره چکان

drought *n* خشک سالی • قحط

drown *vi* غرق شدن

drowned *see* drowning

drowning (& fig) *adj* غریق • غرق
• غرقه • مغروق

drowsy *adj* خواب آلود

drum (mus instr) *n* دهل • دول

→ large drum (arch) کوس

drummer (lit) *n* دهل زن • دهل نواز

drumstick (mus instr) *n* چوب دهل

drunk *adj* مست • نشه
→ (& amorous) مستانه
→ (& carefree) سر شار
→ (colloq) دهلچی
→ habitually drunk دایم الخمر
→ slightly drunk سرگرم • خمار
آلود • پر خمار • مخمور
→ very drunk (& pers) خرمست
drunkenness *n* نشه • مست • مستی
• سکر • خرمستی • خمار
dry *adj* خشک • قاق
→ dry & wet (good & bad) خشک
و تر
dry cleaning *n* خشکه شوی
dry farming *n* للمه • کشت للمی
Du Ab (dist) *n* دو آب
Du Abi (ctr) *n* دو آبی
Du Layna (dist) *n* دو لینه
dual (gram) *adj* تثنیه
Dubai (city) *n* دبی • دوبی
dubious (controversial) *adj* شک
آور • حساس
dubious (suspicious) *adj* مظنون
Dublin *n* دبلین
duck *n* مرغابی
duct *n* مجرا
→ (anat) کانال
due <to sth> *prep* نسبت • بنابر
<چیزی>
duel *n* جنگ تن به تن
dulcimer (mus instr) *n* سنتور
dull (faint) *adj* خیره
dull (slow-witted) *adj* خرفهم
dumbbell *n* وزن بر داری
dumplings (Afgh dish) *n* آشک
dung (& fig) *n* کود • گه
→ (colloq) گو
→ cow dung (for fuel) سرگین
→ sheep dung پشک • پشقل
dungeon *n* سیاه چاه • سیاه چال
duodenum *n* اثناعشر
dupiyaza (Afgh dish) *n* دو پیازه
duplicate *n* نسخه • نقل
Dur Baba (dist) *n* دربابا
durability *n* دوام • داشت • مقاومت
durable *adj* دوام دار • مقاوم
Durand Line *n* خط دیورن • خط
دیورند
during *adv* در وقت • حینی که
390

during *prep* در خلال • ظرف • در
ظرف
Durrani (P tribal confederacy) *n*
درانی • ابدالی
Dushanbe *n* دوشنبه
dusk (& adv) *n, adv* شام
dust *n* خاکه • خاک • گرده • گرد
dust (remove dust) *v* گرد گیری
کردن
dust cloud *n* غبار • گرد
dust jacket (book's) *n* وقایه
dust storm *n* گردباد • خاکباد
duster (brush, cloth) *n* گرد گیر
dusty (neg) *adj* گرد آلود
dutar (mus instr) *n* دو تار
Dutch (& lang, pers) *adj, n* هالیندی
duties (obligations) *n pl* واجبات •
وجایب
duties (servant's) *n* نوکری •
خدمت
dutiful *adj* گپ شنو
duty (excise) *n* محصول
duty (obligation) *n* وظیفه
→ on duty سر وظیفه
→ official on duty موظف • وظیفه
دار
duty (rel/moral) *n* فرض • فریضه
DVD *n* دی وی دی • سی دی
dwell *see* reside
dwelling *see* residence
dye *n* رنگ
→ henna dye حنا
dye with henna *v* حنا بستن
dyed *adj* رنگ شده
dynamic *n* محرک
dynasty *n* خانواده • خانه واده •
فامیل
dysentery *n* اسهال خونی •
دیزانتری • پیچ
Dzadran (ctr, alt Jadran) *n* خدران
Dzadzi (dist, alt Jaji) *n* خاخی

E

each (every) *adj* هر • همه
→ each of us همۀ ما
→ with one weapon each با یک
یک قبضۀ سلاح

each other *pron* • یک دیگر • یک
دگر
ear *n* گوش
→ area behind the ear • بناگوش •
بن گوش
ear canal *n* سوراخ گوش
eardrum *n* پرده گوش
earlier *adv* وقتر • پیشتر
earlobe *n* دلک گوش • بن گوش •
بناگوش • نرمی گوش • نرمه گوش
early *adj* پیش رس • وقت
early *adv* وقت • زود • به زودی
earn *v* کمایی کردن
earnest (& adv) *adj, adv* جدی
earnings *n* درآمد • کمایی
earring *n* گوشوار • گوشواره • زیر
گوش • آویزه
→ slave's earring (hist) حلقه گوش
• غلام حلقه به گوش
earth (soil) *n* خاک • خاکه • گرده •
ثری
→ Earth of Bokhara (mounds
outside Kabul) خاک بخارا
Earth, the *n* دنیا • زمین • جهان
→ Earth (planet) ارض • کره •
ارض
earthen *adj* گلی
earthquake *n* زلزله • زمین لرزه •
زمین جنب
earwax *n* چرک گوش
ease *n see* at ease; comfort (ease)
east *adj* شرق • خاور
→ east wind (pleasant) صبا
→ place of sunrise in east مشرق
East, the *n* شرق • خاور
→ from the east شرقا
eastern *adj* مشرقی
Eastern Shura (hist) *n* شورای
مشرقی
easy *adj* آسان • سهل
eat *v* خوردن • نان خوردن • غذا
خوردن
eavesdrop *v* استراق سمع کردن
eavesdropping *n* استراق سمع
ebony *n* آبنوس
eccentric (math) *adj* مختلف المرکز
echo *n* انعکاس صدا • پژواک •
انعکاس صوت

eclipse *n* گرفتگی
→ lunar eclipse خسوف • مهتاب
گرفتگی
ECO *see* Economic Cooperation
Organization
economic *adj* اقتصادی
Economic Cooperation
Organization *n* اکو • ایکو
economics *n* علم اقتصاد • علم
ثروت
economist *n* اقتصاد دان • اقتصاد
شناس • عالم اقتصاد
economy (frugality) *n* اقتصاد
economy, the *n* • اقتصاد •
اقتصادیات
→ market economy اقتصاد
بازاری
ecstasy *n* جذبه
→ Sufic ecstasy وجد
Ecuador *n* ایکوادور
edema (dropsy) *n* استسقا
edema (of tree) *n* بوغمه
Eden (bibl) *n* عدن
edge *n* دم
→ outer edge دامن
edible (& thing) *adj, n* خوراکه
edict *n* فرمان • حکم
edifice *n* عمارت • تعمیر • آبد
editing *n* تحریر
editor (newspaper) *n* روزنامه
نویس
→ under <sb's> editorship به
اهتمام <کسی>
editorial (article) *n* سر مقاله
editorial board *n* هیئت تحریر
editor-in-chief *n* مدیر روزنامه
educate *vt* تعلیم دادن
educated *adj* تعلیم یافته
→ well-educated تحصیل کرده •
تحصیل یافته
education *n* تعلیم • آموزش
educational *adj* تعلیمی • تحصیلی
→ (cultural) فرهنگی
eel *n* مارماهی
effect (influence) *n* تاثیر • فعالیت
→ in effect نافذ
effect (result) *n* اثر • ثمر • ثمره

391

effective *adj* • سریع • ثمر بخش
الاثر
→ (impressive) موثر • مؤثر
effectiveness *n* خاصیت
effeminate *adj* زنچه
efficacious *adj* نتیجه بخش
effigy *n* تصویر
effort & attempt *phrs* جد و جهد
effort *n* سعی • اهتمام • کوشش •
جهد • تلاش • مجاهدت
→ efforts مساعی
egg *n* تخم
→ (colloq) سفال
→ (ovum) بیضه
→ scrambled eggs خاگینه
→ sunny side up (eggs) نیم رویه
eggplant *n* بادنجان • بادنجان
سوسنی
→ fried eggplant بورانی بادنجان
→ stuffed eggplant دولمه
eglantine (white flower) *n* نسترن
ego *n* خودی
egotism *n* خودی
egotistical (& pers) *adj, n* خود بین
• خود پرست • خود خواه
Egypt *n* مصر
Egyptian (& pers) *adj, n* مصری
Ehsan (m name) *n* احسان
Eid (Musl rel feast) *n* عید
eight *adj, n* هشت
eighteen *adj, n* هژده
eighteenth *adj* هژدهم
→ (lit, used before n) هژدهمین
eighth *adj* هشتم
→ (lit, used before n) هشتمین
eightieth *adj* هشتادم
→ (lit, used before n) هشتادمین
eighty *adj, n* هشتاد
either ... or *conj* خواه ... خواه
ejaculation *n* انزال
EKG *see* electrocardiogram
elaborate *adj* مبسوط
elaboration *n* تدقیق
elapse (time) *vi* گذشتن
elastic *adj* ارتجاعی
elbow *n* آرنج
elder (pers) *n* قریه دار • کلان •
کلانتر • کلان سال • ملک • بزرگ
→ (graybeard) ریش سفید
392

elder *adj* ارشد
elect (have election) *v* انتخاب
کردن • انتخابات کردن
-elect *adj* منتخب
→ governor-elect والی منتخب
elected *adj* منتخب • انتخابی
election *n* انتخابات • انتخاب
electrical current *n* رو برقی
electrician *n* برقی
electricity *n* برق
electrocardiogram *n* گراف قلب
electrode *n* پلیت بتری
electromagnet *n* مقناطیس برقی
electromagnetism *n* مقناطیسیت
برقی
electronics *n* الکترونیکس
electroshock *n* تکان برقی • شوک
برقی
elegant قشنگ
element (& chem) *n* عنصر • اس •
اساس
→ elements (rudiments) الفبا
elementary *adj* ابتدایی
→ elementary school مکتب
ابتدایی
elephant *n* فیل
→ elephant howdah هوده
elevation *n* ارتفاع • بلندی
eleven *adj, n* یازده
eleventh *adj* یازدهم
→ (lit, used before n) یازدهمین
eliminate (get rid of) *vt* رفع کردن
elimination (getting rid of) *n* رفع
eloquence *n* گشاده زبانی
eloquent *adj* • زبان آور • زبان دار
گشاده زبان
else *adj, adv* دیگر • دگر
elucidate *vt* تصریح کردن
elucidation *n* تصریح • تشریح •
توضیح
embalm *see* mummify
embargo <against a country> *n*
تحریم <علیه یک مملکت>
embark on (plane) *vi* سوار شدن
embarrass <sb> *v* خجالت دادن
<به کسی>
→ be embarrassed خجالت کشیدن
embarrassing *adj* خجالت آور
embarrassment *n* خجالت • خجلت

embassy n سفارت • سفارت خانه
→ (chancery) محل پذیرایی مقام
embezzle v حیف و میل کردن
embezzlement n دست برد • اختلاس
embittered adj تلخ کام
embolden v جرئت دادن
embossed work n برجسته کاری
embrace n آغوش • بغل • کنار • کران
embrace vt در آغوش کشیدن • در آغوش گرفتن
embrasure n تیر کش
embroidery (w/beads) n مهره دوزی
→ (kind of Afgh embroidery) خامک دوزی
embroil v درگرفتن • پیچش کردن
embroiled adj درگیر
embryo n نطفه • جنین
embryonic adj جنینی
emerald n زمرد
emerald-colored adj زمردین
emerge v گل کردن
→ (fig, become clear) فوراً ظاهر شدن
emerge; become visible vi پدید آمدن • پدیدار شدن
emergency adj اضطراری
emergency n اضطرار
→ emergency room اتاق عاجل
emetic adj قی آور • دوای قی آور
emigrant n مهاجر
emigrate v مهاجرت کردن • هجرت کردن
emigration n مهاجرت • هجرت
émigré n مهاجر
emir n امیر
emirate n امیری • امارت
emotion n احساس
empathetic adj غمخور • غم خور
emperor n امپراتور • شاهنشاه
→ (Caesar) قیصر
→ (colloq) امپراطور
emphasis n تاکید • شد و مد
emphasize v تاکید کردن
emphatically adv اکیداً • با شد و مد
empire n امپراتوری • شاهنشاهی
→ (colloq) امپراطوری

employ vt استخدام کردن • کار دادن
employed adj مشغول • مصروف
employee n کارمند • دست اندر کار
→ (personnel) کارکنان
employer n کارفرما
employment n استخدام
empower vt گماشتن
empty (deserted) adj خلوت
empty (evacuate) vt خالی کردن • تهی کردن
empty (vacant) adj خالی • تهی
empty (vacate) vt تخلیه کردن • تهی کردن
empty-handed adj دست خالی
emulate v پهلو زدن
enable vt توانا ساختن
enactor n واضع
enamel n لعاب
enameled adj لعابی
enamored <of sb> adj عاشق <کسی>
enchanting adj ساحر • سحر آمیز • افسونگر • جادوگر
encircle <sth/sb> vt دور <چیزی/کسی را> گرفتن
encircled adj محاط
enclosure n محوطه
encompass n احتوا کردن
encompassing n احتوا
encounter <w/sb> vi بر خوردن <با کسی>
encounter n ملاقات • تصادف • دو چار
encourage <sb to do sth> vt تشویق کردن <کسی را به چیزی>
encouragement n تشویق • تشجیع
→ (incentive) مشوق
encroachment n تجاوز
encyclopaedia n دایرت المعارف
end n ختم • خاتمه • آخر • فرجام • نهایت • کران • کرانه • سرانجام
→ (bottom) پایان
→ (result) عاقبت
→ (tip) غایت
→ at the end of در ذیل
→ end of page ذیل
→ in the end سرانجام

393

خاتمه یافتن • پایان دادن • end vi
خلاص شدن • به سر رسیدن •
متوقف شدن
خاتمه دادن • متوقف شدن end vt
به خطر انداختن endanger vt
در معرض خطر endangered adj
→ endangered species نوع حیوان
در معرض نابودی
سعی • اهتمام • endeavor n
مجاهدت • جهد
کوشیدن • در سعی و endeavor v
تلاش به سر بردن
→ (colloq) کوشش کردن
خاتمه ending (conclusion) n
پسوند ending (gram) n
→ ending (1st pers pl poss); (1st
pers sg/pl pres perf) [یم- aft cons]
ایم
→ ending (1st pers sg poss); (1st
pers sg pres & past) [م- aft cons]
ام
→ ending (2nd pers sg poss); (2nd
pers sg obj) [ـت aft cons] ات
→ ending (3rd pers pl pres, past &
pres perf) اند
→ ending (3rd pers sg possessive);
(3rd pers sg direct object) [ـش aft
cons]; (ending, forms n from v root)
[ـش] اش
ختم ending (termination) n
بی کران endless adj
ظهر endorsement (of check) n
نویسی
وقف endowment (Musl rel) n
تحمل • endurance (forbearance) n
برداشت • بردباری • تاب • توان •
طاقت • صبر
دیرپای enduring adj
→ (colloq) مدعی
دشمن • خصم • مخاصم • enemy n
عدو
قوه energy (mil) n
تولید برق energy production n
ضعیف ساختن • enfeeble vt
ضعیف کردن
پیچاندن enfold vt
مجرا کردن enforce vt
تنفیذ • انفاذ enforcement n
→ law enforcement تنفیذ قانون

پای وازی • engagement party n
شیرینی خوری
→ become engaged پای بند شدن
انجن • موتور • ماشین engine n
انجنیر engineer n
انجنیری engineering n
انگلستان • انگلیسستان England n
انگلیسی English (& lang) adj, n
انگلیس English pers n
→ (colloq) انگریز
حک کردن engrave v
حکاک engraver n
ارتقا دادن enhance vt
ارتقا • ارتقاء enhancement n
لغز enigma n
→ speak enigmatically لغز گفتن
انجیل Enjil (dist) n
منع کردن enjoin v
مستفید شدن <از enjoy <sth> vi
چیزی>
مستفید <از enjoying <sth> adj
چیزی>
بر خوردار enjoying o.s. adj
روشن enlightened (& pers) adj, n
فکر • روشن دل
منور enlightened adj
چهره کردن enlist (soldier) v
دشمنی • خصومت • enmity n
مخالفت • عداوت
کافی • وافی • بس enough adj
پرسان کردن • سوال enquire v
کردن • پرسیدن
→ (officially) استعلام کردن
پرسنده enquirer n
→ (official) استعلام
خون به جوش enrage (fig) vt
آوردن
→ become enraged (fig) خون به
جوش آمدن
خشمناک • غضبناک • enraged adj
ارغند
غنا ساختن enrich vt
غنا سازی enrichment n
ثبت نام کردن • نام نویسی enroll v
کردن
شامل • مشمول enrollee n

نام نویسی • ثبت نام enrollment *n*
→ (in school) شمول
→ enrollment directorate (mil)
مدیریت مکلفیت
به زنجیر کشیدن enshackle *vt*
کفن کردن enshroud *v*
به دام افتادن ensnare *vt*
پیچش کردن • درگرفتن entangle *v*
پیچش • درگیر entanglement *n*
وارد شدن • آمدن • در enter *vi*
آمدن • درون شدن
درون کردن enter *vt*
وارد entering *adj*
دست و پایی • enterprising *adj*
متشبث
ساعت تیری entertainment form *n*
حمیت enthusiasm *n*
با حمیت enthusiastic *adj*
مند
فریبنده • سحار enticing *adj*
کامل • تمام • سراسر entire *adj*
سرتاسر • مجهز • مکمل
کاملا • به کلی • بالکل entirely *adv*
• سرتاسر
جمیع • همه entirety *n*
حشره شناس entomologist *n*
دانشمند حشره شناس
حشره شناسی • علم entomology *n*
حشرات • علم الحشرات
دخول • در آمد • ورود entrance *n*
• ادخال
→ for entrance or entry ورودی
لابه کردن • زاری کردن entreat *v*
• تضرع کردن • الحاح کردن
لابه • زاری • تضرع • entreaty *n*
الحاح
سنگر بندی entrenchment *n*
سپردن entrust *vt*
حواله entrusting *n*
داخل شدن entry (entrance) *prep*
ماده • قلم • قید entry (line item) *n*
کفش کن entryway *n*
تلفظ enunciation *n*
پاکت • لفافه envelope *n*
حاسد • envious (& pers) *adj, n*
حسود • بخیل
محیط environment (natural) *n*
زیست • ماحول
محیطی environmental *adj*

پیرامون environs (adjacent area) *n*
• پیرامن • حومه
غبطه • حسودی • حسادت envy *n*
بخل • بخیلی
غبطه خوردن envy *v*
حسد envy, jealousy *n*
→ be envious حسد بردن • حسد
خوردن
انزایم enzyme *n*
پلیت epaulette (mil) *n*
زود گذر ephemeral *adj*
هفتالی Ephthalite (hist) *n*
رزمی epic *adj*
کار نامه • حماسه epic *n*
حماسه سرایی → epic singing
حماسه سرای → singer of epics
وبا epidemic disease *n*
بشره epidermis (anat) *n*
بیماری مرگی epilepsy *n*
صرع • مرگی → epileptic seizure
خاتمه epilogue (book's) *n*
اسقف episcopate *n*
نامه • مکتوب epistle *n*
مترسل epistolarian (lit) *n*
ترسل epistolary art *n*
epoch *see* era
همتا • کفو • همپایه equal (peer) *n*
• همشان • همطراز
ثانی → (rival)
مساوی • برابر equal *adj*
مساوات • تساوی • equality *n*
برابری • استوا
معادله equation (math) *n*
خط استوا equator *n*
سوار کار equestrian *n*
متساوی الاضلاع equilateral *adj*
توازن • موازنه • equilibrium *n*
تعادل
متعادل → in equilibrium
تحویل • اعتدال equinox (vernal) *n*
بهاری
آماده ساختن • حاضر equip *vt*
کردن
مهمات • تجهیزات • equipment *n*
وسایل • ساز و برگ • ساز و سامان
آماده • حاضر • مهیا equipped *adj*
تیار → (colloq)
معادل • هم چند equivalent *adj*
مثل equivalent *n*

395

era *n* عصر • زمان • دوره • دور • تاریخ • روزگار

eradicate *vt* از ریشه کشیدن • قلع و قمع کردن

eradication *n* محو • قلع و قمع کردن

erase (extinguish) *vt* گل کردن

erase (rub, scrape) *vt* تراشیدن • حک کردن

→ erasing & correcting حک و اصلاح

eraser (blackboard) *n* تخته پاک

eraser (for pencil) *n* پنسل پاک

erection (med) *n* نعوظ

erode *v* خوردن

errata list (in book) *n* غلط نامه

error *n* اشتباه • غلطی • تخطی

→ in error غلط

erudite *see* learned

erupt *vi* بخار برآمدن

eruption (volcano) *n* آتش فشانی

erysipelas (med) *n* سرخ باد

escalator *n* زینه دورانی

escape <from sth> *n* فرار • نجات ‹از چیزی› • رستگاری

escape *adj* گریز پای

escape *vi* فرار کردن • پشت دادن • گریختن

→ (fig) سپر انداختن • پریدن

escapee *n* فراری

escort *n* معیت

escort *v* بردن

escheat (revert to waqf if no heirs) *vi* وقف ماندن

→ (colloq) وخم ماندن

→ May the waqf escheat it from you! (insult) از سرت وخم بماند

escorted <by sb> *adj* به معیت ‹کسی›

escrow *n* تامینات

Esfahan (city) *n* اصفهان

Eshkamesh (dist) *n* اشکمش

Eshkashem (dist) *n* اشکاشم

Eshkashemi (pers, lang) *n* اشکاشمی

Eshtarlay (dist) *n* اشترلی

esophagus (anat) *n* مری

especially *adv* مخصوصاً • خصوصاً • بالخصوص • بالاخص • علی الخصوص

396

espionage *n* مخبری • جاسوسی

esprit de corps *n* روحیه هماهنگی

essay *n* مقاله

essayist *n* مقاله نویس

essence *n* نفس • روح • جان • ماهیت • زبته • کنه • خاصه

→ essence of the matter نفس الامر

essentially *adv* اساساً

establish *v* تشکیل کردن • به میان آوردن • بر پای کردن • وضع کردن • تهداب گذاری کردن

established (emplaced) *adj* مستقر • تاسیس شده

established (functional) *adj* برقرار

established (stable) *adj* ثابت

establisher *n* موسس

establishing (founding) *n* تهداب گذاری

establishing (settling) *n* استقرار

establishment (formation) *n* تشکیل

establishment (of rules) *n* وضع

establishment (organization) *n* موسسه • تاسیس

Estalef (dist, village) *n* استالف

estate (property) *n* ملک

esteem *n* احترام • حرمت

esteemed *adj* روی دار

estimate *n* تخمین • برآورد

estimate *v* تخمین زدن • تخمین کردن

et cetera *phrs* و غیره • غیره • وغیره • و قسم علی هذا

eternal (& adv) *adj, adv* جاویدانه

eternal (& n) *adj, n* • جاوید • جاویدان • جاودان

→ (attribute of God) صمد

→ the Eternal (God) قدیم

eternal *adj* • جاویدان • سرمدی • جاودان • جاوید • جاویدانه • سرمد • ازلی

eternity *n* ابد • ازل • سرمد

ethics (field) *n* علم اخلاق

ethics (morals) *n pl* • اخلاق • اخلاقیات

Ethiopia *n* اتوپیا • اتوپیه • حبشه

Ethiopian (& pers) *adj, n* اتوپیایی

ethnic *adj* قومی

ethnicity *n* قوم

ethnography n • مردم شناسی • اتنوگرافی

ethnologist n • نژاد شناس • اتنولوژست

ethnology n • نژاد شناسی • اتنولولوژی

etiquette n • مراسم

etymologist n • ریشه شناس

etymology n • ریشه شناسی • علم اشتقاق

eulogist n • مداح • ستایشگر • ثناخوان • سادو

eunuch (hist) n • خواجه

Euphrates (river) n • فرات

euro (currency) n • یورو

Europe n • اروپا • یوروپا

European (& pers) adj, n • اروپایی • یوروپایی • غربی

European Commission n • کمیسیون اروپا

European Union n • اتحاد اروپایی • اتحادیه اروپا

evacuate vt • خالی کردن

evacuation n • خارج شدن • اضطراری

evade <sth> v <از چیزی> • روی گرداندن

evaluate vt • ارزیابی کردن

evaluation n • ارزیابی

Eve (bibl) n • حوا

even (flat) adj • مسطح • مستوی

even (including) adv • حتی • حتى • اگر

even (number) adj • جفت

even if see even though

even number n • جفت • زوج

even though conj • اگرچه • گرچه • هر چند

evening (dusk) n • شام

→ in the evening • شام

evening (night) n • شب • لیل

→ in the evening (at night) • شب

event n • رویداد • واقعه • آمده • پیش آمد • ماجرا

ever (w/pres perf) adv • گاهی

everlasting adj • سرمدی

every (all) adj • تمام

every (each) adj • هر • همه

every day adv • هر روز • روزمره

every time adv • همواره • همیشه

everybody see everyone

everyday adj • روزمره • روزانه

everyday see & ordinary (common)

everyone pron • هر کس • هر که • همه مردم

→ (fig) the high & low • خاص و عام

everywhere adv • هر جای

→ (fig) in every nook & cranny • در کنج و کنار

evidence n • گواهی • برهان

→ taking evidence • استشهاد

evident adj • ظاهر • واضح • صاف • مبرهن

→ evident matters • واضحات

evidently adv • ظاهراً

evil (doing evil) n • شرارت

evil (misfortune) n • بلا

→ be taken unawares by evil • به بلا دوچار شدن

→ consign to evil • به بلا دادن

→ fall into evil • به بلا افتادن

→ irremediable evil • بلا بی درمان

→ stricken by evil • بلا دیده • بلا زده

evil (wicked) adj • بد • شوم

→ (deed) • شرارت آمیز

→ (pers) • شرارت پیشه

→ be influenced by the evil eye • نظر شدن • چشم شدن

evil (wickedness) n • شر

ewe n • میش

exactly adv • عیناً • بعینه • بی کم و زیاد • بی کم و کاست

exaggerate v • مبالغه کردن

exaggerated adj • مبالغه آمیز

exaggeration n • مبالغه • اغراق

exalted adj • شریف • نجیب • والا • علی • علیه • عالی

→ (said of God) • تعالی • متعال

examination (med) n • معاینه • معاینات

examination (test) n • امتحان • آزمایش • تجزیه

examine (& med) v • معاینه کردن

examine (scrutinize) vt • تصفح کردن

examiner n • ممتحن

مثال • سرمشق • نمونه example n
مقتدا به (esp rel, moral) →
نظایر (examples) the like →
مثلاً • فی المثل • for example →
از قبیل
کاوش کردن excavate v
کاوش excavation n
Excellency (form of address) n
جلالتماب
بهین • نمره اول excellent adj
غیر • به غیر <for sth> prep except
• جز • به جز • الا • مگر • به
استثنای <چیزی>
جز • به جز <از (colloq) →
چیزی>
مگر آن که • جز except that conj
آن که • الا آن که
مستثنی • مستثنا excepted adj
استثنا exception n
مگر (colloq) →
زیادتی excess adj
زیادت excess n
بسیاری • برخی excessive adj
زیاده • افراط
بسیار • زیاده • از excessively adv
حد • بیحد • بی اندازه
تبادل exchange (interchange) n
تبادله (colloq) →
نرخ تبادل • نرخ exchange rate →
تبادله
اسعار • foreign exchange →
اسعار خارجی
به • به عوض • in exchange for →
مقابل
تبادل exchange (interchange) vt
کردن
تبادله کردن (colloq) →
تحویل exchange (replacement) n
تبدیل • عوض • بدل
آلش کردن exchange vt
انگیزش excitation n
به هیجان آوردن excite (agitate) vt
excite (provoke, stimulate) vt
انگیختن
excited (esp sexually) (& pers) adj,
مست n
هیجان excitement (agitation) n
دل انگیزی excitement n
هیجان آمیز exciting (agitating) adj
398

دل انگیز exciting adj
بر زبان راندن exclaim v
ندا exclamation n
علامت ندا • exclamation point n
ندائیه
مستثنی • مستثنا excluded adj
متناقض exclusive (mutually) adj
نقیض
excommunicate (fellow Musl as an
تکفیر کردن apostate) v
excommunication (of fellow Musl
تکفیر as an apostate) n
گه • فضله • کود excrement n
هوا خوری excursion n
هوا خوری go on an excursion →
رفتن
عذر • معذرت • excuse (pardon) n
پوزش
بخشیدن excuse (pardon) vt
بهانه excuse (pretext) n
پلمه (colloq) →
سر تکانی کردن make excuses →
• حجت کردن
بهانه one who makes excuses →
جوی
انجام دادن execute (finish) vt
انجامیدن (lit) →
اعدام execute (put to death) vt
کردن
اعدام execution (putting to death) n
تیر باران • (by firing squad) →
چنداواری
قصاص (of murderer) →
عامل executive adj
وصی executor (of will) n
معافیت exemption <from sth> n
<از چیزی>
قیمت عوضی exemption fee →
ورزش exercise (physically) v
کردن • سپورت کردن
تمرین exercise (practice) n
تطبیقات • حرکت
ورزش • سپورت (physical) →
اعمال exertion n
زفیر exhalation n
خسته exhausted adj
هلاک • تکه تکه (fig) →
بی دست و پای be exhausted →
بودن • از دست و پای ماندن

exhibit (display) v به • دادن نمایش
نمایش گذاشتن • نشان دادن
→ (lit) نمودن
exhibition n نمایش
exhibition space n نمایشگاه
exhibitor n وکیل • نماینده
exigency n مقتضا
exile n تبعید • غربت • غریبی
فقر
exist vi وجود داشتن • وجود بودن
existence (availability) n موجودیت
existence (being) n وجود • بدن
existence (fate) n بوش
existence (philosophical) n کون
existing (ongoing) adj پایا
existing adj موجود
exit adj خروجی
exit n خروج
exodus n هجرت • مهاجرت
exordium n فاتحه
expand vi توسعه یافتن
expand vt وسعت • توسعه دادن
دادن • گستردن • گستراندن
→ (colloq) بزرگ ساختن
expandable (possible) adj توسعه
پذیر
expandable (worthy) adj قابل
توسعه
expansion n توسعه • توسیع
گسترش • تعمیم • انبساط
expansionary adj توسعه یابنده
expansionism n توسعه جویی
توسعه طلبی
expansionist (& pers) adj, n توسعه
جوی • توسعه طلب
expansionist (territorially) adj
توسعه جویانه • توسعه طلبانه
expect <sb> vi منتظر <کسی>
بودن
expectation n توقع
expecting (esp pers) adj, n منتظر
expedition (mil) n لشکر کشی
→ be expelled اخراج شدن
→ be expelled for unspecified
reasons خارج شدن
expel (oust) vt اخراج کردن •
خارج کردن

expenditure n خرج • مصرف
→ (colloq) چرخ
→ expenditures اخراجات
expense see expenditure
expensive adj قیمت • قیمت بها •
گران • گران بها
→ (follows n) قیمتی
experience n تجربه
→ work experience سابقه داری
experience v خوردن
experienced (& pers) adj, n تجربه
دیده • با تجربه • تجربه کار •
مجرب • آزمایش کرده • آزمایش
شده • آزموده
→ (longtime) سابقه دار
→ (skillful) ورزیده • مجرب
experiential adj تجربی
experiment n آزمایش • تجزیه
experimental adj آزمایشی • تجربی
• تجربوی
expert n دانشمند • متخصص
expertise n دانش • تخصص
explain (at length) vt مطرح کردن
explain (clarify) vt توضیح کردن •
توضیح دادن • تفسیر کردن
explain (describe) vt شرح دادن •
شرح کردن
→ explain as to a dummy خرفهم
کردن
explaining n تفهیم • افهام
→ phrs افهام و تفهیم
explanation n تعلیل
→ (clarification) توضیح • ایضاح
→ (description) شرح • تشریح
→ (interpretation) گزارش
explanatory adj توضیحی •
توضیحاتی • تفسیری
→ explanatory remarks تعلیقات
explode vi کفیدن • پراندن
exploit see use
explorer n کاشف • مکتشف
explosion n انفجار
explosive adj منفجره
export n صادر • صدور
→ for export (goods) صادراتی
export v صادر کردن
exporter n صادر کننده

399

expose *see &* reveal

expose (criminal in public) *v* تشهیر کردن

expository *adj* تفسیری

→ expository writings نگارش تفسیری

exposure (of criminal in public) *n* تشهیر

express *vt* اظهار کردن • اظهار داشتن • افاده کردن • ابراز کردن

expression *n* افاده • عبارت • ادا • بیان

expulsion *n* اخراج

extant *see* existing

extension, by *adv* توسعاً

extensive *adj* دامنه دار

extent *n* حسب • اندازه • پهنه • حیز

→ to this extent اینهمه • این همه

exterior *n* خارج

exterminate *vi* از میان بردن • از بین بردن • قلع و قمع کردن • از ریشه کشیدن

external *adj* خارجی

extinguish *v* گل کردن

extort (money) *v* باجسبیل گرفتن

extortion *n* باجسبیل

extra *adj* فالتو

extract *n* جوشانده • عصاره

extract *vt* بیرون کردن • کندن

extraordinary *adj* خارق عادت • خارق العاده • خرق عادت • فوق العاده

extraordinary *pers n* نادره

extravagance *n* افراط کاری

extravagant *adj* افراط

extravagant *pers n* افراط کار

extremely *adv* بسیار • نهایت • به غایت

extremism *n* افراطیت

extremist *n* افراطی • تندرو

exudation *n* ترشح • تراوش

exude *v* ترشح کردن • تراوش کردن • تراویدن

eye *adj* عینی

eye *n* چشم

→ avert one's eyes چشم انداختن

→ circles under the eyes حلقه

→ close one's eyes چشم پت کردن

→ cross-eyed چغر • احول • کنج

→ eye of a needle سوراخ سوزن

→ eye <sb> angrily چشم کشیدن <سر کسی>

→ take shuteye چشم پت شدن

→ eyes closed (blindly) چشم پت

eyeball *n* تخم چشم

eyebrow *n* قاش ابرو • ابرو

→ connected eyebrows پیوسته ابرو

→ eyebrow pencil قلم ابرو

→ unconnected eyebrows گشاده ابرو

eyeglasses *n* عینک

eyelash *n* پلک • مژه

eyesight *n* نور چشم

eyewitness *n* شاهد عینی

Ezat Kheyl (ctr) *n* عزت خیل

F

fabric *n* تکه • قماش

→ (brocade) پارچه

facade (archit) *n* نما • نمای عمارت

face *n* روی • چهره • صورت • سیما

→ (lit) رخسار

→ cause to lose face بی آب کردن

→ face powder سفیده

→ face to face بالمواجهه

→ lose face بی آب شدن

facetious (lit) *adj* هزل آمیز

facilitation *n* تسهیل • سهولت • آسانی

facing (opposite) (adj, prep) مقابل • در مقابل • پیش روی • در مقابل

fact *n* حقیقت • واقعیت

→ in fact • در حقیقت • در واقع • واقعاً • فی الواقع

faction (pol) *n* حزب • گروپ

factor (agent) *n* عامل

factor (math, biology) *n* فکتور

factory *n* فابریکه • کارخانه

→ factory manager رئیس فابریکه

factual *adj* حقیقی • واقعی • واقع

400

faculty (of university) n • فاکولته
شعبه
fade v پژمردن
Fahima (f name) n فهیمه
Fahrenheit adj فارنهایت
fail vi ناکام شدن
failed adj ناکام
failure n ناکامی
faint (black out) vi از حال رفتن
faint (dull) adj خیره
fair (fine) adj لطیف
fair (just) (& adv) adj, adv عادلانه
fair (just) (& pers) adj, n عادل
fair (suitable) adj مناسب
fair (sunny) adj آفتابی
→ (colloq) آفتوی
fair (exhibition) n نمایشگاه
fairness (impartiality) n انصاف
fairness (justice) n عدالت
fairy n پری
→ fairy tale قصه جن و پری
faith (creed) (& rel/pol) n عقیده •
نظریه • اعتقاد • ایمان
→ (rel) دین • کیش • آیین
faithful adj وفا دار
faithful (& adv) adj, adv صادقانه
faithful (& pers) adj, n صادق
faithfulness n وفا داری
fake adj • تقلبی • قلابی
falcon (f) n باز
fall (autumn) n • خزان • تیرماه •
پاییز • برگ ریزان
fall (downfall) n سقوط
fall (collapse) vi • افتادن • غلتیدن
fall (fall down) vi افتیدن • غلتیدن
→ fall out of favor • از چشم افتادن
از نظر افتادن
fall (stumble) vi لغزیدن
fall (tire) vi از پای افتادن
fall behind (in task) v پس افتادن
false (artificial) adj ساختگی
false (erroneous) adj غلط
false (mendacious) adj • دروغی •
دروغ
falsification n تزویر
faluda (pudding) n فالوده
fame n • معروفیت • نام آوری •
شهرت
familial adj فامیلی

familiar (friendly) adj انیس
familiarity n معرفت
family n فامیل • خانواده • خانه واده •
عایله
family tree n سلسله نسب • نسب
نامه • شجره
famine n قحط
famous adj مشهور • شهیر • نامدار
• نام آور • نامور • نامی • معروف
• سر شناس
fan (electric) n بادیکه
→ ceiling fan (punkah) پکه
fanaa (rel, Sufism) n فنا
fanatic (& pers) adj, n متعصب
fanaticism n تعصب
fanciful adj تصوری
fancy (imagination) n • تصور •
تخیل
fang (snake's) n نیش
fantasist n خیال باف • خیال پرست
faqih (expert in Musl law) n فقه
far adv دور
Farah (province, seat, dist) n فراه
Farang wa Gharu (dist) n فرنگ
و غارو
Farashghan (mountains) n فرشغان
• فراشغان
farewell n پدرود • وداع
→ see & bid farewell
Farhad (m name) n فرهاد
Farkhar (dist) n فرخار
farm n مزرعه • کشتزار
farm vi زراعت کردن • کشت کردن
farm worker n خرکار
farmer (landowner) n زمین دار
farmer (peasant) n • دهقان • زارع •
زرع • کشاورز • حارث
farmer n زراعت کار • دهقان
farming (agriculture) n زراعت •
للمه • کشت للمی
→ dry farming
farming (landowning) n زمین داری
farsang (unit of dist) n فرسنگ
Farsi (dist) n فرسی • فارسی
Farsi (lang) n فارسی
fart (colloq) n تیز
→ (vulg) گوز
→ (causing flatulence) adj بادگین
fart (colloq) vi تیز زدن
→ (vulg) vi گوز زدن

401

Faryab (province) *n* فاریاب

Farza (dist) *n* فرزه

fascinating *adj* جذاب • دل فریب

fascination *n* محو

fashion *n* مود

fast (fleet of foot) *adj* تیز دو

fast (not eating) *n* روزه • صیام

→ breaking of fast فطر • افطار

fast (quick) (& adv) *adj, adv* تیز • سریع • تند

fast (quickly) *adv* سریع • سریعاً • به سرعت • در اسرع وقت

fast (right away) *adv* پلک زدنی

fast (soon) *adv* زود

fast (swift as wind) *adj* باد پای

fasten *vt* بستن

→ (colloq) بسته کردن

fasting *see* fast

→ month of fasting ماہِ صیام

fat (grease) *n* شحم • چربی

→ (obesity) چاقی

→ (suet, tallow) پیه

→ fat pers (fig) • بستره خمبک چاتی • خم

→ get fat دنبه کردن • شکم کردن

→ short & fat pers (fig) • بغند بغندی

→ very fat pers (fig) بوغ بند

fat *adj* فربه • چاق

→ (colloq) آباد

Fatah (pol party) *n* فتح

fatal (& fig) *adj* قاتل • کشنده • مهلک

fatalism *n* جبر

fatalist *n* جبری

fate *n* سرنوشت • قسمت • بوش • نصیب • تقدیر

Fateh (m name) *n* فتح

father *n* پدر • آغا • آقا

→ (lit) والد

→ father figure پدر خوانده

→ father of ابو

→ father of medicine (Avicenna) ابو علی • ابن سنیا

→ father of the nation (King Zaher Shah) بابای ملت

→ fathers (lit) آبا

fatherhood *n* پدری

father-in-law *n* خسر

→ father-in-law's sister عمه خشو

fatherland *n* وطن • میهن

fatherly *adj* پدروار • پدرانه • پدری

Fatima (f name) *n* فاطمه

fatten up *see* fat

fatty (greasy) *adj* چرب

fatty (sebaceous) *adj* • شحمی چربی دار

fatwa (law, rel) *n* فتوا

faucet *n* شیردهن

→ (colloq) شیردان

fault *n* گناه • گنه • تقصیر

→ at fault <for a crime> مقصر <از یک جرم>

→ find fault عیب جو(ی) کردن

faultfinder (pers) *n* عیب جو • عیب جوی

fault-finding *n* طعنه • طعن

faulty *adj* عیبناک • شرمناک

favor *n* لطف

→ do a favor لطف کردن

favorable *adj* مساعد

favorite (& pers) *adj, pers* دلخواه

favoritism *n* جانب داری • طرف داری

fawn (& fig) *n* بره

Fayzabad (seat, dist) *n* فیض آباد

Fazil (m name) *n* فضل

fear *n* ترس • هراس • خوف • سهم • رعب • بیم

fear *v* ترس داشتن • هراس داشتن

→ (lit) ترسیدن • هراسیدن

fearful (& pers) *adj, n* ترسو • ترسندوک

feasible *adj* شدنی • صورت پذیر

feast & famine (lit) *phrs* قحطی و قیمتی

feast (celebrate) *vi* جشن کردن

feather *n* پر

→ pluck feathers پر کندن

February *n* فبروری

fecal matter *n* مرداری • مواد غایطه

feces (dung) (& fig) *n* گه

→ (colloq) گو

feces (stool) *n* غایط • مواد غایطه

federal *adj* فدرالی

federation *n* فدرال • فدراسیون

federative see federal

feeble (& pers) adj, n ضعيف

feed bag n توبره

feed vt غذا دادن • نان دادن • خوراندن

feel like (doing sth) <+ subj> vi دل خواستن

feeling n احساس

feline n پشک

→ (lit) گربه

fellow citizen n همشهری

fellow traveler n همسفر

→ (fig, pol) هواخواه

felon n جانی • جنایت کار

felonious(ly) see criminal(ly)

female adj ماده • ماچه • اناث

→ (colloq) ماد

→ family memb; chastity; respect for f chastity ناموس

feminine adj مونث

fen n باتلاق • مرداب

fence (esp w/rail) n کتاره

fencer n شمشیر باز

fencing n شمشیر بازی

fennel seeds (wild) n سیاه دانه

ferment (turn sour) vi ترشیدن

→ (colloq) ترش کردن

Ferris wheel n چرخ فلک

ferrous sulfate n زاج سبز

fertile (fig) adj زرخیز

fertile adj حاصل خیز • آباد

fertility n حاصل خیزی

fertilizer (chem) n کود کیمیاوی

festival n جشن • جشنواره

festivity n ساعت تیری

fetal adj جنینی

fetter n زولانه

fetus n جنین • طفل

feuilleton n پاورقی

fever n تب • اهرم

→ anti-fever medicine • تب شکن تبشکن

feverish adj تب دار • تبدار

few adj چند

fiancé, fiancée n نامزد

→ (colloq) نامزاد • نامزات

fickle adj دم دمی

fiction (& fig) n • داستان • رومان ناول

fictitious adj مستعار

fidelity n وفا

field (& fig) n • عرصه • بخش صحنه

field (& of work) n راستا

field (of study) n رشته • شق

field n کشتزار • چمن

→ (& public space) میدان

field pea n مشنگ

fiendish adj دیوسرشت • دیوسیرت • شیطانی • ابلیسی •اهریمنی

fiendishly adv ابلیسانه

fierce (& pers) adj, n ژیان

fiery (& fig) adj آتشی

→ (lit, used before n) آتشین

fiery adj ناری

fifteen adj, n پانزده

fifteenth adj پانزدهم

→ (lit, used before n) پانزدهمین

fifth adj پنجم

→ (lit, used before n) پنجمین

→ one-fifth • پنج یک • یک پنجم خمس

fiftieth adj پنجاهم

→ (lit, used before n) پنجاهمین

fifty adj, n پنجاه

fight (argue) <w/sb> v مجادله کردن <همرای کسی>

fight (argument) n مجادله

fight (battle) n جنگ • رزم • پیکار • حرب • محاربه

→ (lit) نبرد

fight (battle) vi حرب کردن

fight (campaign) n مبارزه

fight (fig) v زد و خورد کردن

fight (scuffle) n کش و گیر • زد و خورد

fight (scuffle) v کش و گیر کردن

fight (struggle) n جهاد • مجاهدت

fight (struggle) v نزاع کردن

fight (wage war) v پرداختن • تادیه کردن

fighter (champion) n مبارز

fighter (holy warrior) n مجاهد

fighting (flare-up) n درگیر

fighting (militant) adj مبارز

fighting (struggle) n • نزاع • تنازع منازعه

figurative *adj* مجازی
→ figurative expression مجاز
figuratively *adv* مجازاً
figure (body) *n* • قواره • اندام • هیکل
figure (number) *n* عدد
file (submit) *vt* • تقدیم کردن • پیش کش کردن
file *n* دوسیه
filial *adj* پسری
filing (submission) *n* تقدیم
Filipino, Filipina (pers) *n* فلیپینی
fill to the top *v* مالامال کردن
fill *v* پر کردن
→ fill in (holes) بند کردن
→ fill up *vi* سیر شدن
filling (& dental) *v* پرکاری
filling station *n* تانک تیل
film (photo, movie) *n* فلم
filmmaker *n* • فلم ساز
filter *v* پالایش کردن
filth *n* • مرداری • چرک
filthy *adj* • مردار • چرک • آلود • چرک آلوده • چتل • کثیف چرکین
→ (lit)
filtration *n* پالایش
final *adj* • آخر • آخری • غایی
→ (lit, used before n) • واپسین • آخرین
finally *adv* • به آخر • بلاخره • آخرالامر • بالآخر
→ (in conclusion) در خاتمه
finance *vt* تمویل کردن
financial *adj* مالی
→ financial difficulties دست تنگ
→ financial responsibility مسوولیتِ مالی • ابواب جمعی
financing *n* تمویل
find *vt* • پیدا کردن • دستیاب کردن
find (discover) *vt* کشف کردن
find (esp in compound v) *vt* یافتن
find out (about sth) *v* متوجه شدن
finder (procurer) *n* یابنده
finding *n* دستیابی
fine (delicate) *adj* • لطیف • قشنگ • نازک
fine (penalty) *n* • جریمه • جزای نقدی

fine arts *n pl* • فنون ظریفه • هنر های زیبا
fine-tuning *n* تصفیه
finger *n* • انگشت • پنجه • کلک
→ little finger کلک
fingernail (& pl) *n* ناخن
→ untrimmed fingernails ناخن رسیده
fingertip *n* سرانگشت
finish *vi* • پایان دادن • خاتمه یافتن • انجام پذیرفتن
→ (run out) خلاص شدن
finished *adj* خاتمه یافته
Finland *n* • فنلیند • فنلند
Finn (pers) *n* فنلیندی
Finnish *adj* فنلیندی
fiqh (Musl jurisprudence) *n* فقه
fire (artillery) *n* • آتش باری • انداخت • فیر • الو
→ ceasefire آتش بس
fire (cannon, gun) *v* توپ زدن
fire (conflagration) *n* • حریق • سوختگی
fire (flame) *n* • آتش • آذر
→ make a fire در دادن
→ set on fire آتش زدن
→ start a fire آتش افروختن
fire (ignite) *v* آتش کردن
fire (sb from a job) *vt* • خارج کردن • برطرف کردن • برکنار کردن • جواب دادن • سبک دوش کردن • موقوف کردن
fire (weapon) <on sb> *v* • فیر کردن • الو کردن ‹بالای کسی›
fire (weapon) *v* تک کردن
fire extinguisher *n* بالون ضد حریق
fire stone *n* سنگ آتش
fire temple (Zor) *n* آتش کده
fire worshiper (Zor) *n* آتش پرست
firearms *n pl* اسلحه ناریه
firebomb *n* بم آتش زا
firebox (train) *n* آتش خانه
fire-breathing *adj* آتش فشان
fired (from a job) *adj* • برطرف • برکنار • موقوف
→ be fired (from a job) خارج شدن
→ be fired (colloq) افتادن
firefighting; fire station *n* اطفاییه
fireplace (& brazier) *n* آتشدان

fireplace (in bathhouse) *n* آتش خانه

firewood *n* چوب سوخت

firewood seller *n* هیزم کش

firewood, brushwood *n* هیزم

fireworks *n* آتش بازی

firing (from a job) *n* • برطرفی • برکناری • انفصال • انفکاک

firing hammer (musket's) *n* کلنگ

firm (company) *n* شرکت • کمپنی • تجارت خانه • موسسه

firm (solid) *adj* استوار • محکم • مستحکم

firm (stable) *adj* ثابت • با ثبات

firm (sturdy) *adj* قایم • محکم • مستحکم • استوار • مضبوط

firmament *n* آسمان • سما • سپهر

firmness (consistency) *n* قوام

firmness (solidity) *n* • استحکام • استواری

firni (pudding) *n* فرنی

Firoz Nakhchir (dist) *n* فیروز نخچیر

Firozkoh (mountain range; hist, 12th-c capital of Ghorid Kingdom) *n* فیروزکوه

Firozkohi (Aimaq tribe) *n* فیروزکوهی

first (ordinal) *adj* • اول • نخست • یکم

→ at first اصلا

→ at first (colloq) در نخست • اول

→ first aid کمک عاجل

→ first lieutenant لومری څارن

→ first of all اولاً • مقدمتاً

→ first-rate نمره اول

→ for the first time بار اول • برای اولین بار

fiscal *adj* مالی

fish *n* ماهی

→ flying fish ماهی پرنده

→ saltwater fish ماهی بحری

fisherman *n* ماهی گیر

fishhook *n* قلاب • چنگک

fishing boat *n* کشتی ماهیگیری

fishing *n* ماهی گیری

fission *n* تفکیک

fist *n* مشت

fit (healthy) *adj* جور

fit (into a space) *n* جفت

fit (into a space) *vi* جور آمدن

fit (into a space) *vt* جفت کردن

fit (usable) *adj* قابل استعمال • قابل استفاده

fitna (Musl civil war) *n* فتنه

five *adj, n* پنج

fix (problem) *vt* حل کردن • چاره ساز کردن

fix (repair) *vt* ترمیم کردن • جور کردن

fixer *n* چاره ساز

fixing (remedying) *n* چاره سازی

fixing (repair) *n* ترمیم

flag (lose power) *vi* فتور رخ دادن

flag *n* بیرق • پرچم • علم • درفش

→ (lit) رایت

flagrant *adj* فاحش

flame (& fig) *n* نایره

flame *n* شعله • لهیب • لمبه

→ (w/sparks) شرار • شرر

flame *v* شعله زدن

flaming (& fig) *adj* شعله ور

flammability *n* قابلیت احتراق

flammable *adj* قابل احتراق

flank (mil) *n* جناح

flare (blaze) *n* شعله • لهیب

flare (blaze) *v* شعله زدن

flared (diagonal) *adj* اریب • وریب

flashback *n* بازتابی

flashlight *n* برق دستی • چراغ دستی

flask *n* پتک

flat (broad) *adj* پهن • هموار

flat (even) *adj* مستوی

flat (level) *adj* مسطح • تخت • هموار

flat *adj* چپات • قفاق • سلی

flat tire *n* پنچر

→ get a flat tire پنچر شدن

flatness (breadth) *n* پهنا • پهنی • همواری

flatter *v* چوری زدن

→ flatter the powerful مداح کردن

flatterer *n* مداح • سادو • ستایشگر

flattery *n* اغراق • مبالغه • چاپلوسی

→ flattery of the powerful مداحی

flatulence *see* fart

405

flavor n ذائقه • چشایی

→ (fig) نمک • ملاحت

flaw n عیب • نقص • ضرر • زیان • علت

flawed adj عیبناک • شرمناک

flawless adj بی عیب

flax (plant) n زغر

flea n کیک

fleawort (plant, seed) (colloq) n اسپغول • اسفرزه

flee (escape) vi فرار کردن

flee (run away) vi گریختن

→ (fig) سپر انداختن • پشت دادن

flee vi

fleeting (ephemeral) adj زود گذر

flexibility n نرمش • انعطاف • قابلیت انعطاف

→ (in policy, schedule) نرمش پذیری

flexible adj انعطاف پذیر • قابل انعطاف • الاستیکی

→ (in policy, schedule) نرمش پذیر

flier (handbill) n نشریه

flight (aerial) n پرواز

flight (escape) n فرار • گریز پای

flighty adj هوسناک

flimsy adj پوشالی

fling vt انداختن

flint & steel phrs چقماق • چخماق

flip a coin v شیر و خط انداختن

flirtation n غنج • عشوه • ناز • مغازله (lit)

flirtatious adj عشوه گر • عشوه ساز

flirtatiousness n عشوه گری • عشوه سازی

flock (sheep, goats) n رمه

flog (w/stick) v چوب زدن • چوب کاری کردن

→ be flogged چوب خوردن

flood n سیل

→ the Flood (bibl) طوفان نوح

→ flood water سیلاب

→ related to flooding سیلابی

floor (ground) n زمین

→ floor covering فرش • شطرنج

floor (story) n منزل • طبقه • پوشش

florist n گل فروش

406

flour n آرد

flourish (grow well) v رونق دادن

flow n جریان

flower n گل

→ (fig) نو عروس

→ flower bed کرد گل

→ flower garden چمن

→ flower shop گل فروشی

flowing adj جاری

flu n انفلونزا • گریپ

fluency (esp stylistic) n روانی • سلاست • فصاحت

fluent (& adv) adj, adv روان • سلیس

fluent (& pers) adj, n فصیح

fluently adv به راحتی

fluid n مایع , ـات

flurry (snow) n پرخ

flush vi سرخ شدن

flute n فلوت

→ (& similar mus instr) توله • نی • مزمار

flutter vi پریدن

fly (insect) n مگس

→ shoo-fly (w/yak or horse hair) چوری • پشه بران • مگس بران

fly vi پریدن

→ (w/wings) پر افشاندن • پر افشانی کردن • پر کشیدن • پر زدن

fly (cause to fly) vt پراندن

flying adj پرنده • پران • طایر

→ flying saucer بشقاب پرنده

→ flying squirrel موش پران

flyswatter n مگس کش

foal n کره

foam n کف

FOB (mil) n بیز اوپراتیفی پیشرانده شده

focus vt تمرکز دادن

focusing n تمرکز

fodder n علف

foe n دشمن • خصم • مخاصم • عدو

fog n غبار

foggy adj غبار آلود

fold (crease) n چین

fold (layer) n قات

fold vt قات کردن • چین دادن

→ fold in two دوقات کردن

folded *adj* • قات کرده • چین خورده
folder *n* دوسیه
folding *adj* قاتکی
→ folding chair چوکی قاتکی
foliage *n* سر سبزی
folklore *n* ادبیات شفاهی
follow (& fig) *vi* پیروی کردن
follow (obey orders) *vt* اطاعت
کردن
follow (pursue) *vt* دنبال کردن
→ as follows به • از قرار ذیل •
قرار ذیل • ذیلاً • به شرح ذیل
follow blindly (slavishly) *v* تقلید
کردن
follow *v* تعقیب کردن
follower *n* تبعه
Followers, the (2nd generation of
Muslims) *n pl* تابعون
following (& adv) *adj* بدنبال
following (next) *adj* بعد • پس •
مابعد • ذیل • تالی
following (pursuit) *n* تعقیب
following (succeeding) *n* تبعیت
following *adj* آینده • اتباع • آتی
foment war *v* جنگ انداختن
fond <of sth/sb> *adj* خواهان
<چیزی/کسی>
font (typeface) *n* بنت
food (meal) *n* طعام
food (portion) *n* خوراک
food *n* غذا • نان
food poisoning *n* مسمومیت غذایی
foodstuffs *n pl* مواد خوراکه •
خوراکه باب • اغذیه
fool *n* احمق • جاهل • نادان • نافهم
foolhardiness *n* سربازی
foolish *adj* احمق • جاهل • خیله
→ (crackbrained) سبک مغز
→ (crazy) دیوانه
→ (doltish) لوده
→ (ignorant) نادان • غبی
→ (maniacal) جنون آمیز
→ (naive) ساده
→ behave foolishly • حماقت کردن
خرگری کردن

foolishness *n* • احمقی • خیلگی
حماقت • سفاهت • لودگی
→ (colloq) خرگری
→ (craziness) دیوانگی
→ (mania) جنون
foot (& anat) *n* پا
→ (colloq) پای
foot (animal's, as food) *n* پاچه
foot (unit of length) *n* فت
foot soldier *n* عسکر پیاده
foothill *n* دامنه
footnote *n* • پاورقی • حاشیه
foot-operated *adj* • پایکی • پایی
footprint *n* پل پای
footwear *n* پای پوش
→ kind of traditional footwear
پیزار
for (because) *conj* • برای آنکه
برای اینکه
for (purpose) *prep* • برای • بمنظور
جهت • به غرض • از بهر
→ (colloq) بری
for (time period) *prep* • مدت • در
مدت • برای
for *prep* بر • از • نزد • پی
→ for example از قبیل
for the sake of *prep* بهر • از بهر
forbearance *n* حوصله
forbearing *adj* • با حوصله • حوصله
دار
forbidden (by Islam) *adj* حرام
→ sth forbidden (fig) حرام
forbidden *adj* ممنوع
force (compel) *vt* مجبور ساختن
force (compulsion) *n* جبر • اجبار
force (esp pl; & mil) *n* قوه
→ air force قوای هوایی
→ ground forces قوای زمینی
→ naval forces قوای بحری
→ Quick Reaction Force قوای
واکنش سریع • نیروی واکنش سریع
force (power) *n* • زور • قوت •
قدرت
→ by force *see* forcibly
→ in force (in effect) نافذ
force (troop) *n* نیرو
force (violence) *n* عنف
forced (& adv) *adj, adv* • ناچار
ناعلاج

forced (compulsory) *adj* اجباری
forced (to do sth) *adj* مجبور
forceful (strong) *adj* قوی • با قوت
forcefully *adv* به عنف • بشّدت
forcefulness *n* شدت
forcibly *adv* جبراً • به جبر • اجباراً
• به اجبار • به عنف • قهراً
ford (crossing) *n* گذر گاه • گذر •
معبر
forearm bone *n* زند
forecast *n* پیش گویی
forefather *n* نیا , ـکان • جد
→ forefathers • اجداد • آبا و اجداد •
پدران
forehead *n* پیشانی • جبین • جبهه •
سر • ناصیه • پینک
→ (colloq) تقدیر
foreign *adj* خارجی
→ foreign policy سیاسَت خارجی
→ Foreign Service Institute
موسسه خدمات خارجه
foreigner *n* خارجی • بیگانه
→ (esp European) فرنگی
→ (outsider) اجنبی • غیر
foreignness *n* بیگانگی
forelock *n* جعد • طره
foremost *adj* نخست • اول
forerunner *adj, n* پیش قدم
foresighted (prudent) (& pers) *adj,*
n دوراندیش
forest (wilderness) *n* جنگل
→ of the forest (wild) جنگلی
forest ranger *n* جنگل بان
forestalling *n* پیش دستی
forever *adv* برای ابد • تا ابد • الی
الابد
foreword *n* پیش گفتار
forge (counterfeit) *v* جعل کردن •
جعل کاری کردن • ساخته کاری
کردن • ساختن
forge (furnace) *n* کوره
forgery *n* جعل
forget *v* فراموش کردن • از یاد
<کسی> رفتن
→ I completely forgot چور از یادم
رفت
forgive *v* بخشیدن • عذر قبول کردن •
تیر شدن • پوزش پذیرفتن
→ (used only of God) آمرزیدن
408

forgiveness *n* عذر • معذرت •
پوزش
→ (Musl law) عفو
forgiving (esp God) *adj* غفور
fork *n* پنجه
form & meaning *phrs* صورت و
معنی
form (& gram) *n* صیغه
form (comprise) <sth> *vt* تشکیل
دادن <چیزی را>
form (establish) *vt* تشکیل کردن
form (figure) *n* قواره
form (give form) <to sth> *v* شکل
دادن <به چیزی>
form (shape) *n* شکل • صورت
→ in the form of به شکل
form (take form) *v* شکل گرفتن
form *n* شکل
→ (gram) بنا
formal (official) *adj* رسمی
formal (procedural) *adj* شکلی
formal (written) (lang) *adj* نوشته
formalities *n pl* شکلیات • تشریفات
• مراسم
formally (officially) *adv* رسماً
formation (establishment) *n* تشکیل
former (previous) *adj* سابق • اسبق
• قبلی • ماتقدم
formerly (previously) *adv* سابقاً •
قبلا
fornicate *vi* زنا کردن
fornicator *n* زنا کار • حرام کار
fort (outpost) *n* تهانه
fort (stronghold) *n* قلعه
fortieth *adj* چهلم
→ (lit, used before n) چهلمین
fortification *n* استحکام
fortress *n* حصار • قلعه
→ (Presidential Palace complex)
ارگ
fortunate (& pers) *adj, n* طالعمند •
بختور • بختیار • مقبل
fortunate *adj* مسعود • خوش بخت
fortunately *adv* خوشبختانه
fortune (fate; horoscope) *n* طالع
fortuneteller *n* فال بین
fortunetelling *n* فال دیدن

forty *adj, n* چهل
→ 40-day period of Sufi meditation چله
forward (send onward) *vt* پیش کردن
forward *adv* پیشاپیش
forward operating base *see* FOB
fossil *n* فسیل
foster (relationship) *adj* رضاعی
→ foster brother • برادر کوکا رضاعی
→ foster sister کوکی
foster *vt* پروردن • پروراندن
foul-mouthed *adj* فحاش
found (establish) *v* تهداب گذاری کردن
foundation (& charitable) *n* بنیاد
foundation (basis) *n* اساس • طرح • نهاد • تهداب
→ lay a foundation • طرح ریختن طرح افگندن • بنا نهادن
foundation (establishment) *n* تاسیس
foundation stone (building's) *n* غرقه
founder *n* موسس
founding *n* تهداب گذاری
foundry *n* ریخته گری
fountain *n* فواره
fountain pen *n* قلم خودرنگ
four *adj, n* چهار
fourfold (adv, n) چارچند
fourteen *adj, n* چهارده
fourteenth *adj* چهاردهم
→ (lit, used before n) چهاردهمین
fourth *adj* چهارم
→ (lit, used before n) چهارمین
→ one-fourth چارکه
fox (& pers, fig) *n* روباه
foyer *n* کفش کن
fraction (math) *n* کسر • عدد کسری
→ per (used in fractions) بر
fraction (portion) *n* حصه
fracture *n* کسر • رخنه
→ bone fracture کسر استخوان
fracture *vt* کسر کردن
fragile *adj* شکننده • پوشالی
fragility *n* شکنندگی
fragment *n* چره

fragrance *n* رایحه
→ (lit) نگهت
→ fragrant w/ambergris عنبر آگین
frail (in ill health) *adj* نازک اندام
frame (for photo) *n* قاب
→ wooden frame • چارچوب چارچوبه • چوکات
frame *n* چوکات
framework *n* چوکات
France *n* فرانسه
frank (candid) *adj* یک رنگ
→ (colloq) • ترت • دل پاک
→ (lit) پاک دل
frankly *adv* به صراحت • صراحتاً • صریحاً • بالصراحه
frantic (& adv) *adj, adv* دیوانه وار
fraternity (solidarity) *n* همبستگی
fratricide *n* برادر کشی
fraud (deceit) *n* • خیانت • تقلب حقه بازی
fraudster *n* • تقلب کار • متقلب حقه باز
fraudulent *adj* تقلب آمیز
→ (counterfeit) تقلبی • قلابی
free (devoid) <of sth> *adj* عاری <از چیزی>
free (gratis) *adj* • مجانی • رایگان
→ practically free مفت
free (unfettered) *adj* آزاد
→ free time فراغت
free weight *n* وزن بر داری
freedom (if abused) *n* • اباحت
→ freedom of conscience (belief) آزادی عقیده
freedom *n* آزادی • آزادگی
freeing (liberating) *n* ابرا
freely *adv* آزادانه
freeman (not slave) *n* آزاد • آزاده
freethinker (atheist) *n* دهری
freeze *vt* یخ زدن
Fremont (city) *n* فریمانت
French (& pers, lang) *n* فرانسوی
frenzy *n* جنون • دیوانگی
frequently *adv* غالباً
fresh (produce) (& adv) *adj, adv* تازه

409

fresh (water) (& adv) *adj, adv* شیرین

freshness (succulence) *n* طراوت

friction *n* • احتكاک • حک

frictional *adj* • احتكاكی

Friday *n* جمعه
→ Friday prayers نماز جمعه

fried *adj* • بریان • سرخ شده
→ fried chicken مرغ بریان

friend *n* • دوست • رفیق • خلیل
→ (f form) رفیقه
→ (acquaintance) (lit) آشنا
→ (become acquainted) آشنایی حاصل نمودن شدن
→ beloved, dear friend حبیب
→ close friend (f) خواهرخانده
→ close friend (m) برادر خانده

friendliness (cordiality) *n* صمیمیت

friendliness (generosity) *n* کرم

friendliness (kindness) *n* لطف

friendly (& adv) *adj, adv* صمیمانه

friendly *adj* • دوستانه • مودت آمیز • اختلاطی • صمیمی • پیشانی باز
→ quick to make friends زود آشنا

friendship *n* • مودت • دوستی
→ (acquaintance) آشنایی
→ Friendship Bridge (btwn Afgh & Tajikistan) پل دوستی

fright *n* • ترس • هراس • خوف • سهم • بیم • رعب

frighten *see* scare

frightening *adj* بیمناک

frightening *see* scary

frivolous (pers) *adj* سبک سر

frivolous *adj* سبک

frog *n* • قورباغه • بقه

from *prep* از
→ from in btwn/within از بین
→ starting from سر از

front (forward part) *n* • پیش • روی
→ front & back • پیش و پس
→ in front of <sth> • در پیشروی <چیزی> • در برابر <چیزی>
→ at/to the front پیشاپیش

front (preceding) *adj* پیش

front *see* & frontline

frontier pillar *n* پایه

frontiers *n pl* ثغور

frontline *n* • صف پیش • قطار پیش • محاذ • جبهه

frostbite *n* یخ زدگی

frown *adj* پیشانی ترشی

frowning *adj* پیشانی ترش

frugal *see* cheap

frugality *n* اقتصاد

fruit (profit, benefit) *n* • ثمر • ثمره

fruit *n* • میوه • سردرختی
→ bearing fruit میوه دار
→ fruit (pl; in general) میوه باب
→ fruit bowl میوه دانی
→ fruit juice • آب میوه • شربت
→ fruit seller میوه فروش • طواف

fruitful (productive) *adj* • ثمر دار • با ثمر • ثمر بخش • پر عایدات • بارور

fry *vt* سرخ کردن
→ be fried سرخ شدن

FSI *see* Foreign Service Institute

fuck (obs) *n* گای

fuck (obs) *v* • گاییدن • بند کردن
→ (w/f) (obs) کس کردن

fucker (pers) (obs) *n* گای

fuel (cooking) *n* مواد سوخت

fuel (gasoline) *n* • تیل • پترول

fuel (heating) *n* • مواد سوخت • محروقات

fuel (supply w/fuel) *vt* تیل دادن

fugitive *adj* گریز پای

fulfill an order *vt* • به جای آوردن • به جای کردن

fulfill *see* carry out

fulfilled (carried out) *adj* پیش برده

fulfillment (completion) *n* • پیشبرد • ادا • ایفا • ایفاء

full *adj* • پر • مملو
→ (to overflowing) سر شار
→ (not hungry) سیر

full to the top *adj* مالامال

fumitory (med herb) *n* شاه تره

fun (recreation) *n* ساعت تیری
→ (break, free time) تفریح
→ have fun تیر شدن
→ having fun بر خوردار

function (be in effect) *v* • فعالیت داشتن • فعالیت کردن

function (operate) *vi* دایر شدن

functioning (active) *adj* فعال

fund (capital) n سرمایه
fundamental (basic) adj اساسی
fundamental (principled) adj
اصولی
fundamentalist (stickler) n اصولی
fundamentally adv اساساً
funeral see burial
→ funeral prayer for the dead
فاتحه
→ funeral procession تشییع جنازه
→ make funeral arrangements
مرده داری کردن
→ funereal corpse جنازه
fungus n پوپنک
funnel n قیف
funny (amusing) adj • خنده آور
خنده خنداور
→ (colloq) خنداور
funny (ludicrous) adj • مسخره
مسخره آمیز
funny (odd) adj • عجیب و غریب
نخچه
funny (witty) adj فکاهی
furious (& adv) adj, adv جنون آمیز
furious adj • غضبناک • خشمناک
ارغند
furnished adj با مبل و فرنیچر
furniture n مبل و فرنیچر • فرنیچر
→ (accoutrements) سامان
furrier (craftsman) n پوستین دوز
furriery (craft) n پوستین دوزی
furrow (deep wrinkle) n • شیار
شدیار • شدگار
further (additional) adj مزید
furthermore adv علاوتاً • به علاوه
fury n • غضب • قهر • خشم
حمیت • دیوانگی • جنون
fuschia (plant) n گوشواره
fuse (electrical) n فیوز
fuselage (hull) n بدنه
fusillade n شلیک پی در پی •
شلیک پیاپی
fuss (bother; dispute) n جنجال
futile adj ضایع
futile adj; sth futile n لاطایل
future adj آینده
→ (gram) مستقبل • مضارع
→ future tense زمان آینده • زمان
مستقبل

future n آتی • آینده

G

Gabriel (archangel) n • جبرییل
جبریل
→ faithful spirit (epithet of Gabriel)
روح الامین
gabble v اسطوره ها گفتن
gabbling n اسطوره
gain (profit) n • منفعت • نفع • کمایی
→ (acquisition) تحصیل
gain (profit) v کمایی کردن
gall bladder n کیسه صفرا
galled (piqued) adj افگار
→ (colloq) اوگار
gallon n گیلن
gallop vi چارنعل رفتن
gallows n دار
→ hang (sb) from a gallows به دار
آویختن • به دار زدن • به دار
کشیدن • غرغره کردن
gamble (wager) n قمار
gamble v قمار بازی کردن
gambler n قمار باز
gambling n قمار بازی
→ (w/astragali) بجل بازی
game (play) n بازی
game (prey) n • نخچیر • شکار
نخچیر
Gandhara (hist, geog) n گندهارا
Gandharan adj گندهاری
gang n دسته
ganjifa (hist, card game) n گنجفه
gap (& fig) n خلا • خلاء
garage n گراج • گاراج
→ (repair shop) ورکشاپ •
کارخانه
garbage n چتلی
garbanzo bean n نخود
garden adj باغی
garden n باغ • حدیقه • بوستان
garden v باغبانی کردن
garden cress (herb) n تراتیزک
gardener (caretaker) n باغبان • گل
چین
gardening n باغ کاری • باغ داری
• باغبانی
Gardeyz (seat, dist) n گردیز

411

gargle vt غرغره کردن

gargling n غرغره

garish & gaudy phrs زرق و برق
دار • پر زرق و برق

garishness phrs زرق و برق

garlic n سیر

Garmseyr (dist) n گرمسیر

garnet (spinel) n لعل
→ red garnet بدخش

garter n بند جراب

gas (esp fuel) n گاز
→ (chem, not solid/liquid) غاز

gas can n گیلنه

gas see & flatulence

gas station n تانک تیل

gasoline n تیل • پترول

gastric juices n عصاره معده

gate n دروازه

gatekeeper n دروازه بان
→ (colloq) دروازه وان

gather vi تجمع کردن • تجمع نمودن

gather vt فراهم کردن

gathering n تجمع • انجمن • اجتماع
• مجموعه • احتفال • گردهمایی
→ gathering of Musl scholars
اجماع
→ Shiite gathering place تکیه •
تکیه خانه

gaudiness see garishness

gaudy see garish

gauze n گاز

gay see homosexual

Gayan (dist) n گیان

Gayti see Kiti

Gaza Strip (geog) n باریکه غزه

gazelle n غزال

gazette n جریده

gear (horse's) n یراق

Gehenna see hell

geld v خصی کردن • اخته کردن

gelded adj خصی • اخته

gem n گوهر
→ gems احجار کریمه • جواهر
→ principal gem in a ring نگین •
نگینه

gem cutter n حکاک

Gemini (zodiac) n جوزا • دوپیکر

gendarme n ژاندارم

gendarmerie n ژاندارمه

412

gender (& gram) n جنس

gene n فکتور

genealogy (family tree) n شجره

genealogy (lineage) n نسب

general (four-star) n ستر جنرال
→ (head of Mughal army, hist)
خانخانان
→ brigadier general • برید جنرال
مل پاسوال • لوا مشر
→ commanding general جنرال •
فرمانده • قوماندان عمومی
→ lieutenant general دگرجنرال •
لوی پاسوال
→ major general تورن جنرال •
پاسوال

general staff (mil) n ارکان حرب •
ستر درستیز

general, in general see generally

generalization n تعمیم • عمومیت

generally adv عموماً • فی الجمله •
اعم

generation (age group) n نسل

generative power n قوه باه

generator n ماشین مولد برق •
داینمو • دینمو

generic adj جنسی

generosity n گشاده دستی • گشاده
دلی • کرم
→ (beneficence) فیض

generous (& pers) adj, n گشاده
دست • گشاده دل • سخی • مهربانی
• دریا دل
→ (beneficent) پر فیضی

Geneva (city) n جینوا • ژنیو

Genghis Khan (hist) n چنگیز

genie n جن

genital adj تناسلی

genitalia see genitals

genitals (f) n عورت
→ (fig, vulg) اشتق

genitals n شرم گاه • فلان • فلانی •
بعض

genius n نابغه

gentle adj حلیم

gentleness n نرمش • مدارا

genuine (authentic) adj اصیل

genuineness n اصالت

genus n جنس

geography n جغرافیه • جغرافیا

geological *adj* طبقات الارضی

geology *n* • علم طبقات الارض • جیولوجی

geomancer *n* رمال • رمل انداز

geomancy *n* رمالی • رمل

geometrical *adj* هندسی

geometry *n* هندسه

Georgia *n* گرجستان

Georgian (& pers) *adj, n* گرجی

Georgian (pers) *n* گرج • گرجی

geranium (flower) *n* جربین

Gereshk (dist) *n* گرشک

German (pers) *n* جرمنی • آلمان

German *adj* جرمنی • آلمانی

Germany *n* جرمنی • آلمانی

germinate *vt* نیش زدن

germs *n pl* جراثیم

Geronimo (in joint attack) *excl* یا چاریار

gesture *n* اشاره

get (obtain) *vt* حاصل کردن • کسب کردن • اکتساب کردن • دریافت داشتن • دریافت کردن

get (obtain; find) *vt* پیدا کردن

get (obtain; receive) *vt* دستیاب کردن

get (take, catch) *vt* گرفتن

get lost *vi* گم شدن

get on (vehicle, horse) *vi* سوار شدن

get up *vi* برخاستن • خاستن
→ (colloq) خیستن

getting (obtaining) *n* • کسب دریافت • دستیابی

geyser *n* چشمه آب جوشان

Ghafur (m name) *n* غفور

Ghalcha *see* Pamir

Ghani (m name) *n* غنی

Ghani Kheyl (ctr) *n* غنی خیل

Gharjestan (hist, province) *n* غرجستان

ghayn (letter) *n* غین

ghazal (lyric poem) *n* غزل
→ ghazal singer غزل سرای
→ ghazal singing غزل سرایی

Ghazanfar (m name) *n* غضنفر

ghazi (honorific) *n* غازی

Ghazi Abad (dist) *n* غازی آباد

Ghazi Mohamed Jan Khan (market) *n* غازی محمد جان خان

Ghazna *see* Ghazni

Ghaznavids, the (hist, dynasty 962-1187) *n pl* غزنویان

Ghazni (seat, province) *n* • غزنی غزنه

ghee (cul) *n* روغن زرد

Ghiljai *see* Ghilzai

Ghilzai (P tribal confederacy) *adj, n* غلزایی • غلجایی

ghizhdi (tent) *n* غژدی
→ pitch ghizhdi tent غژدی زدن

Ghor (province) *n* غور

Ghorak (dist) *n* غورک

Ghorband (dist) *n* غوربند

Ghorid *adj* غوری

Ghorids, the (hist, dynasty 1148-1215 A.D.; & dist) *n pl* غوریان

Ghormach (dist) *n* غورماچ

Ghoryan (dist) *n* غوریان

ghost *n* سایه • ظل
→ Holy Ghost *see* Holy Spirit

ghoul *n* غول

Ghunday (ctr) *n* غندی

giant *n* غول
→ giant w/o horns or tail غول بی شاخ و دم

gibbet *see* gallows

Gibraltar (geog) *n* جبل الطارق

giddy (dizzy) *adj* گیج
→ (colloq) گنگس

giddyup (to horse) *excl* چو
→ (urge a horse on) *v* چو گفتن

gift (present) *n* تحفه • هدیه
→ votive gift to pers of higher rank پیش کش

gift (talent) *n* سلیقه

gigolo *n* ژیگولو

gilded *see* gilt

Gilan (dist) *n* گیلان • گلان

gilt *adj* مطلا

gilt *v* طلا کاری کردن

gin (alcoholic drink) *n* جن

ginger *n* زنجبیل
→ (colloq) زنجفیل

gird o.s. *v* طرف بستن

girl n دختر • دوشیزه
→ (fig) پرده نشین
→ close girlfriend (not romantic) خواهرخانده • رفیقه • دوست
girlhood (virginity) n دوشیزگی
Giro (dist) n گیرو
Girwan (ctr) n گیروان
gist (vulg) n زبده
give vt دادن
→ (allocate) اختصاص دادن
→ (bestow) بخشیدن • اعتا کردن
→ (entrust, hand over) سپردن
give alms v صدقه دادن
give birth v ولادت کردن
give over (leave) vt واگذار کردن • واگذاشتن
give up (let go) vt تیر شدن <از چیزی>
give up (quit) vt ترک دادن
given that conj در کنار این که ...
giving (allocation) n اختصاص
Gizab (dist) n گیزاب • گزاب
gizzard n سنگ دان
glad see happy
gland n غده
→ (colloq) غدود
→ deer's musk gland نافه
glaringly see gloweringly
glass (for drinking) n گیلاس
glass (pane, material) n شیشه
glass (substance) n آبگینه
glass adj شیشه یی
glass cutter (tool) n شیشه بر
glass cutting n شیشه بر
glasses n عینک
→ wearing glasses عینکی
glaze (& cul) n لعاب
glaze v لعاب دادن
glazed adj لعابی
glib adj چرب زبان • زبان آور
glitter n درخشان • لامح • لامع
globe n کرۀ ارض • کرۀ زمین
globular see spherical
gloom n سایه • ظل
gloomy (depressing) adj دل گیر
→ (murky) ظلمانی • تاریک
glory n افتخار • جلال
glove n دستکش
→ (colloq) دسکش

glow n درخشان • لامح • لامع
gloweringly adv خیره خیره
glue n سرش
gnosis n عرفان
gnostic adj عرفانی
gnostic (pers) n عارف
go vi رفتن • تشریف بردن
→ go back (return) بازرفتن
→ go to school مکتب خواندن عودت کردن
→ go up in smoke دود شدن
→ go w/the flow همرنگ جماعت شدن
goal (destination) n سرمنزل • منزل
goal (intent) n مقصد • مقصود
goal (objective) n هدف • مطلب • مطمح • مرام • غایه • مطمح نظر • مورد نظر
goal (soccer) n گول
goat n بز
→ (kid) بزغاله
→ (young billy goat) جدی
→ male goat that leads flock تکه
→ flock (of goats) رمه
→ goat dragging (game) بزکشی
→ goat dung پشک • پشقل
→ goat fluff کرک
→ goat-hearted (cowardly) بزدل
→ goatskin bag سناچ • انبان
→ ibex (wild goat) بز کوهی
→ markhor (wild goat) مارخور
→ milk a goat بز دوشیدن
gobble (eat fast) v لقمه زدن
goblet n جام

414

God n • الله • خدا • ایزد • خداوند •
خداوندگار • یزدان
→ before God (honestly) عنداالله
→ dear God حبیب
→ far-reaching (attribute of God)
واسع
→ for God's sake به • به لحاظ خدا
رضای خدا
→ God bless! خدا رحمت کنه
→ God willing انشاءاالله • خواست
خدا • اگر خواست خدا باشد
→ God's will be done! ماشاءاالله
→ He who forgives (God) بخشاینده
→ helper of the helpless (God)
چاره ساز بی چاره گان
→ in the name of the Almighty &
Merciful God بسم االله الرحمن
الرحیم
→ Lord (God) مولا
→ Providence (God) پروردگار
→ sublime (attribute of God) تعالی
→ Supreme Being (Zor) مزدا
→ thank God! شکر خدا • شکر
خدا را • خدا را شکر کن • بحمداالله
god (deity) n اله
god (idol) n بغ • معبود •
الهه
goddess n الهه
God-fearing adj متقی • خدا ترس
God-given adj, n خدا داده
godhood n خداوندی
godly adj به خدا
godsend see God-given
Gog (bibl) n یاجوج
→ Gog & Magog یاجوج و ماجوج
goiter n بوغمه
gold n طلا • زر
→ gold (& fig, riches) زر
→ gold leaf/foil زرورق
gold panning n ریگ • زرشویی
شویی
golden adj زرین
goldfinch (bird) n سهره
gold-plated adj طلا کاری شده
→ plate with gold طلا کاری کردن
goldsmith n زرگر
→ goldsmith's shop زرگری
goldsmithing n زرگری
Goliath (bibl) n جالوت
→ David & Goliath داوود و جالوت

Gomal (dist) n گومل
gone (absent) (& pers) adj, n غایب
gone (left) adj غایب
goner (about to die) n مردنی
gong n زنگ • گریال
gonorrhea n سوزاک
good adj خوب • نیک • نیکو
→ do good (render service) خوبی
کردن
→ good (nice) نغز
→ good! (OK!) خیر • بخیر است
→ the good & the bad خوب و
خراب • نیک و بد
→ the good & the wicked خوب و
بد
→ good for nothing ناکاره
→ how good! خوشا
goodbye excl خدا حافظ • به امان
خدا
goods (industrial) n pl مصنوعات
goods (wares) n • اموال • اشیا
اجناس • امتعه
gorge n تنگی
gorilla n گوریلا
Gosfandi (dist) n گوسفندی
Goshta (dist) n گوشته
gospel (bibl) n انجیل
gossip (pers) n چغل
→ (fig) هیزم کش دوزخ
gossiping n خبر چینی • خبر کشی
• غیبت
gout (med) n نقرس
govern (rule) v حکم فرمایی کردن
govern v • حکومت کردن
حکمرانی کردن • حکمرانی داشتن
→ self-governing مستقل
government (institution) n حکومت
government (rule) n حکم فرمایی
government (state) n دولت
→ low-ranking govt employee
نوکر • خدمتگار • چاکر
governmental (official) adj حکومتی
governmental (statal) adj دولتی •
سرکاری
governmental adj سرکاری
governor (dist) n ولسوال
governor (province) n والی
→ (arch) مرزبان
→ (hist, local ruler) حاکم

415

grace (beauty) n • زیبا • جمال • حسن • ادا

graceful (fair) adj لطیف

gradation n تدریج

grade (academic) n صنف

grade (categorize) vt درجه بندی کردن

grade (degree, rank) n مرتبه

grade (score) n • نمره • شماره • نمبر

grade (slope) n • سرپایانی • سراشیبی

gradual adj متدرج • تدریجی

gradually adv متدرجاً • تدریجاً • بتدریج • بالتدریج

→ (colloq) رفته رفته • اندک اندک • جسته جسته • آرام آرام • جو به جو

gradualness n تدریج

graduate (pers) n • فارغ • فارغ التحصیل

graduation (academic) n فراغت

graft (bot) n پیوند

grafted adj پیوندی • التصاقی

grain (cereal) n • حب • دانه • غله

→ grains حبوب

→ grains (colloq) حبوبات

grammar n دستور زبان • صرف و نحو • گرامر

grammatical adj دستوری

grand (high) adj بزرگ • لوی

grandchild n نواسه • نبیره

→ (lit) نواده

→ grandfather & grandchild نیکه و نبیره

grandfather n پدر کلان • بابا • نیا • جد

→ (colloq) نیکه • بابه کلان

→ maternal grandfather جد مادری

→ paternal grandfather جد پدری

grandiloquence n طمطراق • آب و تاب

grandma see grandmother (colloq)

grandmother n مادر کلان

→ (colloq) بی بی

grandpa see grandfather (colloq)

granite n خارا

grant (bestow) vt بخشیدن • دادن

→ grant an audience بار دادن

grant n قرضه بلا عوض • مساعدت بلا عوض • کمک بلا عوض

grape adj انگوری

grape n انگور

→ lal (grape variety) لال

grapefruit n چکوتره

grapevine n تاک • رز

grappling hook n چنگک بلا شدن

grasp firmly vt محکم گرفتن

grass n سبزه • چمن

→ (fodder) علف • گیاه

grasshopper n ملخ

grassland (meadow) n مرغزار

grassland (pasturage) n علفزار

grassland, meadow n چمنزار • سبزه زار

grate v رنده کردن

grated adj رنده شده

grateful adj سپاس گزار • شکر گزار • احسانمند • شاکر • متشکر • قدردان • قدر شناس

grater (tool) n رنده • لیسه

gratify (humor) vt دل به دست آوردن

gratify (satisfy) vt رضا دادن

gratis adj مفت • مجانی • رایگان

gratitude n شکر • تشکر • سپاس گزاری • سپاس • قدردانی

grave n گور • قبر • لحد

→ (mausoleum) مقبره

gravel n سنگ ریزه • جغل • جغله

gravestone n لوح قبر • سنگ قبر

graveyard n قبرستان

→ (fig) وادی خاموشان

gravitation n جاذبیت • جذب

gravity (dignity) n وقار

gravity (force) n جاذبه

gravity (seriousness) n جدیت

gray (ash) adj خاکستری

gray (steel) adj فولادی

gray-bearded (& pers) adj, n ریش سفید

graze vi چریدن

grease (fat) n چربی • شحم

grease (lubricate) v چرب کاری کردن

greasy (fatty) adj چرب

great (grand) adj لوی • بزرگ

great (splendid) *adj* مجید
great *excl* خوشا
greater • بزرگتر *adj* کلانتر
→ (lit) اکبر
great-grandchild *n* کواسه • نبیره
Grecian *see* Greek
Greco-Bactrian (hist) *adj* یونانی
باختری
Greco-Buddhist (hist) *adj* یونانی
بودایی
Greece *n* یونان
greed *n* حرص • آز • طمع
greedily *adv* حریصانه • آزمندانه
greedy (& pers) *adj, n* حریص •
آزمند • طماع
→ greedy pers طمع کار
greedy *adj* گرسنه
→ (colloq) گشنه
Greek (& pers, lang) *adj, n* یونانی
green *adj, n* سبز
→ emerald green زمردین
→ jasper green یشمی
→ pistachio green پسته یی
green bean *n* فاصولیه • فاسولیه
greenery *n* سر سبزی
greenhouse *n* گل خانه • گرین
هوس
grenade *n* بم دستی
greyhound *n* تازی
grief (sorrow) *n* غم • اندوه • حزن
• زاری • عزا • ماتم • ندبه
→ (mourning) سوگ
grief *see* & lament
grieve (sorrow) *vi* خون خوردن •
خون دل خوردن • خون جگر
خوردن
→ (mourn) سوگ داشتن
grill *v* کباب کردن
grille (of chadari) *n* چشمکی
grin & bear sth *v* دندان بر جگر
گذاشتن
grind (crush) *n* تکان • چک
grind *vt* چکیدن
grip (clamp) *n* گیرا
gristle *n* غضروف
gristly *adj* غضروفی
groan (moan) *v* نالیدن
groan (whine) *v* نالش کردن
groaning (whining) *n* نالش

grocer (pers) *n* بقالی
groceries (goods) *n* سودا
grocery (store) *n* بقالی
groom (bridegroom) *n* داماد
groom (stableman) *n* مهتر
groove *n* مادگی
gross (flagrant) *adj* فاحش
grotto *n* غار • مغاره
ground (earth) *n* ثری • زمین
ground meat *n* کوفته
grounds *n* زمینه • سبب • علت
→ on the grounds that به • بعنوان
عنوان
group (bunch) <of sth> *n* • خیلی
بسیار ‹از چیزی›
group (category) *n* دسته
group (circle) *n* محفل
group (faction; party) *n* حزب
group (mil) *n* گروپ
→ group of people • جوپه •
جوقه • زمره
→ in groups دسته دسته • جوپه
جوپه • جوقه جوقه • خیل خیل
group *n* گروه • گروپ • دسته
grow (plant) *vt* روباندن
→ (colloq) کشت کردن
grow (plant, crop) *vi* روئیدن←
(colloq) کشت شدن
grow a beard *v* ریش • ریش کشیدن
ماندن
grow up *vi* کلان شدن • بزرگ شدن
growing (strengthening) *n* • تقویت
تقویه
growth (development) *n* • انکشاف
رشد • نشو
growth (increase) *n* تکثر • زیادت
grub (larva) *n* نوزاد • نورسیده
grudge *n* کینه
guarantee (surety) *n* • تامینات
ضمانت
guarantee (warranty) *n* تضمین
guarantee *v* تضمین کردن
guard (sentry) *n* پهره دار
→ Revolutionary Guards (Iran)
پاسداران انقلاب اسلامی
→ stand guard • نگاهبانی کردن •
پهره کردن • پهره دادن • پهره
داری کردن
guard (watch over) *vt* نگاه کردن

guard (watchman) n • نگاهبان
پاسبان • چوکی دار • محافظ
guardhouse n پهره دار خانه
guardian (legal) n وصی
guardian (of minor) n سرپرست
guardian angel n ملک الحارس
guarding n نگاه • نگه • پاسبانی •
محافظت
guerrilla (mil) adj • گریلایی
گوریلایی
guerrilla (mil) n گریلا • گوریلا
guess (conjecture) v حدس کردن
guess (suppose) v خیال کردن
guess n حدس
guest n مهمان
→ uninvited guest سرباری
guest house n مهمان خانه
guffaw n قهقهه
guidance n • راهنمایی • راهنمونی •
رهنمایی
guide (& book) n راهنما • راه نما • ره نما
رهنما • ره نما
guide (indicator) n نمایانگر
guide (pers) n رهنما • بلد
→ spiritual guide پیر • مرشد
guided missile n راکت رهبری شده
guideline n خط مشی
guild (trade) n صنف
guile n مکر • هنر
guilt (criminal) n • مجرمیت •
مجرمی
guilt (sinfulness) n خطاکاری
guilty (sinful) adj گناه کار • گناه
گار • خطاکار
guilty <of a crime> adj مقصر <از
یک جرم>
guitar n گیتار
Gulab (m name) n گلاب
Gulaley (f name) n گلالی
Gulbadan (hist, Babur's daughter) n گلبدن
Guldara (dist) n گلدره
Gulestan (dist) n گلستان
gulf (body of water) n خلیج
gulf stream n رو گرم
gullet n مری
gullible adj زود باور • خوش باور
gulp (swallow) v قرت کردن
Gulran (dist) n گلران
418

gums n بیره • لثه
gun (handgun, pistol) n تفنگچه
gun (rifle, musket) n تفنگ
→ gun barrel میل تفنگ
→ gun carriage عراده
→ machine gun ماشین دار
→ safety position on gun قید
gunpowder n باروت • دارو
gunshot n شلیک
gunsmith n تفنگ ساز
Gurbuz (dist) n گربز
Gurkani (hist, Timurid) adj
گورکانی
Gurzewan (dist) n گرزوان
gush v فواره زدن • فواره کردن
gut (& guts) n روده
gutsy (fig) adj گرده دار
gutter n آبرو
Guzara (dist) n گزره • گزاره
Guzargah-e Nur (dist) n گزرگاه
نور
gymnast n ورزش کار
gymnastics n • ورزش • جمناستک •
سپورت
gynecologist n داکتر نسایی
gypsum plaster n گچ
gypsy (memb of marginalized grp)
n جت • لولی

H

Habibia High School (Kabul) n
حبیبیه • لیسه حبیبیه
Habibullah (hist, Afgh king 1901-
1919) حبیب الله
habit n عادت • شیوه • خوی
habitat n واحد مسکونی
habitually adv عادتاً
habituated (to sth) adj آموخته
hacksaw n اره آهن بر
hadith (Prophet's saying) n حدیث
Hafiz (m name) n حفیظ
Hafiza (f name) n حفیظه
haggle v چانه زدن • چنه زدن
جگره کردن
Hague, The n هاگ • لاهه
hail n ژاله
hailstones see hail
hair (esp f's) n موی

hair salon n آرایشگاه

hair stylist n آرایشگر

→ style (f's) hair موی تیار کردن

haircut (form) n سر • اصلاح سر تیار

→ give a haircut (tom) سر تیار کردن • اصلاح سر کردن

hairy (hirsute) adj پر موی

→ (neg) پشم آلود

haji (pers, honorific) n حاجی

Haji Kheyl (ctr) n حاجی خیل

hajj n حج • حاج

hakam (mediator, hist) n حکم

Hakim Mirza (hist, Akbar's half-brother, Kabul ruler) n حاکم مرزا

halal (rel) adj حلال

half n نیم • نصف

→ (colloq) نصب

→ at half-mast نیمه افراشته

→ melon half پله

half-asleep adj نیم خواب

half-brother n برادر اندر

half-open adj نیم باز

half-sister n خواهر اندر

halim (Afgh rice dish) n هلیم

Halim (m name) n حلیم

Halima (hist, Prophet's nurse; f name) n حلیمه

hall (audience hall) n بارگاه

hall (auditorium) n تالار

hall (bureau; room) n دیوان

hallway n دهلیز • راه رو

→ down the hallway در آخر دهلیز

halo (lunar) n خرگاه

halter (camel's) n مهار

halter (donkey's) n افسار

halvah (cul) n حلوا

→ (w/nuts) حلوای مغزی

ham (meat) n گوشت ران خوک

Hamal (month) n حمل

Hamas (terrorist group) n حماس

hamburger (meat) n کوفته

Hamed (m name) n حامد

Hamid (m name) n حمید

Hamida (hist, Akbar's mother; f name) n حمیده

hammer (coppersmith's) v چارسو

hammer n چکش • چکوچ • چاکوچ • چکوش • چاکوش

→ sledgehammer پتک

hammer see & firing hammer

Hamza (hist, Prophet's uncle; m name) n حمزه

Hanafite (pers) n حنفی

Hanbalite (pers) n حنبلی

Hanbalitic (school of Sunni rel thought) adj حنبلی

hand n دست

→ hand-operated دستکی • دستی

→ side (fig), hand طرف

hand grenade n بم دستی

hand mill n دستکول • دستاز

handbag n دستکول

handcuffs n اولچک • الچک • ولچک

handful n مشت • مشتی

handgun n تفنگچه

handicap n معیوبیت

handicapped (& pers) adj, n معیوب

handicraft n صناعت • صنعت • کار دستی

handiwork n صنعت دست

handkerchief n دست مال

→ (for sweat) عرق گیر

→ (kerchief) دست مال

hand-knitted adj دست بافت

handle n دسته • دستگیر

handmade adj دستکی • دستی

→ crudely handmade خود ساخت

handover (for safekeeping) n تحویل دهی • تحویل

handover (transfer) n تفویض

handrail n کتاره

handshake n مصافحه

→ shake hands دست دادن

handsome (charming) adj جذاب • وسیم

→ (attractive) جمیل • مقبول

→ (colloq) خوش تیپ

→ (well-formed) شکیل

hand-to-hand (combat) adj تن به تن

hand-to-mouth adv دست و دهان

handwoven adj دست بافت

handwriting n خط • دست نویسی

419

handwritten *adj* • خطی • مخطوط دست نویس

Hanfitic (school of Sunni rel thought) *adj* حنفی

hang (suspend) *vt* • بند کردن • آویختن

→ hang (sb) from gallows به دار آویختن • به دار زدن • به دار کشیدن • غرغره کردن

hanging (suspended) *adj* • معلق • ملاق

hangover *n* خمار

Hanzala (8th-c Dari poet) *n* حنظله

happen *vi* صورت گرفتن

صورت پذیرفتن • واقع شدن • وقوع یافتن • به وقوع پیوستن • وارد آمدن • برگذار شدن • بعمل آمدن • به عمل آمدن • وجود داشتن • رو نما شدن • روی دادن • دایر شدن • حدوث یافتن

→ (lit) رخ دادن

happening (event) *n* آمده

happening (incidence) *n* وقوع

happening (occurrence) *n* تدویر

happiness *n* • خوشی • شادمانی • سرور • سروری • مسرت

happy (content) *adj* خوشنود

happy (friendly) *adj* پیشانی باز

happy (lucky) *adj* خوش • مسعود • بخت

happy (merry) *adj* • دل خوش • خوش دل

happy <at sth> *adj* • خوشحال • خوش <به چیزی> • شاد • شادمان • مسرور

Harakat-e Islami (Shia mvmt) *n* حرکت اسلامی

harass *v* به ستوه آوردن

harassed *adj* ستوه

harassment *n* ستوه

harbor *n* بندر گاه

hard (difficult) *adj* • مشکل • دشوار • سخت

hard (not soft) *adj* سخت

hard (solid) *adj* جامد

hardhearted (& pers) *adj, n* سنگ دل • سنگین دل • سنگ دلی

hardship *n* • تلخی • تشدد

hard-working *adj* • پرکار • کارکن • زحمت کش

hardy (tough) *adj* سخت جان

hare *n* خرگوش

harem *n* • حرم • حرم سرا • سرای • پرده سرا

Haris (m name) *n* حارث

harlot *n* روسپی • فاحشه • قحبه

harm (damage) *n* ضرر • مضرت • صدمه • زیان • حیف • افسوس • دریغ

→ (colloq) نقص

harm (injury) *n* گزند • ایذا • اذیت

harm *v* صدمه زدن • گزند رساندن

harmful *adj* ضررناک • مضر • زیان آور

harmonious *adj* هماهنگ • منسجم

harmonize *v* هماآهنگ دادن

harmony (& mus) *n* هماهنگی

→ in harmony متعادل

harp (mus instr) *n* هارپ

→ glass harp (mus instr) جلترنگ

harpist *n* هارپ نواز

harrowing *adj* جگر خراش • دل خراش

harsh (violent; severe) *adj* شدید

harshly *adv* به شدت

harvest *n* محصولات • برداشت

→ harvested crop in pile خرمن

Hashem (m name) *n* هاشم

Hashemite (family claiming direct descent from Prophet) هاشمی

hashish *n* حشیش • چرس

→ people in a circle smoking hashish پره

hashish user (pers) *n* چرسی

Hassan (Prophet's grandson; m name) *n* حسن

haste *n* عجله

hat *n* کلاه • کله • شپو

→ pakol hat پکول

→ straw hat کلاهِ بوریایی

hatch (sm opening) *n* دریچه

hatchet (small) *n* تبرچه

→ dervish's battle hatchet تبرزین

hateful *adj* نفرت آمیز

hatred <toward sb/sth> *n* نفرت <به کسی/چیزی>

haughtiness *n* افاده

haughty *adj* پر افاده • دماغی
Havana *n* هاوانا
have to <+ subj> (modal v) باید
have to <+ subj> *vi* مجبور بودن
have *vt* داشتَن
→ (own) کار داشتن
having *adj* دارا
hawala (banking system) *n* حواله
hawk (bird) *n* باشه
hay *n* کاه • که
hay barn *n* کاهدان
Haydar (m name) *n* حیدر
Hazar Sumuch (dist) *n* هزار سموچ
Hazara *adj* هزارگی
Hazara (ethn grp) *n* هزاره
Hazaragi (dialect) *n* هزارگی
Hazarajat (region) *n* هزاره جات
hazard *n* خطر • مخاطره
Hazrat-e Sultan (dist) *n* حضرت سلطان
he *pron* او
head (& anat) *n* سر
→ (leader, chief) سرکرده • سرور
→ animal's head کله
→ at the head of (sth) در راس
→ head (single animal) راس
→ head (single camel) زنگیر
→ head of delegation راس
→ heads or tails شیر • خط شیر و خط
head (chief) *n* سرکرده
head for (sw) *v* رو آوردن <به طرف کسی>
→ headed for عازم
head to toe *adv* سر تا پا
headache *n* سردردی • سر دردی
→ have a headache سر درد بودن
→ سر <کسی> درد کردن
→ headache-ridden سر درد
heading (rubric) *n* عنوان
headmaster (rel school) *n* مدرس باشی
headquarters *n* قرارگاه • مقر
→ (mil) قوماندانی • قوماندانی مرکزی • قول اردو • مقر فرمان دهی
headstrong (pushy) *adj* سرزور • سرتنبه
→ (stubborn) خود سر

headword in possessive construction (gram) *n* مضاف
heal up (bone fracture) *vi* جوش خوردن
heal *vt* خوب کردن
healing *n* ابرا
health clinic *n* کلینک صحی • کلنیک صحی
health *n* صحت • حال • جوری • تن درستی
→ good health عافیت
health-related *adj* صحی • صحیه
healthy *adj* جور • صحتمند • سلامت • تن درست
heap *n* توده • کوت
hear (listen) *v* شنیدن
→ able to hear شنوا
hearer (listener) *n* شنونده
hearing (law) *n* سماعت
→ (trial) محاکمه
hearing (sense of hearing) *n* سامعه • شنوایی
hearsay *n* آوازه • افواه
heart (anat; & fig) *n* قلب
heart (cards) *n* تپان • لعل
→ (colloq) لال
heart (mind) *n* باطن • خاطر
heart attack *n* حمله قلبی
heartbroken *adj* دل شکسته • شکسته دل
heart-rending *adj* جگر خراش • دل خراش • جگر سوز
heat *n* گرمی
→ central heating مرکز گرمی
heat (steam) *n* تف
→ (colloq) تفت
heat (food) *v* تف دادن
→ (colloq) تفت دادن
heathen (esp pre-Musl) *adj* جاهلی
heaven (sky) *n* آسمان • سما
→ (Paradise) بهشت • جنت
heavenly (divine) *adj* ملکوتی
heavenly (revelation) *adj* منزل
heavy *adj* سنگین • ثقیل • ثقیله گران • قیمت
Hebrew (& pers, lang) *adj, n* عبرانی • عبری
hectare (unit of area) *n* هکتار
hedge *n* پرچال

hedgehog *n* خارپشت
→ (colloq) خارپشتک
heel (of foot) *n* پاشنه • کری
Hegira *n* هجرت • مهاجرت
→ related to the Hegira هجری
height (altitude) *n* ارتفاع • بلندی
height (peak) *n* اوج
height (stature) *n* قد • بلندی
Hejaz (geog) *n* حجاز
Hekmatyar (insurgent leader) *n*
حکمتیار • گلبدین حکمتیار
helicopter *n* هلیکوپتر • هلی کوپتر
hell (Hell) *n* سقر • جهنم
→ hellfire دوزخ • جحیم • جهنم •
جهنمی • سقر
→ in hell تحت السقر
Hellenic *see* Hellenistic
Hellenism (hist) *n* هلینیزم
Hellenistic (hist) *adj* هلینستی
hello *excl* سلام علیکم
→ (response) و علیکم سلام
→ hello (on phone) بلی • الو
Helmand (province, river) *n* هلمند
help *n* کمک • کومک • مساعدت •
مدد • امداد • معاونت • اعانت
→ (fig) پهلو • بازو
→ (resource) چاره • گزیر
help <sb> *v* <به> کمک کردن
کسی> • مساعدت کردن • پهلو دادن
• بازو دادن • مدد کردن • معاونت
کردن • اعانت کردن
→ (arch) دریافتن
helper *n* دستگیر • بازو
helpless (& pers) *adj, n* درمانده
helplessly *adv* اضطراراً
helpmeet *see* helper
Helsinki *n* هلسنگی
hem (border) *n* حاشیه
→ trouser hem پاچه • دهن پاچه
hem (garment) *v* پس دوزی کردن
hemisphere (& geog) *n* نیم کره
hemlock (poison) *n* شوکران
hemming (garment) *n* پس دوزی
hemorrhage *n* خون ریزی
hemorrhage *v* خون ریختن
hempseed *n* بنگ دانه • شاه دانه
hen *n* ماچه مرغ

henna *n* حنا • خینه
→ henna tray (at wedding) تختِ
خینه
hence *adv* از آن جهت • از آن
سبب • به آن جهت • در نتیجه •
نتیجتاً • بالنتیجه • لذا • لهذا
henceforth *adv* من بعد • منبعد
henchman *n* دست نشانده
henchman *see & trusted agent*
henna *n* حنا
Hephthalite (hist) *n* هفتالی
Her Majesty (title) *n* علیا حضرت
herald *n* قاصد
Herat (province, city) *n* هرات
herb *n* گیاه • نبات • سبزی
herbal *adj* گیاهی
herbivorous (lit) *adj* علف خوار •
گیاه خوار
herd (livestock) *vt* پیش کردن
herd of horses/livestock *n* گله
→ horse herder گله بان
here *adv* این جا
→ (colloq) این جه
→ here is, voila (colloq) اینه
hereafter *adv* بعد از این • پس از
این
hereafter, the *n* عقبی • آخرت
hereditary *adj* میراثی • موروث •
موروثی • ارثی
heredity *n* وراثت
heresy *n* گمراهی
heretic *n* گمراه
heritage *n* میراث
hermaphrodite *n* ذوجنسین
hermit *n* خلوت نشین • تارک دنیا •
تارک الدنیا
→ (ascetic) زاهد
→ (monk) صومعه نشین
hermitage *n* خلوت گاه • جای
خلوت
hernia *n* چره
hero (fighter) *n* جنگ آور • جنگ
آزما • جنگ جو • رزم آزما • رزم
آور • رزم جو • پیکار گر
→ (& fictional) قهرمان
Herodotus (hist) *n* هرودوت
heroin *n* هیروئین
herpes *n* مرداردانه

Hesa-ye Awal-e Behsud (dist) n حصه اول بهسود

Hesa-ye Awal-e Kohestan (dist) n حصه اول کوهستان

Hesa-ye Awal-e Panjsheyr (dist, alt Khenj) n حصه اول پنجشیر

Hesa-ye Duwum-e Kohestan (dist) n حصه دوم کوهستان

Hesa-ye Duwum-e Panjsheyr (hist, dist) n حصه دوم پنجشیر

Hesarak (dist) n حصارک

hesitate vi دل زدن • تردید داشتن

hexagon n مسدس • شش ضلعی

hexagonal see hexagon

Hezb-e Islami (insurgent grp led by Hekmatyar) n حزب اسلامی

Hezb-e Wahdat (Hazarajat-based Shia pol party) n حزب وحدت

hiccough see hiccup

hiccup n هکک

hiccup vi هکک زدن

hidden adj مخفی • مستتر • پنهان • پوشیده
→ (absent) غایب
→ (deliberately) پوشانده
→ (secret) پنهان
→ hidden from view غایب از نظر

hide see conceal
→ hide-and-seek چشم پتکان

hiding place n مخفیگاه • مخفی گاه

high (exalted) adj والا • عالی

high (from drugs/alcohol) n کیف
→ be high کیف داشتن
→ get high کیف کردن

high (grand) adj لوی • بزرگ
→ (arch) برین

high (tall) (& adv) adj, adv بلند • مرتفع

high school n مکتب عالی • لیسه
→ Habibia High School (Kabul) لیسه حبیبیه
→ junior high school مکتب متوسط • مکتب متوسطه
→ Zarghuna (for f, Kabul) زرغونه

higher (better, superior) adj اعلی

highlander n کوه نشین

highness see & majesty
→ His Highness (title) والا حضرت

high-pitched (mus, tone) adj زیر

high-ranking adj عالی رتبه • بلند پایه

high-tech adj عصری

high-threat adj با تهدید بلند • پر مخاطره

highway n شاهراه

highwayman n راگیر

hijack vt ربودن • اختطاف کردن

Hijaz see Hejaz

hike (go hiking) v کوه گردی کردن

hiking n کوه گردی

hill n تپه

hilt n قبضه

hind part n دنبال

Hindi (lang) n هندی

hindrance n کارشکنی • عایق

Hindu (pers) n هندو

Hinduism n هندویزم • اهل هنود

hint (allusion) n ایما • رمز • تلمیح • تلویح

hint (insinuation) n تلمیح • تلویح

hip (anat) n خاصره

hire (appoint) vt مقرر کردن • گماشتن

hire (employ) vt کار دادن • استخدام کردن

hire, be hired, be appointed vi گماشته شدن

hiring (appointment) n تقرر

hiring (employment) n استخدام

hirsute adj پر موی

His Highness see Highness

historian n تاریخ دان
→ (scribe) مورخ

historical adj تاریخی

history n تاریخ

hit vt زدن • ضربه زدن • ضربت زدن • کوفتن <به چیزی>
→ hit & run جنگ و گریز

hitting n ضرب

HIV n اچ آی وی

hive (for bees) n کندو

hoard vt احتکار کردن

hoarded adj احتکاری

hoarding (esp grain) n احتکار

hobble along vi لنگیدن

hockey n هاکی

hog (pig) n خوک

hoist (flag) vt افراختن • افراشتن

423

hold (keep; store) vt نگاه کردن
→ hold down (limit) محدود کردن
holding (meeting) n انعقاد
hole n غار • سوف
→ cavity سوراخ
→ deep hole (well) چاه
→ hole in clothing زدگی
holey (full of holes) adj سوراخی
• سوراخ سوراخ • غار غار
holiday n رخصتی • تعطیل
holiness n تقدس
Holland n هالیند • هالند • هلند
hollow (& fig) adj پوچ مغز
hollow (fig) adj میان تهی • میان
خالی
hollow n شیله • کاواک • پوک
Holuliyya (hist, Musl sect) n حلولیه
• اهل تناسخ
holy adj آسمانی • سماوی
روحانی • مقدس • متبرک
→ (& pers) adj, n مقدس
→ most holy (God) قدوس
Holy Ghost see Holy Spirit
holy man (spiritual guide) n پیر •
مرشد
Holy Spirit (rel) n روح القدس
home economics n تدبیر منزل
home n خانه
→ entertainers' home (old Kabul)
خرابات
homeland n مولد • وطن • زادگاه •
میهن • مسقط • سرزمین • الراس
homeless adj بی خانه • آواره •
آواره گرد • در به در • بیجاشده
homeless pers n خانه به دوش
homelessness n آوارگی • آواره
گردی • بیجاشدگی • در به دری
homeowner n مالک خانه
homeownership n مالکیت خانه
hometown n موطن • وطن
homework n کار خانگی
homicide (lit) n قتل
homogeneity n تجانس
homogeneousness see
homogeneity
homonym n متشابه

homosexual adj, n هم جنس باز
→ (obs) کونی
→ (sodomite) لوطی
→ homosexual's father دله
homosexuality n هم جنس بازی
→ (sodomy) لواطت
Honduran (& pers) adj, n
هاندوراسی
Honduras n هاندوراس
honest (just) (& pers) adj, n درست
• درست کار • راست کار
یک رنگ • صادق →(frank)
honestly (in God's eyes) adv
عنداالله
honey n عسل
honeydew (on leaves) n شکرک
honeymoon n ماه عسل
honeysuckle (flower) n • الی سکن
هنی سکل
Hong Kong (geog) n هانگ کانگ
honk the car horn v هارن کردن
honor n افتخار • عرض • ناموس
→ Your Honor جناب عالی • عالی
جناب • جناب مبارک
honor (Pashtunwali) ننگ
honor (respect) n آبرو
honor v سرافراز کردن • سربلند
کردن
honor guard n گارد تشریفاتی
honorable (deed) adj دانهۀشرافت
honorable (pers) adj شرافتمند
honorable adj محترم • مشرف • با
شرف • کرام
honorable (respectable) adj
آبرومند
honorably (respectably) adv
آبرومندانه
honored (exalted) adj شریف •
سرافراز • سربلند
→ honored (Mecca) مکرم
→ Honored Birthday (Prophet's)
مولود شریف
honorific n لقب
honoring n تشریف
hoodlum (& adj) adj, n بدمعاش •
چاقوکش
hoof n سم
hook n قلاب • چنگک

hookah *n* چلم
→ حقه (arch)
hooker *see* prostitute
hoop *n* چنبر
hoopoe (bird) *n* • اتوتک • هدهد
وتوتک • پیوک • شانه سرک • مرغ
سلیمان
→ پوپک (arch)
hope *n* امید • آرزو • آرمان • چشم
داشت
→ امل (lit)
hope *v* امید کردن • امید داشتن • چشم داشتن
→ خدا کنه که <+ subj> I hope
hopeful (& pers) *adj, n* امیدوار •
آرزومند • خواهشمند
hopefully *adv* امیدوارانه •
آرزومندانه • خواهشمندانه
hopefulness *adv* امیدواری •
آرزومندی • خواهشمندی
hopeless *adj* ناامید
hopelessness *n* ناامیدی • یاس •
مایوس
horizon *n* افق
hormone *n* هورمون
horn (animal's) *n* شاخ
horn (on car) *n* هارن
→ صور (mus instr)
horned *adj* شاخ دار • شاخدار •
شاخی
→ ذوالقرنین two-horned (epithet)
hornet *n* زنبور گاو
horoscope *n* طالع
horrible *adj* خدا ناشناس • خدا
ناترس
horrified *adj* مدهوش
horrifying *adj* مدهش
horror *n* دهشت

horse (& chess) *n* اسپ
→ اسپ قزل bay
→ لخته colt
→ گله herd of horses
→ یراق horse's gear
→ مادیان mare
→ بیتل mare (colloq)
→ یابو pack horse
→ کرنگ • reddish-brown horse
اسپ کرنگ
→ اسپ بوز roan
→ خنگ white horse
horse herder *n* گله بان
horse racing *n* اسپدوانی • اسپ
دوانی
horseman *n* سوار • سوار کار
horseplay (colloq) *n* خرمستی
horseradish (Japanese) *n* ملی
horseshoe *n* نعل
horticulture *n* باغ داری
Hosila *see* Hoziila
hospitable *adj* مهمان نواز • مهمان
دار
hospital *n* شفاخانه
→ بستر شدن be hospitalized
→ بستری be hospitalized (colloq)
شدن
→ سرویس hospital department
→ mental hospital (arch)
دار المجانین
→ شفاخانۀ عقلی و mental hospital
عصبی
hospitality *n* میزبانی • مهمان
نوازی • پذیرایی
Hossein *see* Hussein
host *n* میزبان
hostage *n* گروگان
hostile (& adv) *adj, adv* • خصمانه
دشمنانه
hostile (in conflict) *adj* متخاصم
hostility (enmity) *n* • دشمنی
خصومت • عداوت
hot (burning) *adj* داغ • سوزان •
سرخ
→ hot <for sb> خواهان <کسی>
hot (smuggled) *adj* قاچاقی •
گریزی
hot (spicy) *adj* تند • تند مزه • تیز ؛
تند • تند خوی

Hotak (P tribe) n هوتک
Hotaki (& pers) adj هوتکی
hotel n هوتل
hot-tempered (pers) adj • تند خوی
تند مزاج
hot-water bottle n مشکوله
hound (Afghan) n تازی
hour n ساعت
hourglass n ساعت ریگی
houri n حوری • حور
house n خانه • منزل • بیت • کد
→ (of parliament/Congress) مجلس
→ (residence) منزل
→ House of Commons مجلس
عوام
→ House of Flowers (Presidential
Palace) گلخانه • قصر گل خانه
→ house of mourning ماتم سرا
→ Meshrano Jirga (upper house)
مشرانو جرگه
→ mud house خانه گلی
→ secluded house • خلوت خانه
خانه خلوت
→ Wolesi Jirga (lower house)
ولسی جرگه
house (sons; clan) n بنو
house (Sufi) n خانقاه
housecleaning n خانه تکانی
housefly n مگس
household n عایله • خانومان
فامیل
→ (takes pl verb) n pl خانواده
household members n pl متعلقین
housemate adj, n همخانه
housewarming party n بوریا کوبی
how about...? adv چطور ... ؟
→ (colloq) چطو ... ؟
how many times? adv چند دفعه ؟
how many? adv چند ؟
→ (colloq) چند دانه • چند تا ؟
how much? adv چقدر (= چقه) ؟
how? adv چگونه • چطور • چسان
→ (in excl) ... چی
howdah (on camel) n • هودج
عماری • کجاوی • محمل
howdah (on elephant) n هوده
however, but conj لاکن • لیکن
لکن • ولی • مگر • اما
→ (lit) مع هذا
426

Hozila (hist, central Afgh region) n
هوزیله • هوسیله
hubbub غالمغال • قالمقال • قیل و
قال
huddle (planning grp) n پره
hue (color) n رنگ
hue & cry n هیاهو
hug n آغوش • بغل
hug vt در آغوش کشیدن • در
آغوش گرفتن
hull (fuselage) n بدنه
Huma (f name) n هما
huma (legendary bird) n هما
human being n نفر • آدم • انسان
Human Immunodeficiency Virus
see HIV
human rights n حقوق انسان
→ Human Rights Watch مراقب
حقوق بشر
humaneness n آدمیت
humanitarian adj بشردوستانه
humanity (humankind) n • انسان
بشر • نوع بشر • بشریت • آدمیت
→ (human nature) ناسوت
Humayra (f name) n حمیرا
Humayun (hist, Mughal emperor
1508-56) نصیر الدین همایون
Humayun (m name) n همایون
humble adj • فروتن • خاضع
عاجز
→ (dervish-like) • درویش صفت
درویش نهاد
→ humble pers خاکسار
→ humble pers (fig) گربه مسکین
humbler (lit) adj احقر
humid adj مرطوب
humidity n رطوبت
humility n تواضع • افتادگی
humor (aqueous) n زلانیه
humor n فکاهی
humorist n فکاهی نویس
humoristic (lit) adj هزلی
humorous adj فکاهی
Hun (hist) n هون
→ White Hun (hist) هفتالی
hundred adj, n صد • سد
hundred thousand n لک
hundredth adj صدم
→ (lit, used before n) صدمین

Hungarian (& pers) adj, n مجار

Hungary n مجار

hunger n گرسنگی

hunger strike n قیام گرسنگی

hungry adj گرسنه

→ (colloq) گشنه

hunt n شکار

→ (arch) نخچیر

hunt v شکار کردن

→ (arch) نخچیر افگندن • نخچیر کردن

hunter n شکاری • شکار افگن • صیاد • صید افگن

hurl (cast) vt انداختن

hurricane n طوفان بحری

hurry n عجله

hurry v زودتر شدن • زودتر رفتن • عجله کردن

→ excl هله

hurt n درد

hurt vi درد کردن • درد داشتن

Husayn see & Hussein

Husayn Kheyl (ctr) n حسین خیل

husband n شوهر • زوج

→ (colloq) مرد

→ husband & wife زن و شوی • زوجین

hush money n حق السکوت • حق سکوت

hushed (left unsaid) adj مسکوت

Hussein (Prophet's grandson;m name) n حسین

Hut (month) n حوت

hut (shack) n کلبه

hyacinth (flower) n سنبل

hydrogen n هایدروجن

hydrogenous adj هایدروجنی

hydroxide (chem) n هایدروکساید

hyena n کفتار

hygiene n حفظ الصحه

hygienic (medical) adj صحی • صحیه

hymen (anat) n پرده بکارت

hyperbole n اغراق • مبالغه

hyperbolic adj مبالغه آمیز

hypnotism n خواب مصنوعی • خواب مقناطیسی • تنویم مقناطیسی • هپنوتزم • هپنوسس

hypocrisy n دورویی • دورنگی • ریا • ریاکاری • زرق

hypocrite (fig) n گرگ آتشی

hypocritical adj دورنگ • دوروی • دورویه • ریاکار

hypotenuse (math) n وتر • تار

hypothesis n فرضیه

hypothetical adj فرضی

hypothetically adv فرضاً

I

I pron من

→ (colloq) مه

→ (fig) اینجانب

i.e. adv, pron یعنی

IAW see in accordance with

Ibadat Khana (hist, Akbar's house of rel debate) n عبادت خانه

ibex n بز کوهی

ibid adv ایضاً

IC see international community

ice n یخ

ice chest n یخچال

ice cream n شیر یخ • آیس کریم

ice skate (v) n یخ مالک زدن

ice skating n یخ مالک

Iceland n آیس لیند

Icelander n آیس لیندی

Icelandic adj آیس لیندی

icicle n زنگوله

icterus (med) n یرقان • زردی

ID see identity

idat (Musl law) n عدت

idea n فکر • فکرت • مفکوره • مفهوم • اندیشه • تصور • تخیل

ideal n آرمان

idealism (philos) n اصالت تصور

identical adj یک سان • متحد الشکل

identification see identity

identify (recognize) vt شناختن

identity (identification) n هویت • تذکره • تذکره

→ identity card نفوس • ورقه هویت

identity (reputation) n شهرت

ideological adj ایدیولوژیک

ideology n جهان بینی • طرز تفکر • ایدیولوژی

427

idiom (term) *n* اصطلاح

idiomatic (colloquial) *adj* اصطلاحی • مصطلح

idiot *n* احمق • • جاهل • نادان • نافهم

IDLG, Independent Directorate of Local Goverance *n* ریاست مستقل ارگان های محلی

idol *n* بت • معبود • بغ
→ The Blue Idol & the Red Idol (poem) خنگ بت و سرخ بت

idolater *n* بت پرست

idolatrous *adj* بت پرست

idolatry *n* بت پرستی

IDP see internally-displaced pers

IED *n* آله منفجره تعبیه شده

if <+ subj> *conj* اگر
→ (colloq) اگه • گر

if only <+ past subj> *adv* کاش • کاش که • کاشکی

iftar (meal) *n* افطار • فطر

ignite (light) *v* بل کردن

ignite (set on fire) *vt* آتش زدن • آتش کردن

ignoble *adj* پست • دنی

ignominious *adj* افتضاح آمیز • فتضح آور • رسوا • رسوایی آور • فضیحت آمیز • فضیحت آور

ignominy *n* افتضاح • رسوایی • فضیحت

ignorance (stupidity) *n* غباوت

ignorance (esp in pre-Musl society) *n* جاهلی

ignorant *adj* جاهل • نادان • نافهم • جاهلانه • غول • غبی

ignore *vt* تجاهل کردن • تجاهل نمودن • صرف نظر کردن <از چیزی> • جنگی بودن • جنگی شدن

Ikhwan (hist, Saudi Wahhabist holy warriors; cf. Muslim Brotherhood) *n* اخوان

ill *adj* مریض • بیمار • ناجور • ناخوش

illegal *adj* غیر قانونی

illegitimate child *n* حرامی

illiterate *adj* ناخوان • بیسواد

illness *n* مریضی • بیماری • عارضه
→ slight illness کسالت

illuminate *vt* تاباندن

illusion *n* مجاز

illusory *adj* مجازی

image *n* تصویر

imaginary *adj* مستعار • خیالی

imagination *n* تصور • تخیل • خیال • مفکوره

imaginative *adj* تصوری

imagine (suppose) *vt* تصور کردن

imagine (think) *vt* پنداشتن

imam (rel) *n* امام

Imam Saheb (dist) *n* امام صاحب

imamate (rel) *n* امامت

Imami Shiite see Twelver

imbibe see drink

IMF *n* صندوق وجهی بین المللی

imitate (mimic) *v* تقلید کردن

imitation (manmade) *adj* مصنوعی

imitation (mimicry) *n* تقلید

imitation (substitute) *n* بدل

imitator *n* مقلد

immature (childish) (& adv) *adj, adv* کودکانه • طفلانه

immature (childish) *adj* طفلانه

immature (wine) *adj* نارس • نارسیده

immeasurable *adj* بیکران

immediate *adj* فوری • عاجل

immediately *adv* فوراً • دفعتاً • ناگاه

immigrant *adj, n* مهاجر

immigrate *v* مهاجرت کردن

immigration *n* مهاجرت • هجرت

imminent *adj* قریب الوقوع

immodest woman (insult) *n* توتا • چشم

immolation *n* قربان
→ self-immolation خودسوزی

immortal *adj* فنا ناپذیر
→ immortal (God) لایموت

immortality *n* فنا ناپذیری

immune (& med) *adj* مصون • مصئون • محفوظ
→ immune system سیستم معافیت

immunity (& med) *n* مصونیت

→ immunity to a disease معافیت از یک مرض

impatient *adj* بی حوصله

imperative mood (gram) *n* وجه امری

→ negative imperative نهی

imperfect *adj* ناقص

imperial *adj* • شاهنشاهی • امپراتوری

imperialism *n* استعمار • امپریالزم

imperialist *n* استعمار گر • امپریالست

imperialistic *adj* استعماری • امپریالستی

imperious (& adv) *adj, adv* آمرانه

impermissible *adj* غیر مجاز

impervious (to argument) *adj* نفوذ ناپذیر

implement (tool, device) *n* آله • آلت • افزار • ابزار • دست افزار

→ (colloq) اوزار

implement *vt* تنفیذ کردن

implementation *n* تنفیذ • نفاذ • تطبیق

implication (inclusion) *n* تضمن

implication (metonymy) *n* • کنایه کنتره

→ implication & innuendo کنتره و کنایه

implying *adj* متضمن

import *v* وارد کردن

importance *n* اهمیت

important *adj* مهم

→ important matters مهمات

imported *adj* وارداتی

imports *n pl* واردات

importune *vt* تقاضا کردن

impose <sth on sb> *vt* تحمیل کردن <چیزی را بر کسی>

imposition *n* تحمیل

impossibility *n* • محال • مستحیل • ناممکن

impossible *adj* ناممکن • غیر ممکن • مستحیل • محال

impostor *n* شیاد

impractical (pers) *adj* هیچ کار

impregnate *vt* آبستن • آبستن کردن • نمودن <کسی را>

impregnation *n* تلقیح • القاح

impression *n* اثر • تاثیر

→ (print) طبع • چاپ

→ make an impression <on sth> نشان انگشت کردن <به کسی>

impressionable *adj* سریع التاثر

impressive *adj* تاثیر • مؤثر • موثر • بخش

imprisoned *adj* زندانی

imprisonment *n* قید • حبس

improbable *adj* غیر احتمالی

→ be improbable از ذهن دور بودن • دور از ذهن بودن

improper *adj* بیجا

improve *vi* بهتر شدن

improve *vt* تکامل • تکامل دادن • بخشیدن

improvement *n* پیشبرد • بهبود

improvisation *n* بداهت

→ by improvisation بداهتاً

improvised explosive device *see* IED

imprudent *adj* بی تدبیر

impudence *n* گستاخی • بی رویی

impudent *adj* • گستاخانه • گستاخ خیر

→ (fig) سفید چشم • چشم سفید • بی روی

→ (outspoken) زبان دراز

in (at) *prep* در • به

in (inside) *prep* داخل • درون

in (into) (arch) *prep* اندر

in accordance with *prep* با رعایت <چیزی>

in order to do <sth> *adv* به قصد <چیزی>

in order to *prep* بمنظور • بغرض • تا • که • تا که

in spite of <sth> *prep* علیرغم <چیزی>

in the act *adv* بالفعل

inadvertence *n* خواب خرگوش

inadvertently *adv* نادانسته • ندانسته • سهواً

inanimate (not living) *adj* غیر ذیروح

inaugural *adj* افتتاحی

429

inaugurate (open) vt • گشایش دادن • افتتاح کردن
→ be inaugurated • گشایش یافتن • افتتاح شدن
inauguration (opening) n • گشایش • افتتاح
inauspicious adj بد شگون
incantation (rel) n دم و دعا
incantation (spell) n • جنتر • رقیه • ساحری • افسون • افسونگری • جادوگری
incapable adj • قاصر • بیعرضه
incense n بخور
incentive n • انگیزه • محرک • سائقه • مشوق
→ (reward)
incessantly adv دمادم • دم به دم
inch (unit of length) n انچ
→ one-eighth of an inch سوت
incidence (occurrence) n • وقوع • حدوث
incident (event) n • بر خورد • عارضه
incident (mishap) n • حادثه • واقعه
incidental (occasional) adj عارضی
incidentally (by the way) adv • راستی • نا گفته نمانه
incisors (teeth) n pl ثنایا
incite war v جنگ انداختن
inciter n محرک
inclination n تمایل
→ (fig) نبض
→ (tendency) • میل • میلان
incline (slope) n میلان
inclined adj متمایل
included adj • مندرج • مندمج
including (even, even if) adv حتی
including adj • به شمول • شامل • متضمن • به انضمام <چیزی>
inclusion n • شمول • تضمن
incombustible adj • احتراق ناپذیر • غیر قابل احتراق
income n • درآمد • عایدات
→ source/item of income مدرک
income tax n مالیت بر عایدات
incompatible adj • متناقض • نقیض
incompetent adj بیعرضه
incomplete adj ناقص
inconclusive adj نافرجام
incorrigible adj اصلاح ناپذیر
430

increase n • افزایش • ازدیاد • تکثیر • زیادت • ارتقا • ارتقاء
increase vt • افزودن • ارتقا دادن
→ (upward) • بالا بردن • بالا رفتن
increasing n تزیید
incurable adj • درمان ناپذیر • بی درمان
→ incurable pain درد بی درمان
indebted adj قرض دار
indebtedness n قرض داری
indecency n قباحت
indecision n دو دلی
indefinite (gram) adj • مبهم • نکره
independence n • آزادی • استقلال • حریت
independent adj • آزاد • مستقل • سر پای خود
Independent Directorate of Local Goverance see IDLG
independently adv مستقلاً
index n • فهرست • فهرست اعلام • نشانه • نشانی • اندکس
India n • هندوستان • هند
Indian (national of India) n هندی
Indian (Native American) n • بومی امریکایی
Indian (of India) adj هند
Indian Ocean n بحر هند
indicate vt نمایاندن
indication n • اشاره • نشان دهنده
indicative mood (gram) n • وجه اخباری
indicator n • نمایانگر • نشان دهنده
indifference (fig) n • سردی • برودت
indifferent (depressing) adj • سرد • خنک • یخ
indifferent (unconcerned) adj • بی پروا • خون سرد • دل <کسی>
→ become indifferent سرد شدن
indigenous adj • بومی • محلی
indigent see poor
indignation (anger) n • قهر • خشم • غضب • غیظ
indignation (offense) n رنجش
indigo (plant, dye) n نیل
indigo solution n نیلاب
indirect object (gram) n مفعول غیر مستقیم

indiscreet adj زبان دراز

indisputable adj یقینی

indisputably adv یقیناً • بی گفت و گو • بیسخن • به یقین

indistinct adj سردرگم

individual (person) n نفر • شخص • فرد

Indo-Aramean adj هندی آرامی

Indo-Aryan see Indo-Iranian

Indochina (geog) n هند و چین

Indochinese adj هند و چینی

Indo-European adj هندی اوروپایی

Indo-Iranian adj هندی آریانی • هندی آریایی

Indonesia n اندونیزیا

Indonesian adj اندونیزیایی

indubitably adv بیسخن • بی گفت و گو

Indus (River) n اندس • سند

industrial adj صنعتی

industrious adj پرکار • کارکن

industry (& craft) n صناعت • صنعت

inebriated adj نشه • مست

inebriation n نشه

inefficient adj هیچ کار • بیعرضه

inevitable adj اجتناب ناپذیر • غیر قابل اجتناب

inevitably adv ناچار • بناچار

inexpensive adj ارزان

inexperience n خامی • خام کاری

inexperienced adj بی تجربه
→ خام • خام کار (colloq)

infamous adj نام بد • بد نامی

infamy n نام بدی

infancy n طفلی • طفولیت • کودکی

infant n طفل • اولاد • کودک
→ شیر خوار (nursling)

infantry (mil) n قوای زمینی

infantryman n عسکر پیاده

infect vi سرایت کردن

infectious adj ساری • عفونی • مسری
→ (colloq)

infer v نتیجه گیری کردن • استمنا کردن

inference n استمنا • برداشت

inferior (in rank) adj مادون • زیر دست

inferior adj دنی

inferiority n کهتری

inferiority complex n عقده حقارت • عقده کهتری

inferno see hell

infertile adj عقیم • نازای

infidel (apostate) n ملحد

infidel (unbeliever) n کافر • بی دین
→ declaration of fellow Musl to be an infidel تکفیر

infiltration n نفوذ

infinitival adj مصدری

infinitive (gram) n مصدر

infinitive form n شکل مصدری

infinitive mood (gram) n وجه مصدری

infix (gram) n میان وند

inflammation n سوزش • التهاب
→ be inflamed سوزش کردن

inflate (w/air) vt بر باد دادن • بر باد کردن

inflation (econ) n تورم پولی • تورم قیمتی

inflation (w/air) n باد

inflected (gram) adj تصریفی

inflexibility n جمود

inflexible adj یک پهلو

influence (authority) n نفوذ

influence (effect) n تاثیر • اثر

influence (spiritual) n جذبه
→ have influence <on sb/sth> نفوذ داشتن <سر کسی/چیزی>

influential (authoritative) adj با نفوذ
→ influential people اهل حل و عقد

influential (spiritually) adj با جذبه

influenza n انفلونزا • گریپ

inform <of sth> v معلومات دادن • خبر دادن <از چیزی> • مطلع نمودن • مطلع کردن

information n معلومات • استخبارات • اطلاع • آگاهی • وقوف

information officer n مسئول مطبوعات

informed adj آگاه • با خبر • مطلع • وارد • واقف

informer (spy) n مخبر • جاسوس

infrared adj ماورای حمره • ماورای سرخ

infrastructure n زیر بنا

431

infrequently *adv* دیر دیر • به ندرت
infringement (law, principle) *n*
نقض
infuriate *vt* خون به جوش آوردن
→ become infuriated خون به
جوش آمدن
ingratitude *n* ناسپاسی • کفران
ingredients *n pl* ترکیبات • اجزا
inhabitant (resident) *n* باشنده • اهل
→ inhabitants (population) نفوس
inhalation *n* بخور • شهیق
inherent *adj* ضمنی
inherently *adv* ضمناً
inherit *v* میراث گرفتن • میراث
خوردن • به ارث گرفتن
inheritance *n* میراث • ارثیه •
وراثت
→ by inheritance ارثاً
inherited *adj* میراثی • موروثی •
موروث • ارثی • ارثیه
initially *adv* در اول • درنخست
initiative *n* ابتکار • ابداع • نوآوری •
پیش قدمی
→ taking the initiative
inject (give injection) *v* سوزن زدن
• پیچکاری کردن • زرق کردن
injection (shot) *n* پیچکاری • زرق
• تزریق
injunction *n* منع • ممانعت • قدغن
• حکم
injure *v* صدمه زدن • گزند رساندن
injured (& pers) *adj, n* زخمی •
افگار • مجروح
→ (colloq) اوگار
injury *n* زخم • جراحت • ریش •
آسیب • خساره • گزند • زیان •
صدمه • ضرر
injustice *n* بیداد • جور • ستم • ظلم
• حیف • افسوس • دریغ
ink *n* رنگ
inlaid work *n* خاتم کاری • خاتم
سازی
inn (caravanserai) *n* سرای
innate *adj* غریزی
inner *adj* درونی • داخلی
innkeeper *n* سرایبان • سرای دار
→ (colloq) سرایوان
innocence *n* معصومیت
innocent (& adv) *adj, adv*
معصومانه
432

innocent *adj* معصوم • بیگناه
innovation (rel, neg) *n* بدعت •
کثره
innuendo *n* کنایه • کثره
innumerable *adj* از حصر بیرون
inorganic *adj* غیر عضوی
inquest (official) *n* تحقیق
inquire (officially) *v* استعلام کردن
inquire *v* سوال کردن • پرسان
کردن • پرسیدن • بازپرسیدن • جویا
شدن
inquirer *n* پرسنده
inquiring *adj* جویا
inquiry *n* سوال • پرسان
→ (official) استعلام
→ (search) جستجو
→ inquiry about sb بازخواست
insane (& adv) *adj, adv* جنون آمیز
insane (& pers) *adj, n* دیوانه •
مجنون
insanity *n* اختلال • اختلال دماغ •
خلل دماغ • دیوانگی • جنون
insatiable (hungry) (colloq) *adj*
گرسنه چشم
inscription (stone) *n* سنگ نوشته
insect *n* حشره ٫ -ها/حشرات
insecticide *adj, n* حشره کش
inseminate *v* تلقیح کردن
insemination *n* القاح • تلقیح
inseparable *adj* ملزوم
insert *v* ادغام کردن
inserted *adj* مندرج • مندمج
insertion *n* ادغام
inside *n* درون • داخل • باطن •
مابین • قلب
inside *prep* داخل • درون • در بین
• میان
inside-out *adj* چپه شده
insight (understanding) *n* بصیرت
• بصارت • ژرفبینی
insightful *adj* ژرفبین
insignificant *adj* جزئی • سطحی •
ناچیز
insincere (hypocritical) *adj* دورنگ
• دوروی • ریاکار
insincere (self-interested) *adj*
مطلب آشنا
insincere (w/empty words) *adj*
زبانی • شفاهی
insincere *adj* ریاکار

insincerity *n* • دورویی • دورنگی • ریا • ریاکاری • زرق

insinuating *adj* کنایه آمیز

insist *v* اصرار کردن • اصرار ورزیدن

insistence *n* اصرار

insistent *adj* سر سخت
→ be insistent اصرار داشتن

insofar as *phrs* تاجایکه

insole *n* پتک

insolence *n* گستاخی

insolent *adj* گستاخ • گستاخانه
→ (outspoken) زبان دراز

insolvency *n* ورشکستگی

insolvent *adj* • ورشکست • ورشکسته
→ become insolvent ورشکست شدن • ورشکسته شدن

insouciant *adj* لاابالی • بی پروا

inspect (conduct search) *vt* تفتیش کردن
→ be inspected • بررسی شدن • بازرسی شدن

inspect (examine) *n* معاینه کردن

inspect (investigate) *vt* بررسی کردن • بازرسی کردن

inspection (investigation) *n* • بررسی • بازرسی

inspection (med) *n* • معاینه • معاینات

inspection (search) *n* تفتیش

inspector *n* تفتیش

install (set up) *vt* نصب کردن
→ installation & setup نصب و منتاژ

installation (setup) *n* نصب

installment (payment) *n* قسط

instance (occasion) *n* مورد

instance (repetition) *n* • دفعه • بار • کرت • مرتبه • نوبت

instant *n* • لحظه • دم

instead of *prep* • به عوض • به جای • در عوض • در بدل

instinct *n* • سلیقه • غریزه

instinctive *adj* غریزی

institute *see* institution
→ Dar ul-Ulum (institute for advanced Arabic & rel studies) دار العلوم

institution *n* موسسه

instruct (order) *v* • سفارش دادن • هدایت کردن

instruct (train) *vt* تعلیم دادن

instructed (ordered) *adj* سفارشی

instruction (explanation) *n* تفهیم

instruction (order) *n* • سفارش • هدایت • ارشاد • تلقین
→ (document) هدایت نامه

instructional *adj* تدریسی

instructor *n* • معلم • آموزگار
→ (f) معلمه
→ (in rel school) مدرس

instrument (tool, device) *n* • آله • آلت • افزار • ابزار
→ (colloq) اوزار

instrumentalist (mus) *n* موسیقی نواز

insufficiency *n* کمبود

insufficient *adj* کمبود

insulated *adj* عایق دار

insulation *n* عایق کاری

insulator *n* عایق

insulin (med) *n* انسولین

insult *n* • اهانت • توهین

insult *v* گستاخی کردن

insulting *adj* • اهانت آمیز • توهین آمیز • گستاخانه

insults
→ bag made of whole skin of lamb or goat (form) سناچ
→ blockhead لوده
→ coward شیشه دل
→ hypocrite گرگ آتشی
→ mice-eater موش خور
→ parrot-eye توتا چشم
→ runt لچک
→ son of a bitch بی پدر
→ uncircumcised (m) نابرید

insurance *n* بیمه

insure (underwrite) *vt* بیمه کردن

insurer (underwriter) *n* بیمه کننده

insurgency *n* • بغاوت • یاغیگری
→ (milder) شورش

insurgent *n* باغی
→ (milder) شورشی

integer (math) *n* عدد صحیح

integrity (character) *n* • رشاد • خوی

integrity (wholeness) *n* تمامیت

433

íntellect n هوش • ذهن • عقل
intellectual adj عقلی
intelligence (cleverness) n ذكاوت
• ذكا
intelligence (info) n آگاهی • اطلاع
• وقوف
→ Intelligence Department (hist,
until 1973) ریاست ضبط احوالات
intelligence (prudence) n هوشیاری
intelligence n تیز • خرد • عقل
هوشی
intelligent ("gets it") adj فهیم
intelligent (clever) adj تیز • ذكی
هوش
intelligent (prudent) adj, n هوشیار
• هوشمند
→ be intelligent ذكاوت داشتن
intelligent (quick to learn) adj
تیزفهم
intelligent (wise) (& pers) adj, n
عاقل • خردمند
intelligible adj معقّول
intend v قصد داشتن • خیال داشتن
• تصمیم داشتن
→ intend to do <sth> در صدد
<چیزی> بودن
intense adj شدید
intensity n شدت
intent (law) n مفهوم
intent (purpose) see intention
intention n قصد • صدد • اراده •
مطلب • هدف • منظور • مقصد •
مقصود • مرام
intentionally adv قصداً • ارادتاً •
عمداً
→ (colloq) به قصد
inter (bury) vt دفن كردن • گور
كردن • به خاك سپردن
interagency adj میان اداری
intercession n وساطت •
میانجیگری
intercourse (sex) n مقاربت • جماع
• مجامعت

interest (concern) n علاقه • علاقه
یی • دل چسپی
→ (on loan) مفاد • فایده
→ (usury) ربا • ربح • سود
→ having common interests
مشترك المنافع
→ interests (in sth) منافع
→ pursue one's own interests (fig)
كباب خویش را پختن
→ self-interest غرض • نفع •
منفعت
interested (in sth) (& pers) adj, n
علاقه مند • ذوقمند
interesting adj جالب • شنیدنی •
دلچسپ
interfere <in sth> vi مداخله كردن
<به چیزی>
interference n مداخله
interim adj عبوری • موقت
interior adj درونی • داخلی
interior n داخله • درون • میان •
ضمن • وسط • صمیم • بطن
→ Interior Ministry وزارت داخله
interjection n ندا
interlocutor n همصحبت
intermediary adj رابط
intermediary n میانجی • میانگی •
میان گی
intermediate adj متوسط • مابینی
intermediate v میانجیگری كردن •
میانگی كردن • میان گی كردن
interment n دفن
intermission n تفریح • وقفه
intermittent (fever) adj متناوب •
نوبتی
intermittently adv به تناوب • به
وقفه ها • بالتناوب
internal adj درونی • داخلی
internally-displaced person n
بیجاشده داخلی
international adj بین المللی
→ international community جامعه
بین المللی
International Monetary Fund see
IMF
International Police Coordination
Board n بورد هماهنگی بین المللی
پولیس

International Security Assistance
Force *see* ISAF

Internet *n* انترنت

interpersonal *adj* ذات البيني

interpretation (explanation) *n*
گزارش

interpretation (lang) *n* ترجمه

interpretation (phrasing) *n* تعبیر

interpretation (rel) *n* اجتهاد

interpreter (expounder) *n* شارح

interpreter (expounder) *see &* mufti

interpreter (lang) *n* ترجمان

interrogate *v* سوال کردن • سوال

پیچ کردن • پرسان کردن

interrogative *adj* سوالی • سوالیه •
پرسشی

interrupt *vt* مزاحمت کردن •
مزاحمت ایجاد کردن • اخلال کردن

→ pers who interrupts مزاحم

interrupted (segmental) *adj* مقطع

intersection *n* چاراهی • چارراه •
چهار راهی

→ (math) قاطع

Inter-Services Intelligence *see* ISI

interval (distance) *n* مسافه • فاصله

interval (time) *n* مدت • فاصله •
مسافه

intervene <in sth> *vi* مداخله کردن
<به چیزی>

intervention *n* مداخله

interview (& media) *n* مصاحبه

interview (& media) *vt* مصاحبه
کردن

intestines (anat) *n* روده

intimate (close) *adj* دم ساز

intimate (pers) *n* مقرب

intimidate *v* تخویف کردن

intimidation (threat) <against sth> *n*
تهدید <به ضد چیزی>
تخویف • ارعاب (bullying) ←

intolerable *adj* تحمل ناپذیر • غیر
قابل تحمل

intoxicated (& pers) *adj, n* • مست
نشه

intoxicated *adj* سرشار

intoxicating *adj* سکرآور • مستی
آور

intoxication *n* سکر • مستی • کیف

intractable *adj* گردن کش

intransitive (gram) *adj* غیر • لازم
متعدی

intricate *adj* پیچ در پیچ • پیچیده •
مغلق

intrigue (plot) *n* دسیسه • توطنه

intrinsic (natural) *adj* طبیعی

introduce (rules) *vt* وضع کردن

introduce <sb to sb else> *vt* معرفی
کردن <کسی را به کسی دیگر> •
شناختاندن

→ be introduced <to VIP> پیش
شدن <نزد کسی>

introduced (acquainted) *adj* معرفی

introducer (presenter) *n* معرف

introduction (of rules) *n* وضع

introduction (prologue) *n* مقدمه

introverted *adj* درون گرا

intumescence (med) *n* آماس •
پندیدگی • تورم • ورم

intumescent (med) *adj* متورم •
آماسیده • پندیده • ورم کرده

inventory *n* موجودی

inverse *adj* واژگون • واژگونه •
واژون • معکوس
→ (arch) نگون

inversely *adv* معکوسا

invert *vt* معکوس کردن

inverted *adj* معکوس • واژگون
→ (arch) نگون

invest *vi* سرمایه گذاری کردن

investigate (& research) *v* تحقیق
کردن

investigate (inspect) *vt* بررسی
کردن • بازرسی کردن

investigation (& research) *n* تحقیق

investigation (inspection) *n*
بازرسی • بررسی • بازجویی •
رسیدگی

investment *n* سرمایه گذاری

investor (pers) *n* سرمایه گذار

invigorate *vt* جوان کردن

invisible (mysterious) *adj* غیبی

invitation *n* مهمانی • دعوت •
ضیافت
→ invitation letter دعوت نامه

invite *vt* مهمان کردن • دعوت
کردن

invocation (prayer) *n* دعا

invoice (bill) *n* بل

435

invoice n صورت حساب
involved (embroiled) adj درگیر
involved adj دخیل
→ be involved <in sth> دخالت
داشتن <در چیزی>
involvement n دخالت
iodine (element) n آیودین
→ tincture of iodine تینچر آیودین
IOU (colloq) n حجت • سند
IPCB see International Police
Coordination Board
Iran n ایران
Iranian (& pers) adj, n ایرانی
Iraq n عراق
Iraqi (& pers) adj, n عراقی
Ireland n آیرلیند
iris (flower) n زنبق
Irish (& pers) adj, n • آیرلیندی
آیرلندی
IRoA (Islamic Republic of
Afghanistan) n ج.ا.ا.
iron (flatiron) n اتو
→ (colloq) اطو
iron (metal) n آهن • چونه
→ cast iron چدن
→ made of cast iron چدنی
iron adj آهنین
Iron Curtain n پرده آهنین
iron ore n سنگ آهن
ironclad (armored) adj زره پوش
ironsmith n آهنگر • حداد
irreconcilable adj آشتی ناپذیر
irregular (gram) adj سماعی • غیر
قیاسی
irrelevant adj از بحث خارج
irremediable adj چاره ناپذیر •
درمان ناپذیر • بی درمان
irrevocable adj برگشت ناپذیر •
غیر قابل برگشت
irrigated adj مشروب
→ non-irrigated للمی
irrigation canal n نهر
irritating n ملال انگیز • ملالت
انگیز
irritation (med) n سوزش • التهاب
→ be irritated سوزش کردن
irritation n ملال • ملالت

ISAF, International Security
Assistance Force n آیساف • قوای
امنیتی مساعدت بین المللی
Isfahan (city) n اصفهان
Ishmael (bibl) n اسماعیل
ISI, Inter-Services Intelligence n
آی اس آی
Islam (rel) n اسلام
→ Five Pillars of Islam پنج ارکان
اسلام
Islam Qala (border crossing) n
اسلام قعله
Islamabad (city) n اسلام آباد
Islamic Republic of Afghanistan
(see & IRoA) n جمهوریت اسلامی
افغانستان
Islamic Unity (hist, pol mvmt) n
اتحاد اسلامی
Islamism n مسلمانی
Islamize vt مسلمان ساختن
island n جزیره
islander n جزیره نشین
Ismaili Shiite community
(collectively) n اسماعیلیه • باطنیه
Ismaili Shiite see Sevener
isolated adj خلوت
isolation n خلوت
isosceles adj متساوی الساقین
Israel n اسرائیل
Israeli (& pers) adj, n اسرائیلی
Israelite (& pers) see Hebrew;
Israeli
issuance (export) n صدور
issuance (publication) n • انتشار
نشر
issuance (sending out) n صادر
issue (export) v صادر کردن
issue (matter) n مسئله • قضیه
issue (publish) vt منتشر کردن
issued (printed) adj منتشر
isthmus (geog) n خاکنا
it, he, she pron او
Italian (& pers) adj, n • اتالیایی
ایتالیایی • ایتالوی
Italy n اتالیا • ایتالیا • ایطالیا
itch (itchiness) n خارش
itch (have an itch) vi خارش داشتن
item (entry) n قلم
Ithna Shiite see Twelver

436

itinerary *n* مسیر • سفرنامه
ivory *n* عاج
izar (f garment) *n* ازار

J

Jabal us-Saraj (dist) *n* جبل السراج
jack (cards) *n* غلام
→ jack of diamonds غلام خشت
jack (car, truck) *vt* جک بالا کردن
jack (tire jack) *n* جک تیر
jackal *n* شغال
jackdaw (bird) *n* زاغچه
jacket (waist-length) *n* کرتی
→ sheepskin jacket پوستین
jade (< F) *n* ژاد
Jadi (month) *n* جدی
Jadran (ctr) *n* جدران
Jaghatu (ctr, dist) *n* جغتو
Jaghuri (dist) *n* جاغوری
Jaffa (city) *n* یافا
Jaji (dist) *n* جاجی
Jaji Maydan (dist) *n* جاجی میدان
Jahan Gusha *see* Genghis Khan
Jahangir (hist, Mughal emperor
1605-1627) نور الدین جهانگیر
Jahiliyyah (pre-Musl era) *n* جاهلیت
• دورۀ جاهلی
jail *n* زندان • بندی خانه • محبس
Jakarta *n* جاکارتا
Jalal (m name) *n* جلال
Jalalabad (seat, dist) *n* جلال آباد
Jalalzai (P tribe) *n* جلالزی
Jalreyz (dist) *n* جلریز
jam (preserves) *n* مربا
Jam (hist, Zor legend, king) *n* جم
→ Jam's golden bowl جام جم
Jamaica *n* جمیکا
Jamaican (& pers) *adj, n* جمیکایی
Jamal (m name) *n* جمال
Jamiat-e Islami (Musl pol grp) *n*
جمعیت اسلامی
Jamil (m name) *n* جمیل
Jamsheyd (m name) *n* جمشید
Jamsheydi (Aimaq tribe) *n* جمشیدی
jangling *n* شرنگ
Jangnama (hist) *n* جنگ نامه
Jani Kheyl (dist) *n* جانی خیل
janissary (hist) *n* ینیچری

January *n* جنوری
Japan *n* جاپان
Japanese (& pers) *adj, n* جاپانی
Japheth (bibl) *n* یافث
jasmine (flower) *n* یاسمن • یاسمین
• سمن
→ jasmine-scented سمنبوی
→ jasmine-white سمنبر
jasper (mineral) *n* یشم
jaundice (med) *n* یرقان • زردی
Jauza (month) *n* جوزا • دوپیکر
Java (island) *n* جاوا
javelin *n* نیزه
→ (arch) ژوبین
jaw *n* اَلاشه • چنه
→ pers's nose, mouth, & jaw پوز
و چنه
Jawand (dist) *n* جوند
Jaxartes (hist) سیر دریا
Jaweyd (m name) *n* جاوید
jealous (& pers) *adj, n* حسود
jealousy (envy) *n* حسد • حسودی
→ be jealous حسد بردن • حسد
خوردن
jealousy (rivalry) *n* رقابت
Jeddah (city, port) *n* جده
jeer *vt* نیش زدن
jeering *adj* نیش دار
Jelga (dist) *n* جلگه
→ *see* & Jelga Nahrin
Jelga Nahrin (dist, alt Khaja
Hejran) جلگه نهرین
jeopardize *vt* به مخاطره انداختن
به مخاطره افگندن
jerib (unit of area) *n* جریب
Jerusalem *n* بیت المقدس • القدس
قدس • اورشلیم
jest *n* مزاح
→ (lit) هزل
→ in jest به مزاح
→ in jest (colloq) به مزاق
jest *vi* مزاح کردن
Jesuit (rel) *n* یسوعی
Jesus (bibl) *n* یسوع • عیسی
→ Jesus Christ حضرتِ عیسی
→ spirit of God (epithet) روح الله
jet (plane) *n* جت
Jethro (bibl) *n* شعور

437

jewel n يراق • زيور • گوهر
→ ring's main jewel نگين • نگينه
jeweler n جواهر فروش • گوهری • جوهری
jewelled adj جواهر • جواهر نشان • گوهر نشان نگار
→ (colloq) دانه نشان
→ jewelled articles جواهر آلات
jewelry n يراق • زيور • جواهر
→ jewelry shop جواهر فروشی
Jewish adj يهودی
Jewish pers n يهودی • يهود
→ (colloq) جهود • موسوی • جوود
jihad (rel) n مجاهدت • جهاد
→ related to jihad جهادی
jihadist n جهادگر
jinn n جن
jinni جنی
jirga (council) n جرگه
job n چوکی • شغل
jockey n سوار کار
jocular (lit) adj هزل آميز
John (bibl) n يوحنا
John the Baptist (bibl) n يحیی
join (attach) vi پيوستن
join (become member) v عضويت حاصل کردن
joined (attached) adj ملحق
joiner (carpenter) n نجار
joint (& adv) adj, adv شريکی
→ of joint responsibility تضامنی
joint (anat) n بند • مفصل
→ finger/toe joint بند انگشت
joint (pipe) n زانو خم
joint (shared) adj مشترک
Joint Chiefs of Staff see chairman
Joint Provincial Coordination Center n مرکز هماهنگی مشترک ولايتی
Joint Regional Coordination Center n مرکز هماهنگی مشترک ساحوی
joint responsibility n تضامن
→ of joint responsibility تضامنی
joint venture n شرکت مختلط
jointly adv شريکی • مشترکا
joke n پرزه • فکاهی • مزاح
→ (colloq) مزاق
→ (lit) هزل

joke vi مزاح کردن
joker (& cards; neg) n جيک • جيکر • جوکر
joker n مزاحی • مزاقی
→ (colloq) به مزاح
jokingly adv به مزاح
jonquil (flower) n نسرين
Jordan n اردن
Joseph see Yosuf
Joshua (bibl) يسوع • عيسی
journal (periodical) n مجله • ژورنال
journalism n جريده نگاری • جريده نويسی • روزنامه نويسی • ژورناليزم
journalist n خبرنگار • جريده نگار • جريده نويس • روزنامه نويس • روزنامه نگار • ژورنالست • ژورناليست
journalistic adj مطبوعاتی • ژورناليستی
journey n سفر • مسافرت
jowl (colloq) n کومه • گونه • رخساره
Jowzjan (province) n جوزجان
joy n سرور • مسرت • خوشی • شادمانی • وجد
JPCC see Joint Provincial Coordination Center
JRCC see Joint Regional Coordination Center
Judaic see Jewish
Judaism n يهوديت
Judas tree n ارغوان
judge n قاضی
judgment (law) n قضاوت • حکم
judgment (by eminent Musl jurist) n اجتهاد
judicial adj عدلی • قضايی • قضائی
judiciary see judicial
jug (for water) n کوزه
jug (sm pitcher) n جک
→ broken jug تيکر
juggle (deceive) n حقه بازی کردن
juggler (deceiver) n آدم حقه باز
jugular vein n شاه رگ

438

juice (extract) *n* عصاره
→ cooking juices (korma) لعاب
→ gastric juices عصاره معده
juice (fruit) *n* آب میوه • شربت
→ fruit juice syrup شربت • آب میوه
juicy *adj* پرآب
julep *n* جلاب
July *n* جولای • جولایی
jump *n* خیز • جست
jump *vi* خیز زدن • خیز کردن • جست زدن
→ jumping & leaping جست و خیز • خیز و جست
Junbish-e Meli (pol mvmt) *n* جنبش ملی
June *n* جون
jungle (wilderness) *n* جنگل
junior high school *n* مکتب متوسط
junkman *n* ویران کار
Jupiter (planet) *n* برجیس • مشتری
juridical *see* judicial
jurisprudence (Musl) *n* فقه
jurist (Musl law) *n* فقه
→ (eminent; Musl law) مجتهد
Jurm *n* جرم
just (fair) (& adv) *adj, adv* عادلانه
just (fair) (& pers) *adj, n* عادل • با عدالیت
just (righteous) (& pers) *adj, n* راست کار • درست کار
justice *adj see* judicial
justice *n* عدلیه
→ Justice Ministry وزارت عدلیه
justice (fairness) *n* عدل • عدالت • انصاف • داد
justice (pers) *see* & judge
→ chief justice قاضی القضات
→ chief justice (rel) خان علوم
juvenile *see* childish; youth
juvenile prison *n* دارالتأدیب
Juwayn (town) *n* جوین

K

Kaaba, the (rel) *n* کعبه

kabob (cul) *n* کباب
→ sandal kabob چپلی کباب
→ skewer kabob شش کباب
Kabul (capital, province, dist) *n* کابل
→ (arch) دارالملک
Kabuli (& pers) *adj, n* کابلی
Kajaki (dist) *n* کجکی
→ Kajaki Dam بند کجکی
kahin (pre-Musl soothsayer) *n* کاهن
Kahmard (dist) *n* کهمرد
Kajran (dist) *n* کجران
Kakal (dist, alt Kakar) *n* کاکل
Kakar (dist, alt Kakal) *n* کاکر
Kakar (P tribe) *n* کاکر
Kalakan (dist) *n* کلکان
Kalat *see* Qalat
kaldar (currency) *n* کلدار
Kaldar (dist) *n* کلدار
Kalfagan (dist) *n* کلفگان
Kama (dist) *n* کامه
Kamal (m name) *n* کمال
Kamdeysh (seat, dist) *n* کامدیش
Kan-e Ezat (ctr) *n* کان عزت
Kandahar (province, seat, dist) *n* قندهار
Kang (dist) *n* کنگ
kangaroo *n* کانگرو
Kangihim (hist, Chinese philologist) *n* کنگهم
Kaparay (ctr) *n* کپری
Kapisa (province) *n* کاپیسا
Karachi (city) *n* کراچی
Karaj (city) *n* کرج
karakul sheepskin *n* قره قل • پوست قره قل
Karakum (desert) *n* کاراکم
karat *n* قیراط
→ (lit) عیار
Karim (m name) *n* کریم
Karima (f name) *n* کریمه
Karta-ye Chahar (Kabul city dist) *n* کارته چهار
Karta-ye Naw (Kabul city dist) *n* کارته نو
Karta-ye Sakhi (Kabul city dist) *n* کارته سخی

439

Karta-ye Sey (Kabul city dist) n کارته سه

Karukh (dist) n کرخ

Kashgar (geog; oasis) n کاشغر

Kashmir (province) n کشمیر

Kashmiri (& lang, pers) adj, n کشمیری

Kathmandu n کتمندو

Kawkab (f name) n کوکب

kayak n قایق • زورق

Kazakhstan n قزاقستان

Kazha (ctr) n کاژه

keep vt نگاه داشتن • نگاه کردن • نگاه داشتن • محکم کردن <چیزی را در کجا>

→ keep books محاسبه کردن

→ keep doing <sth> رفتن

keeping n نگاه داری • نگه داری • نگاه داشت • نگه داشت

keepsake n یاد گار • یاد گاری

Keran wa Munjan (dist) n کران و منجان

kerosene n تیل خاک

Keshektan (dist, alt Hesa-ye Duwum-e Kohestan) n کشکتان

Keshem n کشم

Keshem-e Bala (ctr) n کشم بالا

Keshendeh (dist) n کشنده

key (critical) adj کلیدی • بسیار مهم

key n کلید

→ key money (for shop) سرقفلی

key (mus) n سر

KhAD (hist, Afgh secret police) n خاد

Khadija (f name, Prophet's first wife) n خدیجه

Khadir (dist) n خدیر

Khagani see Khaqani

khaja (form of address for descendants of Abu Bakr) n خواجه

Khaja (m name) n خواجه

Khaja Bahawuddin (dist) n خواجه بها الدین

Khaja Du Koh (dist) n خواجه دو کوه

Khaja Ghar (dist) n خواجه غار

Khaja Hejran (dist, alt Jelga Nahrin) n خواجه هجران

Khaja Sabz Posh (dist) n خواجه سبز پوش

Khaja Umari (dist) n خواجه عمری

Khak-e Jabar (dist) n خاک جبار

Khak-e Safeyd (dist) n خاک سفید

khaki-colored adj خاکی

Khakreyz (dist) n خاکریز

Khaled (m name) n خالد

Khalil (m name; P tribe) n خلیل

Khalq (hist, PDPA faction) n خلق

→ adherent of Khalq خلقی

Khalqi (pol, & pers) adj, n خلقی

Khamyab (dist) n خمیاب

khan n خان

Khan Neshin (dist) n خان نشین

Khan-e Charbagh (dist) n خان چارباغ

Khanabad (dist, ctr) n خان آباد

Khanaqa (dist) n خانقاه

Khandud (ctr) n خاندود

Khaqani (12th-c Dari poet) n خاقانی

Kharijite (hist, memb of ancient Musl sect) n خارجی

Khartoum n خرطوم

kharwar (unit of weight) n خروار

Kharwar (dist) n خروار

Khas Kunar (dist) n خاص کنر

Khas Uruzgan (dist) n خاص اورزگان

Khash (dist) n خاش

Khash Rod (dist) n خاش رود

Khatak (P tribe in NWFP) n ختک

Khayr Khana (1-3, Kabul city dists) n خیرخانه

Khayyam see Omar Khayyam

Khazraj (hist, Arabian tribe) n خزرج

→ the Khazraj tribe بنو الخزرج

khedive (hist, Egyptian viceroy) n خدیو

khel (tribal subdivision) n خیل • خل

Khenj (dist) n خنج

Khenjan (dist) n خنجان

Kheyal (m name) n خیال

Khirqa (shrine) n خرقه

Khiva (city) n خیوا

Khorasan (hist, medieval name of Afgh) n خراسان

Khost (province, seat) n خوست

Khost Meyla (ctr) n خوست میله

Khost wa Fereng (dist) n خوست و فرنگ

Khudawandgar-e Balkh (13th-c Sufi & Dari poet) n خداوندگار بلخ

Khugeyani (dist) n خوگیانی

Khujand (city) n خجند

Khulm (dist) n خلم

Khuram (m name; hist, Shah Jahan's birth name) n خرم

Khuram wa Sarbagh (dist) n خرم و سرباغ

Khurasan see Khorasan

Khursheyd (m/f name) n خورشید

Khushhal Khan Khatak (hist, P leader) n خوشحال خان ختک

Khushi (dist) n خوشی

Khusraw (m name; hist, Jahangir's eldest son) n خسرو

Khwahan (dist) n خواهان

khwaja see khaja

Khwarazm (hist, empire 11th c. – 1220 A.D.) n خوارزم

Khyber (geog) n خیبر

→ Khyber Pass کوتل خیبر

KIA, killed in action adj, n شهید در عملیات • شهید در محاربه

kiblah (direction of Mecca) n قبله

→ kiblah indicator قبله نما

kick n لگد

→ kick w/front of foot پیش پایی

kick vt لگد زدن • لگد انداختن • لگد پراندن

→ get kicked لگد خوردن

kid (esp one's own n اولاد • طفل

→ (colloq) اشتک

→ kid (young goat) بزغاله

→ kid stuff اشتک بازی

kid around vi مزاح کردن

kiddie adj اشتکانه • طفلانه

kidnap vt اختطاف کردن • ربودن

→ (colloq, fig) پراندن

kidnapper n رباینده

kidnapping n اختطاف • ربایندگی

kidney n گرده • کلیه

→ related to the kidneys کلیوی

kidney beans (red) n لوبیا

kilim n گلم • گلیم

kill vt کشتن

→ (fig) خون کردن • جان گرفتن • از پای در آوردن • از بین بردن

killed adj قتیل • کشته

→ be killed کشته شدن • هلاک شدن

→ killed in action see KIA

killing n خون

kiln n داش

kilogram n کیلوگرام • کیلو

kin n خویش

kind (type) n نوع • قسم • جنس • رقم • چیز • قبیل • سورت • قماش

kind adj مهربان

→ (compassionate) مشفق • شفیق • خون گرم

kindergarten n کودکستان

kindling n درگیران

kindness n مهربانی

kinetics (mil) n pl حرکات • عملیات

kinfolk n pl اقربا • اقارب • نزدیکان

king (& chess, cards) n شاه • پادشاه • سلطان • ملک

→ King of China (fig, fine rider in procession) فغفور چین

kingdom n شاهی • پادشاهی • سلطنت • شهریاری • ملکوت

kingly see regal

kinship n خویشی

Kirghiz see Kyrgyz

kismet n قسمت

kiss n بوسه

→ (colloq) ماچ

kiss vt بوسیدن

→ (colloq) ماچ دادن • ماچ کردن

kitchen n آشپز خانه

→ (colloq) کار خانه

→ kitchen master (hist, Mughal imperial household) خوان سالار

→ kitchen sink ظرف شوی

kite (bird) n زغن

kite n کاغذ پران

→ (colloq) گدی پران • گدی

kith & kin phrs کس و کوی

Kiti (dist) n کیتی • گیتی

knead (dough) vt خمیر کردن • مشت کردن

knee n زانو

kneecap n عینک زانو

441

kneel *vi* زانو زدن
knickers (for sports) *n* نیکر
knife *n* کارد
→ well-tempered (knife) جوهردار
knight (chess) *n* اسپ
knight (rider) *n* سوار
knit (weave) *v* بافتن
knitter (weaver) *n* بافنده
knob *n* تکمه • دکمه
knock (at door) *v* • دق تق کردن •
دق الباب کردن
knock *see* blow
knocking (at door) *n* دق تق • دق
الباب
knockout blow *n* ضربه فنی
knot *n* عقد • گره
→ (on tree) زخ
know (recognize) *vt* شناختن
know (understand) *vt* فهمیدن
know how to *v* یاد داشتن
know *vt* دانستن
know (recognize) <sb> *vt* به جای
آوردن
knowing (informed) *adj* وارد
knowledge (& mystical) *n* عرفان
knowledge (acquaintance w/) *n*
شناسایی • شناخت • معرفت
knowledge (information) *n*
معلومات • اطلاع • آگاهی • وقوف
knowledge (science) *n* علم • دانش
knowledge (understanding) *n*
بصیرت • بصارت • فهم
knowledge (wisdom) *n* حکمت
→ a little knowledge بضاعت
مزجات
knowledge *n* دانش • عرفانی
knowledgeable (informed) *adj* آگاه
• با خبر • مطلع • واقف
known *adj* معلوم
knuckle (finger/toe) *n* بند انگشت
Kof Ab (dist) *n* کوف آب
Koh Band (dist) *n* کوه بند
Koh-e Safi (dist) *n* کوه صافی
Kohestan (dist) *n* کوهستان
→ *see* & Hesa-ye Awal-e
Kohestan
Kohestanat (dist) *n* کوهستانات
kohl (cosmetic) *n* کحل • سرمه •
الکحل

442

Koran *see* Quran
Koranic *see* Quranic
Korea *n* کوریا
Korean (& pers, lang) *adj, n*
کوریایی
korma (stew) *n* قورمه
Kot (dist) *n* کوت
Kotwal (ctr) *n* کوتوال
Kuala Lumpur *n* کوالا لمپور
Kuchi (once-nomadic grp) *n* کوچی
Kuhsan (dist) *n* کهسان
Kulola Pushta (Kabul city dist) *n*
کلوله پشته
Kunar (province, river) *n* کنر
Kunduz (province, seat, dist) *n*
کندز • قندز
Kurd (ethn grp) *n* کرد
Kurdish (lang) *n* کردی
Kurdistan *n* کردستان
Kurengal (valley) *n* • کرنگل
کورنگل
kuroh (unit of distance) *n* کروه
Kushan (& pers) *adj, n* کوشانی
Kushans, the (hist, dynasty 1st-3rd
c. A.D.) *n pl* کوشانیان
Kushk (dist) *n* کشک
Kushk-e Kohna (geog, dist) *n*
کشک کوهنه • کشک کهنه
kushta-ye tela (aphrodisiac) *n*
کشته طلا
Kuwait *n* کویت
Kuwaiti (& pers) *adj, n* کویتی
Kuz Kunar (dist) *n* کوز کنر
Kyrgyz (& pers, lang) *adj, n*
قرغزی
Kyrgyz *n* قرغز
Kyrgyzstan *n* قرغزستان

L

lab *see* laboratory
labor (toil) *n* رنج
labor (work) *n* کار
→ forced labor بیگار
→ labor market بازار مزدوری
→ labor union اتحادیه کارگاری
labor in vain (fig) *v phrs* به یخ
نوشتن و در آفتاب ماندن

laboratory *n* • لابراتوار • آزمایشگاه
→ related to the laboratory
لابراتواری
laborer *n* • کار گر • رنج بر •
مزدور • مزدور کار • اجوره کار •
زحمت کش
laborer *see* & worker
→ forced laborer بیگاری
→ work as forced laborer بیگاری
کردن
lack (absence) *n* عدم
lack (shortage) *n* • فقدان • کمی
lacking <sth> *adj* فاقد <چیزی>
ladder *n* • زینه • نردبان
ladies & gentlemen *excl* حضار
کرام
ladle *n* • ملاقه • چمچه
→ soup ladle چمچه • ملاقه
lady *n* • خانم • زن
→ lady of the house کد بانو
lady (of rank) *n* بیگم
→ (arch, esp Hazara) خاتون
lag behind *v* • عقب افتادن • پس
ماندن
Laghman (province) *n* لغمان
lake *n* • جهیل • غدیر • تالاب • آب
گیر • حوض • برکه • دریاچه
lal (grape variety) *n* لال
Lal Pur (dist) *n* • لعل پور • لال پور
Lal wa Sarjangal (dist) *n* لال و
سرجنگل
Lalkhanabad (ctr) *n* لالخان آباد
lama (rel) *n* لاما
lamb *n* • حمل • بره
→ lambskin quilt (w/lining) جعفری
lame *adj* لنگ
lamely *adv* لنگان
lameness *n* لنگی
lament *n* • شیون • زاری • عزا •
سوگ • ماتم • ندبه • نالش
lament *v* • شیون کردن • زاری
کردن • سوگ گرفتن • نالیدن
lamp *n* چراغ
lance *n* نیزه
land *n* • بوم • مرز • خشکه
→ hectare (unit of land) هکتار
→ state land(s) اموال خالصه
land (earth) *n* زمین

land (touch down) *v* • پهلو گرفتن •
پیاده شدن
landing (of aircraft) *n* نشست
landlocked *adj* محاط به خشکه
landlord (feudal) *n* خان
landowner (farmer) *n* زمین دار
landowner (large) *n* ملاک
landowning (farming) *n* زمین داری
lands (estates) *n pl* اراضی
landscape *n* منظره
lane (btwn houses) *n* • کوچه •
سرک • جاده
language *n* • زبان • لسان
languid *adj* • پر خمار • خمار آلود •
مخمور • خمار
→ (colloq) خمار
languor *n* فتور
→ (colloq) خمار
lantern w/candle *n* لالتین
Laos *n* لاوس
lapel *n* یخن
lapis lazuli *n* لاجورد
lapping up (as a dog) *n* لق لق
lard *n* روغن خوک
large *adj* • بزرگ • کلان
→ large intestine روده کلان
lark (bird) *n* جل
larkspur (flower) *n* دلفون
larva *n* • نوزاد • نورسیده
laryngeal *adj* حنجروی
larynx (anat) *n* حنجره
→ have laryngitis صدای <کسی>
گرفته بودن
lascivious *adj* شهوت انگیز
lash (for flogging) *n* شلاق
lash (flog) *v* شلاق قرار دادن
Lash wa Juwayn (dist) *n* لاش و
جوین
Lashkar Gah (seat) *n* لشکر گاه
Lashkar-e Taiba (militant org) *n*
لشکر طیبه • جماعت الدعوت
last (final) *adj* • آخر • أخری
→ (lit, placed before n) • واپسین •
آخرین
→ last & the one before پر و پرار
→ next to last پرار
last (previous) *adj* • تیر شده • گذشته
last night *n, adv* دیشب
→ (lit) دوش

443

last night's adj دیشبه

lasting (enduring) adj • دیرپای دوام دار

latch (door) (colloq) n تنبه

late (deceased) adj • مرحوم متأخر

late adv دیر • ناوقت • نوقت

lately adv دراین اواخر • اخیراً

later (colloq) adv پسانتر

later adv بعد • پس • پسان • پسانتر

lathe n ماشین خراطی

→ lathe worker خراط • خراد

→ work at a lathe خراطی کردن

lather (soap up) v کف کردن

lather n کف

Latin (lang) n لاتین

Latin adj لاتینی

latitude n عرض البلد

latrine n چاه بدرفت • چاه تشناب

→ (colloq) مکان

laugh vi خنده کردن • خنده <کسی> آمدن • خندیدن

laughter n خنده

→ (fig) salt of life نمک زندگی

→ laughter (guffaw) قهقهه

launch n پرتاب

launderer n رخت شوی

lavatory n تشناب

Law & Order Trust Fund for Afghanistan see LOTFA

law enforcement n تنفیذ قانون

law n قانون • ناموس

→ customary law عرف

→ law of the land قانون حاکم

→ laws of nature نوامیس طبیعت

law office n دارالوکاله

lawful (Musl rel) n شرعی • مشروع

lawfully (Musl rel) adv شرعاً

lawsuit n دعوا • قضیه

lawyer n وکیل • وکیل مدافع • وکیل دعوا

laxative n مسهل • جلاب

→ laxative manna شیر خشت

lay (cloth) vt هموار کردن

lay (trap) vt نشاندن

lay eggs v تخم دادن • تخم گذاشتن • بیضه گذاشتن • بیضه نهاندن

lay off (from job) vt سبک دوش کردن • گذاشتن

444

layer (& fig) n منزل • طبقه

Layla (f name) n لیلی

layout n نقشه • خریطه

layover n توقف

Lazha Ahmad Kheyl (dist, alt Ahmad Kheyl) n لژه احمد خیل

laze vi نشستن → (colloq) شیشتن

lazy (possessed by evil spirit) (& pers) adj, n دیوزده

lazy adj تنبل • کاهل

lead (metal) n سرب → made of lead سربی

leader n آمر • سر • سرکرده • سردار • سرور • سالار • قاید • مهتر • زعیم • رهبر • کله → (epithet for Prophet) پیشوا • پیشوا

leadership n سروری • سرکردگی • زعامت • رهبری

leading adj عمده

leaf (paper) n ورق

leaf (plant, tree) n برگ

league n جامعه • اجتماع → League of Nations جامعه ملل

leaking (from roof) n چکک

leap n جست • خیز

leap v جست زدن • خیز کردن

learn (memorize) vt حفظ کردن

learn vt یاد گرفتن → (lit) آموختن

learned (& pers) adj, n فاضل • عالم • متبحر → more learned افضل → most learned علامه → the learned men افاضل

learning (education) n • آموزش تعلیم

learning (process) n معرفت • کسب

learning (urbanity) n ادب

lease (hire out) v اجاره دادن

lease (hire) v اجاره کردن

lease n اجاره

leaseholder n اجاره دار

least adj, n کمترین → at least کم از کم • اقلا • دست کم

leather adj چرمی

leather n چرم
leather goods n چرم باب
leather strip n چرمک
leather worker n چرمگر
leather workshop n چرمگری
leatherwork n چرم دوزی
leave (be ousted) vi خارج شدن
leave (go) vi رفتن
leave (quit) vt ترک کردن • ترک دادن • واگذار کردن • واگذاشتن • گذاشتن
leavening n خمیر مایه • مایه خمیر
Lebanese (& pers) adj, n لبنانی
Lebanon n لبنان
lecherous adj شهوت ران
→ (colloq) شهوتی
lecherousness n شهوت رانی
lechery n شهوت
ledge n رف
leech n جوک • شلک • شلوک • زلوک • زالو
leek n گندنه
→ wild leek بولان
leer n نگاه هوس آلود
left (remaining) adj باقی مانده
→ be left (remain) باقی ماندن
left (side) n چپ
left-handed adj چپ دست
leftovers (food) n نان شب مانده
leg (anat) n پا
→ (colloq) پای
leg (chair, table) n پایه
leg (colloq) (anat) n لنگ
legacy n میراث
legal adj قانونی
legal center n مرجع حقوقی
legality n قانونیت
legalize vt قانونی ساختن
legend n افسانه • اسطوره
legendary adj افسانه یی • اساطیری • داستانی • مشهور
legible adj خوانا
legislate v به قانون ماندن • قانون گذاری کردن
legislating n قانون گذاری
legislative adj قانون گذار
→ Legislative Council تقنین
legislator n قانون گذار
legitimacy (Musl law) n مشروعیت

legitimate (& adv) adj, adv عادلانه
legitimate (Musl law) adj حلال
→ legitimate child حلالی
leisure n فراغت • تفرج • تفریح
lemon n لیمو
lemonade n لیموناد
lend vt عاریت دادن
length (of jacket, pants) n قد
→ foot (unit of length) فت
→ full-length (coat) قد نما
length n طول • درازی
lengthy adj دراز • طولانی • طویل
leniency (& see mercy) n مدارا
lens (crystal) n زجاجیه
lens (eye, camera) n عدسیه
lentil n دال • عدس • نسک
Leo (zodiac) n شیر • اسد
leopard n پلنگ
leper n آدم جذامی
leprosy n جذام
leprous adj جذامی
lesion (med) n adj ریش • زخم
less <than sth> adj کمتر <از چیزی>
lessee see leaseholder
lesser adj اقل
lesson n درس • سبق
lessor n اجاره ده • اجاره دهنده
let (allow) phrs بان که • بانین که
lethal (& fig) adj قاتل • کشنده • مهلک
letter (document) n مکتوب • نامه • خط
→ letter of agreement توافق نامه • توافقنامه
→ letter of appreciation تقدیر نامه
Letter (of alphabet) n حرف
letter writer n نامه نگار
→ (lit) مترسل
lettuce n کاهو
leukoma (med) گل
level (raze) vt غلتاندن
level (standard) n سویه
level (surface) n سطح
level (tool) n آب ترازو
level adj مسطح • تخت • هموار
lever n اهرم
lewd (colloq) adj شهوتی
lewdness n قباحت

445

lexicographer *n* لغت شناس
lexicon *n* • قاموس
لغت نامه • دکشنری • فرهنگ
liability *n* جواب دهی
liable *adj* جواب ده
liaison *adj* رابط
liar *n* دروغ پرداز • دروغ باف •
→ (colloq) دروغ گو
liberal *adj* آزادی خواه
liberation (rescuing) <from sth> *n*
نجات <از چیزی> • رستگاری
libertine *n* افسار گسیخته
liberty *n* حریت • آزادی
Libra (zodiac) *n* میزان
library *n* کتابخانه
→ (arch) دارالکتاب
license (freedom if abused) *n*
اباحت • جواز • روایی
license (permit) *n* اجازه نامه •
جواز
license plate *n* نمبر پلیت
lick *vt* لیسیدن
licorice *n* شیرین بویه
lid *n* سر • سر پوش
lie (untruth) *n* دروغ
→ (excuse, false pretext) پلمه
→ lies اکاذیب
lie (tell a lie) *v* دروغ گفتن
lie down (rest) *vi* دراز کشیدن
lie down *vi* افتادن
lieutenant colonel, LTC *n* سمونمل
lieutenant general, LTG *n* لوی
پاسوال
lieutenant, 1LT *n* ضابط • ضابط
اول • بریدمن • لمری بریدمن •
لمری څارن
→ second lieutenant, 2LT دوهم
بریدمن • دوهم څارن • دوهم سارن
→ third lieutenant, 3LT دریم
بریدمن • دریم څارن • دریم سارن
life *n* زندگانی • حیات
→ lose/risk one's life سر باختن
lifejacket *n* واسکت جان
lifestyle *n* طرز زندگی
lifetime *n* عمر
lift *vt* بر داشتن • برگرفتن
→ (colloq) ورداشتن
→ lift weights وزن بر داری کردن
light (bright) *adj* روشن

light (color) *adj* کمرنگ
light (not heavy) *adj* سبک • خفیف
light (ignite) *v* بل کردن
light *n* چراغ • پرتو
→ (& fig) نور • روشنی
→ light bulb گروپ • گروه
light (turn light on) *vt* روشن کردن
light a fire *v* آتش در دادن
lighter (for cigarettes) *n* لایتر
light-fingered (colloq) *adj* تیز بال
lightheaded *adj* سر چرخ
lightning *n* برق
→ (colloq) الماسک • الماسی
like (similar to) *adj* مانند • مثل • به
مثل • مثل از
→ (&) the like نظایر
→ like this (colloq) اینچنین
like <sth> *vt* خوش داشتن <چیزی
را>
→ like <sb> very much خاطر
<کسی را> خواستن
→ take a liking to (sth) خوش آمدن
likeable *adj* دل پسند • خاطر پسند
likelihood *n* احتمال
likely *adj* احتمالی
likely *adv* احتمالاً • محتملاً
likemindedness *n* وحدت فکر
lilac (flower) *n* یاس • یاسمن
انگریزی
lily (flower, dark purple) *n* سوسن
limb (anat) *n* عضو
lime (fruit) *n* لیمو
lime (quicklime) *n* آهک • چونه
limestone *n* سنگ آهک
limit (boundary) *n* کران • کرانه
limit (extent) *n* اندازه
limit (frame) *n* چارچوب • چارچوبه
• چوکات
limit *vt* محدود کردن • مقید ساختن
limitation (state of being limited) *n*
محدودیت
limited (bounded) *adj* محدود
limited *adj* قاصر
limits *see* limit
limp *v* لنگیدن
line (route) *n* خط
→ lines of communication خطوط
مواصلاتی
line (row) *n* قطار • صف • رده

446

line (series) *n* سلسله
line (trace) *n* رده
line up *vi* در لین ایستاده کردن
lineage (genealogy) *n* نسب
linen *adj* کتانی
linen *n* کتان
linguist *n* زبان شناس • دانشمند زبان شناس
linguistic *adj* زبانی • لسانی • شفاهی
linguistics *n* زبان شناسی
link *n* وصل • رابطه • تعلق • علاقه • سروکار
link *v* وصل کردن • پیوستن
linkage *see* link
linked <to sth> *adj* متصل <چیزی / به چیزی>
linseed oil *n* تیل زغر
lion *n* شیر • اسد • غضنفر • ارسلان
lip *n* لب
lipid (med) *n* شحم • چربی
lipstick *n* لب سرین
liquefied *adj* مایع
liquid *n* مایع
liquor *n* شراب • مسکر • باده • می
list (column) *n* جدول
list *n* فهرست • لست • لیست
listen *v* شنیدن • گوش گرفتن • گوش کردن
listener *n* شنونده • مستمع • سامع
listlessness *n* فتور
liter (unit of measure) *n* لیتر
literacy *n* سواد • خوانندگی
→ literacy campaign مبارزه برای سواد
literalism *n* حقیقت بینی • واقع بینی
literalist (pers) *n* شخص حقیقت بین • شخص واقع بین
literally *adv* لفظاً • عیناً • بعینه
literary (style) *adj* فصیح
literate (& pers) *adj, n* با سواد • خواننده
literature *n* ادبیات
lithography *n* چاپ سنگی • طبع سنگی • لتوگرافی
Lithuania *n* لیتوانیا
Lithuanian (& pers, lang) *adj, n* لیتوانیایی

litigation *n* منازعه • نزاع • تنازع
→ under litigation متنازع فیه
litter (palanquin) *n* تخت روان
little *adj* کوچک • خورد
little, a *n* کم • کم کم • یک کمی • اندکی
→ little by little اندک اندک • جسته جسته • جو به جو
live (be alive) *vi* زندگی کردن • زندگی داشتن • زنده بودن
→ may you live long! زنده باشین • زندگی سر شما باشه
live (reside) *v* بود و باش کردن
live *v* به سر بردن
livelihood *see* living *n*
liveliness *n* رونق
liver (anat) *n* کبد • جگر
liver-colored *adj* جگری
livestock *n* گله
→ livestock breeding مال داری
living (& pers) *adj, n* زنده • حی • جان دار • ذی حیات
→ (having a soul) *adj* ذی روح
→ living creature زنده جان
living (livelihood) *n* معاش • تنخواه • نان
→ earn a living امرار معاش کردن
living room *n* اتاق نشیمن • سالون
living together *adj* همخانه
lizard *n* سوسمار • کیلس • چلپاسه • شلند
→ small lizard
llama *n* لاما
LOA *see* letter of agreement
load (burden) *n* بار
load (cargo) *n* محموله
loaded (gun) *adj* پر
loaded (question) *adj* جان دار
loaf of bread (flat, round) *n* قرص
loan *n* قرض • عاریت
→ government loan قرضه
→ interest-free loan قرضه حسنه
→ loan word کلمه دخیل
→ on loan عاریتاً
loan *v* قرض دادن • عاریت دادن
loaned *adj* دخیل • عاریتی • مستعار • ماخوذ
lobe of liver *n* جگر گوشه
lobster *n* خرچنگ دراز
local (& pers) *adj, n* محلی

447

local *adj* منطقوی
locale *n* محل
located *adj* واقع
→ be located <sw> • واقع شدن
قرار داشتن ‹در کجا›
location *n* موقعیت • موقف •
جای • مکان
lock (of hair) *n* زلف • پیچه
→ sidelock (f's) پیچه • زلف
lock (padlock) *n* قفل
→ (colloq) قلف
lock (padlock) *vt* قفل کردن
→ (colloq) قلف کردن
locked (lit) *adj* مقفل
→ be locked قفل شدن
→ be locked (colloq) قلف شدن
locomotive *n* لوکوموتیف
locust *n* ملخ
Lodhi (P tribe) *n* لودهی
Lodi (P tribe) *see* Lodhi
Logar (province, river) *n* لوگر
logical *adj* منطقی
logistical *adj* لوژستیکی
logistics *n* لوژستیک
loincloth *n* لنگ
loins *n* کمر
Lokhi (ctr) *n* لوخی
London *n* لندن
loneliness *n* تنهایی
lonely *adj* تنها
long *adj* دراز • طولانی • طویل
→ (prolonged) متمادی
longevity *n* درازی عمر
longevous *see* long-lived
longing *n* هوا
long-lived *adj* معمر • سال خورده •
طویل العمر
long-range *adj* دوررس • دورمنزل
long-term *adj* دراز مدت • دیررس
• طویل المدت
long-wave *adj* موج دراز
look (appearance) *n* شکل • نما
look (glance) *n* نظر
look around *v* سیر کردن
look for *vt* پالیدن • جستن
look up *v* رجوع دادن • رجوع
کردن
look *vi* به نظر رسیدن • معلوم شدن
lookout (mil) *n* مترصد
448

loop (aviation) *n* ملاق • معلق
loop *v* ملاق خوردن • ملاق زدن
loose (clothes) *adj* گشاد
loose (slack) *adj* سست
loose (tooth) *adj* لق • لقک
loosen *vi* لق شدن
loot *n* غنیمت
loot *v* غارت کردن • چور کردن
looting *n* اغتنام • چور
lopsided *adj* یک بغله
loquat (fruit, tree) *n* لکات
Lord (& God) *n* مولا
lord (hist) *n* خواجه
lord (prince) *n* بیگ
lose (colloq) *vt* از دست دادن
lose (in game) *vi* باختن
lose (time, effort) *vt* ضایع کردن
lose *vt* گم کردن
→ (colloq) از دست دادن
loss (business) *n* نقص • ضرر •
زیان
loss (damage) *n* خساره • تاوان
→ ask compensation for losses
تاوان کردن
→ compensate for losses تاوان
دادن
→ suffer losses تاوان رسیدن •
تاوان شدن
loss (lack) *n* فقدان
loss (waste) *n* ضایعه
losses (casualties) *n pl* تلفات
lost (& pers) *adj, n* گمشده •
گمگشته
→ get lost گم شدن
lost (missing) *adj* گم • مفقود •
مفقود الاثر
lost (wasted) *adj* ضایع
lost *adj* باخت
Lot (bibl) *n* لوط
LOTFA, Law & Order Trust Fund
for Afghanistan *n* لوتفا • صندوق
وجهی برای تنفیذ قانون در
افغانستان
lots *n* قرعه
→ cast lots قرعه انداختن • قرعه
کشی کردن
lottery (for mil draft) *n* پشک
lottery drawing *n* قرعه کشی

lotus (plant) n نیلوفر
→ Indian lotus نیلوفر هندی
lotus-colored adj نیلوفری
loud adj بلند
loudness n بلندی
love (passion) n عشق
→ have a love affair تار داشتن
love n دوستی • محبت • مهر
love vt دوست داشتن
→ fall in love دل دادن • دل از
دست دادن • دل باختن
lovemaking n عشق ورزی
lover (bedmate) n همبستر • هم
بستر
lover n عاشق
lovestruck adj عاشق
low (base) adj گنده
low (in height) adj پخچ • خورد
low (price) adj نازل
low, base adj دنی
low-vision (med) adj کم بین
loya jirga n لویه جرگه
loyal adj صادق • وفا دار • نمک
حلال
loyalty n وفا داری • وفا
lubricant n مواد چرب کاری
lubricate v چرب کاری کردن • تیل
دادن
lubrication n چرب کاری
luck n بخت • طالع
→ bad luck برگشت
→ good luck! برخوردار باشین •
موفق باشین
lucky (& pers) adj, n خوش بخت •
بختیار • بختور • مقبل • طالعمند •
دولتمند • دولت دار • مسعود
ludicrous adj مسخره • مسخره آمیز
luggage n بارجامه • بکس ها
Luke (bibl) n لوک
lukewarm adj نیم گرم • شیر گرم
lullaby n للو
lulling (to sleep) n تنویم
lumber n چوب تعمیر • چوب
luminous adj تابان • تابناک
lunar (year) adj قمری
→ lunar halo خرگاه
lunatic n مجنون • دیوانه
lunch n نان چاشت • طعام چاشت
lung n شش • ریه

lure n جذب • فریبندگی
lush (verdant) adj سرسبز
lust (desire) n هوس
lust (lechery) n شهوت
lustful adj هوس آلود • هوس آمیز •
هوس بار
lute (mus instr) n عود
luxurious adj اعیانی
lymph (node) n لمف
lynx n سیاه گوش
lyre (arch, mus instr) n چنگ
→ lyre player چنگی
→ play the lyre چنگ نواختن •
چنگ زدن
lyric adj غزلی
lyrics (of song) n بیت

M

M.A. n ماستری • دیپلوم ماستری
Macedon (hist) see Macedonia
Macedonia n مقدونیه
Macedonian (& pers) adj, n مقدونی
machine gun n ماشین دار
mad (diacritic) n مد
mad see angry; crazy
madam (form of address) n خانم •
میرمن • مادام
→ (procuress) دلاله • دلال زن
madame see madam
madman n مجنون • دیوانه
madness n جنون • دیوانگی
madrasa n مدرسه
magazine (artillery depot) n جبه
خانه
magazine (journal) n مجله •
ژورنال
magazine (of rifle) n پنجگی
Maghreb (geog) n مغرب
magic (sorcery) n سحر • ساحری •
افسون • افسونگری • جادو •
جادوگری
magic (spell) n افسون • رقیه
magical (& adv) adj, adv ساحرانه
magical adj سحر آمیز • جادویی
magician (sorceror) n ساحر •
افسونگر • جادوگر

449

magician (yogi, supernaturalist) *n*
جوگی • مرتاض

magnet *n* آهن ربا • مقناطیس

magnetic *adj* مقناطیسی

magnificent *adj* مجلل • شاندار
ابهر

magnifying glass *n* ذره بین

Magog (bibl) *n* ماجوج
→ Gog & Magog یاجوج و ماجوج

Magpie (bird) *n* (عکه =) اکک

Magyar *see* Hungarian

maharaja *n* مهاراجه

Mahdawiyya (hist, Musl sect) *n*
مهدویه

Mahdi (rel) *n* مهدی

Mahmud-e Raqi (seat, dist) *n*
محمود راقی

Mahnaz (f name) *n* مهناز

Mahsud (P tribe) *n* محسود

mail *n* پوسته

mailbox *n* صندوق پوستی

main *adj* عمده

mainland *n* براعظم • قاره

mainstay in one's old age عصای
پیری

maintain (sustain) *v* نگاه داشتن •
نگه داشتن

maintenance *n* مراقبت

maize *n* جوار • جواری

majesty *n* حضرت
→ Her Majesty علیا حضرت
→ His Majesty اعلی حضرت

Majid (m name) *n* مجید

major, MAJ (mil) *n* جگرن •
سمونیار • کندک مشر

major general, MG (mil) *n* پاسوال •
تورن جنرال
→ (non-Afgh) میجر جنرال

majority (most) *n* اکثر • اکثریت

majority (quorum) *n* اکثریت

make (build) *vt* ساختن

make (compel) *vt* مجبور ساختن

make (do) *v* کردن
→ (lit) نمودن

make (produce) *vt* ایجاد کردن

make out to be *v* وانمود کردن

make sure *v* علم آوری کردن

make up (comprise) <sth> *vi*
<چیزی را> تشکیل دادن

450

make up (fabricate) *v* بافتن

makeup *n* آرایش
→ the 7 types of makeup هفت قلم
→ put on too much makeup به
هفت قلم آرایش کردن
→ apply makeup آرایش کردن

malachite *n* مرمر سبز

malaria *n* تب • تب نوبتی • ملاریا
لرزه

Malay peninsula *n* ملایا

Malaysia *n* مالیزیا

Malazai (P tribe) *n* ملازی

male *adj* نر • ذکور

male (esp large animal) *adj* نر

Malestan (dist) *n* مالستان

malfunction (mechanical) *n* • بندش
عارضه
→ find the malfunction بندش پیدا
کردن
→ have a malfunction عارضه
داشتن

malice *n* پستی

malicious *adj* دنی • پست

Malikite (school of Sunni rel
thought) (& pers) *adj, n* مالکی

malingering *adj* تمارض

malleable (in argument) *adj* نفوذ
پذیر

mallet *n* چکش چوبی

mallow (med herb) *n* پنیرک

Mama Kheyl (ctr) *n* ماما خیل

Mamluks (hist, caliphate 1250-
1517) *n pl* ممالیک

mammal *n* پستاندار

man *n* مرد

manacle *n* زولانه

management *n* سیاست

manager, director *n* مدیر
→ factory manager رئیس فابریکه
→ general manager رئیس

Manama *n* ال منامه • منامه

mandarin orange *n* کینو

Mando Zayi (dist) *n* مندو زائی

Mandol (dist) *n* ماندول • مندول

mane *n* یال

Manes (hist, 215-276 A.D.) *n* مانی

manganese (element) *n* منگنیز

mange *n* گرگ

manger *n* آخور • آخر

mango n • آنبه • آم نغزک
mangy adj گرگی • گرگین
mania n جنون • دیوانگی
maniacal (& adv) adj, adv جنون
آمیز
Manichaean (& pers) adj, n مانوی
Manichaeanism (hist) n مانویت
manifest (obvious) adj • آشکار
نمایان
manifestation n بروز
Manila n مانیلا • منیلا
mankind n بشر • بشریت • انسان •
نوع بشر
manly (& pers) (brave) adj, n جوان
مرد
manly (brave) (& adv) adj, adv
مردانه وار • مردانه
manner n طور • رویه • روش •
طرز • گونه • چگونگی • نحو
manners n وضعیت • اخلاق
manning (personnel) n پرسونل
mansion n قصر • کاخ • کوشک
mantle (ledge) n رف
man-to-man (combat) adj تن به تن
mantu (cul) n منتو
manufacture vt تولید کردن
manufacturer n سازنده
manufacured adj مصنوع
manure n کود
manuscript n دست نویس • نسخه
خطی • خطی
many adj بسیار • بسیاری • برخی
• خیلی • زیاد • یک تعداد زیاد •
افزون • چندین
many times adv به مراتب
map n نقشه • خریطه
Maqhur (dist, lake) n مقهور
Maqsud (m name) n مقصود
Marawara (dist) n مروره
marble (material) n مرمر
march n قدم رو • پیش روی
March n مارچ
march v قدم رو کردن • پیش روی
کردن
Mardyan (dist) n مردیان
mare (f horse) n مادیان
→ (colloq) بیتل
margin (edge) n • دامن • حاشیه
کران • کرانه

marginal notes n pl تعلیقات
marigold (flower) n جعفری
marijuana n کنب • بنگ
marinate adj اخته
marinate v اخته کردن
maritime adj بحری • اقیانوسی
marjoram (arch) n مرزنگوش
mark (sign) n اثر • علامت • پل
mark (target) n آماج • آماج گاه •
هدف • هدف گاه • نشان • نشان گاه
• نشانه • نشانی
Mark (bibl) n مرقس
Markaz-e Behsud (dist) n مرکز
بهسود
marker (gram) n نشانه • نشانی
market n بازار • مارکیت
→ free market بازار آزاد
→ market economy اقتصاد
بازاری
→ wholesale market مندوی
marketing n بازار یابی
marketplace n بازار
→ (caravanserai) سرای
→ marketplace crossroads
چارسوق
markhor (kind of wild goat) n
مارخور
marksmanship n نشان زنی
Marmul (dist) n مارمول
marriage n تزوج • ازدواج •
عروسی
→ (fig) پیوند
→ bond of marriage عقد
→ child marriage نکاح صغیره
→ give in marriage تزویج کردن •
ازدواج کردن
→ temporary marriage صیغه
→ unmarriageable relative (Musl
law) محرم
marriage certificate n تذکره ازدواج
• نکاح خط
marriage contract n نکاح
marriage proposal n • خواستگاری
طلبگاری
→ propose marriage خواستگاری
کردن • (به) خواستگاری رفتن
married (f) adj شوهر دار
married (m) adj زندار • زن دار
→ get married عروسی کردن

451

married *adj* متاهل • عروسی
marrow (bone) *n* مغز استخوان
marrow (spinal) *n* • حرام مغز
نخاع
marry (unite in matrimony) *v*
وصلت کردن • هم سر کردن
Mars (planet) *n* بهرام • مریخ
marsh *n* • جبه زار • دل دل زار
مرداب
→ marsh gas (methane) متان
→ salt marsh شوره زار
marshal (mil) *n* مارشال
→ field marshal فیلد مارشال
marshmallow *n* خطمی • خیری
marshy *adj* جبه زار • دل دل زار
marten (animal) *n* خز • دله خفک
→ marten pelt پوستِ خز • پوستِ
دله خفک
martial *adj* جنگی
martingale (strap) *n* بند سلبند
martyr *n* شهید
martyrdom *n* شهادت
→ place of martyrdom مشهد
marvel *n* قیامت
→ (dim) نغزک
Marwat (P tribe) *n* مروت
Marxism *n* مارکسزم
Marxist *adj* مارکسستی
Marxist *n* مارکسست
Maruf (dist) *n* معروف • ماروف
Mary (bibl; f name) *n* مریم
masculine *adj* مذکر
Mashhad (city) *n* مشهد
mask *n* نقاب • حجاب
mason *n* سنگ کار • گل کار
معمار • بنا
masonry *n* سنگ کاری • گل کاری
• معماری • بنایی
masquerade *n* مسخره
mass *n* توده
massacre *n* قتل عام • کشتار
massage *n* • مشت و مال • مالش
مساژ
→ (colloq) چاپی
massage *vt* مالیدن
masses, the *n* توده • خلق
→ of the masses توده یی • خلقی

Massoud (P tribe) *n* مسعود
→ Ahmed Shah Massoud
احمد شاه مسعود (hist,1953-2001)
mast (of ship) *n* دیرک
master (sovereign) *n* سرکار
master *n* سرکار • مولا
→ master copy اصل
→ Master of Arts degree ماستری
• دیپلوم ماستری
→ master of Sufi order شیخ
→ master of the house مالک خانه
• کد خدا
mastermind *n* کارگزار اصلی
mastery *n* تسلط
masturbate *v* جلق زدن • استمنا
کردن
masturbation *n* جلق • استمنا
mat (woven) *n* بوریا
→ mat weaver بوریا باف
Mata Khan (dist) *n* مته خان • متا
خان
matam (mourning) *n* ماتم
matches *n* گوگرد
mate (chess) *n* مات
mate (couple) *see* & sex
mate (couple) *v* جفت شدن
mate (spouse) *n* جفت • جوره
material (cloth) *n* تکه
material (substance) *n* ماده
material (substantial) *adj* مادی
→ material world ناسوت
materialist *n* مادی
materiel (mil) *n* مهمات • مهمات
جنگی • مهمات حربی
mathematical *adj* ریاضی
mathematics *n* ریاضی
matrimony (union) *n* وصلت
matrimony *see* & marriage
matter (& law) *n* قضیه
→ matters (general) شئون
→ no matter who... ... هر که
matter (be important) *vi* فرق داشتن
→ it doesn't matter • پروا ندارد
فرق ندارد
Matthew (bibl) *n* متی • متا
mattress *n* توشک • دوشک
→ (colloq) تشک
Matun (dist, alt Khost) *n* متون
maturity (character) *n* رشاد

maturity (perfection) n کمال

matutinal *see* morning *adj*

maulana (rel) n مولوی • مولانا

maulvi *see* maulana

maxim n حکمت

maximum n حد اعظم • حد اکثر

may <+ subj> (modal v) • شاید
ممکن

→ may it not be (w/ or w/o مبادا
dependent clause in subj)
مبادا که

→ may it not be (colloq, excl) نبادا
• نبادا که

May (month) n می

maybe *adv* ممکن

Maydan Wardak (province, alt
Wardak) n میدان وردک

Maydan Shahr (seat, dist) n میدان
شهر

Maymana (seat) n میمنه

mayor n شاروال • رئیس بلدیه

mayoralty n شاروالی

Maywand (dist) n میوند

Mazar-e Sharif (seat, dist) n مزار
شریف

→ (colloq) مزار

me *pron* مرا • من را

→ (fig, colloq) اینجانب

meadow n سبزه زار • چمنزار •
مرغزار

meal n طعام • خوراک • نان • غذا

→ daily meal قوت

mean (base) *adj* پست • دنی • نازل

meaning n معنی • مفهوم •
مضمون • مفاد

meaningful *adj* معنی دار • با معنی

meaningless *adj* پوچ

means n وسایل • سبب • ذریعه

meanwhile *adv* در عین حال • در
این ضمن • در این حالت

measles n حصبه • سرخکان

measure (length) *vt* متر کردن

measure (size) n اندازه • حسب

→ (lit) میزان

measure (step) (esp pl) n تدبیر •
اقدام

→ take measures تدابیر گرفتن

measure (weight) *vt* سنجش کردن
• سنجیدن

measurement (comparison) n قیاس

measurement (weighing) n سنجش

meat n گوشت

→ ground meat کوفته

meatball n کوفته

Mecca (city) n مکه

Mecca (orig name) n یثرب

mechanic n میخانیک • مستری

mechanical *adj* • میخانیکی
میکانیکی

mechanism n • میکانزم • مکانزم
میکانیزم

mechanized *adj* مکانیزه شده

medal n مدال

meddle <in sth> vi مداخله کردن •
فضولی کردن <به چیزی>

meddling n مداخله • فضولی

Medes (hist) n ماد

media n pl رسانه های خبری

mediate v وساطت کردن • واسطه
کردن • میانجی گری کردن •
میانگی کردن

mediation n • وساطت • سفارت
واسطه • وسیله • میانجی گری •
میانگی

mediator n • میانجی • سفیر
میانگی • ثالث بالخیر

mediator (hist) n حکم

medical *adj* صحیه • صحی •
پزشکی

→ (arch) هیئت طبی

medical corps n طبابت

medical profession n • طبابت
پزشکی • داکتری

medical treatment n معالجه •
طبیبی • طبابت

medicine (drug) n دوا • دارو

medicine (practice) (arch) n
پزشکی

medicine (profession) n طب

→ ancient Eastern medicine
حکمت

→ preventive medicine طب
وقایوی

Medina (city) n مدینه

meditation n تفکر

meditative (& pers) *adj, n* متفکر

meditatively *adv* متفکرانه

Mediterranean Sea n بحیره رومی

medium-wave *adj* موج متوسط

meek (humble) *adj* خاضع • خاضع
• فروتن

meek (incapable) (& pers) *adj, n*
عاجز

meek (sheeplike) *adj* گوسفندی

meek pers *n* گربه مسکین •
خاکسار

meet (encounter) <sb> *v* مصادف
<شدن <با کسی>

meet (gather) *v* ملاقات کردن

meet (get acquainted) <w/sb> *v*
آشنا شدن • آشنایی حاصل نمودن
<همرای کسی>

meeting (encounter) *n* • تصادف
ملاقات • دو چار • دچار

meeting (gathering) *n* • مجمع
جلسه • میتنگ

meeting (rendezvous) *n* ملاقات

meeting (session) *n* • نشست
مجلس

Mehtarlam (seat, dist) *n* مهترلام

melancholy (& pers) *adj, n* خاطر
آزرده • آزرده خاطر

melody (mus) *n* آهنگ • ترانه • نوا

melon *n* خربوزه

→ half a melon پله

→ slice of melon قاش • تلم

melt *vi* گداختن

melt *vt* • آب کردن • ذوب کردن
گداختن

melting *n* ذوب

member (m anat) *n* • آلت • اندام
عضو

member (of grp; & anat) *n* عضو

→ member of communist
organization سازمانی

→ members (associates)
مربوطین

→ members (of family) منسوبین

membership *n* عضویت

membrane *n* • غشا • پرده • برقع
حجاب • نقاب

memento *n* • یاد گاری یاد گار

memoir *n* خاطرات

memorandum (note) *n* یاد داشت

memorandum (request) *n* عریضه

→ memorandum of understanding
توافق نامه • توافقنامه

memorial *n* یاد گار

454

memorize *vt* • حفظ به ذهن سپردن
کردن • به حافظه سپردن

memorized *adj* • مصون • محفوظ

→ memorized material محفوظات

memory (mind, heart) *n* خاطر

memory (recall) *n* • حافظه • یاد

memory (recollection) *n* • یاد گار
خاطره

men's *adj* مردانه

menace *n* تهدید

menace *vt* تهدید کردن

mend *vt* ترمیم کردن

mendicant *n* گدا

→ (colloq) گداییگر

mending *n* ترمیم

Mengajek (dist) *n* منگجک

menopausal *adj* یانسه

menopause *n* یانسگی

Menshevik (hist) *n* منشویک

menstruate *v* • حیض داشتن
حایضه بودن

menstruating *adj* • حایض • حایضه

menstruation *v* • حیض • طمث

mental (intellectual) *adj* • عقلی
ذهنی

→ mental development رسیدگی

→ mental hospital شفا خانه عقلی

→ mentally developed رسیده

mental (psychic) *adj* • وجدانی

mental (psychological) *adj* • روانی
نفسانی

mentality *n* • ذهنیت • روحیه

mention *n* ذکر

mention *v* تذکر دادن

mention *vt* • ذکر کردن • به زبان
آوردن • یاد کردن • یاد آور شدن

mentioned *adj* • متذکره • مذکور
مزبور

→ (colloq) در فوق

mentioning *n* تذکار

mentoring *n* مشوره دهی

menu *n* مینو • لست غذا

Meray (ctr) *n* مری

mercantile *adj* • تجارتی • تجاری

mercenary (& mil) *n* اجیر

merchandise *n* • مال • اجناس
سودا • بنجارگی • امتعه

→ stale merchandise • بازار زده
بیع زده

merchant n • تاجر • سوداگر • بازارگان
→ (colloq) تجار

merciful adj مهربان

merciful adj; the Merciful (God) n رحمان

mercilessness n قساوت

Mercury (planet) n • دبیر • عطارد • انجم
→ (arch) تیر

mercury n • سیماب • جیوه

mercy n • مهربانی • رحمت

mere adj • خالی • صرف • تنها

merely adv • خالصاً • صرفاً • تنها

merit n لیاقت

merry adj • دل خوش • خوش دل

Merv (city) n مرو

Mervian adj, n • مروی • مروزی

Meshrano Jirga n مشرانو جرگه

mess hall n طعام خانه

message n • پیغام • پیام

messenger (herald) n • رسول • قاصد

messenger (prophet) n • پیغامبر • نبی

Messiah (esp in Dari poetry) n • مسیح • مسیحا

messy (colloq) adj • گدود • جنگل

metabolism n متابولزم

metal adj فلزی

metal n فلز

metallic (shiny) adj آیینی

metalwork n فلز کاری

metalworker n فلز کار

metamorphosis n مسخ

metaphor (lit) n استعاره

metaphysics n • ماوراء الطبیعه • مابعد الطبیعه • متافیزیک

metathesis n • قلب • تقلیب

metempsychosis n • تناسخ • حلول • تناسخ

meteorogical adj جوی

meteorology n • هوا شناسی • مترولوژی

meter (unit of length) n متر

methane n متان

method (custom; & rel) n • آیین • کیش • دین • مذهب
→ (colloq) آئین

method n • متود • اسلوب • روش • راه • طریقه

methodical adj • متودیک • منظم

methodology n متودولوژی

metonymic adj کنایه یی

metonymy n • کنایه • کتره

Mexican adj مکسیکویی

Mexico City n شهر مکسیکو

Mexico n مکسیکو

Meyan Neshin (dist) n • میان نشین • میه نشین

Meyzan (month) n میزان

mice-eater (insult) n موش خور

Michael (bibl) n میکاییل

microbe n مکروب
→ microbes (bacteria) جراثیم

microbiologist n مکروب شناس

microbiology n مکروب شناسی

microphone n • مکروفون • مکرافون

microscope n • مکروسکوپ • ذره بین

microscopic adj مکروسکوپی

midday n • ظهر • چاشت

middle (central) adj • میانه • مرکزی • وسطی
→ Middle East • شرق میانه • خاور میانه
→ middle school مکتب متوسطه

middle (half) n • نیم • نصف
→ (colloq) نصب

middle (intermediate) adj • متوسط • مابینی
→ Middle English انگلیسی میانه

middle n • میان • مابین • مرکز • وسط • قلب • ناف
→ (fig) • قلب • ناف

middle-aged adj میانه سال

midnight n نصف شب

midriff (anat) n تهی گاه

miffed adj دق

might n • زور • قوت • قوه • نیرو

migraine (colloq) n نیم سری

migrate v مهاجرت کردن

migration n • مهاجرت • هجرت

Mikrorayon (1-4, Kabul city dists) n مکرورایون

mild (moderate) adj • معتدل • اعتدالی

455

mild (weak) *adj* خفیف

mild-mannered *adj* حلیم

mildew *n* پوپنک

mile (unit of distance) *n* میل

milieu *phrs* کس و کوی

militant (& pers) *adj, n* مبارز

→ (colloq) جنگره

military *adj* • نظامی • عسکری

حربی • جنگی • رزمی

military base *n* قشله • قشله

عسکری

military camp *n* اردوگاه

military objectives *n pl* نقاط نظامی

military, the *n* اردو • ارتش

→ memb of military نظامی

milk *n* شیر

→ powdered milk شیر خشک

milk (cow) *v* دوشیدن • دوختن

milk bottle (infant's) *n* شیر چوشک

milkfish *n* شیر ماهی

mill (for wool) *n* پشمینه بافی

mill (hand mill) *n* دستاس • دستاز

mill (water mill) *n* آسیاب • آسیا

mill (grain) *v* آسیا کردن

mill (w/hand mill) *v* دستاس کردن

millenium *n* هزاره

miller *n* آسیابان

millet (grain) *n* ارزن • گال

milliard *see* billion

milling *n* آسیابانی

million *n* ملیون

→ ten million کرور

millionaire *n* ملیونر

millstone *n* آسیا سنگ

mimic *v* تقلید کردن

mimicker *n* مقلد

mimicry *n* تقلید

mind (heart) *n* خاطر • باطن

mind (intellect) *n* خرد • عقل • ذهن

mind (spirit) *n* نفس

mindset *n* طرز تفکر • روحیه

mine (deposit) *n* معدن • کان

mine (explosive) *n* مین • ماین

→ (colloq) منین

→ mine clearing مین پاکی • مین

بی جا کردن

→ mine deactivation خنثی ساختن

مین ها

→ mine laying مین گذاری

456

mine (tunnel) (mil) *n* نقب • سوف

minefield *n* مین دار • کشتزار مین

mineral water *n* آب معدنی

mingling *n* خلط

minimum *n* حد اقل • اقلا • حد

اصغر

miniskirt *n* مینی ژوپ

minister (government) *n* وزیر

minister w/o portfolio *n* وزیر

مشاور

ministerial (meeting) *n* جلسه وزرا

ministry *n* وزارت • وزارت خانه

minor (trivial) *adj* جزئی

minority (being under age) *n*

کهتری

minority (numerical) *n* اقلیت

minstrel (lit) *n* مطرب

minstrelsy (lit) *n* مطربی

mint (coin) *v* سکه زدن

mint (spearmint) *n* نعناع

→ wild mint (pennyroyal) پودینه

mint (coin money) *n* ضراب خانه •

ضرب خانه

minus *adj* منفی

→ (colloq) تحت صفر

minute (time) *n* دقیقه

mir (title) *n* میر

Mir Bacha Kot (dist) *n* میر بچه

کوت

miracle *n* آیت • آیه

miracle (by Messiah) *n* برهان

مسیح

miracle (by Musl saint) *n* کرامت

miracle (by prophet) *n* معجزه

mirage *n* سراب

Miramor (dist) *n* میره مور

Miran (ctr) *n* میران

mirror *n* آیینه • آینه • مرآت

Mirza Suleyman (hist, Babur's

cousin) مرزا سلیمان

miscarriage (med) *n* نقصان • سقط

جنین غیر عمدی

miscarry (a fetus) *v* نقصان کردن

mischief (devilry) *n* شیطانی

mischievous (devilish) *adj*

شیطانی • ابلیس • اهریمن

mischievous (naughty) *n* شوخ •

شیطان

misdemeanor n جنحه
→ petty misdemeanor قباحت
miser n بخیل • پیسه دوست
miserliness n پول دوستی
misfortune (calamity) n • مصیبت
بلا
misfortune (misery) n فلاکت
→ (colloq) برگشت
mislead (beguile) vt اغفال کردن
misleading adj اغفال کننده
misqal (unit of weight) n مثقال
Miss (form of address) n پیغله
miss (long for; takes pers پشت
ending) v پشت دق شدن
missile (less portable) n راکت
missile launcher (& pers) راکت
انداز • راکت لنچر n
missile n مزایل
missing see lost
mission n ماموریت
missionary n مبلغ • مبلغ مذهبی
mist n غبار
mistake n غلطی • تخطی • لغزش
• اشتباه • خطا
→ by mistake see mistakenly
→ make a mistake غلط کردن
تخطی کردن • اشتباه کردن
→ X marking a mistake چلیپا
mistake <sth for sth> v خطا کردن
<چیزی از چیزی>
mistaken adj غلط
mistakenly adv سهواً • اشتباهاً
mister (form of address) adj شاغلی
• اقای • صاحب
mistrust n گمان بد
misty adj غبار آلود
misunderstanding n غلط فهمی
misunderstanding (mutual) n سوء
تفاهم
misuse n سوء استفاده
mix vt مخلوط کردن • لت زدن
mixed adj مخلوط
mixing (& social) n خلط
mixing (cards) n گد
mixing (social) n اختلاط • امتزاج
mixture (solution) n محلول
mixture n مخلوط
Mizan (dist, month) n میزان
moan v نالیدن • نالش کردن

moaning n نالش
mob n ازدحام • بیروبار
mobile phone • تلفون جیبی
تیلفون جیبی
mobilization n سفربری • تجهیز •
بسیج
mobilize (mil) vi سفربری کردن •
بسیج کردن
mobilize <troops> vt سوق دادن
<به نیرو ها>
mock vt ریش خند زدن • ریش خند
کردن • هجو گفتن
mocked adj ریش خند
mockery n ریش خند • ریش خندی
• هجو • هجا
mode (fashion) n مود
mode (mus) n سر • مقام
model (example) n نمونه
→ (for calligraphy practice) مشق
moderate (& pol) adj میانه رو
moderate (& pol) adj میانه روی
moderate adj معتدل • اعتدالی
moderation n میانه روی • اعتدال •
استوا
modern (& adv) adj, adv نو • جدید
modern (current) adj معاصر
modern (high-tech) adj عصری
modernism n تجدد خواهی • تجدد
طلبی • تجدد پسندی
modernist (& pers) adj, n تجدد
خواه • تجدد طلب • تجدد پسند
modernity n تجدد
modesty (civility) n تواضع
modesty (shame) n شرم
modulation (mus) n تلحین
Moghul, Mogul see Mughal
Mohamad Agha (dist) n • محمد آغا
محمد آغه
Mohamed (m name) n محمد
Mohamedzai (P tribe) n محمدزی
moist adj تر • مرطوب • نمدار
moisten vt تر کردن
moisture (esp on surface) n نم
molar (tooth) n دندان الاشگی
mold (fungus) n پوپنک
mole (animal) n کور موش
mole (beauty mark) n خال
molecule n مالیکول
mollusc n حیوان ناعمه • نرمتن

457

molt v پر افگندن • پر انداختن • پر ریختانده • پر ریختن

mom (colloq) n ننه

moment n لحظه • دم

monarch (m) n شاه • پادشاه • سلطان

monarchist adj سلطنت طلب

monarchy n شاهی • پادشاهی • سلطنتی • شهریاری

monastery n دیر • صومعه

monastic order n رهبانیت

monasticism n رهبانیت

Monday n دوشنبه

monetary adj پولی • وجهی

money n پول • پیسه

→ advance money سلم • پول پیشکی

→ blood money خون بها

→ honest money پول حلال

→ hush money حق السکوت • حق سکوت

money-grubbing see miserly

money-maker (pers) n پول ساز

Mongol (& pers) adj, n مغل

Mongolia n مغلستان

Mongolian adj, n مغل

mongrel adj ناجنس • دورگ

monk n راهب • صومعه نشین

monkey n بوزینه • شادی • میمون

monochromatic adj یک رنگ

monologue n مونولوگ

monosyllabic adj یک هجایی

monotheism n یکتا پرستی • یگانه پرستی

monotheist n یکتا پرست • موحد

monotonous adj یک نواخت

monotony n یک نواختی

monster n جناور • جانور • حیوان • هیولا

month n ماه

monthly adj ماهانه • ماهوار

monument n یادگار • منار

mooch n مفت خور

mooch v مفت خوردن

mood (gram) n وجه

moon n ماهتاب • ماه

→ full moon بدر

→ moon's halo خرگاه

moral adj اخلاقی

458

morale n روحیه

morals n pl اخلاق

morbid adj مرضی

more <than sth> adj زیادتر • بیش • بیشتر <از چیزی>

more adj زیاده

more or less phrs کم و بیش • زیاد و کم

moreover adv علاوتاً • به علاوه

mores n وضع • وضعیت

morning adj صباحی • صبحگاهی • پگاهی • سحری

morning n صبح • صباح • قبل از ظهر • پگاه • پگه • سحر

morning (dawn) n بامداد

→ in the morning صبحانه • صباحی • صبح • صبحکی

morning sickness n گدایش • گدازش

Morocco n مراکش

morose adj ترش

morphine n مورفین

morphology & syntax n صرف و نحو • دستور زبان • گرامر

Morse code n الفبای مورس

morsel (piece) n توته • تکه

mortal (perishable) adj فنا پذیر

mortality n فنا

→ mortality rate میزان مرگ و میر • نسبتِ وفیات

mortar (trench mortar) n هاوان

mortar (vessel) n اغر • هاون • هاوان

Mosaic (bibl) adj موسوی

mosaic n موزاییک

Moscow n ماسکو • مسکو

Moses (bibl; m name) n موسی

mosque n مسجد

mosquito n پشه

mosquito net n پشه خانه

mostly (often) adv اکثراً • اکثر اوقات

→ (colloq) بسیاری وخت ها

moth (butterfly) n پروانه

moth (clothes moth) n کویه

mother n مادر

→ (colloq) ننه

→ (lit) والده

motherhood n مادری

mother-in-law *n* خشو • خاش

mother-of-pearl *n* صدف • صدف • مرواريد

motion (movement) *n* • حرکت سير

motion (proposal) *n* پيش نهاد

motivate <sb to do sth> *vt* تشويق کردن <کسی را به چيزی>

motivation *n* تشويق • تشجيع

motive (incentive) *n* انگيزه • سياقه

motive (reason) *n* موجب

motor *n* موتور

motorcycle *n* موترسکل

MOU *see* memorandum of understanding

mound (heap) *n* توده • تپه • کوت
→ dirt mound خاک توده

mount (get on) *vi* سوار شدن

mount (seat, set) *vt* نشاندن

mountain *n* کوه • که

mountain climber *n* کوه نورد

mountain pass *n* کوتل • کتل

Mountain Tajik *see* Wakhi

mountaineer *n* کوه نشين

mountainous *adj* کوهستانی

mountainside کوه سينه

mounted (atop sth) *adj* • سوار سواره

mourn *v* سوگ داشتن • ماتم داشتن • عزا گرفتن

mournful (& adv) *adj, adv* نالان

mourning *n* سوگ • عزا • ماتم • زاری • ندبه
→ in mourning سوگوار • عزا دار • ماتم دار • ماتم ديده • ماتم زده • سياه پوش

mouse *n* موش

moustache *n* بروت

mouth (& fig) *n* دهان • دهن

mouthful (of food) *n* لقمه

move (body part) *vt* حرکت دادن

move (change of residence) *n* کوچ • کوچ کشی

move (change residence) *vi* کوچ کردن • کوچ کشی کردن

move (chess) *n* چال

move (emigrate) *vi* هجرت کردن • مهاجرت کردن

move (emigration) *n* • هجرت مهاجرت

move (get going) *vi* حرکت کردن

move around (stir up fuss) *v* شور خوردن

movement (& mil, social) *n* حرکت • جنبش

movement (change, rotation) *n* گردش

movement (motion) *n* • حرکت سير

movie *n* فلم

movie theater *n* سينما

Mr. *see* mister

Mrs. (form of address) *n* • خانم ميرمن • زن

much (& too much) *adj* بسيار • زياد • خيلی • افزون
→ as much as هرقدر

mucus *n* خلم • لعاب
→ mucous membrane غشای مخاطی

mud *adj* گلی

mud *n* گل • خت
→ mud & straw for surfacing کاه گل
→ mud house خانه گلی

muddy *adj* خت • گل آلود

muezzin (rel) *n* موذين

mufti (law, rel) *n* مفتی

Mughal (hist) *adj, n* مغل

muhaqaq (callig style) *n* • محقق خط محقق

Muharram (month) *n* محرم
→ Shiite chest-beating during Muharram ماتم

muhr (hist, gold coin) *n* مهر

Mujabriya (fatalist school of Islamist thought) *n* مجبريه • جبريه

mujahed (mil, rel) *n* مجاهد
→ Union of Seven (mujahedin grp, 1990s) اتحاد هفت گانه
→ Union of Three (mujahedin grp, 1990s) اتحاد سه گانه

mulberry *n* توت
→ ground dried mulberries تلخان

mule *n* قاطر • قاطر

mullah (rel) *n* ملا
→ head mullah in royal household
ملا باشی • خان ملا خان
→ mullah's assistant چلی
Mullah Mohamed Kheyl (ctr) *n* ملا
محمد خیل
Mullazai *see* Malazai
multiplication (math) *n* ضرب
→ multiplication table جدول
ضرب
multiply (math) *v* ضرب کردن
multitude *n* انبوه
multitudinous *adj* انبوه
Mumand Dara (dist) *n* مومند دره
mummified *adj* مومیایی
mummify *vt* مومیایی کردن
mummy *n* مومیا
Munawar (m name) *n* منور
mung beans *n* ماش
municipality *n* شاروالی
Munj (ethn grp, village) *n* منج
Munji (& lang, pers) *adj, n* • منجی
منجانی
Muqadas (m name) *n* مقدس
Murch (ctr) *n* مرچ
murder (lit) *n* قتل
→ murder victim • قتیل • مقتول
کشته
murder *vt* به قتل رساندن
murderer *n* قاتل • سفاح • سفاک
murderous *adj* قاتل
Murghab (river, dist) *n* مرغاب
murky *adj* تاریک • ظلمانی
murmur *n* شرشر
mursal (rose variety) *n* مرسل
Musa Kheyl (dist) *n* موسی خیل
Musa Qala (dist) *n* موسی قلعه
Musayi (dist) *n* موسینی • موسهی
Muscat *n* مسقط
muscle (anat) *n* عضله
→ (esp calf, arm, forearm) ماهیچه
muscular *adj* عضلاتی
muse *v* خیال کردن
museum *n* موزه • موزیم
mushroom *n* سماروق
music *n* موسیقی • موزیک • آهنگ
• ساز
musical (production) *n* موزیکال

musical instrument *n* • آله موسیقی
ساز
musician *n* موسیقی نواز • نوازنده
• سازنده
musicologist *n* موسیقی دان
musk *n* مشک • نافه
→ deer's musk gland نافه
→ musk-colored (black) مشکین
musky (scent) *adj* مشکین
Muslim (pers) *n* مسلمان • مسلم
→ non-Muslim کافر • بی دین
Muslim Brotherhood (mvmt) *n*
اخوان المسلمین
muslin (for chadar) *n* ململ
must (definitely) *adv* حتماً
must <+ subj> *modal v* باید
→ (formal) بایست
must <+ subj> *v* مجبور بودن
mustard *n* شرشم • اوری • خردل
→ (& plant) اوری
Mutazila (hist, rationalist Sunni
school of theology) *n* • معتزله
المعتزله
Mutazilite (hist, follower of
mutazila) *n* معتزلی
mute *adj* لال • گنگ
→ (& willfully silent) زبان بریده
mutton *n* گوشت گوسفند
mutual (common) *adj* اصلی
mutual (reciprocal) *adj* دوطرفه
muzzle (anat) *n* پوز
muzzle (worn) *n* پوزبند
Myanmar *see* Burma
myrobalan (almond) *n* هلیله • هلیله
کابلی
myrtle (shrub) *n* مورم
mysterious (unseen) *adj* غیبی
mystery (secret) *n* راز • سر
mystic (& Sufi, & pers) *adj, n*
متصوف • صوفی • عارف
mystical (esp Sufically) *adj* عرفانی
mystical (& Sufic) (& adv) *adj, adv*
عارفانه
mysticism (esp Sufic, Shiite) *n*
عرفان
myth (legend) *n* افسانه • اسطوره
mythical (legendary) *adj* افسانه یی
• اساطیری
mythological *adj* اساطیری

mythology n متولوژی • اساطیر

N

Nad Ali (dist) n ناد علی
Nader (m name) n نادر
Nader Shah (hist, Afgh king 1929-1933) n محمد نادر شاه • نادر شاه
Nader Shah (hist, Persian king 1688-1747) n نادر شاه
Nader Shah Kot (ctr) n نادر شاه کوت
Nadera (f name) n نادره
nag (pest) n شوله
nag (whine) v نق زدن
nagging adj سلیطه • لولی
→ (colloq) شلیطه
nagging n نق
Naghlu Dam n بند نغلو
Nahid (f name) n ناهید
Nahr-e Saraj (dist) n نهر سراج
Nahr-e Shahi (dist) n نهر شاهی
Nahrin (dist) n نهرین
nail (peg) n میخ
→ fingernails, toenails ناخن
→ nail clipper ناخنگیر
Naim (m name) n نعیم
naive adj ساده
Najd (geog) n نجد
Najib (m name) n نجیب
Najib ud-Dawla (hist, Rohilla P leader) n نجیب الدوله
Najiba (f name) n نجیبه
Najibullah (hist, last Afgh communist president) n نجیب الله
naked adj لچ • برهنه • عریان
nakhchir (kind of deer) n نخچیر
Namak Ab (dist) n نمک آب
name n نام
→ having the same name هم نام
→ in the name of the Almighty & Merciful God بسم الله الرحمن الرحیم
→ last name عبادی
→ name of the game (fig) بند نغلو
→ taking a new name when converting to Islam نامگذاری
name vt نام گذاشتن

name (nominate) <sb, sth> vt مسمی کردن <کسی / چیزی را> • نام دادن • نام گذاری کردن
named adj بنام • با نام
Nangarhar (province) n ننگرهار
nap v چشم پت شدن
napkin n دستمال کاغذی
→ paper napkin دستمال کاغذی
Naqshbandiyya (Sufi order) n نقشبندیه
Narang (dist) n نرنگ
Naray (dist) n ناری
narcissus (white flower) n نرگس
→ (lit) عبهر
→ yellow narcissus نسرین
narcotics n pl مواد مخدر • مواد مخدره • مخدرات
narcotize vt تخدیر کردن
narghile see hookah
narrate v حکایت کردن • قصه کردن
narrative adj حکایتی • قصصی • روایتی
narrative n حکایت • قصه • روایت
narrator n گوینده • نطاق • سخن گوی • سخن ران
narrow adj باریک • تنگ • کمعرض • کم بر
narrow-minded adj تنگ نظر
NASA n ناسا
nasal adj انفی
Nasim (m name) n نسیم
Nasima (f name) n نسیمه
Nasir (m name) n نصیر
Nasir (P tribe) n ناصر
naskh (callig style) n نسخ • خط نسخ
Nasrin (f name) n نسرین
Nasruddin (fictional mullah) n نصرالدین • ملا نصرالدین
nastaliq (callig style) n نستعلیق
natal adj تولدی
nation (people) n مردم • ملت
nation (state) n مملکت • ملک
national (pers) n تابع • تبعه
national adj ملی
National Aeronautics & Space Agency see NASA

National Directorate of Security *see*
NDS

National Liberation Front (hist,
guerrila mvmt) *n* جبهه نجات ملی

National Military Academy of
Afghanistan *n* اکادمی ملی نظامی
افغانستان

National Military Command Center
n مرکز هماهنگی نظامی ملی

National Police Command Center *n*
مرکز سوق و اداره پولیس ملی •
مرکز هماهنگی پولیس ملی

National Socialist *see* Nazi

nationalist (pers) [cf. ملی] *n*
ناسیونالست

nationalistic *adj* ملی

nationality *n* ملیت

nationwide *adv* در سرتاسر کشور

native (aborigine, & pers) *adj, n*
بومی

native (local, & pers) *adj, n* محلی

native (of nation) *adj* وطنی •
داخلی

NATO *n* ناتو • سازمان پیمان
اتلانتیک شمالی

natural *adj* طبیعی • عیانی • عینی
• سکه

→ natural gas گاز

naturalization (law) *n* تابعیت

naturalize (law) *n* تابعیت ‹دیک
کشور› به دست آوردن

naturally *adv* معلوم دار • طبعاً •
طبیعتاً • بالطبع

nature (disposition) *n* طبع • نهاد •
مزاج • مجاز

nature (essence) *n* نفس

nature (natural world) *n* طبیعت

nature (quality) *n* کیفیت

→ (fig) خمیر

naughty (devilish, & pers) *adj, n*
شیطان • ابلیس • اهریمن

naughty (mischievous) *n* شوخ

nauseous *adj* دل بد

nautical mile *n* میل بحری

naval (mil) *adj* بحری • از قوای
بحری

navel (anat) *n* ناف

navy (mil) *n* قوای بحری

→ navy blue سرمه یی

462

Naw Bahar (dist) *n* نو بهار

Nawa (dist) *n* ناوه

Nawa-ye Barakzai (dist) *n* ناوه
بارکزی

Nawur (dist) *n* ناور

Nawzad (dist) *n* نوزاد

nay (vote) رای مختلف

Nayka *see* Nika

Naypyidaw (capital) *n* نی •
نیپیدو • پنی دو

naysayer *adj,* منفی باف

nayza (unit of meas) *n* نیزه

Nazarene (Christian) *adj, n*
نصرانی

Nazareth (city) *n* نصره

Nazeyan (dist) *n* نازیان

Nazi (f name; & hist) *n* نازی

Nazism (hist) *n* نازیزم • ناسیسم

NCO (mil) بریدگی • خورد ضابط
→ (colloq) ضابط

NCO (police) *n* ساتنمن

NDS *n* ریاست مصونیت ملی

near (to) *prep* نزدیک • در نزدیک
• نزدیک به • قریب

near *adj, adv* نزدیک • قریب

nearly (lit) *adv* عنقریب

nearsighted *adj* عاقبت اندیش •
عاقبت بین • عاقبت نگر • مآل
اندیش

neat (clean) *adj* پاک

→ neat & orderly به نظم و نسق

necessarily (compulsorily) *adv*
ناچار • بناچار • به ناچار • ناگزیر

necessarily *adv* ضرورتاً •
بالضرورت • بالضرور • لابد •
لزوماً

necessary (compulsory) *adj* ناچار

necessary (required) *adj* ضروری
• ضرور • لازم • لازمی

necessary (useful) *adj* کارآمد

→ (lit) واجب

→ as necessary عندالضرورت •
عندالضروره • عندالللزوم

→ if necessary در صورت لزوم •
عند اللزوم

necessity *n* لزوم • مقتضا

→ (necessary thing) لازمه

→ necessities ضروریات • لوازم

neck (anat) *n* گردن

neckerchief *n* گلوبند

necklace *n* • گردن بند • گلوبند • طوق • عقد

neckline (clothes) *n* گریبان • یخن

necktie *n* نکتایی

nectarine *n* شلیل

need (urgent) *n* احتیاج

need (urgently) *v* احتیاج داشتن
→ (colloq) کار داشتن

need <sth> *vt* ضرورت داشتن <به چیزی> • نیاز داشتن

need *n* نیاز • ضرورت
→ because of need به حکم ضرورت

needle (& syringe) *n* سوزن

needlework *n* سوزن دوزی

needy (pers) *n* • نیاز مند • غریب • مستحق

nefarious *adj* شوم

negative *adj* منفی
→ (colloq) تحت صفر

negativist (& pers) *adj, n* منفی باف

neglect (fig) *vt* پس گوش کردن

neglect *v* فرو گذاشت کردن

negligence *n* اهمال • فرو گذاشت
→ (fig) خواب خرگوش

negligent *adj* • بی پروا • لاابالی • غافل

negotiate *v* مذاکرات کردن

negotiation *n* مذاکره

neigh *n* شیهه

neigh *v* شیهه کشیدن

neighbor *n* همسایه
→ neighbor & fellow farmer پلوان شریک

neighborhood *n* جوار

neighboring *adj* همسایه

neither ... nor ... *adv* نه ... نه ...

Nejrab (dist) *n* نجراب

nelumbo (plant, genus) *n* نیلوفر هندی

nenuphar (plant) *n* نیلوفر

neoconservatism *n* نو محافظه کاری

neoconservative (& pers) *adj, n* نو محافظه کار

Nepal *n* نیپال

nephew (by brother) *n* برادر زاده

nephew (by sister) *n* خواهر زاده

nephritic (med) *adj* کلیوی

Neptun (f name) *n* نپتون

Neptune (planet) *n* نپتون

Nerkh (dist) *n* نرخ

nerve (anat) *n* عصب
→ optic nerve عصب باصره

nervous (anxious) *adj n* نگران

nervous (med) *adj* عصبی

nervousness *n* نگرانی

nest *n* • آشیان • آشیانه

Nestor (hist) *n* نسطور

Nestorian (hist) *n* نسطوری

Nestorianism (hist) *n* دین نسطوری

net *n* شبکه
→ net weight وزن خالص

Netherlands, the *n* • هالیند • هالند • هلند

network *n* شبکه

neurologist *n* • داکتر اعصاب • نورولوژست

neurology *n* نورولوژی

neutral *adj* • بیطرف • بیطرفانه • خنثی

neutrality *n* بیطرفی

neutralization *n* خنثی ساختن

neutralize *vt* خنثی ساختن

neutrally *adv* بیطرفانه

neutron *n* نیوترون

never *adv* • هیچ • هیچ وقت • هیچ گاه • هرگز

nevertheless *conj* و اما

new (& adv) *adj, adv* • نو • جدید

New Delhi *n* • دهلی جدید • دهلی نو

New Year's Day *n* نوروز

New York (city, state) *n* نیو یارک

newborn *adj* • نورسیده • نوخاسته

newborn *n* • نوزاد • نورسیده

newcomer *n* تازه وارد

newly-arrived *adj, n* نو وارد

newly-sprouted *adj* نورسته

newlywed (f) *adj, n* نو عروس
→ newlyweds' feast ناشتایی

news *n* • خبر • گزارش • راپور
→ good news; (colloq) reward for bringing good news مژده

newscaster *n* نطاق

newspaper *n* • اخبار • روزنامه • جریده

next (& pers) *adj, n* • دیگر • دگر

463

next <to sth> prep • پهلو • در پهلو • کنار • در کنار • پیوست • نزد • به • نظر • برای <چیزی>
next adj • آینده • مابعد • تالی
next-door adj در به دوار
Neyazi (P tribe) n نیازی
Neysh (dist) n نیش
NGO n سازمان غیر دولتی • سازمان بیرون حکومت • انجو
nice (good) adj خجل
nice (& adv) adj, adv نیکو • نکو
nicety (subtlety) n دقیقه
nickel adj نکلی
nickel (metal, coin) n نکل
nickname n لقب
Nicosia • نیکوسیه نقسیه
nicotine n نکوتین
niece (by brother) n برادر زاده
niece (by sister) n خواهر زاده
nigella seeds n سیاه دانه
Niger نایجیر
Nigeria n نایجیریا
Nigerian (& pers) adj, n نایجیریایی
Nigerien see Nigerois
Nigerois (& pers) adj, n نایجیری
night n شب • لیل
→ night-blind (& pers) شب کور
→ night blindness شب کوری
nightingale (bird) n • مرغ پگاهی • مرغ سحر • عندلیب • بلبل
nightmare (colloq) n سیاهی
nightspot (club) n کلوب
Nika (dist) n نیکه
Nile (river) n نیل
Nili (seat, dist) n نیلی
nimble (speech) n نغز
Nimroz (province) n نیمروز
nine adj, n نه
→ (colloq) نو
nineteen adj, n نزده
nineteenth adj نزدهم
→ (lit, used before n) نزدهمین
ninetieth adj نودم
→ (lit, used before n) نودمین
ninety adj, n نود
Nineveh (hist) n نینوا
ninth adj نهم
→ (lit, used before n) نهمین

nipple n • سر پستان • نوکِ پستان • لاخ
Nishapur (city) n نیشاپور
niter n شوره
nitpicker adj منفی باف
nitrate (chem) n نایتریت
nitrogen n نایتروجن
NMAA see National Military Academy of Afghanistan
NMCC see National Military Command Center
no (w/neg v) adj کدام • هیچ چ
no adv نی
→ (answer to question) نخیر
→ (colloq) نه
no one see nobody
Noah (bibl) n نوح
→ Noah's Ark کشتی نوح
nobility (aristocracy) n نجبا
noble (aristocrat) n • آدم اصل • اصیل زاده • مرزا • میرزا • بدل • شریف
noble (metal) adj نجیبه
noble adj • نجیب • اصل • اصیل • اصیل زاده
→ noble act مکرمت
nobody pron هیچ کس • هیچ چ یک • هیچ کدام
nod v سر تکان دادن
noise n • غالمغال • قالمقال • قیل و قال • غوغا • هنگامه
→ (hue & cry) هیاهو
→ (sound) صدا
noisy (& pers) adj, n • غوغا گر • غوغایی
nomad n • صحرا نشین • بیابان نشین • بیابان گرد
→ Bedouin nomad بادیه نشین
nomadic adj • صحرا نشین • بیابان نشین
nominal (& gram) adj • اسمی • اسمیه
nominally adv اسماً
nominate <sb, sth> vt • مسمی کردن <کسی / چیزی را> • نام دادن • نام گذاری کردن
nominative (gram) adj فاعلی
nominee n کاندید • کاندیدا
non-aligned adj • بیطرف • بی طرف

464

non-believer (law) *n* بیگانه • اجنبی • خارجی

nonchalant *adj* سهل انگار

non-commissioned officer see NCO

nonentity *n* صفر

nonetheless (lit) *adv* مع هذا

non-existence *n* نیستی

non-governmental organization see NGO

non-irrigated *adj* للمی

non-performance *n* عدم اجرا

non-political *adj* غیر سیاسی

non-profit organization *n* سازمان غیر انتفاعی

non-rejectable *adj* غیر قابل تردید

nonsense *n* حرف مفت • جفنگ

nonsensical *adj* پوچ • پوک

noodles (& w/meatballs) *n* آش

nook *n* کنج

noon *n* چاشت • ظهر

→ noon cannon (hist, Kabul) توپ چاشت

Noorzai (P tribe) *n* نورزی

noose *n* ریسمان غرغره

norm *n* معیار • نورم • ستندرد • ملاک • لایحه

normal *adj* نورمال

north *n* شمال

→ from the north شمالاً

→ Shamali (plain north of Kabul) سمتِ شمالی • شمالی

→ the north شمال • شام

North America *n* امریکای شمالی

North Atlantic Treaty Organization see NATO

North Pole *n* قطب شمال

northeast *n* شمال شرق

northeastern *adj* شمال شرقی

Northern Alliance *n* ائتلاف شمالی

northwest *n* شمال غرب

northwestern *adj* شمال غربی

Norway *n* ناروی

Norwegian (& pers, lang) *adj, n* نارویژی

nose (anat) *n* بینی • دماغ

→ tip of the nose پرهِ بینی

nose stud *n* خال بینی • میخک

nostril *n* سوراخ بینی

nosy *adj* کنج کاو

not ... but ... *phrs* نه ... بلکی ... • نه ... مگر ...

not bad *phrs* میگذره

→ (colloq) مگذره

note (mention) *v* یاد کردن • یاد آور شدن

note (mus) *n* سر

note (record) *n* یاد داشت

→ note on sm piece of paper پرزه

notebook *n* کتابچه

noteworthy *adj* قابل توجه

nothing *pron* هیچ • هیچ چیز

→ better than nothing غنیمت

notice (heed) *n* توجه

→ be noticed به مشاهده رسیدن

→ take notice توجه کردن • متوجه کردن

notice (notification) *n* اطلاع • اطلاعیه • آگاهی • وقوف

notice (warning) *n* اخطار • اخطاریه

→ put <sb> on notice اخطار دادن <به کسی>

notification see notice

notify *vt* خاطر نشان کردن • خاطر نشان ساختن

notoriety *n* نام بدی

notorious (& adv) *adj, adv* برملا • آشکار

notorious <for sth> *adj* مشهور <به چیزی>

notorious *adj* نام بد

noun *n* اسم • اسمیه

→ indefinite noun نکره

→ noun phrase اسمیه

→ proper noun علم

nourishing *adj* غذایی

nourishment *n* پرورش

nouveau riche *adj* نودولت • نو به دولت رسیده • نادیده • نوکیسه

nouveau riche *n* نادیده گی • آدم نادیده

novel (new) *adj* طرفه

novel *n* ناول • رومان • داستان

novelist *n* داستان نویس

novella *n* داستان کوچک

November *n* نومبر

novice (of Sufi order) *n* مرید

465

novitiate (in Sufi order) *n* مریدی

now *adv* • حالا • حالی • در حال • اکنون • کنون • اینک • عجالتاً • فعلاً (lit) →

nowhere *adv* هیچ جا • هیچ جای

nozzle (for spraying) *n* ژیکلور

NPCC *see* National Police Command Center

nuclear *adj* • هسته یی • اتمی • ذروی

hostی (colloq) →

nuclear proliferation *n* نشر اسلحه هستوی

nuclear-free *adj* فاقد سلاح ذروی

nude *adj* • برهنه • لچ • عریان

numb *adj* • بی حس • کرخت

قرخت (colloq) →

go numb (limb) → خواب بردن ‹چیزی را›

number (digit, figure) *n* • رقم • عدد

number (quantity) *n* • تعداد • عده

number (score) *n* نمره

number *n* • شماره • نمبر

numerous *adj* • متعدد • بسیاری • برخی

numismatics *n* سکه شناسی

numismatist *n* سکه شناس

nun *n* راهبه

Nurestan (province, seat) *n* نورستان

Nurestani (& pers, lang) *adj, n* نورستانی

Nurgal (dist) *n* نورگل

Nurgaram (dist) *n* • نورگرم • نورگرام

nurse (sb) *v* • تیمار داری کردن • تیمار کردن

nurse *n* نرس

wet nurse → • دایه • دایی

nursery *n* پرورشگاه

nursing (loosely) *n* بیمار داری

nursling (infant) *adj* شیر خوار

nurture *vt* • پروردن • پروراندن

Nurzai *see* Noorzai

Nusay (ctr) *n* نسی

nut (mechanical) *n* نت

nut & bolt *phrs* نت و بولت

nutritious *adj* غذایی

nuts (edible) *n* • خسته باب • مغزیت

466

O

O (w/vocative) *excl* • ای • یا

o'-clock *adj* بجه

oak (tree) *n* بلوط

oath *n* • سوگند • قسم

oath of allegiance → بیعت

Oba (dist) *n* اوبه

obedience (to orders) *n* اطاعت

obedience *n* • انقیاد • پذیرش

obedient (dutiful) *adj* گپ شنو

obedient (following orders) *adj* • فرمان بردار • فرمان دار • مطیع

obese *adj* چاق

obese *see* & fat

obesity *n* • چاقی • فربهی

obey (order) *v* • فرمان بردن • اطاعت کردن

obey an order *vt* • به جای آوردن • به جای کردن

object (goal) *see* objective *n*

object (gram) *n* مفعول

object (thing) *n* • چیز • شی

objectionable *adj* زشت

objective (gram) *adj* مفعولی

objective *adj see* & ocular

objective (goal) *n* • منظور • هدف • مرام • مطلب • غایه

objectivity *n* • عینیت • آفاقیت • واقع بینی

obligation (& rel) *n* وظیفه

obligations (duties) → • واجبات • وجایب

obligation *n* مکلفیت

oblige (sb) *vt* مجبور ساختن

obliged *adj* • مکلف • مجبور

be obliged → مکلفیت داشتن

oblivious (& pers) *adj, n* غافل

oblong *see* rectangular

obscene *adj* • زشت • قبیح

(foul-mouthed) → فحاش

obscenity *n* • فحش • قباحت

obscure (anonymous) *adj* گمنام

obscurity (anonymity) *n* • گمنامی • خمول

observance (of duties) *n* • رعایت • رعایه • مراعات

observant (watching) adj نگران

observation (contemplation) n مشاهده

Observation (supervision) n نگرانی

Observation (watching) n مراقب

observe (rules) vt مراعات کردن

observe (watch) v متوجه کردن

observer n نگران • ناظر

obstacle n مانع • عایق →
چالش (fig)

obstetric adj ولادی

Obstetrician n داکتر ولادی

obstinacy n ستیزه

obstinate (contentious) (& pers)
adj, n ستیزه جو(ی) • ستیزه
خو(ی) • ستیزه کار • ستیزه گر

obstinate (opinionated) adj خود
رای

obstinate (pushy) adj سرزور •
سرتنبه

obstinate (stubborn) adj خیر چشم
• خیره چشم • لجوج

obstruct vt مسدود کردن • بسته
کردن

obstructed adj مسدود • بسته

obstruction n انسداد

obstructionism n کارشکنی

obtain vt دستیاب کردن • دریافت
داشتن • دریافت کردن

obtaining n دستیابی

obtuse (angle) adj منفرجه

obvious (& adv) adj, adv آشکار •
نمایان
→ obvious matters واضحات

obvious adj ظاهر • واضح • صاف
• روشن • مبرهن

occasion (opportunity) n مناسبت

occasional (incidental) adj
عارضی

occasionally adv احیاناً • گاه گاه •
گاهی • وقتاً فوقتاً

occult adj پنهان

occult sciences n pl حکم

occupation (job) n مسلک • شغل •
مشغولیت • مصروفیت
→ (colloq) کسب

occupation (of country) n اشغال •
تصرف

occupation (of territory) adj اشغالی

occupational adj مسلکی

Occupied Territories n pl اراضی
اشغالی • قلمرو فلسطینی

occupying power n تصرف قدرت

occur <to sb> vi به نظر <کسی>
رسیدن

occur see & happen

occurrence n وقوع • وقع

ocean n بحر • اقیانوس

oceanic adj بحری • اقیانوسی

oceanologist n اقیانوس شناس

oceanology n اقیانوس شناسی

octagon (& adj) adj, n مثمن • هشت
ضلعی

octagonal see octagon

October n اکتوبر

ocular adj عینی • آفاقی

odd (number) adj طاق

odd (strange) adj نخچه

ode n چکامه
→ compose an ode چکامه سرودن

odor n بوی

oeuvre (publication) n تالیف

of course adv معلوم دار

off (switched off) adj گل کرده
→ off & on (at intervals) به وقفه ها

offend v تجاوز کردن • بر خوردن

offended adj دل آزرده • آزرده دل

offense (indignation) n رنجش

offense see & offensive n

offensive (& mil) adj حمله ور •
متعرض • تهاجمی • هجومی

offensive (& mil) n حمله • تعرض •
تهاجم • هجوم

offer (bid) n آفر

offer (present) vt تقدیم کردن • پیش
کش کردن

offer (proposal) n پیش نهاد

offer (supply) n عرضه

offer (supply) vt عرضه کردن

office (bureau) n ریاست • شعبه •
اداره • دایره • دیوان

office (position) n منصب •
ماموریت

office (workplace) n دفتر • اداره •
دایره
→ office supplies قرطاسیه
→ office worker کاتب

officer (mil, police) *n* افسر
→ commissioned mil officer
منصب دار • صاحب منصب • افسر
→ NCO خورد ضابط • بریدگی
officer (police) *n* فرد • ساتونکی
→ commissioned police officer
څارنمن
official (pers) *n* مامور • موظف
official *adj* رسمی
officially *adv* رسماً • رسمیاً
offspring *n* نسل • نطفه • ثمره •
ذریه
→ (of an animal) چوچه
often *adv* غالباً
oft-forgiving (God) *adj* غفور
ogle *v* نظر بازی کردن
ogler *n* نظر باز
ogling *n* چشم چرانی • نظر بازی
→ (lit) دلال
oil (cooking oil) *n* روغن
oil (petroleum) *n* نفت • پترول
→ oil & gas نفت و گاز
→ pump oil from ground تیل
کشیدن
oil *see* & lubricant
oilcloth *n* موم جامه
oily (& food) *adj* چرب
ointment *n* مرهم
OK (all right) (colloq) *excl* خو
OK (w/pleasure) *excl* به چشم
OK *adj* خیر
okra *n* بامیه
old (ancient) *adj* قدیم • قدامت دار •
باستان • باستانی
old (esp people) *adj* پیر • معمر •
کلان سال • سال خورده
old (not new; worn-out) *adj* کهنه
old age *n* سن پیری
Old Testament *n* تورات
old-fashioned *adj* قدیمی
→ (conservative) کهنه خیال
olive *n* زیتون
→ Russian olive (oleaster) سنجد
olivine *n* زبر جد
Olympiad *n* اولمپیاد
olympic *adj* اولمپیک
Omar (m name; hist, 2nd caliph) *n*
عمر

Omar Khayyam (12th-c Dari poet) *n*
خیام • عمر خیام
Omarzai (small P grp) *n* عمرزی
omen *n* فال
→ bad omen شگون
→ be an omen افتادن
→ good omen تیمن
omission *n* افتادگی
omitted *adj* محذوف
OMLT (mil) *n* تیم رابط ناتو و
مشاورین
Omna (dist) *n* اومنه
on *prep* بالا • سر • بر
→ on the whole بطور دربست
once *adv* یک بار • یک دفعه
one (of sth) *adj, n* یکی
→ one another یک دیگر • یک
دگر
→ one by one, one each یک یک
→ one-on-one (combat) تن به تن
→ one-way یک طرفه
one *adj, n* یک
oneness (& of God) *n* یگانه گی •
یگانگی • یکتایی
oneself *pron* خویش
→ (takes pers endings) خود
→ by oneself تنها • به تنهایی
ongoing *adj* پیش و پس • پایا
→ be ongoing جریان داشتن
onion *n* پیاز
→ green onions نوش پیاز
→ onion soup (Afgh dish) پیاوه
only (mere) *adj* صرف
only (merely) *adv* تنها • صرفاً •
فقط • خالصاً
only (sole) *adj* یگانه • یکتا
only (solely) *adv* تنها
onomatopoeia *n* تسمیه تقلیدی •
اسم متکی بر صوت
onomatopoeic *adj* تقلیدی
→ onomatopoeic word کلمه تقلیدی
ooze *n see* oozing
ooze *v* تراوش کردن • ترشح کردن
ooze *vi* تراویدن
oozing *n* تراوش • ترشح
OPEC *n* اوپک

468

open *adj* باز
→ (colloq) واز
→ open at one end سرکشاده
→ open to persuasion نفوذ پذیر
→ open-faced (fig) گشاده روی
→ open-handed (fig) گشاده دست
→ open-hearted (fig) گشاده دل
→ open-minded روشن فکر
open (overt) (& adv) *adj, adv* برملا
• آشکار
open *v* باز کردن
→ (colloq) واز کردن
→ (door, window) باز گذاشتن
open (begin) *vt* گشایش دادن • افتتاح کردن
open (begin; reveal) *vt* گشودن
→ be opened گشایش یافتن • افتتاح شدن • بازگشایی شدن
opening (aperture) *n* دهان • دهن
opening (beginning) *n* • گشایش افتتاح
opening *adj* افتتاحی
→ (f form) افتتاحیه
openly (overtly) *adv* • آشکار آشکاراً • برملا
opera *n* اوپرا
operate (function) *vi* دایر شدن
operate (surgery) *v* عمل کردن
Operation & Mentor Liaison Team *see* OMLT
operation (math, med, mil) *n* عملیه
→ operations (esp mil) • عملیات حرکات
operational *adj* عملیاتی
operative (trusted aide) *n* • معتمد تحویل دار نقدی
operator (telephone) *n* تلفون چی
ophite *n* مرمر سبز
ophthalmologist *n* داکتر چشم
opinion (assumption) *n* گمان
opinion (belief) *n* • عقیده • نظریه اعتقاد
opinion (verdict) *n* قضاوت
opinion (viewpoint) *n* نظر • نظریه
opinionated *adj* خود رای
opinon (idea) *n* فکر • فکرت • مفکوره • اندیشه
→ poor opinion سوء ظن
→ public opinion مفکورهٔ عام

opium *n* تریاک • افیون
→ (& poppy) کوکنار
opium addict *n* افیونی • تریاکی
opponent *n* حریف • رقیب • ضد • هم چشم
opportunism *n* پیش پای بینی • ابن الوقتی
opportunist *adj, n* • پیش پای بین ابن الوقت • زمان ساز
opportunity *n* امکان • مجال • فرصت
opposed (resistant) *adj* مخالف
opposite (contrary) *adj* • بر عکس متضاد • ضد
opposite (facing) *adj* مقابل • در مقابل • پیش روی
opposition (contrariness) *n* ضدیت
opposition (contrast) *n* تقابل
opposition (resistance) *n* مخالفت
oppressed (& pers) *adj, n* ستم دیده • ستم رسیده • ستم زده • ستم کش • ستم کشیده
→ be oppressed ستم دیدن
oppression *n* ستم • بیداد • جور • ظلم
oppressive (& adv) *adj, adv* جابرانه
oppressive *adj* زبردست • ستم آمیز • ظلم آمیز
oppressor *n* زبردست • جابر • دست انداز • زور آور • ستمگر • ستم گار • ستم کار • ستم اندیش
opt *v* اختیار فرمودن • اختیار کردن
optic *adj* باصره
→ optic nerve عصب باصره
optical *see* optic
optician *n* عینک ساز
optimism *n* خوشبینی
optimistic *adj* خوشبین
option (choice) *n* اختیار
optional *adj* اختیاری
or *conj* یا
→ and/or و یا
Orakzai (P tribe) *n* اورکزی
oral (verbal) *adj* زبانی • شفاهی
→ oral history • تاریخ دهن به دهن تاریخ سینه به سینه

orange *n* مالته
→ orange-colored نارنجی
→ mandarin orange کینو
→ sour orange نارنج
orate *v* نطق کردن
oration *n* نطق
orator *n* نطاق • خطیب • سخن گوی • سخن ران
orbit (in space) *n* مدار
orbiter (in space) *n* مدار گرد
order (arrange) *v* نظم دادن • چیدن
order (arrangement) *n* • ترتیب قرار • نظم
→ out of order از کار افتاده
order (command) *n* • امر • فرمان امریه • قوماندہ • حکم
→ order & prohibition امر و نهی
order (command) *v* • فرمان دادن قوماندہ دادن
order (direct) *v* هدایت کردن
order (directive) *n* هدایت
order (in restaurant) *v* فرمایش دادن
order (instruct) *v* سفارش دادن
order (instruction) *n* • دستور سفارش
order (medal) *n* مدال
order (rel, Sufi) *n* طریقت • صوفیه • متصوفه • سلسله
order (restaurant) *n* فرمایش
order (system; regime) *n* نظام
ordered (instructed) *adj* سفارشی
ordering (arranging) *n* • ترتیب تنظیم
ordinal number *n* عدد ترتیبی
ordinarily (usually) *adv* معمولاً
ordinary (common) *adj* عادی
ordinary (natural) *adj* طبیعی
ordinary (usual) *adj* معمول
ordnance (mil) *n* مواد منفجره
organ (& anat) *n* • آلت • افزار عضو
organic (& chem) *adj* عضوی
organic *adj* آلی
organism *n* وجود • بدن • عضویت
organization (& mil unit) *n* • قطعه جزوتام
organization (institution) *n* موسسه

organization (regulation) *n* • تنظیم ترتیب
organization *n* سازمان
Organization of Petroleum-Exporting Countries *see* OPEC
organizational *adj* سازمانی
organize (form) *vt* تشکیل کردن
organized (orderly) *adj* منسجم
organized *adj* منظم
Orient *n* شرق • مشرق زمین • خاور
orifice *n* منفذ
origin (source) *n* چشمه • سرچشمه • منبع • مصدر • مایه
original *adj* اصلی
→ original copy اصل
originally *adv* اصلاً
originate <from sth> *vi* سرچشمه گرفتن <از چیزی>
ornament *n* زیور • یراق
ornamentation *n* تزیین
Orozgan *see* Uruzgan
orphan (esp w/o father) *n* • یتیم بی پدر
orphanage *n* یتیم خانه • دارالایتام
Oscar (award) *n* آسکر • جایزه
oscillate *v* آسکر • اسکار نوسان داشتن
oscillation *n* نوسان
Osman *see* Usman
ostentation *n* سامانه • طمطراق
ostrich *n* شتر مرغ
other (& pers) *adj*, *n* دیگر • دگر
→ in other words به اصطلاح دیگر • به عبارت دیگر • به تعبیر دیگر
otherwise *conj* اگرنه
Ottawa *n* اوتاوا • اتاوا
Ottoman (hist) *adj* عثمانی
ouch *excl* آخ • واخ • وخ
ought <+ subj> *v* مجبور بودن
oust *vt* خارج کردن
→ be ousted خارج شدن
out (expose criminal) *v* تشهیر کردن
out of *prep* از خلال
outbreak (& med) *n* ظهور
outburst *n* غلیان

470

outcome n • نتیجه • عاقبت • ماحصل

outhouse n مکان

outing (exposure of criminal) n تشهیر

outlay n مصرف

outline n خاکه

outlook (prospects) n • دورنما • دورنمای

outlook (viewpoint) n جهان بینی

outpost (border, highway) n تهانه

outrage (injustice) n • ستم • بیداد • جور • ظلم

outreach n پیش دستی

outset (start) n • اوایل • آغاز • شروع • ابتدا

outside adj خارج

outside adv بیرون

outside n خارج

outsider n خارجی • اجنبی • بیگانه

outskirts n حومه

outspoken (colloq) adj ترت

outstanding (prominent) adj برجسته

oval adj بیضوی

ovary n تخم دان

oven n داش
→ oven-baked داشی

over (about) prep • بر سر • به سر • در سر • سر

over (finished) adj خاتمه یافته

over (on) prep در بالای

overcoat n بالاپوش

overdo v مبالغه کردن

overeat vi • پر خوری کردن • تخته کردن

overlooking (w/view of) adj مشرف

overseas (fig) n خارج

overseas adv • در خارج • ماورای ابحار

oversee (supervise) v نظارت کردن

overseer n • ناظر • پیش کار

oversensitive (& pers) adj, n • اندک رنج • زود رنج

oversight (supervision) n • نظارت • مراقبت

overthrow (government) vt • سرنگون کردن • از بین بردن

overthrown (government) adj سرنگون

overtime (work) n اضافه کاری

overview (review) n مرور

ovum n بیضه

owl (bird) n • جغد • بوم

own (colloq) v کار داشتن

owner n صاحب
→ property owner مالک

ownership (property) n مالکیت

ox n • گاو • ثور

oxcart n گاو کراچی

oxidation n احتراق

oxide n اوکساید

Oxus (hist, river) n • آمو دریا • دریای آمو • دریای پنج • جیحون

oxygen n اکسیجن

oyster (& shell) n صدف

P

pace (step) n • گام • قدم

pace (step) v گام سپردن

Pachir wa Agam (dist) n • پچیر و اگام • پچیر و آگام • پچیر او اگام • پچیر او آگام

pacific adj • آرام • کاهل • تنبل

Pacific Ocean بحر آرام

pacifier (plastic nipple) n چوشک

pack animal (esp horse) n بارکش
→ pack horse یابو

package n پارسل

packet n بسته

packing list n لست اموال

pact n • پکت • پیمان • میثاق • معاهده • معاهدت

paddy (rice in husk) n شالی

padlock n قفل
→ (colloq) قلف

pagan (esp pre-Musl) adj جاهلی

page (paper) n صفحه

Paghman (dist) n پغمان

pagoda n • بت خانه • بتکده

Pahlavi (lang) n پهلوی

pahlawi (hist, gold coin) n پهلوی

pain n درد
→ pain & suffering phrs • تاب و تب • تب و تاب

471

painful *adj* دردناک • دردآلود
→ very painful (fig) جگر سوز
paint *n* رنگ
paint *v* رنگ کردن
→ paint a picture نقش کردن
painted *adj* رنگ شده
painter *n* نقاش • نگارگر
painting *n* نقش
→ related to painting نقاشی
pair *n* جفت • جوره • زوج
pajamas (f garment) *n* ازار
pajamas (traditional Afgh) *n* تنبان
→ (colloq) تنبا
→ bodkin for drawing pajama
drawcord through waist بند کش
→ pajama drawcord ازاربند
Pajhwok (press agency) *n* پژواک
pakawra (cul) *n* پکوره
Pakistan *n* پاکستان
Pakistani (& pers) *adj, n* پاکستانی
Paktika (province) *n* پکتیکا
Paktiya (province) *n* پکتیا
palace *n* قصر • کاخ • کوشک
→ Delkusha (Palace bldg in Kabul)
دل کشا
palang (decorated bed) *n* پالنگ
palanquin *n* تخت روان
pale (pers) *adj* زعفرانی
paleontologist *n* فوسیل شناس
paleontology *n* فوسیل شناسی
Palestine (geog) *n* فلسطین • قلمرو
فلسطین
Palestinian (& pers) *adj, n* فلسطینی
palm (hand) *n* کف
palm (tree) *n* نخل • نخیل • درخت
خرما
→ palm grove نخلستان
Pamir (region, mtn range) *n* پامیر
Pamiri (& pers, lang) *adj, n* پامیری
→ (Wakhi) واخی
→ Pamiri grps/langs غلچه
pamper *v* ناز دادن
pampered *adj* ناز دانه
pan (saucepan) *n* روغن داغ
pan for gold *v* • زرشویی کردن
ریگ شویی کردن
Panah (ctr) *n* پناه
panegyric (ode) *n* مدیحه

panegyrist *n* • ستایشگر • ثناخوان
مداح • سادو
panic *v* دست و پای خود را گم
کردن
pan-Islamism *n* اتحاد الاسلام • پان
اسلامیزم
Panja Kheyl (ctr) *n* پنجه خیل
Panjab (geog, dist) *n* پنجاب
Panjsheyr (province) *n* پنجشیر
Panjwayi (dist) *n* پنجوایی
panther *n* پلنگ سیاه
pants *n* پتلون
pantyhose (f) *n* جراب زنانه
paper (material) *n* کاغذ
paper *see* & newspaper
paper clip *n* کلپ
parachute *n* پراشوت
parachutist *n* پراشوتست
parade (mil) *n* رسم گذشت عسکری
Paradise *n* بهشت • جنت • دار البقا
→ Paradise (Eden) عدن
paragraph *n* پاراگراف • پره گراف
parallel *adj* متوازی • موازی
parallelogram *n* متوازی الاضلاع
parallelopiped *n* متوازی الاسطوح
paralysis *n* فلج
paralytic (pers) *n* افلیج
paralyzed *adj* فلج • افلیج
→ be paralyzed فلج بودن
→ become paralyzed فلج شدن
parapet *n* مورچل • سنگر
paraphrasing *n* تعبیر مجدد
parasite *n* مفت خور
→ (fig) کاسه لیس
parcel *n* پارسل
Parcham (hist, PDPA faction) *n*
پرچم
→ Parchami adherent پرچمی
parched (very thirsty, fig) *adj* جگر
سوخته
pardon (& under law) *n* • عفو
معذرت • معافی
pardon *vt* بخشیدن • عذر قبول
کردن • بحل کردن
→ (Musl law) عفو کردن
parent *see* father, mother
parenthesis *n* قوس

472

parents *n pl* • والدین • اولیا • ابوین
→ having the same parents عینی
• اعیانی • سکه
Paris *n* پاریس
parity *n* مساوات
park (public space) *n* پارک
park (vehicle) *v* پارک کردن
parliament *n* پارلمان • شورای ملی
→ house of parliament مجلس
→ Meshrano Jirga مشرانو جرگه
→ parliamentary immunity
مصونیت قانون گذاری
→ Wolesi Jirga ولسی جرگه
parrot *n* توتا • طوطا
→ parrot-eye (f, insult) توتا چشم
parrying (defending) *n* دفع
Parsi *see* Farsi
part (mechanical) *n* پرزه
part (portion) *n* قسمت • بخش •
حصه • نصیب • بهره • جزء • جزو
• پارچه
part (role) *n* رول • نقش
part *see* & participation
Parth *see* Parthian
Parthia (hist) *n* پارت
Parthian (hist, & pers) *adj, n* پارتی
• پهلو • پارس
Parthians (hist, 248 BC–224 AD,
empire) *n pl* پارتیان • پهلوان
partial (biased) *adj* طرف دار •
جانب دار • پله بین
partiality (bias) *n* طرف داری •
جانب داری
partially (partly) *adv* قسماً
→ partially-sighted (med) کم بین
participant *n* شامل • مشمول •
مشترک
participate <in sth> *vi* اشتراک
کردن • شرکت داشتن • حصه
گرفتن • سهم داشتن • سهم گرفتن
• سهیم بودن <در چیزی>
participating *adj* شامل • مشمول •
سهم دار
participation *n* اشتراک • شمول •
سهم
participle (gram, verbal adjective) *n*
صفت مفعولی
participle (gram, verbal noun) *n*
اسم مفعولی

particular (special) *adj* مخصوص •
خاص
particularity *n* خصوصیت •
خصیصه
particularly *adv* مخصوصاً •
خصوصاً • خاصتاً • بالاخص •
بالخصوص • علی الخصوص
partisan *n* جانب دار • طرف دار •
هوا خواه • هوا دار
partisanship *n* جانب داری • طرف
داری • هوا خواهی • هوا داری
partition (screen) *n* حاجز • در •
پرده
partner *n* شریک • همدست
partnership (farming) *n* بازگری
partnership *n* همدستی
→ (btwn landowner &
farmworkers) مضارعه
→ limited/silent partnership
مضاربت
party (banquet) *n* مهمانی • ضیافت
• دعوت
party (mvmt) *n* فرقه
→ Independence and Renewal
Party (hist) فرقۀ استقلال و تجدد
party (pol) *adj* حزبی
party (pol) *n* حزب • پارتی
→ party member حزبی
party (to agreement) *n* • جانب •
طرف
party (to lawsuit) *n* طرف دعوا
Parun (dist) *n* پارون
parvenu *n* نادیده گی • نادیدگی •
آدم نادیده • تازه به دوران رسیده •
نو به دولت رسیده • نو کیسه
Parwan (province) *n* پروان
Paryan (dist) *n* پریان
Pasaband (dist) *n* پسابند
pasha (hist, honorific) *n* پاشا
Pashai *see* Pashayi
Pashayi (lang) *n* پشه یی
Pashto (lang) *n* پشتو • افغانی
Pashtun (pers, lang) *n* پشتون
Pashtun Kot (dist) *n* پشتون کوت
Pashtun Zarghun (dist) *n* پشتون
زرغون
Pashtunistan *n* پشتونستان

473

Pashtunwali *n* پشتونوالی
→ giving f away in marriage to compensate for a crime بد دادن
pass (defile) *n* کتل • کوتل • گذر • گذر گاه • معبر
→ Khyber Pass کتل خیبر
pass (go by) *vi* گذشتن
pass (time) *vt* سپری کردن
→ (colloq) تیر شدن
pass away (& fig) *vi* فنا شدن
pass by <sth> *vt* گذشتن <از چیزی>
pass through *vi* عبور و مرور کردن • سپری کردن
passable (road) *adj* قابل تیر شدن
passage (channel) *n* مجرا
passage (going) *n* رو
passage (time, traffic) *n* مرور
passenger *adj* مسافری
passenger *n* مسافر
passion (fervor) *n* حمیت
passion (love) *n* عشق
passion (lust) *n* هوس
passionate (fervid) *adj* با حمیت • حمیت مند
passionate (lusty) *adj* هوسناک
passive (gram) *adj* مجهول
passive resistance (pol) *n* مقاومت منفی
passport *n* پاسپورت
past (gram) *adj* ماضی
→ past tense stem ریشه شماره دو
past (previous) *adj* گذشته • تیر شده
pasta (& w/meatballs) *n* آش
paste (glue) *n* سرش
paste (sauce) *n* رب
pasteboard *see* cardboard
pasteurized *adj* پاستوریزه
pastime *n* ساعت تیری • سرگرمی
pastry *n* حلویات
pastry chef *n* کلچه پز
pastry seller *n* کلچه فروشی
pastry shop *n* کلچه فروشی
pasturage *n* مالچه • مراتع • علف چر • علفزار
pasur (card game) *n* پاسور
patch (clothing) *n* پیوند
→ leather patch for shoe پینه

patch (shoe) *v* پینه زدن • پینه کردن • پینه ماندن
patched (shoe) *adj* پینه یی
→ having many patches پینه پینه
patched *adj* پیوندی • التصاقی
patella (anat) *n* عینک زانو
paternal (fatherly) *adj* پدری
paternity (fatherhood) *n* پدری
path (& fig, rel) *n* راه • طریق • صراط
→ following a spiritual path سیر
→ raised path on edge of farm plot پلوان
pathological *adj* مرضی
pathology *n* علم الامراض
patience (forbearance) *n* حوصله • تحمل • شکیب • طاقت • صبر
patience *n* شکیبایی • برداشت • بردباری
→ be patient برداشت داشتن • بردبار بودن
→ lose patience سر رفتن
patient *adj* با حوصله • حوصله دار • شکیبا
patient (gentle) *adj* حلیم
patient (med) *n* بیمار • مریض
patrimony (heritage) *n* میراث
patriot *n* وطن دوست • وطن خواه
patriotism *n* وطن دوستی
patrol (act, pers) *n* گزمه
patrol *v* گزمه گشتن
patrolman (police officer) *n* ساتونکی
patronage *n* حمایت • حمایه • واسطه • وسیله
pattern *n* نقش
pause (esp in speech) *n* مکث
pause *n* توقف • فصل • وقفه
pause *see* & stop
pause *v* توقف دادن • توقف کردن • مکث کردن
paved *adj* قیر
pavement (stone) *n* سنگ فرش
paw (unit of weight) *n* پاو
pawn (chess) *n* پیاده
pay *vt* پرداختن
→ pay extra to sweeten a deal سر دادن
paying authority *n* مرجع پرداخت

payment (installment) *n* قسط

payment *n* تأدیه • ادا

→ payment in advance پیش خرید

PBIED (mil) *n* مواد منفجره جابجا شده با در شخص انتحار کننده • شخص انتحار کننده

PDC *see* provincial development committee

PDPA (hist, pol) *n* حزب دموکراتیک خلق افغانستان

pea (field pea) *n* مشنگ

pea (green pea) *n* متر

peace *n* صلح • امن • مصالحه • آشتی

→ peace with all (Akbar's rel ideal) صلح کل

peaceful (comfortable) *adj* آرام

peaceful (quiet) *adj* خاموش

peaceful (safe) *adj* امن

peacemaker *n* مصلح

peacock *n* طاووس

→ Peacock Throne تخت طاووس

Peak (top) *n* اوج

pear *n* ناک

pearl *n* مروارید • در • لولو

→ (colloq) مرواری

→ pearl diver غواص مروارید

peasant (farmer) *n* زارع • دهقان • کشاورز

pebble *n* سنگ چل

peck (w/beak) *vt* نول زدن • منقار زدن • چیدن

peculiarities *n pl* غرایب

pedagogy *n* علم تربیه • پداگوژی

pedal (& treadle) *n* رکاب

pedantic (verbose) *adj* لفاظ

pedantry (verbosity) *n* لفاظی

pederast *n* بچه باز

pederasty *n* بچه بازی

pedestal (column base) *n* فیل پایه

pedestrian *n* پیاده

pedigree (family tree) *n* سلسله نسب • نسب نامه

→ not pedigreed (mongrel) ناجنس

pedophile *see* pederast

pedophilia *see* pederasty

peel *vt* پوست کردن

peer (equal) *n* همپایه • همشأن • همطراز • همتا • کفو

peg *n* میخ

pellet (from gun) *n* چره

pelt (skin) *n* پوست

pelvis (anat) *n* لگن خاصره

pen (for animals) *n* آغیل • آغل

pen *n* قلم

→ ballpoint pen قلم خودکار • خود کار

→ fountain pen قلم خودرنگ

→ pen name اسم مستعار • نام مستعار

penal (law) *adj* جزایی

penalty *n* جریمه

→ death penalty جزای مرگ • جزای اعدام

pencil *n* پنسل

pending *adj* موکول

penetrate *v* درون کردن • داخل کردن

penetrating *adj* نافذ

penetration *n* نفوذ • رخنه

peninsula *n* جزیره نما • شبه جزیره

penis *n* قضیب • آلت جنسی

→ (colloq) ذکر

→ (fig) شرم گاه مرد • اندام

→ (obs) ذکر • شرم گاه مرد

→ penis of slaughtered animal نره

penitentiary *see* prison

penknife *n* چاقو

pennyroyal (wild mint) *n* پودینه

pensive (& pers) *adj* متفکر

pensively *adv* متفکرانه

pentagon (shape) *n* پنج ضلعی

penultimate *adj* پرار

people (masses) *n* خلق

people (nation) *n* ملت • مردم • ناس

→ people (subjects of monarchy) رعیت

people (nationality) *n* ملیت

people (of a group) *n* اهل

→ people of the book (Jews, Christians, Muslims) اهل کتاب

people (& nation) *n* مردم

people's *adj* توده یی • تودیی

→ People's Democratic Party of Afghanistan *see* PDPA

pepper (black pepper) n فلفل • پلپل
• مرچ سیاه
pepper (spice, chili) n مرچ
pepperwort (herb) n تراتیزک
per prep فی
per (in fractions) prep بر
per diem n سفر خرج
perceive v دریافتن
percent adv فیصد
percentage n فیصدی
perceptible (visible) adj مرئی
perceptible adj مدرک • محسوس
perception n دریافت • ادراک •
درک • تلقی • دید
perceptive (of perception) adj
مدرکه
perceptive (subtle) adj نازک خیال
• باریک اندیش
percussive (mus instr) adj ضربی
perfect (complete) vt تکمیل کردن
• تکمیل دادن • تکامل بخشیدن
perfect (flawless) adj بی عیب
perfection (completion) n تکمیل •
انجام
perfection (maturity) n کمال
perforated adj سوراخ سوراخ •
غار غار
perform (art) v نواختن • کانسرت
دادن
performance (art) n هنرنمایی
performance (completion) n اجرا •
ایفا • ایفاء
performance (mus) n نوازندگی
performer (art) n هنرمند • هنرور •
بازیگر • آرتست • آرتیست
performer (mus) n سازنده • نوازنده
perfume n عطر
perfume merchant n عطار
perfunctory (& adv) adj, adv
سرسری
perhaps <+ subj> v شاید • ممکن
perianth (plant) n لفافه
perimeter n محیط
perineum (anat, colloq) n چات
period (dot) n نقطه/نقاط
period (era) n دور • دوره • عصر
period (f's) n طمث • حیض
period (interval) n مدت
period (time) n زمان • روزگار

periodic adj ادواری
periodical n مجله • ژورنال
perishing n تلف
perjury n سوگند دروغ
perm (of hair) n تونی
permanent adj دایم • دایمی
permanent wave see perm
permanganate (chem) n پرمنگنیت
permissible adj جایز
permission n اجازه • اذن • اجازت
permit n اجازه نامه • جواز نامه
permitted (by Islam) adj حلال
permitted adj مجاز
perpendicular (line, plane) n عمود
perpendicular adj قایم
perpetrator (law) n عامل • مرتکب
perpetrator n فاعل
perpetual adj جاویدان • جاودان •
جاوید • جاویدانه
perpetuate v ادامه دادن
perpetuation n ادامه • دوام •
مدوامت
perplexed adj سرگشته • سرگردان
• حیران • متحیر
perseverance n ایستادگی
Persian (non-Arab) adj عجمی
Persian (pejor) n عجم
Persian (pers, lang) n فارسی •
پارسی
→ ancient Persian (lang) پارسی
باستان
→ Dari (Persian) فارسی دری •
فارسی • پارسی دری
→ Persian (esp classical) پارسی
→ Persian speaker فارسی بان
Persian adj فارسی • پارسی
persist v اصرار کردن • اصرار
ورزیدن
persistence n اصرار • پافشاری
persistent adj سر سخت
→ be persistent اصرار داشتن
persistently adv سر سختانه
person (& gram) n نفر • کس • آدم
• فرد
→ (& gram) شخص
→ (dignitary) حضور
→ person w/AIDS مبتلا به ایدز •
مبتلای ایدز

476

personage (VIP) n • شخصیت • شخص

personal adj شخصی • خصوصی

personality n شخصیت

personally adv شخصاً • اصالتاً

personification n تشخیص

personnel n • پرسونل • افراد • کارکنان

Personnel-Borne Improvised Explosive Device see PBIED

perspective n • دورنما • دورنمای • دیدگاه

perspiration n عرق

perspire v عرق ریختن

persuade vt راضی کردن <کسی را> • رضایت دادن • قناعت دادن <به کسی>

Peru n پیرو

perusal (study) n مطالعه

Peruvian (& pers) adj, n پیرویی

Peshawar (city) n پشاور

pessimistic adj بدبین

pest (nag) n شوله

pester (annoy) <sb> vt آزار دادن <کسی را> • عذاب کردن • اذیت رساندن

pestering n آزار • عذاب • اذیت

pestilence n pl حشرات

pestle n • اغر سنگ • دسته هاون • هاوان

petal (bot) n • تاس برگ • طاس برگ • گل برگ • جام

petition (supplicate) v عرض کردن • عریضه دادن

petition (supplication) n • عرض • عریضه

petitioner (supplicant) n عارض

petroleum n نفت • پترول

pharaoh (hist) n فرعون

pharmacist n دواساز • کمپودر

pharyngeal adj حلقی

pharynx (anat) n حلق

phase (stage) n مرحله

pheasant n تذرو • مرغ دشتی

phenomenon n پدیده

philanthropic adj انسان دوستانه • بشر دوستانه

philanthropist n انسان دوست • بشر دوست

philanthropy n انسان دوستی • بشر دوستی

Philippine adj فلیپینی

Philippines n فلیپین

philology n فقه اللغه • فلولوژی

philosopher n فیلسوف

philosophy n حکمت

phlebotomist n حجام • رگ زن

phlebotomy n • حجامی • حجامت • رگ زنی

phlegm n بلغم • خلط

Phoenicia (hist) n فنیقیه

Phoenician (hist, & pers) adj, n فنیقی

phone (sound) n صوت

phone (telephone) n تلفون • تیلفون
→ phone book رهنمای تلفون
→ make a phone call تلفون کردن • تیلفون کردن

phoneme n • واحد صوت • آواز • فونیم

phonemic adj واحد صوتی

phonemics n فونیم شناسی

phonetic adj صوتی

phonetics n • علم الاصوات • علم اصوات • آواز شناسی • فونتکس

phonology n فونولوجی

photocopy n فوتوکاپی

photograph n عکس

photograph v عکس گرفتن

photographer n عکاس

photography n عکاسی
→ photography studio عکاس خانه • ستودیوی عکاسی

phrase n عبارت

phrase v عبارت ساختن

phraseology see phrasing

phrasing n • جمله بندی • عبارت سازی • تعبیر

physical (bodily) adj جسمانی

physical (physics) adj فزیکی

physician (arch) n پزشک

physician n طبیب • داکتر • دکتور

physics n فزیک

physiology n • علم وظایف الاعضا • فزیولوژی

pianist n پیانو نواز

piano (mus instr) n پیانو

pick (peck at) v چیدن • کندن

pick (select) *see* choose
pick (w/sharp point) *n* زاغنول
pick *n see* & pickaxe, plectrum
pick up (lift) *vt* برداشتن • برگرفتن
→ (colloq) ورداشتن
pickaxe *n* کلنگ • کلند • کدال
picket (stake) *n* میخ
picking (selection) *n* تصمیم انتخاب
pickle (cucumber, &tc.) *n* • آچار
ترشی
pickle (cucumber, &tc.) *vt* آچار
انداختن
pickpocket *n* کیسه بر
picky *adj* مشکل پسند
picnic *n* میله • پکنک
picnic *v* میله کردن • میله رفتن
pictographic *adj* تصویری
pictography *n* خط تصویر نگاری
خط هیروغلیف
picture (appearance) *n* شکل
picture (photo) *n* عکس
→ take a picture عکس گرفتن
picture (portrait) *n* تصویر
piece (& merchandise) *n* دانه •
عدد
→ (colloq) تا
piece (animal hide) *n* جلد
piece (clothing) *n* ثوب
→ one uniform یک ثوب دریشی
piece (food morsel) *n* توته • تکه
piece (mus) *n* پارچه
piece (paper) *n* شقه
piece (section) *n* قسمت • نصیب •
پارچه
piece (small) *n* ریزه
piece (splinter) *n* پرچه
piece *see* & unit
piecework (esp contract) *n* تیکه
pierce *see* & penetrate
pierce *vt* سنبیدن
pig *n* خوک • خنزیر
→ wild pig جناور • جناور بد
pigeon (& dove) *n* کبوتر
pigeon (dark red) *n* آتشی
→ pigeon droppings پیخال • پیخ
pigment *n* رنگ
pile (heap) *n* توده • کوت
pile (money) *n* پایه
pilgrim *n* زایر

pilgrimage (hajj) *n* حاج • حج
→ place of pilgrimage مزار
→ (shrine) زیارت/زیارات
pill *n* گولی
pillage *v* غارت کردن • چور کردن
pillager *n* غارتگر
pillaging *n* اغتنام • چور
pillar (archit) *n* ستون
→ (support) رکن • عماد
→ frontier pillar پایه
pillow *n* بالش
→ (colloq) بالشت
pillowcase *n* پوش بالش
pilot *n* پیلوت • هوانورد
→ fighter pilot عسکر قوای هوایی
pimple *n* آبله
pimples (acne) *n* • دیگ بخار
جوانی دانه
→ have pimples بخار کشیدن
pin *n* سنجاق
pinch *n* چندی
→ take a pinch چندی کندن •
چندی گرفتن
Pindi *see* Rawalpindi
pine (tree, wood) *n* ارچه • کاج
pink (rosy) *adj* گلابی • گلگون
pinky (anat) *n* خنصر
pinky (finger) *n* کلک
pioneer (forerunner) *adj, n* پیش قدم
→ (standard-bearer) • بیرق دار
پرچم دار
→ (trailblazer) تبر دار • تبردار
pious *adj* خدا پرست • متدین •
بادیانت • دین دار • متعبد • رباعی
pious (& pers) *adj, n* پارسا
pipe *n* پایپ • پیپ • نل
pipe (& mus instr) *n* نی
pipeline *n* پایپلاین
piper *n* نینواز
pipette (chem) *n* قطره چکان
piqued *see* galled
pir (Sufi master) *n* پیر
Pir (m name) *n* پیر
Pisces (zodiac) *n* حوت
piss *see* urine, urinate
pistachio *n* پسته
pistachio-colored *adj* پسته یی
pistil (bot) *n* آله تانیث
pistol (gun) *n* تفنگچه

478

pit (deep hole) *n* چال
→ (dungeon) سیاه چاه • سیاه چال
pit (depth) *n* چقری
pit *n* پرتگاه
pitch (asphalt) *n* قیر
pitch *v see* & throw
→ pitch tent خیمه زدن
pitcher (jug) *n* جک
→ (w/handle, spout, us w/lid) آفتابه
pitchfork *n* شاخی • دوشاخه
pitfall *n* چالش
pitiful *adj* رقت آور • رقت انگیز •
رقت بار
pity (injustice) *n* شرم • حیف •
افسوس • دریغ
pity (regret) *n* افسوس
pity (sympathy) *n* دلسوزی • رقت
→ have pity دلسوزی داشتن
→ what a pity! شرم است
pivot (& orbit) *n* مدار
pivot (axis) *n* محور
place *n* محل • گاه • جایگاه • نقطه
• مکان
→ (colloq) جای • گه • جایگه
→ (lit) جا
→ (position, & mil) موضع
→ birthplace زادگاه • مولد • مسقط
الراس
→ built-up place آباد
→ place where sth is displayed
معرض
place (put) *vt* گذاشتن • ماندن
placement *n* جایگزین
placenta *n* مشیمه • جفت • جوره
plagiarism *n* سرقت ادبی • مسخ
plagiarize *v* سرقت ادبی کردن
plague (& fig) *n* طاعون
plain (simple) *adj* ساده
plaintiff (law) *n* مدعی
plaintive (lightly) *adj* گله آمیز
plaintive (mournful; & adv) *adj, adv*
نالان
plan (design) *v* طرح کردن •
طراحی کردن
plan *n* برنامه • پلان • طرح
→ make plans سازماندهی کردن
plane (airplane) *n* طیاره
plane (surface) *n* سطح
plane (tool) *n* رنده • لیسه

plane geometry *n* هندسه مسطح
plane tree *n* پنجه چنار
planet (& star) *n* فلک • افلاکی
سیاره • نجم • اختر • کوکب
→ planet-worshiper افلاکی
→ the 7 celestial bodies هفت
سیاره • هفت اجرام • هفت کوکب •
هفت کواکب
plank (board) *n* تخته
planner *n* طراح
planning *n* طرح ریزی •
سازماندهی • پلانگذاری • نقشه
کشی
plant *n* گیاه • نبات
plant (set in place) *vt* نشاندن
→ (colloq) شاندن
→ plant fruit trees for the waqf
وقف نشاندن • وخم شاندن
plant (sow) *v* کاشتن
→ (cover with earth) گور کردن
→ plant a sapling غرس کردن
plantain *n* زوف
planting (sowing) *n* کشت • بذر
افشانی • تخم پاشی
→ planting saplings غرس • نهال
شانی • نهال نشانی
plasma *n* پلازما
plaster of Paris *n* گچ
plastering *n* پلستر کاری
plastic *adj* پلاستیکی
plastic *n* پلاستیک
plate (dish) *n* بشقاب • قاب
plate (gild) *v* طلا کاری کردن
plate *see* & plating
plateau *n* سطح مرتفع • نجد
platform (pol) *n* گزارش نامه • مرام •
نامه
plating *n* روی کش • پلیت
platinum *n* پلاتین • طلای سفید
platoon (mil) *n* بلوک
→ (arch) پلتن
platter (serving) *n* غوری
play (& game) *n* بازی
play (on mus instr) *vt* نواختن
→ play music ساز کردن
→ play the flute فلوت نواختن
play (theatrical) *n* نمایش
play *v* بازی کردن
→ play a role نقش بازی کردن

479

playful *adj* بازی گوش

playing card *see* card

playmate *n* همبازی • هم بازی

plaything (& pers) *n* بازیچه

plaything *n* ملعبه

plead *v* لابه کردن • زاری کردن • تضرع کردن • الحاح کردن

pleading *n* تضرع • الحاح • زاری

pleasant *adj* خوب • شیرین • دل پذیر • خوش • خوش آیند • خوش خوی • لطف آمیز • گوارا • گوار

please (w/requests) *adv* لطفاً

please <sb> *vt* خوشنود ساختن • دل <کسی را> خوش کردن

pleasure (delight) *n* لذت • تمتع • حظ

→ (intoxication) کیف

→ (satisfaction) رضا

→ with pleasure! به چشم

pleat *n* پلیت

plectrum *n* مضراب • زخمه

→ (arch) زخمه • مضراب

→ (worn on index finger) ناخنک

pledge *n* تعهد • عهد • پیمان

Pleiades (astron) *n* پروین • ثریا

pliability *n* نرمش

pliers (tool) *n* انبر • پلاس

→ (w/sharp point) زاغنول

plinth *n* پیزاره

plosive (speech) *adj* انسدادی

plot (land) *n* کرد

plot (scheme) *n* دسیسه/دسایس • توطئه

plotter (schemer) *n* دسیسه باز • دسیسه کار • توطئه گر

pluck (of slaughtered animal) *n* جگر بند

pluck (pick) *v* چیدن • کندن

→ pluck feathers پر کندن

plug (spark plug) *n* پلک

plum *n* آلو

plumb line *n* رشتۀ شاقول

plumber *n* نل دوان

plumbing (work) *n* نل دوانی

plume (ornamental) *n* جغه

plunder *v* غارت کردن • چور کردن

plunderer *n* غارتگر

plundering *n* اغتنام • چور

plural (gram) *n* جمع

→ broken plural (Ar) جمع مسکر

→ plural suffix پسوند جمع

→ regular plural (Ar) جمع سالم

plurality *n* تعدد

pluralize (gram) *vt* جمع بستن

plus *adj* مثبت

plus *n* جمع

→ plus sign علامتِ جمع

Pluto (planet) *n* پلوتو

pneumonia (colloq) *n* سینه و بغل • ذات الریه

poached (cul) *adj* نیم جوش

pocket *n* کیسه • جیب

pocketknife *n* چاقو

pod (bot) *n* پلی

poem *n* شعر • نشیده

→ bacchanalian poem خمریه

→ Dari poem w/2 couplets دو بیتی • چار بیتی

→ lyric poem غزل

poet *n* شاعر • ناظم

poet laureate *n* ملک الشعرا

poet's biography *n* تذکره • تذکرت الشعرا • تذکره شاعران

point (decimal) *n* اعشاریه • نقطه

point (needletip) *n* نیش

point <sth> out < to sb> *vt* تذکر دادن • نشان دادن <چیزی را به کسی>

pointing (w/hand, finger) *n* اشاره

pointless *adj* بی فایده

poison *n* سم • زهر

poison *vt* مسموم ساختن • مسموم کردن

poisoned *see* poisonous

poisonous *adj* زهر آگین • زهر آلود • زهرناک • سمی

poisonousness *see* toxicity

poker (fireplace) *n* آتش کاو • سیخ تنور

Poland *n* پولیند • پولند

polar *n* قطبی

pole (axis) *n* قطب

Pole (pers) *n* پولیندی

pole (pillar) *n* پایه

pole (tent) *n* دیرک

pole vault *n* خیز با نیزه

polemic *n* جدل

polemical *adj* جدلی
police *n* پولیس
→ Afghan Border Police پولیس
سرحدی افغان
→ Afghan National Auxiliary Police
پولیس کمکی ملی افغان
→ Afghan National Civil Order
Police پولیس نظم عامه ملی افغان
→ Afghan Uniform Police پولیس
یونفورم دار ملی افغان
→ commissioned police officer
څارنمن
→ mil police on duty انضباط
→ police academy اکادمی پولیس
→ police commissioner سر مامور
• سرمامور
→ police officer ساتونکی • فرد
policy (action) *n* طرز العمل
policy (guideline) *n* خط مشی
policy (politics) *n* سیاست
Polish (for boots) *n* رنگ
Polish *adj* پولیندی
polite (courteous) *adj* خلیق
polite (urbane) *adj* ادیب • شیوه دار
• مودب • مهذب
politely *adv* مودبانه
politeness (urbanity) *n* ادب
political *adj* سیاسی
→ political science علم سیاست
→ political scientist عالم سیاست •
دانشمند سیاست • متخصص سیاست
→ political section (embassy's)
شعبه سیاسی
politician *n* سیاست • سیاست
مدار
politics *n* سیاسَت • زندگی سیاسی
poll tax on non-Muslims *n* جزیه
pollinate *v* تلقیح کردن
pollination *n* تلقیح
pollute *vt* آلودن
polluted *adj* چتل • کثیف • آلوده
poly- (pref) *n* تعدد
polygamy *n* تعدد زوجات
polygon (math) *n* پولی گون •
پولیگون
polytheism (apostasy) *n* شرک
polytheism *n* تعدد آلهه
polytheist *n* مشرک
pomegranate *n* انار

pomp *n* سامانه • طمطراق
pompon *n* پوپک
pond (small) *n* دند
pool (reservoir) *n* حوض
pool (small) *n* دند
poor & content *phrs* خوشحال
poor (distressed) *adj* پریشان
poor (empty-handed) *adj* تهی دست
poor (helpless) *adj* بی چاره • چاره
• فرومانده
poor (indigent) *adj* • فقیر •
مسکین
مفلس • بی بضاعت • محتاج • بی
نوا • فقیر
poor *adj* غریب • نادار
poor house *n* • مرستون •
دار المساکین
→ (arch) دار المساکین • مرستون
→ (esp for Sufis) لنگر
Popalzai (P tribe) *n* پوپلزی
popcorn *n* پله • جواری
Pope, the *n* پاپ
poplar (tree) *n* چنار • سفیدار
→ white poplar خدنگ
poppy (& head/pod) *n* کوکنار
→ poppy seed (& cul) • خشخاش
خاش خاش
poppy *see* & opium
poppy-free *adj* عاری از کوکنار
popular *adj* عوام پسند • محبوب
popularity *n* محبوبیت
popularization *n* تعمیم • گسترش
popularize *vt* گسترش دادن
population *n* نفوس
porch *n* رواق
porcupine *n* سگر • شغر • جیره
pore (anat) *n* منفذ
→ pores مسامات
pork *n* گوشت خوک
porridge (w/dill) *n* اماچ
port (seaport) *n* بندر • بندر گاه
porter (at market) *n* حمال •
جوالی (colloq)
portion (part) *n* قسمت • نصیب •
پارچه
portion (ration) *n* جیره
portion (serving) *n* خوراک
portion (share) *n* بهره
portrait *n* تصویر
portraitist *n* نقاش • نگارگر

481

portray vt ترسیم کردن • نمایاندن
Portugal n پرتگال
Portuguese (& lang, pers) adj, n
پرتگالی
portulaca (flower) n فرشی
position (& mil) n موضع
position (commission) n منصب
position (job) n چوکی • مقام • جای
• وظیفه
position (slot in org table) n بست
positive adj مثبت
possessed (by evil spirit) adj
دیوزده
possessing <sth> adj, n والا •
واجد <چیزی>
possibility n امکان • مجال
possible adj ممکن • شدنی •
صورت پذیر
→ as far as possible حتی الامکان
poster n پوستر
posting (assignment) n ماموریت
post-partum (& pers) adj, n زچه
postpone see & delay
postpone vt پس انداختن • موکول
کردن • عقب انداختن
postponed adj معطل • موکول
→ be postponed vi پس افتادن
postponement n معطلی • تعویق
postposition (gram) n پسینه
pot (for cooking) n دیگ
pot (jug) n کوزه
pot (marijuana) n کنب • بنگ
→ habitual pot user بنگی
potable adj مشروب • آشامیدنی
potassium n پوتاسیم
→ p. carbonate پوتاسیم کاربونیت
potato n کچالو
→ (< F) سیب زمینی
→ pakura (potato dish) پکوره
potential (& adv) adj, adv بالقوه
pothead n بنگی
potsherd n تیکر
potter n کلال
→ potter's shop کلالی
pottery n کلالی • سفال • سیرامیک
→ of/for pottery سفالی • سیرامیک
→ of/for pottery (lit) سفالین
pouch n کیسه
poultry n مرغ
482

poultry farming n مرغ داری
pound (unit of meas) n پاو
pound vt کوفتن
pour (solids) (colloq) vt توده کردن
pour vi ریختن
pour vt ریختاندن • خالی کردن
pouring n ریزش
poverty (bankruptcy) n افلاس
poverty (distress) n پریشانی
poverty (helplessness) n
فروماندگی
poverty (indigence) n غربت •
غریبی • فقر • تهی دستی • مسکنت
• مسکینت
POW n زندانی جنگ • اسیر
powder n گرده • گرد
powder one's face v سفیده کردن
powdered adj سوده
powdered milk n شیر خشک
power (& pol) n قدرت
power (authority) n اختیار
power (output) n قوه
power (strength) n زور • قوت •
توان • نیرو • دستگاه • دم و دستگاه
→ (colloq) شیمه
→ power of attorney وکالت خط •
وکالت خط شرعی
→ power station فابریکه برق
→ motive power عامل
→ purchasing power قوه خرید
powerful (& pol) adj قدرتمند
powerful (persistent) adj سر سخت
powerful (strong) adj قوی • با قوت
• قوتمند • قدرتمند • توانا
practical adj عملی
practically adv عملا
practice (exercise) n تمرین • مشق
• تطبیقات
→ in practice عملا
→ put into practice جامعه عمل
پوشاندن
pragmatic adj عملی
Prague n پراگ
prairie n جلگه • دشت
praise n ستایش • سپاس • شکر
praise vt ستایش کردن • ثنا گفتن
→ self-praiser خود ستایی
praiseworthy adj قابل ستایش •
سزاوار ستایش

Prakrit (lang) *n* پراکرت

prattle *n* حرف مفت

pray (Musl) *v* نماز خواندن

pray *vi* دعا کردن

→ one who prays for others' well-being داعی • دعاگوی

prayer (invocation) *n* دعا

prayer (Musl) *n* صلات

→ (Musl, five times daily) نماز

→ having two genuflections in prayer دو گانه

→ making up a missed prayer قضایی

→ prayer for rain استسقا

→ prayer for the dead ترحیم • اتحاف دعا

→ touching forehead to ground in Muslim prayer سجده • سجود

prayer leader *n* امام

prayer rug *n* سجاده • جای نماز • مصلا

praying mantis *n* گهواره جنبان

preach (sermonize) *v* وعظ کردن

preacher (orator) *n* خطیب

preacher *n* واعظ

→ head preacher in capital میر واعظ

preaching & propagandizing *phrs* وعظ و تبلیغ

preaching (sermon) *n* وعظ

precautionary *adj* احتیاطی

precedence *n* اولویت • افضلیت • تقدم

→ (colloq) الویت

precedent *n* تعامل

preceding *adj* پیش

pre-Christian *adj* قبل المیلاد

precipice *n* لاش

precipitate (chem) *n* رسوب

precipitation (& snow) *n* بارندگی

precipitation (rain) *n* بارش

precise *adj* دقیق • مضبوط

precisely *adv* دقیقاً

predator *n* درنده

predatory (meat-eating) *adj* گوشت خوار

predatory *adj* درنده

predecessor (ancestor) *n* سلف

predestination *n* جبر • سرنوشت

predicate (gram) *n* مسند • گزاره

predicate (logic) *n* محمول

prediction *n* پیش گویی

predominance *n* غالبیت

predominant *adj* غالب

preface *n* پیش گفتار • دیباچه

prefer (choose) *vt* گزیدن • برگزیدن

prefer <sth over sth else> *vt* ترجیح دادن <چیزی را نسبت به چیزی دیگر>

preferable (lit) *adj* ارجح

preference (taste) *n* ذوق • سلیقه • مذاق

preference *n* ترجیح • رجحان • برتری

preferred (& pers) *adj, n* برگزیده

prefix *n* پیشوند • پیش آوند • سابقه

pregnancy *n* آبستنی • حاملگی

→ (colloq) بارداری • شکم داری

pregnant *adj* حامله • آبستن

→ (colloq) باردار • شکم دار • آوست

→ (cow) سر پستان

→ get pregnant (colloq) شکم کردن

prehistoric (after n) *adj* از ماقبل تاریخ

prehistoric *adj* قبل التاریخ

prehistory *n* ماقبل تاریخ

prejudice *n* تعصب

preliminary *adj* مقدماتی

→ preliminaries مقدمات

premature *adj* پیش رس

→ premature baby طفل پیش رس

premier *see* prime minister

prenatal *adj* قبل الولاده

preparation *n* تهیه

→ preparations ترتیبات

prepare *vi* آمادگی گرفتن

prepare *vt* آماده ساختن • تهیه کردن

→ (colloq) تیار کردن

prepared *adj* آماده • حاضر • مهیا

→ (colloq) تیار

→ be prepared تهیه شدن

preparedness *see* readiness

preposition *n* پیشینه

prescribe (med) *v* نسخه را نوشتن

483

prescription (med) n نسخه
presence (of dignitary) n حضور
→ presences (grp of rel scholars,
esp Sufi masters) حضرات
presence n وجود • پیش گاه • بدن
present (current) adj فعلی •
کنونی
→ present tense زمان حال
→ present tense stem ریشه
شماره یک
present (on hand) adj, n • وجود
حاضر
→ be present • وجود داشتن
موجود بودن
present n تحفه • هدیه
→ (to pers of higher rank) پیش
کش
→ giving a present اتحاف
present vt تقدیم کردن • پیش کش
کردن • به میان آوردن • ارائه دادن
• ارائه کردن
presentation n تقدیم • ارائه
presenter n معرف
presently see now
preservation n نگاه داری • نگه
داری • نگاه داشت • نگه داشت
preserve (game, forest) n قرغ
preserve v نگاه داشتن
preserves (fruit) n مربا
presidency n ریاست جمهوری
president n رئیس
→ President of the Republic رئیس
جمهور
presidential adj رئیس جمهوری
→ presidential decree امر رئیس
جمهوری
→ Presidential Palace قصر
ریاست جمهوری
→ Presidential Palace complex
ارگ
press (journalistic) adj مطبوعاتی
press (printing) n مطبعه/مطابع
press (squeeze) vt فشردن
press agency n آژانس خبری
press conference n کنفرانس
مطبوعاتی
press officer n مسئول مطبوعات
press, the n pl مطبوعات
pressure cooker n دیگ بخار
pressure n فشار
484

prestidigitator n چابکدست • ماهر
prestige n نفوذ • حیثیت • پرستیژ
prestigious adj با نفوذ
presumably adv بالفرض • فرضاً
pretend v وانمود کردن
pretending adj تظاهر
pretense n ظاهر سازی
pretentious (colloq) adj خود ساز
pretext (false) n بهانه • پلمه
pretty (& f) adj, n مقبول • زیبا •
جمیل • نیکو
prevailing (usual) adj غالب
prevalence n حاکمیت • حکم
فرمایی • تسلط
prevalent adj حکم فرما • متسلط •
مسلط
→ be prevalent • تسلط داشتن
تسلط یافتن
prevent vt بازداشت کردن •
بازداشتن
prevention (& med) n • جلوگیری
پیشگیری <از بیماری> • جلوگیری
• وقایه • توقیف • مانع
preventive adj وقایوی
previous adj گذشته • تیر شده •
سابق • اسبق • ماتقدم • قبلی
previously adv سابقاً • قبلاً
prey n شکار • نخچیر • نخجیر
price n قیمت • ارزش • بها
→ price of copy of Quran هدیه
→ prices (high cost of living) قیمتی
price list n نرخ نامه
prick vt نیش زدن
→ feel sharp, pricking pain سیخ
زدن
prickle n خار
prickly adj خاردار
pride n افتخار • باد • غرور •
ناموس
primarily adv اصلا
primary adj اصلی
→ the primary & the secondary
اصل و فرع
prime minister n صدر اعظم
prime ministership n صدارت
prime of youth n غرور جوانی
primitive (elementary) adj ابتدایی
primitive (uncouth) adj بدوی
primordial matter n هیولا

primrose (flower) n پریمینا

prince (emir) n امیر

prince (hist, title) n مرزا • میرزا • بیگ

prince (king's son) n شاه پور

→ petty kings & princes ملوک الطوایف

princess (king's daughter) n شاه دخت • شاه دختر

principal (main) adj عمده

principal (of school) n مدیر مکتب • سر معلم

principle n اصل • اساس • ناموس

→ established principle کلیه

→ in principle اصولاً

→ principles of writing اصول نگارش

print (impression) n چاپ • طبع

print v طبع کردن

printed (issued) adj منتشر

printed adj چاپی • مطبوع

printer n طابع

printing adj طباعتی

printing n طباعت • طبع • چاپ

printing press n مطبعه

prior adj مقدم

prior to <+ subj> adv قبل از آن که • قبل بر آن که

prior to <sth> prep قبل از <چیزی> • قبل بر

priority n اولویت • افضلیت

→ (colloq) الویت

prison n زندان • بندی خانه • محبس

→ juvenile prison دار التادیب

prison cell n کوته قلفی

prisoner n زندانی • بندی • اسیر • محبوس

prisoner of war see POW

privacy n خلوت

private (mil) n فرد

private adj شخصی • خصوصی • خاص • مخصوص

→ private security company موسسه امنیتی خصوصی

→ in private (tête-á-tête) دو به دو

privately adv خاصاً • در خلوت

privilege (distinction) n امتیاز

privy (colloq) n مکان

prize n جایزه

→ Nobel Prize جایزۀ نوبل

probable adj احتمالی

probably adv احتمالاً • محتمالاً

probationary adj آزمایشی

problem (& math) n مسئله • قضیه

problem (difficulty) n مشکل • ناآرامی • معضله • معضل • عقده غوامض

→ unsolved problems

problem see & malfunction

problematic see difficult

procedural adj شکلی

procedure n خط مشی

proceeding (on journey) adj رهسپار

process n روند • عملیه • پروسه

proclamation n اعلام • اعلامیه

procrastinate v دفع الوقت کردن

procrastination n دفع الوقت

procreation (biol) n تناسل

procurer (broker) n دلال

procurer (finder) n یابنده

procuress (madam) n دلاله • دلال زن

produce v محصول دادن

produce (manufacture) vt ساختن • تولید کردن

producer (film) n تهیه کننده • کار گردان

product (result) n حاصل • عملکرد • ثمر • ثمره

→ industrial products مصنوعات

production (output) n تولید • محصول

→ production capacity ظرفیت تولید

productive (fertile) adj حاصل خیز • پر بار

productive (of production) adj تولیدی

productivity (fertility) n حاصل خیزی

profanity n کفر

→ speak profanities کفر گفتن

profession (craft) n پیشه • کسب • حرفه

profession (job) n مسلک • شغل • مشغولیت • مصروفیت

professional adj مسلکی • حرفه یی

485

professor *n* • استاد • پوهاند •
پروفیسر
→ associate professor *n* پوهنوال
→ junior assistant professor
پوهنیار
→ senior assistant professor
پوهنمل
proficiency *n* مهارت • تسلط
proficient *adj* با مهارت • ماهر
profile *n* نیم رخ
→ in profile (photo) نیم رویه
profit *n* کمایی • فایده • عملکرد •
بهره • مفاد • ثمر • ثمره • منفعت •
نفع • انتفاع
profit *v* کمایی کردن
→ make a profit طرف بستن
profitable *adj* پر عایدات • با ثمر •
ثمر بخش • مثمر • سودمند • مفید •
نافع • انتفاعی
→ be profitable غنیمت بودن
profiteer *n* سودجو • سودجوی
profiteering *n* سودجویی
profound (deep) *adj* عمیق • چقر
profound (serious) *adj* سنگین
profoundly (deeply) *adv* عمیقاً
progeny *n* ذریه
program *n* پروگرام
→ Program Tahkim-e Sulh
پروگرام تحکیم صلح
progress *n* پیش رفت • پیشرفت •
ترقی • تکامل
progressive *adj* پیش رفته • پیشتر •
مترقی
prohibit *v* منع کردن • بازداشت
کردن • بازداشتن
prohibited *adj* ممنوع • غیر مجاز •
→ (by Islam) حرام
prohibition *n* منع • ممانعت •
بازداشت • توقیف • نهی • قدغن
project *n* پروژه
projectile *n* مرمی • گلوله
projector *n* پروجکتر • پروژکتور
proletarian *adj, n* زحمت کش •
رنج بر
proletariat *n* طبقه رنج بران • رنج
بران
proliferation *n* نشر
prologue *n* مقدمه
prolong *v* ادامه دادن

prolonging *n* ادامه • دوام • مدوامت
prominent *adj* برجسته
promiscuous (sexually) *adj* هر
جای
promise <sth to sb> *vt* وعده دادن •
وعده کردن <چیزی را به کسی> •
قول دادن • زبان دادن • پیمان کردن
promise *n* وعده • عهد • تعهد •
قول • میثاق • پیمان • پکت
→ promise & threat وعده و وعید
→ promise-breaker پیمان شکن •
پیمان گسل
→ promise-maker وعده دار
→ promised meeting place وعده
گاه
promontory (geog) *n* دماغه
promote (enhance) *vt* ارتقا دادن
promote (in rank) *v* ترفیع دادن •
ترفیع کردن
promotion (enhancement) *n* ارتقا •
ارتقاء
promotion (in rank) *n* ترفیع
pronoun (gram) *n* ضمیر
pronunciation *n* تلفظ • ادا
→ correct pronunciation شد و مد
proof (argument) *n* حجت
proof (corroboration) *n* ثبوت
proof (evidence) *n* گواهی • برهان
→ proof of Messiah's identity
(miracle) برهان مسیح
proofreader *n* مصحب
propaganda *n* تبلیغات • پروپاگند
→ preaching & propagandizing
وعظ و تبلیغ
propagandist *n* مبلغ • مبلغ مذهبی
propeller *n* پروانه
proper *adj* درست • صالح • مساعد
proper noun (gram) *n* اسم خاص
properly *adv* عدل • خوب
property (chattels) *n* اموال
property (possession) *n* حق
property (real estate) *n* جای داد •
جایداد
→ property in one's charge ابواب
جمعی
prophet *n* نبی • پیغام بر • رسول
→ heir to the Prophet واسع
proportion (symmetry) *n* تناسب
proportionate *adj* متناسب

486

proportionate to *adj* با تناسب
proposal *n* پیش نهاد
propound *vt* مطرح کردن
proprietor *n* مالک • کارفرما
proprietorship *n* مالکیت
prosaic *adj* نثری
prose *n* نثر
prosecute *vt* تعقیب کردن
prosecution *n* تعقیب
→ public prosecutor مدعی العموم
• څارنوال
prospects *n* دورنما • دورنمای
prosper *v* به نوا رسیدن
prosperity *n* تنعم • برکت • نوا •
رفاه
prosperous (& pers) *adj, n*
پیروزمند • فیروزمند • ظفرمند
prosperous *adj* پیروز • فیروز •
مظفر • مرفه
prostate *n* پروستات
prostate gland *n* غده پروستات
prostitute *n* فاحشه • قحبه • خود
فروش
→ (arch) روسپی
prostitution *n* فحشا • فاحشگی
protect *v* پشتی کردن • پشتیبانی
کردن
protection (support) *n* • حمایت
حمایه • پشتی • پشتیبانی
→ (colloq) پشتیوانی
protection *n* حفظ • محافظت •
حفاظت • دفاع
protective (supportive) *adj* حمایتی
protector (conservator) *n* نگاه دار
• نگه دار
protector (savior) *n* فریاد رس
protector (supporter) *n* پشتیبان
→ (colloq) پشتیوان
protectorate (pol) *n* کشور تحت
الحمایه
protest (objection) *n* اعتراض
protest (revolt) *n* قیام
protest (revolt) *vi* قیام کردن
Protestant (& pers) *adj, n* پروتستان
protocol (ceremony) *n* مراسم •
تشریفات
prototype *n* نمونه • پروتوتایپ
protracted *adj* متمادی
protruding *adj* پیش برآمده

protuberance *n* بینی
protuberant *see* protruding
proud *adj* مفتخر
prove *v* ثبوت کردن • به ثبوت
رساندن
→ prove false دروغ برآمدن
proven *adj* ثبوت شده • به ثبوت
رساندنه • به ثبوت رسیده • مبرهن
proverb *n* مثل • ضرب المثل
provide *vt* فراهم کردن
→ provided that ... مشروط بر این
که • مشروط به این که • به شرط آن
که
Providence (God) *n* پروردگار
Provider (God) *n* رازق • رزاق
province *n* ولایت • صوبه
provincial (regional) *adj* سمتی
provincial *adj* ولایتی
→ provincial council شورای
ولایتی
→ provincial development
committee کمیته انکشاف ولایتی
→ provincial governor والی
→ Provincial Reconstruction Team
see PRT
→ provincial tax office مستوفیت
provision (injunction) *n* حکم
provisionally (temporarily) *adv*
موقتاً
provisioning (supply) *n* اعاشه
provisions (supplies) *n* تدارکات
provocative (arousing) *adj* هوس
انگیز • شهوت آنگیز
provoke (& arouse) *vt* انگیختن
prow (of ship) *n* سینه کشتی • پوزه
proximate *see* near
proximity *n* جوار
proxy *n* نماینده • وکیل
PRT (Provincial Reconstruction
Team) *n* تیم باز سازی ولایتی • تیم
پی آر تی
prudence *n* ملاحظه کاری •
هوشیاری • حزم
prudent (foresighted) (& pers) *adj,
n* دوراندیش
prudent (tactful) *adj* با تدبیر
prudent *adj* ملاحظه کار • محتاط •
احتیاط کار • هوشیار • هوشمند •
عاقل • خردمند

487

prudently *adv* احتیاطاً • محتاطانه

prune *n* آلو بخارا

pry into personal matters (colloq) *v*
پلته و چراغ گرفتن

Psalms (bibl) *n* زبور • مزامیر •
مزامیر داوود

PSC *see* private security company

pseudonym *see* pen name

psyche *n* نفس

psychic (mental) *adj* وجدانی

psychological *adj* روانی • روحی •
نفسی • نفسانی

psychologist *n* روان شناس

psychology *n* روان شناسی •
روحیات • علم النفس

Ptolemy (hist) *n* بطلیموس •
بطلمیوس

PTS *see* Program Tahkim-e Solh

puberty *n* بلوغ

pubes *see* pubis

pubic hair (esp m) (vulg) *n* پشم

pubis *n* زهار

public (common) *adj* عام

public (notorious) (& *adv*) *adj, adv*
برملا • آشکار

→ become public برملا شدن

→ made public منتشر

public, the *n* عامه

→ in public در محضر عامُ

public opinion *n* مفکوره عام

public relations *n* ارتباط عامه

publication (handbill) *n* نشریه

publication (issuance) *n* انتشار •
نشر

publish *vt* منتشر کردن

published *adj* منتشر

→ be published منتشر شدن

publisher *n* ناشر

pudding (faluda) *n* فالوده

→ firni pudding فرنی

→ rice pudding شیر برنج

puddle *n* دند

pudendum (f anat) *n* شرم اندام •
اندام شرم

puerile *adj* کودکانه • طفلانه

puff (& bragging) *n* پف

pugnacious (fig) *adj* شعله ور

puke *see* vomit

pul (unit of currency) *n* پول • پیسه

Pul-e Alam (seat, dist) *n* پل علم

Pul-e Charkhi (prison) *n* پل چرخی

Pul-e Hesar (dist) *n* پل حصار

Pul-e Khumri (seat, dist) *n* پل
خمری

pull (drag) *vt* کشاندن

pull *n see* & influence

pull out *vt* برآورده کردن •
برآوردن

pulley *n* چرخ

pulmonary *adj* ریوی

pulp *vt* چکیدن

pulpit (in mosque) *n* منبر

pulse (med) *n* نبض

pulverize *vt* میده کردن

pump *n* پمپ

→ water pump واتر پمپ

pun (quip) *n* لطیفه

pun *see* & joke

punch (w/fist) *n* مشت

punch *vt* مشت زدن

punctuation *n* تنقیط • نقطه گذاری
• نقطه گذاری

pundit *n* ناظر سیاسی • مبصر

punish *v* به سزا رساندن

punishment *n* جزا • مجازات • سزا
• کیفر

→ discretionary punishment تعزیر

→ punishment as prescribed by
Quran حد

→ punishment beyond that
prescribed by Quran غیر مقدره

Punjab *see* Panjab

punk (insult) *n* لچک

pupil (of eye) *n* حدقه • مردمک

pupil (student) *n* شاگرد • متعلم •
تلمیذ

puppet (& henchman) *n* دست
نشانده

puppy *n* کچک • چوچه سگ •
چوچه سگ • سگ چوچه • پاپی

Pur Chaman (dist) *n* پرچمن

purchase *see* buy

purchasing power *n* قوه خرید

purdah *n* حجاب • برقع • پرده •
روی بند • نقاب

pure (clear) *adj* صاف

pure (in literary style) *adj* فصیح

488

pure (unadulterated) adj • خالص
خالصانه

purebred adj نسلی

purely adv خالصانه

purely (merely) adv خالصاً

purgative n • جلاب مسهل

purity (chastity) n عصمت

purity (clarity) n صافی

purple adj
→ eggplant purple بادنجانی
→ lily purple سوسنی
→ rosy purple ارغوانی
→ violet purple بنفش

purpose • قصد • صدد • غرض •
مرام • مقصد • مقصود
→ on purpose see intentionally

purse (handbag) n دستکول

purslane (edible weed) n خرفه

pursue vt دنبال کردن

pursuer n پیگیر

pursuit n تعقیب

pus (med, & fig) n • چرک • ریم

push n تنبه

push vt تیله کردن • راندن
→ push & shove تیله و تنبه کردن

pushcart n کراچی

Pusht Rod (dist) n پشت رود

Pushtun see Pashtun

pushy adj سرتنبه • برتنبه •
سرزور

pustule n آبله

put (apply) vt قرار دادن

put (lay, place) vt ماندن • گذاشتن
→ put down (throw) پرتافتن
→ put off (delay) موکول کردن
→ put on glasses • عینک گذاشتن
عینک ماندن
→ put out (extinguish) گل کردن
→ put out (obs) کس دادن

put back in place vt به جای کردن

putting (placing) n تعبیه

putting off (parrying) n دفع

puzzle n معما • چیستان

PWA see person with AIDS

pyramid n هرم/اهرام

Pythagoras (hist) n • فیثاغورس
فیثاغور

Q

Qades (dist) n قادس

Qadiriyya (Sufi order) n قادریه

Qadiyan (town) n قادیان

Qadiyani (sect) n قادیانی

Qajar dynasty (hist, Persia, 1794-1925) n سلسله قاجاریه

Qala (ctr) n قلعه

Qala-ye Kah (dist) n قلعه کاه

Qala-ye Naim (ctr) n قعله نعیم

Qala-ye Naw (seat, dist) n قلعه نو

Qala-ye Wazir (Kabul city dist) n قلعه وزیر

Qala-ye Zal (dist) n قعله ذال

Qalandar (dist) n قلندر

Qalat (seat, dist) n قلات • کلات

Qandahar see Kandahar

qanun (mus instr) n قانون

Qarabagh (dist) n قره باغ

Qaramqol (dist) n قرمقول

Qarghayi (dist) n قرغه یی

Qari, Abdullah (20ᵗʰ-c Dari poet laureate) n قاری • عبدﷲ ملک الشعرا

Qarqin (dist) n قرقین

Qasem (m name) n قاسم

Qataghan (hist, province) n قطغن

Qaus (month) n قوس

Qaysar (dist) n قیصار • قیصر

qaysi (sweet apricot) n قیسی

Qizilbash (grp) n قزلباش • قزل باش

Qom (city, river) n قم

QRF (Quick Reaction Force) n قوای واکنش سریع • نیروی واکنش سریع

quadraplegic adj بی دست و پای

quadrilateral n رباعی

quadruple (adv, n) چارچند

quail n بلدرچین • بلدرجین • کرک • بودنه

quake n لرزه

quake see & earthquake

qualification (ability) n قابلیت

qualifications (experience) n شایسته سالاری

489

qualifications (stipulations) *n pl*
شرایط

qualified (able) *adj* قابل • با استعداد
• لایق

qualitative *adj* کیفی

quality (nature) *n* کیفیت

quality (type) *n* جنس • جنسیت

quantity (number) *n* عده • تعداد

quantity *n* • کمیت • قدر • مقدار
مبلغ

quarrel (wrangle) *v* پرخاش کردن

quarrel *n* مجادله • ستیزه • ستیز

quarrel *see* & argument, fight

quarrel *v* مجادله کردن ‹همرای
کسی›

quarreling (wrangling) *n* پرخاش

quarrelsome (& pers) *adj, n* ستیزه
جو(ی) • ستیزه خو(ی) • ستیزه کار
• ستیزه گر

→ (childishly) جنگروک

→ (colloq) جنگره

quarrelsome pers *n* خاش

quarry *see* game, prey

quarter (one-fourth) *n* چارکه

quarter-hour *n* پاو

quarterly *adj* سه ماهه

quartz (mineral) *n* کوارتز

quatrain *n* رباعی

queen (cards) *n* ماتکه

queen (chess) *n* وزیر

queen *n* ملکه • سلطانه

question (issue) *n* قضیه/قضایا

question mark *n* علامت سوالیه •
سوالیه

question marker (gram) (part) آیا

question *n* سوال • پرسان • پرسش

→ pepper w/questions سوال پیچ
کردن

questionnaire *n* پرسش نامه

Quetta (city) *n* کویته • کویته

queue *n* لین

queue *vi* در لین ایستاده کردن

quick of study *adj* سریع الانتقال

Quick Reaction Force *see* QRF

quick *see* fast

quicklime *n* چونه • آهک

quickly *see* fast

quicksilver *n* سیماب • جیوه

quick-tempered *adj* تند مزاج • تند
خوی • تند

quiet (comfortable) *adj* آرام

quiet (silent) *adj* خاموش

quiet ‹sb› down *vt* خاموش ساختن
‹کسی را›

quiet *n* سکوت • خاموشی

quilt *n* لحاف

→ (lambskin, w/lining) جعفری

quince *n* بهی

→ (arch) به

quince seeds (med) *n* بهی دانه

quinine *n* کنین

quip *n* لطیفه

quit *v* ترک دادن

quiver (for arrows) *n* تیر کش

quiver (shudder) *n* لرزه

quivering *adj* لرزان • لرزیده

Qum *see* Qom

quotation mark *n* • قوس خورد
قوس کوچک

quote *n* نقل

quotient *n* خارج قسمت

quoting ‹sb› *prep* • ‹به نقل ‹کسی›
به قول

Quran *n* قرآن

→ price of copy of Quran هدیه •
تحفه

→ reciter of Quran قاری

→ revelation (Quran) تنزیل

→ Word of God (Quran) کلام الله

→ Yasin (Quranic sura) یاسین

Quran reading (art) *n* تجوید

Quranic *adj* قرآنی

Quraysh (hist, Arabian/Prophet's
tribe; f name) *n* قریش

Quraysha (f name) *n* قریشه

Qurayshi (member of Quraysh) *n*
قریشی

Qurayza (hist, Arabian tribe) *n*
قریظه

→ the Qurayza tribe بنو قریظه

Qurghan (dist) *n* قرغان

Qush Teypa (dist) *n* قوش تیپه

490

R

rabbit n خرگوش خانگی • خرگوش اهلی

rabani (divinity scholar) n ربانی

Rabani (m name) n ربانی

Rabeya (f name) n رابعه

race (category) n نژاد • جنس • جنس آدم • جنس بشر • عرق

race (competition) n مسابقه

→ taking lead in a race سبق

racial adj نژادی • قومی

racism n تعصب نژادی

radiance n تاب • تابش

radiate vi تابیدن

radiation n تشعشع

radio adj رادیویی

radio n رادیو

radio transmitter n دستگاه فرستنده رادیو • دستگاه مرسله

radioactive adj رادیواکتیف

radioactivity n تشعشعات ذروی • تشعشعات اتومی

radiology n رادیولوژی

radish n ملی سرخک

radium n رادیوم

radius (anat) n کعبره

radius n شعاع

rage n قهر • خشم • غضب • غیظ • صفرا • حمیت • جنون • دیوانگی

rage vi قهر بودن

Ragh (dist) n راغ

Ragha (ctr) n راغه

Rahim (m name) n رحیم

Rahima (f name) n رحیمه

raid (& mil) n دست برد

railing (& fence) n کتاره

railroad line n خط آهن • خط ریل

railroad train n ریل

rain (precipitation) n بارش

rain n باران

rain vi باریدن

rainbow n قوس قزح • رنگین کمان • کمان رستم (colloq) →

raincoat n بارانی

rainfall n بارندگی • بارش

rainy adj بارانی

raise (animals) vt نگاه کردن

raise (flag) vt افراختن • افراشتن

raise (increase) vt ارتقا دادن

raise (lift) vt برگرفتن • برداشتن • ورداشتن (colloq) →

raisin n کشمش

rally (pol) n تظاهر

ram (m sheep) n گوسفند نر • قچ

ram fighting n قچ جنگی

Ramadan see Ramazan

Ramak (ctr) n رامک

Ramallah n رام الله

Ramazan (month) n ماه رمضان • ماه روزه • ماه صیام

→ song of Ramazan (sung by children) رمضانی

ramrod n سیخ تفنگ

rancor n کینه

range (for shooting) n تیر رس

range (of mountains) n سلسله

range (of projectile) n برد

range (reach, extent) n حیز

rank (grade, degree) n مرتبه

rank (row, line) n صف • قطار

rank (standing) n رتبه • پایگاه • منصب

→ high-ranking عالی رتبه • عالیرتبه • بلند پایه

→ pers of equal rank همپایه • همشان • همطراز

rape n تجاوز به عصمت

rapid see fast

rapidly see fast

rapier n سیف • تلوار • شمشیر

rapist n متجاوز به عصمت

rapprochement n تجدید روابط

Raqya (f name) n رقیه

rare adj نادر

rarely adv به ندرت • دیر دیر

rarity (& pers) adj, n نادره

rash n پت

Rashad (m name) n رشاد

Rashid (m name) n رشید

Rashida (f name) n رشیده

Rashidan (dist) n رشیدان

raspberry n راس بری • راسبری

Rasul (m name) n رسول

rate (cost per unit) n نرخ

→ rate schedule نرخ نامه

rate (percentage) *n* فیصدی

ratification *see* approval

ratify *see* approve

ration (food) *n* جیره • قوت لایموت
→ rations recipient • جیره خور
جیره خوار

rationalist (& pers) *adj, n* واقع بین

rationing (esp food) *n* جیره بندی

raven (bird) *n* زاغ • کلاغ

ravioli (& Afgh dish) *n* آشک

ravish *vt* ربودن • اختطاف کردن

raw (& dough) *adj* نارس • نارسیده

raw (unripe) *adj* خام

Rawalpindi (city, Pakistani mil
headquarters) *n* راولپندی

ray *n* شعاع • پرتو

rayon *n* سند

Razaq (m name) *n* رزاق

raze *vt* غلتاندن

Raziq (m name) *n* رازق

razor blade *n* تیغ • پاکی • پل

re- (pref) • یک بار دیگر •
از سر یک بار دگر

→ reaching one's goal اصابت

reach *vi* رسیدن

reach out *v* پیش دستی کردن

reaction (chem) *n* تعامل

reaction *n* واکنش • انعکاس عمل

reactionary *n* ارتجاعی • مرتجع

reactor (nuclear) *n* کوره

read *v* خواندن
→ able to read خواننده
→ read out loud بلند خواندن
→ read quickly (skim)
مرور کردن
→ read to o.s.
پیش خود خواندن
→ unable to read ناخوان • بیسواد

readable *adj* خوانا

reader (textbook) *n* قرائت

reader *n* خواننده

readiness *n* آمادگی
→ (colloq) تیاری

ready (money) *adj* نقد

ready (prepared) *adj* آماده • حاضر
→ (colloq) مهیا تیار
→ get ready آماده شدن • تیار شدن
→ ready to start رو به راه

real *adj* حقیقی • واقع • واقعی •
برهان

492

real estate *n* جای داد

realism (art) *n* واقعیت گرایی

realism (outlook) *n* واقع بینی

realist (art, phios) (& pers) *adj, n*
واقعیت گرای

realist (in outlook) (& pers) *adj, n*
واقع بین

reality *n* حقیقت • واقعیت

realization (coming true) *n* تحقق

realization (understanding) *n* درک
• ادراک

realize (carry out) *vt* برآوردن
→ (colloq) برآورده کردن
→ be realized برآورده شدن

realize (understand) *v* درک کردن •
پی بردن

really *adv* در واقع • واقعاً • فی
الواقع • حقیقتاً

really? *excl* راستی ؟

realm (kingdom) *n* ملکوت

realm (scope) *n* حیز

realty *n* رهنمای معاملات

reap *v* درو کردن

reaper *n* دروگر

reaping *n* درو

rear (a child) *vt* کلان کردن

rear *adj* عقبی

rear *n* پس • دنبال • عقب

rear *n see* & buttocks

rear guard *n* موخره

reason (cause) *n* سبب • دلیل •
موجب • علت • باعث • روی

reason (proof) *n* حجت

reason (wisdom) *n* خرد • عقل •
وجه

reasonable *adj* مناسب • موجه •
منطقی • معقول

reasoning *n* استدلال

reassure *vt* دل آسا کردن

reassuring *adj* دل آرام

rebel *n* شورشی • باغی • یاغی •
طاغی • خارجی

rebel *v* سرکشی کردن • سرکشیدن

rebellion *n* شورش • بغاوت

rebellious (& pers) *adj, n* سرکش •
گردن کش • عاصی • نافرمان •
یاغی

rebelliousness *n* • سرکشی
یاغیگری

rebuild *vt* از سر آباد کردن

rebuke *see* reproach

recall *v* خاطر نشان کردن • خاطر نشان ساختن • یاد کردن

receipt (bill) *n* رسید

→ enter receipts on books رسید کردن

receive (accept) *vt* پذیرفتن

receive (get) *vt* • دستیاب کردن دریافت داشتن • دریافت کردن

receive (take) *vt* اخذ کردن

received (letter, file) *adj* واصل

received *adj* دریافتی

receiver (radio) *n* آخذه

receiving (for safekeeping) *n* تحویل گیری

receiving (getting) *n* • دستیابی دریافت

receiving (taking) *adj* گیرنده

receiving (taking) *n* اخذ

recent (new) (& adv) *adj, adv* • نو جدید

recently *adv* اخیراً • دراین اواخر • در این وقت ها

→ (colloq) هم این حالا

receptacle *n* ظرف

receptionist *n* نفر پذیرش

receptive to advice *adj* نصیحت پذیر

recession (econ) *n* وقفه اقتصادی

recidivism *n* رجعت

recipe *n* نسخه • ترکیبات

recipient (pers) *n* گیرنده

reciprocal *adj* دوطرفه

recitation (esp Quran) *n* تلاوت • قرائت

→ (at medium speed) تدویر

recite *v* خواندن

reciter of Quran *n* قاری

recline *vi* اتکا کردن

recluse *n* خلوت نشین • زاهد

recognize *vt* شناختن

→ (govt) به رسمیت شناختن

recognize, know <sb> *vt* به جای آوردن

recoil (of gun) *n* لگد

recommend *v* سفارش کردن • صلاح دادن

recommendation *n* سفارش • تجویز • پیش نهاد

→ letter of recommendation سفارش خط

recommendatory *adj* سفارشی

recompensable *adj* جبران پذیر

reconcile *v* صلح کردن

reconciliation *n* مصالحه • صلح • آشتی

reconnaissance (mil) *n* کشف

reconnoiter *v* کشف کردن

reconstitution *n* تشکیل مجدد

reconstruct *vt* از سر آباد کردن

reconstruction *n* باز سازی

record (memo) *n* یاد داشت

record (videotape) <sth> *vt* فلم گیری ویدیویی کردن <از چیزی>

record (write down) *vt* ضبط کردن

record (written entry) *n* ثبت • قید

→ record of mil recruit's description چهره خط

recorded (written) *adj* مکتوب

recording (video) <of sth> *n* فلم برداری ویدیویی <از چیزی>

recording (writing down) *n* ضبط • تحریر • درج

recourse *n* واسطه • وسیله • متوسل

recover (from illness) *v* شفا یافتن

recovery (from illness) *n* شفا

recreation *n* تفریح

recreational *adj* تفریحی

recruit (hire) *vt* استخدام کردن

recruit (mil) *n* جلبی

recruited *adj* جدید الشمول

recruitment (hiring) *n* استخدام

recruitment (mil) *n* جلب

→ hasht-nafari (1 out of 8, hist) هشت نفری

rectangle *n* چهار ضلعی

rectangular *adj* چهار ضلعی • چارکنج • چارکنجه

recur *vi* دور کردن

recurrence (& med) *n* عود

recurrence *n* رجعت

recurrent *adj* ادواری

recognize *vt* • ضبطی • کتبی • تحریری

recorded (written) *adj* ضبطی • کتبی • تحریری

493

red *adj* سرخ
→ (lit) لعل
→ dark red آتشی
→ Red Crescent سره میاشت
→ Red Cross • صلیب سرخ
صلیب احمر
→ Red Sea بحیره احمر
→ red-hot سرخ
→ ruby red یاقوتی
→ watermelon red تربوزی
→ wine red میگون
redbud (tree) *n* ارغوان
reduce *v* • کاهش دادن • تقلیل دادن
تنقیص دادن • تنقیص کردن
reduction *n* کاهش • تقلیل • تنقیص
• تنزیل
reed (for writing) *n* نال
reed (mus instr) *n* نی
reef (coral) *n* تپه مرجان
reel *n* چرخه
refer <to sb/sth> *vt* مراجعه کردن
<به کسی / چیزی>
referee *n* رفری
reference (source) *n* مرجع • ماخذ
• منبع
→ reference book • سر چشمه
ماخذ • منبع
refinement *n* پالایش • تصفیه
refinery (for oil) *n* تصفیه خانه
reflection *n* انعکاس
reflective *adj* قابل انعکاس
reflex *n* انعکاس روحیاتی
reform *n* • اصلاح سازی • اصلاح •
ریفورم • رفورم
reformer *n* اصلاح طلب • مصلح
refrain (song, poem) *n* برگردان
refraining (inaction) *n* • خود داری
نکردن
refreshment *n* تجدید قوا
refrigerator *n* یخچال
→ (room-sized) سردخانه
refuge *n* پناه • پناه گاه
→ take refuge • پناه بردن • پناه
گرفتن
refugee *n* پناه گزین • پناهنده
refurbished *adj* تجدید
refusal *n* ابا • استنکاف • امتناع
refuse (deny harshly) *v* پیخ زدن

refuse (politely) *v* • عذر خواستن
عذر کردن
refuse (to do sth) *v* سر باز زدن
refuse (to help) (fig) *v* جواب دادن
refuse (trash) *n* خاکروبه
refuse *v* ابا ورزیدن
refutation (disproving) *n* تکذیب
regal *adj* • شاهی • پادشاهی •
سلطنتی
regard (consider) *v* مراعات کردن
regard (consideration) *n* • مراعات
رعایت
regard (respect) *n* لحاظ
→ with regard to به حیث
regarding (about) *see* concerning
regent *see* king, monarch
→ vice-regent (arch) مرزبان
regime *n* نظام • رژیم
regiment (mil) *n* غند
region *n* • منطقه • ساحه • ساحت •
حوزه • سمت • طرف • ولا • زون
→ (of city) ناحیه
regional *adj* • منطقوی • ساحوی •
سمتی
→ Regional Training Center مرکز
تعلیمی ساحوی
register *v* • ثبت نام کردن • نام
نویسی کردن
registration *n* ثبت نام • نام نویسی
regret *n* • دریغ • آرمان • تأسف •
افسوس
regular (gram) *adj* قیاسی • باقاعده
regulation (control) *n* • تنظیم •
ترتیب
regulation (rule) *n* مقرره • دستور
rehabilitation *n* احیای مجدد
reign (of ruler) *n* عصر • دوره
reincarnation *n* • تناسخ • حلول •
حلول و تناسخ
→ Holuliyya (hist, Musl sect
believing in reincarnation) • حلولیه
اهل تناسخ
reindeer *n* گوم • گوزن
reinforcement *n* تجدید قوا
reinforcements (mil, sport) *n* تازه
دم • تازه نفس
reins *n* عنان • زمام • لگام • لجام
→ give free rein to سر دادن
reject *v* رد کردن • تردید کردن

rejectable *adj* قابل تردید

rejection *n* رد • تردید

rejuvenate *vt* جوان کردن

related (connected) <to sth/sb> *n* متعلق (به) < چیزی / کسی>

relation <to sb/sth> *n* • ارتباط • وابستگی (به) <چیزی / کسی>

relationship (kinship) *n* خویشی • خون شریکی
→ blood relationship

relationship *n* رابطه • مناسبت

relative (kin) *n* خویش
→ maternal relatives ذوی الارحام
→ paternal relatives اقوام
→ relatives • اقربا • اقارب • نزدیکان • منسوبین
→ relatives & street کس و کوی
→ relatives (dependents) متعلقین • وابسته گان • متعلقان

relative *adj* نسبی
→ relative to نسبت به • با تناسب • نظر به

relatively *adv* نسبتاً • به صورت نسبی

relativity *n* نسبیت

relax *n* استراحت

relaxation (fig) *n* تمدد اعصاب

relaxed (& pers) *adj, n* خاطر آسوده • آسوده خاطر

release (law) *n* ابرا

release *n* رهایی • رهائی

release *vt* رها کردن • گشودن
→ (colloq) ایلا کردن

releaseable (document) <to sb> *adj* قابل نشر <به کسی>

relevant *adj* ذیربط

reliable (credible) *adj* معتبر

reliable (trusted) *adj* معتمد • موثق • موثوق • تحویل دار نقدی

relic *n* عتیقه • انتیک

relief (aid) *n* مدد • کمک • امداد

relief (med) *n* رهایی • رهائی
→ relief in place (mil) تبدیل در محل

relieve (aid) *v* مدد کردن

relieve (med) *vt* رهایی بخشیدن

religion *n* دین • کیش • آیین
→ (sect) مذهب

religious (sectarian) *adj* مذهبی
→ religious leader (imam) امام

religious *adj* دیندار • با خدا

relinquish *vt* درگذشتن

remain (be left) *vi* باقی ماندن

remain (stay) *vi* ماندن

remainder *n* باقی مانده • باز مانده

remaining (left) *adj* سایر • باقی مانده

remark *n* ملاحظه
→ remarks (speech) بیانیه

remark *vt* خاطر نشان کردن • خاطر نشان ساختن

remarkable *adj* قابل ملاحظه

remediable *adj* چاره پذیر
→ irremediable بی درمان

remedy *n* چاره • گزیر • درمان
→ seeking a remedy چاره جویی

remember *v* به یاد داشتن • به یاد آمدن <کسی> • متذکر شدن • تذکر دادن

remind *v* یاد آوردن
→ (colloq) یاد آوری کردن

reminder *n* تذکر • یاد آوری

remittance (transfer) *n* • حواله • تحویل • ارسال

remodeling *n* تجدید ساختمان

remorse *n* آرمان

remote *adj* دوردست

removal (from office) *n* موقوفی

removal *n* ازاله

remove (from office) *vt* موقوف کردن • خارج کردن

removed (from office) *adj* موقوف

renal (med) *adj* کلیوی

renaming (when converting to Islam) *n* نامگذاری

rend *see* tear *vt*

rendezvous *n* میعاد • میعاد گاه

rendezvous *see* & meeting

renege *v* وعده شکستن • عهد شکستن

renew (extend) *vt* تمدید کردن <چیزی را> • تمدید دادن <به چیزی>

renew *vt* تجدید کردن

renewal (extension) *n* تمدید

renewal *n* تجدید

renewed *adj* تجدید • مجدد

rennin (cul) *n* پنیر مایه

renounce (fig) *vt* پشت پا زدن

495

renovate *vt* ترمیم کردن
renovated *adj* ترمیم شده
renovation *n* ترمیم
renown *see* fame
renowned *see* famous
rent (money) *n* کرا • کرایه
→ for rent کرایی
rent <sth from sb> *v* • کرا گرفتن
کرا کردن <چیزی را از کسی>
→ marketplace stall rent ته جایی
rent <sth> out <to sb> *v* کرا دادن
کرایه دادن <چیزی را به کسی>
rental *adj* کرایی • کرایه
→ rental car موتر کرایی • موتر
کرایه
rented *adj* کرایی
renter *n* کرا نشین • کرایه نشین
reorder (order again) *vt* پیش و پس
کردن
repair (china) *vt* بند زدن
→ china repairman چین بند زن
repair (fix) *vt* جور کردن • ترمیم
کردن
repair (patch) *v* پینه زدن • پینه
کردن • پینه ماندن
repair *n* ترمیم
→ repair shop ورکشاپ • کارخانه
reparations (mil) *n* غرامت جنگ •
تاوان جنگ
reparative *adj* تاوانی
repartee *n* حاضر جوابی
→ skilled at repartee حاضر جواب
repeat *vt* تکرار کردن • بازگفتن
repeated *adj* مکرر
repeatedly *adv* مکرراً • تکراراً
repelling *n* دفع
repentance *n* توبه • انابت
repetition (instance) *n* دفعه • بار •
کرت • مرتبه
repetition (reiteration) *n* تکرار
replace (exchange) *n* آلش کردن
replace <sb/sth> *vt* جای <کسی /
چیزی> گرفتن
replacement *n* بدل • بدیل • عوض
• اشتبنی • جانشین
reply *n* جواب • پاسخ
→ in reply جوابی
reply *v* جواب دادن
report (findings) *n* گذارش • راپور
496

report (news) *n* خبر
reporter *n* خبر نگار • نامه نگار •
ژورنالیست • ژورنالست
representative (& leg) *n* وکیل
→ authorized representative
نماینده • گماشته (proxy)
reprint *n* تجدید چاپ
reprint *vt* طبع دوم کردن
reprisal (requital) *n* قصاص
reproach *n* سرزنش • نکوهش •
تعزیر
reproach *v* سر زنش کردن
reproduction (procreation) *n* تناسل
reproductive (procreative) *adj*
تناسلی
republic *n* جمهوریت
→ Czech Republic جمهوریت
چک
→ people's republic جمهوریت
توده یی
republican *adj* جمهوری
republican *n* جمهوریت خواه
republicanism *n* جمهوریت خواهی
repudiate *vt* رد کردن
repudiation *n* رد
repulsion *n* تدافوع
→ (mutual) تنافر داری
repulsive *adj* تدافعی
→ (mutually) تنافر دار
reputable *adj* نیک نام
reputation *n* عرض • اسم و رسم •
ذکر • نام
→ damage one's reputation
عرض خود را بردن
reputation *see* & fame
request (importune) *vt* تقاضا کردن
request <sth from sb> *vt* خواهش
کردن • خواستن <چیزی را از
کسی>
request *n* خواهش
requesting *adj* خواستار
requestor *n* خواستار
require (need) *vt* ضرورت داشتن
<به چیزی> • نیاز داشتن
required (necessary) *adj* ضروری
• ضرور
requirement *n* مقتضا • نیاز مندی
→ requirements • ضروریات
لوازم • واجبات

requisition (for supplies) *n* تقاضا نامه

requital (of murder) *n* قصاص

rescue <from sth> *n* نجات ‹از چیزی› • رستگاری

rescue *vt* نجات دادن

research *n* تتبع • تحقیقات • پژوهش • پژوهندگی
→ (fig) کاوش

research *v* تحقیقات کردن • پژوهش کردن
→ (fig) کاوش کردن

research-related *adj* تحقیقی

researcher *n* پژوهنده • محقق

resemblance *n* see similarity

resemble *vi* مجانست داشتن

reservation *n* ریزرف
→ make a reservation ریزرف کردن

reserve (stockpile) *n* ذخیره/ذخایر

reserve *adj* احتیاطی

reservoir *n* حوض • آب گیر • آبگیر

resettlement *n* اسکان مجدد

reside *vi* اقامت کردن • اقامت داشتن

residence *n* اقامتگاه • مقام • منزل • مسکن • سر پوش • نشیمن • نشیمن گاه • نشیمن گه • جایگاه • جایگه • سکنی • سکونت

resident (local) *n* اهل • باشنده

residential unit *n* واحد مسکونی

resignation *n* استعفا
→ pers who resigns مستعفی

resist *v* مقاومت کردن

resistance *n* مخالفت • ایستادگی • مقاومت
→ passive resistance مقاومت منفی

resistant *adj* مخالف • مقاوم

resolution (decision) *n* تصمیم

resolution (document) *n* فیصله نامه • قطع نامه

resolve (decide) *v* تصمیم گرفتن
→ be resolved تصمیم داشتن

respect *n* احترام • لحاظ • حرمت • پاس

respect (honor) *n* آبرو • کرام

respectable *adj*

respectable (honorable) *adj* آبرومند

respectable (legitimate) *adj* حلال

respectably (honorably) *adv* آبرومندانه

respected (dignified) *adj* با وقار

respected (esteemed) *adj* محترم • روی دار

respectfully (& in correspondence) *adv* محترمانه • با احترام

respirator *n* جهاز تنفس

respond *v* جواب دادن

response *n* جواب • پاسخ • انعکاس عمل

responsibility *n* ذمه • مسئولیت
→ (authority) صلاحیت
→ (liability) جواب دهی
→ joint responsibility تضامن

responsible (& pers) *adj, n* مسئول

responsible (for sth) *adj* ذمه دار • ذمه وار • ذمه وردار (colloq)

responsible (having authority) *adj* صلاحیت دار • با صلاحیت

responsible (liable) *adj* جواب ده

rest (relaxation) *n* استراحت • قرار • تفریح
→ rest break

rest (remainder) *n* سایر • باقی • مانده • بقیه • بازمانده

restaurant *n* رستوران • رستورانت

restoration (& art) *n* احیا

restoration (renovation) *n* ترمیم

restore (renovate) *vt* ترمیم کردن

restored (renewed) *adj* مجدد

restored (renovated) *adj* ترمیم شده

restrict *vt* مقید ساختن

restricted *adj* قاصر • مقید

restriction *n* حضر
→ being restricted محدودیت

restrictive *adj* مقید
→ restrictive interpretation (of rel) اجتهادِ مقید

restroom *n* تشناب

result (effect) *n* اثر • حاصل • ثمر • ثمره

result (outcome) *n* نتیجه • عاقبت • محصول • ماحصل
→ as a result of در اثر • در نتیجه

497

resurrection *n* قیامت
→ be resurrected قیامت شدن
→ Resurrection Day روز
بازخواست • روز بازپرس
retail *n* پرچون
retailer *n* • بنجاره • پرچون فروش
خورد فروش
retailing *n* پرچون فروشی • خورد
فروشی
retaliation *n* • پاداش • پاداشت
قصاص
retaliatory *adj* جوابی
reticence *n* سکوت • خاموشی
reticent *adj* پس رفته
retina *n* شبکیه
retirement *n* تقاعد
→ related to retirement تقاعدی
retreat (mil) *n* عقب نشینی • رجعت
retreat (mil) *v* عقب نشینی کردن •
عقب نشستن
retribution *n* جزا • کیفر • تلافی •
جبران • پاداش • پاداشت
retroactive *adj* رجعی
return (profit) *n* فایده
return *n* • برگشت • بازگشت •
عودت • معاودت • مراجعت
→ (arch) ایاب
→ returning & going
ایاب و ذهاب
return *vi* برگشتن • بازرفتن •
عودت کردن
→ (colloq) پس آمدن
return *vt* برگرداندن
reveal *vt* • افشا کردن • تجلی دادن •
تجلی کردن • گشودن
revelation *n* افشاگری • بروز •
افشا • تجلی
→ (from God) تنزیل
→ (mystical) مکاشفه
→ (of Quranic verse) نزول
→ (rel) وحی
revenge *n* انتقام
→ get one's revenge دل ‹کسی›
یخ کردن • دل خود را خالی کردن
→ one who takes revenge منتقم
→ take revenge • انتقام گرفتن •
انتقام کشیدن
→ take revenge for murder خون
گرفتن

revenue *n* عایدات
→ provincial revenue collector
دیوان (hist)
reverie *n* خیال بافی
review *n* • مرور • بررسی
review *v* • مرور کردن • تجدید نظر
کردن
revile *vt* زبان کردن
revise *vt* تجدید نظر کردن
revival *n* • تجدد • احیا
→ Muslim revival after Six-Day
War صحوه
revocable *adj* • برگشت پذیر • قابل
برگشت
revolt *n* • قیام • بغاوت • شورش •
اغتشاش
revolt *vi* قیام کردن
revolution *n* انقلاب
→ (fig) طوفان انقلابی
revolutionary (& pers) *adj, n*
انقلابی
→ Revolutionary Guards پاسداران
انقلاب اسلامی
revolve *v* چرخ دادن
revolve *vi* گردیدن
revolve *vt* گرداندن
revolving *adj* چرخی
revolving *n* • گردان • صرف •
تصریف
reward *n* • پاداش • پاداشت • ثمره •
مکافات
reward (spiritual) *n* ثواب
Reyg (dist, *see* & Khan Neshin) *n*
ریگ
Reygestan (dist, see Reyg) *n*
ریگستان
reyhan (callig style) *n* • خط
ریحان
rhetoric *n* • بیان • خطابه • علم
بلاغت
rhetorical *adj* بیانی
rheumatism *n* روماتزم
rhinocerous *n* کرگدن
rhubarb *n* • رواش • چکری
rib *n* قبرغه
ribbon *n* • نوار • پتی • فیته

498

rice *n* برنج
→ cooked white rice چلو
→ long-grain rice برنج باریک
→ medium-grain rice برنج لک
→ paddy (rice in husk) شالی
→ pilau (rice dish) پلو
→ qabele (rice dish) قابلی
→ rice field شالیزار
→ rice pudding شیر برنج
→ rice stuck to bottom of pot ته دیگی
→ utensil for serving rice کفچه
rich (& pers) *adj, n* • غنی • پولدار • پیسه دار • دولتمند • دولت دار • متمول • ثروتمند
→ nouveau riche نو به • نودولت دولت رسیده • نادیده • نوکیسه
→ rich & poor دارا و نادار
rich (fertile) *adj* پر • حاصل خیز • بار
riches *n* غنا • ثروت
→ (fig) زر • طلا
riddle *n* چیستان • معما
rider (horseman) *n* سوار
→ fine rider in procession (fig) فغفور چین
→ ride w/the tide همرنگ جماعت شدن
ridicule *n* ریش خند • ریش خندی
ridicule *vt* ریش خند زدن • ریش خند کردن
ridiculed *adj* ریش خند
ridiculous *adj* چتی • مسخره • مسخره آمیز
rifle (automatic) *n* پیشه
rifle (musket) *n* تفنگ
→ rifle sling بندِ تفنگ
right (correct) *adj* درست
→ be right راست گفتن
right (not left) *adj* راست
right (prerogative) *n* حق
right now (lit) *adv* فعلاً
right of way) *n* حق تقدم
righteous (& pers) *adj, n* عادل • راست کار • درست کار
righteousness *n* عدل • عدالت • داد
rightful *adj* ذی حق
rightly-guided (rel) *adj, n* رشید
Rig-Veda (Hinduism) *n* ریگویدا

rind *n* پوست
→ (discarded) پچاق
ring (circle, hoop) *n* حلقه • چنبر
ring (on finger) *n* انگشتر
→ Ring Road • سرک دایروی • سرک دایره وی • سرک حلقی
→ ring w/jewel(s) نگین
→ signet ring خاتم • مهر
ringing (sound) *n* زنگ
ringlet (hair) see curl
rinse *vt* آب کش کردن
riot *n* شورش • طغیان
→ riot police (ANCOP) پولیس نظم عامه ملی افغان
rioter *n* شورشی
rip *n* شقه
rip *v* شقه کردن
ripe *adj* رسیده
ripeness *n* رسیدگی
riqa (callig style) *n* خط • رقاع • رقاع
rise (ascent) • *n* ارتقا • ارتقاء • طلوع
rise (get up) *vi* خاستن • برخاستن
→ (colloq) خیستن
rise (sun) *vi* طلوع کردن • سر زدن
rising *adj* ارتقایی
risk (jeopardize) *vt* به مخاطره انداختن • به مخاطره افگندن
risk (wager) *n* قمار
risk (wager) *v* قمار زدن
risk *n* مخاطره • خطر
rival *n* رقیب • ثانی • حریف • هم چشم
→ s/he has no rival ثانی ندارد
river bank *n* لب دریا • کنار دریا
river *n* دریا • رود
→ of/from a river دریایی
Riyadh *n* ریاض • الریاض
riyal (currency) *n* ریال
road *n* راه
→ (street) سرک
road (& fig) *n* طریق • صراط
→ dirt road راه خامه • سرک خامه
→ fork in the road دوراهی
→ main road (avenue) جاده
→ road construction سرکسازی
roadblock *n* راه بند
→ (order) عبور و مرور منع

499

roan (horse) n بوز
roar (& animal) vi غریدن
roar (& animal's) n غرش
robber n دزد • سارق
robbery n دزدی • سرقت • دست
برد
robe of honor (hist) n ملبوس خاص
• خلعت
robot n آدم میخانیکی
robust adj تناور
rock (boulder) n صخره
rock (sway) v جمبانی گردن
→ rock a cradle گهواره جمبانی
گردن
rock n سنگ • حجر
rocket (larger) n مزایل
rocket (smaller) n راکت
rocket launcher (& pers) راکت
انداز • راکت لنچر
rocket-propelled grenade n راکت
آر پی جی
rod (arch, mus instr) n رود
rod of Moses (bibl) n عصای موسی
Rodat (dist) n رودات
Rohilla (hist, P highlanders) n
روهیلا
role n رول • نقش • سهم
roll (roster) n حاضری
→ take roll حاضری گرفتن
roll vi غلت خوردن
roll vt غلت زدن
roll call see roll n
roller skates n رولت
Roman Empire (hist) روم
Romania n رومانیا • رومانیه
Romanian (& pers) adj, n
رومانیایی
Rome n روما • روم
roof n پوشش
roof vt پوشاندن
→ straw & mud for roofing کاه گل
rook (bird) n زاغ • کلاغ
rook (chess) n رخ
room (hall) n دیوان
room (in inn, fort, prison) n کوته

room (small) n حجره • سلول
→ emergency room (med) اتاق
عاجل
→ have room for <sw> گنجیدن
<در کجا>
→ room & board اعاشه و اباته
→ secluded room • خلوت خانه
خانه خلوت
→ single-occupancy room (hotel)
اتاق یکنفری
→ waiting room (med) اتاق انتظار
room n اتاق
roommate n هم اتاق
rooster n خروس • مرغ سحری
root (math) n جذر
→ irrational root جذر اصم
root (origin) n مایه
root (stem) n ریشه • عرق
rope n ریسمان • رسن
rope (small) n بند • طناب
rope dancer n بند باز
rosary (Muslim) n تسبیح
rose (esp pink) n گلاب • گل
→ (lit) ورد
→ mursal (rose variety) مرسل
→ red rose سوری
→ rose-colored گلگون
rosewater n گلاب
roster see list, roll
rosy adj گلگون
rotate v چرخ دادن • گرداندن
rotation n گردش • گردان • صرف
• تصریف
rotational adj وضعی
rotten (corrupt) adj فاسد
rotten adj گنده • پوسیده
rouge n غازی
rough (& fig) adj درشت
roughly adv تخمیناً • از روی
تخمین
round (circular) adj مدور • گرد
round (curved) adj گول
round see & spherical
round-trip adj دوطرفه
rouse (incite) vt جوش آوردن
rouse (make to rise) vt خیزاندن
→ (colloq) خیستاندن
rout n شکست • انهزام • هزیمت
rout v see defeat

route *n* • خط مسیر
→ en route to • رهی • راهی
route *see &* road
routed *adj* تار و مار
row (line) *n* • قطار • لین
rowboat *n* • زورق • قایق
Roxanne (hist) *n* رخشانه
royal *adj* شاهی
Rozi (m name) *n* روزی
RPG *see* rocket-propelled grenade
RTC *see* Regional Training Center
rub (& massage) *vt* مالیدن
→ (colloq) چاپی کردن
rub *v* احتکاک کردن • حک کردن
rubab (mus instr) *n* رباب
→ rubab player رباب نواز • ربابی
rubber band *n* الاستیک
rubbing (friction) *n* • اصطکاک
احتکاک • حک
ruble (currency) *n* روبل
rubric (heading) *n* عنوان
ruby *n* • یاقوت • یاقوت آتشی
یاقوت احمر • یاقوت سرخ
→ ruby red یاقوتی
ruby *see &* spinel, garnet
ruckus (noise) *n* غالمغال • قالمقال
• قیل و قال
rude (impolite) *adj* بد گذران • بد
گذاره • درشت • خشونت آمیز
→ (uncouth) فاقد تهذیب
→ be rude خشونت کردن
rude (& pers) *adj, n* مزاحم
rudiments *n* الفبا
rue (wild plant) *n* اسپند • سپند
ruffle (of bird, animal) *n* طوق
rug (carpet) *n* قالین
rug (small carpet) *n* قالینچه
rug (w/o pile) *n* گلم • گلیم
→ (colloq) پلاس
ruin *n* خرابی • تخریب
ruin *see &* damage, destruction
ruin *vt* خراب کردن
ruined *adj* ویران • خراب
→ (colloq) بیران
ruinous *adj* مخرب • ویرانگر
Rukha (dist) *n* رخه
rule (axiom) *n* کلیه
rule (custom) *n* رسم • آیین • کیش
• دین • مذهب

rule (dominion) *n* حاکمیت • تسلط
rule (law) *n* قانون
rule (regulation) *n* مقرره
→ obscure rules روایاتِ ضعیفه
rule (govern) <sw> *vi* حکمرانی
کردن <در کجا>
ruler (& governor) *n* • والی
حکمران
→ (hist) حاکم
ruler (master) *n* سرکار • فرمان
روا
ruler (pol) *n* آمر • سرکار
→ the rightful ruler علو الآمر
ruler (straightedge) *n* جدول • خط
کش
ruler *see &* king, lord
ruling circles *n pl* محافل حاکمه
rumba (dance) *n* رمبا
Rumi (13th-c Sufi poet) *n* رومی
rumor *n* آوازه
→ (lit) شایعه
→ by rumor افواهاً
rumored *adj* افواهی
rump (croup) *n* ساغری • سرین
→ (lit) کفل
rump *see &* buttocks
run *vi* دویدن
run (& surrender) *v* سپر انداختن
run (escape) *vi* فرار کردن
→ on the run بدو
run away *v* گریختن
run out (be depleted) *vi* خلاص
شدن • تمام شدن
rung (of ladder) *n* پله • پته
runner (carpet) *n* پای انداز
running *adj* بدو
runny (nose) *adj* جاری
runt (insult) *n* لچک
rupee (currency) *n* روپیه • کلدار
rupiah *see* rupee
rupture (hernia) *n* چره
rural (pers) *adj* روستا زاده
rural *adj* روستایی • دهاتی
Russia *n* روسیه
→ (neg/fig, as invader) ابر جناور
Russian (& pers, lang) *adj, n*
روسی
→ (colloq) اروسی

501

Russian (pers) *n* روس • روسی
→ (colloq) اروس • اروسی
rust *n* زنگ • موریانه
rust *v* زنگ زدن
Rustam (m name, legend) *n* رستم
Rustaq (dist) *n* رستاق
rustling (sound) *n* شرشر
rusty *adj* زنگ زده
Ruy-e Du Ab (dist) *n* روی دو آب
rye *n* جودر

S

Sabari (dist) *n* صبری
sable *n* سمور
sabotage *n* تخریب • خراب کاری
→ related to sabotage تخریبی
saboteur *n* تخریب کار • خراب
کار
sabre *n* سیف • تلوار • شمشیر
Sabz Posh *see* Khaja Sabz Posh
sack (burlap) *n* بوری • بوجی
sack *v see* plunder
sacred *adj* مقدس • روحانی
→ sacred object مقدسه
sacred *see* & holy
sacrifice *n* قربان • فدا
sacrifice *vt* قربانی دادن • قربانی
کردن
→ I would sacrifice my life for you
فدایت شوم
→ one who sacrifices own life
جانباز
sad (& pers) *adj, n* غمگین •
محزون • اندوهگین • حزین • دل
تنگ • خاطر آزرده • آزرده خاطر •
متأثر
sad (bored) *adj* دق
sad *adj* نمکی
saddle *n* پالان • زین
saddle strap *n* سینه بند
saddlebow *n* قاش زین
saddler *n* سراج
Sadeq (m name) *n* صادق
Sadi (Persian poet, 1184-1283?) *n*
سعدی
Safavid (Sufi sect) *n* صفوی
Safavids, the (hist, dynasty 1499-
1736 A.D.) *n pl* صفویان

safe *adj* امن • ایمن • مصون •
مصئون • محفوظ
→ safe & secure خاطر جمع
safety *n* ایمنی • مصونیت • سلامت
safety *see* & security
safety position (on gun) *n* قید
Saffarid (hist) *adj, n* صفاری
Saffarids, the (hist, dynasty 867-
1495 A.D.) *n pl* صفاریان
saffron (herb) *n* زعفران
→ saffron-colored زعفرانی
Safi (P tribe) *n* صافی
sage (plant) *n* گل نافرمان
Saghar (dist) *n* ساغر
Sagittarius (zodiac) *n* قوس
Sahar (f name) *n* سحر
sahib (honorific) *n* صاحب
Sahwa (Muslim revival since Six-
Day War) *n* صحوه
said (title) *see* sayed
sail *n* شراع
→ (lit) بادبان دار
→ having sails شراعی
sailor (mil) *n* عسکر قوای بحری
→ (arch) ملاح
saint (Christian) *n* قدیس
→ (f) قدیسه
sake *n* خاطر
Sakhi (m name) *n* سخی
salad (cul) *n* سلاته
Salafism (mvmt) *n* سلفزم • سلفیزم
• سلفیه • دعوت سلفی
Salafist (& pers) *adj, n* سلفی
Salang (dist) *n* سالنگ
salary *n* تنخواه • معاش
Saleh (m name) *n* صالح
Saleha (f name) *n* صالحه
saline *adj* شور
saliva *n* لعاب دهن • آب دهن •
بزاق • لعاب • تف
salivary *adj* بزاقی
salt *n* نمک • ملاحت
salt *vt* نمک انداختن • نمک پاشیدن
• شور کردن
salt container *n* نمکدان
salt marsh *n* شوره زار
salt shaker *n* نمکدانی
saltiness *n* شوری

502

saltpeter n شوره

salty adj نمکی • شور

salute (mil) n احترام نظامی

salvation n وارستگی • رستگاری

salve n مرهم

salvo, volley, report (of a gun) n شلیک

Samad (m name) n صمد

Saman (f name) n سمن

Samangan (province) n سمنگان

Samanian see Samanid

Samanid (& pers) adj, n سامانی

Samanids, the (hist, dynasty 874-999 A.D.) n pl سامانیان

Samarkand (city) n سمرقند

same adj عین

→ both are the same هردو یک چیز است

→ the very same همان • همو • همین • همی • همین

sample n نمونه

Sanaa n صنعا

Sanaayi Ghaznawi (11th-12th-c Sufi poet) n سنایی غزنوی • ابو المجد مجدود بن آدم

Sanawbar (f name) n صنوبر

sanction <against country> (econ) n تعزیراتِ اقتصادی • تحریم <علیهِ یک مملکت>

→ trade sanction محدودیت تجارتی

sanctity n روحانیت

sanctuary n حریم

sanctum see sanctuary

sand n ریگ

→ made of sand ریگی

sandal (f's) چپلی بوت

sandal (m's) چپلی

sandal n چپلک

→ sandals سر پایی

→ sling for sandals بندِ چپلی

sandalwood n صندل • چوب صندل

sandbag n خریطهِ ریگ

sandpaper n ریگ مال

sandstorm n طوفانِ ریگ • خاک باد • گرد باد

sandy adj ریگی

Sang Atash (ctr) n سنگ آتش

Sang-e Masha (ctr) n سنگ ماشه

Sang-e Takht (dist) n سنگ تخت

Sangar (ctr) n سنگر

Sangar Saray (ctr) n سنگر سرای

Sangcharak (dist) n سنگچارک

Sangin (dist) n سنگین

sanitation n تنظیف • حفظ الصحه

sanj (mus instr) n سنج

santur (mus instr) n سنتور

sap (tunnel) (mil) n نقب • سوف

sapling (tree) n نهال

sapper battalion n کندکِ استحکام

sapphire n یاقوت کبود • یاقوت ازرق

→ yellow sapphire یاقوت زرد • زبرجد هندی

Sar Hawza (dist) n سرحوضه

Sara (f name) n سارا

sarang (mus instr) n سارنگ

Saratan (month) n سرطان

sarcasm n طعنه • طعن

sarcastic adj پهلو دار

Sar-e Pul (province, seat, dist) n سر پل

sari adj ساری

Sarobi (f name) n سروبی

Sarqala (ctr) n سرقلعه

Sassanian see Sassanid

Sassanid (hist, empire 226-651 A.D.) n ساسانی

satellite n مدار گرد

satin adj اطلسی

satin n اطلس

satire (derision) n طنز

satire (esp poem) n هجو • هجا

satiric (derisive) adj طنز آمیز

satiric adj هجایی • هجوی

→ satiric poem هجونامه

satirist n طنز نویس

satisfaction n رضایت • رضا • قناعت

satisfactory adj رضایت بخش • قناعت بخش

satisfied adj راضی • قانع • خوشنود

satisfy vt راضی کردن • رضا دادن • قانع ساختن • خوشنود ساختن

satisfying see satisfactory

satrap (arch) n مرزبان

503

Saturday n شنبه

Saturn (planet) n زحل • کیوان

sauce n رب

saucepan n روغن داغ

Saudi Arabia n عربستان سعودی • عربستان

Saur (month) n ثور

savage (& adv) adj, adv وحشیانه • وحشتناک

savagery n وحشت • وحشیگری

SAVAK (hist, Iranian intel service under Shah) n ساواک

save (keep) vt نگاه کردن

save (rescue) <sb/sth> vt نجات دادن <کسی / چیزی را>

saved (rescued) (& pers) adj, n وارسته

saving (rescuing) <from sth> n نجات <از چیزی> • رستگاری

savings (money) n پس انداز

savings account n حساب پس انداز

savior n فریاد رس

savor see flavor, salt

savory see salty

savvy in business adj کاردان

saw (tool) n اره
→ hacksaw اره آهن بر

sawdust n بوره اره

sawyer n اره کش

saxophone (mus instr) n سکسفون

say (tell, state) vt گفتن
→ (formal) فرمودن
→ (neg imper) مگو • نگو
→ things said & unsaid گفته ها و نگفته ها
→ saying & stating گفتگو • گفت و گو

Sayad (dist) n صیاد

sayed (title for descendants of the Prophet, before name) n سید

Sayed Karam (dist) n سید کرم

Sayed Kheyl (dist) n سید خیل

Sayedabad (dist) n سید آباد

Sayghan (dist) n سیغان

saying n مقوله

scab (colloq) n ارجق

scab (colloq) v ارجق گفتن

scabies n گرگ

scabrous adj گرگی • گرگین

504

scaffold (wooden) n چوب بست

scaffold n خوازه

scale (balance) n ترازوی درجه دار

scale (merchant's) n موازنه تجاری

scalene (math) adj مختلف الاضلاع

scan (read quickly) v مرور کردن

scandal n رسوایی • افتضاح • فضیحت

scandalized adj رسوا

scandalous adj رسوایی آمیز • رسوایی آور • افتضاح آمیز • افتضاح آور • فضیحت آمیز • فضیحت آور

Scandinavia (geog) n سکندیناویا

Scandinavian adj سکندیناوی

scapula (anat) n استخوان شانه • استخوان کتف

scapula (colloq) n بیلک شانه

scare vt ترساندن

scared adj هراسان

scarf (f's, worn on head) n دستمال سر

scarf (muffler) n دستمال گردن

scary adj ترس آور • ترسناک • هراس آور • هراسناک • بیمناک • خوفناک • سهمناک

scatter vt پاشاندن • پاشیدن
→ (colloq) پاش دادن

scatter vt پراگندن

scatterbrained (& pers) adj, n تهی مغز

scattered (destroyed) adj متلاشی

scattered (dispersed) adj پاشان • پراگنده

scenery (theater) n صحنه سازی

scent (fragrance) n رایحه • نسیم

scent (perfume) n عطر

scent (smell, odor) n بوی

schedule n جدول

Scheherazade (1001 Ar Nights; cf Sheyrzad) n شهرزاد

scheme (intrigue) n دسیسه • توطنه

scheme (layout) n نقشه • خریطه

schism (discord; civil war) n فتنه

schist (rock) n شیست

scholar n عالم
→ scholar of divinity ربانی

scholarly adj محققانه

scholarship (aid) n بورس

school n مكتب

→ elementary school مكتب ابتدایی

→ high school لیسه • مکتب عالی

→ language school مکتب زبان

→ middle school مکتب متوسطه

→ rel boarding school مدرسه

→ school transfer document سه پارچه

schoolmate (fellow alumnus) n هم مکتب

schoolmate (in different class or school) n هم دوره

science n علم • دانش • حکمت

scientifically adv علماً

scientist n عالم

scimitar n تیغ

scissors n قیچی

→ (lit) مقراض

sclera (anat) n صلبیه

scoff v هجو گفتن

scoffing n هجا

scope (range) n دامنه • حیز

score (grade) n نمره • شماره • نمبر

score a goal v گول زدن

Scorpio (zodiac) n عقرب • گژدم

scorpion n عقرب • گژدم • کژدم

Scotch adj سکاتس لیندی

Scotland n سکات لیند • سکات لند

Scotsman n سکاتس لیندی

scout (reconnaissance) n کشاف

scowl adj پیشانی ترشی

scowling adj پیشانی ترش

scrape v رنده کردن

scrapmonger n ویران کار

scratch n پرت کردن • خاریدن

scratched adj خراشیده

scratching n پرت

scream vi چیغ زدن • چیغ کشیدن

screen (& film) n پرده

screen (film) vt تماشا کردن

screen (folding) n در پرده

screen (mesh) n جاله

screening (film) n نمایش

screening (vetting) n طی مراحل

screenplay n سناریو

screenplay writer n • سنارست سناریو نویس

screw (bolt) n پیچ

screw (obs) v بند کردن

screw (small) n پیچک

screwdriver n پیچکش • پیچتاب

→ Phillips screwdriver پیچکش چاررخ

scribe n مورخ

script n سناریو

scrofula (med) n خنازیر

scroll n طومار

scrutinize vt تصفح کردن • نظارت کردن

scrutiny n تدقیق • نظارت

scuffle see fight

scuffle v • کش و گیر کردن

sculptor n مجسمه ساز • پیکر تراش • هیکل تراش

sculpture (discipline) n مجسمه سازی • پیکر تراشی • هیکل تراشی

sculpture (statue) n مجسمه • پیکره

Scythian (hist) adj سکایی • سیت

Scythian (pers) (hist) n سکا • سیت

sea n بحر • بحیره

sea level n سطح بحر

seafood n نان بحری

seagull n مرغ نوروزی

seal (stamp) n مهر

seal (stamp) vt مهر کردن

seal off vi محاصره کردن

seaman n عسکر قوای بحری

search (for sth illicit) n تلاشی

search (inquiry) n جستجو • جست و جو

search (inspection) n تفتیش

→ conduct a search تفتیش کردن

search for v پالیدن • جستن

seashore n لب بحر

season (of year) n فصل

seasonal adj فصلی

seasoning n مساله • مساله دیگ

seat (couch) n سیت

seat (headquarters) n مقر

seat (of monarch, judge) n مسند

seat (of province) n مرکز

seat vt نشاندن

seatbelt n کمربند

sebaceous adj چربی دار • شحمی

505

secant (math) *n* قاطع
secluded *adj* خلوت نشین
seclusion *n* خلوت
→ seclusion of women ستر عورت
second (ordinal) *adj* دوم • ثانی
→ second lieutenant دو هم بریدمن
دو هم خُوارن
→ second person (gram) مخاطب
• شخص دوم
second (unit of time) *n* ثانیه
secondary *adj* ثانوی • فرعی
→ secondary component فرع
secondly *adv* ثانیاً
secrecy *n* راز داری
secret (covert) *adj* نهفت • نهفته
→ department of secret services
ریاست استخبارات
secret *adj* پنهان • مخفی • پوشیده •
سربسته • پشت پرده
secret *n* راز • سر • سخن سربسته
→ able to keep secrets راز دار
→ unable to keep a secret تنک
ظرف
secretariat *n* تحریرات • دارالانشا
secretary (& diplomat) *n* کاتب
→ (arch) دبیر
→ (official) منشی
Secretary General *n* • سر منشی
منشی عمومی
secretly *adv* نهفت
sect *n* مذهب • فرقه • پرگنه •
طایفه • عشیره
sectarian *adj* مذهبی • فرقوی
section (office) *n* شعبه/شعبات
section (part) *n* بخش
sector *n* سکتور • ساختار • بخش
secular world *n* ناسوت
secure *adj* ایمن
secured *adj* محفوظ • مصون
securing *n* تامین
security *adj* امنیت
security *n* امنیت • ایمنی • امن
security officer *n* کوتوال
security-related *adj* امنیتی
sedative *adj, n* مسکن • دوای
مسکن
sediment *n* رسوب
→ form sediment ته نشین شدن
sedimentary *adj* رسوبی
506

sedimentation *n* ته نشین
seditionist (& pers) *adj, n* محرک
seduce (deceive) *v* فریفتن
seduced (deceived) *adj* فریب داده
seduction (deception) *n* فریب
see (& visit) *vt* دیدن
seech (plant) *n* سیچ
seed (& sperm) *n* تخم
seed *n* دانه • حب • غله • بذر
→ seeds حبوب • حبوبات
seedling *n* نهالی
seeing *n* دیدن • مشاهده • بینی
seek *vt* پالیدن • جستن
seeker *n* جوینده
→ (esp rel) طالب
→ asylum seeker پناه گزین
seem *vi* معلوم شدن • به نظر
رسیدن • نمودن
seemingly *see* apparently
seesaw (colloq) *n* اندرچو
segment *n* حصه/حصص
segmental (gram) *adj* مقطع
segregated *adj* پرده نشین
segregation (of f) *n* پرده نشینی
seige *n* محاصره
→ beseige محاصره کردن
seismograph *n* زلزله سنج
seismology *n* زلزله شناسی
seize *vt* ضبط کردن
seized *adj* ضبطی
seizing *n* اغتنام
seizure (confiscation) *n* ضبط
seizure (med) *n* صرع • مرگی
select *see* & choose
select *vt* گزیدن • برگزیدن
selected (& pers) *adj, n* برگزیده
→ selected works (of author)
منتخبات
selection (decision) *n* تصمیم
انتخاب
self (takes pers endings) *pron* خود
→ oneself خویش
self (the individual) *n* خویش تن
self-confidence *n* اعتماد به نفس
self-conscious *adj* خود آگاه
self-contradiction *n* متناقض گویی
self-control (fig) *n* عنان اختیار
self-defense *n* دفاع از جان
self-governing *adj* مستقل

self-immolation *n* • خود سوزی • خودسوزی

self-interest *n* خود غرضی

self-interested *adj* • خود غرض • مطلب آشنا

selfish (& pers) *adj, n* • خود بین • خود پرست • خود خواه

self-reliance *n* اعتماد به نفس

self-reliant *adj* مستقل

self-reliantly *adv* مستقلاً

self-sacrifice *n* • از جان گذشته گی • از خود گذری

Seljuks, the (hist, dynasty 11th-14th c.) *n pl* سلجوقیان • سلاجقه

sell *v* فروش کردن • فروختن

seller *n* فروش • فروشنده

semantic *adj* معنایی

semester *n* سمستر

semicircle *n* نیم دایره

semi-colon *n* سمی کلن

Semite (pers) *n* سامی

Semitic *adj* سامی

senate *n* • سنا • مجلس سنا

Senate *n* مجلس سنا

senator *n* سناتور

send (& transmit) *vt* فرستادن

send *vt* • روان کردن • راهی کردن • کسیل کردن

sending *n* ارسال

senile (fig) *adj* ضعیف

senior (in rank) *adj* بلند پایه

senior <to sb> (in experience) *adj* • سابقه دارتر • مافوق • بالا دست <از کسی>

senior *adj* ارشد

seniority (eldership) *n* ارشدیت

seniority (in experience) *n* سابقه داری

seniority (in qualifications) *n* شایسته سالاری

senna (plant) *n* سنا

sensation (feeling) *n* احساس

sense (meaning) *n* • معنی • مفهوم

sense (perception) *n* • حس • حاسه

→ sense of hearing • حس سامعه • حس شنوایی

→ sense of sight • حس باصره • قوه باصره

→ sense of smell حس شامه • حس بویایی

→ sense of taste • حس ذایقه • حس چشایی

→ sense of touch • حس لامسه • حس بساوایی

sensible (reasonable) *adj* معقول

sensitive *adj* • حساس • نازک

→ (tender-hearted) نازک دل

sensitivity (& allergy) *n* حساسیت

sentence (gram) *n* • جمله • کلام

→ complex sentence جملة مختلف

→ compound sentence جملة مرکب

→ simple sentence جملة بسیط

sentence (law) *n* حکم

sentence (law) *vt* محکوم کردن

sentenced (& pers) (law) *adj, n* محکوم

sentencing (law) *n* محکومیت

sentry *n* پهره دار

separate *adj* جدا

separate *vi* • جدا شدن • تجزیه شدن • گسیختن • گسستن → (colloq) سکستن

separate *vt* • جدا افتادن • جدا کردن • تجزیه کردن • گسیختن • گسستن → (colloq) سکستن

separately *adv* • جدا جدا • جداگانه

separation *n* • تفکیک • تجزیه

separatism (pol) *n* تجزیه طلبی

separatist (pol) *n* تجزیه طلب

→ separatist groups (neg) دسته های تجزیه طلب

sepoy *n* • سپاهی • عسکر • لشکری

September *n* سپتمبر

sequel *n* دنباله

sequester *vt* محاصره کردن

Sera Rod *see* Surkh Rod

seraph (bibl) *n* اسرافیل

Serb (pers) *n* • صرب • صربی

Serbia *n* صربستان

Serbian (& pers) *adj, n* صربی

507

Serena (Kabul hotel) n • سرینا
هوتل سرینا

sergeant n ضابط بریدگی • خورد ضابط
→ (colloq) ضابط
→ police sergeant ساتنمن

series n سلسله

serious adj سنگین

serious (& adv) adj, adv جدی

seriously adv به جدیت • جدی

seriousness n جدیت

Serkanay (dist) n سرکانی

sermon (esp Musl, Friday) n خطبه

sermon (preaching) n وعظ

serum n سیرم

servant (domestic) n • خدمتگار
نوکر • چاکر مزدور • مزدور کار •
خادم

servant (slave girl) n کنیز

servant (waiter) n پیش خدمت

servant n خدمتگار • نوکر

serve (food) v پیش کردن •
سرویس کردن

serve v خدمت کردن

service (assistance) n • خدمت
نوکری
→ at your service به خدمت شما •
به چشم

service (rel) n عبادت

serving (portion) n خوراک

sesame n کنجد

session n نشست • جلسه • مجلس •
اجلاس • اجلاسیه

set (of items) n سیت

set (sun, stars) vi غروب کردن

set (put, apply) vt قرار دادن
→ set aside اختصاص دادن
→ set forth (demands) مطرح
کردن
→ set on fire آتش زدن • آتش در
دادن
→ set up (establish) بر پای کردن
→ set up (install) نصب کردن

Setam-e-Meli (party) n ستم ملی
→ Setam-e-Meli member ستمی

setback (colloq) n برگشت

setting (sun, stars) n افول

settle (form sediment) vi ته نشین
شدن

settle (sw) v مسکن اختیار کردن

settled (in new place) adj مستقر

settlement n اسکان

settling (sw) n • مسکن گزین
استقرار

seven adj, n هفت
→ the Seven Sleepers (lit)
اصحاب کهف

Sevener (rel; & pers) adj, n
اسماعیلی

seventeen adj, n هفده

seventeenth adj هفدهم
→ (lit, used before n) هفدهمین

seventh adj هفتم
→ (lit, used before n) هفتمین

seventieth adj هفتادم
→ (lit, used before n) هفتادمین

seventy adj, n هفتاد

sever vt بریدن

several adj چندین

severance (firing) n • انفکاک
انفصال

severe adj شدید

sew v دوختن

sew (tailor) v خیاطی کردن

sewage n گنداب
→ sewer pipes نل های بدرفت
→ sewer system کانالیزاسیون

sewage n pl آب های بدرفت

sewing machine n ماشین خیاطی

sewing n دوزی

sex (gender) n جنس

sex (intercourse) n • مجامعت
جماع • مقاربت
→ have sex <w/f> پیش شدن <به
زن>
→ have sex (couple) جفت شدن

sex appeal n جاذبه جنسی

sexual adj جنسی

sexuality n جنسیت

Seykwa (ctr) n سه کوه

seyr (unit of weight) n سیر

Shabarghan (seat) n شبرغان

shack n کلبه

shackle n زولانه
→ shackles زنجیر

shade n سایه • ظل

shadow see shade

Shafiite (pers) n شافعی

508

Shafiitic (school of Sunni rel thought) *adj* شافعی

shaggy (hairy) *adj* پشم آلود

shah *n* شاه • شه • پادشاه • سلطان

Shah Jahan (hist, Mughal emperor 1628-1658) *n* شاه جهان

Shah Wali Kot (dist) *n* شاه ولی کوت

shahadat (Musl credo) *n* شهادت

Shahed-e Hasas (dist) *n* شاهد حساس

Shahgerd (ctr) *n* شاه گرد

Shahi Kot (ctr) *n* شاهی کوت

Shahjoy (dist) *n* شاه جوی

Shahla (f name) *n* شهلا

Shahnama (hist, 10th-c epic poem) *n* شاه نامه • شهنامه

Shahr-e Buzurg (dist) *n* شهر بزرگ

Shahr-e Kuhna (Kabul city dist) *n* شهر کهنه

Shahr-e Naw (Kabul city dist) *n* شهر نو

Shahr-e Safa (ctr) *n* شهر صفا

Shahrak (dist) *n* شهرک

Shahrestan (dist) *n* شهرستان

Shakardara (dist) *n* شکردره

shake (jolt) *n* تکان • شوک • چک • جتکه → (colloq) جیک

shake *vi* لرزیدن

shake *vt* لرزاندن

shake hands *v* مصافحه کردن

Shakila (f name) *n* شکیلا

shakiness *n* لرزش

shaking *adj* لرزان • لرزیده

shaky *adj* لرزانک → (colloq) لق • لقک

shallow (superficial, & pers) *adj, n* ظاهربین

shallow *adj* کم عمق

sham *n* طاهر سازی

Shamal (dist) *n* شمل

Shamali (geog, north of Kabul) *n* سمتِ شمالی • شمالی

shaman *n* شمن

shame (bashfulness) *n* حیا • خجالت • خجلت

shame (dishonor) *n* ننگ • عار

shame (modesty) *n* شرم → (colloq) خنگ

shameless *adj* بی شرم • بی حیا • بیعار • وقیح

Shamolzai (dist) *n* شمولزی

shampoo *n* شامپو

Shams (m name) *n* شمس

shank (of leg) *n* ساق

shape *n* شکل • قواره • صورت

shapely *adj* خوش قواره

Sharak Hayratan (dist) *n* شهرک حیرتان

Sharan (seat, dist) *n* شرن • شرنه

Sharana *see* Sharan

share (of stock) *n* سهم

share (portion) *n* حصه • قسمت • نصیب • بهره • تقسیم

share (divide) *vt* تقسیم کردن

share (jointly) *vt* شریک کردن

sharecropping contract *n* مزارعه

shared (joint) *adj* مشترک • شریکی

shareholder *n* سهم دار • سهمدار

sharia (Musl law) *n* شرع • شریعت → compliance w/sharia مشروعیت → lawful under sharia مشروع → versed in sharia متشرع

Sharif (m name) *n* شریف

sharp (cutting) *adj* بران

sharp (light) *adj* تیز

sharp (penetrating) *adj* ثاقب → be sharp-witted ذکاوت داشتن

sharpen knives on stone wheel *v* چرخ کردن

sharpshooter *n* نشان زن • نشانچی

sharpshooter (archer) *n* تیر انداز

shatranj (floor covering) *n* شطرنج

shatter *vt* پرچه پرچه کردن

shattered *adj* پرچه پرچه

shave (face) (colloq) *v* کل کردن → unshaven beard ریش رسیده

shave (scrape) *vt* تراشیدن

shaving (of wood) *n* پفک رنده

Shawak (dist) *n* شواک

shawl *n* شال

Shaygal wa Sheltan (dist) *n* شیگل و شلتن

she *pron* او

Sheberghan (seat, dist) *n* شبرغان

509

shed (blood) *vt* ریختاندن
shed (tears) *see* cry, weep
sheep *n* گوسفند
sheep (ram) *n* قچ
sheepish (meek) *adj* گوسفندی
sheepskin *n* قره قل • پوست قره قل
sheet (of paper) *n* ورق • تخته
Sheghnan (dist) *n* شغنان
Sheghni (pers, lang) *n* شغنی
sheik *n* شیخ
Sheki (dist) *n* شکی
shell (crustacean) *n* صدف
→ cowrie shell کودی
shell (projectile) *n* مرمی • گلوله
shell (skin, pelt) *n* پوست
shell (skin, peel) *vt* پوست کردن
shelter (refuge) *n* پناه گاه
shelter *n* سر پناه • سرپوش
shepherd (colloq) *n* چوپان • شبان
shepherding *n* چوپانی • شبانی
Sher Shah Suri (hist, Kakar P leader) *n* شیر شاه سوری
Sheykh Ali (dist) *n* شیخ علی
Sheyrzad (dist; cf Scheherazade) *n* شیرزاد
Sheywa (ctr) شیوه
Shia *n* شیعه
→ Batiniyya (Shia group) • باطنیه اسماعلیه
→ Ismaili Shia • اسماعیلیه • باطنیه
Shib Koh (dist) *n* شیب کوه
Shibar (dist) *n* شیبر
shield *n* سپر
Shighni (pers, lang) *n* شغنی
Shiism *n* تشیع
Shiite (& pers) *adj, n* شیعی
→ Ismaili Shiite اسماعیلی
→ Ithna Shiite اثناعشری
Shikeyb (m name) *n* شکیب
Shindand (dist) *n* شیندند
shine *n* تابش
shine *vi* تابیدن
shining *adj* تابان • تابناک
shining *n* تاب • درخشان • لامح • لامع
Shinkay (dist) *n* شینکی
Shinwar (dist) *n* شینوار
Shinwari (dist, alt Shinwar) *n* شینواری
510

shiny *adj* آیینی
ship *n* کشتی • سفینه • جهاز بحری
Shirin Tagab (dist) *n* شیرین تگاب
shirk (apostasy; < Ar) *n* شرک
shirk (work) *v* شانه خالی کردن
shirk responsibility *v* از مسؤلیت شانه خالی کردن
shirt *n* پیراهن • پیرهن
shirt (for sports) *n* جمپر
shirtcuff *n* کف
shit (& fig) (vulg) *n* گه
→ (colloq) گو
shiver *n* لرزه
shock *n* تکان • شوک • چک
→ (colloq) جتکه • جیک
shocking *adj* تکان دهنده
shoe *n* بوت
→ shoe a horse نعل بندن
→ shoe polish رنگ
→ shoe repairman • پینه دوز موچی
shoelace *n* بند بوت
shoes (esp sandals) *n* سر پایی
shola (Afgh dish) *n* شله
Shola Jaweyd (party) *n* شعله جاوید
Sholgara (dist) *n* شولگره
shoo (to scare cats) *excl* پشت
shoot (film) *v* فلم گیری کردن • فلم برداری کردن
shoot (sprout) *n* نوده
shoot <at sb> *vi* فیر کردن <بالای کسی>
→ practice target shooting نشان زدن
shooting (archery) *n* تیر اندازی
shooting range *n* تیر رس
shop *n* دکان • فروشگاه • بنجارگی
shop *v* خرید کردن • خریدن
shopkeeper *n* دکان دار
shopping *n* خرید
Shorabak (dist) *n* شورابک
shore *n* کنار • کران
short (in length) *adj* کوتاه
short (insufficient) *adj* کمبود
short (of stature) *adj* پخچ • خورد
→ in short به اجمال • فی الجمله
short circuit *n* شارتی • شارتي برق
shortage *n* کمبود • کمی • قحط • فقدان

shortcut n میان بر • راه میان بر
shorten vt اختصار کردن
Shorteypa (dist) n شورتیپه
shortfall see shortage
shorts (for sports) n نیکر
short-term adj کوتاه مدت
shortwave adj موج کوتاه
shot (bullet, arrow) n تیر
shot (injection) n زرق • پیچکاری • تزریق
should <+ subj> phrs باید • بهتر است
→ should have باید داشته باشد • باید داشته باشه
shoulder (of road) n لب سرک
shoulder belt n حمایل
→ (colloq) امیل
shoulder blade n بیلک شانه
shoulder n شانه • دوش
→ (lit) کتف
→ broad-shouldered چارشانه
→ middle of the shoulder تخته شانه
→ shoulder blade استخوان شانه • استخوان کتف
shout n فریاد • نعره • چیغ •نفیر • قیل و قال • قالمقال
shout vi فریاد زدن • چیغ زدن • چیغ کشیدن
shove n تیله • تنبه
shove v تیله کردن • تنبه کردن
shovel n بیل
show (entertainment) n تماشا
show <sth to sb> vt نشان دادن <چیزی را به کسی> • نمودن
→ (film) تماشا کردن
→ show off خود نمایی کردن
shower n شاور
shrapnel n چره
shred v رنده کردن
shredded adj رنده شده
→ shredded carrot خلال
shrew n لولی
shrewd adj مکار • هوشیار • هوشمند • عاقل • خردمند • رند • رندانه
shrewdness n مکاری
shrewish adj سلیطه • لولی
→ (colloq) شلیطه

shrine n مزار • زیارت گاه • مقبره
→ (colloq) زیارت
→ Mazar-e Sharif (shrine) مزار
→ shrine custodian متوالی
→ tie a string at a shrine to seek intercession بند بستن
shrink vi جمع شدن
shroud n کفن
shrub n بته
shrug v شانه بالا انداختن
shudder n لرزه
shuddering adj لرزان • لرزیده
shuffle (cards) v گد کردن
shuffling (mixing) n گد
Shuhada (dist) n شهدا
shun <sth> v روی گرداندن <از چیزی> • روی گشتاندن
shura (council) n شورا
Shuryak (valley) n شوریک
shut (lit) adj مقفل
shut vt قات کردن • پیش کردن
→ shut up! چپ باش • قرا باش
shuttle n شاتل
Shutul (dist) n شتل
shy adj پس رفته
shy see bashful
sick (bedridden) adj جای مانده • بستری
sick (ill) (& pers) adj, n بیمار • مریض
sick (unhealthy) adj ناجور • ناخوش • مریض
→ (colloq) مرضی
sickly adj بیمار غنج
sickness n بیماری • مریضی
side (& direction) n طرف • سمت • سوی • سو • جهت
→ from every side از تمام جوانب
→ on one side یک پهلو
side (flank) (mil) n جناح
side (geometric shape) n ضلع
side (party to agreement) n جانب • طرف
side (road, river) n بغل
side street n سرک فرعی
sideburns n شقیقه
sidelock (f's) n پیچه • زلف
sidewalk n پیاده رو

sieve (wire, silk, horse hair) n ایلک • اللک • پرویزن

sift (flour) vt ایلک کردن

sifter (for flour) n ایلک • اللک • أردبیز

sifter (for grain) n غربال

sight (on gun or surveying instrument) n نشان نگاه

sight (on gun) n نشانه

sight (vision) n باصره • بصیرت • بصارت • بینایی

sightsee v سیر کردن

sightseeing n تماشا • سیر • سِیل

sign (affix signature) v امضا کردن
→ (colloq) دستخط کردن

sign (indication) n نشان دهنده

sign (mark) n اثر • علامت • نشان • نشانه • نشانی

sign (ratify) vt صحه گذاشتن

sign (signboard) n لوحه

sign (symbol) n علامت • نشان • نشانه
→ secret sign رمز

signal (traffic) n اشارات ترافیکی

signature (colloq) n دستخط • امضا

signature (ratification) n توشیح

signature n امضا
→ (colloq) دستخط

signet ring n مهر

significance n معنی • اهمیت

significant adj معنی دار • با معنی

Sikh (& pers) adj, n سک

silence n سکوت • خاموشی
→ forcibly silenced (pers) زبان بسته • دهان بسته

silent (& insult) adj زبان بریده

silica n سیلیکا

silicon (element) n سیلیکان

silk (& raw) n ابریشم
→ (arch) قز
→ (lit, & cloth, garment) حریر
→ silk fabric (plain/painted) پرند
→ silk kabob (dessert) ابریشم کباب
→ silk that changes color بوقلمون

silk adj ابریشمی • ابریشمین
→ (lit) حریر

silken see silk adj

silkworm n کرم ابریشم • کرم پیله • کرم قز

sill (threshold) n آستانه

silliness (foolishness) n نادانی • خیلگی

silly (foolish) adj نادان • خیله

silly (frivolous) adj سبک سر

silver adj نقره یی
→ silver-plated نقره کار
→ silvery نقره یی • نقره گون

silver n نقره • سیم

silversmith n نقره کار • زرگر
→ silversmith's shop زرگری

silversmithing n زرگری

silvery see silver adj

SIM card (phone) n سیم کارت

similar <to sth> adj مانند • مثل • مماثل • هم گون • هم مانند • نظیر • شبیه • مشابه • متشابه <از چیزی>

similar to (sth) adj به سان

similarity n مماثلت • هم گونی • هم مانندی • مجانست

simple adj ساده

simplicity n سادگی

simulating adj تظاهر

simultaneity n همزمانی

simultaneous (& adv) adj, adv همزمان

simultaneously adv عندالموقع

sin n گناه • گنه • اثم

Sinai (peninsula) n سینا

since (& till now) adv از ... به این طرف

since (because) conj چرا که • چونکه • چون که • چون

sincere adj ساده دل • پاک دل • صاف • خالصانه

sincere (frank) (& pers) adj, n صادق
→ (colloq) دل پاک

sincerely adv خالصاً • خالصانه

Sind (geog) n سند

sinew (anat) n پی

sinful adj خطاکار

sinful (esp adulterous) adj بد کار

sinfulness n معصیت • معاصی • خطاکاری

sinfulness see & sin

sing v آواز خوانی کردن • خواندن

singer *n* خنیاگر • آواز خوان
→ (colloq) خواننده
singing *adj* نغمه سرا • نغمه سرای • نغمه خوان • نغمه پرداز
singing *n* نغمه سرایی
single (alone) *adj* یکه
single (unmarried) *adj* مجرد
single-story (house) *adj* یک منزله
singular (gram) *adj* مفرد
sink (& ship) *vi* غرق شدن
sink (in kitchen) *n* ظرف شوی
sinking (& ship) *adj* غرق
sinner *n* گناهگار • گناهکار • گنهگار
sip by sip *adv* جرعه جرعه
sip *n* شپ • قرت • جرعه
sip *v* شپ کردن • قرت کردن
sir (form of address) *n* شاغلی • صاحب
sissoo (tree) *n* شیشم
sister *n* خواهر • همشیره
→ foster sister خواهر رضاعی • کوکی
→ half-sister, stepsister خواهراندر
sister-in-law *n*
→ (brother's wife) ینگه
→ (husband's brother's wife) ایور
→ زن • زن ایور
→ (husband's sister) ننو
→ (wife's sister) خاشنه • خیاشنه
sister-wife in Musl polygamous marriage *n* امباغ
→ (colloq) انباق
sit *vi* نشستن
→ (colloq) شیشتن
→ sit cross-legged چهار زانو نشستن
site *see* place
sitting *n* نشیمن
sitting *see* & session
situation (circumstance) *n* حال
situation (condition) *n* حالت • وضعیت • وضع
situation (location, status) *n* موقعیت • موقف
six *adj, n* شش
sixteen *adj, n* شانزده

sixteenth *adj* شانزدهم
→ (lit, used before n) شانزدهمین
sixth *adj* ششم • ششمی
→ (lit, used before n) ششمین
→ the sixth one ششمی
sixtieth *adj* شصتم
→ (lit, used before n) شصتمین
sixty *adj, n* شصت • شصت
size *n* اندازه
skein (yarn, thread) *n* کلاوه
skeleton *n* استخوان بندی • اسکلیت
skeptical (& pers) *adj, n* دیر باور
sketch *n* رسم
sketch *v* رسم کشیدن • رسم کردن • ترسیم کردن
skewer (for kabob) *n* سیخ
skewered *adj* سیخی
ski *n* سکی
ski *v* سکی بازی کردن
skiing *n* سکی بازی
skill (& ability) *n* صناعت • صنعت • مهارت
skill (craft) *n* کسب • کمال
skilled (capable) *adj* ماهر • با مهارت • تادست • لایق مجرب • ورزیده • آزموده
→ skillful w/hands چابکدست
skilled (expert) *adj* کاردان
skim (read quickly) *v* مرور کردن
skin (anat) *n* بشره
skin (peel) *vt* پوست کردن
skin (pelt, rind) *n* پوست • جلد • مشک
→ inflatable skin
skinny *adj* لاغر • نزار
→ become skinny تار گشتن
→ very skinny تار و نار
skirmish *n* کشمکش • کش مکش
skirt (margin) *n* دامن
Skopje *n* سکوپیه
skull (anat) *n* جمجمه
sky *n* آسمان • سما • گنبد
sky-high *adj* آسمانسا
skyscraper *n* آسمان خراش
slab (of stone) *n* تخته سنگ
slain *adj* قتیل • کشته
slander *n* افترا • بهتان
slander *v* افترا کردن • بهتان زدن • بهتان گفتن
slanted *adj* کج

513

slanting *adj* وریب • اریب
slap *n* سلی • قفاق • چپات
→ slap on back of neck پس گردنی
slap *vt* قفاق زدن • چپات زدن
slaughter (of livestock) *n* کشتار
slave *n* غلام • برده
→ slave girl کنیز
→ slave market (hist) نخاس
slavery *n* بردگی
sledgehammer *n* پتک
sleep *n* خواب
→ sleep deprivation بیدار خوابی
→ sleep-deprived خام خواب • بیدار خواب
sleep *vi* خوابیدن • خواب کردن
→ fall asleep خواب بردن
sleeping bag *n* بستره
sleepy *adj* خواب آلود
sleeve (of shirt) *n* آستین
→ sleeve cuff کف
sleight of hand *n* چالاکی دست
slender (graceful) *adj* لاغراندام
slender (narrow) *adj* باریک
slice (melon) *n* قاش • تلم
slice *vt* قاش کردن • تلم کردن
sliced *adj* تلم تلم
slick (& fig) *adj* لشم
slight *adj* خفیف
slightly *adv* یک کمی
slim (graceful) *adj* لاغراندام
sling (for arm) *n* حمایل • فلاخن
→ (colloq) امیل
slingshot *n* غولک • فلاخن
→ (colloq) پلخمان
slip (error) *n* لغزش • تخطی
slip (stumble) *vi* لغزیدن
slipper (sandal) *n* چپلک
→ slippers کفش
slippery (& fig) *adj* لشم
slit (in clothes) *n* چاک
→ slit at hem چاک دمان
→ slit at neckline چاک گریبان
slogan *n* شعار
sloganeer *v* شعار دادن
slope *n* دامنه • شیوه • سرپایانی • سراشیبی • میلان
→ (steep slope) لاش

sloping *adj* سرپایان • سراشیب • سرازیر
slot (groove) *n* ماده گی
slow *adj* آهسته • سست
→ (sluggish) بطی
slowly *adv* به آهستگی • آهسته • سست
→ (gradually) آرام آرام • اندک اندک
slowness *n* آهستگی
slow-witted *adj* خرفهم • کودن
slow-working *adj* تال کار
sludge *n* لوش
slug (snail) *n* گاوک • لیسک
→ (lit) حلزون
sluggish (lazy) *adj* تنبل • کاهل
sluggish (market) *adj* کاسد
sluggish (slow) *adj* بطی
slump (in prices) *n* نزول
sly *adj* زرنگ • نراد
small *adj* خورد • کوچک • ریزه
→ small piece ریزه • میده
small intestine *n* روده خورد
smallness *n* کوچکی
smallpox *n* چیچک • آبله
→ smallpox pustule آبله
smart (clever) *adj* زرنگ • نراد
smart (intelligent) *adj* تیز هوش
smart (learned) *adj* ادیب
→ (fig) حکاک
→ be smart ذکاوت داشتن
smash *vt* شکستاندن
smear (defame) *vt* گپ ساختن
→ smear campaign <against sb> توطیه جهت بدنامی <کسی>
smell (be perceived) *vi* به مشام رسیدن
smell (scent, odor) *n* بوی
smell (sense of smell) *n* شامه
smell (sth) *vt* بوی کردن
smile *n* لب خند • تبسم
smile *vi* لب خند زدن • متبسم شدن
→ angry smile نیش خند
smiling *adj* متبسم
smith (blacksmith) *n* آهنگر
smoke (cigarettes) *v* سگرت کشیدن
→ smoke (puff on) پف کردن
→ smoke a cigar سیگار کشیدن

smoke <sth> v ‹به چیزی› دود دادن

smoke n دود

smokestack n دود کش

smooth (flat) adj مستوی • هموار

smooth (slippery) (& fig) adj لشم

smuggle v قاچاق بردن

smuggled adj گریزی • قاچاقی

→ smuggled goods اموال قاچاقی

smuggler n قاچاقبر • قاچاقچی

smuggling n قاچاق

snack bar n کانتین

snail see slug

snake n مار

snake charmer n مارگیر

snapdragon n گل نافرمان • نافرمان

snare n دام

→ ensnare به دام افتادن

→ lay a snare دام نشاندن • دام نهاندن

snatch (kidnap) vt ربودن • اختطاف کردن

sneak vi خزندن

sneeze n عطسه

sneeze v عطسه زدن

snicker n پوزخند

snicker v پوزخند زدن • پوزخند کردن

snoopy adj کنج کاو

snore vi خور زدن

snorer n خور خوری

snoring adj خور خوری

snot (mucus) n خلم

snotty adj خلمی • خلموک

snow n برف

→ snow flurry پرخ برف

→ snow-white سمنبر

→ wet snow تربرف

snowflake n پاغنده

snowman n آدم برفی

snowstorm n بوران

→ (colloq) بادکویه

snowy adj برفی

snub see shun

snubbed adj دق

snuff n ناس • نسوار

→ (for oral intake) نسوار دهن

→ snuff addict نسواری

→ snuff-colored نسواری

so (in that way) adv همچنان

so (in this way) adv همچنین

so (introduces clause) excl خی

soak vt آغشته کردن

→ (moisten) تر کردن

→ get soaked تر شدن

soap (sliver) n پچاق

soap n صابون

→ make soapy کف کردن

sober (& pers) adj, n هوشیار

سوبریتی هوشمند • عاقل • خردمند

sobriety (& fig) n هوشیاری

so-called adj نام نهاد

soccer (Afgh game) n توپ بازی

sociable adj زود آشنا • اجتماعی

→ be sociable جوش خوردن

social adj اجتماعی

socialist adj سوسیالستی • سوسیالیستی

socialist n سوسیالست • سوسیالیست

society n اجتماع • ناس

→ (league) انجمن • جوامع

socio-economic adj اجتماعی اقتصادی

sociologist n جامعه شناس • سوسیولوژست

sociology n جامعه شناسی • سوسیولوژی

sock (clothing) n جراب

→ string of socks بندِ جراب

socle (wall support) n پیزاره دیوار

sodium (element) n سودیم

→ sodium nitrate سودیم نایتریت

sodomy n لواطت

sofa n کوچ

Sofia n صوفیه

soft adj نرم • ناعم • سست

→ softening of one's pronunciation تخفیف ادا

Sogdian see Soghdian

Soghd Valley (geog) n سغد • سغدیانه

Soghdian (pers, lang) n سغدی

515

soil (earth) *n* زمین • خاک • ثری
→ uncultivated soil بوره
soil (taint) *n* آلودگی • لوث
solar (of the sun) *adj* شمسی
→ solar system منظومه شمسی
solar (year) *adj* خورشیدی
solder *n* لحیم
solder *v* لحیم کردن
soldering *n* لحیم کاری • لحیم
soldier (& police) *n* عسکر •
لشکری
soldier (risks head) *n* سرباز
soldier (sepoy) *n* سپاهی
soldier (troop) *n* فرد • نفر • شخص
• قوه
→ fellow soldier همرزم
→ Unknown Soldier سپاهی گم نام
soldiering *n* سربازی
sole (foot, shoe) *n* کف
sole (only) *adj* یگانه • واحد • یکتا
solemn *adj* سنگین
solid (firm) *adj* استوار • محکم •
مستحکم • جامد • خلل ناپذیر
solid (mass) *n* جسم
solidarity *n* همبستگی
solidity (firmness) *n* استواری •
استحکام
soliloquy (dramatic) *n* مونولوگ
solitary confinement *n* حبس مجرد
solitude *n* تنهایی
solo (alone) *adj* یکه
Solomon (bibl;m name) *n* سلیمان
Solomon bird *n* مرغ سلیمان
solstice *n* انقلاب
→ winter solstice (1st of Jadi) یلدا
solution (mixture) *n* محلول
solution (to problem) *n* حل • راه •
حل • راه حل و فصل
solve (problem) *vt* حل کردن
Somalia *n* سومال
some (a certain) *adj* فلان • فلانی
→ a certain someone فلان کس
some *adj* بعض • بعضی • فلان
somebody *pron* کسی
→ (anyone) کسانی که
someone *see* somebody
somersault *n* معلق • ملاق
somersault *v* معلق زدن • ملاق
زدن • ملاق خوردن

something *pron* چیزی
→ a certain something فلان چیز
sometimes *adv* بعض اوقات •
بعضاً
→ (colloq) بعض وخت ها • گاه گاه
→ once in a while خال خال
son *n* بچه • پسر
→ son of ابن
→ sons of man & jinn ابنای انس و
جن
→ sons of the age • ابنای زمان
ابنای روزگار
→ sons of the homeland ابنای
وطن
→ sons of the race ابنای جنس
son of a bitch (insult) *n* بی پدر
song (art of singing) *n* نغمه سرایی
song *n* آواز • نشیده •
→ (& nursery rhyme) ترانه
songbird *n* پرنده نغمه سرا
songstress *n* نغمه زن
songwriter *n* نغمه سرا • نغمه
سرای • نغمه ساز
son-in-law *n* داماد
soon *adv* بزودی • زود
→ as soon as همین که
soothsay *v* فال دیدن
soothsayer *n* فال بین
soothsayer (pre-Musl) *n* کاهن
soothsaying *n* فال دیدن
sophist (pers) *n* سوفسطایی
sophistication (urbanity) • ذوق
سلیقه • مذاق
soprano *n* آواز زیر • صدای زیر
sorceress *n* ساحره
sorceror *n* ساحر • افسونگر •
جادوگر
sorcery *n* سحر • افسون • جادو
sordid *adj* زشت • قبیح
sore (& wound) *adj, n* ریش • زخم
sore throat *n* گلودرد
sorrow (depression) *n* غبار خاطر
• غبار دل
sorrow (grief) *n* غم • اندوه • حزن
sorrowful *adj* غمگین • اندوهگین •
حزن آلود • حزین • مفمون
→ making sorrowful حزن آور
sorry (regretful)*adj* متأسف
sort (by type) *v* سورت کردن

sort (type) n • جنس • نوع • قسم •
سورت • قبیل • قماش • چیز
sorting n سورت بندی • سورت
کاری
so-so (not bad) phrs میگذره
→ (colloq) مگذره
soul (spirit) n • نفس • جان • روح •
روان
→ like a soulmate یک دل
sound n صدا • آواز • نوا
→ speech sound (phone) صوت
soup n شوربا
sour (& morose) adj ترش
→ go sour ترش کردن • ترشیدن
sour cherry n آلبالو (=آلوبالو)
sour orange n نارنج
source (origin) n سر چشمه • چشمه
• عین • مایه • منبع • مصدر
→ source (book) مرجع
→ source (reference) ماخذ • مأخذ
→ source of income مدرک
south n جنوب
→ from the south adv جنوباً
→ South America امریکای جنوبی
→ South Pole قطب جنوب
Southeast Asia n آسیای جنوب
شرقی
southeast n جنوب شرق
southeastern adj جنوب شرقی
southern adj جنوبی
southwest n جنوب غرب
southwestern adj جنوب غربی
souvenir n سوغات • ارمغان
sovereign adj see self-governing
sovereign (pol) سرکار
sovereign (ruler) n سرکار
sovereignty n حاکمیت • تسلط
Soviet (& pers) adj, n شوروی
sow (plant) v کاشتن
sow (scatter seeds) v • تخم پاشیدن •
پاش دادن • پاشاندن • پاشیدن
sowing (cultivation) n زرع • کشت
sowing (planting) n • بذر افشانی •
تخم پاشی
Sozma Qala (dist) n سوزمه قلعه
space (blank) n فاصله • مسافه
→ fit in a space <sw> گنجیدن <در
کجا>
space (cosmos) n فضا

space (interstice) n خلال
spaceship n سفینه فضایی • کشتی
فضایی • فضا پیما
spacious (wide) adj فراخ
spade (cards) n قره
spade (shovel) n بیل
Spain n اسپانیا
→ (colloq) هسپانیه
span n وجب
span v وجب کردن
Spanish (& lang) adj, n اسپانیایی
→ (colloq) هسپانوی
spare (extra) adj اشتبنی • فالتو
spare tire n تیر اشتبنی • تیر فالتو
spark n جرقه • شرار
spark plug n پلک
sparrow (bird) n گنجشک
sparse adj تنک
spatula (esp for serving) n طعام
بخش
speak vi تکلم کردن • گپ زدن •
حرف زدن
→ (& breathe) دم زدن
speaker (chair) n رئیس
→ Speaker of Parliament رئیس
پارلمان • رئیس مجلس
speaker (orator) n • سخن گوی •
سخن ران
→ speaking ability قوه افاده
spear n نیزه
spearhead n سنان • پیکان
spearmint n نعاع
special adj مخصوص • خاص
specialist (expert) n متخصص
specialty (expertise) n • تخصص •
اختصاص • خصوصیت • خصیصه
species n نوع حیوان
specific adj مشخص
→ sth specific خصوص
specification n نوعیت
specificity n خصوص
specimen n نمونه
speck n خال
speckled adj خال خالی
spectator n • تماشابین • تماشاچی •
تماشاگر
speculation (theorizing) n
نظریه/نظریات
speculative (theoretical) adj نظری

517

speech (address) *n* • خطاب
خطابه • سخنرانی • نطق
speech (remarks on festive
occasion) *n* بیانیه
speech (spoken language) *n* • گپ
حرف • سخن • کلام • قول
→ faculty of speech قوه • گویایی
گویایی • ناطقه
speed *n* سرعت • تیزی
speed up *v* تیز رفتن
spell (incantation) *n* جنتر
spell (magic) *n* رقیه • افسون
spelling *n* املا • تجی
spend (consume) *vt* مصرف کردن
• به مصرف رساندن
spend (money) *v* • خرج کردن
مصرف کردن
spend (time) *v* سپری کردن
sperm *n* تخم • نطفه
sphere (discipline) *n* صحنه
sphere (shape) *n* کره • دور
spherical *adj* کروی • مدور • گرد
sphericity *n* کرویت
Sphinx *n* ابو الهول
spice *n* مساله • مساله دیگ
spice merchant *n* عطار
spicy *adj* تند • تند مزه • تند خوی • تیز
spider *n* جولاه • جولاهک
جولاگک • تارتنک • عنکبوت
spiderweb *n* تار جولاه • خانۀ
جولاه • تنسته
spill (liquids) *vi, vt* ریختن
spill (liquids) *vt* • ریختاندن • خالی
کردن
spill (solids) *vt* توده کردن
spin (weave) *v* تنیدن
Spin Boldak (dist) *n* سپین بولدک
spinach *n* سبزی پالک • اسفناج
spinal *adj* نخاعی
→ spinal column ستون • فقرات
فقرات
→ spinal cord نخاع شوکی
→ spinal marrow نخاع • حرام
مغز
spindle *n* دوک
spinel (& garnet) *n* لعل
spinning (of head) *n* دوران سر
spinning wheel *n* چرخه
518

Spira (dist) *n* سپیره • سپره
spirit (essence) *n* روح
spirit (evil) *n* دیو
spirit (soul, nature) *n* نفس • جان
spirits (alcohol) *n* شراب
spiritual *adj* روحانی
spiritual leader *n* روحانی
spirituality *n* روحانیت
spit (saliva) *n* تف • آب دهن • بزاق
• لعاب
spit (skewer) *n* سیخ
spit <at sb/sth> *v* تف انداختن <به
کسی / چیزی>
spite (rancor) *n* کینه
→ in spite of <sth> با وجودِ
<چیزی>
spiteful (vindictive) *adj* شتر کینه
splash *vt* پراندن
spleen (anat) *n* تلی • سپرز
spleen (esp animal's) *n* طحال
splendid *adj* • شانداری • مجلل
مجید • ابهر
splendor (glory) *n* جلال
splint (med) *n* تخته شکسته بندی
splinter (wood; piece) *n* • پرچه
توته
splintered (shattered) *adj* پرچه
پرچه • توته توته
split *n* شق
split (tear) *n* شقه
split (tear) *v* شقه کردن
split *vi* شق شدن
split *vt* شق کردن
spoil (disrupt) *vt* • اخلال کردن
اخلال نمودن
spoiled (coddled) *adj* ناز دانه
spoiler (disrupter) *n* • اخلال گر
تباه کار • تبه کار
spoiling (going to waste) *n* تضییع
• ضایع
spoils (booty) *n* غنیمت
spoken (colloquial) *adj* اصطلاحی
• مصطلح • گفتاری
spokesperson *n* سخن گوی • سخن
ران • گوینده • نطاق
sponge *n* اسفنج
sponger (parasite) *n* مفت خور
spongy *adj* اسفنجی

spontaneous (& adv) *adj, adv* خود • به خود • به خودی خود

spool (for yarn or thread) *n* ماسوره • ماشوره • چرخه

spool (w/o thread) *n* گوتک

spool (w/thread) *n* گوت

spoon *n* قاشق
→ serving spoon طعام بخش

sport (athletics) *n* ورزش • جمناستک • سپورت

sports *adj* سپورتی

sportsman *n* ورزش کار • سپورت مین

sportsmanship *n* ورزش کاری • سپورت مینی

spotted *adj* خال خالی • لکه دار
→ spotted fever حمای لکه دار

spouse *n* جفت • زوج • زوجه • همسر

sprain (colloq) *n* مچ

sprain (get a sprain) *v* مچ خوردن
→ she sprained her foot پایش مچ خورد

spray *vt* پاشاندن • پاش دادن

spray *vt, vi* پاشیدن
→ aerial spraying سمپاشی از طریق هوایی • سمپاشی

spray nozzle *n* ژیکلور

spread (disease) *vi* سرایت کردن

spread (dissemination) *n* نشر

spread (expand) *vt* گستراندن • گستردن

spread (expansion) *n* گسترش • تعمیم

spread out (cloth) *vt* هموار کردن

spring (coil) *n* اسپرنگ • فنر

spring (season) *n* بهار
→ in the spring بهاران

spring *see* & source

springtime *adj* بهاری

springtime *n* بهاران

sprinkle *vt, vi* پاشیدن

sprinkle *vt* پاشاندن • پاش دادن

sprinkled *adj* پاشان

spritzer (nozzle) *n* ژیکلور

sprout (germinate) *v* نیش زدن • سر زدن

sprout (shoot) *n* نوده

sprout *n* جوانه

sprout *v* جوانه زدن

spur (& plant's) *n* مهمیز
→ having spurs مهمیز دار

spurt *v* فواره زدن • فواره کردن

spy *n* جاسوس • مخبر

spy *v* مخبری کردن

spying *n* جاسوسی • مخبری

squad (10 soldiers) *n* دلگی

squalid (lit) *adj* چرک • چرکین

squalor (lit) *n* چرک

square (shape) *adj, n* مربع • چهار ضلعی

square (public space) *n* میدان
→ village square میدان قریه

square root *n* جذر مربع
→ squared (math) مجذور

squat *vi* بالا دو زانو نشستن • چند نشستن

squeeze *vt* فشردن • شپلیدن • تنگ گرفتن

squirm *v* پیچ و تاب خوردن

squirrel (brown) *n* موش خرما

squirrel (grey) *n* سنجاب

Sri Lanka *n* سری لانکا • سرندیپ

Srinagar (city) *n* سری نگر

St. Petersburg (city) *n* سنت پتربرگ

stability *n* ثبات

stabilize *vi* تثبیت شدن

stabilize *vt* تثبیت کردن

stable (for horse, donkey) *n* طویله

stable *adj* با ثبات
→ be stable ثبات داشتن • ثبات یافتن

stableman *n* مهتر

staff (personnel) *n* اراکن • هیئت

staffing plan (tashkil) *n* تشکیل

stage (& theater) *n* صحنه

stage (of life) *n* سن

stage (phase) *n* مرحله
→ stages (esp pl) مدارج

stagger *vi* لگد خوردن

stain (& moral) *n* لکه

stair *n* پایه

stairs *n* زینه

stake (bet) *v* داو زدن

stake (picket) *n* میخ

stake (wooden beam) *n* تیر

stale (food) adj • دیر مانده • قاق • خشک

stalk (of plant) n • نره

stall (stop) vi • ایستاد شدن

stamen n • آله تذکیر • نافه

stammer *see* stutter

stamp (postage) n • تکت پوستی

stamp (seal) n • مهر

stamp (seal) vt • مهر کردن

stand (upright position) n • ایستاده

stand n *see* & opinion

stand one's ground v • قد علم کردن

stand up vi • ایستاد شدن

standard (banner) n • بیرق • پرچم • علم • درفش

→ standard-bearer • بیرق دار • پرچم دار

standard (level) n • سویه

standard (literary) adj • فصیح

standard (measure) n • معیار • نورم • ستندرد • ملاک • لایحه • محک

→ standards (criteria) • موازین • معاییر

standing (social) n • جایگاه • جایگه

standing (upright) adj • ایستاد • ایستاده

standing adj • پایا

standing n • قیام

standing *see* & rank

standstill n • جمود

stanza n • بند

star (& planet) n • فلک • افلاکی • نجم • کوکب

→ fixed star • ثابته

→ lucky star • ستارهٔ بخت

→ star chart (horoscope) • ستاره

→ worshiper of stars & planets • افلاکی

star (astron) n • ستاره • اختر • کوکب

starch n • آهار • نشایسته

starched adj • آهار دار

starchy adj • نشایسته یی

stare v • چشم دوختن • نگاه دوختن

starfish n • ستاره

starling (black) (bird) n • قره قش

start (switch on) vt • سوچ کردن

→ start to speak • بسم الله کردن

start n • شروع • آغاز • اوایل • سر • ابتدا • بدو • بنا • آمد آمد

start vi • شروع شدن • آغاز شدن

start vt • شروع کردن • آغاز کردن • درآمدن • به راه انداختن • گشودن • بنا کردن

starter (dough) n • خمیر ترش • خمیر مایه

starting over n • استیناف

starting up n • تدویر

starvation n • گرسنه گی

state (condition) n • حالت • کیفیت

state (country) n • مملکت • ملک • کشور • دولت

state (government) n • دولت

state (in federation) n • ایالت

state (quality) n • کیفیت

state vt • اظهار کردن • اظهار داشتن • تصریح کردن

statement n • اظهار • بیان • گذارش

statement (of account) n • صورت حساب

statement (remarks) n • بیانیه

statesman n • سیاست مدار • شخص سیاسی • زمام دار

static adj • ایستا

stating n • تصریح • تشریح • توضیح

station (stop) n • ایستگاه

stationary adj • ایستا

stationery n • قرطاسیه

→ stationery store • قرطاسیه فروشی

statistical adj • احصایی • احصائیوی

statistics n • احصائیه • احصاییه • آمار

statue n • مجسمه • پیکره

stature (height) n • قد • بلندی

status (situation) n • موقف • موقعیت

status (social) n • جایگاه • جایگه

statute (law) n • قانون

statutory (legal) adj • قانونی

stay vi • ماندن

stay (reside) vi • اقامت کردن • اقامت داشتن

stay put <sw> vt • محکم گرفتن ‹خود را در کجا›

520

steadfast *adj* • محکم • مستحکم
قایم • ثابت قدم • استوار
steady *adj* با ثبات
steal (take by theft) *vt* سرقت کردن
• به سرقت بردن
→ be skillful in stealing سرمه از
چشم دزدیدن • سرمه از چشم زدن
→ be stolen سرقت شدن • به
سرقت رفتن
stealing (theft) *n* دزدی • سرقت
→ (colloq) دزی
steam (heat) *n* تف
→ (colloq) تفت
steam (vapor) *n* بخار
steam *vt* تف دادن
→ (colloq) تفت دادن
→ steamed (cooked) دم پخت
steamroller *n* رول
stearic *adj* شحمی • چربی دار
steel *adj* فولادی
steel *n* فولاد • پولاد
→ rohina (Indian steel) روهینا
steep (soak) *vt* آغشته کردن
steer (bull) *n* ثور
stem (gram) *n* ریشه
stem (of plant) *n* نره
step (measure) *n* اقدام
→ steps (measures) (esp pl)
تدابیر
→ take steps (measures) تدابیر
گرفتن
step- (pref) اندری • ناسکه
step- (relationship) *adj* اوگه یی
step (stage) *n* مرحله
→ steps (stages) (esp pl) مدارج
step (stair) *n* پته • پله
step (stride, pace) *n* قدم • گام
step (stride, pace) *v* گام سپردن
step on sth *vt* لگد کردن
stepbrother *n* برادر اندر
stepmother *n* مادر انداز • مایندر
steppe *n* جلگه • دشت
stepsister *n* خواهر اندر
stepson (lit) *n* پسر اندر
stepson *n* بچه اندر
sterile (infertile) *adj* عقیم • نازای
stern *adj* سختگیر
stew (korma) *n* قورمه
steward (on plane) *see* stewardess

steward (overseer) *n* پیش کار
stewardess *n* مهمان دار
stick (club) *n* دنده
stick (of wood) *n* چوبک
→ stick & carrot (fig) وعده و وعید
stick *vi* چسپیدن
stick (sth to sth) *vt* چسپاندن
stick out *vi* پیش برآمدن
→ sticking out پیش برآمده
stickler *n* اصولی
sticky *adj* چسپناک
→ (colloq) چسپوک
stiffness *n* جمود
stigma (moral) *n* لکه
still *adv* هنوز • باز هم
still (distillery) *n* انبیق
stimulant *n* منبه
stimulus *n* انگیزه • سایقه • منبه
sting (bite) *vt* گزیدن
sting (of insect) *n* نیش
sting (prick) *vt* نیش زدن
stinginess (miserliness) *n* • بخل
بخیلی • امساک • ممسکی • چشم
تنگی • پول دوستی
stingy (& pers) *adj, n* • بخیل
ممسک • چشم تنگ • تنگ چشم •
پول دوست • پیسه دوست
stink *vi* بوی دادن
stinking (rotten) *adj* گنده
stipulate *v* شرط کردن
stipulation *n* شرط • مقرره •
→ stipulations شرایط
stir (mix, whip) *vt* لت زدن
stir up (incite) *vt* جوش آوردن
stirrup *n* رکاب
stitch *n* خام کوک
stitch *v* خام کوک کردن
stock (breed) *n* عرق
stock *see* & race
stock market *n* بورس
→ share of stock سهم
stockpile *n* ذخیره
stomach *n* معده • شکم • بطن
→ having a stomach ache شکم
درد • دل درد
stone *adj* سنگی
stone *n* سنگ • حجر
stone (throw stones) *v* سنگ باران
کردن • رجم کردن

521

stone (to death) vt سنگسار کردن
→ stoning (to death) سنگسار
Stone Age n دوره حجر • دوره
سنگ • عصر حجر
stone throwing n سنگ باران
stonecutter (pers) n سنگ تراش
stonewall v جنگی بودن • جنگی
شدن
stonework n سنگ کاری
stony adj سنگ لاخ • سنگناک •
سنگسار
stool (feces) n غایط • مواد غایطه
stool (low seat) n چارپایه • کرسی
stop (pause) n توقف • وقفه
stop (pause) vt توقف دادن • توقف
کردن • متوقف ساختن
stop (stall) (vehicle) vi ایستاد شدن
stop (station) n ایستگاه
stop by (visit <sb>) v افتاد خانه
<کسی> شدن
stop vi متوقف شدن
stop vt متوقف کردن
stop (to animal) excl ایشه
stop (to pers) excl دریش
stopover n توقف
stopped adj متوقف
storage place n تحویل خانه
store (keep) vt نگاه کردن
store (shop) n دکان
→ department store فروشگاه
store owner n دکان دار
storehouse n گدام
stork (bird) n لگلگ • لکلک
storm n طوفان
→ dust storm گردباد • خاکباد
story (fiction) n داستان • رومان •
ناول
→ related to a story داستانی
→ short story داستان کوتاه
→ story (folk tale, myth, legend)
افسانه • اسطوره
→ story (narration) حکایت
→ story (tale) قصه
→ story in verse منظومه
→ tell a story (brag) داستان
پرداز
→ tell a story see & narrate
story (of building) n منزل • طبقه •
پوشش
522

storyteller (& braggart) adj, n
داستان پرداز
storyteller (narrator) n گوینده •
سخن گوی • سخن ران • نطاق
stove (for heating) n بخاری
stove (oven, kiln) n داش
strabismic adj کانج
strabismic see & cross-eyed
straggle (lag) v عقب افتادن • پس
ماندن
straight (direct) adj مستقیم • روبه
رو
straight ahead adv رو به رو • رو
به روی • مستقیم
straightforward (frank) adj یک
رنگ
strain (filter) v پالایش کردن
strained (tense) adj تیره
strainer n صاف • اللک
straining (filtration) n پالایش
strait (geog) n آبنا • بغاز
strange adj عجیب و غریب • نخچه
stranger n خارجی • اجنبی • بیگانه
• غیر
strangled adj مختنق
strangulation n اختناق
strap (leather) n تسمه
stratagem n حیله
strategic adj استراتژیکی •
ستراتژیک • ستراتیژیک • سوق
الجیشی
strategy n استراتژی •
ستراتیژی • سوق الجیشی
stratum n طبقه • منزل
straw adj پوشالی
→ straw hat کلاه بوریایی
straw n پوشال • کاه • که
→ straw & mud for surfacing کاه
گل
strawberry n توت زمینی
stream (brook) n جوی • نهر
stream (current) n رو
street n سرک
strength n قدرت • قوت • قوه •
توان • زور • استواری • نیرو •
شیمه • دستگاه • دم و دستگاه
strengthen vt تحکیم کردن
strengthening (growing) n تقویت •
تقویه

strengthening (intensification) *n*
تشدید

strengthening *n* • تحکیم • تأمین

stress (accent, pressure) *n* فشار

stress (emphasis) *n* تأکید
→ adjacent & adjoining stress
قرب و جوار

stress (emphasize) *v* • تأکید کردن
تأکید نمودن

stretch *vt* گستراندن • گستردن

stretcher (med) *n* تذکره

stretching *n* تمدد

strict (stern) *adj* سختگیر
→ be strict سختگیری کردن

strictly (emphatically) *adv* اکیداً

stride *n* گام

strife *n* ستیزه • ستیز

strike (hit) *n* ضربه

strike (hit) *v* ضربه زدن • ضربت
زدن • کوفتن

strike (labor) *n* اعتصاب

striker (labor) *n* اعتصابی

string (& on mus instr) *n* تار • وتر
• سیم

string (catgut) *n* زه

string (cord) *n* بند • رشته

string (of socks) *n* بندِ جراب

string (of vegetables) *n* آونگ

string (thread) *n* تار • نخ

string bean *n* فاصولیه • فاسولیه

stringed (mus instr) *adj* تاری

strip (motor for parts) *v* زبده بردن
<از موتر>

strip (naked) *vi* برهنه شدن • برهنه
کردن

strip (naked) *vt* برهنه ساختن

strip *n* باریکه
→ Gaza Strip باریکهٔ غزه

strip of leather *n* چرمک

stripe *n* پارچه

strive (struggle) *v* ستیزه کردن

strive (try) *v* در سعی و تلاش به
سر بردن

stroll (for pleasure) *vi* • قدم زدن
هوا خوری کردن • گردش کردن •
گردیدن

strong (capable) *adj* توانا

strong (oppressive) (& pers) *adj, n*
زبردست

strong (powerful) *adj* قوی • قوتمند
• قدرتمند

strong (solid) *adj* مستحکم • محکم
• استوار

strongman (oppressor) *n* زور آور

structure (building) *n* ساختمان • آبد

structure (composition) *n* • ساختار
سکتور

struggle (campaign) *n* مبارزه

struggle (fighting) *n* • نزاع • تنازع •
منازعه

struggle (jihad) *n* جهاد • مجاهدت

struggle (strife) *n* ستیز • ستیزه

struggle <w/sb> *v* ستیزه کردن •
نزاع کردن • مجادله کردن <همرای
کسی>

strumpet *n* زن هر جایی

stubborn (hardhearted) (& pers)
adj, n سنگ دل

stubborn (headstrong) *adj* خود سر

stubborn (obstinate) *adj* خیر چشم
• خیره چشم • لجوج

stubborn (pushy) *adj* سرتنبه

student (& pupil) *n* • شاگرد • متعلم
تلمیذ

student (esp of Islam) *n* • طالب
طالب العلم

student (Sufi novice) *n* مرید

student (university) *n* محصل

student of hadiths *n* محدث

studio (workshop) *n* ستدیو

study (at university) *vi* تحصیل
کردن

study (perusal) *n* مطالعه

study *v* درس خواندن
→ study a lesson • درس خواندن
سبق خواندن

study *vt* خواندن • یاد گرفتن •
آموختن

studying (esp at university) *n*
تحصیل

stuff *n* مواد • ماده

stumble *vi* لگد خوردن • تکر
خوردن • لغزیدن

stung (bitten) *adj* گزیده

stupid (foolish) (& pers) *adj, n*
احمق • خیله

stupid (ignorant) *adj* غبی • غول •
بیمغز

523

خر • مرکب • کودن stupid (silly) n •
کودن stupid (slow) adj
خرگری stupidity (colloq) n
حماقت • stupidity (foolishness) n •
خیلگی • سقاهت • لودگی
نادانی • stupidity (ignorance) n •
غباوت
بلادت • بلاهت stupidity n
محکم • مستحکم • sturdy adj
استوار • مضبوط • تناور
ماهی خاو یار • sturgeon (fish) n •
سگ ماهی • ماهی خاویار
تتلگی • زبان گرفتگی • stutter n •
لکنت
لکنت داشتن stutter (habitually) v
تتله stuttering (& pers) adj, n
stuttering n see stutter n
سبک style (literary) n
طرز • قسم • style (manner) n •
روش • سبک
قلم style (of writing) n
ناخودآگاه subconscious adj
علاقه subdistrict (see & district) n
داری
علاقه دار subdistrict governor n
شق subdivision n
مضمون subject (academic) n
تبعه • رعیت subject (citizen) n •
مسند الیه • نهاد • subject (gram) n •
فاعل
رعیت subject (of monarch) n
موضوع • سوژه subject (topic) n •
ذهنی • انفصی subjective adj •
انفصیت subjectivity n
زیر نگین آوردن subjugate vt
وجه subjunctive mood (gram) n
التزامی
تعالی sublime (God) adj
شریف sublime (honored) adj
→ (arch) برین
علی • عالی sublime adj •
→ (f form) علیه
تحت البحری submarine n
خاضع • خاشع • submissive adj •
فروتن
→ (like a sheep) گوسفندی
تقدیم کردن • submit (file, offer) vt •
پیش کش کردن

پیش کردن submit <sth to sb> vt
<چیزی به کسی>
تن در دادن submit to v
تقدیم • submitting (filing, offering) n •
تفویض
تابع subordinate (& gram) adj
تابع subordinate (& gram) vt
ساختن
مادون • subordinate (inferior) adj •
زیر دست
فقره subordinate clause (gram) n
تابع
اشتراک subscribe (participate) v
کردن • اشتراک نمودن
subscription (participation) n
اشتراک
آینده • مابعد • بعد subsequent adj •
• پس • متعاقب • تالی
بعداً • بعد از آن subsequently adv •
• متعاقباً • پس از آن • سپس
هم سر subsidiary (of firm) n
اعاشه subsistence n
رزق subsistence (basic needs) n
کنه substance (essence) n
مادی substantial (material) adj n
مدلل substantiated (law) adj
بدیل • substitute (replacement) n •
بدل • عوض • اشتبنی • جایگزین •
جانشین
نازک خیال • subtle (clever) adj •
باریک اندیش • باریک بین • باریک
باریک subtlety (cleverness) n •
اندیشی • باریک بینی
دقیقه subtlety (nicety) n •
لطیفه subtlety (quip) n •
طرح کردن • subtract (math) v •
منفی کردن • وضع کردن
طرح subtraction n
مربوطات suburbs (of city) n pl
مخرب • ویرانگر subversive adj •
نایل شدن <به succeed <at sth> v
چیزی>
کامیاب شدن • موفق succeed vi •
بودن
تبعیت succeeding (coming after) n
موفقیت • برخورداری success n •
کامیاب • موفق • successful adj •
برخوردار

successfully *adv* • به طور موفقانه • موفقانه

succession (caliphate, & Sufi term) *n* خلافت

successive (coming after) (& adv) *adj, adv* • پی هم • پیاپی • پی در پی

successor *n* جانشین

successor (& descendant) *n* خلف

successor (esp caliph) *n* خلیفه

successors (first four to Prophet) *n* چاریار

succinct *see* concise

succulence *n* طراوت

such as *adv* • از قبیل • بدینگونه

suck *vt* • چوشیدن • مکیدن

suckle *see* suck

Sudan *n* سودان

sudden *adj* • ناگهان • ناگهانی • ناگاه • ناگهان

suddenly *adv* • بطور ناگهان • ناگاه • فوراً • بغتتاً • دفعتاً

suede *n* جیر

suet *n* • پیه • چربو • شحم • چربی

Suez (geog) *n* سویز

suffer *v* • رنج بردن • محنت دیدن • محنت کشیدن

suffering (afflicted) *adj* مشقت دیده

suffering <from sth> *adj* <مبتلا <به چیزی>

suffering *n* • رنج • محنت

sufficiency *n* • تکافو • کفایت

suffix (gram) *n* • لاحقه • پسوند • پساوند

suffix *n* پساوند

suffocating *adj* خفک

Sufi (& pers) *adj, n* • صوفی • متصوف • عارف • رند • پشمینه پوش

→ in a Sufic way صوفیانه

Sufi order *n* • طریقت • صوفیه • متصوفه

→ disciple of Sufi order مرید

Sufic *adj* عرفانی

Sufic (& adv) *adj, adv* • صوفیانه • عارفانه

Sufis, the *n* • متصوفه • صوفیه • اهل طریقت

Sufism *n* • صوفیه • تصوف • متصوفه • عرفان • طریقت • اهل طریقت

→ the axis of Sufism قطب

Sufist, Sufistic *see* Sufic

sugar *n* • شکر • بوره

→ brown sugar گر

→ lump sugar قند

→ sugar cane • نیشکر • نی شکر

suggest (recommend) *v* • صلاح دادن

suggestive *adj* القابی

Suhrawardiyya (Sufi order) *n* سهروردیه

suicide *n* • خود کشی • انتحار

suicide bomber *n* • شخص انتحار کننده • مواد منفجره جابجا شده با در شخص انتحار کننده

suit (& m dress suit) *n* دریشی

suit (agree with) *vt* ساختن

suitability (merit) *n* لیاقت

suitable (proper) *adj* • خوب • مساعد • لایق

suitable (reasonable) *adj* مناسب

suitable (useful) *adj* کارروا

suitcase *n* بکس سفر

→ (trunk for clothes) جامه دان

suitor (m) *n* • خواستگار • طلبگار

Suleyman Khel (P tribe) *n* سلیمان خیل

sulfate (chem) *n* زاج

sulfate (chem) *n* سلفیت

sulfur (element) *n* • گوگرد • سلفر

sulfuric acid *n* تیزاب گوگرد

suls (callig style) *n* • ثلث • خط ثلث • قلم ثلث

sultan (king) *n* سلطان

Sultan-e Bakwa (ctr) *n* سلطان بکواه

sultana (queen) *n* سلطانه

Sultana (f name) *n* سلطانه

sultanate *n* سلطنت

Sultani Bakwa (ctr) *n* سلطانی بکواه

Sultanpur (ctr) *n* سلطانپور

sum (of money) *n* • مبلغ • مقدار

sum (total) *n* • مجموع • حاصل

sum (unit of currency) *n* سوم

Sumer (hist, empire about 3500-2500 B.C.) *n* سومر

Sumerian (& pers) adj, n سومری

summary (concise) adj • فشرده اختصاری

summary n اجمال • خلاصه

→ in summary • خلاصه این که خلاصه کلام آن که

→ summary report فشرده گزارش

summary n تلخیص

summer adj تابستانی

summer n تابستان

summon vt خواستن

summons n جلب

sun n آفتاب • شمس • خورشید

Sunbula (month) n سنبله

Sunday n یکشنبه

sunglasses n عینک آفتابی

sunken (ship) adj غرق

Sunna (way/manners of Prophet) n سنه

Sunni (& pers) adj, n سنی

→ the Sunni community اهل سنت • اهل تسنن

sunny (weather) adj آفتابی

→ (colloq) آفتوی

sunny side up (eggs) adj نیم رویه

sunrise n طلوع آفتاب

→ (colloq) آفتاب برآمد

→ place of sunrise مطلع • مشرق

sunset n غروب آفتاب • غروب

→ (colloq) آفتاب نشست

sunstroke n جل

super- (prefix) (pref) ابر

superficial (shallow) (& pers) adj, n ظاهربین

superficial (trivial) adj سطحی

superior (better) adj اعلی

→ superiority بهتری

superior (senior) adj مافوق • بالا دست

superior (strong) (& pers) adj, n زبردست

→ superiority زبردستی

superiority n ترجیح • رجحان • بهتری

superlative (gram) n صفت عالی

Superman n ابر مرد

supermarket n مغازه

supernatural adj • مابعد الطبیعی فوق الطبیعی • خرق عادت • خارق عادت

supernatural, the n • مابعد الطبیعه ماوراءالطبیعه • متافزیک

superpower n ابر قدرت

supersonic adj مافوق سرعت

superstition n خرافه

superstitious adj خرافی

supervise v نظارت کردن

supervision n نظارت • نگرانی

→ under <sb's> supervision تحت نظر <کس> • زیر نظر

supervisor see & boss

→ supervisor of waqfs & rel law صدر شهر

→ supervisor of rel instruction خان علوم

→ supervisor of public morals محتسب

Supervisory Council (hist, 1992-1996) n شورای نظار (1996)

supper n نان شب • طعام شب

supple adj قابل انعطاف • انعطاف پذیر

supplement (esp printed) n ذیل

→ supplements ملحقات

supplementary adj مزید

supplementation n تتمه

suppleness n انعطاف

supplicate prayerfully v رازونیاز کردن

supplication (prayerful) n رازونیاز

supplier (contractor) n تیکه دار

supplies (mil) n pl اکمالات

→ related to supplies تدارکاتی

supplies (provisions) n تدارکات

supply (deliver) vt عرضه کردن

supply (delivery) n عرضه

→ supply & demand عرضه و تقاضا

support (& of own household) n نفقه • نفقات

support (backing) n تایید • تائید

support (materially) vt نفقه دادن

support (patronage) n حمایت • پیش بانی • نگاه بانی

support (pillar) n عماد

support (protection) n • پشتی
پشتیبانی • حمایت
پشتیوانی (colloq) →
support <sb> vt پشتی کردن
پشتیبانی کردن •روی دادن ‹کسی
را›
supporter (fellow traveler) n
هواخواه • هوا دار
supporter (partisan) n • جانب دار
طرف دار
supporter (patron) n • حامی
حمایت گر
supporter (protector) n پشتیبان
پشتیوان (colloq) →
supporter n ظهیر
supporting adj حمایوی
suppose v خیال کردن • تصور
کردن
supposedly adv بالفرض • فرضاً
supposition n تصور • تخیل •
مفکوره
suppository n شیاف
suppress (rights) vt پای مال کردن
• پامال کردن
suppressed adj مختنق
supreme (said of God) adj متعال
Supreme Court n ستره محکمه •
محکمه عالی • محکمه تمیز •
محکمه علیه تمیز • داد گاه عالی
sur (mus instr) n صور
sura (of Quran) n سوره
→ 1st sura of Quran سورۀ فاتحه
Suraya (f name) n ثریا • پروین
sure (certain) adj واثق • اعتمادی
→ be sure یقین داشتن
→ make sure علم آوری کردن
surety (traditional) n گرو
surety n تامینات
surface (front) n روی
surface (plane) n سطح
surface-to-air adj زمین به هوا
→ surface-to-air missile مزایل
زمین به هوا
surge (wave) n موج • موجه
surgeon n جراح
surgery n جراحی • عملیات
surgical adj جراحی
Suri (hist, 12th-c Ghorid ruler) n
سوری • سیف الدین بن عزالدین

Surkh-e Parsa (dist) n سرخ پارسا
Surkh Rod (dist) n سرخ رود
surna (mus instr) n سرنا
surna player n سرنیچی • سرنایچی
Surobi (dist) n سروبی
surplus <to> adj زاید ‹از›
surplus adj زیادتی
surplus n فاضل • مازاد
surprise (amazement) n استعجاب
• تعجب • استعجابه
surprise (sth unexpected) n مفاجا •
مفاجات
surprised adj غافل گیر • حیران •
متحیر • مات
→ be surprised غافل گیر شدن
surrealism n • سورریالزم
سورریالیسم
surrender (capitulate) v تسلیم شدن
• تسلیم کردن
surrender (escape) v سپر انداختن
surround <sth/sb> vt دور
گرفتن ‹چیزی/کسی را›
surrounded adj محاط • احاطه
surroundings n ماحول
surveil v نظارت کردن
surveillance n نظارت
survey (questionnaire) n سروی
surveying n مساحتی
surveyor n مساح
survive vi به سلامت ماندن
survivor (of deceased) n بازمانده
susceptible <to sth> adj دست
خوش ‹چیزی›
susceptible adj حساس
suspect (doubt) v مشتبه بودن
suspect (pers) n متهم • آدم
مشکوک • مظنون
suspect (sth neg to be true) v سوء
ظن داشتن
suspected adj مشکوک
suspend (from duty) vi موقوف
کردن
suspend (hang) vt آویختن
suspended (from duty) adj موقوف
suspended (hanging) adj • معلق
ملاق
suspending (hanging) n تعلیق
suspenseful adj متشنج
suspension (from duty) n موقوفی

527

suspension (hanging) *n* تعلیق

suspicion *n* گمان بد

suspicion (doubt) *n* سوء ظن

suspicious (doubtful) *adj* بد گمان

suspicious (suspected) *adj* مشکوک

sustainment *n* پرورش • مراقبت

sustenance (basic needs) *n* رزق

sut (unit of measure) *n* سوت

suture *n* بخیه

swallow (bird) *n* ابابیل • غچی • پرستو • فراشتروک

swallow *v* قرت کردن

swamp *n* جبه زار • دل دل زار • باتلاق • مرداب

swan *n* قو

Swat (geog, Pakistan) *n* سوات

swear (curse) *v* داو زدن • دشنام دادن • پوچ گفتن • فحش گفتن
→ (colloq) دو زدن

swear (take oath) *v* سوگند خوردن

swear in (by oath) *vt* سوگند دادن

sweat *n* عرق

sweat *v* عرق ریختن

sweater *n* جاکت

sweaty *adj* عرقناک

Swede (pers) *n* سویدنی

Sweden *n* سویدن

Swedish (& lang) *adj* سویدنی

sweet (& adv) *adj, adv* شیرین
→ sweet person بره

sweetbriar (flower) *n* نسترن

sweetheart *n* دل بر • دل ستان • حبیب • محبوب

sweetness *n* شیرینی

sweets *n* حلویات

sweet-talking *adj* چرب زبان

swell *vi* پندیدن • ورم کردن

swelling *n* پندیدگی • تورم • ورم • آماس

swift (bird) *see* swallow

swift *adj* تیز • تیزرو • سبک رفتار • سبک سیر • (fig) →
باد پای

swim *vi* شنا کردن • آب بازی کردن

swimmer *n* شناور • آب باز

swimming pool *n* حوض آببازی • حوض شنا

swimsuit *n* مایو

swindle *n* غبن

swindle *v* حقه بازی کردن

swindler *n* مارگیر • حقه باز

swine *n* خوک • خنزیر

Swiss (& pers) *adj, n* سویسی

switch *n* تکمه • دکمه • سوچ
→ switch off گل کردن
→ switch on سوچ کردن

Switzerland *n* سویس

swivel *adj* چرخکی
→ swivel chair چوکي چرخکي

swollen *adj* پندیده • آماسیده • متورم • ورم کردن

sword *n* شمشیر • تیغ • سیف • تلوار • پولاد
→ well-tempered (sword) جوهردار

swordsman *n* شمشیر زن

sycophant *n* کاسه لیس

syed (title) *see* sayed

syllabic *adj* سیلابی • هجایی

syllable *n* سیلاب • هجا

symbol *n* سمبول • رمز

symmetrical (to) *adj* با تناسب

symmetrical *adj* متناسب

symmetry *n* تناسب • تناظر

sympathetic *adj* دل سوز • مشفق • شفیق • غمخور • غم شریک

sympathize *v* دل سوختن

sympathy *n* دل سوزی • غم شریکی • رقت

symptom *n* عرض • علامت • نشان • نشانه

synagogue *n* کنشت

synonym *n* مترادف • مرادف • هم معنی

synonymous *adj* هم منعی • مترادف • مرادف

synopsis *n* اجمال • خلاصه

syntax (gram) *n* نحو • سنتکس

syphilis *n* آتشک • سفلیس

Syr Darya (river) *n* سیر دریا

Syria *n* سوریه • سوریا • شام

Syriac (hist, lang) *n* سریانی

Syrian *adj* سوریایی

syringe *n* سوزن • پیچکاری

syrup (esp fruit) *n* شربت

system (apparatus) *n* جهاز

528

system (network) *n* شبکه
→ sewer system کانالیزاسیون
→ solar system منظومه شمسی
→ ventilation system روباه خانه
system *n* سیستم • منظومه • نظام
systematic *adj* منظم • متودیک
systole (med) *n* انقباض قلب

T

Tabiun (2ⁿᵈ generation of Prophet's
followers) *n pl* تابعون
table (list) *n* فهرست • جدول
→ table of contents فهرست
مندرجات • فهرست موضوعات
table (surface) *n* میز • میز کار •
دسترخوان
→ (fig)
tablecloth *n* سرمیزی
→ (& on ground) • دسترخوان
سفره
tablet *n* لوح • لوحه
Tabriz (city) *n* تبریز
tabulate *vt* جدول بندی کردن
tabulation *n* جدول بندی
tacit (implied) *adj* ضمنی
tacitly (implicitly) *adv* ضمناً
tack (horse's gear) *n* یراق
tact *n* مردم داری
tactful *adj* با تدبیر
tactic *see* tactics
tactical *adj* تاکتیکی • تکتیکی
tactics *n* تاکتیک • تکتیک
tactless *adj* بی تدبیر
Tagab (dist) *n* تگاب • تگ آب
Tagalog (lang) *n* فلیپینی
Tahmasp I (hist, Safavid Shah
1524-1576) *n* شاه • طهماسپ •
طهماسپ
tail *n* دم • دنبال
→ sheep's tail دنبه • دنبه گوسفند
→ star w/tail (comet) ستاره دنباله
دار
tailor *n* خیاط
tailor *v* خیاطی کردن
taint *n* آلودگی • لوث
Taj (m name) *n* تاج
Tajik (dialect, lang) *n* تاجیکی

Tajik (pers) *n* تاجیک
→ Afghan Tajik دهگان
→ Mountain Tajik (Wakhi) واخی
Tajik *adj* تاجیکی
Tajikistan *n* تاجیکستان
take (for o.s.) *vt* غنیمت گرفتن
take (grab) *vt* گرفتن
take (receive) *vt* • اخذ کردن
خوردن
→ take a pulse نبض دیدن
→ take aim نشان گرفتن
→ take hold of <sth> محکم گرفتن
<چیزی را>
→ take out (extract) • برآوردن
بیرون کردن
→ (colloq) برآورده کردن
→ take place *see* happen
takeoff (of aircraft) *n* برخاست
→ takeoff & landing نشست و
برخاست
Takhar (province) *n* تخار
Takht-e Rustam (stupa) *n* تختِ
رستم
Takht-e Sulayman (mountain) *n*
تختِ سلیمان • تمتِ سلیمانی
taking (receiving) *n* • اخذ • اتخاذ
قبضه
Tala wa Barfak (dist) *n* تاله و
برفک
talcum powder *n* طلق • تلک
tale *see* story
talent *n* استعداد • سلیقه • لیاقت
talented *adj* با استعداد • قابل
ماهر • چابکدست • لایق • ورزیده •
آزمایش کرده • آزمایش شده •
آزموده • مجرب
Taliban *n* طالبیان • طالبان
taliq (callig style) تعلیق • خط تعلیق
talk (converse) *v* مکالمه کردن
talk (speak) *vi* گپ زدن • تکلم
کردن
talk (speech) *n* سخن • سخن رانی
talk *n* گپ • صحبت • محاوره •
گفتار
talkative (sweetly) *adj* بلبلی
talks (negotiations) *n* مذاکرات
tall (elevated) *n* بلند • مرتفع

529

tall (of stature) adj بالا • بلند بالا • بلند قد • بلند قد • بلند
→ grow tall quickly قد کشیدن
tallow n شحم • چربو • چربی
tally n چوب خط
talon (claw) n چنگ • چنگال
Taluqan (seat, dist) n تالقان
tambourine n دایره • دف
tambur (mus instr) n تنبور
tambur player n • تنبور نواز
تنبورچی
tame (domesticated) adj اهلی
→ to be tame (horse) vi پشت دادن
Tamerlane (hist, 1336-1405) n
تیمور
→ Code of Tamerlane تزک
تیموری
Tanay (dist) n تنی
tangelo (fruit) n سنبره
tangerine (fruit) n کینو
tangible adj محسوس
tanner n دباغ
→ tanning of hides دباغی • دباغت
• چرمگری
tap (faucet) n شیردهن
→ (colloq) شیردان
tape n فیته
Taqnin (in Justice Min) n تقنین
Tara Kheyl (ctr) n تره خیل
tardy see late
Tareen see Tarin
target (mark) n • هدف گاه • هدف
آماج • آماج گاه • نشان • نشانه •
نشان گاه • نشان نگاه
tariff (rate) n نرخ
Tarin (P tribe) n ترین
Tarin Kot (seat) n ترین کوت
Tarkhoj (ctr) n ترخوج
Tarnak wa Jaldak (dist) n ترنک و
جلدک
tarnish n لوث • آلودگی
tarp n تریال
Tartar see Tatar
Tarzi, Ghulam Mohamad (19th-c
Dari poet) n طرزی • غلام محمد
Tashkent n تاشکند
tashkil (staffing plan) n تشکیل
task n وظیفه
taste (flavor) n مزه • مذاق

taste (morsel) n چاشنی • چشک
taste (preference) n • ذوق • مذاق
سلیقه
taste (sense of taste) n • ذایقه
چشایی
taste (arch) vt مزیدن
tasty adj مزه دار • خوش مزه • با
مزه • لذیذ
Tatar n تتار • تاتر
tattooed beauty mark n خال
taunt vt نیش زدن
taunting n نیش
Taurus (zodiac) n ثور
tawhid (doctrine of unity of God) n
توحید
tawqi (callig style) n خط • توقیع
توقیع
Tawus (m name) n طاووس
tax n اج • مالیه • مالیت
→ tax payment in cash مالیت
نقدی
→ tax payment in kind مالیت
جنسی
tax collecting n تحصیل داری
→ (when done by village elder for
state) قریه داری
tax collector n • تحصیل دار
باجگیر
→ provincial tax collector مستوفی
tax office (provincial) n مستوفیت
tax return n اظهار نامه
tax v مالیه گرفتن
taxi n تکسی
taxman (provincial) n مستوفی
Taywara (dist) n تیوره
Tbilisi n طبلیسی
tea n چای
→ green tea leaves boiled in milk
w/sugar & cream شیر چای
→ tea strainer چای صاف
→ teacup پیاله • پیمانه
→ teahouse چای خانه
→ teapot چاینک
teach (sb) a lesson v سبق دادن
teach <sb> v درس دادن • یاد دادن
<به کسی>
teach (& train) vt تعلیم دادن • وارد
ساختن
530

teacher n • معلم • آموزگار
→ (arch) دبیر
→ (f) معلمه
→ (in rel school) مدرس
→ teacher training college دارالمعلمین
teaching n تدریس
tear (rip) n شقه
tear (teardrop) n • اشک • آب چشم • آب دیده • سرشک
→ tears (fig) • نم • گریه
tear (be rent) vi شقه کردن • تکه شدن • جدا شدن • گسیختن • گسستن
→ (colloq) سکستن
tear (rend) vt تکه کردن • جدا کردن • جدا افاندن • گسیختن • گسستن
→ (colloq) سکستن
tear gas n گاز اشک آور
tearful adj پر آب
tease (pester) v جور دادن
→ mild teasing remark مطایبه
technical adj تخنیکی
technical school n تخنیکم
→ Jangalak (tech school) تخنیکم جنگلک
→ Mazar-e Sharif (tech school) تخنیکم مزر شریف
technician n تخنیکر
technique (artistic) n فن
technologist n تخنیک دان
technology n تخنیک
tedious adj کسالت آور
teenage (& pers) adj, n • نوخاسته • نوخان • نورسیده • جوانک
Tehran n تهران
Tel Aviv n تل ابیب
telegram n تلگرام
telephone n تلفون • تیلفون
→ telephone book رهنمای تلفون
telephone v تلفون کردن • تیلفون کردن
television n تلویزیون
→ watch television تلویزیون دیدن
tell vt • گفتن • معلومات دادن
temperament n • مزاج • مجاز
temperate adj • معتدل • اعتدالی
temperateness n اعتدال
temperature n • حرارت • گرمی

temple (anat) n شقیقه
temple (place of worship) n • عبادتگاه • عبادت خانه • پرستشگاه
→ Ibadat Khana (hist, Mughal temple) عبادت خانه
temple (synagogue) n کنشت
temporarily adv موقتاً
temporary adj • موقت • سپنج
ten adj, n ده
→ ten million کرور
tenacious adj متشبث
tenant n • کرا نشین • کرایه نشین
tend towards <sth> v • رو به <چیزی> گذاشتن • میل داشتن • میل کردن • میلان داشتن
tendency n • میل • میلان
tender (sensitive) adj نازک
tender (for public works) n مناقصه
tender-hearted adj نازک دل
tenderness n نرمش
tendon (anat) n پی
tennis n • تینس • تنیس
→ play tennis تینس بازی کردن
→ tennis ball توپ بادی
→ tennis court • میدان تینس • میدان تینس
tense (taut) adj • متشنج • کشیده
tense (gram) n زمان
tension n کشیدگی
tension (& fig) n تنش
tent n خیمه
→ black tent of P nomads غژدی
→ pitch tent خیمه زدن
→ tent (for f) • پرده سرا • حرم سرا
→ tent (yurt) • یورت • خرگاه
tentative adj آزمایشی
tenth adj دهم
→ one-tenth ده یک
→ one-tenth (tithe) • عشر • ده یک
Terazayi (dist) n ترازئی
term (& idiom) n اصطلاح
term (semester) n سمستر
term (stipulation) n شرط
→ terms (stipulations) شرایط
term (time period) n دوره
→ term of mil service • دوره مکلفیت
termination (conclusion) n ختم
termination (dismissal) n طرد

531

termite *n* مورِیانه
terrace (of house) *n* تراس • ایوان
terrible *adj* دهشتناک • وحشتناک
terrified (& pers) *adj, n* دهشت آور • دهشت انگیز انگیز • مدهش • جلال
terrified (& pers) *adj, n* دهشت زده • وحشت زده
terrifying *adj* دهشت افگن
terrifying *see* & terrible
territorial *adj* ارضی
→ territorial integrity تمامیتِ ارضی
territory *n* قلمرو • رقبه • ولا
→ Palestinian territories قلمرو فلسطینی • اراضی اشغالی
→ territories اراضی
terror *n* دهشت • ترور
terrorism *n* دهشت افگنی • تروریزم
terrorist *adj* چریکی • تروریستی
terrorist *n* دهشت افگن • تروریست • چریک
terse *adj* موجز
Teshkan (dist) *n* تشکان
test (exam) *n* امتحان • آزمایش
test (experiment) *n* آزمایش • تجزیه
testament (will) *n* وصیت
tested (tried) *adj* آزمایش کرده • آزمایش شده • آزموده
tester (examiner) *n* ممتحن
testify *v* شهادت دادن
testimonial (letter of satisfaction) *n* رضا نامه
testimony *n* شهادت • گواهی
tête-á-tête *adv* دو به دو
text (document) *n* مضمون
text (of document) *n* متن
textbook *n* کتاب درسی
textile *adj* نساجی
texture (of carpet) *n* بافت
teyka (card game) *n* تیکه
than *prep* نسبت به • نظربه
thank (say thanks) *v* ثنا گفتن
thank <sb> *vt* شکر کردن • شکر کردن <از کسی>
thanks (gratitude) *n* تشکر • شکر • سپاس • سپاس گزاری
→ thanks be to God! بحمدالله
532

that (which) *pron* که • یعنی • یعنی که
that *adj, pron* آن • همان
→ (colloq) اون • همو
that is (i.e.) *phrs* یعنی که
theater *n* تماشا خانه • تیاتر
theft *n* دزدی • سرقت
→ (colloq) دزی
theism *n* خدا شناسی
theist *adj, n* خدا شناس
them *pron* انها را • اینان را
→ (colloq) اونا را
→ (lit) ایشان را
then (afterwards) *adv* باز • بعد • پس
then (in that case) *conj* پس • در آن صورت
theocracy *n* تیوکراسی
theologian (Musl) *n* فقیه
theology (discipline) *n* علم الهی
→ (as academic subject) دینیات
→ Musl scholastic theology علم کلام • علم الکلام
theorem *n* برهان
theoretical *adj* نظری
theoretically *adv* ظاهراً
theory (hypothesis) *n* نظریه • فرضیه
theory *n* تیوری
therapeutic *adj* معالجوی
therapy (med) *n* تداوی • معالجه • طبابت
there *adv* آنجا
→ (colloq) اونجه
thereafter *adv* بعد از آن • پس از آن • سپس
therefore *adv* در نتیجه • نتیجتاً • بالنتیجه • بنا بر آن • بنا بر این • از آن جهت • از آن سبب • به آن جهت • لذا • لهذا
thermometer *n* میزان الحراره • ترمامیتر • ترمومتر
these *adj* این
these *pron* اینها • این ها
thesis *n* تیسس
they (& 2ⁿᵈ pers sg for dignitary) *pron* آنها • اینان
→ (colloq) اونا
→ (lit) ایشان

thick (dense) adj انبوه
thick (slow-witted) adj خرفهم
thick (viscous) adj غلیظ • تیره
thicken (syrup) vt به قوام آوردن
thicket n بته زار • بیشه
thief n دزد • سارق
thigh (anat) n ران
thin (skinny) adj لاغر • نزار
thin (sparse) adj تنک
→ become thin due to illness or
suffering تار گشتن
→ very thin تار و نار
thing n چیز • شی
think (suppose) v فکر کردن •
تصور کردن • پنداشتن
thinker n مفکر • متفکر • اندیشمند
thinking n تفکر
third adj سوم • سومی • ثالث
→ (lit, used before n) سومین
third lieutenant (mil) n دریم بریدمن
• دریم خارن
third party (law) n اجنبی/اجانب •
بیگانه • خارجی
third person (gram) n غایب
thirdly adv سوم • ثالثا
thirsty (& pers) adj, n تشنه
→ very thirsty (fig) جگر سوخته
thirteen adj, n سیزده
thirteenth adj سیزدهم
→ (lit, used before n) سیزدهمین
thirtieth adj سی ام
→ (lit, used before n) سییمین
thirty adj, n سی
this adj این • همین • هذا
→ (colloq) همی
thorn n خار
thornapple (med herb) n داتوره
thorny adj خاردار
thorough adj کامل
thoroughbred adj اصیل
thoroughly adv کاملاً • به کلی •
بالکل • بلکل
those adj آنها
→ (colloq) اونا
though (even if) conj اگرچه • هر
چند
thought (idea) n فکر • فکرت •
اندیشه • مفکوره

thought (reflection) n خیال
→ capacity of thought مفکره
thoughtfully adv متفکرانه
thousand adj, n هزار
thousandth adj هزارم
→ (lit, used before n) هزارمین
thrash (w/stick) v چوب زدن •
چوب کاری کردن
→ be thrashed چوب خوردن
thread n تار • نخ
→ thread (gold, silver) گلاتاتون
thread (needle) vt تار کردن • در
کشیدن
threadbare adj تار تار
threat (hazard) n مخاطره
threat (warning) <against sth> n
تهدید <به ضد چیزی> • وعید
→ threat & promise وعده و وعید
threat see & warning
threaten vt تهدید کردن
threatening adj تهدید آمیز
three adj, n سه
threshold n درگاه • آستانه
throat n گلو • حلقوم
→ (colloq) گلون
throne n تخت • اورنگ • اریکه •
سریر
throng n ازدحام • بیروبار
through prep توسط • بتوسط •
بواسطه • طی • از راه • از خلال
throw vt انداختن • پرتافتن
→ throw away پس انداختن • باطل
کردن
→ throw up (vomit) دل بد شدن •
قی کردن • استفراغ کردن • شکوفه
کردن
throwing n پرتاب
thrust (shove) n تنبه
thrust (shove) v تیله کردن
thug (& adj) adj, n بدمعاش
thug (esp w/knife) n چاقوکش
thunder n غرش • رعد
thunder v غرش کردن
thunderous adj رعد آسا
thunderstorm n رعد
Thursday n پنجشنبه
thus (in this way) adv طوریکه •
همچنین
thus see & therefore

Tibet (geog) n تبت
Tibetan (& pers) adj, n تبتی
tick (parasite) n کنه
ticket n تکت
tickle n تختخک • دغدغه
tickle v تختخک دادن
→ be tickled تختخک خوردن
ticklish adj تختخکی
tide n مد
tie (bond) n رشته • قید
→ ties of kinship رحم
tie (necktie) n نکتایی
tie (relationship) n رابطه
tie vt بستن • بسته کردن
Tiflis see Tbilisi
tiger n ببر
tight (close-fitting) adj چسپ
→ be tight <on sb sw> تنگ گرفتن
<کسی را در کجا>
tight (narrow) adj تنگ • کم عرض
• باریک
tightrope walker n بند باز
tightrope walking n بند بازی
Tigris (river) n دجله
Tihamah (geog) n تهامه
tile n کاشی
→ tiled surface کاشی کاری
till (until) adv تا • تا که
tilted adj کج
timber n چوب تعمیر • چوب
time (era) n دوره • دور • زمان •
روزگار
time (instance) n دفعه • بار • کرت
• مرتبه
time (reign) n دوره • عصر
time n وقت • ساعت • گاه
→ at the time of هنگام • در وقت
→ on time به وقت
→ that time آن دفعه
→ time of birth میلاد
→ time period ساعت
times (-fold) adj برابر
timid adj n ترسو • شیشه دل
timidity n ترسویی
Timurid (hist) adj تیموری
→ Andijan Timurids (see &
Chaghatai) اندیجان تیموریان
→ Timurid dynasty (hist) تیموریان
Timurid see & Tamerlane
534

tin (mineral) n قلعی
→ (arch) ارزیز
tip (end) n غایت
→ tip of the nose پرۀ بینی
tipped over adj چپه شده
tipsiness n خمار
tipsy adj خماری • خمار آلود • پر
خمار • مخمور
→ (colloq) خمار
tire (wheel) n تیر
→ get a flat tire پنچر شدن
→ spare tire تیر اشتبنی • تیر فالتو
→ tire jack جک تیر
tire (falter) vi از پای افتادن
tired (exhausted) adj تکه تکه
tired (weary) adj خسته
tithe (Islamic) n عشر/اعشار
title (deed) n سند مالکیت • قباله
title (heading) n عنوان
title (honorific) n لقب
title see & forms of address
(appendix)
to (in time expressions) adv کم
to (until) prep الی • تا
to (up to) prep تا
to prep به • از
to see & toward
toasted adj بریان
tobacco n تنباکو • تمباکو
→ tobacco products دخانیات
Tocharian (hist, lang) n تخاری
today adv امروز
toe (anat) n انگشت • پنجه • کلک
toe (of shoe, boot) n پنجه گی
toenails n ناخن
→ untrimmed toenails ناخن رسیده
together adv با هم
→ (jointly) مشترکاً • جوره
→ (simultaneously) یکجا • یکجای
toil (suffering) n رنج
toilet n تشناب
Tokyo n توکیو
tolerable adj تحمل پذیر • قابل
تحمل
tolerance (of pain) n تاب درد
toll (tribute) n باج
tomato n بادنجان رومی
tomb (grave) n قبر • گور • لحد
tomb (mausoleum) n مقبره

tombstone n • سنگ قبر • لوح قبر

tomorrow adv • صباح • فردا

→ day after tomorrow • دیگر سبا

tonality (mus) n • سر

tone (of voice) n • لهجه • تون

tongs (brazier) n • آتش گیر

tongue n • زبان • لسان

tonic (med) n • غرغون • غرغونی

tonight adv • امشب

tonsillitis n • التهاب لوزتین

tonsils n pl • لوزتین • تانسل ها

too (also) adv • هم • نیز • همچنان

too (excessively) adv • بسیار • بیحد • بی اندازه

tool (implement) n • آله • آلت • افزار • دست افزار • ابزار

→ (colloq) • اوزار

→ tools (utensils) • سامان

→ tools & instruments • ساز و برگ • ساز و سامان

tooth n • دندان

toothpick n • چوبک دندان • دندان خلال • خلال

top n • فوق

top (apex) n • اوج

top (cover) n • سرپوش • سر

top (toy) n • چرخک

→ top to bottom • سرتاپا

→ on top of • در بالای

top bazi (game) n • توپ بازی

top danda (game) n • توپ دنده

topaz (yellow) n • یاقوت زرد • زبرجد هندی

topic n • موضوع

Tora Bora (geog) n • توره بوره

Torah (rel) n • تورات

torment n • چارمیخ

tormenting adj • جان فرسا

torn (ragged) adj • تکه • پاره • چیر

→ torn to shreds • تکه تکه

Toronto (city) n • تورنتو

torso n • بدن • تن

tortoise n • سنگ پشت

→ (colloq) • سنگ بقه

torture n • شکنجه • عذاب • تعذیب

torture vt • شکنجه دادن • شکنجه کردن • عذاب دادن

total n • جمیع • مجمع • مجموعی

→ grand total • جمع کل

totality n • جملگی • همگی

totally adv • بالجمله • جملتاً

touch (contact) n • تماس

→ I'll be in touch w/you • من همرایت به تماس می باشم

touch (sense of touch) n • لامسه • بساوایی

touch v • دست زدن

→ be touched v • دست خوردن

touchstone n • محک • سنگ محک

touchy (& pers) adj, n • اندک رنج • زود رنج

→ touchy pers (fig) • بابونه

tough (hardy) adj • سخت جان

tourism (travel) n • سیاحت

tourist (travel) adj • سیاحتی

tourist (traveler) n • سیاح

tow (car) v • کش کردن

tow truck n • موتر کش کننده

toward prep • سوی • به سوی • جانب • به جانب • طرف • به طرف

towel (bath towel) n • قطیفه • قدیفه

→ face towel • روی پاک

→ hand towel • دست پاک

tower n • برج

town (city) n • شهر

town (small) n • قصبه

toxic adj • سمی

toxicity n • سمیت • زهریت

toxin n • سم • زهر

toy n • بازیچه • ملعبه

tracer bullet n • مرمی رسام

trachea (anat) n • قصبت الریه

trachoma (med) n • تراخم • کوکره

track (trace) n • درک • سراغ

→ railroad track • خط آهن • خط ریل

tract (farmland) n • پرگنه

trade (commerce) n • تجارت • بازارگانی • سوداگری

trade (deal) n • سودا

trade (do business) vi • تجارت کردن

trade (guild) n • صنف

trade (vocation) n • حرفه • پیشه • کسب • کسب و کار

trade see & buying & selling

tradesman (artisan) n • کسبی

535

tradition (custom) n • رسم • عنعنه
رسم و رواج
tradition (heritage) n میراث
traditional adj سنتی • عنعنوی
→ (under customary law) عرفی
traffic n آمد و رفت • عبور و مرور
traffic signal n pl اشارات ترافیکی
tragacanth gum n کتیره
tragedy n تراژیدی
tragic adj تراژیک
trail (tail) n دنباله
train (be instructed) vi تعلیم کردن
train (instruct) vt وارد • تعلیم دادن
ساختن
train (locomotive) n • لوکوموتیف
ریل
trained (& mil) adj تعلیم یافته
training (& mil) n پرورش • تعلیم
training (exercise) n تمرین
training grounds n میدان تعلیم
traitor (to country) n دشمن • وطن
وطن فروش
traitor n خیانت • خاین • خیانت کار
پیشه
traitorous adj خیانت کار
trample (& fig) vt • پای مال کردن
پامال کردن
tranquilizer n مسکن • دوای مسکن
transaction n معامله
transcription (phonetic) n آواز
نویسی
transcription n نسخ
transfer (detainee) vt منتقل کردن
transfer (remittance) n • حواله
تحویل
transfer n ارسال • انتقال • تفویض
transfer vt انتقال دادن
transferred (detainee) adj منتقل
Transfiguration (rel) n تجلی
transfigure (rel) v تجلی دادن • تجلی کردن
transform vt تحول • تحول دادن
کردن
transformation n مسخ • تحول
transformer n ترانسفارمر
transgression n تجاوز
→ minor transgression صغیره
transgressor n تجاوز کار
transistor n ترانزیستور

536

transition n خروج • تحویل
transitional adj انتقالی
transitive (gram) adj متعدی
transitory see transitional
translate v ترجمانی • ترجمه کردن
کردن • گزارش کردن • برگرداندن
translation n • ترجمانی • ترجمه
برگردان
translation office n دارالترجمه
translator n مترجم • ترجمان
transmigration of souls n • تناسخ
حلول • حلول و تناسخ
transmission (mech) n ترانسمیشن
transmission (message) n مخابره
transmit vt روان کردن • فرستادن
transmittable adj انتقالی
transmitter n دستگاه فرستنده •
دستگاه مرسله • ترانسمیتر
transparency adj شفافیت
transparent adj شفاف
transport n • انتقال • نقل • حمل
تفویض
→ transport & transportation حمل
و نقل
transportation see transport
trap n دام • تلک • قیقان
trapezoid n ذوزنقه
trash n خاکروبه • چتلی
travel (journey) n سفر • مسافرت
travel (tourism) n سیاحت
→ traveling to sw عازم
travel office n دفتر مسافرتی
travel v سفر کردن • به سفر رفتن
→ set out on travel راهی شدن
→ travel abroad به خارج سفر
کردن
traveler (fig) n ابن السبیل
traveler (tourist) n سیاح
→ fellow traveler هواخواه
→ traveler of the path (Sufi)
راهرو • سالک
traveler n مسافر
traveling adj پیما
travelogue n سفرنامه
tray (copper, round) n • مجمعه
سینی
tray (grocer's) n تبنگ
tray (small & for food; & for carrying
presents to betrothed) n خوانچه

tray (tea tray) *n* پتنوس

treacherous (disloyal) *adj* خیانت کار • خائن • خیانت پیشه

treacherous (villainous) *adj* شیطانت آمیز • شیطانت بار

treachery (villainy) *n* شیطانت

treachery *see* & treason

treacle (poison antidote) *n* تریاق

treadle *n* رکاب

treason *n* خیانت به وطن • وطن دشمنی • دشمنی وطن • وطن فروشی

treasure (& hidden) *n* گنج • دفینه
→ treasure trove دفینه

treat (a patient) *v* معالجه کردن • شفا دادن

treat kindly *vt* نواختن

treatment (med) *n* تداوی • معالجه • طبابت
→ give med treatment طبابت کردن • طبیبی کردن

treatment (of people) *n* پیشامد • پیش آمد • بر خورد <با/همرای کسی>

treaty *n* پکت • پیمان • معاهده

tree *n* درخت • شجر

trembling *n* ارتعاش

trench (parapet) *n* مورچل • سنگر

trenchmate *n* همسنگر • همرزم • همنبرد

trend (tendency) *n* جهت • میلان

trespasser *n* متجاوز

trestle *n* خرک

trial (hearing) *n* محاکمه
→ put <sb> on trial محاکمه کردن

triangle *n* مثلث • سه ضلعی

triangular *adj* مثلث • سه ضلعی

tribal *adj* قبیله یی • قبیلوی • قومی
→ tribal affiliation قومیت

tribalism *n* تعصب قومی

tribe *n* قبیله • قوم • عشیره • پرگنه

tribe (sons; clan) *n* بنو

tribunal (court) *n* داد گاه • محکمه

tribute (poll tax) *n* جزیه

tribute *n* باج

trick (artifice) *n* حیله • فن

trick (deceive) *v* حقه بازی کردن

trick (deception) *n* چال • غبن

trickery (deceit) *n* تقلب

trickster *n* حیله باز • حیله ساز • حیله گر • محتال • محیل

tricky (deceitful) *adj* تقلب آمیز

tried & true *adj* مجرب • ورزیده • آزمایش کردن • آزمایش شده • آزموده

trigger *n* ماشه

trigonometry *n* مثلثات

trim beard *v* اصلاح ریش کردن

trim nails *v* ناخن گرفتن

Trinity (& doctrine) (rel) *n* تثلیث

trip (journey) *n* سفر • مسافرت
→ have a good trip! سفر بخیر

trip (stumble) *vi* تک خوردن

tripartite *adj, n* ثلاثی

triplicate *adj* سه پارچه

triumph *n* ظفر • پیروزی • فتح

triumph *v* ظفر یافتن • فاتح شدن

triumphant *adj* ظفرمند • مظفر • پیروزمند • پیروز • فیروز • فاتح • فاتحانه • فیروزمند

triumphantly *adv* فاتحانه

trivet (for cooking pot) *n* دیگ پایه

trivial *adj* سطحی • جزئی

troop (mil) *n* نیرو • قوه

troop *see* & soldier

trouble (bother) *n* زحمت • رنج • مشقت

trouble (difficulty) *n* مشقت
→ stir up trouble (fig) آتش در دادن

troublesome *adj* مزاحم

trousers (pajamas) *n* تنبان • ازار
→ (colloq) تنبا

trousers (pants) *n* پتلون
→ trouser leg (& hem) پاچه

trout *n* ماهی خال دار

trove (treasure) *n* دفینه • گنج

trowel (for masonry) *n* دست پناه

trowel (small shovel) *n* بیلچه • بیلک

truancy *n* مکتب گریزی

truant student *n* مکتب گریز • شاگرد گریز پای

truce *n* متارکه
→ establish a truce متارکه کردن

truck (lorry) *n* چکله • لاری

truck (pickup truck) *n* پیکپ

true (correct) *adj* درست • صحیح

537

true (real) adj • واقع • واقعی • حقیقی

true adj درست • برحق

truly adv حقیقتاً

truncated (pyramid) adj ناقص

trunk (chest) n محفظه

trunk (elephant's) n خرطوم

trunk (torso) n تن • بدن

trust (confidence) n <کسی> اعتماد • اطمینان • اعتبار • وثوق • trust n

trust vt اعتماد کردن
→ be trusted اعتماد داشتن

trusted agent n • تحویل دار نقدی معتمد

trustee n امین

trusting (confident) adj • اعتمادی واثق

trustworthy (in cash transfer) adj معتمد • تحویل دار نقدی

trustworthy adj قابل اعتماد • معتمد • موثق • موثوق

truth n حقیقت • واقعیت

truth-seeker n حقیقت جوی

try <+ subj> v • کوشش کردن کوشیدن • در سعی و تلاش به سر بردن

try <sb> (law) vt محاکمه کردن

Tsamkani (dist, alt Chamkani) n څمکنی

tsar (hist) n زار • تزار

tube (duct) (& anat) n کانال

tube (pipe) n نل • نی

tuberculosis n سل • توبرکلوز

Tuesday n سه شنبه

Tukzar (ctr) n تکزار

Tulak (dist) n تولک

tulip (flower) n لاله

tumor (med) n غدود • تومور

tumult (clash) n تلاطم

tumult (turmoil) n قیامت • هرج و مرج

tumult (uproar) n هنگامه

tumultuous adj پر تلاطم

tune (mus) n آهنگ
→ in tune به سر

tunic n کرتی

tuning fork n دیاپزن

tunnel (esp mil) n نقب • سوف

538

turban n لنگی • لنگوته • دستار

turbulent see tumultuous

Turcoman see Turkmen

turf n زمین

Turk (pers) n ترک

turkey (bird) n فیل مرغ • بوقلمون

Turkey n ترکیه

Turkish (& lang) adj, n ترکی

Turkmen (& pers) adj, n ترکمن

Turkmen (lang) n ترکمنی

Turkmenistan n ترکمنستان

Turkoman see Turkmen

turmeric (spice) n زردچوبه

turmoil see tumult

turn (in game) n نوبت

turn (revolution) n چکر

turn (revolve) vi گردیدن • دور خوردن
→ turn a somersault معلق زدن
→ turn around چرخ دادن
→ turn back vt گرداندن
→ turn down (sound) خاموش ساختن <کسی را>
→ turn in (submit) تقدیم کردن
→ turn into (be transformed) درآمدن • در آمدن
→ turn off (switch off) • گل کردن سوچ زدن
→ turn on (switch on) سوچ کردن
→ turn out (end up) (+ adj) تمام شدن • به میان آمدن
→ turn to <sb> (for help) رو آوردن <به طرف کسی>
به میان آمدن (appear) turn up →
→ turn upside-down معکوس کردن

turn (& page) vt گرداندن

turn to (for help) v رجوع کردن

turncoat n زمان ساز

turned off adj گل

turning (return) n برگشت

turning in (submission) n تقدیم

turning to (for recourse) n متوسل

turnip n شلغم

turquoise n پیروزه • فیروزه

turret n برجک

turtle n سنگ آبی

turtledove (bird) n فاخته

Turwo (dist) *n* تروو

tutor (f) *n* معلمه

tutor (rel) *n* آخوند • ملا

tutor *n* مدرس • ادیب • معلم

TV *see* television

twang (nasal) *n* غنه

tweezers (for hair) *n* موی چینک

twelfth *adj* دوازدهم

→ (lit, used before n) دوازدهمین

twelve *adj, n* دوازده

twelve *n* اثناعشر

Twelver (rel) (& pers) *adj, n* اثناعشری • شیعی

twentieth *adj* بیستم

→ (lit, used before n) بیستمین

twenty *adj, n* بیست

twenty-first *adj* بیست و یکم

twenty-one *adj, n* بیست و یک

twice *adv* دو باره • دو دفعه

twice *see* & again

twig (of tree) *n* شاخه • شاخچه

twig (wicker) *n* خمچه

twilight *n* شفق

twin (arch) *n* دو پیکر • جوزا

twin *n* دو گانه گی

twinkle (eyes) *v* چشمک زدن

twinkle (in eyes) *n* چشمک

twist *n* پیچ

→ road full of twists & turns راه پر پیچ و خم

twist *vt* پیچاندن

twitch *vi* پریدن

two *adj, n* دو

→ in twos (arch) دوگان

→ two (sth) ago پرار

→ two years ago پرار سال

→ it takes two to tango (prov) از یک دست صدا نمیآیه

twofold *adj, adv* دوقات • دوقاته • دولا

two-ply *see* twofold

two-story (house) *adj* دو منزله

type *n* جنس • نوع • قبیل • قماش • رقم

→ of the same type همرنگ

typhoid *n* محرقه • تیفوید

typhoon *n* طوفان بحری

typhus *n* تیفوس

→ spotted fever (type of typhus) حمای لکه دار

typo (error) *n* غلطی چاپی • غلطی طباعتی

typography *n* چاپ حروفی • چاپ سربی • طبع حروفی

tyranny *n* ستم • بیداد • جور • ظلم

→ دست اندازی • دست درازی • فرعونی

tyrant *n* مستبد • دست انداز

→ (pharaoh) فرعون

U

U.S. *see* United States

U.S. Agency for International Development *see* USAID

ud (mus instr) *n* عود

udder *n* پستان

ugly (deformed) *adj* بد شکل

→ ugly & coarse man (fig) زخ • بلوط

ugly *adj* بدرنگ • زشت • کریه

UK *see* United Kingdom

ulama (rel scholars) *n pl* علما

→ the progressive mullahs علمای منور

Ulan Bator *n* اولن باتور

ulcer *n* قرحه • قرح

→ (of stomach) قرحه معده

ulna (anat) *n* زند

ultimate (final) *adj* آخر • آخری

ultraviolet *adj* ماورای بنفش

ululate *v* با صدای بلند زاری کردن

Umarzai *see* Omarzai

Umayyads, the (hist, dynasty 656-1492 A.D.) *n* بنو امیه

umbilical cord *n* بند ناف • ناف

umbrella *n* چتری

Umma (rel) *n* امه

UN (United Nations) *n* ملل متحد

Unaba (dist, alt Anaba) *n* انابه

unable *adj* قاصر

unacceptable *adj* غیر قابل قبول

→ (unreasonable) غیر موجه

UNAMA *n* یوناما

unanimity *n* همنوایی • هم آوازی

539

unanimous *adj* • همنوا • هم آواز •
یک زبان
unattractive *adj* بی قواره
unattractive *see* & ugly
unavoidable *adj* اجتناب ناپذیر •
غیر قابل اجتناب
unaware (& pers) *adj, n* غافل
unbearable *adj* طاقت فرسا
unbelief (rel) *n* کفر
unbeliever (rel) *n* کافر • بی دین
uncertain (doubtful) *adj* مشکوک
uncertain (undecided) *adj* دو دل
uncertainty (doubt) *n* شک
uncertainty (indecision) *n* دو دلی
uncircumcised (& pers) *adj, n*
نابرید
unclassified (document) *adj* غیر
محرم
uncle
→ father's brother • کاکا • اودر •
عمو
→ father's brother (lit) عم
→ mother's brother • خال • ماما
→ mother's brother (arch) • خال
ماما
unclean after intercourse or wet
dream (rel) *adj* جنب
unclean state after intercourse or
wet dream *n* جنابت
→ (required ablution) غسل جنابت
unclear (confused) *adj* سردرگم
uncommon *adj* نادر
unconcerned *adj* بی پروا
unconditional *adj* فاقد شرایط •
بدون قید و شرط
unconfirmed *adj* تایید ناشده
unconscious *adj* بی خود
→ become unconscious از خود
رفتن • بی خود شدن
uncontrollable *adj* یاغی • باغی
uncorroborated *adj* تایید ناشده
uncouth *adj* فاقد تهذیب
uncovered (bareheaded) *adj* برهنه
سر
uncovered (f w/o veil) *n* روی لچ
undecided *adj* بر سر دوراهی • دو
دل
under *prep* زیر • در زیر • تحت •
ماتحت • در ذیل
540

underarm *n* زیر بغل
underclothes *n* زیرجامه
underdeveloped *adj* • پس مانده •
عقب افتاده
→ be underdeveloped عقب افتادن
• پس ماندن
underived (gram) *adj* جامد
undershirt *n* زیرپیراهنی • عرق
گیر
understand *vt* فهمیدن
→ make (sb) understand فهماندن
understanding (acceptance) *n*
هضم
understanding (agreement) *n* تفاهم
understanding (comprehending)
adj احاطه
understanding (comprehension) *n*
فهم
understanding (insight) *n* بصیرت
• بصارت
understanding (realization) *n* درک
• ادراک
understood *adj* مستفاد
underwear *n* زیرپوش
underwear (m's) *n* سلدراج
underwrite (insure) *vt* بیمه کردن
underwriter (insurer) *n* بیمه کننده
undoubtedly *adj* بیشک • بیشک و
شبهه • بیشک و ریب
undress *vi* • لچ شدن • برهنه شدن •
برهنه کردن
undress *vt* برهنه ساختن
uneconomical *adj* غیر اقصادی
uneducated (ignorant) *adj* • جاهل
نادان • نافهم
unemployed (fired) *adj* سبک دوش
unemployed *adj* بیکار
unemployment *n* • بیکاری • سبک
دوشی
unenthusiastic *adj* بی حمیت
UNESCO *n* یونسکو
unexpected *adj* • غیر مترقب • غیر
مترقبه
unexploded ordnance *see* UXO
unfaithful *adj* نمک حرام
unfettered *adj* • بی زولانه • آزاد
unfinished *adj* نیم کاره
unforeseen *adj* • ناگهان • ناگهانی •
ناگاه • ناگاهان

unfortunate (& pers) adj, n سیاه بخش • بد بخش • تیره بخت • نگون بخت

unfortunate (star-crossed) (& pers) adj, n فلک زده

unfortunate adj • برگشته بخت بخت برگشته

unfortunately adv • بدبختانه متأسفانه • با تأسف

unfriendly (slow to make friends) adj دیر آشنا

unfriendly see & hostile

ungrateful adj ناسپاس

unhappy (displeased) (& pers) adj, n خاطر گرفته • گرفته خاطر

unhappy (sad) adj • غمگین اندوهگین • حزین • مفمون • ناخوش

UNHCR n کمشنری عالی سازمان ملل متحد در امور پناهنده گان

unhealthy adj ناجور • مریض • ناخوش • غیر صحی

UNICEF n یونیسف

uniform (identical) adj • یک سان متحد الشکل

uniform (mil) n یونیفورم • یونیفارم

uniform (professional) n دریشی

uniformity n یک سانی

unify vt اتحاد کردن

unilateral (& adv) adj, adv یک جانبه • یک طرفه

unintentional adj بی قصد

unintentionally adv بی قصد • سهواً

uninvited adj ناخوانده • سرباری

union (& labor) n اتحادیه

union (matrimony) n وصلت

unique adj یگانه • وحد • یکتا • خاص • مخصوص

unit (& mil) n قطعه • جزوتام

unit (artillery) n میل

unit (blanket) n تخته

unit (book) n جلد

unit (carpet) n تخته

unit (circular object) n حلقه

unit (clothing) n ثوب
→ one uniform یک ثوب دریشی

unit (hide) n جلد

unit (merchandise) n دانه • تا • عدد

unit (quantity) n واحد
→ unit of measurement واحد قیاسی

unit (ship, plane) n فروند

unit (soldier) n قوه

unit (sword) n قبضه
→ two swords دو قبضهٔ شمشیر

unit (telephone) n پایه

unit (timepiece) n قاب

unit (vehicle) n عراده

unit (watermill) n حجر

unite vt اتحاد کردن
→ unite in matrimony وصلت کردن

united adj متحد • متحده

United Arab Emirates n امارات متحده • الامارات العربیه المتحده

United Front (pol party) n جبهه متحد

United Kingdom n شاهی متحد

United Kingdom see & Britain

United Nations see UN

United Nations Assistance Mission in Afghanistan see UNAMA

United Nations Educational, Scientific & Cultural Organization see UNESCO

United Nations High Commissioner for Refugees see UNHCR

United Nations International Children's Emergency Fund see UNICEF

United Nations Security Council Resolution see UNSCR

United States n ایالات متحده • امریکا

unity (accord) n وحدت

unity (agreement) n اتفاق

unity n اتفاق • اتحاد

unity of God (doctrine) n توحید

universal adj جامعی

universal joint n یونیورسل • نیورسل

universality n جامعیت

universe n جهان • عالم • کیهان
→ (the Creation) خلقت

university n پوهنتون
→ university department فاکولته

unjust (cruel) adj ظالم

541

unjust *adj* ناحق
unkempt *adj* مشوش
unknowingly *adv* نادانسته • ندانسته
Unknown Soldier *n* سپاهی گم نام
unleavened *adj* فطیر
unless *conj* الا • الا آن که • جز •
جز آن که • به جز • مگر • مگر آن
که
unlimited *adj* مطلق
unload *vt* خالی کردن • تخلیه کردن
unlucky *see* unfortunate
unmanly *adj* نامردانه وار
unmanly *see* & cowardly
unmarriageable relative (Musl law)
n محرم
unmarried *adj* مجرد
unobtainable *adj* نایاب
unpaved (dirt) *adj* خامه
unpleasant (& depressing) *adj* سرد
• خنک • یخ
unpleasant (pers) *adj* بد قهر •
ناگوار • ناخوش • سرد • خنک •
یخ
unpleasant (sordid) *adj* زشت
unreal (illusory) *adj* مجازی
unreality (illusion) *n* مجاز
unreasonable *adj* غیر موجه
unrecompensable *adj* جبران ناپذیر
unripe *adj* نارس • نارسیده
unsaid *adj* مسکوت
unsaleable (goods) *adj* بازار زده •
بیع زده
UNSCR *n* فیصله نامهٔ شورای
امنیتِ ملل متحد
unscrew *v* پیچک کشیدن
unshaven *adj* رسیده
→ unshaven man آدم رسیده
unskilled *adj* بی مهارت
unskillful *n* خام کار
unsociable *adj* بد گذاران • بد گذاره
unspeakable *adj* مگو
unstable (fragile) *adj* خلل پذیر
unstable (shaky) *adj* متزلزل • بی
ثبات
unsteady *adj* لرزنک • بی ثبات
unsubstantiated *adj* عاری از
حقیقت
unsuccessful *adj* ناکام
untie *vt* باز کردن
542

until *adv* تا • تا که • الی
until now *adv* تا حالا • تا حالی • تا
اکنون • تا کنون
untimely death *n* جوان مرگی
unusual (extraordinary) *adj* غیر
معمول
unusual (not customary) *adj* خارق
عادت • خارق العاده
unutterable *adj* مگو
unwilling (& adv) *adj, adv* دل ناخواه
unwilling *adj* نه خواسته
unwise *adj* نادان
unwise *see* & foolish
unwrap *vt* گشودن
up *adv* بالا • بلند
uphill *adj, adv* سربالا
upper *adj* بالا • فوقانی
→ upper body بالا تنه
uprising *n* قیام • اغتشاش
uproar *n* هنگامه • قیل و قال •
قالمقال • غالمغال • طوفان انقلابی
upset (agitated) *adj* سرخ شده
→ be upset سرخ شدن
→ get upset سرخ شدن • دماغ
سوختن • جلالی شدن
upset <sb> *vt* سرخ کردن <کسی
را>
upshot (outcome) *n* عاقبت •
ماحصل
upside-down *adj* چیه شده
upside-down *adj* واژگون •
واژگونه • واژون • معکوس • نگون
• سرنگون
upstairs *n* منزل بالا • طبقه بالا
→ upstairs room بالا خانه
upstart *n* تازه به دوران رسیده • نو
به دولت رسیده • نو کیسه • نادیدگی
• آدم نادیده
upward *adv* سربالا
uranium *n* یورانیم • یورانیوم •
اورانیوم
Uranus (planet) *n* اورانوس
urbane *adj* انسان
urbanity *n* مدنیت
Urdu (lang) *n* اردو
Urfi (16th-c Dari poet) *n* عرفی •
جمال الدین محمد
urge (drive) *vt* راندن
urgency *n* ضرورت

urgent *adj* فوری • عاجل
Urgun (dist) *n* ارگون
urinate *v* پیشاب کردن • شاش کردن
کردن
urine *n* • شاشه • شاش • ادرار
• پیش آب • شاشی
(fig) ← جواب چای
urology *n* یورولوژی
Ursa Major (constellation) *phrs* بنات النعش
Uruzgan (province) *n* • اورزگان اروزگان
us *pron* ما را
usable *adj* قابل • قابل استعمال استفاده
usage *n* رسم
USAID *n* اداره انکشافی امریکا
use (exploit) <sth> *vt* استفاده کردن • کار گرفتن <از چیزی>
use (exploitation) <of sth> *n* استفاده <از چیزی>
use (utilization) *n* استعمال • اعمال • اطلاق
use (utilize) <sth> *v* استعمال کردن <چیزی را> • مستفید شدن <از چیزی>
use up *vt* تمام کردن
used to *adj* آموخته
← be used to عادت کردن
used up *adj* پیش خور
useful *adj* کارآمد • کارروا • مفید • نتیجه بخش
useful (profitable) *adj* • سودمند • مفید • نافع
useless *adj* ناکاره • بی فایده
useless (absurd) *adj* چتی
useless (pointless) *adj* • بی فایده • نافرجام
using (utilizing) <sth> *adj* مستفید <از چیزی>
Usman (hist, caliph) *n* عثمان
USSR (hist) (colloq) *n* شوروی
usual (customary) *adj* معمول
usual (predominant) *adj* غالب
← as usual • کماکان • کم از کم همچنین
usually (customarily) *adv* معمولاً
usually (most often) *adv* غالباً
usurer *n* سودخوار

usurious *adj* سودخور
usurper (of ruler) *adj, n* غاصب
usury (excessive interest) *n* ربا • ربح • سود
usury (practice) *n* • سودخوری • سودخواری
utensil (for serving rice) *n* کفچه
utensils (tools) *n* سامان
uterus (anat) *n* رحم • زهدان
utilize *see* use
utopian (fig) *adj* خیالی
utter (exclaim) *v* بر زبان راندن
utterly *adv* کاملاً • به کلی • بالکل
UV (ultraviolet) *adj* ماورای بنفش
uvula (anat) *n* ملاج • ملاز • ملازه • ملاژه
(colloq) ← کچکک
UXO *n* مواد منفجرناشده
Uzbek (lang) *n* اوزبکی
Uzbek (pers) *n* اوزبک
Uzbekistan *n* اوزبکستان

V

vacant *adj* خالی
vacate *vt* خالی کردن • تخلیه کردن
vacation *n* رخصتی • تعطیل
vaccinate *see* & inject
vaccinate against smallpox *vt* خال زدن • خال کردن
vaccination against smallpox *n* آبله کوبی • خال کوبی
vaccination *n* تطبیق واکسین • واکسینیشن
vaccination *see* & injection
vaccine *n* واکسین
vacillate *v* نوسان کردن • در نوسان بودن
vacillation *n* نوسان
vacuum (void) *n* خلا • خلاء
vacuum cleaner *n* جاروی برقی
vagina *n* مهبل • فرج
(fig) ← شرم گاه زن
(obs) ← کس
vaginal *adj* مهبلی
vagrant *adj* در به در
vagrant *n* آواره • آواره گرد • بیجاشده

vague *adj* مبهم

vain *see* & conceited

vain *see* & useless

→ in vain به رایگان

→ vain effort تحصیل حاصل

valley *n* دره • وادی

valor (arch) *n* بهرامی

valor *n* رشادت

valor *see* & bravery

valuable *adj* گران • قیمت

valuables *n pl* اموال قیمتی

value *n* قیمت • ارزش • حسب •
بها

valve *n* وال

vandal *n* تخریب کار • خراب کار

vandalism *n* تخریب کاری • خراب
کاری

vanguard *n* پیش قراول

vanilla *n* وانیلا

vanish *vi* غیب شدن

vanishing • نابودی • اضمحلال

vanity *n* غرور • کلان کاری

vanity *see* & conceit

vanquish *vt* مغلوب کردن

→ (lit) هزیمت دادن

vanquished *adj* مغلوب

→ (& pers) هزیمتی

→ vanquisher of infidels غازی

vanquishing (God) *adj* قهار

vapor *n* بخار

variety (diversity) *n* تنوع

variety *see* & type

various *adj* مختلف • متفاوت • ناهم
گون

variously *adv* از اختلاف

vault (archit) *n* گنبد • کمان

veal *n* گوشت گوساله

vector (med) *n* ناقل

Veda (rel) *n* ویدا

→ Rig-Veda ریگویدا

Vedic (rel) *adj* ویدایی

vegetable (green) *n* سبزی

→ vegetables ترکاری

vegetation (plants) *n* نباتات

vehicle *see* unit (vehicle)

→ vehicles وسایط

veil *n* پرده • حجاب • برقع • روی
بند • نقاب

vein *n* ورید • سیاه رگ • رگ

544

velocity *n* سرعت • تیزی

velvet *n* مخمل

→ (colloq) بخمل

venal (corrupt) *adj* حرام خور

venality (corruption) *n* حرام خوری

vendor (on street) *n* فروشنده

→ street vendor's tray • مجمعه
سینی

venerable (honored) *adj* مکرم

venerable (sacred) *adj* مقدس

venerate *vt* پرستش کردن • عبادت
کردن

veneration *n* پرستش • عبادت •
نیایش

venereal *adj* تناسلی • مقاربتی •
جنسی • زهره وی

vengeance *n* انتقام

→ (for murder) خون خواهی

venom *n* سم • زهر

vent *n* هوا کش

ventilation *n* تهیه

ventilation system *n* روباه خانه

ventilator *n* دستگاه تهیه

venture (firm) *n* شرکت • کمپنی

→ joint venture شرکت مختلط

Venus (planet) *n* ناهید • زهره •
ونوس

veranda *n* رواق • ایوان

verb (gram) *n* فعل

→ auxiliary verb فعل معاونت

verbal (oral) *adj* زبانی • شفاهی

verbal adjective *n* صفت مفعولی

verbal noun *n* اسم مفعولی • صفت
مفعولی

verbena (plant) *n* شاه پسند • بربینه

verbose (pedantic) *adj* لفاظ

verbosity *n* اطناب • دراز نویسی

verbosity (pedantry) *n* لفاظی

verdant *adj* سرسبز

verdict *n* قضاوت

verdigris (color) *adj* زنگار

verdure *n* سر سبزی

vermilion (color) *adj* شنگرف

vermin *n pl* حشرات

vernal *adj* بهاری

→ vernal equinox اعتدال بهاری

verse *n* شعر • نشیده

verse (Quranic) *n* آیت • آیه

vertebra (anat) *n* مهره

vertebral *adj* نخاعی
vertebrate *adj* فقاریه
vertical *adj* عمودی • قایم
vertigo *n* دوران سر
very *adv* • بسیار • خیلی • به غایت • نهایت
vessel (receptacle) *n* ظرف
→ (for flour, grain) کندو
→ (earthen, for liquids) خم • چاتی
→ (earthen, for milk/yogurt) خمره
→ (earthen) خمبک • چاتی
vessel (ship) *n* سفینه • کشتی
vest *n* واسکت
→ sheepskin vest پوستینچه
vet (screen) *v* طی مراحل کردن
vetch (beans) *n* ماش
veterinarian *n* بیطار
veterinary *adj* بیطاری
vetting (screening) *n* طی مراحل
via *adv* از طریق • از راه • توسط • به توسط • به وسیله
viability *n* بازتوانی
vibrate *v* ارتعاش داشتن
vibrating *adj* لرزانک
vibration *n* ارتعاش • لرزش
vice (depravity) *n* رذیلت
vice (esp sexual) *n* فساد
vice versa *adv* بالعکس • به عکس • بر عکس
vice-regent (arch) *n* مرزبان
vicissitudes of the world *n* روزگار • زمانه • لیل و نهار
victim *n* قربانی
→ murder victim مقتول • قتیل • کشته
victorious *adj* برنده • مظفر • ظفرمند • پیروز • پیروزمند • فیروز • فیروزمند • فاتح • فاتحانه
victoriously *adv* فاتحانه
victory *n* برد
victory *see &* triumph
video camera *n* کمره ویدیویی
video recording *n* فلم برداری ویدیویی
videotape *vt* فلم گیری ویدیویی کردن
Vienna *n* ویانا
Vientiane *n* وینتیان
Vietnam *n* ویتنام

Vietnamese (& lang, pers) *adj, n* ویتنامی
view (vista) *n* منظره
→ from this view از این نگاه
→ in view of نظر به
viewing (observation) *v* مشاهده
viewpoint *n* درک
vigor *n* جوانی
vigorous (young) *adj* جوان
vigorous *adj* قوتمند • قدرتمند
vilayet *see* province
vile *n* زار
vilify (colloq) *vt* گپ ساختن
village *n* قریه • ده • روستا • قشلاق
→ large village قصبه
village chief *n* قریه دار
village square *n* میدان قریه
villager *n* دهکی • روستایی • روستا زاده • قشلاقی
villainous *adj* شیطانت آمیز • شیطانت بار
villainy *n* شیطانت
vindictive *adj* شتر کینه
vine (for vegetables) *n* بیاره
vinegar *n* سرکه
vineyard *n* باغ انگور • انگورباغ • تاکستان • تاک باغ
violation *n* نقض • تخطی
violence *n* خشونت • عنف • اختناق
violent (harsh) *adj* شدید
violently *adv* به عنف
violet (& color) *adj, n* بنفش
virgin *n* دوشیزه • عذرا
virgin (houri) *n* حوری • حور
virgin (only Mary & Fatima) *n* بتول
virginal *adj* عذرا • بتول
virginity (of f) *n* دختری • دوشیزگی • بکارت
Virgo (zodiac) *n* سنبله
virile *adj* نر
virility *n* باه
virtue *n* خاصیت
→ virtues اخلاق
virtuous *n* صالح
virus *n* ویروس
visa *n* ویزه
→ fiancé(e) visa ویزه نامزدی
→ student visa ویزه تحصیلی

viscous (thick) adj • غلیظ • تیره
visible adj مرئی
→ be visible معلوم شدن
vision (image) n خیال
vision (plan) n دیدگاه
vision (sight) n بصیرت • بصارت • نظر
visit n دیدار • بازدید
→ (formal) زیارت
visit v دیدن • دیدن کردن • باز دید کردن
→ visit for a long time بستره انداختن
visitor (pilgrim) n زایر
visitor n مهمان
→ visitor to prisoner پای واز
visor (of helmet) n نقاب • حجاب
vista n منظره
vital (needed) adj لازم • لازمی
vitriol (blue) n زاج کبود
vitriol (chem) n زاج
vitriol (green) n زاج سبز
vitriol (white) n زاج سفید
vizier (minister) n وزیر
vocal adj صوتی • اوازی • حنجره وی
→ vocal cords رشته های صوتی
vocal see & outspoken, frank
vocalic adj صدایتی
vocation n مسلک • حرفه
vocation see & craft, industry
vocational adj مسلکی • حرفه یی
vogue n مود
voice n صدا • صوت • اواز
→ (fig) حنجره
→ voice of the people آواز مردم • صدای مردم
voiced (consonant) adj صدا دار • طنین دار • با آوا • مصوت
voiceless (consonant) adj بیصدا
volcano n آتش فشان
volley (artillery) n فیر • آتش باری
voltage n ولتیج • ولتاژ
volume (contents) n محتویات • مندرجات
volume (loudness) n بلندی
volume (of book) n جلد
voluntarily adv بالاراده • داوطلبانه
voluntary adj اختیاری • داوطلبانه

volunteer adj داوطلبانه
volunteer n داوطلب • رضا کار
volunteer vi داوطلب شدن • داوطلب بودن
voluptuous young f (fig) n حوری
vomit n قی
vomit v قی کردن • استفراغ کردن
→ (colloq) دل بد شدن • استفراق کردن • شکوفه کردن
vote n رای
vote v رای دادن
voter n رای دهنده
voting adj رای دهنده
votive offering (cash gift) n نذر
vow n تعهد • عهد • وعده • پیمان
vowel n صایت • مصوت • واؤل
vulgar adj زشت گوی
→ (fig) بازاری
vulnerable adj آسیب پذیر
vulture n کرگس
vulva (anat) n شرم گاه زن

W

wage (remuneration) n • معاش • مزد • دست مزد • تنخواه • اجوره • اجرت • دست رنج
→ advance wages معاش پیشکی
→ pay wages تنخواه دادن
→ return of surplus wages بازگشت
Waez Shahid see Jaghatu
wage (war) v پرداختن
→ wage jihad جهاد پرداختن
→ wage war جنگ پرداختن
wage earner (pers) n تنخواه خور
wager n قمار • شرط
wager v قمار زدن • شرط کردن
Waghaz (dist) n واغظ
Wahhabi (pers) n وهابی
Wahhabism (sect) n وهابیت
Wahid (m name) n وحید
Wahida (f name) n وحیده
wail n شیون
wail see & lament
wail v شیون کردن
waist (& of garment) n کمر
waistcoat n واسکت

wait vi انتظار کشیدن • انتظار بودن • صبر کردن
→ for sb منتظر <کسی> بودن
→ be kept waiting معطل بودن
→ make <sb> wait منتظر ماندن <کسی را> • معطل کردن
→ pers who is waiting منتظر
waiter n پیشخدمت
waiting around n منتظریت
waive (relinquish) vt درگذشتن
→ waive immunity مصونیت برآوردن
wake (service) n مجلس ترحیم
Wakhan (dist, geog) n • واخان • واخن
Wakhi (ethn grp; & pers, lang) adj, n واخی
Wali (m name) n ولی
Wali Mohamed Shahid (geog) n ولی محمد شهید
walk n چکر
walk vi به پای رفتن • راه رفتن • پیاده رفتن
→ (for pleasure) قدم زدن • هوا خوری کردن • گردش کردن • گردیدن
→ slow & graceful walk خرام
→ take a walk چکر زدن
→ walking pers رو
walkie-talkie n آله مخابره
walking stick n چوب دست • عصا
walkway n راهرو
wall n دیوال
→ (colloq) دیوار
→ dividing wall حاجز • در پرده
→ straw & mud for surfacing walls کاه گل
wallet n بکس جیبی
walnut n چارمغز
Wama (dist) n واما
wanderer n کوچه گرد • کوچه گشت
wandering (errant) adj سرگردان • سرگشته
wandering n کوچه گردی • کوچه گشتی
want <& + subj> v خواستن
wanton adj کوچه گرد • کوچه گشت

wantonness n کوچه گردی • کوچه گشتی
waqf (charity) n وقف
→ (colloq) وخم
→ deed to waqf's endowment وقف نامه
→ plant fruit trees for the waqf وقف نشاندن • وخم شاندن
war n جنگ • حرب • محاربه • پیکار • رزم
→ (lit) نبرد
→ fitna (Musl civil war) فتنه
→ foment war جنگ انداختن
→ wage war جنگ پرداختن
→ war against infidels غزا • جهاد
→ war narrative (Jangnama) جنگ نامه
→ War on Terror مبارزه علیه تروریزم
war (wage war) vi • جنگ کردن • حرب کردن
Waras (dist) n وارس • ورس
Wardak (province, P tribe) n وردک
wardrobe n الماری
Warduj (dist) n وردوج
warehouse n تحویل خانه • گدام
→ commercial warehouse سرای
warehouse keeper n تحویل دار
wares see goods, merchandise
warfare n محاربه
wariness n احتراز
warlike adj جنگی
warlord n سالار جنگ • جنگ سالار
warm adj گرم
warm-blooded adj خون گرم
warn vt هشدار دادن • هوشدار دادن • اخطار دادن <به کسی>
warning n اخطار • هشدار
→ (written) اخطاریه
warp (in weaving) n تنسته
warp (of wood) n تاب
warranty n تضمین
warrior (champion) n پهلو
warrior (holy) n مجاهد
warrior (valiant) n قهرمان
warrior (vanquisher of infidels) n غازی

warrior *see* & fighter, soldier

Warsaj (dist) *n* ورسج

Warsaw *n* وارسا

wart *n* زخ

warthog *n* خوک وحشی

wary *see* & cautious

→ be wary *vi* احتراز کردن

wash (& clothes) *vt* • شوی کردن
شستن

wash (body) *v* غسل کردن

washbasin (brass, copper) *n* لگن

washbowl تشت

washed away *adj* ششته

washer (of dead) *n* • مرده شوی
غسال

washer (small disc) *n* واشل

Washir (dist) *n* واشیر

washing *n* شست و شو • شست و
شوی

washing machine (for clothes) *n*
ماشین کالا شوی

Washington (capital, state) *n*
واشنگتن

Wasim (m name) *n* وسیم

wasp *n* زنبور

→ wasp's nest خانه • زنبور خانه
زنبور

wastage *n* ضایعه

waste (for throwing away) *adj*
باطله

waste *vt* خاک و دود کردن

waste (time, effort) *vt* ضایع کردن

→ waste time باد پیمودن • باد
پیمانه کردن

→ waste money پول به هوا
انداختن

waste paper *n* کاغذ باطله

wastebasket *n* باطله دانی

wasted *adj* ضایع

wasteland *n* بیابان • بادیه • صحرا

wastepaper *n* کاغذ باطله

wasting (spoiling) *n* تضییع

Watapur (dist) *n* وته پور • وتپور

watch (& TV) *v* سیر کردن

watch (clock) *n* ساعت

watch (guard) *n* پهره

→ stand watch پهره کردن • پهره
دادن • پهره داری کردن

watch (guard) *vt* نگاه کردن

watch (shift, & mil) *n* پاس

watchful *adj* برحذر

watching (guarding) *n* نگاه • نگه •
پاسبانی • محافظت

watching (observation) *adj* مراقب
• محافظ

watchman (guard) *n* •
پاسبان • نگاهبان • نگهبان

→ (bazaar, warehouse) چوکی دار

water *n* آب

→ soda water سودا واتر

water bottle *n* بوتل آب

water flask *n* بتک

water lily *n* نیلوفر آبی

water pipe *n* چلم

water pump *n* واتر پمپ

watercourse *n* مسیر

water-diverting *adj* آب گردان

watered (fabric) *adj* موج دار

waterfall *n* آبشار

watermelon *n* تربوز

waterway *n* آبرو

watery *adj* آبگین

watt *n* شمعه

wave *n* موج • موجه

waver *v* نوسان کردن • در نوسان
بودن

wavering *n* نوسان

wavy *adj* موج دار

wax *adj* مومی

wax *n* موم • شمع

wax paper *n* موم جامه

way (course) *n* • راه • طریق •
طریقه • صراط • اسلوب • نحو •
گونه

→ on the way راهی • رهی

way (manner) *n* • طور • طرز •
رویه • روش • شیوه • گونه • نحو •
وجه

→ in every way هرکدامشه

→ in this way به این ترتیب

Waygal (dist, valley) *n* وایگل

wayward *adj* سرگردان • سرگشته

Waza Kha (dist) *n* وازه خوا

Wazir (P tribe) *n* وزیر • وزیری

Wazir Akbar Khan Mena (Kabul
city dist) *n* وزیر اکبر خان مینه

we *pron* ما

548

weak (& pers) adj, n • ضعیف •
عاجز • خفیف • سست • نحیف •
نزار
weak (in color) adj کمرنگ
weak (neg) adj زار
weak (powerless) adj ناتوان
weaken n ضعیف ساختن • ضعیف
کردن • تضعیف کردن
weakening n تضعیف
weakness (of character) n عیب
wealth (affluence) n بضاعت
wealth (capital) n سرمایه
wealth (fig) n برگ و بار
wealth (power) n دستگاه • دم و
دستگاه
wealth (riches) n • ثروت • تمول
دارایی • غنا
wealthy (& pers) adj, n متمول
wealthy (blessed) (& pers) adj, n
خدا داده
wealthy adj • پولدار • پیسه دار •
غنی • دارا • دولتمند • دولت دار
wealthy pers (benefactor) n منعم
weapon n سلاح
weaponry n اسلحه
→ (colloq) وسله
wear (clothes) vt • پوشیدن • به تن
داشتن
→ wear out (clothes) تار تار شدن
wearisome adj کسالت آور
weasel n موش خرما
weather n آب و هوا • هوا
→ be under the weather کسالت
داشتن
weave (of carpet) n بافت
weave v بافتن • تنیدن
weaver n بافنده • جولا
→ mat weaver بوریا باف
→ mat weaving بوریا بافی
→ weaver's card شانه
weaving adj نساجی

wedding (ceremony) n • عروسی •
ازدواج • نکاح • زفاف • توی •
طوی
→ wedding night شب حنا
→ wedding party توی • طوی
→ wedding ring چله
→ newlyweds' breakfast ناشنایی
→ name of wedding song آهسته
برو
Wednesday n چهارشنبه
weed n علف هرزه • گیاه هرزه
weeding n خیشاوه
week n هفته
weekend آخر هفته
weekly adj هفته گی • هفته وار
→ weekly news magazine هفته
نامه • اخبار هفته وار
weep v گریه کردن • ندبه کردن
weeping n گریه • ندبه
weft (in weave) n پود
weigh vt سنجش کردن • سنجیدن •
وزن کردن
weighing n سنجش • وزن
weight (heaviness) n وزن
→ free weight وزن برداری
→ gain weight وزن گرفتن
→ lift weights وزن برداری کردن
→ lose weight وزن باختن
weightlifting n وزن برداری
weighty adj سنگین
weird adj عجیب و غریب
welcome excl خوش آمدین • مانده
نباشین
→ you're welcome قابل تشکر
نیست
welcome (reception) n استقبال
welcome v خیر مقدم گفتن
welcoming adj • مهمان نواز •
پیشانی باز
welcoming address n خیر مقدم
welfare see well-being
well (for water, oil) n چاه
well (nicely) adv نیکو • نکو
→ get well خوب شدن
well adv خوب • بخوبی • به خوبی
• بخیر
well-being n بهبود
well-informed adj مطلع

well-known adj • سرشناس • شهیر • مشهور • معروف • نامدار
west (& Maghreb) n مغرب
west (& Occident) n غرب
→ from the west غرباً
West Bank (geog, Palestine) n کرانه غربی رود اردن
Westerner (pers) n غربی
wet adj تر
→ get wet تر شدن
wet (damp) adj مرطوب • نمدار
wet (moisten, soak) vt تر کردن
wet dream n
→ have a wet dream محتلم شدن
→ having had a wet dream محتلم
→ unclean after wet dream جنب
→ uncleanness after wet dream جنابت
wet-nursing n ارضاع
whale n ماهی وال • وال • حوت
wharf n باراندز
what pron آنچه
what? pron چه ؟
→ (colloq) چی ؟
→ what nationality? کجایی ؟
→ what number? (ordinal) چندم ؟
whatever pron هر چه
wheat n گندم
wheat-colored adj گندمی • حبشی
wheel (tire) n تیر
→ turn of the wheel چکر
wheel (vehicle's) n عرابه
wheel n چرخ
wheeler-dealer (& pers) adj, n معامله گر
wheezy (& pers) adj, n فش فشی
when conj وقتی که • حین
→ (as soon as) به مجردی که
→ (at the moment of) به مجرد
→ (at the time of) هنگام • در وقت
→ (lit) هنگامی که
→ (on the occasion of) به مناسبت
when? adv چه وقت ؟
→ adv کی ؟
whenever adv هرگاه • هرگه
where conj جایی که
→ where & when needed در مکان و زمان ضرورت
where? pron کجا ؟ • در کجا ؟
550

whet (blade) v چرخ کردن
whether...or... conj چه ... چه ...
which pron یعنی • یعنی که • که
which? adj کدام ؟
while adv در حالی که
while conj در کنار این که ...
whine (groan) v نالش کردن
whine (nag) v نق زدن
whining (groaning) n نالش
whining (nagging) n نق
whip (flog) vt شلاق زدن
→ whip (w/in limits prescribed by Quran) حد زدن
whip (mix) vt لت زدن
whip n شلاق
whipping (as legal punishment) n جزای ضرب
whirlpool n چرخ آب • گرد آب
whirlwind n چرخ باد • گردباد • خاکباد
whiskers n بروت
whisper n پس پس
whisper v پس پس کردن
white adj سفید • ابیض
→ cream-white کریمی
→ gray- or blue-white خنگ
→ jasmine-white سمنبر
→ white pers سفید پوست
White House n قصر سفید
WHO see World Health Organization
who? pron کی • که ؟
whoever (anyone) pron هر که
whoever (someone) pron کسانی که
whole (complete) adj پوره • مجهز • مکمل
whole (entire) adj تمام • سراسر • سرتاسر
whole (total) n جمیع • مجموع
→ on the whole فی الجمله
whole adj دربست
whole n سرتاسر • • سراسر
whole number n عدد صحیح
wholesaler n عمده فروش
whole-wheat adj سبوس دار
wholly adv سرتاسر • بالکل • کلا • کاملا
whore n فاحشه • روسپی • قحبه

why? adv ؟ چرا
→ whys & wherefores چرا ها و چون ها
wick n فتیله • پلته
wicked (& pers) (black-hearted) adj, n سیاه دل
wicked (evil) adj بد • شرارت پیشه
wicked (fiendish) adj • دیوسرشت دیوسیرت
wickedness (evil) n شر
wicker adj نیین • نیی
wicker n خمچه
→ wicker basket see basket
wide (broad) adj وسیع • عریض
فراخ • پهن • بر دار
wide (loose) (clothes) adj گشاد
widen v وسعت دادن
widespread adj هموار
→ being widespread تداول
widow n بیوه • بیوه زن
→ king's widow ملکه
→ waiting period for widow to remarry (Musl law) عدت
widowhood n بیوه گی • بیوگی
width n • وسعت • عرض
پهنی • فراخی • بر
wife n خانم • زن • زوجه
→ (bedfellow) همخوابه
→ (colloq) کوچ
→ (in Hazara dialect) خاتون
→ sister-wife in Musl polygamous marriage امباغ • انباق
wig n موی عاریتی • موی ساختگی
wilayat al-faqih (Iran pol system) n ولایت الفقیح
wild adj جنگلی • وحشی
→ wild boar خوک وحشی
wilderness n جنگل • دشت
will (document) n وصیت نامه
will (volition) n قصد • اراده
willful (obstinate) adj سرتنبه
willing adj, n حاضر
willingly adv آزادانه • با آغوش باز
→ willingly or not • خواه مخواه طوعاً و کرهاً
willow (tree) n بید
→ Egyptian willow مشک بید • بید مشک

willy-nilly adv • طوعاً • خواه مخواه و کرهاً
win (victory) n برد
win v بردن
win (conquer) v فتح کردن
wind adj بادی
wind n شمال • باد
→ east/pleasant wind صبا
windmill n آسیای بادی
window n کلکین
→ window (small) دریچه
window-shop v سیر کردن
windpipe (anat) n قصبت الریه
windy adj باد خیز
wine (arch) n خمر • باده • می
→ (loosely) شراب
→ bowl for drinking wine (lit) ساغر
→ wine-flavored (loosely) میخوش
wine seller (arch) n خمار
wineglass (lit) n پیاله • پیمانه
wineskin n مشک
wing (air force) n غند
wing (bird's) n جناح • بال
wink n چشمک
wink v چشمک زدن • پلکک زدن
winking (meaningfully) n اشاره
→ چشم • اشاره کنج چشم
winner n برنده
winning adj برنده
winter adj زمستانی • شتایی
winter n زمستان • شتا
winter solstice n یلدا
wire (cable) n سیم • لین
wisdom n عقل • حکمت • خرد • بخردی
→ limited wisdom عقل قاصر
wise (& pers) adj, n عاقل • خردمند • بخرد • هوشیار
wise man (hist, mediator) n حکم
wish n خواهش • خواسته • امید • آرزو • امل • نیاز
→ as you wish مطابق خواهش شما
→ I wish that <+ past subj> • کاش کاش که • کاشکی
wish v خواستن • امید کردن • امید داشتن
wishbone n چناق
wishful (& pers) adj, n خواهشمند
wit (repartee) n حاضر جوابی

551

witch *n* ساحره • زن جادوگر

with *prep* با • همراه

→ (colloq) کتی

withdraw (extract) *vt* بیرون کردن

withdraw (retreat) (mil) *vi* عقب نشینی کردن • عقب نشستن

withdrawal (retreat) (mil) *n* عقب نشینی

wither *v* پژمردن

within (during) *prep* در • ظرف • ظرف

within (inside) *prep* از مابین • مابین • در مابین

without friend or home *adj* بی کس و کوی

without *prep* بی • بدون

withstand *v* مقاومت کردن • مقاومت نشان دادن

witness *n* شاهد • گواه

witty (skilled at repartee) *adj* حاضر جواب

wizard *n* ساحر • افسونگر • جادوگر

woad (plant) *n* وسمه

Wolesi Jirga (pol) *n* ولسی جرگه

wolf *n* گرگ

woman *n* زن • عورت

→ (fig) پرده نشین

womanhood *n* زنی

womb (anat) *n* زهدان • رحم

→ (colloq) شکم • معده

wonder (marvel) *n* قیامت

→ (dim) نغزک

wood *n* چوب

→ firewood چوب سوخت

→ wood charcoal زغال چوب

woodcarving *n* چوب کاری • کندن کاری روی چوب

woodpecker *n* دار کوب • نجارک

wool *adj see* woolen

wool *n* پشم

→ cheviot سرج

woolen *adj* پشمی • پشمین

word *n* لغت • لفظ • کلمه • واژه

→ word & deed قول و عمل

→ word for word لفظ به لفظ • کلمه به کلمه

→ Word of God کلام الله

→ word of honor قول شرف

552

word *v* عبارت ساختن

wordiness *n* اطناب • دراز نویسی • عبارت پردازی • عبارت آرایی • داستان پردازی

wording (phrasing) *n* جمله بندی • عبارت سازی • تعبیر • متن

work (& employment) *n* کار

work (oeuvre) *n* اثر

work (published) *n* تالیف

work (toil) *n* رنج

→ at work سر کار

→ go to work سر کار رفتن

→ hard work (fig) توپ کشی

work *v* کار کردن

work briefly (not very hard) *v* نول زدن

work out (lift weights) *v* وزن برداری کردن

worker (employee) *n* دست اندر کار

worker (laborer) *n* کارگر

workmanship *n* صنعت • صناعت

workplace *n* محل کار

workshop *n* ورکشاپ • کارخانه

→ leather workshop چرمگری

world *n* جهان • دنیا • عالم • کیهان • گیهان • گیتی

→ (fig) ازرق • دارالفنا • دارالمکافات

world (material, secular) *n* دهر • ناسوت

→ worldly freethinker دهری

→ vicissitudes of the world روزگار • زمانه • لیل و نهار

World Bank *n* بانک جهانی

world conqueror *n* جهان گشا

World Health Organization *n* سازمان صحی جهان

worldly *adj* جهانی • دنیایی

worm *n* کرم

worn out (clothes) *adj* ژنده

worn out *adj* مندرس • فرسوده • کهنه

worried *adj* نگران • پریشان • مشوش

worry *n* تشویش

worry <about sth> *vi* نگرانی داشتن • پروا داشتن ‹راجع به چیزی›

→ stop worrying *vi* جمع شدن

worse *adj* بدتر

worsen *vi* بدتر شدن

worship (& idolatry) *n* • پرستش
نیایش

worship (rel service) *n* عبادت

worship (in rel service) *v* عبادت
کردن

worship (idolize) *vt* پرستش کردن

worshiper *n* • عابد پرست

→ fire worshiper (Zor) آتش پرست

→ worshiper of stars & planets
افلاکی

worthiness *n* لیاقت

worthless *adj* • خراب • بی قیمت
ناچیز

worthy *adj* • لایق • ماهر • سزا •
چابکدست

worthy of <sth> *adj* قابل <چیزی>

→ worthy of father's name خلف

would that <+ past subj> *adv* کاش
• کاش که • کاشکی

wound *n* • زخم • ریش • جراحت

wounded (& pers) *adj, n* • زخمی •
افگار • مجروح • ریش

→ (colloq) اوگار

wow *excl* • واه واه • په • په • پهه

wow (strange) *excl* شگفتا

wrangle *v* پرخاش کردن

wrangling *n* پرخاش

wrap *vt* پیچاندن

wrapping *n* پیچ

wrath *n* • قهر • خشم • غضب • غیظ

wrench (tool) *n* رنج چ

→ adjustable wrench اسکورنچ

wrestler *n* • پهلوان • گرد • یل

wrestling *n* پهلوانی

wretch (insult) *n* سگ

wrinkle *n* چین

wrinkle (furrow) *n* شیار

wrinkle *vi* چین خوردن

wrinkled *adj* چین خورده

wrist (anat) *n* بند دست

write *v* نوشتن

→ (colloq) نوشته کردن

writer *n* • نویسنده • نویس • مؤلف

writhe *v* پیچ و تاب خوردن

writing *n* • نگارش • نوشتن

writing down *n* درج

written (formally styled) *adj* نوشته

written (recorded) *adj* • مکتوب •
کتبی • تحریری

written *adj* نویس

written <by sb> *adj* قلم <کسی>

→ what's wrong? چی شده ؟

Wur Mamay (dist) *n* • ور ممی • ور
ممای

Wuza Jadran (dist) *n* وزه جدران

X

X mark (marks mistake) *n* چلیپا

xenophile *n* بیگانه پرست

xenophilous *adj* بیگانه پرست

Y

Yaftal-e Sufla (dist) *n* • یفتل سفلی
یفتل

Yahya (m name) *n* یحیی

Yahya Kheyl (dist) *n* یحیی خیل

yak *n* غژگاو

yak's tail *n* پرچم

Yakawlang (dist) *n* یکاولنگ

Yamgan (dist) *n* یمگان

Yangi Qala (dist) *n* ینگی قلعه

yard (courtyard) *n* حویلی

yard (enclosure) *n* محوطه

yard (field) *n* چمن

Yathrib (later Medina) *n* یثرب

Yawan (dist) *n* یاوان

yawn *n* فاژه

yawn *v* فاژه کشیدن

yea (vote) *n* رای موافق

year *n* • سال • سنه

→ last year پارسال

→ last year & the year before پر
و پرار سال

→ last year's پرساله

→ this year امسال

→ the year before last پرار سال

yeast *n* • مایه خمیر • خمیر مایه

yellow *adj* زرد

→ chickpea yellow نخودی

→ lemon yellow لیمونی

→ saffron yellow زعفرانی

553

yelp (as dog when beaten) n چو

→ yelp v چو زدن

Yemen n يمن

yes adv بلی

→ (when answering phone) الو

yesterday adv ديروز

→ day before yesterday پريروز

→ three days ago پيش پری روز

→ three nights ago پيش پری شب

yesterday's adj ديروزی • ديروز

yet (w/neg of pres perf) adv هنوز

yield (income, product) n عملکرد •
بهره بر داری

yield (submit) v تن در دادن

yogi n جوگی • مرتاض

yogurt n ماست • جرغات

→ (colloq) ماس

→ dried yogurt ball قروت

yoke n يوغ

Yosuf (m name) n يوسف

you (informal sg) pron تو

you (pl, formal sg) pron شما

young (animal offspring) n چوچه

young adj جوان

→ young at heart تازه دل

Young Afghans (hist, 1920s) n pl
جوانان افغان

youth (pers) n جوان • برنا

youth (time of life) n سن جوانی

youth (youthfulness) n • برنایی
جوانی

Yüeh-Chih see Yuezhi

Yuezhi (hist) n يونه چی

Yugoslavia (hist, country) n
يوگوسلاويا

Yugoslavian adj يوگوسلاويايی

yurt n يورت • خرگاه

→ pitch yurt يورت زدن

Yusuf see Yosuf

Yusuf Kheyl (dist) n يوسف خيل

Yusufzai (P tribe) n يوسفزی

Z

Zabul (province) n زابل

Zachariah (bibl, m name) n زکريا

Zahir (12th-c Dari poet) n ظهير

Zahir Shah (hist, Afgh king r. 1933-
1973, d. 2007) n محمد • ظاهر شاه
ظاهر شاه

zakat (Musl law) n زکات

Zambar (ctr) n زمبار

Zana Khan (dist) n زنه خان

Zaranj (seat, dist) n زرنج

Zarathustra see Zoroaster

Zardosht see Zoroaster

Zarkharid (ctr) n زرخريد

Zarghun (m name) n زرغون

Zarghun Shahr (dist) n زرغون
شهر

Zarghuna (f name, Kabul f high
school) n زرغونه

Zari (dist) n زاری

Zarkol (lake) n زرکول

Zartosht see Zoroaster

zeal n شور • حميت • حماس •
تعصب

zealous adj با حميت • حميت مند

zebra n گوراسپ

Zechariah (bibl, m name) n زکريا

zedoary (med) n جدوار

Zenda Jan (dist) n زنده جان

zero n صفر

Zeybak (village, dist) n زيباک

Zeybaki (& pers, lang) adj, n
زيباکی

Zeywar (m name) n زيور

Zheri (dist) n ژری • ژيری

zinc n جست

→ (arch) روی

→ zinc sulfate زاج سفيد

zinnia (flower) n زنيه

Zion n صهيون

zipper n زپ

Zipporah (bibl, f name) n صفورا

Ziruk (dist) n زيروک

Zohra (f name) n زهره

zone n منطقه • ساحه • ساحت •
زون

zoo n باغ وحش

zoology n علم حيوانات • حيوان
شناسی • زولوجی

Zoroaster n زردشت • زرتشت

Zoroastrian (& pers) adj, n
زردشتی • زرتشتی • مزدايی • مغ
• آتش پرست

554

Zoroastrianism (fig, arch) *n* بهدين •
دين به
Zubayda (f name) *n* زبيده
zucchini *n* ترايى
Zulfiqar (sword) *n* ذوالفقار
Zuleyka (f name, Potiphar's wife) *n*
زليخا
zuqum (tree) *n* زقوم
Zurmal (dist, alt Zurmat) *n* زرمل
Zurmat (dist, alt Zurmal) *n* زرمت

Appendices

Provinces and Districts

Afghanistan is divided into 34 provinces, each presided over by a governor, who resides in its main city (seat). Provinces are subdivided into districts, each of which has an administrative center (ctr). Below, the name of a district is also the name of its administrative center, unless indicated otherwise. District names and boundaries have shifted often in recent years; the IDLG remains the official arbiter.

BADAKHSHAN بدخشان
Fayzabad (seat) فیض آباد
Arghanj Khwa (dist) ارغنج خواه
Argo (dist) ارگو
Baharak (dist) بهارک
Darayem (dist) داریم
Darwaz (dist, ctr Nusay) درواز
Darwaz-e Bala (dist, ctr Murch) درواز بالا
Eshkashem (dist) اشکاشم
Fayzabad (dist) فیض آباد
Girwan (dist) گیروان see Yamgan
Jurm (dist) جرم
Keran wa Munjan (dist, ctr Seykwa) کران و منجان
Keshem (dist) کشم
Keshem-e Bala کشم بالا see Tagab
Khandud خاندود see Wakhan
Khash (dist) خاش
Khwahan (dist) خواهان
Kof Ab (dist) کوف آب
Kohestan (dist) کوهستان
Murch مرچ see Darwaz-e Bala
Nusay نسی see Darwaz
Ragh (dist) راغ
Seykwa سه کوه see Keran wa Munjan
Shahr-e Buzurg (dist) شهر بزرگ
Sheghnan (dist) شغنان
Sheki (dist) شکی
Shuhada (dist) شهدا
Tagab (dist, ctr Keshem-e Bala) تگاب • تگ آب

Takht-e Sulayman (mountain) تختِ سلیمان • تمتِ سلیمانی
Teshkan (dist) تشکان
Wakhan (dist, ctr Khandud) واخان • واخن
Warduj (dist) وردوج
Yaftal-e Sufla (dist) یفتل سفلی • یفتل
Yamgan (dist, ctr Girwan) یمگان
Yawan (dist) یاوان
Zarkol (lake) زرکول
Zeybak (dist) زیباک

BADGHIS بادغیس
Qala-ye Naw (seat) قلعه نو
Ab Kamari (dist, ctr Sang Atash) آب کمری
Bala Murghab بالا مرغاب see Murghab
Chartaq چارتاق see Jawand
Ghormach (dist) غورماچ
Jawand (dist, ctr Chartaq) جوند
Kushk-e Kohna (area) کشک کوهنه • کشک کهنه
Maqhur (dist) مقهور
Murghab (dist, ctr Bala Murghab) مرغاب
Qades (dist) قادس
Qala-ye Naw (dist) قلعه نو
Sang Atash سنگ آتش see Ab Kamari

BAGHLAN بغلان
Pul-e Khumri (seat) پل خمری
Andarab (dist) اندراب
Baghlan-e Jadid (dist) بغلان جدید
Burka (dist) برکه
Dahana-ye Ghori (dist) دهنه غوری
Deh Salah (dist) ده ساله
Doshi (dist) دوشی
Farang wa Gharu (dist) فرنگ وغارو
Guzargah-e Nur (dist) گزرگاه نور
Jelga Nahrin جلگه نهرین see Khaja Hejran
Khaja Hejran (dist, alt Jelga Nahrin) خواجه هجران
Khenjan (dist) خنجان
Khost wa Fereng (dist) خوست و فرنگ

Nahrin (dist) نهرین
Pul-e Hesar (dist) پل حصار
Pul-e Khumri (dist) پل خمری
Tala wa Barfak (dist) تاله و برفک

BALKH بلخ
Mazar-e Sharif (seat) مزار شریف
Adina Masjed مسجد آدینه see
Charbolak
Balkh (dist) بلخ
Boyna Qara بوینه قره see Sholgara
Charbolak (dist) چاربولک
Charkent (dist) چارکنت
Chemtal (dist) چمتال
Dawlatabad (dist) دولت آباد
Dehdadi (dist) دهدادی
Kaldar (dist) کلدار
Keshendeh (dist) کشنده
Khulm (dist) خلم
Marmul (dist) مارمول
Mazar-e Sharif (dist) مزار شریف
Nahr-e Shahi (dist) نهر شاهی
Sharak Hayratan (dist) شهرک
حیرتان
Sholgara (dist) شولگره
Shorteypa (dist) شورتیپه
Zari (dist) زاری

BAMYAN بامیان
Bamyan (seat) بامیان
Kahmard (dist) کهمرد
Panjab (dist) پنجاب
Sayghan (dist) سیغان
Shibar (dist) شیبر
Waras (dist) وارس • ورس
Yakawlang (dist) یکاولنگ

DAYKUNDI دایکندی • دی کندی
Nili (seat) نیلی
Eshtarlay (dist) اشترلی
Gayti گیتی see Kiti
Gizab (dist) گیزاب • گزاب
Kajran (dist) کجران
Khadir (dist) خدیر
Kiti (dist) کیتی • گیتی
Miramor (dist) میره مور
Nili (dist) نیلی
Sang-e Takht (dist) سنگ تخت
558

Shahrestan (dist) شهرستان

FARAH فراه
Farah (seat) فراه
Anar Dara (dist) انار دره
Bakwa (dist, ctr Sultani Bakwa)
بکواه
Bala Buluk (dist) بالا بلوک
Farah (dist) فراه
Gulestan (dist) گلستان
Khak-e Safeyd (dist) خاک سفید
Lash wa Juwayn (dist) لاش و
جوین
Pur Chaman (dist) پرچمن
Pusht Rod (dist) پشت رود
Qala-ye Kah (dist) قلعه کاه
Sultani Bakwa سلطانی بکواه see
Bakwa
Shib Koh (dist) شیب کوه

FARYAB فاریاب
Maymana (seat) میمنه
Almar (dist) المار
Andkhoy (dist) اندخوی
Belcheragh (dist) بلچراغ
Dawlatabad (dist) دولت آباد
Gurzewan (dist) گرزوان
Khaja Sabz Posh (dist) خواجه سبز
پوش
Khan-e Charbagh (dist) خان
چارباغ
Kohestan (dist, ctr Qala) کوهستان
Maymana (dist) میمنه
Pashtun Kot (dist) پشتون کوت
Qala قلعه see Kohestan
Qaramqol (dist) قرمقول
Qaysar (dist) قیصار • قیصر
Qurghan (dist) قرغان
Sabz Posh see Khaja Sabz Posh
Shirin Tagab (dist) شیرین تگاب

GHAZNI غزنی
Ghazni (seat) غزنی
Ab Band (dist, ctr Haji Kheyl) آب
بند
Ajrestan (dist, ctr Sangar)
اجرستان
Andar (dist, ctr Meray) اندر

Bahram-e Shahid (dist, ctr Jaghatu) بهرام شهید
Dado *see* Zana Khan دادو
Deh Yak (dist, ctr Ramak) ده یک
Du Abi *see* Nawur دو آبی
Gilan (dist) گیلان • گلان
Giro (dist, ctr Panah) گیرو
Haji Kheyl *see* Ab Band حاجی خیل
Jaghatu *see* Bahram-e Shahid جغتو
Jaghuri (dist, ctr Sang-e Masha) جاغوری
Khaja Umari (dist) خواجه عمری
Khugeyani (dist) خوگیانی
Malestan (dist) مالستان
Maqhur (dist, lake) مقهور
Meray *see* Andar مری
Nawa (dist) ناوه
Nawur (dist, ctr Du Abi) ناور
Panah *see* Giro پناه
Qarabagh (dist) قره باغ
Ramak *see* Deh Yak رامک
Rashidan (dist) رشیدان
Sangar *see* Ajrestan سنگر
Sang-e Masha *see* Jaghuri سنگ ماشه
Waez Shahid *see* Jaghatu واعظ شهید
Waghaz (dist) واغظ
Wali Mohamed Shahid (geog) ولی محمد شهید
Zana Khan (dist, ctr Dado) زنه خان

GHOR غور
Chaghcharan (seat, dist) چغچران
Charsada (dist) چارسده
Dawlat Yar (dist) دولت یار
Du Layna (dist) دو لینه
Lal wa Sarjangal (dist) لال و سرجنگل
Pasaband (dist) پسابند
Saghar (dist) ساغر
Shahrak (dist) شهرک
Taywara (dist) تیوره
Tulak (dist) تولک

HELMAND هلمند
Lashkar Gah (seat) لشکرگاه

Baghran (dist) بغران • باغران
Disho (dist) دیشو
Garmseyr (dist) گرمسیر
Gereshk (dist) گرشک
Kajaki (dist, dam) کجکی
Khan Neshin (dist) خان نشین
Lashkar Gah (dist) لشکرگاه
Musa Qala (dist) موسی قلعه
Nad Ali (dist) ناد علی
Nahr-e Saraj (dist) نهر سراج
Nawa-ye Barakzai (dist) ناوه بارکزی
Nawzad (dist) نوزاد
Reyg *see* Khan Neshin ریگ
Sangin (dist) سنگین
Washir (dist) واشیر

HERAT هرات
Herat (seat) هرات
Adraskan (dist) ادرسکن
Chesht-e Sharif (dist) چشت شریف
Enjil (dist) انجیل
Farsi (dist) فرسی • فارسی
Ghoryan (dist) غوریان
Gulran (dist) گلران
Guzara (dist) گزره • گزاره
Islam Qala (border crossing) اسلام قلعه
Karukh (dist) کرخ
Kuhsan (dist) کهسان
Kushk (dist) کشک
Kushk-e Kohna (dist) کشک کوهنه • کشک کهنه
Oba (dist) اوبه
Pashtun Zarghun (dist) پشتون زرغون
Shindand (dist) شیندند
Zenda Jan (dist) زنده جان

JAWZJAN جوزجان
Sheberghan (seat) شبرغان
Aqcha (dist) اقچه
Darzab (dist) درزاب
Fayzabad (dist) فیض آباد
Karakum (desert) کاراکم
Khaja Du Koh (dist) خواجه دو کوه
Khamyab (dist) خمیاب
Khanaqa (dist) خانقاه

Mardyan (dist) مردیان
Mengajek (dist) منگجک
Qarqin (dist) قرقین
Qush Teypa (dist) قوش تیپه
Sheberghan (dist) شبرغان

KABUL کابل
Kabul (seat, national capital) کابل

Kabul City
Afshar (city dist) افشار • افشر
Bibi Mahru (city dist) بی بی مهرو
Chehel Sutun (city dist) چهل ستون
Darulaman (city dist) دارالامان
Dasht-e Barchi (city dist) دشت برچی
Deh Buri (city dist) ده بوری
Karta-ye Chahar (city dist) کارته چهار
Karta-ye Naw (city dist) کارته نو
Karta-ye Sakhi (city dist) کارته سخی
Karta-ye Sey (city dist) کارته سه
Khayr Khana (1-3, city dists) خیرخانه
Kulola Pushta (city dist) کلوله پشته
Mikrorayon (1-4, city dists) مکرورایون
Qala-ye Wazir (city dist) قلعه وزیر
Shahr-e Kuhna (city dist) شهر کهنه
Shahr-e Naw (city dist) شهر نو
Wazir Akbar Khan Mena (city dist) وزیر اکبر خان مینه

Kabul Province
Bagrami (dist, ctr Husayn Kheyl) بگرامی
Chahar Asyab (dist, ctr Qala-ye Naim) چهار آسیاب
Deh Sabz (dist, ctr Tara Kheyl) ده سبز
Estalef (dist, village) استالف
Farza (dist) فرزه
Guldara (dist) گلدره
Husayn Kheyl حسین خیل *see* Bagrami
Kabul (dist) کابل
Kalakan (dist) کلکان
560

Khak-e Jabar (dist) خاک جبار
Mir Bacha Kot (dist) میر بچه کوت
Musayi (dist) موسهی • موسئی
Paghman (dist) پغمان
Qala-ye Naim قلعه نعیم *see* Chahar Asyab
Qarabagh (dist) قره باغ
Shakardara (dist) شکردره
Surobi (dist) سروبی
Tara Kheyl تره خیل *see* Deh Sabz

KANDAHAR کندهار • قندهار
Kandahar (seat) کندهار • قندهار
Arghandab (dist) ارغنداب
Arghestan (dist) ارغستان
Daman (dist) دامان • دامن • دمن
Ghorak (dist) غورک
Kandahar (dist) کندهار • قندهار
Khakreyz (dist) خاکریز
Maruf (dist) معروف • ماروف
Maywand (dist) میوند
Meyan Neshin (dist) میان نشین • میه نشین
Neysh (dist) نیش
Panjwayi (dist) پنجوایی
Reyg (dist) ریگ
Reygestan ریگستان see Reyg
Shah Wali Kot (dist) شاه ولی کوت
Shorabak (dist) شورابک
Spin Boldak (dist) سپین بولدک
Zheri (dist) ژری • ژیری

KAPISA کاپیسا
Mahmud-e Raqi (seat) محمود راقی
Alasay (dist) اله سای • السای
Ezat Kheyl عزت خیل see Hesa-ye Awal-e Kohestan
Haji Kheyl حاجی خیل see Koh Band
Hesa-ye Awal-e Kohestan (dist, ctr Ezat Kheyl, alt Kohestan) حصه اول کوهستان
Hesa-ye Duwum-e Kohestan (dist, ctr Ezat Khey, alt Keshektan) حصه دوم کوهستان
Keshektan کشکتان see Hesa-ye Duwum-e Kohestan
Koh Band (dist, ctr Haji Kheyl) کوه بند

Mahmud-e Raqi (dist) محمود راقی
Nejrab (dist) نجراب
Tagab (dist) تگاب

KHOST خوست
Khost (seat) خوست
Bak (dist) باک
Dadwal دادول see Mando Zayi
Gurbuz (dist) گربز
Jaji Maydan (dist) جاجی میدان
Kaparay کپری see Nader Shah Kot
Khost (Matun) (dist) خوست
Khost Meyla خوست میله see
  Qalandar
Mando Zayi (dist, ctr Dadwal) مندو
  زائی
Matun متون see Khost (dist)
Musa Kheyl (dist) موسی خیل
Nader Shah Kot (dist, ctr Kaparay)
  نادر شاه کوت
Qalandar (dist, ctr Khost Meyla)
  قلندر
Sabari (dist, ctr Zambar) صبری
Shamal (dist) شمل
Spira (dist) سپیره • سپیره
Tanay (dist) تنی
Terazayi (dist) ترازئی
Zambar زمبار see Sabari

KUNAR کنر
Asadabad (seat, dist) اسد آباد
Asmar اسمار see Bar Kunar
Bar Kunar (dist, ctr Asmar) بر کنر
Chapa Dara (dist) چپه دره
Chawkay (dist) چوکی
Dangam (dist) دانگام
Dara-ye Peych (dist) دره پیچ
Ghazi Abad (dist) غازی آباد
Khas Kunar (dist) خاص کنر
Kunar (river) کنر
Kurengal (valley) کرنگل • کورنگل
Marawara (dist) مروره
Narang (dist) نرنگ
Naray (dist) ناری
Nurgal (dist) نورگل
Serkanay (dist) سرکانی
Shaygal wa Sheltan (dist) شیگل و
  شلتن

Shuryak (valley) شوریک
Watapur (dist) وته پور • وتپور

KUNDUZ کندز • قندز • کندوز
Kunduz (seat) کندز • قندز • کندوز
Ali Abad (dist) علی آباد
Archi (dist) ارچی
Chahar Dara چهار دره see
  Chardara
Chardara (dist) چاردره
Imam Saheb (dist) امام صاحب
Khanabad (dist) خان آباد
Kunduz (dist) کندز • قندز
Qala-ye Zal (dist) قعله ذال

LAGHMAN لغمان
Mehtarlam (seat) مهترلام
Alingar (dist, river) علینگار
Alisheng (dist) علیشنگ
Dawlat Shah (dist) دولت شاه
Farashghan (mountains) فرشغان •
  فراشغان
Khanabad خان آباد see Qarghayi
Lalkhanabad لالخان آباد see
  Qarghayi
Mehtarlam (dist) مهترلام
Qarghayi (dist; ctr Khanabad, alt
  Lalkhanabad) قرغه یی

LOGAR لوگر
Pul-e Alam (seat) پل علم
Azra (dist) ازره
Baraki Barak (dist) برکی برک
Charkh (dist) چرخ
Kharwar (dist) خروار
Khushi (dist) خوشی
Logar (river) لوگر
Mohamad Agha (dist) محمد آغا •
  محمد آغه
Pul-e Alam (dist) پل علم

MAYDAN WARDAK میدان وردک
Maydan Shahr (seat) میدان شهر
Behsud بهسود see Markaz-e
  Behsud
Chak-e Wardak (dist) چک وردک
  • چک

561

Daymirdad (dist, alt Jelga; ctr Miran) دایمیرداد

Ghazi Mohamed Jan Khan (market) غازی محمد جان خان

Hesa-ye Awal-e Behsud (dist, ctr Zarkharid) حصه اول بهسود

Jaghatu (dist) جغتو

Jalreyz (dist) جلریز

Jelga جلگه see Daymirdad

Kan-e Ezat کان عزت see Nerkh

Markaz-e Behsud (dist, ctr Behsud) مرکز بهسود

Maydan Shahr (dist) میدان شهر

Miran میران see Day Mirdad

Nerkh (dist, ctr Kan-e Ezat) نرخ

Sayedabad (dist) سید آباد

Zarkharid زرخرید see Hesa-ye Awal-e Behsud

NANGARHAR ننگرهار

Jalalabad (seat) جلال آباد

Achin (dist, ctr Sarqala) اچین

Agam اگام • آگام see Pachir wa Agam

Basawul باسول see Mumand Dara

Bati Kot (dist, ctr Nader Shah Kot) بتی کوت

Behsud (dist) بهسود

Chaparhar (dist) چپرهار

Dara-ye Nur (dist, ctr Panja Kheyl) دره نور

Deh Bala (dist, ctr Kotwal) ده بالا

Dur Baba (dist) دربابا

Ghani Kheyl غنی خیل see Shinwar

Goshta (dist) گوشته

Hesarak (dist, ctr Ragha) حصارک

Jalalabad (dist) جلال آباد

Kama (dist, ctr Sangar Saray) کامه

Kazha کاژه • کژه see Khugeyani

Khugeyani (dist, ctr Kazha) خوگیانی

Kot (dist) کوت

Kotwal کوتوال see Deh Bala

Kunar (river) کنر

Kuz Kunar (dist, ctr Sheywa) کوز کنر

Lal Pur (dist) لعل پور • لال پور

Mama Kheyl ماما خیل see Sheyrzad

562

Mumand Dara, Mo- (dist, ctr Basawul) مومند دره

Nader Shah Kot نادر شاه کوت see Bati Kot

Nazeyan (dist) نازیان

Pachir wa/aw Agam (dist, ctr Agam) پچیر و/او اگام/آگام

Panja Kheyl پنجه خیل see Dara-ye Nur

Ragha راغه see Hesarak

Rodat (dist, ctr Shahi Kot) رودات

Sangar Saray سنگر سرای see Kama

Sarqala سرقلعه see Achin

Sera Rod سره رود see Surkh Rod

Shahi Kot شاهی کوت see Rodat

Sheyrzad (dist, ctr Mama Kheyl) شیرزاد

Sheywa شیوه see Kuz Kunar

Shinwar (dist, ctr Ghani Kheyl) شینوار

Shinwari شینواری see Shinwar

Sultanpur سلطانپور see Surkh Rod

Surkh Rod (Sera Rod) (dist, ctr Sultanpur) سرخ رود

NIMROZ نیمروز

Zaranj (seat) زرنج

Chakhansur (dist) چخانسور

Charburjak (dist) چاربرجک

Kang (dist) کنگ

Khash Rod (dist, ctr Lokhi) خاش رود

Lokhi لوخی see Khash Rod

Zaranj (dist) زرنج

NURESTAN نورستان

Kamdeysh (seat) کامدیش

Barg-e Matal (dist) برگ متال

Du Ab (dist) دو آب

Kamdeysh (dist) کامدیش

Mandol (dist) مندول • ماندول

Nurgaram (dist) نورگرم • نورگرام

Parun (dist) پارون

Wama (dist) واما

Waygal (dist, valley) وایگل

PAKTIKA پکتیکا

Sharan (seat) شرن
Barmal (dist) برمل
Dila (dist) ديله
Gayan (dist) گيان
Gomal (dist) گومل
Jani Kheyl (dist) جانى خيل
Mata Khan (dist) متا خان • متا خان
Nayka نيکه see Nika
Nika (dist) نيکه
Omna (dist) اومنه
Sar Hawza (dist) سرحوضه
Sarobi (dist) سروبى
Sharan (dist) شرن
Sharana شرنه see Sharan
Turwo (dist) تروو
Urgun (dist) ارگون
Waza Kha (dist) واږه خوا
Wur Mamay (dist) ور ممى • ور ممای
Yahya Kheyl (dist) يحيى خيل
Yusuf Kheyl (dist) يوسف خيل
Zarghun Shahr (dist) زرغون شهر
Ziruk (dist) زيروک

PAKTIYA پکتيا
Gardeyz (seat) گرديز
Ahmad Abad (dist) احمد آباد
Ahmad Kheyl (dist) احمد خيل
Ali Kheyl على خيل see Jaji
Chamkani (dist) چمکنى
Dand wa Patan (dist, ctr Ghunday) دند و پتان
Dzadran خدران see Wuza Jadran
Dzadzi خاخى see Jaji
Gardeyz (dist) گرديز
Ghunday (dist) غندى see Dand wa Patan
Jadran جدران see Wuza Jadran
Jaji (dist, ctr Ali Kheyl) جاجى
Jani Kheyl (dist) جانى خيل
Lazha Ahmad Kheyl لژه احمد خيل see Ahmad Kheyl
Sayed Karam (dist) سيد کرم
Shawak (dist) شواک
Tsamkani خمکنى see Chamkani
Wuza Jadran (dist, ctr Jadran) وزه جدران
Zurmal زرمل see Zurmat

Zurmat (dist) زرمت

PANJSHEYR پنجشير
Bazarak (seat, dist) بازارک
Anaba انابه see Unaba
Char Qarya چار قريه see Khenj
Dara (dist) دره
Dara-ye Hazara دره هزاره see Hesa-ye Duwum-e Panjsheyr
Hesa-ye Awal-e Panjsheyr حصه اول پنجشير see Khenj
Hesa-ye Duwum-e Panjsheyr (former dist, ctr Dara-ye Hazara) حصه دوم پنجشير
Khenj (dist, ctr Char Qarya) خنج
Paryan (dist) پريان
Rukha (dist) رخه
Shutul (dist) شتل
Unaba (dist) اونبه

PARWAN پروان
Chaharikar (seat) چاريکار
Bagram (dist, air base) بگرام
Chaharikar (dist) چاريکار
Ghorband (dist, ctr Shahgerd) غوربند
Jabal us-Saraj (dist) جبل السراج
Koh-e Safi (dist, ctr Mullah Mohamed Kheyl) کوه صافى
Mullah Mohamed Kheyl ملا محمد خيل see Koh-e Safi
Salang (dist) سالنگ
Sayed Kheyl (dist) سيد خيل
Shahgerd شاه گرد see Ghorband
Sheykh Ali (dist) شيخ على
Shinwari (dist) شينوارى
Surkh-e Parsa (dist) سرخ پارسا
Tagab (dist) تگاب • تگ آب

SAMANGAN سمنگان
Aybak (dist) ايبک
Dara-ye Suf دره صوف see Dara-ye Suf-e Bala, Dara-ye Suf-e Payin
Dara-ye Suf-e Bala (dist, ctr Dara-ye Suf) دره صوف بالا
Dara-ye Suf-e Payin (dist) دره صوف پايين
Firoz Nakhchir (dist) فيروز نخچير
563

Hazrat-e Sultan (dist) حضرت سلطان

Khuram wa Sarbagh (dist) خرم و سرباغ

Ruy-e Du Ab (dist) روي دو آب

Takht-e Rustam (stupa) تختِ رستم

SAR-E PUL سر پل
Sar-e Pul (seat) سر پل
Balkhab (dist, ctr Tarkhoj) بلخ آب
Gosfandi (dist) گوسفندی
Kohestanat (dist) کوهستانات
Sangcharak (dist, ctr Tukzar) سنگچارک
Sar-e Pul (dist) سر پل
Sayad (dist) صياد
Sozma Qala (dist) سوزمه قلعه
Tarkhoj (dist) ترخوج see Balkhab
Tukzar (dist) تکزار see Sangcharak

TAKHAR تخار
Taluqan (seat) تالقان
Baharak (dist) بهارک
Bangi (dist) بنگی
Chah Ab (dist) چاه آب
Chal (dist) چال
Darqad (dist) درقد
Dasht-e Qala (dist) دشت قلعه
Eshkamesh (dist) اشکمش
Farkhar (dist) فرخار
Hazar Sumuch (dist) هزار سموچ
Kalfagan (dist) کلفگان
Khaja Bahawuddin (dist) خواجه بها الدين
Khaja Ghar (dist) خواجه غار
Namak Ab (dist) نمک آب
Rustaq (dist) رستاق
Taluqan (dist) تالقان
Warsaj (dist) ورسج
Yangi Qala (dist) ينگی قلعه

URUZGAN اورزگان • اروزگان
Tarin Kot (seat) ترين کوت
Chora (dist) چوره
Deh Rawod (dist) ده راود
Khas Uruzgan (dist) خاص اورزگان

Shahed-e Hasas (dist) شاهد حساس

WARDAK see MAYDAN WARDAK

ZABUL زابل
Qalat (seat) قلات
Arghandab (dist) ارغنداب
Atghar (dist) اتغر
Daychopan (dist) دايچوپان see Deh Chopan
Deh Chopan (dist) ده چوپان
Kakal (dist) کاکل see Kakar
Kakar (dist) کاکر
Mizan (dist) ميزان
Naw Bahar (dist) نو بهار
Qalat (dist) قلات
Shahjoy (dist) شاه جوی
Shahr-e Safa (dist) شهر صفا see Tarnak wa Jaldak
Shamolzai (dist) شمولزی
Shinkay (dist) شينکی
Tarnak wa Jaldak (dist, ctr Shahr-e Safa) ترنک و جلدک

Ministries

Ministry of... وزارتِ
Agriculture & Irrigation زراعت و آبياری
Border Affairs امور سرحدات
Commerce & Industry تجارت و صنايع
Communication مخابرات
Counternarcotics مبارزه با موادِ مخدر
Culture & Youth فرهنگ و جوانان
Defense دفاع
Economy & Labor اقتصاد و کار
Education معارف
Energy & Water انرژی و آب
Finance ماليه
Foreign Affairs امور خارجه
Hajj & Endowments حج و اوقاف
Higher Education تحصيلاتِ عالی
Interior Affairs امور داخله

Justice عدلیه
Labor & Social Affairs
کار و امور اجتماعی
Martyrs & Disabled شهدا و معیوبین
Mines معادن
Public Health صحتِ عامه
Public Works فوایدِ عامه
Reconstruction اعمار مجدد
Returnees عودتِ مهاجرین
Rural Revival & Development
احیا و انکشافِ دهات
Urban Development
انکشافِ شهری
Women's Affairs امور زنان

Dari Proverbs & Expressions

آب که از سر پرید چه یک نیزه چه صد نیزه What is one or 100 nayza when the water is over (your) head?

آهن بد شمشیر بران نمیشود Poor iron will not make a good sword.

ارزان بی علت نیست , قیمت بی حکمت Nothing cheap is without flaw nor is an expensive thing without wisdom.

از زیر چکک گریخت و زیر باران نشست S/he ran out from under a leaky roof into the rain.

از سرنیچی چه می رود غیر پف From the surna player comes only the breath.

الو الو به از پلو A good fire is better than pilaf.

انسان بدون خطا نیست No person is without error.

بار کج به منزل نمیرسد A crooked load won't reach its destination.

برادر با برادر حسابش برابر Brothers should keep square accounts.

به خری که کار نداری ایشه مگو Don't say "stop" to a donkey that isn't yours.

به لق لق سگ دریا مردار نمیشود The lapping of a dog doesn't sully the river.

به یک گل بهار نمیشه One flower does not a spring make.

پایت را برابر گلیمت دراز کن Extend your foot (only) as far as (the end of) your blanket.

پنج انگشت برادر است برابر نیست Five fingers are brothers (but) not equal.

پیش کله خر یاسین خواندن to read the Yasin before a donkey's head

تا شمال نباشد درخت شور نمیخورد A tree doesn't move unless there's wind.

تا که طفل گریه نگند مادرش شیر نمیدهدش A child's mother gives it no milk until it cries.

565

جنگل که در گرفت تر و خشک می سوزد When a forest catches fire, the dry and the wet will burn.

جوینده یابنده است Seek and you shall find.

خدا یک دست را محتاج دیگر دست نکند May God not make one hand dependent on the other.

خر خو همو خر است , لاکن پالان اش نو است It's the same old donkey but w/a new saddle.

خنده نمک زنده گی است Laughter is the salt of life.

خون به خون ششته نمیشود Blood cannot be washed away w/blood.

دزد نابلد در کاهدان می درآید A country thief starts out in the hay barn.

دزد نباش پادشاه نترس Be not a thief and fear not the king.

دل به دل راه داره Love will find a way.

دو تربوز در یک دست گرفته نمیشه Two watermelons cannot be held in one hand.

دویدن , افتیدن هم دارد One who runs may also fall.

زخم بد جور میشود , گپ بد نی A bad wound will heal, a bad word will not.

زور کم قهر بسیار دارد Much anger betrays weakness.

زیر کاسه نیم کاسه است Under the bowl is another bowl.

سالی که نیکو است از بهار اش پیدا است You can tell a good year by its spring.

سر زخمم نمک پاش مده Don't sprinkle salt on my wound.

سرگردانی هم سیل است Looking around is also seeing.

سر خر سوار , خر را گم کرده Atop a donkey, [but] lost the donkey.

سگ زرد برادر شغال است The yellow dog is the brother of the jackal.

سیر از دل گرسنه نمیآید , سوار از دل پیاده نمیآید The full man's stomach doesn't make him hungry, the rider's heart doesn't make him walk.

شنیده کی بود ماننده دیده Hearing is not the same as seeing.

شیر خانه , روباه بیرون A lion at home, a fox abroad.

صد سر را تر کرده , یکی را کل نی
S/he has moistened 100 faces (but) hasn't shaved one.

صدا از یک دست نمیبرآید No sound comes from one hand.

صدقه رد بلا است Alms avert calamity.

عقل به سر است , نه به سال
Wisdom is within, not in years.

عقل سلیم در بدن سلیم هست A sound mind is in a sound body.

غم هر چیز میرود لاکن غم شکم نی
There's no forgetting hunger.

قرض مقراض محبت است Debt is the scissors of love.

قصاب که بسیار شد گاو مردار میشود
Too many butchers ruined the cow.

کس ندیدم که گم شد از راه راست
You'll never go wrong by doing right.

کسی که قدر یک سیب را نفهمید , قدر باغ را نمیفهمد One who hasn't appreciated the apple doesn't appreciate the orchard.

کلال در تیکر شکسته آب میخورد
The potter drinks water from a broken jug.

کوه هر قدر که بلند باشد , باز هم سر خود راه داره No matter how high the mountain, there is a path to the top.

گذشته را صلوات آینده را احتیاط
Over the past say a prayer, look to the future.

گوشت که گنده شود نمک می زنند , نمک که گنده شود او را چه بزنند
Rotten meat is salted, but rotten salt is no good.

مار گزیده از ریسمان دراز می ترسد
S/he who is bitten by a snake is afraid of a rope.

مشک آن است که خود ببوید , نه که عطار بگوید Perfume is what smells good, not what the perfume seller says.

نوکر نو آهو را می گیره بدو A new servant catches a deer on the run.

همرنگ جماعت شو Be like the group.

هیچ کس نمیگوید که دوغ من ترش است No one says his (own) buttermilk is sour.

یک روز دیدی دوست , دیگر روز دیدی برادر Friendship becomes brotherhood.

یک سر صد سر را اداره می کند اما
صد سر یک سر را نمیتوانند اداره کند
One chief can keep 100 people
moving, but 100 chiefs cannot
keep even one person moving.

Musical Terms

accompany <sb> همراهی کردن
<کسی را>
barbut (mus instr) بربوط
bridge (mus section) خرک
cymbal (mus instr) سنج
dambura (mus instr) دمبوره
drum (mus instr) دهل
dulcimer (mus instr) سنتور
dutar (mus instr) دو تار
flute فلوت • توله • نی • مزمار
glass harp (mus instr) جلترنگ
guitar (mus instr) گیتار
harmony هماهنگی
→ be in harmony هماهنگی
داشتن
harp (mus instr) هارپ
horn (mus instr) صور
lute (mus instr) عود
lyre (arch, mus instr) چنگ
mode (mus) مقام
modulation تلحین
music موزیک • موسیقی • آهنگ
• ساز
→ make music ساز کردن
→ music & singing ساز و آواز
musical (production) موزیکال
musical instr آله موسیقی • ساز
musician موسیقی نواز • سازنده
musicologist موسیقی دان
note (mus) سر
percussive ضربی
→ percussive instr ساز ضربی
• آله ضربی
perform (on mus instr) نواختن
piano (mus instr) پیانو
play (on mus instr) نواختن

plectrum مضراب
→ (arch) زخمه
pluck چیدن
qanun (mus instr) قانون , -ها
reed نی
rod (arch) (mus instr) رود
rubab (mus instr) رباب
sanj (mus instr) سنج
santur (mus instr) سنتور
sarang (mus instr) سارنگ
saxophone (mus instr) سکسفون
sitar (mus instr) ستار
string (on mus instr) تار • وتر •
سیم
string (catgut) زه
stringed تاری
→ stringed instrument ساز
تاری • آله تاری
sur (mus instr) صور
tambur (mus instr) تنبور
tone (mus) مقام
ud (mus instr) عود
wind instrument ساز دمی • آله
دمی • نای • نی

Flora & Fauna

acacia (tree, flower) اکاسی
aerial spraying سمپاشی از طریق
هوایی • سمپاشی
anise بادیان • رازونیاز
bahar (flower) بهار
bahar (spice) بهارالبر
bakhti (kind of camel) بختی
barberry زرشک • زرغول
bat (mammal) شب پره • شب •
پرک
betel leaf پان
bloom, blossom v گل کردن
blossom n نو عروس
botanical گیاهی
botanist گیاه شناس • نبات شناس
botany گیاه شناسی • نبات شناسی
• علم نباتات
bulbul (songbird) بلبل • عندلیب
calendula see zubayda
camel شتر

castor bean plant ارند
centipede • گوش خزک • چلپایک
chamomile گل بابونه
chicken مرغ
chicory (med herb) کاسنی
cilantro گشنیز
cockscomb (flower) تاج خروس
coriander see cilantro
cormorant زاغ آبی
cowrie shell کودی
crane (bird) کلنگ
crow زاغ • کلاغ
dahlia دلیه
datura (med herb) داتوره
delphinium (flower) دلفون
dove کبوتر
duck مرغابی
eglantine (white) نسترن
fennel see nigella
field چمن
fleawort (& seed) • اسپغول
اسفرزه
flower گل
flower garden چمن
flower petals جام
fragrance (lit) نگهت
fumitory (med herb) شاه تره
fuschia (flower) گل گوشواره
garden باغ
→ tend a garden باغبانی کردن
garden cress (herb) • تراتیزک
گل چین • باغبان
gardener باغبان
gardening باغ کاری • باغ داری
goat بز
→ (kid) بزغاله
→ (young billy goat) جدی
geranium (flower) جریبن
graft (botany) پیوند
grafted پیوندی • التصاقی
grape انگور
→ lal (grape variety) لال
grapefruit چکوتره
grapevine تاک • رز
grass (field) چمن
grass (fodder) علف • سبزه • گیاه
grasshopper ملخ
greenhouse گل خانه • گرین
هوس • گرین هاوس

grow vi کشت شدن
grow vt کشت کردن
hare خرگوش
harvest خرمن • محصولات
hawk باشه
hemlock شوکران
hempseed بنگ دانه • شاه دانه
herb گیاه • نبات • سبزی
herbivorous علف خوار • گیاه
خوار
honeysuckle الی سکن • هنی
سکل
hoopoe هدهد • اتوتک • پیوک •
پوپک • شانه سرک • مرغ سلیمان
horse اسپ
hyacinth سنبله
indigenous محلی
indigo (plant, dye) نیل
ibex (wild goat) بز کوهی
iris (flower) زنبق
jackdaw (bird) زاغچه
jasmine یاسمن • یاسمین
jimson weed (med herb) داتوره
jonquil (plant) نسرین
kite (bird) زغن
lark (bird) جل
larkspur (flower) دلفون
leaf (of plant, tree) برگ
lilac یاس • یاسمن انگریزی
lily (dark purple) سوسن
lotus نیلوفر
→ Indian lotus نیلوفر هندی
magpie (bird) اکک • عکه
mallow (med herb) پنیرک
marigold جعفری
marijuana بنگ • کنب
markhor (wild goat) مارخور
marsh (salt) شوره زار
marten (animal) خز • دله خفک
mursal (rose) مرسل
mustard (plant) • خردل • اوری
شرشم
myrobalan هلیله
myrtle (shrub) مورم
narcissus نرگس
→ (lit) عبهر • نرگس
narcissus (yellow) نسرین
native محلی

569

nelumbo (plant, genus) نیلوفر هندی

nenuphar (plant) نیلوفر

nigella seeds سیاه دانه

nightingale (bird) مرغ پگاهی • مرغ سحر • عندلیب

owl (bird) جغد • بوم

pasha khana (tree) پشه خانه

pepperwort (herb) تراتیزک

perianth لفافه

pheasant تذرو • مرغ دشتی

pigeon کبوتر

pine (tree) ارچه

pistil آله تأنیث

pitchfork دوشاخه

plant n گیاه • نبات

plant vt شاندن • کاشتن • نشاندن • گور کردن

plantain seed (med) زوف

planting (sowing) کشت

pollination تلقیح

pollinate تلقیح کردن

poppy (head, pod) کوکنار

poppy seed (& food) خشخاش • خاش خاش

portulaca (flower) فرشی

prickle n خار

primrose پریمینا

purslane (edible weed) خرفه

quail (bird) بلدرچین • بلدرجین

quince بهی • به

quince seeds (med) بهی دانه

rabbit خرگوش خانگی • خرگوش اهلی

ram (m sheep) گوسفند نر • قچ

raven, rook (bird) زاغ • کلاغ

redbud (tree) ارغوان

rhinocerous کرگدن

rhubarb رواش • چکری

rooster خروس • مرغ سحری

root ریشه , -ها

rose (esp pink) گلاب • گل

rose (mursal) مرسل

rue (wild plant) اسپند • سپند

ruffle (of bird, animal) طوق

sable سمور

saffron (herb) زعفران

570

sage, salvia گل نافرمان

sandalwood صندل • چوب صندل

seagull مرغ نوروزی

see عکاسی اکاسی

seech (vegetable) سیچ

seed بذر • تخم

seedling نهالی

senna plant (med) سنا

sesame کنجد

shell (crustacean) صدف

sissoo (tree) شیشم

snake مار

snapdragon نافرمان • گل نافرمان

Solomon bird مرغ سلیمان

songbird پرنده نغمه سرا

sow پاشاندن • پاش دادن

sparrow گنجشک

species (of animal) نوع حیوان

species (of plant) نوع نبات

spider جولاه • جولاهک • جولاگک • تارتنک • عنکبوت

spinach سبزی

spur (on plant) مهمیز

→ having spurs مهمیز دار

squirrel (brown) موش خرما

squirrel (grey) سنجاب

stalk نره

stamen آله تذکیر

starling (black) قره قش

stem نره

stork (bird) لکلک • لگلگ

strawberry توت زمینی

sturgeon (fish) ماهی خاو یار • سگ ماهی • ماهی خاویار

swallow (bird) ابابیل • غجی • پرستو • فراشتروک

swan (bird) قو

sweetbriar (white) نسترن

swift (bird) see swallow

thorn خار

thornapple (med herb) داتوره

transplant vt نشاندن

trout (fish) ماهی خال دار

trowel بیلچه • بیلک

tulip لاله

turtledove فاخته

vegetable سبزی

vegetation نباتات
verbena شاه پسند • بربینه
violet (flower) بنفشه
vulture (bird) کرگس
water lily نیلوفر آبی
weed علف هرزه • گیاه هرزه
weeding خیشاوه
whale ماهی وال • وال • حوت
willow tree بید
woad (plant) وسمه
yard (field) چمن
zinnia زنیه

Forms of Address

Below is a partial list of forms of address, which vary by region and dialect. Titles of religious learning or distinction (*e.g.*, پیر *pir*) are frequent forms of address. Family relationships ("brother," "sister," "uncle," "aunt") are often used to address non-family members. The suffix جان (*jān*) after a name or title means "dear" or "beloved."

agha jan (respectful, for m) آغا جان
agha saheb (for m descendants of Prophet) آغا صاحب
akhund (rel teacher) • آخوند آخند
akhundzada (akhund born of family of akhunds) آخوند زاده
bibi jan (respectful, for f) بی بی جان

brother برادر
Excellency جلالتماب
ghazi (vanquisher of infidels) غازی
haji (for one who has performed the hajj) حاجی
khaja, khoja (for descendants of Abu Bakr) خواجه
khala (respectful, for f; aunt) خاله
khalifa jan (for driver or workman) خلیفه جان
lala, lalay (respectful, for older m) لالا • لالی
madam, madame خانم • میرمن • بی بی • مادام
majesty
→ Her Majesty علیا حضرت
→ His Majesty اعلی حضرت
mama (uncle) ماما
maulana (rel) مولانا
maulvi (rel) مولوی
Miss پیغله • بی بی
Mr. شاغلی • اقای • صاحب
Mrs. خانم • میرمن • زن
mullah (rel) ملا
pir (Sufi master) پیر
saed *see* sayed
said *see* sayed
sayed (descendant of Prophet, before name) سید
sheik (master of Sufi order) شیخ
sir شاغلی • صاحب
sister خواهر
syed *see* sayed

Other Titles from Hippocrene Books

Beginner's Dari with Audio CD
177 pages · 5½ x 8½ · 0-7818-1139-2 · $21.95pb

Dari Dictionary & Phrasebook
5000 entries · 226 pages · 3¾ x 7 · 0-7818-0971-1 · $12.95pb

Introduction to Pushtu
343 pages · 4¾ x 7 · 978-0-7818-0939-9 · $18.95pb

Pashto Dictionary & Phrasebook
5000 entries · 232 pages · 3¾ x 7 · 0-7818-0972-X · $12.95pb

Farsi (Persian) Dictionary & Phrasebook
4000 entries · 219 pages · 3¾ x 7½ · 0-7818-1073-6 · $13.95pb

Urdu-English/English-Urdu Dictionary & Phrasebook
(Romanized)
3,000 entries · 175 pages · 3¾ x 7½ · 0-7818-0970-3 · $13.95pb

Tajik-English/English-Tajik Dictionary & Phrasebook
1400 entries · 147 pages · 3¾ x 7 · 978-0-7818-0662-X · $11.95pb

Turkmen-English/English-Turkmen Dictionary & Phrasebook
4000 entries · 207 pages · 3¾ x 7 · 978-0-7818-1072-2 · $11.95pb

Uzbek-English/English-Uzbek Dictionary & Phrasebook
3000 entries · 200 pages · 3¾ x 7½ · 978-0-7818-0959-X · $11.95pb

Beginner's Iraqi Arabic with 2 Audio CDs
365 pages · 5½ x 8½ · 0-7818-1098-1 · $29.95pb

Mastering Arabic with 2 Audio CDs
320 pages · 6 x 9 · 0-7818-1042-6 · $29.95pb

English-Arabic/Arabic-English Modern Military Dictionary
11,000 entries · 204 pages · 5½ x 8½ · 0-7818-0243-1 · $16.95p

Arabic-English/English-Arabic Dictionary & Phrasebook
4,500 entries · 220 pages · 3¾ x 7½ · 0-7818-0973-8 · $13.95pb

Arabic-English/English-Arabic Practical Dictionary
18,000 entries · 440 pages · 4½ x 7 · 0-7818-1045-0 · $24.95pb